# WILLS, TRUSTS AND ESTATES

## INCLUDING TAXATION AND FUTURE INTERESTS

### Second Edition


By

**William M. McGovern, Jr.**
*Professor of Law*
*University of California, Los Angeles*

**Sheldon F. Kurtz**
*Percy Bordwell Professsor of Law and Professor of Surgery*
*University of Iowa*



**HORNBOOK SERIES®**

WEST GROUP

A THOMSON COMPANY

ST. PAUL, MINN., 2001

610 Opperman Drive
P.O. Box 64526
St. Paul, MN 55164–0526
1–800–328–9352


Printed in the United States of America

**ISBN** 0–314–23815–8

*TEXT IS PRINTED ON 10% POST CONSUMER RECYCLED PAPER*

# Preface

In most law schools today, the formerly separate courses in Wills, Trusts, and Future Interests have been integrated into a single offering. This book reflects this trend. It covers the same ground (roughly) as Atkinson on Wills, Bogert on Trusts, and Simes on Future Interests. It also introduces students to estate and gift taxes. We think there are clear advantages in a unified treatment of these subjects.

This book does not purport to give an exhaustive treatment. Much of the law of wills is statutory. We emphasize the Uniform Probate Code, even though it has not been adopted as widely as the Uniform Commercial Code. We think in most instances the Code represents the "better view." It has influenced legislation in many states which have not adopted it completely. However, any person who uses this book should make sure that the governing law in the jurisdiction conforms to the statements herein.

Many law school courses in trusts and estates and related casebooks cover the various federal tax laws that affect wealth dispositions. Thus, it is appropriate that this hornbook introduce students to the federal gift, estate and generation skipping transfer tax laws and grantor trust rules affecting the wealth disposition process. Chapter 15 is designed for this end. The more detailed coverage of the estate tax in the first edition of this book has been reduced, because we cannot predict what changes will arise out of the new administration which took office as this book was in its final stages. In exchange we have added a chapter on a subject which is prominent in the minds of many clients: how to ascertain and carry out the wishes of an incompetent patient with respect to end-of-life medical treatment. (Chapter 14.)

*Changes in the Law*

Property law is more stable than other areas of law. Many states still impose the formal requirements for wills which were prescribed by the Wills Act of 1837. In others, statutes based on the Statute of Frauds of 1676 lay down the formal requirements for both wills and trusts.

Nevertheless, property law has undergone numerous changes in recent years. The growing popularity of will substitutes like joint tenancy and revocable trusts has affected the law of wills. Former doubts about whether these devices were valid have largely disappeared (see Chapter 4), but many states allow surviving spouses and creditors to reach assets transferred outside of probate (see Chapters 3, and 13). The difference between the tax treatment of gifts and transfers at death has been minimized (Chapter 15).

Many states have reduced the formal requirements for wills. The Uniform Probate Code allows holographic wills and interested witnesses, and allows witnesses to sign the will outside of the testator's presence. (Sections 4.1-.4) Doubts about the validity of pour-over wills have disappeared. (Section 6.2) The rule that wills cannot be reformed for mistake is being questioned, and in some cases ignored. Many states have permitted a testator's informally expressed wishes to be effectuated by making the drafting attorney liable to the intended beneficiary, despite the "lack of privity" between them .. ( Section 6.1).

Probate avoidance has affected the law governing administration (see Chapter 12). The Uniform Probate Code reflects a widely shared view that costs of court supervision of personal representatives and trustees outweigh the benefits. In order to expedite the settlement of estates, most states have sharply reduced the period allowed for will contests and for filing claims against estates. However, simplification of administration, if carried too far, may run afoul of the requirement of due process. The United States Supreme Court held unconstitutional a nonclaim statute which cut off claims of creditors after notice by publication only.

With regard to trust investments, legal lists have been replaced by the "prudent person" (or "prudent man") rule in nearly all states. This trend has been extended in many to other fiduciaries, such as executors and conservators. Commentators have questioned the traditional practice of scrutinizing individual investments, saying that courts should instead examine the performance of the portfolio as a whole. This view is adopted both by the Third Restatement of Trusts and the Uniform Prudent Investor Act (Section 12.7)

Changes in some of the rules governing principal and income appear in a recently promulgated third Uniform Principal and Income Act (Section 9.4). These rules have become somewhat less important, since trusts today usually allow the trustee to distribute principal to the "income beneficiaries." This has gives added importance to rules governing trustees' discretionary decisions. One aspect of this question relates to the eligibility of beneficiaries of discretionary trusts for governmental welfare benefits. (Section 9.5). Many trusts allow the trustee to accumulate income. Statutory restrictions on accumulations have largely vanished, but their tax advantages have been largely eliminated (Section 11.6).

The tax on generation–skipping transfers (Section 15.4) has reduced the estate–tax advantages of by–pass trusts in large estates. However, the commonest form of trust—one for the life of the settlor's spouse—continues to have tax and other advantages (Section 9.3). Despite improvements in the law of guardianship, a trust is usually the best way to manage property for persons who are incompetent to handle it. However, custodianships under the Uniform Transfers to Minors Act, and durable powers of attorney have become popular substitutes for the trust in some situations (Section 9.2)..

Legal life estates and contracts to make wills continue to crop up in reported cases, although sophisticated estate planners advise against their use. The same is true of contractual wills which are discussed in Section 4.9.

Spendthrift trusts continue to arouse controversy, although their practical importance is less significant than pension plans under ERISA because of the large number of people who participate in the latter. (Section 13.1).

The frequent complaint that the Attorney General's supervision of charities is inadequate may have made courts more liberal in conferring standing on private persons to sue trustees for breach On the other hand, some have urged an expanded use of cy pres to remove restrictions imposed by settlors in charitable trusts. Constitutional law, public opinion, and the Internal Revenue

Code have done more than trust law to eliminate racially discriminatory terms. (Section 9.7).

Sex discrimination in charitable trusts is more problematic. In other areas of property law it is under attack. The constitution has been held to bar preference for males in choosing administrators (Section 12.4). Husbands no longer have sole managerial power over community property. Virtually all states have eliminated distinctions between widows and widowers as to the elective share (Sections 3.7-.8). ) Parties to an invalid marriage and cohabitants who never participated in a marriage ceremony may today be treated as "spouses" for some purposes. "Common law" marriage, which recently seemed to be on the way out, is being revived in an altered form. Some states have extended marriage-like treatment to homosexual couples.(Section 2.11)

The treatment of adopted children and children born out of wedlock has also changed. Adopted persons (even adults) have been largely assimilated into the adoptive family and cut off from their biological relatives in intestate succession and class gifts. (Section 2.10) Children born out of wedlock are much more likely to inherit or take under a class gift today. (Section 2.9)

The differences between separate and community property states with respect to the tax treatment and property division at divorce have been reduced (Section 3.8). Significant differences still exist between the elective share in most separate property states and the spouse's rights in community property, but the latest version of the Uniform Probate Code elective share is modeled on community property concepts. (Section 3.7) Agreements limiting the claims of spouses are becoming common with the increasing incidence of multiple marriages. No consensus on how to deal with such agreements has emerged (Chapter 3.9).

Reform of the Rule against Perpetuities has received much attention in the law reviews and state legislatures, even though litigated cases on the subject are rare. Sophisticated practitioners generally avoid the Rule by a savings clause. The widely adopted Uniform Statutory Rule Against Perpetuities produces in most instances the same result for less competent drafters (Section 11.4).

The law's traditional preference for early vesting of future interests has been questioned by modern commentators. Sophisticated drafters usually postpone vesting and state expressly that "heirs" should be determined as of the date when their interest becomes possessory. Since most future interests today involve trusts where the trustee has a power of sale, postponement of vesting does not impede alienability. Hence, the revised Uniform Probate Code makes this the preferred construction. (Sections 10.2-.2). This may make it harder to get the consent of all the beneficiaries to modify a trust, though some states have sought to address this problem by the use of guardians ad litem. The *Claflin* rule continues to predominate in American law, but some authorities have questioned the traditional assumption that a spendthrift provision in a trust shows a purpose which would be frustrated by early termination.(Section 9.5). Sophisticated drafters continue to urge the use of powers of appointment to provide flexibility in trusts, but their effect on tax objectives and creditors must be considered by a careful drafter. (Section 10.4).

Often a testator's circumstances change after the will is executed. Most states now provide that a divorce revokes any devises to the testator's former spouse (Section 5.4). Anti–lapse statutes deal with devisees who predecease the testator (Section 8.3). These statutes have not traditionally applied to will substitutes, but the revised Uniform Probate Code changes this rule, and also gives a decedent's creditors and spouse rights against non-probate assets. (Sections 3.7, 13.1-.2). It also rejects the traditional rule (still retained in some states) that the compensation of the personal representative and attorney for an estate should be determined by the size of the probate estate, thereby eliminating one ground for avoiding probate. (Section 12.5) Ademption of specific devises where the devised property is not in the estate when the testator dies is reduced under the Uniform Probate Code, which on this point also has been followed by many states. (Section 8.1).

Choice of law problems arise when the law changes. Does the new rule apply to a will previously executed? To a testator already dead? The traditional reluctance to make changes "retroactive" has been questioned, particularly when the old rule is thought to have frustrated the testator's probable intent. (Section 1.3) . Choice of law problems also arise when two or more states (or foreign countries) are involved in an estate or trust. A tendency to make domicile more important than situs in determining the governing law is noticeable in the Uniform Probate Code, which also seeks to reduce the traditional difficulties of probate and administration in several jurisdictions. See Sections 1.2, 12.3.

John Langbein has described what he calls a "revolution in family wealth transmission." Because of the importance of "human capital" in today's technological society, middle–class parents now devote a large proportion of their resources to their children's education. Much of the rest goes into pension plans which usually take the form of annuities which expire when the parents die. As a result, transfer of wealth on death is no longer the dominant mode of wealth transmission of the middle classes.[1] Nevertheless, wealth transmission at death continues to be an important subject, worthy of a lawyer's attention. Despite the popularity of will substitutes, most persons with substantial wealth want wills and hire lawyers to draft them. Indeed, the only contact which many persons have with the legal system arises from the devolution of property at death.

Many wills and trusts are never scrutinized by a court at all except for a cursory examination at probate. This book emphasizes the lawyer's role as drafter or "estate planner." ). All the chapters suggests ways to avoid problems which otherwise lead to litigation.

WILLIAM M. MCGOVERN, JR.
SHELDON F. KURTZ

Revised, March, 2001

1. Langbein, *The Twentieth-Century Revolution in Fancily Wealth* Transmission, 86 Mich.L.Rev. 722 (1988).

# WESTLAW® Overview

*Wills, Trusts and Estates,* Second Edition, offers a detailed and comprehensive treatment of basic rules, principles and issues relating to the law of wills, trusts and estates. To supplement the information contained in this book, you can access Westlaw, a computer-assisted legal research service of West Group. Westlaw contains a broad array of legal resources, including case law, statutes, expert commentary, current developments and various other types of information.

Learning how to use these materials effectively will enhance your legal research abilities. To help you coordinate the information in the book with your Westlaw research, this volume contains an appendix listing Westlaw databases, search techniques and sample problems.

THE PUBLISHER

*

# Summary of Contents

# Table of Contents

# WILLS, TRUSTS AND ESTATES

*

# Chapter 1

# TERMINOLOGY AND CHOICE OF LAW

*Analysis*



## § 1.1 Terminology

This section lists alphabetically several frequently recurring terms that are encountered elsewhere in the book. A brief definition of the term is given, with a reference to the section in the book where the term is more fully discussed.

***abatement***

The reduction of devises in a will in order to pay claims against the estate. The rules on abatement are discussed in Section 8.2.

***ademption***

The defeat of specific devises by transfer of the property after the will is executed. See Section 8.1. The word is also used for gifts made by a testator while still alive to a devisee designated in the will which are intended to replace, in whole or part the devisee's right under the will. See Section 2.6 at note 30 et seq.

***administrator***

Someone appointed to administer the estate of a decedent who died intestate, or whose will failed to designate effectively an executor. An administrator who operates under a will is called an administrator "with will annexed." Sometimes the Latin *cum testamento annexo* (or "c.t.a") is used.[1]

***advancement***

A gift made by a person which is taken into account when the donor later dies intestate. See Section 2.6

***annuity***

A provision for periodic fixed payments to a person, usually for life, but sometimes for a stipulated period. The trustee of a trust may be directed to

**§ 1.1**

1. Cal.Prob.Code § 8440.

pay such an annuity, although this is less common than a direction that the trustee pay the all the trust income to a person or persons, or as much as the trustee deems appropriate out of the income or principal. Often annuities are created by a contract between a company and a person who buys an annuity, either for the benefit of the purchaser or of another. In this situation the annuity usually performs a function like life insurance; the company promises to pay the agreed amount for the life time of the annuitant, thus assuming the risk that the annuitant will live so long that the payments total much more than the original price. Insurance proceeds are often paid out in the form of an annuity after the death of the insured.

***appointment***

See **power of appointment**

***attest***

Bear witness, especially as to a will. See Section 4.3.

***attorney***

See **power of attorney**

***bequeath, bequest***

A somewhat antiquated name for a gift of personal property in a will. See **devise**.

***cestui que trust (use)***

Obsolete term for trust beneficiary, derived from law french.[2]

***charity***

Charitable trusts are subject to certain special rules. The question whether a gift is "charitable" may also be important for tax purposes, but the meaning in this context may be somewhat different. Section 9.7.

***child***

Many problems arise from this simple word. Does it include adopted child? a step child? See Section 2.10. A child born out of wedlock? See Section 2.9. A grandchild? See Section 10.1.

***class gifts***

A gift to a group, like "children", as distinguished from a gift to individuals, like "John and Mary". The consequence of something being a "class gift" can be important, so there is much case law defining the term in borderline situations, such as a gift "to my children, John and Mary." See Section 8.3.

2. "The beneficiary is described in law french as 'cestui a qui use le feoffment fuit fait,' and from this obtains his curious title 'cestui que use.' The plural of this term is often rendered charmingly as 'cestuis que usent,' an expression calculated to give a grammarian bad dreams." A. Simpson, *An Introduction to the History of the Land Law* 163–64 (1961).

***clear and convincing evidence***

A requirement of proof intermediate between a preponderance of the evidence, the ordinary rule in civil cases, and proof beyond a reasonable doubt, which is required to convict in criminal cases.[3] The term recurs frequently. The Uniform Probate Code, for example, allows wills which fail to meet the formal requirements if there is "clear and convincing evidence that the decedent intended the document" to be a will.[4] What is *not* clear is (a) what effect this standard has on juries when it appears in an instruction[5], and (b) in cases tried by the court, whether it is the trial court or the appellate court which must be satisfied that the evidence was clear and convincing.[6] Some courts regard uncorroborated testimony of an interested witness as not "clear and convincing"[7] but there is no general rule to this effect.

***codicil***

A document used to modify a will. From the Latin *codicillus*[8], a diminutive of *codex*, the source for our word code. Codicils are usually shorter than wills, but they are subject to the same formal requirements.[9]

***collateral relatives***

Distinguished from lineal descendants or issue, they are related to a person through an ancestor such as a parent or grandparent. The term includes brothers, sisters, nieces, nephews, cousins, etc. Derived from the Latin *latus*, side.

***community property***

The system of property ownership for spouses in 8 American states and many foreign countries. It affects both intestate succession and the limitations on one spouse's right to devise or give away property, and is discussed in Section 3.8.

***confidential relationship***

This term is used as a basis for a presumption that a will or gift was caused by undue influence. See Section 7.3. It is also the basis for an

3. First Nat. Bank v. King, 635 N.E.2d 755 (Ill.App.1994).

4. Unif. Prob. Code § 2–503. See also *id.* § 6–211(b) (ownership of joint account based on contributions unless clear and convincing evidence of a different intent); Cal. Prob. Code §§ 220 (clear and convincing evidence of survival required), 5302 (right of survivorship in joint account), 6453 (of paternity).

5. In Matter of Estate of Bennett, 865 P.2d 1062 (Kan.App.1993), the court said "we doubt very much that an experienced trial judge is much bothered by euphemisms such as clear and convincing or preponderance of the evidence. * * * it is highly unlikely that the decision in this case would have been any different if the evidence had been weighed by a higher standard." But in Matter of Estate of Mitchell, 623 So.2d 274 (Miss.1993). judgment on a verdict was reversed because a jury had erroneously been instructed that a preponderance of the evidence was sufficient.

6. 2 McCormick, Evidence 340 (4th ed. 1992). In Williams v. Estate of Pender, 738 So.2d 453 (Fla.App.1999) a trial court's finding because expressly based on a mere "preponderance of the evidence" was reversed because the "clear and convincing" standard was appropriate.

7. Ryan v. Ryan, 642 N.E.2d 1028 (Mass. 1994); Hettinga v. Sybrandy, 886 P.2d 772 (Idaho 1994).

8. The word had a somewhat different meaning in Latin, however. "Codicili" were informal instruments which were sometimes used even without a will. W. Buckland and A. McNair, *Roman Law and Common Law* 12 (2d ed. 1965).

9. Uniform Probate Code § 1–201(56) ("'will' includes codicil"); Cal.Prob.Code § 88 (same).

exception to the requirement that trusts of land must be in writing. See Section 6.5. Some courts use "fiduciary relationship" as a synonym, although the two terms are sometimes distinguished.[10]

***conservator***

Some persons accent the first syllable of the word, others the second. There is also inconsistency as to its meaning. Under the UPC a conservator is "person appointed by a Court to manage the estate of a protected person."[11] A "protected person" may be either a minor or an adult who has been judged incompetent to handle property. In any event, the conservator only deals with the conservatee's property.[12]

In California, on the other hand, there may be a conservator of the *person* of an adult.[13] A person who is appointed to manage the property of a minor is called a "guardian of the estate" rather than a conservator, and the minor is referred to as the "ward" rather then the conservatee.[14] In other words the distinction between guardians and conservators in California turns on the age of the protected person, whereas under the UPC the difference is based on whether the person or property is involved.

Both guardians and conservators are fiduciaries, and many of the rules governing trustees also apply to them.[15]

***constructive trust***

Commonly distinguished from "express" trusts which are based on the intent of the settlor whereas constructive trusts are imposed regardless of intent in order to prevent unjust enrichment, e.g. on a thief, who obviously intends only to benefit himself.[16] However, constructive trusts are often imposed to carry out an intent which was informally expressed, as in oral trusts of land. See Sections 6.1, 6.5.

***contingent remainder***

A future interest which is not necessarily going to take effect, as in a gift "to A for life, then to her children who survive her." While A is alive, one cannot know whether or not she will have children who survive her. Contingent remainders are contrasted with "vested" remainders, e.g. "To A for life, then to B." Even though B cannot take possession while A is alive, his remainder is vested; if he dies before A, the property will be part of B's estate. For further discussion see Section 10.1.

***corpus***

Another term for the principal of a trust as distinguished from its income.

**10.** Cleary v. Cleary, 692 N.E.2d 955 (Mass. 1998).

**11.** UPC § 1–201(8). *See also* Unif.Trust Code § 103(4).

**12.** Thus in a UPC state a "guardian" who sold the property of an incompetent was actually acting as a conservator. Matter of Estate of Gardner, 845 P.2d 1247 (N.M.App.1992).

**13.** Cal. Prob. Code § 1800.3.

**14.** Cal. Prob. Code § 1510.

**15.** Cal.Prob.Code § 2101: "The relationship of guardian and ward and of conservator and conservatee is a fiduciary relationship that is governed by the law of trusts ... "Under UPC § 5–423, conservators have all the "powers conferred by law on trustees." However, in many points there are differences between conservators and trustees. See Section 9.2.

**16.** *Restatement (Third) of Trusts* § 1, comm. e (1996).

***custodian***

A fiduciary designated to handle property under the Uniform Transfers to Minors Act.

***cy pres***

From the French *si pres*, as near. The term is used in connection with the modification of charitable trusts which cannot be carried out literally. See Section 9.7. More recently, the term has been used for modifying a private trust which violates the Rule against Perpetuities, but in this case "reformation" is the more common label. See Section 11.4.

***dead man statute***

A rule which in many states bars testimony by an interested witness when the opposing party is dead. The rule has often been criticized and has many variations. Under one, the testimony is allowed but it must be corroborated. For further discussion see 1 McCormick, *Evidence* § 65 (4th ed. 1992).

***death taxes***

The generic term for taxes occasioned by death. The most common types are the estate tax, imposed by the United States and several states, and "inheritance" taxes imposed by some states. Inheritance taxes are based on the amount passing to each successor, with usually different rates for different kinds of successor, *e.g.* children are taxed at a lower rate that unrelated devisees. The estate tax, on the other hand, is based on the estate as a whole, and is not effected by who gets the property, except there are deductions for gifts to spouses and charities. A survey of the federal estate tax appears in Chapter 15. State inheritance taxes vary and the rates are generally much lower.

***deed***

Although in ordinary English, the word can refer to any act, in this area of the law it usually means an written instrument transferring property (usually land).

***descend***

Traditionally land was said to "descend" to the heirs of a person who died intestate, whereas personal property was "distributed" to the intestate's next of kin.[17] Vestiges of this terminology survive[18] but nearly everywhere the rules governing both types of property are the same today.

Do not confuse "descend" and "descendant." Property may "descend" to a collateral relative or spouse who is not a "descendant."

**17.** 2 W. Blackstone, Commentaries *201 (descent is the title to land acquired by an heir), *515 (rules for distribution of an intestate's goods).

**18.** See Mass. Gen. Laws ch. 199 § 1 (realty shall *descend* according to the laws of this commonwealth; personalty shall be *distributed* under the laws of the state of which the owner was an inhabitant); Va. Code § 64.1–1 Fifth (real estate *descends* * * *), § 64.1–11 (*distribution* of personalty is the same).

***descendant***

Synonymous with "issue,"[19] this term includes children, grandchildren, great-grandchildren, etc., but not collateral relatives; the latter are descendants of the decedent's *parents* or other ancestor.

***devise***

Originally this word was used (both as a noun and a verb) to describe a gift of *land* in a will.[20] The proper term for a gift of personal property was "bequest" (a word of Anglo-Saxon origin) or "legacy" (from the Latin *legatum*).[21] Today the Uniform Probate Code uses "devise" to cover both real and personal property.[22]

One who receives a devise is a devisee. This term has in the lexicon of the UPC displaced the older "legatee."[23]

***disclaimer***

A refusal to accept a gift or inheritance. A complex body of law has arisen on the subject, since different consequences can attach to disclaimers as distinguished from accepting property and then giving it away. See Section 2.8. Renunciation is sometimes used as an equivalent term.[24]

***distribute***

See **descend**

***domicil, or domicile (either spelling is acceptable)***

From the Latin *domus*, home. Often used interchangeably with "residence,"[25] but the two terms are also often distinguished.[26] The term is significant in the choice of law, especially for personal property. See Section 1.2. It is also important for venue; under the Uniform Probate Code, for example, proceedings for administration of an estate may be commenced "where the decedent had his domicile at the time of his death."[27]

***donee***

The recipient of a gift, or a person on whom a power of appointment is conferred. See **power of appointment**.

***dower***

The term given by the common law to a widow's rights in her husband's land; the counterpart to the widower's right to "curtesy." See Section 3.2.

**19.** Uniform Probate Code § 1–201(25) (issue means descendant).

**20.** 2 W. Blackstone, Commentaries *372.

**21.** *Id.* 512: "A legacy is a bequest, or gift, of goods and chattels by testament; and the person to whom it was given is styled the legatee." But the distinction was never rigidly followed; the term "bequests" in a will might be construed to cover a devise of land as well. Estate of Lindner, 149 Cal.Rptr. 331 (App. 1978).

**22.** Uniform Probate Code § 1–201(10).

**23.** *Id.* § 1–201(11). *See also* Cal.Prob.Code § 34.

**24.** Cal.Prob.Code § 265: " 'Disclaimer' means any writing which declines, refuses, renounces, or disclaims any interest."

**25.** Uniform Probate Code § 1–201(31) (nonresident means a decedent domiciled in another jurisdiction).

**26.** In re Estate of Tolson, 947 P.2d 1242, 1250 (Wash.App.1997) (statement that decedent was a "resident" of Washington "does not address the issue of domicile" since they are "distinct concepts").

**27.** Uniform Probate Code § 3–201.

***durable power***

A power of attorney which does not terminate when the principal becomes incompetent. It is a modern device to avoid the need for conservatorship. See Section 7.2.

***entireties, tenancy by***

A peculiar form of joint tenancy between spouses, no longer in existence in many states. See Section 13.2.

***equitable conversion***

The word used to describe the fact that when land is sold, the proceeds may be treated as personal property, *e.g.* for applying the rule that personal property is governed by the law of the domicile of the owner. See Section 1.2, note 26.

***ERISA***

Employment Retirement Security Act of 1974, a federal statute governing most pension plans, which subjects them to many of the same rules as trusts. Its impact in the area of probate is problematic, since it expressly supersedes state laws, and yet is silent as to many matters as to which state law would provide detailed rules, *e.g.* as to the effect of homicide on succession.

***escheat***

When a person dies without a will and without heirs, his/her property passes to the state by "escheat."[28]

***estate***

In this course the term is used primarily to describe the property of a decedent. The term sometimes refers only to the "probate" estate, the assets which pass by will or intestacy under the jurisdiction of the probate court. Because of the popularity of will substitutes like joint tenancy and living trusts, much property today passes "outside probate." Most of this property is subject to the federal estate tax, which is based on the "gross" estate. See Section 15.3.

***execute***

Doing what is necessary to make an instrument formally valid, typically signing a will or deed. The place where an instrument was executed may be significant for choice of law, and the time of execution may also be important for various purposes.

***executor***

A person or persons designated in a will to "execute", i.e. carry out the testator's wishes as expressed in the will. The executor may be either an individual or a bank which has a trust department. The term "executrix" for female executors is rarely used today. Executors have no power to act until

**28.** Historically, escheat occurred when land reverted to the lord of the fee, either for lack of qualified heirs or as a forfeiture. 2 W. Blackstone, Commentaries *244.

they are appointed by the court, which usually happens when the will is probated. See Section 14.4.

***executory interest***

A type of future interest distinguishable from a remainder on technical grounds. The distinction was once important but is virtually obsolete today. See Section 11.1, note 16.

***expectancy***

A hope of acquiring property, e.g. by inheritance from a parent who is still alive. Property can be transferred without consideration, but an expectancy cannot. The distinction between property and an expectancy is thin in borderline cases. See Section 4.5, note 82.

***express trust***

A term used in contradistinction to resulting and constructive trusts.[29]

***fee tail***

A form of ownership contrasted with "fee simple" by the fact that a fee tail ceased when the owner died without issue. A serious clog on alienation at one time, the fee tail has been abolished or severely restricted today. See Section 10.2, note 40.

***fiduciary***

Derived from the Latin *fiducia*, trust, the term covers a wide spectrum of persons who are entrusted with property which belongs to another. The Uniform Probate Code defines the term to include personal representatives, guardians, conservators and trustees[30], but custodians and agents are also fiduciaries.[31] The relationship between clients and lawyers is often described as a fiduciary one. The common term can be misleading since not all "fiduciaries" are treated the same way. "The duties of a trustee are more intensive than those of most other fiduciaries."[32] See also **confidential relationship**.

***fraud***

A knowing misrepresentation, which may be the basis for denying probate to a will. See Section 6.1. Also the term is used to describe a promise made without intent to perform, which may cause the imposition of a constructive trust even if the promise is oral. See Section 6.5. Fraud is also sometimes used to get around various defenses, such as statutes of limitations and res judicata. For example, under the Uniform Probate Code, "if a will which is known to be a forgery is probated informally, and forgery is not

**29.** *Restatement (Third) of Trusts* § 2, comm a (1996).

**30.** Uniform Probate Code § 1–201(16). *See also* Cal.Prob.Code § 39.

**31.** For some of the differences and similarities between trustees, custodians, and agents see McGovern, *Trusts, Custodianships, and Durable Powers of Attorney*, 27 Real Prop., Prob. and Trust J. 1, 4 (1992).

**32.** *Restatement (Third) of Trusts* § 2, comm. a (1996).

discovered until after the period for [a will] contest has run, the defrauded heirs could still bring a fraud action."[33]

***fraudulent conveyance***

A gift which is subject to attack by the donor's creditors, *e.g.* because the donor was insolvent when the gift was made.

***future interest***

An interest in property which does not allow present possession or enjoyment, a generic term for remainders, executory interests, reversions, etc.

***general devise***

Contrasted with specific and with residuary devises for purposes of ademption and abatement. See Sections 8.1–8.2. General devises are very often pecuniary, *e.g.*, "$1,000 to my friend, Mary."

***general power***

See **power of appointment**

***gift causa mortis***

A concept borrowed from Roman law which applied special rules to gifts made by persons who were contemplating death at the time. See Section 5.5.

***grantor***

A word often used to describe the person who creates a living trust. Synonymous with settlor and trustor.

***guardian***

See **conservator**

***guardian ad litem***

A person appointed to represent a minor or other incompetent person in litigation (from the Latin *lis, litis*, suit). Under the Uniform Probate Code, for example, "a court may appoint a guardian ad litem to represent the interest of a minor, an incapacitated, unborn or unascertained person."[34] Appointment of a guardian ad litem is optional, since the person(s) may already be adequately be represented by others who have the same interest. A guardian ad litem's role is generally limited to litigation, unlike other guardians.

***heir***

From the Latin *heres*, which can be translated as "heir." But in Latin an heir was often designated in the will of a testator to whom the heir was not related, whereas in English such a person is a "devisee" but not an heir. In correct English usage an heir is a person designated by the law of intestacy to take from a decedent. For example, when a trust provided that property would pass to the "heirs at law" of the settlor's son, it did not pass to a friend of the son whom he had designated as his "heir," but rather to the son's

33. Uniform Probate Code § 1–106, Comment.

34. Uniform Probate Code § 1–403(4). *See also* Cal.Prob.Code § 1003.

cousins who were his closest blood relatives, because "the term 'heir at law' must be defined with reference to the statute of descent and distribution."[35] (However, even in the common law the term is sometimes used to mean devisees or children.)[36]

As we shall see, a decedent's spouse always inherits on intestacy, but whether a spouse is to be deemed an "heir" in construing the words of a will is a more complex issue. See Section 2.4.

When a person dies without issue, the estate passes to collateral relatives, such as brothers and sisters. They can be heirs, but the term "heirs of the body" usually connotes only issue and so collateral relatives would not qualify.

Sometimes the word "heirs" is used as a "word of limitation" as in a deed "to *A* and his heirs." In this case *A*'s heirs acquire no interest at all; the word simply means *A* gets a fee simple. See Section 10.2.

Historically, "heirs" was used to designate those who took the decedent's land. The persons who inherited personal property were called the next of kin.[37] However, in modern usage, the term heir generally covers anyone who takes real or personal property by intestacy.[38]

***holographic***

From the Greek *holos*, whole and *graphein*, write, a will written entirely in the testator's handwriting. See Section 4.4.

***homestead***

A certain amount of property, usually a residence, which is exempt from creditors. There are typically restrictions on voluntary transfer by the owner. See Section 3.4.

***honorary trust***

A name sometimes given to trusts for non-charitable purposes without a definite human beneficiary, like a trust for a pet. See Section 9.7, note 54.

***hotchpot***

Used to describe the way an advancement is taken into account in distributing the estate of an intestate. See Section 2.6.

***illegitimate***

Until recently, this term was used to describe children born out of wedlock. Now it is deemed unfairly degrading, and so avoided in most legal discussions. See Section 2.9.

***inheritance tax***

See **death taxes**

**35.** PNC Bank, Ohio, N.A. v. Stanton, 662 N.E.2d 875 (Ohio App.1995).

**36.** Snyder v. Davis, 699 So.2d 999 (Fla. 1997) ("heirs" in a constitutional provision protecting homestead includes devisees).

**37.** 2 W. Blackstone, Commentaries *515.

**38.** Uniform Probate Code § 1–201(21); Cal.Prob.Code § 44.

***instrument***

A generic term for a document by which an interest in property passes, including wills, deeds, trusts etc.[39]

***intangible***

From the Latin *tangere*, touch, refers to property such as securities, bank accounts, patents, which cannot be touched, in contrast to furniture, cattle, etc. Even if securities are represented by a certificate, they are considered to be intangibles. Wills often distinguish between intangible property, which is put into a trust, and tangible property, which is inappropriate for a trust and so is left outright.[40]

***international will***

A will which is subject to special requirements. When these are followed, the will can be probated in any country which signed a 1973 treaty on the subject.

***in terrorem***

Related to the word "terror," it is often used for a clause designed to deter someone from contesting a will by providing that any devise to him in the will is forfeited by such a contest. See Section 12.1, note 109.

***inter vivos***

Latin "between the living," contrasted with a testamentary gift or trust which is made by a will. "Living" trust is a commonly used synonym for inter vivos.

***intestate***

Without a will, related to the Latin word for will, *testamentum*. The rules governing intestate succession are described in Chapter 2.

***issue***

See **descendants**

***joint tenancy***

A form of co-ownership in which property passes to the surviving owner(s) when a tenant dies. Contrasted with tenancy in common, under which the decedent's interest passes to his/her estate. See Section 4.8.

***joint will***

A will signed by two persons, usually husband and wife, purporting to dispose of the property of both. See Section 4.9.

***laches***

A defense to claims based on delay in asserting them. The equitable counterpart to the statutes of limitations, but laches is discretionary, whereas

**39.** Uniform Probate Code § 1–201; Cal. Prob.Code § 45.

**40.** See Unif.Stat.Will Act § 5(a)(2).

statutes of limitations provide fixed limits, like 2 years. See Section 12.8, note 119.

***lapse***

From the Latin *lapsus*, to fall. In the context of wills it refers to the failure of a devise, usually because the devisee predeceased the testator. Most states have "anti-lapse" statutes to deal with this situation. See Section 8.3.

***latent ambiguity***

From the Latin *latens*, hidden, an ambiguity in a will which is not apparent from reading the will, as contrasted with a "patent" ambiguity which is. A devise "to my cousin, Mary Jones" does not appear to be ambiguous, but it is if the testator has two cousins with that name. See Section 6.1.

***laughing heirs***

A term used to describe remote relatives who inherit intestate property in the absence of closer relatives. They are so named because they are not sorry about the death of the decedent whom they hardly knew, if at all.

***legacy, legatee***

See **devise**

***legal interest, title***

An interest which historically was enforced in the law courts, as distinguished from equitable interests, which were recognized only in the courts of equity. In a trust, the trustee has legal title, while the interests of the beneficiaries are equitable.

***legal list***

Refers to lists of types of investment which are authorized for fiduciaries by statute. See Section 12.7, note 27.

***legitimate***

See ***illegitimate*** Also used as a verb (with the last syllable accented) to describe a procedure whereby a child born out of wedlock may be rendered equivalent to one born in wedlock.

***letters***

An official certification of the appointment of a fiduciary by a court designed to establish his or her authority to deal with third persons. Thus the Uniform Probate Code provides that any restrictions "on the power of a personal representative which may be ordered by the Court must be endorsed on his *letters of appointment* and, unless so endorsed, is ineffective as to persons dealing in good faith with the personal representative."[41] The general term "letters" may refer to letters testamentary (given to an executor), letters

**41.** Uniform Probate Code § 3–504. *See also* Cal.Prob.Code § 8405.

of administration (given to an administrator), letters of guardianship and letters of conservatorship.[42]

***living trust***

See **inter vivos**.

***lineal descendants***

See **collateral relatives**

***living will***

"A relatively short instrument saying * * * that the life of the person signing is not to be artificially prolonged by extraordinary medical measures when there is no reasonable expectation of recovery."[43] See Section 14.5.

***marital deduction***

A deduction permitted under the federal estate and gift taxes for transfers from one spouse to another. See Section Chapter 15.

***marital property***

Roughly the equivalent of community property. A Uniform Marital Property Act has been adopted only in Wisconsin.

***Medicaid Qualifying Trust (MQT)***

A trust which is treated as a resource disqualifying the beneficiary from receiving medicaid. See Section 9.5, note 57.

***mistake***

The law distinguishes between mistake of fact and mistake in execution. If I sign a "will" not realizing it is a will, it may be denied probate, but if my will disinherits my son because I erroneously think he is a drug addict, the will is valid. See Section 6.1.

***mobilia sequuntur personam***

A Latin maxim saying that moveable goods (mobilia) are governed by the law of the domicile of the owner. See Section 1.2, note 35.

***Model Code of Professional Responsibility, Model Rules of Professional Conduct***

Two sets of provisions governing proper conduct by lawyers. Nearly all states have adopted one or the other. Several provisions are particularly relevant to this area of law, *e.g.* lawyers who draft wills from which they benefit. See Section 7.4.

***mortmain***

Statutes which restrict gifts to charity by will. In nearly all states they have been repealed or held unconstitutional. See Section 3.10.

**42.** Uniform Probate Code § 1–201(28). *See also* Cal.Prob.Code § 52.

**43.** Mellinkoff, Dictionary of American Legal Usage 572 (1992).

***mutual wills***

Wills executed by two persons, usually spouses, with reciprocal provisions, *e.g. H* leaves his estate to *W* if she survives, *W* leaves her estate to *H* if he survives. See Section 4.9, note 6.

***next of kin***

See **heirs**

***no contest clause***

See **in terrorem**.

***nonclaim statutes***

Statutes which require that claims against an estate be filed within a specified period. See Section 13.3.

***notary public***

"A person authorized by law to administer oaths, [and] authenticate signatures and documents." Do not confuse the American notary with "the far more significant role and status of notaries public in civil law jurisdictions."[44]

***nuncupative will***

An oral will, allowed in some states in limited circumstances. See Section 4.4, note 40.

***patent ambiguity***

See **latent ambiguity**.

***per capita, per stirpes***

Alternative ways to divide property among heirs or devisees, but this dichotomy oversimplifies the possibilities. See Section 2.2.

***personal representative***

The generic term which covers both executors and administrators.[45]

***possibility of reverter***

A type of future interest reserved in a grant. The technical distinctions between these and rights of entry are discussed in Section 11.6.

***pourover (also pour-over)***

A popular name for a will which leaves property to a trust created by another document. Discussed in Section 6.2.

**44.** Mellinkoff, Dictionary of American Legal Usage 428 (1992).

**45.** Uniform Probate Code § 1–201(36); Cal.Prob.Code § 58.

***power***

Authority conferred on a fiduciary to act, such as an executor's power to sell property of an estate. It may be conferred by the terms of the instrument or implied by law.

***power of appointment***

Authority given to a person (called the donee) to direct where property shall pass. Powers are either testamentary or presently exercisable. The law also distinguishes between general and special powers. All these terms are defined in Section 10.4.

***power of attorney***

Authority given to a person, known as an "attorney in fact," to perform acts on behalf of the principal who confers the authority. Such attorneys should not be confused with attorneys at law.

> Persons holding powers of attorney have historically not been considered attorneys who can appear in the courts. When a principal designates another to transact some business * * *, he appoints an agent to act for him as an "attorney in fact." * * * An "attorney in fact" has been consistently distinguished from an "attorney at law."[46]

Do not confuse powers of attorney with powers of appointment, as some persons have done.[47] See also **durable power**.

***precatory***

Directions in an instrument which are construed not to impose any obligation, from the Latin *precor*, to ask. Disputes about whether particular words are mandatory or only precatory are common. See Section 4.6, note 65.

***presumption***

This "slipperiest of the family of legal terms"[48] is often used in this area of the law. For example, under the California Probate Code if a will is lost, "it is *presumed* that the testator destroyed the will with the intent to revoke it."[49] If the issue is decided by a jury, a presumption means that a verdict must be directed for the party claiming revocation when the basic fact is proved (that the will is lost) unless the other side (the proponents of the will) come up with evidence to the contrary.[50] If such contrary evidence is produced (e.g. indicating that the will was lost by accident), there is disagreement as to whether the presumption should be mentioned to the jury. It is not under the "bursting bubble" view advocated by some[51] but criticized by others.

**46.** Disciplinary Counsel v. Coleman, 724 N.E.2d 402 (Ohio 2000).

**47.** Matter of Estate of Krokowsky, 896 P.2d 247 (Ariz.1995) (holographic will conferring a "power of attorney" did not give a power of appointment).

**48.** 2 McCormick, Evidence 342 (4th ed. 1992).

**49.** Cal.Prob.Code § 6124. A similar presumption exists at common law. See Section 5.2.

**50.** In this respect a presumption differs from a "permissible inference" which would *allow* the jury to find that the will was revoked, but not compel them to do so. McCormick, *supra* note 48, at 342.

Even when a case is tried by the court, if a presumption is not rebutted the court must find accordingly. Matter of Estate of Nelson, 274 N.W.2d 584 (S.D.1978).

**51.** Matter of Estate of McCoy, 844 P.2d 1131 (Alaska 1993) (error to mention presumption to jury since it affects the burden of proof, not the burden of persuasion); Vitacco v. Eck-

Under the Uniform Rules of Evidence, Rule 301, "a presumption imposes on the party against whom it is directed the burden of proving that the nonexistence of the presumed fact is more probable than its existence." Under Federal Rule 301, on the other hand, a presumption merely "imposes on the party against whom it is directed the burden of going forward with evidence to rebut or meet the presumption, but does not shift to such party the burden of proof." In close cases this distinction makes a difference.[52]

***pretermitted***

Used to describe a child or other heir who is omitted from a will by oversight. See Section 3.5. The word "omitted" is synonymous and is also used.[53]

***principal***

The distinction between "principal" and "income" of a trust is discussed in Section 9.4. The relationship between a "principal" and an agent is discussed at Section 7.2. Neither word should be confused with "principle."

***private trust***

Used in contrast to charitable trusts which are governed by special rules. See Section 9.7.

***probate***

From the Latin *probare*, prove, the term often refers to the process of proving that a will is valid. A will which the court finds valid is "admitted to probate." The court which performs this function is usually called the probate court, or the probate division of the court of general jurisdiction in the state.

The court which admits the will to probate also appoints the personal representative to administer the estate, and continues to supervise the administration of the estate. For this reason, the term "probate" is often loosely used to include administration of the estate. For example according to *Restatement, Third, of Property (Wills and Other Donative Transfers)* § 1.1 the " 'probate estate' is the estate subject to administration," but the two concepts are not identical.[54] In an intestate estate no will is probated, but the estate still must be administered. Conversely, in "independent" administration, the probate court may have little to do with administration after it probates the will. Nevertheless, the term "avoiding probate" has come to mean keeping property out of administration. Property which passes outside of administration is not part of the "probate" estate. See **estate**.

Probate courts traditionally had limited jurisdiction, but in recent years there has been a trend to expand their competence. This has tended to reduce disputes about which court has jurisdiction to decide a particular matter.[55]

berg, 648 N.E.2d 1010, 1013 (Ill.App.1995) (presumption disappears when the other party meets its burden).

**52.** Higgs v. Estate of Higgs, 892 S.W.2d 284, 288 (Ark.App.1995).

**53.** Uniform Probate Code § 2–302; Cal. Prob.Code § 6570.

**54.** In re Estate of Kruegel, 545 N.W.2d 684 (Minn.App.1996) (statute allowing "six months after probate" to assert claims did not include the period of administration after the will was probated).

**55.** In re Messer Trust, 579 N.W.2d 73 (Mich.1998) (probate court now has jurisdic-

***prudent man/person rule***

In states which do not have a legal list of proper investments for fiduciaries, the governing standard allows them to make those investments that a prudent man (now person) would make. See Section 12.7. This vague standard has been extended to other aspects of fiduciary conduct. For example, under the Uniform Transfers to Minors Act the custodian "shall observe the standard of care that would be observed by a prudent person dealing with the property of another."[56]

***publication***

An oral statement by the testator that a document is his/her will, so the witnesses understand that the testator knows what he/she is signing. See Section Section 4.3.

The term is also used in its more common sense of notice published in a newspaper, *e.g.* to creditors of an estate. See Section 13.3.

***putative spouse***

A person not legally married, but who is treated as a spouse, *e.g.* for purposes of intestate succession, because he/she in good faith thought there was a marriage even though the other party was already married. See Section 2.11, note 17.

***quasi community property***

Property treated as if it were community property even though it is not, because acquired by someone while living in a separate property state who later moved to a community property state. See Section 3.8, note 77.

***reformation***

Correcting a writing to make it conform to what the signer intended. Long applied to deeds, arguably the same remedy should be available for wills. See Sections 6.1, 6.5. Also used for modifying a trust to avoid a violation of the Rule against Perpetuities. See Section 11.4, note 21.

***representation***

The concept whereby more remote relatives take a share of a decedent's property in place of a parent or other ancestor who is dead. See Section 2.2.

The term is also used when holding that a judgment binds someone who was a minor or unborn when it was rendered on the ground that his/her interests were represented by another. See Section 12.8, note 111.

***res***

From the Latin *res*, thing. A somewhat antiquated term for the property held in a trust.[57]

tion over inter-vivos as well as testamentary trusts).

**56.** Uniform Transfers to Minors Act § 12(b).

**57.** *Restatement (Third) of Trusts* § 3, comm. b (1996).

***residue***

The property remaining in an estate after the payment of claims, specific and general devises. The clause disposing of this property is commonly called a residuary devise. The classification of devises is important for purposes of abatement and for allocating the income of an estate.

***resulting trust***

When a trust fails there is a "resulting trust" for the settlor who presumably did not intend to let the trustee keep the property in this event. The term is used in various situations in which there has been a transfer without an intent that the transferee retain beneficial enjoyment of the property, but there is no beneficiary other than the settlor. It is the equitable counterpart to a reversion.[58] The term is also used for a "purchase money resulting trust" when one person pays for property which is transferred to another. See Section 6.4, note 48.

***Restatement***

Two of the many Restatements are particularly important in this area. The *Restatement (Second) of Trusts* was promulgated in 1959. Portions of a third version have been issued in draft form. The *Restatement (Second) of Property, Donative Transfers* now runs to four volumes, issued between 1981 and 1990, and already a Third Restatement on the subject is being drafted.

The *Restatement (Second) of Conflict of Laws* (1971) is important as to choice of law.

***restraint on alienation***

A rule designed to prevent property from becoming inalienable. It is different from, but associated with, the Rule against Perpetuities. See Section 11.8.

***reversion***

A future interest reserved the grantor, expressly or by implication. When *A* gives *B* a life estate, and the deed says nothing about what happens when *B* dies, the land will "revert" to *A*.

***revival***

When a will which revoked a prior will is in turn revoked, this may "revive" the first will. See Section 5.3.

***Rule against Perpetuities***

A common-law rule designed to prevent property from being tied up by the dead hand for too long. Discussed at length in Chapter 11.

***Rule in Shelley's case***

A virtually obsolete rule dealing with a remainder to the "heirs" of a life tenant. See Section 10.2, note 47.

58. *E.g.* Estate of Hull v. Williams, 885 P.2d 1153 (Idaho App.1994) (trust with indefinite terms). *See also Restatement (Third) of Trusts* §§ 7–8 (1996).

***separate property***

Contrasted with community property.

***settlor***

The term commonly used for a person who creates a trust. "Trustor" and "grantor" are also used occasionally.[59]

***sever***

The term for turning a joint tenancy into a tenancy in common. See Section 5.5, note 46.

***situs***

From the Latin *situs*, location. The situs of property is often important for choice of law. It is also important for venue; an estate can be administered "where property of the decedent was located" if the decedent was not domiciled in the state.[60] Situs is hard to determine in the case of much personal property, like shares of stock. See Section 1.2, note 17.

***specific devise***

A devise of specific property, such as "my house" or "my furniture," contrasted with a general or residuary devise. See Section 8.1.

***spendthrift trust***

A trust which restricts a beneficiary from alienating his/her interest and prevents creditors from reaching it. See Section 13.1.

***Statute of Frauds***

All or parts of the original English statute of 1676 have become part of the law in most American states. It (a) prescribed formal requirements for wills (later superseded in England by the Wills Act of 1837), (b) required a signed writing to convey land, to create a trust of land, and for certain contracts. See Sections 4.1, 4.5, and 4.9.

***testament/ testamentary/ testator***

From the Latin word for will, *testamentum*. In modern English, "will" has largely replaced testament, but the adjective "testamentary" is still current, *e.g.* a trust created by will is a testamentary trust, in contradistinction to a "living" trust.[61]

The person who executes a will is a testator. Testatrix, for a female, is archaic.[62]

***Totten trust***

Trusts of a bank account, named after a leading case which held them valid. See Section 4.6, note 39. They are really will substitutes and have little in common with ordinary trusts, since they terminate when the settlor dies.

**59.** *Restatement (Third) of Trusts* § 3, comm. a (1996); cf. Matter of Estate of West, 915 P.2d 504 (Utah App.1996) (referring to creators of a trust as "trustors")

**60.** Uniform Probate Code § 3–201.

**61.** *Restatement (Third) of Trusts* § 2, illus. 3, 5 (1996).

**62.** Uniform Probate Code § 1–201(52): " 'Testator' includes an individual of either sex."

***trust***

Certain uses of this multi-purpose word have nothing to do with the subject of this book, such as business trusts, and "trust deeds" which are a security device much like a mortgage.[63] The primary purposes of trusts covered in this book are described in Section 9.1.

***trustor***

A word sometimes used to designate the creator of a trust, although "settlor" is more common.

***Uniform Anatomical Gift Act***

Promulgated in 1987, and adopted in 15 states.[64] A 1968 version has been adopted in 35 states.

***Uniform Common Trust Fund Act***

Approved in 1938 and adopted in 34 states.

***Uniform Custodial Trust Act***

Approved in 1987 and adopted in 14 states. It allows standard trust provisions to be incorporated by reference.

***Uniform Disposition of Community Property Rights at Death Act***

Promulgated in 1971, adopted in 13 states. Discussed in Section 3.8, note 81.

***Uniform Fiduciaries Act***

Promulgated in 1922 and adopted in 24 states. The Act deals with situations "where one person deals with another whom he knows to be a fiduciary . . . The liabilities of the fiduciary himself are not dealt with but only the liabilities of the person dealing with the fiduciary." The parts of the Act dealing with the transfer of securities have been superseded by the Uniform Commercial Code and by a Uniform Act for the Simplification of Fiduciaries Securities Transfers. See Section 12.8, note 181.

***Uniform Management of Institutional Funds Act***

Forty six states have adopted this act which was approved in 1972. It deals with the management of funds held by charitable institutions.

***Uniform Principal and Income Act***

A version promulgated in 1931 has 8 adoptions. A revision in 1962 lists 34 adoptions. Revised again in 1997. Discussed in Section 9.4.

**63.** See also the disclaimer in *Restatement (Second) of Trusts* § 1, comm. b (1959); Uniform Probate Code § 1-201(53); Cal.Prob.Code § 82.

**64.** The state adoptions are listed at the beginning of each act in Uniform Laws Annotated, which give a citation to the place in the state statutes where the particular act appears. Some of these lists are problematic, since states often "adopt" an act but make many changes in it. Conversely, a state may not be listed as having adopted an act which has nevertheless been the source for many provisions in the state's code. This is particularly common in the case of the Uniform Probate Code.

***Uniform Probate Code***

Promulgated in 1969 and adopted in 15 states. A revised version of Article II appeared in 1990, and a revised version of Article VI appeared in 1989. The UPC has relatively few provisions dealing with trusts. The UPC incorporated certain existing Uniform acts, and many parts of it appear in free-standing versions, some of which have been more widely adopted than the UPC as a whole. A list of the more important ones follows:

**Disclaimer of Property Interests Act**[65]

Promulgated in 1978. 21 adoptions listed. See Section 2.8.

***Durable Power of Attorney Act***

Promulgated in 1979. 26 adoptions listed. Discussed in Section 7.2.

***Estate Tax Apportionment Act***

Promulgated in 1958, revised in 1964. Adoptions of the two versions total 14.

***Simultaneous Death Act***

Originally promulgated in 1940 and almost universally adopted. The UPC incorporates a revision made in 1991. Discussed in Section 8.3, note 86.

***Statutory Rule against Perpetuities***

Promulgated in 1986, revised and incorporated in the revised UPC. 20 adoptions. Discussed in Section 11.4.

***Testamentary Additions to Trusts Act***

Promulgated in 1960. 39 adoptions listed. Discussed in Section 6.2.

***Uniform Prudent Investor Act***

Approved in 1994 and adopted in over half the states. Discussed in Section 12.7.

***Uniform Statutory Form Power of Attorney Act***

Promulgated in 1988 and adopted in 3 states.

***Uniform Statutory Will Act***

Promulgated in 1984 and adopted in 2 states. It was drafted by knowledgeable estate planners as a model to be used primarily by lawyers less experienced in the field. It is often cited in this book as a reflection of what good drafters can do to handle or avoid many of the problems treated in the book.

***Uniform Supervision of Trustees for Charitable Purposes Act***

Approved in 1954 and enacted in 4 states.

**65.** Appears in UPC as § 2–801. This act was issued with two companions which split transfers at death and inter vivos transfers.

***Uniform Transfers to Minors Act***

Promulgated in 1983 and adopted in 42 states. A revision of the Uniform Gifts to Minors Act. Discussed in Section 9.2.

***Uniform Trustees' Powers Act***

Promulgated in 1964 and adopted in 16 states. Will be superseded by Uniform Trust Code for states which adopt that.

***Uniform Trust Code***

Not to be confused with the Uniform Trusts Act, which is much less comprehensive. Approved in 2000.

***Uniform Trusts Act***

Promulgated in 1937 and adopted in 6 states.

***vested remainder***

See **contingent remainder**.

***wait and see***

A reform of the common-law Rule against Perpetuities based on waiting to see if the interest vests in time. See Section 11.4.

***ward***

A person for whom a guardian has been appointed.

***waste***

Misuse or neglect of property by a life tenant which may be actionable by the remainderman.

***will contest***

A proceeding brought to have a will declared invalid, e.g. for incapacity or undue influence. In many states a contest can be instituted even after the will is admitted to probate. See Section 12.1.

***workers' compensation***

Statutes providing benefits to employees and their dependents for accidental injury or death of an employee.

***worthier title***

An almost obsolete doctrine which held that a gift to the "heirs" of a grantor or testator gave them no interest in the property conveyed. See Section 10.2, note 58.

***wrongful death***

Statutes abrogating the common law rule that death of an injured person abated any claim for the injury. They are discussed in Section 2.5.

## § 1.2 Conflict of Laws

### *Importance*

The law of wills is largely statutory. Although the laws of the American states agree on most basic points, they differ in many details. For example, in all states, when a person dies without a will, the surviving spouse gets a share of the estate, but the size of that share differs.[1] When the law of foreign countries is taken into account, the differences may become greater. Nearly all American states reject a "forced share" for children of a person who dies with a will, but many other countries provide for this.[2] Thus it often becomes important to decide which law applies to a case. A whole Restatement is devoted to the subject of conflict of laws.[3]

Various factors have been used to determine the governing law.

### *Designation by transferor*

Uniform Probate Code § 2–703 says that "the meaning and legal effect of a governing instrument is determined by the local law of the state selected in the governing instrument" with certain exceptions. A similar idea appears in other statutes[4] and in the Restatement.[5] Thus a statement in a will that "this will shall be governed by the law of Virginia" is usually controlling. Sometimes the choice of law designation is inferred. For example, the will of a testator who died in New York was held to show an intent to apply Massachusetts law to a trust created by the will which designated Massachusetts residents as trustees and provided for approval of successor trustees by a Massachusetts court. The court thought that this showed an intent to have Massachusetts law govern.[6]

This makes good sense insofar as the law seeks to effectuate intention, as it generally does. The Uniform Probate Code says that the "legal effect" as well as the "meaning" of a will can be controlled by the testator's designation,[7] but this is qualified in order to prevent a person from avoiding rules which limit freedom of choice, such as the elective share of the surviving spouse.[8] Courts have made similar limitations. A testator's designation of New York law in a will did not bar his spouse from claiming greater rights under the law of Virginia where the spouses were domiciled.[9] However, the same

§ 1.2

1. See Section 2.1.

2. See Section 3.2.

3. *Restatement (Second) of Conflict of Laws* (1971).

4. Cal.Prob.Code § 21103; N.Y.E.P.T.L. § 3–5.1(h); Unif.Trust Code § 109(b).

5. *Restatement (Second) of Conflict of Laws* § 224(1) (construction of conveyance of land), § 264(1) (construction of will of movables), § 268(1) (construction of a trust of movables). *See also* Cantor v. Department of Income Maintenance, 531 A.2d 608 (Conn.Super.1985) (Maryland law applied because trust instrument so provided).

6. Amerige v. Attorney General, 88 N.E.2d 126, 133 (Mass.1949). In Wilmington Trust Co. v. Wilmington Trust Co., 24 A.2d 309, 314 (Del.1942), a power to designate successor trustees was held to include naming a trustee in another state "with a consequent shifting of the controlling law."

7. The Restatement, on the other hand, distinguishes between "construction," as to which the testator's designation controls, (see the sections cited in the previous note), and "validity." *See Restatement (Second) of Conflict of Laws* §§ 239 (wills of land), 263 (wills of movables), 269 (testamentary trusts). However, Section 270 allows the designation of the settlor of an inter vivos trust to control its validity (with qualifications).

8. Uniform Probate Code § 2–703. *See also* Cal.Prob.Code § 21103.

9. Estate of Clark, 236 N.E.2d 152 (N.Y. 1968). *See also Restatement (Second) of Conflict of Laws* § 270, comm. b (1971).

court allowed a designation of New York law to defeat a claim by the testator's child to a forced share under the law of France, the testator's domicile.[10] The UPC provision which allows an instrument to select the governing law does not apply if this would produce a result to a "public policy of this state;" this caveat would not protect a policy of a state other than the forum.[11]

Can a testator (or other transferor) designate the law of a state which has no connection to the testator, the property or the beneficiaries? One court refused to respect a designation of Georgia law in a trust because Georgia had no such tie.[12] However, this is not a stated requirement in the UPC or the Restatement.[13]

Similar problems can arise in interpreting a contract which controls succession to property. For example, a wife waived her right to a share of her husband's estate by an ante-nuptial agreement which recited that it was to be governed by the law of New York, even though the parties were married in Connecticut where the husband later died. A Connecticut court gave effect to the choice of New York law, but only after determining that the provision had not been inserted in the contract by fraud or undue influence, and that New York had a substantial relationship to the parties (the wife was residing there).[14]

If I say "the law of X shall govern my will," I may mean to include X's rules on the choice of law, which may point to another state's substantive rules. Thus a trust provision that Massachusetts law should govern was held to include the Massachusetts rule that the legitimacy of a child was governed by the law of his domicile, which in this case was New Hampshire.[15] However, the Uniform Probate Code assumes that a reference to state law is intended to mean "the local law of the state" named.[16]

### *Situs*

The situs of land is often held to control the choice of law. For example, when a woman domiciled in Germany died owning land in Florida, the court

**10.** Matter of Estate of Renard, 439 N.E.2d 341 (N.Y.1982). *See also* Matter of Estate of Wright, 637 A.2d 106 (Me.1994) (designation of Maine law bars child's claim under Swiss law). In National Shawmut Bank v. Cumming, 91 N.E.2d 337 (Mass.1950), the settlor of an inter-vivos trust defeated his wife's claim to a share by providing that the trust would be governed by Massachusetts law.

**11.** Uniform Probate Code § 2–703; cf. Unif.Trust Code § 109(b) ("contrary to a strong public policy of the state having the most significant relationship to the matter at issue").

**12.** First National Bank v. Daggett, 497 N.W.2d 358 (Neb.1993). *See also* Morris & Leach, *The Rule Against Perpetuities* 25 (1962); Effland, *Will Construction Under the Uniform Probate Code* 63 Ore.L.Rev. 337, 346 (1984).

**13.** *Restatement (Second) of Conflict of Laws* §§ 224, comm. e, 264, comm. e, 268, comm. b. But if the question is the validity of the trust, the designated state must have "a substantial relation to the trust." *Id.* § 270, comm. b. The Hague Convention on the Law Applicable to Succession to the Estates of Deceased Persons, approved in 1989, allows designation only of a state where the designator is or was a "habitual resident." Schoenblum, *Multijurisdictional Estates and Article II of the UPC*, 55 Alb.L.Rev. 1291, 1324 (1992).

**14.** Elgar v. Elgar, 679 A.2d 937 (Conn. 1996) (following *Restatement, Second, Conflict of Law* § 187 (1971).

**15.** Powers v. Steele, 475 N.E.2d 395 (Mass.1985). See also Wilmington Trust Co. v. Annan, 531 A.2d 1209 (Del.Ch.1987) (reference to law of Quebec leads to law of domicile).

**16.** Uniform Probate Code § 2–703.

applied Florida law to determine her heirs as to her land there.[17] Many state statutes, and the Restatement, are similar.[18]

This rule has not gone unchallenged. Scoles and Hay argue that "the law of the situs ... often defeats the superior interests or policy concerns of nonsitus states."[19] A person who leaves property in several states probably considers the "estate and its economic well-being as a unit without regard to where the parts are located," but the situs rule often imposes different laws on the various parts of the estate.[20] Thus when a Virginia resident left her estate to the issue of her children, even though Virginia held this did not include adopted children, a Nebraska court awarded her land in Nebraska to an adopted child under the situs rule.[21]

In certain contexts the situs rule protects legitimate interests. It allows prospective purchasers of land to consult the law with which they will be most familiar.[22] In other situations the interest of the situs is more doubtful, for example, a dispute between members of a family who reside in another state.

The situs rule in the case of land is easy to apply.[23] The leading alternative is to look to the law of the owner's domicile, which, as we shall see, is often hard to determine. But situs can also be hard to determine when the concept is applied to personal property.

Generally the situs rule is confined to land. This raises the question, what is land and what is personal property? If I own a company which owns land, should we focus on the stock which represents my interest (personal property) or the underlying asset, the land?[24] Is a leasehold land or personal property?[25]

**17.** In re Estate of Salathe, 703 So.2d 1167 (Fla.App.1997). *See also* Matter of Estate of Allen, 772 P.2d 297 (Mont.1989); Cohn v. Heymann, 544 So.2d 1242 (La.App.1989)(forced heirship allowed as to Louisiana land); First National Bank v. Daggett, 497 N.W.2d 358 (Neb.1993) (despite designation of Georgia law in trust instrument); In re Estate of Rubert, 651 A.2d 937 (N.H.1994) (right of pretermitted heir).

**18.** Cal. Civil Code § 755 (land within California governed by California law); N.Y.E.P.T.L. § 3–5.1(b)(1); Mass.Gen.Laws ch. 199, § 1; *Restatement (Second) of Conflict of Laws* §§ 223 (conveyance of land), 277–78 (trust of land). The reference to the law of the situs may eventually lead somewhere else. In Matter of Estate of Wright, 637 A.2d 106 (Me. 1994), a treaty referred questions to the law of the situs, but this was held to include the conflicts rules of the situs, which allowed the testator to designate a different law. However, "in most situations the courts of the state of the situs will apply its local law." *Restatement (Second) of Conflict of Laws* § 278, comm. a (1971).

**19.** Scoles & Hay, *Conflict of Laws* 798 (2d ed. 1992). *See also* Weintraub, *Obstacles to Sensible Choice of Law for Determining Marital Property Rights on Divorce or in Probate*, 25 Houston L.Rev 1113, 1122 (1988).

**20.** Scoles and Hay, *supra* note 19, at 796. *See also* Reif v. Reif, 621 N.E.2d 1279 (Ohio App.1993); Howard v. Reynolds, 283 N.E.2d 629 (Ohio 1972) (looking to the law of the owner's domicile in order to treat the estate as a unit). For a case in which the situs rule produced an injustice as to an estate which was "spread around the world" see Re Collens, [1986] 1 All E.R. 611 (Ch. 1985).

**21.** In re Estate of Hannan, 523 N.W.2d 672 (Neb.1994).

**22.** *Restatement (Second) of Conflict of Laws* § 223, comm. b (1971).

**23.** Pfau v. Moseley, 222 N.E.2d 639 (Ohio 1966) (citing the desirability of certainty in applying the law of the situs).

**24.** Cohn v. Heymann, 544 So.2d 1242 (La. App.1989) treated the stock as personal property in this situation. *See also* Blood v. Poindexter, 534 N.E.2d 768 (Ind.Tax 1989); Indiana Department of State Revenue v. Estate of Puschel, 582 N.E.2d 923 (Ind.Tax 1991) (interest in trust holding land is personal property).

**25.** N.Y.E.P.T.L. § 3–5.1(a)(1) defines "real property" to include leaseholds. For a general discussion see *Restatement (Second) of Conflict of Laws* § 278, comm. e (1971).

Classification may be affected by "equitable conversion." For example, a will directed the executor to sell the testator's property and distribute the proceeds to "my heirs at law." The testator owned land in Indiana, but the court determined his heirs under the law of Illinois, the state of his residence, because "a direction in a will to the executor to sell realty converts such realty into personalty."[26] The result would have been different if the will had simply *authorized,* rather than *directed* a sale of his land.[27]

Although the law of the situs is primarily important for land, in some situations it governs personal property as well. For example, a man died intestate without heirs. He was a resident of Illinois but had a bank account in Washington. The account escheated to Washington. When "property goes by escheat ... the country in which the property is located is entitled to the funds rather than the country in which the decedent was domiciled."[28] When a resident of Brazil opened a trust account in a New York bank, a court applied New York law on the theory that the owner had "elected" to have New York law govern when he chose a bank there.[29]

The situs of property may be relevant for purposes other than the choice of law. Tangible property within the United States is subject to our gift taxes even when owned by a nonresident.[30] A will can generally be probated where the testator was domiciled or where she had property.[31] If she owned stock, or had a bank account, where are they located for this purpose? Under the Uniform Probate Code, claims represented instruments (like a stock certificate) are located where the instrument is, and other claims are located "where the debtor resides or, if the debtor is a person other than an individual, at the place where is has its principal office."[32] For federal gift tax purposes, debts owed by an American and stock issued by an American corporation are deemed to be situated within the United States even though owned by a non-resident.[33] The rules are sufficiently murky that more than one state may have a reasonable claim to be the situs of some assets.

### *Domicile*

The law of the owner's domicile is usually determinative as to personal property, or "movables," the term commonly used in conflicts literature.[34] This concept is often expressed by the Latin maxim *mobilia sequuntur*

**26.** Moore v. Livingston, 265 N.E.2d 251 (Ind.App.1970). *See also* In re Estate of Janney, 446 A.2d 1265 (Pa.1982) (N.J. law not controlling because land in N.J. had been sold); Cal.Prob. Code § 21107; *Restatement (Second) of Conflict of Laws* § 225 (1971).

**27.** 5 *Amer. Law of Prop.* § 22.58. Thus in In re Estate of Hannan, 523 N.W.2d 672 (Neb. 1994), the court applied Nebraska law to the sale proceeds of land in Nebraska even though the testator was domiciled in Virginia.

**28.** O'Keefe v. State, Department of Revenue, 488 P.2d 754 (Wash.1971). Some states, however, give intangibles (like a bank account) to the state of the intestate's residence if that state would recognize its claim in the converse case. Cal.Prob. Code § 6805(b).

**29.** Neto v. Thorner, 718 F.Supp. 1222 (S.D.N.Y.1989). *See also* De Werthein v. Gotlib, 594 N.Y.S.2d 230 (A.D.1993); Sanchez v. Sanchez De Davila, 547 So.2d 943 (Fla.App.1989) (applying Florida law on similar facts against children's claim under Venezuela law); Dawson v. Capital Bank & Trust Co., 261 So.2d 727 (La.App.1972) (applying Louisiana law to a bank account owned by a Mississippi resident).

**30.** Internal Revenue Code § 2501.

**31.** *Restatement (Second) of Conflict of Laws* § 314 (1971); Uniform Probate Code § 3-201; Cal.Prob.Code §§ 7051-52.

**32.** Uniform Probate Code § 3-201(d).

**33.** Internal Revenue Code § 2511(b).

**34.** *Restatement (Second) of Conflict of Laws* §§ 260 (intestate succession), 263 (validity and effect of will), 264 (construction of will), 265 (spouse's forced share).

*personam*, movables follow the person. Thus an Ohio court applied Vermont law to determine the inheritance of the assets of a decedent who died domiciled in Vermont.[35] When a man domiciled in New York died owning property in Louisiana, his wife invoked Louisiana law to claim a share as community property. Her claim was allowed as to land, but not as to the personal property, since Louisiana was said to have no interest "in protecting and regulating the rights of married persons residing and domiciled in New York."[36]

The Uniform Probate Code uses domicile to determine the elective share of a surviving spouse as to *all* the decedent's property, including land.[37] California subjects even land outside the state acquired by couples domiciled in California to its community property laws.[38] Conversely, if a couple domiciled elsewhere acquires land in California, the spouse's rights to an elective share in the land are governed by the law of the domicile.[39] Domicile is also an important concept in the assessment of taxes. For example, the estate of a citizen or resident of the United States is subject to United States estate tax regardless where the property is situated.[40]

Some courts refer to the law of the testator's domicile when construing a will even when land is involved.[41] When a couple owned a condominium in Florida, their respective liability on the mortgage was determined by the law of their domicile.

> Even though the property is located in Florida ... the settling of debts between District of Columbia domiciliaries appears to us to be of paramount interest to the District of Columbia.[42]

Since many persons own property located in more than one jurisdiction, but have a single domicile, reference to the law of the domicile has the advantage of treating the owner's property as a unit. It is unlikely that a

**35.** Howard v. Reynolds, 283 N.E.2d 629 (Ohio 1972). *See also* Morris v. Cullipher, 816 S.W.2d 878 (Ark.1991) (applying law of domicile , Arkansas, as to CDs issued by Texas bank); In re Estate of Rubert, 651 A.2d 937 (N.H.1994) (personal property governed by law of Virginia since decedent domiciled there at death); Knight v. Knight, 589 N.Y.S.2d 195 (A.D.1992); Fifth Third Bank v. Crosley, 669 N.E.2d 904, 908 (Ohio Com.Pl.1996) (applying Florida law in construing a will since testator was domiciled there at death). *But cf.* Cal.Civil Code § 946 ("*if there is no law to the contrary, in the place where personal property is situated*, it is deemed to follow the person of its owner, and is governed by the law of his domicile"); note 29 supra.

**36.** Estate of Crichton, 228 N.E.2d 799 (N.Y.1967). *See also Restatement (Second) of Conflict of Laws* § 265 (1971).

**37.** Uniform Probate Code § 2–202(d). *See also* Lotz v. Atamaniuk, 304 S.E.2d 20 (W.Va. 1983) (applying law of domicile to defeat claim). However, Professor Schoenblum suggests that non-UPC states in which land is located will not in fact defer to this choice of law. Schoenblum, *Multijurisdictional Estates and Article II of the UPC*, 55 Alb.L.Rev. 1291, 1315 (1992). In Banks v. Junk, 264 So.2d 387 (Miss.1972), the court refused to apply Mississippi law to land in Louisiana owned by a Mississippi domiciliary.

**38.** Cal. Family Code § 760.

**39.** Cal.Prob.Code § 120. *See also* Estate of Rhoades, 607 N.Y.S.2d 893 (Sup.1994) (refusing to apply N.Y. law since decedent domiciled in Florida). *Contra*, La.Civ.Code art. 10.

**40.** Internal Revenue Code §§ 2001(a), 2031(a). Section 2014 gives a credit for taxes paid to a foreign country "in respect to any property situated within such foreign country" included in the estate. *See* Share, *Domicile is Key to Determining Transfer Tax of Non–Citizens*, 22 Est.Plann. 31 (1995).

**41.** Beauchamp v. Beauchamp, 574 So.2d 18, 20–21 (Miss.1990); Estate of Buckley, 677 S.W.2d 946 (Mo.App.1984); *Restatement (Second) of Conflict of Laws* § 224, illus. 1 (1971).

**42.** Sarbacher v. McNamara, 564 A.2d 701, 707 (D.C.App.1989).

testator intended words in a will to have different meaning when applied to land as distinguished from personalty.

Domicile may also be important in questions of status, which in turn may control inheritance. Thus when a man claimed to inherit a share of his "wife's" estate, the court applied German law to determine the validity of their marriage, because they were domiciled there.[43]

Domicile is often hard to determine. Although the words domicile and residence are often used interchangeably, they are not the same. For example, when a man died in a nursing home where he had lived for 8 years, the court held he was not domiciled there. "A change of domicile requires 'an actual moving with an intent to go to a given place and remain there.' "[44] Conversely, a residence of only a few days may constitute a change of domicile when there was an intent to make the new residence home.[45] A person may have several residences, but only one domicile.[46]

Since reasonable minds can often differ as to where a person was domiciled, courts sometimes reach conflicting decisions on the question. A finding in state *A* that the decedent was domiciled there bars a court in state *B* from finding otherwise only as to parties over whom the court in state *A* had jurisdiction.[47] But under the Uniform Probate Code, when conflicting claims of domicile arise in different states, "the determination of domicile in the proceeding first commenced must be accepted as determinative" on the theory that "the decedent would prefer that his estate be unified under either rule rather than wasted in litigation."[48]

When courts refer to the law of the domicile, they usually mean that of the decedent at the time of death.[49] However, when a testator was domiciled in New York when she executed her will, but moved to New Hampshire before she died, the court refused to look to New Hampshire because the will had been executed with reference to New York law.[50] According to the Restatement, courts "usually construe a given word or phrase [in a will] in accor-

**43.** In re Estate of Salathe, 703 So.2d 1167 (Fla.App.1997).

**44.** Matter of Estate of Brown, 587 N.E.2d 686, 689 (Ind.App.1992). *See also* Nora v. Nora, 494 So.2d 16 (Ala.1986) (decedent who spent the last 36 years of his life in Alabama remained domiciled in Louisiana); Matter of Estate of Marcos, 963 P.2d 1124 (Haw.1998) (Marcos not domiciled in Hawaii although he spent the last 3 1/2 years of his life there); Gellerstedt v. United Missouri Bank, 865 S.W.2d 707 (Mo.App.1993) (move to Missouri nursing home did not necessarily show a change of domicile).

**45.** In re Estate of Elson, 458 N.E.2d 637 (Ill.App.1983).

**46.** Hager v. Hager, 607 N.E.2d 63 (Ohio App.1992); Matter of Estate of Burshiem, 483 N.W.2d 175 (N.D.1992).

**47.** *Restatement (Second) of Conflict of Laws* § 317 (1971); In re Estate of Rubert, 651 A.2d 937 (N.H.1994) (Virginia court's determination contested by interested parties there was entitled to full faith and credit); In re Estate of Tolson, 947 P.2d 1242 (Wash.App. 1997) (California court's determination that decedent was domiciled there entitled to full faith and credit).

**48.** Uniform Probate Code § 3–202.

**49.** *Restatement (Second) of Conflict of Laws* §§ 260, 263, 264 (1971).

**50.** Royce v. Estate of Denby, 379 A.2d 1256 (N.H.1977). In this case, since the testator was incapacitated during her residence in New Hampshire, arguably she never changed her domicile. *See Restatement (Second) of Conflict of Laws* § 23, comm. b (1971). In Matter of Estate of Garver, 343 A.2d 817 (N.J.Super.App.Div.1975), the court also refused to apply the law of the domicile at death on the ground that it would defeat the decedent's intent.

Professor Schoenblum criticizes the UPC using domicile without regard to its duration as the basis for the spouse's elective share. Schoenblum, *Multijurisdictional Estates and Article II of the UPC*, 55 Alb.L.Rev. 1291, 1316 (1992).

dance with the usage prevailing in the state where the testator was domiciled at the time the will was executed, [since] this would presumably be in accord with the expectations of the testator."[51]

In some cases, the court considers the domicile of the decedent's survivors rather than that of the decedent. Thus when a question arose as to the rights to insurance proceeds on a policy on the life of a man who worked in Arkansas, the court looked to Oklahoma law because all of the claimants lived there.[52]

### *Forum*

Sometimes the forum simply applies its own law. According to the Restatement, "a court usually applies its own local rules prescribing how litigation shall be conducted."[53] This is justified by the fact that on such question it may be difficult to apply another state's rules, and the parties do not rely on them in entering transactions since they do not anticipate litigation at all.[54] Thus in a dispute over insurance an Oregon court refused to apply a Washington statute which would have barred the insured's widow from testifying, even though Washington substantive law governed the case.[55] Similarly, an Arkansas court applied its own law as to burden of proof and presumptions in considering probate of a will executed in Tennessee.[56]

Some courts say that in the absence of satisfactory proof of contrary applicable foreign law, the law of the forum should be applied. Thus even though a decedent was domiciled in Mexico when he died, a New York court applied its own law, since it was "reluctant to take upon itself the burden of determining what the law of Mexico is."[57]

### *Interests*

Professor Schoenblum criticizes the Uniform Probate Code's use of domicile for most choice of law questions, arguing for a "broader interests analysis favored in one form or another by many conflicts scholars."[58] The Restatement, while restating the more traditional rules described above on many issues, says that for inter vivos trusts where the governing law is not designated by the settlor, the court should look to "the local law of the state with which, as to the matter at issue, the trust has its most significant

**51.** *Restatement (Second) of Conflict of Laws* § 264, comm. f (1971). *See also id.* § 268, comm. f; Estate of Buckley, 677 S.W.2d 946 (Mo.App.1984). But in Gellerstedt v. United Missouri Bank, 865 S.W.2d 707 (Mo.App.1993), even though the testator was clearly domiciled in Kansas when she executed her will, the court held that if she had changed it to Missouri before she died, Missouri law should control.

**52.** Whirlpool Corp. v. Ritter, 929 F.2d 1318, 1321 (8th Cir.1991). *See also* Matter of Estate of Gilmore, 946 P.2d 1130, 1138 (N.M.App.1997) (interest of state of decedent's domicile is "slight" as against the domicile of the potential beneficiaries of a wrongful death claim).

**53.** *Restatement (Second) of Conflict of Laws* § 122 (1971).

**54.** *Id.* comm. a.

**55.** Equitable Life Assurance Society v. McKay, 760 P.2d 871 (Or.1988), following *Restatement (Second) of Conflict of Laws* § 138 (1971).

**56.** Warner v. Warner, 687 S.W.2d 856 (Ark.App.1985). *See also Restatement (Second) of Conflict of Laws* §§ 133–34 (1971). *But cf.* Matter of Estate of Gilmore, 946 P.2d 1130, 1133 (N.M.App.1997) (the disposition of wrongful death proceeds is not a "procedural" matter governed by the law of the forum).

**57.** Matter of Estate of Edwards, 452 N.Y.S.2d 293 (N.Y.Surr.1982). *See also Restatement (Second) of Conflict of Laws* § 136, comm. f (1971).

**58.** Schoenblum, supra note 13 at 1317.

relationship."[59] This permits consideration of several factors, including the place of execution of the trust, the situs of the assets, the domicile of the settlor and of the beneficiaries.[60]

This flexible approach has had a mixed reception in the courts. A Louisiana court rejected it since the Louisiana Civil Code required reference to the law of the decedent's domicile, but the court added that "even under the interest analysis" the result would probably be the same.[61] Other courts have sometimes expressly "rejected wooden applications of the traditional conflicts rules" in favor of "choices of law based on the relevant policies and interests at stake in given situations."[62] In a case involving a contract to devise property to the promissor's child, the court applied Massachusetts law, even though the promissor died domiciled in New Hampshire, because Massachusetts "has the most significant relationship to the transaction," since the contract was negotiated and executed and the beneficiaries resided there.[63]

### *Favoring Validity*

A recurring theme in discussions of choice of law is fulfilling the expectations of the transferor (testator, settlor, etc.). This underlies a liberal rule as to the formal validity of wills. Under the Uniform Probate Code a will is valid if it complies with the Code *or* with the law of the place where the will was executed *or* where the testator was domiciled, the purpose being "to provide a wide opportunity for validation of expectations of testators."[64] The Uniform Trust Code goes even further for inter-vivos trusts, allowing them to be valid also if they comply with the law of the trustee's domicile or place of business or where any trust property was located.[65] Many states have similar provisions,[66] and courts may reach this result even without a statute "where the requirements of form * * * have been satisfied in substance."[67] Thus when a will attested by interested witnesses was executed in Florida, which allowed

**59.** *Restatement (Second) of Conflict of Laws* § 270(2) (1971). *See also* Uniform Trust Code § 109(b)(2).

**60.** *Restatement, Second, Conflict of Laws* § 270, comm. c (1971). In Fifth Third Bank v. Crosley, 669 N.E.2d 904, 908 (Ohio Com.Pl. 1996), the court applied Ohio law to two living trusts on the ground that they were "executed in Ohio and the situs of each trust is Ohio," presumably because the trustee was an Ohio trust company.

**61.** Cohn v. Heymann, 544 So.2d 1242 (La. App.1989). The court noted that the children who sought to apply Louisiana law to get a forced share were domiciled in New York. In Lewis v. Steinreich, 652 N.E.2d 981 (Ohio 1995), the court, following the Restatement, looked to the state with "the most significant contacts," but this turned out to be the decedent's domicile.

**62.** Royce v. Estate of Denby, 379 A.2d 1256, 1259 (N.H.1977). *See also* Whirlpool Corp. v. Ritter, 929 F.2d 1318, 1321 (8th Cir. 1991).

**63.** Nile v. Nile, 734 N.E.2d 1153, 1161 (Mass.2000).

**64.** Unif.Prob.Code § 2–506, comment. *See also Restatement, Third, of Property (Wills and Other Donative Transfers)* § 3.1, comm. e (1998) (favoring rule "as a principle of decisional law" where no statute).

**65.** Unif.Trust Code § 109(a).

**66.** Cal.Prob.Code § 6113; *Restatement (Second) of Conflict of Laws* § 263, comm. c (1971); Scoles & Hay, *supra* note 19, § 20.9. In Matter of Estate of Zelikovitz, 923 P.2d 740 (Wyo.1996), a codicil was probated under such a statute; since it was valid under Wyoming law, it was not necessary to examine its validity under the law of Oklahoma where it was executed. However, Schoeblum notes that many states with similar statutes "do not go as far as the UPC." Schoenblum, *supra* note 13, at 1294.

**67.** *Restatement (Second) of Conflict of Laws* § 223, comm. e (1971). But in Matter of Estate of Campbell, 673 P.2d 645 (Wyo.1983), the court applied the law of the state of execution to invalidate a will which would have been valid by the law of the state of domicile.

this, it could be probated in Ohio, where the testator was domiciled at death, even though Ohio invalidated devises to interested witnesses.[68]

The UPC is limited to "written" wills, and so would not validate an oral will even if made by a testator in a jurisdiction which allowed them.[69] Nor can the rule be used to escape from limitations of testamentary freedom, such as the spouse's elective share; if a testator executed a will in a state which did not give spouses an elective share, the spouse could claim a share under the law of the testator's domicile even though the will was formally valid.[70]

The choice of law rules on marriage reflect a similar attitude of sustaining its validity if possible. "There is a strong inclination to uphold a marriage because of the hardship that might otherwise be visited upon the parties and their children."[71] Generally a marriage which satisfies the requirements of the state where it took place will be recognized in other states.[72] But even a marriage invalid where contracted may be valid when "it would be valid under the local law of some other state having a substantial relation to the parties," such as their domicile.[73]

The question whether a child is "legitimate" crops up frequently as to succession to property. Here also the choice of law may be determinative. According to the Restatement, "the law favors the status of legitimacy" so that a change of domicile may operate in the child's favor, but not against a claim.[74] Thus when a child was born out of wedlock in Ohio but died domiciled in Washington, the court applied Washington law which allowed her paternal relatives to inherit. Acknowledging that "determinations of personal status" were usually governed by the place of birth, the question here was inheritance, and as to this, Washington had the dominant interest.[75] A child who had been declared legitimate under German law, where his father was domiciled at the time, was deemed legitimate under Illinois law where the child died so that the father's relatives could inherit from the child, because

**68.** Hairelson v. Estate of Franks, 720 N.E.2d 989 (Ohio App.1998).

**69.** Schoenblum criticizes the writing requirement in Uniform Probate Code § 2–506, arguing that an oral manifestation of intent may be more reliable than a writing. Schoenblum, supra note 13, at 1300.

**70.** Uniform Probate Code § 2–202(d).

**71.** *Restatement (Second) of Conflict of Laws* § 283, comm. h (1971). The hardships historically inflicted on children of unmarried parents has been considerably reduced in recent years by the trend to give equivalent rights to children born out of wedlock. See Section 2.9.

**72.** *Id.* § 283(2); Cal. Family Code § 308; Estate of Loughmiller, 629 P.2d 156 (Kan. 1981) (marriage between first cousins valid because celebrated in state which allowed it). This principle is sometimes rejected when the marriage occurred during a brief visit by a couple which was domiciled elsewhere. Vaughn v. Hufnagel, 473 S.W.2d 124 (Ky.1971); Matter of Lamb's Estate, 655 P.2d 1001 (N.M.1982); In re Stahl's Estate, 301 N.E.2d 82 (Ill.App. 1973); Matter of Marriage of Wharton, 639 P.2d 652 (Or.App.1982). *But see* Mott v. Duncan Petroleum Trans., 414 N.E.2d 657 (N.Y. 1980); Estate of Smart v. Smart, 676 P.2d 1379 (Okl.App.1983); Renshaw v. Heckler, 787 F.2d 50 (2d Cir.1986).

**73.** *Restatement (Second) of Conflict of Laws* § 283, comm. i (1971). *See also* In re Estate of Shippy, 678 P.2d 848 (Wash.App. 1984) (marriage valid under Washington law where couple resided when husband died, even though invalid in Alaska where marriage contracted); Unif. Marriage and Divorce Act § 210 (marriages valid by place contracted *or* by domicil of the parties are valid); Allen v. Storer, 600 N.E.2d 1263 (Ill.App.1992) (common-law marriage valid because couple was domiciled in Ohio which allowed them).

**74.** *Restatement (Second) of Conflict of Laws* § 287, comm. d (1971).

**75.** Matter of Estate of Cook, 698 P.2d 1076 (Wash.App.1985). *See also* Buchea v. United States, 154 F.3d 1114 (9th Cir.1998) (even though tribal customary adoption did not terminate parental rights, it has that effect under governing Alaska law).

this result was "consistent with public policy which generally favors the status of legitimacy."[76]

### *Drafting*

One who undertakes to draft a will or trust should be familiar with the choice of law issues discussed above. The client may have property in another jurisdiction either now or later, or may die domiciled in another state or country. A provision in the instrument which specifies the governing law will in most instances be respected and may avoid undesirable rules or uncertainty as to the governing law.

The client should be advised to make his/her domicile clear; otherwise the estate may possibly be subject to litigation on the issue, and to double taxation.[77] A recital in a will as to the testator's domicile is helpful, since domicile is largely a question of intent,[78] but not conclusive, since the testator may have changed domicile after signing the will.[79]

## § 1.3 Change in the Law

Although the law of property has a reputation for being conservative, it has been subject to many changes over time. A question which often arises as to the time when a change in the law becomes effective. The answer to this may depend on whether the change comes about by a judicial decision overruling prior cases or by a statute. Because of the somewhat fictitious notion that judges "discover" the law but do not make it, they ordinarily do not hesitate to apply their rulings to cases which arose earlier. According to Blackstone, when judges find that an older decision "is most evidently contrary to reason," they "do not pretend to make a new law, but to vindicate the old one from misinterpretation. For if it be found that the former decision is manifestly absurd or unjust, it is declared, not that such a sentence was *bad law*, but that it was *not law*.[1]" Despite this comforting rationalization, judges hesitate to overrule precedents on which parties may have relied, and may prefer to leave a questionable rule unchanged. Blackstone, for example, cites the common law rule which barred half blood relatives from inheriting land, saying that "though a modern judge * * * might wish [the rule] had been otherwise settled, yet it is not in his power to alter it."[2] Similar reasoning can be found in modern cases.[3]

**76.** In re Estate of Janussek, 666 N.E.2d 774 (Ill.App.1996). *See also* Powers v. Steele, 475 N.E.2d 395 (Mass.1985); Lucas v. Estate of Stavos, 609 N.E.2d 1114 (Ind.App.1993) (Louisiana judgment establishing paternity is entitled to full faith and credit in Indiana wrongful death suit). *But see* In re Dumaine, 600 A.2d 127 (N.H.1991) (applying New Hampshire law to bar a child born out of wedlock in New York).

**77.** Parks, *Special Estate Planning Strategies to fit the Needs of the Mobile Client*, 18 Est.Plan. 150 (1991). As to double taxation based on inconsistent findings as to domicile see Scoles & Hay, supra note 19, § 4.5.

**78.** The court relied on a will recital in determining domicile in Matter of Estate of Brown, 587 N.E.2d 686 (Ind.App.1992); Cohn v. Heymann, 544 So.2d 1242 (La.App.1989); Le Sueur v. Robinson, 557 N.E.2d 796 (Ohio App. 1988).

**79.** Lotz v. Atamaniuk, 304 S.E.2d 20 (W.Va.1983) (finding of Ohio domicile erroneous even though the will recited it).

§ 1.3

**1.** 1 Blackstone, *Commentaries* *69–70 (1765).

**2.** *Id.* 71. For the modern rules on this question see Section 2.2, note 58.

**3.** Wasserman v. Cohen, 606 N.E.2d 901 (Mass.1993) (adhering to the rules of ademption because "stability in the field of trusts and

However, judges today sometimes overrule precedents prospectively. For example, in 1984 a court announced that "for the future we shall no longer follow the rule announced" in an earlier case, but since "the bar has been entitled reasonably to rely on that rule in advising clients" the new rule would apply only in future cases.[4] Such prospective overruling is rather rare. One court has said that it "should be limited to a case in which the hardship on a party who has relied on the old rule outweighs the hardship on the party denied the benefit of the new rule; and there are few cases where such rigorous demonstrations can be made."[5] On the other hand, it is not unusual for a precedent-breaking decision in one case not to be applied retroactively in similar cases. For example, in 1988 the United States Supreme Court in *Tulsa* held unconstitutional a state statute which barred claims against a decedent's estate after notice by publication to creditors.[6] The next year another case arose involving a claim by a creditor against an estate which had closed in 1987. The relevant state statute "involved the same constitutional infirmities" as the one held invalid in *Tulsa*, but the court refused to apply *Tulsa*, because retroactive application "could cause the disturbance of many property rights" which had "created immeasurable reliance" and were "unexpectedly declared invalid."[7]

When change in law comes through legislation, the effective date usually depends upon the terms of the statute. In most states, for example, the common-law Rule in Shelley's Case has been abolished by statutes which are expressly limited to instruments executed after the statute was passed.[8] The Uniform Trust Code alters the common law by making trusts presumptively revocable, but this rule is expressly inapplicable to trusts created before the Code becomes effective.[9] On the other hand, a statute passed in 1997 was applied to a conveyance made in 1996 because the court accepted the legislature's claim that the statute was "intended as a clarification of existing law and not as a new enactment."[10] Sometimes courts even use statutes which by their terms are prospective only as evidence of a state "policy" which should be applied retrospectively.[11]

estates requires that we continue the doctrine").

**4.** Sullivan v. Burkin, 460 N.E.2d 572, 576–77 (Mass.1984). *See also* Jeruzal's Estate v. Jeruzal, 130 N.W.2d 473 (Minn.1964); Rosenberg v. Lipnick, 389 N.E.2d 385 (Mass.1979).

**5.** Decker v. Meriwether, 708 S.W.2d 390, 394–95 (Tenn.App.1985).

**6.** Tulsa Professional Collection Services v. Pope, 485 U.S. 478 (1988).

**7.** Hanesworth v. Johnke, 783 P.2d 173, 176–77 (Wyo.1989). *See also* Farm Credit Bank v. Brown, 577 N.E.2d 906, 911 (Ill.App.1991). *But see* In re Estate of Reynolds, 970 P.2d 537, 543 (Kan.1998) (applying *Tulsa* retroactively).

**8.** Society Nat. Bank v. Jacobson, 560 N.E.2d 217 (Ohio 1990) (Rule applied even though statute abolished in 1941 because the trust was created in 1931); Toler v. Harbour, 589 S.W.2d 529 (Tex.Civ.App.1979); City Bank and Trust Co. v. Morrissey, 454 N.E.2d 1195 (Ill.App.1983). As to the Rule in Shelley's Case see Section 10.2, at note 47 et seq.

Often such legislation is expressly made prospective because of doubts, not necessarily well founded, about the constitutionality of retroactive legislation. Leach, *Perpetuities Legislation, Massachusetts Style*, 67 Harv.L.Rev. 1349, 1365 (1954).

**9.** Unif.Trust Code § 602(a).

**10.** Premier Property Management, Inc. v. Chavez, 728 N.E.2d 476, 480 (Ill.2000). *See also* Noggle v. Bank of America, 82 Cal.Rptr.2d 829, 834 (App.1999); Department of Social Serv. v. Saunders, 724 A.2d 1093 (Conn.1999); Matter of Estate of Thomas, 998 P.2d 560, 562 (Nev.2000) ("amendment is persuasive evidence of what the legislature intended by the prior statute").

**11.** Warner v. Whitman, 233 N.E.2d 14, 17 (Mass.1968) (perpetuities reform statute); In re Arens' Trust, 197 A.2d 1 (N.J.1964) (Principal and Income Act); Estate of Coe, 201 A.2d 571 (N.J.1964) (inclusion of adopted child in class gift); In re Estate of Hollister, 221 N.E.2d 376, 379 (N.Y.1966) (concurring opinion).

Statutes which do not make clear when they become applicable are usually presumed to be prospective. Courts give "retrospective applications to statutes 'only when the mandate of the legislature [to do so] is imperative.' "[12] Even when a statute is clearly stated to apply retrospectively, a court may hold that this is unconstitutional. For example, a wife put title to a house bought with her funds put into joint tenancy with her husband who agreed orally that the house was to remain her separate property. The legislature later passed a statute providing that property held in joint tenancy was presumed to be community property unless there was a written agreement to the contrary. The statute purported to apply to pending proceedings, but the court held this was an unconstitutional impairment of the wife's property rights. If existing law had required the parties to execute a writing to prove their agreement, they would probably have done so. "The parties' legitimate expectations, therefore, are substantially disregarded in favor of needless retroactivity."[13] On the other hand, many other constitutional attacks on retroactive legislation have failed. For example, a statute which restricted gifts to lawyers in instruments which they drafted was applied to a revocable trust drafted before the statute was enacted. This did not violate due process because the lawyer "did not have a vested right" under the trust so long as it was revocable.[14]

Today there is less reluctance to make changes in the law retroactive than formerly. For example, the first Uniform Principal and Income Act (1931) did not apply to trusts in existence when the Act was adopted, but the second version (1962) does, and has been held constitutional.[15] More recently the Uniform Prudent Investor Act was expressly made applicable to trusts existing at the time of its adoption, though only to "actions occurring thereafter."[16] When in 1955, Illinois changed existing law to presume that adopted children were included in class gifts, it did so only as to instruments thereafter executed, but in 1989, it made the new rule applicable to all instruments, regardless of when they were made.[17]

**12.** Connecticut Bank & Trust Co. v. Brody, 392 A.2d 445, 451 (Conn.1978) (perpetuities reform statute). *See also* Levy v. Crawford, 600 N.E.2d 597, 598 (Mass.App.1992); Estate of Hilton, 52 Cal.Rptr.2d 491 (App.1996) (change in statutory fees of attorney for an estate); Ohio Citizens Bank v. Mills, 543 N.E.2d 1206 (Ohio 1989) (inclusion of adoptees). However, a statute which said that it was "declaratory of existing law" was applied retroactively in Estate of Ridenour v. Commissioner, 36 F.3d 332 (4th Cir.1994) (scope of a durable power). *See also* Matter of OnBank & Trust Co., 688 N.E.2d 245 (N.Y.1997) (statute dealing with trustee's fees found intended to apply retroactively).

**13.** In re Marriage of Buol, 705 P.2d 354 (Cal.1985). For other decisions holding retroactive statutes unconstitutional see Whirlpool Corp. v. Ritter, 929 F.2d 1318 (8th Cir.1991); Willcox v. Penn Mutual Life Ins. Co., 55 A.2d 521 (Pa.1947); Board of Education v. Miles, 207 N.E.2d 181 (N.Y.1965).

Some state constitutions prohibit retroactive legislation in general terms. *E.g.* Colo.Const. art 2, § 11. Query whether this makes any difference.

**14.** Bank of America v. Angel View, 85 Cal.Rptr.2d 117, 121 (App.1999). *See also* Evans v. McCoy, 436 A.2d 436 (Md.1981); First Nat. Bank v. King, 651 N.E.2d 127 (Ill.1995); Hiddleston v. Nebraska Jewish Education Society, 186 N.W.2d 904 (Neb.1971).

**15.** National Geographic Society v. Williams, 497 S.W.2d 908 (Tenn.App.1972) (first UPIA inapplicable to an existing trust); Venables v. Seattle–First Nat. Bank, 808 P.2d 769 (Wash.App.1991) (applying a newer version to an existing trust); Bogert, *The Revised Uniform Principal and Income Act,* 38 N.D.Law 50, 52 (1962). However, one part of the 1962 Act and its counterpart in the 1997 version (§ 411(d)) are made prospective due to "concerns about the constitutionality" of retroactivity. See Comment to § 411.

**16.** Unif.Prud.Inv.Act § 11 (1994).

**17.** Chicago Title and Trust Co. v. Steinitz, 681 N.E.2d 669, 671 (Ill.App.1997).

There are two arguments in favor of making changes retroactive. First, presumably the new rule is better than the old one or it would not have been made. If the new rule is better, why postpone its applicability? Secondly, having the new rule and the old one operate simultaneously makes the law more complicated. Trustees, for example, would have to keep track of different rules applicable to different trusts depending upon the date of their creation.[18] This problem can be avoided if the new rule applies to *all* trusts.

On the other hand, it may be unfair to parties who have relied on existing law when a change is made retroactive. Sometimes this argument focusses on the transferor (testator, settlor, etc.), sometimes on other persons, such as the transferee, or a fiduciary who has acted in reliance on the old rule. For example, even though Illinois now includes adopted children in class gifts, regardless of when a will was executed, a trustee who made a distribution under the old law which excluded adopted children cannot be held liable therefor.[19]

"Retroactivity" is a general term, and courts do not always use it consistently. In the law applicable to wills, several points in time may be deemed relevant.

### *Execution of an Instrument*

Before 1981 many testators executed wills which left property "equal to the maximum marital deduction allowable" under the Internal Revenue Code to their spouse. At that time this amounted to 50% of the estate, but in 1981 the maximum marital deduction was increased to 100%. Recognizing that this change "might have an unintended impact on existing wills, Congress provided a transitional rule" whereby formula clauses in wills executed before 1981 should be construed to provide the more limited gift provided by the prior law even if the testator died after 1981.[20] Some statutes by their terms apply only to instruments executed thereafter.[21] However, the more common effective date for laws affecting wills is the date of the testator's death. Thus when an anti-lapse statute was changed between the time the testator executed his will and his death, the court applied the amended version. "When laws are changed after a will is executed but before it is probated, the parties' rights are determined in accordance with the law in existence at the testator's death."[22] When a change occurs after a testator has executed a will but before the testator dies, he/she can change the will if the change in the law does not

**18.** Levin, *Section 6104(d) of the Pennsylvania Rule against Perpetuities,* 25 Vill.L.Rev. 213, 215 (1980). The Uniform Transfers to Minors Act applies to transfers made under its predecessor because "it will be more orderly to subject gifts * * * under the prior Act to the procedures of this Act, rather than to keep both Acts in force." Uniform Transfers to Minors Act § 22, comm.

**19.** 755 ILCS § 5/2–4(g); Chicago Title and Trust Co. v. Steinitz, 681 N.E.2d 669 (Ill.App. 1997).

**20.** In re Estate of Pouser, 975 P.2d 704, 707 (Ariz.1999). *See also* Reynolds v. Russell, 433 A.2d 699, 702 (Del.Ch.1981); Bank One Ohio Trust Co. v. Hiram College, 684 N.E.2d 1275 (Ohio App.1996) (reference to statutorily authorized investments means statute as it existed when will was executed); Boston Safe Deposit & Trust Co. v. Wilbur, 728 N.E.2d 264, 268 (Mass.2000) (looking to cases decided at the time a will was executed). However, in *Pouser, supra,* and in several other cases courts have decided that the testator actually intended the new rule to apply. Estate of Weeks, 462 A.2d 44 (Me.1983); Matter of Estate of Eversole, 885 P.2d 657 (Okl.1994).

**21.** Cal.Prob.Code § 246(b) (construction of the term "per stirpes").

**22.** Matter of Estate of Micheel, 577 N.W.2d 407, 410 (Iowa 1998).

reflect the testator's desires. This is also true for revocable trusts. Thus a statute restricting donative transfers to attorneys drafting instruments was applied to a revocable trust drafted prior to the statute, because by its terms the statute governed "instruments that become irrevocable" thereafter.[23] However, for an irrevocable instrument the date of execution is more significant.[24] The Uniform Probate Code applies by its terms to "instruments executed before the effective date" of the Code when "executed by decedents dying thereafter."[25] As to wills and revocable trusts, this is the general view, but as to irrevocable instruments it is questionable.[26]

In Whirlpool Corp. v. Ritter[27] a man took out life insurance in 1985 and designated his wife as beneficiary. They were later divorced. In 1987 a statute was passed under which a divorce revoked the benefits to a former spouse. Although the statute by its terms applied to anyone dying thereafter, the court held that its application to a prior contract violated the constitution, because "an individual could rely on the pre-existing law and neither know nor expect that the rules governing his policy have changed."[28] This case has been criticized by the Joint Editorial Board of the UPC[29], and its position has been rejected in some other cases involving similar facts.[30]

For some purposes, however, the UPC looks to the date of execution of a will. A will is valid if it complies "with the law at the time of execution" even if it does not comply with more stringent formalities imposed thereafter.[31] However, if the formal requirements are *relaxed* after the will is executed, this may validate a defective will. The purpose of this rule is "to provide a wide opportunity for validation of the expectations of testators"[32] since presumably no one would expect to execute an invalid will. Similarly a court applied a statute validating non-probate transfers of securities to a contract made prior to the statute's enactment on the ground that it "simply protect[ed] what the parties intended."[33] The Uniform Marriage and Divorce Act validates all marriages which "were valid at the time of the contract or were subsequently validated" by law.[34]

**23.** Bank of America v. Angel View, 85 Cal.Rptr.2d 117 (App.1999).

**24.** Ohio Citizens Bank v. Mills, 543 N.E.2d 1206 (Ohio 1989) (law as of date of execution of trust applied in determining to exclude adoptees); Shortridge v. Sherman, 406 N.E.2d 565 (Ill.App.1980) (1912 deed not affected by 1955 change in the law re adoptees).

**25.** Uniform Probate Code § 8–101(b).

**26.** Compare 12 Del.Code tit. 12 § 213 (in construing a will or trust, determine class by law in effect when instrument becomes irrevocable). In Powers v. Wilkinson, 506 N.E.2d 842, 849 (Mass.1987), the court announced a new rule to apply "only to trust instruments executed after the date of this opinion," apparently without distinction between revocable and irrevocable trusts.

**27.** 929 F.2d 1318 (8th Cir.1991).

**28.** *Id.* at 1323. In Baker v. Leonard, 843 P.2d 1050 (Wash.1993), the court applied the law in effect when a bank account was opened to determine the depositor's intent ignoring a change in the law which occurred before she died.

**29.** Halbach & Waggoner, *The UPC's New Survivorship and Anti-lapse Provisions*, 55 Alb.L.Rev. 1091, 1129 (1992).

**30.** Matter of Estate of Dobert, 963 P.2d 327 (Ariz.App.1998); Mearns v. Scharbach, 12 P.3d 1048 (Wash.App.2000).

**31.** Uniform Probate Code § 2–506. *See also* Cal.Prob.Code § 6113; Matter of Estate of Fitzgerald, 738 P.2d 236 (Utah App.1987); Estate of Grossen v. Vincent, 657 P.2d 1345 (Utah 1983); In re Fernandez' Estates, 413 A.2d 998 (N.J.Super.Law Div.1980).

**32.** Uniform Probate Code § § 2–506, comment. *See also* Cal. Prob. Code § 6113; Succession of Gresham, 506 So.2d 156 (La.App.1987); Uniform Transfers to Minors Act § 22(a) (validating transfers made prior to the Act).

**33.** Bielat v. Bielat, 721 N.E.2d 28, 34 (Ohio 2000).

**34.** Unif. Marriage and Divorce Act § 210. *See also* Matter of Heirship of McLeod, 506 So.2d 289 (Miss.1987); Warren Gen. Hosp. v. Brink, 610 N.E.2d 1128 (Ohio App.1992) (common-law marriage made prior to their abolition

Statutes imposing formal requirements on contracts to make wills do not apply to contracts previously made.[35]

### *Date of Death*

For most purposes the date of death determines the governing law. When changes in status, such as adoption, marriage and divorce affect the distribution of property at death, courts generally look to the date of death rather than the law in effect when the adoption, marriage or divorce occurred.[36]

Sometimes a change in the law occurs shortly after a decedent's death, before the property has been distributed. Here too the courts usually apply the law as of the date of death. For example, when a child was killed in April 1972, the then governing law split the estate between her parents and her husband. In July, the state adopted the Uniform Probate Code which would give a larger share to her husband, but the court held that the new law did not apply.[37] Although by its terms the Code applies to proceedings which are still pending when the Code takes effect,[38] any "accrued right" is protected, and the court held that this included the parents' share under prior law.

### *Unconstitutional Laws*

If the law in effect at the date of death is unconstitutional it may not control.[39] For example, when a father died illegitimate children could not inherit under Texas law. A few months later the United States Supreme Court held a similar statute unconstitutional. The Court said that Texas could not apply its statute to bar an illegitimate child because the administration of the father's estate was still in progress, but "after an estate has been finally distributed, the interest in finality may provide [a] * * * valid justification for barring the belated assertion of claims."[40] While this is only dictum, many cases have refused to upset distributions which have occurred under unconstitutional laws.[41] Even though Ohio's mortmain statute was held unconstitu-

is valid). Compare the validation principle applied in the choice of law between states. Section 1.2, note 64 et seq.

**35.** Cal.Prob.Code § 150(c); Mabry v. McAfee, 783 S.W.2d 356 (Ark.1990); Matter of Estate of Kerr, 918 P.2d 1354, 1357 (N.M.App. 1996); Junot v. Estate of Gilliam, 759 S.W.2d 654, 658 (Tenn.1988); In re Estate of Roccamonte, 735 A.2d 614, 618 (N.J.Super.A.D.1999).

**36.** As to adoption see Matter of Estate of Ryan, 928 P.2d 735 (Ariz.App.1996); Aldridge v. Mims, 884 P.2d 817 (N.M.App.1994); Matter of Estate of Hinderliter, 882 P.2d 1001 (Kan. App.1994); Morgan v. Mayes, 296 S.E.2d 34 (W.Va.1982); In re Raymond Estate, 641 A.2d 1342 (Vt.1994). As to divorce see Morse v. Alley, 638 S.W.2d 284 (Ky.App.1982); Buehler v. Buehler, 425 N.E.2d 905 (Ohio App.1979). *But see* In re Estate of Crohn, 494 P.2d 258 (Or.App.1972) (applying statute in effect at date of divorce); In re Estate of Ralston, 674 P.2d 1001 (Colo.App.1983) (applying law at the date of a marriage).

**37.** Hogan v. Hermann, 623 P.2d 900 (Idaho 1980). *See also* Pazzi v. Taylor, 342 N.W.2d 481 (Iowa 1984) (refusing to apply a new law passed a few months after an intestate died).

**38.** Uniform Probate Code § 8–101(b)(2). However, in Scribner v. Berry, 489 A.2d 8 (Me.1985), this was held to apply only to "procedural rules," since there is an exception for cases where "in the opinion of the Court the former procedure should be made applicable in the interests of justice."

**39.** So also, if a retroactive statute replaces an unconstitutional one, its retroactive application is likely to be upheld. In re Marriage of Bouquet, 546 P.2d 1371 (Cal.1976) (statute providing equal treatment for wives and husbands could be applied retroactively); Cooper v. Harris, 499 F.Supp. 266 (N.D.Ill.1980) (applying statute passed after father died to allow inheritance by illegitimate child).

**40.** Reed v. Campbell, 476 U.S. 852, 855 (1986).

**41.** Turner v. Nesby, 848 S.W.2d 872 (Tex. App.1993) (claim by illegitimate barred by 4 year time limit of review of declarations of heirship); Boan v. Watson, 316 S.E.2d 401 (S.C.1984) (when husband died prior to a case

tional in 1986, it was applied six years later to property under an earlier will.[42]

The probable reliance of persons who receive distributions is protected, and it is not necessary for them to prove actual reliance.[43] An even stronger claim for protection is presented by bona fide purchasers for value[44] and fiduciaries who have made prior distributions. When a will made a gift of income to the testator's "descendants," a statutory presumption that this excluded children born out of wedlock was held to be unconstitutional, but the court refused to hold that a child born out of wedlock was entitled to income from the beginning, since this would "ignore the countervailing interests of the beneficiaries [born in wedlock who had been getting all the income] and the trustee." The child only received income which the trustee had held in reserve pending resolution of the dispute.[45] The California Probate Code protects fiduciaries from liability "for any action taken before the operative date that was proper at the time the action was taken."[46]

### *Future Interests*

Suppose a will gives an interest to *A* for life, and then a remainder to a class, such as *A*'s "issue," when *A* dies. Under the law in effect when the testator dies, an adopted child of *A* would not have taken, nor a child born out of wedlock. After the testator dies but during *A*'s life, the law changes. Does the new rule apply? There are many inconsistent decisions on this issue. Older cases tend to hold the new law inapplicable on the theory that the testator relied on the law in effect at his/her death.[47] The Uniform Probate Code has been held inapplicable to the construction of wills of testators who died prior to its effective date.[48] A Massachusetts decision overruling the presumption that "issue" did not include children born out of wedlock was made prospective only because "the Bar has been entitled reasonably to rely on [the old] rule in advising clients."[49]

The dissenting justices in that case questioned the claim that the testator had relied on the old rule. "It is likely that the donor did not have any

holding a widow's statutory right was unconstitutional, his widow could claim dower); Dooley v. Reimer Farms, Inc., 638 N.E.2d 260 (Ill.App.1994) (since testator died in 1968, a remainder interest did not include illegitimate children); Stallworth v. Hicks, 434 So.2d 229 (Ala.1983).

**42.** Wendell v. AmeriTrust Co., N.A., 630 N.E.2d 368 (Ohio 1994).

**43.** Contrast Uniform Probate Code § 3–909 which allows property which has been improperly distributed to be recovered unless the payment "can no longer be questioned because of adjudication, estoppel, or limitation."

**44.** Levin, *Section 6104(d) of the Pennsylvania Rule against Perpetuities,* 25 Vill.L.Rev. 213, 218–19 (1980) (describing a case of a purchaser of property distributed under a mortmain statute which was later held unconstitutional).

**45.** Estate of Dulles, 431 A.2d 208 (Pa. 1981).

**46.** Cal.Prob.Code § 3(f). Uniform Probate Code § 8–101(b)(4) more generally protects any "act done before the effective date."

**47.** Calhoun v. Campbell, 763 S.W.2d 744 (Tenn.1988) (adoptee excluded because will took effect in 1939 and drafters rely on existing law); Callan v. Winters, 534 N.E.2d 298 (Mass.1989); Continental Bank, N.A. v. Herguth, 617 N.E.2d 852 (Ill.App.1993); Matter of Estate of Jenkins, 904 P.2d 1316 (Colo.1995) (adopted child excluded because of rule existing when testator died); Ohio Citizens Bank v. Mills, 543 N.E.2d 1206 (Ohio 1989) (adoptee excluded under law in effect when trust executed); Newman v. Wells Fargo Bank, N.A., 59 Cal.Rptr.2d 2 (1996) (adopted-out child excluded by applying the law in effect when the testator died).

**48.** Scribner v. Berry, 489 A.2d 8 (Me. 1985).

**49.** Powers v. Wilkinson, 506 N.E.2d 842, 849 (Mass.1987).

'intention at all with respect to the question.' "[50] As one court observed, "surely any scrivener who had those previous cases [excluding adopted children] in mind would not have left" the question open to a court's interpretation, but would have made a clear provision in the will on the subject.[51] Some courts have made changes retroactive, or upheld retroactive statutes, asserting that the testator intended to have whatever law was in effect at the time of final distribution of the trust control.[52]

A related question is raised by the use of the word "heirs" in a will. This is normally construed to incorporate the rules of intestate succession, but as of what date? According to the Restatement of Property, "even though the donor knew at the time the dispositive instrument was drafted that the statute governing intestate succession * * * excluded adopted children and children born out of wedlock, a change in the law of such State, before [the person whose "heirs" are to receive the gift] dies * * * would apply."[53]

Sometimes the discussion focusses on the interests of the devisees rather than the intentions of the testator. As we have seen, once property has been distributed, it will not be taken back from the distributee on the ground that the law has changed. On the other hand, rights which have not yet irrevocably vested may be defeated by a change in the law. When a man created a joint tenancy in land with his son, a subsequent change in the law giving the man's widow a claim to share in the land was held to apply because the father could have destroyed the son's right of survivorship by severing the joint tenancy.

> Although [the son's] ownership rights in the property vested at the deed of conveyance, his right of survivorship to the whole property was not an 'irrevocable accrued right' until [the father's] death. Therefore the subsequent act of the legislature in creating the spouse's elective share rights did not divest [the son] of an irrevocably accrued right.[54]

Some courts say that a future interest which is "vested" is entitled to protection, but this word is variously interpreted. When a will left land to the testator's son for life, remainder to his children, this was held to include an adopted child under a statute which by its terms applied to wills whenever executed unless the estate had already "vested." The statute applied since the remainder did not vest until the son died.[55]

50. *Id.* at 851.

51. Zimmerman v. First Nat. Bank, 348 So.2d 1359, 1366 (Ala.1977). Perhaps this argument is less persuasive when the old rule was embodied in a clear statute. *See* Newman v. Wells Fargo Bank, N.A., 926 P.2d 969 (Cal. 1996).

52. Annan v. Wilmington Trust Co., 559 A.2d 1289 (Del.1989) (inclusion of children born out of wedlock); Brown v. Trust Co., 196 S.E.2d 872 (Ga.1973); In re Sollid, 647 P.2d 1033 (Wash.App.1982) (inclusion of adopted child). In Ohio Citizens Bank v. Mills, 543 N.E.2d 1206 (Ohio 1989) construed a statute allowing adopted children to take as prospective only, but the legislature later amended the statute so that it now applies to instruments previously executed. Fifth Third Bank v. Crosley, 669 N.E.2d 904 (Ohio Com.Pl.1996).

53. *Restatement (Second) of Property, Donative Transfers* § 29.3, comm. d (1987). *See also* Conway v. Childress, 896 S.W.2d 15 (Ky. App.1994) (illegitimate child included as "heir"); Matter of Dodge Testamentary Trust, 330 N.W.2d 72 (Mich.App.1982) (inclusion of spouse as heir); Boatmen's Trust Co. v. Conklin, 888 S.W.2d 347, 354 (Mo.App.1994) (even though the court construed the word "issue" in the same will under the law as of the date of execution); Cal.Prob.Code § 21114; Uniform Probate Code § 2–711.

54. In re Estate of Antonopoulos, 993 P.2d 637, 644 (Kan.1999).

55. Thurston v. Thurston, 363 N.W.2d 298 (Mich.App.1985). *See also* Sola v. Clostermann, 679 P.2d 317 (Or.App.1984) (applying new law to include child born out of wedlock because remainder was contingent); Crumpton v. Mitchell, 281 S.E.2d 1, 6 (N.C.1981) (upholding

Use of the term "vested rights" to explain decisions is dubious because the term means different things in different contexts. In some opinions the term "vested" becomes circular.

> A reviewing court applies the law as it exists at the time of the appeal unless doing so would interfere with a vested right ... A vested right is ... 'an expectation that cannot be taken away by legislation.'[56]

### *Rule against Perpetuities*

The Rule has been changed in many states in recent years. These changes are of two types. The first validates interests which would previously have been invalid.[57] It has been argued with some success that making such changes retroactive promotes rather than defeats the expectations of the testator, since no one would go to the trouble of creating an interest which was invalid.[58] Some statutory reforms of the Rule have been by their terms prospective only,[59] but a Massachusetts court applied such a statute to an earlier will on the ground that it expressed the policy of the state.[60] The Uniform Statutory Rule is partially retroactive, and some statutes are fully so.[61] The Iowa Supreme Court has upheld the retroactive application of that state's statute.[62]

The second type of reform has subjected to time limits interests which were previously exempt from the Rule, such as possibilities of reverter.[63] In this context the argument that no one expects to create an invalid interest argues *against* retroactive application of the statute. In the New York Court of Appeals held unconstitutional a 1958 statute limiting possibilities of reverter when applied to an 1854 deed, saying that "retrospective legislation ... cannot impair vested rights."[64]

But even if possibilities of reverter are "vested," their value when a statute is passed is usually slight, and this, in the view of some courts, justifies imposing retroactive limitations on them.[65]

a retroactive statute because due process does not protect contingent interests). *But see* Billings v. Fowler, 279 N.E.2d 906 (Mass.1972). For the ambiguities inherent in terms such as "contingent and "vested" see Section 10.1, at note 7 et seq.

**56.** Premier Property Management, Inc. v. Chavez, 728 N.E.2d 476, 481 (Ill.2000).

**57.** These reforms are discussed in Section 11.4.

**58.** Morris & Leach, *The Rule Against Perpetuities* 32 (1962); Levin, *Section 6104(d) of the Pennsylvania Rule against Perpetuities,* 25 Vill.L.Rev. 213, 229 (1980).

**59.** Connecticut Bank & Trust Co. v. Brody, 392 A.2d 445, 451 (Conn.1978); Low v. Spellman, 629 A.2d 57 (Me.1993); Mo.Stat. § 442.553(3); Texas Prop. Code § 5.043(d).

**60.** Warner v. Whitman, 233 N.E.2d 14, 17 (Mass.1968). *See also* Juliano & Sons v. Chevron, U.S.A., 593 A.2d 814 (N.J. Super.App.Div.1991); Fleet Nat. Bank v. Colt, 529 A.2d 122 (R.I.1987).

**61.** The "wait and see" aspect of the Uniform Statutory Rule applies only to interests created after the effective date, but prior interests if invalid, can be reformed. Section 5. Compare Cal.Prob.Code § 21202 (statute applies regardless of when interest created, but not if validity has been determined in a proceeding or settlement). The Pennsylvania statute was originally prospective but later amended to make it retroactive. In re Estate of Weaver, 572 A.2d 1249, 1257 (Pa.Super.1990) (applying 1947 statute to will taking effect in 1935).

**62.** Henderson v. Millis, 373 N.W.2d 497, 506 (Iowa 1985).

**63.** For a discussion of this exemption see Section 11.6, at note 22 et seq.

**64.** Board of Education v. Miles, 207 N.E.2d 181, 184 (N.Y.1965). *See* Walton v. City of Red Bluff, 3 Cal.Rptr.2d 275 (App.1991) for a more recent discussion of the authorities on this question.

**65.** Hiddleston v. Nebraska Jewish Education Society, 186 N.W.2d 904 (Neb.1971). *See also* Opinion of the Justices, 151 N.E.2d 475 (Mass.1958) (limitation on dower justified by its slight value).

### *Fiduciary Administration*

Many trusts go on for years, during which questions of allocations between principal and income arise. As we have seen, the Uniform Principal and Income Act of 1962, unlike its predecessor, applies to trusts created prior to its adoption, but it applies only to "any receipt or expense received or incurred after the effective date" of the Act.[66] A similar approach is taken to investments by trustees. "Whether an investment is proper is determined by the terms of the statute in force at the time when the investment is made" rather than by the rules in force when the trust was created.[67]

The Uniform Trustees' Powers Act contains alternate provisions as to its effective date; one version applies to previously established trusts, but this "will not affect the validity of any act of the trustee performed prior to its enactment."[68]

### *Procedural Changes*

It is sometimes said that legislatures are "free to apply changes in rules of evidence or procedure retroactively."[69] For example, a testator died in April; in June of the same year, the statutory period allowed for probating wills was reduced from 9 to 6 months from the date of the testator's death. This was held to bar an attempt to probate the will in December. "The statute in effect when the petition ... is filed should apply if there is a reasonable time in which to commence a proceeding before the expiration of the shortened limitation period provided by the amended statute." Here there was 3 months left to run and that was enough.[70] The Uniform Probate Code recognizes that in some cases it may be appropriate to defer the effectiveness of procedural changes "in the interest of justice."[71] But in a case in which a will contest was pending when the legislature abolished trial by jury in such proceedings, the court applied the new law despite a similar savings clause.[72]

**66.** Unif.Prin. & Inc.Act (1962) § 14. In In re Reznor's Estate, 213 A.2d 791 (Pa.1965), the court refused to apply the Act to stock dividends which had been allocated to principal in 1928 and 1938. Presumably any distributions to an income beneficiary would not be disturbed.

**67.** *Restatement (Second) of Trusts* § 227, comm. p (1959). *See also* Uniform Prudent Investor Act § 11. As to investments by fiduciaries see Section 12.7.

**68.** Uniform Trustees' Powers Act § 8, and comment.

**69.** In re Marriage of Buol, 705 P.2d 354, 358 (Cal.1985). This was the rationale for upholding a limitation of possibilities of reverter in Presbytery of Southeast Iowa v. Harris, 226 N.W.2d 232, 242 (Iowa 1975): the statute "does not abolish or alter any vested right. Rather it modifies the procedure for effectuation of the remedy." In Evans v. McCoy, 436 A.2d 436, 448 (Md.1981), the court upheld a retroactive statute creating a presumption of intent to include adoptees because "this is a rule of evidence and not a rule of substantive law."

**70.** Matter of Estate of Forrester, 762 P.2d 198, 201 (Kan.App.1988).

**71.** Uniform Probate Code § 8–101(b)(2).

**72.** Estate of Gardner, 2 Cal.Rptr.2d 664 (App.1991).

# Chapter 2

# INTESTATE SUCCESSION

*Analysis*



## § 2.1 The Surviving Spouse's Share

What happens to the property of a person who dies without a will? Here we deal with the share that passes to the decedent's surviving spouse if any.[1] The following section deals with the share which passes to the decedent's blood relatives.

Although Blackstone in the 18th century devoted considerable discussion to the common law "canons of descent,"[2] today in every state intestate succession is controlled by a statute.[3]

### *History*

The spouse was never an heir to land at common law. Widows and widowers were relegated to lifetime enjoyment of the marital estates of dower and curtesy.[4] Dower for widows was limited to one third of the husband's land. Curtesy extended to all of the wife's land, but was dependent on issue being born of the marriage; "if a cry was heard within the four walls, as the old writers quaintly put it; it mattered nothing that issue did not survive."[5] Limiting spouses to a life interest stemmed from a fear that if the surviving

§ 2.1

1. As to who is a "spouse" see Section 2.11.

2. W. Blackstone, *Commentaries* Bk 2, Chap. 14. These applied only to land; even in Blackstone's day succession to personal property was governed by a Statute of Distributions.

3. *Restatement, Third, of Property (Wills and Other Donative Transfers)* § 2.1, Introductory Note (1998).

4. For the history of dower and curtesy see 3 W. Holdsworth, *History of English Law* 185–197 (5th ed. 1942).

5. A. Simpson, *An Introduction to the History of Land Law* 66 (1961). *See also* 2 W. Blackstone, Commentaries ** 126, 129 (1766).

spouse inherited land in fee it would be permanently removed from the decedent's family, particularly if the couple had no children or if the surviving spouse remarried or had children by another marriage. The marital life estates in land hindered marketability; land is hard to sell when ownership is divided between a life tenant and remaindermen. Even in the 18th century Blackstone observed "in estates of considerable consequence, tenancy in dower happens very seldom: for the claim of the wife to her dower at the common law * * * became a great clog to alienations" and so was eliminated in wealthy families, usually by ante nuptial agreements.[6]

Personal property was subject to different rules. Under the Statute of Distribution of 1670, a widow took one-third of her husband's personalty if he left surviving issue and one-half if he did not.[7] Intestacy provisions for widowers were unnecessary because a husband acquired all his wife's personal property upon marriage on the theory that "husband and wife ... are one person in law."[8]

Most American jurisdictions today give a spouse an outright (fee simple) share of the decedent's property, but a few states retain vestiges of the historical distinction between land and personalty and give the spouse only a life interest in the former.[9] The Uniform Probate Code, however, like most statutes, gives a surviving spouse the same share in land and personal property.[10] Distinctions between widows and widowers have disappeared, and would be of doubtful constitutionality today.

In virtually all states today surviving spouses receive a larger share on intestacy than was provided by common-law dower and curtesy or the Statute of Distributions. This is partly attributable to the feminist movement, since in a majority of families the surviving spouse is a woman, "not only because women live longer than men, but also because wives tend to be, on the average, nearly three years younger than their husbands."[11] Empirical data suggests that most people want a larger share to pass to the spouse than the former rules provided.[12] This may be based, in part, on the fact that most surviving spouses are "beyond working years" and a large percent of them are "either poor or near poor, ... having income no more than two times the poverty level," especially when the decedent died intestate.[13]

**6.** 2 W. Blackstone, *Commentaries* * 136. As to the legal issues raised by ante nuptial agreements today see Section 3.9.

**7.** 22 & 23 Car. 2, c. 10, § 5.

**8.** 2 W. Blackstone, *Commentaries* *433 (1765). This legal fiction inspired the famous remark in Dickens "if the law supposes that .. then the law is an ass." J. Baker, *An Introduction to English Legal History* 395 (2d ed. 1979).

**9.** West's Ann. Ind. Code 29–1–2–1(c) (if spouse had no children by the decedent); Vernon's Tex. Prob. Code Ann art 38(b). The distinction presents problems in classification. *E.g.,* Parson v. Wolfe, 676 S.W.2d 689 (Tex. App.1984) (land contract treated as personalty).

**10.** Uniform Probate Code § 2–102. In 1890 69% of the common-law states limited the surviving spouse to a life interest in the decedent's land. By 1982 this had dropped to 11.9%. Shammas, et. al., *Inheritance in America* 165 (1987).

**11.** Waggoner, *Marital Property Rights in Transition*, 59 Mo.L.Rev. 21, 31 (1994). *See also* Shammas, supra note 10, at 176.

**12.** *E.g.*, Waggoner, *The Multiple Marriage Society and Spousal Rights under the Revised Uniform Probate Code*, 76 Iowa L. Rev. 223, 230–31 (1991). The use of surveys to shape the intestacy rules is discussed at 2.3, note 1 et. seq.

**13.** Waggoner, *supra* note 11, at 31–33.

### *Division Between Spouse and Issue*

When a decedent leaves both surviving spouse and issue, arguably the entire estate should go to the spouse. If the issue include minor children, giving them a share would require a guardianship or other arrangement for managing the property.[14] If the spouse is the childrens' other parent, awarding the estate to the spouse may be a better way to provide for them. If the decedent's children are adults (as is most commonly true today because of increased life expectancy), they are usually capable of providing for themselves, whereas the spouse is more likely to need the decedent's property. For these reasons the Uniform Probate Code gives the entire estate to the spouse in intestacy "if all the decedent's surviving descendants are also descendants of the surviving spouse and there is no other [surviving] descendant of the surviving spouse."[15] The comment points out that this is more generous to the spouse than the pre–1990 UPC, but is justified by the fact that "testators in smaller estates (which intestate estates overwhelmingly tend to be) tend to devise their entire estates to their surviving spouses, even when the couple has children."

The exception is an important one in today's society when because of multiple marriages a decedent is often survived by children of a prior marriage, or the surviving spouse has children by another marriage. Here, as the story of Cinderella illustrates, the spouse is less likely to provide for children of the decedent. The Uniform Probate Code reduces the spouse's share in this situation, as do many other (but not all) statutes.[16]

Arguably the spouse's share ought to depend upon the length of the marriage. The UPC uses the length of the marriage in determining the spouse's elective share when the spouse is claiming against a will,[17] but not for fixing the spouse's share in intestacy. However, the length of the marriage is an important factor in community property states where the spouse typically receives all the community property and only a fraction of the decedent's separate property upon intestacy.[18] Since community property is generally limited to property acquired during the marriage, there is usually little or no community property accumulated during a brief marriage.[19]

Some states make the spouse's share depend on how many children the intestate has, *e.g.*, the spouse gets one-half if there is only one child (or the issue of one child), but only one-third if more than one child (or child's issue) survives.[20]

**14.** As to the disadvantages of guardianship for managing property see Section 9.2, note 2.

**15.** Uniform Probate Code § 2–102.

**16.** New Hampshire Rev. Stat. Ann. 561:1; Vernon's Tex. Prob. Code Ann. § 45. *See also* Shammas, *supra* note 10, at 166. These special rules do not cover the case where the spouse remarries and has children by another person after the decedent dies.

**17.** See Section 3.7, note 12.

**18.** Cal.Prob.Code § 6401 says the spouse gets "the one half of the community property that belongs to the decedent;" the other half already belongs to the spouse. The spouse's share of separate property is 1/2 or 1/3 depending on the number of children. The surviving spouse also gets all the community property under Uniform Probate Code § 2–102A(b). *See also* Rev.Code Wash. § 11.04.015(1). In Texas this is true only if all the issue are also issue of the spouse. Vernon's Tex. Prob. Code Ann. § 45. In Louisiana, the spouse only gets a usufruct (life interest) in the decedent's half community property. La.Civ.Code art. 890.

**19.** A more complete discussion of community property appears in Section 3.8.

**20.** Cal.Prob.Code § 6401(c) (separate property); Minn.Stat. § 525.16(3); Ohio Rev. Code § 2105.06.

In some states the fraction received by the spouse depends on the size of the estate. Under the Uniform Probate Code, for example, a spouse who has children by a prior marriage receives $150,000 and one half of the balance of the estate, *i.e.* all of a small estate, but only a fraction of a larger one.[21] A spouse may need a larger share of a smaller estate for support, whereas a fraction of a larger estate may suffice. In very large estates, giving everything to the spouse may be disadvantageous for tax reasons,[22] but this is probably not a relevant factor in shaping intestacy rules which are designed for more modest estates, since wealthier persons usually have a will.

### *Spouse's Share in the Absence of Issue*

When a decedent was survived by a widow but no issue, the Statute of Distributions increased the widow's share of personal property from one-third to one-half, but the widow's interest in land remained the same: even if the husband's only relatives were remote cousins, the widow's dower was only one-third. Modern statutes generally increase the spouse's share if the decedent has no issue. Many statutes give all to the surviving spouse if no issue survive,[23] but under some, the decedent's parents share with the surviving spouse. The Uniform Probate Code, for example, gives the spouse the first $200,000, and three-fourths of the estate when the decedent dies without issue, survived by a parent, the parent(s) taking the rest.[24] If no parents survive, the surviving spouse takes the entire intestate estate under the Code, but in some states the spouse must share with the decedent's siblings and their issue.[25]

When a decedent has no issue the property of both spouses may pass ultimately to the relatives of the surviving spouse. California seeks to avoid this result by giving the relatives of the predeceasing spouse a share of the surviving spouse's estate if the latter dies intestate. Thus when W survives H and dies intestate a few years later "the portion of [her] estate attributable to" H will pass to H's relatives rather than to hers.[26] In order to minimize the administrative difficulties of identifying the property of the first spouse in the surviving spouse's estate, a time limit is imposed, so that in our hypothetical, if W survived H by more than 5 years the statute would not apply.[27] Nor would the statute apply if W was survived by a spouse or issue, or if she had a will devising her estate to others. Thus if H wishes to make sure that "his"

**21.** Uniform Probate Code § 2–102(2). *See also* N.Y. EPTL § 4–1.1(a)(1). Statutes which give the spouse a lump sum can present a problem when the law of more than one state applies. *Restatement, Third, of Property (Wills and Other Donative Transfers)* § 2.1, Reporters Note argues that the spouse should only get the lump sum provided by the state of domicile.

**22.** Tax planning for spouses is discussed at Section 15.3, text after note 183.

**23.** Ariz.Rev.Stat. § 14–2102(1) (separate property); Ark.Stat. § 61–149(b) (only applies if the decedent and surviving spouse have been married for three years or more); Colo.Rev. Stat. § 14–11–102(1)(a); Iowa Code §§ 633.211, 633.212; McKinney's New York Est. Pow. Trust Law § 4–1.1(a)(2); Ohio Rev. Code § 2106.06(D); Utah Code Ann. § 75–2–102.

**24.** Uniform Probate Code § 2–102(2). The spouse's share was somewhat smaller in the pre–1990 version. Compare Burk v. Burk, 903 P.2d 914 (Or.App.1995) (applying California law to divide husband's separate property equally between widow and parents); Consedine v. Consedine, 653 N.E.2d 1116 (Mass.App. 1995) (under Pennsylvania law, widow gets first $20,000, splits the rest with the decedent's mother).

**25.** Cal.Prob.Code § 6401 (separate property equally divided between spouse and parents or issue of parents).

**26.** Cal.Prob.Code § 6402.5.

**27.** The limit is 15 years for real property.

property returns to his family when his widow dies, he should put it into a trust for W for life with remainder to his relatives rather than relying on the statute. The English Administration of Estates Act puts the bulk of an intestate estate in trust for the surviving spouse for life if there are no issue, with a remainder to the intestate's collateral relatives.[28]

## § 2.2 Relatives

Normally whatever does not pass to the surviving spouse on intestacy goes to the decedent's blood relatives. Spouses of relatives (e.g. sons-in-law, daughters-in-law) get no share.[1] The issue of a decedent are the first takers. Issue (or descendants—the two terms are synonymous) include children, grandchildren, great-grandchildren, etc.[2] Only if there are no surviving issue do collateral relatives (such as brothers, sisters, nieces, nephews, etc.) or ancestors (parents, grandparents, etc.) inherit. This is true in all states.

### *Exclusion of Issue of Living Ancestor*

Grandchildren and more remote relatives do not take if they have a living ancestor in a generation closer to the decedent. Thus, if the intestate is survived by all her children and by grandchildren, the latter do not get a share.

This exclusion of a living ancestor's issue keeps down the number of takers, and makes it easier to sell property. It also reduces the chances of property going to a minor with the associated complication of guardianship. Moreover, if remoter issue were allowed to share, others born after distribution would be excluded, since only issue living when the intestate dies can inherit.[5] Giving all the property to parents of remoter issue means that any later-born issue will also probably get a share when their parents die and leave their property to their children.

### *Representation*

A child who predeceases the decedent does not get a share of the estate; only persons who survive the intestate can be heirs. Under the Uniform Probate Code and many other statutes, a person who survives the decedent by less than 120 hours would get no share of the estate.[6] However, an heir does not have to survive until the decedent's estate is distributed; if an heir survives the decedent but dies prior to distribution the heir's share passes to his or her estate.[7]

Children of a relative who would have been an heir but for his or her failure to survive the decedent receive the share the relative would have taken

**28.** Administration of Estates Act, c. 23, § 46 (1925).

§ 2.2

**1.** However, such relatives by affinity may ultimately take property of the decedent as heirs or devisees of the spouse.

**2.** Uniform Probate Code § 1–201(9)(25); *Restatement (Third) of Property (Wills and Other Donative Transfers)* § 2.3, comm b (1998).

**5.** This includes children in gestation. Uniform Probate Code § 2–108 (if they live 120 hours after birth); Cal.Prob.Code § 6407 (relatives conceived before decedent died but born thereafter are included). For a general discussion of after-born children see Section 10.3.

**6.** Uniform Probate Code § 2–104; Cal. Prob.Code § 6403. For a general discussion of simultaneous death, see Section 8.3, note 86 et seq.

**7.** Booker v. Lal, 726 N.E.2d 638, 641 (Ill. App.2000).

if he or she had survived. These children are said to "represent" their parent, but they inherit directly from the decedent; their share does not pass through parent's estate and is not subject to the parent's will or claims of the parent's creditors.[8]

At one time the idea of representation was in doubt. When King Richard I died without issue in the 12th century, he was survived by a brother, John, and a nephew, Arthur, the son of John's deceased older brother. John seized the crown, but under the law as it was ultimately settled, Arthur should have succeeded as his father's representative.[9] All states today allow representation. The common law governing land allowed it without limit,[10] but the Statute of Distributions of 1670, which governed personal property, did not allow representation among collateral relatives except in the case of brothers' and sisters' children (the decedent's nephews and nieces).[11] Some American statutes today also bar representation among collaterals after a certain point, *e.g.* children of a deceased aunt or uncle, will not share in an estate if the decedent had surviving aunts or uncles.[12] The Uniform Probate Code, on the other hand, does not limit representation and would give the cousins in this case a share.[13]

A related problem can arise in the construction of instruments. A gift to "A's children" is usually held not to include A's grandchildren since this would be inconsistent with the ordinary understanding of the word children.[14] Sophisticated drafters usually use the word "issue" or "descendants" rather than children in order to include the issue of deceased children. For example, the Uniform Statutory Will leaves the estate (if the testator has no spouse) to "the children of the testator if all of them survive, otherwise to the surviving issue of the testator by representation."[15] Such a devise to "issue" does not include a grandchild or remote descendant whose parent was living.[16]

### *Computation of Shares*

Suppose that Mary has three children, Alice, Andrew and Arthur. Alice predeceases her, but Andrew and Arthur and Alice's three children survive.

**8.** Uniform Probate Code § 2–110; Cal. Prob. Code § 6410.

**9.** 2 F. Pollock & F. Maitland, *History of English Law* 283–86 (2d ed. 1898), T. Plucknett, *Concise History of the Common Law* 717 (5th ed. 1956); J. Baker, *Introduction to English Legal History* 227 (2d ed. 1979).

**10.** 2 W. Blackstone, *Commentaries* *217 (1765).

**11.** Statute of Distributions, 22 & 23 Car. 2, c. 10, § 7 (1670). The Statute of Distributions was drafted by persons familiar with Roman law which did not allow representation among collaterals. Gaius, *Institutes* 3.15; Justinian, *Institutes* 3.1.6, 3.2.4.

**12.** Dahood v. Frankovich, 746 P.2d 115 (Mont.1987); In re Estate of Trask, 543 A.2d 416 (N.H.1988) (first cousins once removed do not share with first cousins).

**13.** Uniform Probate Code § 2–103(4). *See also* Calif.Prob.Code § 6402(d); Estate of McCrary, 62 Cal.Rptr.2d 504 (App.1997)(issue of deceased first cousins share with surviving first cousins); Matter of Estate of Swartz, 870 P.2d 179 (Okl.App.1994); In re Estate of Martineau, 490 A.2d 779 (N.H.1985).

**14.** See Section 10.1, note 61.

**15.** Uniform Statutory Will Act § 7(a)(1).

**16.** *Restatement (Second) of Property, Donative Transfers* § 28.2(2) (1987); Theopold v. Sears, 258 N.E.2d 559 (Mass.1970); Central Trust Bank v. Stout, 579 S.W.2d 825 (Mo.App. 1979). This construction is reinforced if the instrument uses the word "per stirpes." Stowers v. Norwest Bank Indiana, N.A., 624 N.E.2d 485 (Ind.App.1993) (gift "to children and grandchildren per stirpes" goes to children only); Bonney v. Granger, 356 S.E.2d 138 (S.C.App.1987) (gift "to issue per stirpes" goes only to grandchildren, excluding more remote descendants).

Under Uniform Probate Code § 2–708 a gift to "issue" or "descendants" goes to the persons who would take under the rules of intestacy.

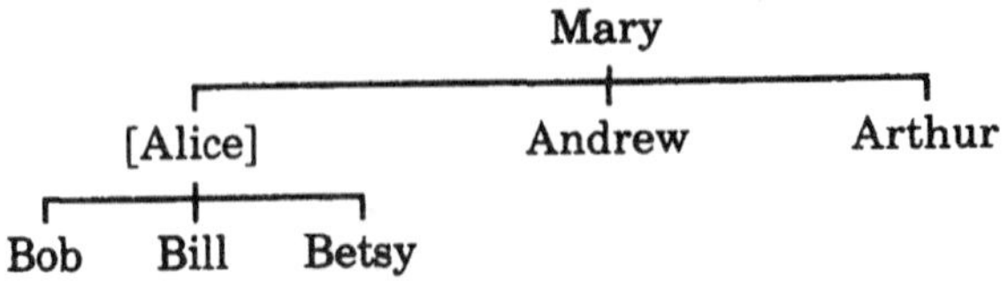


All states agree that Bob, Bill and Betsy would split Alice's one-third and so each takes one-ninth of Mary's estate by representation.

Division among grandchildren when there are no surviving children is more controversial. Suppose all of Mary's children predecease her and that Andrew had one child and Arthur had two.

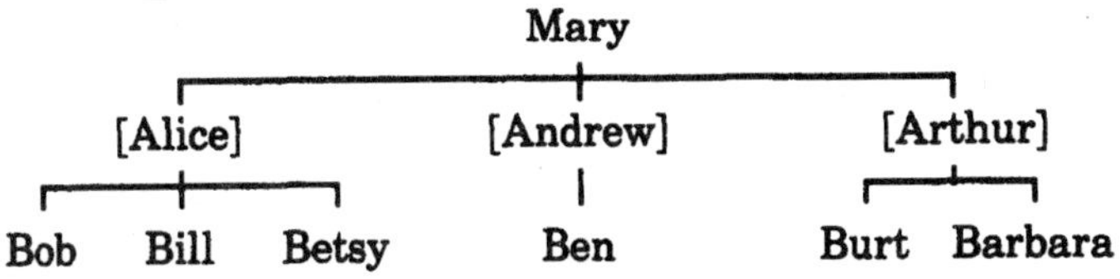


In many states each of the grandchildren would take an equal (1/6) share. In California, for example, the issue "take equally if they are all of the same degree of kinship to the decedent."[17]

The common law, on the other hand, adopted a method of division often called per stirpes, which means "according to the roots; since all the branches [of a family] inherit the same share that their root, whom they represent, would have done."[18] Under this system, Ben takes his father's 1/3, while Burt and Barbara divide their father's 1/3, each getting 1/6. Alice's three children would each take 1/9. Some states still follow this approach.[19]

The same issue can arise when inheritance goes to collateral relatives. If Mary had no issue, parents, or spouse, and her siblings were all dead, her estate would go to their children (Mary's nieces and nephews), equally in some states,[20] per stirpes in others.[21]

In a third type of case, there are surviving children as well as grandchildren by two or more deceased children, *e.g.*, Alice and Andrew predecease Mary but Arthur survives her.

**17.** Cal.Prob.Code § 6402(a). The UPC no longer uses this language, but the result is the same. Uniform Probate Code § 2–103, comment. *See also* Brice v. Seebeck, 595 P.2d 441 (Okl.1979) (division among nieces and nephews).

**18.** 2 W. Blackstone, *Commentaries* *217 (1766). Perhaps a more appropriate metaphor would treat the decedent's children as trunks, and the recipients as roots growing out of the trunk.

**19.** 755 ILCS § 5/2–1(a); Kentucky Rev. Stat. § 391.040.

**20.** Matter of Estate of Kendall, 968 P.2d 364 (Okla.Civ.App.1998) (estate divided equally among 12 nieces and nephews, children of 3 deceased siblings).

**21.** The answer is not necessarily the same for collaterals and descendants. *See* Ga.Code Ann. § 113–903(4) (among descendants distribution is per stirpes), § 113–903(5) (distribution among nieces and nephews is per capita). For a comprehensive listing of the statutes see *Restatement (Second) of Property (Donative Transfers)* § 28.2, Statutory Note (1987).

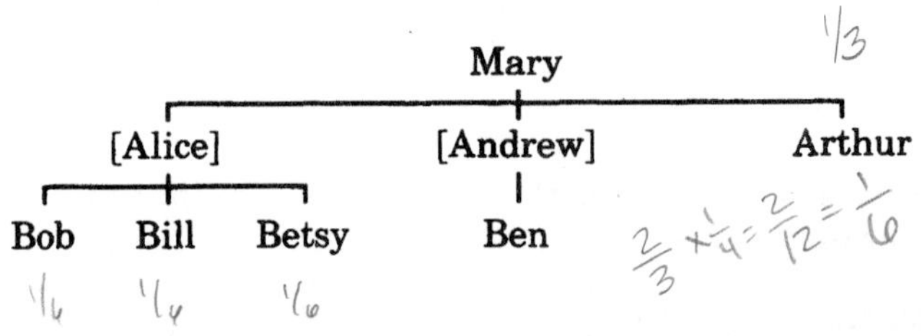


In many states, Bob, Bill, and Betsy will divide Alice's share, each receiving one-ninth of Mary's estate, and Ben will take Andrew's share of one-third.[22] This causes persons in the same generation get unequal shares. Ben gets more than Bob, Bill, and Betsy even though all four are of the same degree of kinship to Mary. Professor Waggoner has argued that persons of the same degree should always take equally.[23] Under his system, which the UPC has now adopted,[24] Arthur would still get one-third, but the remaining two-thirds would drop down to the next generation and be equally divided, so the children of Alice and Andrew would each receive one-sixth of Mary's estate. This system is sometimes called "per capita at each generation."[25]

When there are no surviving children and an estate is to be divided among grandchildren and great-grandchildren (or among nephews and grand-nephews), where does the initial division occur? A leading case on this question arose from a trust created by Clinton Hastings, the founder of the Hastings Law School and the only person to be Chief Justice of two states (Iowa and California). When Hastings' trust was distributed, his living issue were four grandchildren and two great-grandchildren, children of deceased grandchildren.[26]

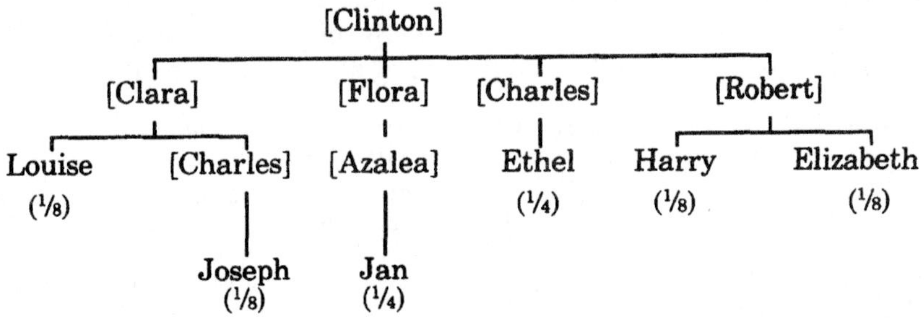


The court divided the estate at the level of Hastings' children even though they were all dead. As a consequence, claimants in the same degree received unequal shares (*e.g.* Ethel and Harry) and a great grandchild (Jan) received more than three grandchildren. The Restatement names this method

**22.** Calif.Prob.Code § 240. This was also true of the pre–1990 UPC.

**23.** Waggoner, *A Proposed Alternative to the Uniform Probate Code's System for Intestate Distribution Among Descendants,* 66 Nw. U.L.Rev. 626, 628 (1972).

**24.** Uniform Probate Code § 2–106.

**25.** *Restatement (Third) of Property (Wills and Other Donative Transfers)* § 2.3, comm. g (1998); Cal.Prob.Code § 247. This method applies in California only if an instrument calls for it.

**26.** Maud v. Catherwood, 155 P.2d 111 (Cal.App.1945).

of division "strict per stirpes."[27] Under the Uniform Probate Code (and present California law), on the other hand, the estate would have been initially divided at the closest level to the intestate where there were living claimants; Hastings' children would be ignored because they were all dead.[28] Louise, Ethel, Harry and Elizabeth would get one-sixth, as would Joseph and Jan, as the representatives of Charles and Azalea respectively.

### *Interpretation of Wills*

The question how to compute shares also arises under wills. If a will devises property to "grandchildren" (or "nieces and nephews"), courts usually require an equal distribution, without regard to the number of children (or brothers and sisters) from which the claimants stem.[29]

If a devise is to "issue" or to "heirs" the UPC would follow the rules of intestacy in determining the shares,[30] but additional language may change the result, since the testator's intent controls. There has been much litigation about what a testator intended by words like "equally" or "share and share alike." For example, a will left land to the testator's son's "heirs, share and share alike." The son was survived by a daughter and by two children of a deceased son. By the law of intestacy, the son's estate would go half to the daughter and half to the children of the deceased son, but the court held that the words "share and share alike" required that each heir take one third.[31] Other courts, however, have held that " 'equally,' referring to a multi-generational class, normally means per stirpes,"[32] *i.e.* each stirps gets an equal share, but not each taker.

The words "per stirpes" are as ambiguous as "equally." When a will gave property "per stirpes to my grand nieces and the issue of any deceased grandnieces" the court had to decide whether the basis of division should be the testator's nieces and nephews or the next generation.[33] The court held that the grandnieces and grandnephews were the roots,[34] but on similar facts other courts have disagreed.[35] In California, if an instrument calls for distribu-

**27.** *Restatement (Third) of Property (Wills and Other Donative Transfers)* § 2.3, comm. d (1998).

**28.** Uniform Probate Code § 2–106; Calif.Prob.Code § 240. *See also* Hockman v. Estate of Lowe, 624 S.W.2d 719 (Tex.App.1981) (when intestate had nine nieces and nephews, each living one gets 1/8 and the ninth share divided between the children of a dead nephew); Estate of McCrary, 62 Cal.Rptr.2d 504 (App.1997) (decedent survived by 4 first cousins and 67 descendants of 14 deceased cousins; each surviving first cousin takes 4/18, balance divided among the others).

**29.** *Restatement (Second) of Property (Donative Transfers)* § 28.1 (1987); Matter of Lopez, 636 P.2d 731 (Haw.1981).

**30.** Uniform Probate Code §§ 2–708, 2–711; Cal.Prob.Code §§ 245, 21114; *Restatement (Second) of Property, Donative Transfers* § 29.6 (1987).

**31.** Black v. Unknown Creditors, 155 N.W.2d 784 (S.D.1968). *See also* Johnson v. Johnson, 468 N.E.2d 945 (Ohio Prob.1984); Old Colony Trust Co. v. Stephens, 190 N.E.2d 110 (Mass.1963); *Restatement (Second) of Property (Donative Transfers)* § 29.6, illus. 3 (1987).

**32.** Dewire v. Haveles, 534 N.E.2d 782, 786 (Mass.1989). *See also* First Illini Bank v. Pritchard, 595 N.E.2d 728 (Ill.App.1992); In re Trust of Woodworth, 492 N.W.2d 818 (Mich. App.1992); Matter of Trust Estate of Dwight, 909 P.2d 561 (Haw.1995) (direction to distribute "equally per stirpes" is not contradictory since it means each branch of the family gets an equal share).

**33.** Estate of Edwards, 250 Cal.Rptr. 779 (App.1988).

**34.** *See also* In re Will of Lewis, 434 S.E.2d 472 (Ga.1993); Bonney v. Granger, 356 S.E.2d 138 (S.C.App.1987); Matter of Estate of Evans, 704 P.2d 35 (Mont.1985); Hartford Nat. Bank and Trust v. Thrall, 440 A.2d 200 (Conn.1981); Matter of Griffin's Will, 411 So.2d 766 (Miss. 1982); Wachovia Bank and Trust Co. v. Livengood, 294 S.E.2d 319 (N.C.1982)

**35.** Teller v. Kaufman, 426 F.2d 128 (8th Cir.1970); *Restatement (Second) of Property (Donative Transfers)* § 28.2, comm. b (1987);

tion "per stirpes" or "by representation" to the issue of X, the division is made at the level of X's children even if they are all dead.[36] This is also the Uniform Probate Code's interpretation of the words "per stirpes," but not "by representation."[37]

Drafters who use words like "by representation" in an instrument should define it in order to make the meaning clear.[38] The California Probate Code offers definitions to which drafters can refer to make the testator's preference clear.[39]

### *Parents and their Issue*

If a decedent leaves no surviving issue, parents or siblings are next in line. Historically, ascendants (parents, grandparents, great-grandparents, etc.), never inherited.[40] The reasons for this rule are mysterious.[41] It was abolished in England in 1833[42] and survives nowhere.

Most American jurisdictions today actually prefer the decedent's parents (or surviving parent) over brothers and sisters.[43] In some states, however, siblings share with parents under a variety of formulas.[44]

### *More Remote Relatives*

Some intestacy statutes name no specific takers after the issue of parents; they simply give the inheritance to the decedent's "next of kin."[45] Collateral relatives always share a common ancestor. To compute the degree of kinship between a decedent and a collateral relative, one must add the number of generations up from the decedent to the common ancestor and then down from the common ancestor to the relative. Thus a brother is in the second degree, a nephew is in the third degree, the common ancestors being the decedent's parents. First cousins are related in the fourth degree: two generations from the first cousin to the common ancestors (the grandparents) and two generations from the grandparents down. The degrees of kinship are illustrated in the following chart:[46, 47]

Bank of New England, N.A. v. McKennan, 477 N.E.2d 170 (Mass.App.1985); Estate of Morton, 222 A.2d 185 (N.J.1966).

**36.** Cal.Prob.Code § 246.

**37.** Uniform Probate Code § 2–709.

**38.** Uniform Statutory Will Act § 1(5).

**39.** Cal.Prob.Code §§ 246–47. Many testators may not have a clear preference. For example, one with 3 healthy children when executing a will may find it hard to think about how she would want her property divided if she were survived only by grand nieces and nephews.

**40.** T. Littleton, *Tenures* § 3.

**41.** Blackstone attributes it to feudalism: "the decrepit grandsire of a vigorous vassal" would not be able to perform the feudal services. 2 W. Blackstone, *Commentaries* * 212 (1765). Maitland rejected this reason but confessed that it was "by no means easy" to explain the rule. Pollock & Maitland, *The History of English Law* 286–93 (2d ed. 1898).

**42.** Statute, 3 & 4 Will. 4, c. 106, § 6 (1833).

**43.** Uniform Probate Code § 2–103(2); Cal. Prob.Code § 6402(b); Conn.Gen.Stat.Ann. § 45a–439(a)(1).

**44.** 755 ILCS § 5/2–1(d) (equal division among parents and siblings); Tex.Prob.Code Ann. § 38(a) (all to parents but if one dead 1/2 to siblings).

**45.** Ala.Code § 43–3–1(7); Conn.Gen.Stat. § 45–276; 12 Del.Code § 503(4); 14 Vt.Stat. § 551(5).

**46.** These persons are often called "second cousins" but this term is more appropriately applied to persons linked by common great-grandparents. This terminology is not important for our purposes, since no statute uses the word "cousin" to describe a taker on intestacy, although the word may occasionally appear in a will.

**47.** For further examples, extending to third cousins once removed see *Restatement (Third) of Property (Wills and Other Donative Transfers)* § 2.4, comm. k (1998).

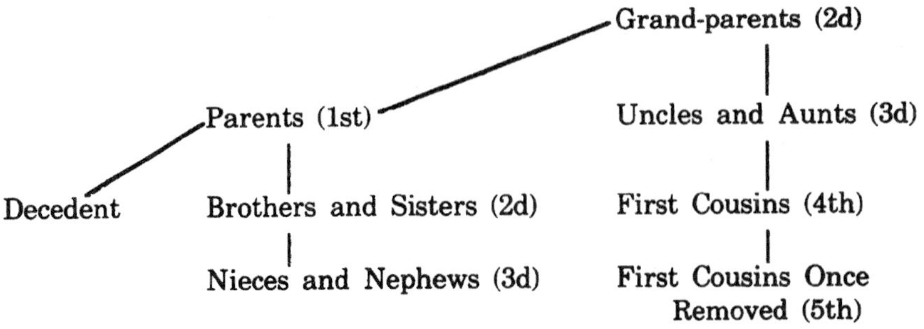


Issue of a nearer ancestor are preferred to issue of a more remote ancestor even if they are not as close in degree. This is sometimes called the parentelic principle. The decedent's issue are in the first parentela, parents and their issue (brothers, sisters, nieces, etc.) are in the second parentela, grandparents and their issue (uncles, aunts, first cousins, etc.) are in the third parentela and so forth. A nephew, even though he is in the third degree of kinship, takes ahead of grandparents who are in the second degree because the nephew is issue of a closer ancestor (the decedent's parents).[48]

The parentelic principle is followed in modern statutes.[49] The Uniform Probate Code designates as heirs first the issue of the decedent (§ 2–103(1)) (the first parentela), then the decedent's parents and their issue (§ 2–103(2)(3)) (second parentela), then the grandparents and their issue (§ 2–103(4)) (third parentela).[50]

Everyone has two sets of grandparents, maternal and paternal. The UPC divides the estate into maternal and paternal halves, and then subdivides each half. Thus if the only surviving relatives were a paternal aunt (father's sister) and three maternal uncles (mother's brothers), the paternal aunt would take one-half of the estate and the maternal uncles would take one-sixth each, in disregard of the principle applied elsewhere that persons of the same degree of kinship to the decedent should take equally.[51] Other states do not split the estate between the maternal and paternal families and would give one-fourth to each of the aunts and uncles.[52]

### *Ancestral Property*

Historically, land returned to the branch of the family from which it

**48.** Pollock & Maitland, *supra* note 9, at 296.

**49.** The parentelic principle is not always followed among remoter relatives. *Restatement (Third) of Property (Wills and Other Donative Transfers)* § 2.4, illus. 1 (1998) (third cousins share with second cousin twice removed in some states).

**50.** See also Cal. Prob. Code § 6402, which provides that if there are no relatives in the first three parentelas, the estate goes "to the next of kin in equal degree, but where there are two or more collateral kindred in equal degree who claim through different ancestors, those who claim through the nearest ancestor are preferred to those claiming through an ancestor more remote." There is no comparable provision in the UPC since it does not allow inheritance beyond the issue of grandparents.

**51.** Uniform Probate Code § 2–103(1), (4).

**52.** Cal.Prob.Code § 6402(d); N.Y.EPTL § 4–1.1(a)(8); Ind.Code § 29–1–2–1(c)(6); Dahood v. Frankovich, 746 P.2d 115 (Mont.1987).

came.[53] If a woman had inherited Blackacre from her paternal grandfather and died without surviving issue of herself or her parents, her paternal collaterals (uncles, aunts, cousins) would take Blackacre to the exclusion of her maternal collaterals. This doctrine never applied to personalty.

The ancestral property idea creates administrative difficulties because it requires tracing the source of land. Therefore it has been discarded by most jurisdictions today, but a few states retain vestiges of it.[54]

### *Half-blood*

Half-bloods are related to each other through only one common ancestor rather than two. If Arthur and Andrew have the same father but different mothers, Arthur being a child of his father's prior marriage, Arthur and Andrew are half-brothers. A son of Andrew would be Arthur's half-nephew.

Historically, half-blood relatives could not inherit land from each other.[55] In 1833 a statute allowed half-bloods to inherit land, but only if no siblings of the whole-blood survived.[56] As to personal property, half-bloods shared equally with whole-blood relatives.[57]

Most modern statutes make no distinction between whole-bloods and half-bloods.[58] A few states give the half-blood only half as much as a whole-blood of the same degree.[59] Others combine the ancestral property rule with a limited exclusion of the half-blood. For example, in Washington, half-blood and whole-blood kindred receive the same share "unless the inheritance comes to the intestate by descent devise or gift from one of his ancestors * * * in which case all who are not of the blood of such ancestors shall be excluded from such inheritance."[60]

A devise of property "to my brothers and sisters" is presumed to include half-brothers and half-sisters.[61]

### *"Laughing Heirs" and Escheat*

If a person dies survived by neither spouse nor close blood relatives, should the decedent's property escheat to the state or be distributed to remote relatives? The latter are sometimes called "laughing heirs" because they are

**53.** 2 W. Blackstone, *Commentaries* *220 (1765).

**54.** Ken.Rev.Stat. § 391.020; Minn.Stat. Ann. § 525.16(5) (property of a minor goes to issue of parent from whom decedent inherited it). *See Restatement (Third) of Property (Wills and Other Donative Transfers)* § 2.4, comm. d (1998).

**55.** 2 W. Blackstone, *Commentaries* *224 (1765). Blackstone ascribed this to the ancestral property rule. If Arthur could inherit from Andrew, he *might* get property which Andrew had inherited from his mother, to whom Arthur was not related. Henry Maine rejected Blackstone's explanation and offered one of his own which Maitland in turn rejected. H. Maine, *Ancient Law* 126 (World Classics ed.); Pollock & Maitland, *supra* note 9, at 305.

**56.** Statute, 3 & 4 Will. 4, c. 106, § 6 (1833).

**57.** 2 W. Blackstone, *Commentaries** 505 (1765).

**58.** Uniform Probate Code § 2–107; Calif.Prob.Code § 6406; Conn.Gen.Stat.Ann. § 45a–439(e); Matter of Estate of Seaman, 583 N.E.2d 294 (N.Y.1991).

**59.** Fla.Stat.Ann. § 732.105; Ken.Rev.Stat. § 391.050; Tex. Prob.Code § 41(b); Curry v. Williman, 834 S.W.2d 443 (Tex.App.1992)(full brother gets 20% of estate, 3 half brothers get 10% each).

**60.** Rev.Cod.Wash. § 11.04.035. Under this statute more remote whole blood relatives are preferred to half-bloods. Matter of Estate of Little, 721 P.2d 950 (Wash.1986).

**61.** *Restatement (Second) of Property (Donative Transfers)* § 25.8, comment d (1987); Uniform Probate Code § 2–705(a); Cal.Prob. Code § 21115.

personally unaffected by the decedent's death and so laugh all the way to the bank. The Uniform Probate Code excludes such remote relatives, limiting inheritance to issue of grandparents.[62] Second cousins of a decedent who were barred from inheriting under a similar statute challenged it as unconstitutional. The court in upholding the statute, cited the following reasons for limiting inheritance:

> (1) It is restricted to relatives whom the decedent probably knew and had an interest in; (2) it solves problems occasioned by * * * the expense and difficulty in locating more remote relatives, the threat of frivolous litigation in will contests by so-called "laughing heirs," and the administrative problems which may be caused by dividing an estate into too many small portions;[63] and (3) the enumerated relatives and * * * the state are more likely to care for decedent than are the decedent's more remote relatives.[64]

Despite these considerations, most statutes permit inheritance by distant blood relatives rather than let the property escheat to the state,[65] under the theory that "escheats are not favored by the law and are to be avoided wherever possible."[66] Many states allow persons related to the decedent's spouse but not to the decedent to inherit if the decedent has no surviving relatives. In California, for example, issue of a predeceased spouse inherit when the decedent has no relatives closer than issue of grandparents.[67]

A person who feels no affection for remote relatives (or close ones) can disinherit them by will.[68] But heirs can contest a will, *e.g.* for incapacity or undue influence, and in most states they must be notified when a will is offered for probate.[69] As a result, an heir tracing industry has evolved. Most firms charge a percentage of the estate to the estate or to the heirs. In a large estate these fees can be quite substantial.[70]

### *Aliens*

At common law an alien could not hold land in England. "If the person to whom land would descend according to the common rules of inheritance, be an alien, it misses him and passes to some remoter kinsman of the dead

**62.** Uniform Probate Code § 2–103. *See also Restatement (Third) of Property (Wills and Other Donative Transfers)* § 2.4, comm. i (1998).

**63.** Blackstone calculated that "if we suppose each couple of our ancestors to have left * * * two children; and each of those on an average to have left two more,* * * all of us have now subsisting near two hundred and seventy millions of kindred in the fifteenth degree." 2 W. Blackstone, *Commentaries* *205 (1765).

**64.** Matter of Estate of Jurek, 428 N.W.2d 774, 777 (Mich.App.1988).

**65.** This includes states which otherwise adhere to the UPC scheme of intestate succession. Minn.Stat.Ann. § 525.16; Utah Code Ann. § 75–2–103.

**66.** Estate of McGuigan, 99 Cal.Rptr.2d 887, 890 (App.2000).

**67.** Cal.Prob.Code § 6402(e). Under paragraph (g) issue of a spouse's parents take if the decedent has no relatives at all. Under Conn. Gen.Stat. Ann § 45a–439(e) the estate goes to stepchildren if a decedent has no spouse or relatives. *See also* Fla. Stat. Ann. § 732.103(5) (kindred of deceased spouse); Ohio Rev. Code § 2105.06(I) (stepchildren or their descendants).

**68.** As we shall see in Chapter 3, in most American states, only the decedent's spouse is protected against disinheritance.

**69.** As to notice and standing to contest wills see Section 12.1. As to incapacity and undue influence see Sections 7.1, 7.3.

**70.** Rodenbush, *Missing Heirs: Put Yourself in their Shoes*, 130 Trusts & Estates (Dec. 1991) p. 53.

man."[71] This rule has been invoked in modern cases, *e.g.* to deny Polish relatives of a decedent any share in his real estate. The right to inherit could be conferred on aliens by treaty or statute, but at that time there was no such treaty between Poland and the United States, and a statute conferred rights only on resident aliens.[72] The Restatement of Property, however, reverses the presumption: unless a statute otherwise provides, noncitizens can acquire and transmit property.[73]

## § 2.3 General Aspects of Intestacy: Statutory Wills

### *Empirical Studies*

American schemes of intestate succession purport to distribute an intestate's estate along the lines that the average person would prefer. However, studies of public preferences regarding the disposition of wealth at death suggest that some common statutory provisions are out of line with today's attitudes. These studies are of two types. The first examines probate court records of decedents' wills.[1] Such studies influenced the Uniform Probate Code.[2] The second type relies on interviews with living persons who say how they would want their property to pass on death in various hypothetical situations.[3] Both types of study have deficiencies.

The examination of wills may be misleading as to the average person's desires because "willmakers tend to be wealthier, better educated, and engaged in higher status occupations than those who die without a will."[4] According to one study 72% of persons with estates under $100,000 have no wills, as compared with 15% of those with estates between $200,000 and $1 million.[5] Also wills usually reflect the influence of lawyers who draft them, and perhaps the law should strive to follow "innate preferences" which are "unadulterated by" such influences. On the other hand, the lawyer's advice is

**71.** Pollock & Maitland, *supra* note 9, at 442. The authors doubt whether this rule existed before the end of the thirteenth century, since William the Conqueror, "a foreigner at the head of an army recruited from many lands conquered England [and] endowed his followers with English lands."

**72.** In re Estate of Constan, 384 A.2d 495 (N.H.1978).

**73.** *Restatement, Third, of Property (Wills and Other Donative Transfers)* § 1.3 (1998). A Statutory Note appended to this section lists many relevant statutes.

§ 2.3

**1.** *See* M. Sussman *et al., The Family and Inheritance* (study of probate court records of estates in Cuyahoga County, Ohio); Browder, *Recent Patterns of Testate Succession*, 67 Mich. L.Rev. 1303 (1969) (study of probate court records of estates in Washtenaw County, Michigan, and London, England); Dunham, *The Method, Process and Frequency of Wealth Transmission at Death,* 30 U.Chi.L.Rev. 241 (1963) (study of probate court records of estates in Cook County, Illinois); Price, *The Transmission of Wealth at Death in a Community Property Jurisdiction*, 50 Wash.L.Rev. 277 (1975) (death certificates, probate records and inheritance tax files of 211 adults who died in King County, Wash. in 1969); Ward & Beucher, *The Inheritance Process in Wisconsin*, 1950 Wis.L.Rev. 393 (study of county court records of estates in Dane County, Wisconsin).

**2.** See Comment to Part 1, § 2–102, comment.

**3.** Fellows *et al., Public Attitudes about Property Distribution*, 1978 Am.B. Found. Research J. 321 (market research organization conducted 750 telephone interviews of respondents in five states); Fellows, Simon, Snapp & Snapp, *An Empirical Study of the Illinois Statutory Estate Plan,* 1976 U.Ill.L.F. 717 (interviews of 182 Illinois residents); *Intestate Succession in New Jersey: Does it Conform to Popular Expectations?,* 12 Colum.J.L. & Soc. Prob. 253 (1976) (telephone survey of randomly selected Morris County residents); Note, 63 Iowa L.Rev. 1041 (1978) (telephone and personal interviews).

**4.** Beckstrom, *Sociobiology and Intestate Wealth Transfers,* 76 Nw.U.L.Rev. 216, 217–19 (1981).

**5.** Waggoner, *Marital Property Rights in Transition*, 59 Mo.L.Rev. 21, 29 (1994).

often sound and brings up factors which the client had not previously considered but which, once mentioned, cause the client to make sensible changes in an initial dispositive plan. Should not the law be modelled on the *informed* wishes of citizens?

### *Why Not Die Intestate?*

Attorneys may be asked why a client should have a will. One reason is that state intestacy laws at best only meet the needs of a 'normal' family and may not fit the client's situation. The spouse of a year is generally treated the same as the spouse of a long time; a wealthy or unloving child is treated the same as a needy and devoted one. Unrelated persons are excluded even if they have enjoyed the same kind of relationship with the decedent as a child. Remote relatives may take an estate which the owner would prefer to leave to a charity or friends.[6] One who dies intestate gives up the opportunity to tailor the dispositions to the particular family situation.

When a client has minor children, intestacy is particularly undesirable. When property passes directly to a minor, a guardian of the minor's property may have to be appointed to manage the minor's property. Many states impose strict court supervision over a guardian's actions. These restrictions are cumbersome and generally antithetical to the child's interest in earning a fair return on the property and reducing costs.[7] Moreover, guardianship ends when a child ceases to be a minor, and many believe that children who are 18 (or sometimes much older) need to have property managed for them. The best method for accomplishing this is a trust. For this reason some states allow wrongful death proceeds awarded to a minor to be placed in a trust, but such provisions do not exist for ordinary intestate succession.[8]

Many testators with minor children avoid guardianship by leaving everything to their spouse in the expectation that the spouse will take care of the children. This solution may not be satisfactory if the surviving spouse is not the parent of the decedent's children, or has other children by a prior marriage. Even if this is not the case, the client may fear that the spouse may remarry and have another family to which the client's property may be diverted. Here too a trust can provide a better solution than any of the intestacy statutes.

Even if a person wants all her property to pass to the heirs designated by the intestacy laws, and even if no trust is needed, a will may still be desirable. A will can designate an executor to administer the estate and can give the executor powers beyond those conferred by law. Administration of an estate is more efficient when the executor has such powers.[9]

**6.** In Estate of Griswold, 94 Cal.Rptr.2d 638, 640 (App.2000) half siblings with whom decedent had had no contact and who were unaware of his existence inherited from him.

**7.** For further discussion of alternatives to guardianship see Section 9.2.

**8.** In Sawyer v. Lebanon Citizens Natl. Bank, 664 N.E.2d 571 (Ohio App.1995) such a trust was created for the decedent's minor children who were to get the funds outright when they reached age 25, whereas in most states a guardianship ends at age 18.

**9.** For examples of how a will can avoid restrictive administrative procedures see Stein & Fierstein, *The Demography of Probate Administration,* 15 U.Balt.L.Rev. 54, 80–81 (1985).

### *Statutory Wills*

Despite the advantages of wills, many persons do not have them.[10] To some extent this is due to the reliance on nonprobate methods of transfer at death, such as living trusts and joint tenancy.[11] To some extent it is based on reluctance to hire lawyers. No state requires that will be drafted by lawyers, but wills which are drafted without lawyers often cause problems, and many lay persons are reluctant (perhaps wisely) to draft their own will.

Some states have promulgated statutory wills which lay persons can use at a very modest cost. Many of the disadvantages of dying intestate can be avoided by using the California statutory will, for example. It allows a testator to leave all the estate to the spouse by signing the appropriate box.[12] The testator can designate a custodian for his/her children, which avoids many of the disadvantages of guardianship.[13] The form allows designation of an executor, and implies powers in the executor which are more extensive than those given to an administrator without a will.[14]

A Uniform Statutory Will Act, promulgated in 1984, allows a testator to create a trust for the spouse for life, and a trust for a child who "cannot effectively manage * * * property by reason of mental illness * * * or other cause."[15] Probably few lay persons are aware of this Act; the drafters primary goal was "to provide attorneys a simple will* * * at minimum cost to the client" rather than one which laypersons would adopt themselves.[16] Lawyers who have little experience or training in probate would be well advised to consult the statutory will before drafting a will "from scratch."

## § 2.4 Gifts to "Heirs"

Most lawyers advise clients not to die intestate, but lawyers often use the intestacy laws in drafting wills and trusts by including a gift to the "heirs" of the testator, settlor or another person. This term is normally interpreted to incorporate by reference the laws of intestate succession.[1]

### *Equivalent Words*

Occasionally an instrument uses the word "next of kin" rather than heirs. Historically this was the term used to describe persons who took personal property while the heirs inherited the land,[2] but the differences between the two have almost universally disappeared. The Uniform Probate Code uses the word "heirs" for all takers by intestacy,[3] and calls for interpret-

**10.** Schoenblum, *Will Contests—An Empirical Study*, 22 Real Prop. Prob. and Trust J. 607 (1987)(only 20% of decedents had wills filed for probate during the period 1976–84); Warren, *Advisors Often Fail to Heed Own Advice*, Trusts & Estates Jan. 1995, p. 6 (38% of accountants and 25% of lawyers surveyed had no will).

**11.** For a discussion of the advantages of avoiding probate see Section 9.1, at note 5 et seq.

**12.** Cal. Prob. Code § 6240, par. 5, Choice One.

**13.** Custodianships are discussed at Section 9.2, at note 5 et seq.

**14.** Cal.Prob.Code § 6241.

**15.** Unif.Stat.Will Act § 6 (trust for spouse), § 9 (trust for disabled individual).

**16.** *Id.*, Prefatory Note. The Act has been adopted in Massachusetts and New Mexico.

§ 2.4

**1.** *Restatement (Second) of Property (Donative Transfers)* § 29.1 (1987); Uniform Probate Code § 2–711; Cal.Prob.Code § 21114.

**2.** In In re Johnson's Will, 301 N.Y.S.2d 174 (App.Div.1969) the court applied the law governing to real estate in 1909 even though the property to be distributed was personal property because the will devised it to "heirs."

**3.** Uniform Probate Code § 1–201(21). *See also* Cal.Prob.Code § 44.

ing the word "next of kin" in an instrument as a gift to the same persons.[4] Occasionally an argument is made that the word "next" excludes more remote relatives who would take by representation on intestacy, but this argument is usually rejected.[5]

Words of more uncertain import, like "relatives" and "family" are also under the Uniform Probate Code construed to mean the takers under intestacy statutes.[6] Some courts have so construed the word "representatives," so that a gift to "children and the representatives of any deceased child" referred to the deceased child's heirs.[7]

### *Other Meanings of Heirs: Devisees*

The word "heirs" does not always refer to the intestacy statutes. Its Latin root, *heres,* in Roman law was used to mean either a person designated by will or someone who took upon intestacy.[8] This usage still survives in Louisiana, where a husband devise of property upon his wife's death "to her heirs," was held to allow her to "will the property to whomever she pleases" because "heirs" included testamentary legatees.[9]

In the common law tradition, however, heirs ordinarily means only those persons designated by law to take upon intestacy.[10] Thus a gift to "the heirs at law" of the testator's son passed to the son's relatives and not to a friend whom the son had designated as his "heir."[11] But sometimes the context shows that the word "heirs" was used to mean devisees. For example, when a will made devises to eight named individuals in paragraph 5, and left the residue of his estate "to the heirs set forth in Item 5," the named individuals, although not heirs of the testator, were awarded the residue.[12]

### *Is the Spouse an "Heir"*

Most courts construe gifts to "heirs" to include spouses because most modern intestacy statutes give spouses a share of the estate on intestacy.[13] The Uniform Probate Code agrees unless the spouse has remarried when the

**4.** Uniform Probate Code § 2–711. *See also* Cal.Prob.Code § 21114.

**5.** Meador v. Williams, 827 S.W.2d 706 (Ky.App.1992)(includes issue of predeceased sibling); *Restatement, Second, of Property (Donative Transfers)* § 29.1, comm. b (1987); Graves v. Hyer, 626 S.W.2d 661, 668 (Mo.App. 1981) ("nearest blood kin").

**6.** Uniform Probate Code § 2–711. *See also* Cal.Prob.Code § 21114; *Restatement, Second, of Property (Donative Transfers)* § 29.1, comm. b (1987) ("relatives"); cf. *Restatement, Second, Trusts* § 415 (1959). Professor Fratcher questioned this construction in situations where the intestacy statute give everything to a spouse and nothing to the decedent's blood relatives. Fratcher, *Class Gifts to "Heirs," "Issue" and Like Groups*, 55 Alb.L.Rev. 1205, 1217 (1992).

**7.** Boston Safe Deposit & Trust Co. v. Wilbur, 728 N.E.2d 264, 268 (Mass.2000).

**8.** Justinian, *Institutes* 2.20.34 (the main purpose of a will is to designate the heir).

**9.** Succession of Dinwiddie, 263 So.2d 739 (La.App.1972).

**10.** Glanville, *Tractatus de Legibus* 71 (G. Hall ed. 1965).

**11.** PNC Bank, Ohio, N.A. v. Stanton, 662 N.E.2d 875 (Ohio App.1995).

**12.** Evans v. Cass, 256 N.E.2d 738 (Ohio Prob.1970). *See also* In re Leake's Estate, 246 N.E.2d 314 (Ill.App.1969); Hancock v. Krause, 757 S.W.2d 117 (Tex.App.1988); *Restatement (Second) of Property (Donative Transfers)* § 29.1, comm. g. (1987).

**13.** *Id.* § 29.1, comm. j; Estate of Calden, 712 A.2d 522 (Me.1998). *But see* Carter v. King, 353 S.E.2d 738 (Va.1987); McLane v. Marden, 277 A.2d 315 (N.H.1971); *Restatement (Second) of Property, Donative Transfers* § 29.3, comm. a (1987) (spouse is not an heir where governing law allows only dower); Daugherty v. Daugherty, 784 S.W.2d 650 (Tenn.1990) (spouse gets personal property but not land); Russell v. Russell, 399 S.E.2d 415 (N.C.App.1991).

disposition takes effect. Thus in a devise "to A for life, remainder to my heirs," if the testator's widow has remarried when A dies, she would not qualify as an heir.[14]

Sometimes "heirs" appears in a context which shows that only blood relatives were intended. A devise to the "heirs per stirpes" of the testator's daughter was interpreted to exclude her husband.[15] Nor would a devise to "the heirs of Mary's body" include her husband.[16]

Sometimes the context shows that the testator used the word "heirs" to mean "children" or "issue." When a testator left land to his grandson's heirs, "and if he should die without heirs to my other Grandchildren," the court construed "heirs" to mean "issue," since the "other Grandchildren" would *be* the grandson's heirs if he had no issue, and a gift to a person's heirs if he dies without heirs is nonsense.[17] An intent to exclude a spouse from the "heir" category may also be found in a direction that "the heirs of a deceased child shall take the share *their parent* would have taken if living."[18]

### *Choice of Law*

A drafter who decides to use a gift to "heirs" in a will should make clear *which* intestacy statute should control, since the laws of different states differ. For example, a trust provided that at the death of the settlor's grandson, his widow "shall receive such portion of the trust estate as she would be entitled to had her husband died intestate." This portion was greater under Maryland law, where the trust was created and administered, than under the law of Texas, where the grandson was domiciled at death. The court held that Maryland law governed,[19] but the Uniform Probate Code looks to the "law of the designated individual's domicile," *i.e.*, Texas on these facts.[20] The Restatement of Property would have looked to the law of Texas including its choice of law rules, which might in turn lead to the situs of any real property involved.[21] These rules are all subject to any express provision accompanying the word "heirs," e.g. the Uniform Statutory Will Act refers to "the individuals who would be entitled to receive the estate as if the property were located in this state and [the ancestor] had then died intestate domiciled in this state."[22]

The governing intestacy statute may change between the time the testator executes the will and the time the property is distributed. Therefore the will should also specify the time of the controlling law.[23] Some states have different rules for different types of property (real and personal, or separate and community), so the will should say which rules apply.

**14.** Uniform Probate Code § 2–711. *See also* Cal.Prob.Code § 21114.

**15.** Varns v. Varns, 610 N.E.2d 440 (Ohio App.1991). *Contra*, Wright v. Brandon, 863 S.W.2d 400 (Tenn.1993).

**16.** *Restatement, Second, of Property (Donative Transfers)* § 29.1, comm. j (1987).

**17.** Cheuvront v. Haley, 444 S.W.2d 734 (Ky.1969). *See also Restatement (Second) of Property (Donative Transfers)* § 29.1, comm. f (1987); Dickson v. Renfro, 569 S.W.2d 66 (Ark. 1978); Estate of Forrest, TC Memo 1990–464.

**18.** *Restatement (Second) of Property, Donative Transfers* § 29.1, comm. e (1987).

**19.** Lansburgh v. Lansburgh, 632 A.2d 221 (Md.App.1993).

**20.** Uniform Probate Code § 2–711. Under Cal. Prob. Code § 21114 the heirs are apparently determined under California law regardless of domicile.

**21.** *Restatement, Second, of Property (Donative Transfers)* § 29.2 (1987).

**22.** Uniform Statutory Will Act § 6(3).

**23.** See Section 10.2, note 28.

### *Planning*

Objections can be raised to using words like "heirs" in drafting. Most testators do not know what the intestacy statutes provide. Even if the drafter describes them, an oral summary may be misunderstood or forgotten. Some testators whose wills left property to "heirs" apparently understood this to mean something different from what the law provides.[24] Nevertheless, the word "heirs" is useful because the intestacy statutes cover a wide variety of situations. Many wills specify a distribution for the situations most likely to prevail, but use a devise to "heirs" as an "end limitation" to cover remote contingencies.[25] This is simpler than spelling out all possible contingencies in the will—e.g. to my parents, if living, otherwise to my brothers and sisters, if living, otherwise to their issue, if living, otherwise etc. However, particularly in a jurisdiction which limits inheritance, like the Uniform Probate Code, a gift to the "heirs" of someone who dies without close relatives or a spouse may produce an escheat.[26] If heirship is *not* limited by the governing law, it may require a costly search for remote relatives.[27] Many testators might prefer an end limitation to charity instead of "heirs."

## § 2.5 Recovery for Wrongful Death

Many decedents who have accumulated little or no property at death may nevertheless provide their families with a valuable claim against a tortfeasor who was responsible for their death. At common law tort claims died with the person, but all states now allow wrongful death actions. The original statute was Lord Campbell's Act, an English statute of 1846.[1] The law on this subject is not generally considered part of the law of wills. For example, wrongful death recovery is not covered by the Uniform Probate Code. In California, the subject is dealt with in the Code of Civil Procedure, not the Probate Code.[2] But wrongful death actions are typically brought by the decedent's personal representative who is appointed by the probate court.[3]

Many statutes refer to the intestacy laws in designating the beneficiaries of a wrongful death. In California, for example, the action is brought on behalf of the "decedent's surviving spouse, children, and issue of deceased children, or, if none, the persons who would be entitled to the property of the decedent

24. *See* Matter of Taff's Estate, 133 Cal. Rptr. 737 (App.1976); Gustafson v. Svenson, 366 N.E.2d 761 (Mass.1977); Brunson v. Citizens Bank and Trust Co., 752 S.W.2d 316 (Ky.App.1988) (testator apparently thought his "heirs" included his sisters even though he had a daughter).

25. Uniform Statutory Will Act § 7(a)(2) (devise to heirs if testator dies without issue).

26. Uniform Probate Code § 2–711 expressly allows the state to take under a gift to "heirs." *Contra, Restatement, Second, of Property (Donative Transfers)* § 29.1, comm. k (1987).

27. See Section 2.2, note 65.

**§ 2.5**

1. An Act for Compensating the families of Persons killed by Accidents, 9 & 10 Vict. ch. 96 (1846).

2. Cal.Code Civ.Proc. § 377.60 et seq.

3. Lord Campbell's Act created an action for the "the Executor or Administrator of the Person deceased." 9 & 10 Vict. ch. 93, § 2. *See also* Cal.Code Civ.Proc. § 377.60 (action may be brought by decedent's personal representative); Ind.Code § 34–1–1–2; Model Survival and Death Act § 3(a); Utah Code § 78–11–7 (action brought by heirs or personal representative). In many jurisdictions the personal representative's right to sue is made exclusive in order to avoid multiplicity of litigation. Weeks v. Cessna Aircraft Co., 895 P.2d 731 (Okl.App. 1994).

by intestate succession."[4] As to "children," courts look to the intestacy statutes to determine who is included, *e.g.* in the case of an adopted child or child born out of wedlock.[5] However, the beneficiaries of wrongful death actions are not always the same as those who take on intestacy. For example, a statute which designated "the heir or heirs of the deceased" was interpreted to include only descendants of the decedent and not collateral relatives who might inherit, because the purpose of the statute was "to compensate those who suffer pecuniary loss by reason of the death" and this would not be generally true of the latter.[6] In Georgia, children of a deceased child of the decedent can inherit, but are not entitled to claim for wrongful death.[7] In other states, certain heirs, such as the surviving spouse and children, are presumed to have been damaged by the death, whereas others, though eligible to claim, must prove that they were damaged.[8]

Conversely, dependent relatives of the decedent have been allowed to recover for wrongful death even though they would not have inherited because there was a closer relative.[9] Lord Campbell's Act allowed recovery by stepchildren and stepparents, even though they do not usually inherit.[10] Parents do not inherit if the decedent was survived by issue, or, in many states, if there is a surviving spouse. But dependent parents have been allowed to recover in a wrongful death action even if they were not heirs.[11] Even unrelated dependents who resided with the decedent can qualify in some states.[12]

**4.** Cal.Code Civ.Proc. § 377.60. *See also* Ohio Rev.Code § 2125.02(A) (for spouse, children, parents, and "other next of kin"); Ind. Code § 34–1–1–2 (for widow or widower, dependent children, or dependent next of kin); Ouellette v. State Farm, 918 P.2d 1363 (Okl. 1994) (parents are not "next of kin" and so cannot recover for wrongful death of child who was married and had children); Baugh v. Baugh ex rel. Smith, 973 P.2d 202 (Kan.App. 1999); Morris v. William L. Dawson Nursing Center, 702 N.E.2d 345 (Ill.App.1998) (same for siblings); Booker v. Lal, 726 N.E.2d 638 (Ill.App.2000) (children of deceased siblings eligible to take by representation). See, however, the cases cited at note 11 infra.

**5.** Cheyanna M. v. A.C. Nielsen Co., 78 Cal.Rptr.2d 335 (App.1998). *But see* Brookbank v. Gray, 658 N.E.2d 724 (Ohio 1996) (illegitimate child can recover for wrongful death even though ineligible to inherit). As to adoption and birth out of wedlock generally see Sections 2.9 and 2.10.

**6.** Ablin v. Richard O'Brien Plastering Co., 885 P.2d 289 (Colo.App.1994) (siblings cannot sue even though they are literally "heirs"); Whitenhill v. Kaiser Permanente, 940 P.2d 1129 (Colo.App.1997) (parents). *Compare* Kelson v. Salt Lake County, 784 P.2d 1152 (Utah 1989) (siblings cannot sue because they are not "heirs" if the decedent is survived by parents).

**7.** Tolbert v. Maner, 518 S.E.2d 423 (Ga. 1999). *But see* Booker v. Lal, 726 N.E.2d 638 (Ill.App.2000) (children of deceased siblings eligible by representation).

**8.** Miller v. Allstate Ins. Co., 676 N.E.2d 943 (Ohio App.1996) (sister of decedent can claim but does not benefit from the statutory presumption of damage); Wolf v. Boren, 685 N.E.2d 86 (Ind.App.1997) (no recovery for parents and siblings who were not "dependent" on decedent).

**9.** Luider v. Skaggs, 693 N.E.2d 593 (Ind. App.1998).

**10.** 9 & 10 Vict. ch. 93, § 5. As to the treatment of stepchildren generally see Section 2.10, note 66.

**11.** Butler v. Halstead, 770 P.2d 698 (Wyo. 1989) (even though a child was the only heir, decedent's mother could share in the wrongful death recovery); Oxendine v. Overturf, 973 P.2d 417 (Utah 1999); Model Survival and Death Act § 1(2) ("survivors" includes ascendants as well as descendants); Ramage v. Central Ohio Emergency Serv. Inc., 592 N.E.2d 828 (Ohio 1992) (grandparents can claim even when there was a surviving parent).

**12.** Cal.Code Civ.Proc. § 377.60. Under the Model Survival and Death Act § 1(2) the beneficiaries can include dependents who "were members of the decedent's household or related to the decedent by blood or marriage." In Lealaimatafoa v. Woodward–Clyde Consl., 867 P.2d 220 (Haw.1994) a woman living with the decedent and her child were allowed to recover under a statute which provided for a spouse, children, parents "or other dependent."

Even if the decedent's heirs and the statutory wrongful death beneficiaries are the same persons, the fixed shares prescribed by the intestacy statutes may not control the allocation of a wrongful death recovery.[13] Under the typical intestacy statute, parents inherit equally, but they often are awarded unequal amounts for wrongful death based on their relationship with the child.[14] In Ohio a parent "who abandoned a minor child" is disqualified altogether.[15]

In California the court allocates the recovery among the eligible claimants.[16] The statute gives no guidance as to how this discretion is to be exercised. In Ohio the court makes the allocation "having due regard for the injury and loss to each beneficiary * * * and for the age and condition of the beneficiaries."[17] A beneficiary guilty of wrongdoing may be disqualified.[18] Under the Model Survival and Death Act the determination is made by the "trier of fact," whether court or jury. If the claim is settled, the court must approve its terms and can control the allocation.[19]

### *Survival Claims*

The flexibility given by most wrongful death actions in allocating the recovery stands in sharp contrast to the fixed shares provided by the intestacy statutes. Perhaps this difference is due to the fact that if the intestacy statute produces a "bad" result in a given case, *e.g.* by allowing an undeserving child an equal share with his siblings, this can be avoided by a will. Wrongful death recoveries, on the other hand, are not governed by the decedent's will. Consequently parents who have accumulated property are free to disinherit their children, but not those who are killed before they have had time to accumulate property.[20]

Most states allow the decedent's estate to recover for some losses, and this recovery can be controlled by the decedent's will.[21] Under the Model Act, for example, damages which "accrued to [the decedent] before his death* * * become part of the decedent's estate and are distributable in the same

**13.** In some states, however, the intestacy statutes control the allocation. Estate of Boyd, 606 P.2d 1243 (Wyo.1980) (applying a statute later repealed); Pogue v. Pogue, 434 So.2d 262 (Ala.Civ.App.1983) (recovery equally divided between mother and father who had failed to support the child because intestacy statute controlled); Ind. Code § 34–1–1–2 (distribution "in the same manner as the personal property of the deceased").

**14.** Jones v. Jones, 641 N.E.2d 98 (Ind.App. 1994) (proper to award 65% to the mother who had custody of the child); Guy v. Johnson, 448 N.E.2d 1142 (Mass.App.1983); Carter v. Beaver, 577 So.2d 448 (Ala.1991) (entire recovery awarded to custodial parent); Matter of Estate of Lande, 567 N.E.2d 668 (Ill.App.1991) (same); In re Estate of Marinelli, 650 N.E.2d 935 (Ohio App.1994) (nothing awarded to father who "failed to maintain any semblance of a father-son relationship" with decedent).

**15.** Ohio Rev. Code § 2125.02(A)(1).

**16.** Cal.Code Civ.Proc. § 377.61.

**17.** Ohio Rev. Code § 2125.03(A)(1); *cf.* Booker v. Lal, 726 N.E.2d 638, 641 (Ill.App. 2000) (allocation on basis of "percentage of dependency").

**18.** Myers v. Robertson, 891 P.2d 199 (Alaska 1995) (parents whose negligence caused the death of a child deemed to have predeceased the child so recovery goes to other heirs). Compare Section 2.7.

**19.** Model Survival and Death Act § 3(f)(g). Cal.Prob.Code § 9835 requires that the settlement of a wrongful death action by a personal representative be approved by the court.

**20.** As to a parents' freedom to disinherit children in American law see Section 3.1.

**21.** *Restatement, Third, of Property (Wills and Other Donative Transfers)* § 1.1, illus. 20 (1998). Under Alaska Stat. § 09.55.580, when a decedent is survived "by no spouse or children or other dependents," the recovery "shall be administered as other personal property of the decedent."

manner as other assets of the estate."[22] These damages usually include medical expenses or pain and suffering by the decedent before death.[23] Arguably they should also include the prospective earnings of the decedent,[24] but the Model Act gives to the statutory beneficiaries rather than the estate "the present monetary value of * * * financial contributions they would have received from the decedent had death not ensued."[25] When a decedent was survived by two children who received only half of his estate under his will, damages for loss of prospective inheritance, based on the decedent's anticipated earnings, went to the children under the statute even though they would not have actually received them under their father's will![26]

Thus a death may produce two types of recovery, one going to the decedent's estate and the other to the statutory beneficiaries. Both claims are usually enforced by the decedent's personal representative, and the Model Act allows the claims to be combined in a single action.[27] It is sometimes hard to allocate a recovery between them.[28]

## § 2.6 Advancements

If Mary has three children, Alice, Arthur and Andrew, in all states they would share equally if Mary died intestate. But suppose that Mary while she was alive gave $10,000 to Alice. If this $10,000 is not taken into account in dividing Mary's estate, Alice will get more of Mary's property than her brothers, contrary to the general assumption that parents want their children to share equally. Many states today have a statute dealing with such "advancements" on an inheritance.[1] These statutes differ from each other on several points.

### *Proof of Intent*

Under the Uniform Probate Code a lifetime gift is treated as an advancement against the donee's share of the donor's intestate estate "only if the decedent declared in a contemporaneous writing or the heir acknowledged in writing that the gift is an advancement."[2] The fact that the gift is in writing

**22.** Model Survival and Death Act § 2(b). See also Cal. Code Civ. Proc. § 377.34; Matter of Estate of Sims, 918 P.2d 132 (Utah App. 1996) (widow who collects for personal injuries suffered by her husband must turn over the proceeds to his estate).

**23.** In re Thornton, 481 N.W.2d 828 (Mich. App.1992) (pain and suffering); Ind. Code § 34–1–1–2 (medical and funeral expenses go into the estate).

**24.** Smedley, *Some Order out of Chaos in Wrongful Death Law,* 37 Vand.L.Rev. 273, 280 (1984). In Brockie v. Omo Const., Inc., 887 P.2d 167 (Mont.1994) a jury awarded no survival damages despite uncontroverted evidence of substantial expected earnings by the decedent, but awarded large damages under the wrongful death action. The court ordered a new trial.

**25.** Model Survival and Death Act § 3(d)(2). See also Ohio Rev. Code 2125.02(B)(4) ("loss of prospective inheritance").

**26.** Kulawik v. ERA Jet Alaska, 820 P.2d 627 (Alaska 1991).

**27.** Model Survival and Death Act § 4. *See also* Cal.Code Civ. Proc. § 377.61–.62.

**28.** Hooks v. Owen, 719 N.E.2d 581 (Ohio App.1998) (abuse of discretion to allocate part of settlement proceeds to wrongful death beneficiaries)

§ 2.6

**1.** Elbert, *Advancements I,* 51 Mich.L.Rev. 665, 674 (1953) (hereinafter cited as *Advancements I* ). The Statute of Distributions of 1670, § 5, had a provision on the subject. For the earlier history see 2 W. Blackstone, *Commentaries* *516–17 (1765).

**2.** Uniform Probate Code § 2–109. *See also Restatement (Third) of Property (Wills and Other Donative Transfers)* § 2.6 (1998); Calif.Prob.Code § 6409; N.Y.EPTL § 2–1.5; Ohio Rev.Code § 2105.051; 20 Pa.Stat. § 2109.1.

(e.g. a check or a deed) does not suffice to make it an advancement unless the writing so describes the gift. The word "advancement" does not have to be used so long as the writing makes the intent clear.[3] Under such a statute few advancements will be legally recognized because persons who die intestate do not usually consult lawyers about their estates and nonlawyers are not likely to know about the writing requirement.[4]

Some have praised the Code because it eliminates "wasteful litigation" about the decedent's intention which is often "either nonexistent or obscure,"[5] and might have to be resolved on the basis of untrustworthy testimony.[6] These difficulties could be eliminated by a contrary presumption, i.e. requiring *all* gifts to be treated as advancements absent written evidence of a contrary intent.[7] Professor Fellows has suggested that "the distribution of a decedent's estate take into account all gifts to lineal descendants of substantial sums not given for maintenance or education of the donee * * * without further inquiry into the decedent's intent" in order to further "the decedent's probable intent to treat children or their families equally."[8] The drafters of the UPC, on the other hand, thought that "most inter vivos transfers today are intended to be absolute gifts" rather than advancements,[9] but there is no empirical evidence for this or the opposite assumption.[10]

Many states do not require a writing to prove that a gift was intended as an advancement. What if there is no evidence at all as to the donor's intent? Some states presume that gifts are not advancements,[11] but many make the opposite presumption.[12]

The intention that a gift be an advancement must have existed when the gift was made; the donor cannot later convert an absolute gift into an advancement; hence the requirement in the UPC of a "contemporaneous writing."[13] However, a change of heart which is *beneficial* to the recipient is allowed; a provision in a will that loans previously made to a child shall be treated only as advancements was given effect.[14] Conversely, the *recipient* can acknowledge that a prior gift be deemed an advancement; the word "contemporaneous" does not apply to such a writing.[15] In states not requiring a

**3.** *Restatement (Third) of Property (Wills and Other Donative Transfers)* § 2.6, comm. c (1998). Unif.Prob.Code § 2–109 is clearer on this point than its predecessor, Section 1–110 of the pre–1990 Code.

**4.** Fellows, *Concealing Legislative Reform in the Common–Law Tradition,* 37 Vand.L.Rev. 671, 678 (1984).

**5.** Chaffin, *A Reappraisal of the Wealth Transmission Process,* 10 Ga.L.Rev. 447, 497, 499 (1976). *See also* Bratt, *Kentucky's Doctrine of Advancements: A Time For Reform,* 75 Ky. L.J. 341, 388 (1986) (proposing a similar statute).

**6.** In Matter of Martinez' Estate, 633 P.2d 727 (N.M.App.1981), the court refused to accept the claim of an advancement on the basis of "self-serving testimony in 1980 [by another heir] to a conversation with [the decedent] in 1953 to prove [his] intent in 1941."

**7.** La.Civ.Code §§ 1227–32.

**8.** *See* Fellows, *supra* note 4, at 704–05.

**9.** Uniform Probate Code § 2–109, Comment.

**10.** Averill, *An Electic History and Analysis of the 1990 Uniform Probate Code,* 55 Alb. L.Rev. 891, 915 (1992).

**11.** Iowa Code § 633.224.

**12.** La.Civ.Code § 1230; *Advancements II,* p. 249; Lee's Estate v. Graber, 462 P.2d 492 (Colo.1969).

**13.** Uniform Probate Code § 2–109(a); *Restatement (Third) of Property (Wills and Other Donative Transfers)* § 2.6, comm. c (1998).

**14.** O'Brien v. O'Brien, 526 S.E.2d 1 (Va. 2000).

**15.** Some statutes requiring a writing are not specific as to the time. 755 ILCS § 5/2–5; Md. Estates and Trusts Code § 3–106.

writing, later declarations may be accepted as evidence of the donor's intent at the time of the gift.[16]

Circumstantial evidence may show that a gift was not intended to be an advancement. Payments for a child's support or education, such as paying college tuition,[17] are not usually held to be advancements. A sale is not an advancement, but if the consideration was inadequate the difference between price and value may be an advancement,[18] A recital of consideration in a deed can be rebutted by proof that in fact there was none.[19]

Will substitutes like insurance, joint tenancy and revocable trusts are often treated as advancements,[20] even though the recipient gets no benefit *in advance* of the decedent's death. Even a bequest in a will which fails to dispose of all the testator's estate operates as an advancement as to the intestate property in some states, but others recognize advancements only in cases of total intestacy.[21]

### *Computation of Shares*

A comment to the Uniform Probate Code illustrates how shares are computed when there is an advancement.[22] Suppose a decedent with a wife (W) and three children, A, to whom he had advanced $50,000, B, who had received $10,000, and C, dies intestate with an estate of $190,000. The advancements are figuratively added back into the estate, bringing it up to $250,000. This increases W's share under the UPC, but in some states advancements only affect descendants of the donor.[23]

The balance passing to the three children would be $75,000, or $25,000 each. A who has already received more than his share is not required to refund the excess, but he gets no more of the decedent's estate.[24] (However, if the $50,000 which A received was a *loan*, it would be set off against A's share[25] and he would have to repay the difference.)

**16.** Matter of Martinez' Estate, 633 P.2d 727 (N.M.App.1981).

**17.** La.Civ.Code § 1244; *Advancements III*, p. 535 (support), p. 538 (education); *Advancements II*, p. 254 (trifling gift). *But cf.* Bratt, *supra* note 5, at 386 (paying for professional school education is an advancement).

**18.** La.Civ.Code § 1248; *Advancements I*, p. 678, *Advancements II*, p. 255. *But see* In re Scott's Estate, 642 P.2d 1287 (Wyo.1982); 3 *Amer.Law of Prop.* § 14.10, at 587 (if consideration substantial, even if inadequate, should be no presumption of advancement).

**19.** Thomas v. Thomas, 398 S.W.2d 231 (Ky.1965).

**20.** Brodrick v. Moore, 226 F.2d 105 (10th Cir.1955); Lee's Estate v. Graber, 462 P.2d 492 (Colo.1969); *Restatement (Third) of Property (Wills and Other Donative Transfers)* § 2.6, comm. f (1998); Uniform Probate Code § § 2–109, comment.

**21.** *Advancements II*, p. 242; Bratt, *supra* note 5, at 344; 20 Pa.Stat. § 2100.1; Tenn.Code § 31–5–102.

**22.** The statute itself "does not specify the method of taking an advancement into account. * * * The process, called the hotchpot method is provided by the common law." Uniform Probate Code § 2–109, comment. *See also Restatement (Third) of Property (Wills and Other Donative Transfers)* § 2.6, illus. 1 (1998).

**23.** Md. Estates and Trusts Code § 3–106(d); Mass. Gen. Laws Ann. c. 196, § 3. In the UPC hypothetical, W is not the mother of the decedent's children. In some situations the spouse would get the entire probate estate even without the advancement. Uniform Probate Code § 2–102.

**24.** O'Brien v. O'Brien, 526 S.E.2d 1 (Va. 2000) (child to whom advancement made cannot be sued for the excess). Several statutes expressly state that the advancee need not make a refund. Iowa Code § 633.224; 755 ILCS § 5/2–5. In Louisiana, however, if the estate of the donor is "insufficient to give the other children their legitimate portion," the donee may be required to refund. La. Civ. Code § 1234. As to forced heirship in Louisiana see Section 3.2.

**25.** Uniform Probate Code § 3–903.

A's advancement and his share are now disregarded, and new calculations are made for a $200,000 estate ($190,000 plus the $10,000 advancement to B). After W takes her share, $50,000 is left to be divided between B and C. B has already received $10,000, so he gets $15,000 more, and $25,000 goes to C.

What if B predeceases the decedent and B's children take by representation? Their share would not be affected by the advancement under the UPC, "unless the decedent's contemporaneous writing provides otherwise,"[26] but some states take the advancement into account as to the descendants of the advancee.[27]

The recipient is not charged with interest for the period between the time of the advancement and the donor's death.[28] If the advancement is in the form of property, any subsequent appreciation or depreciation of the property is ignored; the Uniform Probate Code follows the generally accepted principle that "the property advanced is valued as of the time the heir came into possession or enjoyment of the property or as of the time of the death of the decedent, whichever first occurs."[29]

### *Satisfaction of Devises*

The rules on advancements apply only to intestate succession. If a will leaves an estate "to my children equally," no child's share is reduced by any gifts received from the testator before the will was executed; the law assumes that the testator has taken into account any prior gifts to the extent she intends.[30] On the other hand, a gift by a testator *after* she executed her will might be treated as a partial or total satisfaction of a devise if the testator so intended.[31] The Uniform Probate Code provision on this issue parallels its rule on advancements; lifetime gifts are not taken into account unless the will (or some other writing) so provides.[32] The writing must be contemporaneous with the gift; a later writing by the donor is too late.[33] Here too the writing

**26.** Uniform Probate Code § 2–109. *See also* Cal.Prob.Code § 6409(d); *Restatement (Third) of Property (Wills and Other Donative Transfers)* § 2.6, comm. h (1998). On the other hand, a gift to a grandchild may be an advancement even though the recipient was not a prospective heir at the time of the gift, if the grandchild later turns out to be an heir.

**27.** Md. Estates and Trusts Code § 3–106(c); 755 ILCS § 5/2–5; La.Civ.Code § 1240.

**28.** *Advancements III* p. 561; Ga.Code Ann. § 113–1017.

**29.** Uniform Probate Code § 2–109(b). *See also* Cal.Prob.Code § 6409(b); Md. Estates and Trusts Code § 3–106(b); *Restatement (Third) of Property (Wills and Other Donative Transfers)* § 2.6, comm. d (1998). *But see* N.Y. EPTL § 2–1.5(d) (value it would have for estate tax purposes).

**30.** 3 *Amer.Law of Prop.* § 14.10, at 586; Bratt, *supra* note 5, at 343; *cf.* O'Brien v. O'Brien, 526 S.E.2d 1 (Va.2000) (provision in a will that prior loan be treated as advancement effective). But if a will directs distribution to the testator's "heirs" some cases would take advancements into account in carrying out this direction. *Advancements II*, p. 241; *cf. Restatement of Property* § 316 (1940).

In Louisiana, "collation" is required both in testate and intestate succession. La. Civil Code § 1228.

**31.** N.Y. EPTL § 2–1.5(a) uses the term "advancement" to include gifts to the "beneficiary under an existing will of the donor," but the more common term is "satisfaction" or "ademption by satisfaction" of the prior devise.

**32.** Uniform Probate Code § 2–609. *See also Restatement, Third, of Property (Wills and Other Donative Transfers)* § 5.4 (1998); Cal. Prob.Code § 21135; N.Y. EPTL § 2–1.5(b); Mass.Gen.Laws c. 197, § 25A; Young v. Young, 979 P.2d 338, 344 (Utah 1999).

A specific devise can be adeemed by extinction when the testator gives the devised property to the devisee or someone else. In this case the testator's intent can be effected without a writing. See Section 8.1.

**33.** In In re Estate of McFayden, 454 N.W.2d 676 (Neb.1990), a written statement by the donor that all gifts were to be treated as advances on a devise was ineffective both as to

requirement does not apply to loans. Thus when a will devised property to the testator's sons equally a transfer by the testator to one son was found to be a loan and was set off against his share of the estate, even though there was no note.[34]

Some states allow oral evidence of intent in all cases[35], and even presume that a gift by a testator to a child was intended to satisfy an earlier bequest.[36] Similarities between the devise and the gift may show an intent to substitute one for the other, as when a will left $5,000 to a home in memory of the testator's wife and the testator later gave the same amount to the home for the same purpose.[37] There is authority that "a devise of land cannot be satisfied except by a conveyance of the same land," and so a devise of a share of the testator's real estate is not adeemed by a later gift of a specific parcel to the devisee.[38]

The Uniform Probate Code rules on valuation of gifts in satisfaction of devises are the same as for advancements, but the effect on the issue of a recipient who predeceases the donor differs: a will donor-testator is presumed to have intended that the share of the donee's issue be reduced or eliminated in this situation.[39]

### *Planning*

An attorney drafting a will should ask the testator about any prior gifts. The testator may wish to reduce the share of for a child or spouse who has already received substantial gifts. The law assumes that testators have taken prior gifts into account, and drafters should make sure that this assumption is correct. If the share of a child is reduced because of an advancement, a recital in the will can explain what might otherwise seem to be an unfair disposition of the estate.[40]

Should the will say anything about later gifts? A provision which reduces devises if a later gift is made to the devisee would be effective under the UPC but would require the executor of the will to determine whether the testator had made such gifts and whether the clause was meant to apply to them, *e.g.*

prior and later gifts because it was not contemporaneous with the gifts. A statement in the will itself, or a codicil thereto, could have effectuated the donor's intent.

**34.** In Matter of Estate of Button, 830 P.2d 1216 (Kan.App.1992).

In some states even a loan which has been discharged in bankruptcy can be set off against the debtor's share of the estate, Estate of Randeris v. Randeris, 523 N.W.2d 600 (Iowa App. 1994), but UPC § 3–903 allows the debtor "the benefit of any defense which would be available to him in a direct proceeding for recovery of the debt."

**35.** Kent. Rev. Stat. § 394.370.

**36.** 3 *Amer.Law of Prop.* § 14.11; Carmichael v. Lathrop, 66 N.W. 350 (Mich.1896); *cf.* Chaffin, *The Time Gap in Wills,* 6 Ga.L.Rev. 649, 668 (1972).

**37.** In re Kreitman's Estate, 386 N.E.2d 650 (Ill.App.1979). *See also* Trustees of Baker Univ. v. Trustees of End. Ass'n of Kansas State College of Pittsburg, 564 P.2d 472 (Kan. 1977).

**38.** Maestas v. Martinez, 752 P.2d 1107 (N.M.App.1988).

**39.** Uniform Probate Code § 2–609. The Comment to this section notes the discrepancy but does not purport to explain it. *Restatement (Third) of Property (Wills and Other Donative Transfers)* § 2.6, comm. h (1998) purports to explain the rule in intestacy by saying "the heir must have received the advanced property in order to be charged" but in fact the heir is not charged whether or not he inherited the advanced property from the original recipient.

**40.** A will which seems "unfair" because a child, for example, is disinherited is more likely to be upset if contested for incapacity or undue influence. Sections 7.1, note 27, Section 7.3, note 10 et seq.

should Christmas presents be counted?[41] It is better to keep a will current by periodic revision or codicils so as to reflect the testator's current wishes.

## § 2.7 Homicide

A person who is otherwise eligible to inherit or take by will or will substitute may be barred because of homicide.

### *History*

If a wife murders her husband can she inherit from him? There are no reported decisions on this question before the end of the nineteenth century. This may be partially explained by the fact that, historically, convicted felons forfeited their property, but most states abolished forfeiture for crime long before courts raised the question whether a murderer could inherit. Apparently during this interval courts allowed murderers to inherit without questioning the result. When the argument that a murderer should not be allowed to inherit began to appear, many courts rejected it, saying that any change in the law must come from legislation.[1]

In 1897 Dean Ames suggested that courts should impose a constructive trust on the murderer.[2] The Restatement of Restitution and some courts adopted this suggestion[3] on the grounds that it "avoids the dubious practice of reading implied exceptions into a statute."[4] This reasoning seems questionable. How can a court claim to be applying a statute when it awards property to someone other than the person to whom the statute gives it? Many courts reject the constructive trust approach as "somewhat fictitious."[5]

In states which still maintain separate courts of equity, the constructive trust rationale may require the parties to resort to that tribunal, which traditionally had exclusive jurisdiction over trusts.[6] Under more recent decisions, however, probate courts have the power not to distribute property to the murderer.[7]

### *Statutes*

Most states now have statutes which bar a murderer from inheriting from the victim. Some of these statutes are incomplete. A Vermont statute, for

41. The law relating to advancements has been used to interpret such clauses. *Advancements I*, pp. 679–81.

§ 2.7

1. McGovern, *Homicide and Succession to Property*, 68 Mich.L.Rev. 65–57 (1968).

2. Ames, *Can a Murderer Acquire Title by His Crime and Keep It?*, 36 Am.Law Reg. (n.s.) 225, 228–29 (1897). [This essay was republished in J. Ames, *Lectures on Legal History* 310 (1913).]

3. *Restatement of Restitution* § 187 (1937); Angleton v. Estate of Angleton, 671 N.E.2d 921 (Ind.App.1996) (based on statute); Parks v. Dumas, 321 S.W.2d 653 (Tex.Civ.App.1959); Sikora v. Sikora, 499 P.2d 808 (Mont.1972).

4. G. Bogert, *Trusts* § 478, at 78 (2d ed. 1960). *See also Restatement of Restitution* § 187, comment a at 764 (1937).

5. In re Duncan's Estates, 246 P.2d 445 (Wash.1952). *See also* Wall v. Pfanschmidt, 106 N.E. 785 (Ill.1914); Fellows, *The Slayer Rule: Not Solely a Matter of Equity*, 71 Iowa L.Rev. 489, 550–51 (1986); McGovern, *supra* note 1, at 68–9.

6. In re Estate of Mahoney, 220 A.2d 475 (Vt.1966) (probate court must follow statute literally; constructive trust only enforceable in equity).

7. Mitchem v. First Interstate Bank, 802 P.2d 1141 (Colo.App.1990) (suit to impose constructive trust dismissed because probate court has power to handle the issue); Maine Savings Bank v. Bridges, 431 A.2d 633, 637 (Me.1981). In Angleton v. Estate of Angleton, 671 N.E.2d 921 (Ind.App.1996), the probate court itself imposed a constructive trust, and rejected the argument that the proceeds must be distributed to the killer before the trust is imposed.

example, says that a devisee or heir, if convicted of intentionally killing a decedent, forfeits his share of the decedent's estate.[8] The statute does not cover an insurance policy beneficiary who murders the insured. The cases interpreting such incomplete statutes are hard to reconcile. A court allowed a person convicted of manslaughter to inherit because the governing statute only covered "murder."[9] But another court operating under a like statute barred a person convicted of manslaughter on the theory that the statute did not "completely supplant the common law principle * * * that one should not be allowed to profit by his own wrong."[10] Sometimes a statute which does not literally apply is extended as evincing "a legislative policy to deny the convicted murderer of the fruits of his crime."[11]

The Uniform Probate Code provision on this subject covers a variety of cases and adds a catchall: "A wrongful acquisition of property or interest by the killer not covered by this section must be treated in accordance with the principle that a killer cannot profit from his [or her] wrong."[12] This principle has been applied when someone killed his grandmother, whose heir died a few months later leaving the killer as her heir. "The fact that there is an intervening estate should not * * * thwart the intent of the legislature that the murderer not profit by his wrong."[13] Courts have extended statutes to accessories who did not actually kill the decedent.[14] On the other hand, some courts have refused to apply the principle to wrongful death claims.[15]

The drafters of the UPC feared that the preemption provisions of ERISA which "supersede any and all state laws insofar as they * * * relate to any employee benefit plan"[16] might preclude application of the Code to pension plans,[17] but these fears, at least as to homicide, have so far proved to be groundless.[18]

**8.** 14 Vt.Stat. § 551(6).

**9.** Nable v. Godfrey's Estate, 403 So.2d 1038 (Fla.App.1981). *See also* Estate of Kramme, 573 P.2d 1369 (Cal.1978).

**10.** Quick v. United Benefit Life Ins. Co., 213 S.E.2d 563 (N.C.1975). *See also* Harper v. Prudential Ins. Co., 662 P.2d 1264 (Kan.1983); Wright v. Wright, 449 S.W.2d 952 (Ark.1970).

**11.** Bailey v. Retirement Board of Policemen's Annuity and Ben. Fund, 366 N.E.2d 966, 969 (Ill.App.1977). *See also* Sundin v. Klein, 269 S.E.2d 787 (Va.1980); New Orleans Elec. Pension Fund v. DeRocha, 779 F.Supp. 845, 850 (E.D.La.1991) (statute dealing with insurance is a "guidepost" to treatment of pensions).

**12.** Uniform Probate Code § 2–803(f). The pre–1990 version of this provision simply referred to "the principles of this section" without identifying them. Uniform Probate Code § 2–803(d) (pre–1990). *See also* Cal. Prob. Code § 252. A similar provision appeared in a statute proposed in 1936 which a few states have adopted. Wade, *Acquisition of Property by Willfully Killing Another—A Statutory Solution,* 49 Harv.L.Rev. 715, 750–51 (1936). For a summary description of the various statutes as of 1992 see *Restatement, Second, of Property, Donative Transfers,* § 34.8, Statutory Note (1992).

**13.** In re Estate of Vallerius, 629 N.E.2d 1185, 1189 (Ill.App.1994). *See also Restatement (Second) of Property, Donative Transfers,* § 34.8, illus. 2 (1992) (son who kills sibling cannot thereby increase his share of his mother's estate).

**14.** In re Estate of Walker, 847 P.2d 162 (Colo.App.1992); Matter of Estate of Gibbs, 490 N.W.2d 504 (S.D.1992); Uniform Probate Code § 2–803, comment (criminal accountability "as an accomplice or co-conspirator" is encompassed).

**15.** Aranda v. Camacho, 931 P.2d 757 (N.M.App.1997) (no wrongful death action lies when husband kills his wife since he is the sole statutory claimant); Marks v. Lyerla, 2 Cal. Rptr.2d 63 (App.1991). After the latter case Cal. Prob. Code § 258 was enacted to change the result.

**16.** 29 U.S.C. § 1144(a).

**17.** Uniform Probate Code § 2–803, comment.

**18.** Mendez–Bellido v. Board of Trustees, 709 F.Supp. 329 (E.D.N.Y.1989) (spouse barred

### *Degree of Crime*

Georgia and Virginia at one time barred succession only by those who killed in order to obtain the victim's property,[19] but later amended their statutes to eliminate any reference to motive.[20] Virtually all courts today hold that a killer's motives are immaterial.[21]

Some courts have allowed a killer to take if the crime was less than murder,[22] but Louisiana bars an insurance beneficiary from collecting the proceeds if he is "criminally responsible" for the death of the insured; this includes even an unintentional killing.[23] The Uniform Probate Code takes an intermediate position, barring anyone who "feloniously and intentionally" kills the decedent.[24] This encompasses voluntary manslaughter as well as murder, but not involuntary manslaughter. Most modern cases also disqualify for voluntary manslaughter,[25] but not unintentional homicide even though criminal.[26] Arguably, even a negligent killer should not be allowed "to profit from his wrong," but the existence of profit from the crime is often questionable, since the killer might have survived and inherited from the decedent anyway.

A killer who is guilty of no criminal offense at all, *e.g.*, one who kills in self-defense or by accident, is not disqualified.[27] Juvenile killers may be precluded from inheriting even if their act was not subject to the ordinary criminal law,[28] but a killer who was insane is not disqualified in most states.[29]

### *Proof of Crime*

The problem of proof arises in three different situations. Often the alleged killer has not been tried, either because he committed suicide after the

by killing her husband from taking under pension plan); New Orleans Elec. Pension Fund v. DeRocha, 779 F.Supp. 845 (E.D.La.1991) (same); Metropolitan Life Ins. Co. v. White, 972 F.2d 122 (5th Cir.1992) (federal employees insurance).

**19.** *See* Life & Cas. Ins. Co. v. Webb, 145 S.E.2d 63 (Ga.App.1965); Ward v. Ward, 6 S.E.2d 664 (Va.1940).

**20.** Ga.Code Ann. §§ 56–2506, 113–909; Va.Code § 55–403.

**21.** Francis v. Marshall, 841 S.W.2d 51 (Tex.App.1992). *Compare* Sherman, *Mercy Killing and the Right to Inherit*, 61 U.Cinn.L.Rev. 803 (1993) (mercy killer should be allowed to inherit); *Restatement (Third) of Property (Wills and Other Donative Transfers)* § 8.4, comm. j (Prel.Dft. 2000) (raising the question but giving no answer).

**22.** Nable v. Godfrey's Estate, 403 So.2d 1038 (Fla.App.1981); Aranda v. Camacho, 931 P.2d 757 (N.M.App.1997).

**23.** In re Hamilton, 446 So.2d 463 (La.App. 1984); *cf. Restatement (Second) of Property, Donative Transfers*, § 34.8, illus. 1 (1992).

**24.** Uniform Probate Code § 2–803(b).

**25.** Davis v. Secretary of Health and Human Services, 867 F.2d 336 (6th Cir.1989) (Social security denied to widow convicted of manslaughter); In re Mahoney's Estate, 220 A.2d 475 (Vt.1966); Sikora v. Sikora, 499 P.2d 808 (Mont.1972). *Contra, Restatement of Restitution* § 187, comment e (1937).

**26.** Miller v. Kramarczyk, 714 N.E.2d 613 (Ill.App.1999) (negligent killer not disqualified); Matter of Safran's Estate, 306 N.W.2d 27 (Wis.1981); Hood v. Vandevender, 661 So.2d 198 (Miss.1995).

**27.** State Farm Life Ins. Co. v. Smith, 363 N.E.2d 785 (Ill.1977); Powell v. Powell, 604 S.W.2d 491 (Tex.Civ.App.1980); Huff v. Union Fidelity Life Ins. Co., 470 N.E.2d 236 (Ohio App.1984) (killing in defense of another).

**28.** Huff v. Union Fidelity Life Ins. Co., 470 N.E.2d 236 (Ohio App.1984); Matter of Josephsons' Estates, 297 N.W.2d 444 (N.D.1980); 20 Code Fed.Reg. § 404.35.

**29.** Estate of Artz v. Artz, 487 A.2d 1294 (N.J.Super. 1985); Ford v. Ford, 512 A.2d 389 (Md.1986); Turner v. Estate of Turner, 454 N.E.2d 1247 (Ind.App.1983). *Contra,* Ind.Code § 29–1–2–12.1.

crime, or the criminal case is still pending when the decedent's estate is to be distributed.[30] Many courts operating under a statute which bars one "convicted" of murder have held that the murder can be established only by a criminal conviction.[31] Courts operating under common-law principles conclude, however, usually without even discussing the point, that the absence of a criminal conviction does not prevent them from determining guilt.[32]

Sometimes the accused has been acquitted (or convicted of an offense not serious enough to bar succession). Most courts in this situation admit evidence that the accused was in fact guilty.[33] This can be justified on the ground that proof beyond a reasonable doubt is not necessary to establish the existence of a crime in a civil proceeding, and an acquittal may mean merely failure to meet the higher standard of proof required in criminal proceedings. Under the Uniform Probate Code, "in the absence of a conviction, the court * * * must determine whether, under the preponderance of evidence standard, the individual would be found criminally accountable."[34]

If the killer has been convicted, this proof of guilt beyond a reasonable doubt should *a fortiori* satisfy the preponderance-of-the-evidence test in the civil. Thus the Uniform Probate Code makes a conviction conclusive in determining the right to succession,[35] and some courts have so held even without statutory authority,[36] but some statutes simply make the conviction admissible evidence.[37]

### *Avoiding Forfeiture*

The law no longer imposes forfeiture for crime; indeed, many state constitutions expressly prohibit it.[38] Barring a murderer from inheriting is distinguishable, because it does "not deprive the murderer of any property

**30.** If an heir is convicted of killing the decedent and appeals, should distribution of the estate be postponed while the appeal is pending? Courts have disagreed on this question. *Compare* State Farm Life Ins. Co. v. Davidson, 495 N.E.2d 520 (Ill.App.1986), *with* Prudential Ins. Co. v. Tull, 524 F.Supp. 166 (E.D.Va.1981); Angleton v. Estate of Angleton, 671 N.E.2d 921 (Ind.App.1996) (no abuse of discretion to order immediate distribution). As to the recovery of property which has been wrongfully distributed, see Section 12.10, note 47.

**31.** Holliday v. McMullen, 756 P.2d 1179 (Nev.1988); Button by Curio v. Elmhurst Nat. Bank, 522 N.E.2d 1368 (Ill.App.1988); Bird v. Plunkett, 95 A.2d 71 (Conn.1953).

**32.** *Restatement of Restitution* § 187, comment f (1937); Bernstein v. Rosenthal, 671 P.2d 979 (Colo.App.1983).

**33.** Matter of Congdon's Estate, 309 N.W.2d 261 (Minn.1981); Matter of Eliasen's Estate, 668 P.2d 110 (Idaho 1983); California-Western States Life Ins. Co. v. Sanford, 515 F.Supp. 524 (E.D.La.1981). *But see* Turner v. Estate of Turner, 454 N.E.2d 1247 (Ind.App. 1983).

**34.** Uniform Probate Code § 2–803(g). *See also* Cal. Prob. Code § 254; Matter of Estates of Young, 831 P.2d 1014 (Okl.App.1992) (acquittal not conclusive because of higher standard of proof in criminal cases); Matter of Estate of Gibbs, 490 N.W.2d 504 (S.D.1992). In Federal Kemper Life Assur. v. Eichwedel, 639 N.E.2d 246 (Ill.App.1994), a confession which was inadmissible in criminal proceedings was used to bar the killer from collecting insurance.

**35.** Uniform Probate Code § 2–803(g). *See also* Calif.Prob.Code § 254(a); Metropolitan Life Ins. Co. v. White, 972 F.2d 122 (5th Cir. 1992) (federal employees' insurance). Under the UPC, the conviction is conclusive only "after all right of appeal has been exhausted." But some courts treat a conviction as conclusive even if an appeal is pending. Angleton v. Estate of Angleton, 671 N.E.2d 921 (Ind.App. 1996); Matter of Dorsey, 613 N.Y.S.2d 335 (Surr.1994).

**36.** Travelers Ins. Co. v. Thompson, 163 N.W.2d 289 (Minn.1968); In re Laspy's Estate, 409 S.W.2d 725 (Mo.App.1966); In re Glenn's Estate, 299 A.2d 203 (Pa.1973).

**37.** 20 Pa.Stat. § 8814; Rev.Code Wash. § 11.84.130.

**38.** *E.g.,* Ill. Const. art. 1, § 11; *cf.* United States Constitution, art. 3, § 3 ("no Attainder of Treason shall work * * * Forfeiture except during the Life of the Person attainted").

rights, but [only] prevent(s) his acquisition of *additional* rights."[39] The distinction between depriving someone of what he already owns and barring the "acquisition of additional rights" is fuzzy in some instances. Suppose A and B own land in joint tenancy, and A murders B. Most authorities would allow A to keep his share of income from the property since he did not acquire that interest by his crime.[40] When A dies, some courts would award all the land to B's estate on the theory that but for the murder, B might have taken as surviving joint tenant.[41] Most courts, however, would divide the property equally between the estates of A and B[42] on the theory that no one knows who would have survived but for the killing. The Uniform Probate Code agrees; it terminates the right of survivorship but the killer's half interest is preserved.[43] Courts have reached the same result as to community property; the killer spouse retains a half interest.[44]

Joint bank accounts are treated differently from land. Ownership of joint bank accounts under the UPC (as in many other states) is proportional to contributions. Thus if A contributed all the money in a joint bank account, the account is "his" during his lifetime, even if B is also designated as a party.[45] A could therefore keep the account if he killed B. On the other hand, if *B* killed A, the whole account would be awarded to A's estate.[46] As to land, on the other hand, the source of the funds used to acquire it is irrelevant, because "if one spouse provides all the funds for property conveyed to a married couple jointly, it will be presumed that the provider makes a gift to the other spouse of an undivided one-half interest in the property."[47]

Suppose a parent gives property to A for life, remainder to B, and B kills A. Few statutes cover this case. B's enrichment from accelerating his remainder could be avoided by postponing his enjoyment for the duration of A's normal life expectancy.[48] If B's remainder was vested, he ought not to forfeit

**39.** Sundin v. Klein, 269 S.E.2d 787 (Va. 1980) (emphasis added). *See also* In re Estate of Fiore, 476 N.E.2d 1093, 1097 (Ohio App. 1984) (statute is constitutional because it "only prevented the murderer from inheriting property, rather than divesting him of such property").

**40.** *Restatement of Restitution* § 188, comment b (1937); In re Hawkins' Estate, 213 N.Y.S.2d 188 (1961); *cf.* Homanich v. Miller, 221 S.E.2d 739 (N.C.App.1976). *But see* First Kentucky Trust Co. v. United States, 737 F.2d 557 (6th Cir.1984) (killer forfeits all interest in joint tenancy).

**41.** *Restatement of Restitution* § 188, comment b (1937); Hargrove v. Taylor, 389 P.2d 36 (Or.1964); *cf.* Glass v. Adkins, 436 So.2d 844 (Ala.1983).

**42.** Gallimore v. Washington, 666 A.2d 1200 (D.C.App.1995); Estate of Grund v. Grund, 648 N.E.2d 1182 (Ind.App.1995); Hicks v. Boshears, 846 S.W.2d 812 (Tenn.1993); *Restatement (Second) of Property, Donative Transfers*, § 34.8, comment c (1992).

**43.** Uniform Probate Code § 2–803(c)(2). *See also* Cal. Prob. Code § 251.

**44.** Armstrong v. Bray, 826 P.2d 706 (Wash.App.1992); Matter of Estates of Spear, 845 P.2d 491 (Ariz.App.1992).

**45.** Uniform Probate Code § 6–211(b). If the parties are married, their contributions are presumed to have been equal. *See also* Cal. Prob.Code §§ 5301(a), 5305 (contributions presumed to be community property).

**46.** Uniform Probate Code § 2–803, comment: "any portion of the decedent's contribution to the co-ownership registration running in favor of the killer would be treated as a revocable and revoked disposition." See also Estate of Castiglioni, 47 Cal.Rptr.2d 288 (App. 1995) (error to award funds in joint account traceable to H's separate property to W who killed him). In In re Estate of Fiore, 476 N.E.2d 1093 (Ohio App.1984) where both parties had contributed but the proportions were unclear, the whole account was awarded to the victim's estate.

**47.** Sundin v. Klein, 269 S.E.2d 787 (Va. 1980).

**48.** *Restatement of Restitution* § 188, comment c (1937); *cf.* In re Moses' Estate, 300 N.E.2d 473 (Ill.App.1973).

it,[49] but if it was contingent on his surviving A, he might be deemed to have predeceased her,[50] or the court could wait to see if B outlives A's normal life expectancy.[51]

If B was the beneficiary of an insurance policy on A's life, he will not collect the proceeds if he kills her. But if the premiums were paid with community property, some courts would give him half the proceeds,[52] others would limit him to one half of the *cash surrender value* of the policies.[53]

In some situations the insurance company is not bound to pay *anyone* when the insured is killed. When the beneficiary took out the policy with the intent to kill the insured the policy is voidable for fraud.[54] Even if the intent to kill arose after the policy was taken out, the insurer may escape liability if the killer owned the policy, as distinguished from being merely a beneficiary.[55]

### *Alternate Takers*

If a killer is disqualified, who takes? In most situations, the victim's property is distributed as if the killer predeceased the victim.[56] This principle often allows the children of the killer to take, for example, by representation in case of intestacy or under an anti-lapse statute in case of a will.[57] Wills and insurance policies often designate alternate beneficiaries to take if a devisee or primary beneficiary fails to survive. Usually the fiction that the killer died before the victim is also applied in this situation, and the alternate beneficiary takes.[58] Some courts, however, refuse to allow this when it seems to advantage the killer. For example, when a will left property to the testator's wife, with an alternative gift to her children if she died first, a court refused to allow the

**49.** *Restatement of Restitution* § 188, comment c (1936); *cf.* Moore v. Moore, 201 S.E.2d 133 (Ga.1973).

**50.** *Restatement of Restitution* § 188, comment c (1937); Fellows, *supra* note 5, at 511.

**51.** In re Moses' Estate, 300 N.E.2d 473 (Ill.App.1973).

**52.** New York Life Ins. Co. v. Cawthorne, 121 Cal.Rptr. 808 (App.1975).

**53.** In re Hart's Estate, 185 Cal.Rptr. 544 (App.1982); Aetna Life Ins. Co. v. Primofiore, 145 Cal.Rptr. 922 (App.1978). The present California statute, Cal. Prob. Code § 252, says that the killer "is not entitled to any benefit under the * * * policy." It is not clear exactly what effect this has.

**54.** Federal Kemper Life Assur. v. Eichwedel, 639 N.E.2d 246 (Ill.App.1994); Chute v. Old American Ins. Co., 629 P.2d 734 (Kan.App. 1981); Flood v. Fidelity & Guar. Life Ins. Co., 394 So.2d 1311 (La.App.1981). Contrast Bradley v. Farmers New World Life Ins. Co., 679 N.E.2d 1178 (Ohio App.1996)(refusing to treat murdered wife as her husband's agent in applying for the policies on her life).

**55.** Caliman v. American General Fire & Cas. Co., 641 N.E.2d 261 (Ohio App.1994).

**56.** *Restatement (Second) of Property, Donative Transfers*, § 34.8, comment b (1992). Uniform Probate Code § 2–803 uses the expression "as if the killer disclaimed," but this amounts to the same thing, since under § 2–801(d) property disclaimed "devolves as if the disclaimant had predeceased the decedent."

This provision does not control the killer's own property; the victim's estate takes from the killer's when both are deceased only if the victim actually survived. Mothershed v. Schrimsher, 412 S.E.2d 123 (N.C.App.1992).

**57.** Matter of Estate of Van Der Veen, 935 P.2d 1042 (Kan.1997); Estate of Benson, 548 So.2d 775 (Fla.App.1989); Misenheimer v. Misenheimer, 325 S.E.2d 195 (N.C.1985); *cf.* Heinzman v. Mason, 694 N.E.2d 1164 (Ind. App.1998) (children of killer by another marriage do not take since they were not heirs of the victim-stepmother). Cal.Prob.Code § 250(b)(1) makes the antilapse statute inapplicable in this situation. *See* McGovern, *supra* note 1, at 76–77.

**58.** Bradley v. Bradley, 443 S.E.2d 863 (Ga. App.1994); Francis v. Marshall, 841 S.W.2d 51 (Tex.App.1992); Hulett v. First Nat. Bank and Trust Co., 956 P.2d 879 (Okl.1998). When no alternate beneficiary is designated, insurance proceeds may go to the insured's probate estate. Estate of Chiesi v. First Citizens Bank, 613 N.E.2d 14 (Ind.1993).

children to take when the wife killed the testator.[59] Another court when the policy named the murderer's sister as alternate beneficiary, remanded the case for a trial as to the decedent's intent, saying that if the insured "had an independent relationship of some kind" with the sister, he might have wanted her to take despite the crime. A concurring opinion doubted that such a search for the "hypothetical" intent of the decedent would prove fruitful.[60]

### *Protection of Third Parties*

Sometimes a crime is discovered after a person has acted in reliance on the normal devolution of property, *e.g.* by buying property from the killer. The Uniform Probate Code does not apply its killer-disqualification rules to anyone who "purchases property for value and without notice." [61]Another provision protects "payors" (such as insurance companies) from liability for payments made before they receive "written notice of a claimed forfeiture."[62] One court held that this provision did not protect an insurer who was negligent in paying proceeds to a killer. "If an insurer is on notice of facts suggesting that the primary beneficiary is not entitled to * * * policy proceeds, the insurer has a duty to make a reasonable inquiry and to withhold payment until its suspicion is dispelled."[63]

### *Other Cases of Misconduct*

Courts have refused to make other exceptions to the intestacy statutes to bar persons guilty of misconduct vis a vis the decedent. For example, a mother was allowed to inherit from her 15 year old child although for most of his life "she had "failed to provide any financial support to, maintain any interest in, or display any love and affection for her son." The court noted that there were statutes providing procedures for the termination of parental rights' which had not been pursued here, as well as provisions barring killers and spouses who had abandoned the decedent from claiming an elective share. "If the law is to be changed to make provision for the situation at hand, it is for the legislature to make the change, not the courts."[64] The Uniform Probate Code, however, bars a parent from inheriting from a child unless the parent "has openly treated the child as his [or hers], and has not refused to support the child."[65] The South Dakota Supreme Court cited another provision of the UPC, under which "the principles of law and equity supplement its provisions" (§ 1–103), to bar devisees from receiving a share of the punitive damages which the estate had recovered from them for converting property of the testator. The Court wished to "uphold the public policy of this state that perpetrators of fraud will be deprived of the fruit of their wrongdoing."[66]

**59.** In re Estate of Mueller, 655 N.E.2d 1040 (Ill.App.1995).

**60.** State Farm Life Ins. Co. v. Pearce, 286 Cal.Rptr. 267 (App.1991).

**61.** Uniform Probate Code § 2–803(i)(1). *See also* Cal.Prob.Code § 255; McGovern, *supra* note 1, at 69.

**62.** Uniform Probate Code § 2–803(h)(1). *See also* Cal. Prob. Code § 256.

**63.** Lunsford v. Western States Life Ins., 908 P.2d 79 (Colo.1995).

**64.** Hotarek v. Benson, 557 A.2d 1259, 1263 (Conn.1989).

**65.** Uniform Probate Code § 2–114(c).

**66.** Matter of Estate of O'Keefe, 583 N.W.2d 138, 141 (S.D.1998).

## § 2.8 Disclaimers

### *Tax Consequences*

Suppose that a man dies survived by his wife and a son who would share his property by intestate succession or by his will. The wife may have ample resources and prefer that her share pass to their son who has greater need and is in a lower income tax bracket. (The progressive nature of our tax laws often fosters such altruism among family members.) She could give her share of her husband's estate to the son, but this might require payment of a gift tax.[1] She can avoid a gift tax by making a "qualified disclaimer" under the Internal Revenue Code.[2] On the other hand, a disclaimer by the son may have advantageous tax consequences for the father's estate by increasing the size of his marital deduction, since property passing to a spouse as a result of a disclaimer qualifies for the marital deduction.[3]

These results occur because in theory a disclaimer "relates back" to the time of the testator's or intestate's death, and the share never passes to the disclaimant but rather goes directly to the person who takes as a result of the disclaimer. Some have attacked this result on the ground that the disclaimant can choose to accept the share, and normally someone who fails to exercise a power to take property is treated as making a transfer.[4] Halbach justifies the special tax treatment of disclaimers on the ground that they are used for "post-mortem estate planning," *e.g.* failure to make proper use of the marital deduction. Without recognition of qualified disclaimers there would be "an unwarranted and unrealistic demand for wills to be perfected and updated before a testator's death."[5] Taxpayers who could afford to keep their wills up to date would pay less taxes than those who could not.

Before 1976 a disclaimer was a taxable gift unless it was "effective under the local law,"[6] and state disclaimer laws varied considerably.[7] Many states have liberalized the rules on disclaimer so as not to deprive their citizens of the potential for tax savings. A Uniform Disclaimer of Property Interests Act along these lines is incorporated into the Uniform Probate Code. However, since most disclaimers are motivated by tax considerations, a comment to the Code warns lawyers "to check both the state and federal disclaimer statutes before advising clients."[8]

Congress attempted to avoid unequal treatment of citizens of different states in 1976 by enacting Section 2518 of the Internal Revenue Code which sets forth uniform requirements for a "qualified disclaimer." Now even a disclaimer which is not recognized under state law may escape gift tax if it meets the requirements of the Internal Revenue Code.[9] However, there still are instances where a disclaimer which fails to satisfy state law requirements is ineffective for federal tax purposes.[10]

§ 2.8

1. For an overview of the gift tax, see Section 15.2.

2. Int.Rev.Code § 2518.

3. DePaoli v. C.I.R., 62 F.3d 1259 (10th Cir.1995). As to the marital deduction, see Section 15.3.

4. Martin, *Perspectives on Federal Disclaimer Legislation,* 46 U.Chi.L.Rev. 316, 357 (1979). As to unexercised powers of appointment see Section 10.4, at note 14.

5. Halbach, *Curing Deficiencies in Tax and Property Law,* 65 Minn.L.Rev. 89, 120 (1980).

6. Treas.Reg. § 26.2511–1(c).

7. Martin, *supra* note 4, at 321–22.

8. Uniform Probate Code § 2–802, comment.

9. Internal Revenue Code § 2518(c)(3).

10. Estate of Bennett, 100 T.C. 42 (1993). Cal.Prob.Code § 295 attempts to remedy this problem by a catch-all provision making all disclaimers effective under the Internal Revenue Code also valid under state law.

Lawyers who failed to advise clients about the possible tax advantages of disclaimers are subject to suit for malpractice.[11]

### *Creditors' Rights*

Sometimes a person wishes to disclaim because she is insolvent; her creditors would take her share if she accepted it, and she would prefer to have the property go to members of her family. Some states treat disclaimers made to avoid creditors' claims as a fraudulent conveyance,[12] or bar disclaimers by a person who is insolvent,[13] but most states adopt the "relation-back" idea in this context also, with the result that a disclaimed share passes directly to the new takers, free from the disclaimant's creditors.[14] However, a disclaimer made by a person who has previously thereto filed for bankruptcy is voidable.[15] Also, disclaimers have been held ineffective to defeat federal tax liens.[16]

According to the Restatement of Property, a donee can also avoid responsibility for environmental clean-up responsibilities by a timely disclaimer.[17] But several courts have treated disclaimers like an assignment so as to make the disclaimant ineligible for welfare benefits under need-based programs.[18]

### *Requirements for a Disclaimer*

Unlike the release or assignment of an expectancy which requires consideration, a disclaimer can be gratuitous. In fact if a disclaimant receives consideration for the disclaimer, the disclaimer does not qualify for tax purposes.[19] There is less risk of an improvident disclaimer than in the case of an expectancy, because disclaimers occur after the original transferor is dead. A purported disclaimer by the child of a living parent was held ineffective, because the statute (based on the UPC) allowed disclaimer of an "interest" and an expectancy was not an interest.[20]

**11.** Kinney v. Shinholser, 663 So.2d 643 (Fla.App.1995); Linck v. Barokas & Martin, 667 P.2d 171 (Alaska 1983).

**12.** Stein v. Brown, 480 N.E.2d 1121 (Ohio 1985); Matter of Reed's Estate, 566 P.2d 587 (Wyo.1977).

**13.** Mass.Gen.Laws c. 191A, § 8; Fla.Stat. § 732.801(6); Wash.Rev.Code § 11.86.060.

**14.** In re Atchison, 925 F.2d 209 (7th Cir. 1991); Frances Slocum Bank and Trust Co. v. Martin, 666 N.E.2d 411 (Ind.App.1996); Dyer v. Eckols, 808 S.W.2d 531 (Tex.App.1991); cf. Succession of Neuhauser, 579 So.2d 437 (La. 1991) (creditor of disclaimant can bar disclaimer only in case of "fraud"). A disclaimer can bar even creditors who have attempted to reach the property before the disclaimer, Matter of Estate of Opatz, 554 N.W.2d 813 (N.D. 1996), but under Uniform Probate Code § 2-801(e), a judicial sale of the property cuts off the right to disclaim.

For a good discussion of the policy issues involved, see Hirsch, *The Problem of the Insolvent Heir*, 74 Corn.L.Rev 587 (1989).

**15.** In re Cornell, 95 B.R. 219 (Bktcy.W.D.Okl.1989); In re Detlefsen, 610 F.2d 512 (8th Cir.1979). A disclaimer made on the eve of bankruptcy, on the other hand is not voidable unless it constitutes a fraudulent conveyance under state law. Matter of Simpson, 36 F.3d 450 (5th Cir.1994).

**16.** Drye Family 1995 Trust v. U.S., 152 F.3d 892, 898 (8th Cir.1998). *Contra*, Leggett v. U.S., 120 F.3d 592 (5th Cir.1997).

**17.** *Restatement (Second) of Property, Donative Transfers* § 32.3, comm. e (1990).

**18.** Troy v. Hart, 697 A.2d 113 (Md.App. 1997); Hoesly v. State, Dept. of Social Services, 498 N.W.2d 571 (Neb.1993); Department of Income Maintenance v. Watts, 558 A.2d 998 (Conn.1989).

**19.** Treas.Reg. § 25.2518-2(d)(1); Estate of Allen, TC Memo 1990-514; Estate of Thompson, 89 T.C. 619 (1987). But in Estate of Monroe v. C.I.R., 124 F.3d 699 (5th Cir.1997), disclaimers were held to qualify even though the disclaimants received equivalent gifts from the beneficiary of the disclaimers.

**20.** In Matter of Estate of Baird, 933 P.2d 1031 (Wash.1997), "The common law rule allowing anticipatory disclaimers based on valuable consideration" might still apply, but there was none here.

At common law, a disclaimer recognized oral disclaimers,[21] but under the Uniform Probate Code a disclaimer must be "signed by the disclaimant."[22] Perhaps an unsigned disclaimer could still be valid at common law,[23] but the Internal Revenue Code requires disclaimers to be in writing in order to qualify for tax purposes.

Uniform Probate Code § 2–801 says the disclaimer "must be filed in the [probate] court" where the estate is being administered, and an unfiled disclaimer has been held to be revocable.[24] Internal Revenue Code § 2518 merely requires that the disclaimer be "received by" the legal representative of the transferor.[25]

Once a person has accepted property, it is too late to disclaim it.[26] Mere failure to act for an extended period may amount to acceptance; at common law, a disclaimer must be made within a "reasonable time."[27] The Uniform Probate Code and the Internal Revenue Code are more precise: they allow 9 months from the date of the decedent's death.[28] This creates problems if probate of a will is delayed or contested. For example, if a will was not discovered for nine months after the testator dies, it would be too late for a devisee to disclaim.[29] If a will is contested and declared invalid 9 months after a testator died, an heir could not thereafter disclaim.

The Uniform Probate Code allows future interests to be disclaimed for up to 9 months after they become "indefeasibly vested."[30] This may occur long after the will which created them took effect. For example, if a will creates a trust for "Mary for life, at her death, to her then living issue," the interest of issue would not vest until Mary died.[31] However, the nine months allowed by the Internal Revenue Code starts to run when "the transfer creating the interest ... is made," *i.e.* at the testator's death. Thus a disclaimer by a child of Mary at her death would be effective under the Uniform Probate Code, but it would be treated as a gift for tax purposes (assuming that Mary outlived the testator by 9 months or more).[32]

**21.** 3 *Amer. Law of Prop.* § 14.15, at 630.

**22.** Uniform Probate Code § 2–801(c). In Estate of Allen, TC Memo 1989–111, a disclaimer signed by an orally authorized agent was held to be effective.

**23.** Medlin, *An Examination of Disclaimers Under UPC Section 2–801*, 55 Alb.L.Rev. 1233, 1276 (1992). Cal. Prob. Code § 288 specifically requires that all disclaimers comply with the statute. Uniform Probate Code § 2–801(f), on the other hand preserves the right to disclaim "under any other statute."

**24.** Matter of Estate of Griffin, 812 P.2d 1256 (Mont.1991). In the case of property passing under a "nontestamentary instrument" the disclaimer must be delivered "to the person who has legal title to or possession of the interest disclaimed." Disclaimers affecting land must be recorded. Uniform Probate Code § 2–801(b). *See also* Cal.Prob.Code § 280.

**25.** Estate of Bennett, 100 T.C. 42 (1993) (disclaimer delivered to executor but not filed in court was ineffective under state law).

**26.** Estate of Selby v. United States, 726 F.2d 643 (10th Cir.1984); Uniform Prob. Code § 2–801(e); Internal Revenue Code § 2518(b)(3); Estate of Hall, 456 S.E.2d 439 (S.C.App.1995) (person who had executed a receipt for property cannot thereafter disclaim it).

**27.** In re Nunn's Estate, 518 P.2d 1151 (Cal.1974) (nine years is too late); *Restatement (Second) of Property, Donative Transfers,* § 32.2(2), 32.3(2) (1990); *Amer. Law of Prop.* § 14.15.

**28.** Uniform Prob. Code § 2–801(b); Internal Revenue Code § 2518(b). *See also* Texas Prob. Code § 37A; Ga.Code Ann. § 113–824(b).

**29.** Estate of Fleming v. Commissioner, 974 F.2d 894 (7th Cir.1992) (rejecting claim that time runs from probate of the will).

**30.** Uniform Probate Code § 2–801(b)(1). See also Cal. Prob. Code § 279.

**31.** As to when future interests vest see Section 10.1.

**32.** Internal Revenue Code § 2518(b)(2)(A); United States v. Irvine, 511 U.S. 224 (1994) (disclaimer in 1979 of a future interest created in 1917 was a taxable transfer).

Under Section 2518 the time allowed to a minor to disclaim does not begin to run until the child reaches age 21,[33] presumably because until then a minor is not competent to decide whether or not to disclaim. Most states deal with this problem differently, by allowing a guardian to disclaim on behalf of a minor. Such a disclaimer by a fiduciary raises special problems.

***Disclaimers by Fiduciaries***

Uniform Probate Code § 2–801(a) allows disclaimers by "the representative of a person," including "a conservator of a disabled person" and "a guardian of a minor,"[34] if a court finds that the disclaimer "is in the best interest of the protected person."[35] The comparable provision in the California Probate Code uses slightly different language: the court must find that "the minor . . . as a prudent person would disclaim the interest if he or she had the capacity to do so."[36] Normally guardians have a duty to conserve a minor's property. For example, when a guardian of minor children sought to disclaim part of their share in their father's estate in order to get the maximum marital deduction for the estate, the court refused to allow the disclaimer because the children would lose by it even though it would have saved taxes. "Where an infant is involved there must be a showing that the renunciation would be directly advantageous to him and not merely to the parent."[37] However, a court acting under either the Uniform or California Probate Codes might have approved the disclaimer, since the children's mother would benefit from the disclaimer and she would probably use the funds (augmented by the tax savings) for their support, and so the disclaimer may have been in the children's "best interests."

Uniform Probate Code § 2–801(a) also allows disclaimers by an agent acting under a power of attorney. This may save the expense of court proceedings when a disclaimer for a principal who has been adjudicated incompetent is appropriate.[38] However, if the power of attorney does not authorizes disclaimers expressly, courts hesitate to infer that an agent is empowered to diminish the principal's estate.[39]

If an heir or devisee dies shortly after the decedent, can her executor disclaim her share of the decedent's estate before it is distributed, assuming there has been no acceptance and the allotted time has not run? The Uniform Probate Code allows personal representative to disclaim on behalf of a decedent,[40] but here too fiduciary duties of the personal representative may be an obstacle.[41] In California the court can approve a disclaimer by a personal

33. Internal Revenue Code § 2518(b)(2)(B). Although virtually all states have reduced the age of majority from 21 to 18, the Code does not take this change into account.

34. As to the distinction between "guardians" and "conservators" see Section 1.1.

35. Uniform Probate Code § 5–407(c).

36. Cal.Prob.Code § 277(f). As to conservators, the standard appears in Cal.Prob.Code § 2583, which provides a long list of relevant factors, but the substance is similar.

37. In re Estate of De Domenico, 418 N.Y.S.2d 1012 (Surr.1979). *See also* Matter of Estate of Horowitz, 531 A.2d 1364 (N.J.Super.Law Div.1987).

38. For a discussion of the advantages of a durable power of attorney in avoiding the need for conservatorship see Section 9.2, at note 21 et seq.

39. Cal.Prob.Code § 4264(d)(agent cannot disclaim unless expressly authorized unless court approved).

40. § 2–801(a). In In re Estate of Lamson, 662 A.2d 287 (N.H.1995), the court held that such a power existed even without a statute.

41. E.g., Uniform Probate Code § 3–709: personal representatives must "take possession or control of the decedent's property". § 3–715(11) allows them to abandon property that is "valueless."

representative only if it thinks the decedent would have disclaimed.[42] One court rejected a disclaimer by the executor of a will which had created a trust for children who would receive the property outright under the disclaimer.[43] Another refused to allow an executor to disclaim over an objection from a creditor of the testator, saying that executors have duties to creditors and can only disclaim when this would benefit the estate.[44] On the other hand, a court allowed a trustee to disclaim on behalf of trust beneficiaries when the decision was "made in good faith with the best interests of the trust's beneficiaries in mind."[45] This is possible when the disclaimer reduces taxes, particularly if one looks at the situation from the viewpoint of the family as a unit rather than its individual members.

### *Interests Disclaimable*

Historically, heirs taking by intestacy could not disclaim even though devisees under a will could.[46] There was no good reason for this distinction and most states have abolished it. The Uniform Probate Code expressly allows heirs as well as devisees to disclaim.[47]

One can also disclaim an inter-vivos gift. In this case the time starts to run "when there is a completed gift for Federal gift-tax purposes."[48] Thus, if a person creates a revocable living trust, the time within which the beneficiaries must disclaim does not start to run until the settlor's power to revoke expires (normally at the settlor's death). The same rule applies to joint accounts where the depositor usually retains a right of withdrawal until death.[49]

### *Partial Disclaimers*

The Uniform Probate Code expressly allows a person to disclaim property "in whole or in part,"[50] but the Treasury Regulations require that the interest retained be "severable" from the one disclaimed; they would not allow a person, for example, to disclaim property left to her in fee while retaining a life interest.[51]

**42.** Cal.Prob. Code § 277(f).

**43.** In re Morgan's Estate, 411 N.E.2d 213 (Ill.1980). In Matter of Estate of Schock, 543 A.2d 488 (N.J.Super.Law Div.1988), on the other hand, the court approved an executor's disclaimer when the persons who benefitted thereby agreed to create a trust with the property like the one in the decedent's will.

**44.** In re Estate of Heater, 640 N.E.2d 654 (Ill.App.1994).

**45.** McClintock v. Scahill, 530 N.E.2d 164 (Mass.1988). See also Cleaveland v. United States, 88–1 USTC #13,766, 1988 WL 123836 (C.D.Ill.1988) (trustee disclaims power without objection of adversely affected beneficiaries, thereby saving the marital deduction). But see Rev.Rul. 90–110, 1990–2 C.B. 209 (trustee's disclaimer of power to invade corpus for a grandchild is ineffective without grandchild's consent) .

**46.** Coomes v. Finegan, 7 N.W.2d 729 (Iowa 1943) (disclaimer by heir ineffective); Hardenbergh v. Commissioner, 198 F.2d 63 (8th Cir. 1952) (disclaimer by heir is a taxable gift).

**47.** Uniform Probate Code § 2–801(a). *See also* Texas Prob. Code § 37A; Ga.Code Ann. § 113–824(a); Md. Estates and Trusts Code § 9–101(a). A right to sue for wrongful death of a relative may not be disclaimed, because such claims may not be assigned and a disclaimer would be "the functional equivalent of an assignment." Mayo v. White, 224 Cal.Rptr. 373, 377 (App.1986).

**48.** Treas.Reg. § 25.2518–2(b)(3).

**49.** *Id.* § 25.2518–2(c)(4). The rule is otherwise for joint tenancies in land.

**50.** Uniform Probate Code § 2–801(a). *See also* Cal.Prob.Code § 267; Palmer v. White, 784 P.2d 449 (Or.App.1989) (allowing disclaimer of some but not all devises in a will).

**51.** Treas.Reg. § 25.2518–3.

### *Effect of Disclaimer*

If property is effectively disclaimed, the Uniform Probate Code provides the "disclaimed interest devolves as if the disclaimant had predeceased the decedent."[52] The effect of deeming the disclaimant to have predeceased depends on the circumstances. In the hypothetical described at the beginning of this section, if the son was the decedent's only issue and the decedent died intestate and the local intestacy statute gave the surviving spouse everything in the absence of issue, the son's disclaimer would cause his share to go to the widow. But if the son had children, his children would take his share by representation, even though a statute provides that a disclaimer is binding on persons "claiming through" the disclaimant.[53] Thus the son could not in this situation increase the marital deduction in his father's estate by a disclaimer, since the disclaimed share would not pass to the widow.[54] However, the marital deduction could be increased if *both* the son *and* his children disclaimed.[55]

What if decedent had two children, A and B, and A had no issue when he disclaimed? In this situation, B would take A's share as the only surviving "descendant" of the decedent.[56] If B was dead, survived by one child, and A had three children, what would happen if A disclaimed? Uniform Probate Code § 2–106 would call for an equal division among the four grandchildren if A and B were dead, but § 2–801(d) would prevent A from swelling his children's share of his father's estate by a disclaimer.[57]

Estate planners sometimes draft wills in anticipation of a possible disclaimer by a devisee. If a will devises property "to Mary, but if she predeceases me, to Andrew," Andrew would take if Mary survived John but disclaimed.[58] This might not be the optimal result; Mary may need property for her support for life, but wish to reduce her estate taxes at death. The best solution may be to put the property in a trust in which Mary gets the income for life without the trust property being taxable in her estate when she dies.[59]

**52.** Uniform Probate Code § 2–801(d). *See also* Cal.Prob.Code § 282; Tex.Prob.Code § 37A; Md. Estates and Trusts Code § 9–101(b).

**53.** Estate of Bryant, 196 Cal.Rptr. 856 (App.1983); Estate of Burmeister, 594 P.2d 226 (Kan.1979). *But see* In re Estate of Rohn, 175 N.W.2d 419 (Iowa 1970) (disclaimer bars takers under an anti-lapse statute).

**54.** Hunt v. United States, 566 F.Supp. 356 (E.D.Ark.1983). *See also* Webb v. Webb, 301 S.E.2d 570 (W.Va.1983) (disclaimant intended to benefit his mother but property goes to his children); Ernst v. Shaw, 783 S.W.2d 400 (Ky. App.1990) (disclaimer causes property to pass to disclaimant's children, not his sister, whom he intended to benefit). In In re Estate of York, 727 N.E.2d 607 (Ohio App.1999) a similar error led to a malpractice claim against the attorney who drafted the documents.

**55.** Matter of Guardianship of Kramer, 421 N.Y.S.2d 975 (Surr.1979).

**56.** Under Cal. Prob. Code § 6401, the spouse gets a larger share of a decedent's separate property when there is only one child, so the disclaimer might increase the widow's share too.

**57.** See Uniform Probate Code § 2–801, Comment. Whether the text achieves the intended result is less clear. See Medlin, *An Examination of Disclaimers Under UPC Section 2–801*, 55 Alb.L.Rev. 1233, 1261 (1992). The same idea is expressed more clearly in Cal.Prob.Code § 282(b). The courts which have dealt with this situation without statutory guidance have reached divergent results. *Compare* Estate of Bryant, 196 Cal.Rptr. 856 (App. 1983), *with* Welder v. Hitchcock, 617 S.W.2d 294 (Tex.Civ.App.1981). A similar issue can arise when a child of the intestate is disqualified by homicide. Fellows, *The Slayer Rule: Not Solely a Matter of Equity,* 71 Iowa L.Rev. 489, 525–27 (1986).

**58.** Matter of Estate of Bruce, 877 P.2d 999 (Mont.1994) (secondary beneficiaries of IRA account take when primary beneficiary disclaims). When a life interest under a will is disclaimed, the remainder is accelerated so as to take effect immediately. Uniform Probate Code § 2–801(d); Pate v. Ford, 376 S.E.2d 775 (S.C.1989).

**59.** For a more detailed discussion of optimal marital tax planning see Section 15.3.

A testator when executing a will may be uncertain whether or not the estate at death will be large enough to warrant such a trust, and may therefore prefer to leave all the estate property to a spouse outright with the idea that when the testator dies, the spouse can disclaim all or part of the devise if this is appropriate. A will can provide that any property which a spouse disclaims shall go into a trust for the spouse for life.[60] Such a provision would get around the limitation on partial disclaimers,[61] and general rule that a disclaimant is deemed to have died before the decedent, since this applies only if "the decedent has not provided for another disposition."[62]

### *Agreements Among Successors*

Heirs and devisees can alter the devolution of an estate by agreement as well as by disclaimer. Disclaimed property usually passes as if the disclaimant had predeceased the decedent, but an agreement can provide for whatever distribution the parties desire. A child can agree that his share should go to his mother, even though a disclaimer would give his share to his children. Unlike disclaimers, such agreements constitute transfers and are subject to the rights of creditors and to taxes. Therefore, Uniform Probate Code § 3–912, which provides for such agreements among successors, is prefaced by the words "subject to the rights of creditors and taxing authorities." When a child who owed his ex-wife money agreed to give his share of his mother's estate to his sibling, the ex-wife had the agreement set aside.[63] When one child, to whom a will left most of the estate, agreed that the estate should be divided equally with her siblings, the inheritance tax was based on the will, not on the agreement.[64] Even an agreement increases the surviving spouse's share, the marital deduction will not be increased, since the marital deduction requires that the property pass from one spouse to the other.[65]

The Uniform Probate Code refers to a "written" agreement, and this has been interpreted by some courts to make an oral agreement among successors unenforceable.[66] But a letter which repudiates an agreement while acknowledging its existence may suffice.[67] In some states no writing is necessary.[68]

Some cases speak as if consideration were necessary to make such an agreement enforceable,[69] but it would seem that a person who agrees to take less than she would otherwise receive is making a gift, which, while it may be subject to gift tax, does not require consideration.[70] Sometimes the beneficiary

**60.** Llewellyn, *Estate Planning for the Married Couple,* 28 Vill.L.Rev. 491, 508–09 (1983).

**61.** See note 51 *supra.*

**62.** Uniform Probate Code § 2–801(d)(1). *See also* Cal.Prob.Code § 282(a).

**63.** Matter of Estate of Haggerty, 805 P.2d 1338 (Mont.1990).

**64.** Estate of McNicholas v. State, 580 N.E.2d 978 (Ind.App.1991).

**65.** Jeschke v. United States, 814 F.2d 568 (10th Cir.1987). The result is different if the agreement is made to settle a bona-fide contest.

**66.** Matter of Estate of Leathers, 876 P.2d 619 (Kan.App.1994); Estate of Webster, 920 S.W.2d 600 (Mo.App.1996).

**67.** Matter of Estate of Cruse, 710 P.2d 733 (N.M.1985); *Restatement (Second) of Contracts* § 133, Comment c (1979).

**68.** Gregory v. Rice, 678 S.W.2d 603 (Tex. App.1984).

**69.** Matter of Estate of Wahby, 758 S.W.2d 440 (Mo.1988) (refusing to enforce agreement because of duress, adding there was "little or no consideration"). But courts do no usually examine the adequacy of consideration. Emberson v. Hartley, 762 P.2d 364 (Wash.App.1988); *cf.* Matter of Estate of Grimm, 784 P.2d 1238 (Utah App.1989) (good faith controversy supplies consideration even if not well founded).

**70.** As to the requirements for making a gift, see Section 4.5.

of an estate makes an agreement with an "heir-hunting" firm which locates the beneficiary and informs him of his interest in the estate in return for a large percentage of his share. In California, a court may refuse to distribute a share of an estate to an assignee if it finds that the consideration for the assignment was "grossly unreasonable."[71] But in other states, courts have upheld agreements in which the firm took a high percentage of the heir's share.[72]

## § 2.9 Children Born Out of Wedlock

### *History and Policy Considerations*

According to recent data, one in every four American babies is now born out of wedlock.[1] The legal right to succession of such children has dramatically improved in recent years. In the 12th century, Glanville said "no bastard born outside a lawful marriage can be an heir,"[2] and this remained the law in England until the present century. In 1969 England gave children born out of wedlock the right to inherit.[3] In America, the Uniform Probate Code provides that for purposes of succession "an individual is the child of his [or her] natural parents, regardless of their marital status."[4] Some American statutes are less favorable to children born out of wedlock, but court decisions beginning in 1968 have held many such statutes unconstitutional.[5] Today, the very term "illegitimate" is usually replaced in legal terminology by the phrase "born out of wedlock."[6] A recent judicial opinion expressed "concern over perpetuation of the offensive term 'illegitimate' in [a statute] referring to a child born to parents not married to each other." An "innocent child" should not be "stigmatized by that reference."[7]

What has brought about this great change? What reasons lay behind the historical refusal to allow inheritance by children born out of wedlock? Four reasons can be suggested, but none of them is entirely satisfactory.

(1) *Feudalism.* The rule barring inheritance by out-of-wedlock children has often been ascribed to feudalism.[8] If a feudal tenant died without heirs his

**71.** Cal.Prob.Code § 11604.

**72.** Nelson v. McGoldrick, 896 P.2d 1258 (Wash.1995) (50% fee was not unconscionable as a matter of law); Matter of Estate of Katze–Miller, 463 N.W.2d 853 (Wis.App.1990) (40% fee upheld). Compare Landi v. Arkules, 835 P.2d 458 (Ariz.App.1992) which allowed an heir to rescind a similar contract. Several cases on both sides of this issue are cited in In re Estate of Campbell, 742 A.2d 639, 640 (N.J.Super.Ch. Div.1999).

§ 2.9

**1.** Adoption of Kelsey, 823 P.2d 1216, 1223 (Cal.1992) (citing Census statistics for 1989–90).

**2.** R. Glanville, *Tractatus de Legibus* 87 (G. Hall ed. 1965).

**3.** Family Law Reform Act, § 14 (1969).

**4.** UPC § 2–114(a). *See also* Cal.Prob.Code § 6450; *Restatement (Third) of Property (Wills and Other Donative Transfers)* § 2.5 (1998).

**5.** Levy v. Louisiana, 391 U.S. 68, 88 S.Ct. 1509, 20 L.Ed.2d 436 (1968), involved a wrongful death action on behalf of illegitimate children. In Trimble v. Gordon, 430 U.S. 762, 97 S.Ct. 1459, 52 L.Ed.2d 31 (1977), the Supreme Court first held unconstitutional an intestacy statute which restricted inheritance by illegitimates. For more recent similar decisions by state courts see Estate of Dulles, 431 A.2d 208 (Pa.1981); Talley v. Succession of Stuckey, 614 So.2d 55 (La.1993); Turner v. Nesby, 848 S.W.2d 872 (Tex.App.1993); Estate of Hicks, 675 N.E.2d 89 (Ill.1996).

**6.** Cal.Prob.Code § 6452; 10 Okl.Stat. § 1.1 (all statutory references to "illegitimate" or "bastard" deemed to refer to a child born out of wedlock).

**7.** Guard v. Jackson, 940 P.2d 642, 645–46 (Wash.1997) (concurring opinion).

**8.** Butcher v. Pollard, 288 N.E.2d 204, 207 (Ohio 1972).

land escheated to the overlord. Barring illegitimates from inheriting produced an escheat when an intestate left no other heirs.[9] However, the theory that feudal lords promoted the bar on inheritance in order to increase the incidence of escheat is implausible, because in most situations there are other relatives to inherit if children born out of wedlock are excluded.

(2) *Intent.* Intestacy laws are designed to carry out the decedent's wishes. The bar against inheritance by illegitimates may have reflected the average decedent's intent. However, probably most parents in the past loved their illegitimate children.[10] In the 15th century, John Fortescue assumed that parents wanted their illegitimate children to inherit; the law frustrated this desire in order to punish the parents for their sin.[11]

(3) *Sin.* In the 19th century Kent echoed Fortescue's explanation; the rule was designed "to discourage illicit commerce between the sexes."[12] Today, sexual "commerce" between unmarried persons no longer appears "illicit" or immoral to many. This change in attitudes may have contributed to the change in the law, but this explanation also presents difficulties. Even if sex outside marriage was [or is] regarded as wrong, it was [and is] unfair to punish children for the sins of their parents. Modern courts have said: "No child is responsible for his birth and penalizing the illegitimate child is an ineffectual—as well as an unjust—way of deterring the parent."[13] This idea is not new. Even in the 18th century, the conservative Blackstone thought it "unjust" to impose disabilities on an illegitimate "innocent offspring of his parents' crimes."[14]

The "deterring sin" explanation is also hard to reconcile with the fact that even a secret marriage, unblessed by the church, made the issue of the marriage legitimate. "Parties sinned by marrying without publications of banns and blessing by a priest," but their marriage was valid and their children were legitimate.[15] Modern law, in contrast, generally invalidates such informal "common-law" marriages[16] but has improved the legal position of children born out of wedlock. Many of the "children born out of wedlock" who can inherit today, would also have inherited as "legitimate" children under the older more liberal rules governing marriage.

(4) *Problems of Proof.* For Blackstone, the purpose of marriage "taken in a civil light, abstractly from any religious view" was "to ascertain and fix upon some certain person to whom the care * * * of the children should

**9.** King v. Commonwealth, 221 Va. 251, 269 S.E.2d 793 (1980).

**10.** "Our father's love is to the bastard Edmund

As to the legitimate * * * "

W. Shakespeare, King Lear, Act I, Scene 2, lines 17–18. *See also* L. Tolstoy, *War and Peace,* part 1, Chapter 18.

**11.** J. Fortescue, *De Laudibus Legum Anglie* 94 (S. Chrimes ed. 1949).

**12.** J. Kent, *Commentaries on American Law* 175 (1827).

**13.** Weber v. Aetna Casualty & Surety Co., 406 U.S. 164, 175, (1972). *See also* Succession of Brown, 388 So.2d 1151, 1153 (La.1980); In re Woodward's Estate, 40 Cal.Rptr. 781, 784 (App.1964).

**14.** 1 W. Blackstone, *Commentaries** 459 (1765).

**15.** R. Helmholz, *Marriage Litigation in Medieval England* 27 (1974). *See also* 2 F. Pollock & F. Maitland, *The History of English Law* 379–80 (2d ed. 1898).

**16.** Section 2.11, note 43. For a recent claim by a child to be born in wedlock on the basis of such an informal marriage see Ruscilli v. Ruscilli, 630 N.E.2d 745 (Ohio App.1993).

belong." To allow bastards to inherit would create "very great uncertainty * * * in the proof that the issue was really begotten by" the alleged father.[17]

The problem of proving paternity clearly influenced the common-law rules on inheritance. If a married woman gave birth to a child, her husband was held to be the child's father despite any evidence to the contrary, because "the privity between a man and his wife cannot be known."[18] This presumption of paternity avoided difficult problems of proof as well as serving to legitimate many children who were the fruit of adultery.

Maternity is more easily proved than paternity. In the 18th century Blackstone pointed out that in the civil law a bastard could inherit from his *mother* "the mother being sufficiently certain, though the father is not."[19] At this time English law made no distinction between fathers and mothers, but the first step in protecting inheritance rights generally was to allow children born out of wedlock to inherit from their mother.

### *Proof of Paternity*

Science has recently made great progress in making paternity determinations more accurate.[20] This has undercut the difficulty-of-proof argument against inheritance by non-marital children.[21] Such proof may be available even after the father is dead.[22] Proof of biological paternity is not always determinative of the parent/child relationship, however. If a married woman is inseminated artificially with the sperm of a man who is not her husband, the husband is deemed the child's father and not the sperm donor under the Uniform Parentage Act, if the husband has consented in writing.[23] Even without this statute, or without compliance with its limitations, courts have reached the same result; for example, a husband's oral consent may estop him from denying paternity even though he is clearly not the biological father of the child.[24] According to the Restatement of Property, children produced by assisted reproductive technologies "should be treated as part of the family of

**17.** 1 W. Blackstone, *Commentaries* *455 (1765).

**18.** Y.B. 32 & 33 Edw. 1 (R.S.) 60, 63 (1304) (Hengham J.). For modern vestiges of the idea see Hess v. Whitsitt, 65 Cal.Rptr. 45 (App.1967) (black child born to a white mother deemed to be the child of her white husband); Rumlin v. Lewis, 381 So.2d 194 (Ala.1980) (child born 4 years after husband and wife separated); Estate of Cornelious, 674 P.2d 245 (Cal.1984) (husband deemed to be father even though this was "biologically impossible"). Modern cases have weakened the presumption considerably. Johnson v. Adams, 479 N.E.2d 866 (Ohio 1985); In re Adoption of McFadyen, 438 N.E.2d 1362 (Ill.App.1982); Symonds v. Symonds, 432 N.E.2d 700 (Mass.1982); State ex rel. Munoz v. Bravo, 678 P.2d 974 (Ariz. App.1984); Matter of Marriage of Hodge, 722 P.2d 1235 (Or.1986) (presumption inapplicable if husband and wife not cohabiting).

**19.** 2 W. Blackstone, *Commentaries** 248 (1765).

**20.** *E.g.* Nwabara v. Willacy, 733 N.E.2d 267, 274 (Ohio App.1999) (DNA test identifies father with 99.95% probability). L.A. Times, Feb. 7, 2001: (Paternity claims asserted by alleged children of air crash victim dismissed on the basis of DNA testing).

**21.** S.M.V. v. Littlepage, 443 N.E.2d 103, 110 (Ind.App.1982) (concurring); *cf.* Mills v. Habluetzel, 456 U.S. 91, 98n, 104n, (1982); Pickett v. Brown, 462 U.S. 1 (1983).

**22.** Alexander v. Alexander, 537 N.E.2d 1310 (Ohio Prob.1988) (proper to order body exhumed for DNA testing to establish paternity); Batcheldor v. Boyd, 423 S.E.2d 810 (N.C.App.1992) (same). Contra, Estate of Sekanic, 653 N.Y.S.2d 449 (A.D.1997).

**23.** § 5. this Act was promulgated in 1973 and has been adopted in 18 states.

**24.** In re Marriage of Adams, 528 N.E.2d 1075 (Ill.App.1988); R.S. v. R.S., 670 P.2d 923 (Kan.App.1983); Levin v. Levin, 626 N.E.2d 527 (Ind.App.1993) (no statute). But in Jhordan C. v. Mark K., 224 Cal.Rptr. 530 (App. 1986), the sperm donor was held entitled to a paternity declaration when the statutory procedure requiring a physician's supervision was not followed.

* * * parents who treat the child as their own" even though "one or both of them might not be the child's genetic parent."[25]

Under the Uniform Parentage Act a presumption of paternity is created when a man "receives [a minor] child into his home and openly holds out the child as his natural child" even though this is consistent with the absence of biological paternity.[26] Conversely, claims by biological fathers to parental rights have sometimes been rejected in order to protect a family unit when the mother is married to someone else.[27] Failure to act like a parent may outweigh biological claims. The Uniform Probate Code bars inheritance by a parent or a relative of a parent if the parent has not "openly treated the child as his [or hers]" or has "refused to support the child."[28]

### *Inheritance From and Through Mother*

As early as 1827 several American statutes allowed children born out of wedlock to inherit from their mother;[29] by 1934 this rule was virtually universal.[30] Proof of maternity is rarely an issue. The Uniform Parentage Act has some rather complex rules on proving paternity, but motherhood is simply established "by proof of her having given birth to the child."[31] The picture in recent years has been complicated by the advent of surrogate mothers, but so far they have not figured in inheritance disputes.[32]

When children born out of wedlock seek to inherit *through* the mother from a relative of the mother, the decedent's intent seems more doubtful. If John's daughter has a son out of wedlock, even if the daughter would want him to inherit her property, John might not want him to share in *his* estate. Nevertheless, most statutes would allow the son to inherit from John by representation. For example, under the Uniform Probate Code, "for purposes of intestate succession by, *through*, or from a person, an individual is the child of his [or her] natural parents, regardless of their marital status."[33]

### *Inheritance From Father*

Claims to inherit by, from and through the father present the major area of uncertainty today. Some states do not distinguish between fathers and mothers; illegitimacy has no effect on inheritance in either case, and "paternity is a fact to be proved as any other fact, *i.e.*, by a preponderance of the

**25.** *Restatement (Third) of Property (Wills and Other Donative Transfers)* § 2.5, comm. l (1998).

**26.** Section 4.

**27.** Dawn D. v. Superior Court (Jerry K.), 952 P.2d 1139 (Cal.1998); Matter of Paternity of Adam, 903 P.2d 207 (Mont.1995); Marriage of Matter of Marriage of Ross, 783 P.2d 331 (Kan.1989).

**28.** Section 2–114(c). *See also Restatement (Third) of Property (Wills and Other Donative Transfers)* § 2.5(5) (1998). Under pre–1990 UPC § 2–109(2), this bar applied only to fathers of children born out of wedlock. Such a distinction between fathers and mothers has been held unconstitutional. Rainey v. Chever, 510 S.E.2d 823 (Ga.1999); Guard v. Jackson, 921 P.2d 544 (Wash.App.1996). *Contra*, In Estate of Scheller v. Pessetto, 783 P.2d 70 (Utah App.1989). Cal.Prob.Code § 6452 applies to both parents but only if the child is born out of wedlock.

**29.** J. Kent, *Commentaries on American Law* 176 (1827).

**30.** Vernier & Churchill, *Inheritance By and From Bastards,* 20 Iowa L.Rev. 216 (1934).

**31.** Uniform Parentage Act § 3(1).

**32.** In Johnson v. Calvert, 851 P.2d 776 (Cal.1993), the court rejected the claim of a surrogate mother, holding she was bound by her contract with the couple whose gametes were implanted in her uterus.

**33.** Uniform Probate Code § 2–114(a). *See also* Cal.Prob.Code § 6450(a).

evidence."[34] Some states, however, impose an extra burden on non-marital children who seek to inherit from a father. In some, the child must establish paternity by "clear and convincing" evidence; a mere preponderance of the evidence is not enough.[35] Some states require particular kinds of proof, such as a written acknowledgement of paternity.[36] The Supreme Court upheld against a constitutional challenge a New York statute which allowed children born out of wedlock to inherit from their father only if a court had made an order declaring paternity during the father's life was on the reasoning that "fraudulent assertions of paternity will be much less likely to succeed * * * where proof is put before a court of law at a time when the putative father is available to respond."[37] Meritorious cases might be excluded by the statute, but this is true of any formal requirement, *e.g.,* that wills be in writing. But as a dissenting justice observed, the statute could exclude the *most* meritorious cases; a father who voluntarily supports a child he would probably want the child to inherit, but the child, having no reason to bring paternity proceedings, would not qualify under the statute.[38] The New York statute was later amended to allow a child born out of wedlock to inherit from the father without an adjudication of paternity during the father's lifetime, and most states today agree.[39] A statute requiring a child born out of wedlock to produce a written, signed acknowledgement of paternity in order to inherit from the father was recently held unconstitutional by a state court. "While Washington has a legitimate interest in determining paternity ... [the statute] excluded more illegitimate children from inheriting from their fathers than was necessary to further these interests."[40]

### *Presumptions of Paternity*

In many cases the question of paternity may be resolved by a presumption. The Uniform Parentage Act, to which the Uniform Probate Code refers, creates five such presumptions.[41]

First, if the mother is married and the child is born during the marriage, or within 300 days after the marriage is terminated, the mother's husband is presumed to be the father. This presumption was virtually irrebuttable at common law, but under the Act, it can be rebutted by "clear and convincing evidence."[42] However, the presumption can be rebutted only by the child, the

**34.** Matter of Estate of Cook, 698 P.2d 1076 (Wash.App.1985). *See also* Griffin v. Succession of Branch Through Smith, 479 So.2d 324, 328 (La.1985); Allen v. Bowen, 657 F.Supp. 148 (N.D.Ill.1987) (Social Security benefits).

**35.** Matter of Estate of King, 837 P.2d 463 (Okl.1990) (claim denied because proof of paternity not clear).

**36.** Wis. Stat. § 852.05(1); DePaoli v. C.I.R., 62 F.3d 1259 (10th Cir.1995) (under N.M. statute, since amended); In re Estate of Geller, 980 P.2d 665 (Okl.Civ.App.1999) (statute requires either written acknowledgement or taking into the home).

**37.** Lalli v. Lalli, 439 U.S. 259 (1978). *See also* Estate of Blumreich, 267 N.W.2d 870 (Wis. 1978).

**38.** 439 U.S. at 278.

**39.** N.Y. EPTL § 4–1.2(a)(2); Wood v. Wingfield, 816 S.W.2d 899 (Ky.1991) (can prove paternity after death of the father); Meckstroth v. Robinson, 679 N.E.2d 744 (Ohio Com.Pl.1996) (posthumous child).

**40.** Pitzer v. Union Bank of California, 969 P.2d 113, 118 (Wash.App.1998).

**41.** Uniform Probate Code § 2–114(a): "The parent and child relationship may be established under [the Uniform Parentage Act] [applicable state law]." *See also* Cal.Prob.Code § 6453. The presumptions appear in Uniform Parentage Act § 4. A child without a presumed father under Section 4 can sue to establish paternity under Section 6. Of course, paternity is relevant for many purposes in law other than inheritance.

**42.** Uniform Parentage Act § 4(b). *See also* Green v. Estate of Green, 724 N.E.2d 260, 265

mother, or a man who is presumed to be the father under other provisions of the Act. Thus a sister of the decedent who would inherit in the absence of issue would not be permitted to prove that a child born to her brother's wife was not in fact his.[43]

Second, there is also a presumption of paternity if the mother and man "attempted to marry each other by a marriage solemnized in apparent compliance with law, although the marriage is or could be declared invalid."[44] At common law a child was illegitimate if the marriage of the father and mother was invalid.[45] But the Supreme Court has held it unconstitutional to deny inheritance when the parents went through a marriage ceremony just because one of them was already married.[46]

Historically, a child born during a valid marriage was legitimate regardless of when the child was conceived,[47] but a marriage of the parents after a child was born did not make the child legitimate. England adopted the contrary rule of canon and Roman law only in 1926.[48] Under Uniform Parentage Act a man who marries the mother after the child is born is presumed to be the father if "with his consent, he is named as the child's father on the child's birth certificate," or is obligated to support the child by a "written voluntary promise or by court order."[49] Even without such actions, a step-child relationship between a husband and his wife's children may allow inheritance, but only in rare situations.[50]

Even if a man who never married or attempted to marry the mother is presumed to be the father under the Parentage Act if "he receives the child into his home and openly holds out the child as his" while the child is a minor.[51] A presumption of paternity can also be created if a man files a written acknowledgement of which the mother is informed and which she does not dispute. The last two presumptions, unlike the first three, can be rebutted by "any interested party."[52]

All these presumptions are rebuttable "only by clear and convincing evidence." When two conflicting presumptions apply in the same case, the one

(Ind.App.2000) (child proved that he was not the son of his mother's husband).

**43.** Uniform Parentage Act § 6(a); Matter of Estate of Raulston, 805 P.2d 113 (Okl.App. 1990) (sister can't challenge paternity of her brother's wife's child); Estate of Lamey v. Lamey, 689 N.E.2d 1265 (Ind.App.1997).

**44.** Uniform Parentage Act § 4(b)(2).

**45.** On this basis Richard III claimed that his nephews were illegitimate and so he was entitled to the throne of England. P. Kendall, *Richard the Third* 259 (1955).

**46.** Reed v. Campbell, 476 U.S. 852 (1986). *See also* In re Estate of Bartolini, 674 N.E.2d 74 (Ill.App.1996) (bigamous "marriage" of parents renders child "legitimate" under statute).

**47.** E. Coke on Littleton 244; 1 W. Blackstone, *Commentaries* 454 (1765).

**48.** Legitimacy Act, § 1 (1926). An exception in that statute for a child born of an adulterous union was eliminated by Legitimacy Act, § 1 (1959).

**49.** Section 4. *See also* Green v. Estate of Green, 724 N.E.2d 260 (Ind.App.2000) (person who married mother after child was born and acknowledged child held to be the father). *But see* Garrison v. Smith, 561 N.E.2d 1041 (Ohio App.1988) (man who later married the mother but did not acknowledge the child as his is not the child's father for inheritance purposes).

**50.** See Section 2.10, at note 66 et seq.

**51.** Section 4. Even without this statutory presumption, a man who cohabits with mother and child may be found to have married the mother, thus rendering the child "legitimate." Matter of Estate of Lowney, 543 N.Y.S.2d 698 (App.Div.1989) (cohabitation creates presumption of marriage); Thompson v. Brown, 326 S.E.2d 733 (Ga.1985) (common-law marriage); Ruscilli v. Ruscilli, 630 N.E.2d 745 (Ohio App. 1993) (same).

**52.** Uniform Parentage Act § 6(b).

"founded on the weightier considerations of policy and logic controls."[53] An attempt to rebut the presumption may be barred, however, by failure to act "within a reasonable time after obtaining knowledge of relevant facts" and in any event five years after the child's birth.[54] For example, a man who married a woman with a young child and was named the father on the birth certificate was not allowed to deny paternity when he divorced the mother almost five years later.[55] However, some courts have refused to apply these time limits in inheritance cases.[56]

The Uniform Parentage Act allows a child without a presumed father to sue to establish paternity up to three "years after the child reaches the age of majority." The drafters recognized that this long statute of limitations "will cause problems of proof in many cases" but since a minor could not sue they thought it "unreasonable to bar the child's action by reason of another person's failure to bring a paternity action at an earlier time."[57] However, this liberal rule does not allow claims to inherit to be "asserted beyond the time provided by law relating to distribution and closing of decedent's estates." Thus a child may be barred by the closing of an estate while the child is still a minor.[58] On the other hand, some courts have allowed children who failed to sue to establish paternity after they reached majority to later claim an inheritance on the theory that they "had no reason to judicially establish the decedent's paternity" during his life when he acknowledged it.[59]

A stipulation in a divorce decree which names the children of the marriage has been held to be res judicata as to paternity in proceedings involving inheritance.[60] However, a declaration in the decree that a person was *not* the husband's child does not preclude her from asserting the contrary if she was not a party to the divorce litigation.[61] Nor does a decree designating *A* as the child's father preclude the child from later claiming that *B* was

**53.** Uniform Parentage Act § 4(b). In Gregory v. McLemore, 899 P.2d 1189 (Okl.App. 1995) a dispute between two "presumed fathers" was resolved on the basis of blood tests, but in Steven W. v. Matthew S., 39 Cal.Rptr.2d 535 (App.1995) found for the man who had been acting like a father for several years even though he was not the biological father.

**54.** *Id.* § 6(2). This rule applies only to the presumptions arising from a marriage.

**55.** Mak–M v. SM, 854 P.2d 64 (Wyo.1993). *See also* In re Marriage of Freeman, 53 Cal. Rptr.2d 439 (App.1996).

**56.** Lewis v. Schneider, 890 P.2d 148 (Colo. App.1994) (child can inherit from man other than his mother's husband even after the 5 year limit).

**57.** Section 7. Compare Pickett v. Brown, 462 U.S. 1, 15, 17 (1983) holding unconstitutional a 2 year limitation on actions for support by a child born out of wedlock, noting that the state "tolls most actions during a child's minority" and "scientific advances in blood testing have alleviated the problems of proof surrounding paternity actions."

**58.** In S.V. v. Estate of Bellamy, 579 N.E.2d 144 (Ind.App.1991) it was held constitutional to bar a posthumous child even though the statutory limitation expired before he was born. But in Smith by Young v. Estate of King, 579 So.2d 1250 (Miss.1991), a decree of distribution was set aside on the ground that the administrator was guilty of fraud in failing to disclose the existence of a child born out of wedlock. Contra, Pitzer v. Union Bank of California, 9 P.3d 805 (Wash. 2000).

**59.** Tersavich v. First Nat. Bank & Trust Co., 571 N.E.2d 733 (Ill.1991); Woods v. Harris, 600 N.E.2d 163 (Ind.App.1992). *But see* Matter of Estate of Foley, 925 P.2d 449 (Kan. App.1996) (claim to inherit rejected because 3 year statute had run); Succession of Grice, 462 So.2d 131 (La.1985) (19 year limit on filiation proceedings bars claim of 31 year old child to inherit); Garrison v. Smith, 561 N.E.2d 1041 (Ohio App.1988).

**60.** Estate of Kelm, 70 Cal.Rptr.2d 33 (App. 1997).

**61.** Gonzales v. Pacific Greyhound Lines, 214 P.2d 809 (Cal.1950) (wrongful death claim); Flaherty v. Feldner, 419 N.W.2d 908 (N.D.1988).

actually her father.[62]

### *Inheritance by and through Parents from Child*

The common law deemed a child born out of wedlock to be *filius nullius,* the child of no one, so that such a child who had no spouse or issue had no heirs.[63] Today, however, most statutes allow parents of a child born out of wedlock and their relatives to inherit from the child. The Uniform Probate Code, for example, allows inheritance by and through parents of children born out of wedlock, if they have acknowledged and not refused to support the child.[64] But parents who challenge a statute which bars them from inheriting have a less appealing case than a child who seeks to inherit from a parent. The child's status is involuntary, but the parents are responsible for their situation.[65] Nevertheless, unmarried parents have some constitutional rights. The Supreme Court struck down a statute which did not permit a mother to sue for the wrongful death of her child born out of wedlock.[66] Unmarried fathers may also have constitutionally protected parental rights in certain situations.[67] A state court recently struck down a statute which allowed mothers but not fathers to inherit from children born out of wedlock. Since this involved sex discrimination, the statute was subject to strict scrutiny. The problems of proof did not warrant barring the claimant in this case since he had already been adjudicated the father.[68] Another court allowed the father of a child born out of wedlock to sue for wrongful death of his child even though he had failed to contribute to the child's support. A statute which barred the father's claim was held to violate the state's Equal Rights Amendment, since it contained no comparable bar on mothers.[69]

### *Claims Not Based on Intent*

When children born out of wedlock sue for wrongful death, worker's compensation, Social Security or other benefits over which the decedent has no control, their claim seems particularly strong. Refusal to allow children to inherit may reflect the decedent's intent; if it does not, the decedent can provide for the child by will. But a will cannot dispose of wrongful death claims or Social Security benefits. The "burdens of illegitimacy" seem particularly unfair "when neither parent nor child can legally lighten them."[70] Furthermore, the social interest in deterring wrongs favors tort claims when a

**62.** Estate of Willis, 574 N.E.2d 172 (Ill. App.1991); Simcox v. Simcox, 546 N.E.2d 609 (Ill.1989). *See also* In re Paternity of S.R.I., 602 N.E.2d 1014 (Ind.1992) (claim by another man to be the father).

**63.** Glanville, *supra* note 2, at 88; 1 W. Blackstone, *Commentaries** 459 (1765).

**64.** Uniform Probate Code § 2–114. *See also Restatement (Third) of Property (Wills and Other Donative Transfers)* § 2.5 (1998).

**65.** Parham v. Hughes, 441 U.S. 347 (1979) (upholding a statute barring a father who had not legitimated a child from suing for child's wrongful death); King v. Commonwealth, 269 S.E.2d 793 (Va.1980); Harding v. DeAngelis, 657 N.E.2d 758 (Mass.App.1995). In Gonzales v. Cowen, 884 P.2d 19 (Wash.App.1994) a father's claim was denied on the ground that paternity could only be established during the child's lifetime.

**66.** Glona v. American Guarantee & Liability Ins. Co., 391 U.S. 73 (1968).

**67.** Adoption of Kelsey, 823 P.2d 1216 (Cal. 1992) (unwed father who has tried to maintain contact with child has standing to oppose adoption).

**68.** Estate of Hicks, 675 N.E.2d 89 (Ill. 1996)

**69.** Guard v. Jackson, 940 P.2d 642 (Wash. 1997).

**70.** Weber v. Aetna Casualty & Surety Co., 406 U.S. 164, 173 (1972). However, usually the parent can adopt the child and thereby bring it within the ambit of relevant statutes.

child is the only potential claimant. "[W]hy * * * should the tortfeasors go free merely because the child is illegitimate?"[71] Also, the problem of proof is less acute under statutes which require the claimant to be a dependent who was being supported by the decedent. Spurious "children" would not satisfy this test.[72] Therefore even if a child who cannot inherit may be allowed to sue for wrongful death, or for benefits under Social Security or a worker's compensation statute.[73]

### *Wills*

Claims to take under a will turn on intent. If the will gives no clue to the intent, courts traditionally presumed the testator intended to exclude children born out of wedlock in a devise to "children" or the like.[74] This presumption could be overcome by showing "a contrary intent * * * from additional language or circumstances," such as the fact that the only possible takers under the devise were illegitimate.[75] Some authorities distinguished between fathers and mothers. If a will left property to the "children" of a woman, all were included because of "the natural affection of a mother for her children, whether legitimate or illegitimate." A devise to a man's "children" was different because of the difficulty of proving paternity and because there was usually no "close association between an illegitimate child and his father."[76]

Recently, the law has construed wills more favorably to children born out of wedlock. Under the Uniform Probate Code, unless a will provides otherwise "individuals born out of wedlock and their respective descendants * * * are included in class gifts in accordance with the rules for intestate succession."[77] Even in states which without a similar statute dealing with will construction, intestacy statutes are often cited as evidence of probable intent.[78] The recent more favorable attitude toward inheritance by children born out of wedlock has persuaded some courts to presume that class gifts in wills include them.[79]

**71.** Levy v. Louisiana, 391 U.S. 68, 71 (1968). *See also* Glona v. American Guarantee & Liability Ins. Co., 391 U.S. 73, 75 (1968).

**72.** Weber v. Aetna Casualty & Surety Co., 406 U.S. 164, 173 (1972); Claim of Burns, 435 N.E.2d 390 (N.Y.1982); Brookbank v. Gray, 658 N.E.2d 724 (Ohio 1996). *cf.* Johnson Controls, Inc. v. Forrester, 704 N.E.2d 1082, 1086 (Ind.App.1999) (lack of contact between father and child reduces damages recoverable for father's wrongful death).

**73.** In S.V. v. Estate of Bellamy, 579 N.E.2d 144 (Ind.App.1991), even though a child's claim to inherit was time barred, his suit to establish paternity was not dismissed since he might be able to claim Social Security. But in some states a child who does not qualify to inherit cannot sue for wrongful death either. Cheyanna M. v. A.C. Nielsen Co., 78 Cal. Rptr.2d 335 (App.1998).

**74.** *Restatement of Property* § 286 (1940); Theobald, *Wills* § 851 (12th ed. 1963); Dutra De Amorim v. Norment, 460 A.2d 511 (Del. 1983); Tindol v. McCoy, 535 S.W.2d 745 (Tex. Civ.App.1976).

**75.** *Restatement of Property* § 286(1)(a) (1940) *See also* Theobald, *Wills* §§ 857–58 (12th ed. 1963).

**76.** 5 *Amer. Law of Prop.* § 22.33.

**77.** Uniform Probate Code § 2–705. The comparable provision in the pre–1990 UPC applied only to wills, but the present provision covers all "governing instruments." Uniform Probate Code § 2–701. *See also* Cal.Prob.Code § 21115(a).

As to whether such statutes apply to instruments creating future interests which were executed prior to the statute's effective date see Section 1.3, note 48.

**78.** *Restatement of Property* § 286(2)(c) (1940); *Restatement (Second) of Property (Donative Transfers)* § 25.2, comment a (1988). If the will gives property to "heirs," the intestacy statute is particularly persuasive as to intent. *Id.* § 29.1.

**79.** Matter of Estate of Best, 485 N.E.2d 1010 (N.Y.1985); Vincent v. Sutherland, 691 P.2d 85 (Okl.App.1984); Annan v. Wilmington Trust Co., 559 A.2d 1289 (Del.1989); Butcher v. Pollard, 288 N.E.2d 204 (Ohio App.1972) (insurance).

The second Restatement of Property, unlike the first, agrees, but circumstances or language in the will may show a contrary intent. For example, a gift to "the children of John" would not include a child who John claimed (albeit erroneously) was not his.[80] A court can give effect to a testator's intent to exclude children born out of wedlock without violating the constitution, since this does not involve "state action."[81]

### *Planning*

An attorney who drafts a will should ascertain the testator's intent and make it clear in the will. Some persons would wish children born out of wedlock to share in their estates and some would not. The law will give effect to either intent if specified. Even if there are no such children presently in the testator's family, the question cannot be ignored if a will (as is typical) provides for issue who are as yet unborn. Most testator would probably wish to include children who are "technically" illegitimate because a divorce predating the marriage of their parents was invalid. At the other extreme, they would not want someone who falsely claimed to be a child to share in the estate. Naming the testator's children in a will (or reciting lack of children) can prove useful, but such recitals do not always preclude a child from proving paternity.[82]

The effect of a provision for "lawful" descendants is not clear. Since most states no longer use the term "illegitimate" to describe children born out of wedlock, they might be included in a gift to "lawful" children.[83] A restriction to children "born in wedlock" is clearer, but it might bar persons whom the testator wished to include, such as children of an invalid marriage or of a marriage-like relationship. The language of the Uniform Statutory Will Act probably reflects the views of most testators on this issue: "an individual born out of wedlock is not the child of the father unless the individual is openly and notoriously so treated by the father."[84]

## 2.10 Adoption

### *History*

Although well known in the civil law, the common law did not recognize adoption.[1] England legalized it by statute only in 1926.[2] In America at first

**80.** *Restatement (Second) of Property (Donative Transfers)* § 25.2, comment e, illus. 6, § 25.8, illus. 2 (1988).

**81.** Harris Trust and Sav. Bank v. Donovan, 582 N.E.2d 120 (Ill.1991); In re Dumaine, 600 A.2d 127 (N.H.1991). On the other hand, a statutory presumption that children born out of wedlock were not included in class gifts was held unconstitutional in Estate of Dulles, 431 A.2d 208 (Pa.1981).

**82.** Matter of Padilla's Estate, 641 P.2d 539 (N.M.App.1982); In re Estate of Peterson, 442 P.2d 980 (Wash.1968).

**83.** *Restatement (Second) of Property (Donative Transfers)* § 25.2, illus. 1 (1985) ("lawful" includes child born out of wedlock but legitimated). See also Bell v. Forti, 584 A.2d 77 (Md.App.1991). But see Continental Bank, N.A. v. Herguth, 617 N.E.2d 852 (Ill.App.1993) ("lawful" excludes children born out of wedlock); Decker v. Meriwether, 708 S.W.2d 390 (Tenn.App.1985) (same); In re Dumaine, 600 A.2d 127 (N.H.1991) ("legitimate" excludes child born out of wedlock even though parents later married); *Restatement (Second) of Property (Donative Transfers)* § 25.9, illus. 2 (gift to issue "born in wedlock" excludes child born out of wedlock).

**84.** Uniform Statutory Will Act § 1(1).

**§ 2.10**

**1.** For the history of adoption see Binavince, *Adoption and the Law of Descent and Distribution: A Comparative Study and a Proposal for Modern Legislation*, 51 Cornell L.Q. 152, 154–58 (1966); Kuhlman, *Intestate Succes-*

child placement involved almost no governmental regulation. Homeless children were simply "put-out" to be raised by a suitable blood relative.[3] Some families formalized the arrangement through private statutes. In the middle of the 19th century, state legislatures began to enact general adoption legislation.[4] Formal adoption today has evolved from a relative rarity to a popular means of ushering newcomers into a family. Americans adopt 130,000 or more children annually.[5]

Adoption raises questions both as to intestate succession and the construction of wills and other instruments.

### *Intestate Succession*

When a person adopts another several types of question can arise regarding intestate succession. First, can the adoptee inherit from the adopter if he dies intestate? from the adopter's relatives, *e.g.* if the adopter predeceases his parents? Third, can the adoptee's children inherit from the adopter or his relatives? Fourth, can the adopter or his relatives inherit from the adoptee if the latter dies without a spouse or issue. (This last question is not so common, because usually the adoptee survives the adopter, but not always.) Uniform Probate Code § 2–114 answers yes to all these questions: "for purposes of intestate succession by, through, or from a person . . . an adopted individual is the child of his or her adopting parents." Most states reach the same result today.[6] The trend is certainly in this direction. For example, a court recently held unconstitutional a state statute which did not allow an adopted child to inherit from a half-sister by adoption.

> the Legislature might have concluded that collateral kin would expect intestate succession to be limited to the bloodline and exclude adopted persons. That presumption is no longer reasonable . . . The argument that adoptees should not inherit from adoptive relatives who were not parties to the adoption contract "ignore[s] the fact that a child's birth always imposed a potential heir on the relatives of his biological parents, yet no one would suggest that the child should not inherit from his blood relatives because they had not consented to his conception."[7]

Some states allow adoptees also to inherit from their birth parents as well as

*sion By and From the Adopted Child*, 28 Wash. U.L.Q. 221, 222–24 (1943); Presser, *The Historical Background of the American Law of Adoption*, 11 Journal of Family Law 443 (1971); Huard, *The Law of Adoption: Ancient and Modern*, 9 Vand.L.Rev. 743 (1956).

**2.** Adoption of Children Act, 16 & 17 Geo. 5, ch. 29 (1926).

**3.** *See A Social History of the American Family* 124–27 (1917); Witmer, Herzog, et al., *Independent Adoptions* 33–34 (1963).

**4.** The first comprehensive adoption act providing for the welfare of adopted children was passed by the Massachusetts legislature in 1851. Mass. Acts of 1851, c. 324. Earlier statutes only required the filing of a deed of adoption. Miss. Laws 1846, c. 60; Tex. Acts of 1849–50, p. 36, c. 39.

**5.** Prefatory Note, Uniform Adoption Act (1994). This Act supersedes the Uniform Adoption Act of 1969, which a few states had adopted.

**6.** *E.g.*, Cal.Prob.Code § 6450; Tex.Prob. Code § 40; Tenn. Code § 31–2–105; In re Estate of Brittin, 664 N.E.2d 687 (Ill.App.1996) (children of adopted child inherit from adopter); Estate of Kuhn v. Kuhn, 267 N.E.2d 876 (Ind.App.1971) (half sibling by adoption); McClure v. Noble, 602 So.2d 377 (Ala.1992) (inheritance from relative of adopter); *Restatement (Third) of Property (Wills and Other Donative Transfers)* § 2.5(2) (1998).

**7.** MacCallum v. Seymour, 686 A.2d 935 (Vt.1996). However, in Nunnally v. Trust Co. Bank, 261 S.E.2d 621 (Ga.1979), a similar attack on a Georgia statute was rejected.

their adoptive parents.[8] If the adoptee is a minor (as is usually the case), arguably the child should not be prejudiced by losing a right of inheritance she would otherwise have. One court suggested that if an adoption eliminated the adoptee's inheritance from natural relatives, "fairness, if not due process would require . . . a guardian ad litem to represent the child in every adoption proceeding, unnecessarily complicating the process."[9] This reasoning suggests a distinction between the child and the birth parents; since the latter as adults surrendered the child, they can justifiably be barred from inheriting from the child, but the child should be allowed to inherit from them.[10]

Maintaining inheritance ties between an adoptee and the biological family conflicts with the policy of strengthening the new family unit. Consistent with this policy, adoption records are usually sealed so the adoptee may not even know who the birth parents were.[11] The Uniform Probate Code severs the tie between adopted children and their genetic parents in most cases.[12]

However, in many adoptions the birth parents continue to associate with the child. Over half the adoptions occurring today involve children adopted by step parents or relatives.[13] In this situation, such continued association is more likely to occur. If a man adopts his wife's children by a prior marriage, for example, Uniform Probate Code § 2–114(b) would allow them to inherit not only from him and his relatives but also from their mother and her relatives and from their genetic father and his relatives. The genetic father and his relatives would not inherit from the adopted child however.[14] The Restatement also favors retaining the tie to genetic relatives when the adoption is by a relative of either parent or the spouse of a relative. For example, when after the death of both parents, a child is adopted by a maternal aunt, the child could inherit from relatives of both genetic parents.[15] Some states, however, cut the tie between an adoptee and the genetic parents in all cases.[16]

**8.** Ala. Code § 26–10–5; 15 Vt.Stat. § 488(9); Matter of Estate of Van Der Veen, 935 P.2d 1042 (Kan.1997) (statute to this effect was declaratory of prior law); In re Estate of Reedy, 22 Cal.Rptr.2d 478 (App.1993) the children of a child given for adoption can inherit from genetic grandmother).

**9.** Lockwood v. Adamson, 566 N.E.2d 96, 101 (Mass.1991). *See also* Harrell v. McDonald, 242 N.W.2d 148 (S.D.1976).

**10.** Tex.Prop.Code § 40 draws this distinction. *See also* In re Estate of Fleming, 991 P.2d 128, 132 (Wash.App.2000). In Illinois the natural parents and their kindred can only inherit properties which the adoptee acquired from them by gift, will or inheritance. 755 ILCS § 5/2–4(b).

**11.** See generally Uniform Adoption Act § 6–101 et seq. In Aimone v. Finley, 447 N.E.2d 868 (Ill.App.1983), the court upheld the constitutionality of a statute which barred an adoptee from access to the records of his adoption.

**12.** Uniform Probate Code § 2–114(b). *See also Restatement (Third) of Property (Wills and Other Donative Transfers)* § 2.5, comm. e (1998).

**13.** Prefatory Note, Uniform Adoption Act (1994).

**14.** *See* Matter of Estate of Ryan, 928 P.2d 735 (Ariz.App.1996) (applying UPC to allow child to inherit from father after he was adopted by his stepfather). The Restatement allows inheritance both ways in this situation. *Restatement (Third) of Property (Wills and Other Donative Transfers)* § 2.5(2)(C) (1998).

**15.** *Id.*, comm. f.

**16.** Buchea v. United States, 154 F.3d 1114 (9th Cir.1998) (under Alaska law, child adopted by grandparents cannot recover for wrongful death of biological father); Estate of David v. Snelson, 776 P.2d 813 (Colo.1989) (after adoption by stepparent children no longer inherit from father); Hall v. Vallandingham, 540 A.2d 1162 (Md.App.1988); Kerr v. Kerr, 522 N.E.2d 983 (Mass.App.1988). In re Estate of Luckey, 291 N.W.2d 235 (Neb.1980) a child who was adopted twice was not allowed to inherit from the first adoptive father. *See also In re* Estate of Orzoff, 452 N.E.2d 82 (Ill.App.1983).

An adoptee who can inherit from two sets of relatives (genetic and adoptive), has an advantage denied to other children. Some courts have even allowed a child adopted by a family member to inherit twice from the same decedent, once as an adopted child and once, by representation, through his biological parents.[17] The Uniform Probate Code, however, only gives the child a single share in this situation.[18]

### *Class Gifts*

If a will makes a class gift to someone's "children," or "grandchildren," or the like,[19] can someone who enters the designated class by adoption share? Conversely, does a child of John who has been adopted by someone else still count as John's "child" in construing the will of John or another with a devise to "the children (or issue) of John?" This depends on the testator's intent, not the intestacy statutes. Many courts treat the intestacy statutes as evidence of the average person's intent,[20] but not always. For example a court held that a gift in a trust to "issue" of the settlor's nephew included a child who had been adopted by his stepfather, even though under the applicable intestacy rule the child would not have inherited from the settlor.[21] Construction of the word "heirs" is more closely tied to the intestacy rules. Thus when a will left property to the "issue" of a grandchild, and, in default of issue "to my heirs," an adopted child was held to be included as an "heir" because the intestacy laws so provided, but not as "issue."[22]

Under the Uniform Probate Code, the same rules generally determine the effect of adoption for intestate succession and the construction of class gifts, both for wills and other dispositive instruments, such as living trusts and deeds.[23] The intestacy rules may also control the construction of the word "children" in a wrongful death statute.[24]

The large number of cases on this topic reflect the frequency of adoption in modern life, and the relative wealth of the persons involved in adoption.[25] (Children born out of wedlock appear less often in cases involving the construction of instruments.) Often such gifts appear in instruments which

**17.** In re Estate of Cregar, 333 N.E.2d 540 (Ill.App.1975) (children adopted by an aunt can inherit from another aunt in both capacities).

**18.** Uniform Probate Code § 2–113. *See also Restatement (Third) of Property (Wills and Other Donative Transfers)* § 2.5, comm. i (1998); Cal.Prob.Code § 6413; Unsel v. Meier, 972 S.W.2d 466 (Mo.App.1998) (in construing a gift to "bodily heirs" giving an adoptee a double share would violate public policy).

**19.** Under *Restatement, Second, of Property, Donative Transfers* § 25.8 (1987), the constructional rules for "children" also apply to "grandchildren," "brothers and sisters," "nieces and nephews," and "cousins."

**20.** Estate of Russell, 95 Cal.Rptr. 88 (App. 1971); *In re* Sollid, 647 P.2d 1033 (Wash.App. 1982); Matter of Trust Created Under Agreement with McLaughlin, 361 N.W.2d 43 (Minn. 1985).

**21.** Lockwood v. Adamson, 566 N.E.2d 96 (Mass.1991). *See also* Estate of Garrison, 175 Cal.Rptr. 809 (App.1981); Estate of Dawson, 522 N.E.2d 770 (Ill.App.1988); Connecticut Bank and Trust Co. v. Coffin, 563 A.2d 1323 (Conn.1989).

**22.** Boatmen's Trust Co. v. Conklin, 888 S.W.2d 347 (Mo.App.1994). *See also* Boston Safe Deposit & Trust Co. v. Wilbur, 728 N.E.2d 264, 270 (Mass.2000) (adopted child takes since gift was to "representatives"-construed to mean heirs).

**23.** Section 2–(not.)705. The pre–1990 UPC had a similar rule, but by its terms was limited to wills. Sections 2–603, 2–611.

**24.** In Phraner v. Cote Mart, Inc., 63 Cal. Rptr.2d 740 (App.1997), an adopted child was not allowed to sue for the death of her biological mother, since she was not an heir under the intestacy law.

**25.** In MacCallum v. Seymour, 686 A.2d 935 (Vt.1996), the court noted that adoption petitions in Vermont had increased from 223 in 1945 to 532 in 1996.

were executed many years earlier, when the prevailing construction excluded "strangers to the adoption." That is, if John adopted Mary, she would be his "child" in construing his will, but he could not "foist her" on someone else; thus she would not be John's "child" in construing the will of another person who left property to the "children" of John. This was the presumed meaning under the first Restatement of Property[26], but the second Restatement, like the UPC and most states, has abandoned it.[27] Sometimes this change was effected by statute, sometimes by judicial decisions overruling earlier cases.[28]

What evidence is sufficient to show a contrary intent? Particular language defining or modifying a general reference to "children" or the like may control. According to the Restatement, a gift to "blood descendants" or "natural-born children" manifests an intent to exclude children by adoption.[29] But most cases have held that the word "body" (as in "heirs of his body") does *not* exclude adoptees.[30]

The cases are divided on whether extrinsic evidence can be used to show an intent different from the prevailing presumption. Some statutes say the presumption as to intent can be overcome only by language in the instrument,[31] but the rules of construction in the Uniform Probate Code apply "in the absence of a finding of contrary intent" which can come from any source.[32] One court relied on evidence of the testator's affection for two adopted grandchildren in holding that they were included in a class gift, even though the testator had died in 1943 when the "stranger-to the-adoption" presumption prevailed.[33] In another case evidence of the testator's concern for blood relationships was held to warrant including a child who had been adopted out of the family in a class gift.[34]

The fact that the exclusion of a child would make a gift meaningless may show an intent to include, since words in an instrument are presumably intended to mean something. Suppose for example that a trust provides for the settlor's "children," and his only children have been adopted by his sister. Under the Uniform Probate Code, these children would be presumptively

**26.** Section 287. The exclusion of strangers to the adoption was only a presumption. For example, in In re Bankers Trust Co., 291 N.E.2d 137 (N.Y.1972), the court found that as testator intended to include an adoptee even under the old rules.

**27.** *Restatement, Second, of Property (Donative Transfers)* § 25.4 (1988).

**28.** *E.g.,* Elliott v. Hiddleson, 303 N.W.2d 140 (Iowa 1981).

**29.** *Restatement, Second, of Property (Donative Transfers)* § 25.4, comm. c. *See also* Matter of Will of Paats, 589 N.Y.S.2d 147 (Surr.1992) ("natural children born of the marriage"); Fifth Third Bank v. Crosley, 669 N.E.2d 904 (Ohio Com.Pl.1996) ("issue of the blood"). *But see* Trust Agreement of Jones, 607 A.2d 265 (Pa.Super.1992) ("descendants of the blood" includes adoptees).

**30.** Society Nat. Bank v. Jacobson, 560 N.E.2d 217 (Ohio 1990); Martin v. Gerdes, 523 N.E.2d 607 (Ill.App.1988); McIlvaine v. AmSouth Bank, N.A., 581 So.2d 454 (Ala.1991); Hagaman v. Morgan, 886 S.W.2d 398 (Tex.App. 1994); In re Trusts of Harrington, 250 N.W.2d 163 (Minn.1977). *But see* Hurt v. Noble, 817 P.2d 744 (Okl.App.1991); Schroeder v. Danielson, 640 N.E.2d 495 (Mass.App.1994).

**31.** Martin v. Gerdes, 523 N.E.2d 607 (Ill. App.1988). *See also* Wilmington Trust Co. v. Chichester, 369 A.2d 701 (Del.Ch.1976) (extrinsic evidence inadmissible because a gift to "issue" was "unambiguous"). As to the use of extrinsic evidence generally see Section 6.1.

**32.** Uniform Probate Code § 2–601.

**33.** Connecticut National Bank & Trust Co. v. Chadwick, 585 A.2d 1189 (Conn.1991).

**34.** Connecticut Bank and Trust Co. v. Coffin, 563 A.2d 1323 (Conn.1989). *See also* Estate of Leonard, 514 A.2d 822 (N.H.1986). In DePrycker v. Brown, 358 So.2d 1140 (Fla.App. 1978) extrinsic evidence was relied on to exclude an adopted-away child.

disqualified,[35] since they do not fall under the step-parent exception to the general rule that adoption cuts the tie to the birth parents. But since no one else qualifies as a "child" of the settlor, they should be included.[36] The settlor may have had in mind other children which he might have in the future (but did not); however, this explanation is implausible if the settlor was very old when the instrument was executed.[37]

### *Adult Adoptions*

Adult adoptions pose special problems, both in intestacy situations as well as the construction of class gifts. Some states have no provision for adult adoption[38] and others restrict it by requiring a specified age differential or relationship between the adopter and the adoptee.[39] Most states, however, permit such adoptions with few or no limitations.[40]

Procedures for adult adoptions are generally simpler than for child adoptions. No home investigation is made and consent of the adoptee's parents is not required.[41] Parental support obligations involved in the adoption of a minor do not apply. The adoptee often does not change his name, live with the adopter or change his life in any way. Nevertheless, the legal consequences of the adoption of an adult are generally the same as for the adoption of a minor. This is true for inheritance under the Uniform Probate Code.[42]

In construing class gifts, however, many courts have refused to allow persons adopted as adults to take as "children" of the adopter. For example, a wife who was adopted by her husband was held not to be one of his "issue" under the terms of his parent's trust.[43] However, in some cases adult adoptees have been held to qualify under class gifts.[44]

**35.** Uniform Probate Code §§ 2–114, 2–705.

**36.** *Restatement, Second, Property, Donative Transfers* § 25.2, illus. 1 (1988).

**37.** *Cf. id.* § 25.6, illus. 1 ("my children" includes step-children when at the time she executed her will T had no children and was past the age of childbearing).

**38.** Matter of Adoption of Chaney, 887 P.2d 1061 (Idaho 1995) (refusing to allow an 18 year old to be adopted because statutory procedures contemplated only adoption of minors.)

**39.** N.J.Stat. § 2A:22–2 (adoptee must be at least 10 years younger than adopter); Haw. Rev.Stat. § 578–1.5 (adoptee must be the adopter's niece, nephew or step-child). Some states require a showing that the adoptee lived with the adopter a specified number of years or that he had a filial relationship with the adopter during his minority. Va.Code § 63.1–222 (adoptee must have resided with adopter for one year during minority); Ohio Rev.Code § 3107.02 (adult may be adopted only if disabled, mentally retarded, or established a child-parent relationship while still a minor);

**40.** Under Uniform Adoption Act § 5–101 one cannot adopt one's spouse. In In re Jones, 411 A.2d 910 (R.I.1980), the court refused to allow a married man to adopt his mistress. In Matter of Adoption of Robert Paul, 471 N.E.2d 424 (N.Y.1984), a homosexual was not permitted to adopt his lover.

**41.** Wadlington, *Adoption of Adults: A Family Law Anomaly,* 54 Cornell L.Rev. 566, 571–73 (1969); Note, 1972 Wash.U.L.Q. 253, 257–58 (1972).

**42.** Uniform Probate Code § 2–114(b). *See also* Uniform Adoption Act § 5–102 (1994); In re Estate of Brittin, 664 N.E.2d 687 (Ill.App. 1996) (children of person adopted at age 46 inherit from adopter).

**43.** Matter of Trust Created by Belgard, 829 P.2d 457 (Colo.App.1991). *See also* Matter of Duke, 702 A.2d 1007 (N.J.Super.App.Div.1997); Cox v. Whitten, 704 S.W.2d 628 (Ark.1986) (48 year old adoptee); Cross v. Cross, 532 N.E.2d 486 (Ill.App.1988) (power to appoint to "issue" does not allow appointment to adult adoptee).

**44.** Solomon v. Central Trust Co., 584 N.E.2d 1185 (Ohio 1992) (adoptee had lived with adopter from age 9, even though adopted as an adult); Satterfield v. Bonyhady, 446 N.W.2d 214 (Neb.1989) (adopted stepchild); In re Estate of Joslyn, 45 Cal.Rptr.2d 616 (App. 1995); Hagaman v. Morgan, 886 S.W.2d 398 (Tex.App.1994) (stepdaughter); Evans v. McCoy, 436 A.2d 436 (Md.1981) (adoption of a

A few courts have questioned the motive for the adoption of an adult, but this is hard to determine and is not even discussed in most opinions. The Uniform Probate Code provides a limitation that is easier to apply: in construing class gifts "an adopted individual is not considered the child of the adopting parent unless the adopted individual lived while a minor ... as a regular member of the household of the adopting parent."[45] This is a not uncommon occurrence, particularly when a step-parent wishes to adopt step children but cannot do it so long as the children are minors, because their other parent refuses to consent.[46] The Restatement of Property speaks of the adopter having "raised" the adoptee; this formulation presumably gives the same result as the UPC.[47] All the cases cannot be reconciled on the basis of this distinction, but it is reflected in some decisions.[48]

An adult adoption may be used to create a right to inherit in an intestacy. Suppose John is terminally ill and wants a friend to take a share of the estate of a living parent of John. John can accomplish this by adopting the friend if John dies before the parent and the parent dies intestate.[49] The scheme will not work under the Uniform Probate Code if John's parent executes a will, but the parent may not know about the adoption, since notice is not usually given to the adopter's parents.[50] However, this scenario is not nearly as common as the one in which a will leaves a future interest "to John's issue" and he decides to adopt someone after the will has become irrevocable.

Because adoption can have an impact on succession to property, it is sometimes challenged by persons adversely affected, but such challenges often fail on procedural grounds. For example, a remainder was devised to the issue of the testator's two sons, Leo and Roy. When Leo adopted his stepchildren, Roy's children sought to challenge the adoption so they would take all the devise. The court rejected their challenge because "prospective heirs ... had no standing to challenge the validity of the adoption." Moreover, a statute

53 year old cousin bars a gift over on death without issue).

**45.** Uniform Probate Code § 2–705(c). This limitation applies only when the donor or testator is a stranger to the adoption. Cal.Prob. Code § 21115(b) is similar.

**46.** "An adoption of an adult ... may provide formal recognition of a de facto relationship that has existed for many years—for example, when an individual has been reared by someone other than a parent, but a proceeding for adoption has never been initiated. It may be a belated adoption by a stepparent in a situation in which a child's noncustodial parent never consented to the proposed stepparent adoption. When the noncustodial parent dies, or the child reaches his 18th birthday, the noncustodial parent can no longer block the adoption by the stepparent." Uniform Adoption Act § 5–101, comment.

**47.** *Restatement, Second, Property, Donative Transfers* § 25.4(2) (1987).

**48.** In Solomon v. Central Trust Co., 584 N.E.2d 1185 (Ohio 1992), in allowing an adult adoptee to take, the court pointed out that such adoptions are allowed in Ohio only when the relationship began when the child was a minor. *See also* In re Estate of Joslyn, 45 Cal.Rptr.2d 616 (App.1995); In re Estate of Brittin, 664 N.E.2d 687 (Ill.App.1996) (inheritance through a person adopted at age 46 but raised by adopter from age 3). Conversely in Rhay v. Johnson, 867 P.2d 669 (Wash.App. 1994) a 65 year old adoptee was not treated as a child of the adopter because there was no normal mother-child relationship.

**49.** This actually happened in Harper v. Martin, 552 S.W.2d 690 (Ky.App.1977).

**50.** Uniform Adoption Act § 5–108, comment. If the parent's will simply leaves property "to John" or "to my children," the adoptee would take under the anti-lapse statute. *See* Uniform Probate Code § 2–706. But if the will leaves property to "my issue" or "to John's children" the adoptee would qualify only if he or she met the requirements of Section 2–705(c).

required any challenge to an adoption to be brought within one year of the decree and this had long since expired.[51]

Normally an adoption in one state will be given effect in another, subject to a limitation on adoptions which violate the policy of the forum.[52] For example, a New Jersey court recognized an adoption of an adult which had taken place in California, even though it would not have been permitted in New Jersey.[53] Forum shopping is deterred to some extent by jurisdictional requirements. Under the Uniform Adoption Act,[54] for example, a petitioner for adoption of an adult must have lived in the state for at least 90 days before the petition is filed.

### *Equitable Adoption*

Even a person who was raised from infancy by a collateral relative does not become the relative's "child" for purposes of the intestacy laws if the relative did not adopt him.[55] However, children who have never been formally adopted may be treated as if they had been under the theory of equitable adoption. The rationale usually given for equitable adoption is that the child is the beneficiary of a promise made by the foster parents to adopt him.

> When there is a valid contract for adoption, although not consummated and given effect by adoption proceedings during the lifetime of the adopting parent, the contract may be enforced to the extent of decreeing that the child occupy the status of an adopted child in equity, entitled to rights of inheritance from the adoptive parent.[56]

Even when a child has been raised from infancy, most courts will not find an equitable adoption unless there was a contract to adopt the child,[57] but one court has rejected this requirement,[58] and in any event such a contract can be inferred from conduct.[59]

**51.** Hurt v. Noble, 817 P.2d 744 (Okl.App. 1991). *See also* Estate of Hart, 209 Cal.Rptr. 272 (App.1984) (one year limit bars adoptee's challenge to an adoption which cut off his right to inherit).

**52.** *Restatement (Second) of Conflict of Laws* § 290 (1971). In Kupec v. Cooper, 593 So.2d 1176, 1178 (Fla.App.1992), the court refused to give effect to a German adoption which was "repugnant to the laws and policies of Florida."

The law of the state of adoption does not always control its effect. In Warren v. Foster, 450 So.2d 786 (Miss.1984), an adoption which had taken place in Tennessee was held not to bar inheritance from the birth father under Mississippi law even though it would have had that effect in Tennessee.

**53.** Matter of Estate of Griswold, 354 A.2d 717 (N.J. Super.1976). However, the adoptee was not allowed to take as a matter of construction. In Tsilidis v. Pedakis, 132 So.2d 9 (Fla.App.1961) the court refused to recognize a Greek adoption which would not have been allowed in Florida.

**54.** Section 5–104.

**55.** Tait v. Wahl, 987 P.2d 127 (Wash.App. 1999).

**56.** Board of Education v. Browning, 635 A.2d 373, 376–77 (Md.1994). *See also* Lankford v. Wright, 489 S.E.2d 604 (N.C.1997); Estate of Wilson, 168 Cal.Rptr. 533 (App.1980); *cf.* Williams v. Estate of Pender, 738 So.2d 453 (Fla.App.1999) (clear and convincing proof required).

**57.** O'Neal v. Wilkes, 439 S.E.2d 490 (Ga. 1994) (contract made by unauthorized relative and so did not create equitable adoption); In re Estate of Staehli, 407 N.E.2d 741 (Ill.App. 1980); In re Estate of Castaneda, 687 S.W.2d 465 (Tex.App.1985); Estate of Stewart, 176 Cal.Rptr. 142 (App.1981).

**58.** Wheeling Dollar Sav. & Trust Co. v. Singer, 250 S.E.2d 369, 374 (W.Va.1978). *See also* Welch v. Wilson, 516 S.E.2d 35 (W.Va. 1999) (finding equitable adoption without reference to any contract).

**59.** *Restatement (Third) of Property (Wills and Other Donative Transfers)* § 2.5, comm. k (1998); In re Lamfrom's Estate, 368 P.2d 318, 321 (Ariz.1962).

Although most states recognize equitable adoption in some contexts, courts tend to give it limited effect.[60] Perhaps because of the contract rationale, it does not usually allow the child to take *through* the adoptive parents, unlike a formal adoption,[61]or allow the parents to take from the child.[62] It does not cut off inheritance by the child from birth relatives or their right to inherit from the child.[63] Some courts refuse to give any effect to an alleged equitable adoption.[64]

### *Stepchildren*

Unadopted stepchildren (children of a spouse) are not heirs in most states. For example, the definition of "child" in Uniform Probate Code expressly excludes them.[65] A few states allow stepchildren to inherit if an intestate has no close blood relatives.[66] California also allows a foster or step child to inherit if the (1) the relationship began during the child's minority "and continued throughout the joint lifetimes" of the child and parent, and (2) the foster or step parent "would have adopted the [child] but for a legal barrier."[67] This provision also allows the child's issue to inherit "from or through a foster parent or stepparent" but gives the foster or stepparent no rights. Presumably the "legal barrier" to formal adoption which the statute contemplates is the refusal of a noncustodial parent to consent to the child's adoption. But this refusal ceases to be a barrier when the child reaches majority, [68]so if the stepchild reaches majority before the stepparent dies, the statute does not apply.[69]

A devise "to children" normally does not include a stepchild,[70] but courts sometimes infer from the circumstances that a testator intended to include stepchildren. A will which left property to "my children" was held to include stepchildren whom the testator had raised from infancy and habitually referred to as her children, since she had only one natural child and the will

**60.** McGarvey v. State, 533 A.2d 690 (Md. 1987) (equitably adopted child not a "child" entitled to favorable inheritance tax rate).

**61.** Board of Education v. Browning, 635 A.2d 373 (Md.1994) (claim to inherit from adopter's sister); Matter of Estate of Jenkins, 904 P.2d 1316 (Colo.1995); Estate of Lind, 257 Cal.Rptr. 853 (App.1989). But in Wheeling Dollar Saving & Trust Co. v. Singer, 250 S.E.2d 369 (W.Va.1978), the court allowed an equitably adopted child to take under the will of a relative of the adopter.

**62.** Reynolds v. City of Los Angeles, 222 Cal.Rptr. 517 (App.1986) (parents of equitably adopted child cannot sue for wrongful death of child); Matter of Estate of Edwards, 435 N.E.2d 1379 (Ill.App.1982); Whitchurch v. Perry, 408 A.2d 627 (Vt.1979). *Contra*, Lawson v. Atwood, 536 N.E.2d 1167 (Ohio 1989).

**63.** Curry v. Williman, 834 S.W.2d 443 (Tex.App.1992); Gardner v. Hancock, 924 S.W.2d 857 (Mo.App.1996) (equitably adopted child can inherit from birth father).

**64.** Matter of Estate of Robbins, 738 P.2d 458 (Kan.1987); Maui Land & Pineapple Co. v. Naiapaakai Heirs of Makeelani, 751 P.2d 1020 (Haw.1988); Lindsey v. Wilcox, 479 N.E.2d 1330 (Ind.App.1985); York v. Nunley, 610 N.E.2d 576 (Ohio App.1992) (limited to wrongful death cases).

**65.** Section 1–202(5). *See also Restatement (Third) of Property (Wills and Other Donative Transfers)* § 2.5, comm. j (1998).

**66.** Md.Estates and Trusts Code § 3–104(e); Ohio Stat. § 2105.06(I); Fla.Stat. § 732.103(5).

**67.** Cal.Prob.Code § 6454.

**68.** Uniform Adoption Act § 5–103 (1994) (adoption of adult requires only consent of adoptee and adopter and the latter's spouse).

**69.** Estate of Joseph, 949 P.2d 472 (Cal. 1998). Earlier decisions were divided on this point. *Compare* In re Estate of Stevenson, 14 Cal.Rptr.2d 250 (App.1992) (stepchild can inherit) *with* Estate of Cleveland, 22 Cal.Rptr.2d 590 (App.1993) (foster child cannot inherit on similar facts).

**70.** *Restatement (Second) of Property (Donative Transfers)* § 25.6 (1987); National Home Life Assur. Co. v. Patterson, 746 P.2d 696 (Okl.App.1987) (insurance beneficiary designation).

referred to "children."[71] Similarly, a trust for the settlor's "nephews and nieces" was construed to refer to her husband's nephews and nieces when she had none of her own.[72]

Stepchildren may also be included in a gift to "the family" of a stepparent.[73] They have been awarded damages for the death of a stepparent under a statute allowing recovery to "dependents,"[74] and are covered under many workers' compensation statutes.[75]

### *Planning*

A planner should find out if an adoption has actually occurred in the testator's family and, if so, how the testator wishes to deal with it. Even if there has been no adoption, one may later take place, particularly if the will creates future interests.

Many standard forms used in drafting wills assume that the testator intends to include adopted children in class gifts.[76] Unless qualified, such language includes all adoptees,[77] but some suggested forms expressly exclude persons adopted as adults.[78] This exclusion is too broad if the testator wishes to include those raised from infancy by the adopter and adopted later.[79]

The Uniform Statutory Will Act, like the Uniform Probate Code, treats an adoptee as "the child of the adopting parents and not of the natural parents" except when the adopter is a natural parent's spouse.[80] Perhaps some testators would not want an adoption to break the tie to biological relatives in other cases if the adoptee lived with them for a significant period or continued to associate with them.[81]

## § 2.11 Spouses

For many purposes it becomes necessary to determine whether a person was a decedent's "spouse." Under the Uniform Probate Code, the "surviving spouse" receives among other things a share of an intestate estate, a right to elect against a will, a family allowance, and priority in appointment as a

**71.** In re Gehl's Estate, 159 N.W.2d 72 (Wis.1968). *See also Restatement (Second) of Property (Donative Transfers)* § 25.6, illus. 1 (1987); Transamerica Occidental Life Ins. Co. v. Burke, 368 S.E.2d 301 (W.Va.1988) (stepchildren included as "children" under an insurance policy when insured treated them like his own children); Matter of Estate of Neshem, 574 N.W.2d 883 (N.D.1998) (stepchild described as "our child" elsewhere in will included in devise to "issue").

**72.** Clymer v. Mayo, 473 N.E.2d 1084 (Mass.1985). *See also* Estate of Anderson, 359 N.W.2d 479 (Iowa 1984); Martin v. Palmer, 1 S.W.3d 875 (Tex.App.1999) (error on summary judgment to exclude nephews and nieces of spouse in devise to "my nephews and nieces") .

**73.** *Restatement (Second) of Property (Donative Transfers)* § 25.10, illus. 5 (1987).

**74.** Greer Tank & Welding, Inc. v. Boettger, 609 P.2d 548 (Alaska 1980). The result is otherwise if the statute gives the action to the decedent's "heirs." Steed v. Imperial Airlines, 524 P.2d 801 (Cal.1974); Versland v. Caron Transport, 671 P.2d 583 (Mont.1983). The California statute was later amended to allow recovery by dependent stepchildren. Cal.Code Civ.Proc. § 377.60(b).

**75.** Code of Ala. § 25–5–1(2); Ind.Code § 22–3–3–19; Mid-American Lines, Inc. v. Industrial Commission, 411 N.E.2d 254 (Ill. 1980).

**76.** J. Farr & J. Wright, *An Estate Planner's Handbook* 452–53 (4th ed. 1979).

**77.** Diemer v. Diemer, 717 S.W.2d 160 (Tex.App.1986).

**78.** Martin, *The Draftsman Views Wills for a Young Family,* 54 N.C.L.Rev. 277, 307 (1976).

**79.** T. Shaffer, *The Planning and Drafting of Wills and Trusts* 172–73 (2d ed. 1979).

**80.** Uniform Statutory Will Act § 1(1).

**81.** Halbach, *Issues About Issue: Some Recurrent Class Gift Problems,* 48 Mo.L.Rev. 333, 348 (1983).

decedent's personal representative.[1] A will or other instrument frequently designates a spouse as beneficiary. If the instrument also names the spouse, it is immaterial whether or not the person named is actually a lawful spouse.[2] Therefore the question of the validity of a marriage is less common in probate cases than the question who is a "child" within the meaning of a class gift, because "children" are often not named in a will whereas spouses usually are. But if an instrument simply designates a "spouse" without adding a name, only a lawful spouse qualifies.[3] When a person has been married twice, a question may arise as to *which* spouse was intended. For example, a trust made a provision for "the surviving spouse" of the settlor's son. The son was married to Amelia when the trust was created, but he later married Bette. The court held that Bette was intended, even though the settlor never knew her.[4]

A number of objections can be raised to a person's claim to be a spouse. Such objections may be rejected because of the liberal choice of law rules which are designed to sustain the validity of a marriage if possible.[5] Also, challenges to a marriage are often not allowed after the death of one of the parties, which is the time when the issue of the validity of a marriage becomes relevant in probate cases. For example, the purported marriage may be void as incestuous,[6] but under the Uniform Marriage and Divorce Act, a challenge on this ground may be made only while both spouses are alive.[7]

Since marriage is a contract, it is subject to the standard grounds for avoiding contracts, such as fraud, duress and incapacity.[8] Some states bar such challenges after one of the spouses has died,[9] but others do not. For example, one court allowed a marriage to be declared invalid after the death of a spouse where there was "fraud of the grossest kind, without apparent opportunity to detect or correct the inequity during the lifetime of the deceased spouse" who had been married while she was incapacitated and terminally ill.[10] Another court reached the same conclusion despite a statute

**§ 2.11**

**1.** Uniform Probate Code §§ 2–102, 2–202, 2–404, 3–203(a).

**2.** However, a devise to a "spouse" to whom the testator is not legally married may not qualify for the estate tax marital deduction even if the devisee takes. Estate of Steffke, 538 F.2d 730 (7th Cir.1976) (marriage invalid as bigamous).

**3.** Serradell v. Hartford Acc. and Indem. Co., 843 P.2d 639 (Alaska 1992); Proctor on Behalf of Proctor v. Insurance Co. of North America, 714 P.2d 1156, 1158 (Utah 1986); Metropolitan Life Ins. Co. v. Johnson, 645 P.2d 356 (Idaho 1982); *cf.* Ex parte Creel, 719 So.2d 783 (Ala.1998) (claim of common law marriage in connection with the issuing letters of administration).

**4.** Dillow v. Wagner, 715 So.2d 362 (Fla. App.1998). *See also* Matter of Trust of Killian, 459 N.W.2d 497, 501 (Iowa 1990).

**5.** As to choice of law see Section 1.2, at note 71 et seq.

**6.** In re Levie's Estate, 123 Cal.Rptr. 445 (App.1975) (claim by spouse rejected because marriage between first cousins is invalid); Estate of Loughmiller, 629 P.2d 156 (Kan.1981) (in similar circumstances marriage held valid under choice of law rules).

**7.** Uniform Marriage and Divorce Act § 208(c). This is not true under Alternative B, but the comment suggests disapproval of this alternative. *See also* 1 W. Blackstone, *Commentaries* * 434 (incestuous marriages only voidable during life of the parties).

**8.** In re Marriage of Davis, 576 N.E.2d 972 (Ill.App.1991) (suit by spouse's guardian to avoid marriage for incapacity); Nelson v. Nelson, 878 P.2d 335 (N.M.App.1994) (same); Uniform Marriage and Divorce Act § 208(a)(1) (marriage can be voided for fraud or incapacity).

**9.** Uniform Marriage and Divorce Act § 208(b); Cal. Family Code § 2211; Matter of Estate of Fuller, 862 P.2d 1037 (Colo.App. 1993) (children cannot challenge their father's marriage for incapacity after his death); Hall v. Nelson, 534 N.E.2d 929 (Ohio App.1987).

**10.** Matter of Estate of Lint, 957 P.2d 755 (Wash.1998). *See also* Matter of Estate of Hendrickson, 805 P.2d 20 (Kan.1991); In re Marriage of Goldberg, 27 Cal.Rptr.2d 298 (App.

barring attacks on a marriage for incapacity after the death of a spouse because "at the alleged ceremony the decedent did not respond because of his brain tumor" and this made the marriage void rather than voidable.[11]

Two challenges to a marriage are especially common and usually survive death: (1) bigamy and (2) lack of a marriage ceremony.

### *Bigamy*

Suppose John marries Frances, abandons her without a valid divorce, and then marries Sally who is unaware of the prior marriage, or believes that it has been legally dissolved. When John dies, who is his wife?

Sally can invoke a number of theories to support her claim. A presumption that a marriage is valid may lead a court to assume that John had divorced Frances before he married Sally, or that his marriage to Frances was invalid and thus no bar.[12] But the presumption of validity may be rebutted if Frances never received notice of any divorce proceedings.[13]

If Frances died or divorced John after his marriage to Sally,[14] Sally could argue that her marriage became valid when she and John continued to cohabit with her. This argument is particularly persuasive in jurisdictions which allow common-law marriages,[15] but some other states also provide for this result.[16]

In some states Sally would have rights as a "putative spouse." The Louisiana Civil Code, borrowing from the Napoleonic Code, says that a "marriage which has been declared null, produces nevertheless its civil effects * * * if it has been contracted in good faith."[17] "Good faith" includes reasonable errors of law as well as mistakes of fact.[18] The "civil effects" enjoyed by a putative "spouse" include the right to inherit, sue for wrongful death, and take under an insurance policy payable by its terms to the insured's "widow."[19]

1994) (action to nullify marriage for fraud survives plaintiff's death).

**11.** In re Estate of Crockett, 728 N.E.2d 765, 766 (Ill.App.2000).

**12.** Chandler v. Central Oil Corp., 853 P.2d 649 (Kan.1993); Schall v. Schall, 642 P.2d 1124 (N.M.App.1982); In re Estate of Davis, 640 P.2d 692 (Or.App.1982); Matter of Fray, 721 P.2d 1054, 1058 (Wyo.1986); Matter of Estate of Allen, 738 P.2d 142, 145 (Okl.1987) (concurring opinion); McCormick, *Evidence* 344 (4th ed. 1992).

**13.** Daniels v. Retirement Board, 435 N.E.2d 1276 (Ill.App.1982); Succession of Choyce, 183 So.2d 457 (La.App.1966).

**14.** If John had obtained an *interlocutory* divorce decree from Frances before he married Mary, a final divorce entered nunc pro tunc may validate his marriage. In re Estate of Shippy, 678 P.2d 848 (Wash.App.1984).

**15.** Matter of Estate of Alcorn, 868 P.2d 629 (Mont.1994); Brown v. Carr, 402 S.E.2d 296 (Ga.App.1991); Estate of Smart v. Smart, 676 P.2d 1379 (Okl.App.1983).

**16.** Uniform Marriage and Divorce Act § 207(b); In re Estate of Banks, 629 N.E.2d 1223 (Ill.App.1994). For a case reaching this result even without a statute see Proctor on Behalf of Proctor v. Insurance Co. of North America, 714 P.2d 1156 (Utah 1986). On the other hand, in Batey v. Batey, 933 P.2d 551 (Alaska 1997) refused to treat the second "wife" as married because she had no good faith belief in the validity of the marriage when she entered it, even though the husband later divorced his legal wife.

**17.** La.Civ.Code, art. 117. This is a translation of Code Civil, art. 201. Canon law is the ultimate source of the idea. *See* Blakesley, *The Putative Marriage Doctrine*, 60 Tul.L.Rev. 1, 11 (1985).

**18.** Jones v. Equitable Life Assur. Soc., 173 So.2d 373 (La.App.1965).

**19.** *Id;* King v. Cancienne, 316 So.2d 366 (La.1975); Succession of Choyce, 183 So.2d 457 (La.App.1966).

The common law did not recognize "putative" spouses,[20] but the idea is spreading; according to the third Restatement, "a putative spouse is treated as a legal spouse for purposes of intestacy," unless a statute provides otherwise.[21] California would allow Sally to inherit from John, collect worker's compensation benefits or bring a wrongful death action as his widow.[22] The Uniform Marriage and Divorce Act gives putative spouses all the rights of a legal spouse.[23] The Social Security Act gives benefits to applicants who "in good faith went through a marriage ceremony" which "but for a legal impediment not known to the applicant * * * would have been a valid marriage."[24] If the lawful wife is entitled to social security benefits, the putative spouse gets nothing,[25] but the Uniform Marriage and Divorce Act authorizes courts to "apportion property * * * among the claimants as appropriate in the circumstances and in the interests of justice," and suggests that "a fair and efficient apportionment standard is likely to be the length of time that each spouse cohabited with the common partner."[26] In a recent case in which a husband had lived with a putative wife for about a year, but his only substantial assets at death were pension benefits from employment during his marriage to the lawful wife, the putative wife was held to have "no equitable interest."[27]

### *Separation and Divorce*

Some states bar a lawful spouse from claiming a share of the other spouse's estate under certain circumstances. In Pennsylvania, for example, a spouse who has "willfully and maliciously" deserted or "willfully neglected or refused" to support the other spouse for a year or more cannot share in the spouse's estate.[28] A Kansas statute barring workers' compensation benefits to

**20.** Evans, *Property Interests Arising from Quasi-Marital Relations,* 9 Cornell L.Q. 246, 247 (1924); Tatum v. Tatum, 736 P.2d 506 (Okl.1982). However, according to Blakesley, *supra* note 17, at page 52, most states give some relief on some theory.

In Batey v. Batey, 933 P.2d 551 (Alaska 1997) refused to recognize the claim of a putative spouse who failed to meet a statutory requirement of a good faith belief in the validity of the marriage. A dissenting judge believed the husband who had lived with the claimant for 20 years, should be "estopped" to deny the marriage.

**21.** *Restatement, Third, of Property (Wills and Other Donative Transfers)* § 2.2, comm. e (1998).

**22.** Calif.Fam.Code § 2251; Calif.Code Civ. Proc. § 377.60(b). A putative spouse inherits separate as well as community property, and can administer the decedent's estate, Estate of Leslie, 689 P.2d 133 (Cal.1984), and can claim as an omitted spouse, In re Estate of Sax, 263 Cal.Rptr. 190 (App.1989), but has been denied a family allowance, Estate of Hafner, 229 Cal. Rptr. 676 (App.1986), and benefits under a pension plan designed for persons to whom the employee "was married." Allen v. Western Conference of Teamsters Pension Trust Fund, 788 F.2d 648 (9th Cir.1986).

**23.** Uniform Marriage and Divorce Act § 209; Estate of Whyte v. Whyte, 614 N.E.2d 372 (Ill.App.1993); Williams v. Fireman's Fund Ins. Co., 670 P.2d 453 (Colo.App.1983).

**24.** 42 U.S.C.A. § 416(h)(1)(B).

**25.** Martin v. Harris, 653 F.2d 428 (10th Cir.1981). This is not true if the putative spouse is treated as a spouse by state law. Blakesley, *supra* note 17, at 49–51.

**26.** Uniform Marriage and Divorce Act § 209. *See also Restatement, Third, of Property (Wills and Other Donative Transfers)* § 1.2, comm. e (1998); *cf.* Estate of Hafner, 229 Cal. Rptr. 676 (App.1986) (equal division between legal and putative spouses). For a discussion of alternative methods of equitable division *see* Blakesley, *supra* note 17, at 38–40.

**27.** In re Marriage of Himes, 965 P.2d 1087, 1101 (Wash.1998).

**28.** 20 Pa.C.S. § 2106(a). In Estate of Fulton, 619 A.2d 280 (Pa.Super.1992), the court barred a husband from claiming a share of the estate of a wife who had deserted him. His "acquiescence" in this—he began cohabiting with another woman by whom he had a child, was held to fall under the statute.

Or.Rev.Stat. § 114.135 gives courts discretion to deny or reduce a spouse's elective share if the couple was separated at death.

a spouse who "for more than six months willfully deserted or abandoned the employee" was held to extend to cases of "mutual abandonment of the marital relationship" regardless of who was at fault or instigated it.[29] Modern counterparts appear in some states to the Statute of Westminster of 1285 which barred an adulterous wife from claiming dower.[30] Under the Uniform Probate Code, however, a separation, absent a divorce, does not affect succession rights unless the spouse in a separation agreement waived claims to share in the other's estate.[31] Thus many spouses have successfully asserted claims to share in a decedent spouse's estate even though divorce proceedings between them were pending when the decedent died.[32] However, the New Jersey Supreme Court has held that a surviving spouse in this situation could not claim an elective share, but only an equitable share of the marital property as in a divorce between living spouses.[33]

A legal spouse who contracts a bigamous marriage may be barred from asserting rights under the first marriage "if, under the circumstances, it would be inequitable for him to do so."[34] An "estoppel" to claim rights under the first marriage may exist even if the second marriage is dissolved.[35] However, such claims are sometimes allowed. For example, a deserted wife who had remarried was allowed rights as her legal husband's widow when he died.[36] Under the Uniform Probate Code, estoppel is limited to persons who have obtained or consented to an invalid divorce, or who have remarried after such a divorce.[37] Of course, a *valid* divorce terminates a marriage without

**29.** Redditt v. McDonald's Restaurant, 990 P.2d 759 (Kan.App.1999).

**30.** In Oliver v. Estate of Oliver, 554 N.E.2d 8 (Ind.App.1990), such a statute was used to bar a husband from claiming a devise under his wife's will.

**31.** Uniform Probate Code § 2–802, comment; In re Estate of Zimmerman, 579 N.W.2d 591, 597 (N.D.1998); In re Estate of Salathe, 703 So.2d 1167 (Fla.App.1997) (husband gets a share of wife's estate despite separation agreement). As to waiver, see Matter of Estate of Highgate, 348 N.W.2d 31 (Mich.App.1984); Simpson v. King, 383 S.E.2d 120 (Ga.1989); Section 3.9.

**32.** Hempe v. Hempe, 635 P.2d 403 (Or. App.1981); McClinton v. Sullivan, 430 S.E.2d 794 (Ga.App.1993); In re Estate of Watson, 348 N.W.2d 856 (Neb.1984); Hamilton v. Hamilton, 879 S.W.2d 416 (Ark.1994); Matter of Estate of Duncan, 525 N.E.2d 1212 (Ill.App.1988).

**33.** Carr v. Carr, 576 A.2d 872 (N.J.1990). In Estate of Burford v. Burford, 935 P.2d 943 (Colo.1997), divorce proceedings were bifurcated and a decree of dissolution was entered. The husband died before the property division was adjudicated. The court held that the wife was no longer entitled to the rights of a spouse in probate proceedings, and remanded for consideration of the property issues remaining in the dissolution proceedings. *See also* Estate of Lahey, 91 Cal.Rptr.2d 30 (App.1999) (legal separation terminates right to inherit); Magoon v. Magoon, 780 P.2d 80 (Haw.1989).

**34.** Kosak v. MacKechnie, 505 N.E.2d 579 (Mass.App.1987). *See also* Matter of Estate of Warner, 687 S.W.2d 686 (Mo.App.1985) (husband estopped to challenge validity of Mexican divorce so as to claim property as tenant by the entirety).

**35.** Matter of Estate of Allen, 738 P.2d 142 (Okl.1987).

**36.** Matter of Estate of Kueber, 390 N.W.2d 22 (Minn.App.1986). *But see* In re Estate of Dalton, 647 N.E.2d 581 (Ohio Com.Pl.1995) (remarriage of deserted spouse estops her from claim against husband's estate); In re Estate of Butler, 444 So.2d 477 (Fla.App.1984).

**37.** Uniform Probate Code § 2–208. Cal. Prob.Code § 78 is similar, but Estate of Anderson, 70 Cal.Rptr.2d 266 (App.1997), held that a husband who had remarried was estopped to inherit from his legal wife even though there had been no divorce. In Farrell v. Porter, 830 P.2d 299 (Utah App.1992) a wife's obtaining a divorce not knowing that her husband had died was held not to estop her under the Code. In In re Estate of Newton, 583 N.E.2d 1026 (Ohio App.1989), a wife was allowed to claim a Mexican divorce was invalid; the fact that she lived separate from her husband for 25 years thereafter did not estop her. In In re Estate of Salathe, 703 So.2d 1167 (Fla.App.1997), both spouses had brought divorce proceedings which were dismissed for lack of jurisdiction. The husband was allowed to claim as an heir of his wife's estate.

resort to the idea of estoppel. Thus when a man and woman are divorced, she is not his "surviving spouse" if she survives him.[38]

In some community property states, if spouses separate their subsequent earnings cease to be community property,[39] but in others this is true only in the event of a formal separation agreement or decree.[40]

### *No Ceremonial Marriage*

Some states do not require a ceremony for a valid marriage. Canon law, which governed the law of marriage throughout the Middle Ages, held that consent alone was necessary. Not until the 16th century did the Catholic Church require the presence of a priest for the marriage to be valid.[41] In England, no marriage ceremony was legally required until a statute of 1753.[42] Today a few states still permit non-ceremonial "common-law" marriages, but their number is declining.[43] Nevertheless, all states recognize a common-law marriage if it was valid where contracted.[44]

How is a "common-law" marriage proved? Definitions vary from state to state.[45] Some states require "clear and convincing evidence,"[46] but in others a preponderance of the evidence is enough.[47] Some courts require a specific agreement concerning marriage,[48] but others infer a marriage contract when a couple live together and hold themselves out as man and wife.[49] Even when a

**38.** Parada v. Parada, 999 P.2d 184, 188 (Ariz.2000).

**39.** Aetna Life Ins. Co. v. Bunt, 754 P.2d 993 (Wash.1988); Cal. Family Code § 771. *But see* In re Marriage of von der Nuell, 28 Cal. Rptr.2d 447 (App.1994) (couple not "separated" when they continued to see each other even though H had moved out); Seizer v. Sessions, 940 P.2d 261 (Wash. 1997) (desertion by one spouse does not constitute separation absent acquiescence by the other).

**40.** Forrest v. Forrest, 668 P.2d 275 (Nev. 1983); Keller v. Department of Revenue, 642 P.2d 284 (Or.1982) (parties who are living apart are not "separated" for this purpose if the marriage is still intact); Lynch v. Lynch, 791 P.2d 653 (Ariz.App.1990) (wife shares in $2.2 million lottery winnings while couple separated and divorce pending).

**41.** Donahue, *The Case of the Man Who Fell into the Tiber: The Roman Law of Marriage at the Time of the Glossators,* 22 American J.Legal History 1, 3, 52 (1978).

**42.** 1 W. Blackstone, *Commentaries* 439 (1765); Statute, 26 Geo. 2, c. 33 (1753).

**43.** Younger, *Marital Regimes,* 67 Cornell L.Review 45, 75 (1981). In In re Estate of Hall, 588 N.E.2d 203 (Ohio App.1990), the majority opinion called on the legislature to abolish common law marriage. It did so the following year but the change was not retroactive. Ruscilli v. Ruscilli, 630 N.E.2d 745 (Ohio App. 1993). *See also* Matter of Heirship of McLeod, 506 So.2d 289 (Miss.1987). Idaho abolished common law marriage effective Jan. 1, 1996, Matter of Estate of Wagner, 893 P.2d 211 (Idaho 1995), but Utah adopted it in 1987, Whyte v. Blair, 885 P.2d 791 (Utah 1994).

**44.** Varoz v. Estate of Shepard, 585 N.E.2d 31 (Ind.App.1992) (Indiana must recognize Colorado judgment declaring plaintiff to be decedent's common-law wife); Allen v. Storer, 600 N.E.2d 1263 (Ill.App.1992) (error to reject claim of common-law marriage as against public policy of Illinois).

**45.** Weyrauch, *Informal and Formal Marriage,* 28 U.Chi.L.Rev. 88, 91 (1960).

**46.** In re Estate of Hall, 588 N.E.2d 203 (Ohio App.1990); Mueggenborg v. Walling, 836 P.2d 112 (Okl.1992); *cf.* In re Marriage of Mosher, 612 N.E.2d 838 (Ill.App.1993) (such claims are regarded with suspicion).

**47.** East v. East, 536 A.2d 1103 (D.C.App. 1988); Hansen v. Hansen, 958 P.2d 931 (Utah App.1998); In re Estate of Antonopoulos, 993 P.2d 637, 648 (Kan.1999) (finding of common law marriage affirmed where supported by "substantial evidence").

**48.** Gonzalez v. Satrustegui, 870 P.2d 1188 (Ariz.App.1993); Matter of Peltomaa's Estate, 630 P.2d 215 (Mont.1981).

**49.** Brown v. Carr, 402 S.E.2d 296 (Ga.App. 1991); Mott v. Duncan Petroleum Trans., 414 N.E.2d 657 (N.Y.1980); In re Glasco, 619 S.W.2d 567, 570 (Tex.Civ.App.1981); Estate of Smart v. Smart, 676 P.2d 1379 (Okl.App.1983). *But see* Estate of Wires, 765 P.2d 618 (Colo. App.1988) (no marriage where couple cohabited for years but chose not to marry so W would not lose her Social Security).

contract of marriage exists, some courts hold that cohabitation and reputation as husband and wife are also necessary.[50]

Even if the relevant law does not recognize common-law marriages, the dramatic increase in recent years of cohabitation by unmarried couples, and its increasing social acceptability may bring about a change in the law comparable to the expansion of the rights of illegitimate children.[51] The years between 1970 and 1980 saw a 200% increase in the number of unmarried couples sharing the same household. "Until the last decade, unmarried cohabitation was generally perceived as a lower-class phenomenon. Its adoption by the middle and upper-middle classes, as well as its rising rate of occurrence, has probably been responsible for the new judicial sensitivity to the plight of the cast-off cohabitant."[52] Since these words were written the trend has continued; "from 1970 to 1993 alone, the number of unmarried couple households in the U.S. increased from 523,00 to 3,510,000."[53]

So far, though, protection for unmarried cohabitants has been rather limited. The Restatement calls the right of a "domestic partner" to be treated as a spouse a "developing question," as to which it takes no position.[54] In New Hampshire,

> Persons cohabiting and acknowledging each other as husband and wife, and generally reputed to be such, for the period of three years, and until the decease of one of them, shall thereafter be deemed to have been legally married.[55]

Oregon gives worker's compensation benefits to an unmarried cohabitant who lived with the injured worker for over a year if "children are living as a result of that relation."[56] In other states unmarried survivors have been awarded worker's compensation benefits under more generally worded provisions.[57] An English statute authorizing courts to award a "reasonable financial provision" from an estate to "any person * * * who immediately before the death of the deceased was being maintained * * * by the deceased" has been held to justify an award to a decedent's mistress.[58] But wrongful death claims by surviving unmarried cohabitants have generally been rejected.[59]

**50.** Matter of Estate of Vandenhook, 855 P.2d 518 (Mont.1993) (no marriage if parties do not cohabit or hold selves out as spouses); Hansen v. Hansen, 958 P.2d 931 (Utah App. 1998) (claim of marriage fails where "the parties' closest friends did not consider the two married").

**51.** Prager, *Sharing Principles and the Future of Marital Property Law,* 25 UCLA L.Rev. 1, 19–21 (1977).

**52.** Blumberg, *Cohabitation Without Marriage,* 28 UCLA L.Rev. 1125, 1129 (1981).

**53.** Salzman v. Bachrach, 996 P.2d 1263, 1267 (Colo.2000). However, such cohabitation is for most a temporary status; "the parties either break up or get married fairly quickly." Waggoner, *Marital Property Rights in Transition,* 59 Mo.L.Rev. 21, 63 (1994).

**54.** *Restatement, Third, of Property (Wills and Other Donative Transfers)* § 2.2, comm. g (1998). A provision for giving surviving cohabitants a share upon intestacy was advanced by Professor Waggoner in *Marital Property Rights in Transition,* 59 Mo.L.Rev. 21, 79 (1994), but has not found its way into the UPC.

**55.** N.H.Rev.Stat. § 457.39.

**56.** Or.Rev.Stat. § 656.226.

**57.** Department of Indus.Rel. v. Workers' Comp. Appeals Bd., 156 Cal.Rptr. 183 (App. 1979) ("dependent * * * member of the family or household"); West v. Barton–Malow Co., 230 N.W.2d 545 (Mich.1975). Blumberg, *supra* note 52, at 1141–42, cites cases both ways.

**58.** Inheritance (Provision for Family and Dependents) Act, 1975, § 1; Malone v. Harrison, [1979] 1 W.L.R. 1353 (Fam.D). But in In re Beaumont, [1979] 3 W.L.R. 820 (Ch.D.) a claim by a man who had been living with decedent for 36 years was denied because he had been paying his own way; the statute requires that the claimant have been maintained by the deceased "otherwise than for a full valuable consideration." § 1(3).

The equal protection idea which has used for children born out of wedlock does not protect unmarried cohabitants. The Supreme Court upheld a limitation of Social Security benefits to widows and divorcees on the ground that:

> Congress could reasonably conclude that a woman who has never been married to the wage earner is far less likely to be dependent upon the wage earner at the time of his death * * *
>
> General rules are essential if a fund of this magnitude is to be administered with a modicum of efficiency, even though such rules inevitably produce seemingly arbitrary consequences in some individual cases. * * * A process of case-by-case adjudication that would provide a 'perfect fit' in theory would increase administrative expenses to a degree that benefit levels would probably be reduced.[60]

In the case of children the problem of proving paternity is outweighed by the unfairness of penalizing them for a difficulty which they did not create. Unmarried cohabitants cannot make such an argument.[61]

### *Contract*

Unmarried cohabitants sometimes assert rights under a contract with their partner. Most of these cases arise while both parties are alive. "Claims arising at death are less common because, if the parties remain devoted to one another, the surviving partner is probably provided for in the decedent's will or other parts of the estate plan."[62] The argument that such contracts violate public policy because they involve illicit sex is generally rejected on the ground that sex plays only an incidental role in the relationship.[63] Occasionally cohabiting couples make an express contract concerning the arrangement,[64] but since this is rather unusual,[65] the significant issue is whether courts will infer a contract between them. Professor Waggoner favors giving cohabitants an intestate share under some circumstances but says any implied contract is "a fiction" since generally the parties do not share the same expectations about the arrangement.[66]

**59.** Elden v. Sheldon, 758 P.2d 582 (Cal. 1988) (loss of consortium); Roe v. Ludtke Trucking, Inc., 732 P.2d 1021 (Wash.App. 1987); Hooks v. Owen, 719 N.E.2d 581, 583 (Ohio App.1998); Ford v. Wagner, 395 N.W.2d 72 (Mich.App.1986) (dram shop act); Kulawik v. ERA Jet Alaska, 820 P.2d 627 (Alaska 1991). *But see* Lealaimatafoa v. Woodward–Clyde Consl., 867 P.2d 220 (Haw.1994) (claim as "dependent").

**60.** Califano v. Boles, 443 U.S. 282, 289 (1979). The protection given by the Social Security Act to putative spouses is limited to those who go through a marriage ceremony. Thomas v. Sullivan, 922 F.2d 132 (2d Cir. 1990).

**61.** Sykes v. Propane Power Corp., 541 A.2d 271 (N.J.Super.App.Div.1988) (justifying refusal to allow unmarried cohabitant to sue for wrongful death).

**62.** Waggoner, *supra* note 54, at 65.

**63.** Marvin v. Marvin, 557 P.2d 106 (Cal. 1976); Morone v. Morone, 413 N.E.2d 1154 (N.Y.1980); Kinkenon v. Hue, 301 N.W.2d 77 (Neb.1981); Salzman v. Bachrach, 996 P.2d 1263 (Colo.2000). *But see* Hewitt v. Hewitt, 394 N.E.2d 1204 (Ill.1979).

**64.** Sullivan v. Rooney, 533 N.E.2d 1372 (Mass.1989) (promise to give cohabitant a half interest in a house enforced); Byrne v. Laura, 60 Cal.Rptr.2d 908 (App.1997) (oral agreement to support cohabitant for life and for her to receive defendant's property at death).

**65.** Waggoner, *supra* note 54, at 67–68, notes the "enormous disparity of bargaining power" which often exists and means that any contract is more likely to take the form of the subordinate party waiving all rights.

**66.** *Id.* at 73.

Some critics contend that recognizing an implied contract between cohabitants conflicts with the legislative decision to abolish common-law marriage,[67] but there are differences between the two. Historically, common-law marriages were often used to invalidate a later formal marriage as bigamous,[68] whereas courts can imply a contract which does not eliminate the rights of a lawful spouse.[69] However, a line must be drawn between casual cohabitation and a stable relationship. Commentators have suggested a test based on the birth of children, or the length of the relationship.[70]

Assuming a court implies a contract, what will be its terms? One theory would compensate the plaintiff for services performed during the relationship, less any benefits received,[71] but courts often reject such claims on the ground that the services were rendered without any expectation of payment.[72] A cohabitant who contributes to the acquisition of property in ways other than performing domestic services has more chance of success.[73] For example, a Missouri court rejected a claim for compensation for domestic services, like cooking and laundering. "If two persons live together in the same household concurrently rendering services to each other * * * in the absence of an *express* contract that payment is to be made in addition to the benefit derived from the arrangement * * * the law presumes such benefit to be the full recompense to each for the services rendered." But the same court allowed the claimant compensation for "non-domestic type services she performed for decedent's businesses," and for expenses she had incurred in maintaining a townhouse in which they lived.[74]

Courts sometimes infer an agreement to divide all property acquired during a relationship equally.[75] Washington courts have divided property between separating unmarried cohabitants on principles similar, though not

**67.** Clark, *The New Marriage,* 12 Will.L.J. 441, 449 (1976); In re Estate of Alexander, 445 So.2d 836 (Miss.1984).

**68.** Richard III claimed the throne of England on the basis of an unsolemnized marriage by his brother which made the brother's children illegitimate. P. Kendall, *Richard the Third* 257 (1955).

**69.** "Enforcement of the contract between plaintiff and defendant * * * will not impair any right of" Marvin's wife. Marvin v. Marvin, 557 P.2d 106, 115 (Cal.1976). *See also* Younger, *Marital Regimes,* 67 Cornell L.Rev. 45, 100 (1981); Waggoner, supra note 54, at 79 (under proposed statute for partners only persons not married to another qualify). In Wilkinson v. Higgins, 844 P.2d 266 (Or.App.1992), the court awarded an interest to the decedent's cohabitant "partner" even though he was married to another woman.

**70.** Younger, *Marital Regimes,* 67 Cornell L.Rev. 45, 99 (1981) ("Substantial duration"); Blumberg, *supra* note 52, at 1143 (2 years); Wolk, *Federal Tax Consequences of Wealth Transfers between Unmarried Cohabitants,* 27 UCLA L.Rev. 1240, 1268 (1980) (3 years); Waggoner, supra note 54, at 79 (duration of relationship a factor in establishing "marriage-like" status, presumed when parties have cohabited for 5 years).

**71.** Matter of Steffes' Estate, 290 N.W.2d 697 (Wis.1980).

**72.** Matter of Lamb's Estate, 655 P.2d 1001 (N.M.1982); Osborne v. Boatmen's Nat. Bank, 732 S.W.2d 242 (Mo.App.1987) (disregarding claimant's "self-serving" testimony to the contrary); Neumann v. Rogstad, 757 P.2d 761 (Mont.1988) (rejecting a claim by a husband for compensation for services to his wife).

**73.** Adams v. Jankouskas, 452 A.2d 148 (Del.1982); Brooks v. Kunz, 637 S.W.2d 135 (Mo.App.1982); Waggoner, supra note 54, at 66.

**74.** Estate of Erickson, 722 S.W.2d 330 (Mo.App.1986). *See also* Suggs v. Norris, 364 S.E.2d 159 (N.C.App.1988).

**75.** Western States Construction v. Michoff, 840 P.2d 1220 (Nev.1992); Wilkinson v. Higgins, 844 P.2d 266 (Or.App.1992).

identical to those which control the division between spouses upon a divorce,[76] but they do not allow an unmarried cohabitant to inherit as a spouse.[77]

Professor Blumberg has proposed that the law should "assimilate cohabitants to married persons" for all purposes, since "most cohabitants feel there is no difference between marriage and cohabitation,"[78] but others argue that this would defeat expectations, since cohabitants refrain from marriage because they wish to avoid its legal incidents.[79] Waggoner's proposed statute would give cohabitants "a substantially smaller intestate share than a spouse would take under the UPC" and no right to an elective share or claim to act as the decedent's personal representative.[80]

Thus, the legal position of cohabitants who do not solemnize a marriage is unclear. Recognition of common-law marriage is declining, but the rights of unmarried cohabitants are increasing. Usually, the best theory for a surviving partner is an implied contract. However, some courts do not accept it, and even for those that do, the terms to be implied are unclear.

### *Same Sex Marriages*

Even more problematic are the claims of homosexual cohabitants, who, according to one estimate, number over 3 million.[81] A California court allowed a homosexual lover to sue on an express promise of a share of the defendant's property.[82] But a New York court rejected a claim of a homosexual partner to a spouse's share of an estate, saying that the statutory limitation of marriage to persons of the opposite sex was constitutional.[83] In Hawaii, on the other hand, the constitutionality of the same limitation was thrown in doubt by a court decision;[84] thereafter the legislature passed a statute which accords to "reciprocal beneficiaries" the same rights as spouses, *e.g.* to an intestate or elective share.[85] This status is open to unmarried adults who are legally prohibited from marrying one another and who register their relationship by filing a notarized statement of intent.[86] A Vermont statute allows persons of the same sex to enter into a "civil union" which gives them "all the same benefits, protections and responsibilities under law ... as are granted to spouses in a marriage," including intestate succession, actions for wrongful death, and the right to hold as tenants by the entirety.[87] Because of the general rule which recognizes marriages as valid if valid in the state where

**76.** Connell v. Francisco, 898 P.2d 831 (Wash.1995). *See also* Shuraleff v. Donnelly, 817 P.2d 764 (Or.App.1991); Matter of Marriage of Thomas, 825 P.2d 1163 (Kan.App. 1992).

**77.** Peffley–Warner v. Bowen, 778 P.2d 1022 (Wash.1989). In In re Marriage of Hilt, 704 P.2d 672 (Wash.App.1985), a couple began cohabiting in 1974 and married in 1978. Property which they acquired in 1974 to which both contributed was treated as community property.

**78.** Blumberg, *supra* note 52, at 1166–67.

**79.** Lauper v. Harold, 492 N.E.2d 472, 474 (Ohio App.1985); Connell v. Francisco, 898 P.2d 831, 836 (Wash.1995).

**80.** Waggoner, *supra* note 54, at 80.

**81.** Spitko, *The Expressive Function of Succession Law and the Merits of Non–Marital Inclusion*, 41 Ariz.L.Rev. 1063, 1071 (1999). The author advocates giving "same-sex committed partners" rights to inherit on intestacy.

**82.** Whorton v. Dillingham, 248 Cal.Rptr. 405 (App.1988).

**83.** Matter of Cooper, 592 N.Y.S.2d 797 (App.Div.1993). *See also* Raum v. Restaurant Associates, 675 N.Y.S.2d 343 (A.D.1998) (wrongful death claim by homosexual partner rejected); In re Estate of Hall, 707 N.E.2d 201 (Ill.App.1998) (surviving partner has no standing to challenge constitutionality of bar to single-sex marriage).

**84.** Baehr v. Lewin, 852 P.2d 44 (Haw. 1993). *See also* Baker v. State, 744 A.2d 864 (Vt.1999).

**85.** Haw.Rev.Stat. §§ 560:2–102, 560:2–202.

**86.** Haw.Rev.Stat. § 572C–5.

**87.** 15 Vt.Stat.Ann § 1204.

they took place[88] other states might be forced to recognize marriages between persons of the same sex. In order to avoid this Congress in 1996 passed the Defense of Marriage Act, which provides that states are not "required to give effect" to laws of other states "respecting a relationship between persons of the same sex that is treated as a marriage."[89]

Professor Spitko believes that the Hawaii statute does not go far enough because it does not provide for "many gay men and lesbians" who are "reluctant to publicly acknowledge their relationships with their committed partners" because of discrimination in society. He suggests that the "growing segment of corporate America that offers various benefits to the 'domestic partners' of employees" can provide guidance in establishing rules to determine whether there is "sufficient commitment in a relationship" to warrant providing an intestate share to the survivor.[90]

A few cases have involved transsexuals who claimed to be married. These were summarized in a recent decision involving a person born as a man who claimed to be the widow of a man under a wrongful death statute. The court concluded:

> Medical science recognizes that there are individuals who sexual self-identity is in conflict with their biological and anatomical sex. Such people are termed transsexuals. A transsexual is not a homosexual ... in that transsexuals believe and feel they are members of the opposite sex.
>
> Through surgery and hormones, a transsexual male can be made to look like a woman, including female genitalia and breasts. Transsexual medical treatment, however, does not create the internal sexual organs of a woman ...

The majority concluded that the plaintiff was a male and "cannot be married to another male."[91]

### *Planning*

The Uniform Statutory Will Act defines the term "surviving spouse" of the testator carefully to exclude a person from whom the testator was separated under a decree of separation or a written separation agreement, or if the marriage was dissolved by a divorce even if the divorce is not recognized in the state. Conversely, a person to whom the testator is not legally married because the termination of a previous marriage was not valid is deemed to be the testator's spouse.[92] In an ordinary will in which the testator's spouse is named, such a definition is unnecessary, since the named devisee may take even if designated as a spouse and the marriage is not valid. If the testator after executing the will divorces the spouse or they are separated, the testator should review the will and make appropriate changes, although, as we shall see, the law makes some default provisions to cover this situation.[93]

Some wills provide for the spouse of a child or other relative of the testator. The testator may have a particular spouse in mind, but not always. If

**88.** Section 1.2, note 71.

**89.** 28 U.S.C. § 1738C.

**90.** Spitko, *supra* note 81, at 1088.

**91.** Littleton v. Prange, 9 S.W.3d 223, 230–31 (Tex.App.1999).

**92.** Unif. Statutory Will Act § 1(7).

**93.** See Section 5.4.

the testator wishes to include a future spouse, *e.g.* of a presently unmarried child, the definitions in the Uniform Statutory Will Act could be expanded to cover "spouses" of persons other than the testator. But the testator may prefer more flexibility by giving the child a broad power of appointment. The advantages (and possible risks) of powers of appointment are covered in Section 10.4.

# Chapter 3

# LIMITS ON TESTAMENTARY POWER

*Analysis*



## § 3.1 Policy Considerations

This chapter deals with the question how much freedom an owner should have to dispose of property at death. It has sometimes been argued that society should restrict this freedom in order to prevent excessive inequality of wealth,[1] but this argument is usually rejected today, since there are better ways to deal with the unequal distribution of wealth in society, such as progressive taxation.[2]

A more cogent reason for limiting the power of disposition arises from the duty of parents to support their children and spouses to support each other.[3] These obligations have long been recognized. Blackstone said that the duty of parents to support their children was "a principle of natural law,"[4] and therefore parents should be obligated to leave their children "at least a necessary subsistence."[5] As we shall see, this suggestion has been adopted in many jurisdictions of the British Commonwealth, but it does not represent the law in most American states.[6]

§ 3.1

1. 2 W. Blackstone, *Commentaries* *373–74 (1765). *See also* Succession of Steckler, 665 So.2d 561, 564 (La.App.1995) (forced heirship is designed to prevent "the cummulation [sic] of excessively large fortunes through primogeniture and entailment").

2. Le Van, *Alternatives to Forced Heirship,* 52 Tul.L.Rev. 29, 44 (1977); Nathan, *An Assault on the Citadel: A Rejection of Forced Heirship,* 52 Tul.L.Rev. 5, 6–7 (1977).

3. *E.g.,* Cal.Family Code §§ 3900 (duty of parents to support child); 4300 (duty to support spouse).

4. 1 W. Blackstone, *Commentaries** 447 (1765). However, the common law did not provide adequate remedies to enforce this duty. Foster, Freed & Minodnick, *Child Support: The Quick and the Dead,* 26 Syr.L.Rev. 1157 (1975).

5. 1 W. Blackstone, *Commentaries** 449–50 (1765).

6. See Section 3.2, note 27.

### *Spouses v. Children*

Spouses receive more protection against disinheritance than children in most of the United States, most notably in the "elective share" to which spouses are entitled in nearly all American jurisdictions.[7] In a way this is surprising[8] since spouses can provide for their support by contract when they marry, whereas children enter the parent-child relationship involuntarily and have no such opportunity. Also, young children cannot support themselves, whereas many spouses are able to work when a marriage ends.[9] But the case for protecting children against disinheritance encounters an objection which does not apply to spouses. The duty to support children usually applies only to minors,[10] and they are incapable of managing property. Therefore, any property which they get must be managed by a guardian or conservator. Guardianship is inconvenient and expensive, and many parents seek to avoid it by leaving all their property to the other spouse in the expectation that he or she will use it to bring up the children. A will which leaves all the estate to the testator's spouse technically disinherits the testator's children, but why should the law upset this sensible estate plan?[11]

The surviving spouse, on the other hand, is normally competent to manage any property received from the decedent's estate. Also, spouses have another basis for claiming a share of the decedent's estate, in addition to the obligation of support. Usually both spouses contribute to the accumulation of property during a marriage, even if all the property is held in the name of the decedent spouse. The elective share given to spouses is

> based on two rationales: (1) contribution—which recognizes that no matter what role a spouse plays in marriage, he or she has made some contribution towards the acquisition of the property of the deceased spouse and (2) support—which recognizes that the surviving spouse will need support after the death of his or her spouse.[12]

The decedent's children, on the other hand, normally have made no such contribution.[13]

If the surviving spouse is the other parent of the decedent's children, the claims of the spouse and those of the children usually coincide. The share given to the spouse will indirectly provide for the children; the spouse will, indeed must use the property awarded for the children's support if they are

**7.** Only Georgia permits a spouse to be disinherited. Kwestel & Seplowitz, *Testamentary Substitutes—A Time for Statutory Clarification*, 23 Real Prop.P.T.J. 467, 468 (1988). As to the elective share see Section 3.7. The spouse's claim to half the community property is its counterpart in a number of states. See Section 3.8.

**8.** Batts, *I Didn't Ask to be Born,* 41 Hast. L.J. 1197, 1198 (1990) (finding the American protection of spouses hard to reconcile with the lack of protection to children).

**9.** Rein, *A More Rational System for the Protection of Family Members from Disinheritance,* 15 Gonz.L.Rev. 11, 47 (1979).

**10.** 1 W. Blackstone, *Commentaries* *449 (1765); *cf.* Cal.Family Code § 3910 (duty of parents to support an incapacitated child of whatever age).

**11.** Chaffin, *A Reappraisal of the Wealth Transmission Process,* 10 Ga.L.Rev. 447, 475 (1976); Foster, Freed & Minodnick, *supra* note 4, at 1186.

**12.** Mongold v. Mayle, 452 S.E.2d 444, 447 (W.Va.1994).

**13.** However, there are cases in which a child has helped a parent in a business or provided care. This may give rise to an enforceable claim that the parent has agreed in return to leave property to the child at death. See Section 4.9, note 12.

minors. But with the increase in multiple marriages,[14] the surviving spouse often is not the parent of the decedent's children and there may be hostility between them; at the least a stepparent cannot be counted on to provide for his or her stepchildren.[15] Most litigation today about the spouse's forced share arises in this context.

### *Arguments for Free Disposition*

Arguments against the claims of spouses and children to share in an estate against the decedent's wishes have been made for centuries. Bracton in the 13th century asserted that men would have no incentive to work and save if they were compelled to leave their property at death to their widows and children.[16] Similar arguments have been made in modern times.[17] However, the law compels persons while they are alive to support dependents even though this may also deter work or saving. Moreover, a person's duty to pay debts survives death, so should not the duty to support survive as well?[18]

Bracton also argued that freedom of testation gave wives and children an incentive to treat the testator well.[19] Blackstone made a similar point. When children could not be disinherited they became "disobedient and head-strong."[20] King Lear was mistreated by his daughters as soon as their share of his estate was secure.[21] On the other hand, some parents use their testamentary freedom to control the lives of their children in an unappealing way, for example, disinheriting a child who adopts a religion or marries a person of whom the parent disapproves.[22] Arguably the law should allow a will to disinherit a child or spouse only for certain misconduct.[23]

A better argument for testamentary freedom is that it permits more intelligent estate planning than the rigid rules of intestate succession: "the parent more often than not will know better how to dispose of his property than will the state [which imposes] an inflexible blanket rule."[24] Such planning is not limited to punishing family members for conduct which the testator disapproves. A will may depart from the equal treatment of children mandated by the intestacy laws in order to take account of their differing needs. Or, a testator who has provided for one child by gifts during lifetime may leave this child less than the others; the law of advancements is a crude alternative for reflecting this desire. Or a testator may wish to provide for children equally, but in different ways, for example, by leaving a family

**14.** Only 55% of marriages today are the first marriage for both spouses. Oldham, *Should the Surviving Spouse's Forced Share Be Retained?*, 32 Case West.Res.L.Rev 223, 233 (1987–88).

**15.** Oldham, *What Does the U.S. System Regarding Inheritance Rights of Children Reveal about American Families?* 33 Family L.Q. 265, 269–70 (1999).

**16.** 2 Bracton, *De Legibus et Consuetudinibus Angliae* 181 (Thorne ed. 1968).

**17.** Macey, *Private Trusts for the Provision of Private Goods*, 37 Emory L.J. 295, 297 (1988); Cahn, *Restraints on Disinheritance,* 85 U.Pa.L.Rev. 139, 145 (1936).

**18.** Rein, *supra* note 9, at 18–19.

**19.** *See* note 16 *supra.*

**20.** 2 W. Blackstone, *Commentaries* 12 (1765). *See also* Nathan, *supra* note 2, at 15.

**21.** For a modern case, reminiscent of Lear, *see* Matter of Succession of Chaney, 413 So.2d 936 (La.App.1982).

**22.** *E.g.,* Shapira v. Union Nat. Bank, 315 N.E.2d 825 (Ohio Com.Pl.1974); 1 W. Blackstone, *Commentaries* *449 (1765). For the validity of such provisions see Section 3.10, note 16 et seq.

**23.** *E.g.,* La.Civ.Code art. 1621 (specifying causes for disinheritance).

**24.** Nathan, *supra* note 2, at 19.

business to one child and equivalent bequests of other assets to the others.[25] Or, may wish to leave property in trust for a child or spouse who is unable to handle property.[26] Why should the law allow a child or spouse to upset reasonable wills like these?

### *Fixed–Share v. Discretionary Restraints*

Restraints on testamentary freedom are of two types: (1) fixed share and (2) discretionary. The most important limitation on testamentary freedom in the United States today, the spouse's elective or community property share, is generally a fraction of the estate. The elective share has been justified as designed "to secure a minimal means of sustenance for the surviving spouse, and to relieve the State of providing support in a situation where advanced age or infirmities make the surviving spouse unable to provide his or her own support,"[27] but the fixed share imperfectly fits this rationale.

> [As] a means of assuring a degree of support for the surviving spouse * * * the forced share is a very crude instrument, because the costs of living and financial resources of the widow or widower are irrelevant, as are the lifetime gifts the decedent may have made to the spouse. * * * Also the fraction of the estate to which the surviving spouse is entitled does not vary with the size of the estate. * * * One-third of an estate of $1,000,000 may enable a spouse to live in the accustomed style, but one-third of an estate of $200,000 may not.[28]

A similar objection can be made against the forced share given to children in the civil law. Napoleon proposed it vary with the size of their parents' estate, but his idea was rejected by the drafters of the "Napoleonic" Code because it "would require an expensive and often uncertain appraisal" of the estate.[29]

The fixed-share schemes which protect the surviving spouse in America are easy to administer, but they often give a spouse more or less than is necessary for support. Some states reduce the surviving spouse's share by gifts received from the decedent or by the spouse's other resources, however acquired. Even these statutes correlate only imperfectly with the need for support because they ignore the spouse's earning capacity. Also support needs can change over time, for example, if the spouse remarries or dies. And yet virtually all American statutes give the spouse a lump sum and take no account of later changes in circumstances.[30]

These objections to a fixed share do not all apply to the alternative rationale for the spouse's share, viz., recognition of the spouse's contributions to the estate. A spouse who helped to build up an estate can not properly be denied a share in it on the ground that the spouse is self-supporting. Nor

**25.** *Id.* at 16.

**26.** The advantage of trusts over alternative forms of property management are further explored in Section 9.2.

**27.** Montgomery v. Estate of Montgomery, 677 N.E.2d 571, 581 (Ind.App.1997).

**28.** E. Halbach ed., *Death, Taxes and Family Property* 111–12 (1977). *See also* Odham, *supra* note 14, at 229–30. As we shall see, some of these objections do not apply to the Uniform Probate Code. Section 3.7, at note 12 et seq.

**29.** Lemann, *In Defense of Forced Heirship,* 52 Tul.L.Rev. 20, 23–24 (1977). Professor Paul Haskell has proposed a similar scheme. Haskell, *The Power of Disinheritance: Proposal for Reform,* 52 Geo.L.J. 499, 519 (1964).

**30.** The family allowance provides a relatively unimportant exception to this statement. See 3.4.

should the decedent be allowed to put the spouse's share into a trust without the spouse's consent. However, if the spouse's contribution to the accumulation of property justifies the forced share, the share ought to depend upon the length of the marriage. If a marriage has lasted only a few weeks, the surviving spouse would have contributed very little to the decedent's estate, but would receive a large portion of it under most American statutes.

The family maintenance system which is common in the British commonwealth gives courts discretion to make awards from an estate to a spouse or child for whom the decedent's will fails to make adequate provision. The claimant's need is the primary determinant. The claimants' other resources, including earning capacity, are considered.[31] Awards can take the form of periodic payments which can be altered as needs change.[32] Need, however, is not the only factor; indeed, a spouse does not have to show need at all.[33] The contribution made by a spouse (including "looking after the home and caring for the family") and the length of the marriage are taken into account.[34] The "conduct" of an applicant may also be considered.

Even some fixed-share statutes provide that a claimant who engages in specified types of misconduct forfeits his share. A Louisiana statute allows a parent to disinherit a child for any of ten "just causes."[35] Some states bar spouses who have abandoned a decedent from claiming an elective share in the estate.[36] Such provisions go back to the Statute of Westminster of 1285 which provided that a wife who left her husband and lived in adultery lost her right to dower.[37] Courts tend to construe such statutes strictly, so as to avoid a "forfeiture."[38] And in the absence of a statutory provision, courts have refused to hold that desertion of the decedent bars a spouse's claims to an elective share.[39]

Discretionary statutes avoid many of the traditional objections to limitations on testamentary freedom. They do *not* disrupt intelligent estate plans by imposing an "inflexible blanket rule" modelled on the laws of intestate succession. In fact, they recognize that the intestacy statutes may be unsuitable, and allow courts to vary the statutory disposition in intestate estates.[40] Many American writers have urged that statutes of this type be adopted in the United States.[41] Others object that these statutes would promote litigation

**31.** English Inheritance (Provision for Family and Dependents) Act, 1975, § 3(1)(a), (6).

**32.** Laufer, *Flexible Restraints on Testamentary Freedom,* 69 Harv.L.Rev. 277, 293 (1955); New Zealand Family Protection Act, 1955, § 12; English Inheritance (Provision for Family and Dependents) Act, 1975, § 6.

**33.** *Id.* § 1(2).

**34.** *Id.* § 3(2).

**35.** La.Civ.Code art. 1621.

**36.** N.Y. EPTL § 5–1.2; Ind.Code § 29–1–2–15; N.C.Gen.Stat. § 31A–1.

**37.** Statute of Westminster II, 13 Edw. I, ch. 34.

**38.** In re Harris' Estate, 391 N.W.2d 487 (Mich.App.1986) (husband who occasionally visited his wife was not "absent" for a year, and so could claim an elective share). *See also* In re Estate of Kostick, 526 A.2d 746 (Pa. 1987); Estate of Calcutt v. Calcutt, 576 N.E.2d 1288 (Ind.App.1991); In re Estate of Montgomery, 528 S.E.2d 618 (N.C.App.2000) (wife who left her husband not barred without "repeated" acts of adultery).

**39.** Petition of Shiflett, 490 S.E.2d 902 (W.Va.1997); Estate of Miller v. Miller, 768 P.2d 373 (Okl.App.1988).

**40.** New Zealand, Family Protection Act, 1955, § 4; England, Inheritance (Provision for Family and Dependents) Act, 1975, § 1.

**41.** Laufer, *supra* note 32, at 27; Rein, *supra* note 9, at 47; Cahn, *supra* note 17, at 147; Niles, *Probate Reform in California,* 31 Hastings L.J. 185, 198–99 (1979).

because courts would be "without guideposts or rules."[42] But American courts regularly make similar discretionary determinations when they fix alimony and child support or divide property in divorce proceedings. For example, under the Uniform Marriage and Divorce Act, courts are to "equitably apportion" the spouses' property, considering among other things "the duration of the marriage ... employability, estate, liabilities, needs of each of the parties" and "the contribution or dissipation of each party" in their property.[43] The English Inheritance Act requires courts to treat the division of property at death and divorce in similar fashion.[44]

Discretionary statutes may lead to excessive litigation. But since wills which disinherit children or spouses are much rarer than divorce,[45] there would be few occasions to litigate under a discretionary statute designed to deal with this problem.[46] A statute giving redress to disinherited children might not actually increase the incidence of litigation in American law because disinherited children often contest wills on the ground that the testator was insane or subject to undue influence.[47]

Nevertheless, the drafters of the Uniform Probate Code rejected the idea of modeling the spouse's elective share on divorce law. Professor Waggoner has noted that "although all or most all states now follow the so-called equitable-distribution system upon divorce, there is considerable division among the states in the details," and thus the system was not compatible "with a uniform laws project striving to achieve uniformity within the probate system." Uniformity was important "in order to prevent a spouse bent on disinheritance from domicile shopping by relocating property to a state with fewer safeguards against this sort of behavior." Also, equitable distribution involves giving weight to fault in some states, and this is unfair "when death terminates the marriage [and] only the surviving spouse can testify as to ... fault."[48] Courts have rejected claims that the differences in legal treatment of the division of marital property upon divorce and death violate equal protection guarantees under the constitution.[49]

The drafters of the Uniform Probate Code were probably correct to conclude that "the consensus of national legal thinking would not accept a solution for the problem of spousal disinheritance that conferred so much discretion on the judicial system."[50] American legislatures have failed to adopt discretionary statutes on the model of the British commonwealth which some writers have proposed. The Supreme Court held that a statute requiring wills of Indian land to be "approved by the Secretary of the Interior" did not give the Secretary power to disapprove a will which disinherited the testator's

**42.** Chaffin, *supra* note 11, at 462.

**43.** Uniform Marriage and Divorce Act § 307 Also many American wrongful death statutes give courts broad discretion to distribute damages among the decedent's family. See Section 2.5, note 16 et seq.

**44.** Inheritance (Provision for Family and Dependants) Act, 1975, § 3(2).

**45.** Browder, *Recent Patterns of Testate Succession in the United States and England,* 67 Mich.L.Rev. 1303, 1305–08 (1969).

**46.** Plager, *The Spouse's Nonbarrable Share: A Solution in Search of a Problem,* 33 U.Chi.L.Rev. 681, 715 (1966).

**47.** Rein, *supra* note 9, at 54. As to incapacity and undue influence see Sections 7.1, 7.3.

**48.** Waggoner, *The Multiple Marriage Society*, 76 Iowa L.Rev. 223, 242–44 (1991).

**49.** Hamilton v. Hamilton, 879 S.W.2d 416 (Ark.1994).

**50.** Wellman, *Arkansas and the Uniform Probate Code,* 2 U. of Ark. at Little Rock L.J. 1, 13 (1979).

daughter "simply because of a subjective feeling that the disposition of the estate was not 'just and equitable.' "[51]

### *Inter–Vivos Transfers*

If one thinks that either spouses or children should be able to upset a will which disinherits them, should they also be allowed to attack transfers which the decedent made while alive? One might distinguish between transfers made for consideration and gifts. To upset sales would impede commerce and be unfair to purchasers who paid value. Moreover, the assets available for support of the seller's dependents are not depleted by a sale, since the sale proceeds take the place of the property sold. A right based on a spouse's contribution to the acquisition of property raises different considerations. Community property states, where the spouse's claim rests on a contribution theory, often allow one spouse to attack sales of community real property made by the other.[52] On the other hand, a spouse whose claim is predicated on the duty of support should not be allowed to dictate which assets are used to fulfill that duty so long as adequate support is provided. Thus the Uniform Probate Code allows a surviving spouse to attack only those lifetime transfers for which the decedent did not receive adequate consideration.[53]

Perhaps even donees should be protected from some claims of the donor's family. Small gifts, like ordinary Christmas presents, should not be subject to attack.[54] Even as to more substantial gifts, donees may be unfairly prejudiced if they are made to return property which was given to them many years earlier. Many states, therefore, only allow surviving spouses a share of the property which the decedent owned at death. But the line between transfers during life and those which take effect at death is often blurred. How should one classify a gift made by a husband two days before he died? Or a trust created by a wife under which she reserved the income for her life and a power to revoke the trust until she died? In recent years such "will substitutes," which purport to be present gifts but which have virtually no effect until death, have become increasingly popular. They were originally not encompassed by the family maintenance statutes of the British Commonwealth,[55] but recent amendments have given courts power to reach them.[56] American law in many states now allow spouses to reach transfers made during life which are will-like in substance.[57]

**51.** Tooahnippah v. Hickel, 397 U.S. 598, 610 (1970).

**52.** Neumann v. McMillan, 629 P.2d 1214 (Nev.1981); Padilla v. Roller, 608 P.2d 1116 (N.M.1980); Rev.Code Wash. § 26.16.030; Cal. Fam.Code § 1102 (real property).

**53.** Uniform Probate Code § 2–208(a). *See also* Inheritance Act, 1975, § 10(2) (allowing court to reach property transferred within 6 years of death where the transferee did not give "full valuable consideration").

**54.** Even in community property states, small gifts of community property by one spouse are often allowed. La.Stat.Ann.Civ.Code art. 2349; Horlock v. Horlock, 533 S.W.2d 52 (Tex.Civ.App.1975); Redfearn v. Ford, 579 S.W.2d 295 (Tex.Civ.App.1979).

**55.** Laufer, *supra* note 32, at 299.

**56.** English Inheritance (Provision for Family and Dependents) Act, 1975, § 8–10.

**57.** See Section 3.7, at note 21 et seq.

## § 3.2 Historical and Comparative Law

### *Land*

Wills of land and personal property followed different paths historically. Originally the common law limited a parent's right to give away land. Distinctions were made between land which the parent had acquired as distinguished from inherited, and between gifts within the family and gifts to strangers.[1] These rules disappeared early in the 13th century,[2] probably because the rise of primogeniture, under which all a parent's land descended to the eldest son, created great pressure to allow parents to make gifts to younger children.[3]

The freedom acquired by parents in the 13th century to transfer land did not extend to wills. Land could not be devised by will at common law until the Statute of Wills of 1540.[4] Blackstone attributes this rule to feudalism. "Before the [Norman] conquest [of 1066 which introduced feudalism into England], lands were devisable by will. But, upon the introduction of the military tenures, the restraint of devising lands naturally took place, as a branch of the feodal doctrine of non-alienation without the consent of the lord. * * * The reason of conferring the feud being the personal abilities of the feudatory to serve in war, it was not fit that he should be at liberty to transfer this gift * * * to others who might prove less able."[5] This explanation is reminiscent of the modern rule which allows landlords to restrain alienation by tenants under a lease.[6] However, there are difficulties with Blackstone's explanation. The feudal lord's concern with the personal abilities of tenants would apply to all transfers of land without the lord's consent, but in 1290 the statute Quia Emptores allowed tenants to alienate their land inter vivos without the lord's permission,[7] whereas the prohibition on devises continued for another two and a half centuries.

The feudal opposition to wills existed in the later Middle Ages, but it did not focus on the lord's concern with the "personal abilities" of the tenant, but rather on the feudal incidents such as wardship which gave lords the profits of land when it descended to a minor heir of the tenant. If tenants could make wills they could avoid wardship by devising land away from a minor heir.

For Glanville, the prohibition against wills was a logical consequence of the rule that land could only be transferred by delivery, commonly known as livery of seisin.[8] The law required delivery probably because jury trial originally depended upon neighbors who relied on their own knowledge in rendering verdicts rather than the testimony of witnesses produced in court. If possession of land was not delivered to the donee, the neighbors would not learn of the gift. A will takes effect only when the testator dies, and so is incompatible with delivery. Juries knew who had been in possession of land but were not competent to decide whether a decedent had made a will.[9] Only the church

**§ 3.2**

**1.** R. Glanville, *Tractatus de Legibus 69–71* (G. Hall ed. 1965).

**2.** A claim that a father could not give away all his inheritance seems to have been accepted in 6 Curia Regis Rolls 201 (1212), but was rejected in 13 Curia Regis Rolls pl. 1588 (1229).

**3.** T. Plucknett, *A Concise History of the Common Law* 528 (5th ed. 1956); Simes, *Public Policy and the Dead Hand* 10–11 (1955).

**4.** Glanville, *supra* note 1, at 69–70.

**5.** 2 W. Blackstone, *Commentaries* 57,373 (1765).

**6.** See Section 11.8, notes 32–33.

**7.** 18 Edw. 1, c. 1 (1290). For the background of this statute see D. Sutherland, *The Assize of Novel Disseisin* 86–95 (1973).

**8.** Glanville, *supra* note 1, at 69.

**9.** Plucknett, *supra* note 3, at 736.

courts, which did not employ jury trial, could pass on wills.[10] But the common law never allowed church courts to deal with *land.*[11] Thus the medieval prohibition on wills of land rested on the inadequacy of the jury, the only form of trial known to the common law courts, and the fact that they had exclusive jurisdiction over land.

***Uses***

The prohibition on devises was evaded in the later Middle Ages by uses which were common in the 15th century. If John wanted to devise land to Arthur, he would deliver seisin to Tom and Dick "to the use" of John's last will and declare in his will that the land should pass to Arthur when John died. If Tom and Dick failed to carry out John's will the Chancellor would compel them to do so. Why? Blackstone said the Chancellors enforced wills because they were almost all ecclesiastics who wanted to foster devises for religious purposes: "as the popish clergy then generally sat in the court of chancery, they considered that men * * * at their death would choose to dispose of [their land] to those who, according to the superstition of the times, could intercede for their happiness in another world."[12] However, most 15th century wills were designed to provide for the testator's wife or younger children rather than the church.[13] Landowners wanted to make wills to provide for their families better than the rules of intestate succession, which, because of primogeniture were even worse than today's rules. The inadequacy of juries to try wills was irrelevant because the Chancellor did not rely on juries; he examined witnesses under oath to ascertain the testator's intent.[14]

In the early 16th century, Henry VIII sought to end uses in order to maximize his revenue as a feudal lord from wardships. He induced the judges (who at this time held office at the King's pleasure) to hold that the devise of a use was "void."[15] This decision unsettled titles to much of the land in England, which for more than a century had been passing by such devises, and led Parliament to enact the famous Statute of Uses which validated all wills previously made, but effectually barred wills thereafter by providing that when land was held in use the legal title should pass to the beneficiary of the use.[16] This made it impossible to evade the common-law prohibition on wills.

The preamble of the Statute reiterated many of the arguments which Glanville had made against wills 350 years before. They were "for the most part made by such persons as be visited with sickness, in their extreme agonies and pains * * * at which times they * * * dispose indiscreetly and unadvisedly their lands." They injured both lords and heirs: "many heirs have been unjustly * * * disinherited, the lords have lost their wards" and other feudal incidents.

**10.** Glanville, *supra* note 1, at 81.

**11.** 2 Bracton, *De Legibus* 70, 149; Plucknett, *supra* note 3, at 737.

**12.** 2 W. Blackstone, *Commentaries* *375 (1765).

**13.** *See* K. Digby, *Introduction to the History of the Law of Real Property* 333–36 (4th ed. 1892); A. Kiralfy, *A Source Book of English Law* 266–67 (1957).

**14.** *Ibid.* Juries today are often used to try facts in will contests, see Section 12.1, at note 47, but for centuries juries' knowledge of the facts has depended on evidence produced in court rather than their own knowledge.

**15.** Re Lord Dacre, 93 Sel.Soc. 228 (1536).

**16.** Statute of Uses, 27 Hen. 8, c. 10, § 9 (1536).

The abolition of wills produced a strong outcry. In an uprising in 1536 the rebels demanded that the Statute of Uses be repealed.[17] Henry VIII had to consent to the Statute of Wills of 1540 which allowed wills, but protected the interests of feudal lords to some extent. A person who held land by knight service could only dispose of two-thirds of it; as to the other third, the lord's right to wardship and other feudal incidents was expressly preserved.[18] This limitation on wills became obsolete in 1660 when the feudal incidents were abolished.[19]

### *Personal Property*

Feudal considerations did not apply to personal property, which originally was much less important than land, although today the opposite is true. The common law conceded jurisdiction over testaments of personal property to the church courts, which did not employ jury trial, and allowed wills. There were, however, limitations on a testator's right to disinherit completely his wife[20] and children. In the 12th century a decedent's moveables were divided into three equal parts, one for his children, one for his wife, and a third "over which he has free power of disposition." If the testator died without a wife he could dispose of half of his personalty.[21] Bracton restated these rules in the next century, but said that they did not apply if there was a local custom to the contrary.[22]

In the later Middle Ages the situation described by Bracton came to be reversed. Freedom of testation became the general rule, and a wife or children who sought a forced share had to allege a local custom. This change is puzzling since canon law scholars had accepted the Roman law principle "that a child had a *de iure* share in the estate of his or her parent," but by the end of the fourteenth century this "had been reduced to the level of a local rather than a national custom, and had largely ceased to be in force."[23] All local customs restricting testamentary freedom were eliminated by statutes in the late 17th and early 18th centuries.[24]

Before then, the differing rules in different localities had allowed evasion of local restrictions.[25] A similar problem exists in the United States today. Our 50 jurisdictions offer opportunities for a determined parent or spouse to evade any restrictions on testamentary freedom. This deters states from imposing restrictions which may simply encourage a flight of property to jurisdictions where testamentary freedom is unimpaired.[26]

**17.** Plucknett, *supra* note 3, at 587.

**18.** Statute of Wills, 32 Henry 8, c. 1, § 4 (1540). The power of devising land held by "socage" tenure was not limited because wardship did not apply to socage tenure, since "no military or other personal service being required, there was no occasion for the lord to take the profits in order to provide a proper substitute for his infant tenants." 2 W. Blackstone, *Commentaries* *87–88 (1765).

**19.** Statute, 12 Car. 2, c. 24, § 1 (1660).

**20.** At common law a husband acquired title to his wife's personal property upon marriage, 2 W. Blackstone, *Commentaries* *433 (1765). Therefore there was no occasion to consider the wife's right to disinherit her husband.

**21.** Glanville, *supra* note 1, at 80.

**22.** 2 Bracton, *supra* note 11, at 180–81.

**23.** Helmholz, *Legitim in English Legal History,* [1984] U. of Ill.L.Rev. 659, 660, 667. However, church courts provided some protection to children who were needy. *Id.* at 669–70.

**24.** 2 W. Blackstone, *Commentaries* *492–93 (1765).

**25.** Statute, 11 Geo. 1, c. 18, § 1 (1724).

**26.** As to the rules governing choice of law see Section 1.2.

### *Modern British Law*

In the British Commonwealth, instead of the medieval fixed share, modern legislatures, beginning with New Zealand in 1900[27] have established discretionary controls to protect spouses and children. These have been described in the preceding section. The New Zealand Family Protection Act of 1955 also allows claims by parents. The English statute includes, in addition to spouses and children, step-children who were "treated by the deceased as a child," former spouses, and any other person who was "being maintained" by the decedent.[28]

### *Civil Law*

The fixed share for children which Glanville and Bracton described still exists today in a modified form throughout much of the world. A "testator is required under Islamic inheritance law to leave various heirs, including distant relatives, specified percentages of his wealth."[29] The French Civil Code of 1804 prescribed fixed shares in order to prevent parents from reinstituting primogeniture by leaving all their property to the eldest son; to the leaders of the French Revolution primogeniture was associated with aristocracy and was contrary to their egalitarian ideals.[30] The share reserved for children, known as the *legitime,* varies with the number of children: a parent with one child can dispose of half his estate, but if there are three children the disposable share is only one fourth.[31] Even if a testator has no children, a share is reserved for any surviving ascendants (parents, grandparents, etc.)[32] The *legitime* is protected against *inter vivos* gifts as well as wills,[33]but insurance is exempt; if a parent designates a stranger as beneficiary of an insurance policy, the children cannot claim a share of the proceeds.[34]

Louisiana once had similar rules, but they have been watered down considerably in recent years. Since 1981 only descendants of the decedent, and since 1995, only children who are under age 24 or "who, because of mental incapacity or physical infirmity, are incapable of taking care of" themselves, are protected.[35] In Louisiana, unlike France, a child can be disinherited for twelve specified "just causes" which must be set forth in the will.[36] A parent

**27.** Laufer, *Flexible Restraints on Testamentary Freedom,* 69 Harv.L.Rev. 277, 281 (1955).

**28.** Inheritance (Provision for Family and Dependants) Act, 1975, § 1(1).

**29.** Schoenblum, *The Role of Legal Doctrine in the Decline of the Islamic Waqf: A Comparison with the Trust,* 32 Vand.J. Transnational Law 1191, 1196 (1999).

**30.** H. Maine, *Ancient Law* 187 (World Classics ed. 1931). The original Revolutionary legislation was quite restrictive; a person with children could devise only a tenth of his property. J. Brissaud, *A History of French Private Law* § 518, at 747 (R. Howell tr. 1912).

**31.** French Code Civil art. 913. A larger share can be left to the testator's spouse for life. *Id.* art. 1094–1.

**32.** *Id.* art. 914.

**33.** *Id.* art. 923.

**34.** Amos & Walton, *Introduction to French Law* 338 (3d ed. 1967).

**35.** An earlier attempt by the legislature to limit forced heirship to such children was held unconstitutional in Succession of Lauga, 624 So.2d 1156 (La.1993). The constitutional protection of forced heirship was thereafter limited in 1995. La. Const. Art. 12, § 5. The forced share is one-half if there are two or more children, one-fourth if there is only one child. La.Civ.Code art. 1495.

**36.** *Id.* art. 1621. These have given rise to a considerable amount of litigation. Succession of Del Buno, 665 So.2d 172 (La.App.1995) (disinheritance for failure to communicate with testator upheld); In re Succession of Gray, 736 So.2d 902 (La.App.1999) (same); Succession of Cure, 633 So.2d 590 (La.App.1993) (same); Ambrose Succession v. Ambrose, 548 So.2d 37 (La.App.1989) (disinheritance for "cruelty" allowed); Succession of Steckler, 665 So.2d 561

can put the child's forced share into a trust.[37] Louisiana also restricts inter vivos gifts, but there are several exceptions.[38]

Since forced heirship is common in many other parts of the world, American courts have had to deal with choice of law problems which it raises. They "have displayed a marked propensity to latch on to any respectable theory that will defeat rights of forced heirship."[39] For example, when the will of a French domiciliary executed in Paris disinheriting her son, provided that it should be "regulated by the laws of the State of New York," a New York court denied the son's claim to a *legitime*, saying that there was "a significant distinction between enforcing a * * * spouse's elective share, which differs only in degree from our own law * * * and enforcing a descendant's forced share which runs counter to our local policy." [40]

## § 3.3 Claims for Support

Litigation raising the issue whether a father's duty to support a child survives his death rarely arises when the father is married to the child's mother when he dies. Usually the father leaves all or most of his estate to the mother. If he does not, the mother in most states can claim a share of it. The mother will use the property she receives plus her own property to support the child. Indeed she can be compelled to do so since mothers are also obligated to support their children.[1]

But if parents are divorced when the father dies, or if they were never married, the mother is not a "surviving spouse" entitled to a share of his estate. Fathers' wills often do not provide for children by a former marriage or born out of wedlock. Normally at the time of divorce, the father is ordered or agrees to make payments for the child's support. Does this obligation survive the father's death? This may depend on the terms of the agreement or divorce decree; if it is silent, the obligation to make future payments expires at death in some states, but not in all. For example, a father who was obligated by an Indiana divorce decree to pay child support died in Ohio while the children were still minors.[2] Under Ohio law, his obligation terminated at death[3], since the divorce decree made no provision for this,[4] but under Indiana law, the obligation continued.[5] This gave rise to the further question whether

(La.App.1995) (disinheritance disallowed, since child had sent parent two Christmas cards).

**37.** Lorio, *Louisiana Trusts: The Experience of a Civil Law Jurisdiction with the Trust,* 42 La.L.Rev. 1721, 1735–36 (1982).

**38.** La.Civ.Code art. 1508 (heir can only reach gifts made within 3 years of death); art. 1511 (sales excluded unless price is less than 2/3 of value).

**39.** 1 J. Schoenblum, *Multistate and Multinational Estate Planning* § 12.02.4, at 358 (1982).

**40.** Estate of Renard, 439 N.E.2d 341 (N.Y. 1982). *See also* Sanchez v. Sanchez De Davila, 547 So.2d 943 (Fla.App.1989) (claim to forced heirship under Venezuela law of bank account in Florida); Matter of Estate of Wright, 637 A.2d 106 (Me.1994) (claim under Swiss law rejected where will said Maine law should govern).

§ 3.3

**1.** H. Clark, *The Law of Domestic Relations* § 6.2 (1968); Cal.Family Code § 3900 (father and mother have equal responsibility to support their child).

**2.** Barnett v. Barnett, 619 N.E.2d 38 (Ohio App.1993).

**3.** However, accrued claims for support due at death can be enforced from the obligor's estate. Connin v. Bailey, 472 N.E.2d 328 (Ohio App.1984).

**4.** Compare Gulford v. Wurster, 493 N.E.2d 258 (Ohio App.1983) (construing support obligation in a separation agreement to survive death).

**5.** *See also* Marriage of Perry, 68 Cal. Rptr.2d 445 (App.1997) ("a child support obligation survives the death of a parent and is a charge against his or her estate"); Kiken v.

the Indiana decree would be given effect in Ohio. Ordinarily judgments which are subject to modification (as support orders typically are) are not entitled to full faith and credit, but this limitation did not apply to accrued claims for support which were due at death.[6]

A recent Massachusetts case held that an order in a paternity action against the father of a child born out of wedlock to support the child until he reached majority created an obligation enforceable against the father's estate.[7]

Many of the traditional justifications for freedom of testation do not apply in this situation. The disinheritance of children here is not merely the "technical" one which occurs when a spouse leaves everything to the other parent of the decedent's children. The disadvantage of guardianship for minors is irrelevant since support payments typically go to the mother for the benefit of the children.[8] Reluctance to confer discretion on courts is not a valid objection to enforcing a duty of support which was fixed at the time of the divorce. However, some sort of a discretionary adjustment in a prior support order may be called for by the changed circumstances produced by the parent's death.

Death usually changes the financial circumstances of the parties. Life insurance proceeds or Social Security benefits may render continuation of the support payments no longer necessary. For example, when a father who was obligated to pay monthly child support of $304 died, the child began receiving Social Security payments of $768 as a result of the father's death. Although this was held not to extinguish the father's obligation, the executor of his estate could seek to have it modified because of the changed circumstances.[9] If a father has remarried and incurred obligations to a new family, enforcing his duty to support his children by the prior marriage might deplete his estate at the expense of his new dependents.[10]

The Uniform Marriage and Divorce Act attempts to reconcile these competing considerations: provisions in a divorce decree or agreement for child support are not terminated by the death of the obligated parent (unless the decree so provides), but the "amount of support may be modified * * * to the extent just and appropriate in the circumstances."[11]

This statute only protects children of a testator who has been divorced. A claim that this was an unconstitutional denial of equal protection was rejected

Kiken, 694 A.2d 557 (N.J.1997) (same). For further statutes and cases on both sides of this question see Oldham, *What Does the U.S. System Regarding Inheritance Rights of Children Reveal about American Families?* 33 Family L.Q. 265, 271 (1999).

**6.** *Accord*, Adair v. Martin, 595 S.W.2d 513 (Tex.1980).

**7.** L.W.K. v. E.R.C., 735 N.E.2d 359 (Mass. 2000).

**8.** H. Clark, *The Law of Domestic Relations* § 15.1, at 490 (1968); L.W.K v. E.R.C., 735 N.E.2d 359, 362 (Mass.2000).

**9.** In re Marriage of Bertrand, 39 Cal. Rptr.2d 151 (App.1995). Courts have responded to this situation in various ways. In re Marriage of Meek, 669 P.2d 628 (Colo.App. 1983) (proper to terminate support obligation because of Social Security benefits); Gilford v. Wurster, 493 N.E.2d 258 (Ohio App.1983) (Social Security payments credited to obligation); Berg v. D.D.M., 603 N.W.2d 361, 367 (Minn. App.1999) (same); Pessein v. Pessein, 846 P.2d 1385 (Wash.App.1993) (obligation is not reduced by Social Security payments); Estate of Brummett v. Brummett, 472 N.E.2d 616 (Ind. App.1984) (proper not to reduce support obligation because of Social Security benefits).

**10.** H. Clark, *The Law of Domestic Relations* § 15.3, at 506 (1968).

**11.** Uniform Marriage and Divorce Act § 316(c). In Matter of Marriage of Perry, 68 Cal.Rptr.2d 445 (App.1997) a child support order was revised upward to reflect the end of the father's personal needs with his death.

on the ground that disinheritance by parents who have not been divorced is alleviated by the other parent's right to a share of the decedent's estate.[12] A similar argument was used to justify protection for a child born out of wedlock.[13]

### *Alimony*

The duty to pay alimony to a former spouse usually ceases when the payor dies,[14] but an agreement may provide otherwise, either expressly or by implication.[15] For example, an agreement to pay annual support until a wife remarried or died was held to create a claim against the husband's estate, since the explicit "criteria for termination were remarriage or death of the ex-wife," not the husband's death.[16] But another court rejected this reasoning, saying that when an agreement contains "no unequivocal direction to pay after death, * * * the preference that maintenance obligations terminate upon death of the payor should ordinarily prevail." But the court refused to grant summary judgment for the husband's estate; since the wife had not been represented by counsel when the separation agreement was drafted, "the omission of the recommended and customary explicit clause providing for the circumstance of the death of the payor ... ought not to be deemed ... a complete or reliable manifestation of intent for both contracting parties."[17]

Lawyers who negotiate a divorce settlement which provides for support payments should anticipate that the payor may die while the children or spouse still need support. A provision in an agreement or divorce decree for continuation of payments from the obligor's estate is not an adequate solution, because the estate may be inadequate—even if the obligor currently earns a high income, that income will cease at death. Also, it is generally undesirable to keep an estate open to continue periodic payments. The Uniform Marriage and Divorce Act deals with the latter problem by allowing an obligation to be "commuted into a lump sum payment."[18] Many divorce settlements require a parent to maintain or procure life insurance for the benefit of children whom the divorcing parent is obligated to support.[19] The California Family Code provides that unless otherwise agreed, obligations to support a spouse terminate "upon the death of either party"[20], but a court

**12.** Kujawinski v. Kujawinski, 376 N.E.2d 1382 (Ill.1978).

**13.** L.W.K. v. E.R.C., 735 N.E.2d 359, 366 (Mass.2000).

**14.** Hendricks v. Hendricks, 817 P.2d 1339 (Or.App.1991); Prim v. Prim, 754 S.W.2d 609 (Tenn.1988); Barron v. Puzo, 610 N.E.2d 973 (Mass.1993); Dolvin v. Dolvin, 284 S.E.2d 254 (Ga.1981).

**15.** Dogu v. Dogu, 652 P.2d 1308 (Utah 1982); In re Estate of Dahlstrom, 992 P.2d 1256 (Kan.App.1999); In re Last Will and Testament of Sheppard, 757 So.2d 173 (Miss. 2000).

**16.** Lipe v. Lipe, 728 P.2d 1124 (Wyo.1986). *See also* Cohen v. Cronin, 346 N.E.2d 524 (N.Y.1976); In re Estate of Bartlett, 485 N.E.2d 566 (Ill.App.1985).

**17.** Matter of Riconda, 688 N.E.2d 248, 252–53 (N.Y.1997).

**18.** Uniform Marriage and Divorce Act § 316(c).

**19.** In re Estate of Downey, 687 N.E.2d 339 (Ill.App.1997) (noting a conflict in the cases as to whether a court could order such a provision, but clearly "the parties may voluntarily agree to do so"); Smithberg v. Illinois Mun. Retirement Fund, 716 N.E.2d 316 (Ill.App. 1999) (death benefits under pension plan paid to ex-wife pursuant to divorce decree).

**20.** Cal. Family Code § 4337. However, under § 3952, if a parent with a support obligation dies leaving a *child* "chargeable to the county or ... confined in a state institution," the county or state can get reimbursement from the parent's estate.

Uniform Marriage and Divorce Act § 316 also distinguishes between "maintenance" of a spouse, which terminates on the death of either party, and "support" for a child, which is

may order payment of an amount "sufficient to purchase an annuity ... or to maintain insurance for the benefit of the supported spouse on the life of the spouse required to make the payment of support" or to establish a trust for support.[21] Such a provision can provide security that the claim will be paid,[22] and it also avoids having to keep an estate open.

## § 3.4 Family Allowance and Homestead

### *Family Allowance*

A decedent's assets are frozen for a substantial period while the estate is administered. During this period claims against the estate are ascertained and paid.[1] Until this is done one cannot know how much will be left in the estate; it may prove to be insolvent. But the decedent's family cannot be left to starve while the claims of creditors are ascertained, so the law provides an allowance for their support during administration. The idea is as old as Magna Carta which provided that widows could remain in their husband's home for forty days after his death while their dower was being assigned to them.[2]

The family allowance provides for the decedent's spouse and children. Some statutes give allowances only to minor children,[3] but the Uniform Probate Code covers "minor children whom the decedent was obligated to support and children who were in fact being supported by him."[4] The allowance is paid to the surviving spouse "for the use of" the children, but if a child is not living with the spouse, "the allowance may be made partially to the child or his guardian or other person having his care and custody."[5]

The size of the allowance varies. The Uniform Probate Code gives "a reasonable allowance."[6] According to the comment, "account should be taken of the previous standard of living." An Illinois statute says that the allowance shall be "suited to the condition in life of the surviving spouse and to the

"terminated by the emancipation of the child but not by the death of the parent."

**21.** Cal.Family Code § 4360. *See also* Porter v. Porter, 526 N.E.2d 219 (Ind.App.1988) (proper to order husband to take out insurance on his life for the support of his children); In re Marriage of Perry, 68 Cal.Rptr.2d 445 (App. 1997) (support payments ordered from trust created by father before his death); Benson v. Benson, 977 P.2d 88, 94–5 (Alaska 1999) (proper to order father who had been dilatory in making support payments to create a trust to satisfy them).

**22.** But if the father who is obligated to keep insurance in force nevertheless allows the policy to lapse, it may be necessary to enforce the claim against his probate estate. Tintocalis v. Tintocalis, 25 Cal.Rptr.2d 655 (App.1993); Kiltz v. Kiltz, 708 N.E.2d 600 (Ind.App.1999). For further discussion of this issue see Section 13.2, at note 38.

**§ 3.4**

**1.** For the payment of claims against an estate see Section 13.3.

**2.** Magna Carta cap. 7 (1215). For modern reflections of the widow's "quarantine" see Matter of Estate of Stroh, 392 N.W.2d 192 (Mich.App.1986) (widow entitled to remain in home rent-free until dower assigned); Mass. Gen.Laws ch. 196, § 1 (spouse can remain in house for 6 months rent-free); Cal.Prob.Code § 6500 (spouse and minor children can remain in dwelling until 60 days after inventory is filed).

**3.** Tex.Prob.Code § 286; Ohio Rev.Code § 2106.13; Ga.Code § 53–3–2; Md.Estates and Trusts Code § 3–201(b).

**4.** Uniform Probate Code § 2–404. *See also* 755 ILCS 5/15–1(a) (minor and adult dependent children); Calif.Prob.Code § 6540 (includes adult dependent children and parents); Or.Rev.Stat. § 114.015; *cf.* In re Estate of Degner, 518 N.E.2d 400 (Ill.App.1987) ("dependent" includes a child unable to support herself even though decedent had not been supporting her).

**5.** Uniform Probate Code § 2–404. *Cf.* 755 ILCS 5/15–2(a) (award to child not residing with spouse goes to "such person as the court directs").

**6.** Uniform Prob.Code § 2–404. Cal. Prob. Code § 6540 is similar.

condition of the estate."[7] The allowance can be very substantial if the estate is large and the claimants were accustomed to "the finer things of life."[8]

If the spouse and children have sufficient other resources, the Texas Probate Code bars them from receiving a family allowance.[9] The Uniform Probate Code is less clear on this.[10] Some courts draw a distinction between a spouse's independent means, which do not bar an award, and benefits derived from the decedent which do.[11] Some courts also consider a spouse's earning capacity in fixing the award.[12] A spouse's remarriage precludes receiving an award in some states.[13]

Some statutes fix the amount of the family allowance, leaving nothing to the court's discretion,[14] and others provide for a minimum award.[15] The Uniform Probate Code allows the decedent's personal representative to determine the allowance at up to $18,000, but a court may order a smaller or larger allowance on petition by an interested person.[16] Where statutes designate a specific amount, inflation may make it unrealistic as time goes by unless it is revised.[17]

Once a trial court has fixed the family allowance, appeals from its decision rarely succeed.[18] Since the allowance is designed to meet immediate needs of the decedent's family, extensive and time-consuming appellate review is inappropriate.[19]

The American family allowance resembles family maintenance legislation in the British Commonwealth, but the American allowance provides support only "during the period of administration" of the estate.[20]

**7.** 755 ILCS 5/15–1.

**8.** William Randolph Hearst's widow was awarded an allowance of $10,000 per month. T. Atkinson, *Handbook of the Law of Wills* 134 (2d ed. 1953). Compare Howard v. Howard, 257 S.E.2d 336 (Ga.App.1979) ($25,000 awarded to widow for "year's support"); Matter of Estate of Hamilton, 869 P.2d 971 (Utah App. 1994) ($1,000 a month for 24 months); Matter of Estate of Lettengarver, 813 P.2d 468 (Mont. 1991) ($6,000 award).

**9.** Tex.Prob.Code § 288. *Cf.* Calif.Prob.Code § 6540(c) (claimants "without reasonable maintenance from other sources" are given preference). Compare the consideration of other resources in determining support needs in trusts for support, discussed in Section 9.5, at note 45 et seq.

**10.** "Account should be taken of .. the nature of other resources available ... If the surviving spouse has a substantial income, this may be taken into account. Whether life insurance proceeds ... were intended by the decedent to be used for the period of adjustment or to be conserved as capital may be considered." Uniform Probate Code § 2–404, comment. *Cf.* In re Estate of Wentworth, 452 N.W.2d 714 (Minn.App.1990) (proper to deny allowance to spouse with other means of support); Matter of Estate of Wheat, 955 P.2d 1339 (Kan.App. 1998) (proper to deny allowance to spouse and children who received substantial life insurance proceeds).

**11.** Matter of Estate of Caffrey, 458 N.E.2d 1147 (Ill.App.1983). In Matter of Estate of Parkhill, 548 N.E.2d 821 (Ill.App.1989), a widower was given the minimum allowance because he had received over $249,000 from assets held in joint tenancy with the decedent.

**12.** In re Estate of O'Neill, 432 N.E.2d 1111 (Ill.App.1982); Ga.Code § 53–3–7(c)(1).

**13.** *Id.* § 53–3–2(a).

**14.** Md.Estates and Trusts Code § 3–201 ($5,000 for spouse and $2,500 for each minor child); Ohio Code § 2106.13 ($25,000); Ind. Code § 29–1–4–1 ($8,500).

**15.** 755 ILCS 5/15–1 ($10,000 to spouse plus $5,000 for each eligible child).

**16.** Uniform Prob.Code § 2–404.

**17.** The UPC guideline was raised from $6,000 to $18,000 in 1990. Uniform Probate Code § 2–405, Comment.

**18.** In re Marriage of Meek, 669 P.2d 628 (Colo.App.1983); Matter of Estate of Bowman's, 609 P.2d 663 (Idaho 1980); Matter of Estate of Buhler, 607 P.2d 956 (Ariz.1980); Matter of Estate of Lettengarver, 813 P.2d 468 (Mont.1991).

**19.** *See* Calif.Prob.Code § 6545 (no stay of payment of family allowance pending appeal).

**20.** Uniform Probate Code § 2–404. *See also* Cal.Prob.Code § 6543 (allowance terminates when estate is distributed); Matter of

Many statutes, including the Uniform Probate Code, provide that the allowance may be paid in installments. Payments cease if a recipient dies before all the installments are paid according to the UPC,[21] but in some states any unpaid family allowance passes to the spouse's estate.[22]

The family allowance takes precedence over nearly all claims against the estate; in this respect it provides more protection to spouses than the elective share, which is based on the net estate.[23] However, the family allowance may be limited if an estate is insolvent. Under the Uniform Probate Code the allowance "may not continue for longer than one year if the estate is inadequate to discharge allowed claims."[24]

The family allowance is payable only out of assets which the decedent owned, and if the decedent's property was mortgaged or held in trust, the rights of the mortgagee or trust beneficiary are superior.[25] Although the family allowance is usually payable only out of the probate estate, the Uniform Probate Code allows many non-probate assets (*e.g.* joint bank accounts) to be reached to pay the family allowance if the probate estate is insolvent.[26] Other non-probate assets such as life insurance are not reachable to satisfy the family allowance, however.[27] As we shall see, the rights of a spouse to satisfy the elective share from such assets are more extensive.[28]

The family of a decedent is entitled to an allowance even if they are disinherited by the decedent's will. If the will provides for them, they can take under the will and claim an allowance too, unless the will expressly provides that they must elect between the two.[29] In this respect also, the family allowance differs from the typical elective share.[30]

Estate of Bell, 833 P.2d 294 (Okl.App.1992). This is not true in Maine. *See* Me.Rev.Stat. tit. 18–A, § 2–403.

**21.** Uniform Probate Code § 2–404(b).

**22.** 755 ILCS 5/15–1; Tex.Prob.Code § 287; Matter of Estate of Gray, 505 N.E.2d 806 (Ind. App.1987). This seems inconsistent with the support rationale of the family allowance, but it allows the allowance to qualify for the federal estate tax marital deduction. Estate of Radel, 88 T.C. 1143 (1987).

**23.** Uniform Probate Code § 2–404; *cf.* Cal. Prob. Code § 11420; Estate of Rosenberger, 495 N.W.2d 234 (Minn.App.1993); Timothy C. Wirt, M.D., P.C. v. Prout, 754 P.2d 429 (Colo. App.1988); Matter of Estate of Wilhelm, 760 P.2d 718 (Mont.1988).

**24.** Uniform Prob.Code § 2–404(a). *See also* Calif.Prob.Code § 6543; Or.Rev.Stat. § 114.065. In Matter of Estate of Caffrey, 458 N.E.2d 1147 (Ill.App.1983) an award was reduced when it appeared it would render the estate insolvent.

**25.** Parson v. Parson, 56 Cal.Rptr.2d 686 (App.1996); Matter of Estate of Epstein, 561 N.W.2d 82, 87 (Iowa App.1996); Hughes v. Hughes, 314 S.E.2d 920 (Ga.App.1984).

**26.** Uniform Probate Code § 6–102; Matter of Estate of Wagley, 760 P.2d 316 (Utah 1988). *See also* Kroslack v. Estate of Kroslack, 504 N.E.2d 1024 (Ind.1987). For the right of creditors to reach non-probate assets see Section 13.2.

**27.** In re Estate of Agans, 998 P.2d 449 (Ariz.App.1999). The comment to Uniform Probate Code § 6–102 says that it is designed not to conflict "with existing legislation protecting death benefits in life insurance . . . from claims by creditors." As to this exemption see Section 13.2, at note 32 et seq.

**28.** See Section 3.7. at note 29 et seq.

**29.** Uniform Prob.Code § 2–404(b); 755 ILCS 5/15–1(b); Sanders v. Pierce, 979 S.W.2d 457 (Ky.App.1998) (widow's exemption); Russell v. Hall, 266 S.E.2d 491 (Ga.1980); *cf.* In re Estate of Reddick, 657 N.E.2d 531 (Ohio App. 1995) (will put spouse to an election). If the decedent had no will, the family allowance is not charged against the recipient's intestate share. Matter of Estate of Bowman's, 609 P.2d 663 (Idaho 1980).

**30.** See Section 3.7, at note 46 et seq.

### *Homestead; Exempt Property*

The Uniform Probate Code has two other provisions for spouses and children, a "homestead allowance" and one for "exempt property." Exemptions from execution existed at common law, but homestead is a uniquely American contribution which goes back to a statute of the Republic of Texas enacted in 1839.[31] Homestead and exempt property, like the family allowance, take precedence over claims of creditors and any will of the decedent.[32] The amounts involved are relatively small. The UPC homestead allowance gives the spouse $15,000, and, if there is no surviving spouse, the same amount is divided among the "minor and dependent" children.[33] The award of exempt property is only $10,000.[34] However, these amounts are not dependent upon need.[35]

In some states, homestead is more substantial.[36] The Arkansas Constitution provides a homestead of up to one-quarter acre of land in cities and 80 acres elsewhere without regard to value, but widows only get a life estate and children only a right to the income until they are 21.[37] Moreover, homestead is available only if the decedent owned a residence; a family living in rental property derives no benefit.[38] The homestead and exempt property allowance under the Uniform Probate Code, on the other hand, do not depend on the type of property in the decedent's estate. "The shift to money substitute protects all surviving spouses and minor children, regardless of whether the decedent owned real estate or merely leased it."[39]

Some homestead laws protect children,[40] but under the UPC homestead and exempt property all go to the surviving spouse; children benefit only if no spouse survives.

**31.** Matter of Estate of Dodge, 685 P.2d 260, 263 (Colo.App.1984).

**32.** Uniform Prob.Code §§ 2–402, 2–403; In re Estate of Peterson, 576 N.W.2d 767 (Neb. 1998); Matter of Estate of Dunlap's, 649 P.2d 1303 (Mont.1982) (specifically disinherited child can claim exemption). Florida allows a devisee who is not an heir to take advantage of the homestead exemption. Snyder v. Davis, 699 So.2d 999 (Fla.1997). A constructive trust can be imposed on homestead property which was wrongfully acquired. Kostelnik v. Roberts, 680 S.W.2d 532 (Tex.App.1984).

**33.** This was raised from $5,000 in 1990. Uniform Probate Code § 2–402, Comment.

**34.** Uniform Probate Code § 2–403. Before 1990, it was only $3,500. This amount goes, in the absence of a spouse, to the "children"—it is not restricted to minors and dependent children.

**35.** In re Estate of Wentworth, 452 N.W.2d 714 (Minn.App.1990) (proper to deny family allowance but not homestead and exempt property claim on basis that spouse had sufficient resources of her own).

**36.** Fla. Const. art. 10, § 4 (homestead for residence of up to one half-acre in municipality, and 160 acres elsewhere). Uniform Probate Code § 2–402A preserves the constitutional right of homestead in those states where it exists. In Matter of Estate of Heimbach, 847 P.2d 824 (Okl.App.1993), a widow was awarded an 80 acre farm for life as homestead, even though the decedent had devised it to his children by a prior marriage.

**37.** Ark.Const. art. 9, §§ 4–6. *Cf.* Carolina Production Credit Ass'n v. Rogers, 318 S.E.2d 357 (S.C.1984) (widow loses homestead when she remarries). In contrast, under the UPC if a wife dies before receiving her homestead allowance her executor can claim it. Matter of Estate of Merkel's, 618 P.2d 872 (Mont.1980).

**38.** Brantley & Effland, *Inheritance, the Share of the Surviving Spouse, and Wills: Arkansas Law and the Uniform Probate Code Compared,* 3 U.Ark. at Little Rock L.J. 361, 388 (1980).

**39.** *Restatement, Third, of Property (Wills and Other Donative Transfers)* § 1.1, comm. j (1998); Uniform Probate Code § 2–402. Washington provides a discretionary award "in lieu of" homestead when the decedent does not own a home. In re Estate of Martin, 655 P.2d 1211 (Wash.App.1983). Under Uniform Probate Code § 2–403, exempt property is taken primarily "in household furniture, automobiles, furnishings, appliances, and personal effects," but if necessary, other assets are used to fill up the $10,000.

**40.** In re Estate of Finch, 401 So.2d 1308 (Fla.1981).

Even though homestead and the exemption take precedence over claims of creditors, they may provide less protection than the elective share as to property which is not in the probate estate.[41] But some states protect homestead against inter-vivos conveyances by one spouse without the other's consent.[42]

## § 3.5 Pretermitted Heir Statutes

Most American states today have statutes, commonly known as "pretermitted" or "omitted heir"[1] statutes, which are based on the idea that failure to mention a child in a will was an oversight, so the omitted child should get a share of the estate in order to fulfill the testator's true intent. The idea goes back to Roman law, in which an heir had to be expressly disinherited if the testator intended that he receive no share.[2] The common-law rejected this rule, but held that if a testator married *and* had a child after executing a will, the will was revoked.[3] American pretermitted heir statutes, which began in the 18th century,[4] do not depend on the testator's marrying subsequent to the will.

### *Variations in the Statutes*

Pretermitted heir statutes differ on several points.[5]

1. *Are all children*[6] *covered, or only those born or adopted after the will was executed?* Many statutes, including the Uniform Probate Code, cover only children who were born after the will was executed.[7] Others are not so limited.[8] It is questionable whether statutes which include all children are consistent with the testator's probable intent.

**41.** Estate of Overmire v. American Nat. Red Cross, 794 P.2d 518 (Wash.App.1990) (no award in lieu of homestead out of revocable trust). This result may be changed if a state has adopted Uniform Probate Code § 6–102, as proposed in 1998.

**42.** Fla.Const. art. 10, § 4(c); Sims v. Cox, 611 So.2d 339 (Ala.1992) (deed of homestead to daughter not signed by wife is voidable); Ray v. American Nat. Bank & Trust Co., 894 P.2d 1056 (Okl.1994).

**§ 3.5**

**1.** Although from the Latin *praeter*, the prefix is commonly spelled *preter* in modern English. Uniform Probate Code § 2–302 uses the term "omitted." *See also* Cal.Prob.Code § 21620. "Wyoming remains the only state which does not have some form of pretermitted heir provisions." Averill, *The Wyoming Probate Code of 1980: An Analysis and Critique,* 16 Land & Water L.Rev. 103, 117 (1981).

**2.** Justinian, *Institutes* 2.13. Originally the rule applied only to sons of the testator, but Justinian abolished this discrimination between the sexes.

**3.** 2 W. Blackstone, *Commentaries* 502–03 (1765); Pascucci v. Alsop, 147 F.2d 880 (D.C.Cir.1945).

**4.** Matthews, *Pretermitted Heirs: An Analysis of the Statutes,* 29 Colum.L.Rev. 748, 753 (1929).

**5.** For a comprehensive list of the statutes see Statutory Note to *Restatement (Second) of Property, Donative Transfers* § 34.2 (1990).

**6.** "Children" are defined in the same way as for intestate succession. Uniform Probate Code § 1–201(5). Thus, a child adopted by another may not qualify as a pretermitted heir of the natural parents. Matter of Estate of Couch, 726 P.2d 1007 (Wash.App.1986); see Section 2.10, note 12 et seq. So also, a child born out of wedlock takes under the statute only if he qualifies as an heir. In re Sanders, 3 Cal. Rptr.2d 536 (App.1992); Matter of Estate of King, 837 P.2d 463 (Okl.1990); Section 2.9. In Talley v. Succession of Stuckey, 614 So.2d 55 (La.1993), the statute by its terms covered only legitimate children, but the court held that the constitution required its extension to a child born out of wedlock.

**7.** Uniform Probate Code § 2–302; Tex.Probate Code § 67; Ohio Rev.Code § 2107.34; Cal.Prob.Code § 21620; N.Y. EPTL § 5–3.2.

**8.** Mass.Gen.Laws c. 191, § 20; Matter of Estate of Hilton's, 649 P.2d 488 (N.M.App. 1982).

> A childless testator may occasionally fail to focus on the possibility that he may have children after execution of his will. But * * * forgetting about the existence of a child one already has is on a par with misplacing a house—not very likely.[9]

Statutes which provide for an omitted, existing child may be consistent with intent, however, if the testator mistakenly believed that the child was dead. The Uniform Probate Code also covers such children.[10] Is this distinguishable from a testator's mistaken belief that a child was not his? The law generally provides no relief for such mistakes of fact.[11]

The date of the child's birth, not conception, is controlling for purposes of applying the statute. Even when a testator was five months' pregnant when she executed her will, her child qualified as after-born under a pretermitted heir statute.[12] For an adopted child, the date of adoption rather than the date of birth controls. No inference of intent to disinherit can be drawn from failure to provide for a person who was not the testator's child when the will was executed.[13]

When, after the execution of a will and the subsequent birth of a child, a testator executes a codicil to the earlier will, the child is no longer regarded as after-born. The execution of a codicil is said "republish" the will as of the date of the codicil.[14]

2. *Is the statute limited to children, or are more remote descendants included?* The Uniform Probate Code and many other statutes only protect omitted children,[15] but some statutes also cover issue of a deceased child.[16] The limitation to "children" in the Uniform Probate Code is hard to understand since the Code allows grandchildren of a decedent to take by representation if a decedent dies intestate.[17]

3. *What evidence is admissible to show that the disinheritance was intentional?* Some courts admit any evidence of the testator's actual intent. Thus under a statute which gave a share to an omitted child "unless it appears that such omission was intentional," a claim by three daughters was rejected on the basis of testimony that the testator had had no contact with them for 15 years before he died and had represented himself to the world as

9. Rein, *A More Rational System for the Protection of Family Members Against Disinheritance,* 15 Gonz.L.Rev. 11, 24–25 (1979). *See also* Matthews, *supra* note 4, at 752; Evans, *Should Pretermitted Children Be Entitled to Inherit?,* 31 Calif.L.Rev. 263, 269 (1943); Niles, *Probate Reform in California,* 31 Hast.L.J. 185, 197 (1979).

10. Uniform Probate Code § 2–302(c). *See also* Cal.Prob.Code § 21622; Ohio Rev.Code § 2107.34; *cf.* Wis.Stat. § 853.25(2) (child omitted by "mistake or accident"). A child who claims under this provision has the burden of proving the testator's mistake, at least when there is no reason to suppose the testator thought the child was dead. Estate of Della Sala, 86 Cal.Rptr.2d 569 (App.1999).

11. See Section 6.1, at note 52.

12. DeCoste v. Superior Court, 470 P.2d 457 (Ariz.1970).

13. Uniform Probate Code § 2–302; Tex. Prob.Code § 67(c); N.Y. EPTL § 5–3.2; Estate of Turkington, 195 Cal.Rptr. 178 (App.1983).

14. Azcunce v. Estate of Azcunce, 586 So.2d 1216 (Fla.App.1991). *But see Restatement, Third, of Property (Wills and Other Donative Transfers)* § 3.4, illus. 3 (1998) (disapproving the result in Azunce).

15. Uniform Probate Code § 2–302; Cal. Prob.Code § 21620.

16. Mass.Gen.Laws c. 191, § 20; Ohio Rev. Code § 2107.34; Wis.Stat. § 853.25; Matter of Estate of Woodward, 807 P.2d 262 (Okl.1991) (grandchildren take as pretermitted heirs).

17. Section 2.2, at note 8 et seq. If a will devises property to "my children," and a child predeceases the testator, survived by issue, they will take not as pretermitted heirs, but under the anti-lapse statute. See Section 8.3.

a single man.[18] But under many statutes evidence of an intent to disinherit the child must appear in the will itself.[19]

The Uniform Probate Code says that it must appear "*from the will* that the omission was intentional," unless "the testator provided for the child by transfer outside the will." The transfer bars the child if the testator intended it to "be in lieu of a testamentary provision." This can be "shown by the testator's statements or . . . inferred from the amount of the transfer or other evidence."[20] Thus oral statements by a testator showing an intent to disinherit are admissible if, but only if, they are connected with a transfer to the child.[21]

The Code also bars claims by omitted children when the will devises "all or substantially all the estate to the other parent of the omitted child."[22] Presumably in this situation the devisee will use the property for the benefit of the children, so they are not really disinherited.

Language in the will can also bar claims by a pretermitted heir. Blackstone mentioned a "groundless vulgar error" that a testator had to leave "the heir a shilling or some other express legacy, in order to disinherit him effectually."[23] This belief still persists, since many wills make nominal devises to persons whom the testator wishes to disinherit.[24] But a will which simply says "I do not wish to provide for my son Arthur" is sufficient, because all statutes bar claims by an expressly disinherited heir.[25] It has also been held to bar a claim by Arthur's children in case he predeceases the testator and the statute allows more remote issue to claim as pretermitted.[26]

There has been much litigation about what language is sufficient to bar heirs who are not mentioned by name in the will. The cases are hard to reconcile, and the language of each will differs. Generally speaking, courts are reluctant to treat "boilerplate" provisions as showing an intent to disinherit children, for example, a statement that "all other persons are excluded from receiving anything from my estate."[27] But when a will provides for the testator's "descendants," a child who is not mentioned by name is not deemed

**18.** In re Estate of Blank, 219 N.W.2d 815 (N.D.1974). *See also* Matter of Estate of Flowers, 848 P.2d 1146 (Okl.1993) (remand for consideration of extrinsic evidence of intent). According to *Restatement (Second) of Property, Donative Transfers* § 34.2(2), Comment f (1990) "evidence outside the will as to the testator's intent should be admissible" unless the statute provides otherwise.

**19.** Estate of Jones v. Jones, 759 P.2d 345 (Utah App.1988), reversed on other grounds, Matter of Estate of Jones, 858 P.2d 983 (Utah 1993).

**20.** Uniform Probate Code § 2–302(b). *See also* Cal.Prob.Code § 21621. *But see* In re Estate of Came, 529 A.2d 962 (N.H.1987) (beneficiary of $500,000 trust also takes as pretermitted heir).

**21.** Contrast the rule governing gifts to an heir which the UPC allows to be charged against the heir only if the donor's intent to do so is expressed in writing. See Section 2.6, note 2.

**22.** Uniform Probate Code § 2–302(a)(1); *cf.* Cal.Prob.Code § 21621(b) (applicable only when testator had some children when the will was executed).

**23.** 2 W. Blackstone, *Commentaries* *503 (1765).

**24.** Matter of Estate of Hilton, 649 P.2d 488 (N.M.App.1982); In re Estate of Cooke, 524 P.2d 176 (Idaho 1973).

**25.** Such a clause may not be effective if the will fails to give the property to someone else, however. See Section 3.10, note 9. It may also be desirable to recite the reason for disinheriting a child so that the will not appear "unnatural" and thus subject to claims of incapacity or undue influence. See Section 7.1, note 29.

**26.** In re Estate of Laura, 690 A.2d 1011 (N.H.1997).

**27.** Matter of Estate of Woodward, 807 P.2d 262 (Okl.1991); In re Estate of Cooke, 524 P.2d 176 (Idaho 1973) ($1 to any other person who claims against estate).

to be pretermitted, even if the provision for the child is conditional on an event which does not occur, *e.g.*, "to my wife, Mary, if she survives me, otherwise to my descendants." If Mary survives, the descendants take nothing, but they were not overlooked.[28] If the will had merely left the estate to Mary, the legal effect would be the same, because if she did not survive, the testator's descendants would take by intestacy. But in this case it is hard to argue that the will provided for them.

Even a substantial devise in a will to a person whom the testator later adopts does not bar a pretermitted-heir claim by the devisee; courts assume that the testator's failure to change the will to give the devisee more after the adoption was an oversight.[29]

4. *What does a pretermitted heir take?* In a few states the birth of a child to the testator revokes a previous will.[30] This result seems "too drastic," since an after-born child can be given a share of the estate while leaving the rest of the will intact.[31] In most states, pretermitted heirs receive their intestate share.[32] This may amount to the whole estate,[33] but this depends on the facts. In community property states all the community property usually passes to the spouse on intestacy, so the share of a pretermitted child may be zero.[34]

Giving pretermitted heirs an intestate share may produce a questionable result. Suppose that a will leaves $3,000 each to the testator's two children, A and B, and the rest of the large estate to charity. A daughter C is born later, and all three children survive the testator. C's intestate share would give her more than her older siblings, but it is doubtful that testator would have intended this.[35] The Uniform Probate Code would only give C a share equal to that of her siblings, whose shares would abate ratably to make up C's share, so each child would get $2,000.[36] A Wisconsin statute gives courts discretion to "make such provision for the omitted child or issue out of the estate as it deems would best accord with the probable intent of the testator."[37]

5. *Non-probate property* A man had insurance on his life which designated his "children, Robert and Tamara" as the beneficiaries. He later had a third child who claimed a share of the insurance proceeds. This situation fits within the rationale of the pretermitted heir statutes, but is not covered by them because they refer only to *wills,* and so the after-born child takes

**28.** Leatherwood v. Meisch, 759 S.W.2d 559 (Ark.1988); Estate of Norwood, 443 N.W.2d 798 (Mich.App.1989); Matter of Estate of Broughton, 828 P.2d 443 (Okl.App.1991). *But see* Robinson v. Mays, 610 S.W.2d 885 (Ark. 1981); In re MacKay's Estate, 433 A.2d 1289 (N.H.1981).

**29.** Brown v. Crawford, 699 P.2d 162 (Okl. App.1984); Estate of Marshall, 621 P.2d 187 (Wash.App.1980); Estate of Turkington, 195 Cal.Rptr. 178 (App.1983).

**30.** Ga.Code § 53–4–48; Conn.Gen.Stat. § 45a–257; Talley v. Succession of Stuckey, 614 So.2d 55 (La.1993). This was also the effect at common law of marriage and birth of issue subsequent to the will. See note 3 *supra.*

**31.** Chaffin, *A Reappraisal of the Wealth Transmission Process,* 10 Ga.L.Rev. 447, 473 (1976).

**32.** Cal.Prob.Code § 21620; 755 ILCS 5/4–10.

**33.** Even if the intestate share of the pretermitted heirs is 100%, the will may contain administrative provisions which make its admission to probate significant. *See* Estate of Shimun, 136 Cal.Rptr. 668 (App.1977).

**34.** Rein, *supra* note 9, at 35.

**35.** Matthews, *supra* note 4, at 751–52; Rein, *supra* note 9, at 34.

**36.** Uniform Probate Code § 2–302(a)(2). *See also* Md.Estates and Trusts Code § 3–302; N.Y. EPTL § 5–3.2(a)(1)(B).

**37.** Wis.Stat. § 853.25(5). *See also* Rev. Code Wash. § 11.12.091(3).

nothing.[38] Although the Uniform Probate Code extends many rules of construction for wills to will substitutes, it does not do this in the case of after-born children.[39] But the Restatement of Property states that the policy of the controlling pretermitted heir statute "should be applied by analogy to the omitted issue" in a will substitute.[40]

### *Drafting Suggestions*

Although pretermitted heir statutes are designed to carry out the testator's probable intent, they often fail to do so. The harm which they can cause is reduced by the limitations in the Uniform Probate Code version, which restrict claims to after-born children, and provides an exception for wills which leave everything to the other parent of the children. But these limitations may not apply if the testator dies domiciled in a state where a broader statute controls.[41]

Lawyers usually guard against the problem at which pretermitted heir statutes are aimed—unintended omission of an after-born child—by using class gifts. If a will leaves the estate "to my issue"[42] instead of "to Arthur and Andrew," an after-born child would not have to (and could not) invoke a pretermitted heir statute. Some testators object to an impersonal reference to "issue" but a will can name the testator's existing children, while making it clear that after-born children are also included in a devise.

## § 3.6 Omitted Spouse

At common law a *woman's* will was revoked by her marriage but a *man's* will was not unless he also had after-born children. The distinction was based on a rule which has disappeared today—the incapacity of a married woman to make a will.[1] It was eliminated in England by the Wills Act of 1837 which provided that marriage revoked any existing will of either spouse.[2] This rule prevails in some states today,[3] but in others a will is revoked only if the testator (of either sex) later marries *and* has a child.[4]

**38.** Penn Mutual Life Ins. Co. v. Abramson, 530 A.2d 1202 (D.C.App.1987). *See also* Matter of Guardianship of Koors, 656 N.E.2d 530 (Ind. App.1995); Matter of Estate of Cayo, 342 N.W.2d 785 (Wis.App.1983) (refusing to apply statute to a living trust).

**39.** McGovern, *Nonprobate Transfers Under the Revised Uniform Probate Code*, 55 Alb. L.Rev. 1329, 1339–46 (1992).

**40.** *Restatement (Second) of Property, Donative Transfers* § 34.2(2) (1990). According to Comment g, this policy does not apply to a "one-item substitute for a will, such as a joint bank account." Cal.Prob.Code § 21620 applies to revocable living trusts as well as wills.

**41.** In Royce v. Estate of Denby, 379 A.2d 1256 (N.H.1977), a will was saved from claims by a child only because the court applied the law of New York, where the testator was domiciled when she executed the will, rather than the law of New Hampshire, where she died.

**42.** A common mistake is to use the word "children" in place of issue. "Issue" (or "descendants") provides for the children of a child who dies prematurely, which is presumably what most testators desire.

**§ 3.6**

**1.** Parker v. Hall, 362 So.2d 875 (Ala.1978) (holding unconstitutional a statute which made the same distinction).

**2.** Wills Act, 1 Vict. c. 26, § 18 (1837). This rule still prevails in England, unless when the will was made the testator was expecting to marry. Administration of Justice Act, 1982, § 18.

**3.** Ky. Rev. Stat § 394.090; R.I.Gen.Laws § 33–5–9. A statute which simply says that marriage revokes a will applies even though the spouse predeceases the testator. Lessard v. Lessard, 273 A.2d 307 (R.I.1971), and, arguably, even when the will leaves the estate to the future spouse. Erickson v. Erickson, 716 A.2d 92 (Conn.1998). But under Ore.Rev.Stat. § 112.305, a subsequent marriage revokes the will only if the spouse survives the testator. In Knott v. Garriott, 784 S.W.2d 603 (Ky.App. 1989) a marriage which was later annulled was held not to revoke a prior will.

**4.** Kan.Stat. § 59–610; Md.Estates and Trusts Code § 4–105(c); Tenn.Code § 32–1–201(4).

Many statutes give an intestate share to an omitted spouse like an omitted child. This is not the same as revoking the will, even when the spouse's intestate share amounts to the entire estate, since administrative provisions in the will are still effective.[5] Also, any omitted spouse claim disappears if the new spouse predeceases the testator or they are divorced before the testator dies.

There are many similarities between Uniform Probate Code § 2–301, giving an intestate share to a spouse who marries the testator after a will is executed, and § 2–302, protecting after-born children.[6] In both situations, a codicil which "republishes" the will after the marriage or birth has been held to bar the claim of the spouse or child.[7] There are also curious differences between the two provisions. A spouse who is omitted from a will because the other spouse mistakenly believes he/she is dead is not covered by Uniform Probate Code § 2–301, but a child in the same situation is. The Code bars the spouse where "the will was made in contemplation of the testator's marriage,"[8] but there is no comparable bar on a child whose birth was contemplated when the will was executed.

An omitted-spouse statute has been held to apply to a remarriage,[9] but according to a comment to the Uniform Probate Code the statute applies only if the will was "executed by the decedent at any time when [the spouses] were not married to each other but not a will executed during a prior marriage."[10]

Since the underlying theory in the provisions for omitted spouses and children is the correction of an oversight, both rules are subject to evidence that the omission was in fact intentional. Both sections use virtually identical language covering a "transfer outside the will" intended to "be in lieu of a testamentary provision."[11] Under this proviso a widow who had received a $230,000 gift from the testator was held not to be an omitted spouse[12], but a widow who got survivorship rights in her husband's pension automatically without any action by him was also allowed an intestate share of the testator's estate.[13]

**5.** Matter of Estate of Coleman, 718 P.2d 702 (N.M.App.1986); Matter of Estate of Groves, 788 P.2d 127 (Ariz.App.1990).

**6.** *See also* Cal.Prob.Code § 21610 (omitted spouse) and § 21620 (omitted child). Both were modelled on earlier versions of the UPC.

**7.** In re Estate of Wells, 983 P.2d 279 (Kan. App.1999); Matter of Estate of Ivancovich, 728 P.2d 661 (Ariz.App.1986). *But see* Matter of Will of Marinus, 493 A.2d 44 (N.J.Super.App.Div.1985) (later codicil which does not refer to earlier will does not bar spouse's claim).

**8.** Uniform Probate Code § 2–301(a)(1). Similar language appears in Mass.Ann. Laws c. 191 § 9; R.I.Gen.Laws § 33–5–9; Wis.Stat. § 853.11(2), but not in Cal.Prob.Code § 21610, which was based on an earlier version of the UPC. In Estate of Dennis, 714 S.W.2d 661 (Mo.App.1986), the court rejected a claim by an omitted spouse when the will was executed on the same day as the marriage. *See also* Erickson v. Erickson, 716 A.2d 92 (Conn.1998) (will executed 2 days before marriage). *But see* Matter of Estate of Wagley, 760 P.2d 316 (Utah 1988) (claim allowed where marriage took place 5 days after will executed).

**9.** Stevenson v. United States National Bank, 695 P.2d 77 (Or.App.1985).

**10.** Presumably this means "a prior marriage to the surviving spouse." In any event, one may wonder if the text supports the comment.

**11.** Uniform Probate Code §§ 2–301(a)(3), 2–302(b)(2).

**12.** Matter of Estate of Bartell, 776 P.2d 885 (Utah 1989). *See also* Matter of Estate of Taggart, 619 P.2d 562 (N.M.App.1980).

**13.** Noble v. McNerney, 419 N.W.2d 424 (Mich.App.1988). *See also* Estate of Shannon, 274 Cal.Rptr. 338 (App.1990).

An intent not to provide for the spouse may also be manifested in the will itself. (Such an express disinheritance would not preclude a claim to an *elective share*. See the next Section). The relevant language in the UPC is similar, though not identical, for spouses and children[14]. General language disinheriting heirs is not sufficient.[15] A frequent source of litigation is a provision (usually relatively small) for a friend whom the testator later marries. Most courts have held that such a devise does not bar an omitted spouse claim unless the will was made in contemplation of the marriage,[16] but there are also contrary decisions.[17] The comment to Uniform Probate Code § 2–301 says the section should apply even "if the person the decedent later married was a devisee in his or her premarital will," but "the value of any such devise . . . must be counted toward and not be in addition to the ultimate share" which the spouse receives.

The UPC also bars an omitted spouse from taking property which the testator's premarital will leaves to children of a prior marriage, on the theory that the failure to provide for the spouse in this situation is not likely to be an oversight.[18] Here the spouse can still claim an elective share,[19] but, as we shall see, the size of the elective share depends upon the length of the marriage, and so is rather small if the later marriage is of short duration.

In several states a testator's marriage has no effect on a will.[20] Arguably spouses need no other protection than the elective share. But the elective share is usually smaller than the intestate share which an omitted spouse receives. Under the Uniform Probate Code, for example, on intestacy a spouse in many situations takes all of the estate.[21] However, most omitted spouse statutes only give a share of the decedent's *probate* estate, and so do not apply to property held in a living trust, for example,[22] whereas non-probate transfers are often included in the computation of the elective share, as we shall see.

**14.** Uniform Probate Code § 2–301(a)(2) ("the will expresses the intention that it is to be effective notwithstanding any subsequent marriage"). Compare § 2–302(b)(1) ("it appears from the will that the omission was intentional").

**15.** Estate of Katleman, 16 Cal.Rptr.2d 468 (App.1993). A spouse has even been allowed a share despite a provision that "this will shall not be affected by any subsequent marriage." Estate of Green's, 174 Cal.Rptr. 654 (App. 1981).

**16.** Miles v. Miles, 440 S.E.2d 882 (S.C. 1994); In re Estate of Deoneseus, 906 P.2d 922 (Wash.1995); In re Estate of Gaspelin, 542 So.2d 1023 (Fla.App.1989); In re Stephenson, 1999 WL 510776 (Mo.App.1999).

**17.** Estate of Christensen v. Christensen, 655 P.2d 646 (Utah 1982); Matter of Estate of Keeven, 716 P.2d 1224 (Idaho 1986); Porter v. Porter, 726 P.2d 459 (Wash.1986). See also Ky.Rev.Stat. § 394.090 (will not revoked by marriage if it provides for the person who later becomes the testator's spouse). In D'Ambra v. Cole, 572 A.2d 268 (R.I.1990) a will left all the estate to a woman whom the testator married 6 months later. The court held that the will was not revoked by the marriage, which would have given the testator's brothers a share of his estate.

**18.** Waggoner, *The Multiple Marriage Society*, 76 Iowa L.Rev. 223, 254 (1991).

**19.** Mongold v. Mayle, 452 S.E.2d 444 (W.Va.1994).

**20.** McKnight v. McKnight, 267 So.2d 315 (Miss.1972); 755 ILCS 5/4–7(b); N.Y.E.P.T.L. § 5–1.3(a) (omitted spouse share applies only if will executed before 1930).

**21.** Uniform Probate Code §§ 2–102, 2–102A. In Hellums v. Reinhardt, 567 So.2d 274 (Ala.1990), an omitted spouse took the entire estate. Under Cal.Prob.Code § 21610, however, an omitted spouse gets no more than one half of the decedent's separate property even if on a true intestacy all would go to the spouse. The omitted spouse's share is also, like the elective share, but not the family allowance, subject to claims of creditors. Labayog v. Labayog, 927 P.2d 420 (Haw.App.1996) (claim of omitted spouse is subject to decedent's obligation in divorce decree).

**22.** Kirksey v. Teachers' Ret. System, 302 S.E.2d 101 (Ga.1983); Estate of Heggstad, 20 Cal.Rptr.2d 433 (App.1993) (revocable trust not covered by omitted spouse claim); Riccelli

Omitted spouse statutes have been the cause of malpractice actions against a lawyer who drafted a will which failed to include a provision as to the testator's impending marriage.[23] Even no marriage is impending, the testator should be advised to review the will if this should occur. Such a warning appears in the California Statutory Will.[24]

## § 3.7 Elective Share

### *Historical Introduction; Gender Discrimination*

At common law the rights of surviving spouses depended on their sex. A widow received *dower,* a life estate in one-third of lands which her husband owned at any time during the marriage.[1] A widower received *curtesy,* a life estate in *all* the lands which his wife owned during the marriage, but only if issue were born of the marriage.[2] Maitland attributed the unequal treatment of husbands and wives to the interest of feudal lords in seeing that services were performed: the widow's share was smaller because she could not perform military service.[3]

In most states today distinctions between the sexes have been eliminated. Statutes which differentiate between the rights of widows and widowers have been held to be an unconstitutional denial of equal protection.[4] Some states still retain the name "dower," but the husband and wife usually receive equivalent shares by that name.[5]

### *Deficiencies of Dower*

Dower did not adequately protect the surviving spouse. It attached only to land, but the chief or only form of wealth in many families is personal property.[6] Because dower attached to all land which the husband owned at any time during marriage, it gave the wife a "veto * * * over all her husband's transactions involving his real property."[7] Since dower was only a

v. Forcinito, 595 A.2d 1322 (Pa.Super.1991) (joint tenancy). However, the California statute was subsequently amended to include revocable trusts. Cal.Prob.Code § 21601, 21610. *See also* White v. McGill, 585 N.E.2d 945 (Ohio App.1990) (marriage revokes beneficiary designation under a pension); *Restatement, Third, Trusts* § 25, Comment *e* (Tent. Draft 1996); *Restatement, Second, Property (Donative Transfers)* § 34.1(3) (1990).

**23.** Heyer v. Flaig, 449 P.2d 161 (Cal.1969). *See also* McAbee v. Edwards, 340 So.2d 1167 (Fla.App.1976).

**24.** Calif.Prob.Code § 6240.

**§ 3.7**

**1.** 2 W. Blackstone, *Commentaries* *129 (1765).

**2.** *Id.* at 126. For a brief history of dower and curtesy see A. Simpson, *An Introduction to the History of Land Law* 65–66 (1961).

**3.** 2 F. Pollock & F. Maitland, *History of English Law* 419 (2d ed. 1898).

**4.** Montgomery v. Estate of Montgomery, 677 N.E.2d 571 (Ind.App.1997); Stokes v. Stokes, 613 S.W.2d 372 (Ark.1981); Hall v. McBride, 416 So.2d 986 (Ala.1982); In re Estate of Reed's, 354 So.2d 864 (Fla.1978) (family allowance to widow only). *But see* Matter of Baer's Estate, 562 P.2d 614 (Utah 1977) (greater rights for widows justified by "the disparity between economic capabilities of" men and women).

**5.** Mass.Gen.Laws c. 189 § 1; N.J.Stat. § 3B:28–1.

**6.** Chaffin, *A Reappraisal of the Wealth Transmission Process,* 10 Ga.L.Rev. 447, 457 (1976); Haskell, *The Premarital Estate Contract and Public Policy,* 57 N.C.L.Rev. 415, 421 (1979); Matter of Estate of Cole, 491 A.2d 770 (N.J.Super.Ch.Div.1984).

**7.** Clark, *The Recapture of Testamentary Substitutes to Preserve the Spouse's Elective Share,* 2 Conn.L.Rev. 513, 516–17 (1971). In Sterling v. Wilson, 621 N.E.2d 767 (Ohio App. 1993), a contract to sell land was held unenforceable because the seller's wife refused to release her dower rights. This problem can also occur in community property states. See Section 3.8, note 50.

life estate, widows could not sell the land without the consent of the persons who would succeed to it after her death.[8]

For these reasons modern statutes usually give a surviving spouse (husband or wife) a fee interest instead of a life estate,[9] but only in property which the decedent owned at death. Some statutes continue to use the name dower but it give it a meaning different from common-law dower.[10] Others, like the Uniform Probate Code, have abolished dower and curtesy and replaced it with an "elective share."[11]

### *Size of Elective Share*

The elective share is computed in various ways in different states. Sometimes it equals the spouse's intestate share, or is a fraction thereof, but in the Uniform Probate Code the two are computed differently. The size of a spouse's intestate share under the Code depends on whether the decedent was survived by issue, or issue of a prior marriage. This is irrelevant in the UPC[12] elective share which is based primarily on the length of the marriage. It rises in stages from 3% for a marriage which lasted less than 2 years to 50% for marriages of 15 years or more.[13] The greater complexity of the elective share under the UPC as compared with the spouse's intestate share is due to the fact that "intestacy affects so many estates of small size" whereas "elections are the exception in estate practice" and so "a more individuated system" can be accommodated.[14]

The two systems can produce similar results, but the elective share can be quite different from an intestate share. Both give the spouse a percentage of the estate, with a minimum amount for small estates. In the case of the elective share, this is fixed at $50,000. But in the elective share, unlike intestacy, the surviving spouse's own assets are taken into account. Thus even in a long marriage, if the surviving spouse is wealthier than the decedent, the

8. However, in some states dower can be commuted into a cash equivalent. Rev.Rul. 72–7, 1972–1 Cum Bull 308.

9. *But see* R.I.Gen.Laws § 33–25–2 (surviving spouse gets life estate in land); Ind.Code § 29–1–3–1(a) (spouse gets only a life estate in land if decedent is survived by issue of a prior marriage); In re Seifert's Estate, 242 A.2d 64 (N.H.1968) (direction to sell land in will did not convert it into personal property, so husband who took elective share got only a life interest).

10. Mass.Gen.Laws c. 189, § 1 ("dower" confined to land owned by decedent at death); Ky.Rev.Stat. § 392.020 (dower is a fee interest as to land owned at death). In England, the Dower Act, 3 & 4 Will. 4, c. 105, § 4 (1833), exempted land which the husband disposed of inter-vivos or by will so that dower became simply the widow's share of land on intestacy.

11. Uniform Probate Code § 2–112. *See also* Md. Estates and Trusts Code § 3–202; 755 ILCS § 5/2–9.

12. But not in all states. See In re Estate of White, 651 N.E.2d 324 (Ind.App.1995) (widow limited to life estate where decedent had children by a prior marriage); N.C.Gen.Stat. § 30–1(a).

Many states give a larger elective share if the decedent has no issue. N.Y. EPTL § 5–1.1(c); Ohio Rev.Code § 2106.01(c); 755 ILCS § 5/2–8.

13. Uniform Probate Code § 2–202(a). Apparently years in which the spouses were living separately still count as years of marriage. Cf. *id.* § 2–802 (divorce but not decree of separation terminates spousal status). In In re Estate of Antonopoulos, 993 P.2d 637, 647 (Kan.1999) a spouse increased her elective share from 15 to 30% by proving a common law marriage preceded the formal marriage by 5 years.

In Arkansas a spouse who was married to the decedent for less than a year can claim no elective share, but otherwise the length of the marriage is irrelevant. Shaw v. Shaw, 989 S.W.2d 919 (Ark.1999).

14. Waggoner, *Marital Property Rights in Transition*, 59 Mo.L.Rev. 21, 55 (1994).

elective share may amount to nothing.[15]

The UPC elective share is atypical in several respects, and it remains to be seen how many states will adopt it. However, many states have already adopted the partnership theory which it espouses in the case of divorce.[16] It is also similar in many ways to the community property system which we will discuss in the next Section.

The UPC elective share is the same for real and personal property. This is consistent with the trend to eliminate distinctions between the two, but they survive in a few states.[17]

Unlike the family allowance, the spouse's elective share is subject to claims against the decedent's estate.[18] In this respect, common-law dower was more advantageous; even though it gave the widow only a life estate, her interest came ahead of the husband's creditors.

### *Non-probate Assets*

Common-law dower gave a widow a share of lands of which her husband was seised at any time during the marriage, including land which the husband had conveyed away before he died.[19] Many modern elective share statutes only include assets owned by the decedent at death, the so-called "probate" estate. This has allowed spouses to evade the elective share by using will substitutes or inter-vivos gifts to deplete the estate before they die.[20]

Some cases have subjected property which the decedent transferred before death to the elective share if the transfer was "illusory." Revocable living trusts are frequently so characterized.[21] The second Restatement of Property and the third Restatement of Trusts both allow a surviving spouse to reach the assets of any revocable trust created by the decedent.[22]

A second approach to non-probate transfers focuses on "fraud." A Tennessee statute makes voidable "any conveyances made fraudulently * * * with an intent to defeat the surviving spouse of his * * * elective share."[23]

**15.** In re Estate of Karnen, 607 N.W.2d 32 (S.D.2000) (H's elective share in 50 year marriage was 0 in part because he had substantial assets of his own).

**16.** Uniform Probate Code, Part 2, General Comment.

**17.** Iowa Code § 633.238; Ky.Rev.Stat. § 392.020.

**18.** Uniform Prob.Code § 2–204; Winkelfoos v. Mann, 475 N.E.2d 509 (Ohio App.1984); N.Y. EPTL § 5–1.1(c) (net estate); 755 ILCS § 5/ 2–8(a) (after payment of all just claims); Md. Estates and Trusts Code § 3–203(a) (net estate).

**19.** 2 W. Blackstone, *Commentaries* 132 (1765). For a modern application see Matter of Estate of Stroh, 392 N.W.2d 192 (Mich.App. 1986).

**20.** Briggs v. Wyoming Nat. Bank, 836 P.2d 263 (Wyo.1992) (concurring opinion); Dalia v. Lawrence, 627 A.2d 392 (Conn.1993); Dumas v. Estate of Dumas, 627 N.E.2d 978 (Ohio 1994); Friedberg v. Sunbank/Miami, N.A., 648 So.2d 204 (Fla.App.1994); Soltis v. First of America Bank, 513 N.W.2d 148 (Mich.App.1994).

**21.** Johnson v. Farmers & Merchants Bank, 379 S.E.2d 752 (W.Va.1989); Newman By and Through Ausemus v. George, 755 P.2d 18 (Kan.1988); Seifert v. Southern Nat. Bank, 409 S.E.2d 337 (S.C.1991). In Pezza v. Pezza, 690 A.2d 345 (R.I.1997), the court adopted the "illusory transfer" test, but held that a trust was not subject to the elective share when the settlor had surrendered his right to revoke the trust before he died.

**22.** *Restatement (Second) of Property (Donative Transfers)* § 34.1(3) (1990); *Restatement, Third, Trusts* § 25, Comment d (1996). Contra, *Restatement, Second, Trusts* § 57, Comment c (1959).

**23.** Tenn.Code § 31–105. *See also* Wis.Stat. § 861.17; 755 ILCS § 25/1; Mo.Stat. § 474.150; 14 Vt.Stat.Ann § 473 (real estate); *cf.* In re Estate of Weitzman, 724 N.E.2d 1120 (Ind. App.2000) (result turns on whether husband in creating revocable trust intended to defeat wife's elective share).

Since anyone who makes a gift knows that it will reduce his estate and thereby partially "defeat" the elective share of the donor's spouse this seems to be a questionable criterion.[24]

"Fraud" suggests the idea of fraudulent conveyances which creditors can set aside if they render the transferor insolvent. But since the elective share is usually a percentage of the estate, if a husband reduces his estate by transfers, his estate can still literally satisfy the elective share. Thus the analogy to a fraudulent conveyance is hard to apply.

The term "fraud" might suggest that the result turns on whether the transfer was concealed from the other spouse, but this is only occasionally mentioned in the cases.[25]

Some courts interpret the "fraud" test as allowing "reasonable" transfers which do not "substantially" deplete the probate estate.[26] Even if nearly all a settlor's property is put into a living trust, the trust may still be upheld if it makes a substantial provision for the settlor's spouse.[27] On the other hand, fraud may be "implied in law from transfers of a disproportionate and unreasonable amount of assets by the decedent."[28]

Some statutes explicitly include certain non-probate property in computing the elective share. The Uniform Probate Code gives spouses a share of the "augmented estate," which includes the probate estate and property transferred by the decedent if the transfers was made within two years of death,[29] if the decedent reserved the right to revoke or the income for life,[30] and joint tenancies, to the extent of the "decedent's fractional interest" therein.[31] The fractional interest is presumptively based on the number of joint tenants; *e.g.* if there are two, the decedent's interest is assumed to be one half, but this

**24.** In re Estate of Mocny, 630 N.E.2d 87 (Ill.App.1993) (intent to defeat elective share is irrelevant under "fraud" statute); *But see* Harris v. Rock, 799 S.W.2d 10 (Ky.1990).

In re Estate of Defilippis, 683 N.E.2d 453 (Ill.App.1997), the court said "intent to defraud the surviving spouse ... does not involve the traditional meaning of fraud," but rather "refers to a transfer that is illusory." This is a curious interpretation of the Illinois statute which expressly rejects an "illusory" transfer test.

**25.** Clay v. Woods, 487 N.E.2d 1106 (Ill. App.1985) (no fraud because decedent informed his spouse); Matter of Estate of Froman, 803 S.W.2d 176 (Mo.App.1991) (fraud found where transfer concealed from spouse). In many cases, however, it is unclear (and apparently considered irrelevant) whether the other spouse knew about the transfer before the decedent died.

**26.** Windsor v. Leonard, 475 F.2d 932 (D.C.Cir.1973) ($190,000 transferred to trust, $110,000 left in probate estate). *See also* Warren v. Compton, 626 S.W.2d 12, 18 (Tenn.App. 1981) ("the amount of the transfers in relation to the total estate is not so great as to infer fraudulent intent").

**27.** Methodist Episcopal Church v. Hadfield, 453 A.2d 145 (Md.App.1982); Richards v. Worthen Bank & Trust Co., 552 S.W.2d 228 (Ark.1977).

**28.** Russell v. Walz, 458 N.E.2d 1172, 1185 (Ind.App.1984).

**29.** Uniform Probate Code § 2–205(3). *See also Restatement, Second, Property (Donative Transfers)* § 34.1(2) (1990) (transfers in contemplation of the imminent death of the donor); Dunnewind v. Cook, 697 N.E.2d 485 (Ind. App.1998) (irrevocable trust created after settlor learned she was terminally ill subject to elective share).

**30.** Uniform Probate Code § 2–205(2). *See also* N.Y. EPTL § 5–1.1(b); 20 Pa.Stat. § 2203.

**31.** Uniform Probate Code § 2–205(1)(ii). *Restatement (Third) of Property (Wills and Other Donative Transfers)* § 9.1(c) (Prel.Dft. 2000) purports to restate the same rules as part of the common law, but this is somewhat wide of the mark. Absent a statute, a surviving spouse cannot reach property held in joint tenancy by the decedent and another. In re Estate of Mocny, 630 N.E.2d 87 (Ill.App.1993); Smith v. McCall, 477 S.E.2d 475 (S.C.App.1996); *cf.* Estate of Bruce, 538 A.2d 923 (Pa.Super.1988) (widow can reach husband's half of *tenancy in common*); In re Estate of Tyler, 536 N.E.2d 1188 (Ohio App.1987) (joint account created only for convenience included in probate estate).

may be altered due to the respective contributions of the parties. Thus if the surviving party to a joint bank account contributed all the funds in it, the decedent would have no fractional interest therein.[32]

The UPC list is modelled after the Internal Revenue Code which includes such life-time transfers in a decedent's "gross" estate for tax purposes.[33] Before 1990 the Probate Code exempted life insurance and pensions from the augmented estate[34], but now insurance is expressly included if the decedent owned the policy at death.[35] Most pensions are subject to federal law (ERISA) which requires that they be taken in the form of a joint and survivor annuity which passes to the employee's surviving spouse.[36] Individual retirement accounts (IRAs) are not subject ERISA, but they have been held subject to the elective share in many states.[37]

The Uniform Probate Code formerly included in the augmented estate only property which was transferred "during marriage,"[38] but the present version includes assets subject to the decedent's control at the time of death, regardless of when they were transferred.[39] Some courts have upset conveyances made by a spouse to a third party on the eve of marriage as fraudulent.[40]

The Code excludes from the augmented estate property transferred "to the extent that the decedent received adequate and full consideration in money or money's worth" for the transfer.[41] Thus, unlike common-law dower and community property (in some states), the elective share is not an obstacle to sales of land. Also if the recipient of property in the augmented estate sells it to a third party, the latter is not subject to claims by the spouse.[42]

### *Other Benefits Conferred on Spouse*

**32.** Uniform Probate Code § 2–205, Comment, Examples 4, 6–7; In re Estate of Antonopoulos, 993 P.2d 637 (Kan.1999) (remand to consider contributions of surviving joint tenant, a child of the decedent by a prior marriage).

**33.** Compare 12 Del.Code § 902 which bases the spouse's share on the "gross estate for federal estate tax purposes." As to what this includes see Section 15.3.

**34.** Uniform Probate Code § 2–202(1) (pre–1990). Insurance is excluded from the New York and Pennsylvania statutes N.Y. EPTL § 5–1.1(b)(2); 20 Pa.Stat. § 2203(b)(2). *See also* Taliaferro v. Taliaferro, 843 P.2d 240 (Kan.1992); Graham v. Farmers New World Life Ins. Co., 841 P.2d 1165 (Okl.App.1992).

**35.** Uniform Probate Code § 2–205(1)(iv).

**36.** 29 U.S.C. § 1055(a); Matter of Estate of Harrison, 967 P.2d 1091 (Kan.App.1998); In re Lefkowitz, 767 F.Supp. 501 (S.D.N.Y.1991) (death benefits under pension plan must go to widow even though daughter named as beneficiary).

**37.** Matter of Estate of Luken, 551 N.W.2d 794 (N.D.1996); McCarty v. State Bank, 795 P.2d 940 (Kan.App.1990).

**38.** Uniform Probate Code § 2–202(1) (pre–1990). *See also* Estate of Kotz, 406 A.2d 524 (Pa.1979) (spouse can't attack a joint tenancy created 8 years prior to marriage).

**39.** Uniform Probate Code § 2–205(1); In re Estate of Antonopoulos, 993 P.2d 637 (Kan. 1999) (property put in join tenancy prior to marriage included in augmented estate).

**40.** Estate of Tomaso v. Tomaso, 402 N.E.2d 702 (Ill.App.1980); Efird v. Efird, 791 S.W.2d 713 (Ark.App.1990); Wis.Stat. § 861.17. *Contra,* Perlberg v. Perlberg, 247 N.E.2d 306 (Ohio 1969); Matter of Estate of Scheiner, 535 N.Y.S.2d 920 (Surr.1988). *See generally* Seplowitz, *Transfers Prior to Marriage and the UPC's Redesigned Elective Share—Why the Partnership is not yet Complete*, 25 Ind.L.Rev. 1 (1991).

**41.** Uniform Probate Code § 2–208(a).

**42.** Uniform Probate Code § 2–210(a); Limb v. Aldridge, 978 P.2d 365 (Okl.Civ.App. 1998) (bona fide purchaser from beneficiary of revocable trust not subject to claim by settlor's spouse).

If a husband's will leaves Blackacre to his wife, what effect will this devise have on her elective share? The law might allow her to take *both* her elective share *and* Blackacre unless the will made the devise conditional on waiving the elective share. This was the common-law rule as to dower,[43] and the same rule still applies to the family allowance,[44] homestead, and Social Security benefits.[45]

A second position would require the wife to elect between the will and her statutory share. This is the rule in most states today; hence the term *elective* share.[46] A third approach, adopted by the Uniform Probate Code, simply reduces the spouse's statutory share by the value of any devise to the spouse.[47] If the value of devises to a spouse equal or exceed the statutory share the spouse receives nothing more under the Code, but if the devise is worth $100,000, for example, and the elective share amounts to $150,000, the spouse gets the devise and an additional $50,000 from other assets in the augmented estate.

Many wills create a trust in which the testator's spouse gets the income for life with a remainder to another. Valuation of the spouse's interest under such a trust is problematic, since no one knows how long the spouse will live, and if the trustee has discretion over payments to the spouse, no one knows how the trustee will exercise this discretion. In one case a widow's interest, based on her age, was valued by referring to tax tables at 86% of the value of the trust assets despite her objection that much of the trust consisted of assets which were producing no income.[48] Since 1993, the Code has allowed spouses to avoid this valuation problem by disclaiming any devises; if they do so, they are not charged with benefits provided by the will which they disclaim.[49]

What if a husband instead of devising Blackacre to his wife, puts it into joint tenancy with her? Many states ignore nonprobate transfers to the spouse and would allow the widow to take her full elective share in addition to Blackacre.[50] The Uniform Probate Code, on the other hand, includes all property owned by the surviving spouse at the decedent's death in the calculating the elective share.[51] The theory of the Code is that marriage is a

**43.** Brown v. Parry, 21 Eng.Rep. 438 (1787) (Ch.). However, an intent to make the spouse elect may be inferred from the will. Carolina Production Credit Ass'n v. Rogers, 318 S.E.2d 357 (S.C.1984); In re Estate of Switzer, 599 A.2d 358 (Vt.1991).

**44.** Uniform Probate Code § 2–404(b). This Section also allows a spouse to claim both the family allowance and an elective share. *Accord,* Estate of Calcutt v. Calcutt, 576 N.E.2d 1288 (Ind.App.1991). This is not true in all states. Brown v. Sammons, 743 S.W.2d 23 (Ky.1988).

**45.** Uniform Probate Code §§ 2–206, 2–402; In re Estate of Antonopoulos, 993 P.2d 637, 646 (Kan.1999).

**46.** Matter of Estate of Spurgeon, 572 N.W.2d 595 (Iowa 1998) (wife's election bars her from taking devise under will even though she was not entitled to a statutory share because of waiver); Hannah v. Hannah, 824 S.W.2d 866 (Ky.1992). This is made clear in most statutes. *E.g.,* 755 ILCS § 5/2–8(a) ("if a will is renounced" spouse gets a share).

**47.** Uniform Probate Code § 2–209(a).

**48.** In re Estate of Myers, 594 N.W.2d 563, 570 (Neb.1999) *See also* In re Estate of Karnen, 607 N.W.2d 32 (S.D.2000).

**49.** Uniform Probate Code § 2–209, Comment. See Bloom, *The Treatment of Trust and other Partial Interests of the Surviving Spouse under the Redesigned Elective–Share System,* 55 Alb.L.Rev. 941 (1992); Matter of Estate of Grasseschi, 776 P.2d 1136 (Colo.App.1989) (disclaimer is effective if made within the time allotted for the spouse's election). Not all UPC states have adopted this change. In re Estate of Karnen, 607 N.W.2d 32, 37 (S.D.2000).

**50.** Plue v. Hill, 666 P.2d 835 (Or.App. 1983); Estate of Harper, 93 T.C. 368 (1989). King v. King, 613 N.E.2d 251 (Ohio App.1992).

**51.** Uniform Probate Code § 2–207.

"unspoken bargain" in which the spouses "agree that each is to enjoy a half interest in the fruits of the marriage, *i.e.*, in the property nominally acquired by and titled in the sole name of either partner during the marriage (other than in property acquired by gift or inheritance)." The parenthetical exception for property acquired by gift or inheritance is also found in community property systems, but is actually ignored in the Code in the interest of ease of administration. The Code uses a "mechanically determined approximation system [in] which ... there is no need to identify which of the couple's property was earned during the marriage and which was acquired prior to the marriage or acquired ... by gift or inheritance."[52]

The Restatement of Property, on the other hand, in computing the elective share only considers assets that the spouse acquired from the decedent, including irrevocable gifts during life.[53] This requires tracing the source of the surviving spouse's property; if the spouse can show that an asset was his or her own acquisition, it is not considered.[54]

### *Making the Election*

Spouses have a limited period in which to choose whether or not to take the elective share. Under the Uniform Probate Code the spouse must claim an elective share within 9 months after the date of death, or within 6 months after the probate of the decedent's will, whichever comes last.[55] The court may give an extension of time. Even after the time has expired, courts have allowed an election where the spouse's failure to elect was deemed excusable.[56] A spouse who fails to act in time only gets the benefits provided in the decedent's will,[57] but courts have given relief to spouses who made an unwise election in ignorance of relevant facts, such as the size of the decedent's estate.[58]

A lawyer's advice may help a surviving spouse to choose intelligently whether or not to claim the elective share. If the lawyer advising the spouse also drafted the will, an ethical problem is raised by Rule 1.9 of the Model Rules of Professional Conduct: "a lawyer who has formerly represented a client in a matter shall not thereafter (a) represent another person in the same or a substantially related matter in which the other person's interests are materially adverse to the interests of the former client * * *." One court has held that an attorney who drafted a will could properly advise the testator's widow of her right to an elective share,[59] but another reprimanded a

**52.** Uniform Probate Code, Part 2, General Comment.

**53.** *Restatement (Second) of Property, Donative Transfers* § 34.1, Comments h and i (1990). This was the approach of the pre–1990 Uniform Probate Code.

**54.** In re Estate of Ziegenbein, 519 N.W.2d 5 (Neb.App.1994) (joint account excluded from calculation because widower was the sole contributor); *cf.* Matter of Estate of Lettengarver, 813 P.2d 468 (Mont.1991) (land held in joint tenancy bars elective share because decedent spouse had contributed to its acquisition).

**55.** Section 2–211.

**56.** Matter of Estate of Hessenflow, 909 P.2d 662 (Kan.App.1995) (executor incorrectly informed widow that she was precluded from election by prior waiver); cf. In re Estate of Kruegel, 551 N.W.2d 718 (Minn.1996) (no abase of discretion to deny late petition).

**57.** In re Estate of Goodlett, 588 N.E.2d 367 (Ill.App.1992); Hutton v. Rygalski, 574 N.E.2d 1128 (Ohio App.1989); Matter of Estate of Lingscheit, 387 N.W.2d 738 (S.D.1986).

**58.** Matter of Estate of Epstein, 561 N.W.2d 82, 85 (Iowa App.1996). For further discussion of the extent to which a waiver of spousal rights is binding see Section 3.9.

**59.** Walton v. Davy, 586 A.2d 760 (Md.App. 1991).

lawyer who had drafted a will for a husband and wife and then represented the husband's estate against which the wife claimed an elective share.[60] It may be advisable for the surviving spouse to have independent counsel in considering whether or not to elect against a will, since the attorney for the estate may feel an obligation to preserve the testator's estate plan.[61] If the spouse does not have independent counsel, the attorney for the estate may run afoul of Model Rule 4.3: "in dealing on behalf of a client with a person who is not represented by counsel, a lawyer shall not state or imply that the lawyer is disinterested."

What factors should the spouse (and the lawyer) consider? A simple comparison between the size of the elective share and the benefits given to the spouse by the will is clearly relevant but not always determinative. Suppose that the decedent's will creates a trust which gives a widow the income for her life, with the corpus to be distributed at her death to their children. If the widow's estate will be large enough to generate an estate tax when she dies, she may decide not to take an elective share which would give her more money, because the additional money would be taxed in her estate at death. The widow's failure to take an elective share, like a disclaimer, does not constitute a taxable transfer.[62] On the other hand, if the decedent husband's estate is large enough to incur an estate tax and his will does not qualify for the marital deduction, the widow may wish to elect against the will in order to reduce the taxes on her husband's estate.

If the beneficiaries of the husband's will are also objects of the widow's bounty, such as their common children, the widow's decision whether or not to take an elective share will probably turn on such tax considerations, but she may also be affected by the form of the devise in her husband's will. If it creates a trust for her, is she happy with the designated trustee, or would she prefer to manage the assets herself? (This is not an issue if the widow herself is designated the trustee, as is often the case). Is she happy with the allocation of assets in the will? Some wills provide a substantial share for the spouse, but allocate particular assets, like a family business, to others.[63] A surviving spouse may wish to elect against the will simply because the spouse does not want assets to go to the decedent's devisees. This is not uncommon when the marriage was childless and/or the spouses have children by prior marriages.

### *Election by Conservator*

If the surviving spouse is legally incompetent, a conservator (guardian) must decide on the spouse's behalf.[64] If the spouse has no conservator, the

60. Matter of Robak, 654 N.E.2d 731 (Ind. 1995).

61. Benjamin, *Post-Mortem Strategies Extend Planning Prospects*, 19 Est.Plan. 24 (1992); Link, *Developments Regarding the Professional Responsibility of the Estate Administration Lawyer: The Effect of the Model Rules of Professional Conduct*, 26 Real Prop.Prob. and Trust L. 1, 73 (1991). For a more extensive discussion of the ethical problems when lawyers represent both spouses, see Section 3.9, at note 36.

62. As to disclaimers see Section 2.8. As we shall see in the next section, the rule is otherwise with respect to the surviving spouse's share of community property.

63. In this situation, she may not be able to use the elective share to obtain a portion of each asset in the estate. In re Estate of Murphy, 464 N.E.2d 1057 (Ill.1984). Uniform Probate Code § 2–210(a) allows persons who have received nonprobate transfers and who must contribute to making up the elective share an option "to pay the value of the amount for which he [or she] is liable."

64. In In re Estate of Disney, 550 N.W.2d 919 (Neb.1996), a devisee claimed that the

time for making an election may be tolled until one is appointed,[65] but an agent under a durable power of attorney has been allowed to make the election.[66] A conservator's decision to claim an elective share requires court approval, which may be withheld if the conservatee does not need the additional money for support.[67] But some states allow conservators to elect against a will whenever this is in the conservatee's "best interests."[68] The Uniform Probate Code allows conservators to claim the share, but the funds thereby acquired go into a trust for the spouse's support, and when the spouse dies, they return to the decedent's estate to pass under the will.[69] This removes any incentive to claim an elective share in order to benefit the conservatee's children by a prior marriage or other relatives.

In most states if a spouse dies before making the election, the right to elect disappears and cannot be exercised by the spouse's personal representative.[70] But if the spouse files the election and dies while the claim is being litigated, it can be pursued by the spouse's personal representative in most states.[71] The latter result is arguably inconsistent with the support rationale of the elective share, but not if the elective share is designed to recognize the spouse's contributions to the decedent's wealth, as in community property states.

The right of election cannot be asserted by a creditor of the spouse even if the spouse is insolvent.[72] However, failure to exercise a right to an elective share has been held to render the spouse ineligible for state welfare benefits based on need.[73]

### *Choice of Law*

Differences between state laws on the spouse's elective share may raise the question which law to apply. Different laws may apply to a single estate when land is governed by the law of the situs and personal property by the law of the decedent's domicile.[74] When a state in which land is situated

spouse who elected against the will lacked capacity, but the court rejected the claim.

**65.** In re Estate of Owens, 450 S.E.2d 2 (N.C.App.1994).

**66.** In re Estate of Reifsneider, 610 A.2d 958 (Pa.1992); In re Estate of Schriver, 441 So.2d 1105 (Fla.App.1983); Uniform Probate Code § 2–212(a). As to durable powers see Section 7.2, note 37 et seq.

**67.** In re Estate of Wentworth, 452 N.W.2d 714 (Minn.App.1990); In re Lynch's Estate, 421 N.E.2d 953 (Ill.App.1981); Matter of Guardianship of Scott, 658 P.2d 1150 (Okl. 1983); Uniform Probate Code § 2–203 (pre–1990) (for the present UPC solution see note 69 *infra*); *cf.* In re Estate of Cross, 664 N.E.2d 905 (Ohio 1996) (proper to elect against will even though spouse being supported by Medicaid).

**68.** McElroy v. Taylor, 977 S.W.2d 929, 932 (Ky.1998); Spencer v. Williams, 569 A.2d 1194 (D.C.App.1990).

**69.** Uniform Probate Code § 2–212. This provision applies also if the election is made by an agent under a durable power for an incompetent spouse.

**70.** Kirkeby v. Covenant House, 970 P.2d 241, 248 (Or.App.1998); Sarbacher v. McNamara, 564 A.2d 701 (D.C.App.1989); Matter of Estate of Thompson, 475 N.E.2d 1135 (Ill.App. 1985). *But see* Estate of Bozell, 768 P.2d 380 (Okl.App.1989).

**71.** Will of Sayre, 415 S.E.2d 263 (W.Va. 1992); Smail v. Hutchins, 491 So.2d 301 (Fla. App.1986). *But see* In re Estate of Bilse, 746 A.2d 1090 (N.J.Super.Ch.Div.1999) (heirs of widower only entitled to amount needed for his support for the balance of his life).

**72.** Matter of Savage's Estate, 650 S.W.2d 346 (Mo.App.1983).

**73.** Tannler v. DHSS, 564 N.W.2d 735 (Wis.1997) (medical assistance). *See also* Estate of Wyinegar, 711 A.2d 492 (Pa.Super.1998) (guardian of incompetent spouse must elect since otherwise he would be ineligible for benefits). *But see* Bradley v. Hill, 457 S.W.2d 212 (Mo.App.1970).

**74.** See Section 1.2, at notes 17 et seq. & 34 et seq.

provides an elective share of 1/2, for example, should it in computing this take into account what the spouse is getting from the decedent's personal property or land in other states? The authorities disagree on this question.[75] A spouse is not usually allowed to take under a will in one state and elect against it in another.[76] The Uniform Probate Code avoids such problems by providing that the law of the decedent's domicile governs the elective share as to all a decedent's property.[77] However, when a decedent has made nonprobate transfers in another state, the state of the decedent's domicile may not have jurisdiction over the transferees.[78] If ancillary proceedings in another state are necessary, that state may not agree that the law of the decedent's domicile at death controls.[79]

Change in the law may also raise problems. Most courts apply the law in effect when the testator dies in determining the elective share.[80] But when a Massachusetts court decided to subject revocable trusts to the surviving spouse's elective share, it did so only as to trusts created after the date of the opinion in order to protect persons who had relied on older cases to the contrary.[81] Statutes abolishing dower provide an exception for rights already vested.[82]

## § 3.8 Community Property

### *Significance of Community Property*

In eight states, Arizona, California, Idaho, Louisiana, Nevada, New Mexico, Texas, and Washington, the community property system provides a counterpart to the elective share. In California, for example, when a married person dies, "one-half of the community property belongs to the surviving spouse and the other half belongs to the decedent."[1] This often produces the same result as the spouse's elective share of 50% of the augmented estate under the Uniform Probate Code for long-term marriages. But this depends on how a couple's property is classified, since a spouse in a community property state usually has no rights in the other spouse's separate property if the other spouse devises or gives it to a third person.[2]

The classification of property as either community or separate is relevant for several purposes. The rules of intestate succession distinguish between community and separate property. In most community property states, the

75. Schoenblum, *Multistate and Multinational Estate Planning* § 10.12 (1982).

76. *Id.* §§ 10.08, 10.10; In re Estate of Conrad's, 422 N.E.2d 884 (Ill.App.1981) (failure to renounce will in state of domicile bars claim to elective share of land in Illinois).

77. Uniform Probate Code § 2–202(a)(d).

78. Matter of Estate of Ducey, 787 P.2d 749 (Mont.1990); Toledo Trust Co. v. National Bank of Detroit, 362 N.E.2d 273 (Ohio App. 1976).

79. National Shawmut Bank v. Cumming, 91 N.E.2d 337 (Mass.1950) (applying Massachusetts law to deny widow a share of living trust of Vermont domiciliary).

80. In re Estate of Peterson, 381 N.W.2d 109, 115 (Neb.1986).

81. Sullivan v. Burkin, 460 N.E.2d 572 (Mass.1984). *See also* Jeruzal's Estate v. Jeruzal, 130 N.W.2d 473 (Minn.1964); Matter of Novitt's Estate, 549 P.2d 805 (Colo.App.1976). For a more extended discussion of change in the law see Section 1.3.

82. Tenn.Code § 31–2–102; Haw.R.S. § 533–1; N.J.Stat. § 3B.28–1 (preserving dower in land if husband was seised in 1980).

§ 3.8

1. Cal.Prob.Code § 100.

2. Cal.Fam.Code § 752. However, a surviving spouse receives a substantial share of the decedent's separate property if the decedent died intestate.

surviving spouse gets both halves of their community property if the decedent left no will; the spouse's intestate share of the decedent's separate property is normally smaller.[3]

Community property states usually restrict inter-vivos transfers as well as devises of community property, so courts may have to decide whether property transferred by one spouse was community or separate in the context of a challenge to a conveyance by one spouse.

Even if a testator leaves all his or her property to the other spouse, it may make a difference whether this property was separate or community. Since one-half of the community property already belongs to each spouse, there is no taxable transfer of this half. If either spouse earns income during the marriage, one-half of it is attributed to the other for income tax purposes. Some litigation involving community property concerns taxes.[4] However, this is less common than formerly, because the marital deduction very often produces the same tax result for separate property. In fact, the marital deduction was designed to eliminate the disparity between the tax treatment of residents of community and separate property states.[5]

The classification of a couple's property as community or separate often affects the way it is allocated in a divorce. The division of community property at divorce varies in different states. California divides community property equally between the spouses, but in Arizona community property is "equitably" divided at divorce.[6] In any event, the classification of property may be important.[7] Since divorce is much more common today than disinheritance of a spouse by will when a couple remains married until death, most classification cases arise in the context of a divorce.

The classification of property may also affect the rights of creditors with claims against a spouse. For example, the expenses of a husband's last illness were held to be a "community debt" which could be satisfied out of his widow's share of the community property but not her separate property.[8]

**3.** Calif.Prob.Code § 6401; Uniform Prob. Code § 2–102A. The surviving spouse may get all of the separate property if the decedent had no issue or other close relatives, but the division of community property is not affected by the presence of issue.

Even if the decedent had a will, the surviving spouse may claim an intestate share of the estate as an "omitted" spouse if the will fails to mention the spouse. See Section 3.6; cf. Matter of Estate of Hansen, 910 P.2d 1281 (Wash.1996) (rejecting such a claim on basis of testator's contrary intent).

**4.** Keller v. Department of Revenue, 642 P.2d 284 (Or.1982) (half of H's income attributed to W for tax purposes, since it was community property); Estate of Cavenaugh v. Commissioner, 51 F.3d 597 (5th Cir.1995) (error to include all insurance proceeds in H's taxable estate, since W had a CP interest).

**5.** H.Weinstock, *Planning an Estate* § 4.2 (4th ed. 1995).

**6.** *Compare* Calif.Fam.Code § 2550 *with* Ariz.Rev.Stat. § 25–318.

**7.** Hatcher v. Hatcher, 933 P.2d 1222 (Ariz. App.1996) (division of property in divorce reversed due to erroneous classification of property as separate). *But cf.* Matter of Marriage of Olivares, 848 P.2d 1281 (Wash.App.1993) (erroneous classification of property is not ground for reversal where court has discretion in division of both separate and community property).

**8.** Samaritan Health System v. Caldwell, 957 P.2d 1373 (Ariz.App.1998); Abbett Elec. Corp. v. Storek, 27 Cal.Rptr.2d 845 (App.1994) (distinguishing between community property and joint tenancy with regard to rights of H's creditors);. Nichols Hills Bank v. McCool, 701 P.2d 1114 (Wash.1985) (contract creditor of H cannot reach his share of community property).

### *History and Rationale*

Most of our community property states were once under the rule of Spain, but the ultimate origin of community property is the customs of some of the Germanic tribes which overran the Roman Empire at the end of the ancient world. Community property today exists in many countries of Europe which were never under Spanish rule.[9] It never took hold in England, however, for reasons which are not clear.[10]

The American states which were once under Spanish rule chose to adopt community property even though they rejected everything else in the civil law tradition (with the exception of Louisiana). They adopted community property because they considered the common law rules governing marital property at the time to be unfair. The common law then held that upon marriage a woman's property passed to her husband. The choice of community property improved the status of married women.[11]

At first American courts treated the wife's interest in community property as only an expectancy until her husband died. This was a perversion of the Spanish community property system, which ended when the tax advantages of the Spanish system were recognized.

> If the community was equally owned by the spouses, then only one-half the community would be includible in the decedent spouse's estate. If, however, the husband was regarded as owner of all the community his wife taking no interest until his death, 100 percent of the community would be part of the husband's taxable estate. A similar problem was presented in the income tax context * * * To the extent that state law regarded the spouses as equal owners, the spouses could divide the community [income] for tax purposes, each separately reporting one half. This allowed the use of a considerably lower tax rate * * *.[12]

To achieve these tax advantages community property states began to say that spouses had "present, existing" interests in community property.[13] This has made it difficult to alter the rules of community property retroactively.[14]

From the foregoing history one might infer that community property is a "tax gimmick" and no longer useful under present law since the marital deduction confers similar advantages in separate property states. However, community property continues to flourish. In fact, there is a trend in all states toward the community property approach in dividing marital assets at divorce.[15] Many states now give special treatment to "marital property," which is much like community property.[16] In 1983 a Uniform Marital Property Act

9. Rheinstein, *Division of Marital Property,* 12 Wil.L.J. 413, 419–20 (1976).

10. Donahue, *What Causes Fundamental Legal Ideas,* 78 Mich.L.Rev. 59 (1979).

11. Prager, *The Persistence of Separate Property Concepts in California's Community Property System, 1849–1975,* 24 UCLA L.Rev. 1, 6, 10 (1976).

12. *Id.*, at 60.

13. *Id.* at 63.

14. *E.g.*, In re Marriage of Fabian, 715 P.2d 253 (Cal.1986); In re Marriage of Buol, 705 P.2d 354 (Cal.1985). *See also* Uniform Marital Property Act, Prefatory Note: "A provision effecting automatic reclassification of [property owned when the Act takes effect] would amount to retroactive legislation and would risk constitutional attack."

15. Note, 28 UCLA L.Rev. 1365, 1369 (1981); Reppy, *Community Property in the U.S. Supreme Court,* 10 Comm.Prop.L.J. 93, 119 (1983).

16. Uniform Marital Property Act, Prefatory Note. *See also* In re Marriage of Smith, 405 N.E.2d 884 (Ill.App.1980) (citing cases from community property states in defining "marital property.")

was promulgated, which Wisconsin has adopted.[17] Community property thinking also had an impact on the provisions of the Uniform Probate Code governing the elective share.[18]

The community property system recognizes the contributions to marital wealth of a spouse who does not earn wages, such as a housewife. "Why should a wife working as keeper of the home and nurse of the children be in a less favorable position than the married woman who works outside the home * * * and accumulates her own savings? Does not the housewife through her work enable the husband to earn money and accumulate his savings?"[19] Community property rules do not always benefit a spouse; when a couple has little community property, the spouse has few rights, but arguably this is as it should be. Property which "was not acquired because of the performance of marital duties * * * should not be available for the survivor to share."[20] However, some have criticized the community property system for failing to give a needy surviving spouse any rights in the decedent's separate property.[21] The Uniform Probate Code attempts to meet this objection by including in the elective share an additional amount to reflect the "spouses' mutual duties of support."[22]

The community property system has also been criticized because it raises difficult factual questions. The classification of property as community or separate gives rise to much litigation. The drafters of the Uniform Probate Code, while adopting the basic rationale of community property, preferred to implement it by using "a mechanically determined approximation system" which only considers the length of the marriage without having "to identify which of the couple's property was earned during the marriage and which was acquired prior to the marriage or acquired during the marriage by gift or inheritance."

As more wives enter the work force, problems have arisen in separate property states comparable to those involved in identifying community property. When both spouses are employed and commingle their earnings, a wife for example may claim that assets held in the husband's name were actually hers because she paid for them.[23] The increasing number of married women employed outside the home has reduced the disparities between the two marital property systems. The housewife whom community property is praised for protecting is ceasing to exist, while wage-earning wives are putting an end to the simplicity of the separate property system.

**17.** Wis.Stat. § 766.001 et seq.

**18.** See Section 3.7, at note 16.

**19.** Rheinstein, *supra* note 9, at 420. *See also* Uniform Marital Property Act, Prefatory Note ("marriage is a partnership to which each spouse makes a different but equally important contribution").

**20.** Greene, *Comparison of the Property Aspects of the Community and Common Law Marital Property Systems*, 13 Creighton L.Rev. 71, 110 (1979). *See also* 84 Okl.Stat. § 44 (elective share limited to property "acquired by the joint industry of the husband and wife during coverture").

**21.** Niles, *Probate Reform in California*, 31 Hast.L.J. 185, 193 (1979).

**22.** Uniform Probate Code § 2–202(b). The quoted rationale for this provision appears in the General Comment to Part 2 of the Code.

**23.** Parks v. Zions First National Bank, 673 P.2d 590 (Utah 1983); Adams v. Jankouskas, 452 A.2d 148 (Del.1982).

### *Classification of Property*

In some European countries all the assets of both spouses are community property, but under the Spanish system, the basis of the rules in the eight American community property states, community property is limited to acquisitions due to the gainful activity of either spouse during marriage. What a spouse owned prior to marriage or acquired during marriage by inheritance or donation remains separate property.[24] This principle is common to all American community property systems, but the answer to many specific questions varies in different states.

Assume a wife owns land as separate property and leases it to a tenant after she is married. Spanish law would treat the rent as community property if it was earned during the marriage and so would some American states,[25] but in others income from separate property is also separate.[26] If the land increases in value during marriage, this appreciation will be separate property in all states,[27] unless the increase in value was due to the expenditure of community funds or labor on improvements. In a case in which a wife owned land prior to marriage, and $20,000 in community funds were used to build a home on the land which enhanced its value by $54,000, the community was awarded an interest measured by this enhancement in value.[28] Another court in a similar case adopted a flexible approach: "in most cases simple reimbursement without interest is the appropriate measure for . . . improvements . . . [but] where the improvements actually decrease the value of the property reimbursement may be too generous a measure. Alternatively, reimbursement may be too stingy where the vast bulk of appreciation is due to the improvements."[29] In California in the converse case when separate funds are used to improve community property, the spouse whose funds were used is "reimbursed without interest or adjustment for change in monetary values."[30]

If a spouse's separate property is subject to a mortgage at the time of the marriage and community funds are used to reduce the mortgage, some states simply reimburse the community for the amount paid,[31] but others give the community an interest in the property proportional to its contribution to the total price paid.[32]

**24.** Rheinstein, *supra* note 9, at 419; Calif.Fam.Code §§ 760, 770; Idaho Code § 32–903, 32–906; Lay, *A Survey of Community Property,* 51 Iowa L.Rev. 625, 626, 629–30 (1966). *See also* Uniform Marital Property Act § 4(f), (g).

**25.** Swope v. Swope, 739 P.2d 273 (Idaho 1987); Tabassi v. NBC Bank-San Antonio, 737 S.W.2d 612 (Tex.App.1987).

**26.** Lay, *supra* note 24, at 630; Bayer v. Bayer, 800 P.2d 216, 222 (N.M.App.1990) (contrasting Arizona and New Mexico rules); Cross, *Community Property: A Comparison of the Systems in Washington and Louisiana,* 39 La. L.Rev. 479, 484 (1979); *cf.* Uniform Marital Property Act § 4(d) (all income earned during marriage is marital property).

**27.** *Cf.* Note, 28 UCLA L.Rev. 1365, 1386 (1981) (arguing that "all appreciation in the value of [a] home since the date of the marriage" should be community, but noting that "this rule is not followed anywhere today."). *See also* Uniform Marital Property Act § 4(g)(3). However, in Marshall v. Marshall, 253 B.R. 550 (2000), the court held that "where income from separate property is reinvested instead of distributed, under Texas law the increase in value of the property during the marriage is community property."

**28.** Anderson v. Gilliland, 684 S.W.2d 673 (Tex.1985). *See also* Portillo v. Shappie, 636 P.2d 878 (N.M.1981); Honnas v. Honnas, 648 P.2d 1045 (Ariz.1982); Elam v. Elam, 650 P.2d 213 (Wash.1982).

**29.** Malmquist v. Malmquist, 792 P.2d 372, 382–83 (Nev.1990).

**30.** Cal.Fam.Code § 2640. The reimbursement "shall not exceed the net value of the property at the time of the division." This provision applies only in dividing property at divorce.

**31.** Pringle v. Pringle, 712 P.2d 727 (Idaho App.1985); In re Marriage of Wakefield, 763 P.2d 459 (Wash.App.1988).

**32.** Drahos v. Rens, 717 P.2d 927 (Ariz. App.1985); Dorbin v. Dorbin, 731 P.2d 959 (N.M.App.1986); Malmquist v. Malmquist, 792 P.2d 372 (Nev.1990).

Sometimes a spouse owns a business at the beginning of a marriage and works for it during the marriage. If the spouse was not adequately compensated by the business for the services, and they increased the value of the business, the community acquires a share of the business according to some courts.[33] Others only reimburse the community for the value of the services.[34]

Classification issues also arise when a spouse owns life insurance prior to marriage and premiums are paid during the marriage. Many courts hold that the proceeds "will be separate property or community property in proportion to the percentage of total premiums which have been paid with separate or community funds."[35] In Texas, however, if a policy began as separate property it remains so, and the community is only reimbursed for the premiums paid with community funds.[36] For term insurance, the source of the funds used to pay the most recent premium on the policy is determinative.[37]

If a couple separate but do not divorce, are their earnings during separation separate or community? States differ on this issue. For example, a husband deserted his wife in the '50's, "married" another woman in 1984 and thereafter won $2.5 million in a lottery before he died. Under Washington law, where the husband died, a legal wife has no community property interest in the earnings after the couple's separation indicates that the marriage is defunct,[38] but arguably Texas law governed under which the community continues until a divorce.[39] Although this rule seems inconsistent with the rationale of community property, it "avoids the factual issue of when the couple began living apart, and provides appropriate treatment for the on-again-off-again manner in which some couples try to resolve their differences and patch up their marriages."[40]

If a spouse recovers damages for personal injury, compensation for pain and suffering is regarded as separate property, but amounts given to replace lost earnings during the marriage are community property because the earnings themselves would have been community.[41] Many states treat work-

**33.** Lindemann v. Lindemann, 960 P.2d 966 (Wash.App.1998) (increase in value of husband's separate business attributable to his labor during marriage divided upon separation); Smith v. Smith, 837 P.2d 869 (N.M.App. 1992); *cf.* Josephson v. Josephson, 772 P.2d 1236 (Idaho App.1989) (community has no interest in business where husband was paid an adequate salary for his services); Rowe v. Rowe, 744 P.2d 717 (Ariz.App.1987).

**34.** Jensen v. Jensen, 665 S.W.2d 107 (Tex. 1984).

**35.** Porter v. Porter, 726 P.2d 459 (Wash. 1986). *See also* Lay, *supra* note 24, at 637.

**36.** Rev. Rul. 80–242, 1980–2 Cum.Bull 799; McCurdy v. McCurdy, 372 S.W.2d 381 (Tex.Civ.App.1963).

**37.** Matter of Estate of Bellingham, 933 P.2d 425 (Wash.App.1997); Phillips v. Wellborn, 552 P.2d 471 (N.M.1976).

**38.** *See also* Cal.Fam.Code § 771 (earnings of a spouse "while living separate and apart from the other spouse" are separate property); *cf.* Aetna Life Ins. Co. v. Boober, 784 P.2d 186 (Wash.App.1990) (community continues even though spouses are living apart if their conduct does not show an intent to renounce the community).

**39.** Seizer v. Sessions, 940 P.2d 261 (Wash. 1997). The court noted that Texas would also give a share to the putative spouse. See Section 2.11, at note 17 et seq. The court held that Washington law governed, but remanded for a trial as to whether *both* spouse's conduct showed that the marriage was over; mere desertion by one did not indicate a defunct marriage.

**40.** Lynch v. Lynch, 791 P.2d 653, 655 (Ariz.App.1990). *See also* In re Marriage of von der Nuell, 28 Cal.Rptr.2d 447 (App.1994) (couple not "separated" under Family Code when they continued to go out even though living apart).

**41.** In re Marriage of Hilt, 704 P.2d 672, 676 (Wash.App.1985); Hatcher v. Hatcher, 933 P.2d 1222 (Ariz.App.1996) (distinguishing between earnings during marriage and those after divorce). It may be difficult to allocate an award between these elements. In Brown v.

er's compensation benefits and disability pensions the same way, but some classify them as community property if they are attributable to premiums paid during the marriage.[42]

Questions of fact in classifying property are often resolved by a presumption that everything acquired during a marriage is community property.[43] This presumption applies even though title to an asset (*e.g.* a stock certificate) is in the name of only one spouse.[44] But a spouse can establish that property is separate by tracing its source.[45] For example, a man owned Texaco stock prior to marriage, sold it during the marriage, deposited the proceeds in a bank account which he later used to buy other stock. This stock was held to be his separate property even though acquired during the marriage.[46] But when a wife had a savings account prior to marriage into which community property was deposited, the whole account was held to be community at divorce because she "did not sustain her burden of demonstrating what portion of the monies in the account retained their separate character."[47]

Classification may be altered by agreement between the spouses. In California, a couple may, with or without consideration "transmute separate property of either spouse to community property" or vice versa. This requires an "express declaration" accepted by the spouse adversely affected thereby.[48] But such an agreement is sometimes inferred from conduct. If a husband, for example, uses his separate property to buy a house and takes title in the names of both spouses, many courts would infer that he intended the house to be community property.[49]

### *Non–Probate Transfers*

Because each spouse has a present interest in community property, transfers of community property by one spouse may be voidable by the other. Thus a deed by a husband of a home to his children by a former marriage was held voidable by his widow because the home was community property.[50] This

Brown, 675 P.2d 1207 (Wash.1984), an action for personal injury was pending when a couple divorced. The court said that "allocation of the damages should proceed upon special interrogatories" to the jury.

**42.** Douglas v. Douglas, 686 P.2d 260 (N.M.App.1984).

**43.** Gagan v. Gouyd, 86 Cal.Rptr.2d 733, 738 (App.1999). In Estate of Hull v. Williams, 885 P.2d 1153 (Idaho App.1994), the court applied this presumption even though the marriage lasted only 8 years and the date of acquisition of the property was unclear.

**44.** Matter of Estate of Mundell, 857 P.2d 631 (Idaho 1993) (H owns half interest in IRA accounts listed in W's name); C & L Lumber and Supply, Inc. v. Texas American Bank, 795 P.2d 502 (N.M.1990) (land conveyed by deed "to H as his separate property" is community property, since deed not signed by W).

**45.** Cooper v. Cooper, 635 P.2d 850 (Ariz. 1981); Cal.Prob.Code § 5305 (bank accounts); *cf.* Uniform Marital Property Act §§ 4(b), 14(a).

**46.** Estate of Hanau v. Hanau, 730 S.W.2d 663 (Tex.1987). *See also* Estate of Kenly, TC Memo 1996–516.

**47.** Cooper v. Cooper, 635 P.2d 850 (Ariz. 1981).

**48.** Cal.Fam.Code §§ 850, 852. *See also* Bosone v. Bosone, 768 P.2d 1022 (Wash.App. 1989) (separate property converted to community by agreement).

**49.** In re Estate of Hansen, 892 P.2d 764 (Wash.App.1995); Schmanski v. Schmanski, 984 P.2d 752, 767 (Nev.1999) (separate property put into a joint brokerage account). In California the presumption that property held in both spouses' names is community property can only be rebutted by a writing in divorce cases. Calif.Fam.Code § 2581. If someone gives property "to H and W," it may be classified as community on the ground that the donor so intended. Matter of Marriage of Olivares, 848 P.2d 1281 (Wash.App.1993).

**50.** Bosone v. Bosone, 768 P.2d 1022 (Wash.App.1989); Estate of Hull v. Williams, 885 P.2d 1153 (Idaho App.1994); Ackel v. Ack-

gives more protection to spouses than the elective share, which encompasses only a decedent spouse's probate estate in some states. Even the UPC "augmented estate" would not have included the home in this case if the transfer occurred more than 2 years before the husband died. Many separate property states exclude insurance proceeds from the elective share,[51] but spouses who show that an insurance policy was purchased with community funds can get half the proceeds even if the insured designated someone else as beneficiary.[52]

However, there are limits on a spouse's rights to upset transfers of community property. Third persons who deal in good faith with one spouse may be free from claims by the other spouse. An insurance company which pays a beneficiary designated by an insured spouse is not liable if it had no notice of the community property rights of the other spouse.[53] Purchasers of community real property held in the name of one spouse are protected if they bought "in good faith without knowledge of the marital relation."[54]

A transfer may also be upheld as a legitimate exercise of the spouse's managerial powers. Thus a widow's attack on a transfer of beehives by her husband to his son was rejected, because they were compensation for the son's work in the business, and either spouse could bind the community property by contract.[55] Similarly, a court rejected a husband's challenge of his wife's selection of a payment option under her pension plan which increased payments during her lifetime but gave nothing to the husband when she died.[56]

This rationale may produce the same result as the UPC's exclusion from the augmented estate of transfers made by a spouse for consideration.[57] But the parallel is not complete. Many community property states require the consent of both spouses for all transfers of real estate, even sales.[58] On the other hand, some states permit gifts of community property by one spouse if they are not "excessive."[59]

***Differences Between Community Property and Elective Share***

el, 595 So.2d 739 (La.App.1992) (gift of stock voidable by nonconsenting spouse).

**51.** See Section 3.7, at note 34.

**52.** Emard v. Hughes Aircraft Co., 153 F.3d 949, 955 (9th Cir.1998); Aetna Life Ins. Co. v. Boober, 784 P.2d 186 (Wash.App.1990).

**53.** Leonard v. Occidental Life Ins. Co., 106 Cal.Rptr. 899 (App.1973). *See also* Cal.Fam. Code § 755 (payment under an employee retirement plan discharges payor who has received no written notice of community property rights).

**54.** Calif.Fam.Code § 1102; *cf.* Uniform Marital Property Act § 9.

**55.** Mundell v. Stellmon, 825 P.2d 510 (Idaho App.1992).

**56.** O'Hara v. State ex rel. Public Employees Retirement Board, 764 P.2d 489 (Nev. 1988); Brown v. Boeing Co., 622 P.2d 1313 (Wash.App.1980).

**57.** Uniform Probate Code § 2–208(a).

**58.** Cal.Fam.Code § 1102; Arch Ltd. v. Yu, 766 P.2d 911 (N.M.1988) (contract to exchange land signed by only one spouse is unenforceable).

**59.** Street v. Skipper, 887 S.W.2d 78 (Tex. App.1994) (designation of estate as beneficiary of insurance upheld because not "unfair" to the spouse); Fernandez v. Fernandez, 806 P.2d 582 (N.M.App.1991). Compare Unif. Marital Property Act § 6 allowing gifts of marital property by one spouse up to $500 a year, or more if "the gift is reasonable in amount considering the economic position of the spouses." *See also* La.Civ.Code art 2349 (allowing a "customary gift of a value commensurate with the economic position of the spouses"); Succession of Caraway, 639 So.2d 415 (La.App.1994).

All community property states give each spouse one-half of the community property, regardless of whether or not the decedent spouse had surviving children. Children may provide a reason to reduce a spouse's claim for support, since children are also entitled to support, but community property claims are based on the spouse's contribution to the acquisition of property.

Other peculiar aspects of community property law grow out of this contribution rationale. Separate property states only give an elective share to a *surviving* spouse, and the right to elect is lost if the survivor dies before exercising it.[60] Community property rights, on the other hand, do not usually turn on survival. Thus the estate of a wife who predeceased her husband was awarded one half of the retirement benefits provided by the husband's employer because they were community property.[61]

In separate property states the conservator of a spouse who is incompetent may be denied an elective share if it is not necessary for the spouse's support.[62] Under a community property system, a failure to claim the spouse's share of the community would be regarded as a gift, and the spouse's lack of need would not by itself justify such a gift.[63]

If a will devises property to a spouse, in most separate property jurisdictions the spouse would have to renounce the devise in order to get the elective share, or the value of the devise would be charged against it.[64] In a community property state, however, normally the spouse can keep half of the community property and get the devise too. Each spouse already *owns* half of the community property and normally a devisee does not have to surrender property which she owns in order to take under a will.[65]

If a will leaves "one half my estate to my wife," courts normally assume that the testator "intended only to dispose of his own interest (his separate property and one-half of the community property), and no election is necessary, no matter how liberal the provision is for the wife." However, "if the testator purported to dispose of both his and his spouse's share of the community property," the spouse is put to an election, just as when A's will purports to devise B's property to C and leaves other property to B, B must allow her property to pass to C if she wishes to take under A's will.[66]

If a testator owns community property, the will should make clear what it is disposing of and whether or not the spouse must elect. Some testators want to put both halves of the community into a trust, either because they do not think the spouse can manage property, or because they want to have a unified management of all the community property, or in order to save probate costs

**60.** See Section 3.7, at note 70.

**61.** Allard v. Frech, 754 S.W.2d 111 (Tex. 1988); In re Estate of MacDonald, 794 P.2d 911 (Cal.1990). However, this result is precluded as to plans governed by ERISA. Boggs v. Boggs, 520 U.S. 833 (1997); Ablamis v. Roper, 937 F.2d 1450 (9th Cir.1991).

**62.** See Section 3.7, at note 67.

**63.** As to gifts by conservators see Section 7.2, at note 28.

**64.** See Section 3.7, at note 46.

**65.** In Chesnin v. Fischler, 717 P.2d 298 (Wash.App.1986), a wife used community property to create two joint accounts, one with her husband, the other with her sister. The husband was allowed to keep his account while claiming a share in the one for his sister-in-law. Contrast Uniform Probate Code § 2-209(a).

**66.** Burch v. George, 866 P.2d 92 (Cal. 1994); Smith v. Smith, 657 S.W.2d 457 (Tex. App.1983); In re Estate of Patton, 494 P.2d 238 (Wash.App.1972). As to equitable election outside the community property context see *Restatement (Third) of Property (Wills and Other Donative Transfers)* § 6.1, comm. d (Prel.Dft. 2000).

when the spouse dies.[67] Although a testator cannot dispose of all the community property against the wishes of the other spouse, the spouse often does not object to this, particularly if he or she was used to letting the decedent manage their property and does not wish to undertake the burdens of management now. Acquiescence by the surviving spouse is less likely if the will leaves community property to the decedent's children by another marriage or other relatives, but even in this case, the benefits to the surviving spouse from taking under the will may exceed the spouse's community property rights if the spouse must elect. Unless a widow, for example, is quite old, the income from all the community property for life (as a typical trust provides) may be worth substantially more than her half the community property.[68]

### *Choice of Law*

Although many people move to or from one of the eight community property states, there is an "astonishing dearth of case law" on how conflicts between the laws of separate and community property states should be resolved.[69]

The traditional rule that the law of the situs governs land may apply here,[70] but there is a trend to have domicile control even land. California, for example, defines community property as "all property, real or personal, *wherever situated*, acquired by a married person during the marriage *while domiciled in this state*."[71] If a non-domiciliary buys land in California, the law of the owner's domicile governs the rights of the owner's surviving spouse.[72]

Everyone agrees that domicile should control personal property, but couples often change domicile. In England, domicile at the time of marriage controls. If a couple marries in France all their property is community even though they later move to England.[73] In America, on the other hand, domicile at the time property is acquired determines whether it is community or separate. [74] Thus if a couple buys stock while living in a separate property state, it remains the separate property of the acquiring spouse if they later move to a community property state.[75] This rule may leave a spouse "caught between two radically different systems and protected by neither."[76] The

**67.** Kahn & Gallo, *The Widow's Election,* 24 Stan.L.Rev. 531, 536–38 (1972).

**68.** The income, estate and gift tax consequences of a "widow's election" will are complicated and still not entirely clear. For an extended discussion see H. Weinstock, *Planning an Estate* §§ 5.18–5.31 (4th ed. 1995).

**69.** J. Dukeminier & S. Johanson, *Family Wealth Transactions* 609 (2d ed. 1978).

**70.** In In re Crichton's Estate, 228 N.E.2d 799 (N.Y.1967), a husband died domiciled in New York, owning land in Louisiana. His widow's claim to half the Louisiana land as community property was conceded. *See also* Millikin Trust Co. v. Jarvis, 180 N.E.2d 759 (Ill. App.1962).

**71.** Cal.Fam.Code § 760.

**72.** Calif.Prob.Code § 120. *See also* Uniform Prob. Code § 2–201.

**73.** De Nichols v. Curlier, [1900] A.C. 21 (1899); Juenger, *Marital Property and the Conflict of Laws,* 81 Colum.L.Rev. 1061, 1072 (1981).

**74.** If the couple have separate domiciles, that of the acquiring spouse controls. Seizer v. Sessions, 940 P.2d 261, 265 (Wash.1997) (following *Restatement, Second, Conflicts of Law* § 258, comm. c (1971).

**75.** Brenholdt v. Brenholdt, 612 P.2d 1300 (N.M.1980); *Restatement (Second) of Conflict of Laws* §§ 258, 259 (1969); Nationwide Resources Corp. v. Massabni, 694 P.2d 290 (Ariz. App.1984); Estate of Hanau v. Hanau, 730 S.W.2d 663 (Tex.1987).

**76.** Rein, *A More Rational System for the Protection of Family Members Against Disinheritance,* 15 Gonz.L.Rev. 11, 42 (1979).

elective share of the separate property state is unavailable if the decedent spouse was domiciled elsewhere at death, and the community property system is of no use if all the decedent's assets are classified as separate property. California and Idaho have solved this dilemma by the concept of "quasi-community" property, which treats property acquired in another state "as if" the decedent acquirer had been domiciled in the community property state.[77] Quasi-community property is treated like community property in that the other spouse is entitled to half of it despite the decedent's will, and inherits all of it if the decedent had no will.[78] But unlike true community property, if the acquiring spouse gives away quasi-community property during life, the surviving spouse has no claim unless the transfer had testamentary characteristics; the test is similar to the one for including property in the augmented estate under the Uniform Probate Code.[79]

When the move is in the other direction, from a community property to a separate property state, the spouse may receive *too much* protection rather than too little. If a couple acquires stock while domiciled in a community property state, the stock continues to be community property if they move to a separate property state.[80] Can a surviving spouse also claim an elective share in the decedent's half of the community? Probably not. The Uniform Disposition of Community Property Rights at Death Act would preserve the surviving spouse's share of the community property, but would bar a claim to an elective share in the decedent's half of the community.[81]

The community property interest of a spouse may be preempted by federal law. Several decisions of the United States Supreme Court have dealt with the relationship between federal and state law in this area, but the underlying principles remain unclear. When a husband used community funds to purchase United States Savings Bonds payable on death to his brother, the Court held that this did not deprive the widow of her rights under state law.[82] But the Court rejected a claim by an Army officer's widow to half the proceeds of a National Service Life Insurance Policy purchased with community funds; a federal statute which said the proceeds went to the named beneficiary was held to supersede state community property law.[83] The Court also rejected community property claims asserted against military retirement pay[84] and benefits under the Railroad Retirement Act,[85] but here the Court apparently misread congressional intent, for the relevant statutes were later amended to

**77.** Calif.Prob.Code § 66; Idaho Code § 15–2–201. This does not apply to real property located outside the state.

**78.** Cal.Prob.Code §§ 101, 6401(b).

**79.** Calif.Prob.Code § 102. This section is modelled on the pre–1990 UPC, and thus it excludes life insurance and pensions. *Cf.* Idaho Code § 15–2–202.

**80.** Devine v. Devine, 711 P.2d 1034 (Wash. App.1985); People ex rel. Dunbar v. Bejarano, 358 P.2d 866 (Colo.1961); Scoles & Hay, Conflict of Laws § 14.9 (2d ed. 1992)

**81.** Uniform Disposition of Community Property Rights at Death Act § 3. This act has been adopted in Colorado, Hawaii, Kentucky, Michigan, New York, Oregon, and Virginia.

**82.** Yiatchos v. Yiatchos, 376 U.S. 306 (1964).

**83.** Wissner v. Wissner, 338 U.S. 655 (1950). The California Supreme Court was able to perceive a distinction between this and a very similar insurance program for civilian employees of the federal government in Carlson v. Carlson, 521 P.2d 1114 (Cal.1974).

**84.** McCarty v. McCarty, 453 U.S. 210 (1981).

**85.** Hisquierdo v. Hisquierdo, 439 U.S. 572 (1979). *See also* Wisner v. Wisner, 631 P.2d 115 (Ariz.App.1981) (Social Security).

change the result.[86] ERISA has been held to supersede community property claims when a non-employee spouse who predeceased the employee purported to devise a share of the employee's pension.[87]

## § 3.9 Waivers

Agreements between spouses to limit the survivor's claim to an elective share are increasingly common as more persons enter into second marriages and wish to protect the inheritance of children of a prior marriage from the new spouse. (Nearly all the cases involving waivers arise from a second marriage where one or both spouses has children by a prior union). Even in community property states, where property owned prior to the marriage is not subject to a forced share, parties may wish to provide by agreement that property which would otherwise be community shall be separate, or allow one spouse to dispose of all the community assets.

Such agreements are sometimes made prior to the marriage, sometimes while the couple are married. The rules governing the two situations are not necessarily the same. Historically, any agreement made by a woman after marriage did not bind her; marriage took away her capacity to contract on the theory that "everything that a married woman does [is] done through dread of her husband."[1] On the other hand, ERISA allows the "spouse" of a participant to waive rights to an annuity,[2] and one court has held that an antenuptial waiver of ERISA rights is ineffectual because a fiancee is not a spouse.[3]

Many states have adopted a Uniform Premarital Agreement Act. It does not cover post nuptial agreements,[4] but the standards in the Act are incorporated in Uniform Probate Code, which by its terms applies to agreements made "before or after marriage."[5] California, on the other hand, has adopted both the Uniform Premarital Agreement Act[6] and somewhat different provisions governing postnuptial agreements.[7] The California Family Code express-

**86.** Uniformed Services Former Spouses' Protection Act, 10 U.S.C. § 1408. This Act has been held to exclude retirement pay which a spouse receives as a result of waiving disability benefits, despite the Court's inability to perceive a policy reason for the distinction. Mansell v. Mansell, 490 U.S. 581 (1989). See also In re Marriage of Kraft, 832 P.2d 871 (Wash. 1992).

**87.** Boggs v. Boggs, 520 U.S. 833 (1997). *But see* Emard v. Hughes Aircraft Co., 153 F.3d 949 (9th Cir.1998) (second wife can assert community property rights in pension and insurance which employee left to prior spouse.) As to the possible conflict between community property and copyright laws see Nimmer, *Copyright Ownership by the Marital Community*, 36 UCLA L.Rev. 383 (1988).

**§ 3.9**

**1.** Y.B. 7 Edw. 4, f. 14, pl. 8 (1467). *See also* 2 W. Blackstone, *Commentaries* *138 (1765); Statute of Uses, 27 Hen. 8, c. 10 §§ 4, 7 (waiver of dower effective only if made prior to marriage).

**2.** 29 U.S.C. § 1055(c)(2).

**3.** Hurwitz v. Sher, 789 F.Supp. 134 (S.D.N.Y.1992). In affirming, the Court of Appeals left this question open. 982 F.2d 778, 781 (2d Cir.1992). In In re Estate of Hopkins, 574 N.E.2d 230 (Ill.App.1991), the court upheld a premarital waiver of ERISA rights.

**4.** Uniform Premarital Ageement Act § 1.

**5.** Uniform Probate Code § 2–213. *See also Restatement (Third) of Property (Wills and Other Donative Transfers)* § 9.4 (Prel.Dft. 2000); Day v. Vitus, 792 P.2d 1240 (Or.App. 1990), applying the Act by analogy to a postnuptial agreement.

**6.** Cal.Fam.Code §§ 1600 *et seq.*

**7.** Cal.Prob.Code §§ 140–47. Section 140 indicates that these provisions apply to all agreements "whether signed before or during marriage" but Section 147(c) indicates that premarital agreements are *not* covered. In re Estate of Gagnier, 26 Cal.Rptr.2d 128 (App. 1993), holds that different rules apply to pre- and postnuptial agreements. *See also* Fla.Stat. § 732.702(2) (disclosure required for postnuptial agreements only).

es an idea which can also be found in judicial opinions in other states: spouses occupy "confidential relations with each other ... and neither shall take unfair advantage of the other."[8] The situation of parties who are about to be, but not yet married, is, according to California authority, different.

> Although persons, once they are married, are in a fiduciary relationship to one another * * * so that * * * the advantaged party bears the burden of demonstrating that the agreement was not obtained through undue influence * * * a different burden applies under the Uniform Act in the premarital setting. Even where the premarital agreement clearly advantages one of the parties, the party challenging the agreement bears the burden of demonstrating that the agreement was not entered into voluntarily.[9]

In any event, agreements made after a couple has separated and are anticipating divorce are less likely to be affected by undue confidence in the other spouse.[10] As one court noted in upholding such an agreement, the wife "was in a position of knowledge that is far superior to that of a young bride signing an agreement *before* the marriage."[11]

Some surviving spouses waive rights in the estate after the other spouse has died. Although this situation is not covered by any statute, it can produce abuses of a confidential relationship. In a recent case a widow's release of any claims against her husband's estate was held not binding because the husband's executor, his child by a prior marriage, "failed to disclose the facts which would enable [the widow] to make a free and understanding consent."[12] On the other hand, a husband's waiver of rights in his deceased wife's estate without consideration was held binding, since he before signing the waiver he "was advised of his legal rights" and had "thoroughly reviewed" the inventory of her estate.[13]

### *Formal Requirements*

An oral or unsigned waiver in most states is unenforceable under the Statute of Frauds as an agreement in consideration of marriage,[14] or under a special provision like Uniform Probate Code § 2–213 that the spouse's right of election can only be waived "by a written contract * * * signed by the surviving spouse."[15] However, oral agreements are sometimes enforced on an "estoppel" theory despite such a statute.[16]

**8.** Cal.Fam.Code § 721(b).

**9.** In re Marriage of Bonds, 5 P.3d 815, 831 (Cal.2000).

**10.** Estate of Gibson, 269 Cal.Rptr. 48 (App.1990).

**11.** Davis v. Miller, 7 P.3d 1223, 1233 (Kan. 2000).

**12.** Matter of Estate of Hessenflow, 909 P.2d 662, 672 (Kan.App.1995). *See also* Matter of Estate of Geer, 629 P.2d 458 (Wash.App. 1981); Matter of Estate of Epstein, 561 N.W.2d 82 (Iowa App.1996).

**13.** In re Estate of Ferguson, 730 N.E.2d 1205, 1211 (Ill.App.2000).

**14.** Clark, *Antenuptial Contracts,* 50 U.Colo.L.Rev. 141, 142 (1979); *Restatement (Second) of Contracts* § 124, illus. 3 (1979).

**15.** *See also* Unif. Premarital Agreement Act § 2 (agreement must be signed by both parties); *Restatement (Third) of Property (Wills and Other Donative Transfers)* § 9.4(a) (Prel.Dft. 2000); Ind.Code § 29–1–3–6; Calif.Prob.Code § 142; Estate of Calcutt v. Calcutt, 576 N.E.2d 1288 (Ind.App.1991) (oral waiver unenforceable).

**16.** Estate of Sheldon, 142 Cal.Rptr. 119 (App.1977); Brown v. Boeing Co., 622 P.2d 1313, 1317 (Wash.App.1980).

ERISA requires that a spouse's waiver of rights in the other spouse's pension be "witnessed by a plan representative or a notary public."[17] Historically, married women could waive dower only before a judge who would examine them to make sure they were acting voluntarily.[18] This is not necessary today,[19] but New York requires that a waiver of the spouse's elective rights be acknowledged like a deed.[20]

Uniform Probate Code § 2–208, on the other hand, excludes from the augmented estate (and thus the elective share)[21] property which the decedent transferred "with the written joinder of" the surviving spouse. This section says nothing explicitly about a signature or the disclosure requirements for waivers, to be discussed presently.

California also provides for a "spouse's written consent to a provision for a nonprobate transfer of community property on death." Such consent is revocable during the marriage, in contrast to a "declaration" transmuting community into separate property.[22] The California Supreme Court in 1990 held that a wife's consent to her husband's designation of a beneficiary of community property did not bind her estate because she did not expressly declare an intent to transmute the property.[23] The relevant statutes were thereafter amended to provide that even without such an express declaration, a consent to a transfer could not be revoked after the death of either spouse.[24] However, such a consent can be avoided for fraud or undue influence.[25] Presumably this is also true of a consent to transfers under the Uniform Probate Code, since "the principles of law and equity supplement its provisions."[26]

### *Disclosure*

A common theme in both the statutes and case law concerning waivers is the need for disclosure. The Uniform Premarital Agreement Act and UPC say that an agreement which is "unconscionable" is valid only if the party challenging it was "provided a fair and reasonable disclosure of the property or financial obligations of the other party" or waived such disclosure or otherwise had or could have had adequate knowledge thereof.[27] Many judicial opinions also suggest that disclosure is necessary only if the agreement is unfair. For example, one court denied that an antenuptial agreement must "make reasonable provision *and* [be] entered into after full and fair disclosure ... An agreement can survive if *either* (but not necessarily both) of these requirements is satisfied."[28] Under the Third Property Restatement, however,

**17.** 29 U.S.C. § 1055(c)(2)(A).

**18.** Y.B. 18 Edw. 4, f. 4, pl. 11 (1478); 2 W. Blackstone, *Commentaries* *351 (1765).

**19.** However, in Louisiana an agreement made during marriage to alter the community property regime needs court approval. La.Civ. Code art. 2329.

**20.** N.Y.EPTL § 5–1.1(f)(2). *See also* Wash. Rev.Code § 26.16.120 (agreement on disposition of community property must be acknowledged like a deed).

**21.** See Section 3.7, at notes 29 et seq.

**22.** Cal.Prob.Code §§ 5022, 5030; Cal.Fam. Code §§ 850, 852.

**23.** In re Estate of MacDonald, 794 P.2d 911 (Cal.1990).

**24.** Cal.Prob.Code § 5030(c).

**25.** Cal.Prob.Code § 5015.

**26.** Uniform Probate Code § 1–103.

**27.** Unif. Premarital Agreement Act § 6. Uniform Probate Code § 2–213 is similar.

**28.** In re Estate of Geyer, 533 A.2d 423, 427 (Pa.1987). *See also* Sasarak v. Sasarak, 586 N.E.2d 172 (Ohio App.1990) (even though amount received was "disproportionate" to widow's rights, valid because of full disclosure).

an "unconscionable" agreement is unenforceable even if voluntary.[29]

Sometimes a party attacks an agreement which recites such disclosure, denying that it actually occurred. Many courts view such claims with suspicion,[30] but others hold that the recital of disclosure is not conclusive.[31] The drafter can deal with this problem by attaching a schedule of assets to the agreement itself; this should be effective even if the spouse signing the waiver failed to read it,[32] and even if the value of the listed assets is not given.[33]

In community property states, a spouse's knowledge about the other spouse's separate property seems irrelevant, since spouses have no rights in the other's separate property regardless of any waiver.[34] In all states, one may question whether a spouse's knowledge of the other spouse's wealth should matter unless the spouse understands his or her rights in that wealth, *i.e.* what is actually being surrendered by the waiver. Some courts in passing on waivers have stressed the business experience (or lack thereof) of the party who challenges it. For example, a wife was bound who had "been involved in various businesses ... and was not unaware of the importance or effect of binding legal documents."[35] Conversely, a wife who was "extremely unsophisticated" in business was not bound by prenuptial agreement.[36] Some opinions suggest that a waiver is valid only if the signer was aware of the rights which were being waived.[37] Arguably, unless one indulges in the fiction that everyone knows the law, the party who executes the waiver must have received legal advice.[38] The California Probate Code makes waivers binding when the spouse was "represented by independent legal counsel at the time of signing the waiver," but they can also be upheld without this.[39] Courts are beginning to question the propriety of waivers prepared by a lawyer for one spouse when

**29.** *Restatement (Third) of Property (Wills and Other Donative Transfers)* § 9.4(b) (Prel.Dft. 2000). *See also* Ind.Code § 29–1–3–6 (both "full disclosure" and "fair consideration" needed).

**30.** In Matter of Estate of Thies, 903 P.2d 186 (Mont.1995), a widow attacking the agreement lost because the trial court found her story not credible. *See also* Matter of Baggerley's Estate, 635 P.2d 1333, 1335 (Okl.App. 1981).

**31.** Bohnke v. Estate of Bohnke, 454 N.E.2d 446 (Ind.App.1983).

**32.** Wiley v. Iverson, 985 P.2d 1176 (Mont. 1999); Sasarak v. Sasarak, 586 N.E.2d 172 (Ohio App.1990); *Restatement (Third) of Property (Wills and Other Donative Transfers)* § 9.4, comm. g (Prel.Dft. 2000).

**33.** Matter of Marriage of Yager, 963 P.2d 137 (Or.App.1998).

**34.** Section 3.8, note 24.

**35.** Matter of Estate of Ascherl, 445 N.W.2d 391, 393 (Iowa App.1989). *See also* Elgar v. Elgar, 679 A.2d 937, 943 (Conn.1996) ("both parties were experienced business people"); Wiley v. Iverson, 985 P.2d 1176, 1181 (Mont.1999) (wife was "a relatively experienced businesswoman, well educated").

**36.** Sogg v. Nevada State Bank, 832 P.2d 781, 785 (Nev.1992). *See also* In re Estate of Grassman, 158 N.W.2d 673, 675 (Neb.1968) (husband "inexperienced in business and legal affairs").

**37.** Jarvis v. Jarvis, 824 P.2d 213 (Kan. App.1991).

**38.** Matter of Estate of Crawford, 730 P.2d 675, 678 (Wash.1986) (unfair prenuptial agreement invalid unless entered "upon the advice of independent counsel"). *Contra*, Matter of Estate of Lebsock, 618 P.2d 683, 686 (Colo. App.1980); Wiley v. Iverson, 985 P.2d 1176 (Mont.1999) (waiver prepared by husband's attorney upheld although wife had no counsel).

**39.** Cal.Prob.Code § 143–44; In re Estate of Gagnier, 26 Cal.Rptr.2d 128 (App.1993). In other states the fact that a spouse had independent counsel is often mentioned as a factor in upholding the agreement. Matter of Marriage of Yager, 963 P.2d 137, 140 (Or.App. 1998); Davis v. Miller, 7 P.3d 1223, 1231 (Kan. 2000). Under *Restatement (Third) of Property (Wills and Other Donative Transfers)* § 9.4 (b) (Prel.Dft. 2000) a rebuttable presumption of voluntariness arises if the spouse "was represented by independent legal counsel or was advised to obtain independent legal counsel."

the other has no lawyer. An Ohio court refused to enforce such a waiver, saying

> The agreement was prepared entirely by decedent's counsel ... To have upheld this agreement, the court would have had to have found that Blair, her fiance's lawyer, adequately advised her. [The court cites EC 5-15 of the Code of Professional Responsibility limiting a lawyer's representation of clients with conflicting interests.] Blair did not fully explain the potential conflict or recommend that appellant obtain other counsel before signing the agreement.[40]

A lawyer who advised his stepmother to waive her right to take against her husband's will was held to have violated the Rules of Professional Conduct and was suspended from practice, because his interest as a beneficiary of his father's will "jeopardized his ability to provide objective legal advice to his stepmother."[41] The California Supreme Court, however, recently rejected a claim that "a premarital agreement in which one party is not represented by independent counsel should be subjected to strict scrutiny for voluntariness." In this case the lawyer for the prospective husband had suggested to his finance that she get her own counsel but she had declined to do so. He had then explained to her that she was giving up her community property rights under the agreement. The "rule of professional conduct prohibiting counsel for one party from giving legal advice to an opposing party who is unrepresented" did not preclude enforcement of the contract. It was proper "for the attorney to take steps to ensure that the premarital agreement be enforceable" and this he had done.[42]

Most spouses in deciding whether or not to waive their rights would want to know who would benefit thereby. A widow may be willing to allow her husband to leave property to his children, but not to his mistress. In California a spouse's consent to a nonprobate transfer of community property is revoked if the beneficiary is later changed by the other spouse.[43]

### *Fairness*

According to the Uniform Premarital Agreement Act, an agreement requires no "consideration" but may be unenforceable if it was "unconscionable," absent adequate disclosure.[44] Even without a statute, courts often say that the marriage itself provides consideration for the waiver in premarital agreements.[45] Even in postnuptial agreements, courts usually have no difficulty in finding consideration,[46] but they sometimes refuse to enforce agreements because they consider them "unfair." This may mean an agreement which

**40.** Rowland v. Rowland, 599 N.E.2d 315 (Ohio App.1991). *See also* Matter of Marriage of Leathers, 789 P.2d 263, 266 (Or.1990) (dissenting opinion); Briggs v. Wyoming Nat. Bank, 836 P.2d 263, 268–72 (Wyo.1992) (dissenting opinion). For more discussion of the ethical issues see McGovern, Undue Influence and Professional Responsibility, 28 Real Prop. Prob. and Trust J. 643, 665–68 (1994).

**41.** Matter of Taylor, 693 N.E.2d 526, 528 (Ind.1998).

**42.** In re Marriage of Bonds, 5 P.3d 815, 827, 833 (Cal.2000).

**43.** Cal.Prob.Code § 5023. *See also* Internal Revenue Code § 417(a)(2).

**44.** Uniform Premarital Agreement Act §§ 2, 6.

**45.** Beatty v. Beatty, 555 N.E.2d 184 (Ind. App.1990).

**46.** Matter of Estate of Brosseau, 531 N.E.2d 158 (Ill.App.1988) (consideration in mutual release of rights in the other spouse's estate); Matter of Estate of Beesley, 883 P.2d 1343 (Utah 1994) (benefits to spouse in agreement supplied consideration).

gives the spouse substantially less than his or her share of property under the law.[47] But many agreements which substantially curtail the spouse's legal rights are sustained, particularly when they protect the decedent's children. "Antenuptial agreements are favored by the law ... It was no more than equitable that the prospective husband should, at the time he made the contract, provide that his estate should go to his children by a former marriage."[48] This argument is especially persuasive when the legal rights of a spouse are considered unduly favorable, *e.g.* a large share of an estate after a short term marriage.

This does not occur in community property states, so courts appear to be less friendly to waivers of community property rights. One court, for example, found unfair and unenforceable an agreement by which the wife waived all rights "by virtue of the expenditure of community funds or community labor" on the husband's separate property, since this allowed the husband "effectively to foreclose the accumulation of any significant community property" in a 10 year marriage.[49] On the other hand, an agreement which allowed the husband to put his wife's half of the community into a trust which made "ample provision" for her and over which she had a power of appointment, was found to be "fair" and enforceable even though she had no independent counsel.[50]

Although the Uniform Probate Code says that an "unconscionable" waiver, absent disclosure, is "not enforceable," the California counterpart allows courts to modify an agreement; courts are not limited to either enforcing or invalidating it altogether.[51] This flexible approach to antenuptial agreements is followed in England's family maintenance scheme[52] and by American courts in divorce cases.[53]

A decedent's failure to perform the consideration promised for a spouse's waiver does not necessarily make the waiver ineffective. Thus when a husband failed to name his wife as beneficiary of an insurance policy as promised, the court nevertheless enforced her waiver, since the husband's breach could be "remedied by a money judgment."[54]

### *Construction*

An enforceable agreement may give rise to problems of construction. For example, an agreement saying that "all property owned by each party at the

**47.** In re Estate of Geyer, 533 A.2d 423 (Pa.1987); Estate of Mader, 89 Cal.Rptr. 787, 792 (App.1970) (presumption of undue influence when agreement gives wife "less than what she would receive by way of her community property rights"). But in Davis v. Miller, 7 P.3d 1223 (Kan.2000), the court rejected a claim that a settlement which gave the wife over $1 million was unconscionable, without discussing what she might have received without the agreement.

**48.** Beatty v. Beatty, 555 N.E.2d 184, 188–89 (Ind.App.1990). *See also* Matter of Baggerley's Estate, 635 P.2d 1333 (Okl.App.1981) ("the antenuptial pact was aimed at achieving a natural and entirely appropriate end—the protection of the inheritance rights of his daughter").

**49.** Matter of Marriage of Foran, 834 P.2d 1081, 1086 (Wash.App.1992).

**50.** Whitney v. Seattle–First Nat. Bank, 579 P.2d 937 (Wash.1978).

**51.** Calif.Prob.Code § 144(b); *cf.* Uniform Commercial Code § 2–302.

**52.** (English) Inheritance (Provision for Family and Dependants) Act § 2(1)(f) (1975).

**53.** Osborne v. Osborne, 428 N.E.2d 810 (Mass.1981); Gross v. Gross, 464 N.E.2d 500 (Ohio 1984).

**54.** Brees v. Cramer, 586 A.2d 1284, 1289 (Md.1991). *See also* In re Estate of Cummings, 425 A.2d 340 (Pa.1981); Gillilan's Estate v. Gillilan's Estate, 406 N.E.2d 981 (Ind.App. 1980).

time of the marriage would remain the separate property of each" was held not to bar the husband from claiming a statutory surviving spouse's allowance from his wife's estate.[55] The Uniform Probate Code, however, gives a broad construction to "a waiver of 'all rights,' or equivalent language, in the property or estate of a present or prospective spouse." Such language is presumed to cover claims to a family allowance, an elective or intestate share[56] or any devise under a will executed before the waiver.[57]

## § 3.10 Negative Limitations

We have heretofore discussed rights given to a spouse or child to take part of an estate when they are disinherited. A few rules are negative in character. They invalidate particular types of devises and may operate in favor of heirs other than a spouse or child.

### *Mortmain*

In the 13th century when the feudal system was in full sway, lords complained against tenants who alienated land into "mortmain" by giving it to religious institutions such as monasteries. These complaints culminated in the Statute of Mortmain of 1279.[1] Though the term mortmain literally means "dead hand" (Latin: *mortuus manus* ), the basis of the lords' complaint was that religious corporations did *not* die, so the lord had no chance to profit from wardship which arose when a tenant left a minor heir, or escheat when a tenant died without heirs. The feudal basis for the original Statute of Mortmain was made clear by the remedy, forfeiture to the lord of whom the land was held. The donor's heirs had no standing to complain of the gift.[2]

A statute of a different sort was enacted in 1736. It reflected the law's historic concern with death-bed wills. The statute provided that all gifts of land to charity had to be made by a deed sealed and delivered at least twelve months before the donor died.[3]

Both of these statutes have been repealed in England, and neither became part of the common law in America,[4] but several American states once had "mortmain" statutes based on these historical models. The underlying purpose is to prevent wills made by dying persons under undue influence, but they operate very arbitrarily. In recent years most have been repealed or held

**55.** Estate of Calcutt v. Calcutt, 576 N.E.2d 1288 (Ind.App.1991). *See also* Matter of Estate of Zimmerman, 579 N.W.2d 591 (N.D.1998) (elective share); Steele v. Steele, 623 So.2d 1140 (Ala.1993) (wrongful death proceeds); Hunter v. Clark, 687 S.W.2d 811 (Tex.App. 1985) (homestead). *But see* Estate of Dennis, 714 S.W.2d 661 (Mo.App.1986).

**56.** This applies even though the agreement is not executed with the formalities prescribed for a will. Matter of Estate of Beesley, 883 P.2d 1343 (Utah 1994). In Matter of Estate of Lindsay, 957 P.2d 818 (Wash.App.1998), a broadly worded separation agreement was held to bar a spouse's claim to homestead even though homestead was not specifically mentioned.

**57.** Uniform Probate Code § 2–213(d). *See also* Cal.Prob.Code § 145. In Matter of Estate of Hansen, 910 P.2d 1281 (Wash.1996), such an agreement was held to bar a claim as an omitted spouse; whether or not the agreement was valid, it was enough to showed that the decedent did not intend to provide for the spouse.

**§ 3.10**

**1.** 7 Edw. 1, stat. 2, c. 13 (1279). For the background of the statute see D. Sutherland, *The Assise of Novel Disseisin* 88 (1973).

**2.** Y.B. 20 & 21 Edw. 1 (R.S.) 262 (1292).

**3.** Statute, 9 Geo. 2, c. 36 (1736).

**4.** *Restatement (Second) of Trusts* § 362 (1959).

unconstitutional.[5] For example, when a daughter invoked a mortmain statute to attack her mother's will leaving property to a hospital, the court held that the statute violated the state constitution.

> The statute does not protect against overreaching by unscrupulous lawyers, doctors, nurses, housekeepers, companions or others with a greater opportunity to influence a testator ... Nor is it rational to apply the statute in cases where the testator dies suddenly due to an accident during the six-month period after making a charitable bequest ... Artful will drafting easily defeats the effect of the statute: If the testator names anybody other than a spouse or lineal descendant to take the charitable devise in the event that the charitable devise fails, nobody would have standing to petition to avoid the charitable devise.[6]

Another traditional way to circumvent mortmain statutes was to use will substitutes. The original mortmain statutes covered any form of conveyance, but the American counterparts cover only wills. Revocable trusts and even death-bed gifts are immune.[7]

Despite the virtual disappearance of mortmain statutes, modern law continues to invalidate transfers made under undue influence. Undue influence will be discussed in Section 7.3.

### *Negative Wills*

A testator's will left his estate to his wife and declared his intention to exclude his children. The wife predeceased the testator and so could not take.[8] The testator's children were allowed to take despite the disinheritance clause in the will on the ground that "a testator cannot disinherit his heirs by words alone, but in order to do so, the property must be given to somebody else."[9] The Uniform Probate Code, on the other hand, specifically authorizes "so-called negative wills, [reversing] the usually accepted common-law rule, which defeats a testator's intent for no sufficient reason."[10] Under the Code, the disinherited heirs' shares pass as if they had disclaimed, i.e., they are deemed to have predeceased the testator.[11] It is often unclear what the testator actually intended in such cases. In above-described case, the estate would under the Code pass to the issue of the testator's children, if any, or to his collateral relatives, or if he had none, escheat. Maybe this is what the testator

**5.** The Ohio statute was repealed in 1985 and held unconstitutional in 1986, but prospectively only. It was used in Wendell v. AmeriTrust Co., N.A., 630 N.E.2d 368 (Ohio 1994), to invalidate a charitable remainder created in 1942.

**6.** Shriners Hospitals v. Zrillic, 563 So.2d 64, 69–70 (Fla.1990). For other decisions holding mortmain statutes invalid see In re Cavill's Estate, 329 A.2d 503 (Pa.1974); Estate of French, 365 A.2d 621 (D.C.App.1976); Shriners' Hospital for Crippled Children v. Hester, 492 N.E.2d 153 (Ohio 1986).

**7.** In re Estate of Katz, 528 So.2d 422 (Fla. App.1988); Matter of Estate of Kirk, 907 P.2d 794 (Idaho 1995); Bible Ministry Ass'n v. Merritt, 391 So.2d 641 (Miss.1980). *Contra, Restatement (Third) of Trusts* § 25, comment d (Tent.Draft 1996).

**8.** The effect of a devisee predeceasing the testator is discussed in Section 8.3.

**9.** Estate of Baxter, 827 P.2d 184, 187 (Okl. App.1992). *See also* Cook v. Estate of Seeman, 858 S.W.2d 114 (Ark.1993); Matter of Estate of Krokowsky, 896 P.2d 247 (Ariz.1995); In re Estate of Jackson, 793 S.W.2d 259 (Tenn.App. 1990).

**10.** Uniform Probate Code § 2–101, Comment. *See also Restatement, Third, of Property (Wills and Other Donative Transfers)* § 2.7 (1998).

**11.** Uniform Probate Code § 2–801(d). *See also Restatement, Third, of Property (Wills and Other Donative Transfers)* § 2.7, comm. c (1998).

would have wanted, but it seems more likely that he disinherited his children only to make sure his wife took.[12] If this was the reason why the children were disinherited, the testator would probably have wanted them to take when his wife could not. One court accepted this view in a similar case despite a statute based on the UPC.

> The plain language of the will indicates that [the testator] wanted to disinherit his other heirs if [his brother, the sole devisee] was alive, but there is no indication that [the testator] wanted to disinherit them if [his brother] predeceased [the testator]. * * * Can it honestly be said * * * that [the testator] intended the State to have his property if his brother did not survive him? If he had had such a bizarre intent, would he have left any doubt?[13]

Even without a statute like the UPC, some courts construe disinheritance clauses as implied gifts to another person in order to give them effect. For example, a will which said "I leave nothing to my husband" was held to be an implied devise to the testator's children.[14]

### *Conditions Relating to Marriage and Divorce*

Some parents try to use wills to control the lives of their children. Roman jurists disputed whether "penal" legacies, such as a legacy contingent on the legatee's marrying Titus' daughter, were valid.[15] American courts have had to deal with similar provisions. For example, a will left a house to the testator's fiancee "so long as she remains unmarried."[16] This arguably violates public policy because it may induce the devisee to remain unmarried. The Restatement of Property invalidates restrictions in instruments which are "designed to prevent the acquisition or retention of" property "in the event of any first marriage of the transferee."[17] The idea has roots in Roman and canon law, but "what may have been the Roman policy—encouraging the growth of the population—can hardly be a strong policy today; nor in the light of our separation of church and state would we feel comfortable following a rule ... striking down marriage restraints because they encourage immoral cohabitation." Still, "we are reluctant to brook any interference with the marriage choice of the parties to the marriage."[18] However, such conditions are valid if "the dominant motive of the transferor is to provide support until marriage" rather than to induce the transferee to remain unmarried.[19] Any evidence as to motive is admissible, and a recital in the instrument itself is not conclusive.[20] The Restatement of Trusts, noting that "a provision may reflect a mixture of motives," says that in some cases it should be "judicially reformed to accomplish the permissible objectives * * * while removing or minimizing

12. In many states they might have taken as omitted heirs if they had not been mentioned in the will. See Section 3.5.

13. Matter of Estate of Jetter, 570 N.W.2d 26, 31 (S.D.1997).

14. In re Thomas, (1984) 1 W.L.R. 237 (1983).

15. Gaius, *Institutes* 2.235; Justinian, *Institutes* 2.20.36.

16. Matter of Estate of Romero, 847 P.2d 319 (N.M.App.1993).

17. *Restatement (Second) of Property, Donative Transfers* § 6.1 (1981).

18. *Id.*, Introductory Note.

19. Thus the court in *Romero, supra* note 16, remanded for a determination of the testator's motive.

20. *Restatement (Second) of Property (Donative Transfers)* § 6.1, comment e (1981).

socially undesirable effects," for example, by replacing a condition with a provision allowing a trustee to exercise discretion to provide for needs.[21]

Regardless of motive, some restraints on marriage are acceptable. Devises conditioned on the testator's spouse remaining unmarried are allowed.[22] Although this rule is supported by case law,[23] the drafters of the Restatement appear to be uncomfortable with it; they note that its "possible harshness" is alleviated by the right of a spouse to take against the will. Also, the fact that such devises do not qualify for the federal estate tax marital deduction operates to deter them. The only legitimate justification for such a condition is to preserve property for the testator's children, and so the rule "may come to be applied" only if the testator is survived by issue.[24]

The Restatement also allows partial restraints, *i.e.* those which restrict "some, but not all, first marriages" of the devisee so long as they do not "unreasonably limit" the freedom to marry. Under this theory a court allowed a devise to the testator's son "only if he is married ... to a Jewish girl."[25] Restrictions which impose difficult problems of interpretation on the courts may be rejected. Thus a court in upholding a devise to issue who were "members in good standing of the Presbyterian Church," distinguished a will which required the devisees to "remain faithful" to a specified religion.[26] Such problems of interpretation can be alleviated by using a trustee to decide if the condition has been met, but this technique has been held invalid when it created a conflict of interest since the trustees would take the property themselves if they refuse to consent to the marriage.[27]

The Restatement invalidates conditions where the testator's "dominant motive" was to break up a family relationship.[28] When a will devised a house to the testator's children on condition that their mother not live in it, the court remanded the case for a finding as to the testator's motive, suggesting that the prohibition may have been only "a recognition of ... 'almost an impossible situation' ", *i.e.* the testator's fiancee and his ex-wife living in the same house.[29]

Conditions designed to induce divorce or separation are also invalid, but there is an exception if the "dominant motive ... is to provide support in the

**21.** *Restatement, Third, Trusts* § 29, comm. e (1999).

**22.** *Restatement, Third, Trusts* § 29, illus. 1 (1997); *Restatement (Second) of Property (Donative Transfers)* § 6.3 (1981).

**23.** Matter of 1942 Gerald H. Lewis Trust, 652 P.2d 1106 (Colo.App.1982); Wilbur v. Campbell, 192 So.2d 721 (Ala.1966). For state statutes dealing with this question and the cases construing them, see Statutory Note to Section 6.3, *Restatement (Second) of Property, Donative Transfers* (1981).

**24.** *Id.*, comment c, e (1981).

**25.** Shapira v. Union Nat. Bank, 315 N.E.2d 825 (Ohio Com.Pl.1974). *See also* Taylor v. Rapp, 124 S.E.2d 271 (Ga.1962) (daughter disinherited if she marries a named individual); In re Keffalas' Estate, 233 A.2d 248 (Pa. 1967) (to daughter if she marries a Greek). *But see Restatement (Second) of Property, Donative Transfers* § 6.2, illus. 1 (restraint invalid when child was already engaged to designated individual), 3 (restraint invalid when child unlikely to marry someone of the designated religion) (1981); *Restatement (Third) of Trusts* § 29, illus. 3 (1997).

**26.** In re Estate of Laning, 339 A.2d 520 (Pa.1975). *See also Restatement (Second) of Property, Donative Transfers* § 6.2, illus. 4 (1981) (requirement that daughter marry "her social equal" is too vague).

**27.** In re Liberman, 18 N.E.2d 658 (N.Y. 1939); *Restatement (Second) of Property, Donative Transfers* § 6.2, comment e (1981).

**28.** *Id.* § 7.2. *See also Restatement, Third, Trusts* § 29, comment e (1997); Jiles v. Flegel, 291 N.E.2d 300 (Ill.App.1972) (devise to adopted children on condition they use name of their biological father).

**29.** Matter of Estate of Romero, 847 P.2d 319, 322–23 (N.M.App.1993).

event of separation or divorce."[30] The Restatement says that today's more liberal rules for divorce do not "indicate an abandonment of the policy of preventing outsiders from inducing the break-up of a marriage by offers of wealth."[31] But some recent cases suggest that courts are willing to countenance attempts to do just that if it seems appropriate under the circumstances. A court sustained a trust under which the settlor's daughter got nothing until she reached 65 or her husband died or they were divorced. The court noted that the daughter's husband "had tricked [the settlor] into investing $10,000 in a worthless venture" and his "financial affairs were under Federal investigation."[32] Another court in a similar case said "not every encouragement of divorce is objectionable;" parents can do this when they seek to advance what they "reasonably believe to be their child's welfare."[33] The Third Restatement of Trusts says that a "reasonable concern over the spouse's financial irresponsibility or apparent gambling or substance addiction" may provide a legitimate motive for such a provision, and that courts may modify objectionable provisions so as to satisfy the settlor's reasonable objectives without invalidating a provision completely.[34]

Conditions designed to control the custody of children may also be invalid. Thus, a trust for the testator's grandchildren provided that the funds should pass to another if certain persons became their guardian. This was held to be against a public policy to choose guardians on the basis of the best interests of the child.[35]

Some conditions are allowed on the ground that they do not affect the beneficiary's conduct after the testator's death. For example, a devise to a daughter to take effect only if "at the time of my death, she is married to and living with her husband" was upheld, since "public policy regarding restraints on marriage should only be concerned with continuing inducements" whereas in this case the "rights become absolutely fixed at [the testator's] death."[36]

The Restatement of Property allows conditions designed to affect other types of conduct, such as religious practices, choice of education or career[37], unless they are too indefinite to be enforced.[38] The Third Restatement of Trusts is somewhat more guarded, suggesting that the "risk of excessive influence on a serious and fundamentally personal decision" may justify a policy restraint. Recent cases of this type are too infrequent to derive firm conclusions.

### *Destruction of Property*

**30.** *Restatement, Second, Property, Donative Transfers* § 7.1 (1981); In re Gerbing's Estate, 337 N.E.2d 29 (Ill.1975) (to son if he divorces his wife); In re Keffalas' Estate, 233 A.2d 248 (Pa.1967) (to married daughter if she remarries a Greek).

**31.** *Restatement, Second, Property, Donative Transfers* § 7.1, Comment b (1981).

**32.** Matter of Estate of Donner, 623 A.2d 307 (N.J.Super.App.Div.1993).

**33.** Hall v. Eaton, 631 N.E.2d 805 (Ill.App. 1994).

**34.** *Restatement, Third, Trusts* § 29, comment e (1997).

**35.** Stewart v. RepublicBank, Dallas, N.A., 698 S.W.2d 786 (Tex.App.1985).

**36.** In re Estate of Heller, 159 N.W.2d 82, 85 (Wis.1968). *See also Restatement, Second, Property, Donative Transfers* § 6.1, comment c (1981); *Restatement, Third, Trusts* § 29, comment d (1997).

**37.** *Restatement, Second, Property, Donative Transfers* §§ 8.1–8.3 (1981).

**38.** *Id.*, § 8.1, comment e, § 8.2, illus. 4.

Virgil's will directed his executors to destroy his poem, the Aeneid. They refused to do so, and it has become a classic of world literature.[39] The law will not assist a decedent in carrying out eccentric wishes. "A settlor may destroy his own Rembrandt. But he cannot establish a trust and order his trustees to destroy it. Society will not assist him to waste economic assets."[40] Such restraints on ownership rights are not needed for the living who have a natural desire to preserve what they own, but the law must impose checks on a decedent's "extravagance and eccentricity."[41] Testators who seek to devote an immense fortune to the erection of a tomb like the pyramids or the Mausoleum[42] would run afoul of the restrictions on trusts for noncharitable purposes, to be discussed in Section 9.7.

Provisions in a will restricting a devisee's use of land may be enforced only if the "the restrictions are confined within reasonable bounds." If not, a court "may refashion the restrictions so that they are reasonable."[43]

Courts may refuse to respect provisions for trust administration which they find "capricious," such as a requirement that the trustees and their spouses be Protestants. "Public policy does not permit a settlor to burden the judicial system with the responsibility to keep watch over every one of his personal vagaries that is unrelated to any proper trust purpose."[44] From this perspective, the trust purpose is all important. Presumably a requirement that the trustees of a trust to run a school for training protestant ministers be Protestants would not be unrelated to the trust purpose.

**39.** Zabel, *The Wills of Literary Figures*, 128 Trusts and Estates, Sept. 1989, p. 59.

**40.** E. Halbach ed., *Death, Taxes, and Family Property* 126 (1977).

**41.** Eyerman v. Mercantile Trust Co., N.A., 524 S.W.2d 210, 215, 217 (Mo.App.1975).

**42.** Erected for King Mausolus by his widow about 350 B.C. and one of the seven wonders of the ancient world.

**43.** Crowell v. Shelton, 948 P.2d 313 (Okl. 1997) (restriction that land "never be used for residential or commercial purposes"). As to restraints on alienation see 11.8.

**44.** In re Estate of Coleman, 317 A.2d 631, 633 (Pa.1974). *See also Restatement, Third, Trusts* § 29, comment h (1997).

# Chapter 4

# FORMALITIES

*Analysis*



## § 4.1 History and Policy

Historically wills have been subjected to an increasing number of formal requirements until recent years. In the Middle Ages, the ecclesiastical courts allowed oral wills of personal property.[1] Although wills of land were not allowed by the law courts before 1540, equity enforced oral devises of uses.[2] The Statute of Wills of 1540 authorized wills of land at law, but required that they be in writing.[3] The writing did not have to be signed by the testator; oral instructions written down before the testator died were sufficient.[4] The Statute of Frauds of 1677, however, required that devises of land be signed by the testator and subscribed by witnesses. Unsigned and unwitnessed wills of personal property remained valid[5] until the Wills Act of 1837 imposed the same requirements for both types of property, and added a few new ones, such as that the signature be at the "end" of the will, and that the witnesses must be present at the same time.[6] The Statute of Frauds and the Wills Act have been the models for many American statutes, but an important American development is the authorization of unwitnessed holographic wills.[7]

§ 4.1

**1.** 3 W. Holdsworth, *History of English Law* 537 (5th ed. 1942).

**2.** K. Digby, *History of the Law of Real Property* 335–36 (4th ed. 1892); Kiralfy, *A Source Book of English Law* 266–67 (1957).

**3.** Statute of Wills, 32 Hen. 8, c. 1 (1540).

**4.** Brown v. Sackville, 73 Eng.Rep. 152 (1552).

**5.** "Though written in another man's hand, and never signed by the testator . . . it hath been held a good testament of the personal estate . . . I speak not here of devises of land, which are quite of a different nature." 2 W. Blackstone, *Commentaries* *501–2 (1766).

**6.** Wills Act, 1 Vict. c. 26, § 9 (1837).

**7.** As to holographic wills see Section 4.4.

***Functions of Formalities***

The most obvious function of formal requirements is evidentiary. If wills did not have to be in writing, witnesses might either misremember or deliberately lie about alleged statements of intention by the testator. The weakness of oral testimony is "especially serious" in the case of wills, as distinguished from contracts, because the testator is "unavailable to testify, or to clarify or contradict other evidence" concerning intention.[8] A few states allow oral wills in special situations, but they typically require that the testator's statements be reduced to writing shortly after they are uttered in order to reduce the faulty memory problem.[9]

Even if the testator actually said (or wrote) particular words, they may not have been intended to effectuate a disposition.

> People are often careless in conversation and in informal writings. Even if the witnesses are entirely truthful and accurate, what is a court to conclude from testimony showing only that a father once stated that he wanted to give certain bonds to his son John? Does this remark indicate finality of intention to transfer, or rambling meditation about some future disposition. * * * Possibly, the remark was inadvertent, or made in jest. Or suppose that the evidence shows, without more, that a writing containing dispositive language was found among papers of the deceased at the time of his death? Does this demonstrate a deliberate transfer, or was it merely a tentative draft of some contemplated instrument, or perhaps random scribbling? * * * Dispositive effect should not be given to statements which were not intended to have that effect. The formalities of transfer therefore generally require the performance of some ceremonial.[10]

This ceremonial makes the testator realize the seriousness of the enterprise, and allows courts to decide whether or not words were uttered or written with testamentary intent. Thus when an instrument "was executed in full accord with the formalities of the statute of wills," a court had no trouble finding that the author had testamentary intent even though it was not labelled a "Will."[11] These functions are more important than the evidentiary one, as is shown by the fact that courts probate lost wills, even though in this situation the writing has no evidentiary value.[12]

More than one ceremonial might fulfill these functions. Even an oral will might do so if the testator used a certain form of words to show seriousness of intent. Statutes which allow oral wills require that the testator "call on a person to take notice or bear testimony that such is his will."[13] As Blackstone explained, "the testamentary words must be spoken with an intent to bequeath, not any loose idle discourse in his illness; for he must require the bystanders to bear witness of such his intention."[14] Such words are not likely

**8.** Gulliver & Tilson, *Classification of Gratuitous Transfers,* 51 Yale L.J. 1, 4 (1941).

**9.** Ohio Rev.Code § 2107.60; Ga.Code § 53–2–49; Miss.Code § 91–5–19. These provisions go back ultimately to the Statute of Frauds.

**10.** Gulliver & Tilson, *supra* note 8, at 3–4.

**11.** Matter of Catanio, 703 A.2d 988 (N.J.Super.App.Div.1997). *See also* Langbein, *Substantial Compliance With the Wills Act,* 88 Harv.L.Rev. 489, 494–6 (1975).

**12.** As to the probate of lost wills Section 5.2, at note 38 et seq.

**13.** Tex.Prob.Code § 65; Ohio Rev.Code § 2107.60; Ga.Code § 53–2–48(2); Miss. Code § 91–5–15. This idea also goes back to the Statute of Frauds.

**14.** 2 W. Blackstone, *Commentaries* *501 (1766).

to be used inadvertently or in jest. On the other hand, writings are often so casual in our society that some have argued that holographic wills (written and signed by the testator but not witnessed) do not involve sufficient ceremonial.[15]

### *Liberalizing Trend*

Many today believe that the requirements for wills are too strict. The trend to impose more formal requirements, which culminated in the Wills Act of 1837, has recently begun to flow in the other direction. Some suggest that the stricter formalities emanate from a time when most wills were made on the testator's deathbed and are no longer needed because wills today are usually made "in the prime of life and in the presence of attorneys."[16] Also, today when form-free will substitutes like joint tenancy are widely used to pass property at death, the more rigorous formalities laid down for wills seem "incongruous and indefensible."[17] Technological changes have made the appropriateness of some formalities questionable. The advent of the computer and tape recorder has raised questions about the need for a writing. The Restatement of Property would treat "a process that produces words on a screen [or] a recording of spoken words" as equivalent to a writing,[18] but the Uniform Electronic Transactions Act, which says that an electronic record satisfies any writing requirement expressly excludes wills from its operation.[19]

Some requirements, like the one that witnesses be disinterested, probably do more harm than good; for every attempted fraud which these rules prevent, hundreds of genuine wills may be defeated by them. This hypothesis has not been empirically verified—it is hard to imagine how it could be. Nevertheless, some intelligent observers have concluded that "the remedies are employed more frequently against innocent parties who have accidentally transgressed the requirement than against deliberate wrongdoers."[20]

Many recent statutes have reduced the formal requirements for wills. The Uniform Probate Code, for example, has dropped the requirements that the witnesses sign in the testator's presence, or that the testator sign the will at the end.[21] Many states which have not adopted the complete UPC have followed it in liberalizing the formal requirements for wills.[22] The trend away from formalism also appears in judicial opinions. Several recent cases have overruled earlier decisions which had rejected wills due to formal defects.[23]

**15.** Gulliver & Tilson, *supra* note 8, at 14; Bird, *Sleight of Handwriting: The Holographic Will in California,* 32 Hast.L.J. 605, 610 (1981); Langbein, *supra* note 11, at 494–96.

**16.** Langbein, *supra* note 11, at 497. *See* Stein & Fierstein, *The Demography of Probate Distribution,* 15 U.Balt.L.Rev. 54, 86 (1985) (average testator executes a will 5 to 7 years prior to death).

**17.** Langbein, *supra* note 11, at 504; Lindgren, *Abolishing the Attestation Requirement for Wills,* 68 N.C.L.Rev. 541, 543 (1990); *Restatement (Second) of Property, Donative Transfers* § 33.1, comm. g (1990). The formal requirements for various will substitutes are discussed in Sections 4.5–4.8.

**18.** *Restatement (Second) of Property, Donative Transfers* § 32.1, comm. b (1990). *But see* Matter of Reed's Estate, 672 P.2d 829 (Wyo.1983).

**19.** Uniform Electronic Transactions Act §§ 3(b)(1), 7.

**20.** Gulliver & Tilson, *supra* note 8, at 12.

**21.** Uniform Probate Code § 2–502.

**22.** *E.g.*, Cal.Prob.Code § 6110.

**23.** Estate of Black, 641 P.2d 754 (Cal. 1982); Waldrep v. Goodwin, 195 S.E.2d 432 (Ga.1973).

In 1975 Professor John Langbein proposed a rule of "substantial compliance" whereby a noncomplying document which sufficiently approximated the prescribed formalities to fulfill their underlying purposes should be admitted to probate.[24] The Uniform Probate Code accepts this idea; it allows probate of a document if the proponent "establishes by clear and convincing evidence that the decedent intended the document" to be a will.[25] The Restatement of Property prescribes a similar approach for courts "in the absence of a legislative corrective" such as that provided by the UPC.[26]

It remains to be seen how far courts will accept and apply this idea. One commentator has suggested that American courts have given the "substantial compliance" idea a "cool reception" despite nearly "uniform support" from academic commentators.[27] English courts of Chancery traditionally exercised a similar dispensing power for the exercise of powers of appointment which failed to literally comply with formal requirements, but they did so only for the benefit of a person who was "a natural object of the donee's affection."[28] Ordinarily, however, courts do not (at least expressly) consider who the devisees are in passing upon its formal validity.

One court invoked the substantial compliance notion in upholding a will when the witnesses signed an affidavit attached to the will rather than the will itself.[29] But another rejected a defectively attested will saying;

> "substantial compliance" does not mean noncompliance, and the fact that the testator's and witnesses' signatures may be genuine does not obviate other express statutory requirements.[30]

A comment to the Uniform Probate Code suggests that some statutory requirements are more important than others in assessing substantial compliance. In dealing with similar legislation in Australia and Israel, courts "lightly excuse breaches of the attestation requirements, [but] they have never excused noncompliance with the requirement that a will be in writing."[31] Professor James Lindgren suggests that so long as "attestation is going to be lightly excused," it should be legislatively abolished.[32] However, courts have refused to treat unattested documents which do not qualify as holographs as valid. *A fortiori* they are not likely to treat an unsigned will as being in substantial compliance with the requirements.[33]

**24.** Langbein, *supra* note 11, at 489. For earlier expressions of this idea in some judicial opinions see Bonfield, *Reforming the Requirements for Due Execution of Wills: Some Guidance from the Past*, 70 Tul.L.Rev. 1893, 1900–01 (1996).

**25.** Uniform Probate Code § 2–502.

**26.** *Restatement (Second) of Property, Donative Transfers* § 33.1, comm. g (1990); *Restatement, Third, of Property (Wills and Other Donative Transfers)* § 3.3 (1998).

**27.** Bonfield, *supra* note 24, at 1906.

**28.** *Restatement (Second) of Property, Donative Transfers* § 18.3 (1984).

**29.** Matter of Will of Ranney, 589 A.2d 1339 (N.J.1991).

**30.** Kirkeby v. Covenant House, 970 P.2d 241, 247 (Or.App.1998). *See also* Burns v. Adamson, 854 S.W.2d 723, 724–5 (Ark.1993); Stevens v. Casdorph, 508 S.E.2d 610 (W.Va. 1998).

**31.** Uniform Probate Code § 2–503, comment. *See also Restatement, Third, of Property (Wills and Other Donative Transfers)* § 3.3, comm. b (1998).

**32.** Lindgren, *The Fall of Formalism*, 55 Alb.L.Rev. 1009, 1025 (1992). *See also* Lindgren, *Abolishing the Attestation Requirement for Wills*, 68 N.C.L.Rev. 541 (1990).

**33.** BankAmerica Pension Plan v. McMath, 206 F.3d 821, 831 (9th Cir.2000) (unsigned beneficiary designation "did not substantially comply with" requirements of pension plan).

Attestation itself, unlike the ceremonies associated with it, has been nearly as fundamental in the statutory schemes as signature and writing ... [T]he attestation requirement may seem to set the level of cautionary and evidentiary functions unreasonably high, *but that is the legislature's policy choice.*[34]

Advocates of allowing probate of defectively executed wills do not deny that cautionary procedures for wills are desirable, but they argue that the sanction of invalidating noncomplying wills is often inappropriate. Professor Lindgren cites a New York statute which requires witnesses to write their addresses on the will. This is a sensible requirement which helps to locate the witnesses when the will needs to be probated, but noncompliance does not invalidate the will. Along the same line he contends that "supervising a will execution other than one's own without using witnesses could subject the lawyer or other professional to a fine" or damages, "but the will itself would not be invalidated by the drafter's ignorance or carelessness."[35]

The second Restatement of Property recommends 8 steps to follow in executing a will. This checklist goes beyond the minimum formalities prescribed by statute, and includes a colloquy between the lawyer and the testator in which the latter states that the will reflects his or her desires.[36] Such precautionary measures are particularly important for wills which may have to be probated in several states. However, as we have seen, many states have liberal choice of law rules which allow wills to be probated if they were executed in compliance with the law at the time and place of execution.[37]

## § 4.2 Signature

The requirement that wills be signed was introduced by the Statute of Frauds in the 17th century. It is found today in all states. The signature helps to identify the will with the testator. It also serves to show finality; the distinction between tentative scribblings and a consummated product is symbolized by the act of signing. The second function is more significant than the first, as shown by the fact that virtually all statutes allow someone else to sign for the testator. The Uniform Probate Code, for example, says that the will must be signed "by the testator or in the testator's name by some other individual."[1] When another person signs the testator's name, the signature by

**34.** Catch v. Phillips, 86 Cal.Rptr.2d 584, 591 (App.1999) (quoting Langbein). *See also* Norton v. Hinson, 989 S.W.2d 535, 537 (Ark. 1999) (no substantial compliance when one of the attesting witnesses was under age).

**35.** Lindgren, *The Fall of Formalism*, 55 Alb.L.Rev. 1009, 1026–7 (1992).

**36.** *Restatement (Second) of Property, Donative Transfers* § 33.1, comm. c (1990). Compare the "publication" requirement imposed in some states, discussed at Section 4.3, at note 39.

**37.** See Section 1.2, note 64, and Section 1.3, note 32.

**§ 4.2**

1. Uniform Probate Code § 2–502. *See also* Cal.Prob.Code § 6110(b)(2); Tex.Prob.Code § 59; Ohio Rev.Code § 2107.03; Walker v. Walker, 929 P.2d 316 (Or.App.1996); *Restatement, Third, of Property (Wills and Other Donative Transfers)* § 3.1, comm. n (1998); *cf.* Muhlbauer v. Muhlbauer, 686 S.W.2d 366 (Tex.App.1985) (will signed by the testator's wife was denied probate for failure to prove she signed "by his direction.").

For international wills, another person is allowed to sign for the testator only "when the testator is unable to sign" and a note of this is made on the will. Uniform Probate Code § 2–1003; *cf.* 20 Pa.Stat. § 2502(3).

itself does not show that the testator approved the will, but if the signer acted at the testator's request, this shows that the testator considered the will to be complete.

By similar reasoning, a partial signature, even initials or an "X" suffices,[2] since they can indicate the will was complete, whereas the testator's full name on pre-printed stationery does not. In this situation a court refused to apply by analogy the definition of "signed" in the Uniform Commercial Code ("it may be found ... in a ... letterhead"), saying "much more formality has historically been required in the execution of wills than in the execution of everyday business and commercial papers."[3] Similarly, the federal Electronic Signatures Act which provides that "an electronic signature satisfies the law" as to contracts is inapplicable by its terms to wills.[4]

### *Place of Signature*

Most of the controversy regarding the signature centers on its place in the will. The Statute of Frauds was silent on this point. Courts held that the testator's name at the beginning of a will was a valid signature.[5] This was a dubious rule if the signature is designed to indicate finality, so the 1837 Wills Act required wills to be signed at the end.[6] This gives rise to a host of problems if taken literally, *e.g.*, is a will signed at the end if a blank space appears between the writing and the testator's signature? In 1852 Parliament amended the Wills Act in order to prevent courts from taking the "end" requirement too literally.[7] In 1982 England eliminated the requirement altogether; now it suffices "that the testator intended by his signature to give effect to the will."[8]

Some American statutes still require that wills be signed at the end.[9] A similar requirement has been inferred from the word "subscribe" in other statutes,[10] but many, including the Uniform Probate Code, do not specify where the signature must appear.[11] Differences in the governing statutes are not always determinative. Courts have upheld wills which were not literally signed "at the end" even when these words appeared in the controlling statute. Thus when there was no room at the bottom of a will and the signature appeared in the margin at the top, the court upheld the will on the theory that the statute meant "the logical end," not "the point which is farthest removed from the beginning."[12] On the other hand, even under the

**2.** Orozco v. Orozco, 917 S.W.2d 70 (Tex. App.1996) (X); Trim v. Daniels, 862 S.W.2d 8 (Tex.App.1992) (initials); Mitchell v. Mitchell, 264 S.E.2d 222 (Ga.1980) (X); Uniform Probate Code § 2–502, Comment; cf. Succession of Squires, 640 So.2d 813 (La.App.1994) (initials constitute "substantial compliance" with signature requirement). But placing an "X" on a will is not a signature if the writer does not intend it as such. Williams v. Overton, 709 P.2d 1115 (Or.App.1985).

**3.** Matter of Reed's Estate, 625 P.2d 447, 452 (Kan.1981).

**4.** 15 U.S.C. §§ 7001, 7003.

**5.** 2 W. Blackstone, *Commentaries** 376 (1765).

**6.** Wills Act, 1 Vict. c. 26, § 9 (1837).

**7.** Wills Act Amendment, 15 & 16 Vict. c. 24, § 1 (1852).

**8.** Administration of Justice Act, 1982, § 17.

**9.** 20 Pa.Stat. § 2502; Ohio Rev.Code § 2107.03; N.Y.E.P.T.L. § 3–2.1.

**10.** Matter of Estate of Rowell, 585 So.2d 731 (Miss.1991); Matter of Reed's Estate, 625 P.2d 447 (Kan.1981); *cf.* Matter of Estate of Wedeberg, 589 N.E.2d 1000 (Ill.App.1992) (will not "signed" when testator's name appeared at the top).

**11.** Uniform Probate Code § 2–502; Cal. Prob.Code § 6110; Tex.Prob.Code § 59.

**12.** In re Estate of Stasis, 307 A.2d 241 (Pa.1973). *See also* In re Powell's Will, 395 N.Y.S.2d 334 (Surr.1977) (page following the signature "constructively inserted" above it).

Uniform Probate Code the testator's putting his or her name on a will does not necessarily constitute a sufficient signature. In rejecting a will a court noted that although the Code:

> does not require the that the signature appear at the end of the instrument ... the problem of signatory intent is more difficult where, as here, the signature appears somewhere other than at the end ... The instrument does not have sufficient indicia of completeness to support an inference that Erickson intended his name in the exordium [the beginning of the will] to be his signature.... The instrument as we have it before us contains nothing to indicate that Erickson had finished his writing.[13]

Other courts, however, have probated wills which they regarded as complete documents even though the testator's name did not appear at the end.[14] Such a finding is easier if there is extrinsic evidence that the testator viewed the document as finished. The UPC expressly allows extrinsic evidence to be used to show testamentary intent.[15] Such intent may be inferred from the testator's asking the witnesses to sign.[16]

Many wills contain several pages. For "international wills" the Uniform Probate Code says that "each sheet will be signed," but failure to do so does not invalidate the will.[17] American courts routinely uphold wills which are signed only on the last page, but careful lawyers have the testator sign (or at least initial) each page.[18] At the least, the connection between the signature page and the preceding ones should be shown by numbering the pages, attaching them with staples, or run-over sentences.[19] For example, a purported will consisting of 5 sheets, some of which were signed and others not, was rejected when some sheets did not appear to relate to the others.[20]

Most wills contain an attestation clause at the end, designed for the witnesses' signature. If the testator signs below the attestation clause, the signature, though removed from the body of the will proper, is usually held sufficient.[21] the Uniform Probate Code explicitly so provides, in order "to counteract an unfortunate [contrary] interpretation ... in a few states."[22]

**13.** Matter of Estate of Erickson, 806 P.2d 1186, 1189–90 (Utah 1991). *See also* Matter of Estate of Wedeberg, 589 N.E.2d 1000 (Ill.App. 1992); Matter of McKellar's Estate, 380 So.2d 1273 (Miss.1980).

**14.** In re Estate of Carroll, 548 N.E.2d 650 (Ill.App.1989) (exordium); Clark v. Studenwalt, 419 S.E.2d 308 (W.Va.1992) (exordium); Draper v. Pauley, 480 S.E.2d 495 (Va.1997) (testator signed before will written out); Estate of Hand, 684 A.2d 521 (N.J.Super.Ch.Div.1996).

**15.** Uniform Probate Code § 2–502(c). *See also* Cal.Prob.Code § 6111.5.

**16.** *Restatement, Third, of Property (Wills and Other Donative Transfers)* § 3.1, illus. 2 (1998).

**17.** Uniform Probate Code § 2–1004; *cf.* La. Stat. § 9:2442(B) (testator must sign every page of statutory will); Successions of Eddy, 664 So.2d 853 (La.App.1995) (noncomplying will rejected).

**18.** *Restatement, Second, Property, Donative Transfers* § 33.1, comm. c (1990).

**19.** *Restatement, Third, of Property (Wills and Other Donative Transfers)* § 3.5, comm. b and c (1998).

**20.** In Matter of Estate of Rigsby, 843 P.2d 856 (Okl.App.1992), two pages were found folded together after the testator's death. Because they did not refer to each other, only the signed page was probated. *See also* In re Estate of Foreman, 984 P.2d 258 (Okl.App.1999).

**21.** Matter of Estate of McKay, 802 P.2d 443 (Ariz.App.1990); Gardner v. Balboni, 588 A.2d 634 (Conn.1991); Hickox v. Wilson, 496 S.E.2d 711 (Ga.1998). *But see* Orrell v. Cochran, 695 S.W.2d 552 (Tex.1985) (signature on self-proving affidavit does not suffice).

**22.** Uniform Probate Code § 2–504, comment.

## § 4.3 Witnesses

### *Number and Competency*

The Statute of Frauds required that wills be attested by "three or four credible" witnesses. The Wills Act reduced the number to two,[1] and the Uniform Probate Code, like most American states today, requires only two.[2] Professor Langbein argues that "attestation by two witnesses where the statute calls for three, or by one where it asks for two" should be deemed "substantial compliance,"[3] but many courts would not agree.[4] In any event, if a will is attested by 2 witnesses, it can be probated even if only one (or none) of them is available to testify when the will is offered for probate.[5]

The Uniform Probate Code says that "any person generally competent to be a witness may act as a witness to a will."[6] This is the prevailing rule.[7] A few states have minimum age requirements for witnesses of wills,[8] but most only demand that they be able to understand the significance of an oath.[9] At common law someone who had been convicted of an infamous crime could not be a witness, but the modern trend is to remove such disabilities. Even a witness who had been convicted of perjury was held to be "credible" and thus sufficient for a will.[10]

In Europe the profession of notary public is closely regulated, and wills executed before a notary are difficult to challenge.[11] An American counterpart is the "international will," authorized by the Uniform Probate Code, based on a Washington Convention of 1973 which several countries have signed. It requires two witnesses and an "authorized person," which means a lawyer who is "in good standing" as an active practitioner.[12] Witnesses to ordinary wills need no special qualifications, however.

Most litigation concerning the competency of witnesses involves witnesses who benefit from the will. The Statute of Frauds said that the witnesses must

§ 4.3

**1.** Statute of Frauds, 29 Car. 2, c. 3, § 5 (1677); Wills Act, 1 Vict. c. 26, § 9 (1837).

**2.** *E.g.*, Uniform Probate Code § 2–502; Cal.Prob.Code § 6110. Some cautious drafters nevertheless recommend using three witnesses. *Restatement, Second, of Property, Donative Transfers* § 33.1, comm. c (1990).

**3.** Langbein, *Substantial Compliance With the Wills Act*, 88 Harv.L.Rev. 489, 521–22 (1975).

**4.** Matter of Estate of Brooks, 927 P.2d 1024 (Mont.1996) (will with one witness denied probate); In re Estate of Carmedy, 642 N.E.2d 1170 (Ohio App.1994) (same); Estate of Whitlatch v. Richardson, 783 P.2d 46 (Or.App. 1989). However, in Estate of McNeill, 463 A.2d 782 (Me.1983), a will signed by only two witnesses although the law required three was held effective to exercise a power of appointment. South Australian courts have probated wills attested by one witness. Langbein, *Excusing Harmless Errors in the Execution of Wills*, 87 Colum.L.Rev. 1, 22 (1987).

**5.** Estate of Burdette, 97 Cal.Rptr.2d 263 (App.2000); Uniform Probate Code § 3–406(a).

**6.** Uniform Probate Code § 2–505(a).

**7.** Chaffin, *Execution, Revocation, and Revalidation of Wills*, 11 Ga.L.Rev. 297, 313 (1977).

**8.** Tex.Prob.Code § 59 (witness must be over 14); Norton v. Hinson, 989 S.W.2d 535 (Ark.1999) (will witnessed by a 14 year old is invalid under a like statute); La.Civ.Code art. 1591 (witness must have attained age 16).

**9.** Chaffin, *supra* note 7, at 312–13; *cf.* Grossen's Estate v. Vincent, 657 P.2d 1345 (Utah 1983) (will with 16 year old witness valid, even though after the will was executed minimum age raised to 18).

**10.** McGarvey v. McGarvey, 405 A.2d 250 (Md.1979); Chaffin, *supra* note 7, at 314.

**11.** 1 J. Schoenblum, *Multistate and Multinational Estate Planning* § 15.02.2 (1982); Bonfield, *Reforming the Requirements for Due Execution of Wills*, 70 Tul.L.Rev. 1893, 1918 (1996) ("by requiring written wills to be drafted by notaries, continental europeans essentially eliminated the will contest").

**12.** Uniform Probate Code §§ 2–1003, 2–1009.

be "credible" which courts in the 18th century construed to mean disinterested. The decision that use of an interested witness rendered the entire will void[13] "threatened to shake most of the titles in the kingdom." So Parliament passed a statute which "declar[ed] void all legacies given to witnesses, thereby removing all possibility of their interest affecting their testimony."[14] Many American jurisdictions today have similar statutes,[15] even though the common law bar against interested witnesses has disappeared.

Some statutes apply to a devisee's spouse as well as the devisee,[16] but other relatives of the devisee are not disqualified.[17] A devise to a church whose minister was a subscribing witness has been upheld on the ground that even though the witness was not "disinterested," this was not a devise "to a subscribing witness" within the meaning of the governing statute.[18]

Persons designated in a will as executor or trustee have can act as witnesses on the theory that they earn their fee, unlike devisees who receive an unearned benefit.[19] However, when a will specified a generous compensation for an executor-witness, the compensation was denied.[20]

A witness who is both a devisee and an heir of the testator may have no interest in having the will probated and should not be disqualified. If the devise exceeds what the witness would take by intestacy only the excess is void.[21]

Many statutes also except supernumerary (extra) witnesses. If three persons witness a will which leaves property to one of them, and the statute requires only two witnesses, the devise to the witness is valid.[22] Similarly, if a will can be probated as a holograph, a devise to a subscribing witness is valid.[23] But if the will makes devises to two witnesses, neither can take by

**13.** Holdfast v. Dowsing, 93 Eng.Rep. 1164 (1747). Until recently, a devise to a witness also rendered the entire will void in Louisiana. Succession of Mitchell, 524 So.2d 150 (La.App. 1988).

**14.** 2 W. Blackstone, *Commentaries* *377 (1765).

**15.** *E.g.*, 755 ILCS § 5/4–6; Tex.Prob.Code § 61; Ohio Rev.Code § 2107.15; Ga.Code § 53–2–45.

**16.** Wills Act 1 Vict. c. 26, § 15 (1837); Conn.Gen.Stat. § 45a–258; Wis.Stat. § 853.07(2); Dorfman v. Allen, 434 N.E.2d 1012 (Mass.1982) (devise to spouse of a witness is void); Matter of Estate of Webster, 574 N.E.2d 245 (Ill.App.1991). However, in Matter of Estate of Harrison, 738 P.2d 964 (Okl.App. 1987), the court refused to invalidate a devise to a witness's spouse, since "neither husband nor wife has any legal interest in the separate property of the other." *See also* In re Estate of Livingston, 999 S.W.2d 874, 877 (Tex.App. 1999); *Restatement, Third, of Property (Wills and Other Donative Transfers)* § 3.1, comm. o (1998).

**17.** Succession of Harvey, 573 So.2d 1304, 1308 (La.App.1991) (granddaughter of devisee can serve as witness). In Dorfman v. Allen, 434 N.E.2d 1012 (Mass.1982), voiding the devise to the witnesses spouse caused the property to pass to the devisee's children.

**18.** Estate of Tkachuk, 139 Cal.Rptr. 55 (App.1977). *See also* Conn.Stat. § 45a–258; Guidry v. Hardy, 254 So.2d 675 (La.App.1971) (witness represented devisee as attorney).

**19.** In re Longworth, 222 A.2d 561 (Me. 1966); Wills Act, 1 Vict. c. 26, § 17 (1837); Wis.Stat. § 853.07(3); 755 ILCS § 5/4–6(b); *Restatement, Third, Trusts* § 32, comm. b. However, naming the drafter of a will as executor or trustee may raise ethical and other problems. See Section 7.4, at note 26 et seq.

**20.** In re Small's Estate, 346 F.Supp. 600 (D.D.C.1972).

**21.** Wis.Stat. § 853.07(2); Tex.Prob.Code § 61; Ohio Rev.Code § 2107.15; Ky.Rev.Stat. § 394.210(2). *But see* Rosenbloom v. Kokofsky, 369 N.E.2d 1142 (Mass.1977).

**22.** N.Y. EPTL § 3–3.2(a)(1); Wis.Stat. § 853.07(2); Brickhouse v. Brickhouse, 407 S.E.2d 607 (N.C.App.1991); *cf.* King v. Smith, 302 A.2d 144 (N.J.Super.Ch.Div.1973) (devise validated when will republished by codicil signed by disinterested witnesses).

**23.** Maines v. Davis, 227 So.2d 844 (Miss. 1969).

claiming that *he* is a supernumerary witness.[24]

The statutory bar "looks solely to the time of execution and attestation of the will." Therefore, a subsequent disclaimer by a witness does not "transform an interested witness into a 'disinterested' one."[25]

Many commentators have criticized the statutes which invalidate devises to witnesses as an outmoded vestige of the old rules against interested witnesses. A similar hold-over exists today in the "dead-man" statutes which exclude interested witnesses in proceedings involving decedents on the theory that the decedent can not rebut their testimony. "Dead man statutes are widely condemned among commentators and practitioners" on the theory that "cross examination and the other safeguards for truth are a sufficient guaranty" of truth without any such "artificial barriers."[26] Today the law allows interested witnesses in ordinary litigation because they may provide the only available testimony.[27] Testators can get disinterested persons to witness a will, but most laymen and not a few lawyers are unaware of the rule and so many "accidental" infringements occur. The deterrent effect of the rule is questionable; "in most cases of fraud or undue influence, the wrongdoer would be careful not to sign as a witness" but would find an apparently "disinterested" witness, who might be bribed without this appearing on the face of the will.[28]

The Uniform Probate Code breaks with tradition by providing that "the signing of a will by an interested witness does not invalidate the will or any provision of it."[29] California has replaced the bar against devises to witnesses by a rebuttable "presumption that the witness procured the devise by duress, menace, fraud, or undue influence."[30] Of course, a careful drafter will always use disinterested witnesses, since, if the will is contested, testimony from a disinterested witness will carry more weight with the fact finder.

### *Must Witnesses See Testator Sign?*

Normally the testator signs the will in the presence of the witnesses, but the will may be valid even if the testator signed before the witnesses appeared. The courts interpreted the Statute of Frauds to mean that "the witnesses must all see the testator sign, *or* at least acknowledge the signing, yet they may do it at different times."[31] The 1837 Wills Act, however, required that the testator's signature "shall be made or acknowledged by the Testator in the Presence of Two or more Witnesses *present at the same Time*,"[32] and some American statutes also so provide.[33] The requirement that the witnesses

**24.** Matter of Watts' Estate, 384 N.E.2d 589 (Ill.App.1979); In re Lubbe's Estate, 142 So.2d 130 (Fla.App.1962). *But see* Rogers v. Helmes, 432 N.E.2d 186 (Ohio 1982).

**25.** Estate of Parsons, 163 Cal.Rptr. 70 (App.1980).

**26.** Langbein, *supra* note 3, at 502.

**27.** *See, e.g.,* Matter of Succession of Calhoun, 674 So.2d 989 (La.App.1996) (devisees can testify as to the authenticity of a holographic will).

**28.** Chaffin, *supra* note 7, at 317. *See also* Gulliver & Tilson, *Classification of Gratuitous Transfers,* 51 Yale L.J. 1, 12–13 (1941); Uniform Prob.Code § 2–505, comment; Langbein, *supra* note 3, at 516.

**29.** Uniform Probate Code § 2–505(b).

**30.** Calif.Prob.Code § 6112. The presumption does not apply when the witness is simply named as a fiduciary, or if there are two other disinterested subscribing witnesses.

**31.** 2 W. Blackstone, *Commentaries* *377 (1765).

**32.** Wills Act, 1 Vict. c. 26, § 9 (1837).

**33.** Calif.Prob.Code § 6110; Va.Code § 64.1–49; Tenn Code § 32–1–104.

be present together adds to the ceremonial nature of the execution, but it is hard to imagine any fraud which it might prevent.

If a witness does not see the testator sign, what sort of acknowledgement must a testator make? Merely telling a witness that "this is my will" has been held insufficient,[34] but the Uniform Probate Code simply requires that the witnesses see either the testator's signing "or the testator's acknowledgement of that signature or acknowledgement of the will" as a whole.[35] Someone who does not see any of these cannot qualify as a witness.[36] One court has held that a testator's acknowledgement of her signature over the telephone does not suffice, because "an 'acknowledgement' made to a witness who cannot perceive what is being 'acknowledged' is meaningless."[37]

### *Publication and Request*

A testator might sign a paper in the presence of witnesses without realizing that it was a will. Roman law at one time required testators to hold the tablets on which the will was written and ask the witnesses to bear witness that they contained the will.[38] Some American statutes require such "publication." In New York, for example, the testator must "declare to each of the attesting witnesses that the instrument * * * is his will" and request them to sign.[39] Courts are usually lax about this requirement, so long as they are satisfied that the testator knew she was signing a will.[40] However, a careful lawyer supervising a will execution should ask the testator whether the document being signed "is your will, its terms have been explained to you, and [it] expresses your desires as to the disposition of your property on your death" in order to remove any doubts about testamentary intent.[41]

The law does not in general require the will to be read aloud or orally explained to the testator,[42] but in some cases this might be a desirable way to assure the testator understood what the will said. But reading the will in the presence of witnesses would reveal its contents and many testators want them kept secret until they die.[43]

**34.** Matter of McKellar's Estate, 380 So.2d 1273 (Miss.1980); In re Groffman, [1969] 1 W.L.R. 733. *But see* In re Estate of Mowdy, 973 P.2d 345, 350 (Okl.Civ.App.1998).

**35.** Uniform Probate Code § 2–502(a)(3); Matter of Estate of Lindsay, 957 P.2d 818, 821 (Wash.App.1998).

**36.** Estate of Allcott, 912 P.2d 671 (Idaho App.1995); Matter of Estate of Brooks, 927 P.2d 1024 (Mont.1996); Stevens v. Casdorph, 508 S.E.2d 610 (W.Va.1998).

**37.** Kirkeby v. Covenant House, 970 P.2d 241, 246 (Or.App.1998). However, the governing statute in this case required the testator to acknowledge the signature "in the presence of each of the witnesses," words which do not appear in Uniform Probate Code § 2–502.

**38.** Gaius, *Institutes* 2.104. This requirement was later eliminated. *Id.* 149a.

**39.** N.Y. EPTL § 3–2.1(a)(3), (4). Uniform Probate Code § 2–1003(b) requires publication for international wills.

**40.** Matter of Estate of Bearbower, 426 N.W.2d 392 (Iowa 1988); Faith v. Singleton, 692 S.W.2d 239 (Ark.1985); Matter of Estate of Burke, 613 P.2d 481 (Okl.App.1979).

**41.** *Restatement, Second, of Property, Donative Transfers* § 33.1, comm. c (1990).

**42.** *Restatement, Third, of Property (Wills and Other Donative Transfers)* § 3.1, comm. h (1998). *But see* La.Rev.Stat. § 9:2443 (will must be read to a blind or illiterate testator).

**43.** When wills are probated after the testator dies, they normally become public documents. See Section 9.1, at note 13 et seq.

### *Signing in Testator's Presence*

The Statute of Frauds required wills of land to be "subscribed [by the witnesses] in the presence of" the testator as well as by the testator.[44] Most modern statutes impose a similar requirement for all wills.[45] Even when the statute only requires the witnesses to "attest" the will, this has been construed to require them to sign it too.[46] The requirement is supposed "to prevent a fraud's being perpetrated * * * by substituting another for the true will,"[47] but dishonest witnesses could falsely swear they signed a spurious will in the testator's presence.[48] The rule may allow *honest* witnesses to spot a substitution by someone else for the document they saw the testator sign. However, this does not require them to sign *in the testator's presence;* they could simply keep custody of the will.

Many commentators have attacked the "presence" requirement.[49] Langbein argues that it should be ignored under the substantial compliance concept.[50] A will is not invalid simply because the testator did not see the witnesses sign because of poor vision or because of their positions if they were all in the same room.[51] Even if a witness takes the will into another room to sign, some courts uphold the will if the testator was aware that the witness was signing the will,[52] but not if the only contact between a witness and the testator was over the telephone.[53]

The Uniform Probate Code dispenses with the presence requirement altogether; the witnesses must sign the will but it does not matter where they do so.[54] Several courts have rejected wills which the witnesses signed only after the testator died,[55] but the present version of the UPC would allow this so long as the signing occurs "within a reasonable time."[56] At this point the requirement of the witnesses' signature seems totally meaningless.

**44.** 29 Car. 2, c. 3, § 5 (1676). *See also* Administration of Justice Act 1982 § 17 (witnesses must sign or acknowledge signature in testator's presence).

**45.** Ga.Code § 53–240; Ohio Rev.Code § 2107.03; Md.Estates and Trusts Code § 4–102; Matter of Estate of Norton, 410 S.E.2d 484 (N.C.1991) (will rejected because the witnesses did not sign it). A witness' acknowledging to the testator a signature previously made elsewhere has been held sufficient. Brammer v. Taylor, 338 S.E.2d 207 (W.Va. 1985).

**46.** In re Estate of Lum, 699 N.E.2d 1049 (Ill.App.1998).

**47.** Glenn v. Mann, 214 S.E.2d 911 (Ga. 1975). *See also* Taylor v. Estate of Taylor, 770 P.2d 163, 166 (Utah App.1989).

**48.** O'Connell & Effland, *Intestate Succession and Wills,* 14 Ariz.L.Rev. 205, 240 (1972).

**49.** *Ibid.;* Gulliver & Tilson, *supra* note 28, at 10–11; Chaffin, *supra* note 7, at 318–22.

**50.** Langbein, *supra* note 3, at 517. *But see* Flagle v. Martinelli, 360 N.E.2d 1269 (Ind.App. 1977); Taylor v. Estate of Taylor, 770 P.2d 163 (Utah App.1989); In re Estate of McDevitt, 755 So.2d 1125 (Miss.App.1999).

**51.** In re Lynch's Estate, 431 N.E.2d 734 (Ill.App.1982).

**52.** In re Demaris' Estate, 110 P.2d 571 (Or.1941); In re Politowicz' Estate, 304 A.2d 569 (N.J.Super.App.Div.1973). This is sometimes referred to as "conscious presence," a term used in Uniform Probate Code § 2–502(a)(2) with respect to someone who signs in place of the testator. *See also Restatement, Third, of Property (Wills and Other Donative Transfers)* § 3.1, comm. p (1998).

**53.** Matter of Jefferson's Will, 349 So.2d 1032 (Miss.1977); Matter of Estate of McGurrin, 743 P.2d 994 (Idaho App.1987).

**54.** Uniform Prob.Code § 2–502. *See also* Calif.Prob.Code § 6110. For an international will the witnesses must sign in the testator's presence. Uniform Prob.Code § 2–1003(e).

**55.** Matter of Estate of Royal, 826 P.2d 1236 (Colo.1992); Matter of Estate of Peters, 526 A.2d 1005 (N.J.1987); Gonzalez v. Satrustegui, 870 P.2d 1188 (Ariz.App.1993). In Disciplinary Counsel v. Bandy, 690 N.E.2d 1280 (Ohio 1998) a lawyer who induced a witness to sign a will after the testator died was suspended from practice.

**56.** Uniform Probate Code § 2–502(a)(3), Comment; *cf.* In Matter of Estate of McGrew, 906 S.W.2d 53 (Tex.App.1995) (will allowed even though 2 years elapsed between the testator's and the witnesses' signing).

Normally the witnesses sign after the testator, but if they sign first, most cases uphold the will, at least if the signatures are part of a continuous transaction.[57] Most statutes do not prescribe any particular place for the witnesses' signatures.[58]

"One who signs his name to a will is not an attesting witness unless he signs with that intention and not for some other purpose."[59] However, a notary who signs a will is usually held to count as a witness.[60]

### *Attestation Clauses and Affidavits*

Even though the wills acts reflect distrust of oral testimony, wills often stand or fall on the basis of it. Even if a will appears regular on its face, it may be denied probate if the witnesses testify that it was not duly executed.[61]

The standard way to deal with this problem is to append an attestation clause reciting that all the formalities were duly performed. For example,

> On October 14, 1984, Mary Jones declared to us that the foregoing instrument, consisting of 14 pages including this one, was her will and she requested us to act as witnesses to it. She then signed the will in our presence, all of us being present at the same time. We now subscribe our names as witnesses in her presence and in the presence of each other.[62]
>
> *Walter Witness*
>
> *Francis True*
>
> *John Jones*

No state requires that wills contain such a clause, but everyone recommends its use.[63] An attestation clause is not conclusive; wills have been denied probate on the strength of testimony that the acts described in the clause did not actually take place.[64] However, many wills have been sustained on the basis of such a clause even though the witnesses' testimony contradicted it.[65]

**57.** Gardner v. Balboni, 588 A.2d 634, 639 (Conn.1991); Waldrep v. Goodwin, 195 S.E.2d 432 (Ga.1973); *Restatement, Third, of Property (Wills and Other Donative Transfers)* § 3.1, comm. m (1998). *But see* Burns v. Adamson, 854 S.W.2d 723 (Ark.1993).

**58.** Casson v. Swogell, 500 A.2d 1031 (Md. 1985). *But see* 84 Okl.Stat. § 55 (witnesses must sign "at the end").

**59.** In re Estate of Alfaro, 703 N.E.2d 620, 626 (Ill.App.1998).

**60.** In re Friedman, 6 P.3d 473 (Nev.2000); Brickhouse v. Brickhouse, 407 S.E.2d 607 (N.C.App.1991); Matter of Estate of Zelikovitz, 923 P.2d 740 (Wyo.1996). *Contra,* Estate of Overt, 768 P.2d 378 (Okl.App.1989).

**61.** Young v. Young, 313 N.E.2d 593 (Ill. App.1974); Matter of Estate of Mackaben, 617 P.2d 765 (Ariz.App.1980); Burns v. Adamson, 854 S.W.2d 723 (Ark.1993); Pool v. Estate of Shelby, 821 P.2d 361 (Okl.1991).

**62.** Attestation clauses often add a statement that the testator was of sound mind and not under undue influence. As to the significance of testimony of the subscribing witnesses on these issues when a will is contested see Sections 7.1, at note 21, Section 7.3, at note 23.

**63.** "No self-respecting draftsman would omit it." Chaffin, *supra* note 7, at 310. Similar clauses appear in the California statutory will, Calif.Prob.Code § 6240, and the Uniform Statutory Will Act, App. 7; *Restatement, Second, of Property, Donative Transfers* § 33.1, comm. c.

**64.** Matter of Estate of Johnson, 780 P.2d 692 (Okl.1989); In re Groffman, [1969] 1 W.L.R. 733; In re Birkeland's Estate, 519 P.2d 154 (Mont.1974).

**65.** In re Estate of Carroll, 548 N.E.2d 650 (Ill.App.1989); Matter of Estate of Collins, 458 N.E.2d 797 (N.Y.1983); Fitch v. Maesch, 690 N.E.2d 350 (Ind.App.1998); *Restatement, Third, of Property (Wills and Other Donative Transfers)* § 3.1, comm. q (clause raises a "rebuttable presumption of the truth of the recitals").

If the witnesses sign an affidavit, under the Uniform Probate Code as in many states, the will can be probated without producing the witnesses in court.[66] This streamlines probate proceedings for uncontested wills, and in contested cases "compliance with signature requirements is conclusively presumed" when the witnesses have signed an affidavit.[67]

Some courts have held that if the witnesses sign only an affidavit they have not signed "the will" as required by law,[68] but most courts reject this hypertechnical interpretation of the wills act, as does the latest version of the UPC.[69]

## § 4.4 Holographic Wills

The word "holograph" comes from two Greek words meaning "whole" and "written."[1] Holographic wills are wholly handwritten by the testator. Because they provide a more generous sample of the testator's handwriting[2] than just a signature, there is less risk of an undetected forgery. Therefore, no witnesses are needed for them.[3]

Holographic wills were first recognized in the fifth century.[4] They came into America via the Napoleonic Code, the model for Louisiana's Civil Code.[5] The Uniform Probate Code allows them, as do many other states, but not all.[6]

Litigation about holographic wills has centered on three points: (1) a requirement in many states that holographic wills be dated; (2) the requirement in many states that they be "entirely" in the testator's handwriting; and (3) testamentary intent.

### *Date*

**66.** Uniform Probate Code § 2–504 which suggests a form of affidavit suitable for this purpose.

**67.** *Id.* § 3–406(b).

**68.** Wich v. Fleming, 652 S.W.2d 353 (Tex. 1983) (but see note 69); In re Sample's Estate, 572 P.2d 1232 (Mont.1977); In re Estate of Ricketts, 773 P.2d 93 (Wash.App.1989). For a critique of these cases see Mann, *Self-proving Affidavits and Formalism in Wills Adjudication,* 63 Wash.U.L.Q. 39 (1985).

**69.** In re Estate of Livingston, 999 S.W.2d 874 (Tex.App.1999) (based on amended Texas Probate Code § 59(b)); In re Cutsinger's Estate, 445 P.2d 778 (Okl.1968); Matter of Petty's Estate, 608 P.2d 987 (Kan.1980); Matter of Will of Ranney, 589 A.2d 1339 (N.J.1991); Uniform Probate Code § 2–504(c).

§ 4.4

**1.** Bird, *Sleight of Handwriting: the Holographic Will in California,* 32 Hast.L.J. 605 (1981).

**2.** In Estate of Hand, 684 A.2d 521 (N.J.Super.Ch.Div.1996), the court probated an hand-printed will as a holograph, saying that it was a susceptible to analysis as cursive writing. In Estate of Brenner, 91 Cal.Rptr.2d 149 (App. 1999) the court allowed a photocopy of a handwritten will as a holograph on the ground that it would provide "the same assurance of assurance of authenticity as original ink." But American law has not recognized typewritten wills as holographs, although they are so treated in some foreign countries. 1 J. Schoenblum, *Multistate and Multinational Estate Planning* § 15.02.1 n. 4 (1982).

**3.** Pennsylvania is unique in allowing unwitnessed wills which are *not* in the testator's handwriting. 20 Pa.Stat. § 2502.

**4.** R. Villers, *Rome et le Droit Prive* 466 (1977).

**5.** Bird, *supra* note 1, at 606. Holographic wills were not generally accepted in Roman or canon law, but were allowed in the ecclesiastical courts of England (which had jurisdiction over testaments of personal property) beginning around 1600, until they were abolished by the Wills Act of 1837. Helmholz, *The Origin of Holographic Wills in English Law*, 15 J. Leg. Hist. 97 (1994).

**6.** Uniform Probate Code § 2–502(b); Cal. Prob.Code § 6111; Tenn.Code § 32–1–105. *Compare* In re Estate of Salathe, 703 So.2d 1167 (Fla.App.1997) (holograph has no effect in Florida).

It may be necessary to ascertain the date of a will (1) to determine which of several inconsistent wills was the testator's last, and (2) to establish that the will was made while the testator was competent in case he lacked capacity at any time before death. In theory, the witnesses to an attested will can establish the date of its execution, but since holographic wills have no witnesses, many states require that they be dated.[7] Holographic wills in such states have been rejected for lack of a date even though the date was irrelevant in the particular case or was otherwise known. The Uniform Probate Code does not require that holographic wills be dated.[8] California has also eliminated the requirement, but provides that an undated will may be invalid if the date is important and cannot be established by other proof.[9]

If a statute requires that a will be dated, abbreviations are allowed but the date must be complete; the month and year are not enough.[10] Thus the validity of a will dated "Monday 26, 1978" has been held to depend on whether Monday fell on the 26th in more than one month during that year.[11] Extrinsic evidence can be used to clarify an ambiguous date like "10/4/84"—does this mean October 4 or May 10? [12]A will is not invalidated by the fact that the date is incorrect.[13]

### *Printed Matter*

Often a testator writes out a holographic will on a sheet of paper containing printed or typewritten words, such as preprinted stationery or a will form in which the testator fills in the blanks. Sometimes words are added to a holograph by another person with the testator's consent. Even if the governing statute requires that the will be "entirely" in the testator's handwriting, some cases have overlooked other writing on the page as "surplusage."[14] Some courts, however, reject the will if the testator intended the nonholographic material to be part of it.[15]

It is hard to see what purpose is served by rejecting such wills. A substantial sample of the testator's handwriting provides a safeguard against forgery whether or not other words appear on the same page. Moreover, the

**7.** *E.g.,* La.Civ.Code art. 1588.

**8.** Uniform Probate Code § 2–502; Matter of Grobman's Estate, 635 P.2d 231 (Colo.App. 1981).

**9.** Calif.Prob.Code § 6111(b). In Matter of Estate of Harrington, 850 P.2d 158 (Colo.App. 1993), an undated holograph was rejected where an attested will revoked all prior wills, but in In re Estate of Kleinman, 970 P.2d 1286 (Utah 1998), the case was remanded to determine whether the holograph was made subsequent to the will.

**10.** In re Carson's Estate, 344 P.2d 612 (Cal.App.1959); Bird, *supra* note 1, at 612; Succession of Holloway, 531 So.2d 431 (La. 1988). *But see* In re Estate of Wells, 497 N.W.2d 683 (Neb.1993) (accepting a will dated "Oct. 85").

**11.** *Compare* Estate of Rudolph, 169 Cal. Rptr. 126 (App.1980) *with* Succession of Raiford, 404 So.2d 251 (La.1981).

**12.** Succession of Bacot, 502 So.2d 1118 (La.App.1987); *Restatement, Third, of Property (Wills and Other Donative Transfers)* § 3.2, comm. e (1998).

**13.** Bird, *supra* note 1, at 612.

**14.** Charleston Nat. Bank v. Thru the Bible, 507 S.E.2d 708, 712 (W.Va.1998); Succession of Burke, 365 So.2d 858 (La.App.1978); Fairweather v. Nord, 388 S.W.2d 122 (Ky. 1965); In re Mulkins' Estate, 496 P.2d 605 (Ariz.App.1972); *Restatement, Third, of Property (Wills and Other Donative Transfers)* 3.2, comm. b (1998). The California Supreme Court has adopted this view, overruling earlier cases which rejected wills containing insubstantial printed matter. Estate of Black, 641 P.2d 754 (Cal.1982).

**15.** Bird, *supra* note 1, at 621; Matter of Estate of Dobson, 708 P.2d 422 (Wyo.1985); Matter of Estate of Krueger, 529 N.W.2d 151 (N.D.1995) (will invalid when the name of one devisee was not in testator's handwriting).

printed-form wills involved in many of these cases serve the channeling policy especially well, since unlike many handwritten letters, the use of a will form shows testamentary intent.

The Uniform Probate Code only requires that the "signature and material portions" of the will be in the testator's handwriting.[16] This may permit a printed will form with handwritten insertions to be probated as a holograph.[17]

### *Testamentary Intent*

The absence of a ceremonial like attestation often creates doubt whether a writing was intended to be a will. A paper need not be labelled "will" in order to have that effect: "it is immaterial what label the testator places on her writing."[18] Use of the word "will," however, does help to show testamentary intent.[19] Some courts regard language of present gift as inconsistent with an intent to make a *will,* for example a hand-written paper which said "I would like Maymie Gilson to have all my personal effects, furniture, and belongings."[20]

A writing which appears to be notes for a contemplated will rather than a will itself, such as a paper listing "names and addresses of those to be named in my will," and a letter to the testator's attorney listing "changes to be made in my will" have been denied probate.[21] In the law of contracts, the fact that the parties contemplated executing a formal contract in the future is evidence that they did not yet regard the deal as complete, but it is not conclusive.[22] So also a court probated a letter written to the testator's attorney, saying that "even if decedent intended that the attorney draft a formal will for execution, she would also have intended that her property pass in accordance with her recorded wishes if she died before execution of a formal will."[23]

Some courts insist that the document offered for probate show testamen-

**16.** Uniform Probate Code § 2–502(b). The older version of the UPC used the words "signature and the material provisions." *See also* Calif.Prob.Code § 6111. The change was "to leave no doubt about the validity of a will in which immaterial parts of a dispositive provision—such as 'I give, devise and bequeath'—are not in the testator's handwriting." *Restatement, Third, of Property (Wills and Other Donative Transfers)* § 3.2, comm. b (1998).

**17.** Matter of Estate of Muder, 765 P.2d 997 (Ariz.1988); In re Estate of Cunningham, 487 A.2d 777 (N.J.Super.Law Div.1984); *Restatement, Third, of Property (Wills and Other Donative Transfers)* § 3.2, illus. 4 (1998).

**18.** In re Estate of Kleinman, 970 P.2d 1286, 1289 (Utah 1998). *See also* Succession of Bacot, 502 So.2d 1118 (La.App.1987) ("I leave all to Danny"); Seifert v. Sanders, 358 S.E.2d 775 (W.Va.1987); Matter of Estate of Ramirez, 869 P.2d 263 (Mont.1994) (letter); Trim v. Daniels, 862 S.W.2d 8 (Tex.App.1992) (back of greeting card).

**19.** Thomas v. Copenhaver, 365 S.E.2d 760 (Va.1988); *cf.* Matter of Rogers, 895 S.W.2d 375 (Tex.App.1994) ("codicil").

**20.** Dahlgren v. First National Bank, 580 P.2d 478 (Nev.1978). *See also* In re Gasparovich's Estate, 487 P.2d 1148 (Mont.1971); In re Estate of Ike, 454 N.E.2d 577 (Ohio App.1982); *cf.* Ayala v. Martinez, 883 S.W.2d 270 (Tex. App.1994) (probating a paper saying property "shall be divided").

**21.** Matter of Will of Smith, 528 A.2d 918 (N.J.1987); (instructions to attorney for preparing will); Estate of Southworth, 59 Cal. Rptr.2d 272 (App.1996) (statement that "I am not taking action now but my intent is to leave my estate to . . ); Matter of Estate of Erickson, 806 P.2d 1186 (Utah 1991) (note cards intended as a draft).

**22.** *Restatement (Second) of Contracts* § 27 (1981).

**23.** Will of Smith, 507 A.2d 748, 750 (N.J.Super.App.Div.1986). *See also* Maines v. Davis, 227 So.2d 844 (Miss.1969) (probating a paper which said "I will finish this later" on the ground that the signature showed finality); In re Estate of Kuralt, 981 P.2d 771 (Mont. 1999).

tary intent without resort to extrinsic evidence.[24] The Uniform Probate Code, however, allows testamentary intent to be proved by extrinsic evidence,[25] and many courts have done the same. For example, a letter was probated as a will in part because it was consistent with the decedent's oral statement that "he was leaving everything to" the person named in the letter.[26] The place where the paper is found may also be relevant. A North Carolina statute requires that holographic wills be found among the testator's "valuable papers" or in the custody of someone with whom it was "deposited by him * * * for safekeeping."[27] The fact that the testator once executed an attested will arguably shows that an unattested paper was not written with testamentary intent.[28] Nevertheless, courts have found testamentary intent in a holograph written after an attested will.[29]

Testamentary intent is usually treated as a question of fact, so a trial court's findings are affirmed if not clearly erroneous.[30] Some courts, however, call it a question of law if the issue turns on the writing alone.[31]

### *Are Holographic Wills Desirable?*

Some commentators object that holographic wills provide no protection against undue influence.[32] This objection seems weak, since undue influence is usually exerted at times other than the moment of execution of a will.[33] A stronger argument against holographic wills is the difficulty of determining testamentary intent. "If a document has been executed with the usual testamentary formalities, a court can be reasonably certain that * * * it was seriously intended as a will," whereas a holograph leaves this question "open to doubt."[34] On the other hand, reported cases of holographs where testamentary intent is doubtful are probably rarer than those in which a testator's clear intent to devise property was frustrated because the jurisdiction did not recognize holographs.

**24.** Mallory v. Mallory, 862 S.W.2d 879 (Ky.1993); Wolfe v. Wolfe, 448 S.E.2d 408 (Va. 1994).

**25.** Uniform Probate Code § 2–502(c). *See also* Cal.Prob.Code § 6111.5; *Restatement, Third, of Property (Wills and Other Donative Transfers)* § 3.2, comm c (1998).

**26.** Blake's Estate v. Benza, 587 P.2d 271, 274 (Ariz.App.1978). *See also* In re Teubert's Estate, 298 S.E.2d 456 (W.Va.1982); Will of Smith, 507 A.2d 748 (N.J.Super.App.Div.1986); In re Estate of Kuralt, 981 P.2d 771 (Mont. 1999). *But see* Estate of Southworth, 59 Cal. Rptr.2d 272, 277 (App.1996) (extrinsic evidence overcome by language of instrument showing no present intent to devise).

**27.** N.C.Gen.Stat. § 31–3.4(a). The statute has been rather liberally interpreted. *E.g.*, Matter of Will of Church, 466 S.E.2d 297 (N.C.App.1996) (will found in pocketbook); Stephens v. McPherson, 362 S.E.2d 826 (N.C.App. 1987) (jewelry box).

**28.** *Cf.* Williams v. Springfield Marine Bank, 475 N.E.2d 1122 (Ill.App.1985) (fact that decedent executed a will on the same day indicates another paper was written without testamentary intent).

**29.** Blake's Estate v. Benza, 587 P.2d 271 (Ariz.App.1978); In re Laurin's Estate, 424 A.2d 1290 (Pa.1981).

**30.** In re Teubert's Estate, 298 S.E.2d 456 (W.Va.1982); Blake's Estate v. Benza, 587 P.2d 271 (Ariz.App.1978); Matter of Martinez' Estate, 664 P.2d 1007 (N.M.App.1983).

**31.** McDonald v. Petty, 559 S.W.2d 1 (Ark. 1977); Wolfe v. Wolfe, 448 S.E.2d 408 (Va. 1994).

**32.** Gulliver & Tilson, *Classification of Gratuitous Transfers,* 51 Yale L.J. 1, 14 (1941). See also Bird, *supra* note 1, at 609.

**33.** As to undue influence see Section 7.3. The subscribing witnesses are more likely to play an important rule when the testator's capacity is at issue. See Section 7.1.

**34.** Estate of Brown, 218 Cal.Rptr. 108, 110 (App.1985). However, getting witnesses to subscribe a document does not preclude claims that there was no testamentary intent. In re Estate of Ike, 454 N.E.2d 577 (Ohio App.1982); Williams v. Springfield Marine Bank, 475 N.E.2d 1122 (Ill.App.1985); *cf.* Currier Gallery of Art v. Packard, 504 N.E.2d 368 (Mass.App. 1987)

Few lawyers would advise clients to write a holographic will, since the costs of attestation are slight compared with the benefits of reducing the risk of contest by using witnesses. Since holographic wills are primarily the work of lay persons, they are often ill-considered and ambiguous.[35] Indeed, some make so little sense that they fail for "uncertainty" even though they were duly executed.[36] However, since "the public plainly insists on being permitted to use a 'do-it-yourself' approach to will making, as is permitted in virtually every other enterprise," denying effect to holographic wills appears "to force the public to rely on lawyers," and hurts the image of the profession.[37]

### *Oral Wills*

Roman law relaxed the formal requirements for soldiers' wills. Perhaps this was regarded as a reward for military service, or perhaps it was thought that soldiers engaged in active service could not easily comply with the formalities prescribed for ordinary wills.[38] In order to prevent casual statements from being mistaken for wills, informal soldiers' wills were recognized only when the testator used formal language "calling together men to witness his will."[39]

These ideas have influenced modern law. The Statute of Frauds of 1676 permitted nuncupative (oral) wills when they were made "in the time of the last sickness of the deceased" when there might be no time to draft and execute a written will. The testator must "bid the persons present * * * bear witness that such was his will."[40] Blackstone says this was to assure that the words were not "loose idle discourse," but he added that the requisites for oral wills were "so numerous" that they had "fallen into disuse."[41] The Wills Act of 1837 abolished them with a proviso that "any Soldier being in actual Military Service, or any Mariner or Seaman being at Sea, may dispose of his Personal Estate" as permitted under prior law.[42]

Some American states have provisions for oral wills modeled on the Statute of Frauds.[43] Others have special rules for wills of soldiers and seamen.[44] Neither provision is often used. Courts require the evidence of an oral will to be of the "clearest and most convincing character,"[45] and they insist on strict compliance with the statutory limitations.[46] The Uniform

**35.** Chaffin, *Execution, Revocation, and Revalidation of Wills,* 11 Ga.L.Rev. 297, 325 (1977); Bird, *supra* note 1 at 631–32.

**36.** In re Estate of Casselman, 364 N.W.2d 27 (Neb.1985); Matter of Estate of Lewis, 738 P.2d 617 (Utah 1987).

**37.** Wellman, *Arkansas and the Uniform Probate Code,* 2 U.Ark.L.R.L.J. 1, 15 (1979). *See also* In re Teubert's Estate, 298 S.E.2d 456, 460 (W.Va.1982).

**38.** Gaius, *Institutes* 2.109 attributes the rule to the "ignorance" (*imperitiam* ) of soldiers.

**39.** Justinian, *Institutes* 2.11.1.

**40.** Statute of Frauds, 29 Car. 2, c. 3, § 19 (1676).

**41.** W. Blackstone, *Commentaries* 501 (1765).

**42.** Wills Act, 1 Vict. c. 26, §§ 9, 11 (1837).

**43.** Ohio Rev.Code § 2107.60; Ga.Code §§ 53–2–47 et. seq.; Tex.Prob.Code § 65; Miss. Code § 91–5–15.

**44.** Va.Code § 64.1–53; N.Y. EPTL 3–2.2(b) (holographic and nuncupative will allowed if testator in armed services); Md. Estates and Trusts Code § 4–103.

**45.** Dabney v. Thomas, 596 S.W.2d 561, 563 (Tex.Civ.App.1980).

**46.** In re McClellan's Estate, 189 A. 315 (Pa.1937) (will rejected because no explicit request to witnesses); Kay v. Sandler, 718 S.W.2d 872 (Tex.App.1986) (will rejected because only one witness heard it).

Probate Code does not allow oral wills, and its liberal choice-of-law rule only applies to "written" wills.[47]

## § 4.5 Gifts

### *History*

*(1) First Stage: Delivery of Property Required*

The history of the formal requirements for gifts is marked by four stages. Originally, an effective gift required delivery of the property. A writing purporting to transfer property was ineffective if the donor stayed in possession of the property, even if the writing was delivered to the donee.[1]

Two reasons underlay this rule. An actual change of possession was necessary because the legal system depended on juries who originally were expected to know the facts before they were impanelled. If a donor stayed in possession of land, the jury from the neighborhood would not know that the gift had taken place. Second, delivery prevented frauds on third parties. A donor who stayed in possession of property might later sell it to *B* who would be unaware of the prior gift to *A*. The delivery requirement protected *B* by making the transfer to *A* invalid.[2]

*(2) Second Stage: Deed as a Substitute for Delivery*

In the 15th century it was suggested that goods could be transferred without delivery; the buyer in a sale of personal property got title even before the goods were delivered, unlike land which would "not pass without livery."[3] A few years later a deed of gift was said to be effective even though the donor kept possession of the goods.[4] These ideas were later extended to land in Equity. When land was sold, the buyer acquired the use (*i.e.* became the equitable owner) by virtue of the bargain and sale.[5] Later, any deed supported by "consideration" was sufficient to transfer the use. Consideration for this purpose was broadly defined to include affection for a relative or spouse.[6] A leading case of the 16th century involved a man who executed a deed purporting to transfer land to his brother after the donor's death. The deed was challenged with an argument restating the traditional rationale for requiring delivery of land:

> Livery of seisin was first invented as an act of notoriety, whereby people might have knowledge of estates, and be more able to try them, if

**47.** Uniform Probate Code § 2–506. In the Matter of Buffi's Estate, 564 P.2d 150 (Idaho 1977) the court held that the "common law doctrine of nuncupative wills" was irrelevant when testator died after the adoption of the UPC, even though the will was made prior thereto.

§ 4.5

**1.** Bracton's Note Book pl. 1971 (1221); 2 H. Bracton, *De Legibus* 124 (1968); T. Littleton *Tenures* § 59; R. Glanville, *Tractatus de Legibus* 69–70 (G. Hall ed. 1965).

**2.** 3 W. Holdsworth, *A History of English Law* 224 (5th ed. 1942). Glanville makes this point in discussing mortgages: if the mortgagor remained possession, the same property could be mortgaged to several creditors. Glanville, *supra* note 1, at 123–24.

**3.** Shipton v. Dog, reprinted in A. Kiralfy, *A Source Book of English Law* 192, 196 (1957) (Fortescue, C.J.).

**4.** Mich. 7 Edw. 4, f. 20, pl. 21 (1467).

**5.** Y.B.Hil. 21 Hen. 7, f. 18, pl. 30 (1505). *See also* Y.B.Pas. 27 Hen. 8, pl. 22, at f. 8 (1535); C. St. Germain, *Doctor & Student* (1530), 91 Sel.Soc. 225.

**6.** R. Brooke, *Abridgement,* Feffements and Uses ¶ 54 (1573). Consideration is defined more narrowly today. *Restatement, Second, Contracts* § 17 (1971).

they should be empaneled on a jury; and by the like reason when a use shall pass, there ought to be * * * a public and notorious consideration * * * which may cause the country to have knowledge of the use for the better trial thereof. * * * And if uses might be so easily raised by covenants * * * where no act or thing apparent is done whereof the country may have notice it would * * * make it very difficult for the people to know who were the owners of lands.

But the court upheld the deed, saying that the donor's affection for his brother was "sufficient consideration" to support it.[7] By this date the reasons for the law's earlier insistence on delivery of land had disappeared. By the 16th century juries could be informed by witnesses and other evidence produced in court (like deeds). The expansion of literacy also contributed to the law's recognition of deeds as a means of conveyance. "In the days when few people could write, * * * livery of seisin was necessary to transfer ownership of real estate. As people became more literate and writing became more common, deeds and written instruments * * * were found to be more reliable in demonstrating the intentions of the parties."[8]

*(3) Third Stage: Writing Required for All Transfers of Land*

By the end of the 16th century land could be transferred *either* by a written deed,[9] *or* by livery of seisin without any writing. The Statute of Frauds of 1676, however, provided that livery of seisin of land conveyed only an estate at will absent a signed writing.[10] As a result, a writing, which was originally ineffective to transfer land, became the *only* effective method of transfer.

Nearly all American states today have legislation based on the Statute of Frauds requiring a signed writing to convey land.[11] Thus when the grantee named in a deed added the name of his wife, she acquired no interest because he "never signed the altered instrument."[12] The writing must also identify the subject matter of the gift; the delivery of a signed blank deed does not suffice unless the donor gives the recipient authority in writing to fill in the blanks.[13] "Except to the extent allowed by the Statute of Frauds, the owner of an interest in land cannot make an effective donative transfer thereof . . . by delivering the land to the donee," although short term oral leases are commonly permitted.[14]

These statutes do not apply to personal property; for chattels, an oral statement of donative intent plus delivery still suffices.[15] This leads to some technical distinctions. For example, the owner of a condominium has an

**7.** 75 Eng.Rep. 457 (1564).

**8.** Lewis v. Burke, 226 N.E.2d 332, 335 (Ind.1967).

**9.** Callard v. Callard, 72 Eng.Rep. 841 (1594) (a use is "not raised upon natural affection without a deed").

**10.** Statute of Frauds, 29 Car. 2, c. 3, § 1 (1676).

**11.** *Restatement (Third) of Property (Wills and Other Donative Transfers)* § 6.3 (Prel.Dft. 2000). According to comm. d, an electronic signature suffices and it can appear anywhere in the document. Compare Section 4.2, note 4 as to the signature on wills.

**12.** Julian v. Petersen, 966 P.2d 878, 881 (Utah App.1998).

**13.** McCormick v. Brevig, 980 P.2d 603, 616 (Mont.1999); *Restatement, Second, of Property (Donative Transfers)* § 32.1 (1990).

**14.** *Id.* § 31.4, comm. a.

**15.** However, many contracts for the *sale* of personal property are also subject to a writing requirement. *See Restatement, Second, Contracts* §§ 110, 125 et seq (1979).

interest in land which must be transferred in writing, whereas an interest in a cooperative apartment is represented by shares of stock which can be transferred orally.[16]

Despite the Statute of Frauds, courts give effect to oral gifts of land if the donee has taken possession and made valuable improvements on the land.[17] It is not enough that the donee has taken possession unless substantial improvements have been made,[18] and even then, a court may simply require reimbursement for the value of the improvements.[19]

The Statute of Frauds does not bar giving effect to a lost deed, if there is clear proof that it once existed.[20]

*(4) Modern Recording Statutes*

American states today all have recording statutes. These statutes cover donative conveyances of land as well as sales. Under these statutes an unrecorded deed is ineffective as against a later bona fide purchaser from the transferor.[21] Unrecorded deeds are still valid between the parties. Thus when a mother deeded land to her daughter, the fact that the deed was not recorded did not bar the daughter from keeping the land as against the mother's estate.[22] Even third parties are usually not protected if they had notice of the unrecorded prior conveyance.[23]

Most recording statutes require special formalities in addition to the transferor's signature as a prerequisite to recording a deed; for example, deeds in California must be "duly acknowledged" before a notary public or other official before they can be recorded.[24]

Most personal property is not covered by a recording system. However, if a transfer is "not accompanied by an immediate delivery" it may be deemed "fraudulent and void" against subsequent bona fide purchasers from the transferor.[25]

### *Personal Property: Tangibles*

**16.** *Id.*, comm. f. An interest under a contract to sell land must be transferred by a writing. First Nat. Bank v. Gregory, 468 N.E.2d 739 (Ohio App. 1983).

**17.** Montoya v. New Mexico Human Services Dept., 771 P.2d 196 (N.M.App.1989); Ortmeyer v. Bruemmer, 680 S.W.2d 384 (Mo.App. 1984); Conradi v. Perkins, 941 P.2d 1083 (Or. App.1997); *Restatement (Second) of Contracts* § 129, illus. 4 (1979).

**18.** Isaak v. Smith, 848 P.2d 1014 (Mont. 1993).

**19.** *Restatement (Second) of Property, Donative Transfers,* § 31.4, comm. e (1990); *cf. Restatement, Second, Contracts* § 129, illus. 5 (1979).

**20.** Cole v. Guy, 539 N.E.2d 436 (Ill.App. 1989).

**21.** The statutes differ as to who exactly is protected against an unrecorded deed. *Compare* Cal.Civ.Code § 1214 (unrecorded deed is "void as against any subsequent purchaser or mortgagee ... in good faith and for a valuable consideration, whose conveyance is first duly recorded, and as against any judgment affecting the title") *with* Siegel Mobile Home Group, Inc. v. Bowen, 757 P.2d 1250 (Idaho App.1988) (unrecorded deed effective against judgment creditor of donor).

**22.** Estate of Blettell v. Snider, 834 P.2d 505 (Or.App.1992). *See also* In re Estate of Ault, 609 N.E.2d 568 (Ohio App.1992).

**23.** Calhoun v. Higgins, 797 P.2d 404 (Or. App.1990).

**24.** Cal.Civ.Code §§ 1170, 1181; *cf.* Galloway v. Cinello, 423 S.E.2d 875 (W.Va.1992) (notary should be disinterested, but use of an interested notary does not invalidate the instrument).

**25.** Calif.Civ.Code § 3440. *See also Restatement (Second) of Property, Donative Transfers* § 34.9 (1990); Center v. Hampton Affiliates, Inc., 488 N.E.2d 828 (N.Y.1985) (based on Uniform Commercial Code § 8–302).

A person can give away tangible personal property either by delivering the property itself,[26] or by executing and delivering a written instrument of gift. For example, a father's letter to his son saying "I wish to give you as a present the oil painting by Gustave Klimt which now hangs in the New York living room" was effective even though the son did not take possession of the painting during his father's lifetime.[27] Conversely, an oral gift of a horse was held to be effective despite a statute requiring "a written and acknowledged bill of sale from the vendor to the purchaser" for "the transfer of livestock." This did not mean "that the transfer of livestock without a bill of sale is ineffective."[28]

### *Intangibles*

Most wealth today is in the form of intangible property, like bank accounts, shares of stock and bonds. Gifts of intangibles can be made in several ways. If they are represented by a paper like a stock certificate or a passbook, the donor may simply deliver it to the donee.[29] Even for a registered security delivery of the certificate without the donor's endorsement is effective.[30] However, intangibles usually represent a claim against an institution and the rules of the institution may require that it receive notice of the transfer. For example, when a woman delivered United States Savings Bonds to her granddaughters her intent to give the bonds was ineffective because she failed to have the bonds reissued in the donees' names as required by Treasury regulations.[31] Some courts hold that such rules are only designed to protect the institution from liability if it pays without notice of the transfer, and should not control who owns the claim,[32] just as an unrecorded deed is effective when no third-party's rights are involved. However, failure to notify the institution of the transfer casts doubt on donative intent. For example, a court found that a father who had delivered certificates of deposit to his son did not intend a gift since he had not "bothered to change the names of the payees."[33]

A donor may also give intangibles by having them re-registered in the donee's name, even if nothing is delivered, and even if the donee is not aware

**26.** Barham v. Jones, 647 P.2d 397 (N.M. 1982) (diamond rings); In re Estate of Kremer, 546 N.E.2d 1047 (Ill.App.1989) (cameras); *Restatement (Second) of Property, Donative Transfers* § 31.1 (1990).

**27.** Gruen v. Gruen, 496 N.E.2d 869 (N.Y. 1986). *See also* Carey v. Jackson, 603 P.2d 868 (Wyo.1979); Lewis v. Burke, 226 N.E.2d 332 (Ind.1967); *Restatement (Second) of Contracts* § 332, comment b (1981); *Restatement (Second) of Property, Donative Transfers* §§ 32.1–.2 (1990).

**28.** Milner v. Colonial Trust Co., 6 P.3d 329, 332 (Ariz.App.2000).

**29.** Mashburn v. Wright, 420 S.E.2d 379 (Ga.App.1992) (certificate of deposit); Rogers v. Rogers, 319 A.2d 119 (Md.1974) (stock); In re Watson's Estate, 256 N.E.2d 113 (Ill.App.1970) (passbook); *Restatement (Second) of Contracts* § 332, illus, 4 (1981); *Restatement (Second) of Property, Donative Transfers* § 31.1, comm. a (1990).

**30.** Estate of Novetzke, TC Memo 1988–268; Andrews v. Troy Bank and Trust Co., 529 So.2d 987 (Ala.1988).

**31.** United States v. Chandler, 410 U.S. 257 (1973).

**32.** *Restatement (Second) of Property, Donative Transfers* § 31.1, comm. b (1990); Abney v. Western Res. Mut. Cas. Co., 602 N.E.2d 348 (Ohio App.1991) (gift of boat effective despite failure to get new title certificate).

**33.** Gibson v. Boling, 622 S.W.2d 180 (Ark. 1981). *See also* Cassiday v. Cassiday, 259 A.2d 299 (Md.1969) (failure to change designated beneficiary on insurance policy); Matter of Estate of Casey, 507 N.E.2d 962 (Ill.App.1987) (failure to endorse CD indicates no gift intended); *Restatement (Third) of Property (Wills and Other Donative Transfers)* § 6.2, comm. i (Prel.Dft. 2000).

of the gift. The Uniform Transfers to Minors Act expressly sanctions this method for making gifts.[34]

Third, the donor may sign a writing indicating an intent to give stock (for example), and deliver the writing but retain the stock certificate. Thus a donor of stock was held to have made an effective gift of it by executing and delivering a deed of gift to the donees; her "failure to deliver the stock certificates did not invalidate her gift."[35]

Signing and delivering a check to a donee is not effective as an assignment of the drawer's funds in the bank.[36] A payee who cashes the check before the drawer dies can keep the money, but if the drawer dies before the check is paid, the check is not enforceable against the drawer's estate.[37] The bank is protected if it pays the check without knowledge of the drawer's death, but in this case the drawer's estate can recover the funds from the payee.[38]

### *Delivery*

The idea of delivery often recurs in the law of gifts. A person can convey land while retaining possession of it,[39] but the donor must deliver a *deed* to the donee; an undelivered deed is ineffective.[40] If a deed has been recorded, delivery is presumed,[41] but the presumption of delivery can be rebutted.[42] Similarly a gift of personal property may fail for lack of delivery. Thus when the owner of a company endorsed stock certificates intending to give them to certain employees but died before they were delivered, the stock was held to belong to his estate.[43] Parents who had loaned money to their daughter later

**34.** Uniform Transfers to Minors Act § 9(a)(1)(i). *See also* Estate of Ross v. Ross, 626 P.2d 489 (Utah 1981); Barham v. Jones, 647 P.2d 397, 399 (N.M.1982) (trailer registered in donee's name); Parson v. United States, 460 F.2d 228 (5th Cir.1972) (policy taken out in another's name); Matter of Carroll, 474 N.Y.S.2d 340 (A.D.1984). Sending stock to the issuer for reissue in the donee's name may be treated as delivery to the donee's agent. Kintzinger v. Millin, 117 N.W.2d 68 (Iowa 1962).

**35.** Estate of Davenport v. C.I.R., 184 F.3d 1176, 1186 (10th Cir.1999). *See also Restatement (Second) of Property, Donative Transfers* § 32.2, illus. 4 (1990); Grau v. Dooley, 431 N.E.2d 1164 (Ill.App.1981); Tanner v. Robinson, 411 So.2d 240, 242 (Fla.App.1982). *But see Restatement (Second) of Contracts* § 332, illus. 3 (1981).

**36.** Uniform Commercial Code § 3–408; Hieber v. Uptown Nat. Bank, 557 N.E.2d 408 (Ill.App.1990).

**37.** Estate of Gagliardi, 89 T.C. 1207 (1987); Creekmore v. Creekmore, 485 S.E.2d 68 (N.C.App.1997); McCarthy v. United States, 806 F.2d 129 (7th Cir.1986); Dillingham v. C.I.R., 903 F.2d 760 (10th Cir.1990). *But see* Sinclair v. Fleischman, 773 P.2d 101 (Wash. App.1989). *Restatement (Third) of Property (Wills and Other Donative Transfers)* § 6.2, comm. r (Prel.Dft. 2000) says that delivery of a "bank check" can be a gift, and even an ordinary check given to a charity may represent an enforceable promise.

**38.** Uniform Commercial Code § 4–405; *Restatement (Second) of Contracts* § 332, illus. 9 (1981).

**39.** Matter of Estate of Williams, 496 N.E.2d 547 (Ill.App.1986).

**40.** Matter of Estate of Dittus, 497 N.W.2d 415 (N.D.1993); Julian v. Petersen, 966 P.2d 878 (Utah App.1998). However, *Restatement (Third) of Property (Wills and Other Donative Transfers)* § 6.3 (Prel.Dft. 2000) dispenses with delivery when a gift is by document.

**41.** Giefer v. Swenton, 928 P.2d 906 (Kan. App.1996); Matter of Estate of Rohrer, 646 N.E.2d 17 (Ill.App.1995); Gross v. Gross, 781 P.2d 284 (Mont.1989).

**42.** Matter of Estate of Shedrick, 462 N.E.2d 581 (Ill.App.1984); Barlow Soc. v. Commercial Sec. Bank, 723 P.2d 398, 400 (Utah 1986); Johnson v. Ramsey, 817 S.W.2d 200 (Ark.1991). However, under the Uniform Transfers to Minors Act § 9(a)(5), recording alone is sufficient.

**43.** Lauerman v. Destocki, 622 N.E.2d 1122 (Ohio App.1993). *See also* Matter of Estate of Hoyle, 866 P.2d 451 (Okl.App.1993) (alleged intent to forgive loans ineffective since notes retained); Young v. Young, 393 S.E.2d 398 (Va.1990); *Restatement (Second) of Contracts* § 332(1) (1979).

told her that the loan was forgiven, and this was supported by an entry in the mother's diary. But this release was held ineffective in a suit by the father's executor to collect the debt. Absent consideration, a release required "the delivery of some instrument in writing."[44]

Delivery performs a function like the formal requirements for wills. It "forces upon the most thoughtless and hasty at least a moment's consideration of the effects of what he is planning to do." It also has evidentiary value in that a donee's possession supports the claim of gift.[45] Nevertheless the value of the delivery requirement has been questioned. The second Restatement of Property suggests that the law should recognize a gifts of personal property "without a delivery by proof of the donor's manifested intention to make a gift."[46] Courts are usually less strict about delivery than about the statutory requirements for wills; they often uphold gifts on the basis of a "constructive" delivery.[47] Even this fiction is occasionally dispensed with: some cases say there is no reason to insist on delivery when donative intent is clear and no third party is affected.[48]

The same physical facts may or may not constitute delivery depending on intent. A donor who puts a deed in a safe-deposit box has "delivered" it but only if he intended "to relinquish control over it and to effect delivery."[49] In such cases "delivery" seems to describe a result reached on other grounds, *i.e.* a finding of "no delivery" reflects a belief that no gift was intended.[50]

Courts tend to excuse delivery in situations where it was impossible or very difficult. For example, a woman two days before she died told the donee that he was to have certain securities which were not in her possession. Because the donor was "physically incapable of" delivering the property, the "unequivocal evidence" of her intent to give constituted "constructive delivery."[51]

Even if delivery is possible, it may be inconvenient to leave the donee in possession. Sometimes a donor delivers a deed to the donee who returns it to the donee "to hold for her," *e.g.* because the donee has no safe-deposit box. This is deemed delivery, even though the donee's claim is not corroborated by possession, because the original handing over of the deed shows a serious intent to give,[52] as distinguished from the case in which the donor simply

**44.** Gartin v. Taylor, 577 N.W.2d 410, 413 (Iowa 1998).

**45.** Mecham, *The Requirement of Delivery,* 21 Ill.L.Rev. 341, 348–49 (1926). *See also Restatement (Third) of Property (Wills and Other Donative Transfers)* § 6.2, comm. b (Prel.Dft. 2000).

**46.** *Restatement (Second) of Property, Donative Transfers* § 31.1, comm. k (1990).

**47.** Whisnant v. Whisnant, 928 P.2d 999 (Or.App.1996) (instructions to broker); Tierce v. Macedonia United Meth. Church, 519 So.2d 451 (Ala.1987) (symbolic delivery in recording); Estate of Davenport v. C.I.R., 184 F.3d 1176, 1185 (10th Cir.1999) (Oklahoma law). *Restatement (Second) of Property, Donative Transfers* § 31.1, comm. b (1990).

**48.** Hengst v. Hengst, 420 A.2d 370 (Pa. 1980); Estate of O'Brien v. Robinson, 749 P.2d 154 (Wash.1988).

**49.** Bennion v. Hansen, 699 P.2d 757, 759 (Utah 1985). *See also* Lenhart v. Desmond, 705 P.2d 338 (Wyo.1985).

**50.** *Cf.* Gulliver & Tilson, *Classification of Gratuitous Transfers,* 51 Yale L.J. 1, 16 (1941).

**51.** McCarton v. Estate of Watson, 693 P.2d 192 (Wash.App.1984). *See also* Brown v. Metz, 393 S.E.2d 402 (Va.1990) (terminally ill donor tells donee to take bonds from his safe deposit box).

**52.** Barham v. Jones, 647 P.2d 397, 399 (N.M.1982); Hocks v. Jeremiah, 759 P.2d 312 (Or.App.1988); In re Estate of Kelly, 608 N.E.2d 423 (Ill.App.1992); *Restatement (Second) of Contracts* § 332, comment e (1981); *Restatement (Second) of Property, Donative Transfers* § 31.1, illus. 12, § 31.2, illus. 12 (1990).

executes a deed and tells the donee that he will hold it for her but never hands it over.[53]

If the donee is already in possession of the property, *e.g.* as a custodian or borrower, when the donor decides to make the gift, the law dispenses with delivery.[54] A similar exception is made when donor and donee live in the same household, *e.g.* a husband gives his wife a piano in their living room.[55]

Delivery can be made to someone other than the donee. Thus when a man executed a deed of land to his wife and her son and handed the deed to his wife, the conveyance to the son was held effective, even though he was unaware of it.[56] However, gifts may fail if the person to whom delivery was made is deemed to be the donor's agent if the donor dies before the donee gets possession, since the agent's authority to complete the transfer expires when the donor dies.[57]

### *Testamentary Transfers*

When gifts are challenged after the donor's death, the problems of proof of the decedent's intent resemble those which arise in proving wills. Some gifts are held to be "testamentary" and thus subject to the statutory requirements for a will. For example, when a father executed deeds of land to two sons and put them in his safe deposit box, the land was included in the father's estate on the ground that he "intended the deed to operate as testamentary transfers."[58] On the other hand, deeds have been held valid even though they had the practical effects of a will because the donor reserved a life estate, or a power to revoke.[59] Even a document which was labelled "LAST WILL" was held to be effective as a deed since it said "I hereby grant" the property involved and was delivered to the donee.[60]

The question whether a transfer is "testamentary" is often linked with the delivery requirement. In a case where deeds to land were challenged as testamentary and for lack of delivery, the court upheld them on the basis of Uniform Probate Code § 6–101 which says that provisions for "transfer on death" in a deed are "nontestamentary."[61] A later comment to this UPC

**53.** *Restatement (Second) of Property, Donative Transfers* § 31.2, illus. 10 (1990).

**54.** Justinian, *Institutes* 2.1.44; *Restatement (Second) of Contracts* § 332, comment e (1981); *Restatement (Second) of Property, Donative Transfers* § 31.1, illus. 1 (1990); Little City Foundation v. Capsonic Group, 596 N.E.2d 146 (Ill.App.1992).

**55.** *Restatement (Third) of Property (Wills and Other Donative Transfers)* § 6.2, comm. e (Prel.Dft. 2000).

**56.** Matter of Estate of Ashe, 753 P.2d 281 (Idaho App.1988). *See also* In re Estate of Kremer, 546 N.E.2d 1047 (Ill.App.1989); *Restatement (Second) of Property, Donative Transfers* § 31.1 (1990). When the same person is both donor and one of the donees, as in a joint tenancy, this theory may dispense with delivery altogether. Kresser v. Peterson, 675 P.2d 1193 (Utah 1984).

**57.** Kesterson v. Cronan, 806 P.2d 134 (Or. App.1991); Smith v. Levy, 558 N.E.2d 282 (Ill. App.1990); Huskins v. Huskins, 517 S.E.2d 146 (N.C.App.1999) (mailing letter to third party, donor dies before letter received). *Restatement (Second) of Trusts* § 57, comm b (1959). *But see* Herron v. Underwood, 503 N.E.2d 1111 (Ill.App.1987); Poling v. Northup, 652 A.2d 1114 (Me.1995) (delivery to donor's lawyer suffices, since intent controls).

**58.** Matter of Estate of Dittus, 497 N.W.2d 415 (N.D.1993). *See also* Kesterson v. Cronan, 806 P.2d 134 (Or.App.1991); Wright v. Huskey, 592 S.W.2d 899 (Tenn.App.1979); Succession of Young, 563 So.2d 502 (La.App.1990).

**59.** Hamilton v. Caplan, 518 A.2d 1087 (Md.App.1987).

**60.** Ex parte Rucker, 702 So.2d 456 (Ala. 1997). *See also* Vigil v. Sandoval, 741 P.2d 836 (N.M.App.1987); Black v. Poole, 196 S.E.2d 20 (Ga.1973).

**61.** Estate of O'Brien v. Robinson, 749 P.2d 154 (Wash.1988).

provision criticized the decision, saying that the provision is not intended to "relieve against the delivery requirement in deeds."[62] The Restatement of Property, like the UPC, validates documents of transfer even when they are used "as a substitute for a will in that the donor's current beneficial enjoyment of the gift property is not significantly curtailed during the donor's lifetime."[63] Unlike the UPC, however, the Restatement also eliminates the delivery requirement for deeds, as distinguished from gifts made without a document.[64]

When a decedent's intention is manifested by a signed writing, this provides almost as much protection against fraud as an attested will. Even more protection is afforded by the formalities prescribed for recorded deeds in many jurisdictions.[65] A comment to the Uniform Probate Code observes:

> the benign experience with such familiar will substitutes as the revocable inter-vivos trust, the multiple party bank account, and United States government bonds payable on death to named beneficiaries all demonstrated that the evils envisioned if the statute of wills were not rigidly enforced simply do not materialize ... Because these provisions often are part of a business transaction and are evidenced by a writing, the danger of fraud is largely eliminated.[66]

The "business transaction" mentioned in this comment presumably refers to such transactions as opening a banking or brokerage account, in which the donor deals with a disinterested person who performs a function analogous to that of the witnesses to an attested will.

### *Clear and Convincing Evidence*

The Uniform Probate Code allows probate of defectively executed wills only if there is "clear and convincing evidence" that they represent the decedent's intent.[67] Many courts use similar language when examining claims that a decedent had made a gift prior to death. For example, in rejecting such a claim a court said that "the burden of showing an *inter vivos* gift was made is on the donee by clear and convincing evidence."[68] Sometimes this burden cannot be satisfied because a Dead Man statute bars testimony by the donee,[69] but in some cases gifts have been proved by the donee's own testimony.[70] It is difficult to ascertain what "clear and convincing evidence" really means, since appellate courts usually defer to trial courts' findings. Conflicting evidence does not preclude a finding that a gift was made.[71] Evidence of donative intent

**62.** Uniform Probate Code § 6–101, Comment. This section departs somewhat from the earlier version which the court in *O'Brien* construed.

**63.** *Restatement (Second) of Property, Donative Transfers* § 32.4 (1990).

**64.** *Compare id.* § 32.3 *with* § 31.1.

**65.** *Id.* § 32.3, comm. *a.*

**66.** Uniform Probate Code § 6–101, Comment. Many non-UPC states have adopted a similar provision. *E.g.*, Cal.Prob.Code § 5000.

**67.** Uniform Probate Code § 2–503.

**68.** Smith v. Shafer, 623 N.E.2d 1261, 1263 (Ohio App.1993). *See also* Wright v. Union Nat. Bank, 819 S.W.2d 698 (Ark.1991); Succession of Young, 563 So.2d 502 (La.App.1990); Duggan v. Keto, 554 A.2d 1126 (D.C.App.1989).

**69.** Matter of Collier, 381 So.2d 1338 (Miss. 1980); Judson Post Estate v. Commonwealth Bank and Trust Co., 456 A.2d 1360 (Pa.1983); Hamilton v. Caplan, 518 A.2d 1087 (Md.App. 1987).

**70.** Grau v. Dooley, 431 N.E.2d 1164 (Ill. App.1981); In re Watson's Estate, 256 N.E.2d 113 (Ill.App.1970).

**71.** Rogers v. Rogers, 319 A.2d 119, 121 (Md.1974).

need not be contemporaneous with the gift itself.[72]

### *Distinction Between Gifts and Promises*

The need for "consideration" in conveyances by deed has disappeared in modern law, although consideration is customarily recited.[73] Promises, on the other hand, must be supported by consideration. A note promising to pay money, even if delivered, is unenforceable by the payee,[74] unless (in some states) the note is under seal, or unless action in reliance makes it enforceable by promissory estoppel, *e.g.* a woman who quit her job and moved to another state in reliance on her friend's promise to give her a house was able to enforce the promise.[75] Courts are prone to find some sort of consideration or to say it is not needed when promises to charity are involved. For example, Martin Luther King wrote a letter stating that upon his death papers which he had deposited with Boston University "shall become ... the absolute property" of the university. The court held that BU's care of the papers amounted to enough "consideration or reliance" to make this promise enforceable against King's estate.[76]

The law normally refuses to enforce donative *promises* because they are "more likely to be uncalculated than deliberative."[77] Delivery and a signed writing are not *enough* protection against rash promises because persons tend to be less cautious about future commitments.

Whether a transaction is treated as a gift or as a promise requiring consideration may depend on the form of words used. For example, a woman who owned land subject to a life estate in her mother agreed to convey it "at the expiration of the outstanding life estate." This was held to be ineffective without consideration because "the property was not to be transferred until some future date,"[78] but a deed purporting to transfer the land immediately subject to a life estate is an effective gift of a remainder.[79]

The nature of the interest given is also important. Even when words indicating a present transfer are used, a person cannot give property which she expects to inherit from a parent. An effective transfer of such an "expectancy" can be made only if it is supported by adequate consideration.[80] So also "a purported assignment of a right expected to arise under a contract not in existence operates only as a promise to assign the right."[81] The restriction on gifts of expectancies guards against improvident transfers, since

**72.** In re Estate of Deahl, 524 N.E.2d 810 (Ind.App.1988).

**73.** 3 *Amer. Law of Prop.* § 12.43; Rubenstein v. Sela, 672 P.2d 492 (Ariz.App.1983).

**74.** Matter of Wetmore's Estate, 343 N.E.2d 224 (Ill.App.1976); Unthank v. Rippstein, 386 S.W.2d 134 (Tex.1964). *See also* Dementas v. Estate of Tallas, 764 P.2d 628 (Utah App.1988) (promise to leave money at death).

**75.** Brown v. Branch, 733 N.E.2d 17, 24 (Ind.App.2000). *See also Restatement, Second, Contracts* §§ 90, 95 (1981).

**76.** King v. Trustees of Boston University, 647 N.E.2d 1196 (Mass.1995). *See also Restatement, Second, Contracts* § 90(2) (1971).

**77.** Eisenberg, *Donative Promises,* 47 U.Chi.L.Rev. 1, 5 (1979).

**78.** Larabee v. Booth, 437 N.E.2d 1010 (Ind.App.1982). *See also Restatement (Second) of Contracts* §§ 330, 332, comment b (1981).

**79.** *Restatement (Second) of Property, Donative Transfers* § 32.1, illus. 4 (1990).

**80.** Johnson By and Through Lackey v. Schick, 882 P.2d 1059 (Okl.1994) (expected inheritance assigned to satisfy assignor's debts); Scott v. First Nat. Bank, 168 A.2d 349 (Md.1961); *Restatement, Third, of Property (Wills and Other Donative Transfers)* § 2.6, comm. j (1998).

**81.** *Restatement (Second) of Contracts* § 321(2) (1981).

expectancies are often undervalued by the donor, like Esau who sold his inheritance for beans.[82] The line between "expectancies" and "property" is a wavering one. At one time, contingent remainders were regarded as expectancies, but in modern law they are property.[83] The distinction is arbitrary. The expectation of inheriting from a parent can be less speculative than many contingent remainders, *e.g.*, "to Clara if Alice (who has seven healthy children) dies without issue." Rights under an existing contract may be more uncertain than a contract which the assignor expects to make in the future.[84] Instead of distinguishing between "expectancy" and "property," perhaps the law should weigh the speculativeness of the particular right transferred, or the improvidence of the transfer, but these would be hard tests to apply.[85]

## § 4.6 Trusts

The modern trust arose from the medieval use. Like uses, trusts were enforced by the court of equity when this was separate from the law courts. An often-cited maxim of equity says that "equity follows the law." This means that the rules governing trusts are usually (though not always) the same as those which govern legal interests. A person who creates a trust, usually called the settlor, is simply making a gift of a special type.

A settlor can create a trust in one of two ways.[1] First, she can declare herself trustee of property; in this case the same person is both settlor and trustee.[2] Second, the settlor can transfer the property to a another person (or corporation) as trustee. If the settlor does this by a will, the trust is a testamentary trust. If the settlor transfers the property to the trustee during life, or declares herself trustee, the trust is an *inter-vivos* or living trust. Such trusts are often used as will substitutes. In older cases the beneficiary of a trust was called the *cestui que use* but this expression from old French is rarely encountered today.

### *Consideration and Delivery*

A declaration of trust, like an outright gift, requires no consideration.[3] Delivery can be regarded as a substitute for consideration in outright gifts, but delivery is not required for a declaration of trust.[4] Nor does the law require "formal change in ownership records or documents of title," such as

82. *Id.* comment b; Genesis 25:29–34.

83. *Compare* Calif.Civ.Code § 1044 *with* 2 W. Blackstone, *Commentaries* *290 (1765).

84. The New York Court of Appeals upheld a gratuitous assignment of a contractual right to the profits of "My Fair Lady," made before the musical was even written. Speelman v. Pascal, 178 N.E.2d 723 (N.Y.1961).

85. Eisenberg, *supra* note 77, at 15.

§ 4.6

1. *Restatement, Third, of Trusts* § 10 (1996); Unif.Trust Code § 401. Not all trusts are created by a settlor. For example, Uniform Probate Code § 2–212(b) puts the elective share of an incapacitated spouse into a custodial trust for the spouse.

2. "No trust exists when the same individual is the sole settlor, sole trustee, *and sole beneficiary*." Vittands v. Sudduth, 730 N.E.2d 325, 334 (Mass.App.2000) (italics added). However, this rarely happens because most trusts have several beneficiaries. *Restatement, Third, of Trusts* § 32, comm. b (1999).

3. *Restatement, Third, of Trusts* § 15 (1996); Cal.Prob.Code § 15208. Compare promises to create trusts in the future discussed at 23 et seq. *infra*.

4. Estate of Heggstad, 20 Cal.Rptr.2d 433 (App.1993); Taliaferro v. Taliaferro, 921 P.2d 803 (Kan.1996).

recording a deed or reregistration of stock certificates, assuming no rights of third parties are affected.[5]

Why is delivery not necessary for declarations of trust? Courts of equity did not use juries, and the delivery requirement was associated with jury trial.[6] Delivery is "an act of notoriety," required for the jury's edification, which can be dispensed with in equity. A feeling that juries are less sophisticated fact finders than judges is reflected in other rules of law, such as the parol evidence rule, which does not apply to equitable proceedings, where courts operating without a jury reform mistakes in written instruments on the basis of oral testimony.[7]

Gulliver and Tilson suggest that the absence of a delivery requirement for trusts was unimportant because "laymen would not normally think of using a declaration of trust."[8] Since the words "I declare myself trustee of this property" are unusual in normal discourse, they perform a channelling function similar to delivery.[9] But this reasoning supposes that courts actually insist on the use of such technical words to create a trust. Two lines of authority on this issue are hard to reconcile. The Restatement of Trusts says that a "property arrangement may constitute a trust ... even though such terms as 'trust' or 'trustee' are not used."[10] Thus a woman who signed a piece of paper stating that "in the event of my death" certain stock "belongs to Miss Peck" was held to have created a trust.[11] A father who manifested an intent to give stock to his children but retain the power to manage it was held to have created a trust. "The law will delineate a trust where, in view of a sufficiently manifested purpose or intent, that is the appropriate instrumentality, even though its creator calls it something else, or doesn't call it anything."[12]

On the other hand, the Restatement also says that an unsuccessful attempt to make an outright gift as distinguished from a trust "will not be given effect by treating it as a declaration of trust."[13] For example, a court refused to impose a trust on a woman who had signed a deed but never delivered it, saying that no trust is created "when a property owner merely intends to give his property to another but the gift is never completed."[14]

**5.** *Restatement, Third, of Trusts* § 10, comm. e (1996); Taliaferro v. Taliaferro, 921 P.2d 803 (Kan.1996).

**6.** See Section 4.5, note 7.

**7.** *Restatement, Second, Contracts* § 214, comm. d (1971); Section 6.4, at note 4.

**8.** Gulliver & Tilson, *Classification of Gratuitous Transfers,* 51 Yale L.J. 1, 16–17 (1941).

**9.** The "technical phraseology" required for a *stipulatio* in Roman law was similar in that it prevented "the attention from gliding over a dangerous pledge." H. Maine, *Ancient Law* 272–73 (1861).

**10.** *Restatement, Third, of Trusts* § 5, comm. a (1996). *See also* Marshall v. Grauberger, 796 P.2d 34 (Colo.App.1990).

**11.** Mahoney v. Leddy, 223 A.2d 456 (Vt. 1966). *See also* Underwood v. Bank of Huntsville, 494 So.2d 619 (Ala.1986) (deposit "as custodian" creates a trust); Cohen v. City of Lynn, 598 N.E.2d 682 (Mass.App.1992) (conveyance of land to city "for park purposes" creates a trust).

**12.** Elyachar v. Gerel Corp., 583 F.Supp. 907, 922 (S.D.N.Y.1984). *See also* Hatton v. Meade, 502 N.E.2d 552 (Mass.App.1987).

**13.** *Restatement (Third) of Trusts* § 16(2) (1996).

**14.** French v. French, 606 P.2d 830, 833 (Ariz.App.1980). *See also* Duggan v. Keto, 554 A.2d 1126 (D.C.App.1989) (letter authorizing removal of bonds from box did not show intent to create a trust); Sussman v. Sussman, 392 N.E.2d 881 (N.Y.1979).

### *Transfer to Trustee*

A settlor who wishes to use another person as trustee must effectively transfer the property to the trustee. If the settlor does not have power to transfer the property, the trust fails.[15] If "title does not pass to the intended trustee for want of delivery of the property or the deed, no trust is created." For this purpose the rules governing transfer of legal title control.[16] Thus no enforceable trust was created when a settlor executed a trust agreement with a bank as trustee which provided for the disposition of her condominium but she never transferred title to the condominium to the bank.[17] Even when a settlor designated himself as one of several trustees and failed to deliver a deed to the other trustees, the trust was held ineffective.[18] Lawyers who draft a trust but fail to make sure that the property is properly transferred to the trustee may be sued for malpractice.[19]

The delivery requirement has been watered down in this context just as in non-trust cases. For example, when a settlor who wished to convey valuable drawings to a trust earmarked them but kept them in her possession, her "placing labels and stamps on the drawings and sequestering them in special containers" was held to constituted "a form of symbolic delivery" since the evidence of donative intent was strong.[20] Delivery of a deed of land to a trustee is effective even though the settlor retains possession of the land itself.[21]

### *Words of Futurity; Expectancies*

Present gifts require no consideration, but promises to make a future transfer do.[22] A similar distinction applies to trusts. A declaration that the settlor "will" create a trust is not sufficient without consideration or some recognized substitute therefor.[23] Thus a letter stating that "in the event of a sale" of specified land, the writer "will hold the sale proceeds in trust" did not create a trust.[24] A man cannot create a trust of property which he does not yet own, any more than he can make an outright gift of an expectancy. A man who agreed to acquire football tickets for another person did not thereby create an enforceable trust because he had no contractual right to the tickets when he made the agreement; "mere expectancies cannot be held in trust."[25]

**15.** Jewish Community Ass'n v. Community First Nat. Bank, 6 P.3d 1264 (Wyo.2000) (purported transfer by board of association without the requisite approval of its members).

**16.** *Restatement, Third, Trusts* § 14, comm. d (1996).

**17.** Dahlgren v. First Nat. Bank, 580 P.2d 478 (Nev.1978). *See also* In re Estate of Wittmond, 732 N.E.2d 659, 662 (Ill.App.2000); Ballard v. McCoy, 443 S.E.2d 146 (Va.1994); Papale–Keefe v. Altomare, 647 N.E.2d 722 (Mass. App.1995); McCormick v. Brevig, 980 P.2d 603, 612 (Mont.1999).

**18.** Pizel v. Pizel, 643 P.2d 1094 (Kan.App. 1982). *But see* Aiello v. Clark, 680 P.2d 1162 (Alaska 1984) (declaration of trust effective despite lack of delivery to co-trustee).

**19.** In Pizel v. Whalen, 845 P.2d 37 (Kan. 1993), lawyers in such a suit escaped liability because of a finding of contributory negligence by the plaintiffs.

**20.** Edinburg v. Edinburg, 492 N.E.2d 1164, 1169 (Mass.App.1986). *See also* Poling v. Northup, 652 A.2d 1114 (Me.1995) (delivery of deed to settlor's lawyer sufficient even though he was settlor's agent); *Restatement, Third, Trusts* § 16, comm. b (1996) (delivery may be "constructive or symbolic").

**21.** Golleher v. Horton, 715 P.2d 1225 (Ariz.App.1985).

**22.** See Section 4.5, at note 74 et seq.

**23.** *Restatement (Third) of Trusts* § 15, comm. b (1996); Calif.Prob.Code § 15208; Tierce v. Macedonia United Meth. Church, 519 So.2d 451, 457 (Ala.1987).

**24.** Kavanaugh v. Dobrowolski's Estate, 407 N.E.2d 856 (Ill.App.1980).

**25.** Kully v. Goldman, 305 N.W.2d 800, 802 (Neb.1981); *Restatement, Third, Trusts* § 41 (1999).

Also claims for personal injury are generally held to be not transferable and thus they cannot be put into a trust.[26]

A trust of an expectancy, or a promise to create a future trust, is binding if supported by consideration.[27] Even without consideration, the trust becomes effective if it begins to operate with the settlor's tacit consent.[28]

Sometimes the only asset put into a trust is an insurance policy on the settlor's life. The policy may have little present value so long as the settlor is alive, especially if the settlor reserves the right to change the beneficiary. Nevertheless, courts routinely uphold such "insurance trusts," and many state statutes confirm their validity.[29]

### *Is the Revocable Trust Testamentary?*

Many living trusts are the functional equivalent of wills; the settlor retains the right to control and enjoy the property for life, and the beneficiary's interest becomes meaningful only when the settlor dies. Some older cases and the first Restatement of Trusts held such trusts were testamentary and invalid unless executed with the formalities prescribed for wills.[30] The *Second* Restatement, however, says that a trust is not testamentary "merely because the settlor reserves a beneficial life interest or because he reserves a power to revoke the trust * * * and a power to control the trustee as to the administration of the trust."[31] This more liberal attitude also appears in recent case law; a claim that a trust is invalid as "testamentary" is unlikely to succeed today.[32] The Uniform Probate Code reflecting the modern attitude provides that trusts (and other) provisions "for a nonprobate transfer on death" are "nontestamentary."[33]

Why should a transfer which has so many characteristics of a will not be treated like one? A common explanation is that a living trust gives the beneficiary a "present interest."[34] It is true that a testator has somewhat more freedom to deal with property while alive than the settlor-trustee of a revocable trust, because the latter has some responsibilities to the beneficiaries. But these responsibilities are minimal so long as the settlor can revoke the trust.[35] Moreover, any such limitations on the settlor-trustee's freedom to

**26.** Vittands v. Sudduth, 730 N.E.2d 325, 333 (Mass.App.2000); *Restatement, Third, of Trusts* § 40, comm. d (1999).

**27.** In re Estate of Chaitlen, 534 N.E.2d 482 (Ill.App.1989) (promise to create trust at death); Bemis v. Estate of Bemis, 967 P.2d 437 (Nev.1998) (promise to create a trust for children in divorce settlement); Bednar v. Bednar, 485 N.E.2d 834 (Ohio App.1984).

**28.** Estate of Brenner, 547 P.2d 938 (Colo. App.1976); Sundquist v. Sundquist, 639 P.2d 181 (Utah 1981).

**29.** Huff, *Life Insurance Trusts for Everyman,* 39 U.Colo.L.Rev. 239, 147 (1967); Gordon v. Portland Trust Bank, 271 P.2d 653 (Or. 1954); *cf.* Rosenblum v. Gibbons, 685 S.W.2d 924 (Mo.App.1984) (benefits under retirement plan); Ind.Code 27–1–12–16(B); N.Y. EPTL § 13–3.3(a); N.C.Gen.Stat. § 36A–100(a); Mo. Rev.Stat. § 456.030.

**30.** *Restatement of Trusts* § 57(2) (1935). *See also* Osborn v. Osborn, 226 N.E.2d 814, 822–25 (Ohio Com.Pl.1966).

**31.** *Restatement (Second) of Trusts* § 57 (1959). *See also Restatement, Third, of Trusts* § 25 (1996). However, if the trustee or the property "cannot be identified until the transferor's death" the instrument must comply with the wills act. *Id.,* § 17, comm. a.

**32.** In re Estate of Zukerman, 578 N.E.2d 248 (Ill.App.1991); Zuckerman v. Alter, 615 So.2d 661 (Fla.1993); Matter of Estate of Groesbeck, 935 P.2d 1255 (Utah 1997).

**33.** Uniform Probate Code § 6–101. *See also* Cal.Prob.Code § 5000.

**34.** Farkas v. Williams, 125 N.E.2d 600 (Ill. 1955); Blue Valley Federal Savings and Loan Ass'n v. Burrus, 617 S.W.2d 111, 114 (Mo.App. 1981).

**35.** Cal.Prob.Code § 16064(c) (trustee has no duty to account to beneficiary of a revocable trust).

deal with the trust property have little to do with the purposes behind formal requirements for wills.

A more persuasive rationale was offered by Gulliver and Tilson. Normally in a living trust "a formal instrument will be prepared and delivered even though it is not doctrinally essential to do so. As a result, the main objectives of the statute of wills seem to be satisfied."[36] This rationale suggests that the law should distinguish between formal and informal trusts. The authorization of nonprobate transfers in Uniform Probate Code § 6–101 is limited to those in a "written instrument," but the Comment to this section says this was not intended to "invalidate other arrangements" such as oral trusts by implication. A trust drafted by an attorney and signed by the settlor and an independent trustee certainly seems to satisfy the purposes of the wills act formalities. More questionable is a declaration of trust like a "Dacey" trust, so called after the author of *How to Avoid Probate,* a phenomenally successful book of the 60's, which contains "simplistic tear-out trust and will forms." Arguably the functions of will formalities are *not* fulfilled when a settlor "sits down in the privacy of his living room, fills in several blanks on a printed form" like Dacey's and signs it with no "active participation of another party to the transaction."[37] Nevertheless, Dacey trusts have been upheld, perhaps because they are hard to distinguish from printed forms which can be probated as holographic wills in many states.[38]

Many persons open bank accounts as "trustee" for another. Such trusts are often called "Totten" trusts after a leading case decided at the beginning of the century.[39] Use of the word "trustee" indicates that the depositor meant to create a trust but there is often little other evidence of intent. The terms of the trust, the trustee's duties and the beneficiary's rights are not specified. Nevertheless, courts hold that trusts were intended and are effective to pass the account to the designated beneficiary when the trustee dies.[40] Several state statutes permit banks to pay the money in such accounts to the designated beneficiary after the depositor dies. Although these statutes literally only protect banks, they have been held to support the beneficiary's right to the account.[41] Other statutes make clear that the account belongs to the beneficiary when the trustee dies.[42] Some cases suggest that this arrangement will also be recognized for forms of property other than bank accounts.[43]

Bank account trusts have been called "the poor man's will," even though substantial amounts occasionally pass under them.[44] According to the Restate-

**36.** Gulliver & Tilson, note 8 *supra,* at 24. *See also* Roberts v. Roberts, 646 N.E.2d 1061, 1065 (Mass.1995). A "delivery," however, is not customary for a declaration of trust.

**37.** Johanson, *Revocable Trusts and Community Property,* 47 Tex.L.Rev. 537, 538 (1969).

**38.** Barnette v. McNulty, 516 P.2d 583 (Ariz.App.1973); Wilkerson v. McClary, 647 S.W.2d 79 (Tex.App.1983). As to holographic wills see Section 4.4, at note 17.

**39.** In re Totten, 71 N.E. 748 (N.Y.1904).

**40.** Sanchez v. Sanchez De Davila, 547 So.2d 943 (Fla.App.1989); Estate of Bischof, 770 S.W.2d 474 (Mo.App.1989); Byrd v. Lanahan, 783 P.2d 426 (Nev.1989); *Restatement, Third, of Trusts* § 26 (1999).

**41.** Blue Valley Federal Savings and Loan Ass'n v. Burrus, 617 S.W.2d 111 (Mo.App. 1981); Matter of Estate of Stokes, 747 P.2d 300 (Okl.1987).

**42.** Calif.Prob.Code § 5302(c). The Uniform Probate Code now assimilates Totten Trusts to POD accounts. Section 6–201(8). As to these see Section 4.6, at note 38.

**43.** In re Estate of Zukerman, 578 N.E.2d 248 (Ill.App.1991) (bond); Tomlinson v. Tomlinson, 960 S.W.2d 337 (Tex.App.1997) (pension benefits). *But see* Matter of Estate of Gagliardi, 432 N.E.2d 774 (N.Y.1982) (refusing to extend Totten trust idea to land).

**44.** McGovern, *The Payable on Death Account and Other Will Substitutes,* 67 Nw. U.L.Rev. 7, 11–12 (1972).

ment of Trusts revocable trusts are "widely used as a legitimate means of avoiding the costs and delays typically associated with the processes of administering decedents' estates."[45] Because such trusts are "widely used," the expectations of many settlors would be defeated if courts were to hold them invalid.[46] On the other hand, because they are so much like wills, they are treated like wills for many purposes other than formal requirements, such as the rights of the settlor's spouse and creditors.[47]

### *Need for a Writing*

A living trust does not have to be executed like a will, but Section 7 of the Statute of Frauds of 1676 required that "all declarations or creations of trust * * * of any lands * * * shall be manifested and proved by some writing signed by the party who is by law enabled to declare such trust." Section 8 excepted trusts which "arise or result by the implication or construction of law." The requirement of a signed writing was not limited to trusts; Section 1 of the Statute also required a signed writing to convey a legal interest in land.[48]

Most American states have provisions like § 7 of the original Statute of Frauds.[49] The writing requirement arises in two contexts. First, a person may declare herself trustee of land for another. Even in states which have not copied § 7 of the English statute, such oral declarations may be held subject to Section 1 as an attempt to convey land orally.[50] It is not enforceable under the exception in § 8 for constructive trusts[51] unless the beneficiary improves the land, or otherwise changes his position in reliance on the trust.[52]

Second, the settlor may convey land to another by a deed which does not indicate that the transferee was intended to hold the land in trust for another. Such a deed, although in writing and signed, does not satisfy the Statute since it does not refer to the trust.[53] But the transferee, if allowed to keep land which was intended for another, would be unjustly enriched, so courts frequently impose a constructive trust in this situation.[54]

To satisfy the Statute of Frauds, the writing must indicate the terms of the trust. A deed which simply conveys land "to *T* as trustee" is not enough,[55]

**45.** *Restatement, Third, Trusts* § 25, comm. a (1996). *See also* Westerfeld v. Huckaby, 474 S.W.2d 189 (Tex.1971). For the disadvantages of probate see Section 9.1.

**46.** Johanson, *supra* note 37, at 557; Gulliver & Tilson, *supra* note 8, at 24.

**47.** As to the rights of the settlor's spouse see Section 3.7, note 21. As to rights of creditors see Section 13.1, at note 4.

**48.** See Section 4.5, note 10.

**49.** *Restatement (Third) of Trusts* § 20, comment a (1996); Calif.Prob.Code § 15206; Fla.Stat. § 689.05. In states which have not adopted this section, some courts treat it as part of the common law, Aragon v. Rio Costilla Cooperative Livestock Asso., 812 P.2d 1300 (N.M.1991), whereas others do not. Ellis v. Vespoint, 403 S.E.2d 542 (N.C.App.1991).

**50.** Brame v. Read, 118 S.E. 117 (Va.1923).

**51.** French v. French, 606 P.2d 830 (Ariz. App.1980).

**52.** *Restatement (Third) of Trusts* § 24, comm. c (1996).

**53.** *Id.* § 22(1).

**54.** See Section 6.4, at note 21 et seq.

**55.** Gammarino v. Hamilton Cty. Bd. of Revision, 702 N.E.2d 415, 418 (Ohio 1998); Jordan v. Exxon Corp., 802 S.W.2d 880 (Tex. App.1991); Hickman v. Trust of Heath, House & Boyles, 835 S.W.2d 880 (Ark.1992); *Restatement (Third) of Trusts* § 22 (1996). However, a *devise* to "X, as trustee" may be the basis for imposing a *constructive* trust if there is extrinsic evidence of the trust terms. See Section 6.1, note 74.

but a deed "to *T* in trust for *B*" may be sufficient. Thus the designation of a trustee and beneficiaries for death benefits in a pension plan was held sufficient to create a trust because "all necessary details are supplied by" statutory provisions governing trusts.[56]

The writing may be signed[57] by either the settlor or by the trustee, depending upon the circumstances. If *S*'s deed to *T* sets forth the terms of the trust, *T* is bound even though she did not sign it, but *S* cannot impose a trust by signing a writing after title to the land has passed to *T*.[58] *T*, on the other hand, can satisfy the Statute by signing a writing prior to, or subsequent to the transfer to her.[59] The writing need not have *created* the trust; a later written acknowledgement of the trust is sufficient. The "writing" may be a series of documents, as where a woman conveyed land by deed "to hold in trust" and a later will directed the trustees how to dispose of the property.[60]

The Statute of Frauds applies only to trusts of land.[61] A few states also require a writing for trusts of personal property. In most states oral trusts of personal property are valid,[62] but they are rare. Even in informal bank-account trusts the settlor usually signs a card indicating that the account is held in trust. The Uniform Trust Code says that "the creation of an oral trust ... may only be established by clear and convincing evidence."[63] Many courts use similar language in cases rejecting claim of an trust for insufficient proof.[64]

### *Precatory Language*

Wills which contain language suggesting that a devisee should use property for someone else raise the question whether the testator intended to create a trust or other legal obligation, or whether the words were precatory, *i.e.,* intended to impose only a moral obligation. For example, a will left property to the testator's father "for the reason that I feel confident that any property which ... my father ... receive[s] from my estate will be used in the best interests of my said children." The children claimed that this created a trust, but the court disagreed. "This language does not impose any sort of clear directive or obligation (other than perhaps a moral or ethical one) ... The purported trustee is given no direction as to how the supposed settlor intends

In Osswald v. Anderson, 57 Cal.Rptr.2d 23 (App.1996), the settlors signed a trust agreement but it failed to adequately describe the land so the statute was not satisfied.

**56.** Tomlinson v. Tomlinson, 960 S.W.2d 337 (Tex.App.1997). *See also* Goytizolo v. Moore, 604 A.2d 362 (Conn.App.1992).

**57.** For this purpose, initials constitute a "signing." In re Estate of Dotterrer, 579 A.2d 952 (Pa.Super.1990). See also Section 4.2.

**58.** Trustees of Presbytery v. Hammer, 385 P.2d 1013 (Or.1963); *Restatement (Third) of Trusts* § 23(1) (1996).

**59.** *Restatement (Third) of Trusts* § 23(2)(b) (1999); McCaffrey v. Laursen, 697 P.2d 103 (Mont.1985); Schaneman v. Wright, 470 N.W.2d 566 (Neb.1991).

**60.** Ramage v. Ramage, 322 S.E.2d 22 (S.C.App.1984). *See also* Hall v. World Savings and Loan Asso., 943 P.2d 855 (Ariz.App.1997); *Restatement (Third) of Trusts* § 22, comm. c (1996).

**61.** As to what is "land" for this purpose see *Restatement, Third, of Trusts* § 22, comm. b (1996).

**62.** Barnette v. McNulty, 516 P.2d 583 (1973) (dictum); In re Trbovich's Estate, 413 A.2d 379 (Pa.1980).

**63.** Unif.Trust Code § 406; *cf.* Calif.Prob.Code § 15207.

**64.** Spearman v. Estate of Spearman, 618 So.2d 276 (Fla.App.1993); Kurtz v. Solomon, 656 N.E.2d 184, 189 (Ill.App.1995) (evidence "must be so unequivocal as to lead to only one conclusion").

his estate to be used to further 'the best interests' of the children." [65]Such vagueness as to the beneficiaries and their interests "tends to suggest that the transferor did not intend to create a trust."[66] In contrast, when a will "requested" that the devisees to pay the testator's sister-in-law "$208.33 per month as long as she shall live," these "precise and explicit terms" were held to be mandatory.[67]

"Wish," "hope," and "desire" are usually construed as precatory,[68] but not always; a statement in a will that "it is my desire that Lee Davis . . . be allowed to purchase" property of the testator was held to give him an enforceable option.[69] Courts sometimes compare different parts of the will in construing ambiguous language. For example, the word "request" in a will was held not to create a trust when other provisions in the same will showed that the testator "was aware of how to leave assets in trust."[70]

It may make a difference who drafted the will. In construing a will which used "wish and desire" a court thought it "worthy of note that the testator in his lifetime was a professor of law" who "operated a well known bar review" course in which wills "received an appropriate share of attention" and so must have been "familiar with the leading cases wherein the term 'wish and desire' was held to be precatory."[71] In contrast, the word 'want' in a home-drawn will was held to be mandatory because "informal language used by a layman who did not have legal advice in drawing his will" should not be construed "technically" but rather "liberally" to carry out the testator's intent.[72]

The financial situation of the affected parties can be a factor. Thus a devise of the testator's estate to his wife with a "request that she use whatever of it she thinks necessary for the support and care of my brother," imposes a duty "upon W as trustee to make reasonable provision for B's support and care" if the brother is needy and the wife is independently wealthy. These circumstances "overcome the inference normally drawn from precatory words."[73]

### *Charge and Condition*

Language which creates a legal obligation does not necessarily create a trust. For example, a man left a building to his son "subject to the provision

**65.** Matter of Estate of Bolinger, 943 P.2d 981, 987 (Mont.1997). *See also* Cickyj v. Skeltinska, 417 N.E.2d 699 (Ill.App.1981); Dwyer v. Allyn, 596 N.E.2d 903 (Ind.App.1992).

**66.** *Restatement, Third, Trusts* § 13, comm. d (1996).

**67.** Spencer v. Childs, 134 N.E.2d 60 (N.Y. 1956). *See also* Levin v. Fisch, 404 S.W.2d 889 (Tex.Civ.App.1966) ("desire" that testator's children pay her sister an annuity of $2,400).

**68.** Dwyer v. Allyn, 596 N.E.2d 903 (Ind. App.1992); Chandler v. Chandler, 292 S.E.2d 685 (Ga.1982); Langston v. Hunt, 601 S.W.2d 833 (Ark.1980); *Restatement (Third) of Trusts* § 13, illus. 5–7 (1996).

**69.** Gillespie v. Davis, 410 S.E.2d 613 (Va. 1991). *See also* Snider v. Wood, 531 So.2d 864 (Ala.1988) ("wish"); Saunders v. Callaway, 708 P.2d 652 (Wash.App.1985).

**70.** Estate of Lowry, 418 N.E.2d 10, 12 (Ill.App.1981). *See also* Page v. Buchfinck, 275 N.W.2d 826 (Neb.1979).

**71.** Matter of Sparacio's Estate, 402 N.Y.S.2d 857 (A.D.1978). *See also* Dwyer v. Allyn, 596 N.E.2d 903 (Ind.App.1992) ("desire" is precatory in a will drafted by experienced lawyer).

**72.** First United Methodist Church v. Allen, 557 S.W.2d 175 (Tex.Civ.App.1977). *See also* Stephens v. McPherson, 362 S.E.2d 826 (N.C.App.1987) (construing "wish" in a holographic will as mandatory).

**73.** *Restatement, Third, of Trusts* § 13, illus. 8 (1996).

that for two (2) years after my death, ... the net rental monies ... shall be divided equally amongst my three (3) children." The son's sister claimed that this created a trust so that the building after the first two years passed under the residuary clause of the will. The court disagreed, finding that the son received the property "outright, subject to a charge for two-thirds of the income for two years."[74] The Restatement of Trusts explains the difference between a charge and a trust:

> A transfer subject to an equitable charge is beneficial to the transferee as well as to the person to be benefited by the charge. Although this may also be true in the case of a trust, the intention to confer a beneficial interest ... upon a trustee is not readily inferred, the usual inference being that a resulting trust arises with respect to the remaining beneficial interest.[75]

Some instruments are construed to impose a condition rather than a trust. When land was conveyed to a town "in trust for" a library, the question arose what should happen to the land when the town closed the library many years later. Had this been a trust, the property might have been applied the property to a related purpose under the *cy pres* doctrine.[76] But the court held that the property should return to the grantors' heirs (the grantors having died in the interim), because the town held "subject to a condition subsequent" rather than in trust. Even though the deed used the word "trust," other language in the deed showed "an intent to divest the transferee of its interest if it fails to maintain a library, indicating no trust was intended."[77] On the other hand, the word "condition" is not always read literally. Even when property is transferred "on condition"

> a trust is created if the transferor manifested an intention (a) that the transferee should be subject to a duty to use the specific property for the transferor's or a third person's benefit rather than (b) that the transferee's interest should be divested upon failure to perform the act specified.[78]

Courts are especially reluctant to read the word condition literally when this might frustrate the transferor's intent to benefit a third person. For example, a testator left his estate to his son Barnard "on the condition" that he support his incompetent brother, James. The court refused to construe this as a condition, since to impose a forfeiture for Barnard's failure to support James would cause the estate to pass by intestacy to the testator's disinherited children, and this would "make less of the assets of the estate available for the support of James."[79]

## § 4.7 Payable-on-Death Contracts

A payable-on-death (POD) account is created when a person deposits money in a bank under an agreement which provides that upon his death the funds in the account will be paid to another. Trust accounts are almost universally held valid, but the validity of P.O.D. accounts is more doubtful in

**74.** In re Estate of Krotz, 522 N.E.2d 790, 793 (Ill.App.1988).

**75.** *Restatement, Third, of Trusts* § 5, comm. h (1996).

**76.** State v. Rand, 366 A.2d 183 (Me.1976); Section 9.7, at note 100.

**77.** Walton v. City of Red Bluff, 3 Cal. Rptr.2d 275 (App.1991).

**78.** *Restatement, Third, of Trusts* § 5, comm. h (1996).

**79.** Whicher v. Abbott, 449 A.2d 353, 355 (Me.1982).

the absence of a statute, perhaps because they have arisen more recently. One court explained the distinction as follows: the depositor in a P.O.D. account retains "*sole* and complete ownership and control of the account during her lifetime" and so the transfer is "in the nature of a testamentary disposition and, not having been made in the manner prescribed by statute for the execution of wills," is invalid.[1] However, the policy reasons discussed in the previous section for upholding Totten trusts—the convenience of avoiding probate, the small amounts usually involved, widespread popular use, and the lack of serious doubt as to the decedent's intent when manifested in a written instrument—apply equally to P.O.D. accounts.

POD accounts are valid under the Uniform Probate Code and many other state statutes.[2] Some statutes protect banks, permitting them to pay the deposit to the designated beneficiary, but not requiring them to do so. But even such statutes have been interpreted as making P.O.D. accounts "a valid method of transferring property upon death, irrespective of the * * * the Statute of Wills."[3] Some statutes govern only one type of financial institution, banks, for example, but not savings and loan associations.[4] Some courts have interpreted such statutes narrowly; a statute authorizing POD accounts was held not to apply to an Individual Retirement Account (IRA), for example.[5] However, a decision by another court upholding a POD designation in an IRA is typical of the more recent cases. The court noted that:

> courts have upheld beneficiary designations in a variety of contractual arrangements analogous to IRA's. For example, the proceeds from an insurance policy are generally payable to the named beneficiary of the policy outside of the insured's probate estate.[6]

Insurance contracts, despite their obvious testamentary aspects, have long been allowed. Their widespread use and "the high probability that they do not present an evil at which the Statute of Wills is aimed" may explain this.[7] In insurance beneficiary designations, as in POD bank accounts, evidence of the decedent's intention appears in the written records of a disinterested institution.

Another analog to the P.O.D. account is an installment sale contract or note which provides for a change in payments when the payee dies. Most cases

§ 4.7

1. Waitman v. Waitman, 505 P.2d 171, 175 (Okl.1972). *See also* Milliken v. First Nat. Bank, 290 A.2d 889 (Me.1972); Truax v. Southwestern College, 522 P.2d 412 (Kan.1974); Matter of Collier, 381 So.2d 1338 (Miss.1980); McGovern, *The Payable on Death Account and other Will Substitutes*, 67 Nw.U.L.Rev. 7, 9 (1972).

2. Uniform Probate Code §§ 6–212(b), 6–214; Cal.Prob.Code §§ 5302(b), 5304. The prefatory note to Article VI of the UPC says that this part of the Code "is one of the most broadly accepted, having been adopted ... by over half the states."

3. Virginia National Bank v. Harris, 257 S.E.2d 867 (Va.1979). *But see* In re Hoffman's Estate, 195 N.E.2d 106 (Ohio 1963) (involving bank account trusts).

4. McGovern, *supra* note 1, at 10. The Uniform Probate Code, on the other hand covers all accounts at financial institutions. These terms are broadly defined in § 6–201.

5. McCarty v. State Bank, 795 P.2d 940 (Kan.App.1990). *See also* Powell v. City Nat. Bank & Trust Co., 440 N.E.2d 560 (Ohio App. 1981) (church cannot be a POD beneficiary, since statute authorizes them only for individuals).

6. E.F. Hutton & Co. Inc. v. Wallace, 863 F.2d 472, 473 (6th Cir.1988). *See also* Matter of Estate of Lahren, 886 P.2d 412 (Mont.1994).

7. Zimmerman v. Mutual Life Ins. Co., 156 F.Supp. 589 (N.D.Ala.1957).

give effect to such provisions.[8] Even though no financial institution acts as an independent witness, a signed writing is usually involved.

In 1989 the Uniform Probate Code was revised to extend the P.O.D. concept to securities. The drafters noted that distinctions between bank accounts and securities made little sense when banks were "offering certificates of deposit of large value" while brokerage houses were providing "cash management accounts."[9] Nevertheless, the provisions in the Code for securities and bank accounts are not identical.[10] As to securities the Code uses the term TOD or "transfer on death" rather than POD in order to avoid the implication that "the investment is to be sold or redeemed at the owner's death so that the sums realized may be 'paid' to the beneficiary."[11]

Legislation in Missouri has gone even further. It authorizes deeds of land and certificates of title to motor vehicles to effect transfers at death without a will.[12] This result might also be reached under the more general terms of Uniform Probate Code § 6–101 which allow nonprobate transfers on death in a "deed of gift . . . or other written instrument of a similar nature."

The Missouri statute allowing nonprobate transfers requires that the beneficiary designation be in writing, subscribed by the owner and witnessed by a disinterested person.[13] An Ohio statute authorizing POD accounts created by a "written contract" was interpreted to require a writing signed by the owner of the funds:

> One of the basic requirements of the Statute of Wills cannot be ignored; that is, the requirement of a writing signed by the testator evidencing his intent. Since a P.O.D. account is testamentary in nature, it follows that the term 'written contract' means a writing signed by the owner of the funds.[14]

However, other cases have upheld oral designations of a beneficiary.[15] The Uniform Probate Code by its terms requires a signed writing to *change* an account, but not to establish one.[16]

## § 4.8 Joint Tenancy

Like the trust, joint tenancy has roots in medieval law, having been used

8. Valenzuela v. Anchonda, 527 P.2d 109 (Ariz.App.1974); Tierce v. Macedonia United Meth. Church, 519 So.2d 451 (Ala.1987); Herman v. Herman, 707 P.2d 1374 (Wash.App. 1985); Williams v. Williams, 438 So.2d 735 (Ala.1983) (partnership agreement). *But see* Martinson v. Holso, 424 N.W.2d 664 (S.D.1988) (provision in land sale that on seller's death payments should go to his sister invalid as testamentary).

9. Uniform Probate Code Art. VI, Prefatory Note.

10. The differences are examined in McGovern, *Nonprobate Transfers under the Revised Uniform Probate Code*, 55 Alb.L.Rev. 1329 (1992).

11. Uniform Probate Code § 6–305, comment.

12. Mo.Stat.Ann. §§ 301.681, 461.025. *See also* Cal.Veh.Code § 4150.7.

13. Mo.Stat. § 461.062. *See also* N.Y. EPTL § 13–3.2(e) (designation of beneficiary of pension or insurance). A bank has been held liable to the intended beneficiary for failure to advise a customer that a writing was necessary to effectuate his intent. Corning Bank v. Rice, 645 S.W.2d 675 (Ark.1983).

14. Witt v. Ward, 573 N.E.2d 201, 207 (Ohio App.1989). *See also* In re Estate of Waitkevich, 323 N.E.2d 545 (Ill.App.1975) (POD designation ineffective when added after decedent signed the ledger card for the account).

15. Union Nat. Bank v. Ornelas–Gutierrez, 772 F.Supp. 962 (S.D.Tex.1991).

16. Uniform Probate Code § 6–213.

as early as the 13th century.[1] In the 15th century, Littleton stated rules for joint tenancy substantially in their modern form. "The nature of joint tenancy is that the one who survives will have the whole tenancy." This applied to both land and personal property, but not where two or more persons held as tenants in common.[2] In modern times joint tenancy has become a common way to avoid probate, particularly for bank accounts and land.[3]

### *Differences Between Historical and Modern Joint Tenancy*

There are differences between modern joint tenancy and its medieval antecedent. Historically, if *A* wished to put property into joint tenancy with *B*, he had to deliver it to a third person who would reconvey the property to *A* and *B*.[4] Modern statutes allow persons to create a joint tenancy for themselves and another without any conveyance to a straw man.[5] Even without such a statute, challenges to joint tenancy for lack of delivery usually fail.[6] Some courts say that joint bank accounts are created by a contract between the depositor and the bank, and so the requirements for gifts do not apply.[7] Even as to deeds of land, delivery has been held unnecessary on the ground that "delivery to one cotenant or reservation of an estate connotes delivery to all cotenants, where the grantor is also the grantee."[8]

A more frequently litigated issue in modern cases is the language needed in an instrument to create a joint tenancy. Historically, courts held that a joint tenancy was created whenever property was conveyed "to *A* and *B*." Blackstone reaffirmed this rule in the 18th century,[9] but the courts had already begun to question it, saying that joint tenancies "are not favoured," because they "do not make provision for posterity," *i.e.*, when land passes to the surviving joint tenant(s), the dead tenant's heirs get nothing, whereas in a tenancy in common, they would inherit the decedent's share (or it would pass under the decedent's will). The common-law had favored joint tenancies because feudal lords wanted to keep land undivided, but this reason had ceased with the end of feudalism.[10]

Today, many statutes reverse the common-law presumption in favor of joint tenancy. For example, in Missouri "every interest in real estate granted

§ 4.8

1. J. Bean, *The Decline of English Feudalism* 87–88 (1968); Spitzer, *Joint Tenancy with Right of Survivorship,* 16 Texas Tech.L.Rev. 629 (1985).

2. T. Littleton, *Tenures* §§ 280–82.

3. Hines, *Personal Property Joint Tenancies* 54 Minn.L.Rev. 509, 517, 521 (1970); Hines, *Real Property Joint Tenancies,* 51 Iowa L.Rev. 582, 586–87 (1966).

4. T. Plucknett, *A Concise History of the Common Law* 577 (5th ed. 1956); McGovern, *The Enforcement of Oral Covenants Prior to Assumpsit,* 65 Nw.U.L.Rev. 576, 589 (1970).

5. Neb.Rev.Stat. § 76–118; Kan.Stat. § 58–501; 33 Me.Rev.Stat. § 901 (stocks and bonds); Cal.Civ.Code § 683; Helmholz, *Realism and Formalism in the Severance of Joint Tenancies,* 77 Neb.L.Rev. 1, 5 (1998).

6. *But see* Estate of Grove v. Selken, 820 P.2d 895 (Or.App.1991) (attempt to create joint tenancy in books by a signed writing fails for lack of delivery).

7. Malek v. Patten, 678 P.2d 201, 205 (Mont.1984); Vetter v. Hampton, 375 N.E.2d 804, 806 (Ohio 1978); Campbell v. Campbell, 175 S.E.2d 243, 245 (Va.1970).

8. Kresser v. Peterson, 675 P.2d 1193, 1194 (Utah 1984). *See also* Matter of Estate of Rohrer, 646 N.E.2d 17 (Ill.App.1995); Andrews v. Troy Bank and Trust Co., 529 So.2d 987 (Ala. 1988); Winterton v. Kaufmann, 504 So.2d 439 (Fla.App.1987).

9. 2 W. Blackstone, *Commentaries* * 180 (1765).

10. Hawes v. Hawes, 95 Eng.Rep. 552 (1747). *See also* Choman v. Epperley, 592 P.2d 714 (Wyo.1979). This explanation, though often repeated, is questionable since joint tenancy deprived lords of their feudal incidents. See note 1 *supra*.

or devised to two or more persons * * * shall be a tenancy in common unless expressly declared, in such grant or devise, to be in joint tenancy."[11] These statutes differ in their terms and have led to some curious distinctions which probably do not reflect the understanding of the parties. This is unfortunate, since joint tenancy is typically created without the benefit of legal advice. For example, a court held that registering cattle in the names "*A* or *B*" did not create a joint tenancy, since a statutory presumption of joint tenancy with right of survivorship applied only to motor vehicles.[12] Under some statutes even a statement that property is held "jointly" is not enough, unless a right of survivorship is expressly mentioned.[13] Some statutes distinguish between the words "*A* and *B*" and "*A* or *B*."[14] Others presume a joint tenancy was intended if *A* and *B* are married to each other.[15] Many courts allow an ambiguous registration of title to be clarified by extrinsic evidence of intent,[16] but some do not. One court has recently said that failure to provide for survivorship rights in a joint account "will be conclusive evidence of an intent not to transfer any right of survivorship to the survivor."[17]

The Uniform Probate Code provides that a bank account which by its terms is payable to two or more parties passes to the survivor "whether or not a right of survivorship is mentioned" unless "the terms of the account" negate a right of survivorship.[18] This may reflect most depositors' probable intent because it avoids probate and administration for the whole account when one party dies. Under the Code if there are *two* surviving parties, one of whom was the decedent's spouse, the spouse takes the entire account. This is a questionable assumption; we do not usually presume that someone who gives property "to my spouse and *X*" intends that *X* get nothing.[19] The Code also provides model forms, which, if used intelligently, provide better evidence of the parties' wishes than phrases like "joint tenancy," the meaning of which

**11.** Mo.Stat. § 442.450. *See also* Kan.Stat. § 58–501; 765 ILCS § 1005/1; Cal.Prob.Code § 21106. Even with a presumption in favor of tenancy in common, a deed may be reformed to turn it into a joint tenancy if there is clear proof that this was intended. Matter of Estate of Vadney, 634 N.E.2d 976 (N.Y.1994).

**12.** Matter of Estate of Shaw, 855 P.2d 105 (Mont.1993). *See also* Starr v. Rousselet, 877 P.2d 525 (Nev.1994) (presumption of joint tenancy only in accounts in credit unions); Matter of Estate of Holloway, 515 So.2d 1217 (Miss. 1987) (statutory presumption of joint tenancy for accounts not applicable to certificates of deposit).

**13.** In re Estate of Hill, 931 P.2d 1320 (Mont.1997); Hoover v. Smith, 444 S.E.2d 546 (Va.1994); Stauffer v. Henderson, 801 S.W.2d 858 (Tex.1990); Wright v. Bloom, 635 N.E.2d 31, 39 (Ohio 1994). *But see* Matter of Estate of Epstein, 561 N.W.2d 82, 86 (Iowa App.1996).

**14.** Fla.Stat. § 319.22 (2)(a). Under Cal.Vehicle Code § 4150.5 both "or" and "and" create a right of survivorship, but "and" requires all living parties to sign when title is transferred.

**15.** Mich.Comp.L. § 557.151 (stocks and bonds); Mo.Stat. § 442.450 (real estate); Sarbacher v. McNamara, 564 A.2d 701, 707 (D.C.App.1989) (applying Florida law, noting that in D.C. tenancy in common would be created); Lutz v. Lemon, 715 N.E.2d 1268 (Ind. App.1999) (household goods acquired during marriage); *cf.* Voss v. Brooks, 907 P.2d 465 (Alaska 1995) (joint tenancy deed creates tenancy in common when parties are not married).

**16.** Matter of Estate of Briley, 825 P.2d 1181 (Kan.App.1992); Matter of Estate of Vadney, 634 N.E.2d 976 (N.Y.1994) (deed reformed to show intent to create joint tenancy); Matter of Estate of Epstein, 561 N.W.2d 82 (Iowa App.1996).

**17.** Robinson v. Delfino, 710 A.2d 154, 161 (R.I.1998). *See also* Starr v. Rousselet, 877 P.2d 525 (Nev.1994); In re Estate of Hill, 931 P.2d 1320 (Mont.1997).

**18.** Uniform Probate Code § 6–201(5), 6–212.

**19.** McGovern, *Nonprobate Transfers under the Revised Uniform Probate Code*, 55 Alb. L.Rev. 1329, 1331 (1992). The presumption applies only to amounts contributed by the decedent; if *X* had contributed to the account, his or her contribution would not pass to the spouse.

is not clear to many persons. Under the Code's suggested forms, depositors can check boxes labelled, e.g. "MULTIPLE–PARTY ACCOUNT WITH RIGHT OF SURVIVORSHIP" or "MULTIPLE–PARTY ACCOUNT WITHOUT RIGHT OF SURVIVORSHIP".[20]

The foregoing provisions apply to accounts at a "financial institution" (including checking and savings accounts and certificates of deposit at banks, savings and loans and credit unions),[21] but not to securities or accounts with a broker—the Code provisions dealing with the latter provide only for TOD registration which the drafters preferred to the "frequently troublesome joint tenancy form of title."[22] Nor does the Code apply to deeds of land, as to which the presumption arising from the words "to *A* and *B*" may differ from that for bank accounts. California, for example, follows the UPC as to bank accounts, but otherwise presumes that two or more persons hold title property as tenants in common.[23] Perhaps this distinction is justified by the fact that land is usually worth more than the typical bank account, so the survivor's taking the whole property can have more serious consequences. In this respect, securities are more like land, but there are obviously exceptions both ways; certificates of deposit, which are treated as bank accounts, may be quite large, whereas cash-management accounts administered by brokers can be rather small. Still another set of rules or presumptions may apply in a state to motor vehicles.

### *Safe Deposit Boxes*

Deposit of articles in a jointly leased safe-deposit box usually has no effect on succession to the contents of the box. The joint-tenancy language in the lease is generally construed to apply only to use of the box.[24] However, a contract which provided that "upon the death of either [party, the] * * * entire contents ... shall belong exclusively to the survivor" was held to pass currency in a box to the survivor.[25] But when $600,000 worth of registered securities was left in such a box, the court refused to award them to the surviving tenant of the box.[26] In California a contract which purports to create a joint tenancy in the contents of a box is void.[27]

A safe-deposit box differs from a bank account in that it usually contains most of the lessee's valuable title documents. A surviving joint tenant's claim to the contents of a box may conflict with the form of registered securities in the box. If *A* and *B* jointly lease a box and *A* deposits stock certificates registered in the names of "*A* and *C* as joint tenants," the ownership of the stock would be in doubt if joint tenancy in the contents of a box were recognized.

**20.** Uniform Probate Code § 6–204. The form does not reveal that the decedent's spouse, if one of the "surviving parties," will get the entire account under § 6–212(a).

**21.** *Id.* § 6–201

**22.** Uniform Probate Code, Prefatory Note to Article VI. For a criticism of this omission see McGovern, *supra* note 19, at 1332.

**23.** Calif.Prob.Code §§ 5130, 5302 (as to bank accounts, like the UPC but without the provision favoring the decedent's spouse), § 21106 (presumption of tenancy in common).

**24.** In re Estate of Finkelstein, 817 P.2d 617 (Colo.App.1991); Wright v. Union Nat. Bank, 819 S.W.2d 698 (Ark.1991); In re Estate of Silver, 1 P.3d 358, 362 (Mont.2000); Hines, *Personal Property Joint Tenancies,* 54 Minn. L.Rev. 509, 525 (1970).

**25.** Matter of Estate of Langley, 546 N.E.2d 1287 (Ind.App.1989). *See also* Steinhauser v. Repko, 285 N.E.2d 55 (Ohio 1972).

**26.** Estate of Matelich v. Matelich, 772 P.2d 319 (Nev.1989).

**27.** Calif.Civ.Code § 683.1.

***Validity of Joint Tenancy***

Attacks on joint tenancy as a testamentary transfer are rare. But courts occasionally hold that if the decedent did not intend to give the other joint tenant a "present interest" in the property there can be no right of survivorship.[28] Other courts, however, have acknowledged that joint tenancy is regarded by many who use it as a will substitute. "We see no harm in that. * * * The formal requisites of wills serve two main purposes: to insure that dispositions are carefully and seriously made, and to provide reliable evidence of the disposition. Those purposes are adequately served by the institutional setting and the signed writing normally involved."[29] A court has also upheld a joint tenancy in stock certificates, characterizing it as the designation of a third party beneficiary to a contract between the shareholder and the corporation; this rationale dispenses with the need for delivery.[30]

Although the validity of join tenancy is rarely challenged today, it is frequently claimed that a purported joint tenancy was not intended to give the other party a beneficial interest, but rather only to allow the other party to make deposits and withdrawals on behalf of the depositor.[31] A person who has this purpose in mind should use a power-of-attorney instead. The forms suggested by the Uniform Probate Code call attention to this option.[32]

A few states require a signed writing to create a joint account,[33] but most do not.[34] Even a statute which required "a written instrument" in order to create a joint tenancy was held to be satisfied by a form filled out by a broker on oral instructions from his clients.[35] The Uniform Probate Code allows joint accounts to be opened orally but requires a signed writing to alter the form of the account thereafter.[36]

## § 4.9 Contracts to Make Wills

Contracts to devise property appear often in litigation. Sometimes they are made in return for services to be performed by the promisee, but commonly the contract is for the benefit of a third party, as when spouses promise each other that the survivor will leave their property to relatives of both. Even jurisdictions which do not ordinarily allow third party beneficiaries to enforce contracts make an exception in this case.[1]

**28.** Lewis v. Steinreich, 652 N.E.2d 981 (Ohio 1995). *See also* Matter of Bobeck, 531 N.Y.S.2d 340 (A.D.1988)

**29.** Blanchette v. Blanchette, 287 N.E.2d 459, 463–5 (Mass.1972).

**30.** Matter of Estate of Evanco, 955 P.2d 525, 528 (Alaska 1998).

**31.** Litigation on this issue is quite common. It is further treated at Section 6.3, at note 3 et seq.

**32.** Uniform Probate Code § 6–204. As to the risk that creditors of all parties to a joint account may reach it see Section 13.2, note 18.

**33.** Rynn v. Owens, 536 N.E.2d 959 (Ill. App.1989) (right of survivorship exists only between persons who sign); Tex.Prob.Code §§ 46, 439(a); Chopin v. Interfirst Bank, 694 S.W.2d 79 (Tex.App.1985); Magee v. Westmoreland, 693 S.W.2d 612 (Tex.App.1985).

**34.** Morris v. Cullipher, 816 S.W.2d 878 (Ark.1991) (applying Arkansas law which does not require a writing rather than Texas law which does); Martinson v. Holso, 424 N.W.2d 664 (S.D.1988) (oral agreement that partnership assets will go to survivor enforced); Simmons v. Foster, 622 S.W.2d 838 (Tenn.App. 1981) (orally created joint account).

**35.** Estate of Tressel v. Tressel, 986 P.2d 72 (Or.App.1999).

**36.** Uniform Probate Code § 6–213. For a discussion of cases dealing with this problem see McGovern, *supra* note 19, at 1335–7.

**§ 4.9**

**1.** Bettencourt v. Bettencourt, 284 N.E.2d 238 (Mass.1972); Youdan, *The Mutual Wills Doctrine,* 29 U.Tor.L.J. 390, 401 (1979).

### *Joint and Mutual Wills*

Some courts infer the existence of a contract when two spouses execute a "joint" will. For example, a husband and wife executed a joint will which said "It is our intention that this Will shall be binding." The husband survived the wife and executed a new will leaving his estate to one of their two children. The other child successfully claimed that the new will was a breach of contract.

> A joint will . . . may by its language evidence an irrevocable agreement between the parties. . . . The [earlier] will evidences a definite, clear and unequivocal intention to establish a binding, irrevocable agreement.[2]

Many courts, however, have refused to infer the existence of a contract in joint wills with somewhat different wording.[3] The Uniform Probate Code provides that "the execution of a joint will * * * does not create a presumption of a contract not to revoke the will."[4] Even a joint will providing that "we agree that the provisions hereof shall not be changed" was held insufficient to show a contract barring the survivor from changing it since the will left the testators' property to the survivor "absolutely."[5]

More common than joint wills are "mutual" wills, separate documents executed by spouses at the same time with reciprocal provisions. Most courts say that whatever inference may be derived from a *joint* will, the mere execution of mutual wills does not indicate a contract.[6] The Uniform Probate Code agrees, but courts have found on the basis of extrinsic evidence that mutual wills were made pursuant to a contract.[7]

### *Statute of Frauds*

The Statute of Frauds may bar oral evidence of such a contract. Contracts to devise land have been held to fall under the provision of the original Statute of Frauds which required contracts to sell land to be in writing.[8] Many states today have provisions which specifically deal with contracts to make wills. The Uniform Probate Code requires either

> (i) provisions of a will stating the material provisions of the contract, (ii) an express reference in a will to a contract and extrinsic evidence proving the terms of the contract, or (iii) a writing signed by the decedent evidencing the contract.[9]

Simply signing a written will does not satisfy the statute unless the will refers to or states the terms of the contract. Even a recital in a joint will that the parties had "heretofore agreed, for valuable consideration * * * to make joint and mutual wills giving to the survivor of us all property" was held

**2.** Adkins v. Oppio, 769 P.2d 62, 64 (Nev. 1989). *See also* In re Estate of Kaplan, 579 N.E.2d 963 (Ill.App.1991); Kitchen v. Blue, 498 N.E.2d 41 (Ind.App.1986); Wetzel v. Watson, 328 S.E.2d 526 (W.Va.1985).

**3.** King v. Travis, 524 N.E.2d 974 (Ill.App. 1988); Matter of Estate of Di Siena, 576 N.Y.S.2d 952 (A.D.1991).

**4.** Uniform Probate Code § 2–514. *See also* Calif.Prob.Code § 150(b).

**5.** In re Estate of Armijo, 995 P.2d 487 (N.M.App.1999).

**6.** Smith v. Turner, 477 S.E.2d 663 (Ga. App.1996); Estate of Maher, 606 N.E.2d 46 (Ill.App.1992); Junot v. Estate of Gilliam, 759 S.W.2d 654 (Tenn.1988); Pearce v. Meek, 780 S.W.2d 289 (Tex.App.1989).

**7.** Todd v. Cartwright, 684 S.W.2d 154 (Tex.App.1984).

**8.** B Sparks, *Contracts to Make Wills* 41–43 (1956).

**9.** Uniform Probate Code § 2–514.

insufficient to bind the survivor not to revoke the will after the first party died.[10]

Refusal to enforce a contract after one party has performed it leads to unjust enrichment. Courts sometimes avoid this by granting restitutionary relief. A comment to the UPC says that the writing requirement does "not preclude recovery in quantum meruit for the value of services rendered the testator."[11] In such actions, courts have used the value of the promisor's estate as evidence of the value of the services performed by the plaintiff, so that the result is nearly equivalent to enforcing the contract. For example, a father had promised to leave his son a share of a company if he continued to work for him. The son proved that the value of the promised share was worth $463,965 and recovered $443,985 "in quantum meruit for the value of his services in reliance on the unenforceable oral promise."[12] On the other hand, services rendered by one family member to another are presumed to have been intended as gifts and are not compensable if this presumption is not rebutted.[13]

Many courts hold that part performance by a promisee satisfies or excuses a statutory writing requirement.[14] The Uniform Probate Code contains no part-performance exception, but courts may nevertheless recognize one, just as they did for the original Statute of Frauds without any warrant in the statutory language.[15] But some courts have taken the Code's tightened proof requirements seriously, saying that "application of the equitable principle of part performance * * * would nullify the purpose of the statute."[16]

A promise which was made without intent to perform it, has been held to be actionable as fraud without a writing.[17] A lost or destroyed writing has been held to satisfy the statute.[18]

### *Executory Contracts*

Parties who have made a contract that a will shall be irrevocable may agree to rescind it.[19] Most authorities also allow either party to repudiate the contract *unilaterally* before there has been any performance. For example, a

**10.** Matter of Lubins, 673 N.Y.S.2d 204 (A.D.1998).

**11.** Uniform Probate Code § 2–514, Comment.

**12.** Slawsby v. Slawsby, 601 N.E.2d 478 (Mass.App.1992). *See also Restatement, Second, Contracts* § 375 (1979); *cf.* Williams v. Mason, 556 So.2d 1045 (Miss.1990) (error to award promised estate, remand for recovery for value of services).

**13.** Clark v. Gale, 966 P.2d 431, 439 (Wyo. 1998).

**14.** Shepherd v. Mazzetti, 545 A.2d 621 (Del.1988); Estate of Von Wendesse, 618 N.E.2d 1332 (Ind.App.1993); *Restatement, Second, Contracts* § 129, illus. 10 (1979).

**15.** Estate of Housley, 65 Cal.Rptr.2d 628 (App.1997). California for many years had a statute modelled on the UPC, but it was recently changed to allow an oral agreement to be proved by "clear and convincing evidence." Cal.Prob.Code § 21700(a)(4).

**16.** Rieck v. Rieck, 724 P.2d 674, 676 (Colo. App.1986). *See also* Cole v. Rivers, 861 S.W.2d 551 (Ark.App.1993); Olesen v. Manty, 438 N.W.2d 404 (Minn.App.1989).

**17.** Brody v. Bock, 897 P.2d 769 (Colo. 1995). *Cf.* Taylor v. Johnson, 677 S.W.2d 680 (Tex.App.1984) (no fraud absent finding intent not to perform when promise was made); Section 6.4, at note 24 et seq.

**18.** Murphy v. Glenn, 964 P.2d 581, 585 (Colo.App.1998); Baker v. Mohr, 826 P.2d 111 (Or.App.1992). *Accord, Restatement, Second, Contracts* § 137 (1979).

**19.** Matter of Estate of Cohen, 629 N.E.2d 1356 (N.Y.1994) (wife's accepting appointment as administrator of her husband's estate was a tacit consent to his revocation of a contractual will); *cf. Restatement, Second, Contracts* § 311 (1979) (limiting ability of parties to a contract to discharge duties to a third party beneficiary in some situations).

couple agreed to leave their property at the death of the survivor to their son. The wife later sued for divorce, repudiated the contract, and made a new will. A suit by the son to enforce the contract was dismissed. "While ... the parties to such an agreement are yet alive, any party may recede therefrom, and revoke his will or make a different disposition of his property, on giving proper notice to the other party."[20] Courts usually enforce contracts even though they have not been partly performed (assuming that the Statute of Frauds is no bar). But since contracts to make wills are usually between family members, perhaps courts feel that the parties did not intend that they should be enforceable to the same extent as a regular commercial contract.

### *Clear and Convincing Evidence*

Even if the Statute of Frauds is not a bar, claims under a contract often fail because the plaintiff's evidence is not considered to be clear and convincing. For example, a daughter's claim that her parents had contracted to leave her a share of their property was rejected because "the proof failed to establish an agreement by clear and convincing evidence ... [Plaintiff] and the witnesses called in her behalf were all related [to her] by blood or marriage did not have that degree of disinterest which would render it obligatory on the fact finder."[21]

Even evidence in writing may not suffice if the terms are too vague. "At best, the documents prove that, at one point in time, decedent planned to leave his house to appellant's family, but changed his mind ... There was no reference to any contract."[22] A claim of an alleged contract has also been rejected because the terms "were extremely vague."[23] Testimony of discrepant versions of the contract terms may also lead a court to conclude that the proof is insufficient.[24]

### *Fairness*

Contracts to make a will must be supported by consideration. Past consideration is not enough; a promise to devise in return for services previously rendered by the promisee is not enforceable.[25] Technical consideration may not suffice. Plaintiffs usually seek what amounts to specific performance[26] and this brings into play equity's traditional reluctance to

**20.** Boyle v. Schmitt, 602 So.2d 665, 667 (Fla.App.1992). *See also* Matter of Estate of Edington, 489 N.E.2d 612, 615 (Ind.App.1986). *But cf.* Matter of Estate of Lilienthal, 574 N.W.2d 349 (Iowa App.1997) (unilateral rescission not allowed when other party was alive but incompetent); In re Estate of Johnson, 781 S.W.2d 390 (Tex.App.1989) (refusing to allow unilateral rescission).

**21.** Mabry v. McAfee, 783 S.W.2d 356, 358 (Ark.1990). *See also* Smith v. Turner, 477 S.E.2d 663 (Ga.App.1996); Matter of Estate of Konow, 506 N.E.2d 450 (Ill.App.1987); Matter of Estate of Stratmann, 806 P.2d 459 (Kan. 1991).

**22.** Olesen v. Manty, 438 N.W.2d 404, 407 (Minn.App.1989). *See also* Kahn v. First Nat. Bank, 576 N.E.2d 321, 325 (Ill.App.1991) ("statements of testamentary intent" do not create "a specific contract capable of enforcement").

**23.** In re Nelson's Estate, 431 N.E.2d 1103 (Ill.App.1981). *See also* In re Estate of Dilling, 633 P.2d 1273 (Okl.App.1981); Estate of Boothby, 532 A.2d 1007 (Me.1987).

**24.** In re Layton's Estate, 323 N.W.2d 817, 823 (Neb.1982).

**25.** In re Estate of Casey, 583 N.E.2d 83 (Ill.App.1991); Rowell v. Plymouth–Home Nat. Bank, 434 N.E.2d 648 (Mass.App.1982); DeMentas v. Estate of Tallas, 764 P.2d 628 (Utah App.1988); *cf. Restatement, Second, Contracts* § 86 (1979) (promises made in recognition of benefit previously received are "binding to the extent necessary to prevent injustice").

**26.** This is often called "quasi-specific performance ... since the making of a will cannot

enforce unfair contracts.[27] Nevertheless, contracts are often enforced despite the lack of an equal exchange. The value of one party's performance may be hard to measure in monetary terms, for example, the promisee's "emigration to this country and the consequent disruption this caused to both himself and his family."[28] Moreover, fairness is determined as of the date of the contract; subsequent events which make the exchange unequal in hindsight are not considered.[29] Many contracts are between spouses with estates of very different size. One court refused to enforce such a contract against the husband's estate because the wife had left him no property. "Although the mutual promises may have amounted to technical consideration, * * * certainly there was great inequality of consideration moving from the two makers. Thus the agreement was not sufficiently fair."[30] However, in many cases a great disparity between the consideration received and the value of the promise has not prevented enforcement.[31]

### *Inter–Vivos Transfers*

Sometimes a promisor who is still living seeks to undercut the contract by conveying property to others. The beneficiaries of the contract often succeed in setting aside such conveyances on the theory that the contract confined the promisor to a life estate in his or her property with a remainder in the beneficiaries of the contract,[32] or the agreement not to change a will "carried with it an implicit agreement ... to make no disposition of that estate property inconsistent with that intent."[33] Other courts are not so strict in enforcing the contract. A husband's promise to execute a will leaving his estate to his children was held to give them no claim to assets he put in joint tenancy, since the contract did not require that he "have property at the time of his demise."[34] Some courts apply a rule of reason. The contract

> does not prohibit the [promisor] from using her property for the necessities and comforts of life.[35] .. from changing the form of the property[36] and ... from making reasonable gifts of estate property to third parties.

be compelled." Walton v. Walton, 36 Cal. Rptr.2d 901, 905 (App.1995).

**27.** *Restatement (Second) of Contracts* § 364 (1979).

**28.** In re Beeruk's Estate, 241 A.2d 755, 759 (Pa.1968).

**29.** Matter of Marriage of Ellinwood, 651 P.2d 190, 192 (Or.App.1982). However, this inequality may persuade a court to find that no contract existed. *See* In re Estate of Trobaugh, 380 N.W.2d 152 (Minn.App.1986) (plaintiff cared for decedent for less than 2 months).

**30.** Levis v. Hammond, 100 N.W.2d 638 (Iowa 1960).

**31.** Kitchen v. Estate of Blue, 498 N.E.2d 41, 45 (Ind.App.1986) (promisor's receipt of his wife's $300 estate was sufficient consideration for his promise to dispose of $130,000 estate).

**32.** Young v. Young, 569 N.E.2d 1, 5 (Ill. App.1991). *See also* Foulds v. First Nat. Bank, 707 P.2d 1171, 1174 (N.M.1985).

**33.** Robison v. Graham, 799 P.2d 610, 615 (Okl.1990). *See also* Matter of Estate of Kerr, 918 P.2d 1354 (N.M.App.1996) (putting property into joint tenancy was a breach); In re Estate of Gibson, 893 S.W.2d 749 (Tex.App. 1995).

**34.** Duran v. Komyatte, 490 N.E.2d 388 (Ind.App.1986). *See also* Blackmon v. Estate of Battcock, 587 N.E.2d 280 (N.Y.1991) (revocable trust).

**35.** *See also* Matter of Ciochon's Estate, 609 P.2d 177, 183 (Kan.App.1980); Pyle by Straub v. United States, 766 F.2d 1141, 1144 (7th Cir.1985) ("she may invade corpus only for health, support and comfort"); Westbrook v. Superior Court, 222 Cal.Rptr. 317, 323 (App. 1986) ("reasonably necessary living expenses").

**36.** The promisor can sell the property if the consideration is adequate. Long v. Buehler, 648 P.2d 270 (Kan.App.1982); *cf.* Pyle by Straub v. United States, 766 F.2d 1141, 1144 (7th Cir.1985) (can exchange for assets "of equal or greater value").

Reasonableness of a gift would depend upon the proportion that the value of the gift bears to the value of the estate.[37]

Even changes in a will have been allowed if the court finds them not inconsistent with the spirit of a contract. For example, a couple's contractual will left their estate in trust for their daughters with a remainder to the grandchildren. After the wife died, the husband made a new will which left the property to the daughters outright. The court rejected a challenge filed on behalf of the grandchildren on the ground that the later will "substantially complied with the contract ... To the extent that the grandchildren had an expectancy under the contract, that expectancy was realized in the form of benefits flowing directly to their mothers and indirectly to them as dependents of their mothers and as the natural heirs of their mother's estates."[38]

### *Third Parties*

The promisor is usually dead when the action to enforce a contractual will is brought, and the action is brought either against the promisor's estate or against a third party. Courts often impress a trust upon the promisor's property in favor of the contract beneficiaries.[39] A bona fide purchaser of property prevails over the equitable claims of the contract beneficiaries,[40] but the contract beneficiaries can recover property in the hands of donees and devisees from the promisor.[41]

Claims of the promisor's spouse in this situation have been variously treated. Some courts have rejected claims to an elective share on the ground that it only applies to the decedent's estate after payment of claims.[42] This reasoning would allow the spouse at least a family allowance which is not subject to the decedent's creditors,[43] but not if the promisor is viewed as only a life tenant or trustee of the property subject to the contract.[44] On the other hand, some courts have allowed a promisor's spouse to prevail over the contract beneficiaries because of "the public policy surrounding the marriage relationship."[45] Other courts have reached intermediate solutions to this dilemma.

**37.** Powell v. American Charter Fed. S. & L., 514 N.W.2d 326, 334 (Neb.1994). *See also* Humphries v. Whiteley, 565 So.2d 96, 100 (Ala. 1990); Murphy v. Glenn, 964 P.2d 581, 586 (Colo.App.1998); Peirce v. Peirce, 994 P.2d 193, 200 (Utah 2000); Nile v. Nile, 734 N.E.2d 1153, 1160 (Mass.2000).

**38.** Kerper v. Kerper, 780 P.2d 923, 937 (Wyo.1989). *See also* In re Estate of Espey, 729 S.W.2d 99, 102 (Tenn.App.1986) (survivor could dispose of her estate "in such a manner as befits the circumstances").

**39.** Robison v. Graham, 799 P.2d 610 (Okl. 1990); Dickie v. Dickie, 769 P.2d 225 (Or.App. 1989); Chapman v. Citizens & Southern Nat. Bank, 395 S.E.2d 446 (S.C.App.1990).

**40.** Olive v. Biggs, 173 S.E.2d 301 (N.C. 1970). As to the rights of a bona fide purchaser from a trustee see Section 12.8, note 163 et seq. In Dickie v. Dickie, 769 P.2d 225 (Or.App. 1989), after the promisor sold the property to a bona fide purchaser, the court imposed a constructive trust on the sale proceeds.

**41.** Musselman v. Mitchell, 611 P.2d 675 (Or.App.1980); O'Connor v. Immele, 43 N.W.2d 649 (N.D.1950).

**42.** Johnson v. Girtman, 542 So.2d 1033 (Fla.App.1989); In re Beeruk's Estate, 241 A.2d 755 (Pa.1968); Schaefer v. Schuhman, [1972] 2 W.L.R. 481 (P.C. 1971); Section 3.7, note 18.

**43.** Kinne v. Kinne, 617 P.2d 442 (Wash. App.1980); Matter of Estate of Harper, 486 N.E.2d 295 (Ill.App.1985); Section 3.4, note 23.

**44.** Gregory v. Estate of Gregory, 866 S.W.2d 379 (Ark.1993); In re Estate of Stewart, 444 P.2d 337 (Cal.1968); Rubenstein v. Mueller, 225 N.E.2d 540 (N.Y.1967).

**45.** Shimp v. Huff, 556 A.2d 252, 263 (Md. 1989); *cf.* Sheldon v. Sheldon, 987 P.2d 1229 (Or.App.1999).

> In determining whether to award specific performance to contract beneficiaries, courts have considered several different factors, including whether the surviving spouse had notice of the contract prior to the marriage, ... the length of the marriage and ... whether the surviving spouse would be deprived of the entire estate by enforcement of the contract.[46]

The contribution of the spouse to the accumulation of the decedent's property is also relevant; the spouse should get half of any community property of the marriage.[47] In a case where the promisor and his second wife had "made substantial financial contributions to the construction of a house and to a joint savings account," the court refused to subject these assets to a constructive trust for the beneficiary of an earlier contract, which it enforced only with respect to the husband's "separate estate."[48] Some cases construe contracts as not intended to include *any* property acquired by the second spouse after the death of the first.[49]

After-born children of the promisor may also be protected if full enforcement of a contract would deprive them of any share of their father's estate.[50]

### *Remedies*

Because probate courts traditionally had no jurisdiction to enforce contracts, a will executed in breach of a contract is often admitted to probate; the contract beneficiary's only remedy is in a court of general jurisdiction.[51] Admitting a will to probate in one court and denying its effect in another seems inefficient, and a breach of contract has sometimes been accepted as a basis for refusing to admit an will to probate if made in breach of contract.[52]

Where law and equity are still separated, actions to enforce contracts to make wills are usually classified as equitable, which means there is no right to jury trial.[53] The statute of limitations starts to run normally when the promisor dies, regardless of when the contract was made.[54] However, a claim may be barred shortly after the promissor's death by virtue of a "non-claim" statute requiring claims against the decedent to be filed within a brief period after administration of the estate begins.[55]

**46.** Shimp v. Huff, 556 A.2d 252, 259 (Md. 1989).

**47.** Perl v. Howell, 650 S.W.2d 523, 525 (Tex.App.1983); Porter v. Porter, 726 P.2d 459 (Wash.1986). *But see* Cal.Fam.Code § 910 (community property is liable for a debt incurred by either spouse before or during the marriage).

**48.** Kassahn v. Kassahn, 868 P.2d 9 (Or. App.1994).

**49.** In re Estate of Gibson, 893 S.W.2d 749 (Tex.App.1995).

**50.** Matter of Estate of Sherry, 698 P.2d 94 (Wash.App.1985).

**51.** Lewis v. Tanner, 312 S.E.2d 798 (Ga. 1984); Perino v. Eldert, 577 N.E.2d 807 (Ill. App.1991); Coffman v. Woods, 696 S.W.2d 386 (Tex.App.1985).

**52.** Estate of McKusick, 629 A.2d 41 (Me. 1993); In re Estate of Gibson, 893 S.W.2d 749 (Tex.App.1995).

**53.** Walton v. Walton, 36 Cal.Rptr.2d 901 (App.1995); In re Layton's Estate, 323 N.W.2d 817 (Neb.1982); Peirce v. Peirce, 994 P.2d 193, 197 (Utah 2000).

**54.** Estate of Brenzikofer, 57 Cal.Rptr.2d 401 (App.1996) (agreement made in 1981, promisor died in 1991, action filed in 1994 was timely).

**55.** McEwen v. McEwen, 529 N.E.2d 355, 359 (Ind.App.1988); In re Estate of Leavitt, 733 A.2d 348 (Me.1999); Matter of Estate of Nichols, 544 N.E.2d 430 (Ill.App.1989); Matter of Estate of Pallister, 770 P.2d 494 (Kan.App. 1989). However, there is contrary authority. In Matter of Estate of Green, 516 N.W.2d 326 (S.D.1994); Murphy v. Glenn, 964 P.2d 581, 584 (Colo.App.1998). For a general discussion of nonclaim statutes see Section 13.3, at note 15 et seq.

Suit is sometimes brought against a promisor who has repudiated while still alive.[56] Courts in this situation have enjoined the promisor from transferring the property, vacated conveyances previously made, and even appointed a trustee to take charge of the property.[57] However, a trust is imposed only if the promisor has attempted to dispose of property improperly, since this would curtail the promisor's extensive rights over the property while alive.[58]

### *Planning*

Although contracts to make wills are common, most commentators think they are a bad idea. "The uncertain federal and state tax consequences of contractual wills * * * makes them generally undesirable.[59] * * * [A] trust is almost invariably a better way to provide for survivors" because "a trust may avoid the uncertainty that inheres in contractual arrangements."[60] Many courts share this feeling. As one judge has said:

> If a young husband and wife sign a [contractual] will when they are about twenty-five years of age and then one of them dies, the survivor is bound (even if he or she lives another fifty years) [to] leave all of his or her property exactly as required by the joint will. In other words, the concrete once poured, is permanently set ... The vicissitudes of life are such that ... we ought not to presume such an intent ... [61]

There is no objective of a contractual will which could not be better accomplished by a trust. An independent, financially responsible trustee provides more security that the plan desired by the parties will be carried out. Even without an independent trustee, trust law itself provides generally effective remedies against breach of trust.[62] The rights of trust beneficiaries are not subject to claims of the trustee's spouse or creditors as is often true under a contract. A discretionary trust can provide flexibility so the plan is not "set in concrete." Spouses who wish to establish a common plan governing the property of both can create a joint trust, but they should make clear the extent to which either can revoke the trust. When a husband and wife jointly created a trust, reserving the "right at any time during our lifetime to revoke" it, this was interpreted (over a strong dissent) to allow the wife after the husband died to amend the trust to cut out his children by a prior marriage.[63]

**56.** Wyrick v. Wyrick, 349 S.E.2d 705 (Ga. 1986); Dickie v. Dickie, 769 P.2d 225 (Or.App. 1989); Thompson v. Thompson, 495 A.2d 678 (R.I.1985); *Restatement, Second, of Contracts* § 253 (1979).

**57.** Lawrence v. Ashba, 59 N.E.2d 568 (Ind. App.1945); Turley v. Adams, 484 P.2d 668 (Ariz.App.1971).

**58.** In re Marriage of Edwards, 45 Cal. Rptr.2d 138 (App.1995).

**59.** Among these uncertainties are (1) whether benefits accruing under the contract are taxable income. Getty v. Commissioner, 913 F.2d 1486 (9th Cir.1990); (2) whether a gift tax is payable when the first party dies, making the will of the other irrevocable. Grimes v. Commissioner, 851 F.2d 1005 (7th Cir.1988). (3) Whether the estate tax marital deduction is allowed when a spouse receives property under a contractual will. Bartlett v. Commissioner, 937 F.2d 316 (7th Cir.1991).

**60.** J. Price, *Contemporary Estate Planning* 167–68 (1983). *See also* Browder, *Recent Patterns of Testate Succession in the United States and England,* 67 Mich.L.Rev. 1303, 1343 (1969).

**61.** In re Hoeppner's Estate, 145 N.W.2d 754, 760 (Wis.1966) (concurring opinion). *See also* Craddock v. Berryman, 645 P.2d 399 (1982) ("contracts to make wills are looked upon with disfavor"); Moore v. Harvey, 406 N.E.2d 354 (Ind.App.1980).

**62.** For remedies against breach of trust see Section 12.8.

**63.** Perrenoud v. Harman, 8 P.3d 293 (Utah App.2000).

Because of the risk of false claims that mutual wills were made pursuant to a contract, wills which two spouses execute at the same time should expressly state that they are not being executed pursuant to a contract.[64]

**64.** T. Shaffer, *The Planning and Drafting of Wills and Trusts* 237 (2d ed. 1979); Martin, *The Draftsman Views Wills for a Young Family*, 54 N.C.L.Rev. 277, 308 (1976).

# Chapter 5

# REVOCATION

*Analysis*



---

## § 5.1 Subsequent Instrument

A will can be revoked even if a power of revocation is not expressly reserved,[1] but all states impose formal requirements for revocation. Wills can be revoked (1) by a subsequent instrument, (2) by a physical act, (3) by a change of circumstances.[2]

As to the first, the Uniform Probate Code is typical. "A will or any part thereof is revoked (1) by a subsequent will which revokes the prior will or part expressly or by inconsistency."[3] A "will" can revoke prior wills even though it contains no other provisions and so the testator dies intestate.[4] The subsequent instrument must be executed with the formalities prescribed for wills. Thus a will which was invalid for lack of publication was not effective to revoke earlier wills.[5]

In a jurisdiction which allows holographic wills, a holographic will may revoke an attested one,[6] but handwritten changes by the testator on a typewritten will may not be effective if the handwritten words by themselves do not show testamentary intent. Thus when a testator crossed out the name of a deceased devisee in a typewritten will and wrote "her share to be divided

**§ 5.1**

**1.** 2 W. Blackstone, *Commentaries* * 502 (1765); T. Littleton, *Tenures* § 168. This was also true in Roman law. R. Villers, *Rome et le Droit Privé* 471 (1977). However, the power to revoke may be limited by a contract. See Section 4.9.

**2.** This today does not usually cause a total revocation of the will. See Section 5.4.

**3.** Uniform Probate Code § 2–507(a)(1). *See also* Calif.Prob.Code § 6120.

**4.** Uniform Probate Code § 1–201(56) ("will" includes "any testamentary instrument that merely ... revokes ... another will"). *But see* In re Estate of Martinez, 985 P.2d 1230 (N.M.App.1999). In Coussee v. Estate of Efston, 633 N.E.2d 815 (Ill.App.1994), a will expressly revoked former wills but failed to dispose of all the testator's property and so a partial intestacy resulted.

**5.** Matter of Estate of Beal, 769 P.2d 150 (Okl.1989). *See also* Flagle v. Martinelli, 360 N.E.2d 1269 (Ind.App.1977) (witnesses did not sign in testator's presence); In re Estate of Laura, 690 A.2d 1011 (N.H.1997); In re Estate of Martinez, 985 P.2d 1230 (N.M.App.1999) (only one witness).

**6.** Matter of Estate of Custick, 842 P.2d 934 (Utah App.1992).

between her siblings," the change was held to be ineffective.[7] However, the Restatement allows testators to make handwritten changes in a will if the statute allows holographic wills; changes in an attested will must be signed, but not alterations in a holograph.[8] The basis for the distinction is not explained. Of course, all wills must be signed, but the question is whether the testator's signature in the original will suffices. An affirmative answer to this question is hard to reconcile with the assumption that a signature is required to show finality of intent.[9]

Oral wills, even in states which allow them, have been held ineffective to revoke a written one.[10]

### *Inconsistency*

Even if a will does not expressly revoke prior wills, an implied revocation may occur if it contains provisions which are inconsistent with an earlier will. Testators who intend to revoke prior wills usually say so expressly, so courts are reluctant to find such revocation by inconsistency. Thus "a grant of an option to one son to purchase certain real estate at below market price is not inconsistent with a bequest of all the assets to all the testator's children in equal shares," and the provisions in both wills were to be carried out.[11] On the other hand, under the Uniform Probate Code a "testator is presumed to have intended a subsequent will to replace rather than supplement a previous will if the subsequent will makes a complete disposition of the testator's estate."[12] The presumption is reversed when the later document does not purport to dispose of all the estate.[13] In a case in which a testator executed 4 wills on the same day, each disposing of only part of his estate but containing a boiler-plate form revoking prior wills, the court ignored the clause and probated all four wills.[14]

The reluctance to find revocation by inconsistency is particularly strong when the subsequent instrument is called a "codicil," since this word suggests a supplement to a prior will rather than an abrogation of it.[15]

The appropriateness of implying a revocation may depend on the nature of the gift. If will #1 gives "my gold watch to Alice" and will #2 leaves the same gold watch to Barbara, the devise to Alice is impliedly revoked. But if will #1 leaves $30,000 to Alice and will #2 leaves $20,000 to Barbara, the two

7. Estate of Sola, 275 Cal.Rptr. 98 (App. 1990); In re Estate of Foxley, 575 N.W.2d 150 (Neb.1998).

8. *Restatement, Third, of Property (Wills and Other Donative Transfers)* § 3.2, comm. f and g (1998). *See also* Estate of Nielson, 165 Cal.Rptr. 319 (App.1980) (will effectively changed by crossing out devisees and inserting others when changes initialed by testator). In Hancock v. Krause, 757 S.W.2d 117 (Tex.App. 1988), the court gave effect to similar changes on the theory that the testator "adopted" his prior signature when he made them.

9. Section 4.2.

10. In re Estate of Mantalis, 671 N.E.2d 1062 (Ohio App.1996); In re Estate of Carlton, 221 So.2d 184 (Fla.App.1969). A contrary decision in the 17th century led to the enactment of the Statute of Frauds. Whitman, *Revocation and Revival: An Analysis of the 1990 Revision of the Uniform Probate Code and Suggestions for the Future*, 55 Alb.L.Rev. 1035, 1038 (1992).

11. Matter of Estate of Hoffman, 375 N.W.2d 231, 235 (Iowa 1985). *See also* Smith v. United States, 801 F.2d 975 (7th Cir.1986); In re Estate of Francoeur, 290 N.E.2d 396 (Ill. App.1972).

12. Uniform Probate Code § 2–507(c). *See also Restatement, Second, Property (Donative Transfers)* § 33.2, comm. b (1990); Blake's Estate v. Benza, 587 P.2d 271 (Ariz.App.1978).

13. Uniform Probate Code § 2–507(d).

14. deGraaf v. Owen, 598 So.2d 892 (Ala. 1992).

15. Starratt v. Morse, 332 F.Supp. 1038 (D.S.C.1971).

devises are not inconsistent.[16] However, if will #2 had left $20,000 to *Alice*, the question arise whether the testator wanted her to get a total of $50,000 or just $20,000?[17] A drafter should make the relationship between a codicil and an earlier will clear.

## § 5.2 Physical Act

### *Nature of Act*

The Statute of Frauds allowed devises to be revoked "by burning, cancelling, tearing or obliterating the same."[1] American states today have similar provisions.[2] The slight differences in wording among the statutes are not usually important.[3]

A will can be effectively revoked by physical act even though it remains legible,[4] but throwing a will in the trash is not enough to revoke it.[5] Nor, according to some courts, is it enough to make marks on a will which do not touch any words.[6] The Uniform Probate Code, however, provides otherwise if the intent to revoke is clear.[7]

Under many statutes, the act upon the will must be done "by either (1) the testator or (2) another person in the testator's presence and by the testator's direction."[8] This limitation may frustrate a testator's clear intent to revoke if the testator's directions to destroy a will are carried out in another place.[9] The Uniform Probate Code requires only the "testator's conscious presence" which, according to the comment "need not be ... in the testator's line of sight."[10]

Sometimes a testator's directions to destroy a will are not carried out, *e.g.* his wife pretended to tear up the will according to his instructions, but

**16.** However, if the testator's estate contains less than $50,000, the devises in this cased would have to be abated. See Section 8.2.

**17.** *Compare* In re Estate of Lund, 110 Cal.Rptr. 183 (App.1973) (devises are cumulative) *with* Anderson v. Dubel, 580 S.W.2d 404 (Tex.Civ.App.1979). Uniform Probate Code § 2–507, comment raises this question but does not answer it.

§ 5.2

**1.** Statute of Frauds, 29 Car. 2, c. 3, § 6 (1676). The Statute of Wills used the terms "burning, tearing or otherwise destroying." 1 Vict., c. 26, § 20 (1837).

**2.** *E.g.*, Uniform Probate Code § 2–507(a)(2); Cal.Prob.Code § 6120.

**3.** *But see* Estate of Eglee, 383 A.2d 586 (R.I.1978) (drawing a line through every word in a will is insufficient where statute only mentions "burning tearing or otherwise destroying").

**4.** Matter of Cox's Estate, 621 P.2d 1057 (Mont.1980); Matter of Estate of Ausley, 818 P.2d 1226 (Okl.1991) (VOID written over parts of will); In re Estate of Dickson, 590 So.2d 471 (Fla.App.1991); Board of Trustees of University of Alabama v. Calhoun, 514 So.2d 895 (Ala. 1987) (signature page removed).

**5.** SouthTrust Bank v. Winter, 689 So.2d 69 (Ala.Civ.App.1996).

**6.** Kronauge v. Stoecklein, 293 N.E.2d 320 (Ohio App.1972).

**7.** Uniform Probate Code § 2–507(a)(2). *See also Restatement, Third, of Property (Wills and Other Donative Transfers)* § 4.1, comm. g (1998); Kroll v. Nehmer, 705 A.2d 716, 717 (Md.1998) (will revoked by writing VOID on the back).

**8.** Calif.Prob.Code § 6120(b); Ind.Code § 29–1–5–6; S.C.Code § 21–7–210; Estate of DeWald v. Whittenburg, 925 P.2d 903 (Okl. App.1996) (cancellation by a friend of testator at his direction).

**9.** In re Estate of Bancker's, 232 So.2d 431 (Fla.App.1970); In re Haugk's Estate, 280 N.W.2d 684 (Wis.1979).

**10.** Uniform Probate Code § 2–507(a)(2), comment. Even when the destruction did not occur in the testator's "conscious presence," the intent to revoke may be effectuated under the "harmless error" rule according to *Restatement, Third, of Property (Wills and Other Donative Transfers)* § 4.1, illus. 9 (1998). See Section 4.1, at note 24 et seq.

produced it unharmed after the testator died. The court probated the will, but said that a constructive trust might be imposed on the widow.[11] Another court used a constructive trust rationale to carry out a testator's intent when the testator, intending to revoke a codicil, tore up a copy instead of the original. "A constructive trust is properly imposed when, as a result of a mistake in a transaction, one party is unjustly enriched at the expense of another ... Although this equitable remedy is usually limited to circumstances in which fraud or a breach of confidence has occurred, it is proper in cases in which one party has benefited by the mistake of another."[12]

The revocatory act must be done with the intent to revoke; an accidental destruction does not revoke a will.[13]

### *Partial Revocation*

Cases in which a testator intends to revoke only part of a will by physical act have given courts much trouble. The Uniform Probate Code allows a will "or any part thereof" to be revoked, but a testator cannot make a new will without a signed writing. The line between revocation and making a new will can be hazy. For example, a will left the estate to the testator's sons, Michael and Edward. He later crossed out Edward's name, but the court refused to give this effect "because this amounted to an enlargement of the bequest to Michael."[14] Another court reached the same result as to the testator's striking out the name of a residuary legatee, but it gave effect to the cancellation of a pecuniary devise in the same will, saying that this was only a "minor" change.[15]

In some cases markings on a will have been deemed to show an intent to revoke it entirely, even if the will is not destroyed.[16]

A testator cannot add words to a will without re-executing it.[17] Alterations made in a will *prior* to execution, on the other hand, are valid. For example, a five-page will was offered for probate. The testator had revised the will before executing it by substituting a new fifth page. All five pages were admitted to probate. "There is no requirement in law that each page of a testament must be * * * typed at the same time, only that the document be complete at the time it is signed."[18] Correcting typographical errors in a will by hand is risky, since someone may argue that the change was made after the will was executed in an ineffective attempt to alter it informally. However, some courts

**11.** Morris v. Morris, 642 S.W.2d 448 (Tex. 1982). *See also Restatement (Third) of Property (Wills and Other Donative Transfers)* § 8.3, comm. m (Prel.Dft. 2000).

**12.** In re Estate of Tolin, 622 So.2d 988, 990–91 (Fla.1993). *See also Restatement, Third, of Property (Wills and Other Donative Transfers)* § 4.1, comm. f (1998).

**13.** Evans v. May, 923 S.W.2d 712 (Tex. App.1996); McKenzie v. Francis, 197 S.E.2d 221 (Va.1973).

**14.** In re Estate of Eastman, 812 P.2d 521 (Wash.App.1991). *See also* Hansel v. Head, 706 So.2d 1142 (Ala.1997) (even though the statute, like the UPC allowed a will "or any part thereof" to be revoked by physical act); Matter of Estate of Malloy, 949 P.2d 804 (Wash.1998). *Restatement, Third, of Property (Wills and Other Donative Transfers)* § 4.1, comm. i (1998) disapproves these cases, as drawing "a distinction without a difference."

**15.** Patrick v. Patrick, 649 A.2d 1204 (Md. App.1994). *See also* Walpole v. Lewis, 492 S.W.2d 410 (Ark.1973).

**16.** Matter of Brune's Estate, 606 P.2d 647 (Or.App.1980).

**17.** Hansel v. Head, 706 So.2d 1142 (Ala. 1997).

**18.** Succession of Norton, 451 So.2d 1203 (La.App.1984).

have given effect to changes made by a testator in a holographic will after it was signed.[19]

### *Presumption of Revocation*

Contestants of a will have the burden of proving that a will was revoked,[20] but when a will which was in the testator's possession cannot be found, or is found in a mutilated condition, after the testator dies, courts presume that the testator intended to revoke the will. This presumption comes from the common law,[21] but in California it has been codified. The California statute applies only if "the testator was competent until death."[22] Even without such a statute, if a testator became incompetent prior to death, a court may assume that she destroyed it while she was incompetent and so there was no effective revocation.[23]

In cases to which the presumption applies, if the proponents of the will produce no contrary evidence, the fact finder must find that the will was revoked.[24] Proponents of the will therefore usually offer evidence to rebut the presumption, and findings of no intent to revoke are routinely affirmed even though the original will cannot be found.[25] Such evidence may include the fact that persons other than the testator had access to the will.[26] Some courts have inferred from evidence of a testator's sloppy habits that the will was simply lost in the mess.[27] Courts admit even alleged oral declarations by the testator indicating that the lost will reflected her wishes or that she continued to feel affection for the devisees or hostility to persons disinherited by the will.[28]

The presumption of revocation is sometimes overcome by the preservation of a duplicate.[29] The California statutory presumption does not apply if "a duplicate original of the will can be found."[30] But some courts have found a will was revoked despite the production of a duplicate, particularly when the duplicate was not in the testator's possession.[31] Conversely, the presumption of revocation applies only when the missing will was once in the testator's possession.[32]

**19.** Charleston Nat. Bank v. Thru the Bible, 507 S.E.2d 708, 712 (W.Va.1998); cf. Section 5.1, note 8.

**20.** Uniform Probate Code § 3–407; Cal. Prob.Code § 8252.

**21.** *Restatement, Third, of Property (Wills and Other Donative Transfers)* § 4.1, comm. j (1998).

**22.** Cal.Prob.Code § 6124.

**23.** In re Fuller's Estate, 399 A.2d 960 (N.H.1979).

**24.** Perez v. Gilbert, 586 N.E.2d 921 (Ind. App.1992). Query, however, if this is true when the mark on the will is "a blemish that could easily have occurred accidentally." *Restatement, Third, of Property (Wills and Other Donative Transfers)* § 4.1, comm. j (1998).

**25.** E.g., McBride v. Jones, 494 S.E.2d 319 (Ga.1998).

**26.** Lonergan v. Estate of Budahazi, 669 So.2d 1062 (Fla.App.1996); Matter of Estate of Wiarda, 508 N.W.2d 740 (Iowa App.1993); Thomas v. Thomas, 784 S.W.2d 173 (Ark.App. 1990).

**27.** Tucker v. Stacy, 616 S.W.2d 473 (Ark. 1981); Hanners v. Sistrunk, 264 S.E.2d 224 (Ga.1980); Matter of Estate of Kasper, 887 P.2d 702 (Kan.App.1994).

**28.** Succession of Altazan, 682 So.2d 1320 (La.App.1996); Matter of Estate of Borom, 562 N.E.2d 772 (Ind.App.1990); Matter of Estate of Kasper, 887 P.2d 702 (Kan.App.1994). But in In re Will of Bonner's, 214 N.E.2d 154 (N.Y. 1966), the court held that declarations of the decedent were inadmissible to show lack of intent to revoke unless they were made in connection with the alleged revocatory act.

**29.** Matter of Estate of Shaw's, 572 P.2d 229 (Okl.1977).

**30.** Cal.Prob.Code § 6124.

**31.** Estate of Fowler v. Perry, 681 N.E.2d 739 (Ind.App.1997); Harrison v. Bird, 621 So.2d 972 (Ala.1993); Matter of Estate of Day, 753 P.2d 1296 (Kan.App.1988).

**32.** Golini v. Bolton, 482 S.E.2d 784 (S.C.App.1997).

The loss or preservation of an *unexecuted* copy of the will has no significance in determinations as to whether there was a revocation. Presumably this applies also to photocopies of an executed original, although there has been little case law as to them. Many lawyers advise testators to sign only one copy of a will in order to reduce the risk that accidental loss of an executed copy would create a presumption that the will was revoked.[33] The lawyer can keep the executed will in a safe place[34] (giving the client a conformed copy for reference), but this practice raises ethical problems because it may be construed as an attempt to give the drafter an edge in being hired to handle the testator's estate. One court expressly disapproved of attorneys' "safekeeping" wills.

> There is little justification [for this] today because most people do have safekeeping boxes, and if not, [a statute] provides for the deposit of a will with the register in probate for safekeeping during the lifetime of the testator.[35] The correct practice is that the original will should be delivered to the testator and should only be kept by the attorney upon specific unsolicited request of the client.[36]

Professor Johnston would prohibit attorneys from safekeeping wills altogether on the ground that "attempting to determine whether the drafting attorney or the testator requested the safekeeping" is too difficult.[37]

### *Lost Will Statutes*

Normally when a will cannot be found and the fact-finder (court or jury) determines that it was not revoked, a copy of the will is probated or other proof is used to establish its contents.[38] The matter may be complicated, however, by a state statute governing the proof of "lost wills." One allows lost wills to be probated if they were "destroyed subsequent to the death of the testator, or before the death of the testator if the testator's lack of knowledge of such ... destruction can be proved." This provision was held to bar the probate of a will even though the testator had destroyed it while under undue influence.

> While a lost will or destroyed will could be admitted to probate if ... a third party surreptitiously destroyed it, that same will could not be admitted to probate if the third party instead held a gun to the testator's head and instructed her to destroy it ... This would certainly seem to reflect a deficiency in the statute. Unfortunately it is a deficiency that the legislature must remedy.[39]

**33.** Beyer, *The Will Execution Ceremony,* 29 S.Tex.L.Rev. 413, 442–43 (1988).

**34.** Cal.Prob.Code §§ 701–35 deal with the liability of a lawyer who loses a will entrusted to the lawyer for safekeeping.

**35.** *See* Uniform Probate Code § 2–515; Mass.Laws ch. 191, § 10.

**36.** State v. Gulbankian, 196 N.W.2d 733 (Wis.1972).

**37.** Johnston, *An Ethical Analysis of Common Estate Planning Practices,* 45 Ohio St.L.J. 57, 133 (1984). Compare *Developments Regarding the Professional Responsibility of the Estate Planning Lawyer,* 22 Real Prop., Prob. and Trust L.J. 1, 28 (1987) (attorney safekeeping is ethical if he "makes it clear that his safekeeping is only an alternative to safekeeping by the client").

**38.** *Restatement, Third, of Property (Wills and Other Donative Transfers)* § 4.1, comm. k (1998); Cal.Prob.Code § 8223 (probate of lost wills).

**39.** Sheridan v. Harbison, 655 N.E.2d 256, 258 (Ohio App.1995).

A similar statute was held to bar probate of a will which the testator had accidentally lost.[40]

Some lost wills cannot be probated even though there is no evidence that the testator wished to revoke them, simply because the contents cannot be satisfactorily proved. For example, an alleged lost will of Howard Hughes was denied probate because a statute required proof of lost wills by two witnesses and the proponents produced only one.[41] Even in a state which does not allow partial revocation by physical act, if the obliterated words cannot be read, the property may pass intestate.[42]

Because of the problems raised by physical act revocations, one wonders why the law allows them,[43] or infers a revocation from circumstances so ambiguous as a missing will. No lawyer should advise a client to revoke a will by tearing it up since this act, even though legally effective, can be easily misinterpreted after the testator dies. If the testator keeps the will, the lawyer should warn the testator to keep it in a safe place and not to try to change the will without professional assistance. The location of the original should be noted on the copies, one of which should be retained by the drafter.[44]

## § 5.3 Revival and Dependent Relative Revocation

Destruction of a will revokes it only if the testator does it "with the intent and for the purpose of revoking" the will.[1] Even an intentional act may not revoke the will if the circumstances indicate that the testator would not want this. This may be the case when the destruction of a will is linked with an abortive attempt to make a new will. For example, when a marked-up will was found together with another unsigned will of a later date, the court probated the marked-up will under the doctrine of dependent relative revocation. "If it is clear that the cancellation and the making of the new will were parts of one scheme, and the revocation of the old will was so related to the making of the new as to be dependent upon it, then if the new will be not made, or if made is invalid, the old will, though canceled, should be given effect." The question is one of intent; here the testator "would have preferred * * * the earlier will over the only other alternative—intestacy."[2] This is a reasonable inference if the dispositive provisions of the two wills are similar[3] and both disinherited the testator's heirs who would take if neither will were probated. But if the two wills are dissimilar, the court may infer that the testator would have preferred to die intestate.[4] Since the question of the

**40.** Matter of Estate of Wheadon's, 579 P.2d 930 (Utah 1978).

**41.** Howard Hughes Medical Institute v. Gavin, 621 P.2d 489 (Nev.1980). *See also* Matter of Estate of Wilson, 875 P.2d 1154 (Okl. App.1994); In re Parker's Estate, 382 So.2d 652 (Fla.1980).

**42.** Hansel v. Head, 706 So.2d 1142 (Ala. 1997).

**43.** Roman jurists hesitated on whether to allow revocation by physical act. Gaius, *Institutes* 2.151.

**44.** Beyer, *supra* note 33, at 442–43.

§ 5.3

**1.** Uniform Probate Code § 2–507(a)(2); Calif.Prob.Code § 6120; *cf.* Ind.Code § 29–1–5–6; Ark.Stat. § 60–406.

**2.** Carter v. First United Methodist Church, 271 S.E.2d 493 (Ga.1980). *See also* Churchill v. Allessio, 719 A.2d 913 (Conn.App. 1998).

**3.** Deducing the testator's intent from the provisions of an unsigned will might seem counter to the wills act, but as we have seen in physical act revocations *any* evidence of the testator's intent is admissible when a will is missing or mutilated. Section 5.2, at note 28.

**4.** *Restatement, Third, of Property (Wills and Other Donative Transfers)* § 4.3, comm. c

testator's intent is one of fact, it may be decided by a jury, and the fact-finder's decision is accorded deference on appeals.[5]

Dependent relative revocation sometimes is applied to partial revocations. For example, a will devised 12 shares (out of 100) to the testator's mother and 7 each to his sisters and brother. The testator later crossed out the number 12 in the bequest to his mother and put "24" in its place, while reducing his sisters' shares to 3 and his brother's to 1. The court, finding that the cancellations "were made with conditional revocatory intent," admitted the original provisions to probate.[6] Since the testator wanted to double his mother's share, he certainly would have preferred her to get the original devise rather than nothing, but the decision as to the sisters and brother is more doubtful. Since he tried to reduce their shares by more than 50%, the testator might have preferred they get nothing rather than the original amount.[7]

### *Subsequent Instrument*

Dependent relative revocation has also been applied to revocation by subsequent instrument. Sometimes the expression is used incorrectly to describe a defectively executed revocation or amendment to a will, even though in this situation there is no revocation at all, not a "dependent" one.[8] The term is more properly used when a valid later will is linked with an ineffective devise. For example, a codicil revoked a bequest to the testator's son, but went on to say that if the son "over comes his laziness disinterest in property and management, sloppy and slothful living * * * then he maybe come a joint administrator of" a trust. The terms of the "trust" were too uncertain to be given effect. The court also refused to give effect to the revocation clause because it thought this would defeat the testator's intent.[9]

Courts have also applied dependent relative revocation when a devise in the revoking will was invalid under the Rule against Perpetuities[10] or a mortmain statute.[11]

(1998); Estate of DeWald v. Whittenburg, 925 P.2d 903 (Okl.App.1996); Kroll v. Nehmer, 705 A.2d 716, 723 (Md.1998). In Matter of Estate of Ausley, 818 P.2d 1226 (Okl.1991) the beneficiaries of the old and new will were the same but their shares were different. The majority rejected dependent relative revocation but a dissent thought that "this evidence strongly indicates .. the testator would have preferred the cancelled will over no will."

**5.** Churchill v. Allessio, 719 A.2d 913 (Conn.App.1998); Estate of Lyles, 615 So.2d 1186, 1190 (Miss.1993) (issue on review was whether the trial judge "was clearly and manifestly wrong").

**6.** Estate of Uhl, 81 Cal.Rptr. 436 (App. 1969). The changes might have been effective if the testator had initialed them, since California allows holographic wills. On the other hand, some courts might have ignored the changes as a partial revocation by physical act. See Section 5.2, at note 14.

**7.** *Cf. Restatement, Third, of Property (Wills and Other Donative Transfers)* § 4.3, illus. 7 (1998).

**8.** Kirkeby v. Covenant House, 970 P.2d 241, 243 (Or.App.1998).

**9.** In re Estate of Casselman, 364 N.W.2d 27 (Neb.1985).*See also* Anderson v. Griggs, 402 So.2d 904 (Ala.1981) (lost will, where witness recalled only clause of revocation, does not revoke prior will). *But see* Estate of Lopes, 199 Cal.Rptr. 425 (App.1984) (contrary result on similar facts).

**10.** In re Bernard's Settlement, [1916] 1 Ch. 552; In re Jones' Estate, 352 So.2d 1182 (Fla.App.1977); *Restatement, Third, of Property (Wills and Other Donative Transfers)* § 4.3, illus. 17 (1998).

**11.** Linkins v. Protestant Episcopal Cathedral Foundation, 187 F.2d 357 (D.C.Cir.1950); In re Kaufman's Estate, 155 P.2d 831 (Cal. 1945); *Restatement, Third, of Property (Wills and Other Donative Transfers)* § 4.3, illus, 14 (1998). *Contra,* Crosby v. Alton Ochsner Medical Foundation, 276 So.2d 661 (Miss.1973). As to mortmain statutes see Section 3.10, note 1 et seq.

Dependent relative revocation has also been applied when a testator revoked a devise under the supposition that the devisee was dead. Other claims that the revocation was produced by a mistake of fact have been rejected,[12] but would be allowed under the third Restatement of Property "if the false belief was recited in the terms of the revoking instrument or is established by clear and convincing evidence."[13]

### *Revival*

When a testator executes two wills and then revokes the second, is the first one revived or does the testator die intestate? The solution to this question is typically governed by a statute, in contrast to dependent relative revocation, which is a common law doctrine.[14] For example, a will left the residuary estate to one child. A subsequent will left it to three children equally. The testator later destroyed the second will. The court held that it did not matter whether by so doing she intended to revive her prior will, because a statute, derived from the English Wills Act of 1837, provided that a "revoked will ... shall not be revived except by reexecution of by a duly executed codicil expressing an intention to revive it."

> The formalities of the statute were neither observed nor attempted. We appreciate that our holding results in partial intestacy and that the resulting distribution ... is the very distribution provided by the destroyed codicil. John [the child favored in the first will] argues that that cannot have been his mother's intent ... We do not reach that question.[15]

In a similar case another court invoked dependent relative revocation and probated the destroyed will when the testator mistakenly thought she was reviving her earlier will.[16] But this result makes sense only if the two wills are substantially similar.

The Uniform Probate Code allows the testator's intent to revive an earlier will to be given effect. Revocation of a second will by physical act revives the first if "it is evident from the circumstances of the revocation of the subsequent will or from testator's contemporary or subsequent declarations that the testator intended" this.[17] Presumably even testimony by interested witnesses would be admissible, *i.e.,* the beneficiaries of the first will could testify that the testator told them she wished to revive it.[18] A Wisconsin

**12.** Palmer, *Dependent Relative Revocation and Its Relation to Relief for Mistake*, 69 Mich. L.Rev. 989, 991 (1971). As to mistake generally see Section 6.1, at note 52 et seq.

**13.** *Restatement, Third, of Property (Wills and Other Donative Transfers)* § 4.3, comm. i (1998). This applies only to "objective" facts, not to a belief about the devisee's affection for the testator.

**14.** Dependent relative revocation is not mentioned in the text of the Uniform Probate Code, but a comment to § 2–507 says "each court is free to apply its own doctrine of dependent relative revocation."

**15.** Matter of Estate of Lagreca, 687 A.2d 783, 785 (N.J.Super.App.Div.1997). *See also* Matter of Estate of Greenwald, 584 N.W.2d 294 (Iowa 1998); Parker v. Mobley, 577 S.W.2d 583 (Ark.1979).

**16.** In re Alburn's Estate, 118 N.W.2d 919 (Wis.1963). *See also Restatement, Third, of Property (Wills and Other Donative Transfers)* § 4.3, comm. b (1988) (approves this result, but argues that the intent to revive should be given effect directly).

**17.** Uniform Probate Code § 2–509(a). *See also* Calif.Prob.Code § 6123(a). When a will is revoked is by a subsequent instrument, any intent to revive an earlier will must be manifested by the instrument. Uniform Probate Code § 2–509(c).

**18.** *Cf.* Bailey v. Kennedy, 425 P.2d 304 (Colo.1967) (adopting an anti-revival rule to avoid this result).

statute is similar to the UPC but it requires "clear and convincing" evidence of the intent to revive, as does the third Restatement of Property.[19]

The Code presumes against an intent to revive; thus if there is *no* evidence as to intent, the testator dies intestate.[20] However, the presumption is reversed when the second instrument only partially revoked the first. Thus if a codicil alters a will and then is destroyed, the provisions of the original will which the codicil had revised are reinstated, unless there is evidence that the testator did not so intend.[21]

Courts may infer an intent to revive from a codicil which simply refers to a will which the testator had previously revoked. Thus a codicil "to my Will executed by me on July 16, 1948" was held to revive it.[22] But when the codicil was executed soon after the will, one might infer that the testator subsequently destroyed the will but forgot about the codicil and so neither should be probated.[23]

Revival and dependent relative revocation are sometimes confused, not only by law students. For example, a finding that a testator's destruction of a will "was a revocation conditional upon his making a new will" which the testator died before executing, was reversed, the supreme court holding that the state's anti-revival statute precluded application of dependent relative revocation. A concurring opinion points out that this reasoning was fallacious; the anti-revival statute "only comes into effect if there has been a revocation. It is to determine precisely that question, *i.e.,* whether there has been a revocation" that the doctrine of dependent relative revocation is applied.[24] Nevertheless, the court probably reached the correct result; since the testator had destroyed his will even before the new one was prepared and the new will was to be "quite a bit different" from the old, he probably intended an unconditional revocation.

## § 5.4 Divorce

Roman law at one time provided that all wills were automatically revoked after ten years.[1] Anglo–American law has no such rule, but a change of circumstances after a will is executed may lead to doubts whether the will continues to reflect the testator's wishes. The Uniform Probate Code provides that a divorce or annulment of a marriage revokes any disposition of property "made by a divorced individual to his [or her] former spouse."[2] Although this

**19.** Wis.Stat. § 853.11(6); *Restatement, Third, of Property (Wills and Other Donative Transfers)* § 4.2, comm. i (1998). See also White v. Wilbanks, 393 S.E.2d 182 (S.C.1990).

**20.** *See also* May v. Estate of McCormick, 769 P.2d 395 (Wyo.1989) (intestacy where there is no evidence of an intent to revive).

**21.** Uniform Probate Code § 2–509(b). *See also* Fla.Stat. § 732.508(2); Wis.Stat. § 853.11; Matter of Hering's Estate, 166 Cal.Rptr. 298 (App.1980). *Contra,* Will of Lake, 560 N.Y.S.2d 966 (Surr.1990).

**22.** In re Barrett's Estate, 260 N.E.2d 107 (Ill.App.1970). *See also* In re Estate of Stormont, 517 N.E.2d 259 (Ohio App.1986).

**23.** *Cf.* In re Estate of Smith, 378 N.W.2d 555 (Mich.App.1985) (dissenting opinion); *Restatement, Third, of Property (Wills and Other Donative Transfers)* § 4.1, comm. n (1998).

**24.** Larrick v. Larrick, 607 S.W.2d 92, 96 (Ark.App.1980). *See also* Matter of Estate of Greenwald, 584 N.W.2d 294 (Iowa 1998).

§ 5.4

**1.** R. Villers, *Rome et le Droit Privé* 472 (1977).

**2.** Uniform Probate Code § 2–804(b). It also revokes any nomination of the former spouse to serve as a fiduciary, such as executor or trustee. The related problem of the effect of a marriage or birth of children on a prior will are discussed at Sections 3.5 and 3.6.

was not the rule at common law,[3] many states today have similar statutes. In a few states a divorce revokes the whole will,[4] but more commonly only the provisions relating to the former spouse are affected.[5]

Courts have applied such statutes even when the devisee was not married to the testator when the will was executed.[6] The fact that the testator cohabited with the ex-spouse after the divorce does not matter.[7] Under the Uniform Probate Code, extrinsic evidence of a contrary intent is generally irrelevant,[8] but the provisions for the spouse are revived if the testator remarries the former spouse.[9]

Divorce only revokes a devise to the *testator's* spouse. Devises to an in-law who later divorced a relative of the testator are not affected. Thus when property was devised to a nephew and "his wife Shirley," Shirley took even though she had divorced the nephew after the will was executed. "The designation of Shirley as [the nephew's] wife is merely descriptive and Shirley was an intended beneficiary ... regardless of her marital status."[10] However, if Shirley had not been named in the will, many courts would have construed the devise to refer to a "wife" of the nephew whom he married after divorcing Shirley.[11]

The Uniform Probate Code revokes also devises to "a relative of the divorced individual's former spouse" who is not also related to the testator. Statutes without such provision have been construed to leave devises to the testator's step-children or former in-laws in effect despite a later divorce between the testator and the spouse,[12] but the Restatement of Property calls for construing all statutes so as to reach the same result as the revised UPC.[13]

**3.** Rasco v. Estate of Rasco, 501 So.2d 421 (Miss.1987) (provisions in a will for wife not revoked by later divorce); *cf.* Estate of Reap v. Malloy, 727 A.2d 326 (D.C.1999) (divorce revokes will only when accompanied by property settlement).

**4.** Winebrenner v. Dorten, 825 S.W.2d 836 (Ky.1991); In re Crohn's Estate, 494 P.2d 258 (Or.App.1972); Estate of Liles, 435 A.2d 379 (D.C.App.1981).

**5.** Matter of Seymour's Estate, 600 P.2d 274 (N.M.1979); Roeske v. First Nat. Bank, 413 N.E.2d 476 (Ill.App.1980).

**6.** In re Estate of Forrest, 706 N.E.2d 1043 (Ill.App.1999); In re Marriage of Duke, 549 N.E.2d 1096 (Ind.App.1990); Estate of Reeves, 284 Cal.Rptr. 650 (App.1991). *Contra,* In re Estate of Carroll, 749 P.2d 571 (Okl.App.1987).

**7.** Estate of Reeves, 284 Cal.Rptr. 650 (App.1991); Pekol v. Estate of Pekol, 499 N.E.2d 88 (Ill.App.1986).

**8.** Uniform Probate Code § 2–804(b) allows for a contrary express provision in the will or "a court order, or a contract relating to the division of the marital estate made between the divorced individuals."

**9.** Uniform Probate Code § 2–804(e). *See also* N.Y.EPTL § 5–1.4; Calif.Prob.Code § 6122(b).

**10.** Estate of Kelly v. Stambaugh, 724 N.E.2d 1285, 1287 (Ill.App.2000). *See also* First Interstate Bank of Washington v. Lindberg, 746 P.2d 333 (Wash.App.1987); In re Estate of McGlone, 436 So.2d 441 (Fla.App.1983). *But see* Grady v. Grady, 395 So.2d 643 (Fla.App. 1981). Compare devises to a named "spouse" who is not legally married. Section 2.11, note 2.

**11.** Matter of Trust of Killian, 459 N.W.2d 497 (Iowa 1990); Wells Fargo Bank v. Marshall, 24 Cal.Rptr.2d 507 (App.1993). *But cf.* In re Erny's Trust, 202 A.2d 30 (Pa.1964) (trust for settlor's "wife" refers to his present wife, not the woman he later married).

**12.** Bloom v. Selfon, 555 A.2d 75 (Pa.1989) (substitute devise to testator's ex-husband's uncle); Porter v. Porter, 286 N.W.2d 649 (Iowa 1979) (ex-wife's son); In re Estate of Kerr, 520 N.W.2d 512 (Minn.App.1994). Other courts have avoided this result on various theories. Estate of Hermon, 46 Cal.Rptr.2d 577 (App. 1995); Estate of Liles, 435 A.2d 379 (D.C.App. 1981).

**13.** *Restatement, Third, of Property (Wills and Other Donative Transfers)* § 4.1, illus. 12 (1998).

Under the Code the disqualified spouse and/or relatives are deemed to have disclaimed the devise.[14]

A separation that does not terminate the status of husband and wife does not revoke a devise to the spouse,[15] but a separation agreement may by its terms bar a spouse from claiming under the other spouse's will. This depends on how the agreement is drafted and construed. An agreement releasing "all claims or rights * * * by reason of the marriage between the parties with respect to any property" belonging to each other was held not to preclude the wife from taking under a will which the husband had executed ten years before. The court said that a separation agreement, in order to revoke a prior devise must "employ language which clearly and unequivocally manifests" such an intent.[16] The Uniform Probate Code, however, presumes that "a waiver of 'all rights' or equivalent language" in the other spouse's property in a settlement entered into "after or in anticipation of separation" is a renunciation of provisions of a prior will of the other spouse.[17]

The Uniform Probate Code and many other statutes provide that apart from divorce "no change in circumstances * * * revokes a will."[18] We shall later discuss the effect of the death of a devisee or the transfer of property after a will is executed.[19]

## § 5.5 Gifts and Will Substitutes

### *Power to Revoke Gifts*

A testator can revoke a will even though it contains no express power to revoke. Inter-vivos gifts, on the other hand, are irrevocable unless they were made in expectation of imminent death.[1] This rule comes from Roman law which allowed gifts "causa mortis" to be revoked because they were so much like wills.[2] According to the Restatement of Property, gifts made "in apprehension of immediate death" are presumed to be revocable.[3]

A donor who repents of a gift which is not causa mortis may be able to have it set aside on grounds that the donor lacked capacity, or was subject to undue influence, or fraud; these possibilities will be discussed later.[4] Also,

**14.** Uniform Probate Code § 2–804(d). As to disclaimer see Section 2.8.

**15.** Uniform Probate Code § 2–804(a)(1); Calif.Prob.Code § 6122(d). *But cf.* Estate of Lahey, 91 Cal.Rptr.2d 30 (App.1999) (legal separation terminates spouse's right to inherit on intestacy).

**16.** Matter of Estate of Maruccia's, 429 N.E.2d 751 (N.Y.1981).

**17.** Uniform Probate Code § 2–213(d). *See also* Calif.Prob.Code § 145; Matter of Estate of Highgate, 348 N.W.2d 31 (Mich.App.1984).

**18.** Uniform Prob.Code § 2–804(f). *See also* Mo.Stat. § 474.420; Calif.Prob.Code § 6122(e); Ind.Code § 29–1–5–8.

**19.** See Sections 8.1 and 8.3.

**§ 5.5**

**1.** Welton v. Gallagher, 630 P.2d 1077 (Haw.App.1981) (bonds given to defendant cannot be recovered where gift was not in contemplation of death); GME, Inc. v. Carter, 817 P.2d 183 (Idaho 1991); *Restatement (Second) of Contracts* § 332(1) (1981) (gratuitous assignment is irrevocable if proper formalities observed).

**2.** Justinian, *Institutes* 2.7.1–2. Gifts which were made "without any thought of death" could not be revoked unless the donee proved to be "ungrateful" in specified ways. Some modern European codes also allow gifts to be revoked for ungrateful conduct by the donee. French Code Civil art. 955; German Civil Code art. 530. *See also* note 6, infra.

**3.** However, if the donor survives and fails to revoke within a reasonable time thereafter, the right to revoke lapses. Also the circumstances, *e.g.* a pattern of making irrevocable gifts to save taxes, may show an intent that the gift be irrevocable. *Restatement, Second, Property, Donative Transfers* § 31.3 (1990). *Cf.* Cal. Prob.Code § 5704.

**4.** As to incapacity see Section 7.1. As to undue influence see Section 7.3. As to fraud see Section 6.1, at note 58.

gifts require donative intent, and statements indicating lack of such intent emanating from a time after the alleged gift, may serve to show no gift ever occurred. Thus a friend's claim that the decedent had given her a watch was rejected because he had "considered taking the watch with him to the nursing home, long after he purportedly gave it to" the claimant, and this was inconsistent with any donative intent.[5]

Courts also allow gifts to be revoked on the basis of an unsatisfied condition.[6] Such a condition is implied for gifts connected with a contemplated marriage. The Restatement of Property allows a donor to recover an engagement ring if the donee breaks the engagement, or the donor does so for a justified reason.[7] Many courts allow the donor to recover gifts made in contemplation of marriage regardless of which party refused to go through with the marriage and the reason. As one court recently said:

> It is difficult to see how the public policies involving divorce and the division of marital property are best served by no-fault principles, but broken engagements should require a fault-based determination as to the ownership of the engagement ring.[8]

Most of the cases involve engagement rings, but other forms of property may be recovered if they were given in contemplation of a marriage which never took place.[9] Wedding presents may be recoverable by the donors.[10] Conditions other than marriage are also enforced.[11] Parents sometimes give property to a child on the understanding that the donee will support and care for them. If the child fails to do this, the donor can get the property back even if the deed of gift was not expressly conditional.[12]

### *Trusts*

In most jurisdictions living trusts cannot be revoked unless the trust instrument reserves a power to revoke. The Restatement of Trusts so states.[13] Some state statutes, on the other hand, say that trusts are revocable unless they otherwise provide.[14] Since many trusts are created with tax considerations in mind, and these are radically different for revocable and irrevocable

**5.** In re Estate of Wittmond, 732 N.E.2d 659, 666 (Ill.App.2000).

**6.** In Louisiana gifts can also be revoked for "ingratitude" by the donee, but this is narrowly defined, *e.g.* "cruel treatment, crimes or grievous injuries." La.Civ.Code art. 1559–60.

**7.** *Restatement, Second, Property, Donative Transfers* § 31.2, illus. 5–8 (1990)

**8.** Heiman v. Parrish, 942 P.2d 631, 638 (Kan.1997). *See also* Fierro v. Hoel, 465 N.W.2d 669 (Iowa App.1990); Patterson v. Blanton, 672 N.E.2d 208 (Ohio App.1996); Vigil v. Haber, 888 P.2d 455 (N.M.1994).

**9.** Boydstun v. Loveless, 890 P.2d 267 (Colo.App.1995) (land put in joint tenancy with "wife").

**10.** *Restatement (Third) of Property (Wills and Other Donative Transfers)* § 6.2, comm. o (Prel.Dft. 2000).

**11.** Wilkin v. Wilkin, 688 N.E.2d 27 (Ohio App.1996) (money given for a course which the donee never took). *See also* Section 4.6, note 77.

**12.** Trout v. Parker, 595 N.E.2d 1015 (Ohio App.1991); Almeida v. Almeida, 669 P.2d 174 (Haw.App.1983); Vincent v. Torrey, 417 N.E.2d 41 (Mass.App.1981); *Restatement (Second) of Contracts* § 372, illus. 3 (1981).

**13.** *Restatement, Second, Trusts* § 330 (1959). *See also* Goytizolo v. Moore, 604 A.2d 362 (Conn.App.1992); Nicosia v. Turzyn, 624 P.2d 499 (Nev.1981). Revocation with the consent of all the beneficiaries is discussed in Section 9.6, at note 28 et seq. Reformation may allow a power of revocation which was omitted by mistake to be enforced. Reformation is discussed at Section 6.3, at note 17 et seq.

**14.** Cal.Prob.Code § 15400; Uniform Trust Code § 602 (applicable only to instruments executed after the effective date of the Code).

trusts[15], most trust instruments make clear whether or not the trust was intended to be revocable.[16]

Many trusts are created by two or more settlors, *e.g.* a husband and wife. This gives rise to the question whether one of the settlors can revoke. In California "if a trust is created by more than one settlor, each settlor may revoke the trust as to the portion of the trust contributed by that settlor."[17] However, a trust which provided that during the life of the settlors it could be revoked "by the Settlors" was held to imply that the surviving settlor could not revoke it.[18] The Uniform Trust Code suggests that when the revocation of a trust by less than all the settlors "breaches an implied agreement not to revoke the trust," persons harmed thereby can sue for breach of contract.[19]

Bank account or Totten trusts[20] are presumed to be revocable. The terms of such trusts are typically so sketchy that it is reasonable to infer that a power to revoke was intended even if none was expressed.[21]

Courts require a settlor who wishes to revoke a trust to comply with any method of revocation specified in the trust instrument. For example, a settlor reserved the right to alter a trust "by an instrument in writing signed by her and delivered during [her] life to the Trustees." After she died an unsigned slip of paper found clipped to the trust instrument was held ineffective to change the beneficiary. "The term 'instrument in writing' suggests ... substantially more than an unsigned scrap of paper." Moreover the settlor had not delivered the writing to her co-trustee.[22] A court construed another trust which allowed changes by a signed writing "delivered to the Trustee" to require delivery during the settlor's lifetime, and thus an amendment delivered the day after the settlor died was invalid.[23] In another case, a person executed a will and a trust at the same time. The latter provided that it could be revoked by an instrument in writing. When the person died, neither the will nor the trust instrument could be found. The court held that the will was revoked pursuant to the presumption which arises when an executed will is missing[24] but not the trust, since no there was no signed writing showing an intent to revoke.[25] However, under the Uniform Trust Code, "substantial

**15.** See Section 15.2, note 36.

**16.** In Ike v. Doolittle, 70 Cal.Rptr.2d 887, 910 (App.1998), the court found that a trust which was stated to be revocable was actually intended to be irrevocable in order to reduce taxes, and reformed the trust accordingly. As to reformation in order to accomplish a better tax result see Section 6.1, note 41.

**17.** Cal.Prob.Code § 15401(b); cf. Unif. Trust Code § 602(b). As to community property, either spouse can revoke, but the property withdrawn from the trust remains community property. Cal.Fam.Code § 761.

**18.** L'Argent v. Barnett Bank, N.A., 730 So.2d 395 (Fla.App.1999). *But see* Perrenoud v. Harman, 8 P.3d 293 (Utah App.2000) (power to revoke passes to surviving settlor).

**19.** Unif.Trust Code § 602, comment. Compare the many claims that joint wills were made pursuant to an agreement not to revoke them. Section 4.9, at note 2.

**20.** See Section 4.6, at note 39 et seq.

**21.** *Restatement (Third) of Trusts* § 26 (1996); Terner v. Rand, 417 So.2d 303 (Fla. App.1982); Cal. Prob. Code § 5301(c). *But see* Underwood v. Bank of Huntsville, 494 So.2d 619 (Ala.1986) (deposit "as custodian" creates an irrevocable trust). Payable on death accounts are also revocable. Uniform Prob.Code § 6–213.

**22.** Northwestern University v. McLoraine, 438 N.E.2d 1369 (Ill.App.1982). *See also Restatement, Second, Trusts* § 330, comm. j (1959); In re Estate of Tosh, 920 P.2d 1230 (Wash.App.1996).

**23.** Lourdes College v. Bishop, 703 N.E.2d 362 (Ohio Com.Pl.1997).

**24.** See Section 5.2, note 21 et seq.

**25.** Matter of Estate of Pilafas, 836 P.2d 420 (Ariz.App.1992).

compliance" with the prescribed method of revocation is sufficient,[26] and some case law agrees.[27]

If no method is specified in the instrument, a power to revoke "can be exercised in any manner which sufficiently manifests the intention of the settlor."[28] A letter directing the trustee to deliver the trust assets to another has been held to effectively revoke a trust even though it did not use the word.[29] Oral revocations have occasionally been recognized[30], but California requires a writing signed by the settlor and delivered to the trustee.[31]

### *Insurance*

Most modern policies expressly give the insured, who is usually the owner of the policy, the right to change the beneficiary.[32] The absence of such a provision in a policy may show an intention that there is no such right.[33] The right to designate the beneficiary is an incident of ownership of the policy, so if an insured assigns the ownership of the policy, the insured can no longer change the beneficiary but the new owner can.[34] However, if the assignment was simply given as security for a loan, the beneficiaries designated by the insured are entitled to any surplus after the loan is paid.[35]

Policies typically require that written notice be received by the insurer when the beneficiary is changed. This protects the company from liability for paying the wrong person.[36] "Substantial compliance" with this requirement is enough. For example, when an insured signed a form to change the beneficiary, but died suddenly before delivering the form, the change was held effective. "When an insured has done everything within his power to effectuate a change of beneficiary, equity will not require exact compliance with all stated conditions" of the policy. Failure to deliver the form was not significant under the circumstances.[37] On the other hand, an insured who requested forms to change the beneficiary, but died 6 months later without ever filling them out, was held not to have substantially complied with the policy, and so the original beneficiary received the proceeds.[38]

**26.** Uniform Trust Code § 602(c)(1).

**27.** Hauseman v. Koski, 857 P.2d 715 (Mont.1993) (signed and recorded instrument revoked a trust even though not mailed to the co-trustees until after the settlor died); Matter of Trust Estate of Doang, 953 P.2d 959 (Haw. App.1998) (informal letter signed by settlor satisfied requirement of "another instrument" to amend trust).

**28.** *Restatement, Second, Trusts* § 330, comm. i (1959).

**29.** Estate of Noell v. Norwest Bank Wyo., N.A., 960 P.2d 499 (Wyo.1998).

**30.** Polz v. Tyree, 705 P.2d 1229 (Wash. App.1985); Gabel v. Manetto, 427 A.2d 71 (N.J.Super.App.Div.1981); Barnette v. McNulty, 516 P.2d 583 (Ariz.App.1973).

**31.** Cal.Prob.Code § 15401(a)(2); *cf.* Unif. Trust Code § 602(c)(B) (any method manifesting clear and convincing evidence of intent).

**32.** *E.g.*, Graham v. Farmers New World Life Ins. Co., 841 P.2d 1165 (Okl.App.1992).

**33.** *Restatement (Second) of Contracts* § 311, comm. c (1981).

**34.** American Western Life Ins. Co. v. Hooker, 622 P.2d 775 (Utah 1980).

**35.** Prudential Ins. Co. of America v. Glass, 959 P.2d 586 (Okl.1998).

**36.** Mass.G.L. c. 175, § 123 requires in addition that a change of beneficiary form be "witnessed by a disinterested person."

**37.** Connecticut Gen. Life Ins. Co. v. Gulley, 668 F.2d 325 (7th Cir.1982). *See also* Bergen v. Travelers Ins. Co., 776 P.2d 659 (Utah App.1989); In re Estate of Knickerbocker, 912 P.2d 969 (Utah 1996); Strauss v. Teachers Ins. & Annuity Ass'n, 639 N.E.2d 1106 (Mass.App. 1994).

**38.** Eschler v. Eschler, 849 P.2d 196 (Mont. 1993). *See also* Webber v. Olsen, 971 P.2d 448 (Or.App.1998); Penn Mutual Life Ins. Co. v. Abramson, 530 A.2d 1202 (D.C.App.1987) (oral expressions of intent to change the beneficiary insufficient).

Insurers sometimes interplead competing claimants to the proceeds of a policy, and this has been held to constitute a "waiver" by the insurer of strict compliance with policy terms,[39] but not always.[40]

Similar rules have been applied to the designation of beneficiaries under pension plans. Here the issue is complicated by the claim that ERISA, the federal statute which governs most pensions, supersedes state law. This claim was recently rejected by one court on the ground that "the doctrine of substantial compliance ... affects only the ultimate ownership of the benefits" and its "connection with ERISA is too tenuous ... to trigger preemption."[41]

### *Joint Tenancy: Land*

A person who puts land into joint tenancy is not usually allowed to get it back. For example, when a husband bought a residence and took title in joint tenancy with his wife, she was awarded a half interest in the house when they later divorced. "When property is taken in joint tenancy by husband and wife, that property is marital property even when the purchase money is supplied by one spouse, unless the presumption that a gift was intended is overcome * * * by clear, convincing, and unmistakable evidence."[42] Courts are skeptical of claims that a person who put title in joint form had no intent to make a gift thereby.[43] In California whenever a spouse takes title to property in joint form with the other spouse, the property belongs to the community unless there is a written agreement or statement in the deed showing a contrary intent.[44]

A joint tenant can destroy the right of survivorship and convert the title into a tenancy in common under which each tenant's share passes to his or her estate at death.[45] Thus when a father put land into joint tenancy with his son, the latter was held to have an "irrevocably accrued right" only as to half the land so long as the father was alive because of the father's right to sever the joint tenancy.[46]

Historically a joint tenant had to convey his or her interest to a third party in order to effectuate such a "severance," but modern courts have eliminated this requirement. Thus a joint tenant's deed purporting to convey

**39.** Burkett v. Mott, 733 P.2d 673 (Ariz. App.1986); Kane v. Union Mut. Life Ins. Co., 445 N.Y.S.2d 549 (A.D.1981); State Employees' Retirement System v. Taylor, 476 N.E.2d 749 (Ill.App.1985).

**40.** McCarthy v. Aetna Life Ins. Co., 704 N.E.2d 557, 561 (N.Y.1998); Webber v. Olsen, 971 P.2d 448 (Or.App.1998) (intent to change beneficiary ineffective for lack of substantial compliance with policy requirements even though insurer interpleaded claimants).

**41.** BankAmerica Pension Plan v. McMath, 206 F.3d 821, 830 (9th Cir.2000).

**42.** In re Marriage of Wingader, 419 N.E.2d 611, 612 (Ill.App.1981). *See also* Helton v. Helton, 683 N.E.2d 1157 (Ohio App.1996); Graham v. Graham, 760 P.2d 772 (Nev.1988). *But see* Hughes v. Hughes, 678 P.2d 702 (N.M. 1984).

**43.** Gross v. Gross, 781 P.2d 284 (Mont. 1989). *See also* Schulz v. Miller, 837 P.2d 71 (Wyo.1992) (attempt to reform deed to eliminate joint tenant's name fails); Cunningham v. Hastings, 556 N.E.2d 12 (Ind.App.1990) (when land in joint tenancy sold on partition, person who paid for it is not entitled to be reimbursed for the price paid). However, the person who paid for the land may be able to impose a resulting trust on a joint tenant who did not if donative intent can be disproved. See Section 6.4, at note 48 et seq.

**44.** Cal.Fam.Code § 2581. This is stronger than the general presumption that all property acquired during the marriage is community. Section 3.8, note 43.

**45.** *Restatement, Second, Property, Donative Transfers* § 31.1, illus. 16 (1990); Estate of Zoglauer, 593 N.E.2d 93 (Ill.App.1992); Crowther v. Mower, 876 P.2d 876 (Utah App. 1994).

**46.** In re Estate of Antonopoulos, 993 P.2d 637, 644 (Kan.1999).

land from herself as grantor to herself as grantee "to dissolve any and all rights of survivorship" was held effective after her death against a claim by the other joint tenant. The court said that the traditional requirement of conveyance to a third person in order to sever a joint tenancy was based on livery of seisin, and "just as livery of seisin has become obsolete, so should the ancient vestiges of that ceremony give way to modern conveyancing realities."[47] In California a severance deed must be recorded to be effective. This requirement is designed to obviate the risk that a tenant might execute such a deed, keep it secret, and then destroy it if he turned out to be the surviving joint tenant.[48]

When both joint tenants join in selling land, does the right of survivorship attach to the proceeds or are they held as tenants in common? The cases on this issue are divided, except in generally saying that the result turns on what the parties intended, although this is often hard to ascertain.[49]

Some states do not allow one spouse to sever when two spouses hold jointly; they hold as "tenants by the entirety" and "being considered as one person in law * * * neither the husband nor the wife can dispose of any part without the assent of the other but the whole must remain to the other."[50] This form of tenancy can exist only between spouses; a deed purporting to create a "tenancy by the entirety" creates only an ordinary joint tenancy if the parties are not legally married.[51] Some states no longer recognize tenancy by the entirety. Thus one court upheld a wife's severance of a joint tenancy with her husband on the ground that tenancy by the entirety was "a peculiar and anomalous estate" which had been abolished by a statute "setting out and defining creation of other interests in detail" without mentioning tenancy by the entireties.[52]

A joint tenant's right to sever may be barred by contract[53] or by the terms of the document which created the joint tenancy. For example, when land was devised to children "as joint tenants and to the survivor of them," a conveyance by one child did not bar her surviving siblings from succeeding to the land when she died.[54]

**47.** Minonk State Bank v. Grassman, 447 N.E.2d 822 (Ill.1983). *See also* Hendrickson v. Minneapolis Federal Savings & Loan Ass'n, 161 N.W.2d 688 (Minn.1968); Riddle v. Harmon, 162 Cal.Rptr. 530 (App.1980); Helmholz, *Realism and Formalism in the Severance of Joint Tenancies*, 77 Neb.L.Rev. 1, 10–13 (1997).

**48.** Cal.Civ.Code § 683.2; In re Estate of England, 284 Cal.Rptr. 361 (App.1991) (unrecorded severance deed ineffective); Fetters, *An Invitation to Commit Fraud: Secret Destruction of Joint Tenant Survivorship Rights*, 55 Ford. L.Rev. 173 (1986).

**49.** Helmholz, *supra* note 47, at 15–20.

**50.** 2 W. Blackstone, *Commentaries* *182 (1765). In Shwachman v. Meagher, 699 N.E.2d 16 (Mass.App.1998), the court cited and followed Blackstone in holding that a deed by the wife alone was void. It noted that the peculiar features of tenancy by the entirety had been abolished by statute, but the statute did not apply to existing tenancies.

**51.** Riccelli v. Forcinito, 595 A.2d 1322 (Pa.Super.1991).

**52.** Schimke v. Karlstad, 208 N.W.2d 710 (S.D.1973).

**53.** Alexander v. Snell, 424 N.E.2d 262 (Mass.App.1981). *But see* Register v. Coleman, 633 P.2d 418 (Ariz.1981) (enforcement of oral agreement barred by Statute of Frauds); Smolen for Smolen v. Smolen, 956 P.2d 128 (Nev. 1998) (provision in divorce decree that land "remain in joint tenancy" did not bar severance by one party).

**54.** Williams v. Studstill, 306 S.E.2d 633 (Ga.1983). *See also* Albro v. Allen, 454 N.W.2d 85 (Mich.1990) (no severance possible when deed expressly refers to right of survivorship).

### *Joint Tenancy: Personal Property*

Courts are more likely to regard joint tenancy in personal property as a will substitute rather than an irrevocable gift to joint tenant(s) who did not contribute to acquisition of the property. For example, a woman bought certificates of deposit in the names of herself and her husband jointly. When her husband later changed the CDs into his own name, she sued him for conversion and prevailed. Although the agreement under which the CDs were issued allowed either party to withdraw the funds, this only discharged the bank from liability. "A deposit by one spouse into an account in the names of both, standing alone, does not constitute a gift to the other. The depositor is still deemed to be the owner of the funds" unless there is "evidence of donative intent."[55] In California, a joint account is presumed to be community property, but either spouse can show that the funds in it came from his or her separate property.[56] The Uniform Probate Code provides that joint accounts belong to the party who contributed the funds while the parties are alive "unless there is clear and convincing evidence of a different intent."[57] This means that the contributing party while still alive can withdraw the funds or change the form of the account,[58] but the latter requires a signed written notice "received by the financial institution during the party's lifetime."[59] Many banks impose similar rules, which are like the standard clauses in insurance policies for change of beneficiary, so perhaps case law will develop a doctrine of "substantial compliance" in this area too.[60]

As to other forms of joint tenancy in personal property the rules are unclear. One court has said that a brokerage account was like a bank account,[61] but the common claim that a joint bank account was created simply for convenience in making deposits and withdrawals without donative intent seems less persuasive for other types of property.[62] The Uniform Probate Code has different rules for securities than for accounts, but they are unclear on this issue.[63]

### *Divorce*

In most states provisions in a will in favor of the testator's spouse are revoked if they later divorce.[64] The assumption as to intent which underlies

**55.** Myers v. Myers, 314 S.E.2d 809 (N.C.App.1984). *See also* In re Estate of Mayer, 664 N.E.2d 583 (Ohio App.1995); Vitacco v. Eckberg, 648 N.E.2d 1010 (Ill.App.1995). *But see* Estate of Vogel, 684 N.E.2d 1035 (Ill.App. 1997) (contributions are irrelevant where terms of agreement allows either party to withdraw funds).

**56.** Cal.Prob.Code § 5305(b) (expressly trumping Family Code § 2581). Under Uniform Probate Code § 6–211(b) the contributions of spouses to a joint account are presumed to be equal.

**57.** Uniform Probate Code § 6–211(b). *See also* In re Thompson's Estate, 423 N.E.2d 90 (Ohio 1981); Kinney v. Ewing, 492 P.2d 636 (N.M.1972).

**58.** Campbell v. Black, 844 P.2d 759 (Kan. App.1993).

**59.** Uniform Probate Code § 6–213. For a criticism of this requirement, see McGovern, *Nonprobate Transfers under the Revised Uniform Probate Code*, 55 Alb.L.Rev. 1329, 1335 (1992).

**60.** Cf. In re Estate of Anderson's, 217 N.E.2d 444 (Ill.App.1966) (will ineffective to change terms of account).

**61.** Parker v. Kokot, 793 P.2d 195, 200 (Idaho 1990).

**62.** In In re Marriage of Orlando, 577 N.E.2d 1334 (Ill.App.1991), a wife's putting stock into joint tenancy was held to create a presumption of a gift which could be rebutted only by clear proof. *See also* Schmanski v. Schmanski, 984 P.2d 752 (Nev.1999) (separate property put into joint brokerage account becomes community, giving W a share upon divorce).

**63.** McGovern, *supra* note 59, at 1349. Cal. Prob.Code § 5305 applies only to accounts.

**64.** See Section 5.4.

this rule seems to apply also to will substitutes like insurance, but most courts do not treat them the same way. For example, an ex-wife who had been named as beneficiary of her husband's POD account during the marriage was awarded the account after he died despite the fact that they had been divorced.[65]

Claims by ex-spouses are sometimes defeated by virtue of a waiver executed at the time of the divorce.[66] Despite the standard policy requirements of notice to the insurer, courts have barred a spouse from claiming insurance when a separation agreement specifically mentioned it even though the company was not notified.[67] But waiver arguments are often rejected on the ground that the language in the divorce settlement was too general.[68] A wife's agreement to waive all claims "in, to, or against the property" of her husband was held to preclude her from claiming as beneficiary of a trust which was listed in the agreement, but not as beneficiary of an insurance policy which was not so listed.[69] Even a provision in a divorce decree awarding a particular account to the husband was held not to bar his ex-wife's claim as the designated POD beneficiary after his death.[70] The Uniform Probate Court calls for a broad construction of a waiver of "all rights" in a separation agreement, but this does not apply to benefits to the former spouse in a living trust as distinguished from a will.[71]

In many states divorce ends the right of survivorship between spouses who own property jointly.[72] Here too the result may turn on the terms of the decree; thus a surviving husband was held to succeed to a house which, by the terms of the divorce, was to remain in joint tenancy,[73] but other courts have found an agreement to sever "from language that is ambiguous at best, and sometimes even from the conduct of the parties."[74]

Some statutes have extended the rule that divorce revokes devises to a former spouse to will substitutes as well as wills. Under the Uniform Probate Code, a divorce "severs the interests of the former spouses in property held by them" as joint tenants, and revokes any revocable disposition made by one spouse to the other in a "governing instrument" which is defined to include

**65.** Matter of Estate of Leone, 860 P.2d 973 (Utah App.1993). *See also* Leahy v. Leahy-Schuett, 570 N.E.2d 407 (Ill.App.1991); Christensen v. Sabad, 773 P.2d 538 (Colo.1989); Schultz v. Schultz, 591 N.W.2d 212 (Iowa 1999).

**66.** Fox Valley & Vic. Const. Wkrs. Pension Fund v. Brown, 897 F.2d 275 (7th Cir.1990); Estate of Anello v. McQueen, 953 P.2d 1143 (Utah 1998) (IRA); Lelux v. Chernick, 694 N.E.2d 471 (Ohio App.1997) (insurance and pension); Robson v. Electrical Contractors Ass'n, 727 N.E.2d 692 (Ill.App.1999) (pension).

**67.** Curley v. Giltrop, 496 N.E.2d 224 (N.Y. 1986); Conn v. Trow, 715 S.W.2d 152 (Tex. App.1986); Life Ins. Co. v. Cassidy, 676 P.2d 1050 (Cal.1984); Johnson v. Johnson, 746 P.2d 1061 (Idaho App.1987) (IRA account).

**68.** Eschler v. Eschler, 849 P.2d 196 (Mont. 1993); Christensen v. Sabad, 773 P.2d 538 (Colo.1989); Deida v. Murphy, 647 N.E.2d 1109 (Ill.App.1995).

**69.** In re Marriage of Velasquez, 692 N.E.2d 841 (Ill.App.1998).

**70.** Schultz v. Schultz, 591 N.W.2d 212 (Iowa 1999).

**71.** Matter of Estate of Groesbeck, 935 P.2d 1255 (Utah 1997).

**72.** Matter of Estate of Ikuta, 639 P.2d 400 (Haw.1981); Goldman v. Goldman, 733 N.E.2d 200 (N.Y.2000) (divorce turns tenancy by the entirety into tenancy in common); 68 Pa.Stat. § 501; Va.Code § 6.1–125.4 (joint account). *But see* Matter of Estate of Sander, 806 P.2d 545 (Mont.1991) (joint tenancy unaffected by divorce).

**73.** In re Marriage of Dudek, 559 N.E.2d 1078 (Ill.App.1990). *See also* Estate of Dompke v. Dompke, 542 N.E.2d 1222 (Ill.App.1989) (joint account becomes husband's by terms of the decree).

**74.** Helmholz, *supra* note 47, at 23.

trusts, insurance policies, POD accounts, and pension benefits as well as wills.[75] This presumption of intent, unlike many others in the Code is not rebuttable by oral evidence of contrary intent. Thus an ex-wife was cut out as beneficiary of an insurance policy by a divorce, despite the insured's statement that "he wanted to leave the designation the way it was."[76] As to pension benefits, there is conflicting authority as to whether ERISA preempts a state statute like this.[77] The effect of the UPC provision on joint bank accounts is unclear.[78]

Some courts have applied statutes which by their terms provide for revocation of a wills only to will substitutes by analogy. For example, provisions in a revocable trust for the settlor's husband were held to be revoked when the settlor divorced him on the ground that it would be "incongruous" not to apply the statutory rule governing wills to this trust.[79]

### *Wills*

Provisions in a will that purport to deal with property which is disposed of by a will substitute are often not given effect. For example, a purported devise of property held in joint tenancy is void, "for no testament takes effect till after the death of the testator and by such death the right of the survivor is already vested."[80] This rule, though ancient, seems questionable. Since a joint tenant can devise her interest "by using two pieces of paper (the instrument of severance and then the will), then logic dictates that one piece of paper (the will) suffices where the election to sever is clearly expressed."[81]

A will may sometimes control joint tenancy property under the theory of an election if the will devises other property to the surviving joint tenant. "If a testator by his will assumes to dispose of the property of another person who is also made a beneficiary under the will," the devisee's acceptance of benefits under the will estops him from objecting to the disposition of his own property, including property acquired as surviving joint tenant.[82]

**75.** Uniform Probate Code §§ 1–201(19), 2–804(b). In Henley v. Henley, 974 P.2d 362 (Wash.App.1999), the statute was held inapplicable to a divorce obtained in another jurisdiction.

**76.** Mearns v. Scharbach, 12 P.3d 1048 (Wash.App.2000). Contrast the rules of construction in part 7 which apply "in the absence of a finding of a contrary intention." Uniform Probate Code § 2–701.

**77.** *Compare* Metropolitan Life Ins. Co. v. Hanslip, 939 F.2d 904 (10th Cir.1991) *with* In re Estate of Egelhoff, 989 P.2d 80 (Wash.1999), cert. granted, 120 S.Ct. 2687 (2000).

**78.** McGovern, *supra* note 59, at 1340.

**79.** Clymer v. Mayo, 473 N.E.2d 1084 (Mass.1985). *See also Restatement, Third, Trusts* § 25, illus. 11 (1996); Miller v. First Nat. Bank & Trust Co., 637 P.2d 75 (Okl. 1981); In re Estate of Davis, 589 N.E.2d 154 (Ill.App.1992).

**80.** 2 W. Blackstone, *Commentaries* *186 (1765). *See also* T. Littleton, *Tenures* § 287; In re Estate of England, 284 Cal.Rptr. 361 (App. 1991) (will cannot sever joint tenancy); Matter of Estate of Ingram, 874 P.2d 1282 (Okl.1994) (CDs held in joint tenancy); Matter of Estate of Kokjohn, 531 N.W.2d 99 (Iowa 1995) (joint account).

**81.** Mattis, *Joint Tenancy: Notice of Severance Mortgages and Survivorship,* 7 N.Ill. L.Rev. 41, 46 (1986). *See also* McGovern, *The Payable on Death Account and Other Will Substitutes,* 67 Nw.U.L.Rev. 7, 22 (1972).

**82.** Citizens Nat. Bank v. Stasell, 408 N.E.2d 587 (Ind.App.1980). This theory has also been applied where the provisions of a will were inconsistent with the designation of an insurance beneficiary. Estate of Stalnaker, 479 A.2d 612 (Pa.Super.1984); Wis.Stat. § 853.17. *But see* Williamson v. Williamson, 657 N.E.2d 651 (Ill.App.1995) (refusing to require an election where the will did not require it expressly).

The Restatement of Trusts allows settlors of bank account trusts to revoke them by will.[83] This can create a construction problem. A devise of "all funds on deposit to my credit in any bank" was held not to revoke the testator's bank account trusts since she had bank accounts in her name alone to which the devise might refer.[84] Even when the intent to revoke a living trust is clear, it may be rejected for failure to satisfy a requirement in the trust terms that amendments be delivered to the trustee during the settlor's lifetime.[85] The Uniform Trust Code allows living trusts to be revoked by will, but only if the trust does not provide an "exclusive" method of revocation.[86]

The Uniform Probate Code does not allow beneficiary designations in a P.O.D. account or a right of survivorship in a joint account to be altered by will.[87] Similarly a will directing who is to receive the proceeds of insurance has been held ineffective to change the beneficiary designation in the policy.[88] This rule allows the bank or insurer to pay the funds promptly after a depositor/insured's death without worrying about a possible will.

> It is in the public interest that an insurance company may pay a loss to the beneficiary designated in the policy as promptly after the death of the insured as may reasonably be done .. If paid to the beneficiary, a will might later be probated designating a different disposition of the fund, and it would be a risk that few companies would be willing to take.[89]

This concern is legitimate, but could be better addressed by simply protecting any bank or insurer which makes payment without notice of the will. The Uniform Probate Code has several provisions protecting banks and other third parties who pay claims in good faith.[90] The Third Restatement of Property provides that payors who pay the beneficiary of record should be protected, but if they receive notice of the change of beneficiary designation in the will, they should comply with it.[91]

A lawyer who drafts a will should ascertain what will substitutes the testator has made. These are often made without legal advice by persons who use lawyers to draft their wills. The testator is powerless to revoke irrevocable gifts, but with proper attention to formalities joint tenancies can be severed and revocable trusts revoked and insurance beneficiaries changed so as to reflect the testator's current wishes. But this requires more than a duly

**83.** *Restatement (Second) of Trusts* § 58, comm. c (1959); *Restatement, Third, Trusts* § 26, comm. c (1996).

**84.** In re Krycun's Estate, 249 N.E.2d 753 (N.Y.1969). *See also* Neto v. Thorner, 718 F.Supp. 1222 (S.D.N.Y.1989); Matter of Estate of Sanders, 929 P.2d 153 (Kan.1996) (trust not revoked by general language in will which did not refer to the trust); *Restatement, Third, Trusts* § 26, illus. 7 (1999).

**85.** However, in In re Estate of Davis, 671 N.E.2d 1302 (Ohio App.1996), where the trust allowed the settlor to amend it during his lifetime, his will was held to be effective to do so since it "operated as an *in praesenti* instrument."

**86.** Unif.Trust Code § 602(c).

**87.** Uniform Probate Code § 6–213(b). *See also* Calif.Prob.Code § 5302(e); Graves v. Summit Bank, 541 N.E.2d 974 (Ind.App.1989) (POD account); Matter of Estate of Ingram, 874 P.2d 1282 (Okl.1994) (CD in joint form); Matter of Estate of Kokjohn, 531 N.W.2d 99 (Iowa 1995) (joint account).

**88.** Estate of Norwood, 443 N.W.2d 798 (Mich.App.1989); McCarthy v. Aetna Life Ins. Co., 704 N.E.2d 557 (N.Y.1998).

**89.** *Id.*, at 560–61.

**90.** Uniform Probate Code §§ 2–803(h), 2–804(g), 6–221–6–227. *See also* Unif.Trust Code § 602(g), protecting trustees who distribute without knowing that a trust has been revoked or amended.

**91.** *Restatement (Third) of Property (Wills and Other Donative Transfers)* § 7.2, comm. e (Prel.Dft. 2000).

executed and properly drafted will. Lawyers who ignore this run the risk of being sued for malpractice.[92]

**92.** In Matter of McCoy, 419 N.W.2d 301 (Wis.App.1987) a settlor told the trustee she wanted to amend the trust. The trustee did not advise her that this required a writing. The trustee was held subject to suit by the intended beneficiary after the settlor died.

# Chapter 6

# EXTRINSIC EVIDENCE

*Analysis*



---

## § 6.1 Wills: Mistake and Ambiguity

### *Policy and General Rules*

Suppose that a will leaves property "to *A*." *B* attempts to show by evidence extrinsic to the will that the testator intended that she rather than *A* should get the property. There are two possible bases for denying *B*'s claim. The first is the parol evidence rule which applies to wills as well as other written documents.[1] A major reason for excluding parol evidence in construing contracts is that someone may have relied on the terms of the writing. Even when courts override the parol evidence rule to reform a writing, they protect persons who have relied on the writing.[2] This problem does not arise for wills, since when extrinsic evidence is offered before an estate is distributed, strangers are not likely to have relied on the language of the will.[3]

The statute of wills provides another theoretical basis for excluding any evidence of the testator's intent that is not in writing, signed, and attested. Courts admit oral evidence to correct mistakes in written contracts which the Statute of Frauds requires to be in writing and signed.[4] But in the case of wills, the best evidence of the testator's intent, the testator, is dead when the will is probated. Therefore, the statute imposes more stringent formal requirements for wills, *viz.* attestation as well as a signed writing. For the same reason, courts have traditionally been reluctant to allow extrinsic evidence in interpreting wills. A "will cannot be reformed to conform to any intent of the

§ 6.1

1. *E.g.,* Or.Rev.Stat. § 41.740: "When the terms of an agreement have been reduced to writing by the parties * * * there can be * * * no evidence of the terms of the agreement other than the contents of the writing * * * The term 'agreement' includes deeds and wills as well as contracts * * *."

2. *Restatement, Second, Contracts* § 155 (1981).

3. Matter of Kalouse's Estate, 282 N.W.2d 98, 108 (Iowa 1979) (dissent); Langbein & Waggoner, *Reformation of Wills on the Ground of Mistake,* 130 U.Pa.L.Rev. 521, 569 (1982).

4. *Restatement (Second) of Contracts* § 156 (1981); World of Sleep, Inc. v. Seidenfeld, 674 P.2d 1005 (Colo.App.1983).

testator not expressed in it, no matter how clearly a different intent may be proved by extrinsic evidence ... [I]f the rule were otherwise, ... property would pass without a will in writing, which the law demands."[5]

### *Mistake*

Nevertheless, courts admit extrinsic evidence of a testator's intent in some situations. The typical wills act says that wills must be in writing and signed, but it does not say that every signed writing must be probated. Thus the statute does not bar courts from refusing to probate a will which was signed by mistake, or a part of a will which was included by mistake.[6] Courts sometimes say that words inserted in a will by mistake may be struck out but words omitted by mistake may not be added. Thus, if a will leaves property "to my brothers and sisters," and the word "brothers" was included by mistake, a court can delete it,[7] but if a devise to the testator's son was left out in error, the court can not add it.[8]

The distinction between adding and deleting words offered for probate can be explained by the wording of the wills act, but the policy considerations in both cases are the same.[9] Whether words are added or deleted, the same threat exists of untrustworthy evidence, unrebuttable by the testator. Moreover, striking words may have the same practical effect as adding them. For example, a will left property to the testator's nephew and "Mabel Schneikert, his wife." The nephew's present wife was named Evelyn. The court awarded the property to Evelyn, finding that she was the intended devisee, since this did not require adding her name to the will. It was possible to achieve the desired result by striking the words "Mabel Schneikert," leaving "a bequest to 'Raymond Schneikert and his wife.' * * * A mistake in description may be corrected by rejecting that which is shown to be false, but no words may be inserted."[10]

Some courts refuse to probate an attested will on the basis of extrinsic evidence that it was not actually meant to operate as a will. According to the Restatement of Property, a clear expression of testamentary intent in a document "raises a strong (but not irrebuttable) presumption" of testamentary intent, which can be rebutted by clear contrary evidence.[11] Other courts disagree; one refused to admit evidence from a contestant that the testator "didn't really mean it; he was merely bluffing," because this "would leave every will open to attack as to the alleged testator's 'real' intent, and would

5. Matter of Estate of Frietze, 966 P.2d 183, 186 (N.M.App.1998). *See also* In re Reynette–James, [1976] 1 W.L.R. 161, 166 (Ch. 1975).

6. In re Estate of Herbert, 979 P.2d 39, 51–52 (Haw.1999); Matter of Estate of Smelser, 818 P.2d 822 (Kan.App.1991). *But see* Estate of Smith, 71 Cal.Rptr.2d 424 (App.1998) (will probated although testator allegedly intended a different distribution).

7. In re Fenwick, [1972] V.R. 646.

8. Knupp v. District of Columbia, 578 A.2d 702 (D.C.App.1990) (name of residuary devisee omitted by mistake); First Interstate Bank v. Young, 853 P.2d 1324 (Or.App.1993); In re Estate of Smith, 599 N.E.2d 184 (Ill.App.1992).

9. Warren, *Fraud, Undue Influence, and Mistake in Wills,* 41 Harv.L.Rev. 309, 333–34 (1928).

10. Breckheimer v. Kraft, 273 N.E.2d 468 (Ill.App.1971).

11. *Restatement, Third, of Property (Wills and Other Donative Transfers)* § 3.1, comm. g (1998). *See also* Cal.Prob.Code § 6111.5 ("extrinsic evidence is admissible to determine whether a document constitutes a will"); *cf.* Fine v. Cohen, 623 N.E.2d 1134, 1138 (Mass. App.1993) (parol evidence admissible to show a trust was not intended to be binding).

deprive testators of any certainty as to the eventual disposition of their estates."[12]

### *Ambiguity*

The rule which bars adding words omitted from a will is sometimes displaced by another rule which allows courts to use extrinsic evidence in order to resolve a "latent ambiguity" in a will. For example, a will left the estate "to my nieces and nephews." The testator had only one niece and one nephew, but his wife had nineteen. He had told his lawyer that he wanted his estate to go to his 21 nephews and nieces including those of his wife. The court construed the will to include them even though words like "nieces and nephews" are normally construed to include only blood relatives. "A latent ambiguity surfaced when the language of the bequest did not square with the actual number of blood nieces and nephews," and extrinsic evidence could be used to resolve it.[13] So also when a will expressed the testator's "desire" that an individual be allowed to buy property, the court used extrinsic evidence to decide whether this language was simply precatory.[14]

A will which purports to devise property which the testator does not own may be found "ambiguous." For example, a testator who devised "all of the lots that I own on Suber Street" did not own any such land but owned other land known as "the Suber property." The court held that this "latent ambiguity" allowed extrinsic evidence of her intent to devise this property.[15] A similar mistake sometimes crops up in the designation of a devisee, as in a will which left property "Mary Beverly Peters of Spottsylvania." The testator had a niece named Mary *Beaumont* Peters in Spottsylvania, and a great niece named Mary Beaumont Peters who lived somewhere else. The court used extrinsic evidence to identify the person intended.[16]

The foregoing examples represent "latent" ambiguities; they were not apparent until one looked outside the will and discovered that no devisee (or property owned by the testator) fit the description in the will. Some courts refuse to consider extrinsic evidence when the ambiguity is patent, *i.e.* apparent on the face of the will.[17] But the distinction between latent and patent ambiguities seems irrelevant to the policy issues involved, and many courts reject it. For example, when a will left the residue to nine persons, each of whom was to receive one-eighteenth of the estate, a court used extrinsic

**12.** Matter of Estate of Duemeland, 528 N.W.2d 369 (N.D.1995). *See also* Taliaferro v. Taliaferro, 921 P.2d 803 (Kan.1996) (living trust).

**13.** Matter of Estate of Anderson, 359 N.W.2d 479 (Iowa 1984). *See also* Clymer v. Mayo, 473 N.E.2d 1084 (Mass.1985) (devise to "my nieces" construed to include step-nieces since testator had none); In re Estate of Fabian, 483 S.E.2d 474 (S.C.App.1997) (evidence that T intended a nephew included in a devise "to my brothers and sisters").

**14.** Gillespie v. Davis, 410 S.E.2d 613 (Va. 1991). As to the distinction between precatory and mandatory terms see Section 4.6.

**15.** Fenzel v. Floyd, 347 S.E.2d 105 (S.C.App.1986). *See also* Matter of Estate of Frietze, 966 P.2d 183 (N.M.App.1998) (same lot devised to two people; extrinsic evidence shows which was the intended devisee). *But see* Matter of Estate of Greenfield, 757 P.2d 1297 (Mont.1988) (devise of property which did not exist held unambiguous).

**16.** Trustees of Wheaton College v. Peters, 677 N.E.2d 25 (Ill.App.1997). *See also* In re Black's Estate, 27 Cal.Rptr. 418 (App.1962) (devise to "University of Southern California known as The U.C.L.A."); Legare v. Legare, 490 S.E.2d 369 (Ga.1997).

**17.** Gafford v. Kirby, 512 So.2d 1356 (Ala. 1987); In re Estate of Corrigan, 358 N.W.2d 501, 503 (Neb.1984); Breckner v. Prestwood, 600 S.W.2d 52 (Mo.App.1980).

evidence to resolve this dilemma, saying that "whenever an ambiguity in a will exists, be it latent or patent, extrinsic evidence is admissible."[18]

Sometimes extrinsic evidence is rejected because (at least in the eyes of the court) the will is not ambiguous at all. For example, a will left property to the "blood heirs" of the testator. The court excluded evidence that the testator thought that his heirs were his sisters and his child, saying "there was no ambiguity in the will" because " 'blood heirs' meant those persons who were related by blood who would take his real estate if he died intestate," *i.e.* only the testator's child.[19] The law has created rules of construction to deal with questions which crop up frequently, like what "heirs" means, whether "children" includes adopted children, children born out of wedlock, etc. Do such rules render a term unambiguous, or can extrinsic evidence be used to show that the testator intended something contrary to the rule of construction? The many cases raising this issue are hard to reconcile.[20] When the rule of construction appears in a statute, the statutory language may make a difference. In California the construction rules govern where a contrary "intention of the transferor is not indicated by the instrument."[21] The comparable provision in the Uniform Probate Code simply says the rules apply "in the absence of a finding of a contrary intention;" this formulation was intended to allow extrinsic evidence to rebut the rules.[22]

Even if a will is ambiguous, extrinsic evidence showing an intent totally at odds with the language of the will may be rejected. For example, a will left paintings "to the New York Museum of Fine Arts" which does not exist. Evidence indicating that the testator meant the Boston Museum of Fine Arts was admitted. But other evidence indicating that she wanted her cousin to have the paintings was not, since the will clearly showed a bequest to a museum, not a person.[23]

The Second Restatement of Property adopts a more liberal position with respect to extrinsic evidence, one which allows a "drafting error in carrying out * * * a testator's intention" to be reformed.[24] This goes farther than most case law today, but there are signs of a trend in this direction which is followed in the proposed Uniform Trust Code.[25]

Professors Langbein and Waggoner, who have long advocated this position, say that the risk of false testimony can be reduced by requiring clear and convincing evidence, a standard which is "pitched above the ordinary prepon-

**18.** In re Gibson's Estate, 312 N.E.2d 1, 3 (Ill.App.1974). *See also* Matter of Estate of Brown, 922 S.W.2d 605 (Tex.App.1996); Board of Regents v. Bates, 418 S.E.2d 8 (Ga.1992); Succession of Neff, 716 So.2d 410 (La.App. 1998).

**19.** Brunson v. Citizens Bank and Trust Co., 752 S.W.2d 316 (Ky.App.1988). *See also* Estate of Straube v. Barber, 990 S.W.2d 40, 47 (Mo.App.1999). As to the meaning of "heirs" see Section 2.4.

**20.** *Compare* Connecticut Bank and Trust Co. v. Coffin, 563 A.2d 1323 (Conn.1989) (extrinsic evidence used to show that "issue" included children adopted by others); Estate of Wilson, 542 A.2d 838 (Me.1988) (extrinsic evidence used to show intent to include adoptees) *with* Godfrey v. Chandley, 811 P.2d 1248 (Kan. 1991) (no consideration of beneficiary's resources in determining what is needed for support); Matter of Estate of Winslow, 934 P.2d 1001 (Kan.App.1997) (lapsed devise passes to other residuary devisees).

**21.** Cal.Prob.Code § 21102.

**22.** Uniform Probate Code § 2–601.

**23.** Phipps v. Barbera, 498 N.E.2d 411 (Mass.App.1986). *See also* Estate of Taff, 133 Cal.Rptr. 737, 742 (App.1976).

**24.** *Restatement, Second, Property, Donative Transfers* § 34.7, Comment d (1990). *See also* England, Administration of Justice Act 1982, § 20.

**25.** Uniform Trust Code § 414.

derance-of-the-evidence standard characteristic of most civil litigation."[26] Also, they find comfort in the fact that reformation of mistakes is an equitable matter, and thus the questions are tried by the court rather than a jury.

### *Nature of the Evidence*

The nature of the evidence offered to show the testator's intent seems to be determinative in many cases. Although the question posed is whether extrinsic evidence is "admissible,"[27] the trial court usually hears it, and the strength of the evidence may determine the outcome. In some cases the evidence of a mistake is overwhelming, as when a husband and wife, executing their wills at the same time, by mistake each signed the other's will. The court reformed the two wills by substituting the proper names, saying that what had occurred was "so obvious, and what was intended so clear" that there was "absolutely no danger of fraud."[28]

Many courts distinguish between evidence of the circumstances and evidence of the testator's declarations. In a will which created a trust to support the testator's wife, the question arose whether the trustee should consider the wife's own resources in deciding her needs.[29] The will was ambiguous on this point, but testimony that according to the testator's instructions the will should have contained the phrase "having in mind [the wife's] separate income" was excluded, because this would "subvert the very purpose of the Statute of Wills." However, the same court held it proper to consider the amount which the testator had contributed to his wife's support while he was alive.[30] A similar distinction is suggested by some statutes, for example, the rules of construction control unless the intent of the testator "as indicated by the will and relevant circumstances is contrary."[31] Some courts say that the circumstances should be considered in deciding whether a will is ambiguous: "a court cannot determine whether the terms of a will are clear and definite in the first place until it considers the circumstances under which the will was made."[32]

Evidence of the circumstances, *e.g.* the age of the testator's children when he executed his will, is hard to manufacture. From this circumstance, one may infer that the testator must have meant "youngest" when a will referred to the time when his "oldest" child should reach 30, because his oldest child already was already 30 when the will was signed.[33] Or, when a will left "all to

**26.** Langbein & Waggoner, *supra* note 3, at 579. *See also* Uniform Trust Code § 414. *But cf.* Phipps v. Barbera, 498 N.E.2d 411 (Mass. App.1986) (preponderance of evidence suffices when resolving a latent ambiguity).

**27.** Even if evidence has been admitted without objection, it may be disregarded on the theory that the bar on parol evidence is a rule of substantive law. Matter of Kalouse's Estate, 282 N.W.2d 98, 105 (Iowa 1979); Tuttle v. Simpson, 735 S.W.2d 539 (Tex.App.1987).

**28.** Matter of Snide, 418 N.E.2d 656, 658 (N.Y.1981). *But see* In re Pavlinko's Estate, 148 A.2d 528 (Pa.1959) (denying probate to both spouses' wills in this situation).

**29.** This is a recurring issue. See Section 9.5, at note 45 et seq.

**30.** Estate of Utterback, 521 A.2d 1184 (Me.1987). *See also* Matter of Estate of Palizzi, 854 P.2d 1256 (Colo.1993).

**31.** N.J.Stat.Ann. § 3B:3–33. According to Ga.Code Ann. § 53–2–94, a court may hear evidence of "the circumstances surrounding the testator at the time of execution" to explain ambiguities, but courts have not felt restricted by this language. Legare v. Legare, 490 S.E.2d 369 (Ga.1997).

**32.** Estate of Anderson, 65 Cal.Rptr.2d 307, 316 (App.1997).

**33.** Matter of Ikuta's Estate, 639 P.2d 400 (Haw.1981).

Danny'' and three persons with that name claimed it, the court heard evidence as to which one had the ''closest relationship to'' the testator.[34] A devise to ''my nieces and nephews'' included nieces and nephews of the testator's spouse when ''there had been a warm friendly relationship between'' them in which the testator ''did not distinguish between nieces and nephews by consanguinity and those by affinity.''[35]

The identity of the drafter may affect the construction of technical words in a will.[36] Thus if a will was drafted by a non-lawyer, a devise of ''all my money'' may be construed to include all the testator's assets,[37] whereas a testator who worked in a county recording office did not mean to include real estate in a bequest of ''personal effects.''[38] A ''peculiar vocabulary'' of the testator may be considered, *e.g.,* the testator ''customarily designated a particular person by a name other than'' his real one, or customarily spoke of an unrelated person as his ''niece.''[39]

Even when the circumstantial evidence is uncontroverted, its bearing on the question of intent is not always clear. Circumstantial evidence may show that one construction of a will treats all the testator's children equally, but some testators do not want this.[40] Courts in recent years have been willing to construe or reform wills to achieve tax reductions which (it is assumed) the testator would have desired. For example, a court reformed a trust in order to make it qualify for the federal estate tax marital deduction.[41] However, some courts have refused to make such changes, doubting whether the testator was so focussed on tax savings.[42] One court approved the division of a trust into separate trusts in order to minimize the generation skipping tax, assuming there was ''an intent on the part of most testators to save taxes,''[43] but refused to change a will in order to confer a general power of appointment on the testator's sons ''even though this would save'' ''very substantial federal taxes'' because this would allowed the testator's grandchildren to lose their

**34.** Succession of Bacot, 502 So.2d 1118 (La.App.1987). *See also* Transamerica Occidental Life Ins. Co. v. Burke, 368 S.E.2d 301 (W.Va.1988) (''children'' includes stepchildren whom transferor treated as his own); Connecticut National Bank & Trust Co. v. Chadwick, 585 A.2d 1189 (Conn.1991) (adoptees for whom testator manifested affection are included); Estate of Christensen, 461 N.W.2d 469 (Iowa App.1990) (''children'' does not include a child from whom testator was estranged).

**35.** Martin v. Palmer, 1 S.W.3d 875, 880 (Tex.App.1999).

**36.** Cal.Prob.Code § 21122 (technical words to be interpreted in their technical sense unless ''the instrument was drawn solely by the transferor [who] was unacquainted with their technical sense'')

**37.** *Restatement of Property* § 242, comm. f (1940). *See also* Transamerica Occidental Life Ins. Co. v. Burke, 368 S.E.2d 301 (W.Va.1988) (''children'' includes stepchildren when will is not drawn by a lawyer).

**38.** Kaufhold v. McIver, 682 S.W.2d 660 (Tex.App.1984). *See also* Boston Safe Deposit & Trust Co. v. Wilbur, 728 N.E.2d 264, 269 (Mass.2000) (presume that technical terms used correctly in will drafted by a lawyer).

**39.** *Restatement of Property* § 242 comm. d (1940).

**40.** *Compare* In re Estate of Seaton, 481 P.2d 567 (Wash.App.1971) *with* Steinke v. Novak, 441 N.E.2d 883 (Ill.App.1982).

**41.** Griffin v. Griffin, 832 P.2d 810 (Okl. 1992). *See also* Loeser v. Talbot, 589 N.E.2d 301 (Mass.1992) (changing a general power into a special to avoid taxation in donee's estate); Simches v. Simches, 671 N.E.2d 1226 (Mass.1996) (gift to grandchildren changed to children in order to avoid generation skipping tax); Uniform Trust Code § 415 (court may modify trust in order to achieve settlor's tax objectives).

**42.** Estate of Heim v. Commissioner, 914 F.2d 1322 (9th Cir.1990); Estate of Nicholson, 94 T.C. 666 (1990); Wisely v. United States, 893 F.2d 660 (4th Cir.1990).

**43.** *See also* BankBoston v. Marlow, 701 N.E.2d 304 (Mass.1998).

inheritance. The court did not believe that the testator intended "to evade taxes at the cost of the dispository scheme."[44]

Some declarations of intent by testators are more reliable than others. A court while remanding a case for consideration of extrinsic evidence to resolve an ambiguity, said that "self-serving statements by [devisees] as to their understanding of the testator's intent would not be admissible."[45] On the other hand, courts often rely on testimony by the attorney who drafted a will as to what the testator intended,[46] even though the drafting attorney may have an interest in avoiding liability for malpractice if the testator's intent is frustrated. Written extrinsic evidence seems more reliable than oral. But these distinctions have not crystallized into firm rules.[47]

### *Scope of Appellate Review*

Questions of construction of a will are often resolved simply on the basis of the language of the will plus any applicable rules of construction, either because no extrinsic evidence of the testator's intent is offered or because such evidence is held inadmissible. Such cases are viewed differently on appeal from those in which a fact finder partly relied on extrinsic evidence. "Interpretation of a will generally is a question of law as long as the court determines the meaning of the document solely from its language and not from any surrounding circumstances."[48] But when a trial court properly considers extrinsic evidence in interpreting an ambiguous will, the appellate court does not "reweigh conflicting evidence," and examines "the record only to determine whether substantial evidence exists to support the trial court's action."[49]

### *Malpractice*

Malpractice suits have added a new dimension to the extrinsic evidence problem. Disappointed devisees have successfully sued attorneys for drafting wills which allegedly omitted a devise which the testator intended for them. "A lawyer who admits that he omitted from a will a residuary clause requested by the testator * * * has facially demonstrated an obvious lack of care and skill." The intended devisee was not required to seek reformation of the will since generally "the doctrine of reformation is not applicable to wills," but the court could look at evidence outside the will to establish the testator's intent in a malpractice action.[50] However, other courts have refused

**44.** Matter of Estate of Branigan, 609 A.2d 431, 438 (N.J.1992).

**45.** District of Columbia v. Estate of Parsons, 590 A.2d 133, 138 (D.C.App.1991).

**46.** Danelczyk v. Tynek, 616 A.2d 1311 (N.J.Super.App.Div.1992); Baker v. Linsly, 379 S.E.2d 327 (Va.1989); Matter of Estate of Holmes, 821 P.2d 300 (Colo.App.1991); Skinner v. Moore, 940 S.W.2d 755 (Tex.App.1997); *cf.* Ike v. Doolittle, 70 Cal.Rptr.2d 887, 903 (App.1998) (drafter of living trust).

**47.** *Compare* In re Reynette–James, [1976] 1 W.L.R. 161, 168 (Ch. 1975) (reformation of wills should be allowed if there is "written contemporaneous evidence supporting the claim") *with* Matter of Estate of Bergau, 684 P.2d 734, 738 (Wash.App.1984) (ban on declarations includes testator's "written declarations not executed under the statute of wills"). In Matter of Estate of Frietze, 966 P.2d 183 (N.M.App.1998), the court allowed testimony by the drafting attorney to resolve an ambiguity in the will, but as to an issue where the will was clear, evidence from the same attorney was not allowed.

**48.** Schreiber v. Kellogg, 50 F.3d 264, 266–67 (3d Cir.1995).

**49.** In re Estate of Pouser, 975 P.2d 704, 709 (Ariz.1999). *See also* Matter of Estate of Klein, 434 N.W.2d 560 (N.D.1989).

**50.** Hamilton v. Needham, 519 A.2d 172 (D.C.App.1986). *See also* Simpson v. Calivas, 650 A.2d 318 (N.H.1994).

to hold a drafter liable on the basis of evidence of the testator's intent which would be inadmissible in probate proceedings.[51]

### *Mistake of Fact*

Courts do not usually give relief when a will is alleged to have been made under a mistake of fact, such as the paternity of a child.[52] Materiality is the great difficulty. If a clause was omitted from a will by mistake, presumably the testator would have wanted it to be inserted if the omission had been noticed. But when a testator is mistaken as to a fact, it may be doubtful what she would have desired had she known the truth. Mistakes of fact in a contract are distinguishable because they usually result in a markedly unequal exchange—*e.g.,* a $100,000 claim settled for $1,000 because the plaintiff mistook the extent of his injuries.[53] In wills it is much harder to determine what the testator would have done but for the mistake.

Under the Uniform Probate Code, if a testator fails to provide in a will "for a living child solely because he believes the child to be dead," the child gets an intestate share.[54] This is probably the strongest case for believing that a mistake was material, but even here the testator might have disinherited a child with whom she had no contact even had she known that her child was alive.[55]

According to the second Restatement of Property, a donative transfer, including a will, should be set aside if it was caused by a mistake of fact. However, the illustrations to this provision suggest that it will be hard to prove sufficient materiality when the mistake is one of fact, as distinguished as a mistake in the terms of the will, like an omitted devise.[56]

If a mistake amounts to an "insane delusion" the rule is different; it will be discussed in treating incapacity.[57]

### *Fraud*

Courts are more receptive to claims of fraud than mistake. It is necessary to show that the fraud induced the testator to make the devise,[58] but someone who misrepresents a fact to a testator probably considered the fact was material and it is not implausible to assume he was right. Thus a will which left the testator's property to her daughters was set aside because her daughters had told her that their father had left all his property to his sons.

**51.** Mieras v. DeBona, 550 N.W.2d 202 (Mich.1996); Espinosa v. Sparber, Shevin, et al, 586 So.2d 1221 (Fla.App.1991); Glover v. Southard, 894 P.2d 21 (Colo.App.1994); Miller v. Mooney, 725 N.E.2d 545, 550 (Mass.2000) (Statute of frauds bars enforcement of oral contract for lawyer to draft a will by which plaintiffs would benefit).

**52.** In re Estate of Angier, 552 A.2d 1121 (Pa.Super.1989); York v. Smith, 385 So.2d 1110 (Fla.App.1980); Witt v. Rosen, 765 S.W.2d 956 (Ark.1989) (gifts made to relatives).

**53.** *Restatement, Second, Contracts* § 152, illus. 12 (1981).

**54.** Uniform Probate Code § 2–302(c). *See also* Calif.Prob.Code § 21622.

**55.** Matter of Araneo, 511 A.2d 1269 (N.J.Super.Law Div.1985).

**56.** *Restatement (Second) of Property, Donative Transfers* § 34.7, comm. e, illus. 9 (no rescission of gift to stepson when donor was unaware that his marriage was invalid), illus. 11 (omitted devise added by reformation) (1990). Compare Uniform Trust Code § 414 (trust can be reformed for a mistake of fact in expression or inducement by settlor).

**57.** See Section 7.1, at note 6 et seq.

**58.** Edwards v. Shumate, 468 S.E.2d 23 (Ga.1996) (claim of fraud rejected because not shown to have affected will).

While a mistake as to an extrinsic fact made by the testator on his own affords no ground for setting aside a will, the situation is different when the mistake is caused by a misrepresentation made to him by a beneficiary. * * * It has also been generally held that in order to invalidate a will resulting from a misrepresentation of an extrinsic fact, it must be shown that the beneficiary knew the representation to be false. * * * We hold that there was no requirement under the facts of this case for the proof to show that [the daughters] knew that the statement * * * was false. * * * [I]t was made in reckless disregard of its truth or falsity, and no more should be required.[59]

Even nondisclosure may amount to fraud if there is a confidential relationship between the testator and another.[60] Claims of fraud are usually linked with undue influence; misrepresentations are regarded as type of undue influence on the testator.[61] Other aspects of undue influence will be discussed in Chapter Seven.

### *Constructive Trusts*

The bar against adding words to a will does not apply to cases of wrongful conduct. For example, a testator expressed a desire to make a new will leaving property to *A*, but *B*, the beneficiary of her existing will prevented her from doing so by false representations and physical force. *A*'s suit against *B* after the testator died alleging those facts was upheld. A devisee who "prevents the testator by fraud, duress, or undue influence from revoking the will and executing a new will in favor of another * * * holds the property thus acquired for the intended legatee." The statute of wills was no bar because "the will has full effect" but "equity, in order to defeat fraud, raises a trust in favor of those intended to be benefited by the testator."[62]

Constructive trusts (like other trusts) were historically enforced in equity and thus there is no right to trial by jury in suits to enforce them. This may explain why courts allow oral evidence of a decedent's intent in such suits. The hostility to such evidence is partly based on the fear that inexperienced juries cannot assess it adequately. However, the jurisdictional boundaries between law and equity are increasingly ignored, as probate courts become courts of general jurisdiction.[63] Also, the Restatement of Torts allows a suit in tort against anyone who "by fraud, duress or other tortious means intentionally prevents another from receiving from a third person an inheritance or gift that he would otherwise receive" if there is reasonably certain proof that such a devise or bequest would have been made.[64]

**59.** Matter of Estate of Vick, 557 So.2d 760, 768–69 (Miss.1989). *See also* Geduldig v. Posner, 743 A.2d 247, 260–61 (Md.App.1999); *Restatement, Second, Property, Donative Transfers* § 34.7, comm. c (1990).

**60.** Rood v. Newberg, 718 N.E.2d 886, 893 (Mass.App.1999) (because of confidential relationship daughter had a duty to disclose to testator that she was mistaken in believing son had stolen from her); *Restatement (Third) of Property (Wills and Other Donative Transfers)* § 8.3, comm. i (Prel.Dft. 2000).

**61.** In re Estate of Berry, 661 N.E.2d 1150, 1152 (Ill.App.1996); Matter of Estate of Lint, 957 P.2d 755, 765 (Wash.1998) (findings of fraud support conclusion of undue influence).

**62.** Latham v. Father Divine, 85 N.E.2d 168 (N.Y.1949). *See also Restatement (Third) of Property (Wills and Other Donative Transfers)* § 8.3, comm. m (Prel.Dft. 2000).

**63.** In re Will of Artope, 545 N.Y.S.2d 670 (N.Y.Surr.1989) (probate court has jurisdiction over claim that devisee had agreed to transfer property to another). *See also* Matter of Lembach's Estate, 622 P.2d 606 (Colo.App.1980).

**64.** *Restatement, Second, Torts* § 774B (1979). Followed in Davison v. Feuerherd, 391 So.2d 799 (Fla.App.1980).

### *Promises*

Constructive trusts are also imposed on devisees who promised the testator that they would give the devised property to another person. For example, a mother with an incompetent child, Mary, left half her estate to Mary's sister, Emily, who agreed to look after Mary. When Emily refused to do so, the court imposed a constructive trust on her. The devisee's promise, on which the constructive trust is based, can be inferred from silence; in this case the testator expressed her wishes in a conversation at which Emily said nothing.[65]

The trustee's promise need not be connected with making a will. If a decedent leaves a will unchanged in reliance on a devisee's promise, or makes no will at all, relying on an heir's promise to give property to another, courts will impose a trust.[66] However, the decedent's wishes must indicate an intent to impose an obligation on the devisee, rather than being merely precatory.[67] Furthermore, they must be communicated to the devisee or heir during the decedent's lifetime.[68] This restriction seems odd, since a devisee would seem to be unjustly enriched by taking property which was intended for another, even if she learned of this intent only after the decedent's death.

It is difficult to reconcile the enforcement of constructive trusts based on oral statements of a testator with the statutory requirements for wills or the requirement of a writing in most states for contracts to make a will.[69] Courts sometimes say that "the operation of the Wills Act is not obstructed * * * since title passes to [the devisee] as stated in the will, but equity acts on [the devisee's] title after the will has given it to him."[70] This reasoning seems specious, but courts impose a high standard of proof for a constructive trust. "The agreement to hold property in trust must be show by clear and convincing evidence * * * because the proof must * * * substitute for the normal statutory requirements of the Wills Act."[71] Interested testimony may be excluded by a Dead Man's Act.[72]

The term "trust" is somewhat misleading in this context, since the devisee upon whom the trust is imposed does not act like a normal trustee who manages property for the beneficiaries. A devisee who has refused to act as agreed, thus making the litigation to impose the trust necessary, is usually replaced by another trustee, if continuing management duties are contemplated.[73]

**65.** Kauzlarich v. Landrum, 274 N.E.2d 915 (Ill.App.1971).

**66.** Kramer v. Freedman, 272 So.2d 195 (Fla.App.1973); *Restatement (Third) of Trusts* § 18(2) (1996).

**67.** *Id.* comm. d. As to precatory language see Section 4.6, at note 65 et seq.

**68.** *Id.*, comm. f. However, the trust is enforceable if the devisee knows that she is to hold property in trust even if she learns the identity of the beneficiary only after the testator dies. *Id,* comm. e.

**69.** See Section 4.9, at note 9 et seq.

**70.** Chapman v. Citizens & Southern National Bank, 395 S.E.2d 446, 452 (S.C.App. 1990).

**71.** *Restatement, Third, Trusts* § 18, comm. h (1996).

**72.** Kamberos v. Magnuson, 510 N.E.2d 112 (Ill.App.1987).

**73.** *Restatement, Third, Trusts* § 18, comm. b (1996). Often the "trustee" is simply ordered to turn the property over to the beneficiary.

### *Semi-secret Trusts*

Some wills show on their face that a devisee was intended to give the devise to others who are not identified in the will. This is sometimes called a "semi-secret" trust as contrasted with a "secret" trust in which the will gives no clue that any trust was intended. Arguably they semi-secret trusts provide a stronger case for relief because the extrinsic evidence showing the intended beneficiaries is not inconsistent with the will but rather supplements it, rather like resolving a patent ambiguity. The Restatement of Trusts makes semi-secret trusts enforceable, and dispenses with the higher burden of proof required for constructive trusts in this situation.[74] However, some courts refuse to enforce semi-secret trusts. For example, when a will directed the executor to distribute the estate "in accordance with the verbal guidelines last given by me," the court held this was invalid, since the "guidelines" were not "in writing and attested in conformity with the statute of wills." Refusal to enforce a semi-secret trust does not leave the devisee unjustly enriched because he does not get to keep the property.[75]

When there is no evidence of the testator's wishes in a semi-secret trust, the property ordinarily passes intestate,[76] but if the will indicates that some kind of charitable trust was intended, the property will be applied to charitable purposes generally if the specific purpose which the testator intended cannot be identified.[77]

## § 6.2 Incorporation by Reference, Facts of Independent Significance and Pour–Over Wills

A multi-page will can probated even though only the last page is signed. The earlier pages are admitted on the theory that they were integrated into the will if they were present when the will was executed.[1] Other writings can also be probated with a will under the theory that they were incorporated by reference.[2] For example, a will recited that the testator wished to leave shares of stock to certain relatives and would place them "in envelopes bearing the name of each such relative and leave [the envelopes] in my Safe Deposit Box." Although the writing on the envelopes was not signed and attested, it was probated as having been incorporated by reference in the will.[3]

**74.** *Restatement (Third) of Trusts* § 18, comm. c, h (1996).

**75.** Matter or Reiman's Estate, 450 N.E.2d 928 (Ill.App.1983). *See also* In re Estate of Liginger, 111 N.W.2d 407 (Wis.1961). Arguably this result leaves the *testator's heirs* unjustly enriched, since they will get property which was not intended for them. *Restatement, Third, Trusts* § 18, comm. a (1996).

**76.** Estate of Bruner, 691 A.2d 530 (Pa.Super.1997); *Restatement, Third, Trusts* § 18, comm. e (1996).

**77.** Estate of Carper, 415 N.Y.S.2d 550 (A.D.1979); *Restatement, Second, Trusts* § 358, comm. e (1959). For the application of cy pres in other situations to save a charitable gift see Section 9.7, at note 44.

**§ 6.2**

1. Estate of Beale, 113 N.W.2d 380 (Wis. 1962); *Restatement, Third, of Property (Wills and Other Donative Transfers)* § 3.5 (1998). For techniques to assure that all the pages will be integrated see Section 4.2, note 19.

**2.** This is the normal effect of incorporation by reference, but according to *Restatement, Third, of Property (Wills and Other Donative Transfers)* § 3.6, comm. h (1998) the incorporated document is "treated as part of the will for purposes of" distributing the estate, but "need not be offered for probate nor be made part of the public record."

**3.** Smith v. Weitzel, 338 S.W.2d 628 (Tenn. App.1960). *See also* Clark v. Greenhalge, 582 N.E.2d 949 (Mass.1991); Matter of Estate of Sneed, 953 P.2d 1111 (Okl.1998). New York is one of the few states which does not recognize incorporation by reference. In re Philip, 596 N.Y.S.2d 146 (A.D.1993). *But cf.* In re Estate of Schmidt, 619 N.Y.S. 2d 245 (Surr. 1994) (statutory exception for published fee schedules).

Attempts to incorporate by reference falter if the identification in the will is not sufficiently precise. Thus an attempt by the proponents of an unexecuted will to have it incorporated by reference in a duly executed codicil failed; although the codicil was stapled to the will and both were inserted in an envelope that had typed on the outside "WILL OF LAWRENCE NORTON AND CODICIL OF LAWRENCE NORTON," there was no reference within the codicil itself that clearly designated the will as the document to be incorporated.[4]

Other courts have been less strict in permitting incorporation on the basis of extrinsic evidence showing that the document in question was the one mentioned in the will.[5] Even a misdescription in the will is not necessarily fatal: a will referring to a letter "dated March 25, 1932" was held to incorporate a letter dated July 3, 1933, because the letter was found with the will, its terms fit the will, and no other letter was found. This provided "reasonable certainty" that the letter was the one referred to in the will.[6]

### *Republication by Codicil*

A codicil which refers to an earlier will is said to "republish" it. This can have the effect of incorporation by reference, allowing probate of a will which was not duly executed.[7] Incorporation of a typewritten document into a holographic codicil does not destroy its holographic character. Even when a holographic "codicil" appeared on the same page as the typewritten will, both were probated under the theory of incorporation by reference.[8]

### *Future Documents*

An important limitation on incorporation by reference prevents testators from using it to change their wills informally: any document to be incorporated by reference must have been in existence at the time the will was executed. Thus when a will left property to a friend to distribute "to the persons named in a letter or memorandum of instructions which I shall leave addressed to her," the letter of instructions could not be admitted to probate.[9] It is not enough that the document *might have been* in existence before the will; its prior existence must be proved,[10] but according to the Restatement of Property this is presumed, even if the will refers to it as a document that "will be found with my important papers."[11] Courts sometimes say that the incorpo-

4. Matter of Estate of Norton, 410 S.E.2d 484, 488 (N.C.1991). *See also* Estate of Sweet, 519 A.2d 1260 (Me.1987).

5. In re Estate of McGahee, 550 So.2d 83 (Fla.App.1989) (paper clipped to the will).

6. Simon v. Grayson, 102 P.2d 1081, 1083 (Cal.1940). In Clark v. Greenhalge, 582 N.E.2d 949 (Mass.1991), a will referring to a "memorandum" was held to incorporate a notebook of the testator.

7. *Restatement, Third, of Property (Wills and Other Donative Transfers)* § 3.6, comm. d (1998); Allen v. Maddock, 14 Eng.Rep. 757 (1858). In *Maddock*, only one will was found. If there had been several, identifying which one was meant would have been a problem. *See* In re Erbach's Estate, 164 N.W.2d 238 (Wis. 1969).

Compare use of a codicil to revive a will which has been revoked. Section 5.3, note 22.

8. Johnson v. Johnson, 279 P.2d 928 (Okl. 1954). *See also* In re Foxworth's Estate, 50 Cal.Rptr. 237 (App.1966); *Restatement, Third, of Property (Wills and Other Donative Transfers)* § 3.6, comm. f (1998).

9. Hastings v. Bridge, 166 A. 273 (N.H. 1933).

10. Tierce v. Macedonia United Meth. Church, 519 So.2d 451, 456 (Ala.1987).

11. *Restatement, Third, of Property (Wills and Other Donative Transfers)* § 3.6, comm. b (1998).

rated document must also *be referred to in the will* as an existing document,[12] but the Uniform Probate Code does not require this.[13]

When a codicil "republishes" an earlier will, a document produced between the time of execution of the will and the codicil can be incorporated. For example, when a will executed in May referred to a letter which was written the following July, the letter was admitted because a codicil executed in November had republished the will.[14]

### *Lists of Tangible Personalty*

The Uniform Probate Code, pursuant to its "broader policy of * * * relaxing formalities of execution," allows a will to refer to a "written statement or list to dispose of items of tangible personal property" if the list is signed by the testator, even if it was prepared or altered after the execution of the will.[15] The restriction to tangible personal property reflects the idea that less formality should be required for property of relatively small value.[16] The requirement that the list be signed by the testator distinguishes this from incorporation by reference; a will can incorporate a writing by someone other than the testator. The Uniform Statutory Wills Act, for example, is designed to be incorporated by reference in wills.[17]

### *Facts of Independent Significance*

If a will leaves property "to my wife" without naming her, a court must resort to evidence outside the will in order to identify the wife. This may even be a marriage which occurred after the will was executed. The Uniform Probate Code follows the common law in allowing wills to "dispose of property by reference to acts and events that have significance apart from their effect upon the dispositions made by the will, whether they occur before or after the execution of the will."[18] The rationale is that such facts are not likely to be seriously disputed. Courts have allowed devises even of the contents of a house or of a safe-deposit box under this theory, but not an unattested writing of the testator.[19]

**12.** Bryan's Appeal, 58 A. 748, 750 (Conn. 1904). *See also* Estate of Sweet, 519 A.2d 1260 (Me.1987) (the "will must describe the extrinsic writing as an existing document"); Ohio Rev.Code § 2107.05; *Restatement (Second) of Trusts* § 54, comm. c (1959).

**13.** Uniform Probate Code § 2–510, comment; Calif.Prob.Code § 6130; *Restatement, Third, of Property (Wills and Other Donative Transfers)* § 3.6, comm. a (1998).

**14.** Simon v. Grayson, 102 P.2d 1081 (Cal. 1940). *See also* Clark v. Greenhalge, 582 N.E.2d 949 (Mass.1991); *Restatement, Third, of Property (Wills and Other Donative Transfers)* § 3.5, illus. 1 (1998).

**15.** Uniform Probate Code § 2–513. For the slight differences between the original and revised version of this provision see *Restatement, Third, of Property (Wills and Other Donative Transfers)* § 3.9, comm. b and c (1998).

**16.** Compare the exemption of sales of goods for less than $500 from the Statute of Frauds. Uniform Commercial Code § 2–201. In Burkett v. Mott, 733 P.2d 673 (Ariz.App.1986), a $10,000 insurance policy was held to be covered by § 2–513, a questionable result. *Cf.* Matter of Estate of Harrington, 850 P.2d 158 (Colo.App.1993) (note attempting to devise $25,000 not covered).

**17.** Uniform Statutory Wills Act § 3.

**18.** Uniform Probate Code § 2–512. *See also Restatement (Second) of Trusts* § 54(c) (1959); Calif.Prob.Code § 6131.

**19.** *Restatement (Second) of Trusts* § 54, illus. 5 (1959); Matter of Estate of Nelson, 419 N.W.2d 915 (N.D.1988) ("personal items used in connection with my farm"); *Restatement, Third, of Property (Wills and Other Donative Transfers)* § 3.7, comm. c, e (1998).

### *Pour–Over Wills*

Both ideas, incorporation by reference and facts of independent significance, have been used to validate a common estate planning device, the "pour-over" will. For example, a couple who had created a revocable trust later executed wills which left property to the trustees of the revocable trust to be held pursuant to its terms. The ultimate beneficiaries of the will could only be ascertained by looking at the trust which was not executed with the formalities prescribed for wills. The couple amended the trust after executing their wills. Could property passing under their wills be governed by the terms of this subsequent amendment of the trust? Earlier cases had refused to allow this, based on the restrictions against incorporating future documents.[20] But this court upheld the pour-over devise by treating the trust as a fact of independent significance; because the trust contained assets other than those which the will poured into it, its terms had independent significance.[21] This theory may presents problems. If the assets in the revocable trust have only nominal value prior to the pour-over, the "independent significance" of the trust is questionable.[22]

The difficulties posed by the doctrines of incorporation by reference and facts of independent significance have led most states to adopt statutes which directly authorize pour-over wills. The Uniform Probate Code allows such devises "regardless of the existence, size, or character of the corpus of the trust."[23] Theoretically a pour-over even to an oral trust could be justified if the trust had independent significance, but the UPC requires that the trust terms be "set forth in a written instrument." However, the trust instrument can be amended after the will is executed.[24] In an earlier version of the UPC, unchanged in some states, the trust instrument must be "executed before or concurrently with the testator's will,"[25] but even a later-executed trust, if funded, might be accepted as a fact of independent significance.[26]

The pour-over device has been accepted by courts and legislatures because it performs a useful function in estate planning, being used to consolidate the various parts of a plan. Many persons wish to put some of their assets in a living trust[27] and have other assets pass to a trust for the same beneficiaries when they die. Or a testator may wish to add assets to a trust created by another person. Both spouses may wish to put their respective

**20.** Koeninger v. Toledo Trust Co., 197 N.E. 419 (Ohio App.1934); Old Colony Trust Co. v. Cleveland, 196 N.E. 920 (Mass.1935).

**21.** Second Bank–State Street Trust Co. v. Pinion, 170 N.E.2d 350 (Mass.1960). *See also* Canal Nat. Bank v. Chapman, 171 A.2d 919 (Me.1961); *Restatement, Third, of Property (Wills and Other Donative Transfers)* § 3.8, comm. d (1998). *But see* South Carolina Nat. Bank of Charleston v. Copeland, 149 S.E.2d 615 (S.C.1966).

**22.** *Restatement (Third) of Trusts* § 19, comm. h (1996).

**23.** Uniform Probate Code § 2–511. This provision is copied from the Uniform Testamentary Additions to Trusts Act which has been widely adopted. *See* Estate of Harper, 93 T.C. 368, 376 (1989) (pourover to a nominally funded trust is valid under statute). In Tyson v. Henry, 514 S.E.2d 564 (N.C.App.1999) the terms of a trust were given effect as having been incorporated by reference in a pour-over will even though no property had been transferred to the trust.

**24.** Uniform Probate Code § 2–511(a).

**25.** Cal.Prob.Code § 6300; Tierce v. Macedonia United Meth. Church, 519 So.2d 451 (Ala.1987) (devise to a trust "to be made" fails).

**26.** *Restatement, Third, of Property (Wills and Other Donative Transfers)* § 3.8, illus. 1 (1998).

**27.** The advantages of avoiding probate by using a living trust rather than a will to dispose of assets are discussed at Section 9.1, at note 5 et seq. Despite these advantages, it is often inconvenient to put *all* settlor's assets into a living trust, particularly assets acquired after the trust is executed.

assets into a trust for their common children. Administrative costs can be reduced by consolidating the trusts of the two spouses.[28] The wife can leave her estate to the trust created by her husband's will and vice versa, depending on who dies first. Or a parent may wish to add property to a trust created by a child for the parent's grandchildren. The Uniform Probate Code allows a pour-over to a trust created by "another individual's will" if the will maker predeceased the testator of the pourover devise.[29]

The usefulness of pour-over wills may be hampered if they are allowed only under the theory of incorporation by reference. Many states subject testamentary trusts to close court supervision. Under the theory of incorporation by reference, the assets poured over by the will would in a testamentary trust subject to such supervision.[30] The Uniform Probate Code avoids this problem by providing that property passing under a pour-over devise "is not held under a testamentary trust of the testator, but it becomes a part of the trust to which it is devised."[31] However, for some purposes, the will and trust are treated together. For example, the probate court has been held to have jurisdiction to determine the validity of both when they are challenged for undue influence.[32] A provision in a trust for a spouse has been used to bar her claim to have been pretermitted in the will which poured assets into the trust.[33]

If a settlor revokes the receptacle trust before dying, the Uniform Probate Code provides that the pour-over devise lapses unless the will otherwise provides.[34] In Illinois, however, the devise takes effect "according to the terms * * * of the trust as they existed at the time of the termination" if the trust is terminated before the testator dies.[35]

### *Pour-up Trusts*

The parts of an estate plan can also be merged by going in the other direction, *i.e.* by making an insurance policy or death benefit under a pension plan payable to the trustee under a will.[36] This can have the advantage of

**28.** Cf. Cal.Prob.Code § 15411 (court can authorize combining two trusts which are "substantially similar"). In Matter of Will of Marcus, 552 N.Y.S.2d 546 (Surr.1990), the court authorized such a consolidation, emphasizing its advantages, without statutory authority. *See also* Matter of Will of Daniels, 799 P.2d 479 (Kan.1990).

**29.** Uniform Probate Code § 2–511. *See also* Cal.Prob.Code § 6300.

**30.** Note, 48 Mo.L.Rev. 523, 528 (1983). As to court supervision of testamentary trusts see Section 12.10, at note 19 et seq.

**31.** Uniform Probate Code § 2–511(b). *See also Restatement (Second) of Trusts* § 54, comm. k (1959); *Restatement, Third, of Property (Wills and Other Donative Transfers)* § 3.8, comm. e (1998).

**32.** Sun Bank/Miami, N.A. v. Hogarth, 536 So.2d 263 (Fla.App.1988). *See also* Davisson v. Indiana Nat. Bank, 493 N.E.2d 1311 (Ind.App. 1986) (trust instrument discoverable for a will contest).

**33.** In re Estate of Norem, 561 So.2d 434 (Fla.App.1990). *But see* Estate of Harper, 93 T.C. 368 (1989) (wife can take under trust and elect against the will).

**34.** Uniform Probate Code § 2–511(c). *See also* Cal.Prob.Code § 6300; *cf. Restatement, Third, Trusts* § 19, comm. f (1996). In Estate of Rose v. Loucks, 772 S.W.2d 886 (Mo.App. 1989), this was held to apply even though the testator had created a similar trust after revoking the original one.

**35.** In re Estate of Stern, 636 N.E.2d 939 (Ill.App.1994).

**36.** *Restatement, Third, of Trusts* § 19, comm. a (1996); *Restatement, Third, of Property (Wills and Other Donative Transfers)* § 3.8, comm. f (1998). Use of this device will not cause the loss of some of the probate-avoidance advantages available to insurance and pensions under statutes like Cal.Prob.Code §§ 6323–24.

avoiding drafting two lengthy documents; the drafter and testator can focus their attention on the terms of the will.

## § 6.3 Will Substitutes

### *Comparison With Wills*

In cases involving wills, extrinsic evidence is generally excluded because the testator is unable to contradict possibly perjured testimony about his or her intent. Will substitutes present a similar problem, but a more liberal admission of extrinsic evidence may be appropriate for them. Most wills are made to order for the testator, but the terms of multiple party accounts (joint, trust or P.O.D.) usually appear on printed forms drafted primarily to protect the bank rather than to express the depositor's intention.[1] As one court said of a bank account signature card, "it can hardly be expected to accurately express the intention and relationships between the joint tenants about which the depository [bank] typically has little if any knowledge."[2] Many persons open joint accounts simply for the convenience of having another party who can make deposits and withdrawals for them, without any intent that the other party succeed to the account at death.[3] Nevertheless, some statutes exclude extrinsic evidence of intent in this situation. For example, a woman added the name of a friend to a joint account, but her will, executed at about the same time, recited that the joint accounts were "for convenience purposes only and without the intent of conveying any interest therein to the joint signator." Nevertheless, the friend was awarded the money in the account after the testator died on the basis of a statute which said that a deposit in a joint account "shall in the absence of fraud or undue influence, be conclusive evidence" of the depositor's evidence to vest title to the deposit in the survivor.[4] Some courts reach this result without a statute on the basis of the parol evidence rule.[5] One court, after reviewing the case law, concluded:

> Our efforts to determine survivorship rights by a *post-mortem* evaluation of extrinsic evidence of depositor intent are flawed to the point of offering no predictability. * * * [I]t is imperative that the depositor know that the opening of such an account is conclusive of his intent to transfer a survivorship interest.[6]

§ 6.3

1. Anderson v. Baker, 641 P.2d 1035, 1039 (Mont.1982). When handwritten words conflict with the printed portion of a form, the handwritten words control. Isbell v. Williams, 738 S.W.2d 20 (Tex.App.1987). The distinction between wills and will substitutes is undercut to some extent by the growing use of printed forms for wills.

2. In re Estate of Silver, 1 P.3d 358, 361 (Mont.2000). *See also* Blaircom v. Hires, 423 N.E.2d 609, 612 (Ind.1981) (dissent).

3. McGovern, *The Payable on Death Account and Other Will Substitutes,* 67 Nw. U.L.Rev. 7, 17 (1972); Hines, *Personal Property Joint Tenancies,* 54 Minn.L.Rev. 509, 530–51 (1970); James v. Elder, 368 S.E.2d 570 (Ga. App.1988) (finding that joint account just set up for convenience); Matter of Estate of Savage, 631 N.E.2d 797 (Ill.App.1994) (same).

4. Baker v. Leonard, 843 P.2d 1050 (Wash. 1993). The statute had later been altered but the court said the statute in effect when the account was opened controlled. *See also* In re Estate of Hill, 931 P.2d 1320 (Mont.1997); *cf.* Childs v. First National Bank, 410 S.E.2d 17 (S.C.App.1991) (account goes to survivor unless written evidence of contrary intent). In Seidl v. Estate of Michelsen, 487 So.2d 336 (Fla.App. 1986), the court avoided a similar result by a strained reading of the statute.

5. Cooper v. Crabb, 587 So.2d 236 (Miss. 1991); Blaircom v. Hires, 423 N.E.2d 609, 611 (Ind.1981); Jeschke v. United States, 814 F.2d 568, 574 (10th Cir.1987).

6. Wright v. Bloom, 635 N.E.2d 31, 37 (Ohio 1994). Followed in Robinson v. Delfino, 710 A.2d 154 (R.I.1998), at least if "survivorship rights are specifically provided for" in the

The Uniform Probate Code says that sums in a joint account on death of a party "belong to the surviving parties."[7] This might be thought to make the form of the account conclusive, since there is no language in the text comparable to that appearing in an early version of the Code (still in effect in some states) saying that the survivor got the funds "unless there is clear and convincing evidence of a different intention."[8] However, a comment to the present Code says that it "permit[s] a court to implement the intentions of the parties to a joint account * * * if it finds that the account was opened solely for the convenience of a party who supplied all of the funds reflected by the account and intended no present gift or death benefit for the other party."[9]

The dichotomy between "gift" and "convenience" is found in many opinions. For example, "if the intent to transfer a present interest to the named survivors at the making of the contract is lacking, it will reduce the account to one of convenience only, and no survivorship right will be found."[10] This can mislead, since persons creating a joint account often want the other party to be able to make deposits and withdrawals for them *and* receive the balance in the account when they die.[11] However, the absence of any possible convenience motive may reinforce the belief that the survivor was intended to enjoy the property where stock is put into joint tenancy. "Unlike a bank account, stocks may be liquidated only with the signature of both joint tenants. * * * Thus, stocks registered in joint tenancy are substantially less 'convenient' than joint bank accounts."[12]

Courts sometimes use a constructive trust rationale in order to effectuate a decedent's intent. For example, when a father with six children put property into joint tenancy with one daughter, a court imposed a trust on the daughter after the father died. Although parol evidence was not admissible "to explain or vary the terms of the instrument" which created the joint tenancy, the daughter held the property in trust since the father intended to benefit all his children and she had "accepted title on that basis."[13] This theory is usually held to require proof of wrongdoing by the "trustee" and thus not to apply if the survivor was unaware of the decedent's wishes.[14] However, when an

terms of the account and there is no "evidence of fraud, undue influence, duress, or lack of mental capacity." Where there is evidence of undue influence or incapacity, however, the terms of the account are not conclusive. Gotthardt v. Candle, 723 N.E.2d 1144 (Ohio App. 1999).

**7.** Uniform Probate Code § 6–212(a).

**8.** Uniform Probate Code (pre–1989) § 6–104(a). *See also* Cal. Prob. Code § 5302(a). The old UPC had certain anomalies, *e.g.* it distinguished between joint and POD accounts. *See* Graves v. Summit Bank, 541 N.E.2d 974 (Ind. App.1989) (can show contrary intent in a joint account, but not a POD account); McGovern, *Nonprobate Transfers under the Revised Uniform Probate Code*, 55 Alb.L.Rev. 1329, 1338 (1992).

**9.** Uniform Probate Code § 6–212, comment. For a commentary on this comment, see McGovern, *supra* note 8, at 1339.

**10.** Offret v. DiDomenico, 623 N.E.2d 128, 130 (Ohio App. 1993).

**11.** In re Estate of Blom, 600 N.E.2d 427, 431 (Ill.App.1992) (dissenting opinion); Matter of Estate of Savage, 631 N.E.2d 797, 802 (Ill. App.1994) (dissenting opinion).

**12.** In re Estate of Flecken, 640 N.E.2d 1329, 1332 (Ill.App.1994). *See also* Matter of Estate of Savage, 631 N.E.2d 797, 802 (Ill.App. 1994) (convenience explanation inapplicable to CDs); Rood v. Newberg, 718 N.E.2d 886, 894 (Mass.App.1999) (convenience explanation rejected for POD account).

**13.** Winsor v. Powell, 497 P.2d 292 (Kan. 1972). *See also* Estate of Zins by Kelsch v. Zins, 420 N.W.2d 729 (N.D.1988); Brand v. Brand, 811 F.2d 74 (2d Cir.1987); In re Estate of Vittorio, 546 N.W.2d 751 (Minn.App.1996).

**14.** Baker v. Leonard, 843 P.2d 1050, 1054 (Wash.1993); cf. Section 6.1, note 68.

insured named his brother beneficiary of life insurance and left an unwitnessed will stating that the brother should hold the proceeds for the insured's wife and children, the court held that an effective express trust was created even if the brother had not known the insured's wishes before the insured died.

> It was not necessary * * * to have notified the trustee and obtained his consent to act before designating him as such in the policies. Having accepted the trust, which he might have disclaimed, it was the duty of the [brother] * * * to carry out its provisions.[15]

Courts are more likely to reject extrinsic evidence of intent when they construe a "custom-made" trust rather than a printed form. Even though the statute of wills does not apply to inter-vivos transfers, the parol evidence rule does. Therefore, when construing a living trust "the settlor's intention * * * must be ascertained by analyzing the trust instrument. * * * Only when the trust instrument is ambiguous can a court consider extrinsic evidence."[16]

It is hard to reconcile this idea with the equally well-accepted principle, that trusts, like contracts, can be reformed to correct a mistake in the writing.[17] For example, when "due to a scrivener's error" a trust would have been "subject to nearly $400,000 in otherwise avoidable taxes," a court reformed it "to effectuate the actual intent of the settlor."[18] Another court reformed a trust for a mistake, saying even though "wills cannot be reformed," living trusts "may be reformed after the death of the settlor for a unilateral[19] drafting mistake."[20]

### *Type of Evidence*

Trusts can be reformed only if there is " 'full, clear, and decisive proof' of mistake."[21] Similarly, it is often said that evidence of an intent inconsistent with the form of a bank account must be "clear and convincing."[22]

Similar principles apply to gifts under the Uniform Transfers to Minors Act. For example, a father who had established accounts for his children later claimed that he had never intended to make a gift and did not understand the effect of signing the signature cards. The court held that his signature "did not create an irrebuttable presumption of intent," but "clear, convincing,

**15.** Duncan by Duncan v. Duncan, 884 S.W.2d 383, 388 (Mo.App.1994).

**16.** First Nat. Bank v. Anthony, 557 A.2d 957, 960 (Me.1989). *See also* Matter of Frank & Lotus Huxtable Living Trust, 757 P.2d 1262 (Kan.1988); Malachowski v. Bank One, Indianapolis, 590 N.E.2d 559 (Ind.1992); Mercury Bay Boating v. San Diego Yacht, 557 N.E.2d 87 (N.Y.1990); *Restatement, Second, Trusts* § 164, comm. e (1959).

However, in the case of "Totten" trusts, the written evidence of intent is so sketchy that extrinsic evidence is admissible to rebut the inferences of intent made by the law. *Restatement, Third, Trusts* § 26, comm. a (1999).

**17.** *Restatement, Second, Trusts* § 333 (1959); *Restatement, Second, Contracts* § 155 (1981).

**18.** Loeser v. Talbot, 589 N.E.2d 301 (Mass. 1992). *See also* Griffin v. Griffin, 832 P.2d 810 (Okl.1992).

**19.** In contracts, the mistake must usually be "mutual," shared by both parties, *Restatement, Second, Contracts* § 155 (1981). Donative transfers are different. See Section 6.4, note 14.

**20.** In re Estate of Robinson, 720 So.2d 540, 541, 543 (Fla.App.1998).

**21.** Loeser v. Talbot, 589 N.E.2d 301, 304 (Mass.1992). *See also Restatement, Second, Contracts* § 155, comm. c (1981).

**22.** Calif.Prob.Code § 5302; Matter of Estate of Martin, 559 N.E.2d 1112, 1114 (Ill.App. 1990); In re Estate of Combee, 583 So.2d 708 (Fla.App.1991).

unequivocal and unmistakable evidence'' was required to overcome it and the father's testimony failed to meet this standard.[23]

Courts tend to view with suspicion extrinsic evidence offered by an interested party. Thus when a man opened a joint account with his sister, and after he died, an affidavit by one of his brothers stating that the decedent had told him that he wanted his estate divided equally among his brothers and sisters and had created the account only for convenience was held to be ''inadmissible without corroboration.''[24]

Declarations of intention by the decedent are admissible,[25] but courts usually give greater weight to the circumstances. The fact that a written disposition appears unnatural may indicate that the decedent intended something else. Thus when a person with minor children named his father beneficiary of an insurance policy, the court found that he intended the father to hold the proceeds in trust for the insured's children; it would have been ''unnatural for the insured to have designated his father as beneficiary without having a corresponding intent that these proceeds be used for the benefit of his minor sons.''[26] When a father put one child's name on a joint bank account, the account, which amounted to over two-thirds of the father's assets was awarded to the father's estate, since ''no reason is shown why he would make such a sizeable gift'' to one child.[27] But a child was allowed to take as surviving joint tenant when he ''had a very close relationship'' with his mother whereas his sisters ''seldom helped his mother'' and they '' 'fought like cats and dogs.' '' Also, in this case the disputed property constituted a relatively small fraction of the mother's estate. She ''could well have intended to favor the child closest to her by giving him the two CDs [held jointly] while still giving substantial benefits to the others.''[28]

Some courts focus exclusively on evidence of a depositor's intent at the time when the account was created. The fact that a ''controversy [between the parties] began *after*'' the accounts were established is irrelevant.[29] Subsequent evidence of a settlor's intent has been held inadmissible to resolve an ambiguity in a trust because this ''would allow a settlor to revoke or modify a trust at his pleasure.''[30] But most courts are not so strict. ''The critical question is the intent of the alleged donor at the time the account was created * * * but subsequent events may be considered as having a bearing on'' this.[31] When a father put his daughters' names on a brokerage account in 1980 and

**23.** Heath by Heath v. Heath, 493 N.E.2d 97, 101 (Ill.App.1986). *See also* Golden v. Golden, 434 So.2d 978 (Fla.App.1983); Gordon v. Gordon, 419 N.Y.S.2d 684 (A.D.1979). But in State v. Keith, 610 N.E.2d 1017 (Ohio App. 1991) extrinsic evidence was successfully used to show lack of donative intent in a transfer under the Act.

**24.** Sawyer v. Lancaster, 719 S.W.2d 346, 350 (Tex.App.1986). *See also* Matter of Estate of Abbot, 510 N.E.2d 619 (Ill.App.1987) (interested testimony barred by Dead Man statute); James v. Elder, 368 S.E.2d 570, 572 (Ga.App. 1988) (''the trial judge was authorized, if not required, to reject [testimony] as self-serving'').

**25.** Pontius v. Nadolske, 584 N.E.2d 1228 (Ohio App.1989).

**26.** Rosen v. Rosen, 167 So.2d 70, 71 (Fla. App.1964).

**27.** Estate of Stanley v. Sandiford, 337 S.E.2d 248, 251 (S.C.App.1985). *See also* Matter of Estate of Abbot, 510 N.E.2d 619 (Ill.App. 1987) (joint account would create ''a gross disparity'' among children).

**28.** Matter of Estate of Lewis, 549 N.E.2d 960, 961, 964 (Ill.App.1990).

**29.** Rasmussen v. LaMagdelaine, 566 N.E.2d 864, 870 (Ill.App.1991).

**30.** Bonney v. Granger, 356 S.E.2d 138 (S.C.App.1987).

**31.** In re Estate of Blom, 600 N.E.2d 427, 429 (Ill.App.1992).

in 1984 executed a will which left the accounts in trust for his wife, the court said that the will showed that he had put his daughters' names on the account "simply for his business or personal convenience" rather than as a gift to them.[32]

### *Protection of Third Parties*

When extrinsic evidence of intent contradicts a writing, third parties who have reasonably relied on the writing are protected.[33] Thus under the Uniform Probate Code a bank is not liable if it pays sums in a multiple party account according to the terms of the account, even if they do not reflect the decedent's intention, unless the bank has previously received written notice not to do so.[34]

## § 6.4 Deeds of Land: Reformation, Constructive and Resulting Trusts

If *A* executes a deed which by its terms conveys land to *B*, can *A* or a third person show by evidence outside the deed that *B* was not intended to keep the land? The parol evidence rule may bar such evidence.[1] However, there are theories which can be used to get around the rule.

Just as a will may be denied probate on the basis of extrinsic evidence that the maker had no testamentary intent,[2] parol evidence can be used to show that a deed was not intended to operate according to its terms. For example, a mother who had deeded land to her daughter was allowed to cancel the deed on the ground that she had signed the deed only to avoid probate with no intent to give the daughter a present interest.[3] Parol evidence can also show that a deed was given conditional on a promise of support of the grantor.[4] A fortiori, someone who is induced by fraud to sign a paper which he does not realize is a deed can have it set aside.[5]

### *Reformation*

Another well-settled exception to the parol evidence rule allows mistakes in a deed to be reformed. For example, when a deed was intended for a

**32.** Parker v. Kokot, 793 P.2d 195, 201 (Idaho 1990). *See also* Matter of Estate of Savage, 631 N.E.2d 797 (Ill.App.1994); Derman v. Dreznick, 546 A.2d 1091 (N.J.Super.App.Div.1988). This reasoning undercuts to some extent the rule that a will cannot alter the terms of a joint account. Section 5.5, note 80 et seq. An earlier will of the depositor was used to show that he did not intend to give the survivor the proceeds of a joint account in Hopper v. Rech, 375 N.W.2d 538, 542 (Minn. App.1985).

**33.** *Restatement (Second) of Contracts* § 155, comm. f (1981).

**34.** Uniform Probate Code § 6–226. *See also* Calif.Prob.Code § 5405.

**§ 6.4**

**1.** Rubenstein v. Sela, 672 P.2d 492 (Ariz. App.1983); Mahrenholz v. County Board of School Trustees, 466 N.E.2d 322 (Ill.App.1984). Parol evidence may be admissible to resolve an ambiguity in the deed. Bledsoe v. Hill, 747 P.2d 10 (Colo.App.1987); cf. Section 6.1, note 14.

**2.** *Id.*, note 11.

**3.** Myers v. Weems, 876 P.2d 861 (Or.App. 1994). *See also* Anderson v. Brinkerhoff, 756 P.2d 95 (Utah App.1988); *cf.* Fine v. Cohen, 623 N.E.2d 1134 (Mass.App.1993) (parol evidence showed "trust" was not intended to be binding).

**4.** Trout v. Parker, 595 N.E.2d 1015 (Ohio App.1991).

**5.** Pedersen v. Bibioff, 828 P.2d 1113 (Wash.App.1992). *See also Restatement, Second, Contracts* § 163 (1981) (no effective assent to a contract where its character is misrepresented); *Restatement, Second, of Property (Donative Transfers)* § 34.7 (1990) (donative transfer induced by fraud may be set aside).

husband alone but was made out by mistake to the husband and his wife, the husband's executor was able to have it reformed.[6]

Some cases say the mistake must be as to the words in the deed rather than their legal effect; for example, the fact that the maker of a deed did not understand the legal significance of joint tenancy does not warrant reformation.[7] But the Restatement of Contracts says that "if the parties are mistaken with respect to the legal effect of the language that they have used, the writing may be reformed to reflect the intended effect."[8]

Relief may be denied if the mistake was the product of "supine negligence." A person cannot claim "he did not understand what he was signing when there was nothing to prevent him from merely reading the deed to discover its contents."[9] But grantors who had "great difficulty in communicating in the English language and did not understand the legal implications of the term 'life estate' " were able to have a deed reformed.[10]

Opinions differ as to whether or not the mistake must be mutual. The Restatement of Contracts generally gives relief only when "*both* parties as to" a writing are mistaken.[11] An uncle who deeded land to his niece, thinking that he was signing a will, got no relief because she did not share his mistake.[12] When a husband put a house in joint tenancy with his wife, his executor was not allowed to recover the house on proof that he had not intended to create a joint tenancy; his "hidden intention," undisclosed to his wife was irrelevant.[13] However, some courts allow reformation of unilateral mistakes in a gratuitous transfer on the ground that "the expectations of a donee are less worthy of protection than are those of a transferee who gives value for the property" (unless the donee has changed position in reliance upon the transfer).[14]

Reformation is equitable relief and "equity will not ordinarily aid a volunteer." This means that the recipient of a gift may be barred from seeking reformation.[15] But when a father deeded land to his children "for $10 and love and affection," the children were able to have the deed reformed to

**6.** Geissel v. Galbraith, 695 P.2d 1316 (Nev. 1985). *See also* Matter of Estate of Vadney, 634 N.E.2d 976 (N.Y.1994) (deed reformed to add "as joint tenants"); *Restatement, Second, of Property (Donative Transfers)* § 34.7, comm. d (1990). *But see* Groh v. Ballard, 965 S.W.2d 872 (Mo.App.1998) (interpreting a statute which made deeds voidable for "fraud, duress, or undue influence" as precluding reformation for mistake).

**7.** Boone v. Grier, 688 P.2d 1070 (Ariz.App. 1984).

**8.** *Restatement, Second, Contracts* § 155, comm. a (1981). *See also* West One Trust Co. v. Morrison, 861 P.2d 1058 (Utah App.1993) (reformation allowed where parties did not understand meaning of "joint tenants").

**9.** Yohe v. Yohe, 353 A.2d 417, 420 (Pa. 1976). *See also* Briggs v. Liddell, 699 P.2d 770, 773 (Utah 1985) (no reformation unless "the error occurred despite exercise of due care"); Wright v. Blevins, 705 P.2d 113 (Mont.1985) (no relief to party who signs a deed without reading it); Henkle v. Henkle, 600 N.E.2d 791 (Ohio App.1991).

**10.** Yano v. Yano, 697 P.2d 1132, 1134–35 (Ariz.App.1985).

**11.** *Restatement, Second, Contracts* § 155 (1981).

**12.** Felonenko v. Siomka, 637 P.2d 1338, 1341 (Or.App.1981). *See also* Briggs v. Liddell, 699 P.2d 770 (Utah 1985) (unilateral mistake does not allow reformation of an insurance policy); Henkle v. Henkle, 600 N.E.2d 791 (Ohio App.1991).

**13.** Estate of Levine, 178 Cal.Rptr. 275 (App.1981). *See also* Schulz v. Miller, 837 P.2d 71 (Wyo.1992); Estate of Gallio, 39 Cal.Rptr.2d 470 (App.1995).

**14.** Yohe v. Yohe, 353 A.2d 417, 424 (Pa. 1976) (concurring opinion). *See also* Yano v. Yano, 697 P.2d 1132 (Ariz.App.1985); Shoemaker v. Estate of Freeman, 967 P.2d 871, 876 (Okl.1998); *Restatement (Second) of Trusts* § 333, comm. e (1959); *Restatement, Second, Contracts* § 155, comm. b (1981).

**15.** *Restatement, Second, Contracts* § 155, comm. d (1981).

include property which had been omitted by mistake; "any nominal consideration accompanied by 'love and affection' is sufficient."[16] Also, a donee has been permitted to sue the donor's heirs for reformation where the donor himself would not have opposed it.[17]

Courts distinguish between mistakes as to the contents of a deed and mistakes of fact; they refuse to upset deeds just because the grantor acted under an erroneous factual supposition. For example, a father gave his son land under which gas was later discovered. The donee's sister claimed that "had the father known of the valuable oil and gas deposits he would have divided them equally between son and daughter," but her claim was rejected as resting on "speculation or conjecture."[18] However, the Second Restatement of Property provides that a mistake of fact may be significant enough to justify setting aside or reforming a transfer, whether by deed or will.[19]

### *Constructive Trusts*

Constructive trusts are imposed on devisees who promised the testator to give the property to another person and refuse to do so.[20] A similar rule applies to inter-vivos transfers where the transferee at the time of the transfer[21] promised to hold the land for the transferor or for a third person. The Restatement of Trusts distinguishes between inter-vivos and testamentary transfers. A devisee or heir always "holds the property upon a constructive trust for the person for whom he agreed to hold it,"[22] but a constructive trust is imposed on inter-vivos transferees only in certain circumstances. As Professor Scott noted, the distinction seems perverse, since "there is less danger of perjured testimony where the transaction is inter vivos than where it is testamentary in character."[23]

However, the categories of cases in which a constructive trusts are imposed on transfers by deed are so broadly defined that the distinction between deeds and wills has limited practical significance. First, a constructive trust will be imposed on a grantee who was guilty of fraud.[24] In England, *any* breach of promise constitutes "fraud,"[25] but American courts define fraud to include promises only when they were made without any intent to perform

**16.** Snyder v. Peterson, 814 P.2d 1204 (Wash.App.1991). *See also* Roots v. Uppole, 400 N.E.2d 1003 (Ill.App.1980).

**17.** Zabolotny v. Fedorenko, 315 N.W.2d 668 (N.D.1982).

**18.** Thomas v. Reid, 608 P.2d 1123, 1124 (N.M.1980). *See also* Harmston v. Harmston, 680 P.2d 751 (Utah 1984); Getty v. Getty, 232 Cal.Rptr. 603, 614 (App.1986); *cf.* § 6.1. But in Berger v. United States, 487 F.Supp. 49 (W.D.Pa.1980), a settlor was allowed to rescind a trust which he had created under the mistaken belief he was going to obtain a government position.

**19.** *Restatement, Second, Property, Donative Transfers* § 34.7, comm. d (1990). The same conclusions are even more strongly stated in the case of fraudulent representations.

**20.** Section 6.1, at note 62 et seq.

**21.** A promise made *after* the transfer does not give rise to a constructive trust. Walsh v. Walsh, 841 P.2d 831 (Wyo.1992).

**22.** *Restatement (Second) of Trusts* § 55 (1959). A transfer made in contemplation of death is treated like a will for this purpose. *Id.* § 45(1)(c); Person v. Pagnotta, 541 P.2d 483 (Or.1975).

**23.** 1A A. Scott, *Trusts* § 55.9, at 93 (4th ed. Fratcher 1987).

**24.** *Restatement, Second, Trusts* § 44(1)(a) (trust for settlor), § 45(1)(a) (trust for 3d person); *Restatement, Third, Trusts* § 24(2)(a) (1996); Guy v. Guy, 411 S.E.2d 403 (N.C.App. 1991).

**25.** Davies, *Constructive Trusts, Contracts and Estoppels,* 1 Adelaide L.Rev. 200, 207 (1980); F. Maitland, *Equity* 59 (1913); *cf.* Masino v. Sechrest, 66 N.W.2d 740 (Wis.1954) (to hold property contrary to the terms of an agreement is "constructive fraud").

when the promise was made. Fraud can be inferred from refusal to perform a promise,[26] but a grantee who intended to perform and later changed his mind is not guilty of fraud,[27] although this distinction is sometimes blurred in cases that impose a trust on the basis of "constructive fraud."[28]

A constructive trust is also imposed if the grantor and grantee were in a "confidential relationship".[29] Arguably, such a relationship exists whenever a transferor intended to create a trust, for trust and confidence are synonyms. But courts usually "require additional evidence of confidence in the relation between [the settlor and trustee] before they will impose a constructive trust."[30] However, confidential relationship is an elastic term. Many cases involve transfers between members of the same family. In New York a confidential relationship is always held to exist among family members, but this is not true in Massachusetts.[31] A confidential relationship has been found between unrelated friends,[32] whereas close relatives are sometimes found not to have had such a relationship.[33]

Some opinions suggest that a confidential relationship must be an unequal one. Thus a court refused to impose a constructive trust on land which a woman conveyed to her fiance/cohabitant, saying that "the doctrine of confidential relationship * * * implies a position of superiority occupied by one of the parties over the other" and here the parties had an "equal relationship."[34] This seems to confuse undue influence (where the idea of a "confidential relationship" also plays an important role)[35] with the question whether oral promises should be enforced. Another court got it right, when it held that while there was no confidential relationship between a father and daughter to support a claim of undue influence, "for the purpose of imposing a constructive trust, a confidential relationship can be based on an agreement between the owner of property and another who will distribute the owner's property in a specified manner."[36] A rationale for enforcing such promises is that the confidential relationship renders plausible a claim that the parties made an agreement without reducing it to writing. "The existence of the

**26.** *Restatement (Second) of Trusts* § 44, comm. b (1959); March v. Gerstenschlager, 436 S.W.2d 6 (Mo.1969).

**27.** Nessralla v. Peck, 532 N.E.2d 685 (Mass.1989); *Restatement, Third, Trusts* § 24, comm. e (1996) (refusal to perform promise is "some but not conclusive evidence of" fraud).

**28.** Baizley v. Baizley, 734 A.2d 1117, 1118 (Me.1999).

**29.** *Restatement (Second) of Trusts* §§ 44(1)(b), 45(1)(b) (1959); *Restatement, Third, Trusts* § 24(2)(b) (1996); Estates of Kalwitz v. Kalwitz, 717 N.E.2d 904, 913 (Ind.App. 1999) (confidential relationship creates "constructive fraud").

**30.** *Restatement (Second) of Trusts* § 44, comm. c (1959). *See also Restatement, Third, Trusts* § 24, comm. f (1996).

**31.** Rudow v. Fogel, 426 N.E.2d 155, 157 (Mass.App.1981). In Gulack v. Gulack, 620 A.2d 181 (Conn.App.1993) the court found a confidential relationship between two brothers in "a close knit family"). *See also* Baizley v. Baizley, 734 A.2d 1117, 1119 (Me.1999) ("familial relationship" creates "a relationship of trust"). A confidential relationship is commonly found between spouses. Rajanna v. KRR Investments, Inc., 810 S.W.2d 548 (Mo.App. 1991); Matter of Estate of McKim, 807 P.2d 215 (N.M.1991).

**32.** David v. Russo, 415 N.E.2d 531 (Ill. App.1980); Thomasi v. Koch, 660 P.2d 806 (Wyo.1983); Klein v. Shaw, 706 P.2d 1348 (Idaho App.1985).

**33.** Beelman v. Beelman, 460 N.E.2d 55 (Ill.App.1984); Meskell v. Meskell, 243 N.E.2d 804 (Mass.1969).

**34.** Mattes v. Olearain, 759 P.2d 1177, 1179 (Utah App.1988). *See also* Estates of Kalwitz v. Kalwitz, 717 N.E.2d 904, 913 (Ind.App. 1999) (confidential relationship arises "where one party dominates a weaker party"); Badger Bldg. Corp. v. Gregoric, 430 N.E.2d 561 (Ill. App.1981).

**35.** See Section 7.3, note 27 et seq.

**36.** Heck v. Archer, 927 P.2d 495, 502 (Kan.App.1996).

confidential and fiduciary relationship * * * was precisely the reason for their failure to have an express agreement to convey. Strength of this relationship is shown by lack of the existence of such an agreement."[37] The argument becomes circular: the absence of a writing indicates the existence of a confidential relationship which makes a writing unnecessary.

Constructive trusts are also imposed when oral evidence shows that a deed was intended only as a mortgage.[38] This may be explained by the fact that mortgagors are usually needy, and so they may sign anything in order to get the loan, including a deed which incorrectly states the intent of the parties.[39]

Oral trusts are also enforced on an "estoppel" theory when a beneficiary has relied on the trust. For example, after a father deeded a farm to his two oldest children with the intent that they hold it for all his children, the younger children worked to improve the farm. The trust was enforceable because the trustees had "induced others to change their position."[40]

When a deed conveys land from *A* to *B*, any attempt to show that *C* was actually supposed to enjoy the land would seem to violate the parol evidence rule, but courts hold that an understanding about beneficial ownership is not inconsistent with a deed which conveys legal title. "Where realty is conveyed by a deed which * * * does not stipulate * * * that the grantee therein named shall take the equitable as well as the legal title, the parol evidence rule does not preclude the establishment of a parol trust."[41] Section 7 of the Statute of Frauds, with its requirement that trusts of land "shall be manifested and proved" by a signed writing poses a more serious problem to the enforcement of oral trusts. Most American jurisdictions have adopted this (with minor variations in language), along with Section 8 which excepts trusts which "arise or result by the implication or construction of law."[42] Courts have made such extensive use of the exception in Section 8 for "resulting" and "constructive" trusts that the rule of section 7 has become almost, but not quite meaningless.

Decisions in the few American states which have not adopted sections 7 and 8 of the Statute of Frauds are inconsistent. Some courts hold that these provisions are part of the common law,[43] but in other states the failure to enact them has led courts to enforce oral trusts of land.[44]

The Uniform Trusts Act provides that if land is conveyed "by deed to a person on a trust which is unenforceable on account of the Statute of Frauds," a trustee who fails to perform the trust "shall be under a duty to convey the real property to the settlor or his successor in interest."[45] This

**37.** Thompson v. Nesheim, 159 N.W.2d 910, 918 (Minn.1968).

**38.** Beelman v. Beelman, 460 N.E.2d 55 (Ill.App.1984); McGill v. Biggs, 434 N.E.2d 772 (Ill.App.1982); *Restatement (Second) of Trusts* § 44(1)(c) (1959).

**39.** 1A A. Scott, *Trusts* § 44.3 (4th ed. Fratcher 1987).

**40.** Potucek v. Potucek, 719 P.2d 14, 18 (Kan.App.1986). *See also Restatement, Third, Trusts* § 24, comm. c (1996).

**41.** Kelley v. Kelley, 575 S.W.2d 612, 616 (Tex.Civ.App.1978). *See also Restatement, Third, Trusts* § 21 (1996); Schaneman v. Wright, 470 N.W.2d 566 (Neb.1991).

**42.** *Restatement, Third, Trusts* § 22, comm. a (1996); Cal.Prob. Code §§ 15003, 15206.

**43.** Bassett v. Bassett, 798 P.2d 160, 163 (N.M.1990).

**44.** Ellis v. Vespoint, 403 S.E.2d 542 (N.C.App.1991); Linger v. Rohr, 383 S.E.2d 825 (W.Va.1989). *See also* Section 4.6, note 49.

**45.** Uniform Trusts Act § 16. This Act promulgated in 1937 is not to be confused with the Uniform Trust Code of 2000.

prevents the trustee from being unjustly enriched but does not effectuate the settlor's intent to benefit a third party. The Third Restatement of Trusts adopts a modified form of this rule, which provides "an appropriate balance between competing policies. It prevents unjust enrichment and yet gives force to the Statute of Frauds" by not enforcing the trust absent fraud, confidential relationship or estoppel. Under the Restatement, if the original settlor has died without repudiating the trust, "the transferee can be compelled to hold the * * * property upon constructive trust for the beneficiaries."[46]

### *Resulting Trusts*

The Statute of Frauds allows enforcement of resulting as well as constructive trusts which contradict the written evidence of title. Resulting trusts arise in several situations. For example, when an express trust fails to provide what to do with property in a certain situation, there may be a resulting trust for the settlor.[47] Here we are focussing on what is commonly called the "purchase money" resulting trust. "Where the property is purchased and the title is taken in the name of one person, but the purchase price is paid by another, * * * [the person] who furnished the consideration money is presumed to intend to acquire a corresponding beneficial interest in the lands purchased."[48] Some courts apply the same rules to resulting and constructive trusts or confuse the two,[49] but the Restatement distinguishes between them, requiring fraud or a confidential relation to enforce a constructive trust but not for enforcement of a resulting trust.[50] Professor Scott suggested that resulting trusts were more readily enforced because the intention of the parties "is evidenced by the circumstances of the transaction rather than by the language of the parties" and thus there was not "the same danger of perjured testimony."[51] However, the inference that should be derived from circumstances is not obvious. At one time whenever deeds were given without consideration, courts presumed that the donee was intended to hold the land in trust, but today they presume that the transferor intended to make a gift to the transferee,[52] whereas they presume a trust was intended in favor of a person who pays for land which is deeded to another.

Perhaps the distinction is based on the fact that a deed normally means what it says and the signer should understand this. But when a buyer of land instructs the seller to put title in the name of a third person, this instruction is often not reflected in a signed writing; the grantor signs the deed but not the person who pays the price.[53]

**46.** *Restatement, Third, Trusts* § 24, comm. h (1996).

**47.** *Restatement, Third, Trusts* § 8 (1996).

**48.** Browder v. Hite, 602 S.W.2d 489, 492 (Tenn.App.1980). *See also* Hofferkamp v. Brehm, 652 N.E.2d 1381, 1388 (Ill.App.1995); Hilliard v. Hilliard, 844 P.2d 54 (Mont.1992); *Restatement (Third) of Trusts* § 9 (1996). When the parties intend to give a beneficial interest to a third party, other than the payor, this is treated as a constructive trust. *Id.*, comm. c.

**49.** Leonard v. Counts, 272 S.E.2d 190, 195 (Va.1980); Yates v. Taylor, 791 P.2d 924, 926 (Wash.App.1990) ("constructive trust" arises when one person pays and title is taken in the name of another).

**50.** *Compare Restatement (Third) of Trusts* § 9 *with id.* § 24 (1996).

**51.** 5 A. Scott, *Trusts* § 440 (4th ed. Fratcher 1989).

**52.** *Restatement (Third) of Trusts* § 9, comm. a (1996).

**53.** The payor "was not the grantor, and we do not have the evidentiary protection of his signing a deed before independent witnesses." Hofferkamp v. Brehm, 652 N.E.2d 1381, 1389 (Ill.App.1995).

The differing legal treatment of resulting and constructive trusts is not of great practical significance. If a gratuitous conveyance was intended to create a trust, the beneficiary can usually prove "fraud" or a "confidential relation" and thereby enforce the trust. Conversely, the presumption of a purchase-money resulting trust can be rebutted by evidence that the payor intended to give the land to the person in whose name title was placed.[54]

When the person who pays for land and the transferee named in the deed are related by blood or marriage, courts presume that the payor intended a gift rather than to create a trust. According to the Restatement of Trusts, the presumption of a gift arises when the transferee was a "spouse,[55] descendant, or other natural object of the bounty" of the person who paid the price.[56] The presumption of a gift has also been applied to a mother-in-law who paid for a house which was conveyed to her son-in-law,[57] but not an aunt who bought a home for her nephew.[58] These distinctions seem arbitrary, but they are not very important because evidence of the parties' actual intent is admissible.[59] However, the presumption of a gift is not overcome by one party's "after-the-fact testimony that the property was * * * not an intended gift"; proof of a "common understanding" of the parties is required.[60]

Some state statutes appear to abolish the purchase-money resulting trust. In Kentucky "when a deed is made to one person, and the consideration is paid by another no use or trusts results in favor of the latter."[61] But this has been held to bar only trusts which arise "from the naked fact that a person has furnished consideration to buy land," and not proof of "an express parol agreement establishing a trust."[62]

A purchase money resulting trust can arise from a sale on credit. For example, a court imposed a trust when a mother and son agreed that a house would be deeded to the son in order to qualify for a veteran's loan, but the mother would make all the payments and own the house. Where the price is not paid at the time of purchase, "the party seeking imposition of the trust

**54.** *Restatement (Third) of Trusts* § 9(1)(a) (1996); Thor v. McDearmid, 817 P.2d 1380 (Wash.App.1991); Erb v. Kohnke, 824 P.2d 903 (Idaho App.1992).

**55.** In the Second Restatement § 442, the comparable words were "*wife*, child, or other natural object." *See* Tarkington v. Tarkington, 272 S.E.2d 99 (N.C.1980) (no gift presumed when wife buys land in names of both spouses). However, more recent cases generally reject any such gender-based distinction. In re Estate of Koch, 697 N.E.2d 931, 933 (Ill.App. 1998).

**56.** *Restatement, Third, Trusts* § 9(2) (1996). *See also* Wachter v. Wachter, 357 S.E.2d 38 (W.Va.1987) (gift presumed when wife pays for land put in husband's name); Matter of Estate of Lettengarver, 813 P.2d 468 (Mont.1991) (joint funds used to buy house put into W's name); Durward v. Nelson, 481 N.W.2d 586 (N.D.1992) (parents pay for land deeded to their son and his wife).

**57.** Matter of Estate of Hock's, 655 P.2d 1111 (Utah 1982).

**58.** Peterson v. Kabrich, 691 P.2d 1360 (Mont.1984). *See also* Blalak v. Mid Valley Transp., Inc., 858 P.2d 683 (Ariz.App.1993) (no gift presumed when daughter pays for land put in mother's name); Hofferkamp v. Brehm, 652 N.E.2d 1381 (Ill.App.1995) (no presumption when parties are engaged but not married); *cf.* Rakhman v. Zusstone, 957 S.W.2d 241 (Ky. 1997) (gift presumed between unmarried cohabitants).

**59.** *Restatement (Third) of Trusts* § 9, comm. c (1996); Treschak v. Yorkville Nat. Bank, 604 N.E.2d 1081 (Ill.App.1992); Hilliard v. Hilliard, 844 P.2d 54 (Mont.1992).

**60.** Valladee v. Valladee, 718 P.2d 206, 209 (Ariz.App.1986). Under Cal.Fam.Code § 2581 property held jointly by spouses is presumed to be community unless there is evidence in writing to the contrary.

**61.** Ky.Rev.Stat. § 381.170. *See also* Minn. Stat. § 501.07.

**62.** Horn v. Horn, 562 S.W.2d 319, 320 (Ky.App.1978). *See also Restatement (Second) of Trusts* § 440, comm. i (1959).

must have incurred an absolute obligation to pay [it] as a part of the original transaction," but she "need not be obligated directly to the grantee's lender; it is sufficient if [she] is obligated to the grantee, pursuant to a promise made before title passes, to make payments to the grantee."[63] However, if there is no such agreement before title passes, a resulting trust does not arise in favor of someone who furnishes funds to the owner subsequent to the purchase.[64]

If someone pays part of the price of land, the resulting trust presumptively arises only as to part,[65] but the land is not beneficially owned in proportion to contributions if the parties intended otherwise. For example, when two brothers contributed to the acquisition of land and title was taken in the name of one, he held half in trust for his brother, since even though they had not paid equal portions, the evidence showed that "from the inception * * * the brothers looked upon themselves as equal partners."[66]

### *Nature of Proof*

Before granting reformation courts require that the evidence of mistake in a deed be clear and convincing. Reformation is denied, for example, if the donor's testimony is equivocal and unsupported by disinterested witnesses.[67] Claims to a resulting or constructive trust also require evidence that is "clear, convincing, unequivocal, and unmistakable."[68] Appellate courts generally defer to findings by a trial court, however. For example, an appellate court, while saying that "proof of an oral trust must be [of] the clearest and most convincing character," affirmed a decision imposing a trust because "this case turns primarily on the credibility of witnesses" and "a court of review which cannot view the witness * * * ought not to reverse that finding absent 'clear, concrete, and convincing evidence to the contrary.' "[69] It is the *trial* court which must be satisfied that the proof was clear and convincing.[70]

Testimony by interested witnesses can be "clear and convincing,"[71] but it may be excluded under a Dead Man statute.[72] Proof sometimes falls short of

**63.** Watkins v. Watkins, 351 S.E.2d 331, 334 (N.C.App.1986). *See also Restatement (Second) of Trusts* § 448, comm. a (1959); Stone v. McCarthy, 511 N.E.2d 780 (Ill.App.1987); Simmons v. Smith, 482 N.E.2d 887 (Mass.App. 1985).

**64.** Leicht v. Quirin, 558 N.E.2d 715 (Ill. App.1990); Workman v. Douglas, 419 N.E.2d 1340, 1345 (Ind.App.1981); Gitto v. Gitto, 778 P.2d 906 (Mont.1989); *Restatement (Second) of Trusts* § 457 (1959).

**65.** *Restatement (Third) of Trusts* § 9, comm. c (1996); Bassett v. Bassett, 798 P.2d 160 (N.M.1990); Yates v. Taylor, 791 P.2d 924 (Wash.App.1990).

**66.** Bassett v. Bassett, 798 P.2d 160, 168 (N.M.1990).

**67.** In re La Rocca's Trust Estate, 192 A.2d 409 (Pa.1963). *See also Restatement, Second, Contracts* § 155, comm. c (1981).

**68.** In re Estate of McCormick, 634 N.E.2d 341, 345 (Ill.App.1994). According to *Restatement, Third, Trusts* § 24, comm h (1996), clear and convincing evidence is needed to show that a trust was intended (when the deed does not indicate such an intent), but "a preponderance of the evidence is then sufficient to establish the intended interests of the beneficiaries." *See also id.* § 9, comm. f (as to resulting trusts).

**69.** Browder v. Hite, 602 S.W.2d 489, 495 (Tenn.App.1980). *See also* Bassett v. Bassett, 798 P.2d 160, 164 (N.M.1990); Greenwald v. Spring Hill Ford, Inc., 527 N.E.2d 1095 (Ill. App.1988).

**70.** Thomasi v. Koch, 660 P.2d 806, 811 (Wyo.1983). *But cf.* Matter of Estate of Hock's, 655 P.2d 1111, 1114 (Utah 1982) ("smaller quantum of contrary evidence" suffices to upset trial court's finding when "based upon a clear and convincing standard").

**71.** Fenton v. Walter, 612 S.W.2d 17 (Mo. App.1981).

**72.** Thompson v. Nesheim, 159 N.W.2d 910 (Minn.1968); Parks v. Zions First Nat. Bank, 673 P.2d 590, 606 (Utah 1983).

the clear and convincing standard, not because the testimony is conflicting but because the parties' intentions were indefinite or vague.[73]

Proof is often circumstantial. The fact that a deed was given for an inadequate consideration is evidence that it was intended as a mortgage.[74] A grantor's staying in possession is evidence that he intended to retain a beneficial interest in property. Thus a father who had put land in his son's name was able to impose a resulting trust, despite the presumption of a gift which arises in this situation, because he had collected the rents, paid the insurance and taxes, maintained the property and otherwise treated it as his own.[75]

Statements of intent are also admissible if they relate to the time when the property was transferred. A person who conveys land with the intent that the grantee own it beneficially cannot later declare that the grantee holds in trust; this would be tantamount to revoking an irrevocable gift. When a mother conveyed land to her daughter, the daughter's brothers were unable to have a trust imposed on her when their evidence of the mother's intent came from conversations which occurred after the deed to the daughter was delivered.[76] However, many courts admit statements of intent after a deed was executed on the theory that "while intention at the time of the conveyance of the property controls * * * subsequent acts and conduct are admissible to show intention at the time of the transaction."[77]

Litigation concerning oral trusts can arise long after the trust was created, because the statute of limitations does not start to run at that time. For example, land was conveyed by a couple in 1986, and suit was brought to impose a constructive trust in 1995. The action was not barred by a six-year statute of limitations because the statute did not start to run until the transferee "disclosed his intention not to return the land."[78]

### *Clean Hands*

Courts of equity may deny relief to plaintiffs who have "unclean hands." This defense is frequently asserted in suits to enforce constructive and resulting trusts because they often involve title put in the trustee's name in order to disguise ownership. For example, a man who had land titled in his brother's name in order to avoid attachments under outstanding judgments was not allowed to enforce a resulting trust. "A party who conveys property in

**73.** Workman v. Douglas, 419 N.E.2d 1340, 1346 (Ind.App.1981) ("the agreement was not sufficiently definite to enforce"); Engel v. Breske, 681 P.2d 263 (Wash.App.1984) (intent was "very loose, very indefinite").

**74.** McGill v. Biggs, 434 N.E.2d 772, 774 (Ill.App.1982).

**75.** Hilliard v. Hilliard, 844 P.2d 54, 58 (Mont.1992). *See also* In re Estate of Koch, 697 N.E.2d 931 (Ill.App.1998); (husband's continued management of property in wife's name shows no gift intended); Levin v. Smith, 513 A.2d 1292, 1298 (Del.1986) (grantee's treating his sister as half owner for years confirms claim of a constructive trust for her).

**76.** Fowler v. Montgomery, 326 S.E.2d 765, 766–67 (Ga.1985). *See also* Groden v. Kelley, 415 N.E.2d 850, 853 (Mass.1981) (statements of settlor after trust execution inadmissible to show his intent).

**77.** Ashbaugh v. Ashbaugh, 152 S.E.2d 888, 892 (Ga.1966). *See also* Key v. Key, 443 N.E.2d 812 (Ill.App.1982); Beelman v. Beelman, 460 N.E.2d 55 (Ill.App.1984); *Restatement (Second) of Trusts* § 443, comm. a (1959).

**78.** Estates of Kalwitz v. Kalwitz, 717 N.E.2d 904, 914 (Ind.App.1999). *See also* Granado v. Granado, 760 P.2d 148, 150–51 (N.M. 1988); Rajanna v. KRR Investments, Inc., 810 S.W.2d 548 (Mo.App.1991); *Restatement, Second, Trusts* § 409 (laches may bar beneficiary who knows of repudiation by trustee).

order to keep it from judgment creditors cannot * * * seek assistance from the courts" after his "fraudulent purpose * * * has been accomplished."[79] Many courts reject the clean-hands defense, however, sometimes on the ground that even if the settlor intended to defraud creditors, none were actually harmed by the transaction.[80] Others say that harm to third persons such as creditors is irrelevant to a suit against the trustee.[81] Others say that the defendants' fault was greater than the plaintiff's,[82] *e.g.,* because the defendant suggested the transfer,[83] or there was "great inequality of condition" between the parties.[84] Sometimes they simply say that refusing to enforce the trust would "compound the defendant's wrong."[85] The result in a particular case may depend on how "seriously against public policy" the transaction appears to be.[86] The Third Restatement states the question as whether "the policy against unjust enrichment of the transferee is outweighed by the policy against giving relief to a person who has entered into an illegal transaction."[87]

Since acceptance or rejection of the clean-hands defense is a discretionary matter,[88] the result in a given case is hard to predict.

### *Third Parties*

The law often protects third person who have relied on a deed which does not reflect the intention of the parties. Thus reformation of mistakes in a deed is not granted if "rights of third parties, such as good faith purchasers for value will be unfairly affected."[89] However, when because of fraud, the grantor did not understand that the document was a deed, it is void and even a bona fide purchaser from the grantee does not acquire title to the land.[90]

If *A* conveys property to *B*, or pays for land which is put in *B*'s name, even if they intended that *B* hold it in trust, if *B* sells the property, a bona fide purchaser for value takes free of the beneficiary's claims.[91] However, the beneficiary can impress a trust on the sale proceeds, or hold the trustee personally liable.[92] The trust can also be enforced against a transferee who

**79.** American Nat. Bank and Trust v. Vinson, 653 N.E.2d 13, 15 (Ill.App.1995). *See also* Pappas v. Pappas, 320 A.2d 809 (Conn.1973); *Restatement (Second) of Trusts* § 444 (1959); Senter v. Furman, 265 S.E.2d 784 (Ga.1980).

**80.** Garcia v. Marquez, 684 P.2d 513, 516 (N.M.1984); Thomasi v. Koch, 660 P.2d 806 (Wyo.1983); Hilliard v. Hilliard, 844 P.2d 54 (Mont.1992).

**81.** Beelman v. Beelman, 460 N.E.2d 55, 58 (Ill.App.1984); Fenton v. Walter, 612 S.W.2d 17 (Mo.App.1981); Kostelnik v. Roberts, 680 S.W.2d 532 (Tex.App.1984).

**82.** Locken v. Locken, 650 P.2d 803, 805 (Nev.1982).

**83.** Samuelson v. Ingraham, 77 Cal.Rptr. 750, 753 (App.1969).

**84.** Hinson v. Hinson, 343 S.E.2d 266, 274 (N.C.App.1986). *See also* Estates of Kalwitz v. Kalwitz, 717 N.E.2d 904, 913–14 (Ind.App. 1999).

**85.** Chapman v. Citizens and Southern Nat. Bank, 395 S.E.2d 446, 454 (S.C.App.1990).

**86.** *Restatement (Second) of Trusts* § 444, comm. e (1959); Granado v. Granado, 760 P.2d 148, 152 (N.M.1988) (policy against felons holding liquor licenses had been "relaxed" by the legislature); Leeks v. Leeks, 570 A.2d 271, 276 (D.C.App.1989).

**87.** *Restatement, Third, Trusts* § 9(1)(b) (1996).

**88.** Carter v. Carter, 210 So.2d 800 (Ala. 1968); Key v. Key, 443 N.E.2d 812, 817 (Ill. App.1982); Kostelnik v. Roberts, 680 S.W.2d 532, 536 (Tex.App.1984).

**89.** *Restatement, Second, Contracts* § 155 (1979).

**90.** Pedersen v. Bibioff, 828 P.2d 1113 (Wash.App.1992); *Restatement, Second, Contracts* § 163, comm. c (1979).

**91.** *Restatement (Second) of Trusts* § 284 (1959); N.Y. EPTL, § 7–3.2.

**92.** McMahon v. McMahon, 422 N.E.2d 1150, 1153 (Ill.App.1981).

had notice of the trust. For example, a person put title in his brother's name and the brother later sold it to another whose claim to be a bona fide purchaser was rejected, because the settlor's "continuous, open and obvious possession of the property" gave him "constructive notice" of the trust.[93] Even a person who acquires property from the trustee without notice is not protected unless he paid value for the purchase.[94]

Creditors of a trustee who relied on the trustee's apparent ownership may be allowed to satisfy their claims out of the trust property. "The actual owner of trust property will be estopped from claiming a resulting trust in the property where the record owner obtained credit upon the strength of ownership,"[95] but some say this applies only if the beneficial owner knew of the creditors' action in reliance.[96] If the trustee fulfills the oral trust by conveying the property to the beneficiary, the trustee's creditors cannot attack this as a fraudulent conveyance. The Statute of Frauds "only precludes judicial enforcement of the oral trust; it does not render it void as between parties to the trust who desire to abide by the terms of their oral agreement."[97] However, courts view with suspicion claims that a debtor's property was held in trust for another member of the debtor's family.[98]

If a trustee becomes bankrupt the equitable interests of the beneficiaries are preserved,[99] but the trustee in bankruptcy has powers of avoidance equivalent to those of a bona fide purchaser for value which may defeat the rights of the beneficiaries.[100] But a beneficiary's possession of property may give constructive notice which defeats a claim of bona fide purchase, and thus the avoidance power of the bankruptcy trustee.[101]

### *Personal Property*

The rather complex rules discussed in this section involve only land. When the beneficial ownership of personal property is at stake, it is relatively easy to show that the form of title is not conclusive, because the Statute of Frauds requirement of a writing to show a trust applies only to land. For example, two sisters orally agreed that they would own their assets jointly. Even though stock certificates were held in the name of one sister, the other was able to make an effective gift of her one-half share.

> It is quite possible, and often happens for reasons of convenience or otherwise, that stock held in the name of one person really belongs to another. In such a case the certificate, though prima facie evidence of

**93.** American Nat. Bank and Trust v. Vinson, 653 N.E.2d 13, 16 (Ill.App.1995).

**94.** Granado v. Granado, 760 P.2d 148 (N.M.1988); French v. French, 606 P.2d 830 (Ariz.App.1980); Ashton v. Ashton, 733 P.2d 147 (Utah 1987). For further discussion of the defense of bona fide purchase for value see Section 12.8, at note 163 et seq.

**95.** Gary–Wheaton Bank v. Meyer, 473 N.E.2d 548, 555 (Ill.App.1984). *See also Restatement (Third) of Trusts* § 9, comm. f (1996); N.Y. EPTL § 7–3.2.

**96.** John Deere Indus. Equipment Co. v. Gentile, 459 N.E.2d 611 (Ohio App.1983). Beneficiaries of a resulting trust prevailed over the trustee's creditors in Armendaris Water Dev. Co. v. Rainwater, 781 P.2d 799 (N.M.App. 1989); Treschak v. Yorkville Nat. Bank, 604 N.E.2d 1081 (Ill.App.1992).

**97.** Ward v. Grant, 401 N.E.2d 160, 163 (Mass.App.1980). *See also* In re Gustie, 36 B.R. 473 (D.Mass.1984).

**98.** Anderson v. Ferris, 470 N.E.2d 518 (Ill. App.1984); Gary–Wheaton Bank v. Meyer, 473 N.E.2d 548 (Ill.App.1984).

**99.** 11 U.S.C. § 541(d).

**100.** *Id.* § 544; *cf.*In re Crabtree, 871 F.2d 36 (6th Cir.1989) (equitable interest voided under a state statute because not recorded).

**101.** In re Sale Guaranty Corp., 220 B.R. 660 (9th Cir.BAP Cal.1998).

ownership in the person to whom it has been issued, poses no such magic or sacredness as to prevent an inquiry into the facts.[102]

**102.** Estate of Davenport v. C.I.R., 184 F.3d 1176, 1184 (10th Cir.1999).

# Chapter 7

# INCAPACITY AND UNDUE INFLUENCE

*Analysis*



## § 7.1 Incapacity

### *Age Requirements*

Modern American statutes typically require that a testator be at least 18 years old in order to execute a valid will.[1] The same limitation applies to inter vivos gifts. If a minor fails to disaffirm a donative transfer within a reasonable time after reaching majority, it becomes valid through ratification.[2]

### *Mental Capacity*

Most American statutes do not define testamentary capacity for adults; they simply say that the testator must be of "sound mind."[3] However, the California Probate Code defines capacity in words which reflect the common law on the subject:

> An individual is not mentally competent to make a will if at the time of making the will *either* of the following is true:
>
> (1) The individual does not have sufficient mental capacity to be able to (A) understand the nature of the testamentary act, (B) understand and recollect the nature of the individual's property, or (C) remember and understand the individual's relations to living descendants, spouse, and parents, and those whose interests are affected by the will.[4]

§ 7.1

1. Uniform Probate Code § 2–501; Calif.Prob.Code § 6100; *Restatement (Second) of Property (Donative Transfers)* § 34.4, comm. a (1990).

2. *Id.* comm. b, § 18.1, illus. 5.

3. Uniform Probate Code § 2–501. Although the provision refers to "making" a will, the same standard applies to revoking one. Wood v. Bettis, 880 P.2d 961 (Or.App.1994) (destruction of will by testator who lacked capacity did not revoke it); *Restatement (Third) of Property (Wills and Other Donative Transfers)* § 8.1, comm. c (Prel.Dft. 2000).

In Louisiana, a testator must be literate in order to execute a "statutory" will. In re Succession of McClinton, 736 So.2d 906 (La.App. 1999) (will rejected because testator was illiterate).

4. Compare Bland v. Graves, 620 N.E.2d 920 (Ohio App.1993) (error to find incapacity from the testator's failure to know the names of her only relatives, second cousins with whom she had little contact).

(2) The individual suffers from a mental disorder with symptoms including delusions or hallucinations, which delusions and hallucinations result in the individual's devising property in a way which, except for the existence of the delusions or hallucinations, the individual would not have done.[5]

### *Insane Delusion*

The second type of incapacity mentioned in the statute generally goes under the name "insane delusion." A testator with an otherwise high degree of intelligence may suffer from such a delusion.[6] However, such claims do not often succeed in upsetting a will, because a testator's mistaken belief is not an "insane delusion" if there was some rational basis for it. Thus a testator's false belief that a child was not his was not an insane delusion, because it did not defy "rational explanation" and could not be "the product of a mental disorder."[7] On the other hand a testator's belief that her nephews and niece were trying to kill her justified rejection of her will, because her belief was "without foundation or basis in fact . . . too bizarre to be real."[8]

In order for the challenge to succeed the will must be the product of the delusion.[9] Thus a will, allegedly motivated by an insane delusion that contestant intended to harm the testator, was probated when the court found that the testator had other reasons for the will: she wished a family business to continue and left most of her estate to a child who was also interested in its continuation.[10]

### *General Incapacity*

Many more wills are rejected for general mental incapacity; if this is found, the contestants need not show that the will was produced by a delusion.[11] Mental incapacity may be congenital, or it may be brought on by disease or old age. The percentage of elderly in the population has dramatically increased and many challenges to capacity today arise from wills made by testators of advanced years.[12] However, a diagnosis of "senile dementia" and evidence of peculiar behavior are not incompatible with a finding of testamen-

**5.** Cal.Prob.Code § 6100.5(a).

**6.** Contestants can assert both grounds, general incapacity and an insane delusion. Breeden v. Stone, 992 P.2d 1167 (Colo.2000).

**7.** Akers v. Hodel, 871 F.2d 924, 935 (10th Cir.1989). *See also* Dillon v. Phillips, 756 P.2d 1278 (Or.App.1988) ("at least a slight basis" for testator's belief that his children had stolen from him); Goodman v. Zimmerman, 32 Cal. Rptr.2d 419 (App.1994); Matter of Estate of Raney, 799 P.2d 986 (Kan.1990); In re Estate of Kottke, 6 P.3d 243, 247 (Alaska 2000). As to a simple mistaken belief by the testator, see Section 6.1, at note 52.

**8.** Matter of Estate of Killen, 937 P.2d 1368, 1373 (Ariz.App.1996). *See also* Matter of Estate of Watlack, 945 P.2d 1154 (Wash.App. 1997) (no rational basis for testator's belief that his daughter had stolen from him).

**9.** Benjamin v. Woodring, 303 A.2d 779 (Md.1973); In re Agostini's Estate, 457 A.2d 861 (Pa.Super.1983); Spruance v. Northway, 601 S.W.2d 153, 157 (Tex.Civ.App.1980) (approved jury instructions).

**10.** Matter of Yett's Estate, 606 P.2d 1174 (Or.App.1980). *See also* Goodman v. Zimmerman, 32 Cal.Rptr.2d 419 (App.1994); In re Estate of Nicholson, 644 N.E.2d 47 (Ill.App.1994); Breeden v. Stone, 992 P.2d 1167, 1173 (Colo. 2000) (will probated despite testator's insane delusion).

**11.** In re Estate of Washburn, 690 A.2d 1024 (N.H.1997).

**12.** *See* Smith and Hager, *The Senile Testator: Medicolegal Aspects of Competency,* 13 Clev.–Mar.L.Rev. 397 (1964).

tary capacity since "the appropriate inquiry is whether the decedent was lucid and rational at the time the will was made."[13]

Medical evidence is often used to determine capacity. Experts who never saw the testator can render opinions based on the testator's medical records.[14] More common is testimony by doctors who treated the testator,[15] although this may encounter objections based on the doctor-patient evidentiary privilege. One court denied a contestant permission to discover the testator's medical records on the ground that only the patient's executor could waive the privilege,[16] but another removed an executor who refused to do this.[17] Some contestants have unsuccessfully sought to have the testator's body disinterred for examination.[18]

Medical testimony is often either rejected or discounted because the doctor's contact with the patient was too far removed from the time when the will was executed. For example, testimony that the testator lacked capacity two years after the will was executed was rejected as "too remote," and a psychiatrist's testimony that the testator had "degenerative dementia" several weeks after the execution was admitted but deemed outweighed by witnesses to the will who testified affirmatively as to the testator's capacity.[19] Some estate planners advise that physicians be used as witnesses to a will if the testator's capacity is likely to be challenged.[20]

Courts often rely on the testimony of the subscribing witnesses; even if they are not experts, they can offer an opinion about the testator's capacity.[21] The force of their testimony is enhanced if they know the testator well, or at least have a substantial conversation with the testator when the will is signed.[22] Courts discount the testimony of witnesses whose contact with the testator was minimal.[23] Proponents of a will have used attestation clauses to undercut subscribing witnesses who testify that the testator *lacked* capacity.[24]

**13.** In re Estate of Schlueter, 994 P.2d 937, 940 (Wyo.2000).

**14.** Roberts v. Baker, 463 S.E.2d 694 (Ga. 1995); Matter of Estate of Kesler, 702 P.2d 86 (Utah 1985). In other cases contests based on such evidence have failed, however. Lucero v. Lucero, 884 P.2d 527 (N.M.App.1994); Morse v. Volz, 808 S.W.2d 424 (Mo.App.1991).

**15.** E.g. Estate of Verdi by Verdi v. Toland, 733 N.E.2d 25 (Ind.App.2000) (summary judgment for contestants reversed on basis of medical diagnosis of testator's suffering from "dementia of Alzheimer type").

**16.** Cline v. Finney, 594 N.E.2d 1100 (Ohio App.1991).

**17.** Pio v. Ramsier, 623 N.E.2d 174 (Ohio App.1993).

**18.** Camilli v. Cemetery, 583 A.2d 417 (N.J.Super.Ch.Div.1990); Holm v. Superior Court (Misco), 232 Cal.Rptr. 432 (App.1986).

**19.** Bishop v. Kenny, 466 S.E.2d 581 (Ga. 1996). *See also* Sanders v. Brooks, 611 So.2d 336 (Ala.1992); Quarterman v. Quarterman, 493 S.E.2d 146 (Ga.1997) (summary judgment for proponents when only evidence of incapacity related to a time years before will executed). However, in Jones v. LaFargue, 758 S.W.2d 320 (Tex.App.1988) a will was rejected on the basis of testimony by doctors who had examined the testator 4 months after the will was executed.

**20.** H Tweed & W Parsons, *Lifetime and Testamentary Estate Planning* 115 (10th ed. 1988); Wohl, *Guidelines for Avoiding Estate Litigation*, 19 Est.Plann. 67 (1992); Estate of Crossmore, TC Memo 1988–494 (discounting value of contestant's claim where doctors familiar with the testator had witnessed the will).

**21.** In re Estate of Schlueter, 994 P.2d 937, 940 (Wyo.2000) (summary judgment for proponents based on affidavits of witnesses that testator had testamentary capacity); In re Estate of Elam, 738 S.W.2d 169 (Tenn.1987); Lawrence v. First Nat. Bank, 516 So.2d 630 (Ala.1987).

**22.** Beyer, *The Will Execution Ceremony*, 29 S.Tex.L.Rev. 413, 432 (1988).

**23.** Bigej v. Boyer, 817 P.2d 760, 763 (Or. App.1991).

**24.** In re Estate of Chlebos, 550 N.E.2d 1069 (Ill.App.1990).

Some lawyers make a tape recording of the execution to show that the testator was "making sense" at the relevant time.[25]

### *Naturalness of Will*

Roman law allowed a testator's children to assert claims that they had been unjustly disinherited "on the pretext that the testator was of unsound mind when he executed the will," although the real basis for the complaint was that the will showed "lack of family feeling."[26] Observers of American law have suggested that our rules on capacity represent a similar veiled limitation on testamentary freedom.[27] Juries are thought to be particularly prone to reject wills which they find unfair where will contests are tried by jury.[28] However, references to "unnaturalness" as evidence of incapacity are often found in judicial opinions. For example, a court upheld a finding of incapacity based upon the testator's

> failure to understand the natural objects of his bounty. On the day the will was executed [testator] twice denied that he had a son ... [The] devise to Dow [a non-relative] was unexpected and unnatural ... The fact that the decedent made such an unlikely disposition of his one-third share of the family farm may be given significant weight by the factfinder.[29]

A will which on its face seems unnatural may be upheld when a reason for the disposition appears. Thus a will which disinherited the testator's grandchildren was probated after her attorney testified that the testator wanted to leave everything to her sister-in-law "because [she] had been good to her."[30] Naturalness, one court has said, should be judged from the perspective of the testator, not the court or jury. "A will is unnatural when it is contrary to what *the testator,* from his known views, feelings, and intentions would have been expected to make"; a will "may differ from ordinary actions of men" and nevertheless not be "unnatural."[31]

Sudden changes in a testator's wishes are viewed with suspicion. Thus a deed and will which altered an "estate plan of long standing" were voided for incapacity as "unnatural."[32] A testator who executed wills "just over three weeks apart [which] contained vastly different provisions" and differed from

**25.** Central Bank–Granite City v. Ziaee, 544 N.E.2d 1121 (Ill.App.1989); Hauck v. Seright, 964 P.2d 749, 755 (Mont.1998) (audiotape used to rebut claim of undue influence); In re Estate of Peterson, 439 N.W.2d 516 (Neb. 1989).

**26.** Justinian, *Institutes* 2.18.

**27.** Fellows, *The Case Against Living Probate,* 78 Mich.L.Rev. 1066, 1070–73 (1980); Epstein, *Testamentary Capacity, Reasonableness and Family Maintenance: A Proposal for Meaningful Reform,* 35 Temp.L.Q. 231 (1962); Green, *Proof of Mental Incompetency and the Unexpressed Major Premise,* 53 Yale L.J. 271 (1944).

**28.** Schoenblum, *Will Contests: An Empirical Study,* 22 Real Prop. Prob. and Trust J. 607, 626 (1987) (jury finds for contestants more often than judges do). Jury verdicts may be avoided or controlled by summary judgment or judgment n.o.v. Matter of Last Will of Dickey, 542 So.2d 903 (Miss.1989); Morse v. Volz, 808 S.W.2d 424 (Mo.App.1991); Quarterman v. Quarterman, 493 S.E.2d 146 (Ga.1997) (summary judgment); In re Estate of Wagner, 522 N.W.2d 159 (Neb.1994) (same).

**29.** Estate of Record, 534 A.2d 1319, 1322–23 (Me.1987).

**30.** Doyle v. Schott, 582 N.E.2d 1057, 1060 (Ohio App.1989). *See also* In re Estate of Elam, 738 S.W.2d 169, 172 (Tenn.1987); Taylor v. Koslosky, 814 P.2d 985 (Mont.1991) (excluding child who had already received benefits); Hodges v. Genzone, 724 So.2d 521, 524 (Ala.Civ. App.1998) (will disinherited testator's daughters "because they had evicted [him] from his house").

**31.** Matter of Estate of Bouchat, 679 P.2d 426 (Wash.App.1984).

**32.** Matter of Guardianship & Conserv. of Estate of Tennant, 714 P.2d 122, 129 (Mont. 1986).

her contemporaneous statements of how she wished to dispose of her property was found to be incapacitated.[33] Conversely, the fact that a disputed will is similar to prior wills helps to refute claims of incapacity, since this shows "that the testator (and grantor) had a constant and abiding scheme for the distribution of his property."[34]

## § 7.2 Conservatorship and Durable Powers of Attorney

All states have procedures for appointing a conservator or guardian for someone who is unable to manage property. (Such a person is sometimes referred to as a "ward," sometimes as a "conservatee.") The standard for appointment of a conservator found in the Uniform Probate Code is typical; a conservator is appointed for adults who are

> unable to manage property and business affairs effectively for such reasons as mental illness, mental deficiency, physical illness or disability, chronic use of drugs, chronic intoxication, confinement, detention by a foreign power, or disappearance.[1]

Can a person for whom a conservator has been appointed make a will? In virtually all states the answer to this question is "yes."

> Ability to transact ... business is not the legal standard of testamentary incapacity ... While ... the existence of a conservatorship at the time a will was executed may have some bearing on the question of testamentary capacity, [it] .. is not an adjudication of testamentary incapacity.[2]

Some courts consider a conservatorship as at least some evidence of testamentary incapacity,[3] but others treat findings in the conservatorship proceedings as inadmissible hearsay in a will contest.[4] Conversely, the fact that proceedings to appoint a conservator for a testator were dismissed because he was found competent is not conclusive as to his testamentary capacity.[5]

**33.** In re Estate of Washburn, 690 A.2d 1024, 1027 (N.H.1997); *cf.* Hauck v. Seright, 964 P.2d 749, 756 (Mont.1998)(inconsistent wills executed three days apart).

**34.** *In re* Estate of Camin's, 323 N.W.2d 827, 836 (Neb.1982). *See also* Matter of Estate of Luger, 797 P.2d 229 (Mont.1990); Costello v. Hall, 506 So.2d 293 (Miss.1987); Matter of Estate of Alexander, 749 P.2d 1052 (Kan.App. 1988). Such a series of consistent wills may even deprive the heirs of standing to contest the last one. See Section 12.1, at note 93.

§ 7.2

**1.** Uniform Probate Code § 5–401.

**2.** Conservatorship of Bookasta, 265 Cal. Rptr. 1, 3 (App.1989). *See also* Estate of Ioupe, 878 P.2d 1168 (Utah App.1994); Matter of Estate of Oliver, 934 P.2d 144 (Kan.App.1997). In Oklahoma, however, a will of a person under guardianship must be signed in the presence of a judge. Myers v. Maxey, 915 P.2d 940 (Okl. App.1995).

**3.** Wood v. Bettis, 880 P.2d 961 (Or.App. 1994) (guardianship creates a rebuttable presumption of incapacity to revoke a will); Estate of Verdi by Verdi v. Toland, 733 N.E.2d 25 (Ind.App.2000) (court refers to appointment of guardian for testator in reversing summary judgment for contestants); Fulkroad v. Ofak, 463 A.2d 1155 (Pa.Super.1983); *Restatement (Third) of Property (Wills and Other Donative Transfers)* § 8.1, comm. h (Prel.Dft. 2000).

**4.** In re Estate of Mask, 703 So.2d 852 (Miss.1997). *See also* Matter of Estate of Kesler, 702 P.2d 86, 96 (Utah 1985) (appointment based on physical infirmities has no probative value on testamentary capacity); In re Estate of Prescott, 8 P.3d 88, 94 (Mont.2000) (conservatorship "has no bearing on the issue" of testamentary capacity).

**5.** Estate of Brown v. Fulp, 718 S.W.2d 588, 597 (Mo.App.1986); In re Estate of Wagner, 522 N.W.2d 159 (Neb.1994) (refusal to appoint conservator is not res judicata in will contest); Matter of Bo, 365 N.W.2d 847 (N.D.1985) (finding of incapacity despite termination of guardianship).

When the question of capacity arises as to an inter vivos gift made by a conservatee, on the other hand, the conservatorship is in many states conclusive, and any gift thereafter made is voidable.[6] This is true even when the conservatorship was voluntary and thus involved no finding of incapacity.[7] Under the Uniform Probate Code appointment of a conservator "vests in the conservator title as trustee to all property ... of the protected person," and the conservatee's interest therein "is not assignable or transferable by the protected person."[8]

The distinction between wills and gifts raises the question of will substitutes. A court held that a statute depriving wards of power "to dispose of property in any manner other than by will" applied to putting money in a joint certificate of deposit, rejecting the claim that the statute did not cover transfers which took effect at death.[9] But other courts have equated will substitutes with wills for this purpose. For example, changing the beneficiaries of a P.O.D. accounts was held to be "in effect, a testamentary disposition similar to a will" and so the guardianship was "only prima facie evidence" of incapacity.[10]

The question of incapacity may also arise when the settlor of a revocable trust seeks to revoke it. Some trusts provide a mechanism for determining capacity in order to avoid expensive and embarrassing court proceedings on the issue. For example, a settlor's attempt to amend a trust after she had moved into a nursing home was held ineffective because the trust by its terms was amendable only while the settlor was "competent," and said that her admission into a nursing home would render her incompetent for this purpose.[11]

### *Gifts Without a Conservatorship*

Even when no conservatorship has been created, gifts made by an incapacitated person may be set aside. A conservator later appointed for the donor can sue to rescind gifts made previously.[12] So may the donor's personal representative after the donor has died.[13] Such a suit may be barred, however,

**6.** Matter of Conservatorship of Marcotte, 756 P.2d 1091 (Kan.1988); O'Brien v. Dudenhoeffer, 19 Cal.Rptr.2d 826 (App.1993); Huntington Nat. Bank v. Toland, 594 N.E.2d 1103 (Ohio App.1991) (note signed by ward is unenforceable). The relevant statute may provide otherwise. Matter of Conservatorship of Spindle, 733 P.2d 388 (Okl.1986) (statute bars contracts but not gifts by conservatee). *Restatement (Third) of Property (Wills and Other Donative Transfers)* § 8.1, comm. h (Prel.Dft. 2000) speaks only of a "rebuttable presumption" of incapacity.

**7.** Zobel by Hancox v. Fenendael, 379 N.W.2d 887 (Wis.App.1985).

**8.** Uniform Probate Code § 5–419. An order for a limited conservatorship may specify that only part of the conservatee's property passes to the conservator. Compare Cal. Prob. Code § 1872: appointment "is an adjudication that the conservatee lacks the legal capacity to enter into or make any transaction" with certain exceptions, such as making a will, but the terms of the court order may broaden or restrict the conservatee's powers. *Id.* §§ 1871, 1873.

**9.** Matter of Conservatorship of Rininger, 500 N.W.2d 47 (Iowa 1993).

**10.** Witt v. Ward, 573 N.E.2d 201 (Ohio App.1989). *See also* Campbell v. Black, 844 P.2d 759 (Kan.App.1993).

**11.** Manning v. Glens Falls Nat. Bank, 697 N.Y.S.2d 203 (A.D.1999). *See also Restatement (Third) of Property (Wills and Other Donative Transfers)* § 8.1, comm. l (Prel.Dft. 2000); Uniform Custodial Trust Act § 10.

**12.** Central Bank–Granite City v. Ziaee, 544 N.E.2d 1121 (Ill.App.1989) (guardian recovers damages from a person who persuaded ward to sell him property for a fraction of its value).

**13.** Howe v. Johnston, 660 N.E.2d 380 (Mass.App.1996). In Olson v. Toy, 54 Cal. Rptr.2d 29 (App.1996), the devisees of the settlor of a living trust were allowed to bring suit to set aside the trust.

if the donor later recovered capacity and ratified the gift.[14]

In determining the donor's capacity, courts usually apply the same standards for will substitutes as for wills.[15] The Restatement of Trusts agrees,[16] but suggests "a standard slightly higher than that for a will" for irrevocable gifts and trusts; as to these, the donor or settlor must be able to "understand the effects the disposition may have on the future financial security of the settlor/donor" and his or her dependents.[17] Certainly a gift which renders the donor a pauper is likely to appear "unnatural,"[18] whereas this is not an issue in transfers which take effect at death.

Wills are generally probated shortly after the testator dies and their validity is determined before the estate is distributed. In contrast, a long time may elapse between the making of an inter vivos gift and a determination of the donor's capacity.[19] During this interval the donee may transfer the property to others, or change position in reliance on the gift. If the donee sells the property to a bona fide purchaser for value, the latter is protected.[20] But persons to whom the donee had given the land are subject to suit.[21] And when a transfer occurs after the transferor has been adjudicated incompetent, the judgment may constitute constructive notice.[22] Even if a defendant is not a bona-fide purchaser, however, equitable adjustments may be made to protect reasonable reliance when a transfer is rescinded.[23]

### *Transfers by Conservators*

Some persons cannot meet even the relatively low standard which the law sets for capacity. Distribution of their property under the intestacy laws or under an out-of-date will executed when they had capacity may produce an unsatisfactory solution.[24] Can a conservator make a will for such a person? The answer in nearly all jurisdictions is no. Uniform Probate Code, in listing conservator's powers over the conservatee's estate, expressly denies the power

14. *Restatement (Third) of Property (Wills and Other Donative Transfers)* § 8.1, comm. g (Prel.Dft. 2000).

15. Bergen v. Travelers Ins. Co., 776 P.2d 659, 664 (Utah App.1989) (change of insurance beneficiary); Akerman v. Trosper, 420 N.E.2d 1148, 1151 (Ill.App.1981) (deed with life estate reserved); Lah v. Rogers, 707 N.E.2d 1208, 1214 (Ohio App.1998) (revocable trust amendment).

16. *Accord,* Uniform Trust Code § 601.

17. *Restatement, Third, Trusts* § 11, comments b and c (1996). *See also* Bigej v. Boyer, 817 P.2d 760 (Or.App.1991); Hilbert v. Benson, 917 P.2d 1152 (Wyo.1996); *Restatement (Third) of Property (Wills and Other Donative Transfers)* § 8.1(c) (Prel.Dft. 2000).

18. Christensen v. Britton, 784 P.2d 908, 912 (Mont.1989) (gift of house without reserving a place to live unnatural).

19. Howe v. Johnston, 660 N.E.2d 380 (Mass.App.1996) (suit brought to rescind transfer 6 years later; statute of limitations was tolled during donor's incompetency); Robertson v. Roberston, 654 P.2d 600 (Okl.1982) (similar).

20. First Interstate Bank v. First Wyo. Bank, 762 P.2d 379 (Wyo.1988) (mortgagee from buyer of land protected even though sale was voidable for incapacity); Cal.Fam.Code § 6713 (BFP of goods transferred by a minor protected). *But see* Keville v. McKeever, 675 N.E.2d 417 (Mass.App.1997) (mortgagee of transferee not a bona-fide purchaser).

21. Robertson v. Robertson, 654 P.2d 600 (Okl.1982).

22. Huntington Nat. Bank v. Toland, 594 N.E.2d 1103 (Ohio App.1991); *cf.* Cal.Prob. Code § 1875 (adjudication does not constitute notice until recorded in county where land located); Uniform Probate Code § 5–420(b) (letters of conservatorship may be recorded).

23. Keville v. McKeever, 675 N.E.2d 417 (Mass.App.1997); Citizens State Bank & Trust Co. v. Nolte, 601 P.2d 1110 (Kan.1979); *Restatement, Second, Contracts* § 15(2) (1979); Cal.Civ.Code § 1692.

24. For the deficiencies of the intestacy statutes in many situations see Section 2.3, at note 6 et seq.

to make a will.[25] However, the Code allows conservators to create revocable trusts, which are the functional equivalent of a will for conservatees. According to the Restatement of Trusts, "prohibitions against will making are generally to be strictly construed" so as not to prohibit "other methods of . . . properly justified post-death disposition of estates of persons under disability."[26]

A conservator may be authorized to make gifts of a conservatee's property. Irrevocable gifts can save income taxes (when the donee is in a lower tax bracket than the donor) and transfer taxes as well.[27] Many statutes expressly mention tax savings as a justification for such gifts,[28] but these are not the only reason for them.[29] A court upheld the gift of a ward's property by his guardian-spouse to herself which would make the ward eligible for Medicaid. "There can be no quarreling with the [trial] court's determination that any person in Mr. Shah's condition would prefer that the costs of his care be paid by the state as opposed to his family."[30] A conservator may create a trust for the conservatee and her incompetent spouse who would otherwise take outright when the conservatee died.[31] The basic test, as expressed in an early case, is "what it is likely the Lunatic himself would do, if he were in a capacity to act,"[32] or, as formulated more recently, "the likelihood from all the circumstances that the conservatee as a reasonably prudent person would take the proposed action if the conservatee had the capacity to do so."[33] This requires consideration of the relationship of the proposed donees to the donor; dependent family members have a strong claim, but others may also be included if the conservatee while competent had made gifts to them or they are named in the conservatee's will.[34] Of course, such gifts should be authorized only if they leave enough property for the conservatee's prospective needs.

It has been held that the power to revoke a trust is "personal to the settlor" and thus cannot be exercised by a conservator, so in effect a revocable

**25.** Uniform Probate Code § 4–523. *See also Restatement, Second, Property (Donative Transfers)* § 34.5, comm. b (1990). *But see* Cal.Prob.Code § 2580(b)(13); [England] Mental Health Act, 1983, § 96(1).

**26.** *Restatement, Third, Trusts* § 11, comm. f (1996). *See also Restatement, Second, Property (Donative Transfers)* § 34.5, comm. b (1990); Matter of Jones, 401 N.E.2d 351 (Mass.1980).

**27.** For example, by taking advantage of the annual exclusion. See Section 15.2, note 9.

**28.** Conn.Gen.Stat. § 45a–655(e)(C) (minimization of income and estate taxes); 30 Okl. Stat. § 3–121A(3) (tax or estate planning); Cal. Prob.Code § 2580(a)(2) (minimizing current or prospective taxes). However, gifts made to qualify for welfare benefits are expressly disallowed by the Connecticut statute. Probate of Marcus, 509 A.2d 1 (Conn.1986). In Matter of Estate of Berry, 972 S.W.2d 324 (Mo.App.1998) the court disapproved proposed gifts which would have reduced both income and estate taxes where there was "no established pattern of giving" by the ward.

**29.** Boone County State Bank v. Andrews, 446 N.E.2d 618, 620 (Ind.App.1983). *But cf.* Matter of Murray, 563 N.E.2d 217 (Mass. 1990); Conservatorship of Hart, 279 Cal.Rptr. 249 (App.1991) (reversing approval of gifts which was based on a misunderstanding of conservatee's tax situation).

**30.** In re Shah, 733 N.E.2d 1093, 1099 (N.Y.2000). *But see* note 28.

**31.** *Restatement, Third, Trusts* § 11 illus. 3 (1996).

**32.** Ex parte Whitbread, 35 Eng.Rep. 878 (1816).

**33.** Cal.Prob.Code § 2583 (k).

**34.** Cal.Prob.Code § 2583; *Restatement, Second, Property (Donative Transfers)* § 34.5, illus. 5 (1990) (gift to nephew of ward whom ward had supported in the past); In re Guardianship of Bohac, 380 So.2d 550 (Fla.App.1980) (disapproving proposed gifts to non-relative devisees to whom ward had made no prior gifts); Conn. Gen Stat. § 45a–655(e) (gifts to non-relatives or charities if "the ward has made a previous gift").

trust becomes irrevocable if the settlor becomes incompetent.[35] However, this result seems inconsistent with the broad powers conferred on conservators by the Uniform Probate Code.[36]

### *Durable Powers of Attorney*

Most statutes require prior court approval for gifts by conservators of a conservatee's property.[37] Because court proceedings are expensive and time consuming, as well as embarrassing to family members when they involve proof of a relative's incapacity, in recent years people have used durable powers of attorney as a better way to manage have their affairs managed if they become incompetent.[38] Agents, like conservators, are fiduciaries, but unlike conservators they are created and usually function without the need for court proceedings. The agent is designated and empowered to act in a "power of attorney" signed by the principal. An "attorney" is not necessarily or even usually a lawyer; to avoid confusion, a distinction is often made between "attorneys-in-fact" and "attorneys at law."[39]

Traditionally the powers of an agent/attorney ceased whenever the principal became incompetent.[40] This rule made agency useless as a device for managing an incompetent's property, and so it was changed by a Uniform Durable Power of Attorney Act which was included in the Uniform Probate Code[41] and adopted (with variations) in most states. A power of attorney is durable when it states that it "shall not be affected by the subsequent disability or incapacity of the principal" or words to that effect.[42] Some prefer a "springing" power, which only comes into effect when the signer becomes incompetent. In order to avoid the need for a court determination of incompetence, a springing power may "be framed to confer authority commencing when two or more named persons ... concur that the principal has become incapable of managing his affairs in a sensible and efficient manner."[43] A durable power is effective only if it is executed when the principal is legally competent; someone who is already incompetent can not confer a power.[44]

Conservators have such powers as are conferred by statute, sometimes modified by the terms of the court order appointing them. The powers conferred by a power of attorney, on the other hand, depend on its terms. Traditionally powers have been strictly construed.[45] They are often interpret-

**35.** In re Guardianship of Lee, 982 P.2d 539, 541 (Okl.Civ.App.1999).

**36.** Uniform Probate Code § 5–407(3). Cal. Prob.Code § 2588(a)(11) expressly allows conservators to exercise a power to revoke unless the trust shows an intent to reserve the right exclusively to the settlor.

**37.** Matter of Conservatorship of Rininger, 500 N.W.2d 47 (Iowa 1993) (conservator surcharged for transfers made without court approval); Matter of Estate of Leone, 860 P.2d 973 (Utah App.1993) (change of beneficiary by conservator without court approval ineffective).

**38.** McGovern, *Trusts, Custodianships and Durable Powers of Attorney*, 27 Real Prop. Prob. and Trust J. 1 (1992).

**39.** Cal.Prob.Code § 4014(a): " 'Attorney-in-fact' means a person granted authority to act for the principal in a power of attorney, regardless of whether the person is known as an attorney-in-fact or agent."

**40.** *Restatement, Second, Agency* §§ 120, 122 (1958).

**41.** Uniform Probate Code § 5–501 et seq.

**42.** Powers of attorney over bank accounts are durable unless they provide otherwise under Uniform Probate Code § 6–205.

**43.** Uniform Probate Code § 5–501, Comment. *See also* Cal.Prob.Code § 4129.

**44.** Hagan v. Shore, 915 P.2d 435 (Or.App. 1996); Testa v. Roberts, 542 N.E.2d 654 (Ohio App.1988).

**45.** McGovern, *supra* note 38, at 33; In re Guardianship of Mabry, 666 N.E.2d 16 (Ill. App.1996) (power to manage real estate did not include power to sell).

ed not to allow the attorney to make gifts.[46] The problem is exacerbated when the power is held by a family member who wishes to make gifts to himself or his family, because of the general prohibition against fiduciaries engaging in transactions in which they have a conflict of interest.[47] Thus when a daughter used a power of attorney to convey her father's property to a trust in which she and her siblings had interests, the court held the trust invalid.

> Such self dealing by an agent, in the absence .. of distinct authority from the principal expressly granted in the empowering instrument, has been continuously and uniformly denounced as one of the most profound breaches of fiduciary duty, irrespective of the agent's good faith ... [48]

Some more recent opinions have been more accommodating toward such transactions. When children under a power of attorney conferred by their mother made gifts to themselves and their families, the court approved this, saying that

> the actions taken by the attorneys-in-fact ... continue the grantor's practice of giving monetary gifts to the natural objects of her bounty and affection; ... [and do] not deplete the grantor's of the assets necessary for her to live her accustomed life-style [she died with an estate in excess of $1 million]; and ... minimize the estate transfer tax, a goal the grantor desired.[49]

An Alabama statute dictates that general powers be construed to allow the attorney to make gifts of the principal's property "to any individuals [or charitable organizations] including the attorney in fact" if the gifts will reduce the principal's estate tax and are "in accordance with the principal's personal history of making ... lifetime gifts."[50] In California, on the other hand, any gifts of the principal's property by an agent must be "expressly authorized in the power of attorney."[51] Thus attorneys advising clients who wish to avoid conservatorship in case they become incompetent and to minimize estate taxes may want to use durable powers but should exercise care in drafting them.

## § 7.3 Undue Influence

Wills and inter-vivos transfers are often challenged as being the product of undue influence. The standards applied to the two types of transfers are generally the same.[1] Sometimes inter-vivos and testamentary transfers are challenged in the same proceedings, usually with the same result.[2] Sometimes

**46.** Estate of Casey, 948 F.2d 895 (4th Cir. 1991); Townsend v. United States, 889 F.Supp. 369 (D.Neb.1995).

**47.** Kunewa v. Joshua, 924 P.2d 559 (Haw. App.1996) (constructive trust imposed on child who used power to convey property to himself). See also Section 12.9.

**48.** Gagnon v. Coombs, 654 N.E.2d 54, 62 (Mass.App.1995).

**49.** LeCraw v. LeCraw, 401 S.E.2d 697, 699 (Ga.1991). *See also* Estate of Ridenour v. C.I.R., 36 F.3d 332 (4th Cir.1994); Estate of Neff, TC Memo 1997–186.

**50.** Ala.Code 1975 § 26–1–2.1. Compare Va. Code § 11–9.5; England, Enduring Powers of Attorney Act, 1985, §§ 3, 8 (attorney may make "reasonable" gifts, court may authorize attorney to benefit himself).

**51.** Cal.Prob.Code § 4264; Estate of Huston, 60 Cal.Rptr.2d 217 (App.1997) (oral ratification of gift ineffective).

§ 7.3

**1.** In re Guardianship of Mowrer, 979 P.2d 156, 161 (Mont.1999). Compare the test(s) for incapacity. Section 7.2, note 15 et seq.

**2.** McKee v. Stoddard, 780 P.2d 736 (Or. App.1989) (will and joint tenancy); Sun Bank/Miami, NA v. Hogarth, 536 So.2d 263 (Fla.App.1988) (will and trust); *cf.* In re Estate

only a particular provision is challenged. For example, a devise of $100,000 was found invalid because of the devisee's undue influence over the testator, but the rest of the will was probated because the tainted devise was "severable."[3] However, courts may conclude that the testator's intent would be better effectuated by invalidating the whole will when undue influence is found.[4]

Undue influence may also invalidate the revocation of a will.[5] When it prevents the making of a will or gift the intended beneficiaries have a tort action against the person whose influence frustrated the gift or will, despite the objection that this requires ascertaining the decedent's intent on the basis of evidence which does not comply with the statutory requirements for a will.[6]

Claims of undue influence and incapacity are commonly combined. The same evidence may be relevant to both issues, since findings of undue influence are often predicated on the mental weakness of the testator/donor. For example,

> One who is infirm and mentally weak is more susceptible to influence than one who is not ... At the time the will was executed [the testator] suffered a debilitating and painful arthritic condition [and] ... had a very severe problem with alcohol abuse.[7]

Conversely, the fact that a testator was strong minded and intelligent is often cited in finding no undue influence.[8] Expert testimony is occasionally heard, although this is less common in undue influence than in incapacity challenges.[9]

As in claims of incapacity, courts often stress the naturalness or unnaturalness of the disposition. For example, in finding undue influence a court noted "the substantial bequest to Christianson is ... suspicious, [since] ... he was no more than a casual acquaintance" of the testator.[10] Conversely, in

of Lemke, 561 N.E.2d 350 (Ill.App.1990) (when will and deed challenged, trial court had discretion to sever the trials). In Estate of Wenzel–Gosset by Gaukler v. Nickels, 575 N.W.2d 425 (N.D.1998), on the other hand, a change in bank accounts will was found valid, but a will executed three days later was rejected for incapacity.

**3.** Estate of Lane, 492 So.2d 395 (Fla.App. 1986). *See also* Rood v. Newberg, 718 N.E.2d 886 (Mass.App.1999); Matter of Jones' Estate, 320 N.W.2d 167 (S.D.1982).

**4.** In re Estate of Marsh, 342 N.W.2d 373 (Neb.1984); Matter of Estate of Keeney, 908 P.2d 751, 755 (N.M.App.1995); *Restatement (Third) of Property (Wills and Other Donative Transfers)* § 8.3, comm. d (Prel.Dft. 2000). Some jurisdictions, moreover, do not recognize partial invalidity. In re O'Loughlin's Estate, 183 N.W.2d 133 (Wis.1971).

**5.** Cook v. Loftus, 414 N.E.2d 581 (Ind.App. 1981); Griffin v. Baucom, 328 S.E.2d 38 (N.C.App.1985).

**6.** *Restatement, Second, Torts* § 774B (1977); Allen v. Hall, 974 P.2d 199 (Or.1999) (decedent's intent to devise property to plaintiff blocked by defendant's misrepresentations); Doughty v. Morris, 871 P.2d 380 (N.M.App.1994); Hammons v. Eisert, 745 S.W.2d 253 (Mo.App.1988). Compare the cases imposing a constructive trust in this situation. Section 6.1, note 52.

**7.** Boehm v. Allen, 506 N.W.2d 781, 784 (Iowa App.1993). *See also* Christensen v. Britton, 784 P.2d 908 (Mont.1989) (donor in a weakened emotional state after wife's death); In re Panek, 667 N.Y.S.2d 177 (App.Div.1997).

**8.** Pascale v. Pascale, 549 A.2d 782 (N.J. 1988) (donor was a shrewd businessman); Matter of Estate of Webb, 863 P.2d 1116 (Okl. 1993) (testator/donor was "strong-minded); Anderson v. Meadowcroft, 661 A.2d 726 (Md. 1995) (claim dismissed for failure to allege that testator was "susceptible" to influence).

**9.** In re Estate of Hoover, 615 N.E.2d 736 (Ill.1993); Matter of Estate of Keeney, 908 P.2d 751 (N.M.App.1995). *But see* Mache v. Mache, 578 N.E.2d 1253 (Ill.App.1991) (no abuse of discretion not to hear expert testimony).

**10.** Matter of Estate of Dankbar, 430 N.W.2d 124, 131 (Iowa 1988). *See also* In re Panek, 667 N.Y.S.2d 177 (App.Div.1997) (will gave proponents far more than their intestate share even though they were not close to testator); Montoya v. Torres, 823 P.2d 905 (N.M. 1991) (gift to step-grandchild unnatural when

rejecting a claim of undue influence courts often note that "the will's terms were reasonable and natural."[11] One observer has even suggested that the undue influence doctrine acts "as a form of forced heirship" requiring that property be left to a spouse or blood relatives.[12] However, relatively few wills are successfully challenged. According to one survey only about one in a hundred wills are contested at all, and of those which are, the proponent has a "statistically overwhelming likelihood of success ... Judges and juries are quite skeptical of" allegations of undue influence.[13] A substantial devise to a non-relative is not necessarily so "unnatural" as to warrant an inference of undue influence,[14] nor is unequal treatment of relatives, especially if there appears to have been a reason for it.[15]

Courts often focus on the impropriety of the influencer's conduct. They admit evidence of the influencer's bad character,[16] or emphasize that "improper devices" were used to sway the testator, such as taking advantage of a belief in the supernatural by transmitting purported advice from dead relatives.[17] Claims of undue influence often involve misrepresentations made to the testator.[18] In contrast, courts distinguish between undue influence and "reasonable persuasion." Thus a will was upheld even though the testator's sons had discussed the will with her and helped her to change it; "theirs were the acts of dutiful sons [whose] mother ... was aging and needed helpful information and even advice." If this were deemed to be undue influence, we would "have finally abolished the family ties of love and natural affection."[19] Another court said in upholding a devise to a wife said

> If a wife by her industry and virtue, and by the assistance which she has rendered her husband, has gained an ascendancy over the mind of her

donor had children of her own); In re Guardianship of Mowrer, 979 P.2d 156, 163 (Mont. 1999) ("unnatural disposition of essentially all of" donor's property to donees).

**11.** In re Estate of Shumway, 3 P.3d 977, 983 (Ariz.App.1999); In re Estate of Kottke, 6 P.3d 243, 249 (Alaska 2000).

**12.** Madoff, *Unmasking Undue Influence*, 81 Minn.L.Rev. 571, 611 (1997). However, *Restatement (Third) of Property (Wills and Other Donative Transfers)* § 8.3, comm. e (Prel.Dft. 2000) is careful to state that gifts to "unmarried partners" are not to be considered "unnatural."

**13.** Schoenblum, *Will Contests: An Empirical Study*, 22 Real Prop.Prob. and Trust J. 607, 625, 655 (1987). However, most of the wills studied left the estate to relatives of the testator; when the devise was to nonrelatives, the chances of a contestant's success were greater. *Id.* at 634, 659.

**14.** Matter of Estate of Gersbach, 960 P.2d 811 (N.M.1998); In re Estate of Squire, 6 P.3d 1060 (Okl.Civ.App.1999) (devise to charities, disinheriting cousins upheld).

**15.** Matter of Estate of Eggebrecht, 967 P.2d 388, 392 (Mont.1998) ("natural" to favor a grandson on whom decedent "primarily relied to assist her")

**16.** In re Estate of Herbert, 979 P.2d 39, 56 (Haw.1999); Bryan v. Norton, 265 S.E.2d 282, 284 (Ga.1980); Warner v. Warner, 687 S.W.2d 856 (Ark.App.1985). *But see* Estate of Garrett, 906 P.2d 254 (Nev.1995) (error to admit evidence of drug use by devisee).

**17.** Estate of Baker, 182 Cal.Rptr. 550 (App.1982).

**18.** Matter of Brown's Estate, 640 P.2d 1250 (Kan.1982) (beneficiary criticized other heirs and tried to prevent contact between them and the testator); Bryan v. Norton, 265 S.E.2d 282, 283 (Ga.1980) (pastor of testatrix's church told her "that her children did not care anything about her"); Rood v. Newberg, 718 N.E.2d 886 (Mass.App.1999) (failure to correct testator's mistaken belief that son had stolen from testator); cf. Allen v. Hall, 974 P.2d 199 (Or.1999) (defendant lied to decedent's lawyer about his ability to execute will).

**19.** Carter v. Carter, 526 So.2d 141, 143 (Fla.App.1988). *See also* Nease v. Clark, 488 P.2d 1396 (Or.App.1971) (influence arising from "gratitude and affection" is proper). *But see* Anderson v. Brinkerhoff, 756 P.2d 95 (Utah App.1988) (deed voidable for undue influence by children despite their good motives and belief they were acting in mother's interest).

> husband; * * * such influence, though it result in procuring a will in her favor * * * would not amount to undue influence.[20]

Duress, which is related to undue influence, requires an "unlawful" threat. When a husband induced his wife to give him property by threatening to leave her, she could not avoid the deed for duress because he had not threatened to do an unlawful act.[21]

The person exerting undue influence need not be a beneficiary. Thus when a husband induced his wife to deed land to his sisters, the wife could avoid the deed without proving that the sisters had been involved in the undue influence.

> A deed procured by undue influence is voidable regardless of whether the undue influence was exerted by the grantee or by someone else ... If, before the grantor takes steps to avoid the deed, the grantee therein conveys the premises to an innocent purchaser, a court of equity will extend protection to such a purchaser ... However, while an innocent purchaser is protected by equity, the initial grantee is not.[22]

The testimony of the subscribing witnesses plays a less important role in claims of undue influence than where the issue is the testator's capacity, since the witnesses would normally be unaware of influence exerted on the testator at times other than the moment of the will's execution.[23] When the execution of challenged documents had been video taped, the court held that "while the tapes constitute strong evidence of capacity," they did not warrant a summary judgment for the contestants on the question of undue influence.[24] "Undue influence need not by exerted at the time a will is made; it is enough that it be operative at that time."[25] Since influence is typically exerted in secret, it may be established by circumstantial evidence.[26]

### *Presumption of Undue Influence*

The burden of proving undue influence is on the contestants, but they can rely on a presumption of undue influence if a person in a "confidential relationship" with the testator participated in preparing the will.[27] Both

**20.** In re Estate of Mowdy, 973 P.2d 345, 347 (Okl.Civ.App.1998). According to *Restatement, Second, Torts* § 774B, comm. c (1977), persuasion "by legitimate means" is not actionable. Similarly, in *Restatement, Second, Contracts* § 177 (1979) undue influence involves "unfair" persuasion.

**21.** Rubenstein v. Sela, 672 P.2d 492 (Ariz. App.1983). *See also* Bailey v. Arlington Bank & Trust Co., 693 S.W.2d 787 (Tex.App.1985); *Restatement, Second, of Property (Donative Transfers)* § 34.7, illus. 4 (1990). However, *Restatement (Third) of Property (Wills and Other Donative Transfers)* § 8.3, comm h (Prel.Dft. 2000) suggests that this might constitute *undue influence.*

**22.** Bedree v. Bedree, 528 N.E.2d 1128, 1130 (Ind.App.1988). *See also* Matter of Estate of Keeney, 908 P.2d 751, 755 (N.M.App.1995); Matter of Estate of Maheras, 897 P.2d 268 (Okl.1995); *Restatement, Second, Property (Donative Transfers)* § 34.7, comm. a (1990). *Restatement, Second, Contracts* § 177(3) (1979) protects a third party who "without reason to know of the undue influence either gives value or relies materially on the transaction."

**23.** Succession of Hamiter, 519 So.2d 341, 347 (La.App.1988) (testimony of subscribing witnesses discounted because they were unaware "of Mrs. Cox's relationship with" testator). *See also* In re Estate of Pedrick, 482 A.2d 215, 227 (Pa.1984) (dissenting opinion).

**24.** Geduldig v. Posner, 743 A.2d 247, 259 (Md.App.1999).

**25.** Erb v. Lee, 430 N.E.2d 869, 872 (Mass. App.1982).

**26.** Montoya v. Torres, 823 P.2d 905, 910 (N.M.1991); Moore v. Smith, 582 A.2d 1237 (Md.1990); Crump v. Moss, 517 So.2d 609, 612 (Ala.1987).

**27.** This presumption has also been applied in cases involving transfers other than wills. Doughty v. Morris, 871 P.2d 380 (N.M.App. 1994) (joint bank accounts).

elements must be present for the presumption to arise. Thus summary judgment was given to the proponents of a will despite the fact that they had a confidential relationship with the testator, when there was no evidence that they "were in any manner active or participated in the preparation or execution of the will."[28] However, some courts talk more generally about "suspicious circumstances" as the second ingredient in creating the presumption. The third Restatement of Property uses this term, and participation in preparing the will is only one of many possible "suspicious circumstances."[29]

Conversely, a will was upheld even though a child of the testator had participated in its preparation because "the normal relationship between a mentally competent parent and an adult child is not *per se* a confidential relationship."[30] Confidential relationship in this context usually means an unequal one in which one party dominates the other.[31] Some relationships are confidential *per se,* such as that between conservator and ward,[32] doctor and patient,[33] and pastor and parishioner.[34] Surprisingly, in view of the casual way in which powers of attorney are often given to relatives, they have been held to establish a confidential relationship between the parties.[35] Courts sometimes distinguish between "confidential" and "fiduciary" relationships; they are particularly prone to avoid gifts made to a fiduciary.[36]

Statements concerning the relationship between spouses are hard to reconcile. In California "a husband and wife are subject to the general rules governing fiduciary relationships,"[37] and courts in other states sometimes use similar language,[38] but one suggested that such a presumption "must be applied with caution as to marital relationships, because of the unique

**28.** Matter of Estate of Brodbeck, 915 P.2d 145, 154 (Kan.App.1996). *See also* Higgs v. Estate of Higgs, 892 S.W.2d 284 (Ark.App. 1995); In re Estate of Julian, 592 N.E.2d 39 (Ill.App.1991); Matter of Estate of Gersbach, 960 P.2d 811 (N.M.1998); In re Estate of Coleman, 738 So.2d 773 (Miss.App.1999); In re Estate of Kottke, 6 P.3d 243, 247 (Alaska 2000) (no undue influence found despite confidential relationship because only slight participation in will making).

**29.** *Restatement (Third) of Property (Wills and Other Donative Transfers)* § 8.3, comm. g (Prel.Dft. 2000.)

**30.** In re Estate of Elam, 738 S.W.2d 169, 173 (Tenn.1987). *See also* Heck v. Archer, 927 P.2d 495, 500 (Kan.App.1996); Estate of Jones v. Jones, 759 P.2d 345 (Utah App.1988) (even though beneficiary drafted the will); Matter of Estate of Neu, 588 N.E.2d 567 (Ind.App.1992) (niece).

**31.** *Restatement, Second, Contracts* § 177 (1979) refers to a person "under the domination of another *or* [one who] is justified, by virtue of his relation with another in assuming that the other will not act inconsistently with his welfare." Compare the use of the term in cases involving constructive trusts. Section 6.4, at note 29 et seq.

**32.** Matter of Basich's Estate, 398 N.E.2d 1182 (Ill.App.1979); Estate of Verdi by Verdi v. Toland, 733 N.E.2d 25 (Ind.App.2000).

**33.** Estate of McRae, 522 So.2d 731 (Miss. 1988) (deed from patient to doctor set aside).

**34.** Bryan v. Norton, 265 S.E.2d 282 (Ga. 1980); Matter of Estate of Maheras, 897 P.2d 268 (Okl.1995) (devise to pastor's church); Roberts–Douglas v. Meares, 615 A.2d 1114 (D.C.App.1992) (solicitation of contributions). *But see* Estate of Osborn, 470 N.E.2d 1114 (Ill.App.1984).

**35.** Smith v. Shafer, 623 N.E.2d 1261 (Ohio App.1993) (gift to attorney voided); White v. Raines, 574 N.E.2d 272 (Ill.App.1991) (same); Mitchell v. Smith, 779 S.W.2d 384 (Tenn.App. 1989) (devise to attorney).

**36.** Cleary v. Cleary, 692 N.E.2d 955 (Mass. 1998) (insurance agent); *Restatement, Second, Trusts* § 2, comm. b (1959); Cal.Prob.Code § 16004(c) (transaction between trustee and beneficiary "by which the trustee obtains an advantage ... is presumed to be a violation of the trustee's fiduciary duties").

**37.** Cal.Fam.Code § 721(b); In re Marriage of Haines, 39 Cal.Rptr.2d 673 (App.1995) (deed from W to H subject to presumption of undue influence).

**38.** Matter of Estate of Banko, 622 N.E.2d 476, 479 (Ind.1993) (but presumption held inapplicable to a joint bank account); Krebs v. Krebs, 759 P.2d 77 (Idaho App.1988) (same); Hughes v. Hughes, 634 P.2d 1271, 1275 (N.M. 1981) (presumption was rebutted).

relationship between spouses."[39] Very few of the vast number of wills which leave all or a large share of the estate to the testator's spouse are challenged, let alone set aside for undue influence.[40] Madoff suggests that where a confidential relationship between spouses is recognized, it is "generally limited to second marriages where the children of the first marriage are disinherited."[41] The third Restatement would extend the same protection to devises to the testator's "unmarried partner."[42]

If a presumption of undue influence arises, the contestant can escape a summary judgment or a directed verdict.[43] The presumption can be rebutted,[44] but some say that the fact finder must find undue influence unless the proponent produces contrary evidence,[45] while others assert that the presumption merely "makes a case which must be submitted to the jury," but does not "*compel* a finding for the contestant."[46] Thus a will was probated on a jury's finding that even though the devisee was in a confidential relationship with the testator and "was active in procuring the will," he was not "unduly benefited."[47] In another case a trust was upheld against a claim of undue influence by a trust officer who enjoyed a "confidential relationship" with the settlor and who assisted in the preparation of the trust, because the "trust officer testified that the decedent provided all instructions regarding" the terms of the trust.[48]

## § 7.4 Role of Lawyers

### *Lawyer as Witness*

Decisions in will contests upholding wills often rely on the testimony of a lawyer who drafted the will and supervised its execution.[1] This creates a problem when the drafting attorney seeks to represent the estate in a will contest. A lawyer in this situation was disqualified under DR 5–102 of the Code of Professional Responsibility:[2]

**39.** In re Estate of Glogovsek, 618 N.E.2d 1231, 1237 (Ill.App.1993). *See also* Morse v. Volz, 808 S.W.2d 424, 432 (Mo.App.1991); Womack v. Womack, 622 N.E.2d 481 (Ind. 1993).

**40.** In Bratton v. Owens, 794 P.2d 423 (Okl.App.1990) a deed from H to W was unsuccessfully challenged. In Matter of Estate of Montgomery, 881 S.W.2d 750, 756 (Tex.App. 1994), a will favoring a wife was upheld, the court noting that this was "not unusual." Occasionally, however, devises to a spouse are found invalid for undue influence. *See* Matter of Waters' Estate, 629 P.2d 470 (Wyo.1981); Fields v. Mersack, 577 A.2d 376 (Md.App. 1990); McKee v. Stoddard, 780 P.2d 736 (Or. App.1989).

**41.** Madoff, *supra* note 12, at 602.

**42.** *Restatement (Third) of Property (Wills and Other Donative Transfers)* § 8.3, comm. e (Prel.Dft. 2000).

**43.** In re Estate of Jessman, 554 N.E.2d 718 (Ill.App.1990); Allen v. Dutton's Estate, 394 So.2d 132 (Fla.App.1980).

**44.** Estate of Wenzel–Gosset by Gaukler v. Nickels, 575 N.W.2d 425 (N.D.1998).

**45.** Taliaferro v. Green, 622 S.W.2d 829 (Tenn.App.1981); McDowell v. Pennington, 394 So.2d 323 (Miss.1981); Franciscan Sisters Health Care Corp. v. Dean, 448 N.E.2d 872 (Ill.1983); In re Last Will of Melson, 711 A.2d 783 (Del.1998) (burden shifts to proponent of will).

**46.** Watson v. Warren, 751 S.W.2d 406, 410 (Mo.App.1988). *See also* Bryan v. Norton, 265 S.E.2d 282, 284 (Ga.1980).

**47.** Estate of Sarabia, 270 Cal.Rptr. 560, 562 (App.1990).

**48.** In re Estate of Squire, 6 P.3d 1060, 1063 (Okl.Civ.App.1999).

§ 7.4

**1.** *E.g.*, Matter of Last Will of Dickey, 542 So.2d 903 (Miss.1989); Gala v. Magarinos, 665 N.Y.S.2d 95 (A.D.1997); Morse v. Volz, 808 S.W.2d 424 (Mo.App.1991).

**2.** Matter of Estate of Seegers, 733 P.2d 418 (Okl.App.1986). *See also* Matter of Estate of McCoy, 844 P.2d 1131 (Alaska 1993); Matter of Will of O'Malley, 534 N.Y.S.2d 854 (Surr.1988).

(A) If after undertaking employment in contemplated or pending litigation, a lawyer learns * * * that he * * * ought to be called as a witness on behalf of his client, he shall withdraw from the conduct of the trial * * *.[3]

The rationale for the rule is that combining the disparate functions of witness and advocate may be confusing to the fact finder. It does not preclude the drafting attorney from representing the estate in administration after the contest is over.[4]

### *Undue Influence*

A factor often mentioned in undue influence cases is whether or not the testator had "independent advice." The independent advisor most often mentioned in this connection is the lawyer who drafted the will.[5]

Lawyers often appear in a *negative* light in undue influence cases. In many rejected wills, the drafting lawyer was selected by the devisee rather than the testator. For example, the devisees "met with an attorney of their choice, not [the testator's], and discussed the planning of his estate." The drafter did not speak with the testator until the will was signed.[6]

Sometimes lawyers who draft a will represent both the testator and a devisee, for example when a lawyer represents several members of a family. In one such case the contestants argued that "a lawyer who drafts for one client a will that benefits another ... creat[es] a strong presumption of undue influence."[7] The court rejected this argument, since the drafting lawyer "had known [the testator] for a number of years ... [She] was clearly the client." The devisees, on the other hand, never discussed the will with the lawyer or the testator. To find an impermissible conflict of interest in this situation "would make it impossible for any lawyer .. to draft a will for any family with which he was half-way familiar."[8] Another court, in rejecting a claim of undue influence, found that a lawyer had provided a father with "independent legal advice" even though he had also done work for the daughter-beneficiary.[9] Another court criticized a lawyer who had failed to disclose to his client,

3. Model Rules of Professional Conduct 3.7 is similar:"A lawyer shall not act as advocate at a trial in which the lawyer is likely to be a necessary witness [with exceptions inter alia] where disqualification of the lawyer would work substantial hardship on the client." *See* Matter of Estate of Waters, 647 A.2d 1091 (Del.1994).

4. Matter of Will of O'Malley, 534 N.Y.S.2d 854 (Surr.1988); Link, *Developments Regarding the Professional Responsibility of the Estate Administration Lawyer: The Effect of the Model Rules of Professional Conduct*, 26 Real Prop. Prob. and Trust L.J. 1, 98 (1991).

5. Matter of Estate of Wessels, 561 N.E.2d 1212, 1217 (Ill.App.1990); Langford v. McCormick, 552 So.2d 964, 969 (Fla.App.1989); Higgs v. Estate of Higgs, 892 S.W.2d 284, 287 (Ark. App.1995); Matter of Estate of Gonzales, 775 P.2d 1300, 1303 (N.M.App.1988).

6. Matter of Estate of Bolinder, 864 P.2d 228, 232 (Kan.App.1993). *See also* Matter of Estate of Carano, 868 P.2d 699 (Okl.1994) (assignment prepared by donee's lawyer who never talked with donor); Christensen v. Britton, 784 P.2d 908 (Mont.1989) (beneficiary took donor to her lawyer and was present in their discussions); McKee v. Stoddard, 780 P.2d 736, 740 (Or.App.1989).

7. Matter of Estate of Koch, 849 P.2d 977, 995 (Kan.App.1993) (quoting Charles Wolfram who appeared as an expert witness for the contestants).

8. *Id.* at 996. *See also* Blissard v. White, 515 So.2d 1196 (Miss.1987).

9. Matter of Estate of Wessels, 561 N.E.2d 1212, 1217 (Ill.App.1990).

the donor, that he was representing the donee in an another matter, but the gift was nevertheless valid because the donor "knew what he was doing."[10]

Particularly troubling are wills which benefit the drafting lawyer. Here the basis for a presumption of undue influence exists—a confidential relationship between attorney and client plus the lawyer's activity in preparing the will. Nevertheless, several such wills have been upheld, since the presumption of undue influence is rebuttable.[11]

### *Rules of the Profession*

The rules of conduct governing the legal profession have become an important factor in this situation. The Model Code of Professional Responsibility[12] Disciplinary Rule (hereinafter DR) 5–101(A) provides: "Except with the consent of his client after full disclosure, a lawyer shall not accept employment if the exercise of his professional judgment on behalf of his client will be or reasonably may be affected by his own financial, business, property, or personal interests." The Code's Ethical Consideration (hereinafter EC) 5–5 appended to this Rule states that a lawyer should urge any client to "secure disinterested advice from an independent, competent person" before accepting a gift from a client, and "[o]ther than in exceptional circumstances, a lawyer should insist that an instrument in which his client desires to name him beneficially be prepared by another lawyer selected by the client." These provisions raise the question whether Ethical Considerations, as distinguished from the Rules have obligatory force.[13]

The Model Rules of Professional Conduct, promulgated by the American Bar Association in 1983, include a clearer prohibition in Rule 1.8(c): "a lawyer shall not prepare an instrument giving the lawyer or a person related to the lawyer as parent, child, sibling, or spouse any substantial gift from a client, including a testamentary gift, except where the client is related to the donee." This rule was the basis for suspending a lawyer who drafted a codicil by which a company was given an option to buy shares of stock held by the testator in a company in which the drafter's mother was also a large shareholder. Although it was not clear whether the option price was lower than the value of the stock at the time the codicil was drafted, "it was reasonably foreseeable" that the the drafter's mother would substantially benefit, which in fact she did by selling her stock at more than twice the price per share fixed by the option.[14]

These rules have been cited in undue influence cases to show that a lawyer's conduct was improper or "undue."[15] Model Rule 1.8(c) was the model for a provision in the California Probate Code that "no provision ... of any instrument shall be valid to make any donative transfer to ... the person who drafted the instrument" with exceptions.[16] Although this provision, like the

**10.** Pascale v. Pascale, 549 A.2d 782, 791–92 (N.J.1988).

**11.** McGovern, *Undue Influence and Professional Responsibility*, 28 Real Property, Probate and Trust J. 643, 645 (1994).

**12.** The Model Code of Professional Responsibility was promulgated by the American Bar Association in 1972, and adopted in one form or another in 49 states.

**13.** McGovern, *supra* note 11, at 651.

**14.** In re Watson, 733 N.E.2d 934, 937 (Ind. 2000).

**15.** Matter of Estate of Dankbar, 430 N.W.2d 124 (Iowa 1988); Krischbaum v. Dillon, 567 N.E.2d 1291 (Ohio 1991); Pascale v. Pascale, 549 A.2d 782 (N.J.1988); *cf.* In re Succession of Parham, 755 So.2d 265 (La.App.1999) (will ipso facto valid because of lawyer's violation of Rule).

**16.** Cal.Prob.Code § 21350. Note that although the Model Rule only governs members

Model Rule, applies only to drafting an instrument, other gifts from clients to lawyers are subject to challenge for undue influence.[17] The Restatement of Law Governing Lawyers expressly bans (with exceptions) both preparing any instrument effecting a gift or devise from client to lawyer and mere accepting such a gift.[18]

The exception in the Model Rule "except where the client is related to the lawyer" has been defined somewhat more precisely in the California counterpart,[19] but still raises troubling questions. Does it exempt a relative who drafts an instrument giving the drafter more than his or her intestate share, *e.g.* one of several children who drafts a will for a parent giving him the whole estate? Case law makes some allowances for kinship between the testator and the drafter. Thus, a trust drafted by the settlor's grandson under which he was given a remainder was upheld, the court saying that because they were related, there was no presumption of undue influence.[20] But kinship is not an absolute defense to a claim of undue influence.[21] The Restatement also makes an exception where the lawyer is related to the client, but only if "the gift is not significantly disproportionate to those give to donees similarly related to the donor."[22]

Friends are *not* covered by the exception for relatives, but some courts have upheld wills in which a drafter-devisee was a close friend of the testator,[23] and the Restatement puts "other natural object[s] of the client's generosity" in the same category as relatives.[24] When a lawyer drafted a will for a family friend which included a devise to himself, the court found no undue influence, but the lawyer was nevertheless reprimanded for violating a disciplinary rule.[25] In another case in which a lawyer was suspended for only 60 days for violating Model Rule 1.8(c), his "very close relationship" with the testator was cited as a "mitigating factor."[26]

Both the Model Rule and the California statute (but not the Restatement) bar devises to certain persons connected with the drafter, such as a spouse or child, but the terms differ. For example, a grandchild or employee of the

of the legal profession, the California provision is not so limited. *See also* In re Estate of Marks, 957 P.2d 235 (Wash.App.1998) (applying Rule 1.8(c) to non-lawyers who helped testator draft will).

**17.** McGovern, *supra* note 58, at 658; In re Estate of Mapes, 738 S.W.2d 853 (Mo.1987) (joint bank account).

**18.** *Restatement, Third, of Law Governing Lawyers* § 208 Prop.Fin.Draft 1996)

**19.** Cal.Prob.Code § 21350(b).

**20.** Lah v. Rogers, 707 N.E.2d 1208, 1213 (Ohio App.1998). *See also* Matter of Will of Wasson, 562 So.2d 74 (Miss.1990) (will drawn by testator's sister-in-law benefitting her children is upheld); In re Estate of Alexander, 749 P.2d 1052 (Kan.App.1988) (will drawn by testator's daughter-in-law benefiting her husband upheld); Matter of Estate of Unke, 583 N.W.2d 145 (S.D.1998) (testator's son participated in drafting will).

**21.** Parker v. Marshall, 549 So.2d 463 (Ala. 1989) (will rejected for undue influence by testator's lawyer-grandchild); Cleary v. Cleary, 692 N.E.2d 955 (Mass.1998) (fiduciary must justify benefit from transaction with beneficiary even though they were related); Clarkson v. Whitaker, 657 N.E.2d 139 (Ind.App.1995); In re Last Will of Melson, 711 A.2d 783 (Del.1998) (presumption of undue influence when testator's son drafts will benefitting son's children).

**22.** *Restatement, Third, of Law Governing Lawyers* § 208(1) Prop.Fin.Draft 1996). This qualification does not appear in (2) involving a lawyer who accepts a gift without preparing an instrument.

**23.** McGovern, *supra* note 11, at 659–60.

**24.** *Restatement, Third, of Law Governing Lawyers* § 208(1) Prop.Fin.Draft 1996).

**25.** Clermont Cty. Bar Ass'n v. Bradford, 685 N.E.2d 515 (Ohio 1997).

**26.** In re Watson, 733 N.E.2d 934, 937 (Ind. 2000).

drafter is covered in California[27] but not under the Model Rule. Benefits to family members of the drafting attorney have been held to raise a presumption of undue influence at common law.[28]

Neither the Model Rule nor the California statute cover instruments which designate the drafter as executor or trustee. This is not a "gift" or "donative transfer," since such fiduciaries are compensated for services rendered. "Such earned fees," as one court remarked, "do not constitute the type of substantial economic benefit which gives rise to a presumption of undue influence."[29] But EC 5–6 of the Code of Professional Responsibility provides that "a lawyer should not consciously influence a client to name him as executor, trustee or lawyer in an instrument." When a will named the drafter and his son as co-executors, a court refused to appoint them, citing EC 5–6. In this case the appointment of co-executors would have increased the fees,[30] which the testator wished to keep low. Furthermore, since the testator had not previously known the drafter, his designation as executor was suspicious.[31] In California the drafter of a trust instrument who is designated as sole trustee in the instrument is subject to removal unless the court finds no undue influence.[32]

In some cases, lawyers have refused to draft a will from which they would benefit, but have been involved in the preparation of such a will by another lawyer. EC 5–5 provides that any will benefitting a lawyer should be "prepared by another lawyer selected by the client." Even this may not be enough. In one case a lawyer refused to draft a will naming himself as a devisee, but prepared a memorandum outlining the client's estate plan. The client found another lawyer who "prepared the will based principally upon [the first lawyer's] memo and a brief meeting" with the client. The court held that it was error to dismiss the contestants' challenge to the will, because "it could be inferred that [the testator] did not receive the benefit of counselling by an independent attorney."[33] In California use of a second lawyer immunizes the transaction only if this lawyer certifies that

> I am so disassociated from the interest of the transferee as to be in a position to advise my client impartially and confidentially as to the consequences of the transfer. On the basis of this counsel, I conclude that

**27.** Cal.Prob.Code § 21350(a)(2).

**28.** Zachary v. Mills, 660 N.E.2d 1301, 1308 (Ill.App.1996). In Estate of Auen, 35 Cal. Rptr.2d 557 (App.1994), a will and deed benefitting an attorney, her family and friends was voided for undue influence without reference to the statute.

**29.** Burke v. Kehr, 876 S.W.2d 718, 722 (Mo.App.1994) (directed verdict for proponents of will which named drafter as executor). *See also* Kuster v. Schaumburg, 658 N.E.2d 462, 466 (Ill.App.1995).

**30.** This is not always true when several fiduciaries are designated. See Section 12.5, at note 127 et seq. In Matter of Bales, 608 N.E.2d 987 (Ind.1993), a drafter was named executor in a will which designated high fees. The lawyer was reprimanded and her fees reduced. *See also* Disciplinary Counsel v. Galinas, 666 N.E.2d 1083 (Ohio 1996); Matter of Eisenhauer, 689 N.E.2d 783 (Mass.1998). In Estate of Gerard v. Gerard, 911 P.2d 266 (Okl.1995), a designated trustee who would earn "substantial fees" was held to have exercised undue influence on a testator.

**31.** Matter of Weinstock's Estate, 351 N.E.2d 647 (N.Y.1976). *See also* McGovern, *supra* note 11, at 668–73.

**32.** Cal.Prob.Code § 15642(b)(6).

**33.** Matter of Henderson, 605 N.E.2d 323, 326 (N.Y.1992). *See also* In re Will of Moses, 227 So.2d 829 (Miss.1969). In Matter of Estate of Kern, 716 P.2d 528 (Kan.1986), a similar case, the will was upheld over a strong dissent, even though the first lawyer had also recommended the drafting attorney to the client. *See also* Vaupel v. Barr, 460 S.E.2d 431 (W.Va. 1995).

> the transfer .. [is] not the product of fraud, menace duress, or undue influence.[34]

Under the Restatement, however, it is enough if the client "has received independent advice, or has been encouraged and given a reasonable opportunity" to do so.[35]

Because of the perceived injury to the image of the bar when a lawyer benefits from a client's generosity, some courts conduct hearings over such wills even if no heir challenges them.[36] Furthermore, lawyers may be disciplined for violating the rules of the profession, regardless of the result of any probate proceedings.[37]

### *Malpractice*

Lawyers who do sloppy work in guarding against claims of incapacity and undue influence can be liable for malpractice. A devisee who won a will contest thereafter sued the drafter for negligence "in failing to firmly establish [the testator's] testamentary capacity and free will" thereby causing the plaintiff's expenses in defending the will to be "at least double what they should have been." The court held the complaint stated a cause of action, even though the devisee was not the defendant's client.[38]

**34.** Cal.Prob.Code § 21351(b).

**35.** *Restatement, Third, of Law Governing Lawyers* § 208(2)(c) Prop.Fin.Draft 1996). This does not apply, however, if the lawyer-donees drafts the instrument effecting the transfer.

**36.** Matter of Delorey, 529 N.Y.S.2d 153 (A.D.1988) (will not probated even though uncontested); Estate of Lind, 257 Cal.Rptr. 853 (App.1989).

**37.** Akron Bar Ass'n v. Parker, 557 N.E.2d 116 (Ohio 1990) (will contest settled, lawyer suspended); Matter of Eisenhauer, 689 N.E.2d 783 (Mass.1998).

**38.** Rathblott v. Levin, 697 F.Supp. 817 (D.N.J.1988).

# Chapter 8

# ADEMPTION, ABATEMENT AND LAPSE

*Analysis*



## § 8.1 Ademption

Sometimes after a will is executed but before the testator dies a change occurs which makes distribution of the estate problematic. For example, a will leaves "my IBM stock to my sister, Elizabeth," and the testator later sells her IBM stock. The devise of the stock is usually held to be "adeemed" (from the Latin *adimere:* to take away), so Elizabeth gets nothing.[1] Why? The testator's executor could buy IBM stock for Elizabeth with the money in the estate. Under Roman law, legacies were adeemed only when the testator so intended,[2] but Chancellor Thurlow in the 18th century set the common law on a different path. Holding that the devise of a bond was adeemed when it was paid off before the testator died, the Chancellor said "there is nothing upon which the bequest may operate. And I do not think that the question ... turns on the intention of the testator."[3] Similar statements can be found in modern judicial opinions, e.g. "the testator's intent is not relevant where the property devised or bequeathed in his will is not part of his estate at death."[4] Such statements are misleading when one examines the cases more closely.[5]

§ 8.1

1. Such "ademption by extinction" is sometimes contrasted with "ademption by satisfaction" when a testator gives something to a devisee, intending thereby to satisfy the devise. In re Estate of Hume, 984 S.W.2d 602, 604 (Tenn.1999); Uniform Probate Code § 2–609; *Restatement, Third, of Property (Wills and Other Donative Transfers)* § 5.4 (1998). The latter problem is discussed in Section 2.6, at note 31 et seq.

Sales of property by an executor after the testator's death are discussed in Section 12.6.

2. Justinian, *Institutes* 2.20.12. Earlier Roman lawyers, however, had assumed that there was an intent to adeem in this situation. Gaius, *Institutes* 2.198.

3. Stanley v. Potter, 30 Eng.Rep. 83 (1789). So also in In re Estate of Warman, 682 N.E.2d 557 (Ind.App.1997) the devise of a claim held by the testator was held to be adeemed when it was settled by the payment of money to him.

For a brief survey of the law before Thurlow see Lundwall, *The Case against the Ademption by Extinction Rule: A Proposal for Reform*, 29 Gonz.L.Rev. 105, 106 (1993).

4. In re Estate of Balter, 703 A.2d 1038, 1041 (Pa.Super.1997) (devise of ring adeemed when it could not be found after testator died). *See also* Wasserman v. Cohen, 606 N.E.2d 901, 902 (Mass.1993); In re Estate of Hume, 984 S.W.2d 602, 606 (Tenn.1999).

5. "Courts purportedly following the identity theory frequently manipulate doctrine to effectuate intent." *Restatement, Third, of Property (Wills and Other Donative Transfers)* § 5.2, comm. b (1998). In some (more recent) cases there are explicit statements that ademption turns on intention. *E.g.* In re Estate of Poach, 600 N.W.2d 172, 177 (Neb.1999).

The result often turns on how the devise is worded. For example, a will devised "my home located at 19 Holly Ridge" and the testator had moved to another home when he died. The court held the devise was adeemed, distinguishing a devise of "the homestead upon which we are living;" the latter was held to mean the testator's home at the time of his death.[6] When a devise uses general language to describe property, the devisee gets any property owned by the testator at death which meets the description even though the testator did not own it when the will was executed.[7]

The Uniform Probate Code attempts to avoid the "harsh results" of ademption, in cases where (in the view of the drafters) it would frustrate the testator's intent. Among other things, the Code gives a specific devisee any property which the testator "acquired as a replacement for" the specifically devised asset. This would presumably have changed the result in the "19 Holly Ridge" case.[8]

### *Classification of Devises*

Only "specific" devises are subject to ademption. If a devise of stock is deemed "general," the executor must buy the shares for the devisee if the testator does not own them at death.[9] There is sometimes said to be a presumption that gifts of securities are general rather than specific,[10] but some devises of stock can only be classified as specific, *e.g.*, "all my IBM stock." A devise of a designated number of shares, on the other hand, is ambiguous. A devise of "my 147 shares of the stock of Wales Brothers" was held to be specific (and thus partially adeemed when the testator only owned 103 shares at death) because of the "reference to the securities as belonging to the testator."[11] Even without the word "my" in the devise, since the testator owned exactly 147 shares when she executed her will, some courts would classify the devise as specific.[12]

There is a third type of legacy, called "demonstrative," which is not subject to ademption. For example, a will left devises totalling $500,000 to eight individuals, designating a stock fund as the source of payment. The fund had only $46,000 in it when the testator died, but the designated individuals were paid in full, because the devise was classified as demonstrative.

> A demonstrative legacy is designated by a particular source and may be satisfied by other sources if the identified source is insufficient ... 'Courts disfavor specific bequests, for if the designated property is not part of the estate at death, the gift will generally be lost through

**6.** Matter of Estate of Brown, 922 S.W.2d 605, 608 (Tex.App.1996). For cases avoiding ademption by the "date-of-death" construction, see Lundwall, *supra* note 3, at 113.

**7.** *Restatement, Third, of Property (Wills and Other Donative Transfers)* § 5.2, comm. e (1998). *But cf.* Succession of Mydland, 653 So.2d 8 (La.App.1995)(devise of "all my interest" in a corporation does not include a corporate asset distributed to the testator when the corporation was dissolved).

**8.** Uniform Probate Code § 2–606(a)(5).

**9.** In re Blomdahl's Will, 257 N.W. 152 (Wis.1934); Matter of Fitch's Will, 118 N.Y.S.2d 234 (A.D.1952).

**10.** Lundwall, *supra* note 1, at 110; *Restatement, Third, of Property (Wills and Other Donative Transfers)* § 5.2, comm. c (1998).

**11.** Estate of Wales, 727 P.2d 536, 537 (Mont.1986). *See also* Estate of Bestwick, 426 A.2d 580 (Pa.1981); Boerstler v. Andrews, 506 N.E.2d 279 (Ohio App.1986).

**12.** Matthews v. Matthews, 477 So.2d 391 (Ala.1985); In re Estate of Soles, 304 A.2d 97 (Pa.1973).

ademption by extinction.' ... An intention to create a specific legacy was not shown with clarity.[13]

### *Change in Form*

Courts sometimes avoid an ademption on the theory that what occurred was a mere "change in form." For example, a devise of "my interest in the investment plan with the United States National Bank" was not adeemed when the interest was distributed to the testator in the form of cash and stock, since this was a change "of form and not of substance."[14] An important basis for the decision was the fact that the distribution to the testator "was an event over which he had no control."[15] On similar grounds, the Uniform Probate Code gives specific devisees of stock any securities which the testator later acquires in the company "by reason of action initiated by the organization" and any securities acquired in another company by reason of a merger.[16] On the other hand, the testator's shift of a savings account to a certificate of deposit was held to cause an ademption.[17]

In most cases where the court finds a mere "change in form" the substitute for the devised property is identifiable in the testator's estate.[18] Even under the UPC, a specific devisee does not get a distribution of *cash*, as distinguished from securities, resulting from a merger.[19]

The mere fact that the proceeds of a sale can be identified in the testator's estate does not always prevent an ademption. Thus the devise of a house was adeemed even though the sales proceeds were paid only after the testator's death. The sale constituted "a 'material alteration' to the subject matter of the specific bequest" so that the proceeds passed under the residuary clause of the will.[20] However, the Uniform Probate Code gives specific devisees "any balance of the purchase price * * * owing from a purchaser to the testator at death by reason of a" sale of the devised property.[21] One court reached this result without a statute on the theory that when the testatrix died, "the property was in existence and owned by her;"

**13.** In re Estate of Lung, 692 A.2d 1349 (D.C.App.1997). *See also* Smith v. Estate of Peters, 741 P.2d 1172 (Alaska 1987); Lavender v. Cooper, 285 S.E.2d 528 (Ga.1982); Leaver v. McBride, 506 S.W.2d 141, 145 (Tenn.1974). *But see* Estate of Norwood, 443 N.W.2d 798 (Mich.App.1989) (bequest of $6,000 from life insurance fails when no insurance in the estate).

**14.** Stenkamp v. Stenkamp, 723 P.2d 336, 338 (Or.App.1986). *See also* Johnston v. Estate of Wheeler, 745 A.2d 345 (D.C.2000) (no ademption in roll-over of pension benefits to an IRA).

**15.** "The fact that a testator did not initiate a change makes the application of the change-in-form principle more likely." *Restatement, Third, of Property (Wills and Other Donative Transfers)* § 5.2, comm. d (1998). Compare the discussion of involuntary transfers infra.

**16.** Uniform Prob.Code § 2–605.

**17.** Estate of Mayberry v. Mayberry, 886 S.W.2d 627 (Ark.1994). *See also* Church v. Morgan, 685 N.E.2d 809 (Ohio App.1996).

**18.** Johnston v. Estate of Wheeler, 745 A.2d 345, 351 (D.C.App.2000) (emphasizing that funds in question "remained segregated" from testator's other property).

**19.** Opperman v. Anderson, 782 S.W.2d 8 (Tex.App.1989); Uniform Probate Code § 2–605(b).

**20.** In re Estate of Hume, 984 S.W.2d 602, 605 (Tenn.1999). *See also* Jennings v. National Bank of Commerce, 606 S.W.2d 130 (Ark.App.1980); Baybank Harvard Trust Co. v. Grant, 504 N.E.2d 1072 (Mass.App.1987); Opperman v. Anderson, 782 S.W.2d 8 (Tex.App.1989); *Restatement, Third, of Property (Wills and Other Donative Transfers)* § 5.2, comm. d (1998) (sale for cash is "too substantial" to be treated as a change of form even if tracing is possible).

**21.** Uniform Probate Code § 2–606(a)(1).

her executor was bound to convey title to the purchaser pursuant to the contract of sale, but the devisee was entitled to the net proceeds.[22]

Events occurring after a will is executed sometimes increase the value of a specific devise. Thus a devise of "my shares in the Putnam High Yield Trust" was held to include shares the testator bought after the will was executed.[23] Even when a will specifies a number of shares, the devisee may receive more as the result of a stock split. For example, a devisee of "200 shares Exxon" was awarded an additional 200 shares which the testator subsequently received in a stock split.[24] Some courts give a devisee of stock the additional shares only if the devise is characterized as specific,[25] but under the Uniform Probate Code a devisee gets the additional securities regardless of how the devise is characterized.[26] Dividends paid in stock, like stock splits, also go a devisee of securities under the UPC, but not *cash* dividends paid to the testator during life.

### *Involuntary Transfers*

Specifically devised assets are sometimes disposed of after the testator has become incompetent by a conservator appointed to manage the testator's property. The Uniform Probate Code gives the specific devisee in this situation "a general pecuniary devise equal to the net sale price" of the asset sold on the theory that an incapacitated testator could not have intended to adeem a devise.[27] Some courts reach this result without a statute,[28] but others only give the specific devisee whatever remains of the sales proceeds when the testator dies.[29]

The Uniform Probate Code provision applies only to devises, but a similar rule has been applied to will substitutes.[30] For example, when a conservator closed joint accounts that the conservatee had previously established for her

**22.** Kelley v. Neilson, 727 N.E.2d 82, 85 (Mass.App.2000). *See also* In re Estate of Poach, 600 N.W.2d 172 (Neb.1999) (property sold pursuant to exercise of an option after the testator died).

**23.** Estate of Russell, 521 A.2d 677 (Me. 1987). *See also Restatement, Third, of Property (Wills and Other Donative Transfers)* § 5.2, comm. e (1998).

**24.** Shriners Hosp. for Crippled Children v. Coltrane, 465 So.2d 1073 (Miss.1985). *See also* Watson v. Santalucia, 427 S.E.2d 466 (W.Va. 1993). In Matter of Estate of Holmes, 821 P.2d 300 (Colo.App.1991), the court even gave a devisee the benefit of a stock split which took place *before* the will was executed on the basis that the testator actually intended to include all of her stock in the company.

**25.** Boerstler v. Andrews, 506 N.E.2d 279 (Ohio App.1986).

**26.** Uniform Probate Code § 2–605, Comment. *See also* Bostwick v. Hurstel, 304 N.E.2d 186 (Mass.1973); In re Estate of Howard, 393 So.2d 81 (Fla.App.1981); Watson v. Santalucia, 427 S.E.2d 466 (W.Va.1993). *Compare* Calif.Prob.Code § 21332 (based on an earlier version of the UPC, applicable only if the "a specific gift" was intended).

**27.** Uniform Probate Code § 2–606(b). *See also* Matter of Estate of Gardner, 845 P.2d 1247 (N.M.App.1992); Cal.Prob.Code § 21134. The rule does not apply if the testator is judicially restored to capacity and survives thereafter by a year. Uniform Probate Code § 2–606(d); Oliver v. Estate of Oliver, 554 N.E.2d 8 (Ind.App.1990) (ademption found when testator's confusion "cleared up" after sale by conservator).

**28.** Matter of Estate of Warren, 344 S.E.2d 795 (N.C.App.1986); Lundwall, *supra* note 3, at 115.

**29.** Matter of Estate of Swoyer, 439 N.W.2d 823 (S.D.1989); In re Graham's Estate, 533 P.2d 1318 (Kan.1975); Grant v. Banks, 155 S.E.2d 87 (N.C.1967).

**30.** Uniform Probate Code § 2–606 appears in Part 6, "Rules of Construction Applicable only to Wills," whereas Part 7 covers "Rules of construction Applicable to Wills and Other Governing Instruments." However, *Restatement, Third, of Property (Wills and Other Donative Transfers)* § 5.2, comm. i (1998) indicates that almost identical rules should "also apply to a will substitute, such as a revocable trust."

niece and nephew, they got the funds after the conservatee died on the ground that the conservator in closing the account had exceeded his authority.

> The conservator's duty is to manage the estate during the conservatee's lifetime. It is not his function ... to control disposition after death ... A conservator may withdraw funds from a joint account only to provide what is necessary for the conservatee's maintenance.[31]

The Uniform Probate Code requires conservators to "take into account any estate plan" of the conservatee in utilizing funds for the conservatee's support.[32]

Today many persons use durable powers of attorney in order to avoid conservatorship.[33] The Uniform Probate Code applies the same rule to sales by an agent with a durable power for an incapacitated principal.[34] Without such a statutory mandate courts have split over whether the rule for conservators should apply to agents as well.[35] Application of the UPC rule requires a determination of the capacity of the principal at the time of the sale; if the principal was then competent, the rule does not apply, but acts of an agent under a durable power are "presumed to be for an incapacitated principal."[36]

Involuntary loss may also arise from accident. When a specifically devised house was damaged by fire after the will was executed, the devisee was awarded the proceeds of an insurance policy on the house. Since the fire "did not occur through any voluntary act" of the testator, it "showed no change" in the testator's intention.[37] The Uniform Probate Code gives a specific devisee any insurance proceeds which are paid to the estate after the testator's death. Even if the loss was uninsured, or the insurance has been paid and dissipated, the devisee may recover the value of the missing property "unless the circumstances indicate that an ademption was intended by the testator or ... is consistent with the testator's manifested plan of distribution."[38] The examples given in the accompanying comment distinguish between property stolen by a burglar (no ademption) and property given away by the testator (devise is adeemed). The Code thus reflects an overall "mild presumption against ademption,"[39] but the narrower exceptions to ademption provided in an earlier version of the Code, are still law in some states.[40]

**31.** Matter of Estate of Briley, 825 P.2d 1181, 1183–84 (Kan.App.1992). *See also* Witt v. Ward, 573 N.E.2d 201 (Ohio App.1989); *Restatement, Second, of Property (Donative Transfers)* § 18.1, illus. 1 (1984). *But see* In re Conservatorship of Gobernatz, 603 N.W.2d 357, 360 (Minn.App.1999) (conservator properly terminated joint account of conservatee).

**32.** Uniform Probate Code § 5–426. *See* Matter of Estate of Reinwald, 834 P.2d 1317 (Idaho 1992) (improper for conservator to eliminate POD beneficiary in renewing CD). For the circumstances in which a conservator can properly affect the conservator's estate plan see Section 7.2, at note 27 et seq.

**33.** See Section 7.2, at note 38 et seq.

**34.** Uniform Probate Code § 2–606(b).

**35.** *Compare* Funk v. Funk, 563 N.E.2d 127 (Ind.App.1990) (no equitable conversion from sale by agent while principal was comatose) *with* In re Estate of Hegel, 668 N.E.2d 474 (Ohio 1996) (devise adeemed by sale by agent under durable power).

**36.** Uniform Probate Code § 2–606(e); *cf.* Chapman v. Chapman, 577 A.2d 775 (Me.1990) (finding ademption when there was no proof that the testator was incompetent when property was sold by an agent).

**37.** White v. White, 251 A.2d 470, 473 (N.J.Super.Ch.Div.1969). *See also* In re Estate of Kolbinger, 529 N.E.2d 823 (Ill.App.1988); Lundwahl, *supra* note 3, at 118 (citing cases both ways).

**38.** Uniform Probate Code § 2–606.

**39.** These words come from the comment to Uniform Probate Code § 2–606, but the text was altered in 1997 to be consistent with *Restatement, Third, of Property (Wills and Other Donative Transfers)* § 5.2, comm. g (1998): "the party opposing ademption bears the burden of proof" in cases not covered by the more specific rules of § 5.2(a) and (b).

**40.** *E.g.*, Cal.Prob.Code §§ 21133–34. For other statutes dealing with ademption in a

### *Other Factors*

Even a testator who voluntarily disposes of a specifically devised asset may not intend to adeem the devise. For example, a testator's shifting money from a savings account to a certificate of deposit in order to get a higher interest rate probably shows an intent to get more money, not to adeem. But even the Uniform Probate Code in creating only a "mild presumption" against ademption, recognizes that in some cases ademption does reflect the testator's probable intent. The reason for a specific devise may disappear when the property is disposed of. When a business is devised to employees in the hope that they will carry on the business, and the testator later sells the business, it seems reasonable to infer an intent to adeem.[41] The same applies to devises of items of sentimental value, like paintings or jewelry.[42] Many wills specifically devise the testator's house and tangible personal property in order to avoid having them go into a trust which holds the residue of the estate.[43] The fees paid to a professional trustee for managing investments of securities are usually an unnecessary expense as to a house. If the testator later sells the house there is no reason why the sale proceeds should not go into the residuary trust, so ademption seems the proper result. Ademption can avoid administrative problems, *e.g.* requiring the executor to determine the value of property which is no longer in the estate or the net sale price of property which the testator sold years before.

Drafters can avoid such problems by a using a different type of devise. Professor Ascher has noted that "competent estate planners generally try to avoid using specific bequests when the testator's real desire is simply to allocate quantities of wealth among a group of individuals. General bequests and fractional shares of the residuary estate are much more apt" for this purpose.[44] There is usually no good reason why a testator would want her sister to get her IBM stock rather than an equivalent amount of money or a fraction of the estate.

### *Income and Appreciation During Administration*

The classification of devises also affects the allocation of income received during the administration of an estate. For example, a will devised a motel to the testator's children, and the residue of his estate to his wife. The motel produced a profit of $10,000 during administration. This was held to pass to the testator's children as part of their specific devise.[45] All the Uniform

limited way see Lundwahl, *supra* note 3, at 119–22.

**41.** Matter of Morrissey, 684 S.W.2d 876 (Mo.App.1984). *See also* Douglas v. Newell, 719 P.2d 971, 982 (Wyo.1986) (dissent); Alexander, *Ademption and the Domain of Formality in Wills Law*, 55 Alb.L.Rev. 1067, 1081 (1992).

**42.** Ascher, *The 1990 Uniform Probate Code: Older and Better, or More like the Internal Revenue Code*, 77 Minn.L.Rev. 639, 644 (1993); Johnston v. Estate of Wheeler, 745 A.2d 345, 352 (D.C.App.2000) (finding no ademption because devise was not "an heirloom of primarily sentimental value"). *But see Restatement, Third, of Property (Wills and Other Donative Transfers)* § 5.2, illus. 4–6 (1998) (no ademption when specifically devised jewelry is stolen).

**43.** Uniform Statutory Will Act § 5.

**44.** Ascher, *supra* note 42, at 644. *See also* Leach, *Cases and Text on the Law of Wills* 148 (2d ed. 1960).

**45.** Estate of Lindsey v. Taylor, 300 N.E.2d 572, 573 (Ill.App.1973). *See also* Matter of Estate of Meyer, 668 N.E.2d 263, 266 (Ind.App. 1996) (growing crops pass to specific devisee of

Principal and Income Acts provide that specific devisees receive the income from the property devised which accrues during the period of administration in addition to the property itself.[46] General or pecuniary devises, on the other hand, do not normally share in the income earned by an estate during administration, but rather get interest, normally specified in a statute. For example, Uniform Probate Code gives such devisees "interest at the legal rate." This interest begins to run one year after the personal representative is appointed and does not depend on whether the estate actually realized income.[47]

Income of an estate which is not attributable to specifically devised property is divided among the residuary devisees and the trustee of any pecuniary devise in trust in proportion to their respective shares of the estate.[48] The question as to how a devise should be classified sometimes arises in this context. For example, a will devised "25% of my estate remaining after debts, funeral expenses and expenses of administration, but before taxes." Was this a pecuniary devise or a fractional share of the residue?

> There are numerous decisions on [this] question. Most appear to turn on the language of the disposition.... When the disposition is a specific amount, such as $10,000, it is clearly pecuniary. A disposition "determinable by means of a formula which is stated in the instrument" is also pecuniary. For example, a bequest of one-half of $20,000 can clearly be determined by means of a formula and is therefore a pecuniary disposition.

Also relevant was the position of the devise in the will. This one appeared in Article Third; in Article Fourth the testator "disposed of her residuary estate in fractions, i.e., 70 per cent to her son and 30 per cent to her son's issue. Obviously if she had intended that the beneficiary of the bequest in Article THIRD should share in increases during estate administration, she could have provided for that result by placing this disposition within her residuary, the next clause in her will. She did not do so."[49]

Even pecuniary devises share in the estate income if they are "in trust." But the court held that this "pour over bequest" did not create a trust, but merely added to an existing trust and so did not qualify. On the other hand, a devise of "such portion of my estate which shall result in an amount equal to one-half of my adjusted gross estate" to the testator's wife, followed by a devise of "the remaining undivided one-half of my estate" to the testator's

farm); Matter of Estate of Niehenke, 818 P.2d 1324, 1332 (Wash.1991).

**46.** Unif.Prin. and Inc. Act (1962) § 5(b)(1); (1997 Act) § 201(1); (1931 Act) § 3–A(3)(a). *But see* Matter of Estate of Hafferman, 442 N.W.2d 238, 240 (S.D.1989) (statute allows executor to use first 10 months' income from specifically devised farm to pay debts of the estate).

**47.** Uniform Probate Code § 3–904. The comment to this section notes that at common law interest runs from the date of the testator's death. In In re Estate of Miller, 437 N.W.2d 793, 797 (Neb.1989), the court interpreted such a statute not to apply when payment of the devise was postponed during a will contest. *Contra*, Matter of Estate of Vaden, 677 P.2d 659 (Okl.App.1983) (citing authority both ways).

**48.** Unif.Prin. and Inc.Act § 210(4) (1997), § 5(b)(2) (1962 Act).

**49.** Estate of McKee, 504 N.Y.S.2d 394, 395–96 (Surr.1986). *See also* Hanna v. Hanna, 619 S.W.2d 655 (Ark.1981) (devise of "assets which will equal one-half of my adjusted gross estate" is "clearly a true pecuniary bequest").

children, was held to give the wife a "fractional residuary bequest" so she could share in the appreciation of the estate.[50]

### *Other Constructional Problems*

Specific devises sometimes give rise to litigation concerning their scope. A common devise is of a house and "its contents." Claims have been made, generally unsuccessful, that this includes cash and securities found in the house.[51] But a similar phrase was construed to include many valuable paintings in the house of artist Mark Rothko.[52]

Does a bequest of "cash on hand" include money in a checking account?[53] Do "the funds in my bank account" include a certificate of deposit?[54] Does "automobiles" include a pick-up truck and a motor home?[55] Is an automobile included in "personal effects?"[56] Cash found on the testator's person when he died?[57]

The interpretation of words may be affected by their context. The words "personal property" normally encompass intangibles such as securities,[58] but when they appeared in a phrase following "household furniture and furnishings, books, pictures, silverware, my automobiles," etc., they were given a restricted construction under "the rule of eiusdem generis," *i.e.,* "general words following the enumeration of specific meaning are not to be construed in their widest extent but only as applying to things of the same kind," and thus did not include intangibles.[59]

Courts sometimes look to the identity of the devisees in resolving such questions of construction. A devise of "all shares of common or preferred stock which I may own" to the testator's financial advisor was held not to include a cooperative apartment.

> Indisputably, for many commercial purposes the law treats a shareholder's interest in a cooperative apartment primarily as an interest in a corporation. Here, however, ... the document manifests decedent's intent that her relatives take the interest in her residence.[60]

It is not usual in modern wills to describe each item of a testator's property, as in Shakespeare's famous devise of his "second-best bed" to his

**50.** In re Estate of Parker, 180 N.W.2d 82 (Mich.App.1970).

**51.** Matter of Clark, 417 S.E.2d 856 (S.C. 1992) (cash); In re Lamb's Estate, 285 A.2d 163 (Pa.1971); *cf.* May v. Walter, 956 S.W.2d 138 (Tex.App.1997) ("tangible personal property contents" of a safe does not include a CD).

**52.** In re Estate of Rothko, 352 N.Y.S.2d 574 (Surr.1974).

**53.** Yes, according to Matter of Estate of Farone, 482 N.E.2d 556 (N.Y.1985). *See also* Scott v. Wallace, 686 So.2d 1241 (Ala.Civ.App. 1996); Matter of Estate of Mitchell, 519 So.2d 430 (Miss.1988) ("cash" includes CDs); Matter of Estate of Flasted, 741 P.2d 750 (Mont.1987) ("cash and savings" includes a $150,000 note).

**54.** Yes, according to Estate of Cushman, 501 A.2d 811 (Me.1985) (one dissent); Matter of Estate of Srubar, 728 S.W.2d 437 (Tex.App. 1987).

**55.** Yes, according to Riggs v. Riggs, 507 So.2d 462 (Ala.1987). *See also* Matter of Estate of Crist, 434 N.W.2d 904 (Iowa App.1988) ("household goods and other chattels" includes excavating equipment).

**56.** No, according to Matter of Estate of Roddy, 784 P.2d 841 (Colo.App.1989).

**57.** Yes, according to Huskins v. Huskins, 517 S.E.2d 146, 151 (N.C.App.1999).

**58.** Emmert v. Hearn, 522 A.2d 377 (Md. 1987).

**59.** Breckner v. Prestwood, 600 S.W.2d 52, 57 (Mo.App.1980). *See also* Sverid v. First Nat. Bank, 693 N.E.2d 423 (Ill.App.1998); In re Estate of Mildrexter, 971 P.2d 758 (Kan.App. 1999); Turner v. Reed, 518 S.E.2d 832 (Va. 1999).

**60.** Matter of Estate of Carmer, 525 N.E.2d 734, 736 (N.Y.1988).

wife. However, objects of great value should be specifically mentioned, since they may be construed not to pass under general references to "household furnishings" or "personal effects."[61]

Specific devises of part of a larger tract of land have also generated litigation. When a husband left his wife thirty acres out of a tract of 164 acres, the court allowed the wife to select thirty acres because she was "the principal object" of the testator's bounty, but such devises have also been construed to make the devisee a tenant in common of the entire tract.[62]

Bequests of property owned by a corporation which the testator controls have been held effective if this does not impair the rights of the corporation's creditors and minority shareholders.[63]

## § 8.2 Abatement

Sometimes there are insufficient assets in an estate to carry out the testator's directions. Suppose a will leaves (1) "my IBM stock to my sister Elizabeth," (2) "$10,000 to the First Presbyterian Church" and (3) "the residue of my estate to my issue." When the testator dies her estate contains the IBM stock (hence there is no ademption problem), but the rest of her assets are worth only $8,000. Or suppose that her assets, apart from the IBM stock, are worth $48,000 but there are claims against the estate amounting to $40,000. The claims must be paid. Which of the devises should be abated to do this?

### *Hierarchy of Devises*

The Uniform Probate Code provides that "shares of distributees abate * * * in the following order: (1) property not disposed of by will; (2) residuary devises; (3) general devises; (4) specific devises."[1] This hierarchy of devises (specific, general and residuary) comes from the common law[2] and is found in many statutes.[3] If the will disposes of the entire estate (as it usually does by virtue of a residuary devise), there is no property in the first category,[4] and so the property which would have passed under the residuary clause is first used. In the foregoing hypothetical, therefore, the testator's issue get nothing, the $10,000 general devise to the Presbyterian Church is partially abated, and Elizabeth's specific devise is unaffected.

Abatement among devises within each category is pro-rata.[5] Thus if the will had made two general devises, of $10,000 and $6,000, and only $8,000

**61.** *Cf.* Matter of Brecklein's Estate, 637 P.2d 444 (Kan.App.1981) (gold coins not included in "belongings"); Griffin v. Gould, 432 N.E.2d 1031 (Ill.App.1982) (extrinsic evidence admissible to determine whether valuable statues were included as "articles of household ornament").

**62.** Stephenson v. Rowe, 338 S.E.2d 301 (N.C.1986).

**63.** Matter of Estate of Hatfield, 730 P.2d 696 (Wash.App.1986).

**§ 8.2**

**1.** Uniform Probate Code § 3–902. *See also Restatement, Third, of Property (Wills and Other Donative Transfers)* § 1.1, comm. f (1998).

**2.** 2 W. Blackstone, *Commentaries* *512–13 (1765)

**3.** Some statutes list devises in accordance with the "priority of *distribution*" as (1) specific, (2) general, (3) residuary, (4) intestate, 20 Pa.Stat. § 3541, but the result is the same.

**4.** Contrary to what you might think on first reading the statute, property passing by non-probate transfers is not in this category. Such property is dealt with elsewhere. See note 6 et seq. infra.

**5.** Uniform Probate Code § 3–902(a); Matter of Estate of Wales, 727 P.2d 536 (Mont. 1986); In re Estate of Oberstar, 709 N.E.2d 872 (Ohio App. 1998).

was available to pay them, each devisee would receive half of the amount designated.

What if a person owns property which does not pass through the probate estate, such as a house or bank account in joint tenancy? In some jurisdictions such property is not subject to claims of creditors at all. Under the Uniform Probate Code the decedent's creditors could reach the joint account, but only if other assets of the estate are insufficient. Thus if there is enough in the probate estate to pay claims, a surviving joint tenant would not have to contribute.[6] Similarly the Restatement of Property states that usually "non-probate property ... is not used to satisfy creditors' claims except to the extent that probate property is not sufficient."[7]

In most wills the residuary devisees are the persons closest to the testator's heart; often pecuniary or specific devises go to friends, collateral relatives or charities, while the testator's spouse and issue get the residue. But to abate residuary devises last, or abate all devises pro-rata, would present administrative problems. Often property which is specifically devised can not readily be sold, or the testator does not want it to be sold. If specific devisees had to contribute to the payment of claims against the estate, they might be forced to sell the property. The residuary estate usually contains cash or liquid assets more suitable for sale.

Pecuniary devisees could contribute to the payment of claims simply by a reduction in the amount. However, when a will leaves "$10,000 to the Presbyterian Church" the testator probably expected the Church to get that amount and no less. This usually happens if the residuary estate is the primary source for paying claims. Rarely do claims exhaust the residuary estate. Thus, the testator's wishes are fulfilled in ordinary cases by making the residue the primary source for paying claims.

### *Apportionment*

The Uniform Probate Code departs from the normal order of abatement when a spouse claims an elective share; the spouse's claim is "equitably apportioned" among all the recipients of the decedent's estate, including non-probate transferees.[8] In most estates the claims are small enough that even if they are all charged to the residue there will be plenty left over for the residuary devisees. The elective share, on the other hand (particularly when based on non-probate assets as it is under the Code), may seriously deplete the residue if liability is not apportioned. Some states nevertheless follow the normal abatement rules in this situation,[9] but others like the UPC apportion liability among all devisees.[10] The Restatement of Property suggests an open-

**6.** See Section 13.2, at note 8 et seq.

**7.** *Restatement, Second, of Property (Donative Transfers)* § 34.3, comm. j (1990). *See also* Cal.Prob.Code § 19001 (revocable trusts); *Restatement, Third, Trusts* § 26, comm. d (1999).

**8.** Uniform Probate Code § 2–207. An exception is made for property irrevocably transferred by the decedent within two years of death. This is included in the calculation of the spouse's share under § 2–205(3), but is postponed in the apportionment under § 2–207(b).

**9.** In re Estate of Brinkman, 326 N.E.2d 167 (Ill.App.1975); Winters National Bank & Trust Co. v. Riffe, 206 N.E.2d 212 (Ohio 1965); Iowa Code § 633.436; Fla.Stat. § 732.209.

**10.** Kilcoyne v. Reilly, 249 F.2d 472 (D.C.Cir.1957); Wilkinson v. Brune, 682 S.W.2d 107 (Mo.App.1984).

ended rule: courts should allocate "liability as the decedent would probably have done had the decedent specifically addressed the question."[11]

The Uniform Probate Code generally follows the normal order of abatement when a pretermitted child or spouse claims a share,[12] but in California, the share is taken from all devisees pro-rata unless "the obvious intention of the testator * * * would be defeated" thereby.[13]

Liability for death taxes, such as the federal estate tax, is often apportioned among beneficiaries of an estate.[14]

### *Classification*

The classification of devises for purposes of abatement can be crucial and it is sometimes problematic. For example a will left 1) $10,000 in cash to designated individuals, 2) an undivided one-half interest of all mineral interests to a nephew and the other half to the nephew's children, 3) 23.521 acres of land to named individuals, 4) all real estate not covered by the foregoing to the nephew, 5) the balance of all cash and accounts to charities, and 6) the residue to two named individuals. The court's classification of 1) as general and 6) as residuary devises respectively is conventional, but its labelling 2), 4) and 5) as specific is more questionable.[15] Another will left $15,000 to the testator's son, and "all the rest of the my property, including the rights to receive royalty distributions from the American Society of Composers, Authors and Publishers," to his wife. The only asset in the estate was the testator's right to royalties. The wife claimed that her devise was specific, but the court classified it as residuary so the son's devise was preserved.[16] In another will a devise of "a sum equal to 10% of the value of my estate" was held to be general devise of 10% of the estate before deducting claims and prior to a devise of the residue.[17]

### *Contrary Intent*

The specific/general/residuary order of abatement does not reflect the testator's intent in some cases. Under the Uniform Probate Code, the hierarchy can be overcome by an express provision, or by showing that it would defeat "the testamentary plan or the express or implied purpose of the devise."[18] Thus a specific devise of personal property was held to abate prior to the residuary devises when the will specified "all debts ... shall be paid from the personal property of my estate."[19]

11. *Restatement, Second, of Property (Donative Transfers)* § 34.1, comm. j (1990).

12. Uniform Probate Code §§ 2–301(b), 2–302(d). *See also* Iowa Code § 633.436; *Restatement (Third) of Property (Wills and Other Donative Transfers)* § 9.5, comm. f (Prel.Dft. 2000).

13. Cal.Prob.Code §§ 21612, 21623. *See also* N.Y.EPTL § 5–1.3(b).

14. See Uniform Probate Code § 3–916(b).

15. Hurt v. Smith, 744 S.W.2d 1 (Tex. 1987). *Contrast* Matter of Estate of Brannan, 569 N.E.2d 104 (Ill.App.1991) ("all personal property not otherwise devised" held to be residuary).

16. Matter of Deutsch's Estate, 644 P.2d 768 (Wyo.1982).

17. Williams v. Faucett, 579 So.2d 572 (Ala. 1989).

18. Uniform Probate Code § 3–902(b). *See also* Cal.Prob.Code § 21400; N.Y.EPTL § 13–1.3(e); *cf.* Matter of Estate of Routh, 524 N.E.2d 46 (Ind.App.1988) (extrinsic evidence to show contrary intent is inadmissible).

19. In re Estate of Ohrt, 585 N.W.2d 259 (Iowa 1998).

Determining the testator's intent may be difficult. For example, a will left a farm to the testator's son, and "a portion of my estate equal in value to the value of the property passing to my son" to the testator's daughter. The son's devise was held to be specific and the daughter's general, with the result that the son ended up with more than his sister.[20] Perhaps the testator's "implied purpose" to treat his children equally should have led the court to ignore the preference for specific devises. In another case a will left 30% of the residue, including the testator's funeral home stock, to the testator's wife. The stock was worth more than 30% of estate. The court said the wife got only 30% of the estate because the testator "obviously intended" his children to get 70% of the estate.[21]

### *Other Factors*

Factors other than the type of devise may affect the order of abatement. Historically, personal property of a decedent was exhausted before real estate in paying claims. A few states retain vestiges of this idea,[22] but the Uniform Probate Code treats both types of property the same way.[23]

Some states favor certain devisees in abatement, regardless of the type of devise. In Iowa gifts to the testator's spouse abate last; even a specific devise to a daughter abates before a residuary devise to a wife.[24] No such preference appears in the text of the Uniform Probate Code, but the comment to § 3–902 states that "it is commonly held, even in the absence of a statute, that general legacies to a wife, or to persons with respect to which the testator is in loco parentis, are to be preferred to other legacies *in the same class* because this accords with the probable purpose of the legacies."[25]

### *Exoneration*

At common law, a specific devisee could, if the devised property was subject to a mortgage, insist that the property be "exonerated", *i.e.*, the mortgage be paid from the assets in the residuary estate.[26] The Uniform Probate Code, however, provides that "a specific devise passes subject to any mortgage," absent evidence of a different intent.[27] A direction to the executor

**20.** Matter of Estate of Hale, 704 S.W.2d 725 (Tenn.App.1985). *See also* Koch v. James, 670 N.E.2d 113 (Ind.App.1996); Matter of Wernet's Estate, 596 P.2d 137 (Kan.1979).

**21.** West v. Francioni, 488 So.2d 571 (Fla. App.1986).

**22.** 2 F. Pollock & F. Maitland, *A History of English Law* 345 (2d ed. 1898); Hurt v. Smith, 744 S.W.2d 1 (Tex.1987); Kan.Stat. § 59–1405; 3 *Amer.Law of Prop.* § 14.23, at 659.

**23.** Uniform Probate Code § 3–902. *See also* Iowa Code § 633.436; N.Y. E.P.T.L. § 13–1.3(b); 20 Pa.Stat. § 3541(a); In re Estate of Oberstar, 709 N.E.2d 872, 874 (Ohio App. 1998).

**24.** Folkerds v. United States, 494 F.2d 749 (8th Cir.1974); Iowa Code § 633.436. *But see* In re Estate of Kraft, 186 N.W.2d 628 (Iowa 1971) (contrary intent shown).

**25.** Emphasis added. Compare Cal.Prob. Code § 21402 (preference for relatives within specific and general devises). *Compare* In re Estate of Oberstar, 709 N.E.2d 872, 875 (Ohio App.1998) (refusing to give preference to general devise to relative over general devise to non-relative).

**26.** Martin v. Johnson, 512 A.2d 1017 (D.C.App.1986); Ashkenazy v. Ashkenazy's Estate, 140 So.2d 331 (Fla.App.1962); Paulus, *Exoneration of Specific Devises: Legislation vs. the Common Law*, 6 Will.L.J. 53, 55 (1970); 3 *Amer.Law of Prop.* § 14.25. However, this could be altered by a contrary direction in the will. Gaymon v. Gaymon, 519 S.E.2d 142, 146 (Va.1999) (devise "subject to encumbrances").

**27.** Uniform Probate Code § 2–608. *See also* Cal.Prob.Code § 21131; Or.Rev.Stat. § 115.255; Egner v. Egner, 443 A.2d 1104 (N.J.Super.Ch.Div.1982). These provisions go back to a New York statute of 1830. 3 *Amer. Law of Prop.* § 14.25.

to "pay all my debts" is not enough to show an intent to exonerate specific devises.[28]

Often land subject to a mortgage was held in joint tenancy by the decedent and another. The above-mentioned UPC provision applies only to specific devises, but some courts have denied claims for exoneration or contribution against the decedent's estate by the surviving joint tenant.[29] But others hold that if both tenants were obligated on the mortgage, the survivor who pays the debt is entitled to contribution.[30]

If an insurance policy is pledged as collateral for a loan some courts reimburse the beneficiary from the insured's estate if the pledgee collects the debt from the policy unless there is "evidence of an unequivocal intention on the part of the [decedent insured] that the proceeds of [the] policy be utilized as the primary fund for satisfaction of his indebtedness."[31]

## § 8.3 Lapse

A will leaves Blackacre "to Alice." If Alice dies before the testator, who will get Blackacre? Several solutions are possible.

### *Vested Interest*

If Alice is dead, she can not literally enjoy the devise—"you can't take it with you," but the property might "vest" in Alice's estate and pass to her devisees (if she died testate) or her heirs (if she died intestate). Some hold that a will cannot dispose of property which the testator did not own when she died, and thus would disregard her will.[1] The Uniform Probate Code, however, rejects this restriction,[2] and some courts have held that a express devise to "the estate of A" passes the devised property to the takers under A's will.[3]

A vested construction is not uncommon in the case of inter-vivos instruments. For example, when a man had a bond registered in his name "as trustee for Audrey" who later predeceased him, the bond was held to pass to Audrey's estate.[4] A similar result is often reached in construing wills made

28. Uniform Probate Code § 2–609; Griffin v. Gould, 391 N.E.2d 124 (Ill.App.1979); Or. Rev.Stat. § 115.001; 3 *Amer.Law of Prop.* § 14.25.

29. Matter of Estate of Zahn, 702 A.2d 482 (N.J.Super.App.Div.1997); Mellor v. O'Connor, 712 A.2d 375 (R.I.1998); Wis.Stat. § 863.13 (if estate pays mortgage, can get subrogation from surviving joint tenant).

30. Estate of Perry, 978 S.W.2d 28 (Mo. App.1998); Sarbacher v. McNamara, 564 A.2d 701 (D.C.App.1989); Estate of Leinbach v. Leinbach, 486 N.E.2d 2 (Ind.App.1985). In Goldstein v. Ancell, 258 A.2d 93 (Conn.1969), where the survivor was not liable on the mortgage, she was allowed total exoneration therefrom. *See also* Ogan v. Ogan, 702 N.E.2d 472 (Ohio App.1997). In Matter of Estate of Brown, 764 P.2d 373 (Colo.App.1988), a direction in the will that "bequests be conveyed free of encumbrances" was held to extend to property passing in joint tenancy.

31. Matter of Estate of Winstead, 493 N.E.2d 1183, 1189 (Ill.App.1986).

See also Falk v. Vreeland Trading Corp., 325 S.E.2d 333 (S.C.App.1985).

§ 8.3

1. In re Estate of Braman, 258 A.2d 492 (Pa.1969). Compare the inability to give an expectancy. Section 4.5, at note 82 et seq.

2. Uniform Probate Code § 2–602.

3. Hudson v. Hopkins, 799 S.W.2d 783 (Tex.App.1990); In re Will of Steel, 556 N.Y.S.2d 557 (A.D.1990); *Restatement, Third, of Property (Wills and Other Donative Transfers)* § 1.2, comm. g (1998).

4. In re Estate of Zukerman, 578 N.E.2d 248 (Ill.App.1991). *See also* Hinds v. McNair, 413 N.E.2d 586 (Ind.App.1980); Detroit Bank & Trust Co. v. Grout, 289 N.W.2d 898 (Mich. App.1980); First Nat. Bank v. Anthony, 557 A.2d 957 (Me.1989).

pursuant to a contract. For example, a husband and wife executed a joint contractual will which contained devises to several individuals who died after the wife but before the husband. Their interests were held to have vested as soon as the wife died, and so passed to their estates.[5] On the other hand, a deed purporting to transfer land to a person who is dead when the deed is executed is generally held to be void, conveying no interest at all.[6]

There are administrative costs incurred in adding property to the estate of a decedent.[7] Perhaps for this reason, the common law refused to hold that devises vested before the testator died. Devises to a person who predeceased the testator lapsed, just as in intestacy, a person who predeceases the decedent cannot inherit as heir.[8]

### *Anti-Lapse Statutes*

All states today have "anti-lapse" statutes on this question. Most of them provide that if a devisee predeceases the testator the devised property passes to the any issue of the devisee who survive the testator.[9] Under these statutes, issue of the devisee more remote than children take only by representation.[10] Suppose that Alice has three children, Barbara, Ben, and Bill, each of whom has two children, and Alice predeceases the testator, but Barbara, Ben and all six of Alice's grandchildren survive the testator. Under the typical anti-lapse statute, the property devised to Alice would pass one third to Barbara, one third to Ben and one sixth to each of Bill's children.[11] They would take directly from the testator, and so the devise would not be taxed in Alice's estate or be subject to claims of her spouse or creditors.[12]

Most anti-lapse statutes give the devised property to the issue of the deceased devisee; if she has no issue who survive the testator, the statute is inapplicable.[13] The Maryland statute, however, gives a lapsed devise to the persons who take by testate or intestate succession from the devisee. Thus if

**5.** Matter of Estate of Anderson, 865 P.2d 1037, 1042 (Kan.App.1993). *See also* Young v. Young, 569 N.E.2d 1 (Ill.App.1991); Fiew v. Qualtrough, 624 S.W.2d 335 (Tex.App.1981). But in Rape v. Lyerly, 215 S.E.2d 737 (N.C. 1975), the rights of a promisee in who predeceased the testator were held to pass to her issue under the anti-lapse statute.

**6.** Julian v. Petersen, 966 P.2d 878, 881 (Utah App.1998).

**7.** Fellows, *In Search of Donative Intent*, 73 Iowa L.Rev. 611, 636 (1988); *Restatement, Second, of Property (Donative Transfers)* § 27.3, comm. b (1990) (estate tax costs of vested interests). *Restatement, Third, of Property (Wills and Other Donative Transfers)* § 1.2, comm. g (1998) seeks to avoid these costs in a devise to a decedent's estate by "passing the devised property directly to the beneficiaries of the [devisee's] estate."

**8.** 2 W. Blackstone, *Commentaries** 513 (1765); *Restatement, Third, of Property (Wills and Other Donative Transfers)* § 1.2 (1998). The English Wills Act of 1837 distributed the devised property as if the devisee had survived the testator, but in 1982 the Act was amended to give the devised property to the devisee's issue, as is typical under American statutes. Administration of Justice Act, 1982, § 19.

**9.** *E.g.,* Uniform Probate Code § 2–603; N.Y. EPTL § 3–3.3; Calif.Prob.Code § 21110. A list of the anti-lapse statutes appears in a Statutory Note to *Restatement, Second, of Property (Donative Transfers)* § 27.1 (1990).

**10.** See Section 2.2, at note 8.

**11.** The rules governing intestate distribution for children who were adopted or born out of wedlock also apply to anti-lapse statutes. Uniform Probate Code § 1–201; Meckstroth v. Robinson, 679 N.E.2d 744 (Ohio Com.Pl.1996) (child of devisee born out of wedlock takes under anti-lapse statute).

**12.** *Restatement (Second) of Property (Donative Transfers)* § 27.1, comm. e (1987). However, if Alice owed money to the testator, some authorities would allow the executor to set off this debt against the share which passes to her issue under the statute. Chaffin, *The Time Gap in Wills: Problems under Georgia's Lapse Statutes,* 6 Ga.L.Rev. 268, 276 (1971).

**13.** Estate of Micheel, 577 N.W.2d 407 (Iowa 1998).

the devisee had left her estate to her husband by her will, he would take the devise under the testator's will.[14]

Some anti-lapse statutes apply only if the devisee is a descendant of the testator.[15] Others include devises to collateral relatives. The Uniform Probate Code version applies to devises to "a grandparent or a lineal descendant of a grandparent of the testator."[16] The Ohio statute covers *any* "relative of the testator."[17] A devise to the testator's spouse or a relative of a spouse does not qualify under such a statute,[18] but some statutes include devises to the testator's spouse,[19] and some cover all devises.[20]

If a devise is made to a trust, the beneficiary rather than the trustee should be treated as the devisee for purposes of the statute.[21] If a trustee designated in a will predeceases the testator, normally another trustee is appointed to administer the trust.[22]

Anti-lapse statutes have been applied to living trusts by analogy. For example, a revocable trust provided that when the settlor died, the assets were to go to his mother. When she predeceased him, the court gave the property to her mother's granddaughter on the theory that "a gift to be enjoyed only upon or after the death of the donor is in practical effect a legacy," so the policy of the anti-lapse statute should control.[23] The Restatement of Property agrees that "the antilapse statute should be construed to apply to revocable trusts as well as to wills whenever that is possible."[24]

The Uniform Probate Code implies a condition of survival to the time of distribution in any "future interest under the terms of a trust," whether or not the trust is revocable.[25] The Code also provides a substitutional gift to the issue of a beneficiary who fails to meet a condition of survival of the decedent if the beneficiary is one of the group protected by the anti-lapse statute, viz. "a grandparent, a descendant of a grandparent, or a stepchild of the decedent." This substitutional gift applies not only to trusts but also to life

**14.** Rowe v. Rowe, 720 A.2d 1225 (Md.App. 1998). However, even in Maryland the devise is not subject to claims of the devisee's creditors. Also, the administrative costs of passing property through the estate of a decedent are minimized because the property passes "directly * * * to those persons who would have taken the property" from the devisee. Md. Estates & Trusts Code § 4–403. cf. note 7.

**15.** Matter of Estate of Ross, 604 N.E.2d 982 (Ill.App.1992) (devise to siblings not covered); Matter of Will of Shannon, 587 N.Y.S.2d 76 (Sur.1992) (devise to cousins); Texas Prob. Code § 68; Miss.Code § 91–5–7.

**16.** Uniform Probate Code § 2–603. *See also* Matter of Estate of Worsham, 859 P.2d 1134 (Okl.App.1993) (devise to sister covered).

**17.** Ohio Rev.Code § 2107.52.

**18.** Matter of Estate of Hillman, 363 N.W.2d 588 (Wis.App.1985) (devise to brother-in-law not covered). However, the Uniform Probate Code § 2–603 now covers step-children of the testator. Cal.Prob.Code § 21110 covers all kindred of a spouse or former spouse of the testator.

**19.** In re Thompson's Estate, 518 P.2d 393 (Kan.1974). *Contra*, Matter of Estate of Baxter, 798 P.2d 644 (Okl.App.1990).

**20.** Tenn.Code § 32–3–105; Ky.Rev.Stat. § 394.400.

**21.** *Restatement, Second, Trusts* § 112, comm. f (1959). The contrary result reached in Portales Nat. Bank v. Bellin, 645 P.2d 986 (N.M.App.1982), was based on a provision of the UPC which has since been changed.

**22.** See Section 12.4, at note 5 et seq. as to the appointment of trustees.

**23.** In re Estate of Button, 490 P.2d 731 (Wash.1971). *See also* Dollar Savings & Trust Co. v. Turner, 529 N.E.2d 1261 (Ohio 1988).

**24.** *Restatement, Second, of Property (Donative Transfers)* § 27.1, comm. e (1987). *See also Restatement, Third, Trusts* § 25, comm. e (1999).

**25.** Uniform Probate Code § 2–707(b). This provision is limited to trusts, according to the Comment, so as not to impede the alienability of land.

insurance policies, pension plans, and POD or TOD registrations. Joint tenancies and joint bank accounts, on the other hand, are excluded.[26]

In states which have not adopted the Code, courts have reached various results in construing inter-vivos instruments. Some cases hold that a beneficiary of a revocable trust who fails to survive the settlor has a vested interest,[27] while others imply a condition of survival with no substitutional gift to the issue of the deceased beneficiary.[28]

### *Contrary Intent*

Anti-lapse statutes, like other rules of construction, do not apply if the will (or other governing instrument) shows that the testator (transferor) intended a different result.[29] If a will, for example, says "to Alice if she survives me, otherwise to Arthur," Arthur takes rather than Alice's issue, if Alice predeceases the testator.[30] The same result has been reached if the devise is more cryptic, such as "to Alice and/or Arthur."[31] If the will simply says "to Alice if she survives me," many courts would interpret this language also to mean the testator did not want the anti-lapse statute to apply,[32] but the Uniform Probate Code disagrees.[33] Although the UPC position has been criticized by some commentators,[34] several courts have reached this result, particularly where refusal to apply the anti-lapse statute would cause a devise to fail. For example, a will left property "to my two brothers, or the survivor," and both brothers predeceased the testator, survived by issue. The court awarded the property to the issue of both brothers.

> Had either [brother] outlived Testator, the anti-lapse statute would clearly not be applicable and the surviving brother would have received the entire estate.[35] . . . The language does not indicate, in the event of the death of both brothers before the death of the testator, an intent . . . to give a preference to the children of either.[36]

**26.** Uniform Probate Code § 2–706. The statutory language is far from clear on this question. See McGovern, *Nonprobate Transfers Under the Revised Uniform Probate Code*, 55 Alb.L.Rev. 1329, 1340 (1992). Cal.Prob.Code § 21110 is similar in many ways to the UPC, but does not mention joint tenancy.

**27.** First Nat. Bank v. Anthony, 557 A.2d 957 (Me.1989).

**28.** In re Estate of Mendelson, 697 N.E.2d 1210 (Ill.App.1998) (land trust).

**29.** As to the admissibility of extrinsic evidence of contrary intent see Section 6.1, notes 21–22.

**30.** *Restatement, Third, of Property (Wills and Other Donative Transfers)* § 5.5, illus. 4 (1998). However, if Arthur also predeceases the testator, the statute may apply. *See id.*, comm. g.

**31.** In re Estate of Massey, 721 A.2d 1033 (N.J.Super.Ch. Div.1998).

**32.** Erlenbach v. Estate of Thompson, 954 P.2d 350 (Wash.App.1998) (trust for two sons "or the survivor of them"); Matter of Estate of Farris, 865 P.2d 1275 (Okl.App.1993); Estate of Berdrow, 7 Cal.Rptr.2d 37 (App.1992); Roberts v. First State Bank, 774 S.W.2d 415 (Tex. App.1989); *Restatement (Second) of Property (Donative Transfers)* § 27.1, illus. 6 (1987).

**33.** Uniform Probate Code §§ 2–603(b)(3), 2–706(b)(3).

**34.** Ascher, *The 1990 Uniform Probate Code: Older and Better, or More like the Internal Revenue Code*, 77 Minn. L. Rev. 639, 650 (1993); Begleiter, *Article II of the Uniform Probate Code and the Malpractice Revolution,* 59 Tenn.L.Rev. 101, 128 (1991).

**35.** *Accord*, Marrer of Estate of Burruss, 394 N.W.2d 466 (Mich.App.1986); Erlenbach v. Estate of Thompson, 954 P.2d 350 (Wash.App. 1998). However, this would not be true under Uniform Probate Code § 2–706. *See also* In re Will of Bybee, 896 S.W.2d 792 (Tenn.App. 1994); In re Estate of Bulger, 586 N.E.2d 673 (Ill.App.1991); Estate of Kehler, 411 A.2d 748 (Pa.1980).

**36.** Early v. Bowen, 447 S.E.2d 167, 172 (N.C.App.1994). *But cf.* Matter of Estate of Simpson, 423 N.W.2d 28 (Iowa App.1988) (statute inapplicable in devise to siblings or the survivor of them when all predecease the testator).

In construing a will with similar language another court said that since the testator did not contemplate that both devisees would predecease her, the words of survivorship were "to be effective only if there are survivors. Since there are no survivors, the anti-lapse statute is free to operate."[37]

Some courts have held that the words "per capita" in a devise to a class show an intent not to apply the statute,[38] but others disagree.[39] A clause giving the residue of the estate "including lapsed gifts" was held to make the statute inapplicable.[40] But the fact that a will contains another devise to a devisee's children does not preclude them from also taking under the anti-lapse statute.[41] Nor does a statement in a will that "I intentionally make no provision for persons not named herein."[42]

### *Class Gifts*

A devise "to my daughters" without naming them is a class gift. A class gift implies a right of survivorship: if any daughter dies without issue before the testator, her share will go to the others. But if the deceased daughter had issue, they take her share under most anti-lapse statutes, including the Uniform Probate Code, which expressly includes class gifts.[43] Even when the statutes are not clear, most courts apply them to class gifts, but some do not.[44]

If a class member was already dead when the testator signed the will, some statutes and cases do not give her share to her issue, on the theory that if the testator had intended to include them, the will would have said so; a devisee's death *after* the will is executed is distinguishable because the testator may not have contemplated it.[45] But under the Uniform Probate Code, even the share of a class member who was already dead when the will was signed goes to her issue,[46] on the theory that strong evidence should be required before assuming a testator intended to disinherit a branch of the family (the issue of the deceased class member) because of the time of death of one member.

Similar questions arise in construing a substitutional gift in a will or trust. For example, a trust provided for distribution to the settlor's children "with a share by right of representation for the surviving children of a deceased child." The court held that "deceased child" referred only to

**37.** In re Estate of Ulrikson, 290 N.W.2d 757, 759 (Minn.1980).

**38.** Matter of Estate of Wetsel, 546 N.Y.S.2d 243 (A.D.1989).

**39.** Rowe v. Rowe, 720 A.2d 1225 (Md.App. 1998); Estate of Renner, 895 S.W.2d 180 (Mo. App.1995); Matter of Estate of Kinnamon, 837 P.2d 927 (Okl.App.1992).

**40.** Estate of Salisbury, 143 Cal.Rptr. 81 (App.1978); *Restatement, Third, of Property (Wills and Other Donative Transfers)* § 5.5, illus. 7 (1998).

**41.** In re Robert's Estate, 88 Cal.Rptr. 396 (App.1970). *But see Restatement (Second) of Property (Donative Transfers)* § 28.4, illus. 4 (1987).

**42.** South Shore Nat. Bank v. Berman, 294 N.E.2d 432 (Mass.App.1972).

**43.** Uniform Probate Code § 2–603(a)(4); *Restatement (Second) of Property (Donative Transfers)* § 27.1, Statutory Note 1 (1987).

**44.** Matter of Kalouse's Estate, 282 N.W.2d 98 (Iowa 1979). England at one time did not apply the statute to class gifts, but the rule has now been changed. Administration of Justice Act, 1982, § 19.

**45.** Haynes v. Williams, 686 S.W.2d 870 (Mo.App.1985); N.Y. EPTL § 3–3.3(a)(3); Calif.Prob.Code § 21110(a) (if testator knew of the death).

**46.** Uniform Probate Code § 2–603(a)(4). *See also* Tenn.Code § 32–3–105; N.J.Stat. § 3B.3–35; *Restatement (Second) of Property (Donative Transfers)* § 27.2, illus. 4 (1987).

children living when the trust was executed who died thereafter.[47] However, the Restatement of Property interprets such language to include the children of an already deceased child in order to "to treat [the settlor's] equal lines equally."[48] Such an intent can be unambiguously stated by a gift to "my then living issue," a simple phrase which gives a share both to children and the issue of any deceased child.[49]

### *Substitute Gifts*

If the anti-lapse statute does not apply, either because a devisee is not within the group of persons encompassed by it (*e.g.* was not related to the testator), or because the devisee had no surviving issue, the property may pass under a substitute gift in the will. A devise "to Alice or her issue" is usually interpreted as a gift to Alice's issue if she fails to survive the testator, even if Alice is not covered by an anti-lapse statute.[50] A devise "to Alice *and* her *heirs,*" on the other hand, is usually held to mean that Alice takes the property if she survives the testator, but her heirs take nothing if she does not.[51] But such language has occasionally been construed to create a substitutional gift to the devisee's heirs, for example when the drafter of the will admitted "that he did not know the difference between the words 'and heirs and assigns' and 'or heirs and assigns.' "[52]

Wills sometimes provide a gift if the testator and devisee die simultaneously. Some courts construe this gift to take effect even if the devisee predeceases the testator by a substantial period.[53] More commonly, however, the provision is construed literally even if this results in property going intestate.[54]

A class gift contains an implied substitutional gift to the surviving members of the class (if the decedent class member's share does not go to his issue under an anti-lapse statute).[55] It is often unclear whether or not a devise is a "class gift." A gift to a group like "children" or "issue" clearly is, but a gift "to Alice and Arthur" is probably not, even if Alice and Arthur *could be* described as a class, *e.g.,* as the children of John. The argument against a class gift construction is even stronger if Alice and Arthur could not be so described, or if their parents had other children as well.[56]

**47.** Chipman v. Spitznagel, 728 P.2d 971 (Or.App.1986).

**48.** *Restatement, Second, of Property (Donative Transfers)* § 27.1, illus, 3 (1987). *See also* Estate of Elmer, 959 P.2d 701 (Wash.App. 1998).

**49.** *Restatement, Second, of Property (Donative Transfers)* § 28.2 (1987).

**50.** In re Sibley's Trusts, L.R. 5 Ch.Div. 494 (1877); 3 *Amer.Law of Prop.* § 14.14, at 616.

**51.** Estate of Straube v. Barber, 990 S.W.2d 40 (Mo.App.1999); Forester v. Marler, 228 S.E.2d 646 (N.C.App.1976); In re Dumas' Estate, 379 A.2d 836 (N.H.1977); *Restatement (Second) of Property (Donative Transfers)* § 18.5, illus. 1 (1984) (appointment "to Mary and her heirs").

As to a devise "to A and his issue" see Section 10.3, at note 22 et seq.

**52.** In re Estate of Mangel, 186 N.W.2d 276 (Wis.1971). *See also* Estate of Calden, 712 A.2d 522 (Me.1998) (devise to stepson "and his heirs" passed to stepson's widow when he predeceased testator).

**53.** Chambers v. Warren, 657 S.W.2d 3 (Tex.App.1983); New Mexico Boys Ranch, Inc. v. Hanvey, 643 P.2d 857 (N.M.1982); *cf.* Helmer v. Voss, 646 S.W.2d 738 (Mo.1983).

**54.** Naylor v. Koeppe, 686 S.W.2d 47 (Mo. App.1985); Wright v. Benttinen, 226 N.E.2d 194 (Mass.1967); In re Estate of Corrigan, 358 N.W.2d 501 (Neb.1984); Larison v. Record, 512 N.E.2d 1251 (Ill.1987).

**55.** *Restatement (Second) of Property (Donative Transfers)* § 27.1(2) (1987).

**56.** *5 Amer.Law Prop.* §§ 22.5–22.7.

A devise "to Alice and Arthur" *may* be held to create a joint tenancy; if so, the right of survivorship is more extensive than in an ordinary class gift. If two joint tenants survive the testator and one dies later, the other takes her share, whereas the right of survivorship in a class gift lasts only until the gift takes effect; the share of a class member who dies thereafter passes to her estate.[57] Modern law generally presumes against joint tenancy,[58] but not against class gifts. Under the Uniform Probate Code, for example, a P.O.D. account for "Alice and Arthur" is treated like a class gift; if only Alice survives the creator of the account (Arthur having died without issue), Alice will take it all, but if both survive the creator and one dies thereafter there is no right of survivorship.[59]

A devise "to my children, Alice and Arthur" points in different directions: "children" suggests a class gift, but the designation of names suggests otherwise. Some cases hold that "where legatees are named as individuals and are also described as a class, the gift by name" controls, so that in a devise "to my sisters Ruth and Mary" Mary's share does not pass to Ruth if Mary dies without issue.[60] But there is also authority to the contrary.[61] The Restatement of Property waffles, saying that the result depends upon "the facts and circumstances."[62] A devise "to Arthur and the children of Alice" is usually held to be a class gift, with Arthur being treated as a member of the class, even though he is not a child of Alice.[63]

Even without names, a devise which states the number of recipients, *e.g.*, "to my *two* children," or designates the shares, *e.g*, "one-half to each," is often held to negate an intent to make a class gift.[64] But not always. A devise "to Bessie Sothman and Louise Fournier, to be equally divided between them" was held to be a class gift[65] as was a devise to a group of named relatives "share and share alike."

> The fact that the testator named the members does not compel the conclusion that it was not a class gift ... Nor does the addition of the phrase to "share and share alike." .. That the testator intended a devise to a class is supported by the presumption that he did not intent to die partially intestate, [the result if this were not construed as a class gift][66]

Courts often cite a preference for a construction which avoids intestacy,

**57.** Cooley, *What Constitutes a Gift to a Class,* 49 Harv.L.Rev. 903, 922 (1936).

**58.** See Section 4.8, at note 11 et seq.

**59.** Uniform Probate Code § 6–212(b)(2). *See also* Cal.Prob.Code § 5302(b); Morton v. McComb, 662 S.W.2d 471 (Ark.1983); King v. William M. King Family Ent., Inc., 515 So.2d 1241 (Ala.1987) (devise to children creates a tenancy in common among those who survived the testator).

**60.** McGill v. Johnson, 775 S.W.2d 826, 826 (Tex.App.1989).

**61.** Matter of Estate of Webster, 574 N.E.2d 245, 248 (Ill.App.1991); Sullivan v. Sullivan, 529 N.E.2d 890 (Mass.App.1988).

**62.** *Restatement (Second) of Property (Donative Transfers)* § 27.1, comm. b (1987).

**63.** Matter of Kalouse's Estate, 282 N.W.2d 98 (Iowa 1979) ("to my first cousins and to Frank"); Allemand v. Weaver, 305 N.W.2d 7 (Neb.1981) (to named siblings "and the children of my deceased sister, Pearl").

**64.** Henderson v. Parker, 728 S.W.2d 768 (Tex.1987) ("our three sons"); Dawson v. Yucus, 239 N.E.2d 305 (Ill.App.1968) ("one-half to Stewart, a nephew, and one half to Gene, a nephew").

**65.** Iozapavichus v. Fournier, 308 A.2d 573 (Me.1973). *See also* Estate of Frailey, 625 S.W.2d 241 (Mo.App.1981); In re Dumas' Estate, 379 A.2d 836 (N.H.1977).

**66.** Estate of Frailey, 625 S.W.2d 241, 243 (Mo.App.1981).

but they often ignore it too.[67]

Courts sometimes compare different parts of the will in order to deduce the testator's intention. For example, a devise to two named persons "or to the survivor of them should either predecease me" was used to show that the testator did not intend a class gift in another devise; she "knew how to manifest an intent to create a class or survivorship gift" when she wanted it.[68]

### *Residuary Clause*

Suppose a will devises Blackacre "to Alice, Arthur, and Andrew." Alice predeceases the testator and has no issue, or is not in the group covered by the anti-lapse statute. Assuming that this language is not construed to create a class gift or a joint tenancy, Alice's share will pass under the residuary clause of the will, if there is one, as is usually the case. The Uniform Probate Code so provides,[69] and courts usually reach this result even without statutory authority.[70]

If the devise was itself in the residuary clause, even though not expressed as a class gift, Arthur and Andrew would take Alice's share under the Uniform Probate Code: "If the residue is devised to two or more persons and the share of one of the residuary devisees fails for any reason, his share passes to the other residuary devisee, or to the other residuary devisees in proportion."[71] Many courts have reached the same result without a statute, either as a general rule,[72] or because they think that the particular testator so intended.[73] The dispute over whether particular language creates a "class gift" is thus irrelevant in many jurisdictions when the devise appears in a residuary clause. However, a dispute may arise as to what is a "residuary devise." A comment to the Uniform Probate Code says that a devise "of all my estate" constitutes a residuary devise for this purpose,[74] but what about a devise of

**67.** For cases in which courts rejected a class gift construction even though this created an intestacy see Brown v. Leadley, 401 N.E.2d 599 (Ill.App.1980); Moffett v. Howard, 392 So.2d 509 (Miss.1981). McGovern has argued elsewhere that the weight given to this factor should depend upon the circumstances, since intestacy is not necessarily a bad result. McGovern, *Facts and Rules and the Construction of Wills*, 26 UCLA L.Rev. 285, 307–10 (1978).

**68.** Dawson v. Yucus, 239 N.E.2d 305, 310 (Ill.App.1968); *cf.* Estate of Kehler, 411 A.2d 748 (Pa.1980) (devise to "surviving" siblings did not show intent to bar the antilapse statute where another devise was expressly stated to be void if the devisee predeceased); Estate of Straube v. Barber, 990 S.W.2d 40, 46 (Mo.App. 1999) (devise "to H and her heirs" not a substitutional gift to heirs; other devises showed that testator "knew how to address the possibility that a legatee would predecease her").

**69.** Uniform Probate Code § 2–604(a). *See also* Cal.Prob.Code § 21111(a).

**70.** 2 W. Blackstone, *Commentaries** 513 (1765); Wilkins v. Garza, 693 S.W.2d 553 (Tex. App.1985). Historically, a lapsed devise of land passed intestate instead of falling into the residue, but this rule is virtually obsolete. 5 *Amer. Law of Prop.* § 21.30.

**71.** Uniform Probate Code § 2–604(b). *See also* Estate of Straube v. Barber, 990 S.W.2d 40 (Mo.App.1999); Calif.Prob.Code § 21111(b); *Restatement, Third, of Property (Wills and Other Donative Transfers)* § 5.5, comm. o (1998). Section 2–604 is subject to the anti-lapse provision, so if a residuary devisee has issue they would take her share, assuming the devisee is in the group covered by the provision. *Id.*, illus. 15.

In Matter of Estate of Fryer, 874 P.2d 490 (Colo.App.1994), a will left the residue to a niece and three friends, and said that if any friend predeceased the testator her share would go to the niece. This was held not to show a contrary intent when a niece and one friend predeceased the testator; the residue passed to the two surviving friends.

**72.** Matter of Estate of Winslow, 934 P.2d 1001 (Kan.App.1997); In re Leavy's Estate, 442 A.2d 588 (N.H.1982).

**73.** In re Dammann's Estate, 191 N.E.2d 452 (N.Y.1963); In re Estate of Kugler, 190 N.W.2d 883 (Wis.1971); Davis v. Anthony, 384 S.W.2d 60 (Tenn.App.1964).

**74.** Uniform Probate Code § 2–604, Comment. *Accord*, North Carolina Nat. Bank v. Apple, 383 S.E.2d 438 (N.C.App.1989). *But see*

"all of the contents of my apartment, furniture, rugs, silverware, china, jewelry, and other personal property?" A court was unsure whether this was a residuary devise and remanded to hear extrinsic evidence of the testator's intent.[75]

### *Intestacy*

Some courts would give a lapsed residuary devise to the testator's heirs rather than the surviving residuary devisees on the theory that since the heirs are the natural objects of the testator's bounty, any intent to exclude them should be more explicit.[76] Even under the Uniform Probate Code, the heirs take if *all* the residuary devisees die without issue prior to the testator.

In the case of a nonprobate transfer, such as a living trust, a joint bank account, or an insurance beneficiary designation, if a designated beneficiary fails to meet a condition of survival and no anti-lapse provision or substitutional gift applies, the property falls into the probate estate and ultimately passes to the heirs or devisees of the transferor (settlor, creator of the account, insured).[77]

### *Other Causes of Lapse*

A devise may fail for reasons other than the death of the devisee. A devise to an animal may be held invalid.[78] One to a witness to a will may be void under a statute.[79] A devisee who disclaims or who divorces or murders the testator may be disqualified.[80] In such cases a provision for a substitute gift in case a devisee predeceases the testator may be held to apply, even when the disqualified devisee actually survived. For example, a will left the estate to the testator's husband, or if he predeceased her, to his uncle. The testator and her husband were later divorced. This revoked the devise to him. The court held that the property passed to the uncle.

> The only reason for the predecease clause was to provide a fallback beneficiary in case the husband was no longer able to take under the will. Once the husband is barred by divorce from taking the gift, the time of his death no longer has any apparent significance.[81]

The Uniform Probate Code also provides that the rules governing predecease should also apply in cases of divorce, homicide, or disclaimer.[82] Some courts have held, however, that a substitutional gift "if A predeceases me" does not apply applies if the gift fails for another reason.[83]

---

Matter of Estate of Allen, 388 N.W.2d 705 (Mich.App.1986).

**75.** District of Columbia v. Estate of Parsons, 590 A.2d 133 (D.C.App.1991).

**76.** Betts By and Through Parker v. Parrish, 320 S.E.2d 662 (N.C.1984). This argument is less persuasive in wills which expressly say that the heirs should get nothing or a specified limited amount. Some courts rationalize the result simply by saying there can be "no residue of a residue." Block v. Edge, 608 S.W.2d 340 (Tex.Civ.App.1980); Moffett v. Howard, 392 So.2d 509 (Miss.1981); Matter of Estate of Hillman, 363 N.W.2d 588 (Wis.App.1985).

**77.** *Restatement, Third, Trusts* § 8, comm. a (1996); Uniform Probate Code §§ 6–212(b)(2), 6–307.

**78.** In re Estate of Russell, 444 P.2d 353 (Cal.1968).

**79.** Dorfman v. Allen, 434 N.E.2d 1012 (Mass.1982); Section 4.3, at note 14 et seq.

**80.** See Sections 2.7 (homicide), 2.8 (disclaimer), 5.4 (divorce).

**81.** Bloom v. Selfon, 555 A.2d 75, 78 (Pa. 1989). *See also* Bowling v. Deaton, 507 N.E.2d 1152 (Ohio App.1986).

**82.** Uniform Prob.Code § 2–804(d), § 2–801(d) (disclaimer), § 2–803(e) (homicide).

**83.** Ray v. Tate, 252 S.E.2d 568 (S.C.1979); *cf.* Jones v. Bransford, 606 S.W.2d 118 (Ark. App.1980) (revoked devise does not "fail" and so does not pass into residue).

### *Planning*

A devise "to my issue who survive me, by representation" duplicates the result of most anti-lapse statutes when a devise is made to children of the testator; the descendants of any child who predeceases the testator will take the child's share.[84] Such language is useful because the drafter cannot be sure what anti-lapse statute will apply, since the law may change or the testator may change domicile or acquire land in another state.

Many wills provide for lapse but fail to cover all the possibilities. For example, "to Alice if she survives me, otherwise to Arthur," does not provide direction if neither survives the testator. Even a bequest "to my issue," may lapse if they all predecease the testator. A substitute gift to charity should be added if the testator does not wish to provide for the relatives who would inherit in an intestacy.

### *Simultaneous Death*

Simultaneous, or nearly simultaneous death is not uncommon; for example, family members die in the same plane crash or automobile collision. When this occurs it may be necessary to determine which one(s) lived the longest. For example, a wife was the designated beneficiary of an insurance policy on her husband's life if she survived him. Both were poisoned and were unconscious on arrival at the hospital, where they never recovered. The insurance proceeds were awarded to the wife's estate based on a finding that she had survived her husband by a few hours, because her EEG on arrival at the hospital "was not flat but rather it showed some delta waves of extremely low amplitude."[85] The result in the case would have been different under the Uniform Probate Code which says that a person who is required to survive under the terms of an instrument must survive by 120 hours.[86] This provision has also been separately promulgated as the Uniform Simultaneous Death Act of 1993. An earlier version of this statute simply said that if "there is no sufficient evidence that the two [persons] have died otherwise than simultaneously, the beneficiary shall be deemed not to have survived."[87] This version was in force in the state where the above described case arose and led to a judgment for the wife's estate, since she had survived, albeit only briefly.

The UPC, like the USDA, provides that for joint tenancies the property is split equally between the estates of the joint tenants. If the above-described case of the poisoned spouses had involved a joint bank account rather than an insurance policy, half the account would have gone to the husband's probate estate and half to the wife's.[88]

**84.** *Cf.* Uniform Statutory Will Act § 7(a)(1). Representation should be defined to make clear what proportion each person takes. *Id.* § 1(5). This language can be adapted easily for the will of testator who has no issue and wishes to provide for collateral relatives, *e.g.,* "to the issue of my parents."

**85.** Janus v. Tarasewicz, 482 N.E.2d 418, 423 (Ill.App.1985). *See also* Estate of Fletcher, 94 T.C. 49 (1990) (H's bond POD W included in W's estate when she survived him by 3 hours).

**86.** Uniform Probate Code § 2–702(b). A similar provision in the pre–1990 Code was limited to intestate succession and wills. § 2–104, 2–601. *Cf.* Cal.Prob.Code § 6403 (intestate succession).

**87.** Uniform Simultaneous Death Act § 2 (1940). At one time this version was in force in 45 states.

**88.** Uniform Probate Code § 2–702(c); Uniform Simultaneous Death Act (1993) § 4. In Estate of Jenkins, 504 N.E.2d 1178 (Ohio App. 1985), the court interpreted an earlier version of the UPC to require that the parties' respec-

### *Provisions in Instrument*

Many wills and other instruments have provisions dealing with simultaneous death, which may be held to supersede the statute. For example, a husband's will left his estate to his wife, with alternative devisees designated if she "dies at the same time I do." The wife survived the testator by 38 hours, and his property passed to her estate; the will was held to override a statutory requirement of 120 hour survival.[89] The 120 hour survival requirement in the present UPC, on the other hand, applies unless the language about simultaneous death in the instrument "is operable under the facts of the case." Here the alternative devise was inoperable since the wife did survive the testator, but by less than 120 hours.[90] Therefore, the alternative devisees would take.

The 120 hour provision in the UPC was designed to cover most cases of virtually simultaneous death without unduly delaying distribution.[91] Some wills require survival by more than 120 hours. The Uniform Statutory Will, for example, says that any devisee who does not survive by 30 days or more is deemed to have predeceased the testator.[92] A longer period might delay distribution by creating uncertainty as to who should take, but estates are hardly ever distributed within 30 days of the decedent's death in any event. Some wills require devisees to survive until the property is distributed to them. This can avoid the disadvantages of distribution to a devisee's estate, but it raises problems of interpretation. For example, in one case the executor had made partial distributions to the devisee before he died. The court held that the devise nevertheless failed, since requirement in the will referred to a "final, court-approved distribution or settlement of the estate."[93] Another litigated issue under such provisions is whether an estate *should have been* distributed earlier; beneficiaries of the devisees' estates have argued successfully that they should take despite failure to survive distribution because distribution had been unreasonably delayed.[94]

The Uniform Probate Code's 120 hour survival requirement "avoids multiple administrations and in some instances prevents property from passing to persons not desired by the decedent."[95] The latter can occur when a will leaves property to the testator's spouse who survives briefly and the property of both spouses thereby passes to the survivor's children by a prior marriage or collateral relatives.[96] On the other hand, a requirement of survival in a devise to a spouse may render it ineligible for the estate tax marital deduction, and in larger estates this may be an overriding consideration in plan-

tive contributions to a joint account be the basis of allocation between their estates.

**89.** Estate of Acord v. C.I.R., 946 F.2d 1473 (9th Cir.1991). *But cf.* Bratley v. Suburban Bank, 515 A.2d 236 (Md.App.1986) (similar will provision did not trump a statutory 30 day survival requirement).

**90.** The example given in the Comment to Uniform Probate Code § 2–702 has similar facts but no case is actually cited.

**91.** Halbach & Waggoner, *The UPC's New Survivorship and Antilapse Provisions*, 55 Alb. L.Rev. 1091, 1098 (1992).

**92.** Uniform Statutory Will Act § 11.

**93.** Hintze v. Black, 873 P.2d 909 (Idaho App.1994). *See also* In re Estate of Long, 918 P.2d 975 (Wash.App.1996).

**94.** Matter of Estate of Johnson, 811 P.2d 360 (Ariz.App.1991); Estate of Justesen, 91 Cal.Rptr.2d 574 (App.1999); Estate of Carlson, 700 P.2d 771 (Wash.App.1985).

**95.** Uniform Probate Code § 2–104, Comment.

**96.** Matter of Estate of Villwock, 418 N.W.2d 1 (Wis.App.1987) (wife survives husband by a few minutes, so all property passes under her will to members of her family).

ning.[97] Therefore some wills provide that in case of simultaneous death the spouse shall be deemed to have survived the testator. Such a provision would override the Uniform Simultaneous Death Act and Uniform Probate Code,[98] and save the marital deduction if the spouses die simultaneously.[99]

### *Definition of Death*

Some cases turn on when death actually occurs for legal purposes. For example, a will left property to a friend of the testator. The friend died on May 4. The testator's death occurred on May 6 according to the death certificate, but the friend's widow argued that the testator had died previously; even though "a mechanical life support system was able to create a heart beat in [the testator] he in fact suffered a total and irreversible cessation of all functions of his brain, and was legally dead."[100] A death certificate is only prima facie evidence of the facts therein stated,[101] but the widow's claim was nevertheless rejected, since she had no expert testimony to support it. "How can a lay person whether judge or juror, be expected to reach a cogent and reliable conclusion from technically complex symptoms ... without the assistance of expert knowledge of the brain's function and pathology?"

### *Disappearance*

The time of death can present a problem when a person disappears. The Uniform Probate Code provides that a person who has not been heard from for five years and whose absence "is not explained after diligent search or inquiry" is presumed to have died at the end of the 5 year period.[102] A similar common-law presumption operates only after 7 years.[103]

**97.** See Section 15.3, note 165.

**98.** Uniform Simultaneous Death Act § 6. According to *Restatement, Third, of Property (Wills and Other Donative Transfers)* § 1.2, comm. e (1998), any "tax advantage in treating the other decedent as the survivor" should be a factor in judicial determinations even without such a clause.

**99.** Treas.Reg. § 20.2056(e)–2(e); Estate of Gordon, 70 T.C. 404 (1978).

**100.** Estate of Sewart, 602 N.E.2d 1277, 1279 (Ill.App.1991). According to Uniform Probate Code § 1–107(1) death occurs when a person has sustained "irreversible cessation of all functions of the entire brain." The same phrase appears in the widely-adopted Uniform Determination of Death Act § 1.

**101.** *Id.*, at 1285. *Accord*, Uniform Probate Code § 1–107(2); Uniform Simultaneous Death Act § 5(2); In re Estate of Price, 587 N.E.2d 995 (Ohio Com.Pl.1990) (deaths treated as simultaneous despite death certificates showing they were 27 minutes apart).

**102.** Uniform Probate Code § 1–107(5). *See also* Cal.Prob.Code § 12401.

**103.** In re Estate of King, 710 N.E.2d 1249 (Ill.App.1999).

# Chapter 9

# TRUSTS

*Analysis*



## § 9.1 Uses of the Trust: Avoiding Probate

The word "trust" is used for many property arrangements which have little in common with each other apart from the fact that they were historically enforced by the Chancellor in the court of Equity. Courts, for example, have imposed "constructive trusts" to avoid unjust enrichment when a person would otherwise profit from having murdered a decedent.[1] The trusts to be discussed in this chapter, on the other hand, are deliberately created by a person normally called the settlor. The word settlor is related to the words "settle" and "settlement," which at one time were commonly used to describe dispositions of property.[2]

Trusts are a form of transfer, usually gratuitous,[3] either *inter vivos* (from the Latin: "between the living"), or testamentary if created by will. People can make gifts without using a trust, but in many situations use of a trust has important advantages. The Restatement of Trusts mentions common reasons for using trusts: "[1]the avoidance of probate, [2] providing property management for those who cannot, ought not or wish not to manage for themselves, [3] providing for the limited and successive enjoyment of property over several generations, ... [4] the saving of taxes and [5] the insulation of the trust property from the claims of the beneficiaries' creditors."[4] The first three will be discussed in this Section.

§ 9.1

1. See Section 2.7, at note 2 et seq.

2. A Simpson, *An Introduction to the History of the Land Law* 218–24 (1961) (discussion of "the family settlement").

3. Trusts are also used as devices for conducting business or investment activities, but this book does not deal with such trusts. They are also excluded from the Restatement of Trusts. *Restatement, Third, Trusts* § 1, comm. b (1996).

4. *Restatement, Third, Trusts* § 27, comm. b (1996). Creditors' rights with respect to trusts is discussed in Section 13.1.

### *Avoiding Probate*

Norman Dacey's best seller *How to Avoid Probate!* described living trusts as "a magic key to probate exemption; a legal wonder drug which will give you permanent immunity from the racket."[5] Dacey regarded lawyers as leading players in the "probate racket," but many lawyers today use living trusts more often than wills in estate planning.[6] Why this concern for "avoiding probate"?

Living trusts do not have to be executed with all of the formalities prescribed for wills,[7] but this is not a significant advantage since compliance with these formalities is not burdensome. In fact, Dacey's living trust forms have spaces for signature by two witnesses, and so could be probated as wills if necessary.[8]

Living trusts may be challenged for incapacity or undue influence just like wills, and the standards are virtually the same. However, many states require that heirs be notified before a will is admitted to probate, whereas no such notice is given to persons adversely affected by a living trust. "The publicity of probate invites attack upon a will; the privacy of an inter-vivos trust discourages it."[9] In many states will contests are tried by jury, and juries may be more prone than judges to reject wills which they find "unnatural." Professor Langbein has suggested that "trusts are more resistant to capacity challenges" than wills because they "belong to the jury-free realm of equity law."[10] However, wills and inter vivos transfers are often challenged in the same proceedings with the same result, and in any event successful contests of either wills or living trusts are rare.[11] Wills have one advantage over trusts in that the time limits on contesting wills are much shorter than those governing non-probate transfers.[12]

Even when wills are not contested, when they are probated after the testator dies. They become public documents open to inspection by all.[13] To a publicity-shy family this can be a cause of concern. After Patty Hearst was kidnapped her family sought to seal the probate records relating their wills, alleging that members of the family "would be in grave danger of their lives and property if their identities were discovered through the use of the probate files." The court noted that "no statute exempts probate files from the status of public records," but persons "can protect themselves from the disadvantages of publicity by ... eschew[ing] court-regulated devices for transmission of inherited wealth and rely[ing] on ... inter vivos ... trusts."[14] Another

5. N. Dacey, *How to Avoid Probate* 31 (updated edition 1983).

6. Prestopino, *Strategies Recommended by Experienced Estate Planners,* Trusts & Estates, Jan. 1994 p. 47.

7. See Section 4.7, at note 29 et seq. A *testamentary* trust, on the other hand, is not valid if the will which purports to create it cannot be probated.

8. *E.g.* Dacey, *supra* note 5, at 42.

9. Dacey, *supra* note 5, at 31. As to the necessity for notice when a will is probated, see Section 12.1, at note 25 et seq.

10. Langbein, *Living Probate: the Conservatorship Model,* 77 Mich.L.Rev. 63, 67 (1978).

11. See Section 7.3, at note 13.

12. Anderson v. Marquette Nat. Bank, 518 N.E.2d 196 (Ill.App.1987) (attack on amendment to revocable trust allowed even though time limit for contesting settlor's will had expired). As to the time limits on contesting wills see Section 12.1, at note 51 et seq.

13. During the testator's lifetime, the will is a secret document, unless the testator chooses to reveal its contents. Cf. Cal.Prob.Code § 2586 (court may order production of the will of a living conservatee when relevant to exercising its powers of substituted judgment).

14. Estate of Hearst, 136 Cal.Rptr. 821, 823–24 (App.1977).

court held that even a will poured assets into a living trust, the trust did not have to be probated, since one purpose of *inter-vivos* trusts was "to avoid publicity concerning family and business plans."[15] However, such publicity is not a concern in most families, and the public is rarely interested in ascertaining the estate plan of the average citizen.

Probate may be costlier than nonprobate transfers.[16] In some states the fees charged by executors and their attorneys are based on the size of the "probate" estate, and thus can be reduced by nonprobate transfers. However, there is a growing trend against basing fees simply on the size of the probate estate.[17] A living trust often requires additional work by lawyers, such as transferring title of assets to the trust, and the fees for this work and for drafting the trust may offset any savings in probate costs.[18] Also, if a family member serves as the executor of a will, it usually makes no sense to avoid probate in order to reduce the executor's fee. Even if a professional executor is named, the fees charged are deductible for tax purposes so some of the cost of probate in larger estates is borne by the government rather than the beneficiaries of the estate.

The delay involved while property of a decedent is being administered is an a source of popular dissatisfaction with probate,[19] but its significance should not be exaggerated. An estate in administration continues to earn income, since the executor must keep the assets productively invested for the ultimate benefit of the beneficiaries.[20] The needs of the beneficiaries of the estate during the period of administration can be met by the family allowance and by partial distributions.

Living trusts are occasionally used to escape limitations on testamentary freedom imposed by mortmain statutes or the spouse's elective share.[21] However, only a few states today have mortmain statutes[22] and many states allow surviving spouses to claim a share of assets in a revocable trust by the decedent as well as the probate estate.[23]

Creditors of a testator can reach the probate estate to satisfy their claims. In some states creditors of the settlor of a revocable trust have no comparable right, but this is no longer true in many jurisdictions today. In any event creditors are not a major consideration in the vast majority of estates which are solvent.[24]

Another possible reason for using living trusts is that some states subject testamentary trusts to close court supervision and this can create costs and delays. A comment to the Uniform Probate code notes

**15.** In re Meskimen's Estate, 235 N.E.2d 619, 622 (Ill.1968).

**16.** Dacey relates a series of horror stories to illustrate this point—*e.g.* "Fees Eat Up Nearly Half of an Estate of $19,425." Dacey, *supra* note 5, at 16.

**17.** See Section 12.5, at note 10 et seq.

**18.** Weinstock, *Planning an Estate* § 6.7 (4th ed. 1995).

**19.** Dacey estimates that it takes from two to five years to clear the average estate through probate. Dacey, *supra* note 5, at 14. *See also* Weinstock, *supra* note 18, § 6.8. As to steps some states have taken to avoid such delays see Section 12.10, at note 70 et seq.

**20.** As to the investment responsibilities of executors and trustees see Section 12.7.

**21.** Matter of Estate of Kirk, 907 P.2d 794 (Idaho 1995); In re Estate of Katz, 528 So.2d 422 (Fla.App.1988) (mortmain statute inapplicable to living trust).

**22.** See Section 3.10, at note 5.

**23.** See Section 3.7, at note 21 et seq.

**24.** As to the rights of creditors against probate and non-probate assets see Sections 13.1–13.3.

> In a substantial number of states, statutes now extend probate court control over decedents' estates to testamentary trustees, but the same procedures rarely apply to inter vivos trusts ... Twenty four states impose some form of mandatory court accountings on testamentary trustees, while only three seem to have comparable requirements for inter vivos trustees.
>
> From an estate planning viewpoint, probate court supervision of testamentary trustees causes many problems ... Regular accountings in court have proved to be more expensive than useful in relation to the vast majority of trusts ...
>
> The various restrictions applicable to testamentary trusts have caused many planners to recommend use of revocable inter vivos trusts.

The Code seeks "to eliminate procedural distinctions between testamentary and inter vivos trusts" and "to eliminate routinely required court accountings" for both.[25] It directs that the administration of trusts "shall proceed expeditiously ... free of judicial intervention."[26] Thus the Code has eliminated or reduced the incentives for avoiding probate by simplifying the process.

The reasons for avoiding probate are stronger in some states than in others. They depend on the client's objectives and situation.[27] One should *not* assume that avoiding probate for all assets of all clients is desirable.

Many persons wish to have some assets pass at death by nonprobate transfer and others pass under their will. In this situation it is important to coordinate the various parts of the estate plan. Pourover wills can be used for this purpose.[28] But the cases show many instances of uncoordinated or inconsistent documents. For example, a man executed a will disposing of insurance in a way which was inconsistent with his designation of insurance beneficiaries executed an hour later.[29] The problem of coordination of probate and nonprobate transfers is exacerbated by the widely followed view that a person cannot control the devolution of nonprobate property by a will.[30]

### *Saving Taxes*

Revocable living trust have no tax advantages. If the settlor retains the power to revoke the trust the trust income continues to be taxed to the settlor, and the trust property is taxed in the settlor's gross estate at death. Irrevocable transfers, on the other hand, can save both income and transfer taxes.[31] These savings do not require the use of a trust; an outright irrevocable gift has the same effect, but an irrevocable trust may be more advantageous than other forms of irrevocable gift for non-tax reasons.

### *Other Ways to Avoid Probate*

**25.** Uniform Prob.Code, Article VII, Comment.

**26.** Uniform Probate Code § 2–701. *See also* Unif.Trust Code § 201(b): trusts are not "subject to continuing court supervision unless ordered by the court."

**27.** For a good discussion see Jones, *Putting Revocable Trusts in their Place,* Trusts and Estates, Sept. 1990 p. 8.

**28.** See Section 6.2, at note 21 et seq.

**29.** Acklin v. Riddell, 856 S.W.2d 322 (Ark. App.1993).

**30.** See Section 5.5, at note 80 et seq.

**31.** See Chapter 15.

Living trusts are not the only device which is available to avoid probate. Joint tenancy is often used for the same reason.[32] Nevertheless most estate planners warn against its use.[33]

Joint bank accounts are often created or alleged to have been created only for convenience, with no intent that the survivor own the account when the depositor dies. This has caused courts much difficulty. A court recently remarked that there were two ways to begin civil litigation, filing a law suit and opening a joint bank account.[34] Revocable trusts are less open to such disputes. Even the simple forms provided in Dacey's book are clear about the settlor's intent to pass the property at death to the designated beneficiary.[35]

The often expressed idea that joint tenancy gives a "present interest" to both (all) parties creates additional problems.[36] If the other joint owner(s) become(s) incompetent, a conservatorship may be needed in order to deal with the property,[37] and creditors of any joint tenant may have claims against the property.[38] If the parties have a falling out, the ability of the creator of the joint tenancy to revoke it is unclear, whereas the power to a settlor to revoke a trust is usually expressly reserved (or negated) in the trust instrument.[39]

Because of the problems with joint tenancy, the drafters of the Uniform Probate Code did not include it among provisions for nonprobate transfers of securities as distinguished from bank accounts. They explained:

> The TOD registration ... give[s] the owner of securities who wishes to arrange for a nonprobate transfer at death an alternative to the frequently troublesome joint tenancy form of title. Because joint tenancy registration of securities normally entails a sharing of lifetime entitlement and control, it works satisfactorily only so long as the co-owners cooperate. Difficulties arise when co-owners fall into disagreement, or when one becomes afflicted or insolvent.[40]

TOD registration of securities, POD bank accounts, and the designation of beneficiaries of insurance policies and death benefits under pension plans allow nonprobate transfer without a trust or the disadvantages of joint tenancy.[41] Nevertheless, securities, bank accounts, and insurance benefits are

**32.** Hines, *Real Property Joint Tenancies,* 51 Iowa L.Rev. 582, 596 (1966); Campfield, *Estate Planning for Joint Tenancies,* 1974 Duke L.J. 669, 672–73; Powell, *Joint Ownership in Estate Planning,* 22 Ohio St.L.J. 292, 294–95 (1961); Wenig, *Joint Property,* 116 Trusts & Estates 516, 520 (1977).

**33.** H. Weinstock, *Planning an Estate* § 6.22 (4th ed. 1995); Prestopino, *supra* note 6.

**34.** Robinson v. Delfino, 710 A.2d 154, 160 (R.I.1998). As to the admissibility of extrinsic evidence to show the depositor's intent see Section 6.3, at note 4 et seq.

**35.** Totten trusts (see Section 4.6, note 39) have some of the same ambiguity as joint accounts. See *Restatement, Second, Trusts* § 58, comm. a (1959) (evidence admissible "to show either that the depositor intended to create an irrevocable trust or that he did not intend to create a trust"). However, litigation about them is relatively uncommon.

**36.** The court in Robinson v. Delfino, *supra* note 34, said that one who opens a joint account creates "immediate possessory as well as survivorship rights." This is not untypical.

**37.** Johnson, *Survivorship Interests with Persons Other Than a Spouse,* 20 Real Prop. Prob. and Trust L.J. 985, 996 (1985).

**38.** See Section 13.2, at note 18 et seq.

**39.** As to attempts to revoke joint tenancies see see Section 5.5, at note 42 et seq.

**40.** Uniform Probate Code, Prefatory Note to Article VI. The failure of the UPC to provide for joint tenancy in securities will not prevent its use and the incumbent problems. McGovern, *Nonprobate Transfers Under the Revised Uniform Probate Code,* 55 Alb.L.Rev. 1329, 1332 (1992).

**41.** As to the validity of these forms see Section 4.7.

often put into a trust in order to accomplish objectives other than avoiding probate.

Insurance proceeds can be put into a trust in several ways. They can be made payable to the insured's estate and pass with other assets into a testamentary trust. Another alternative is to have the proceeds paid directly to trustees named in the insured's will. In some states this has some of the advantages of avoiding probate.[42] Or a living trust can be created and designated as the beneficiary of the insurance policy.[43]

## § 9.2 Management of Property

Trusts are frequently used to manage property for persons who are legally incompetent, either minor children or adults who has been adjudicated incompetent, or for persons who are legally competent but unable (in the settlor's opinion) to handle property well. Many parents want property held in trust for children until they reach an age well beyond eighteen, the age of majority today. A living trust can also provide a solution for persons who are concerned about their own possible future incompetence. In this case someone other than the settlor must be designated as trustee, either initially or upon defined circumstances, such as whenever a physician certifies that the settlor is no longer capable. This can avoid the expense and embarrassment of judicial proceedings to have the settlor declared incompetent.[1]

Virtually all knowledgeable estate planners prefer trusts to guardianship or conservatorship for minors or incompetent adults. Guardians/conservators typically must file a bond, periodically account to a court, and obtain court approval for sales, investments and distributions.[2] Trustees are also fiduciaries who handle property belonging to others, and so the law regulates their activities as well, but trustees are generally freer from court control than guardians. A settlor can choose to take risks with property which he puts into a trust, *e.g.*, by waiving bond,[3] whereas the rules for guardians cannot generally be waived.

Guardianship for minors has the additional disadvantage that it terminates when the child reaches the age of majority[4] even though many, probably most parents do not think an 18–year–old is mature enough to manage property. Trusts can, generally speaking, continue for as long as the settlor wishes.

### *Custodianships*

The Uniform Transfers (Gifts) to Minors Act provides a third alternative for having property managed for minors. Under this Act, the donor designates

**42.** *E.g.*, Cal.Prob.Code § 6323 (insurance payable to testamentary trustee is not subject to administration).

**43.** As to the validity of such insurance trusts see Section 4.6, at note 28.

§ 9.2

1. McGovern, *Trusts, Custodianships, and Durable Powers of Attorney*, 27 Real Prop., Prob. and Trust J. 1, 4 (1992).

**2.** *Ibid.;* Cal.Prob.Code §§ 2320 (bond), 2520 (sales), 2620 (accounting biennially in court), 2570 (investments). The Uniform Probate Code reduces some of these differences between trusts and conservatorships. *E.g.*, § 5–423 (conservator has "all of the powers ... conferred by law on trustees"). *See Restatement (Third) of Property (Wills and Other Donative Transfers)* § 2.3, comm. h (1998).

**3.** As to bond see Section 12.5, at note 124 et seq.

**4.** Uniform Probate Code § 5–424(c).

a "custodian" for a minor to whom the donor gives property. A custodian "has all the rights, powers, and authority over the custodial property that unmarried adult owners have over their own property," to be held, however, in a fiduciary capacity.[5] Custodians are not required to give a bond or make periodic court accountings.[6]

The Act was first promulgated in 1956. In 1983 a new version appeared, now called the Uniform Transfers to Minors Act, because it includes transfers other than gifts. For example, a person can create a custodianship by a will.[7] Someone who owes money to a minor can be forced to pay again if direct distribution to the minor is made, since the minor cannot give a valid receipt. Now the property can be transferred to a custodian. For example, if an insurance beneficiary is a minor when the policy matures, or if a minor has a tort claim, payment to a custodian is authorized.[8] The Act also allows personal representatives and trustees to distribute to a custodian when this is "in the best interests of the minor" to whom property is due to be distributed.[9] For example, an administrator of an intestate decedent could distribute the share of a minor heir to a custodian and thereby avoid the need for appointment of a guardian.

Custodians operate very much like trustees.[10] According to the Restatement of Trusts, they "are subject to the rules of trust law" except where the statute otherwise provides.[11] Custodianship is a useful alternative to a trust for handling smaller amounts of property, because one can establish a custodianship without drafting a trust instrument. If a father, for example, wants to give his daughter a few shares of stock, he can simply have the stock registered in the name of custodian (who can be himself or another adult) "as custodian for [the daughter] under the [state] Uniform Transfers to Minors Act."[12] This designation incorporates by reference the provisions of the Act and thereby confers all necessary powers on the custodian,[13] including discretion to "expend for the minor's benefit so much of the custodial property as the custodian considers advisable" without court order.[14]

A custodianship can be created only for one person,[15] whereas a person can create a single trust for a group of persons and give the trustee discretion to make unequal distributions among them on the basis of differing need, conduct or other factors deemed relevant.[16] The possible advantages (and problems) connected with such discretionary trusts will be discussed in Section 9.5.

Custodianships normally end when the beneficiary reaches age 21.[17] For the many parents who wish to postpone distribution until their children are

**5.** Uniform Transfers to Minors Act § 13(a).

**6.** *Id.* §§ 15(c), 19. As to accountings by other fiduciaries see Section 12.10.

**7.** *Id.* § 5.

**8.** *Id.* § 7.

**9.** *Id.* § 6. This requires court approval if the transfer involves more than $10,000.

**10.** McGovern, *supra* note 1, at 6–10, discusses the similarities and differences between custodians and trustees.

**11.** *Restatement, Third, Trusts* § 5, comm.a (1996).

**12.** *Id.* § 9.

**13.** *Id.* § 11(c).

**14.** *Id.* § 14.

**15.** *Id.* § 10.

**16.** McGovern, *supra* note 1, at 14–16.

**17.** Termination may occur at 18 in some circumstances. Uniform Transfers to Minors Act § 20. The California version allows extension to age 25 in some circumstances. Cal.Prob. Code § 3920.5.

older, a trust is better than custodianship. If a minor dies during a custodianship, the property passes to the minor's estate.[18] A trust can provide for distribution to others when a beneficiary dies—indeed one purpose of many trusts is to keep the trust assets out of the beneficiary's estate at death.[19]

### *Durable Powers of Attorney*

Children are legally incompetent until the age of majority. Legal incompetence at the other end of life is increasingly frequent as people live longer. Many persons use living trusts to provide a better way than conservatorship for handling their property in case they become incompetent before they die. Another alternative is to designate an agent.

Agents, like trustees, are fiduciaries who act for others. Traditionally an agent's powers ceased when the principal became incompetent. This made agency useless for managing property for an incompetent, so a Uniform Durable Power of Attorney Act was promulgated in 1979. The term "attorney" in this context is equivalent to agent, and has nothing to do with being a "attorney at law."[20] Its provisions are included in the Uniform Probate Code and have been adopted (with variations) in most states. They provide "a form of senility insurance comparable to that available to relatively wealthy persons who use funded, revocable trusts."[21]

A durable power of attorney is one which states that it "shall not be affected by the subsequent disability or incapacity of the principal."[22] Some persons wish the agent's powers to begin *only if* they become incompetent. Such "springing powers" should state that "this power of attorney shall become effective upon the disability or incapacity of the principal," and should provide a method for determining when this has happened so as to avoid the expensive legal proceedings which are required to determine capacity. For example, the power might be "framed to confer authority when two or more persons, possibly including the principal's lawyer, physician or spouse concur that the principal has become incapable of managing his affairs in a sensible and efficient manner and deliver a signed statement to that effect to the attorney in fact."[23]

A durable power must have been executed while the principal was legally competent; a person who is already incapacitated can not confer a power.[24]

Agents are like trustees in many respects; they manage property on behalf of the principal just as a trustee manages property for the beneficia-

**18.** Uniform Transfer to Minors Act § 20.

**19.** See Section 9.3.

**20.** " 'Attorney-in-fact' means a person granted authority to act for the principal in a power of attorney, regardless of whether the person is known as an attorney-in-fact or agent." Cal.Prob.Code § 4014(a).

**21.** Uniform Durable Powers of Attorney Act (Uniform Probate Code, Part 5), Prefatory Note.

**22.** These words are quoted from Uniform Probate Code § 5–501 which indicates that "similar words" will suffice but they must be "in writing." Without such language in most states the power terminates upon the principal's incompetence. Matter of Ciervo, 507 N.Y.S.2d 868 (A.D.1986). In California a durable power must be dated, signed by or in the presence of the principal, and by two witnesses, or acknowledged before a notary public. Cal.Prob.Code § 4121.

**23.** Uniform Probate Code § 5–501, Comment.

**24.** Golleher v. Horton, 715 P.2d 1225 (Ariz.App.1985); Testa v. Roberts, 542 N.E.2d 654 (Ohio App.1988); Hagan v. Shore, 915 P.2d 435 (Or.App.1996). But see note 31 infra. As to capacity in general see Section 7.1.

ry(ies). But trustees (like custodians) have many powers implied either by common law or a statute like the Uniform Trustees' Powers Act.[25] In contrast

> Most statutes authorizing durable powers confer no power on the agent. Instead [they] simply state that powers possessed by the agent are not lost when the principal becomes incapacitated. Therefore, to determine the scope of the agent's authority, one must look to the terms of the power and to the law of agency ... Agency law only sparingly implies powers and strictly construes express powers.[26]

Thus a power "to manage and lease my real estate ... and ... to do all other acts ... whatsoever in and about the specified premises ... as I could do in my own proper person" was held not to include the power to sell the land.[27] Courts are particularly hesitant to construe powers to allow the agent to make gifts of the principal's property even when these would produce substantial tax benefits.[28]

In order to simplify the problem of drafting a comprehensive list of powers for an agent, a Uniform Statutory Power of Attorney Act has been promulgated and adopted in some states, but the statutory forms "are so prolix that they intimidate anyone who tries to read them," and "leave important issues unresolved."[29] Because of the tradition of strict construction of agency powers, third persons such as banks and transfer agents have been reluctant to recognize the authority of agents to act for the principal. The Uniform Probate Code contains provisions designed to encourage them to do so by protecting them from liability if they erroneously but in good faith recognize a power in specified circumstances.[30] The protection of third parties and the general freedom from court supervision of agents creates risks. For example, a woman gave her nephew and his wife a power of attorney (cut out of Family Circle magazine) which they used to withdraw and dissipate $135,000 from her bank account. The agents were apparently judgment proof, so the woman sued the bank but it was protected since it had acted in good faith.[31]

Even a "durable" power of attorney terminates when the principal dies, although acts of an agent without actual knowledge of the principal's death may be binding.[32] Since trusts can continue to operate after the settlor dies, they can also function as a will substitute, but power of attorney cannot.

On the other hand, an agent can act under a power of attorney even though the principal has not transferred title to property to the agent; the simple execution of a power of attorney suffices whereas a living trust may fail if the trustee does not obtain title to the property.[33] The respective

**25.** Trustees' powers of sale, investment, etc. are discussed in Sections 12.6 and 12.7.

**26.** McGovern, supra note 1, at 32–33.

**27.** In re Guardianship of Mabry, 666 N.E.2d 16, 20 (Ill.App.1996).

**28.** See Section 7.2, at notes 46 et seq.

**29.** McGovern, *supra* note 1, at 34.

**30.** Uniform Probate Code §§ 5–504, 5–505. For a discussion of these and similar provisions see McGovern, *supra* note 1, at 39–40.

**31.** Bank IV, Olathe v. Capitol Federal S & L, 828 P.2d 355 (Kan.1992). *See also* Johnson v. Edwardsville Nat. Bank & Trust Co., 594 N.E.2d 342 (Ill.App.1992) (bank protected by statute even if principal incompetent when power executed, but not if power was forged and bank was negligent).

**32.** Uniform Prob.Code § 5–504.

**33.** See Section 4.6, at notes 14–17.

advantages of trusts and agency can be combined by executing a power authorizing the attorney to transfer the principal's assets into a trust.

> 'In order to transfer all the client's property into trust, it definitely costs the client time, money and hassle today.' By using an agent to fund the trust only if the settlor becomes incapacitated, the 'costs associated with funding are delayed until the last possible minute.'[34]

## § 9.3 Bypass Trusts

Many persons want to create a trust for a spouse, but not because they lack confidence in the spouse's ability to manage property, but because they do not wish the property to be taxable (or subject to probate costs) when the spouse dies. Avoiding tax in the spouse's estate must be balanced against the advantages of the federal estate and gift tax marital deductions. Achieving the appropriate balance is a fine art which will be discussed hereafter.[1] A person may also have non-tax reasons for confining a spouse to a life interest, particularly if the couple has no children, or if either has children by another marriage, so that the surviving spouse is likely to leave property to persons unrelated to the other spouse. A decedent can prescribe the future devolution of property by confining the spouse to a life interest.

Similar reasons may induce a parent to provide a trust for a child: desire to keep property "in the family" and fear that if the child gets it outright, it may pass to the child's spouse or others outside the family. Tax motives may also operate here, *e.g.* keeping property out of the child's taxable estate at death. However, a trust for a child's life may be subject to an equivalent (or even higher) generation-skipping tax when the child dies.[2] Trusts for the life of a child are less common than trusts for the life of a spouse. Children usually have a longer life expectancy when the parent dies, and the costs of a trust for their lifetime often outweighs the benefits.

### *Legal Life Estates*

A testator or donor can create a life or other limited interest without using a trust. Many use legal life estates. But most knowledgeable estate planners do not recommend them. Professor Browder, for example, says that "the division of ownership into present and future legal estates is a practice that should be avoided whenever possible, particularly when personal property is involved. * * * If the value of the property involved does not justify resort to a trust administration, the property should be bequeathed outright."[3]

The law imposes duties on life tenants to protect the remainder interests; if they allow property to deteriorate they can be sued for waste.[4] In some circumstances they may be required to post a bond.[5] But "unlike a trustee, a

34. McGovern, *supra* note 1, at 42–43.

§ 9.3

1. See Chapter 15.

2. For the generation-skipping tax see Section 15.4.

3. Browder, *Recent Patterns of Testate Succession in the United States and England,* 67 Mich.L.Rev. 1303, 1430 (1969). *See also* J. Price, *Contemporary Estate Planning* 189 (1983).

4. Moore v. Phillips, 627 P.2d 831 (Kan. App.1981).

5. *Cf.* Matter of Estate of Jud, 710 P.2d 1241, 1248 (Kan.1985) (rejecting a demand for a bond "in the absence of a showing of danger of loss or waste").

life tenant as such does not stand in a fiduciary relationship to the other beneficiaries of successive legal interests."[6] Trustees who are independent and financially responsible provide better protection for remainder beneficiaries than the legal restrictions on legal life tenants, but professional trustees cost money. The testator may wish to avoid trustee's fees, particularly in smaller estates or for property which does not require the management skills of a professional trustee, such as a residence. This expense can be avoided either by a legal life estate or by using a family member as trustee. Designating a person, even a nonprofessional, as trustee has the advantage that the word incorporates by reference a body of trust law that deals with problems that recur when property is divided between present and future interests. The law governing legal life estates is less well developed than the law of trusts.[7]

Trustees have extensive powers over property held in trust, but life tenants and remaindermen "may deal only with their own respective interests" in the property.[8] If a third party injures the property, the life tenant may only recover for the damage to her interest, leaving the remaindermen with a separate claim. A trustee, on the other hand, can sue on behalf of all the beneficiaries.[9] A life tenant cannot commit "waste" but has no duty to take out insurance to cover the remainder interests,[10] whereas a trustee is bound to insure the property for the benefit of all.[11] Trustees must furnish information to the beneficiaries as to their administration of the trust,[12] whereas legal life tenants have no comparable obligation to the remaindermen unless the remaindermen can show "there is real danger of destruction of the estate."[13]

Remedies against a life tenant who commits waste are problematic when the succeeding interests are contingent. For example, parents left land to their daughter for life, with a remainder to her surviving issue. When the daughter sold timber standing on the property, her grandson sought relief. The court refused to give him damages since his interest was uncertain; he would have none if he failed to survive the life tenant. An injunction against cutting the timber would avoid the problem of ascertaining damages, but it might also prevent the property being exploited advantageously. Hence, courts refuse to grant an injunction to persons who have only a remote chance of succeeding to the property.

> Injunctive relief to prevent damage or waste has been commonly granted to contingent remaindermen, but an assessment of damages for timber

6. *Restatement (Third) of Trusts* § 5, comm. b (1996).

7. Casner, *Legal Life Estates,* 45 Neb. L.Rev. 342, 346 (1966). This is not true in the civil law, where in the absence of trusts, a large body of law dealing with "usufructs" developed. *See* La.Civ.Code art. 535–629; *cf.* Matter of Estate of Panzeca, 543 N.E.2d 161 (Ill.App.1989) (looking to Louisiana law to construe a will which designated the testator's wife as "usufructuary" of the estate).

8. *Restatement (Third) of Trusts* § 5, comm. b (1996).

9. *Restatement of Property* § 118 (1936); 1 *Amer. Law of Prop.* §§ 2.16(e), 4.107; *Restatement (Second) of Trusts* § 280 (1959).

10. Ellerbusch v. Myers, 683 N.E.2d 1352 (Ind.App.1997) (life tenant who insures property can keep all the proceeds when property is destroyed by fire); 1 *Amer. Law of Prop.* § 2.23; Casner, *supra* note 7, at 351.

11. *Restatement (Second) of Trusts* § 176, comment b (1959).

12. *Restatement, Second, Trusts* § 173 (1959); Section 12.10, at note 1 et seq.

13. Holley v. Marks, 535 S.W.2d 861, 862 (Tenn.1976). *See also* Thomas v. First Nat. Bank, 479 N.E.2d 1014, 1028–29 (Ill.App.1985).

already taken has been infrequent ... If the chances are remote that the contingency vesting the interest will occur, courts will not give relief of any kind to the contingent remainderman.[14]

While the remedies available to remainder interests are thus restricted, life tenants' ability to exploit land is also limited. For example, a life tenant was barred from executing an oil and gas lease under the "open mine" doctrine. "If the pits or mines were open before [the life estate was created], it is no waste for the tenant to continue digging them [but] to open the land to search for mines of metal, coal, etc. is waste."[15] The best use of land may require a long-term lease. Trustees can execute leases which extend beyond the term of the trust,[16] but a life tenant can convey only what she has; if she dies during the term of a lease, the remaindermen can expel the tenant.[17] Legal life estates "shackled much of the land in England" in the 19th century. "The tenant for life could not without special powers exercise the normal functions of leasing, mining and felling timber which belonged to an absolute owner." This prevented "the proper exploitation of the landed wealth" and led to the enactment of legislation which gave broad powers to life tenants.[18]

American law has followed a similar path, but not so far. Many state statutes allow courts to authorize life tenants to sell property. In Massachusetts, for example, a sale binding upon all parties can be authorized if it appears "necessary or expedient" to the court.[19] Some courts have ordered a such a sale even without statutory authorization.[20] Court proceedings are expensive, however. They can be avoided if the instrument that creates the life estate gives the life tenant a power of sale,[21] but a narrowly drafted power may be insufficient. A power to "sell such portion of the real property which may be necessary to remove the mortgage indebtedness" did not allow a sale of property for $108,000 when the mortgages on it amounted to only $25,000. "A power granted by a will to a life tenant to dispose of the property must be strictly construed, and it must be exercised in the manner and for the purpose stated in the will."[22] A power to sell whenever the life tenant "shall deem it necessary for his comfort and support" allows a sale only if the life tenant is in need, but a sale may be desirable for other reasons. If property is expected to appreciate, a mortgage might be more appropriate way to raise funds, but a power to mortgage is not necessarily included in a power to sell.[23]

On the other hand, a broadly drafted power may allow the tenant to destroy the remainder. A tenant with "full and unrestricted power to sell, convey, dispose of, or expend all or any part of said property" was allowed to

**14.** Pedro v. January, 494 P.2d 868, 875 (Or.1972).

**15.** Nutter v. Stockton, 626 P.2d 861, 862 (Okl.1981) (quoting Blackstone's Commentaries). *See also Restatement of Property* § 138, comment b (1936); 5 *Amer. Law of Prop.* § 20.6.

**16.** *See* Section 12.6, at note 36 et seq.

**17.** *Restatement of Property* § 124 (1936).

**18.** J. Baker, *An Introduction to English Legal History* 247 (2d ed. 1979).

**19.** Mass.Gen.Laws c. 183, § 49. *See also* N.C.Stat. § 41–11; N.H.Stat. § 477.39; *Restatement of Property* § 124, comment i (1936); 1 *Amer.Law of Prop.* § 4.99.

**20.** Alsup v. Montoya, 488 S.W.2d 725 (Tenn.1972); Ball v. Curtis, 637 S.W.2d 571 (Ark.1982); Jackson v. Breton, 484 A.2d 256 (Me.1984).

**21.** Ware v. Green, 691 S.W.2d 167 (Ark. 1985).

**22.** Matter of Estate of Hookom, 764 P.2d 1001, 1005 (Wash.App.1988).

**23.** Brunton v. Easthampton Savings Bank, 145 N.E.2d 696 (Mass.1957).

give the property away.[24] Very broad powers given to a tenant, even if they are not exercised, may render a succeeding gift void. Property was devised to the testator's brother, with a gift to others if "such property [is] not ... used, sold, consumed or expended by him." The brother did not sell or consume the property but the gift over was nevertheless ineffective, because the devise to the brother "conveys a fee simple absolute" which made the gift over void "because there is no interest remaining to be devised."[25]

Trustees usually have power to sell trust property whenever appropriate, but they cannot give it away without adequate consideration.[26] When property in a trust is sold, the sale proceeds are retained in the trust. Legal life tenants with a power of sale, unlike trustees, are not obligated to keep the sale proceeds separate from their own property, and if the proceeds cannot be identified when the life tenant dies, the remainder fails.[27] Some drafters therefore stipulate that if assets are sold, the life tenant becomes a trustee of the proceeds.[28]

Since trusts and legal life estates are used for the same purpose, an instrument which creates a life estate may be construed to create a trust. Thus a will which left property to the testator's wife for life accompanied by a direction that the executors "handle my estate during the wife of my life," was held to create a trust by implication.[29] A Pennsylvania statute provides that a life tenant of personal property "shall be deemed to be a trustee of such property * * * with the ordinary powers and duties of a trustee."[30] English legislation converts all life estates to trusts even for land.[31] This tendency to force legal life estates into the trust mold coincides with the common advice of estate planners to use a trust whenever one creates successive interests in property.

### *Trust Purposes*

Trusts can serve more than one objective. A drafter must understand the reason for a trust in order to draft it intelligently. Who should be trustee? If the trust is being used because of doubts about the beneficiary's capacity to handle property, the beneficiary should not be named as the trustee. But the beneficiary may be an ideal trustee for a by-pass trust. How long should the trust continue? This depends on whether a trust is designed to manage

**24.** Kelly v. Lansford, 572 S.W.2d 369 (Tex. Civ.App.1978). *See also* Rawlings v. Briscoe, 197 S.E.2d 211 (Va.1973); Hobbs v. Wilson, 614 S.W.2d 328 (Tenn.1980). *But see* Childs v. Hutson, 545 A.2d 43 (Md.1988) (life tenant's power to "sell or dispose of" the property did not allow gift to her daughter). In Caldwell v. Walraven, 490 S.E.2d 384 (Ga.1997) such a power was held to allow the life tenant to give away the property but not to devise it.

**25.** Langille v. Norton, 628 A.2d 669, 671 (Me.1993). *See also* Sterner v. Nelson, 314 N.W.2d 263 (Neb.1982). However, not all courts follow this view. *E.g.*, In re Estate of Rider, 711 A.2d 1018 (Pa.Super.1998); Matter of Estate of Taylor, 646 P.2d 776 (Wash.App. 1982).

**26.** On trustee's powers of sale see Section 12.6, note 6.

**27.** South Side T. & S. Bank v. South Side T. & S. Bank, 284 N.E.2d 61 (Ill.App.1972). However, traceable property in life tenant's estate goes to the remaindermen. Caldwell v. Walraven, 490 S.E.2d 384 (Ga.1997); Matter of Estate of Taylor, 646 P.2d 776 (Wash.App. 1982); Matter of Estate of Polley, 444 N.E.2d 714 (Ill.App.1982).

**28.** *Restatement (Third) of Trusts* § 5, comm.b (1996).

**29.** Perfect U. Lodge v. Interfirst Bank, 748 S.W.2d 218 (Tex.1988). *See also* Jorge v. Da Silva, 218 A.2d 661 (R.I.1966).

**30.** 20 Pa.Stat. § 6113.

**31.** Maudsley, *Escaping the Tyranny of Common Law Estates,* 42 Mo.L.Rev. 355 (1977).

property until the beneficiaries are mature, or rather to keep property in the family or avoid estate taxes for as long as possible.[32]

Other rules of trust law turn on the purposes of the trust, but courts often have difficulty in discerning them, because the settlor and drafter never thought clearly about the question.

## § 9.4 Principal and Income

Suppose that a woman creates a trust which provides that the trustee shall pay the income to her husband for life, and upon his death, convey the principal to her issue. The trustee will receive dividends, interest, rent, proceeds of property sold, etc. Are these receipts income to be distributed to the husband, or principal to be retained in trust for the settlor's issue? When the trust incurs expenses, such as trustee's fees or taxes, which account is charged with them?

These problems arise repeatedly in the administration of trusts. Trustees need a clear answer. In case of doubt, they can apply to a court for instructions, but this is expensive. In most states a statute answers most questions. There are no less than three Uniform Principal and Income Acts. The first was promulgated in 1931 and is still law in 6 states. The second came out in 1962 and has been adopted by 31 states. A third version dating from 1997 has 7 adoptions.[1] There are often differences between the versions of any given Act in states which adopt it, so the title "Uniform" is misleading.

### *General Principles*

The law of principal and income consists of many detailed rules, not all of which can be treated here. A few general principles underlie these rules. First, the settlor's intent controls. All the Acts expressly state that their provisions are subject to contrary directions in the trust.[2] However, it is sometimes not clear whether a testator or settlor actually intended to depart from the established rules. For example, a will devised a life estate in the testator's residence to his wife with remainder to his children and said "the mortgage remaining shall be paid by the remainder persons." The court refused to construe this language to mean that "the testator intended to deviate from well-established common law principles regarding the obligation of a life tenant ... to pay interest due on encumbrances on the property." He intended to burden the remainder only with payment of the mortgage principal.[3] A provision in another will for payment of the income to the testator's wife "after deduction for the costs and expenses of the trustee" was held not to override the general rule of the governing Act that trustees' fees should be charged half to income and half to principal, and that capital gains taxes and brokerage commissions be charged entirely to principal.[4] On the

32. A settlor must respect the limits imposed by the Rule against Perpetuities. See Chapter 11.

§ 9.4

1. These figures are taken from 7B Uniform Laws Annotated (2000 Annual Pocket Part).

2. 1931 Act § 2; 1962 Act § 2; 1997 Act § 103(a)(1).

3. Gaymon v. Gaymon, 519 S.E.2d 142, 146 (Va.1999). *See also* 1997 Act § 501(a)(3) (interest is payable from income).

4. Venables v. Seattle–First Nat. Bank, 808 P.2d 769 (Wash.App.1991). The decision was based on the 1962 Uniform Act, § 13.

other hand, the proceeds of a sale of timber were allocated to principal under a provision that if the trustee sold "any of the corpus of the estate, the consideration paid therefor shall become a part of the trust property and not an income," even though under the relevant Act proceeds for a timber lease could be deemed income; the will provision overrode the statute.[5]

Some wills give the trustee discretion in making allocations between principal and income. The 1997 Act says that a fiduciary may exercise such a discretionary power "even if the exercise of the power produces a result different from" the one dictated by the Act.[6] Similar provisions appeared in earlier versions of the Act.[7] It is not clear how far such discretion extends. A trustee was not allowed to allocate capital gain to an income beneficiary under a provision empowering the trustee to determine "whether any money coming into its hands shall be treated as" principal or income. "Proceeds from the sale of trust securities are principal. Where proper allocation is not a matter of honest doubt the trustees are not authorized to make allocations contrary to law."[8] On the other hand, another court upheld a trustees' decision to allocate litigation expenses to income rather than corpus.[9]

The definition of income for other purposes may influence the allocation of trust receipts. The 1962 Act provides that the income of an unincorporated business shall be "computed in accordance with generally accepted accounting principles."[10] However, capital gains are treated as "income" for tax purposes but are allocated to principal in trust accounting.[11] The disparities between trust accounting and income taxation sometimes give rise to claims for "equitable adjustment." For example, trustees incurred a capital gain in a sale, paid the resulting income tax out of principal as prescribed by law, but used the state income tax as a deduction against federal income taxes, thereby reducing the amount of taxable trust income reportable by the income beneficiaries. A guardian ad litem for the remaindermen argued that the trustees should make an equitable adjustment but the court refused, saying that "equitable adjustments should be applied only in response to inequities resulting from a trustee's discretionary decisions which favor one beneficiary or class of beneficiaries over another," whereas here the trustee was required by statute to pay the capital gains tax out of principal,[12] and an "equitable adjustment would in effect apportion the capital gains tax.[13] The 1997 Act allows trustees to make "adjustments between principal and income to offset the shifting of tax benefits between income beneficiaries and remainder beneficiaries" in some instances, and requires them in others.[14] Some alloca-

**5.** Hardin v. McPhearson, 569 So.2d 319 (Ala.1990). The relevant statute in this case was § 9 of the 1931 Act. *See also* Hudspeth v. Hudspeth, 756 S.W.2d 29, 32 (Tex.App.1988) (testator did not intend to limit life beneficiary to "income as it is used in a strictly legal sense").

**6.** 1997 Act § 103(a)(2).

**7.** 1962 Act § 2(b). Section 2 of the 1931 Act is similar but the language is less strong.

**8.** Englund v. First Nat. Bank, 381 So.2d 8, 11 (Ala.1980). *Accord,* Donahue v. Watson, 411 N.E.2d 741, 748 (Ind.App.1980); Robinson v. Commissioner, 75 T.C. 346, 354 (1980).

**9.** duPont v. Southern Nat. Bank, 771 F.2d 874, 887 (5th Cir.1985).

**10.** 1962 Act § 8.

**11.** *Id.* § 3(b)(1); 1931 Act § 3(2); 1997 Act § 404(2); *Restatement (Second) of Trusts* § 233, comm. b (1959).

**12.** 1962 Act § 13(c)(4): "any tax levied upon profit, gain, or other receipts allocated to principal notwithstanding denomination of the tax as an income tax by the taxing authority" allocated to principal.

**13.** Harris Trust & Sav. Bank v. MacLean, 542 N.E.2d 943, 948 (Ill.App.1989).

**14.** 1997 Act § 506.

tion decisions are motivated in part on obtaining favorable tax consequences.[15]

A common theme is that receipts should be allocated so that the value of the principal is preserved and everything else is income. The 1931 Act provides that income of a business shall be computed so as not to decrease the principal.[16] The Restatement of Trusts allocates receipts from oil and gas "in such a way as will preserve the value of the principal."[17] Under the 1997 Act proceeds from the sale of timber are allocated to income "to the extent that the amount of timber removed does not exceed the rate of growth of the timber."[18] A court allocated a stock dividend to principal on the ground that otherwise the value of the principal would shrink.[19] This approach is not always followed, however. Unrealized appreciation is not treated as income, even when it reflects undistributed earnings of a corporation whose stock is held in the trust.[20] However, with respect to charitable trusts, the Uniform Management of Institutional Funds Act allows "the net appreciation, realized and unrealized in the fair value of assets of an endowment fund over [its] historic dollar value" to be treated as income.[21]

Courts sometimes suggest that doubtful allocation questions should be resolved in favor of the income beneficiaries because they are "the primary objects of [the settlor's] bounty."[22] The 1997 Act, however, provides that in cases for which no rule is provided receipts shall be added to principal, noting that this serves the long-term interest of all beneficiaries since additions to principal will produce more income in the future.[23]

Administrative convenience is an important factor in allocation. Since trustees must make decisions frequently, an easily applicable rule is better than one which requires difficult calculations or knowledge which is not readily available. The 1962 Act adopted "an arbitrary allocation" of 27 1/2% of the gross receipts from natural resources to principal because apportioning them on the basis of the ratio of minerals extracted to minerals remaining in the ground was too difficult.[24] The 1931 Act adopted the "Massachusetts" rule allocating cash dividends to income and stock dividends to principal in preference to the "Pennsylvania" rule which required apportionment since "experience has shown that, however praiseworthy the intent, the [Pennsylvania] rule is unworkable, since neither trustee or court has the means to value the corporate assets in such way as to secure the fair adjustment aimed

**15.** Estate of Richardson, 89 T.C. 1193, 1203 (1987)(allocation made in order to obtain the maximum possible marital deduction); 1997 Act § 413(a) (adjustments made to preserve marital deduction).

**16.** 1931 Act § 7(3).

**17.** *Restatement (Second) of Trusts* § 239, comm. g (1959).

**18.** 1997 Act § 412(a)(1).

**19.** Estate of Reynolds, 432 A.2d 158, 165 (Pa.1981). *See also* Matter of Estate of Dawson, 641 A.2d 1026, 1034 (N.J.1994) (distributions which were accompanied by "a significant decrease in the market price of the share" allocated to principal).

**20.** *Restatement (Second) of Trusts* § 236, comm. y (1959).

**21.** Unif.Man.Inst.Funds Act § 2.

**22.** Matter of Kuehn, 308 N.W.2d 398, 400 (S.D.1981). *See also* Matter of Jane Bradley Uihlein Trust, 417 N.W.2d 908, 913 (Wis.App. 1987); In re Estate of Warner, 570 A.2d 544 (Pa.Super.1990).

**23.** 1997 Act § 103(a)(4), comment. *See also* In re Trust of Warner, 117 N.W.2d 224, 232 (Minn.1962); In re Talbot's Estate, 74 Cal. Rptr. 920, 927 (App.1969); In re Arens' Trust, 197 A.2d 1, 11 (N.J.1964).

**24.** 1962 Act, Prefatory Note. 1997 Act § 411 rejects this formula, but provides one which is equally easy to apply—90% of receipts allocated to principal, the rest to income.

at."[25] The 1997 Act allows trustees to rely on statements by a corporation as to the character of the distribution which it makes.[26]

Another underlying concept is the desirability of a relatively steady stream of "income," rather than wide fluctuations from year to year. Even when a trust provided that "realized appreciation" should be treated as income, a court refused to treat $900,000 arising from a leveraged buyout as income, since this would conflict with the settlor's intent "to provide a modest monthly income for the beneficiaries for their lives."[27] The 1997 Act allocates any corporate distributions amounting to more than 20% of the company's gross assets to principal.[28] It charges "ordinary repairs" and "regularly recurring" property taxes to income, but "disbursements relating to environmental matters" are charged against principal "on the assumption that they will usually be extraordinary in nature."[29] The 1962 Act allows trustees to "regularize distributions" by amortizing charges against income which were "of unusual amount."[30]

### *Specific Rules: Proceeds of Sale*

When property is sold the proceeds are allocated to principal, including capital gains which are taxed as income under federal law. However, part of the proceeds of a sale may be treated as income in trust accounting if the property had not been producing adequate income before it was sold. For example, when a trustee sold some land, the court allocated part of the proceeds to income. "Where assets are unproductive or underproductive * * * the trustee is under a duty to the income beneficiaries to sell such assets within a reasonable time."[31] The income from this land had "ranged from 1% to 2% of the values of the property at a time when the * * * return achieved by trust institutions in Sioux Falls ranged from 5.02% to 5.86%." Thus the property was "underproductive." The court applied a formula in the Restatement of Trusts to determine the portion of the proceeds to be treated as income.[32] The 1962 Uniform Act has a similar provision, but only for property "which has not produced an average net income of at least 1% per year of its inventory value,"[33] whereas the Restatement rule applies whenever the income from an asset is "substantially less than the current rate of return on trust investments."

The 1997 Act rejects any special treatment for an underproductive asset because it "conflicts with the basic precept" of the Prudent Investor Act which requires one to consider the trust portfolio as a whole.[34] Instead the Act

**25.** 1931 Act, Prefatory Note. *See also* In re Arens' Trust, 197 A.2d 1 (N.J.1964) (abandoning Pennsylvania rule as unworkable); In re Trust of Warner, 117 N.W.2d 224 (Minn.1962) (same).

**26.** 1997 Act § 401(f).

**27.** McMillan v. McLean, 582 So.2d 466, 468 (Ala.1991).

**28.** 1997 Act, § 401(d)(2). *See also* Matter of Estate of Dawson, 641 A.2d 1026, 1034 (N.J.1994) (presumption that distributions exceeding 25% are stock splits, allocable to corpus).

**29.** 1997 Act §§ 501(3), 502(a)(7), comment.

**30.** 1962 Act § 13(b). 1997 Act § 504 is similar.

**31.** As to a trustee's duty to make only income-producing investments see Section 12.7, at note 80 et seq.

**32.** Matter of Kuehn, 308 N.W.2d 398 (S.D. 1981). *See also* Perfect U Lodge v. Interfirst Bank, 748 S.W.2d 218 (Tex.1988); Sturgis v. Stinson, 404 S.E.2d 56 (Va.1991).

**33.** 1962 Act § 12(a). Section 11 of the 1931 Act is similar.

**34.** 1997 Act § 413, comment. As to the Prudent Investor Act see Section 12.7, note 49 et seq.

empowers trustees to make adjustments between principal and income in order to be "fair and reasonable to all beneficiaries." An example in the comment involves a trustee who decides to invest the trust assets entirely in growth stocks that produce little dividend income. The trustee may do this and at the same time transfer (an unspecified amount) of cash from principal to income in order to provide the income beneficiary "the degree of beneficial enjoyment normally accorded a person who is the income beneficiary of a trust."[35] This provision leaves much to the trustee's discretion (subject to judicial review for "abuse of discretion"),[36] but has the advantage that the income beneficiaries do not have to wait until unproductive property is sold in order to get their "fair share." This provision is restricted where it would create a conflict of interest because the trustee is also a beneficiary, or raise tax problems.

### *Corporate Distributions*

The Uniform Acts and the Restatement of Trusts have similar but not identical rules for allocating corporate distributions, including dividends, stock splits, liquidations, etc.[37] Generally speaking, cash dividends are income and other distributions including stock dividends are principal, but there are exceptions. A trust which, contrary to the general rule, provided that "all stock dividends ... shall be treated as income,"[38] received various distributions in stock, *e.g.* 600 shares from a company in which the trust held 300 shares. The court treated these distributions as "stock splits" and allocated them to principal, based on a "rebuttable presumption that a distribution of less than twenty-five percent is a stock dividend and distribution of twenty-five percent or more is a stock split." The court said one should look at all the circumstances, including the effect of the distribution on the stock's market price. In this case the distributions had been accompanied by a significant decrease in the market price of each share.[39] Under the 1997 Act all distributions in "property other than money" are principal,[40] and also those in money which exceed 20% of the distributor's assets.[41]

Cash dividends are generally income, but the 1962 and 1997 Acts allocate cash dividends paid from capital gains by mutual funds to principal.[42] No such provision appears in the 1931 Act or the Restatement, but a court made the same allocation on the ground that a trustee's investment in mutual funds was "in substance nothing more than a fractional ownership in a diversified

**35.** 1997 Act § 104, comment, Example 3.

**36.** 1997 Act § 105.

**37.** 1962 Act § 6; 1931 Act § 5; *Restatement (Second) of Trusts* § 236 (1959).

**38.** A New York statute treats stock dividends of 6% or less as income. N.Y. EPTL § 11–2.1(e)(2). *See also* N.J.Stat. § 3B: 19–7(a) (4% or less); 20 Pa.Stat. § 8105(a); *cf.* South Carolina Nat. Bank v. Arrington, 165 S.E.2d 77, 81 (S.C.1968) (distinguishing between stock splits and stock dividends).

**39.** Matter of Estate of Dawson, 641 A.2d 1026, 1034 (N.J.1994). *See also* Estate of Reynolds, 432 A.2d 158 (Pa.1981) (distribution of 1 share for each 2 held allocated to principal).

**40.** Under this Act even distributions of the stock of a subsidiary company would be principal, but the 1931 and 1962 Acts treat distributions of securities other than those of the distributing corporation as income. 1931 Act § 5(1); 1962 Act § 6(d). *See also Restatement, Second, Trusts* § 236 (1959); First Wyoming Bank, N.A. v. First Nat. Bank, 628 P.2d 1355, 1365 (Wyo.1981). *But see* In re Anthony's Estate, 223 A.2d 857 (Pa.1966) (DuPont's distribution of General Motors' stock allocated to principal).

**41.** 1997 Act § 401.

**42.** 1962 Act § 6(c); 1997 Act § 401(b)(4).

portfolio of securities, as to which the trustee should account as if he held the portfolio securities directly."[43]

A distribution made on total liquidation of a corporation is usually principal even if paid in cash.[44] However, when a trust held stock in a company which earned substantial income but paid no dividends for several years and was eventually liquidated, the court upheld the trustee's decision to allocate part of the liquidation proceeds to income, partly on the basis of a provision in the will giving the trustee power to allocate receipts, partly because of the general duty of trustees "to make the trust property produce income."[45] The 1997 Act would have allowed a comparable transfer of cash from principal to income in this case, even if the trust had given the trustee no discretion to allocate.[46]

The 1997 Act gives trustees holding an unincorporated business leeway to decide the extent to which receipts should be allocated to income, "just as the board of directors of a corporation owned entirely by the trust would decide the amount of annual dividends to be paid to the trust."[47] This discretion is not unlimited. When a trust holds a controlling interest in a corporation, courts can "pierce the corporate veil" and treat corporate earnings as income of the trust even though they have not been declared as dividends. A probate court held that trustees had not generated enough earnings for the income beneficiaries and should "justify in the future any retention in excess of 25%" of the companies' net income. The appellate court upheld the court's power to make such an order, but only if "accumulation of retained earnings were so excessive as to amount to a breach of fiduciary duties."[48]

Interest paid on bonds is income. Proceeds received on redemption or sale are principal. Bonds which carry interest below the currently prevailing rate sell at a discount, whereas if they pay higher than market interest they sell at a premium. If trustees purchase high-interest bonds at a premium, the Restatement of Trusts allows them to allocate part of the interest to principal,[49] but the Uniform Acts reject this rule in order to simplify administration.[50] The 1962 Act makes a special provision for United States Series E bonds, which nominally pay no interest but provide for redemption at a fixed schedule of appreciation in excess of the price at which the bond was issued: this appreciation is treated as income.[51] The 1997 Act eliminates this provision, except in the case of bonds which mature within one year of their purchase.[52]

**43.** Tait v. Peck, 194 N.E.2d 707, 712 (Mass.1963). *See also* In re Latour's Estate, 260 A.2d 123 (N.H.1969); In re Estate of Rosenbloom, 452 A.2d 249 (Pa.Super.1982) (personal holding company).

**44.** 1962 Act § 6(b)(3); 1997 Act § 401(c)(3); 1931 Act § 5(3).

**45.** In re Frances M. Johnson Trust, 320 N.W.2d 466, 469 (Neb.1982).

**46.** 1997 Act § 104, comment, Examples 3 and 6.

**47.** 1997 Act § 403, comment.

**48.** Matter of Estate of Butterfield, 341 N.W.2d 453, 462 (Mich.1983). *See also* Russell v. Russell, 427 S.W.2d 471, 479 (Mo.1968); *cf.* In re Trust of Warner, 117 N.W.2d 224 (Minn. 1962) (holding company's entity disregarded); Jennings v. Speaker, 571 P.2d 358 (Kan.App. 1977).

**49.** *Restatement (Second) of Trusts* § 239, comm. f (1959). No comparable adjustment is made for bonds purchased at a discount. *Id.* § 240, comm. h.

**50.** 1931 Act § 6; 1962 Act § 7(a); 1997 Act § 406(a).

**51.** 1962 Act § 7(b).

**52.** 1997 Act § 406(b).

### *Wasting Assets*

Some property is destined to lose its value over time. Oil wells, for example, eventually run dry. If all the receipts from such a "wasting asset" are classified as income, principal would not be preserved. Nevertheless under the common-law "open mines" rule, "if mines were opened prior to the creation of the estates the life tenant is entitled to continue to work the mines and to take the proceeds as his own without deduction for depletion. On the other hand, where no mines were opened prior to the creation of the estates * * * the proceeds will be treated as principal" if mines are opened thereafter.[53] The 1962 Uniform Act, on the other hand, apportions oil royalties: 27 1/2% go to principal as an allowance for depletion, and the remainder is income.[54] The 1997 Act replaces this with a 90% allocation of receipts to principal and expressly rejects the "open mines" doctrine.[55]

The 1962 Act uses a different formula for other wasting assets, such as patents and copyrights: receipts up to 5% per year of the inventory value of the asset are income, and the balance is principal.[56] The 1997 Act rejects this approach, since it "can produce an unfair result" (to income) when there is an "unexpected growth in the value of the asset" or (to principal) "if the receipts diminish more rapidly than expected." Instead the Act dictates the same 90/10 allocation of receipts used for mineral resources.[57]

Can trustees establish a reserve for depreciation for buildings? Must they? One court held that a testator who devised "net rental monies" to his children "did not intend that depreciation be deducted from the gross rental income ... since depreciation is an accounting adjustment which does not decrease the cash available to the lessor."[58] The 1962 Uniform Act, however, requires trustees to set up "a reasonable allowance for depreciation * * * under generally accepted accounting principles" for property acquired by trustees after the Act took effect.[59] The 1997 Act, on the other hand, simply permits trustees to create a reserve for depreciation. The comment notes that such a reserve "has been resisted by many trustees" because it is "not needed to protect the remainder beneficiaries if the value of the land is increasing."[60]

### *Apportionment Over Time*

**53.** First Wyoming Bank v. First Nat. Bank, 628 P.2d 1355, 1365 (Wyo.1981) (quoting Scott on Trusts). *See also Restatement (Second) of Trusts* § 239, comm. g (1959); Section 9.3, note 15. In McGill v. Johnson, 775 S.W.2d 826, 833 (Tex.App.1989) the court gave an income beneficiary royalties even on leases executed after the testator's death where the trustee had explicit power to execute the lease.

**54.** 1962 Act § 9(a)(3). The 1931 Act, § 9, allocates all oil royalties to principal. See Millikin Trust Co. v. Jarvis, 180 N.E.2d 759 (Ill. App.1962). The figure in the 1962 Act was derived from the rule then used for computing income for tax purposes. Some statutes refer directly to the governing tax rule as it changes from time to time. Neb.Rev.Stat. § 30–3110(c).

**55.** 1997 Act § 411.

**56.** 1962 Act § 11. A similar apportionment formula is in the 1931 Act § 10, but it applies only if the trustee has a duty to change the form of the investment.

**57.** 1997 Act § 410.

**58.** In re Estate of Krotz, 522 N.E.2d 790, 794 (Ill.App.1988).

**59.** 1962 Act § 13(a)(2). There are many local variations in adopting states on this issue. New York for example did not adopt the depreciation provision of the 1962 Act. Matter of Will of Diamond, 519 N.Y.S.2d 788 (Sur.1987). In Florida, depreciation is taken only when the trust instrument so requires. Florida Coast Bank v. Mayes, 437 So.2d 160 (Fla.App.1983).

**60.** 1997 Act § 503. A reserve for depreciation is not even allowed in the case of a residence held for the enjoyment of a beneficiary. *See also Restatement, Second, Trusts* § 239, comm. h (1959).

Items like interest and rent are clearly income but they may be partially allocated to principal if the income beneficiary dies between payments. For example, a trust for the testator's wife provided that at her death, the corpus should pass to designated remaindermen. When the wife died the trustee held income which it had collected but not yet distributed, an asset on which interest was due to be paid after her death, and a dividend declared a few days before her death but paid thereafter. The trial court held that all undistributed income should be paid to the wife's estate, but on appeal this was reversed because the will said that "the trust property then [at the wife's death] remaining, including all accumulated income" went to the remaindermen.[61] Under the 1962 and 1931 Uniform Acts, unless the instrument provides otherwise, periodic payments like rent and interest are "accrued from day to day" and the estate of a deceased income beneficiary gets a share when they are ultimately paid.[62] Under the 1997 Act, on the other hand, if the will had been silent, the wife's estate would have received no accrued interest, but undistributed income which the trustee had received prior to her death would go to her estate in order "to avoid disputes about whether the trustees should have distributed collected cash before the income beneficiary died."[63]

Apportionment problems can also arise at the beginning of a trust. For example, a trust provided that the settlor's husband should receive the income for his life. She died owning E Bonds with over $343,000 in accrued interest. Under the controlling 1962 Act, this accrued interest was treated as income.[64] The husband was entitled to income from the date of his wife's death, but not interest which had accrued before that date. The 1997 Act also provides that an income beneficiary of a testamentary trust gets income from the date of the testator's death "even if there is an intervening period of administration of the testator's estate."[65]

Suppose that a testator holds stock on which a dividend is declared before she dies, but paid after her death. If the will puts the stock into a trust, does the dividend go to the income beneficiary? This depends upon the "record date," the date fixed by the company for determining who is entitled to receive the dividend "or, if no date is fixed, on the declaration date of the dividend." If the relevant date occurred prior to the testator's death, the dividend is assigned to principal.[66]

**61.** Hedrick v. West One Bank, 853 P.2d 548 (Idaho 1993).

**62.** 1962 Act § 4(d); 1931 Act § 4. The court in *Hedrick* did not apply the Act because the trust document controlled.

**63.** 1997 Act § 303(b), comment. Under *Restatement, Second, Trusts* § 235 (1959) interest is apportioned but not rent.

**64.** Under the 1997 Act, however, as we have seen, the money received when the bond was redeemed would be treated as principal. See note 51, *supra*.

**65.** 1997 Act § 301. *See also* Matter of Estate of Hall, 469 N.E.2d 378 (Ill.App.1984) (income beneficiary of testamentary trust entitled to income during estate administration); *Restatement (Second) of Trusts* § 234 (1959).

**66.** 1997 Act § 302(c). *See also Restatement, Second, Trusts* § 236, comm. i (1959); 1962 Act § 4(e); 1931 Act § 5(5); McIlvaine v. AmSouth Bank, N.A., 581 So.2d 454 (Ala.1991) (estate of income beneficiary gets dividend where record date was the day of beneficiary's death); Estate of Wetherby, 197 Cal.Rptr. 689, 693 (App.1983) (income beneficiary's estate entitled to dividend when record date fell in the brief period during which he survived the testator).

### *Planning*

Most principal and income questions have been settled by statute, although the many differences in the statutes may present a choice-of-law problem.[67] Settlors or testators who do not like the statutory rules can provide otherwise, but to ascertain a client's views on all allocation issues would require a good deal of time which could better be spent on other questions.

Farr and Wright suggest a clause which allows trustees to make allocations "fairly and equitably."[68] This does not make clear what factors trustees should consider in such determinations. The 1997 Act, on the other hand, provides a long list of factors which trustees are supposed to consider in making "adjustments."[69]

Trusts can be drafted so that distributions do not depend on classification of items as income or principal. Most trusts allow invasion of principal to meet the needs of the "income" beneficiaries. A settlor may wish to have *all* distributions based on need, but, as we shall see in the next section, controversies about "need" may be harder to resolve than questions about what is "income." On the other hand, making distributions depend on "income" may distort investment decisions. Professor Bogert, for example, thought that "no reasonably prudent trustee * * * mindful of his duty to act impartially between income and remaindermen beneficiaries" could invest in shares of mutual funds because they produced so little income.[70] Conversely, trustees traditionally could not invest in wasting property because of their duty to preserve the principal, even though "wasting property may produce such high income that its net return—income less depreciation—is comparatively sound."[71] The allocation between principal and income required in many trusts is "profoundly inconsistent with the portfolio paradigm" of modern investment theory.[72] The 1997 Act attempts to avoid this problem by empowering trustees to make the necessary adjustments between principal and income "if the trustee manages trust assets as a prudent investor."[73]

It is also possible to allocate benefits from a trust wholly without regard to either income or need.

> [A] constant percentage rule allocates all receipts to principal, and on each payment date distributes as income a fixed percentage of the value of the principal. The annuity rule pays out a fixed dollar amount [which can be] corrected for changes in purchasing power. Both of these approaches * * * permit investment decisions to be made without regard to the form of return on the investment. * * * Furthermore, both rules are easy to administer.[74]

Trusts *must* use one of these two formulas, commonly called "unitrust" and "annuity," if a charitable remainder is to qualify for a federal income,

**67.** 1997 Act § 411, comment. For a general discussion of choice of law see Section 1.2.

**68.** J.Farr & J. Wright, *An Estate Planner's Handbook* 472 (4th ed. 1979).

**69.** 1997 Act § 104(b).

**70.** Bogert, *The Revised Principal and Income Act*, 38 N.D.Law. 50, 54 (1962).

**71.** Comment, 50 Texas L.Rev. 747, 763–64 (1972).

**72.** Gordon, *The Puzzling Persistence of the Constrained Prudent Man Rule,* 62 N.Y.U.L.Rev. 52, 101 (1987).

**73.** 1997 Act § 104(a). *See also* the Prefatory Note.

**74.** Note, 33 U.Chi.L.Rev. 783, 789 (1966). The fixed percentage formula requires periodic valuation of the trust assets; this may be difficult in some cases.

estate or gift tax deduction.[75]

## § 9.5 Discretionary Trusts

### *Reasons for Discretion*

A major advantage of trusts over guardianship is that trustees can be given discretion to make distributions to different beneficiaries. Most trusts give the trustee some such discretion. A power to distribute principal (sometimes called corpus) to an income beneficiary is very common. A power to accumulate income and add it to principal, or to "sprinkle" income and principal among a group of beneficiaries is also used with increasing frequency.

The Uniform Statutory Will contains several such provisions. It creates a trust under which the testator's spouse gets all the income[1], and the trustee may at any time pay to the spouse "amounts of principal which the trustee deems advisable."[2] Another trust directs the trustee to pay "the income and principal of the trust to ... one or more of the issue of the testator in amounts the trustee deems advisable for their needs for health, education, support or maintenance. Income not so paid may be added to principal."[3] When the beneficiaries of a trust are minors, it is advisable to direct that any income in excess of their current needs be accumulated and reinvested by the trustee, since otherwise it would have to be distributed to a guardian. A similar direction may also be advisable for adult beneficiaries who are or may become incompetent.

The financial needs of children vary as they grow up. One who is entering college usually needs more than siblings who are living at home attending public schools. Parents typically consider such differences in need in allocating their resources. If the parents die before their children are grown, a trustee can do the same. In this situation the question arises whether the trustee should take any excess distributions to one child into account when all the trust assets are finally distributed upon termination. If the settlor intends this, the trust instrument should make this clear, since courts may assume the settlor intended otherwise.[4]

Discretionary trusts offer income tax advantages. Since income of a trust is normally taxed to the person who receives it, trustees can reduce the total taxes paid by a family by distributing income to family members who are in lower tax brackets—children instead of their parents, for example, if the children are still in school and the parents have well-paying jobs. "It is normally appropriate, and often necessary, for a trustee to take tax consider-

**75.** See Section 15.3, note 156.

§ 9.5

1. Trustees who are directed to pay all the income to a beneficiary can do so "at reasonable intervals ... but at least annually." *Restatement, Third, Trusts* § 49, comm. c (1996).

**2.** Uniform Statutory Will Act § 6. In State Bank v. Cordes, 522 N.E.2d 783 (Ill.App.1988), a power to use principal for the beneficiary's support was inferred from language directing the trustee to "alleviate any needs" of the income beneficiaries.

**3.** *Id.*, § 8(b).

**4.** If the trust is silent, distributions are not treated as advancements. New England Merchants Nat. Bank v. Morin, 449 N.E.2d 682 (Mass.App.1983); *Restatement, Third, Trusts* § 50, comm. f (1998). However, trustees can make loans or advances to beneficiaries in lieu of outright distributions. *Id.*, comm. d.

ations into account in determining what discretionary decisions to make."[5] Tax rules are complex, however, and will be considered elsewhere—poorly drafted discretionary trusts can have adverse tax consequences.[6]

Giving trustees discretion over distributions of income is not usually advisable when a beneficiary is likely to need all the trust income, since disputes may arise between the beneficiaries and trustee as to how this discretion is exercised. One court, in approving a settlement of litigation over alleged abuse of discretion by a trustee, doubted that the settlor contemplated that "giving such broad discretion to [the trustee] would create such great dissension within [the settlor's] family and threaten to consume a substantial part of the trust corpus in litigation expenses."[7]

### *Judicial Review of Trustee's Discretion*

Judicial review of trustees' decisions takes several forms. Sometimes a remainderman seeks to enjoin a trustee from distributing corpus to an income beneficiary,[8] or to surcharge the trustee for distributions previously made.[9] Conversely, a beneficiary may complain of a trustee's refusal to make distributions. Courts may order trustees to make distributions,[10] or make up for payments which should have been made in the past,[11] including payments to the estate of a beneficiary who has since died.[12] Courts may also "issue instructions to clarify the standards or guidelines applicable to" discretionary powers,[13] "deny or diminish the trustee's compensation, ... or even remove the trustee for repeated or serious abuse of the discretionary power."[14]

Reported cases involving claims by beneficiaries that trustees were too stingy or overly generous in exercising discretion are relatively uncommon, because courts rarely overrule trustees' decisions. For example, when a trust allowed distributions of corpus "if it should become necessary or desirable, in the judgment and discretion of the Trustees," the trustee's decision not to invade principal was upheld, the court saying that "a trustee's exercise of discretion should not be overruled by a court unless the trustee has clearly

5. *Id.*, comm. e.

6. As to the income taxation of trusts and trust distributions see Section 15.1. As to the possible loss of the marital deduction from discretionary provisions in trusts see Section 15.3. As to the risk that a trustee with discretionary powers may be deemed to have a general power of appointment see Section 15.3. As to the possibility that discretionary distributions may trigger a generation skipping tax see Section 15.4

7. Connecticut Bank and Trust Co. v. Coffin, 563 A.2d 1323, 1337 (Conn.1989).

8. Ballenger v. Ballenger, 694 S.W.2d 72 (Tex.App.1985).

9. Austin v. U.S. Bank of Washington, 869 P.2d 404 (Wash.App.1994); Dunkley v. Peoples Bank & Trust Co., 728 F.Supp. 547 (W.D.Ark. 1989); Feibelman v. Worthen Nat. Bank, N.A., 20 F.3d 835 (8th Cir.1994). As to the possibility that a trustee may claim reimbursement from a beneficiary to whom the trustee has made wrongful distributions see Section 12.10, at note 49 et seq.

10. Kolodney v. Kolodney, 503 A.2d 625 (Conn.App.1986).

11. Matter of Estate of Lindgren, 885 P.2d 1280, 1283 (Mont.1994); Matter of Estate of McCart, 847 P.2d 184 (Colo.App.1992).

12. Marsman v. Nasca, 573 N.E.2d 1025 (Mass.App.1991); Third Nat. Bank v. Brown, 691 S.W.2d 557 (Tenn.App.1985).

13. Barnett Banks Trust Co. v. Herr, 546 So.2d 755 (Fla.App.1989); Godfrey v. Chandley, 811 P.2d 1248 (Kan.1991) (declaratory judgment). In Windishar v. Windishar, 731 P.2d 445 (Or.App.1986), the beneficiary did not ask that the trustee be ordered to make specific payments, so the court gave only the "very general" instruction that "the discretion has been exercised less liberally than the trustors intended."

14. *Restatement, Third, Trusts* § 50, comm. b (1998). As to the compensation and removal of trustees and other fiduciaries see Sections 12.4–12.5.

abused the discretion granted him under the trust instrument or acted arbitrarily."[15] If a trial court upholds the trustee, the chances of success on appeal are limited, since the question of whether the trustee has abused discretion is one of fact.[16] However, courts do occasionally overturn trustees' decisions, even if the trust instrument gives the trustee "sole discretion." For example, a trust provided an annuity for the settlor's sister "and such additional sums as may be required for any emergency or need in the sole discretion of the trustee." Despite the "sole discretion" language, the court held that the trustee had acted improperly in paying the sister $1,000 a month: "A trustee should not increase trust payments based upon 'need' or 'emergency,' where the beneficiary has accumulated assets" of her own."[17] Conversely, another trustee was ordered to increase payments to a beneficiary from $1,000 to $2,500 a month. Reference in the trust instrument to the beneficiary's "comfortable maintenance and support" showed that the "trustee's discretion was not intended to be absolute" despite the words "sole discretion."[18] Another trustee who was authorized to distribute income to the settlor's daughter and her descendants, was held to have acted improperly in distributing all the income to the daughter without investigating the needs of her descendants. Although the trust terms gave the trustee with "wide discretion," but it had "to act reasonably" and "should have taken into consideration the financial needs" of the other beneficiaries.[19]

A clause which purports to relieve a trustee from accountability for its decisions is ineffective.[20] A "trustee" who is not subject to account makes no sense. A settlor who really intended a trustee to be absolutely free of supervision would make an outright gift. A *trust* connotes *some* control over the trustee.[21]

Courts do *not* defer to a trustee's interpretation of ambiguous language in a trust instrument. When a company construed the terms of its pension plan as not to provide benefits to employees who lost their jobs when plants were sold, the court refused to apply "a deferential standard of review appropriate when a trustee exercises discretionary powers ... Courts construe terms in trust agreements without deferring to either party's interpretation."[22]

**15.** NationsBank of Virginia v. Estate of Grandy, 450 S.E.2d 140, 1433 (Va.1994). *See also Restatement, Third, Trusts* § 50 (1998); Matter of Roberts, 461 N.E.2d 300 (N.Y.1984).

**16.** In the Matter of Campbell's Trusts, 258 N.W.2d 856 (Minn.1977). Conversely, a trial court's decision that a trustee abused its discretion "will be disturbed on appeal only if * * * manifestly wrong." Gulf Nat. Bank v. Sturtevant, 511 So.2d 936 (Miss.1987); Matter of Estate of McCart, 847 P.2d 184 (Colo.App. 1992).

**17.** Austin v. U.S. Bank of Washington, 869 P.2d 404 (Wash.App.1994). Further discussion as to the consideration of a beneficiary's own resources in determining "need" appears below.

**18.** Kolodney v. Kolodney, 503 A.2d 625, 627 (Conn.App.1986). *See also* Pollok v. Phillips, 411 S.E.2d 242 (W.Va.1991); Unif.Trust Code § 814(a) (despite "absolute" discretion, trustee must act "in good faith and with regard to the purposes of the trust").

**19.** In re Estate of Winograd, 582 N.E.2d 1047, 1050 (Ohio App.1989).

**20.** Briggs v. Crowley, 224 N.E.2d 417 (Mass.1967); *Restatement (Third) of Trusts* § 50, comment c (1998); Matter of Estate of Thomson, 487 N.E.2d 1193 (Ill.App.1986); *cf.* Uniform Trust Code § 104(b) (limiting the Code provisions which the trust terms can override).

**21.** When the terms of a "trust" are extremely vague, a court may find that in fact no trust was intended, and the "trustee" can keep the property. See Section 4.6, note 65.

**22.** Firestone Tire and Rubber Co. v. Bruch, 489 U.S. 101, 111–12 (1989).

In reviewing a trustee's action, the language of the trust instrument is important, *i.e.,* the "existence or non-existence, the definiteness or indefiniteness, of an external standard by which the reasonableness of the trustee's conduct can be judged."[23] If a trust instrument directs a trustee to pay whatever amount it "deems necessary for the support" of a beneficiary, a court will order the trustee to increase payments if the court finds that they were inadequate for support.[24] On the other hand, if the trustees are to make distributions as they "deem best," judicial review is very limited.[25] Thus a trustee's decision to distribute to a beneficiary so he could provide for his step-children was upheld where the instrument allowed the trustee to invade principal "for the benefit of" the designated beneficiaries. "The word 'benefit' ... is more comprehensive than the word 'support.' "[26] Under the Restatement, "benefit" may "authorize discretionary expenditures that fall beyond the usual scope of a support-related standard," but it does not necessarily authorize courts to *compel* such distributions when a trustee does not choose to make them.[27]

The word "support"[28] is defined by reference to the beneficiary's station in life; the trustee is bound to maintain the beneficiary "in accordance with the standard of living which was normal for him before he became a beneficiary of the trust."[29] A trustee was held to have abused its discretion in paying a beneficiary only $700 a month when the settlor "was clearly well to do * * * travelled frequently," lived in a house that stood on 8 acres of land and "had several domestic servants."[30] The size of the trust may also be relevant in determining the appropriate level of support. Where a beneficiary over time comes to enjoy a higher standard of living, this "may become the appropriate standard of support if consistent with the trust's level of productivity." Conversely, "a lower level of distributions may be justifiable if the trust estate is modest relative to the probable future needs of the beneficiary."[31]

If the trust instrument refers to the beneficiary's "comfort" or "happiness," it is not clear how much weight these expressions carry. Any words may be limited by their context. When a trust allowed corpus to be invaded "for the support, maintenance, *benefit* and education" of a beneficiary, the beneficiary requested $4.5 million to buy a jet plane, the court rejected his claim that "benefit" was an independent basis for invading principal.[32] The word "comfort," when "part of a clause referencing the support, maintenance

**23.** *Restatement (Second) of Trusts* § 187, comment d (1959).

**24.** Kolodney v. Kolodney, 503 A.2d 625 (Conn.App.1986); Matter of Estate of Lindgren, 885 P.2d 1280 (Mont.1994); Marsman v. Nasca, 573 N.E.2d 1025 (Mass.App.1991).

**25.** American Cancer Soc. v. Hammerstein, 631 S.W.2d 858 (Mo.App.1981); First Nat. Bank v. Department of Health, 399 A.2d 891 (Md.1979).

**26.** Ewing v. Ruml, 892 F.2d 168, 172–73 (2d Cir.1989). *See also* Estate of Hartzell, T.C.Memo 1994-576 ("well-being" standard allows distributions in order to enable gifts by beneficiary).

**27.** *Restatement, Third, Trusts* § 50, comm.d (1998).

**28.** Often joined with "maintenance;" the two words are synonymous. *Restatement, Third, Trusts* § 50, comm. d (1998).

**29.** Marsman v. Nasca, 573 N.E.2d 1025, 1030 (Mass.App.1991).

**30.** Gulf Nat. Bank v. Sturtevant, 511 So.2d 936 (Miss.1987).

**31.** *Restatement, Third, Trusts* § 50, comm. e (1998).

**32.** Stuart v. Wilmington Trust Co., 474 A.2d 121 (Del.1984).

and education of the beneficiary" means only what is "reasonably necessary to maintain the beneficiary in his accustomed manner of living."[33]

Review of trustees' discretionary decisions sometimes reflects assumptions that the settlor preferred certain beneficiaries. A trustee's denial of a payment requested by the settlor's widow was upheld when the settlor's "children were his primary concern and any provision for his wife * * * was clearly secondary,"[34] whereas invasion of principal for a widow was approved where "the testator was concerned primarily with his wife's comfort and any residue to others was secondary."[35] The trust instrument may indicate the settlor's preferences; for example, "my primary concern in establishing this trust is my wife's welfare and the welfare of my children while they are under age twenty-one and the interests of others in the trust are to be subordinate to theirs."[36] Even without such a clause, a spouse or child of the settlor is more likely to prevail than other beneficiaries.[37]

Courts may distinguish between income and principal even when the trust instrument gives the trustee the same powers over both. A trustee who was directed to "distribute to my spouse ... as much of the income and principal ... as the trustee believes desirable" for his support, was surcharged for excessive distributions of principal whereas the income payments were not considered unreasonable.[38] Conversely, a trustee under a similar clause was rebuked for "niggardliness" when it accumulated much of the trust income.[39] A refusal to invade principal can be thought to serve the long term interests of a beneficiary who requests it, since "a reduction of principal could leave the beneficiary in want later in life."[40]

Many trusts name a beneficiary as trustee. The resultant conflict of interest may affect judicial review of trustees' decisions. A trustee who refused to make payments to the settlor's spouse was held to have "acted with improper motives and with a clear conflict of interest ... by seeking to preserve the trust funds for himself and his heirs as remaindermen."[41] Some jurisdictions even prohibit trustees from participating in decisions in which they have such a conflict of interest; a disinterested co-trustee must act in their place.[42] But most courts defer to the judgment of the settlor who created the conflict of interest in the apparent belief that the beneficiary-trustee would act fairly, and approve exercise of discretionary powers from which the trustee benefits if they are deemed reasonable.[43] However, because of the

**33.** Estate of Vissering v. C.I.R., 990 F.2d 578, 581 (10th Cir.1993).

**34.** In re Flyer's Will, 245 N.E.2d 718, 720 (N.Y.1969).

**35.** Hart v. Connors, 228 N.E.2d 273, 275 (Ill.App.1967).

**36.** Uniform Statutory Will Act § 8(a).

**37.** *Restatement, Third, Trusts* § 50, comm. f (1998).

**38.** Dunkley v. Peoples Bank & Trust Co., 728 F.Supp. 547, 564 (W.D.Ark.1989).

**39.** Old Colony Trust Company v. Rodd, 254 N.E.2d 886, 890 (Mass.1970).

**40.** Emmert v. Old Nat. Bank, 246 S.E.2d 236 (W.Va.1978). *See also* In Matter of Campbell's Trusts, 258 N.W.2d 856 (Minn.1977); Barnard v. U.S. Nat. Bank, 495 P.2d 766 (Or. App.1972).

**41.** Matter of Estate of McCart, 847 P.2d 184, 186 (Colo.App.1992). *See also* Firestone Tire and Rubber Co. v. Bruch, 489 U.S. 101, 115 (1989); Pollok v. Phillips, 411 S.E.2d 242 (W.Va.1991).

**42.** Matter of Estate of Seidman, 395 N.Y.S.2d 674 (A.D.1977); First Union Nat. Bank v. Cisa, 361 S.E.2d 615 (S.C.1987). Some conflict of interest exists in all trusts in which the trustee's compensation is based on the size of the trust (as is common), but this is rarely mentioned by courts.

**43.** *E.g.* Bracken v. Block, 561 N.E.2d 1273 (Ill.App.1990); *Restatement, Third, Trusts* § 50, illus. 1 (1998).

adverse tax consequences of a power of a trustee-beneficiary to distribute to him or herself, the Uniform Trust Code allows such distributions "only in accordance with an ascertainable standard relating to the trustee's health, education, support or maintenance within the meaning of ... the Internal Revenue Code" unless the terms of the trust expressly indicate that a broader discretion was intended.[44]

### *Other Resources*

Claims for support raise the question whether other resources of the beneficiary should be considered. If a trust provides for the support of a person who needs $50,000 a year and has a job which pays $35,000 a year, should the trustee take the beneficiary's earnings into account? potential earnings if the beneficiary refuses to maximize his or her earning potential? income from assets which the beneficiary owns outside the trust? Should the trustee require the beneficiary to sell such assets before resorting to the trust?

The judicial opinions which discuss this issue are hard to reconcile, because the language of the governing instrument and the circumstances vary in every case. One court upheld a trustee's refusal a consider a beneficiary's request for a distribution until the beneficiary provided information regarding his outside sources of income.[45] But another held that since the trust instrument "does not provide for the expenditure of the Beneficiary's estate before any payments are to be made from the Trust, we will not read into the instrument this limitation."[46] The Restatement of Trust presumes that the trustee "is to consider other resources but has some discretion in the matter."[47] However, a trustee who distributed principal to a beneficiary without determining what other funds she might have was held to have shown "reckless disregard" for the rights of the remaindermen.[48]

Some courts distinguish between income and principal; a trustee should consider the beneficiary's income from all sources but the beneficiary's own principal need not be depleted before resorting to the trust.[49] However, there may be tax advantages in a beneficiary's depleting his own assets if they will be subject to estate tax at death before using the trust funds (if they will not be subject to tax). On the other hand, it is undesirable to force beneficiaries to sell assets which are not readily marketable to raise needed funds. Yet sometimes it is the trust which holds illiquid assets which would have to be sold to satisfy a request for a distribution of principal.

**44.** Uniform Trust Code § 814(b). As to the tax problem at which this is directed see Section 15.3, note 125.

**45.** NCNB Nat. Bank v. Shanaberger, 616 So.2d 96 (Fla.App.1993). *See also* Matter of Estate of Winston, 613 N.Y.S.2d 461 (A.D. 1994); NationsBank of Virginia v. Estate of Grandy, 450 S.E.2d 140 (Va.1994). According to the Restatement, the trustee "generally may rely on beneficiary's representations" as to other resources unless "the trustee has reason to suspect that the information thus supplied is inaccurate or incomplete." *Restatement, Third, Trusts* § 50, comm. e (1998).

**46.** Matter of Estate of Lindgren, 885 P.2d 1280, 1283 (Mont.1994). *See also* Godfrey v. Chandley, 811 P.2d 1248 (Kan.1991); Matter of Estate of McNab, 558 N.Y.S.2d 751 (A.D.1990).

**47.** *Restatement, Third, Trusts* § 50, comm. e (1998).

**48.** Feibelman v. Worthen Nat. Bank, N.A., 20 F.3d 835 (8th Cir.1994).

**49.** Barnett Banks Trust Co. v. Herr, 546 So.2d 755 (Fla.App.1989); Hart v. Connors, 228 N.E.2d 273 (Ill.App.1967).

Should trustees consider a beneficiary's right to support from a parent or spouse of the beneficiary? One court allowed use of trust funds to support a child on the ground that the parents' duty to support the child was reducible by the child's other resources.[50] But the Restatement presumes that "the trustee is to take account of a parental duty to support a youthful beneficiary" on the ground that "only the parents would be likely to be benefited if the trustee provides what the child is entitled to in any event."[51]

### *Welfare Eligibility*

A frequently litigated issue in recent years has been the effect of a discretionary trust on a beneficiary's eligibility for governmental welfare benefits. For example, the mother of a man who was receiving health care from a state agency created a trust for him. The agency terminated his benefits, saying that the trust rendered him ineligible. The court disagreed, because this was a "discretionary" trust.

> Courts usually conclude that a support trust is an available asset, while a discretionary trust is not ... because a beneficiary of a support trust can legally compel the trustee to distribute trust assets to him or her, but a beneficiary of a discretionary trust has no such power.[52]

The distinction between "discretionary" and "support" trusts is often repeated,[53] but is not really workable, since trusts which provide "support" for a beneficiary give the trustee some discretion in determining how much the beneficiary should get.

Some courts have said that trust assets should be considered in determining welfare eligibility because "public assistance funds are ever in short supply, and public policy demands they be restricted to those without resources of their own."[54] Many courts, however, reject this analysis. For example, one said that the settlor was under no "obligation to provide for the support of his adult child ... [He] intended to provide his daughter with a source of supplemental support that would not jeopardize her access to basic assistance from Medicaid ... We decline ... to hold the ... trust provision unenforceable on public policy grounds."[55] Another court has said that "it would be a divorce from the reality of life to presume that [the settlor] would

**50.** McElrath v. Citizens & Southern Nat. Bank, 189 S.E.2d 49 (Ga.1972).

**51.** *Restatement, Third, Trusts* § 50, comm. e (1998). *See also* In re Estate of LaRose, 1 P.3d 1018, 1023 (Okl.Civ.App.1999) (parents' funds should be used to support child before guardianship estate); In re Marriage of Hoak, 364 N.W.2d 185 (Iowa 1985).

**52.** Matter of Leona Carlisle Trust, 498 N.W.2d 260, 264 (Minn.App.1993).

**53.** Chenot v. Bordeleau, 561 A.2d 891 (R.I. 1989); Kryzsko v. Ramsey County Social Services, 607 N.W.2d 237, 239 (N.D.2000); Myers v. Kansas Dept. of Social & Rehab. Serv., 866 P.2d 1052 (Kan.1994).

**54.** State ex rel. Sec'y of SRS v. Jackson, 822 P.2d 1033, 1040 (Kan.1991). *See also* Department of Mental Health v. First Nat. Bank, 432 N.E.2d 1086, 1089 (Ill.App.1982); In re Trust of Holmquist, 357 N.W.2d 7 (Wis.App. 1984) (trustee ordered to pay principal to county health care center to cover beneficiary's expenses).

**55.** Young v. Ohio Dept. of Human Serv., 668 N.E.2d 908, 911–12 (Ohio 1996). *See also* Myers v. Kansas of Social & Rehab. Serv., 866 P.2d 1052, 1056 (Kan.1994) (policy does not override settlor's intent). *But see* Estate of Rosenberg v. Department of Public Welfare, 679 A.2d 767 (Pa.1996) (discretionary trust renders beneficiary ineligible for Medicaid); Kryzsko v. Ramsey County Social Services, 607 N.W.2d 237 (N.D.2000).

intend the amount of the trust to be paid to [the state] in preference to having society share the burden."[56]

The result is different when the beneficiary of a discretionary trust is also the settlor. Congress enacted in 1986 a statute dealing with "medicaid qualifying trusts." The name is odd, since such trusts actually *dis*qualify the beneficiary from medicaid. MQTs are defined as trusts created "by an individual (or an individual's spouse) under which the individual may be the beneficiary of ... payments from the trust" in the trustee's discretion, "whether or not the discretion ... is actually exercised."[57] In an MQT "whatever is the most the beneficiary might receive in the full exercise of [the trustee's] discretion is ... counted as available for Medicaid eligibility."[58] However, the statute allows "supplemental needs" trusts which are not counted in determining medicaid eligibility "if the State will receive all amounts remaining in the trust upon the death of upon the death of" the beneficiary to the extent the beneficiary has received medical assistance from the state.[59]

The statute sometimes gives rise to the question who the settlor of a trust actually was. For example, a man settled a claim arising from a disabling injury. The settlement proceeds were placed in a discretionary trust, which was later held to be a MQT. "The fact that the trust ... was established ... by a probate court, as settlor, is inconsequential ... The trust property already belonged to the beneficiary."[60] A discretionary trust established by the beneficiary's spouse is also an MQT—for this purpose the old treatment of spouses as one person governs.[61] But a trust created by a parent for a child, for example, is exempt.

### *Drafting*

The drafter ought to deal with the question of outside resources. One possibility is to give the trustee leeway to consider "to the extent the trustee deems advisable, any income or other resources of that beneficiary known to the trustee and reasonably available."[62]

A clause which authorizes a trustee to use funds for a number of persons, such as the settlor's children, ought to make clear that (1) not every member of the group must receive a distribution,[63] and (2) the income need not all be

**56.** Maul v. Fitzgerald, 432 N.Y.S.2d 282, 284 (A.D.1980). *See also Restatement, Third, Trusts* § 50, comm. e (1998).

**57.** 42 U.S.C. § 1396a(k).

**58.** Cohen v. Commissioner of Div. of Med. Asst., 668 N.E.2d 769, 777 (Mass.1996) ; Oxenhorn v. Fleet Trust Co., 722 N.E.2d 492 (N.Y. 1999) (Medicaid benefits paid by mistake to beneficiary of MQT can be recovered).

**59.** 42 U.S.C. § 1396p(d)(4)(A). *See also* Department of Social Serv. v. Saunders, 724 A.2d 1093 (Conn.1999) (authorizing the use of settlement proceeds to create such a trust on behalf of an incompetent claimant).

**60.** Barham by Barham v. Rubin, 816 P.2d 965, 967 (Haw.1991). *See also* Cohen v. Commissioner of Div. of Med. Asst., 668 N.E.2d 769 (Mass.1996); Forsyth v. Rowe, 629 A.2d 379 (Conn.1993); Matter of Kindt, 542 N.W.2d 391 (Minn.App.1996).

A similar problem arises with respect to spendthrift trusts. See Section 13.1, at note 78 et seq.

**61.** Gulick v. Department of Health & Rehab. Serv., 615 So.2d 192 (Fla.App.1993); Prior v. Ohio Dept. of Human Serv., 704 N.E.2d 296 (Ohio App.1997). However, the statute does not apply to a trust created by will, so a *testamentary* trust created by one spouse for another is not an MQT.

**62.** *cf.* Uniform Statutory Will Act § 6(2).

**63.** As to the distinction between "exclusive" and "non-exclusive" powers see Section 10.4, at note 73 et seq.

distributed, assuming that the settlor wishes maximum flexibility. The Uniform Statutory Will Act, for example, directs the trustee to pay income and principal to "one or more of the issue of the testator * * * Income not so paid may be added to principal."[64]

If the settlor is concerned that the trustee may be too conservative in making distributions, language indicative of generosity may help, *e.g.*, a recital that the income beneficiaries are settlor's "primary concern." Or an income beneficiary can be made a co-trustee, or be given power to remove the trustee and appoint another. If there are co-trustees, there may be a deadlock if they cannot agree, but a beneficiary co-trustee who sues to resolve a deadlock will not encounter the typical judicial deference for trustees' decisions. In some states it may be necessary to make clear that the beneficiary can participate in a decision to make distributions to himself.

Another alternative is to give the *beneficiary* a power to invade principal. This is common when the settlor has confidence in the beneficiary's judgment and puts the assets in trust simply to avoid having them taxed in the beneficiary's estate. Of course, in this situation the tax rules should be carefully studied, in order to make sure that the beneficiary's power does not defeat the tax objective.[65]

### *Factors Other than Need*

Discretion usually involves an assessment of beneficiaries' needs, but the settlor may want other factors considered as well. Clauses framed in terms of "support" may not be adequate in such cases. Even if all the beneficiaries have more income than they need for support, it may be desirable to distribute trust income to one who is in a lower income-tax bracket than the others. A discretionary power which is not limited by any standard can avoid the "troublesome question whether distributions can properly be made purely for tax reasons to selected beneficiaries."[66] There may be other reasons for a distribution as well. For example, trustees distributed the stock of a company to an income beneficiary because they feared "chaos" would result from dividing it among the remaindermen. The court allowed this because the will authorized the trustees to terminate the trust if they "should deem it best" to do so.[67]

Settlors may also wish a trustee to consider the beneficiary's ability to handle funds. Many trusts provide for distribution when a beneficiary attains a certain age. Since settlors can rarely predict when beneficiaries will achieve maturity, it may be better to let the trustee decide when a beneficiary is mature enough to receive the principal. The Uniform Statutory Will Act

**64.** Uniform Statutory Will Act § 8(b).

**65.** As to the income and estate tax consequences of such powers see Section 15.3. A beneficiary's power may also give creditors of the beneficiary greater rights to reach the interest. See Section 13.1, at note 29.

**66.** *Restatement, Third, Trusts* § 50, comm. e (1998).

**67.** American Cancer Soc'y v. Hammerstein, 631 S.W.2d 858 (Mo.App.1981). *See also Restatement, Third, Trusts* § 50, illus. 4 (distribution to enable B to "acquire a home and to advance her career and investment objectives" proper under "best interests" standard) (1998) *But see id*, illus. 3 (similar distribution improper under a "support" standard); Kemp by Buchanan v. Paterson, 159 N.E.2d 661 (N.Y.1959) (power to pay principal for "best interest" of beneficiary does not allow termination of trust for tax savings); Wright v. Trust Co. Bank, 396 S.E.2d 213 (Ga.1990) ("reasonable need" does not allow accommodation of beneficiary's wish to make an investment).

allows trustees to retain property which would otherwise be distributable "to an individual who * * * the trustee determines cannot effectively manage the property." The property becomes distributable "upon removal of the (individual's) disability."[68]

### *Single versus Separate Trusts*

Related to the question of discretionary versus fixed-benefit trusts is the question *how many* trusts should be created. Is it better to create a single trust for all the beneficiaries (the testator/settlor's children, for example), or separate trusts for each? This depends on whether the settlor wants the children to receive equal benefits, or prefers to allow the trustee to give more to one child than to another based on need or some other criterion. This choice often depends upon the ages of the children and on the size of the trust estate. If a modest fund is being used to provide for young children, since one child may have greater need than the others in a particular year, a single trust with discretion in the trustee is usually desirable. At the other extreme is a large estate held in trust for children of full age. Most parents want their children to receive equal shares in this situation, so separate trusts for each child are more suitable (assuming that the childrens' shares are held in trust and not distributed to them outright). With separate trusts, the trustee can satisfy reasonable requests by one child for early distribution of his or her share (*e.g.* in order to buy a house or start a business), without affecting the shares of the child's siblings.

Some settlors provide for single and separate trusts at different stages; a single trust for the children so long as they are all young in which the trustee distributes income and principal as necessary for their support and education, accumulating any excess income. When all of the children have reached a specified age, the trustee divides the property into separate trusts for each child (or distributes the trust assets outright at that point).

### *Indefinite Beneficiaries*

A trust is sometimes held invalid if the trustee has *too much* discretion in choosing beneficiaries on the theory that a trust must have ascertainable beneficiaries to enforce it.[69] For example, a woman left her estate to her sister "to distribute among my heirs, named legatees, and such other persons she may deem deserving in such proportion as she shall deem just." This language was held to create a trust which failed because there were "no named beneficiaries to enforce" it.[70] When a will directed the residuary estate to "be divided among my close friends in such a way * * * as my trustee in her discretion should determine," the gift failed and the residue passed intestate to the testator's heirs, because the words "close friends * * * are too uncertain."[71]

The vice in these cases was the lack of ascertainable beneficiaries, not the absence of a standard to govern the trustee's discretion. A will can authorize

**68.** Uniform Statutory Will Act § 9.

**69.** *Restatement, Third, Trusts* § 44 (1999).

**70.** In re Kradwell's Estate, 170 N.W.2d 773 (Wis.1969). *See also* Matter of Estate of Boyer, 868 P.2d 1299 (N.M.App.1994).

**71.** Re Connor, 10 Dom.L.R.3d 5, 11 (Alberta 1970). *See also* Klassen v. Klassen, [1986] 5 W.W.R. 746 (Sask.Q.B.).

trustees to distribute property "among my surviving children * * * in such manner as [they] * * * consider to be most appropriate."[72] The trust beneficiaries need not be named in the trust instrument; a trust for a class like "my children" is clearly valid, even if they are not born when the trust is created.[73]

Courts have resorted to various techniques to save trusts from invalidity on the grounds of uncertainty. Vague terms when appended to more definite ones may be ignored. When a will directed trustees to distribute to "worthy charities, institutions and individuals," the court avoided invalidity by a limiting construction.

> The word "worthy," as used by the testatrix, was meant by her to refer only to an institution which would fall within the legal definition of charity. * * * If there be any doubt, a testator is presumed to intend the meaning which makes his gift legally effective rather than one which renders it nugatory and void.[74]

But other courts on similar facts have refused to perform such surgery.[75]

The term "relatives" is construed to mean heirs in order to avoid uncertainty; the limits of the class are fixed by the laws of intestate succession.[76] The word "family" may also be construed in this way.[77]

Invalidity can also be avoided if the troublesome language is construed as an outright devise with precatory suggestions rather than a trust. When a will left the estate to a woman "to divide and disperse as she sees fit," the court held that she took the property outright.[78] But other courts have rejected this solution in similar situations. When a will devised the residue to the executors to distribute "to whatever persons and/or charitable organizations they shall determine," the court refused to construe this as a gift to the executors. "It was [the testator's] intention to bequeath the residue to the executors for their individual benefit she could simply have said so. She did not."[79]

*Trusts* must have definite beneficiaries but no such requirement exists for *powers of appointment*.[80] The Restatement of Trusts holds that a direction to *A* to distribute property among an indefinite group of persons gives *A* "power but no duty to distribute the property" to the person(s) *A* may select.[81] The fear that *A* may appropriate the property if there are no beneficiaries to enforce the trust is illusory, because the settlor's heirs can compel *A* to convey

**72.** Deal v. Huddleston, 702 S.W.2d 404 (Ark.1986).

**73.** *Restatement, Third, Trusts* § 45 (1999).

**74.** Newick v. Mason, 581 A.2d 1269 (Me. 1990). *See also* Armington v. Meyer, 236 A.2d 450 (R.I.1967) (employees and acquaintances construed to mean employees); Section 9.7, note 49.

**75.** Klassen v. Klassen, [1986] 5 W.W.R. 746 (Sask.Q.B.) (devise to "persons and/or charitable organization" determined by executors fails).

**76.** *Restatement, Third, Trusts* § 45, comm. d (1999).

**77.** McLendon v. Priest, 376 S.E.2d 679 (Ga.1989) (contract to leave property to spouse's "family" construed to mean heirs).

**78.** Tucker v. Bradford, 599 So.2d 611 (Ala. 1992). *See also Restatement, Third, Trusts* § 13, illus. 5–7 (1999); Section 4.6, at note 64 et seq.

**79.** Klassen v. Klassen, [1986] 5 W.W.R. 746, 756 (Sask.Q.B.). *See also Restatement, Second, of Property (Donative Transfers)* § 12.1, comm. e (1984).

**80.** For a general discussion of powers of appointment see Section 10.4.

**81.** *Restatement (Third) of Trusts* § 46 (1999). *See also Restatement (Second) of Property (Donative Transfers)* § 12.1, comm. e (1984); Cal.Prob.Code § 15205.

the property to them if *A* does not make distribution within a reasonable period.[82] This position is also adopted in the Uniform Trust Code.[83]

Trusts (or powers) for an uncertain group of beneficiaries raise other problems, however. The person named by the settlor may fail to act, *e.g.*, predecease the settlor. When a designated trustee fails to act, courts usually appoint a successor with all the powers conferred on the original trustee, but not if the settlor intended otherwise. A settlor who gives a close relative or friend a broad power to choose beneficiaries may not want some other person to make the selection. The Restatement presumes that "the power of selection * * * (like the typical power of appointment) was intended by the settlor to be personal to the designated trustee."[84] However, when a will requested three named friends of the testator to specify how certain property was to be distributed, and one of them predeceased her, the court concluded that the testator "intended the power to survive" in the remaining two.[85]

Another question is whether the person with power to choose can designate him or herself to receive the property. When conflicts of interest exist in trusts with definite beneficiaries, courts assume that the settlor was aware of them and assumed the trustee would nevertheless act fairly in choosing who should get distributions. But where a person is authorized to distribute property among the testator's "friends" and chooses herself, one wonders whether the settlor actually contemplated this. According to the Restatement of Property, a person who is related to the testator should be treated differently in this case from one who is not.[86]

## § 9.6 Modification and Termination of Trusts

Most trusts are set up to last for a considerable period after the settlor has died; they extend "the dead hand [of the settlor] into the future where needs and circumstances cannot be predicted."[1] If circumstances change after a trust is created, the trust terms may not reflect what the settlor would have wanted under the new circumstances. Arguably courts should have power to allow deviations from the terms of the trust when this occurs. Courts have this power for charitable trusts under the *cy pres* doctrine,[2] but they have been more hesitant to allow deviations from the terms of a private trust. For example, a trust created in 1935 provided annuities for designated individuals. Over the years inflation sharply reduced the value of the annuities, and a beneficiary sought a court order to have hers increased from $5,000 to $14,034 to reflect changes in the Consumer Price Index. The charitable remaindermen refused to consent, and the court said that it was "without power to modify the trust ... in the absence of the agreement of all the

**82.** *Restatement (Third) of Trusts* § 46, comment g (1999).

**83.** Uniform Trust Code § 402(c).

**84.** *Restatement, Third, Trusts* § 46, comm. d (1999). For a more general discussion of whether a trustee's powers are "personal" see Section 12.4, at note 104 et seq.

**85.** Estate of Worthley, 535 A.2d 433 (Me. 1988).

**86.** *Restatement, Second, of Property (Donative Transfers)* § 12.1, illus. 10–11 (1984).

§ 9.6

**1.** Haskell, *Justifying the Principle of Distributive Deviation in the Law of Trusts,* 18 Hast.L.J. 267, 291 (1967). *See also* Frolik, *Adjustment for Inflation for Fixed–Income Trust Beneficiaries,* 54 N.D.Law 661 (1979). An important limitation on the dead hand is the rule against perpetuities, which will be discussed in Chapter 11.

**2.** See Section 9.7, note 88 et seq.

parties in interest" even though it was "difficult to conceive * * * any rational argument that such an adjustment would be contrary to the wishes of the testatrix."[3] Another court refused to allow a trustee to accumulate trust income which exceeded the needs of an income beneficiary who had become incompetent, so that a guardian had to be appointed to receive the excess income.[4] "When the intention of a settlor is plainly expressed * * * the Court will not go outside the instrument in an attempt to give effect to what it conceives to have been the actual intent or motive of the settlor."[5]

On the other hand a New York statute allows courts to "make an allowance from principal to any income beneficiary whose support or education is not sufficiently provided for" if this would "effectuate the intention" of the settlor.[6] The statute literally applies only to an "income beneficiary," but a similar Pennsylvania statute applies to any beneficiary.[7] However, a relative who was not a designated trust beneficiary but who became needy after the trust was created is not covered by the statute.

Some deviations in a trust do not affect the interests of remaindermen. Suppose a trust calls for distributing principal to a person at a specified age, and the person needs support before reaching the designated age. The Restatement allows the use of trust assets for support of a beneficiary "before the time when by the terms of the trust he is entitled to the enjoyment" thereof, "if the interest of no other beneficiary of the trust is impaired thereby."[8] This provision is of limited applicability since most trusts designate a substituted taker in case the primary beneficiary dies prior to reaching the age for distribution. This substitute taker has a beneficial interest which cannot be impaired.[9]

### *Administrative Provisions*

The Restatement allows trustees to deviate from administrative provisions of a trust, if owing to circumstances unanticipated by the settlor, compliance with the trust terms "would defeat or substantially impair the accomplishment of the purposes of the trust."[10] Some trusts prohibit sale of

**3.** New England Merchants Nat. Bank v. Kann, 294 N.E.2d 390, 392–93 (Mass.1973). *See also* Fifth Third Bank v. Simpson, 730 N.E.2d 406, 410 (Ohio App.1999); Estate of Van Deusen, 182 P.2d 565, 571 (Cal.1947); Werbelovsky v. Manufacturers Trust Co., 209 N.Y.S.2d 564 (A.D.1961); Staley v. Ligon, 210 A.2d 384 (Md.1965).

**4.** As to the problem of distributions by a fiduciary to an incompetent see Section 12.10, at note 51 et seq.

**5.** Taylor v. Hutchinson, 497 P.2d 527, 530 (Ariz.App.1972). *See also* Appeal of Harrell, 801 P.2d 852 (Or.App.1990) (refusal to extend duration of a trust for a retarded child).

**6.** N.Y. EPTL § 7–1.6(b). This statute applies only to trusts created after its enactment in 1966, but similar statutes in Pennsylvania and Wisconsin apply to previously created trusts. 20 Penn.Stat. § 6102(a); Wis.Stat. § 701.13(2).

**7.** Pa.Stat. § 6102(a).

**8.** *Restatement (Second) of Trusts* § 168 (1959). A number of statutes allow a invasion of a fund being accumulated for a person who has become "destitute." Ala. Code § 35–4–253; Minn.Stat. § 500.17(4); Calif.Civ.Code § 726; Ind.Code § 32–1–4–5; N.Y. EPTL § 9–2.2; Wis. Stat. § 701.13(1).

In Givens v. Third Nat. Bank, 516 S.W.2d 356 (Tenn.1974), however, a court refused to order distribution of income being accumulated for charities even though this would have saved taxes. The taxation of the undistributed income did not "justify a deviation from * * * the clear and unambiguous terms of the trust instrument."

**9.** *Restatement, Second, of Trusts* § 168, illus. 4 (1959).

**10.** *Restatement, Second, Trusts* § 167 (1959).

the trust assets, or of a particular asset by the trustee. Although such a restriction is valid, courts may overrule it when the circumstances change. For example, a will left a farm in trust, and authorized the trustees to lease the land but not to sell it. Years later new highways turned the land into highly desirable commercial property. A buyer offered $473,960 for the land which was producing an income from farming of only $3,000 a year. The court authorized a sale, since under the changed circumstances "no landowner * * * in his right mind would continue to use this land for agricultural purposes."[11]

Strong evidence is required before courts overrule a prohibition on sale in a trust. Another court refused to order a sale, saying that

> judicial intervention is appropriate only when there has been a change in circumstances affecting the trust which was unforeseen by the donor, and any resulting order must be tailored to implement the intention of the donor * * * In the instant case there has been no change in circumstances * * * The beneficiary's sole reason for desiring the conversion is that she has not been receiving satisfactory distribution payments.[12]

The conservative attitude of courts toward deviations is illustrated by a case in which the instrument required the approval of the settlor's wife before the trustee could sell trust property. The wife turned out to be "impossible to work with" and "not reasonable or rational in her reactions to ... explanations or in her accusations or statements." The court held that it was therefore proper to remove the wife from the position of advisor, but not to eliminate the requirement of an advisor's consent since this would go "beyond what is necessary to correct the circumstances which threaten the purpose of the trust."[13]

Courts may also remove restrictions on trust investments if circumstances change after the trust is created. For example, a trust created in 1977 limited investments to interest-bearing bank accounts and certificates of deposit. Twenty years later a court removed this limitation, saying

> The settlor executed the trust instrument when interest rates were unusually high which strongly suggests that the purpose of the restriction was to ensure a steady, low risk income stream for his wife. Current economic conditions are far different from the unusual conditions that prevailed in 1977. Bank account investments now yield radically lower returns. Furthermore, investment theory has progressed. * * * The settlor's purpose may best be achieved by relaxing the investment restrictions.[14]

During the course of operation of an English trust created in 1936, courts intervened twice to successively expand the scope of permitted investments.[15]

**11.** Ex parte Guaranty Bank & Trust Co., 177 S.E.2d 358, 360 (S.C.1970). *See also* Wisc. Stat. § 701.19(2); Wachovia Bank & Trust Co. v. John Thomasson Const. Co., 168 S.E.2d 358 (N.C.1969); Carroll v. Carroll, 464 S.W.2d 440 (Tex.Civ.App.1971).

**12.** Durdle v. Durdle, 585 N.E.2d 1171, 1175 (Ill.App.1992). *See also* Matter of Will of Killin, 703 P.2d 1323 (Colo.App.1985); Kapiolani Park Pres. Soc. v. Honolulu, 751 P.2d 1022 (Haw.1988) (constitution bars removal of restrictions on leasing in charitable trust).

**13.** Papiernik v. Papiernik, 544 N.E.2d 664, 672 (Ohio 1989).

**14.** Matter of Siegel, 665 N.Y.S.2d 813, 815 (Surr.1997). *See also* 105 N.W.2d 900 (Minn. 1960); Davison v. Duke University, 194 S.E.2d 761 (N.C.1973).

**15.** Steel v. Wellcome Custodian Trustees, [1988] 1 W.L.R. 167 (Ch.D.1987).

Courts do not remove such restrictions on investment, however, "merely because [it] would be more advantageous to the beneficiaries."[16] A court denied a similar request for removing investment restrictions, refusing to assume that the settlor would have done so if he had foreseen the inflation which took place from 1940 to 1960.[17]

Professor Langbein predicts that new trends in trust investment law[18] "will result in less deference to the wishes of the trust settlor [who] ... attempts to impose a manifestly stupid investment restriction on the trust," even in cases in which there has been no unanticipated change of circumstances, based on the idea that the terms of "a private trust must be for the benefit of the beneficiaries."[19] However, the recent Uniform Prudent Investor Act, though innovative in many respects, restates the traditional view that the permissible investments may be restricted by the provisions of a trust.[20]

Several statutes allow premature termination of trusts whose continued operation has become uneconomical because the value of the trust assets is so low. When a professional trustee is used, the costs of a trust can outweigh the advantages when only a small amount is left in the trust. In California when "continuation of a trust under its existing terms will defeat or substantially impair the accomplishment of its purposes," a court may terminate or modify the trust or appoint a new trustee.[21] If a suitable person can be found who will serve without compensation, it may no longer be uneconomic to continue the trust. If termination is necessary, the assets are to be distributed in a manner "that conforms as nearly as possible to the intention of the settlor as expressed in the trust instrument."[22] If the trust has less than $20,000 in it, the trustee can terminate even without a court order.[23]

Another type of deviation which does not alter the shares of the beneficiaries is the consolidation of separate trusts or the division of a trust into separate trusts. California authorizes courts to permit this "for good cause" when the change "will not defeat or substantially impair ... the interests of the beneficiaries."[24] Division of trusts may achieve significant tax advantages, facilitate making appropriate investments, and allow the trustee to make distributions to one beneficiary without affecting the shares of the others. Consolidation on the other hand may reduce trustee fees where the trustee

**16.** *Restatement (Second) of Trusts* § 167, comm. b (1959).

**17.** Toledo Trust Co. v. Toledo Hospital, 187 N.E.2d 36 (Ohio 1962). *See also* Stanton v. Wells Fargo Bank & Union Trust Co., 310 P.2d 1010 (Cal.App.1957); Matter of Estate of Murdock, 884 P.2d 749, 754 (Kan.App.1994) (refusing to remove investment restrictions in charitable trust "in the absence of compelling evidence to indicate that [they were] 'obsolete' ").

**18.** To be discussed in Section 12.7.

**19.** Langbein, *The Uniform Prudent Investor Act and the Future of Trust Investing*, 81 Iowa L.Rev. 641, 663 (1996). *See also Restatement, Third, of Trusts* § 27(2) (1996); Unif. Trust Code § 403.

**20.** Unif.Prud.Inv.Act § 1(b).

**21.** Cal.Prob.Code § 15408(a). *See also* Conn.Gen.Stat. § 45a–520 (charitable trust with assets under $150,000); Ga.Code § 53–12–152(a); R.I.Gen.Laws § 18–4–24 (a) (corporate trustee where trust assets under $100,000); Uniform Trust Code § 413 (where trust assets under $50,000 or "the value of trust property is insufficient to justify the cost of administration").

**22.** Cal.Prob.Code § 15410(c).

**23.** *Id.* § 15408(b); cf. Uniform Trust Code § 413(a).

**24.** Cal.Prob.Code § 15411 (combination), 15412 (division). *See also* Ga.Code § 53–12–152(b); R.I.Gen.Laws § 18–4–25; Uniform Trust Code § 416; Tex.Prop.Code § 112.057.

charges a minimum fee for each trust. Such advantages have persuaded courts to allow it even without statutory authorization.[25]

The Uniform Trusts Code has an open-ended provision which allows courts to modify the administrative *or dispositive* provisions of a trust when this "will further the purposes of the trust" due to "circumstances not anticipated by the settlor."[26] The few reported cases under similar legislation in some states[27] suggest that courts will not often utilize it.[28]

### *Consent of All Beneficiaries*

Very often trust beneficiaries are members of the same family and get along with one another. They may all agree that a trust should be modified or terminated. However, many trusts have minor, unborn or unascertained beneficiaries whose existence makes unanimous consent impossible. For example, a court refused to terminate a trust for the settlor's son with a reminder to his children, because "the vested remainder held by * * * appellant's now living children * * * is subject to divestment *pro tanto* in favor of any of appellant's after-born children. Thus the conveyance by appellant's *present* children is insufficient to convey presently to appellant the *entire* future fee simple interest."[29] Various legal doctrines may help to overcome such obstacles.

Some courts accept proof negating the possibility of future children. For example, a trust provided for termination when all of the settlor's grandchildren were 30. The beneficiaries sought to terminate the trust when the settlor's existing grandchildren were over 30 and her only children were daughters aged 65 and 70. The trustee resisted termination, citing the possibility of later grandchildren under a "presumption that the birth of a child is possible throughout the life of a woman." The court, however, said that the presumption "had its origin at a time when medical knowledge was meager" and should be rebuttable today.[30] This modern view, which is widely though not universally followed,[31] rarely suffices to allow trusts to be modified. It is not enough that a potential parent is unmarried and expresses an intent to have no further children.[32] Also, if a trust gives a remainder to "the issue of A," even if A is incapable of bearing further children and the possibility of adoption is disregarded,[33] if A has children, *their* children are

**25.** Matter of Estate of Branigan, 609 A.2d 431 (N.J.1992); Matter of Will of Kaskel, 549 N.Y.S.2d 587 (Surr.1989).

**26.** Uniform Trust Code § 411(a).

**27.** Cal.Prob.Code § 15409; Tex.Prop.Code § 112.054; Ga.Code § 53–12–153.

**28.** Ivey v. Ivey, 465 S.E.2d 434 (Ga.1996); Wils v. Robinson, 934 S.W.2d 774 (Tex.App. 1996).

**29.** In re Testamentary Trust of Hasch, 721 N.E.2d 1111, 1113 (Ohio App.1999). *See also* Fleisch v. First American Bank, 710 N.E.2d 1281 (Ill.App.1999).

Consent by a minor beneficiary may be valid if ratified by the beneficiary after coming of age. Rosner v. Caplow, 432 N.Y.S.2d 577 (Surr.1980).

**30.** Korten v. Chicago City Bank and Trust Co., 533 N.E.2d 102, 103 (Ill.App.1988).

**31.** *Compare Restatement (Second) of Trusts* § 340, comment e (1959); In re Ransom's Estate, 214 A.2d 521 (N.J.Super.App.Div.1965); Estate of Weeks, 402 A.2d 657 (Pa.1979); Tenn.Code § 24–5–112; Cal. Prob.Code § 15406 *with* Walton v. Lee, 634 S.W.2d 159 (Ky.1982); Clark v. Citizens & So. Nat. Bank, 257 S.E.2d 244 (Ga.1979).

**32.** In re Testamentary Trust of Hasch, 721 N.E.2d 1111, 1114 (Ohio App.1999).

**33.** As to whether adoptees are "issue" of the adopter see Section 2.10.

potential trust beneficiaries whose consent is needed in order to modify the trust.[34]

Some trusts provide for the "heirs" of the settlor or another person. A person's heirs can only be determined at his or her death. Historically the interest of such "heirs" might be eliminated by the Rule in Shelley's Case or the Doctrine of Worthier Title. Although these rules are largely rejected today,[35] certain modern substitutes for them allow the modification of some trusts. In Tennessee the consent of the heirs of a living settlor is not needed to terminate a trust.[36] California allows potential heirs who have only a remote possibility of taking to be disregarded.[37] However, this applies only to the settlor's "heirs," not "issue" or the "heirs" of another individual.

Future interests can sometimes be limited by acceleration. According to the Restatement of Property when an income beneficiary disclaims an interest, "succeeding interests are accelerated." Thus when property is held "to S for life, remainder to S's children, and S "makes a qualified disclaimer[38] of his life interest, * * * the remainder to S's children is accelerated, [and] * * * any child of S that is conceived or adopted" thereafter is excluded.[39] The same notion appears in the Uniform Probate Code: a renunciation causes succeeding future interests to take effect "as though the person renouncing had predeceased the decedent."[40] However, such an acceleration does not occur if the court finds that it would defeat the settlor's intent. When a trust was created for the settlor's son for life with a remainder to his children, the son's renunciation of his interest did not allow termination of the trust. Although the son "may renounce his life estate, he may not renounce the interests of his unborn children or accelerate the remainder."[41]

A guardian ad litem may be appointed to represent minor, unborn or unascertained trust beneficiaries and may approve a modification of the trust terms.[42] However, a guardian's duties to the persons represented may preclude such approval. A court refused to allow a trust to be modified despite a guardian's "pro forma consent," since the modification "would not sufficiently protect the unborn contingent beneficiaries' interests."[43] Where a guardian

**34.** Alcott v. Union Planters Nat. Bank, 686 S.W.2d 79 (Tenn.App.1984).

**35.** See Section 10.2, at note 45 et seq.

**36.** Tenn.Code § 66–1–111(b).

**37.** Cal.Prob.Code § 15404(c). *Cf.* N.C.Gen. Stat. § 41–6 (limitation to "heirs" presumed to mean children).

**38.** As to the requirements of a "qualified disclaimer" see Section 2.8.

**39.** *Restatement (Second) of Property (Donative Transfers)* § 26.1, comm. j (1987). *See also* Pate v. Ford, 376 S.E.2d 775 (S.C.1989); Weinstein v. Mackey, 408 So.2d 849 (Fla.App. 1982). Even without a qualified disclaimer, the same result can occur when a life estate terminates by "merger." *Restatement (Second) of Property (Donative Transfers)* § 26.2, comm. i (1987). As to when a class closes generally see Section 10.3.

**40.** Uniform Prob.Code § 2–801(d); Cal. Prob.Code § 282.

**41.** Stewart v. Johnson, 362 S.E.2d 849, 851 (N.C.App.1987). *See also* Linkous v. Candler, 508 S.E.2d 657 (Ga.1998); Matter of Estate of Ikuta, 639 P.2d 400, 406–07 (Haw. 1981); *Restatement, Second, of Property (Donative Transfers)* § 26.1, comm j (1987).

**42.** Connecticut Bank and Trust Co. v. Coffin, 563 A.2d 1323 (Conn.1989); Matter of Edwards Irrevocable Trust, 966 P.2d 810 (Okla. Civ.App.1998) (error not to allow termination of trust with consent of GAL for remainderman); In re Mark K. Eggebrecht Irrevocable Trust, 4 P.3d 1207, 1210 (Mont.2000) (modification of trust with consent of GAL for minor approved).

**43.** Friedman v. Teplis, 492 S.E.2d 885, 887 (Ga.1997). *Compare* Appeal of Gannon, 631 A.2d 176, 187 (Pa.Super.1993) where a GAL approved a settlement because "his wards had only remote and contingent interest with little likelihood of vesting."

refuses to consent, a court may overrule the decision but will not do so if there is a rational basis for it.[44] Some statutes authorize guardians to consent on the basis of "general family benefit accruing to living members of the beneficiary's family" without focussing solely on the immediate interests of the persons they represent.[45]

Lack of consent by a beneficiary is no bar if a modification will have no effect on the nonconsenting beneficiary.[46] Thus when all the beneficiaries except one annuitant sought to terminate a trust, the court directed the trustee to retain enough funds to pay the annuity and to distribute the rest of the trust assets, saying it was not "necessary to maintain intact a trust corpus of more than $900,000 to fund" a $12,000 annuity.[47]

### *Purposes of the Settlor*

Even if all the beneficiaries consent, termination is not allowed "if the continuance of the trust is necessary to carry out a material purpose of the trust."[48] This limitation does not exist in England[49] or in a few of the United States,[50] but most American jurisdictions follow the leading case, Claflin v. Claflin.[51] This involved a testamentary trust for the settlor's son who was to get the corpus at age 30. The son sought to compel the trustees to give him the trust assets when he was only 24. The court dismissed his suit, even though he was the sole beneficiary, because "the purposes of the trust have not been accomplished."

The dominant idea of *Claflin* is the fulfillment of the settlor's wishes. If circumstances not contemplated by the settlor arise after the trust was created, courts recognize that the settlor's intent might best be carried out by departing from the terms of the trust. In *Claflin,* "nothing [had] happened which the testator did not anticipate," but in another case, where "the testator did not foresee the bountiful accumulations" which the trust was accruing, the court held that early termination would "serve the testator's ultimate objective."[52] Some judges, however, apply the *Claflin* rule rather strictly and refuse to "speculate on what the settlor might have done" under changed circumstances.[53]

The result turns on what the court decides are the "purposes of the trust." A trust may have multiple purposes, and, at least in some states, a weighing of their relative importance is required; the beneficiaries can compel

**44.** Matter of Schroll, 297 N.W.2d 282, 284 (Minn.1980).

**45.** Cal.Prob.Code § 15405; Wis. Stat.§ 701.12(2); Unif.Trust Code § 305(c).

**46.** Musick v. Reynolds, 798 S.W.2d 626, 630 (Tex.App.1990).

**47.** Matter of Boright, 377 N.W.2d 9, 13 (Minn.1985). *See also Restatement (Second) of Trusts* § 340(2) (1959); *Restatement (Second) of Property (Donative Transfers)* § 2.1, comm. i (1983); Uniform Trust Code § 410(e); Calif.Prob.Code § 15404(b). *But see* Probasco v. Clark, 474 A.2d 221 (Md.App.1984); In re Gilliland's Estate, 118 Cal.Rptr. 447 (App.1974).

**48.** *Restatement, Second, Trusts* § 337(2) (1959).

**49.** F. Maitland, *Equity* 53 (1913); Whitman v. Hudgins, 65 N.S.R. 2d 64 (1985) (N.S.).

**50.** Fisher v. Ladd, 268 S.E.2d 20 (N.C.App.1980); *cf.* Calif.Prob.Code § 15403(b) (termination allowed where reason for it "outweighs the interest in accomplishing a material purpose of the trust").

**51.** 20 N.E. 454 (Mass.1889). Prior to *Claflin,* American courts had followed the English view. Alexander, *The Dead Hand and the Law of Trusts in the Nineteenth Century,* 37 Stan. L.Rev. 1189, 1201 (1985).

**52.** In re Bayley Trust, 250 A.2d 516 (Vt. 1969).

**53.** Trabits v. First Nat. Bank, 345 So.2d 1347 (Ala.1977); Frost Nat. Bank of San Antonio v. Newton, 554 S.W.2d 149 (Tex.1977).

a modification unless it "would frustrate a material purpose of the trust and the reason for modification are outweighed by such material purpose."[54] Occasionally trust purposes are recited in the trust instrument, *e.g.* a trust "for the education of the children,"[55] but usually they must be deduced from the beneficial interests created by the trust.[56] Extrinsic evidence may also be used.[57] For example, the beneficiaries of a trust were allowed to terminate it when they produced testimony that the settlor had created the trust in order "to keep the money away from [her daughter's] alcoholic husband." Since the husband was now dead "that purpose no longer exists and termination of the trust was proper."[58]

If a trust calls for distribution when a beneficiary reaches a specified age, the settlor's purpose was probably to postpone distribution until the beneficiary was mature enough to handle the money.[59] In a bypass trust, *e.g.* "to A for life, remainder to her children," on the other hand, it is presumed "in the absence of circumstances indicating a further purpose" than providing for successive enjoyment, the beneficiaries (if they can be ascertained and are sui juris) can compel termination.[60] But a spendthrift provision in the trust may be deemed to show a purpose which bars early termination, because this would frustrate "the testator's obvious purpose to protect the [beneficiary] against his own improvidence."[61] Conversely, the absence of a spendthrift clause is often cited in cases allowing early termination of trusts.[62] According to the Restatement, however, even if the trust has no spendthrift provision and the beneficiary actually transfers his interest, the transferee will not be allowed to terminate the trust.[63]

If a purpose of the trust was to protect against a beneficiary's improvidence, can the beneficiary show that the settlor was mistaken about this? When a trust was created for the settlor's son until he reached age 35, he sought to terminate it at 23, alleging that "he had invested his private funds so successfully that his personal estate had enhanced three hundred per centum in thirteen months." But the court found that this did not justify termination of the trust.[64] According to the Restatement, however, if a trust

**54.** In re Mark K. Eggebrecht Irrevocable Trust, 4 P.3d 1207, 1210 (Mont.2000) (position of trust advisor eliminated). *See also* Cal.Prob. Code § 15403(b).

**55.** Appeal of Gannon, 631 A.2d 176, 186 (Pa.Super.1993).

**56.** *Restatement, Third, Trusts* Ch. 6, Int. Note (1998).

**57.** *Restatement (Second) of Trusts* § 337, comment e (1959).

**58.** Matter of Harbaugh's Estate, 646 P.2d 498 (Kan.1982).

**59.** Rhode Island Hospital Trust Co. v. Smith, 198 A.2d 664 (R.I.1964); Collins v. First Nat. Bank, 251 N.E.2d 610 (Ohio App.1969); *Restatement (Second) of Trusts* § 337, comment j (1959). Even in this case, however, an earlier distribution may be ordered if the beneficiary needs the funds. See note 8 *supra*.

**60.** *Restatement, Second, Trusts* § 337, comm. f (1959); In re Trust of Lane, 592 A.2d 492 (Md.1991); American National Bank v. Miller, 899 P.2d 1337 (Wyo.1995).

**61.** In re Estate of Davis, 297 A.2d 451, 455 (Pa.1972). *See also* Mahan v. Mahan, 577 A.2d 70, 77 (Md.1990); *Restatement (Second) of Trusts* § 337, comment *l* (1959); Fleisch v. First American Bank, 710 N.E.2d 1281 (Ill. App.1999) (termination denied where it would "defeat the spendthrift provisions of the trust"); Neeley v. Neeley, 996 P.2d 346, 348 (Kan.App.2000).

For a general discussion of spendthrift provisions see Section 13.1, at note 32 et seq.

**62.** Johnson v. First Nat. Bank, 386 So.2d 1112 (Miss.1980); Appeal of Gannon, 631 A.2d 176, 186 (Pa.Super.1993); American National Bank v. Miller, 899 P.2d 1337 (Wyo.1995).

**63.** *Restatement (Second) of Trusts* § 337, comment k (1959). *See also Restatement (Second) of Property (Donative Transfers)* § 2.1, illus. 6 (1983).

**64.** Collins v. First Nat. Bank, 251 N.E.2d 610, 614 (Ohio App.1969). *See also* Moxley v. Title Ins. & Trust Co., 165 P.2d 15 (Cal.1946).

was created "solely on account of a physical or mental disability of the beneficiary," removal of the disability warrants termination of the trust.[65] Many drafters routinely insert spendthrift provisions without real consideration of the abilities of the beneficiaries, who are often infants or unborn when the trust is drafted. Therefore, the to make them a litmus test of trust purposes is unfortunate. The California Probate Code makes them "a factor" but not conclusive in deciding whether to modify or terminate a trust.[66] In Louisiana, perhaps because of its civil law tradition, courts have allowed trusts to be terminated when the beneficiary has "demonstrated that he could handle the funds just fine on his own."[67]

Sometimes a will creates a trust for an heir who contests the will, alleging, for example, that the testator lacked capacity. If the interested parties agree on a settlement by which the child will receive property free of trust, the settlement may be approved, despite *Claflin*.[68] A spendthrift clause does not bar a timely disclaimer by the beneficiary.[69] Moreover, if the will (including the spendthrift provision) is threatened with destruction by the contest, the testator would probably approve the settlement. As one court observed:

> We cannot believe that [the settlor] either anticipated or intended that the corpus of the * * * Trust should be eaten up by lawyer's fees, trustee's commissions and other costs associated with the protracted litigation guaranteed to ensue should the beneficiaries * * * be prevented from amicably settling the will contest.[70]

The Uniform Probate Code allows courts to approve settlements "even though [they] may affect a trust or an inalienable interest."[71] However, some courts deny requests for early termination of trusts even in this situation.[72]

### *Settlor Consents*

If the settlor of a living trust consents to early termination, the fact that a "material purpose" of the trust remains unaccomplished is no bar. The *Claflin* rule is designed to carry out the settlor's intent and does not apply if the settlor's current intent is to end the trust.[73] Thus even an "irrevocable" trust may be revoked by the settlor, if the settlor is the sole beneficiary or if

**65.** *Restatement, Second, Trusts* § 337, comm. h (1959).

**66.** Cal.Prob.Code § 15409(b). *See also* Uniform Trust Code § 410(c); 20 Pa.C.S.A. § 6102(a).

**67.** Martin, *Louisiana's Law of Trusts 25 Years After Adoption of the Trust Code*, 50 La.L.Rev. 501, 520 (1990).

**68.** Budin v. Levy, 180 N.E.2d 74 (Mass. 1962).

**69.** Commerce Trust Co. v. Fast, 396 S.W.2d 683 (Mo.1965); *Restatement, Third, Trusts* § 58, comm. c (1999); Uniform Probate Code § 2–801(a); Cal.Prob.Code § 286.

**70.** Appeal of Gannon, 631 A.2d 176, 189 (Pa.Super.1993).

**71.** Uniform Probate Code § 3–1101; Matter of Estate of Grimm, 784 P.2d 1238 (Utah App.1989); *Restatement (Second) of Trusts* § 337, comment *o* (1959).

**72.** St. Louis Union Trust Co. v. Conant, 499 S.W.2d 761 (Mo.1973); Adams v. Link, 145 A.2d 753 (Conn.1958); In re Gilliland's Estate, 118 Cal.Rptr. 447 (App.1974); Fleisch v. First American Bank, 710 N.E.2d 1281 (Ill.App. 1999) (denying termination based on a settlement in the absence of "a *bona fide* family dispute").

**73.** Matter of Edwards Irrevocable Trust, 966 P.2d 810 (Okl.Civ.App.1998); Phillips v. Lowe, 639 S.W.2d 782 (Ky.1982); Johnson v. First Nat. Bank, 386 So.2d 1112 (Miss.1980); *Restatement (Second) of Trusts* §§ 338–39 (1959); Calif.Prob.Code § 15404; Uniform Trust Code § 410(a).

the other beneficiaries agree. The consent of the trustee is not necessary.[74] If there is more than one settlor, it is unclear whether they all must consent.[75]

### *Standing*

The trustee's interest in continuing a trust in order to earn more fees is not a legitimate reason for refusing to terminate it.[76] However, if a court orders termination, the trustee has standing to appeal pursuant to its duty to see that the settlor's intent is carried out.[77]

A trustee who accedes to a request for termination by some beneficiaries can be surcharged by other beneficiaries for a wrongful distribution, but the recipient(s) of the distribution (if not legally incapacitated) can not claim more money on the ground that the earlier distribution was improper, even if they were spendthrifts and dissipated the funds.[78] A settlor who wishes to make sure that a trust will not be terminated prematurely must select a trustee who has enough "backbone" to refuse the beneficiary's requests.

### *Statute of Uses*

The Statute of Uses of 1536 was designed to end *all* trusts of land by transforming the equitable interest of the beneficiaries into legal title. The reasons for the original Statute disappeared long ago,[79] but it has been held to be part of the common law, and applicable by analogy to personal property.[80] The statute "executes" (*i.e.* terminates) "passive trusts" in which the trustee has no duties to perform.[81] Most trustees have active duties to perform, so the Statute of Uses does not apply to them.[82]

### *Planning*

The *Claflin* rule makes it possible in most American states to have a trust continue for as long as the settlor desires up to the limits imposed by the Rule against Perpetuities.[83] Cases in which beneficiaries seek to terminate trusts may be a product of bad planning. When a court terminates a trust because its purposes have ceased, better drafting might have created a more flexible

**74.** Hein v. Hein, 543 N.W.2d 19, 20 (Mich. App.1995).

**75.** *Compare* Sundquist v. Sundquist, 639 P.2d 181, 187 (Utah 1981) (objection by one settlor bars termination) *with* Cal.Prob.Code § 15401(b) (each settlor of a revocable trust "may revoke the trust as to the portion of the trust contributed by that settlor"). See also Section 5.5, note 19.

**76.** Papale–Keefe v. Altomare, 647 N.E.2d 722 (Mass.App.1995); Siegel v. Cherry, 502 N.Y.S.2d 735 (A.D.1986); *Restatement (Second) of Trusts* § 337, comment b (1959). *But see* In re Guardianship of Lombardo, 716 N.E.2d 189, 196 (Ohio 1999) (where voting trust of stock allowed trustee to control company, trustee was a beneficiary who could bar termination of the trust).

**77.** American National Bank v. Miller, 899 P.2d 1337 (Wyo.1995).

**78.** Hagerty v. Clement, 196 So. 330 (La. 1940); *Restatement (Second) of Trusts* § 342 (1959). One who distributes to a minor, however, may have to pay again if the minor squanders the money. See Section 12.10, note 52 et seq.

**79.** See Section 3.2, at note 15 et seq.

**80.** Daugherty v. Daugherty, 784 S.W.2d 650, 654 (Tenn.1990).

**81.** Board of Cooperative Educational Services v. County of Nassau, 524 N.Y.S.2d 224, 225 (A.D.1988) (trust terminated when County "had no further duties as trustee").

**82.** Rentz v. Polk, 228 S.E.2d 106 (S.C. 1976); Hatcher v. Southern Baptist Theological Seminary, 632 S.W.2d 251 (Ky.1982); Rogerson v. Wheeling Dollar Sav. & Trust Co., 222 S.E.2d 816 (W.Va.1976).

**83.** For limits posed by the Rule Against Perpetuities see Chapter 11. A trust can be terminated after the period allowed by the Rule has expired. *Restatement (Second) of Trusts* § 62, comm. e (1959).

trust which could be terminated without litigation. Particularly the thoughtless insertion of a spendthrift provision may cause a trust to be needlessly prolonged. Perhaps courts should be more liberal in authorizing deviations from trusts. But whenever changed circumstances arise, if the trust instrument fails to provide for them the settlor's intention is inevitably open to doubt.

## § 9.7 Charitable Trusts

Charitable trusts are an exception to the general rule that a trust must have definite beneficiaries.[1] Identifiable beneficiaries are not needed to enforce charitable trusts because a public official, the attorney general, does this. Charitable trusts are allowed to go on forever, despite the Rule against Perpetuities.[2] Since terms laid down by the settlor often become out of date over the centuries, courts authorize deviations from the terms of charitable trusts under a power known as *cy pres,* the old French spelling of *si près,* "as near."[3] The name refers to the fact that such modifications stay "as near" to the trust terms as possible under the changed circumstances, although in modern times courts do not always "adopt that scheme which is as nearly as possible like that designated by the terms of the gift."[4]

### *Definition of Charitable*

Because of the peculiar rules governing charitable trusts, courts sometimes must decide whether a particular trust is charitable. According to the Restatement a trust is charitable "if its accomplishment is of such social interest to the community as to justify permitting the property to be devoted to the [designated] purpose in perpetuity."[5] However, courts have often classified trusts which provided little or no social benefit as charitable. For example, a will left property in trust to have the testator's book published. An English professor testified that the book was "without aesthetic merit," and even the drafter of the will said it was "ungodly bad." Nevertheless, the court found that the trust was charitable, saying it "should not hold the trust to be noncharitable merely because it does not approve of the objectives of the settlor and does not consider his trust will bring about social benefits."[6] Although a trust "for the dissemination of beliefs or doctrines which are irrational" is not charitable,"[7] courts are reluctant to characterize a belief as irrational for fear that they may not recognize ideas ahead of their time. "If we exclude trusts which are eccentric, * * * the opportunity for scientific and social experiment by means of charitable trusts would be largely eliminated." For example, "reputable scientists of the day were convinced" that the Wright brothers' flight at Kitty Hawk was impossible.[8]

§ 9.7

1. *E.g.,* Cal.Prob.Code § 15205: "A trust, other than a charitable trust, is created only if there is a beneficiary."

2. See Section 11.6.

3. Because of its French origin, the first word rhymes with "sea" rather than "sigh" and the final "s" in the second word is not pronounced.

4. *Restatement, Second, Trusts* § 399, comm. b (1959).

5. *Id.,* § 368, comment b.

6. Rosser v. Prem, 449 A.2d 461, 470 (Md. App.1982).

7. *Restatement (Second) of Trusts* § 370, comment h (1959).

8. L. Simes, *Public Policy and the Dead Hand* 133 (1955).

Charity is sometimes defined by a list of purposes recognized as charitable. Such a list appeared in the preamble of the Statute of Charitable Uses of 1601. Although "never intended to provide an exhaustive definition," this list "still exerts a strong pull on the modern concept of charity."[9] Some items on this list appear rather quaint today, such as the "marriages of true maids."[10] Conversely, some purposes not on the 1601 list are counted as charitable today, such as the prevention of cruelty to animals.[11] A more current list appears in the Restatement of Trusts: "(a) the relief of poverty; (b) the advancement of education; (c) the advancement of religion; (d) the promotion of health; (e) governmental or municipal purposes; (f) other purposes the accomplishment of which is beneficial to the community."[12]

Even purposes on this list are not charitable if they do not benefit the public. "A college for pickpockets is no charity."[13] An English court refused to hold that a trust under George Bernard Shaw's will to reform the alphabet to make spelling phonetic was charitable. "I do not think that the fact that the testator and a number of other people are of the opinion that the step would be a benefit proves the case, for undoubtedly there are a great many more people * * * who think the exact contrary." Shaw's trust was like those "which advocate a change in the law. Such objects have never been considered charitable."[14]

American courts define charity more broadly. Trusts to promote change in the law, such as one to promote the Equal Rights Amendment or to advance the cause of socialism, have been held charitable.[15] The definition of "charity" for private law purposes is broader than the tax definition.[16] A trust to promote socialism was deemed charitable even though the trustees were authorized "to use the trust assets for non-charitable purposes," since this phrase merely meant that the trust "not be limited to those entities or causes which would * * * qualify as tax-exempt."[17]

There are limits to how far even American courts go in finding trusts to be charitable, however. A trust to distribute the income to children in the first three grades of a school, to further their education was held not to be charitable, since the "admonition to the children" to use the money for education "would be wholly impotent" in the light of "childhood impulses."[18] Nor could the trust be regarded as one for the relief of poverty because distributions were not limited to needy children.[19] The social benefit in the

**9.** Bright, *Charity and Trusts for the Public Benefit—Time for a Re-think?*, The Conveyancer 28, 31 (1989). An historical error led American courts for a time to believe that enforcement of charitable trusts originated with this statute. A. Scott, *Trusts* § 348.2 (4th ed. 1987).

**10.** Statute, 43 Eliz. I, c. 4 (1601).

**11.** Green's Will Trusts, [1985] 3 All E.R. 455 (Ch. 1984).

**12.** *Restatement (Second) of Trusts* § 368 (1959). *See also* Uniform Trust Code § 404(a); Wis.Stat. § 701.10; Ga.Code § 53–12–110.

**13.** Re Shaw, [1957] 1 All E.R. 745, 752 (Ch.).

**14.** On this basis, Amnesty International was held not to be a charity in McGovern v. Attorney–General, [1982] Ch. 321 (1981).

**15.** Estate of Breeden, 256 Cal.Rptr. 813 (App.1989); Register of Wills v. Cook, 216 A.2d 542 (Md.1966); *Restatement (Second) of Trusts* § 374 comment j (1959). However, a trust for a particular political party is not charitable. *id.*, comment k.

**16.** As to the tax benefits of charitable giving see Section 15.

**17.** 256 Cal.Rptr. at 818. The federal estate tax charitable deduction is discussed at Section 15.3.

**18.** Shenandoah Valley Nat. Bank v. Taylor, 63 S.E.2d 786, 791 (Va.1951).

**19.** However, a trust can be "for the relief of poverty" even though it does not state specifically that the beneficiaries must be poor. A trust for the benefit of 'widows and orphans' is

scheme was not sufficient "to justify its existence in perpetuity as a charitable trust."

A trust cannot qualify as charitable if the class of potential recipients is too narrow, *e.g.*, a trust "for the education of John's descendants."[20] But a settlor can select a favored group, such as a small community.[21] Even payment to one individual may involve enough social benefit to make the trust charitable, as in a trust to provide medical education for a person who agreed to practice in a small town, or a prize for an individual who has done something useful.[22]

A trust to maintain the tomb of the testator or his family is not charitable, but the perpetual upkeep of a *public* cemetery or a monument to a "notable person" is.[23] A trust to provide for the settlor's pets is not charitable, but one for the prevention of cruelty to animals in general is.[24]

### *Racial, Gender and Religious Limitations*

The will of Stephen Girard in 1831 created a college for "poor white male orphans," naming the city of Philadelphia as trustee. The Supreme Court held that the college's refusal to admit Negroes was state action forbidden by the 14th Amendment's equal protection clause.[25] A few years later the Court had to deal with a park "for white people only" which had been left to a city. The city resigned as trustee and was replaced by private individuals, but this made no difference, because the "momentum" which the park had "acquired as a public facility" was "not dissipated by the appointment of private trustees."[26]

Arguably, the state's involvement in the supervision and enforcement of charitable trusts should subject them all to the 14th Amendment. No court has yet so held,[27] but they have been quick to find unconstitutional state action when racially restrictive trusts are challenged.[28] When a private trustee sought instructions from a court on whether to abide by racial restrictions,

ordinarily interpreted as meaning "poor widows and orphans." *Restatement (Second) of Trusts* § 369, comment c (1959).

**20.** In re Compton, [1945] Ch. 123; *Restatement, Second, Trusts* § 375 (1959). *But cf.* Runser v. Lippi, 664 N.E.2d 1355 (Ohio App. 1995) (trust for scholarships for needy persons, with preference given to settlor's nieces and nephews); Schoenblum, *The Role of Legal Doctrine in the Decline of the Islamic Waqf: A Comparison with the Trust*, 32 Vand.J. of Transnational Law 1191, 1207 (1999) (quoting Mohammed's view that one's descendants are a fitting object of charity).

**21.** *Restatement, Second, Trusts* § 370, comm. c, d (1959).

**22.** *Id.* comments h, j; In re Carlson's Estate, 358 P.2d 669 (Kan.1961); Estate of Bunch v. Heirs of Bunch, 485 So.2d 284 (Miss.1986).

**23.** *Restatement, Second, Trusts* § 374, comm. h (1959). Even though not charitable, many state statutes allow gifts for the perpetual care of graves if limited in amount. Foshee v. Republic Nat. Bank, 617 S.W.2d 675 (Tex. 1981); Eaton v. Miller, 250 A.2d 220 (Me.1969); Wis.Stat. § 701.11 (trust for perpetual care of tomb is valid unless "capricious").

**24.** In re McNeill's Estate, 41 Cal.Rptr. 139 (App.1964); *Restatement (Second) of Trusts* § 374, comm. c (1959). Trusts for the care of an animal or a grave may be sustained as "honorary." See note 53 et seq. *infra*.

**25.** Commonwealth of Pennsylvania v. Board of Directors, 353 U.S. 230 (1957).

**26.** Evans v. Newton, 382 U.S. 296, 301 (1966). *See also* Commonwealth of Pa. v. Brown, 392 F.2d 120 (3d Cir.1968).

**27.** Adams, *Racial and Religious Discrimination in Charitable Trusts,* 25 Clev.State L.Rev. 1, 13 (1976); *cf.* Lockwood v. Killian, 375 A.2d 998, 1005 (Conn.1977).

**28.** Trammell v. Elliott, 199 S.E.2d 194 (Ga.1973); Dunbar v. Board of Trustees, 461 P.2d 28 (Colo.1969); Connecticut Bank & Trust Co. v. Cyril and Julia C. Johnson Mem. Hosp., 294 A.2d 586 (Conn.Super.1972).

the court said that any advice it gave to comply with them would constitute state action.[29]

Nevertheless, courts have held that racially discriminatory charities can be charitable for purposes of trust law.[30] Such trusts are rare, however, because they do not qualify for federal tax benefits[31] and most charitable giving today is tax-motivated, at least in part.

A trust which provides benefits only for blacks perhaps can be upheld by analogy to affirmative action programs. When a will created a scholarship fund for a "white female student," the racial restriction was stricken but the limitation to females was upheld on the ground that this "benign discrimination * * * does not subvert equal opportunity but rather promotes it by compensating for past acts of discrimination."[32] Another court upheld a trust for "Negro children" but did not comment on the racial limitation.[33]

The Restatement of Trusts allows beneficiaries of a charitable trust to be "limited to the inhabitants of a particular place" or "to persons of a particular sex or religion."[34] A court refused to invalidate the gender restriction in a trust for "five young men who shall have graduated from the Canastosa High School."[35] The result may be different, however, where the court finds state action is involved, *e.g.* when school officials participate in the selection of scholarship recipients.[36]

Courts have also avoided gender limitations by construction. A devise of income to Worcester Academy so long as it "continues to be operated as a boys preparatory school," was not terminated when the Academy became coeducational because the will did not say "boys only."[37] Gender limitations have been removed under *cy pres* when they caused a dearth of eligible claimants, *e.g.*, a scholarship designated for a "male member" of a church was expanded to include females when no qualified male applied.[38] Still, judicial hostility toward sex discrimination is not so marked as in the case of racial discrimination. When a scholarship fund was created for boys graduating from high schools in Hartford County who were "members of the Caucasian race and * * * professed * * * to be of the Protestant Congregational Faith," the court removed the racial restriction, but upheld the religious restriction as an exercise of the settlor's rights under the First Amendment.[39] It also held the

**29.** Bank of Delaware v. Buckson, 255 A.2d 710 (Del.Ch.1969).

**30.** Swanson, *Discriminatory Charitable Trusts: Time for a Legislative Solution,* 48 U.Pitt.L.Rev. 153, 158 (1986).

**31.** Bob Jones University v. United States, 461 U.S. 574 (1983); Estate of Clopton, 93 T.C. 275 (1989).

**32.** Trustees of the University of Delaware v. Gebelein, 420 A.2d 1191 (Del.Ch.1980). *See also* Swanson, *supra* note 30, at 188. *But see* Mississippi University for Women v. Hogan, 458 U.S. 718 (1982) (state nursing school limited to women is invalid).

**33.** In re Robbins' Estate, 371 P.2d 573 (Cal.1962).

**34.** *Restatement (Second) of Trusts* § 370, comment j (1959).

**35.** Matter of Estate of Wilson, 452 N.E.2d 1228 (N.Y.1983). *See also* Shapiro v. Columbia Union Nat. Bank & Trust Co., 576 S.W.2d 310 (Mo.1978); Matter of Cram's Will, 606 P.2d 145 (Mont.1980).

**36.** In re Certain Scholarship Funds, 575 A.2d 1325 (N.H.1990); In re Crichfield Trust, 426 A.2d 88 (N.J.Super.Ch.Div.1980); Luria, *Prying Loose the Dead Hand of the Past,* 21 U.S.F.L.Rev. 41, 48 (1986) (gender restriction in Girard College removed).

**37.** Matter of Edwards' Estate, 446 N.Y.S.2d 551 (A.D.1982). *See also* Ebitz v. Pioneer Nat. Bank, 361 N.E.2d 225 (Mass.1977).

**38.** Wesley United Methodist Church v. Harvard College, 316 N.E.2d 620 (Mass.1974).

**39.** Lockwood v. Killian, 375 A.2d 998 (Conn.1977).

sex restriction should be maintained if the desired increase in the number of applicants could be achieved by broadening the geographical base beyond Hartford County.[40] A California court saw "no Fourteenth Amendment or other problem" in a will which left an estate to a "Protestant" engineering school, but the "all white" designation in the same will was assumed to be invalid even though the trustee was not a public entity.[41]

### *Salvaging Non–Charitable Trusts*

Courts often remove racial restrictions if they find the settlor had a general charitable intent,[42] but a few have allowed the trust to fail when the constitution barred enforcement of the restriction. For example, when the racial restriction in a devise of land for a park was held unenforceable, the land reverted to the testator's heirs because "the park's segregated character was an essential and inseparable part of the testator's plan."[43]

When a will created a trust to teach political science in accordance with the testator's peculiar principles, the court refused to implement the terms of the will literally because "no legitimate institution of higher learning could permit this kind of control of the classroom from the grave," but a plan should be formulated "consistent with academic freedom" to teach a course dealing with the testator's conservative philosophy.[44] On the other hand, when a woman left money to purchase flowers for the graves of her family, the court refused to "rewrite the bequest so that the money will go for charitable purposes," since the testator had no "charitable purpose."[45]

If the words "benevolent" or "philanthropic" were used to describe the trust purposes, an old case held the trust was invalid because these terms are broader than "charitable,"[46] but courts today construe such terms as synonymous with charitable.[47]

A trust which has both charitable and non-charitable objectives may be sustained in part if a clear part can be allocated to each. For example, a will left property to a foundation which was to pay specified amounts to certain individuals and use the rest "to aid the blind." The devises to individuals were held "no impediment to the remaining portion of the trust." Such a "mixed trust" failed only where "there is no method of apportionment" between the charitable and other purposes, whereas here there was an "identifiable separation between" them.[48] Other courts have sustained

**40.** However, when trial court followed this suggestion on remand, it was reversed again on a second appeal. Lockwood v. Killian, 425 A.2d 909 (Conn.1979).

**41.** In re Vanderhoofven's Estate, 96 Cal. Rptr. 260 (App.1971). *See also* In re Zahn's Estate, 93 Cal.Rptr. 810 (App.1971) (rest home "for Christian women" upheld).

**42.** Trammell v. Elliott, 199 S.E.2d 194 (Ga.1973); In re Certain Scholarship Funds, 575 A.2d 1325 (N.H.1990)(removal of gender and religious restriction).

**43.** Evans v. Abney, 396 U.S. 435, 439 (1970). *See also* La Fond v. City of Detroit, 98 N.W.2d 530 (Mich.1959); Connecticut Bank & Trust Co. v. Cyril and Julia C. Johnson Mem. Hosp., 294 A.2d 586 (Conn.Super.1972) (invalid racial restriction causes trust property to fall into residuary estate); Hermitage Meth. Homes v. Dominion Trust, 387 S.E.2d 740 (Va.1990).

**44.** In re Estate of Rood, 200 N.W.2d 728 (Mich.App.1972).

**45.** Foshee v. Republic Nat. Bank, 617 S.W.2d 675 (Tex.1981).

**46.** Morice v. Bishop of Durham, 32 Eng. Rep. 656, 947 (Ch. 1805).

**47.** Wilson v. Flowers, 277 A.2d 199 (N.J. 1971); *cf. Restatement (Second) of Trusts* § 398, comments c, d (1959).

**48.** In re Teubert's Estate, 298 S.E.2d 456, 463–64 (W.Va.1982). *See also Restatement, Second, Trusts* § 398(3) (1959).

"mixed" trusts by disregarding the references to noncharitable objects.[49] But a will directing the executors to distribute the residue to "whatever person or charitable organization they determine" was held to fail for indefiniteness.[50]

Devises which are restricted to charitable purposes, on the other hand, can be quite open-ended, such as "to charity" or "to such charitable organizations as my trustee shall select."[51] Even if the will fails to name a trustee, or if the designated trustee fails to act, the court normally appoints a trustee. If the testator intended that the trust fail if the designated trustee does not serve, this intent will be followed, but this is not the usual construction.[52]

### *Honorary Trusts*

A trust for a non-charitable purpose is sometimes sustained as an "honorary trust." For example, a testator left money to a friend to be applied "towards the promotion and furthering of fox-hunting." The court held that although this purpose was not charitable,[53] it had been "defined with sufficient clearness" and should be given effect. If the friend failed to apply the money to promote fox-hunting, the residuary devisees, to whom the money would otherwise pass, could bring suit.[54]

The term "honorary trust" arises from the idea that there is no beneficiary who can sue to compel the trustee to perform its terms.[55] However, the Uniform Probate Code allows such trusts to be enforced by an individual designated for this purpose in the trust instrument, or by a court.[56]

The Restatement distinguishes between trusts for "a specific noncharitable purpose" (like fox-hunting) and those for "indefinite" purposes, not limited to charities. In the latter case the trust is "presumptively personal," *i.e.* can only be exercised by the designated trustee, and so if he or she is unable or unwilling to serve, the trust fails.[57] If the power is *not* personal and can be exercised after the death of the designated trustee, how long can the trust go on? The Restatement allows "a reasonable period of time, normally not to exceed 21 years."[58] The purpose must not be "capricious" and the amount of the property devoted to it must not be "unreasonably large."[59] The Uniform Probate Code has a similar provision with somewhat different

**49.** Newick v. Mason, 581 A.2d 1269 (Me. 1990); *Restatement, Second, Trusts* § 389(2) (1959); English Charitable Trusts (Validation) Act, 1954, § 1.

**50.** Klassen v. Klassen, [1986] 5 W.W.R. 746 (Sask.Q.B.). *But cf.* Section 9.5, at note 81.

**51.** Lancaster v. Merchants Nat. Bank, 961 F.2d 713 (8th Cir.1992); *Restatement (Second) of Trusts* § 396 (1959).

**52.** *Id.* § 397. Contrast the rule as to trusts for non-charitable purposes, *infra* note 54.

**53.** Query. Under some circumstances, promotion of sports may be deemed charitable in America. Mercury Bay Boating Club v. San Diego Yacht Club, 557 N.E.2d 87, 95 (N.Y. 1990) (sailing race prize); *Restatement, Second, Trusts* § 374, comm f (1959) (trust to provide public facilities for swimming). *But see* Barton v. Parrott, 495 N.E.2d 973 (Ohio Com.Pl.1984) (trust to establish harness race is not charitable).

**54.** In re Thompson [1934] 1 Ch. 342.

**55.** *Restatement (Second) of Trusts* § 124, comment c (1959); Uniform Probate Code § 2–907(a).

**56.** Uniform Probate Code § 2–907(c)(4); *cf.* Unif.Trust Code § 408. For an explanation of the "self-contradictory" language of the UPC see Hirsch, *Trusts for Purposes: Policy, Ambiguity, and Anomaly in the Uniform Laws*, 26 Fla.St.L.Rev. 913, 925 (1999).

**57.** *But cf.* Uniform Probate Code § 2–907(c)(7) (court shall appoint a trustee if "no designated trustee is willing or able to serve").

**58.** *Restatement, Third, Trusts* § 47 (1999).

**59.** *Id,* comm.e. The "capricious" limitation actually applies to all trusts. *Id.*, § 29, comm. h.

details.[60] Reported cases on these questions are rare, perhaps because of the liberal definition of "charitable" purposes by American courts, and probably the most common example of a trust for a specific noncharitable purpose, those for the care of a cemetery plot, are governed in many states by specific statutes. A trust for to provide flowers on specified days for the graves of the testator and her parents was upheld under such a statute.

> Such trust standing alone is in violation of the common law against perpetuities. It is equally clear, however, that by the language used [allowing trusts for the perpetual care and embellishment of tombs] the legislature * * * intended to abrogate the common law rule. * * * "Respect for the dead is a sentiment desirable of cultivation in a civilized community."[61]

Many of these statutes impose limitations on "respect for the dead," and devises which exceed these limits may be void. Thus a devise to construct a "mausoleum" for the testator and specified relatives was held invalid under the Rule because it fell outside the statutory exemption.[62]

### *Standing to Enforce Charitable Trusts*

The Attorney General's standing to enforce charitable trusts existed at common law has been confirmed by statute in many states.[63] The Attorney General has standing even when charitable organizations are named as beneficiaries. When trustees of a trust for the Federation of Jewish Agencies of Greater Philadelphia made allegedly improper investments, even though the Federation itself did not challenge them, the Attorney General was permitted to do so because "the Attorney General represents a broader interest than that of the charity alone. He must protect the interests of the public at large."[64] A suit by the Attorney General is not precluded by a prior judgment approving the conduct of a charitable trustee if the Attorney General was not a party.[65]

The Attorney General has the same right to information from the trustees of a charitable trust as the beneficiary of a private trust.[66] In addition, a Uniform Supervision of Trustees for Charitable Purposes Act requires charitable trustees to register with the Attorney General and file

**60.** Under Uniform Probate Code § 2–907(a), trust may be performed by trustee "for [21] years but no longer" apparently even if the trust will terminate when the trustee dies. A trust for pets under (b) terminates "when no living animal is covered by the trust." The Code says nothing about "capricious" purposes but, "the court may reduce the amount" if it "substantially exceeds the amount required for the intended use."

**61.** Perry v. Twentieth Street Bank, 206 S.E.2d 421, 423 (W.Va.1974).

**62.** Eaton v. Miller, 250 A.2d 220, 227 (Me. 1969).

**63.** *Restatement (Second) of Trusts* § 391 (1959); Cal.Gov.Code § . 12598; Wis.Stat. § 701.10(3). In State of Delaware v. Florida First Nat. Bank, 381 So.2d 1075 (Fla.App. 1979), the Delaware Attorney General was allowed to sue in Florida to enforce a charitable trust.

**64.** In re Estate of Feinstein, 527 A.2d 1034, 1036n (Pa.Super.1987). *See also* In re Estate of Cappetta, 733 N.E.2d 426, 433 (Ill. App.2000) (both AG and charities have standing in case involving devise to named charities).

**65.** In re Los Angeles County Pioneer Soc'y, 257 P.2d 1 (Cal.1953). *But see* Loring v. Marshall, 484 N.E.2d 1315 (Mass.1985) (adverse will construction binding on charities even though Attorney General not a party); Israel v. National Board of YMCA, 369 A.2d 646 (R.I.1977) (N.Y. judgment binding even though R.I. Attorney General not a party).

**66.** State v. Taylor, 362 P.2d 247 (Wash. 1961). As to a trust beneficiary's right to information see Section 12.10, at note 1.

periodic reports. Four states have adopted this Act, and nineteen others have enacted similar legislation.[67] These statutes exempt many charities, such as educational and religious institutions. Their effectiveness is also limited by inadequate staffing. In California, for example, three auditors had to monitor 29,000 registrants.[68]

The standing of persons other than the Attorney General to enforce charitable trusts is restricted. For example, a suit by residents and taxpayers of San Francisco alleging breaches of trust by the trustees of the city's fine arts museums was dismissed.

> Because the beneficiaries of charitable trusts * * * are ordinarily indefinite, the attorney General has primary responsibility for the supervision of charitable trusts, and generally he is the proper party to enforce them. * * * This limitation on standing arises from the need to protect the trustee from vexatious litigation, possibly based on an inadequate investigation, by a large, changing, and uncertain class of the public to be benefited.[69]

Another court dismissed a suit by an unsuccessful applicant for a scholarship; since there were over 930 contenders, "this action would only open the door to similar actions by other unsuccessful nominees."[70]

Even the settlor has no standing absent a statute to enforce a charitable trust,[71] but the settlor, or the settlor's successors, may recover trust property if the trust terminates.[72]

The Restatement allows beneficiaries who have a "special interest" in a charitable trust to sue.[73] Where a trust instrument "suggested" that trust funds be allocated to certain charities, one of them which had been rejected by the trustee was held to have such a "special interest." The plaintiff was "entitled to some kind of minimal review" as to whether the trustee had abused its discretion.[74] An unsuccessful bidder for timber rights held in trust by a state university was likewise held to have standing as a "citizen-taxpayer."

> The issues themselves, relating to the disposition of state resources, are of substantial general importance. [Plaintiff] has a sufficient economic interest to assure that it is not a sham plaintiff with no true adversity of interest.[75]

**67.** Bell & Bell, *Supervision of Charitable Trusts in California,* 32 Hast.L.J. 433, 438 (1980).

**68.** *Id.* at 443, 448.

**69.** Hardman v. Feinstein, 240 Cal.Rptr. 483, 485 (App.1987). *See also* Miller v. Alderhold, 184 S.E.2d 172 (Ga.1971); Weaver v. Wood, 680 N.E.2d 918 (Mass.1997) (church members); Russell v. Yale University, 737 A.2d 941 (Conn.App.1999) (donors and students have no standing).

**70.** Kania v. Chatham, 254 S.E.2d 528, 530 (N.C.1979).

**71.** Carl J. Herzog Foundation v. University of Bridgeport, 699 A.2d 995 (Conn.1997); *Restatement (Second) of Trusts* § 391, comment e (1959). *Contra,* Uniform Trust Code § 404(c); Wis.Stat. § 701.10(3).

**72.** *Restatement, Second, Trusts* § 391, comm. f (1959); Evans v. Abney, 396 U.S. 435 (1970); *cf.* Board of Selectmen v. Attorney General, 447 N.E.2d 677 (Mass.App.1983) (suit by residuary legatee of settlor).

**73.** *Restatement (Second) of Trusts* § 391 (1959).

**74.** St. John's–St. Luke Evangelical Church v. National Bank of Detroit, 283 N.W.2d 852 (Mich.App.1979). *See also* Matter of Village of Mount Prospect, 522 N.E.2d 122 (Ill.App.1988) (neighbors can object to sale of land given to village "for public purposes" even though AG approved the sale).

**75.** Aloha Lumber Corp. v. University of Alaska, 994 P.2d 991, 999 (Alaska 1999).

Standing may depend on the nature of the wrong alleged. A court denied plaintiffs standing to claim that the board of directors had mismanaged a charitable corporation, but upheld their right to claim that the defendants had wrongfully denied them voting rights, because this interest was "distinct from those of the general public."[76]

When there are several trustees, charitable trustees can act by a majority vote,[77] but the minority can sue for a breach of trust, even when the Attorney General has refused to act because he believes that the challenged conduct is not "detrimental to the public interest." Standing is restricted in order to avoid harassing litigation, but a suit by co-trustees poses no such threat since they are few in number.[78]

Some courts are more liberal in conferring standing on the ground that otherwise breaches of trust may go unremedied. "The manifold duties of [the Attorney General] makes * * * supervision necessarily sporadic * * * While supervision of the administration of charities remains inadequate, a liberal rule as to the standing of a plaintiff to complain about the administration of a charitable trust * * * seems decidedly in the public interest."[79] One way to deal with the problem of over-worked Attorneys General without opening the door to a flood of litigation is to allow individuals to sue "on the relation of" the Attorney General with the latter's permission, or to bring a petition for mandamus to require the AG's office to perform its duty.[80] Another may be a class action.[81]

### *Restricted Gifts to Charitable Entities*

Many charitable gifts are made to established organizations. Often, the donors impose restrictions on the use of the money or property given. Such restrictions are sometimes enforced on the theory that the organization holds in trust even though the word "trust" was not used.[82] But even if the gift is not classified as a trust, a donee who "is directed by the terms of the gift to devote the property to a particular one of its purposes is under a duty, enforceable at the suit of the Attorney General" to do so.[83] Even if the gift was by its terms unrestricted, the donated property must not be diverted from the purposes of the organization as set forth in its articles of incorporation.[84] The constitution may bar the removal of such restrictions by legislation.[85]

**76.** Lopez v. Medford Community Center, 424 N.E.2d 229, 232 (Mass.1981).

**77.** Richards v. Midkiff, 396 P.2d 49 (Haw. 1964); *Restatement (Second) of Trusts* § 391 (1959). As to private trusts see Section 12.4, at note 89 et seq.

**78.** Holt v. College of Osteopathic Physicians & Surgeons, 394 P.2d 932 (Cal.1964); Takabuki v. Ching, 695 P.2d 319 (Haw.1985); Belcher v. Conway, 425 A.2d 1254 (Conn.1979).

**79.** Jones v. Grant, 344 So.2d 1210, 1212 (Ala.1977). *See also* Kapiolani Park Pres. Soc. v. Honolulu, 751 P.2d 1022 (Haw.1988) (attorney general "actively joined" in supporting the breach of trust).

**80.** The court suggested these alternatives in rejecting a petition brought by an individual to have a successor trustee appointed for a charitable trust in Arman v. Bank of America, N.T., S.A., 88 Cal.Rptr.2d 410, 416 (App. 1999). *See also* Bell & Bell, *supra* note 66,at 447–48 (1980); *Restatement (Second) of Trusts* § 391, comment a (1959).

**81.** Gaubatz, *Grantor Enforcement of Trusts: Standing in One Private Law Setting*, 62 N.C.L.Rev 905, 926 (1984).

**82.** Board of Selectmen v. Attorney General, 447 N.E.2d 677 (Mass.App.1983).

**83.** *Restatement, Second, Trusts* § 348, comm. f (1959).

**84.** In re Connolly's Estate, 121 Cal.Rptr. 325 (App.1975); Greil Memorial Hospital v. First Ala. Bank, 387 So.2d 778 (Ala. 1980); Blocker v. State, 718 S.W.2d 409 (Tex.App. 1986). However, in Trustees of L.C. Wagner Trust v. Barium Springs Home, 401 S.E.2d 807 (N.C.App.1991), a devisee was allowed to take even though its "purpose, function and services" had changed.

However, courts are reluctant to find that a donor intended to restrict the use of property. When property was devised to the YWCA "to be used by it exclusively for the upkeep and maintenance of the MOOREHEAD HOUSE," the YWCA was allowed to keep it even after it closed Moorehead House on the theory that the will had merely stated the testator's "motive in making the bequest."[86] Courts are especially reluctant enforce restrictions when considerable time has elapsed since the date of the gift. For example, land was given in 1827 to a church "on condition that the same * * * shall be used for * * * the erection and maintenance thereon of a house of public worship." A century and a half later a court held that the donee was no longer subject to the condition. "Because a reasonable time has passed, the condition on the use of the tract has been fulfilled."[87]

### *Removing Restrictions Under Cy Pres Power*

Courts also often remove restrictions under *cy pres*. Because charitable trusts can be perpetual, circumstances often arise during their long existence which render the settlor's scheme impracticable. For example, a will probated in 1899 left property for a home for "orphans between the ages of 6 and 10, an orphan being defined as one whose father is dead." Seventy years later a court expanded this so as to include children between the ages of 6 and 18 who had been deprived of parental care for any reason. The number of applicants who qualified under the will had been declining.

> Today the prevalent trend in child welfare work is to try to place children who are between the ages of 6 and 10 in individual foster homes or provide the means necessary for the parents to retain the child in the home. It is generally only the older child, the one who cannot adjust to a home atmosphere, who is recommended for open institutional care. * * * This is in sharp contrast to the situation when George Clayton wrote his will * * * In the 1890s the main source of needy children was from homes where the father had died. * * * Today only 3.4% of the children eligible for aid to dependent children are so eligible because of the death of the father. * * * The overwhelmingly greatest need at present relates * * * to the care of other children, often older, who have been deprived of parental care for such reasons as divorce, separation or desertion by the father.[88]

Similarly, a trust for "defraying the cost of hospitalization" was modified to allow use "for broader health care purposes" because "today, third-party

**85.** Cohen v. City of Lynn, 598 N.E.2d 682 (Mass.App.1992); Kapiolani Park Pres. Soc. v. Honolulu, 751 P.2d 1022 (Haw.1988).

**86.** Young Women's Christian Ass'n v. Morgan, 189 S.E.2d 169 (N.C.1972). *See also* St. Vincent de Paul Soc. v. Mullen, 562 So.2d 232 (Ala.1990) (devise to Society "for their use as a retail outlet" does not impose a condition); Wood v. Board of County Com'rs of Fremont County, 759 P.2d 1250 (Wyo.1988) (land deeded "for the purpose of constructing and maintaining a hospital" cannot be recovered when hospital moved).

**87.** Independent Congregational Soc. v. Davenport, 381 A.2d 1137 (Me.1978). According to *Restatement, Second, Trusts* § 401, comm. e (1959), provisions for termination of a charitable trust upon the happening of an event are "strictly construed." *See also* Powell, *Defeasible Fees and the Nature of Real Property*, 40 U.Kan.L.Rev. 411, 421 et. seq. (1992)

**88.** Dunbar v. Board of Trust. of George W. Clayton Col., 461 P.2d 28, 31 (Colo.1969).

payment of hospitalization costs is nearly universal."[89]

Courts are generally more willing to deviate from the terms of an old gift as compared with a more recent one,[90] but the latter are also modified on occasion. For example, when a will devised property to a hospital which ceased to operate while the testator's estate was still in administration, the executor was directed to distribute the property to another hospital, "so that the charitable purpose of the testator will not fail."[91]

Courts have used *cy pres* to eliminate racial restrictions in gifts even where no state action was involved. The founder of Rice University said that it was to be for the "white inhabitants" of Texas. The limitation was removed because "under present conditions no university that discriminates * * * on the basis of race could attain or retain the status of a university of the first class."[92] When a will left money to Amherst for scholarships for "Protestant, Gentile" boys, the restriction was eliminated because Amherst refused to accept the gift otherwise.[93]

Courts have also used *cy pres* to accommodate trusts to changes in the tax laws, for example, after the 1969 Tax Reform Act imposed severe penalties on charitable foundations which accumulated income, many trusts were modified so as to avoid the penalty.[94] The Uniform Trust Code allows courts to modify the terms of a trust in order "to achieve the settlor's tax objectives."[95]

When trust funds exceed what is necessary for the stated purpose of the trust, the excess can be applied *cy pres,* as when a will left money for two annual scholarships and the fund produced enough income for more.[96] Conversely if funds are insufficient for the project designated by the settlor, they may be applied *cy pres* for a similar but more modest purpose. For instance, a will left $150,000 for the erection of a hospital. Since "the average capital expenditure to construct and equip one hospital *bed* * * * is between $150,-000–$180,000," the money was used "to renovate and equip existing facilities."[97]

Sometimes *cy pres* is used when the settlor's original purpose has been accomplished. A testator who died in 1861 left money "to create a public sentiment that will put an end to negro slavery." After the Thirteenth

**89.** Matter of Estate of Vallery, 883 P.2d 24, 29 (Colo.App.1993).

**90.** *Restatement (Second) of Trusts* § 399, comment i (1959); *cf.* English Charities Act, 1960, § 14(3) (even property given for specific purpose can be applied *cy pres* where "it would be unreasonable, having regard to * * * the lapse of time since the gifts were made, for the donor to expect the property to be returned").

**91.** Stockert v. Council on World Service, 427 S.E.2d 236 (W.Va.1993). *See also* Matter of Estate of Crawshaw, 819 P.2d 613 (Kan.1991) (when college named as devisee closed a few months after testator's death, devise awarded *cy pres*).

**92.** Coffee v. William Marsh Rice University, 408 S.W.2d 269, 286 (Tex.Civ.App.1966). *See also* Colin McK. Grant Home v. Medlock, 349 S.E.2d 655, 659 (S.C.App.1986) (racial restriction removed because "in the past sixty years racial relations have changed significantly").

**93.** Howard Savings Inst. v. Peep, 170 A.2d 39 (N.J.1961).

**94.** Canal Nat. Bank v. Old Folks' Home Ass'n, 347 A.2d 428 (Me.1975). *See also* Edmisten v. Sands, 300 S.E.2d 387 (N.C.1983); Matter of Booker, 682 P.2d 320 (Wash.App.1984).

**95.** Unif.Trust Code § 415. *See also* Cal. Prob.Code § 17200(a)(15) (courts can amend trust "in the manner required to qualify a decedent's estate for the charitable estate tax deduction").

**96.** Estate of Puckett, 168 Cal.Rptr. 311 (App.1980); *Restatement (Second) of Trusts* § 400 (1959).

**97.** Matter of Estate of Craig, 848 P.2d 313, 317, 322 (Ariz.App.1992). *See also Restatement, Second, Trusts* § 399, comm. j (1959); In re Estate of Thompson, 414 A.2d 881 (Me.1980).

Amendment did this, the money was applied to support the education of freedmen.[98]

*Cy pres* has also been invoked when money is left to an entity, such as the "Cancer Research Fund," which does not exist. Since the testator intended to benefit cancer research, the money was given to the American Cancer Society.[99] *Cy pres* has also been applied when a charitable corporation goes out of existence.[100] On the other hand, when a charity is dissolved in a merger, the funds may pass to the successor organization.[101] When a will left money "to the Cordele Area Y.M.C.A." which had ceased operation but remained in existence, it was held improper to assign the money to another Y.M.C.A. "A bequest to a charitable corporation is given effect if the named entity is still in existence when the time for vesting arrives, even though the corporation meanwhile has become entirely inactive."[102]

Just as judges may classify a purpose as charitable even if they feel the purpose is unwise, they are also reluctant to modify a charitable trust simply because they disagree with its terms. For example, thy rejected the petition of the trustee of a trust "for the inhabitants of the City of Oshkosh" to extend benefits to persons living in adjacent areas. "Cy-pres does not warrant a court substituting a different plan for that set forth in the trust instrument solely because the trustee, or court, or both, believe the substituted plan to be a better plan."[103] The *cy pres* power is exercised "sparingly," because "a settlor must have assurance that his solemn arrangements and instructions will not be subject to the whim or suggested expediency of others after his death."[104] If courts are too liberal in applying *cy pres*, it is said that donors may refrain from making charitable gifts.[105] Others reject this argument on the ground that a donor can always prevent courts from applying cy pres by so stipulating in the trust.[106]

Simes thought that courts were too hesitant to apply *cy pres*, citing the history of Benjamin Franklin's trust. Established in 1790, and designed to last for 200 years, the funds were to be "loaned out to such young married artificers under the age of twenty-five years as have served an apprentice-

**98.** Jackson v. Phillips, 96 Mass. 539 (1867). *See also* Board of Trustees v. Heirs of Prince, 319 S.E.2d 239 (N.C.1984).

**99.** In re Tomlinson's Estate, 359 N.E.2d 109 (Ill.1976).

**100.** In re Connolly's Estate, 121 Cal.Rptr. 325 (App.1975); Alexander v. Georgia Baptist Foundation, Inc., 266 S.E.2d 165 (Ga.1980); *Restatement, Second, Trusts* § 399, comm. o (1959).

**101.** Washington Hospital v. Riggs Nat. Bank, 575 A.2d 719 (D.C.App.1990); Colgan v. Sisters of St. Joseph, 604 N.E.2d 989 (Ill.App. 1992); Cowden v. Sovran Bank/Central South, 816 S.W.2d 741 (Tenn.1991). *But see* In re Estate of Beck, 649 N.E.2d 1011 (Ill.App.1995) (devise to orphanage fails when it conveys its assets to an organization which provides foster care, counseling and adoption services).

**102.** Crisp Area YMCA v. NationsBank, N.A., 526 S.E.2d 63, 66 (Ga.2000). *See also* In re Estate of Lind, 734 N.E.2d 47 (Ill.App.2000) (devise to "Northwestern University, Dental School" did not lapse when trustees voted to close the Dental School).

**103.** In re Oshkosh Foundation, 213 N.W.2d 54, 57 (Wis.1973). *See also* Matter of Estate of Murdock, 884 P.2d 749, 753 (Kan. App.1994) (rejecting cy pres where no evidence that restrictions "made it impossible, impractical, or illegal to carry out the donor's stated charitable purpose").

**104.** First Nat. Bank v. Brimmer, 504 P.2d 1367, 1371 (Wyo.1973).

**105.** Malone, McEachron & Cutter, *The Buck Trust Trial: A Litigator's Perspective*, 21 U.S.F.L.Rev. 585, 638 (1987).

**106.** Johnson & Taylor, *Revolutionizing Judicial Interpretation of Charitable Trusts*, 74 Iowa L.Rev. 545, 575 (1989).

ship."[107] The rate of interest, security and maximum loan were specified. Because of these restrictions, the funds were not always loaned out, and courts authorized modifications from time to time, but only when "the original purpose and plan was demonstrably impossible or impracticable. Moreover, when modification was made, the adherence as nearly as possible to the original purpose resulted in failure of the modification."[108] Simes proposed that after thirty years courts should have an enlarged *cy pres* power to modify charitable trusts "not only if the original purpose was found impracticable but also if * * * the amount to be expended is out of all proportion to its value to society."[109] The Uniform Trust Code allows the use of *cy pres* when a particular trust purpose is "wasteful."[110] Some statutes focus on the welfare of the community rather than the intentions of the donor.[111]

Arguably, courts should also focus on benefit to society rather than the settlor's intent, because the special privileges conferred on charitable trusts are justified only if they provide such a benefit.[112] An extreme example of a court ignoring the settlor's intent illustrates the risks in this idea; pursuant to then current notions of social benefit (among the judiciary) an 18th century court directed that a Jewish testator's devise for "instructing people in our holy religion" should be used to instruct Christianity![113]

Even if literal compliance with the settlor's direction is out of the question, *cy pres* is used only if the settlor had a "general charitable intent"; if not, the trust property reverts to the settlor, or the settlor's successors. When a will left property to the Good Shepherd's Home, an institution for disturbed teen-age girls, which ceased to exist before the testator died, the court refused to give the property to another home operated for the same purpose. The will expressed no charitable purpose and the court refused to infer one from the prior activities of the Good Shepherd's Home.[114] Money was raised for a bone marrow transplant for a victim of leukemia who died before the operation could be performed. The money was returned to the donors, since the solicitation for donations "was solely directed to a solicitation of donations to defray one operative procedure for one specified beneficiary."[115] This result was reached despite the "administrative difficulties in locating the present whereabouts of some contributors," many of whom were anonymous.[116] On the other hand, language in a gift purporting to create a "condition" is not always construed to require return to the donor when the condition is not fulfilled. For example, land was deeded to a city "upon the condition that" it be used as a park. When the land was later condemned for a highway, the donor's heirs' claim to the proceeds was rejected. The court held

**107.** Simes, *supra* note 8, at 129.

**108.** *Id.* at 131–32. For later litigation when the time for termination of the trust arrived see Franklin Foundation v. Attorney General, 623 N.E.2d 1109 (Mass.1993).

**109.** Simes, *supra* note 8, at 139.

**110.** Unif.Trust Code § 412.

**111.** *Restatement, Second, Trusts* § 399, comm. q (1959); Forrest v. Attorney General, [1986] Vict.R. 187 (1985).

**112.** Di Clerico, *Cy Pres: A Proposal for Change,* 47 B.U.L.Rev. 154, 158 (1967); Johnson & Taylor, *supra* note 105, at 577.

**113.** Da Costa v. De Pas, 27 Eng.Rep. 150 (Ch. 1754).

**114.** In re Staab's Estate, 173 N.W.2d 866 (Iowa 1970).

**115.** Matter of Gonzalez, 621 A.2d 94, 96–97 (N.J.Super.Ch.Div.1992).

**116.** Compare the English Charities Act, 1960, § 14 (even property given for specific purpose can be applied *cy pres* if donor cannot be found); N.Y.E.P.T.L. § 8–1.1(j) (if more than 1,000 contributors, unexpended funds after 5 years shall be applied *cy pres*).

the donor intended "to create a charitable trust rather than * * * a fee simple determinable" and the proceeds were applied *cy pres* to a park in another location.[117]

The question whether a settlor had a "general charitable intent" beyond the specific purpose mentioned is just another way of asking what the settlor would have done under the circumstances. This question is hard to answer because the settlor did not contemplate the circumstances which have come to pass.[118] The Uniform Trust Code directs the use of *cy pres* unless the trust explicitly provides to the contrary.[119]

The presumption against intestacy is sometimes used to support *cy pres*,[120] especially when the will expressly disinherits the testator's heirs.[121] This argument is inapplicable when the failure of a charitable gift causes the property to go to another devisee under the will. Even if a gift over is invalid under the Rule against Perpetuities, it may show that the testator did not want *cy pres* to apply.[122] If the substituted legatee is a charity the argument against *cy pres* even stronger, since the public will benefit in any event. For example, a will left the estate to the American Society for the Prevention of Cruelty to Animals on condition that it build a shelter in Joliet, or if the Society "shall fail to qualify," to other charitable organizations. When the ASPCA disclaimed the gift, the Humane Society's petition to be substituted was rejected. The gift over in the will showed that the testator had no general charitable intent to benefit animals.[123]

Most courts admit extrinsic evidence of the testator's intent when this issue is raised. When a will left money to Amherst for a scholarship with religious restrictions which Amherst rejected, the court removed the restrictions rather than have the money pass intestate on the basis of evidence that the testator's heirs were distant relatives with whom he had little contact, he regularly contributed to Amherst and attended reunions of his graduating class, and was not actively interested in any church.[124] On the other hand, a donor's long-term association with Syracuse Medical College was held to show he intended the property to revert rather than go to another school when the designated college went out of existence.[125]

**117.** State v. Rand, 366 A.2d 183 (Me. 1976). *See also Restatement, Second, Trusts* § 399, comm. c (1959). However, in Walton v. City of Red Bluff, 3 Cal.Rptr.2d 275 (App. 1991), land conveyed "to hold in trust for a library, if not so used to revert to grantor" was held to revert when it ceased to be used for a library.

**118.** In re Estate of Thompson, 414 A.2d 881, 886 (Me.1980). In National Soc. of Daughters of American Revolution v. Goodman, 736 A.2d 1205 (Md.App.1999), when the testator learned that the charity she intended to benefit did not exist, she instructed her attorney to prepare a new will eliminating the devise, but she died before executing the new will. The court held that this showed a lack of general charitable intent.

**119.** Unif.Trust Code § 412(b). *See also* Mass.Ann.Laws c. 12, § 8K.

**120.** In re Estate of Rood, 200 N.W.2d 728 (Mich.App.1972).

**121.** In re Tomlinson's Estate, 359 N.E.2d 109, 112 (Ill.1976).

**122.** Nelson v. Kring, 592 P.2d 438, 444 (Kan.1979).

**123.** Matter of Estate of Offerman, 505 N.E.2d 413 (Ill.App.1987). *See also* Hermitage Meth. Homes v. Dominion Trust, 387 S.E.2d 740 (Va.1990); *Restatement, Second, Trusts* § 399, comm. c (1959).

**124.** Howard Savings Inst. v. Peep, 170 A.2d 39, 46 (N.J.1961). *See also* Estate of Klinkner, 151 Cal.Rptr. 20, 26 (App.1978); Board of Trustees v. Heirs of Prince, 319 S.E.2d 239, 244 (N.C.1984). *But see* Board of Selectmen v. Attorney General, 447 N.E.2d 677, 682 (Mass.App.1983).

**125.** Application of Syracuse University, 148 N.E.2d 671 (N.Y.1958).

The language of the will may indicate how significant the modification would be to the settlor. The gift which established Rice University said that instruction was to be for whites, but did not say "for whites solely," and it also said that instruction should be "open to all."[126] In contrast, a court refused to remove a racial restriction in another will which said that it should "be carried out to the letter."[127]

The degree of deviation requested also makes a difference. The Restatement distinguishes between *cy pres* and "deviation" from the terms of a trust with respect to administration.[128] A will devised a house and land in trust for use as a convalescent home, "and if used for any other purpose [it] shall revert to my heirs." A later destruction of the house, which had become unsuitable for use as a home, was approved.

> Authorizing sensible changes in the prescribed, but no longer appropriate mechanics of achieving a testator's primary charitable objective is within the general power of courts of equity * * * to permit deviation short of cy pres applications. * * * The inapplicability of the cy pres doctrine to the testamentary trust here involved due to the existence of the reversionary provisions in the will * * * should not prevent reasonable deviation from the trust's subordinate provisions.[129]

Even in private trusts courts sometimes authorize deviations with respect to administrative provisions when unanticipated circumstances arise,[130] and they may be even readier to do so in charitable trusts. For example, a trust to provide scholarships restricted investments to bank accounts and Kansas municipal bonds. A trustee's petition to be relieved of this restriction was rejected by the trial court on the ground that it did not "frustrate the purpose of the Trust." This was reversed on appeal. Under the Uniform Management of Institutional Funds Act it was enough to show that the restriction was "obsolete, inappropriate or impracticable."[131] A tougher standard was applied to the same trustee's request to modify the prescribed method of awarding scholarships; this could be done only if it was "impossible, impractical, or illegal to carry out the donor's stated charitable purpose."[132]

Courts can usually modify a trust under *cy pres* without the donor's consent, but a few statutes provide otherwise.[133] A settlor's consent to a change is sufficient to remove "minor restrictions."[134] The Uniform Management of Institutional Funds Act makes it sufficient to remove any restriction.[135]

The trustee are not supposed to deviate from trust terms without first obtaining court approval,[136] but courts sometimes ratify deviations which have

**126.** Coffee v. William Marsh Rice University, 408 S.W.2d 269, 279 (Tex.Civ.App.1966).

**127.** La Fond v. City of Detroit, 98 N.W.2d 530, 532 (Mich.1959).

**128.** *Restatement (Second) of Trusts* §§ 381, 399 (1959).

**129.** Wigglesworth v. Cowles, 648 N.E.2d 1289, 1294 (Mass.App.1995).

**130.** Section 9.6, at note 10 et seq.

**131.** Uniform Management of Institutional Funds Act § 7(b).

**132.** Matter of Estate of Murdock, 884 P.2d 749, 752 (Kan.App.1994).

**133.** *Restatement (Second) of Trusts* § 399, comment g (1959); N.Y.E.P.T,L. § 8–1.1(c) (consent of donor required).

**134.** *Restatement, Second, Trusts* § 367, comment c (1959).

**135.** Section 7(a), comment.

**136.** Cinnaminson Tp. v. First Camden Nat. Bank & Trust Co., 238 A.2d 701 (N.J.Super.Ch.Div.1968); *Restatement (Second) of Trusts* § 399, comment e (1959).

already occurred.[137] In exercising their *cy pres* powers, courts give great weight to the trustee's views, but they are not bound to follow the views of either the trustee or of the Attorney General.[138] Appellate review of trial court decisions is not limited to the "clearly erroneous" standard applied to findings of fact.[139]

### *Planning*

A trust may not be the best vehicle for administering a charitable gift. The gift may be too small to justify the cost of a professional trustee. Trustees may be subject to burdensome restrictions which do not apply to not-for-profit corporations.[140] A court has rejected the argument that trust rules should be applied by analogy to charitable corporations because they "are created for the same purpose." By using the form of a charitable corporation, the donor intends to "invoke the far more flexible and adaptable principles of corporate law."[141] On the other hand, some states require state approval to create a corporation, or otherwise subject charitable corporations to restrictions from which trusts are exempt, such as limits on land holdings.[142]

If the donor's purpose does not qualify as charitable, a not-for-profit corporation is better than a trust.[143]

If the donor intends to impose an enforceable restriction, the instrument should make this clear so as to avoid the traditional strict construction of such restrictions. However, donors should be aware that such restrictions may hamper the fulfillment of their charitable objectives, perhaps necessitating court proceedings to remove them.

**137.** Wigglesworth v. Cowles, 648 N.E.2d 1289 (Mass.App.1995).

**138.** *Restatement (Second) of Trusts* § 399, comment f (1959); Belcher v. Conway, 425 A.2d 1254, 1257 (Conn.1979). In Matter of Multiple Sclerosis Service, 496 N.E.2d 861 (N.Y.1986), the court contrasted *cy-pres* with a statute governing not-for-profit corporations, which "accords greater authority" to the views of the corporation's board of directors than to those of a trustee.

**139.** In re Estate of Thompson, 414 A.2d 881 (Me.1980).

**140.** *Restatement (Second) of Trusts* § 348, comment f (1959).

**141.** Oberly v. Kirby, 592 A.2d 445, 466–67 (Del.1991).

**142.** Fisch, *Choosing the Charitable Entity*, 114 Trusts and Estates 875 (1975).

**143.** Fratcher, *Bequests for Purposes*, 56 Iowa L.Rev. 773, 798 (1971).

# Chapter 10

# FUTURE INTERESTS

*Analysis*



---

## § 10.1 Conditions of Survival

Many wills and trusts create future interests in property, for example, "to my spouse for life, remainder to our children." If a child fails to survive the testator, this presents a question of lapse which we discussed in Section 8.3. In this Section we discuss what happens if a remainderman survives the testator or settlor[1] but dies during the life of the life beneficiary, or prior to some other time fixed for distribution, such as "when she reaches age 25."[2] If a court treats the child's interest as vested, it passes to his or her estate to be disposed of by the child's will[3] or to the child's heirs if the child died intestate. But a court may find or infer a condition that any remainderman must survive the life beneficiary in order to take. If so, it must decide what happens to the share of any remainderman who fails to survive. Most anti-lapse statutes[4] apply only to devisees who predecease the testator and so would be irrelevant in this situation. A remainder "to our children" is a class gift so any children who survived would take the shares of children who did not. If no class member survives, or if the remainder was an individual who failed to survive, the remainder might go to the (other) residuary devisees under the testator's will or by intestacy to the testator's heirs if no residuary devisee qualified.[5] If a remainder created by a living trust fails, this may lead to a "resulting trust" for the settlor, or the settlor's successors.[6]

§ 10.1

**1.** Generally speaking, the rules are the same whether the instrument is a will or a living trust, Trackman v. Ringer, 529 N.E.2d 647, 649 (Ill.App.1988), and whether the future interest is legal or equitable, with some exceptions. See note 44 *infra.*

**2.** Normally the question is whether the remainderman survived the life beneficiary, but in National City Bank v. Beyer, 729 N.E.2d 711 (Ohio 2000), the interest of a remainderman who died a few months after the life beneficiary was held to be divested by the terms of a gift over "if such beneficiary dies before the assets have been fully distributed."

**3.** It is also possible, but rare, for remainders to be transferred inter-vivos. *Restatement, Third, of Trusts* § 51 (1999).

**4.** As to anti-lapse statutes see Section 8.3, at note 9 et seq.

**5.** As to what constitutes a "class gift", and whether a failed residuary gift passes intestate or to other residuary devisees, see Section 8.3, at note 56 et seq. and 69 et seq.

**6.** *Restatement, Third, of Trusts* § 7, illus. 1 (1996).

### *Vested or Contingent*

The question whether a remainderman must survive the life interest in order to take is often posed as "was the remainder vested or contingent?" This terminology is convenient, but it can be misleading, because (1) even vested remainders may be conditioned on survival, and (2) not all contingent remainders are conditioned on survival. As to the first point, if a will provides "remainder to my children, but if any child dies before my spouse, his or her share shall go to his or her children," the children's remainder is not contingent on survival, but rather *vested subject to divestment* for failure to survive.[7] In contrast, a remainder "to our then living children," is *contingent.* In the first case the condition of survival is *subsequent;* in the second, the condition is *precedent.*[8] The distinction between precedent and subsequent conditions has practical significance in (the few) jurisdictions which still prohibit the transfer of contingent remainders. For example, when a remainder was devised to "the then-living descendants of my son," a transfer by a child of the son during his father's lifetime was held to be ineffective.

> Whether a remainder is contingent or vested depends upon the language employed. If the conditional element is incorporated into the description of the * * * remaindermen, then the remainder is contingent, but if after words giving a vested interest, a clause is added divesting it, the remainder is vested. Thus, on a devise to A for life, remainder to his children, but if any child dies in the lifetime of A his share is to go to those who survive, the share of each child is vested, subject to be divested by his death. But a devise to A for life, remainder to such of his children as survive him, the remainder is contingent.[9]

Most courts today reject such verbal niceties, and allow both vested and contingent remainders to be transferred. "The holder of a contingent future interest in a clear and growing majority of states * * * has property of which present disposition can be made."[10]

Contingent remainders are not necessarily conditioned on survival of the remainderman. For example, a will left land to the testator's granddaughter for life, with a remainder to her issue if she had any, "and if not, then to Asbury Fletcher." The granddaughter died without issue. Asbury predeceased her. The court held that Asbury did not get the property because his remainder was "contingent."[11] However as a dissenting opinion observed, a remainder may be subject to a condition (the death of the granddaughter without issue) which renders it contingent, without being subject to a further

7. *Restatement of Property* § 253, illus. 1 (1940); National City Bank v. Beyer, 729 N.E.2d 711, 716 (Ohio 2000). *But see* Webb v. Underhill, 882 P.2d 127, 130 (Or.App.1994).

8. Language about survival can come after the designation of the takers and still be deemed "precedent." A remainder "to B's children who survive B" is contingent, *id.* § 278, illus. 1. A condition can be both precedent and subsequent, *e.g.*, "to Arthur if he survives, but if Arthur does not survive, to charity." *See* 5 *Amer.Law of Prop.* § 21.32.

9. Goodwine State Bank v. Mullins, 625 N.E.2d 1056, 1074 (Ill.App.1993).

10. *Restatement, Third, Trusts* § 41, comm. a (1999).

The "central question is not whether the interest is 'vested' or 'contingent,' but rather * * * whether the future interest is so remote that it should not have been included." Moyars v. Moyars, 717 N.E.2d 976, 979 (Ind.App.1999).

11. Fletcher v. Hurdle, 536 S.W.2d 109 (Ark.1976). *See also* Rushing v. Mann, 910 S.W.2d 672 (Ark.1995).

condition that the devisee survive the termination of the life estate. Most courts avoid the confusion of thought of the majority opinion in this case.[12]

### *Preference for Early Vesting*

Some courts give little weight to precedents in construing wills on the ground that the language of every will differs. "Cases construing remainders created by wills are almost as countless as grains of sand on the seashore," but they have little "controlling force * * * because no two wills are alike."[13] Other courts, however, often refer to general rules of construction, either statutory or common law. One commonly cited rule says that the law favors the early vesting of estates.[14] Coke expressed this idea in the 17th century: "the law always delights in the vesting of estates, and contingencies are odious in the law, and are the causes of troubles."[15] Some states have codified the preference for a vested construction,[16] but several writers have attacked it,[17] and courts have begun to question it. For example, "the maxim favoring early vesting of remainders frequently * * * frustrates what the ordinary settlor would have intended" and "should no longer be followed without question."[18] The Uniform Probate Code follows this view by presuming that "a future interest under the terms of a trust is contingent on the beneficiary's surviving to the distributions date."[19]

*(1) Taxes*

One argument against early vesting is that it subjects property to an estate tax when the remainderman dies before the life beneficiary, whereas no such tax accrues when a contingent remainderman dies without satisfying a condition of survival.[20] Administrative costs may also be incurred by adding property to the estate of a deceased remainderman.[21] The Uniform Probate Code's justifies a survivorship requirement as avoiding "cumbersome and

**12.** *See Restatement of Property* § 261 (1940); 5 *Amer. Law of Prop.* § 21.25; Temple Beth Israel v. Feiss, 2 P.3d 388, 390–91 (Or. App.2000); Evans v. Giles, 415 N.E.2d 354 (Ill.1980); In re Ferry's Estate, 361 P.2d 900 (Cal.1961).

**13.** Clark v. Strother, 385 S.E.2d 578, 582 (Va.1989). *See also* In re Estate of Long, 918 P.2d 975, 978 (Wash.App.1996).

**14.** Summers v. Summers, 699 N.E.2d 958, 962 (Ohio App.1997); Warren v. Albrecht, 571 N.E.2d 1179, 1181 (Ill.App.1991); Matter of Estate of Sprinchorn, 546 N.Y.S.2d 256, 258 (A.D.1989); McGovern, *Facts and Rules in the Construction of Wills*, 26 UCLA L.Rev. 285 (1978).

**15.** Roberts v. Roberts, 80 Eng.Rep. 1002, 1009 (K.B. 1613).

**16.** 84 Okl.Stat. § 175; Calif.Prob.Code § 21116.

**17.** Chaffin, *Descendible Future Interests in Georgia: The Effect of the Preference for Early Vesting*, 7 Ga.L.Rev. 443 (1973); Rabin, *The Law Favors the Vesting of Estates. Why?* 65 Colum.L.Rev. 467 (1965); Schuyler, *Drafting, Tax, and Other Consequences of the Rule of Early Vesting*, 46 Ill.L.Rev. 407 (1951).

**18.** Harris Trust and Savings Bank v. Beach, 513 N.E.2d 833, 840 (Ill.1987).

**19.** Uniform Probate Code § 2–707(b). This and all other rules of construction in the Code is subject to "a finding of contrary intention." *Id.*, § 2–701,

**20.** Huggins v. United States, 684 F.2d 417 (6th Cir.1982). Since the remainderman's estate might not have the money needed to pay the tax, the Internal Revenue Code allows payment of the tax to be deferred until the property is distributed, but the estate must pay interest on the deferred tax and may have to post a bond. Internal Revenue Code §§ 6163, 6165, 6601.

**21.** However, some courts avoid these administrative costs by distributing the property directly to the recipients of the remainderman's estate. Dukeminier, *The Uniform Probate Code Upsets the Law of Remainders*, 94 Mich.L.Rev. 148, 161–2 (1995); French, *Imposing a General Survival Requirement on Beneficiaries of Future Interests*, 27 Ariz.L.Rev. 801, 804 (1985); Cunningham, *The Hazards of Tinkering with the Common Law of Future Interests*, 48 Hast.L.J. 676, 698–99 (1997).

costly distributions to and through the estates of deceased beneficiaries of future interests."[22] A court construed a remainder as contingent with the remark that "unfortunate tax consequences may follow a determination that an interest is vested and most transferors who consider all the consequences which attach to a vested interest are inclined to postpone vesting until the time set for enjoyment of the interest in possession."[23]

On the other hand postponing vesting does not always produce tax advantages. Many estates of remaindermen are too small to incur any estate tax; in others, avoiding an estate tax may be more than offset by incurring a generation-skipping tax at a higher rate.[24] Also, the estate tax disadvantage of including a remainder in an estate may be outweighed by income tax savings, since the assets included in an estate get a step up in basis to their date-of-death value.[25]

*(2) Keeping Property in the Bloodline*

Many rules of law are based on an assumption that persons want their property to go to blood relatives when they die. Intestacy statutes generally provide only for blood relatives, except for the decedent's spouse.[26] Most anti-lapse statutes apply only to relatives and make a substitutional gift to the devisee's issue, so that a lapsed devise will pass to relatives of the testator.[27] Courts sometimes refer to "the common desire" to favor blood relatives as a relevant factor in construing instruments.[28]

A vested remainder may pass to a spouse or other devisees of the remainderman who were not related to the testator. This has been used as an argument for construing a remainder as contingent. For example, a remainder to the testator's grandnieces and grandnephews was held to be contingent on survival because otherwise "persons not of testatrix's bloodline, or even corporate institutions, might be the ultimate distributees."[29]

This reasoning has been challenged. Even if a remainder is contingent on survival, a remainderman who does survive can give or devise the property to a person unrelated to the testator. Testators who are disturbed by this possibility can limit the remainderman's interest to a life estate.[30]

**22.** Uniform Probate Code § 2–707, Comment.

**23.** Browning v. Sacrison, 518 P.2d 656, 658 (Or.1974) (quoting 5 *Am.L.Prop.* § 21.3). *See also Restatement, Second, of Property (Donative Transfers) §* 27.3, Reporter's Tax Note (1987); Halbach & Waggoner, *The UPC's New Survivorship and Anti–Lapse Provisions*, 55 Alb.L.Rev. 1091, 1133 (1992). *But see* In re Benson's Estate, 285 A.2d 101, 106 (Pa.1971) (refusing to construe will to avoid estate taxes).

**24.** Dukeminier, *supra* note 21, at 163; Cunningham, *supra* note 22, at 696; Garvey, *Drafting Wills and Trusts: Anticipating the Birth and Death of Possible Beneficiaries*, 71 Or.L.Rev. 47, 62 (1991). Professor Waggoner, on the other hand, doubts "that many trusts covered by section 2–707 will exceed the GST exemption amount of $1 million per donor. Waggoner, *The Uniform Probate Code Extends Antilapse–Type Protection to Poorly Drafted Trusts*, 94 Mich.L.Rev. 2309, 2345 (16). As to the generation-skipping tax see Section 15.4

**25.** See Section 15.

**26.** See Section 2.2.

**27.** See Section 8.3, at notes 13–15.

**28.** 5 *Amer. Law of Prop.* § 21.13, at 131–32.

**29.** In re Trust of Walker, 116 N.W.2d 106, 109 (Wis.1962). *See also* Lamb v. Nationsbank, N.A., 507 S.E.2d 457, 460 (Ga.1998); National City Bank v. Beyer, 729 N.E.2d 711, 716 (Ohio 2000) (testator wanted property to "remain in the family"). In Browning v. Sacrison, 518 P.2d 656, 659 (Or.1974), this general feeling was reinforced by expressions of hostility in the will to an in-law.

**30.** Cunningham, *supra* note 21, at 700.

Furthermore, any constructional preference for blood relatives is questionable today when (1) the law usually allows adopted children to inherit from their adoptive but not their blood relatives, and (2) intestacy laws give the surviving spouse a fee simple even though this often causes property to end up in the hands of non-relatives.[31] Professor Dukeminier has asked why the law should "assume that the decedent would want to be generous with his or her spouse" but not the spouse of a remainderman?[32] Certainly many testators would not object to having property pass to a son-or daughter-in-law,[33] but Professor Waggoner says "in today's divorce-prone * * * world, the evidence indicates that settlors incline toward substituting the descendant, not the spouse, of a remainder beneficiary who predeceases the distribution date."[34]

### *Arguments Supporting Vested Construction*

*(1) Promoting Alienability*

An argument *in favor of* a vested construction is that it "enables property to be freely transferred at the earliest possible date."[35] Conversely, the presence of a spendthrift restraint is sometimes advanced as an argument that the settlor/testator wanted an interest to be contingent.[36] However, the question whether a remainder was contingent on survival usually arises after the life tenant has died, at which time, the property is alienable whichever construction is chosen. Moreover, even before the life estate expires, the ability to transfer property burdened with a remainder does not necessarily turn on whether the remainder is vested or contingent. Nearly all jurisdictions allow contingent as well as vested remainders to be assigned.[37] However, when remainders are contingent on survival, other persons must take if the remaindermen do not survive, and this increase in the number of persons with potential interests may make property harder to sell.[38] For example, land was left to the testator's daughter for life, with a remainder "to such of her children as survive her." A sale of timber by the daughter and her children was successfully challenged by a grandchild who was held to have a contingent interest in the land.[39] On the other hand, even vested remainders can render property virtually inalienable. If the remainder in this case had been vested in the daughter's "children," the property would still be hard to sell because she could have given birth to (or adopted) more children thereafter.[40] "The fluidity of property is impaired to some extent by the existence of *any*

**31.** As to the spouse's intestacy share see Section 2.1. As to adoptees see section 2.10.

**32.** Dukeminier, *supra* note 21, at 152.

**33.** Professor Chaffin, who argues for construing remainders as contingent to keep property in the bloodline, also recommends that wills provide for the widow of a deceased child. Chaffin, *supra* note 16, at 490. *See also* H.Tweed & W.Parsons, *Lifetime and Testamentary Estate Planning* 88 (10th ed. 1988) (recommends a provision for in-laws).

**34.** Waggoner, *supra* note 24, at 2336.

**35.** In re Krooss, 99 N.E.2d 222, 224 (N.Y. 1951).

**36.** Natl. City Bank v. Beyer, 729 N.E.2d 711, 716 (Ohio 2000).

**37.** See note 9 *supra*.

**38.** *Restatement of Property* § 243, comm. i.

**39.** Pedro v. January, 494 P.2d 868 (Or. 1972).

**40.** In re Testamentary Trust of Hasch, 721 N.E.2d 1111 (Ohio App.1999) (court refuses to terminate trust because vested remainder in life beneficiary's children remains open to after-born children for his lifetime). As to the possibility of proving that the birth of further children is impossible, see Section 9.6, note 30.

future interest in it and the extent to which it is further impaired if the interest is contingent is at most a matter of degree."[41]

Most future interests today are beneficial interests in a trust, under which the trustee has power to sell the trust assets.[42] Although courts have traditionally applied the preference for early vesting to trusts as well as legal remainders,[43] the Uniform Probate Code distinguishes between the two. It implies a condition of survivorship only for future interests in a trust, because "the ability of the parties to sell the land would be impaired if not destroyed" if legal remainders were contingent[44]. Even as to trusts, however, a vested construction can reduce the number of beneficiaries whose consent is needed to modify or terminate the trust. For example, when grandchildren who were designated remaindermen sought to modify a trust, the trial court refused, holding that "their interests were contingent upon their surviving" the income beneficiaries, and if they did not, "the trust property would revert to the testator's estate." The appellate court reversed, holding that the grandchildren had a vested interest, and therefore "all the beneficiaries" had consented.[45]

*(2) Avoiding Intestacy*

Courts sometimes hold remainders vested in order to avoid an intestacy. "The abhorrence of courts to intestacy under a will may be likened unto the abhorrence of nature to a vacuum."[46] If a remainder devised to "children" in the residuary clause of a will is contingent on surviving the life beneficiary, the property will pass to the testator's heirs by intestacy if all the children predecease the life tenant unless a substitutional devise is added.[47] The property may even escheat to the state if the testator has no surviving relatives.[48]

However, contingent remainders which are given to a class do not create an intestacy if at least one member of the class survives the life beneficiary. Some courts treat *all* class gifts as contingent on survival: if "a gift to a class is postponed until after the termination of a preceding estate, those members of the class, and those only, take who are in existence when * * * the time for distribution comes."[49] Most courts, however, treat class gifts the same way as gifts to individuals. The Second Restatement of Property says that in a gift to "children" or the like, a child who dies prior to distribution "is not excluded

**41.** Schuyler, *supra* note 17, at 425–26 (emphasis added).

**42.** As to sales by trustees see Section 12.6, at note 2 et seq.

**43.** Summers v. Summers, 699 N.E.2d 958 (Ohio App.1997); In re Trust Under Will of Holt, 491 N.W.2d 25 (Minn.App.1992); Trackman v. Ringer, 529 N.E.2d 647 (Ill.App.1988).

**44.** Uniform Probate Code § 2–707, Comment; Halbach & Waggoner, *The UPC's New Survivorship and Anti–Lapse Provisions*, 55 Alb.L.Rev. 1091, 1132 (1992).

**45.** In re Trust of Lane, 592 A.2d 492, 496–97 (Md.1991). Further discussion of the problem of obtaining consent of all beneficiaries in order to terminate a trust is found in Section 9.6, at note 29 et seq.

**46.** Coddington v. Stone, 9 S.E.2d 420, 424 (N.C.1940). *See also* Matter of Estate of Sprinchorn, 546 N.Y.S.2d 256, 258 (A.D.1989); In re Trust of Lane, 592 A.2d 492, 496 (Md. 1991); *Restatement of Property* § 243, comm. e, § 255 (1940).

**47.** However, if the remainder is devised in a pre-residuary devise, its failure may simply cause the property to pass under the residuary clause of the will. Temple Beth Israel v. Feiss, 2 P.3d 388, 395 (Or.App.2000); Section 8.3, at note 69 et seq.

**48.** Dukeminier, *supra* note 21, at 157. As to escheat see Section 2.2, at note 62 et seq.

**49.** Wilkes v. Wilkes, 488 S.W.2d 398, 405 (Tex.1972). *See also* In re Trust of Walker, 116 N.W.2d 106, 109–10 (Wis.1962).

from the class by reason of such death" absent language or circumstances indicating a contrary intent.[50]

If a particular construction leads to an intestacy, is this a bad thing? Intestate succession statutes represent reasonable surmises of how decedents want their property to pass. They are often used to infer probable intent in construing wills, *e.g.* in deciding whether adopted children should be included in a devise to "children."[51] A constructional preference against disinheriting the testator's heirs is sometimes cited, which seems to cancel out any presumption against intestacy.[52]

In some cases, however, intestacy may distort an estate plan. Suppose a testator has three children, Alice, Andrew and Arthur. Arthur dies survived by two children, Burt and Barbara. The testator's will creates a trust with a remainder "one third to Alice, one third to Andrew, and one sixth each to Burt and Barbara," indicating an intent to treat all three branches of the family equally. If Burt predeceases the life beneficiary, and his share passes to the testator's heirs as intestate property, Alice and Andrew will take more than their 2/3 share under the will. The intended equal division can be effectuated by treating Burt's interest as vested.[53]

An intestacy may also increase taxes and take property out of the testator's bloodline. For example, a testator died in 1944, leaving his estate in trust with a contingent remainder to the descendants of an aunt, who died without issue before the last income beneficiary died in 1965. Since the contingent remainder failed, the property was distributed to the estates of the testator's heirs, who had all died in the interim.[54] Such a distribution can be "as expensive and cumbersome as distribution to the estate of the deceased [remainderman], and it is just as likely to carry property outside of the family."[55]

Intestacy may also give property to an heir whom the testator wished to disinherit. A court construed a remainder as vested when an intestacy would have frustrated "the testator's expressed intention that his three daughters should each receive $1 'and no more.' "[56]

**50.** *Restatement, Second, of Property (Donative Transfers)* § 27.3 (1987). *See also* Hofing v. Willis, 201 N.E.2d 852, 856 (Ill.1964) (overruling earlier cases); Walker v. Applebury, 400 S.W.2d 865 (Tenn.1965); Hartford National Bank & Trust Co. v. Birge, 266 A.2d 373 (Conn.1970); Halbach, *Issues about Issue: Some Recurrent Class Gifts Problems,* 48 Mo. L.Rev. 333, 363 (1983).

**51.** Cal.Prob.Code § 21115; Uniform Probate Code § 2–705(a); In re Coe's Estate, 201 A.2d 571, 574 (N.J.1964); *Restatement of Property* § 286, comm. g, § 287, comm. d, § 288, comm. b (1936).

**52.** In re Rouse's Estate, 87 A.2d 281, 283 (Pa.1952); Matter of Estate of Walters, 519 N.E.2d 1270, 1274 (Ind.App.1988).

**53.** An intestacy can also be avoided in this situation by treating the gift to the brothers as a class gift, despite the use of names. Abrams v. Templeton, 465 S.E.2d 117, 121 (S.C.App. 1995).

**54.** In re Trust of Wehr, 152 N.W.2d 868 (Wis.1967). *See also* Theodore Short Trust v. Fuller, 7 S.W.3d 482, 493 (Mo.App.1999) (remainder fails so property passes to estate of settlor's husband and then to estate of settlor's son).

**55.** French, *supra* note 21, at 816. Roman law avoided this problem by determining the heirs in this situation as of the time when their interest became possessory. Justinian, *Institutes* 3.2.6. Some American cases do the same in construing an express gift to "heirs," see Section 10.2, note 12, but not in an intestacy. Estate of Roulac, 136 Cal.Rptr. 492, 495 (App. 1977). *But see* Uniform Probate Code § 2–711.

**56.** In re Ferry's Estate, 361 P.2d 900, 905–06 (Cal.1961). However, in In re Gautier's Will, 146 N.E.2d 771, 774 (N.Y.1957) the court rejected a similar argument.

*(3) Protecting Remoter Issue*

Although Professor Rabin attacks the preference for a vested construction he concedes that it has one virtue in that it:

> tends to prevent unintended disinheritance of the issue of a deceased remainderman. Suppose that *T* devises Blackacre to his wife W for life, remainder to his son *S*. Suppose further that *S* dies after T but before *W*, leaving a daughter *GD* who survives *W*. * * * Probably *T* would want *GD* to take Blackacre if her father predeceased *W*. Vesting Blackacre at *T*'s death serves a useful purpose in materially increasing the likelihood that *GD* will eventually enjoy it.[57]

Our intestacy laws and anti-lapse statutes assume that decedents want the children of a deceased relative to take in their place.[58] A vested construction may also produce the same result, but not if the remaindermen leave their estates to someone else or die insolvent. A deceased remainderman's estate may be diminished by claims of creditors, a spouse, and death taxes. A remainderman's children can be better protected by a direct substitutional gift to them in the manner of the anti-lapse statutes. The Uniform Probate Code provides such a substitutional gift.[59]

Courts sometimes achieve the same result by construing the word "children" in a will or trust to include the children of a deceased child.[60] This result is particularly attractive if the gift would otherwise fail because there are no eligible children,[61] or where the gift is to "children per stirpes," where if "children" is interpreted literally "per stirpes" makes no sense.[62] But courts usually follow "normal usage" under which "the term 'children' does not include grandchildren or more remote descendants."[63] Nor does "grandchildren" include great-grandchildren, and "cousins" does not even include first cousins once-removed.[64]

A gift to "issue," on the other hand, encompasses descendants of all generations, children, grandchildren, etc.[65] Courts have traditionally construed remainders to "issue" or "descendants," in contrast to one-generation classes like "children," as conditioned on survival of the preceding interests, since this not risk disinheriting descendants of deceased class members.[66]

The idea in the UPC of extending the anti-lapse statute to future interests has not escaped criticism. Professor Dukeminier says that it leads to a "loss of flexibility." If B has a vested remainder

**57.** Rabin, *supra* note 17, at 483–84.

**58.** See Sections 2.2, note 8 and Section 8.3, note 9.

**59.** Uniform Probate Code § 2–707(b)(2).

**60.** Cox v. Forristall, 640 P.2d 878 (Kan. App.1982).

**61.** Matter of Estate of Jenkins, 904 P.2d 1316 (Colo.1995).

**62.** Matter of Estate of Broughton, 828 P.2d 443 (Okl.App.1991); *Restatement (Second) of Property (Donative Transfers)* § 28.1, comm. i (1987).

**63.** *Restatement (Second) of Property (Donative Transfers)* § 25.1, comm. a (1987). *See also* Matter of Gustafson, 547 N.E.2d 1152 (N.Y.1989); Lamb v. NationsBank, N.A., 507 S.E.2d 457, 459 (Ga.1998).

**64.** *Restatement (Second) of Property (Donative Transfers)* § 25.8 (1987); Matter of Shields, 552 N.W.2d 581 (Minn.App.1996); Harris Trust and Sav. Bank v. Beach, 495 N.E.2d 1173 (Ill.App.1986).

**65.** *Restatement, Second, of Property (Donative Transfers)* § 25.9 (1987). As to how property is divided among "issue" or "descendants" see Section 2.2, at note 17 et seq.

**66.** *Restatement, Second, of Property (Donative Transfers)* § 28.2 (1987); Webb v. Underhill, 882 P.2d 127 (Or.App.1994).

> B can devise the remainder to B's children is such shares and upon such terms as appear wise. If B's children are minors, B can devise the remainder in trust in trust for the children until they reach majority, avoiding conservatorship.[67] If one of B's children is disabled and supported by the state in a state institution, B can devise the child's share in a trust, * * * thus avoiding the state's seizure of the child's full share as the child's creditors,[68] as section 2–707 would allow.[69]

Professor Waggoner counters that there is no evidence that "beneficiaries of transmissible future interests do any of the things that Dukeminier's article suggests," and even if they did, "circumstances might change in unpredictable ways between [B's] death and the distribution date" (at the death of the life beneficiary).[70]

### *Drafting Errors*

Most future interest cases arise because the will or trust did not deal adequately with the problem of survival. It apparently never occurred to some drafters that a remainderman might die before the life tenant, but silence on this subject may be deemed to show an intent that the remainder be vested; otherwise the will would have said "if then living" or the like.[71] The argument is strengthened when another gift in the same will expressly requires survival.[72] On the other hand, implying a condition of survival in class gifts can be justified on literalistic grounds: if a gift to "children" is deemed vested, persons who are not "children" may take a share through the estate of a deceased child.[73]

Gifts of future interests typically are expressed in words which look to the future like "then." Such words are not usually construed to postpone vesting. For example, a will gave the testator's son a life estate and "at his death the remainder shall vest in his children." A daughter of the son who predeceased him was held to have a vested interest; the phrase about vesting at the son's death was said to refer only to the date when the remainder would be distributed.[74]

A spendthrift clause is sometimes held to show that beneficiaries did not have vested interests, on the theory that allowing a remainder to pass through the beneficiary's estate would violate the prohibition on alienation.[75]

**67.** For the advantages of a trust over conservatorship see Section 9.2, note 2 et seq.

**68.** As to the effect of a trust for a child who is receiving state aid, see Section 9.5, at note 52 et seq.

**69.** Dukeminier, *supra* note 21, at 151. Professor Waggoner himself expressed similar views originally. Waggoner, *Future Interests Legislation: Implied Conditions of Survivorship and Substitutionary Gifts Under the New Illinois 'Anti–Lapse' Provision,* 1969 U.Ill.L.F. 423, 437–38. *But see* the following note.

**70.** Waggoner, *supra* note 24, at 2331–32.

**71.** Professor Waggoner, contrary to the assumption underlying Uniform Probate Code § 2–707, once contended that at least "as to wills which are written by lawyers, the assumption should be that * * * an express condition of survivorship was omitted because none was intended." Waggoner, *supra* note 69, at 438. *See also* Matter of Estate of Ruhland, 452 N.W.2d 417, 421 (Iowa 1990).

**72.** In re Estate of Benson, 285 A.2d 101, 106 (Pa.1971).

**73.** In re Trust of Walker, 116 N.W.2d 106, 109 (Wis.1962). *See also* Temple Beth Israel v. Feiss, 2 P.3d 388, 391–92 (Or.App.2000) (vested construction rejected because, in the court's view it could not literally be carried out).

**74.** Rudy v. Wagner, 198 N.W.2d 75, 79 (Neb.1972). *See also* Dauer v. Butera, 642 N.E.2d 848, 851 (Ill.App.1994); Hinds v. McNair, 413 N.E.2d 586, 601 (Ind.App.1980).

**75.** In re Robinson's Estate, 68 Cal.Rptr. 420, 425 (App.1968). As to spendthrift provisions see Section 13.1, at note 32 et seq.

This argument, however, is often rejected.[76] The second Restatement of Property says that a spendthrift clause prevents an inter-vivos transfer of the beneficiary's interest,[77] but would apparently not bar the devise of a vested remainder.[78]

### *"To Alice at 30"*

Many trusts provide for distribution of the trust assets when a beneficiary reaches a specified age such as 30. What if the beneficiary dies before she reaches 30? A famous 17th century case said that if money was "to be paid" to the beneficiary at age 30 her interest was vested, but a bequest to her "at age 30" was not.[79] This subtle distinction has little to recommend it,[80] but it found its way into the Restatement of Property.[81]

Some courts say if the trust provides the beneficiary income from the trust before she reaches 30, this indicates that her interest in the corpus is vested,[82] but one may question whether this really affects decisions, since remainders are often held to be vested though the remaindermen had no prior right to income.

### *"Surviving"*

Many wills use the word "surviving" in a remainder. The word is ambiguous, since every person who is born alive survives *someone. Whom* must the remaindermen survive? A will left a remainder to three named sisters-in-law, with the proviso that if any "is not in life, * * * their share be added to the share of any surviving sister-in-law." All three sisters-in-law survived the testator but only one was still living when the life beneficiary died. The court held that she took the whole remainder, deeming the word "surviving" to refer to the death of the life beneficiary, despite a statute saying that "words of survivorship shall refer to the death of the testator in order to vest remainders unless a manifest intention to the contrary shall appear."[83] Some cases interpret "surviving" to refer to the time of the testator's death,[84] but the Uniform Probate Code "codifies the predominant * * * position that survival relates to the distribution date;"[85] even words of survivorship that expressly "relate to * * * an earlier time" (such as the testator's death) do not prevent the implied condition that remaindermen must survive to the date of distribution.[86] A well drafted instrument, like the

**76.** In re Benson's Estate, 285 A.2d 101, 106 (Pa.1971); Trugman v. Klein, 226 N.E.2d 521, 527 (Ill.App.1967).

**77.** *Restatement (Second) of Property (Donative Transfers)* § 25.1, illus. 4 (1987).

**78.** *Restatement, Third, of Trusts* § 58, comm. g (1999).

**79.** Clobberie's Case, 86 Eng.Rep. 476 (Ch. 1677).

**80.** McGovern, *supra* note 14, at 316.

**81.** *Restatement (Second) of Property (Donative Transfers)* § 27.3, comm. f (1987).

**82.** Brown v. American Fletcher Nat. Bank, 519 N.E.2d 166, 168 (Ind.App.1988).

**83.** Lemmons v. Lawson, 468 S.E.2d 749, 750–51 (Ga.1996). *See also* Matter of Gustafson, 547 N.E.2d 1152 (N.Y.1989); Harris Trust and Sav. Bank v. Beach, 495 N.E.2d 1173 (Ill. App.1986); Theodore Short Trust v. Fuller, 7 S.W.3d 482, 490 (Mo.App.1999).

**84.** Swanson v. Swanson, 514 S.E.2d 822, 825 (Ga.1999) (decision in *Lemmons*, see previous note, was "flawed"); Pechin v. Medd, 476 N.E.2d 526, 529–30 (Ind.App.1985); Matter of Mulholland's Estate, 432 N.Y.S.2d 76, 78 (Surr.1980).

**85.** Uniform Probate Code § 2–707, Comment.

**86.** Uniform Probate Code § 2–707(b)(3). *Contra*, DiFilippo v. DiFilippo, 640 N.E.2d 1120, 1123 (Mass.App.1994) (remainder vests at testator's death when a substitutional gift provided "should my brother predecease me").

Uniform Statutory Will Act, avoids ambiguity by using the term "then living," which refers back to the specified date of distribution. Thus

> On the death of the surviving spouse, the principal, * * * must be paid, * * * to the children of the testator in equal shares if all the children are *then living*, otherwise to the *then living* issue of the testator * * *[87]

### *Gifts on Death Without Children or Issue*

References to "death" in a will, like "surviving," often fail to make clear the point in time to which they refer. This problem arises in three kinds of cases.

(1) *Remainderman dies before life tenant.* A will left a remainder "to my sister, and in case of her predecease, to her son." The sister survived the testator but not the life tenant. The court held that her remainder failed.[88] Despite the general preference for early vesting, most courts would agree.[89]

(2) *Remainderman dies after life tenant.* A will left a remainder to the testator's stepsons and "in the event that any of them should die without issue," his share should go "to the survivors." When one of them survived the life tenant and died without issue years later, the court held that his share was not divested and passed under his will. A "devise over if the remainderman should die without issue * * * is to be taken as referring to the remainderman's death prior to the termination of the intervening estate," since otherwise he would have in effect only a life estate, whereas the will gave him a remainder in fee simple.[90] Some courts have reached the opposite result on the ground that if the testator had wanted the substitutional gift to apply only if the remainderman predeceased the life tenant, the will would have said so.[91]

(3) *Immediate devise.* A woman devised a farm to her son Alvin, but if "Alvin should die without leaving children, I devise the farm to my two daughters." Alvin died without issue 27 years after the testator. The court held that the gift over applied only if Alvin predeceased the testator[92]. The California Probate Code agrees; "a transfer of a present or future interest that refers to a person's death 'with' or 'without issue' * * * refers to that person's being dead at the time the transfer takes effect in enjoyment."[93] The Restatement of Property would construe the gift over in this case to apply whenever Alvin died,[94] but not if the will had said "if Alvin should die, the farm shall go to his sisters." The reasoning is that the word "if" would have no meaning in the second case unless it was limited to the devisee's death

**87.** Uniform Statutory Will Act § 6(3).

**88.** Mueller v. Forsyth, 235 N.E.2d 645 (Ill. App.1968).

**89.** Canoy v. Canoy, 520 S.E.2d 128 (N.C.App.1999); Ruth v. First Nat. Bank, 197 S.E.2d 699 (Ga.1973); Browning v. Sacrison, 518 P.2d 656 (Or.1974); *Restatement of Property* § 264 (1940).

**90.** Stanley v. Brietz, 612 S.W.2d 699, 701 (Tex.Civ.App.1981). *See also Restatement of Property* § 269 (1940); Thomas v. Thomas, 294 S.E.2d 795 (Va.1982).

**91.** Adams v. Vidal, 60 So.2d 545, 548 (Fla. 1952); Ford v. Thomas, 633 S.W.2d 58 (Ky. 1982).

**92.** Lones v. Winzer, 486 S.W.2d 758 (Tenn.App.1971).

**93.** Cal.Prob.Code § 21112.

**94.** *Restatement of Property* § 267 (1940). *See also* Neb.Rev.Stat. § 76–111; Minn.Stat. § 500.14(1); Kan.Stat. § 58–504, 5 *Amer. Law of Prop.* § 21.52.

before the testator, since a person may or may not have issue, but everyone is sure to die.[95]

Historically, gifts over upon a devisee's death without issue were deemed to apply if the devisee *or any descendant of his* ever died without issue. With respect to realty this "indefinite failure of issue" construction gave the devisee a fee tail followed by a remainder. As to personal property, a fee tail was not recognized, and the succeeding interest was invalid under the Rule against Perpetuities, since a descendant of the devisee might die without issue centuries later.[96] The indefinite failure of issue construction fostered the alienability of property, but modern law rejects it in favor of the "definite" failure of issue construction under which "death" refers only to the named devisee and not to any of his descendants.[97]

Other ambiguities lurk in the apparently simple phrase "if Alvin should die without leaving children." What if is survived by a *grandchild* but not a child? In this context most courts equate "children" and "issue."[98] If Alvin has children who predecease him, has he died "died without leaving children?" Most courts, but not all, would say yes; the gift over applies unless the devisee's issue survive.[99]

Sometimes a life estate is followed only by a gift over "if the life tenant dies without issue." What happens if the life tenant is survived by issue? Most courts imply a gift to the issue in order to avoid an intestacy.[100] However, in a devise "to A *in fee,* and if he dies without issue, to B," no gift to A's issue is implied because there is no gap to be filled; the property becomes part of A's estate if he is survived by issue.[101]

### *"To A or His Children (Heirs)"*

A remainder to "my children, or their issue (or heirs)," is usually construed to give the share of any child who fails to survive the life beneficiary to his or her issue (or heirs).[102] Such language should not be confused with devises "to A *and* his heirs" or "to A *and* his children."[103]

Some wills provide a substitutional gift to the children of a remainderman who fails to survive the life tenant, but do not say what should happen if a remainderman dies *without* children. Many courts hold that in this situation

**95.** Matter of Estate of Klein, 434 N.W.2d 560 (N.D.1989); In re Magoon's Estate, 247 A.2d 188 (N.H.1968); Dei Cas v. Mayfield, 508 A.2d 435 (Conn.1986); *Restatement of Property* § 263 (1940).

**96.** Hayes v. Hammond, 143 N.E.2d 693, 697 (Mass.1957); *Restatement of Property* § 243, illus. 3 (1940). For a full discussion of the Rule against Perpetuities see Chapter 11. The fee tail is discussed in the next Section at note 40 et seq.

**97.** *Restatement of Property* § 266; Goldberger v. Goldberger, 102 A.2d 338 (Del.Ch.1954); Minn.Stat. § 500.14(1); Kan.Stat. § 58–504.

**98.** 5 *Amer. Law of Prop.* § 22.32, at 321; *Restatement of Property* § 243, illus. 1 (1940).

**99.** *Restatement of Property* § 267 (1940); Calif.Prob.Code § 21112; Minn.Stats. § 500.14(1); Neb.Rev.Stat. § 76–111; N.C.Gen. Stat. § 41–4; N.Y. EPTL § 6–5.6; Clark v. Strother, 385 S.E.2d 578, 582 (Va.1989).

**100.** *Restatement, Property* § 272; 5 *Amer. Law of Prop.* § 21.34.

**101.** *Restatement of Property* § 272, comm. c (1940); Erickson v. Reinbold, 493 P.2d 794 (Wash.App.1972).

**102.** Rowett v. McFarland, 394 N.W.2d 298 (S.D.1986); *Restatement of Property* § 252 (1940) (survival condition implied in a gift "to B or his children").

**103.** As to "A and his heirs" see the next Section at note 37. As to "A and his children" see Section 10.3, at note 22 et seq. As to present interests devised "to A or his children (heirs)" see Section 8.3, at note 50 et seq.

the interest of the remaindermen is vested,[104] but the second Restatement of Property says that "because of the undesirability of having the gift pass through the deceased [class] member's estate" it should go to the other members of the class.[105]

Some wills impose a requirement of survival on the primary remaindermen but not on the persons designated as substitute takers. For example, a will devised a remainder to the descendants of the testator's nephew, or to "the other beneficiaries of the will if no such descendants are then living." The express condition of survival as to the nephew's descendants was deemed to show an intent to impose the same requirement on the other beneficiaries as well,[106] but other courts have drawn the opposite inference, and hold that the substitute takers do not have to survive.[107]

***Planning***

One court has suggested that "a pervasive cloud of uncertainty" surrounds the law of future interests, leading courts to "determine an equitable distribution and thereafter fill in the blanks with appropriate bits and pieces of the law * * * in order to reach the desirable result."[108] One or more of the above mentioned arguments may apply to a particular case and point to an appropriate solution. If so, it seems entirely proper for courts to adopt a "desirable result."[109] But often the relevant considerations point in different direction, *e.g.* a vested construction increases taxes but prevents a descendant from being disinherited because her parent predeceased the life tenant.

Drafters can avoid such dilemmas. The above quoted model from Uniform Statutory Will Act[110] postpones vesting of the remainder without excluding any children of a deceased child. Although the remaindermen will be uncertain while the spouse is alive, the property will be alienable because the trustee is given a power of sale.[111] The remaindermen may turn out to be minors, but the Statutory Will allows retention in trust of any property which would be distributed to any person who "cannot effectively manage or apply the property."[112] Testators who prefer to let any children who predeceases the life beneficiary "decide how best to provide for their own family" can accomplish this by giving the children a special power of appointment over their share if they die before it is distributed to them.[113]

Lawyers should use formulas like the one suggested above in preparing wills and trusts with future interests. It is inefficient and risky to draft wills

**104.** Swanson v. Swanson, 514 S.E.2d 822 (Ga.1999); Matter of Estate of Sprinchorn, 546 N.Y.S.2d 256 (A.D.1989) (remainder to niece and her daughter or the survivor vests in their estates when both predecease life beneficiary); Matter of Blough's Estate, 378 A.2d 276 (Pa. 1977); *Restatement of Property* § 254 (1940).

**105.** *Restatement (Second) of Property (Donative Transfers)* § 27.3, comm. e, illus. 1 (1987). *See also* Warren Boynton State Bank v. Wallbaum, 493 N.E.2d 21 (Ill.App.1986).

**106.** Irish v. Profitt, 330 N.E.2d 861, 871–72 (Ill.App.1975). *See also* Lamb v. NationsBank, N.A., 507 S.E.2d 457, 459 (Ga.1998).

**107.** Mueller v. Forsyth, 235 N.E.2d 645, 649 (Ill.App.1968); *Restatement of Property* § 250, illus. 4, § 252, comm. f (1940).

**108.** Warren–Boynton State Bank v. Wallbaum, 528 N.E.2d 640, 643 (Ill.1988).

**109.** McGovern, *supra* note 14, at 321.

**110.** See note 87 *supra*.

**111.** Uniform Statutory Will Act § 13.

**112.** *Id.* § 9. This withholding of distribution does not delay vesting; if such a beneficiary dies during the trust, the share is paid to his or her estate.

**113.** As to powers of appointment see Section 10.4.

"from scratch;" the many chances for error are demonstrated by the cases strewn though the reports.

### *Income Interests*

Similar construction problems arise when income is payable to several beneficiaries and one dies. For example, a trust called for the payment of income to the "child or children" of the settlor's daughter "during their lives." One of the daughter's children died without issue after receiving income for several years. What was to be done with the income she had been receiving?

> When faced with this problem, courts in other jurisdictions have reached a variety of solutions. * * * Some courts have ordered the income to be paid to the surviving income beneficiaries under the doctrine of implication of cross remainders, as a gift to a class, or as an implied joint tenancy. Other courts have ordered the income paid to the deceased beneficiary's estate until the death of the last income beneficiary.[114] Other courts have ordered the income to be paid to the remaindermen. Finally, some courts have ordered the income to be accumulated until the death of the last income beneficiary.[115]

The court in this case adopted the first mentioned possibility.[116] Would it have done so if the child had been survived by issue who would thereby be cut out? Not under the Restatement of Trusts which presumes that "the settlor intended the income share to be paid to the issue (if any) of the deceased income beneficiary,"[117] a solution like that of the Uniform Probate Code with respect to future interests.

It is hard to predict the result a court will choose in this situation. The best *drafting* solution is probably to allow the trustee to sprinkle income among the beneficiaries. The Uniform Statutory Will Act, for example, allows the trustee to pay income to "one or more of the issue of the testator" as needed for their support.[118] This would permit the trustee to refrain from distributing income to a decedent's estate and to give it directly to the decedent's children or the decedent's siblings in the trustee's discretion.

## § 10.2 Gifts to Heirs

A well-drafted instrument which creates future interests contingent on survival should leave no gaps in case the designated remaindermen fail to survive.[1] Many drafters use the intestacy statutes for this purpose. The

**114.** Oak Park Trust & Savings Bank v. Baumann, 438 N.E.2d 1354 (Ill.App.1982); Prince v. Prince, 239 N.E.2d 18 (Mass.1968); Matter of Lopez, 636 P.2d 731, 738 (Haw. 1981); Wing v. Wachovia Bank & Trust Co., 272 S.E.2d 90 (N.C.1980).

**115.** Trust Agreement of Westervelt v. First Interstate Bank, 551 N.E.2d 1180, 1185 (Ind.App.1990).

**116.** *See also* Svenson v. First Nat. Bank, 363 N.E.2d 1129, 1134 (Mass.App.1977); Littwin v. Littwin, 498 N.E.2d 544, 547 (Ill.App. 1986).

**117.** *Restatement, Third, of Trusts* § 49, comm. c (1999). This differs from *Restatement, Second, Trusts* § 143(2) (1959), which gave the income to the other beneficiaries as an implied cross remainder. However, Dewire v. Haveles, 534 N.E.2d 782 (Mass.1989) came to the same conclusion as the Third Restatement.

**118.** Uniform Statutory Will Act § 8(b). As to the problems of controlling the trustee's discretion in such a trust see Section 9.5, at note 8 et seq.

§ 10.2

**1.** For the disadvantages which can accrue from an intestacy caused by a gap, see Section 10.1, note 53 et seq.

Uniform Statutory Will Act provides that if the remainder to the testator's issue fails, the property passes "to the individuals who would be entitled to receive the estate as if the * * * the testator had then died intestate."[2] A simple gift to the "heirs" of the testator or of another person also incorporates the intestacy statutes,[3] but it raises problems of construction which will be discussed in this section.

A reference to the intestacy statutes has the disadvantage that they usually include very remote relatives (if no closer relatives survive),[4] whereas the testator may prefer that the estate go to a charity. On the other hand, intestacy statutes list descendants and collateral relatives of a decedent in the order which most testators prefer. They incorporate a requirement of survival of the ancestor, but provide for representation of deceased relatives by their issue. Thus, if a will leaves property "to Alice for life, remainder to her heirs," a child of Alice who predeceased her would get no share,[5] but any children of the deceased child would take the share by representation.[6] In this respect a devise to "heirs" is like one to "issue," but "heirs" normally includes a spouse[7] and collateral relatives if the designated ancestor is not survived by issue.

### *Time of Determination*

Often wills and trusts create a remainder to the heirs of someone who dies before the life tenant. For example, a trust gave a remainder "to the heirs of my children" when the last child of the settlor died. Many of the settlor's children had been dead for years when the last one died and the trust terminated. The court held that the remainder vested in each child's heirs as the child died because "vested estates are to be favored. * * * Unless a contrary intention appears, a gift in a will to the heirs of a person * * * will be construed as a gift to such heirs determined as of the time of death of that person," not when the interest became possessory.[8] Courts have reached similar conclusions in construing remainders to the heirs of the testator; the heirs were to be determined as of the testator's death, with the result that a share passed to the estate of any heir who had died before the termination of the trust.[9]

The second Restatement of Property agrees: in a gift to "heirs" the intestacy statute is applied as of the ancestor's[10] death unless a contrary intent is found in "additional language and circumstances."[11] The Uniform Probate Code, on the other hand, says that the "heirs" are to be determined as if the ancestor "died when the disposition is to take effect in possession and enjoyment."[12]

**2.** Uniform Statutory Will Act § 6(3).

**3.** See Section 2.4, note 1.

**4.** Section 2.2, note 65.

**5.** Tootle v. Tootle, 490 N.E.2d 878, 882 (Ohio 1986).

**6.** Representation is discussed in Section 2.2, at note 8 et seq.

**7.** Section 2.4, note 13.

**8.** Matter of Dodge Testamentary Trust, 330 N.W.2d 72, 81 (Mich.App.1982). *See also* Estate of Woodworth, 22 Cal.Rptr.2d 676 (App. 1993).

**9.** Tate v. Kennedy, 578 So.2d 1079 (Ala. 1991).

**10.** We shall refer to the person whose heirs are designated as the "ancestor," even though "heirs" can include collateral relatives as well as descendants.

**11.** *Restatement (Second) of Property (Donative Transfers)* § 29.4 (1987).

**12.** Uniform Probate Code § 2–711. *See also* Cal.Prob.Code § 21114.

The arguments on this question echo those discussed in the previous Section about early vesting. An early date for determining heirs makes property alienable sooner. Thus when land was devised to the testator's daughter, Doris, in fee, with a gift "to my other heirs" if Doris died without issue, Doris was able to sell the land with the consent of the testator's other children and widow.[13] The testator's heirs as of Doris' death might include persons yet unborn and so the sale would have been impossible.[14] The UPC provision postponing the determination of heirs can thus impede alienability, because, unlike the implied condition of survival in class gifts to persons other than "heirs", the provision which postpones the determination of heirs is not restricted to trusts.[15]

The desire to keep property in the bloodline, a standard argument for postponing vesting, is also invoked in cases involving the time for determining heirs.

> There is no inference to be drawn from the testamentary plan that the testator meant for the ownership of any part of his estate to stray outside the family if one of the beneficiaries were to die without descendants before [the trust terminated.] Yet that is what could and did happen if the heirship is determined as of the time of the testator's death rather than at a time when a determination becomes necessary.[16]

When a remainder is given to "children," the keep-property-in-the-bloodline argument against early vesting may be outweighed if a contingent construction would cut out issue of a deceased child.[17] When a remainder is given to "heirs," however, remoter issue take by representation. In this respect gifts to "heirs" are like gifts to "issue," which are generally held to be contingent on survival.[18]

Even without a general presumption as in the Uniform Probate Code, an intent in a particular will to postpone the determination of heirs can be expressed, as in the Uniform Statutory Will Act's devise to "the individuals who *would be* entitled to receive the estate *as if* * * * the testator had *then* died intestate."[19] A frequently asserted argument for *inferring* a similar intent to postpone the determination is the "incongruity" which would result if the heirs were determined when the ancestor died and (as often happens) an heir is given a life interest in the same property. For example, a woman conveyed land to her daughter, Annis, for life, remainder to Annis' issue, if Annis died without issue, to her siblings if living, if none "to my heirs." Annis died without issue and her siblings predeceased her. The donor's heirs as of the time of the donor's death were the donor's children. Determining the heirs at her death would create the "salient incongruity" of (1) giving Annis part of the remainder even though the deed gave her only a life estate, and (2) giving her siblings an interest even though they did not survive Annis as the deed required. Therefore the court determined the heirs as of Annis' death, thereby

13. Cole v. Plant, 440 So.2d 1054 (Ala. 1983).

14. In many states, however, a life tenant can sell land under a court order protecting the remaindermen.*See* Section 9.3, at note 19 et seq.

15. Compare Section 10.1, note 44.

16. Sutton v. Milburn, 711 S.W.2d 808, 813 (Ark.1986). *See also* Matter of Symonds Will, 434 N.Y.S.2d 838, 840 (A.D.1981); Harris Trust & Savings Bank v. Beach, 513 N.E.2d 833, 840 (Ill.1987); Section 10.1, at note 28 et seq.

17. Section 10.1, at note 57 et seq.

18. Section 10.1, note 65.

19. Uniform Statutory Will Act § 6(3).

eliminating Annis and her siblings and giving the land to a collateral relative.[20]

The Restatement of Property adopts the incongruity argument, but only when the ancestor's *sole* heir receives a prior interest under the same will.[21] Some courts avoid an incongruity without postponing the determination of heirs. A woman left her home to her husband for life, remainder "to my nearest (relatives) heirs." The husband was the testator's sole heir, but he did not get the remainder, since the word "relatives" showed an intent to exclude him.[22] The heirs were nevertheless determined as of the testator's death. "If we exclude [the husband] from the class of 'heirs,' others step forward to qualify," so it was unnecessary to "postpone the class closing until the life tenant's death."[23]

The time for determining heirs may turn on the word "then." When a will gave a remainder to the life tenants' "then living" children "and if both shall die leaving no child or children then said fund is to be distributed among my heirs at law," the court construed this as an intent to postpone the determination of heirs.[24] According to the Restatement, however, the word "then" in this context simply sets the time for distribution, not the time for determining the heirs.[25] A devise of a remainder to the "then living" heirs, on the other hand, does postpone the time of determining heirs. Although these words might be construed to mean that the heirs should be determined when the ancestor dies but they must survive the life tenant, but this would make the gift a nullity if all the heirs died before the life tenant whereas when the determination of heirs is postponed there will usually be an eligible taker.[26]

An immediate devise "to the heirs of Alice" can also raise the question when they should be determined. If Alice predeceased the testator, and was survived by children who also predeceased the testator, even though these children would inherit from Alice, they would not take under the devise because courts usually determine "heirs" in this situation as of the time of the testator's death.[27] If in this case Alice survives the testator, courts usually give the property to those persons who *would be* Alice's heirs if she were dead; otherwise distribution would have to be postponed until Alice died.[28] But if Alice has no children when the testator dies, determination of her heirs may be postponed.[29]

**20.** Wells Fargo Bank v. Title Ins. & Trust Co., 99 Cal.Rptr. 464 (App.1971).

**21.** *Restatement (Second) of Property (Donative Transfers)* § 29.4 comm. f (1987).

**22.** Said the court. But see Uniform Probate Code § 2–711 which equates a gift to "relatives" with one to takers on intestacy.

**23.** Rawls v. Rideout, 328 S.E.2d 783 (N.C.App.1985).

**24.** Wheeling Dollar Sav. & Trust Co. v. Singer, 250 S.E.2d 369, 374 (W.Va.1978).

**25.** *Restatement (Second) of Property* § 29.4, illus. 14 (1987). *See also* Nicholson v. Nicholson, 496 S.W.2d 477, 479 (Tenn.1973).

**26.** *Restatement (Second) of Property (Donative Transfers)* § 29.4, comm. h (1987); Matter of Evans' Estate, 334 N.E.2d 850, 853 (Ill.App.1975).

**27.** *Restatement (Second) of Property (Donative Transfers)* § 29.4, comm. g (1987); Uniform Probate Code § 2–711 (which also applies to present gifts to heirs).

**28.** *Restatement (Second) of Property (Donative Transfers)* § 29.4, comm. c (1987).

**29.** *Id.* illus. 3.

### *Change in Law*

Since the statutes governing intestate succession vary, an undefined reference to "heirs" may raise the question which state's statute should control.[30] Also, the intestacy law of a given state may change. For example, when a testator died with a will leaving a remainder to the "heirs of my children," the relevant state law did not give husbands an intestate share of their wife's land, but when the testator's daughter later died, it did. The court found the testator intended to apply the intestacy laws in effect when each child died.[31] But another court, construing a trust created in 1929 which gave a remainder to the heirs of the settlor's grandson, determined heirs as of the grandson's death but used the law in effect in 1929 in doing so.[32]

If the testator designates the relevant law, this may affect the time when the heirs are determined as well as the choice of law. A devise "to my heirs according to the Statute * * * of the State of Illinois in effect at the time of death" of the life tenant was held to show an intent that the heirs be determined as of the life tenant's death.[33]

### *Heirs as a Word of Limitation*

Historically, one had to use the word "heirs" in order to convey land in fee simple; a conveyance "to John in fee simple" gave him only a life estate.[34] This is no longer true,[35] but many drafters still use "heirs" to indicate that a donee or devisee should have a fee simple. In this case "heirs" is called a word of "limitation" because it limits (*i.e.,* defines) John's estate. Heirs acquire an interest only if "heirs" is used as a "word of purchase."[36]

In a gift "to John and his heirs" John's heirs get no interest,[37] but slightly different wording can change the result. Thus a devise to the testator's grandson "and *at his death* to his heirs" was held to give the grandson a life estate with a remainder in his children.[38] A devise "to A and his heirs" is sometimes construed as a substitutional gift to the heirs if A predeceases the testator; *a fortiori* if the will says "to A *or* his heirs."[39]

Construing "heirs" as a word of limitation rather than a word of purchase makes property more marketable, since it is not necessary to wait until the ancestor dies to determine who the heirs are. However, future interests which operate to impede alienation are allowed if they stay within

**30.** See Section 2.4, at note 19 et seq.

**31.** Matter of Dodge Testamentary Trust, 330 N.W.2d 72, 83 (Mich.App.1982). *See also Restatement (Second) of Property (Donative Transfers)* § 29.3 (1987).

**32.** National City Bank v. Ford, 299 N.E.2d 310, 314 (Ohio Com.Pl.1973). *See also* In re Johnson's Will, 301 N.Y.S.2d 174 (A.D.1969); *cf.* In re Matter of Estate of Hughlett, 446 N.E.2d 887, 891 (Ill.App.1983) (law at date of execution of will).

**33.** Spaugh v. Ferguson, 264 N.E.2d 542, 549 (Ill.App.1970). *See also Restatement (Second) of Property (Donative Transfers)* § 29.4, illus. 15 (1987).

**34.** T. Littleton, *Tenures* § 1; 2 W. Blackstone, *Commentaries* *107 (1765); *cf. Restatement of Property* § 27 (1936).

**35.** Lewis v. Searles, 452 S.W.2d 153 (Mo. 1970); Neb.Stat. § 76–104; *Restatement (Second) of Trusts* § 128, comm. a (1959).

**36.** *Restatement, Second, of Property (Donative Transfers)* Introductory Note preceding Chapter 29 (1987). Purchase in this context does not mean "acquire for money." Even if land is given "heirs," they are "purchasers" if they were intended to get an interest. 2 W. Blackstone, *Commentaries* *241 (1765).

**37.** *Restatement (Second) of Property (Donative Transfers)* § 29.7, comm. a (1987). *See also* Estate of Straube v. Barber, 990 S.W.2d 40, 45 (Mo.App.1999); In re White's Estate, 238 A.2d 791 (Vt.1968).

**38.** Cheuvront v. Haley, 444 S.W.2d 734 (Ky.1969).

**39.** Rowett v. McFarland, 394 N.W.2d 298 (S.D.1986). *See also* Section 8.3, note 52.

the limits of the Rule against Perpetuities. Therefore, courts usually construe heirs as a word of purchase if they think it was intended as such, even though this may impede a transfer of property.

### *Fee Tail*

The tension between the law's desire to promote alienability and the desire of some donors to keep property in the family surfaced in the 13th century with limitations of the type "to *A* and the heirs of his (her) body." The courts construed such words as giving *A* a fee simple conditional on having issue; if *A* had no issue, the land would revert to the donor (or pass to a remainderman if one was designated), but if *A* had issue s/he could transfer the property.[40] The statute *De Donis Conditionalibus* of 1285 rejected this construction as contrary to the donor's intention, and allowed *A*'s issue to recover the land if *A* had alienated it.[41] The interest created by limitations "to *A* and the heirs of his (her) body" became known as a "fee tail." The statute *De Donis* did not make clear how far the restraint on alienation in a fee tail extended. *A* could not convey the land, but could her children? her grandchildren? Eventually the courts held that a fee tail was perpetual; if, for example, *A*'s *great grandson* sold the land, *his* children could upset the sale.[42] Courts soon regretted this perpetual restraint on alienation, and allowed fee tails to be conveyed by a complex legal proceeding involving many fictitious allegations. In the 18th century Blackstone praised "the unriveting the fetters of the estate tail, which were attended with a legion of mischiefs to the commonwealth," but he lamented the "awkward shifts [necessary] * * * to get the better of that stubborn statute *de donis*".[43]

Most American states have adopted a statutory solution to the problem.[44] These statutes vary, but in general they allow alienation to be restrained, if at all, for only one generation. For example, a devise to the testator's daughter "and the heirs of her body" was held to give her a fee simple by virtue of a statute, but one which was defeasible if she died without issue, since the will contained a gift over "in the event of the death of my said daughter without bodily heirs."[45] In some states these words would have given the daughter a life estate with a remainder to her issue.[46]

Since the phrase "heirs of her body" is subject to so many possible constructions, drafters should avoid it. If a donor wishes to keep property in the family, a gift "to my daughter for life, remainder to her issue who survive her" makes this clear. (The instrument should also provide an alternative remainder in case the daughter dies without issue.)

### *The Rule in Shelley's Case*

**40.** 2 Bracton, *De Legibus* 68 (Woodbine ed.). In Prichard v. Department of Revenue, 164 N.W.2d 113 (Iowa 1969), the court applied the same rule to hold that if A had issue, the property was taxable in her estate at death.

**41.** Statute of Westminster II, 13 Edw. 1, c. 1 (1285).

**42.** T. Plucknett, *A Concise History of the Common Law* 552–54 (5th ed. 1956).

**43.** 2 W. Blackstone, *Commentaries* *360 (1765).

**44.** *Restatement, Second, of Property (Donative Transfers)* § 30.1, Statutory note par. 7 (1987).

**45.** Russell v. Russell, 399 S.E.2d 415 (N.C.App.1991). *See also* Cal.Civ.Code §§ 763–64.

**46.** Williams v. Kimes, 949 S.W.2d 899 (Mo. 1997); Sligh v. Plair, 569 S.W.2d 58, 60 (Ark. 1978).

A settlor created a trust for his grandson for life, "and upon his death to the heirs of his body." The court held these words gave the grandson a fee tail under the notorious Rule in Shelley's Case.

> Where a freehold is limited to one for life, and, by the same instrument, the inheritance is limited * * * to his heirs, or to the heirs of his body, the first taker takes the whole estate, either in fee simple or in fee tail; and the words "heirs," or "heirs of his body" are words of limitation, and not words of purchase.[47]

Applying the Rule in this case probably produced a good result; it allowed an adopted child of the grandson to take, because a statute converted his fee tail into a life estate with a remainder to his "issue," and "issue" included adoptees even though "heirs of his body" did not.[48] The original Rule in Shelley's was created by courts for a very different purpose, to prevent evasions of the medieval equivalent of the estate tax.[49] It has also been invoked by the Internal Revenue Service in modern cases.[50] However, this is no reason for retaining the Rule since artful drafters can easily avoid it, and generating tax revenue by creating traps for clients of unskilled drafters seems unfair.

A better rationale for the Rule is that it promotes alienability.[51] For example, when land was left to the testator's son for life and "at his death his heirs take the fee simple title," the Rule gave the son a fee simple which he could convey over the protest of his children.[52] The promotion of alienability is a worthy purpose, but the Rule is nevertheless in disrepute because it is so arbitrary. A devise "to my son for life, remainder to his heirs," imposes no greater restriction on alienability than one "to my son for life, remainder to his issue." But the Rule in Shelley's Case does not apply to the latter because it only covers remainders to "heirs."[53]

The Rule in Shelley's Case has been abolished in most states by statute, and, according to the second Restatement of Property, "should be abolished prospectively by judicial decision" if a statute has not already done so.[54] Because abolition of the Rule is prospective, it continues to crop up occasionally in recent cases involving older instruments.[55]

Most rules of construction apply both to land and to personal property,

**47.** Society Nat. Bank v. Jacobson, 560 N.E.2d 217, 221 (Ohio 1990).

**48.** *But see* Section 2.10, note 30.

**49.** 2 W. Blackstone, *Commentaries* *242 (1765); *Restatement (Second) of Property (Donative Transfers)* § 30.1, comm. a (1987). Some have questioned this theory of the Rule's origin. Ziff & Litman, *Shelley's Rule in a Modern Context,* 34 U.Tor.L.J. 170, 175–76 (1984). One thing is clear: the Rule is much older than the 17th century case which gave it its name.

**50.** Estate of Forrest, TC Memo 1990–464. The rule was held inapplicable, however, because the word "heirs" was construed to mean "children." See Section 2.4, note 17.

**51.** *Restatement (Second) of Property (Donative Transfers)* § 30.1, comm. a (1987).

**52.** Toler v. Harbour, 589 S.W.2d 529 (Tex. Civ.App.1979). If the remainder in this case had been to "the heirs of the body" of the son, the effect of the Rule would depend on how the jurisdiction treated estates in fee tail.

**53.** Harper v. Springfield, 578 S.W.2d 824 (Tex.Civ.App.1979); *Restatement (Second) of Property (Donative Transfers)* § 30.1, comm. g (1987); Estate of Forrest, TC Memo 1990–464.

**54.** *Restatement (Second) of Property (Donative Transfers)* § 30.1 (1987).

**55.** City Bank and Trust Co. v. Morrissey, 454 N.E.2d 1195 (Ill.App.1983) (1952 will); Society Nat. Bank v. Jacobson, 560 N.E.2d 217 (Ohio 1990) (1931 trust).

but the Rule in Shelley's Case applies only to land.[56] But it applies both to wills and deeds, and to legal interests as well as trusts. In this respect the Rule in Shelley's Case is unusual, since many old intent-frustrating rules, like the need to use "heirs" to create a fee simple, did not apply to wills as to which "a more liberal construction is allowed."[57]

### *Doctrine of Worthier Title*

The Doctrine of Worthier Title, like the Rule in Shelley's Case, holds that the word "heirs" is not a word of purchase. It thereby preserved the feudal incidents which accrued when land passed by descent rather than purchase.[58] (Acquisition by descent was considered a "worthier title," hence the name). Both rules promote alienability, and may permit early termination of trusts by eliminating an interest in the heirs of a living person.[59]

Whereas the Rule in Shelley's Case applies to remainders to the "heirs" of a life tenant, the Doctrine of Worthier Title applies to the "heirs" of the grantor in a deed or the settlor of a living trust.[60] Many commentators condemn both rules,[61] but the Doctrine of Worthier Title has some defenders,[62] and it has been extended to personal property whereas the Rule in Shelley's Case generally applied only to *land*.[63]

The Rule in Shelley's Case overrides the donor's intention whereas the Doctrine of Worthier Title is today regarded as a rule of construction which gives way to an expression of contrary intent.[64] But the Uniform Probate Code abolishes it both "both as a rule of law and as a rule of construction."[65] Its principal use in modern cases has been to allow settlors to modify or terminate a trust which purports to give an interest to their "heirs." This aspect of the Doctrine is still recognized in some jurisdictions. New York, for example, has abolished the Doctrine but it also allows settlors to revoke a trust regardless of any interest given to the settlor's heirs.[66]

**56.** *Restatement (Second) of Property (Donative Transfers)* § 30.1(3) (1987). *But see* Society Nat. Bank v. Jacobson, 560 N.E.2d 217 (Ohio 1990) (local version of rule covers personal property as well).

**57.** 2 W. Blackstone, *Commentaries* *108 (1765).

**58.** 1 *Amer. Law of Prop.* § 4.19. Similarly, both rules may cause property to be subject to death taxes today. McGovern, *Facts and Rules in the Construction of Wills,* 26 UCLA L.Rev. 285, 304 (1978).

**59.** *Restatement (Second) of Property (Donative Transfers)* § 30.2, comm. a (1987); Bixby v. California Trust Co., 202 P.2d 1018 (Cal. 1949).

**60.** The Doctrine of Worthier Title, like the Rule in Shelley's Case, originally applied to wills as well as inter vivos conveyances, so that if a will left property to the testator's heir, the heir took by descent as if the testator died intestate. At one time, the difference between taking by will and by descent was often significant. Today it rarely is. Where it is significant, courts have rejected the Doctrine of Worthier Title as to wills on the ground that it would frustrate the testator's intent. *Restatement, Second, of Property (Donative Transfers)* § 30.2, comm. j (1987); City Nat. Bank v. Andrews, 355 So.2d 341 (Ala.1978); Matter of Campbell, 319 N.W.2d 275 (Iowa 1982).

**61.** "There is no more reason" for the Doctrine of Worthier Title than for "its close cousin, the Rule in Shelley's Case." Bostwick, *Loosening the Grip of the Dead Hand,* 32 Vand. L.Rev. 1061, 1075 (1979). *See also* W. Leach, *Property Law Indicted!* 9, 54 (1967).

**62.** Morris, *The Inter Vivos Branch of the Worthier Title Doctrine,* 2 Ok.L.Rev. 133, 174 (1949); Warren, *A Remainder to the Grantor's Heirs,* 22 Tex.L.Rev. 22, 23 (1943); 3 R. Powell, *The Law of Real Property* ¶ 381, at 316 (1977).

**63.** *Restatement (Second) of Property (Donative Transfers)* § 30.2 (1987).

**64.** *Ibid.*

**65.** Uniform Probate Code § 2–710. *See also* Cal.Prob.Code § 21108.

**66.** N.Y. EPTL § 6–5.9, 7–1.9(b). Compare Cal.Prob.Code § 15404(c).

The Doctrine of Worthier Title, even where it is still recognized, does not apply if the settlor's "heirs" are to be ascertained at a point in time other than the settlor's death. For example, a trust for the settlor's wife provided that upon her death the property was to be distributed "among my heirs." Devisees under the settlor's will claimed the trust assets under the Doctrine of Worthier Title. The court rejected their claim, construing the trust to require that the heirs be determined at the wife's death rather than the settlor's, and this made the Doctrine inapplicable.[67]

Nor does the Doctrine apply to gifts to the settlor's "issue" as distinguished from "heirs." Modern substitutes for the Doctrine make the same distinction. The New York statute which provides that "persons described only as the heirs, next of kin or distributees" of the settlor have no interest in a trust, was held inapplicable to a trust which gave a remainder to the settlor's "issue;" even though the settlor's issue would have been his heirs, the two terms were not considered to be alike.[68]

## § 10.3 Rule of Convenience; Rule in Wild's Case

The primary concern of this chapter so far has been remaindermen who die too soon, *i.e.,* before the preceding interest terminates. The present section deals with the opposite problem: persons who are born too late to be included in a class gift even though they literally fall within its terms. For example, a will created a trust for "the children of Ralph," the son of the testator. The trustee was to use income and principal for the children's support and education, and to distribute a share of the principal to each child at age 25. When the testator died Ralph had five children, but he later adopted another. The 6th child was held to be entitled to share in the trust.

> If a testamentary gift is to a class in general terms * * * , the death of the testator will, as a general rule, fix the time for distribution, and close the class.[1] * * * However, if the gift is * * * to be distributed at a later determinable date, the class members who are in being at the testator's death take a vested interest in the fund then, subject to the addition of members of the class who are born after the testator's death but before the time of distribution.[2]

Ralph's 6th child was adopted before his oldest child reached 25. Any child born or adopted thereafter would be excluded according to some authorities,[3] even though it would be possible to divide the trust assets each time a child reached age 25 based on the number of children of Ralph then living. This

67. Harris Trust and Sav. Bank v. Beach, 513 N.E.2d 833 (Ill.1987). *See also Restatement, Second, of Property (Donative Transfers)* § 30.2, illus. 1 (1987).

68. In re Dodge's Trust, 250 N.E.2d 849 (N.Y.1969).

§ 10.3

1. Thus if there had been a simple devise to "the children of Ralph," the after-born 6th child would have been excluded. *Accord, Restatement, Second, of Property (Donative Transfers)* § 26.1 (1987).

2. Central Trust Co. v. Smith, 553 N.E.2d 265, 271 (Ohio 1990). *Accord,* In re Testamentary Trust of Hasch, 721 N.E.2d 1111, 1113 (Ohio App.1999); South Carolina Nat. Bank v. Johnson, 197 S.E.2d 668 (S.C.1973).

3. In re Estate of Evans, 80 N.W.2d 408 (Wis.1957); *Restatement, Second, of Property (Donative Transfers)* § 26.2, comm. m (1987); *cf.* In re Silberman's Will, 242 N.E.2d 736, 742 (N.Y.1968) (will provided class would close when eldest grandchild reached 21).

might give the eldest child more than younger siblings, but that seems preferable to giving the later born children nothing at all.

The rule excluding after-born class members is usually called the "rule of convenience" because it avoids "the otherwise necessary complex safeguards in favor of possible but not as yet conceived or adopted takers."[4] It does not arise often because most class gifts are to groups which close naturally at the time of distribution. For example, when a will devises property "to my children" no class members will be born after the will takes effect.[5] But in an outright devise "to my grandchildren," if the testator is survived by children, grandchildren may be born after the testator dies, but they would be excluded by the rule of convenience.

The rule turns on the time when distribution is made. In a future interest, the class does not close until the gift takes effect in enjoyment, *e.g.* at the end of any preceding life estate(s). In some instruments the time of distribution is ambiguous, *e.g.* "when my youngest grandchild reaches [or when all of my grandchildren have reached] age 21." When all of the transferor's *living* grandchildren have reached twenty-one, if children of the transferor are still alive, a later grandchild may turn out to be the "youngest," so one might want to postpone distribution until all the children are dead when the youngest grandchild can be identified with certainty.[6] However, the quoted language is generally read to call for distribution when there is no living grandchild under 21.[7] Although this cuts off any after-born grandchild, few parents have children after their youngest living child reaches 21.

A direction to distribute "when the youngest grandchild reaches 21" also presents a problem if the youngest grandchild dies before reaching 21. Does the trust terminate then, or only when the grandchild *would have* reached 21, or when the *next* youngest grandchild reaches 21? The last is the most sensible solution,[8] since the testator's probable purpose was to avoid distribution to persons under 21. This is achieved if distribution is put off until no living distributee is under 21, but no longer.

If an interest preceding the class gift is disclaimed, many courts hold that the disclaimer "accelerates" the remainder and closes the class.[9]

### *Income*

Many trusts provide for the distribution of income to or among a class. A distribution of an income installment does not close the class because "there is no * * * real inconvenience in allowing the class to remain open to those children born after the distribution of income begins. * * * Each distribution of income can be made to the children * * * living at that time,"[10] treating

**4.** *Restatement, Second, of Property (Donative Transfers)* § 26.1, comm. a (1987).

**5.** As to posthumous children see note 12 *infra*.

**6.** 5 *Amer. Law of Prop.* § 22.44, at 370; Sheridan v. Blume, 125 N.E. 353 (Ill.1919).

**7.** South Carolina Nat. Bank v. Johnson, 197 S.E.2d 668 (S.C.1973); Lux v. Lux, 288 A.2d 701, 707 (R.I.1972); *Restatement (Second) of Property (Donative Transfers)* § 26.2, comm. o (1987). The idea can be expressed by the phrase "when no living grandchild is under the age of 21." See Uniform Statutory Will Act § 8(b).

**8.** *Restatement, Second, of Property (Donative Transfers)* § 26.2, comm. o (1987).

**9.** Pate v. Ford, 376 S.E.2d 775 (S.C.1989); *Restatement, Second, of Property (Donative Transfers)* § 26.1, comm. j (1987). As to disclaimers see Section 2.8.

**10.** Hamilton Nat. Bank v. Hutcheson, 357 F.Supp. 114, 119–20 (E.D.Tenn.1973). *See also*

the income interest as "a series of" gifts.[11]

### *Posthumous and Adopted Children*

When a class "closes" under the rule of convenience, any child who has then been *conceived* is included if the child is later born alive. This may delay the fixing of shares for a few months, but this is not a significant inconvenience.[12] Similarly intestacy statutes include as heirs persons who were conceived before but born after the decedent's death.[13] A recent decision allowed children born over 18 months after their father's death to inherit from him, saying

> After born children who come into existence because of modern reproductive techniques pose special challenges to society and out legal system. * * * Estates cannot be held open for years simply to allow for the possibility that after born children may come into existence. * * * In our present case, [however,] * * * there are no competing interests of other persons who were alive at the time of [the father's] death which would be unfairly frustrated by recognizing [the children] as his heirs.[14]

If a person enters a class by adoption, the crucial date is the adoption, not birth, *i.e.*, any child adopted after the class closed is excluded regardless of the date of birth.[15]

### *Exceptions to the Rule of Convenience*

The rule of convenience does not apply if "a contrary intent of the donor is found from additional language or circumstances."[16] Courts rarely find such a "contrary intent;" the rule of convenience creates a "stronger" presumption of intent than the preference for early vesting. A court applied the rule of convenience even to a trust for "all" of the settlor's children who attained the age of 21 "whether now living, or hereafter to be born." The quoted words were held to refer only to children born after the trust was executed but before the date of distribution.[17] Devises to children "who may hereafter be born or adopted" may also be construed to refer only to children born after the will is executed and before the testator dies.[18]

### *No Class Members In Being*

To avoid rendering a gift totally ineffective, courts do not apply the rule of convenience when no class member is alive at the time of distribution. In such cases all class members get a share whenever born.[19] Thus if a will devises property "to the children of Charles" and Charles has two children when the testator dies, a third child born a year later is excluded, but if

Central Trust Co. v. Smith, 553 N.E.2d 265, 273 (Ohio 1990).

**11.** *Restatement, Second, of Property (Donative Transfers)* § 26.1, comm. f (1987).

**12.** *Restatement (Second) of Property (Donative Transfers)* § 26.1, comm. c (1987).

**13.** Uniform Probate Code § 2–108; Cal. Prob.Code § 6407; Wis.Stat. § 852.13(4).

**14.** In re Estate of Kolacy, 753 A.2d 1257, 1262 (N.J.Super.Ch.Div.2000). *But see* Hecht v. Superior Court, 20 Cal.Rptr.2d 275, 290 (App. 1993) (dictum).

**15.** In re Silberman's Will, 242 N.E.2d 736, 742 (N.Y.1968).

**16.** *Restatement, Second, of Property (Donative Transfers)* § 26.1.

**17.** In re Wernher's Settlement Trusts, [1961] 1 All E.R. 184, 189–90 (Ch. 1960).

**18.** *Restatement (Second) of Property (Donative Transfers)* § 26.1, illus. 22–23 (1987).

**19.** *Id.* §§ 26.1(2), 26.2(2).

Charles has no children when the testator dies and three are born thereafter, they all get a share in spite of any inconvenience this creates.

### *Intent to Limit the Class*

An instrument may limit a class more narrowly than the rule of convenience does. For example, when a will divided the estate "equally between my three grandchildren Francis, Manley, and Willie," a fourth grandchild was not allowed a share even though he was born prior to distribution, because the use of names and the number "three" showed that the testator did not intend a class gift.[20]

Even a class gift may be restricted by its terms. For example, a trust provided for distribution when the youngest grandchild reached 21 "to such of my grandchildren as may be living at the time of my death." Two grandchildren were born after the testator died but before the youngest reached 21. They would not have been barred by the rule of convenience, but the court excluded them as a matter of interpretation.[21]

### *Wild's Case: "To Charles and His Children"*

A devise "to Charles and his children" invokes Wild's Case,[22] a 16th-century decision almost as celebrated as Shelley's Case. The devise in Wild's Case was actually "to Rowland Wild and his wife, and after their decease to their children." The court held that "every child which they shall have after may take by way of remainder." Courts would reach the same result under the rule of convenience. The *dicta* in Wild's Case are more controversial. They consist of two resolutions. First, "if A devises his land[23] to [Charles] and to his children or issues, and [Charles] hath not any issue at the time of the devise,"[24] Charles gets a fee tail. Second, if Charles has issue at the time of the devise, Charles and they take together, cutting out any after-born children.

These resolutions reflect a tension between the "manifest intent" that Charles' children take, and the inconvenience of giving an interest to unborn children. The first resolution, if applied today in states where a fee tail is turned into a fee simple,[25] would give the children no interest, just like a devise "to Charles and his *heirs*" or "Charles *or* his children," *i.e.,* as if "children" was intended as a word of limitation, or as a substitutional gift in case Charles died before the testator.[26] If the transferor actually intended to give Charles' children an interest, this can best be accomplished by interpreting the words as creating a life estate in Charles with a remainder to his

**20.** Platt v. Romesburg, 348 S.E.2d 536 (S.C.App.1986). *See also* Penn Mutual Life Ins. Co. v. Abramson, 530 A.2d 1202 (D.C.App. 1987).

**21.** Estate of Houston, 421 A.2d 166 (Pa. 1980). *See also* Estate of Grove, 138 Cal.Rptr. 684 (App.1977) ("all grandnieces & grand nephews" interpreted to mean those alive at testator's death in order to avoid a violation of the Rule against Perpetuities).

**22.** 77 Eng.Rep. 277 (K.B. 1599).

**23.** Although these resolutions apply by their terms only to *devises* of *land,* they have also been applied to deeds and to gifts of personal property. Link, *The Rule in Wild's Case in North Carolina,* 55 N.C.L.Rev. 751, 773, 783 (1977).

**24.** Modern American cases apply this test at the time of the testator's death rather than when the will was executed. Link, note 23 *supra,* at 771.

**25.** See Section 10.2, note 45.

**26.** Estate of Murphy, 580 P.2d 1078 (Or. App.1978); Link, note 23 *supra,* at 762.

children. The Restatement of Property adopts this solution.[27] An immediate gift to the children would exclude after-borns under the rule of convenience, whereas the life-estate-remainder construction includes them all by postponing distribution until Charles dies.

The second resolution in Wild's Case, which gives Charles and his children (if he has any) immediate interests, is still widely followed,[28] but the Restatement adopts the life-estate-remainder construction here too.[29] This postpones alienability during Charles lifetime,[30] but it allows later-born children to share. This is only a theoretical advantage if Charles is unlikely to have more children when the gift takes effect. As Professor Halbach has observed, the children who are excluded by the rule of convenience are often only a "faint possibility."[31]

### *Planning*

Most commentators agree with the rule of convenience, unlike the Rule in Shelley's Case and the preference for early vesting.[32] It represents a reasonable attempt to reconcile the inclusiveness indicated by a class gift with the inconvenience of preserving an interest for unborn children, but it may not be the best solution to the problem in a particular situation. The exception for cases where no class members exist at the time of distribution is logical, given the desire to avoid nullifying a gift, but other factors might be considered too. Suppose land is devised land to "the children of Charles" or "to Charles and his children," and Charles has one child, but plans to have more. Why should his later children be excluded? Conversely, suppose that Charles is fifty, and a bachelor who has no intention of marrying. Why should the title to the land be kept in abeyance for his lifetime to protect children who are not likely to materialize? Some courts would allow proof that Charles cannot have further children,[33] but even if he can, the possibility of issue might be too remote to justify the inconvenience of protecting their interest.

Gifts "to Charles and his children" raise additional problems. In what proportions should they share? If Charles or one of his children dies, is this a class gift? a joint tenancy?[34] A life estate in Charles, followed by a remainder to his children avoids these problems but it raises others. A trust for Charles with remainder to his "issue" who survive him is preferable.[35]

**27.** *Restatement (Second) of Property (Donative Transfers)* § 28.3 (1987).

**28.** In re Parant's Will, 240 N.Y.S.2d 558, 564 (Surr.1963); Link, *supra* note 23, at 820.

**29.** *Restatement (Second) of Property (Donative Transfers)* § 28.3 (1987). *See also* Neb. Rev.Stat. § 76–113; Kan.Stat. § 58–505.

**30.** In Ellingrod v. Trombla, 95 N.W.2d 635 (Neb.1959), land was devised "to Polly and her descendants." Polly was unable to sell the land because under the governing statute (like the Restatement) she only got a life estate.

**31.** Halbach, *Issues About Issue,* 48 Mo. L.Rev. 333, 359 (1983). *See also Restatement (Second) of Property (Donative Transfers)* § 26.1, comm. a (1987).

**32.** Halbach, *supra* note 31, at 361.

**33.** See Section 9.6, at note 30.

**34.** Wild's Case said that Charles and his children would take a "joint estate," but under modern cases they would hold as tenants in common, In re Parant's Will, 240 N.Y.S.2d 558 (Sur.1963), because of the modern preference for a tenancy in common over joint tenancy. See Section 4.8, note 11.

**35.** For the advantages of a bypass trust over a legal life estate see Section 9.3, note 3 et seq.

## § 10.4 Powers of Appointment

### *Definitions*

We have previously discussed certain powers, such as the power to revoke a trust.[1] Powers can also be conferred by one person on another. If John gives Mary a power of appointment, John is called the "donor" of the power and Mary is the "donee" (even if she cannot benefit from exercise of the power).[2] If a power is reserved, the donor and the donee are the same person.

A trustee who has discretion in distributing income or principal has a kind of power of appointment,[3] but the donee of a power is often not a fiduciary and in making appointments can be "dictated by considerations other than the welfare" of the possible appointees,[4] whereas trustees should not be motivated by self-interest. Trustees' decisions are subject to court control whereas the appointments made under a power are generally not reviewable.[5]

Powers of appointment are divided into two types: "general" and "special."[6] If the donee can appoint to herself or to her estate she has a general power. If she can appoint to anyone in the world *except* herself, her estate or her creditors, her power is special.[7] Most special powers are more limited, *e.g.*, to appoint among her issue. If no limits are expressed in the instrument which creates a power, it is construed to be general. Thus a beneficiary who was given power to appoint "to such person or persons as she may designate," was held to have power to appoint to creditors even though the trust also had a spendthrift provision.[8]

A power is "testamentary" when the donee can appoint only by a will. If powers are "presently exercisable," the donee can make an appointment by deed.[9]

### *Relation Back*

The exercise of a power of appointment is often said to "relate back" to the donor, so that the appointee takes directly from the donor. The donee of the power is regarded as only an agent who "fills in the blanks" in the donor's will or trust, and not as the owner of the appointed assets. For example, when the executors of a donee of a power sought to include the appointed assets in the donee's probate estate,[10] the court rejected their claim, saying that to treat a donee's power as "an interest in property" would hinder

§ 10.4

1. Section 5.5, at note 13 et seq. *Restatement, Second, of Property (Donative Transfers)* § 11.1, comm. c (1984) classifies this as a type of power of appointment.

2. *Id.* § 11.2. *See also* Cal.Prob.Code § 610.

3. *Restatement, Second, of Property (Donative Transfers)* § 11.1, comm. d (1984).

4. *Id.* § 20.2, comm. h.

5. As to judicial review of trustee decisions, see Section 9.5, at note 8 et seq. As to the (relatively rare) cases where the exercise of other powers are invalidated for exceeding the limits of the power see note 70 *infra*.

6. Cal.Prob.Code § 611; N.Y. EPTL § 10–3.2. The Restatement makes the same distinction but prefers the term "non-general" to special. *Restatement (Second) of Property (Donative Transfers)* § 11.4 (1984).

7. The line closely tracks the one made for tax purposes. See Section 15.3, note 119.

8. Dickinson v. Wilmington Trust Co., 734 A.2d 605 (Del.Ch.1999). *See also* First Union Nat. Bank v. Ingold, 523 S.E.2d 725, 728 (N.C.App.1999); Mittleman's Estate v. C. I. R., 522 F.2d 132 (D.C.Cir.1975); Wis.Stat. § 702.01(3); Mich.Comp.Laws § 556.112(h).

9. *Restatement (Second) of Property (Donative Transfers)* § 11.5 (1984); Cal.Prob.Code § 612; N.Y. EPTL § 10–3.3.

10. Since often the fees of executors are based on the size of the probate estate. See Section 12.5, note 7.

"one of the most useful tools in estate planning, in addition to giving credence to an unjust method of assessing executor's fee and attorneys' fees."[11]

For centuries courts have used the relation back concept of powers to avoid rules they dislike. It was "an ingenious trick by which conveyancers circumvented the declared policy of the law or a device by which the courts assisted progress during a period when statutory reform was slow."[12] Many of these historical uses of powers are no longer relevant. Courts still invoke relation back, but they do not apply it consistently to answer all questions concerning powers.[13]

### *Taxes*

Before 1942, powers were distinguished from property under the federal estate tax. Appointive assets were not taxed in the donee's estate unless the power was exercised. Today, however, appointive assets are taxed in the donee's estate, whether or not the power is exercised, if the power is general and was created after 1942. Special powers, however, are not taxed even if exercised.[14]

Powers may be treated as equivalent to ownership for income tax purposes. A person with "a power exercisable solely by himself to vest the corpus or the income" of a trust in himself is taxed on the trust income even if it is accumulated or paid to someone else.[15] Even special powers, if reserved by the settlor, may cause the settlor to be taxed on the trust income.[16]

### *Rights of Creditors*

State laws vary as to the rights of creditors of the donee of a power. For example, a court rejected an attempt by creditors to reach a trust beneficiary's right to withdraw money from a trust, saying that her "unexercised right to withdraw, a general power of appointment, * * * is neither property nor a property right."[17] The Restatement of Property agrees,[18] but many states have changed the rule by statute. In New York, for example, "property covered by a general power of appointment which is presently exercisable * * * is subject to the payment of claims of creditors of the donee" even if the power is not exercised.[19] If a donee becomes a bankrupt, the donee's trustee in bankruptcy can reach the trust assets.[20] But if a power is only testamentary, creditors

**11.** In re Wylie's Estate, 342 So.2d 996, 999 (Fla.App.1977). *Accord,* Aurora Nat. Bank v. Old Second Nat. Bank, 375 N.E.2d 544 (Ill. App.1978); *Restatement, Third, of Property (Wills and Other Donative Transfers)* § 1.1, comm. b (1998).

**12.** *Am.Law of Prop.* § 23.13.

**13.** *Restatement (Second) of Property (Donative Transfers),* Part V, Introductory Note (1984); Mahoney, *Elective Share Statutes: The Right to Elect Against Property Subject to a General Power of Appointment in the Decedent,* 55 N.D.Law. 99, 107–10 (1979).

**14.** See Section 15.3, note 119. However, appointive assets are not always subject to state inheritance tax when the donee dies even if the power is general. In re Estate of Nelson, 571 N.W.2d 269 (Neb.1997).

**15.** Internal Revenue Code § 678.

**16.** *Id.* § 674.

**17.** University Nat. Bank v. Rhoadarmer, 827 P.2d 561, 562 (Colo.App.1991). *See also* Irwin Union Bank & Trust Co. v. Long, 312 N.E.2d 908 (Ind.App.1974).

**18.** *Restatement (Second) of Property (Donative Transfers)* § 13.2 (1984).

**19.** N.Y. EPTL § 10–7.2. *See also* Cal.Prob. Code § 682. For a list of similar statutes see *Restatement (Second) of Property (Donative Transfers)* § 13.2, Statutory Note (1984).

**20.** *Id.* § 13.6, comm. c.

cannot reach the trust assets while the donee is alive even under the New York statute or the Bankruptcy Code.[21]

Even without a statute, creditors of a donee who exercises the power can reach the appointed assets if the appointment was a fraudulent conveyance, *e.g.*, made while the donee was insolvent. If the donee appoints to a creditor, however, other creditors can not object since (outside of bankruptcy) a debtor can prefer one creditor over another.[22] But exercise of a *testamentary* power makes the assets subject to division pro rata among all the testator's creditors.[23]

Creditors have greater rights over appointive assets if the debtor created the power.

> A settlor, who has reserved to himself the income for life and a general power of appointment over the remainder * * * has retained 'all the substantial incidents of ownership' and therefore it would be contrary to public policy to allow him by this formal change to prevent creditors from reaching the property.[24]

Even states which allow creditors of the donee of a general power to reach the appointive assets do not apply the same rule to special powers; even in bankruptcy creditors of the donee of such a power cannot reach the appointive assets.[25]

### *Spouse's Rights*

The relation back concept has been used to prevent a donee's spouse from including appointive assets in the elective share.[26] The second Restatement allows spouses to reach appointive assets only if "the deceased spouse was both the donor and donee of a general power,"[27] but the terms of the relevant statute may change this. The Uniform Probate Code, for example, includes in the assets subject to the elective share (1) property over which the decedent spouse "held a presently exercisable general power of appointment" regardless who created it, and (2) property transferred during the marriage in which the decedent reserved a general power, including a testamentary power.[28]

The powers held by a decedent spouse are less important in community property states. Spouses have no claim to the decedent's separate property in any event, whereas they can upset gifts of community property even if the donor reserved no power at all.[29]

**21.** *Ibid. See also* Bynum v. Campbell, 419 So.2d 1370 (Ala.1982).

**22.** *Restatement (Second) of Property (Donative Transfers)* § 13.5 (1984).

**23.** *Id.* § 13.4.

**24.** United States v. Ritter, 558 F.2d 1165, 1167 (4th Cir.1977). *Accord, Restatement, Second, of Property (Donative Transfers)* § 13.3 (1984); Cal.Prob.Code § 683.

**25.** *Restatement, Second, of Property (Donative Transfers)* § 13.1 (1984); Cal.Prob.Code § 681; N.Y. EPTL § 10–7.1; 11 U.S.C § 541(b)(1). In Ahern v. Thomas, 733 A.2d 756, 769 (Conn.1999), a reserved special testamentary power was held not to make the trust principal available to the settlor for purposes of qualification for medicaid.

**26.** Reno v. Reno, 626 P.2d 552 (Wyo.1981).

**27.** *Restatement (Second) of Property (Donative Transfers)* § 13.7 (1984).

**28.** Uniform Probate Code § 2–205. In Matter of Reynolds, 664 N.E.2d 1209 (N.Y. 1996), a similar statute was construed to allow a widower to reach a trust created by his wife in which she had reserved a broad special power.

**29.** As to community property see Section 3.8, note 50 et seq.

### *Capacity*

Today the law governing capacity is generally the same for the exercise of a power and for the transfer of property. A donee can make an effective appointment "if the donee has capacity to make an effective transfer of similar owned property."[30] We have noted a tendency to set a lower standard for capacity for wills than for inter-vivos gifts.[31] A woman who had a power to appoint the corpus of a trust by a writing "delivered to the trustee during her lifetime," made an appointment while she was under a conservatorship. Even though conservatees were not competent to make present gifts, this appointment was considered to be "testamentary in nature" since it took effect only after the donee died, even though it was not made by a will.[32]

When the donee of a presently exercisable power is under conservatorship, a conservator can exercise the power on the donee's behalf, although this generally requires court approval.[33] Testamentary powers are more problematic since many states deny conservators the power to make a will for the conservatee.[34]

### *Formalities*

The instrument granting a power usually specifies that it shall be exercised "by will" or "by deed." This means a will or deed which complies with the legal requirements prescribed for such instruments,[35] but substantial compliance may suffice. Thus when the donee of a testamentary power exercised it by a will which had only two witnesses instead of the three required by law, the court upheld her appointment, citing the Restatement of Property which allows "approximate" compliance with "the manner of appointment prescribed by the donor."[36] The Restatement distinguishes between requirements imposed by the donor and those imposed by law: as to the latter, "approximation is never sufficient."[37] Some argue that substantial compliance with even the legal requirements for wills should suffice,[38] but it is not clear how far courts will accept or apply this idea. A court recently refused to give effect to an unwitnessed document which purported to exercise a testamentary power.[39]

A donor sometimes adds formal requirements to those imposed by the law,[40] for example, that any instrument exercising the power be delivered to the trustee during the donee's lifetime. Here substantial compliance may suffice. When a donee signed an instrument exercising a power and gave it to

**30.** *Restatement (Second) of Property (Donative Transfers)* § 18.1 (1984). *See also* Cal. Prob.Code § 625. As to the general requirements for capacity see Section 7.1.

**31.** Section 7.2, note 17.

**32.** In re Wood's Estate, 108 Cal.Rptr. 522, 534 (App.1973).

**33.** Cal.Prob.Code § 2580(b)(3); Uniform Probate Code § 5–407(c); *Restatement (Second) of Property (Donative Transfers)* § 18.1(2) (1984); Wilhelm v. Zepp, 447 A.2d 123 (Md. App.1982). As to gifts by conservators see Section 7.2, note 27 et seq.

**34.** Uniform Probate Code § 2–507(c). *Contra*, Cal.Prob.Code § 2580(b)(13). *Restatement, Third, of Trusts* § 11, comm. f (1996), suggests that any prohibition against making wills for a conservatee should be "strictly construed."

**35.** *Restatement (Second) of Property (Donative Transfers)* § 18.2, comm. b, d (1984).

**36.** Estate of McNeill, 463 A.2d 782, 784 (Me.1983); *Restatement, Second, of Property (Donative Transfers)* § 18.3 (1984).

**37.** *Id.* § 18.3, comm. b.

**38.** See Section 4.1, note 23.

**39.** Catch v. Phillips, 86 Cal.Rptr.2d 584 (App.1999).

**40.** *Restatement (Second) of Property (Donative Transfers)* § 18.2, comm. f (1984). *See also* Cal.Prob.Code § 630.

her attorney, who failed to deliver it to the trustee until after the donee died, the court upheld the exercise, saying that all possible purposes of the delivery requirement had been satisfied since the trustee had not distributed the funds before receiving the instrument.[41]

### *Contracts to Exercise Powers*

If the donee of a testamentary power promises for consideration to exercise the power in a particular way the promise is unenforceable. The Restatement justifies this rule on the ground that a testamentary power indicates "an intent that the selection of the appointees be made in the light of the circumstances" existing when the donee dies.[42] This reasoning is questionable, since a requirement that a power be exercised "by will" may simply be designed to forestall claims that an oral statement or casual letter constituted an exercise. If so, a formal contract should be an acceptable substitute for a will.[43]

The Restatement position is anomalous because it allows donees to *release* a testamentary power by deed. A release is supposed not to defeat the donor's intent because it "operates negatively" whereas an appointment "operates affirmatively."[44]

### *Intent to Exercise*

The question whether or not a donee intended to exercise a power is often litigated. For example, a husband gave his wife a general power of appointment. The wife's will left "all the residue of my estate of every kind and nature to a trust." The court, noting that in many jurisdictions a general residuary clause like this would be deemed to exercise any power held by the testator, followed the contrary rule in the Uniform Probate Code, which is based on the idea that "most powers of appointment are created in marital deduction trusts[45] and the donor would prefer to have the property pass under his trust instrument" to the designated takers in default of appointment.[46] The Restatement also adopts the presumption that a residuary clause in the donee's will does not exercise a power because "the donee does not own the property subject to the power."[47] Some statutes make the opposite presump-

**41.** In re Wood's Estate, 108 Cal.Rptr. 522 (App.1973). *See also* In re Meyer, 987 P.2d 822 (Ariz.App.1999) (power effectively exercised even though donee's will was not probated within three months of death as required by power); *Restatement, Second, of Property (Donative Transfers)* § 18.3, illus. 5 (1984) (appointment by will of power exercisable by inter-vivos instrument).

**42.** *Restatement (Second) of Property (Donative Transfers)* § 16.2, comm. a (1984). *See also* In re Brown's Estate, 306 N.E.2d 781 (N.Y.1973) (promise in divorce settlement to exercise power in favor of a son unenforceable); Cal.Prob.Code § 660.

**43.** In the converse case Cal.Prob.Code § 630(b) allows a power "stated to be exercisable by a an inter-vivos instrument" to be also exercised by will.

**44.** *Restatement (Second) of Property (Donative Transfers)* § 14.1, comm. a, § 16.2, comm. a (1984). *See also* Wood v. American Security & Trust Co., 253 F.Supp. 592 (D.D.C. 1966); Cal.Prob.Code § 661; cf *Restatement, Third, of Trusts* § 58, comm. c (1999) (beneficiary can release an interest even though a spendthrift provision bars its transfer).

**45.** At one time in order to qualify for the marital deduction, a trust had to give the spouse a general power of appointment.

**46.** Matter of Estate of Allen, 772 P.2d 297, 299 (Mont.1989). In the present version of the Uniform Probate Code, Section 2–608, the presumption of non-exercise does not apply if the instrument which created the power makes no gift in default of appointment.

**47.** *Restatement (Second) of Property (Donative Transfers)* § 17.3, comm. a (1984). But illustration 2 of this section finds an intent to exercise in a will devising "all property which I am entitled to dispose of." This slight differ-

tion. In New York, a power is exercised if the donee "leaves a will disposing of all of his property" unless a contrary intention "appears expressly or by necessary implication."[48]

Many instruments conferring powers state that they can only be exercised if the donee specifically refers to the power. Such provisions have been strictly construed by some courts, more liberally by others. A will which devised all the donee's property "including all property over which I may have a power of appointment" was held a sufficient exercise, even though it did not identify the source of the power.[49] Other courts on similar facts have held the power was not exercised on the ground that "where the controlling requirements are clearly stated in the donor's will, the donee's intent is irrelevant if she fails to comply with those requirements."[50] The Uniform Probate Code presumes that such provisions are designed only "to prevent an inadvertent exercise," and are therefore satisfied by general language "if the donee had knowledge of and intended to exercise the power."[51]

Some courts consider extrinsic evidence in ascertaining the donee's intent, *e.g.* evidence of the donee's discussions with the drafting attorney.[52] According to the Restatement "direct declarations by the donee as to whether the donee intended a will to exercise the power may not be considered,"[53] but the Uniform Probate Code seems to be contrary on this point.[54]

The Restatement allows evidence of "circumstances existing at the time of the execution of the donee's deed or will" to show the donee's intent.[55] These include the adverse tax consequences of exercising the power,[56] "an extremely close and affectionate relationship" between the donor, donee and the beneficiary of the donee's will,[57] and the extent of the donee's own property. For example, a court concluded that a donee must have intended to exercise a power when her will made pecuniary devises totalling $90,000 and left the residue to five individuals, since the pecuniary devises alone would have exhausted the donee's owned assets.[58] A specific devise of property over

ence in wording seems slim evidence of an intent to exercise powers.

**48.** N.Y. EPTL § 10–6.1(a)(4). *See also* First Union Nat. Bank v. Ingold, 523 S.E.2d 725 (N.C.App.1999) (based on a N.C. statute). For a list of both types of statutes see *Restatement (Second) of Property (Donative Transfers)* § 17.3, Statutory Note (1984).

**49.** McKelvy v. Terry, 346 N.E.2d 912 (Mass.1976). *See also* Wright v. Greenberg, 2 S.W.3d 666, 672 (Tex.App.1999).

**50.** Matter of Smith's Estate, 585 P.2d 319, 321 (Colo.App.1978). *See also* Murstein v. Central Nat. Bank, 495 N.E.2d 37 (Ohio App. 1985); First Nat. Bank v. Walker, 607 S.W.2d 469 (Tenn.1980); Yardley v. Yardley, 484 N.E.2d 873 (Ill.App.1985); Estate of Eddy, 184 Cal.Rptr. 521 (App.1982); Matter of Estate of Burgess, 836 P.2d 1386 (Utah App.1992).

**51.** Uniform Probate Code § 2–704 and Comment thereto.

**52.** Motes/Henes Trust v. Motes, 761 S.W.2d 938 (Ark.1988); McKelvy v. Terry, 346 N.E.2d 912, 916 (Mass.1976).

**53.** *Restatement (Second) of Property (Donative Transfers)* § 17.5, comm. a (1984). *See also* Schwartz v. Baybank Merrimack Valley, N.A., 456 N.E.2d 1141, 1146 (Mass.App.1983).

**54.** Kurtz, *Powers of Appointment under the 1990 Uniform Probate Code*, 55 Alb.L.Rev. 1151, 1167 (1992).

**55.** *Restatement (Second) of Property (Donative Transfers)* § 17.5 (1984).

**56.** *But see* In re Jaekel's Estate, 227 A.2d 851 (Pa.1967) (finding an exercise despite adverse tax consequences).

**57.** Bank of New York v. Black, 139 A.2d 393, 400 (N.J.1958).

**58.** Little Red Schoolhouse v. Citizens & Southern Nat. Bank, 197 S.E.2d 342 (Ga.1973). *See also* Illinois State Trust Co. v. Southern Ill. Nat. Bank, 329 N.E.2d 805 (Ill.App.1975); First Nat. Bank v. Ettlinger, 465 F.2d 343 (7th Cir. 1972); *Restatement (Second) of Property (Donative Transfers)* § 17.5, illus. 3 (1984). *But see* Di Sesa v. Hickey, 278 A.2d 785 (Conn.1971).

which the donee has a power of appointment, *e.g.,* "I leave Blackacre to Alice" will be deemed an exercise.[59] Conversely, an intent not to exercise a special power may be inferred in a devise which includes persons who are not permissible appointees.[60]

The fact that the donee's will was executed before the power was created is not determinative as to the intent to exercise a power. For example, a woman executed a will leaving her estate to a trust. Two years later her mother died leaving her a power. The court held that daughter's will had exercised the power, just as a devise of "all my property" includes property which a testator acquired after executing her will.[61]

### *Lapse*

If a will confers a power of appointment on a donee who predeceases the testator, the power never comes into existence, but the will may be construed to incorporate the terms of the donee's will by reference.[62]

If the donee appoints to a person who predeceases her, the appointment lapses, but an anti-lapse statute may apply. A testator gave his wife a special power of appointment, which she exercised to appoint to the donor's brother. The appointment failed because the brother predeceased the donee; he had survived the testator, but (despite the relation back theory) an appointee must survive the donee as well as the donor in order to take.[63] The brother's children claimed the property under an anti-lapse statute, but the statute applied only if a devisee who was "a relative of the testator" and the brother was not related to the donee.[64] Also, the brother's children were not permissible appointees, since the donee was only authorized to appoint to the brother.[65] The Uniform Probate Code and the second Restatement of Property would remove both these difficulties. The anti-lapse statute applies if the appointee is related to "either the testator or the donor" of the power, and, unless the power expressly provides otherwise, "a surviving descendant of a deceased appointee * * * can be substituted for the appointee * * * whether or not the descendant is an object of the power."[66]

### *Limitations on Special Powers*

Special powers often restrict appointments to a relatively small group such as "children." Courts interpret such words the same way they would construe a gift to the same class. Thus a power given to the testator's son to

**59.** *Restatement (Second) of Property (Donative Transfers)* § 17.4 (1984); Brouse v. Old Phoenix Nat. Bank, 495 N.E.2d 42 (Ohio App. 1985).

**60.** MacLean v. Citizens Fidelity Bank & Trust Co., 437 S.W.2d 766 (Ky.1969). *But see* United California Bank v. Bottler, 94 Cal.Rptr. 227 (App.1971).

**61.** In re Buck Trust, 277 A.2d 717 (Del. 1971) *See also* Motes/Henes Trust v. Motes, 761 S.W.2d 938 (Ark.1988); Wetherill v. Basham, 3 P.3d 1118 (Ariz.App.2000) (attempt to amend trust held to exercise a later acquired power of appointment); *Restatement (Second) of Property (Donative Transfers)* § 17.6 (1984). However, the terms of the power may preclude exercise by an earlier instrument. *Id.* comm. c. *See also* Cal.Prob.Code § 642.

**62.** *Restatement (Second) of Property (Donative Transfers)* § 18.4 (1984).

**63.** *Id.* § 18.5.

**64.** Dow v. Atwood, 260 A.2d 437, 441 (Me. 1969). As to the anti-lapse statutes see Section 8.3, note 9 et seq.

**65.** *See also* Daniel v. Brown, 159 S.E. 209, 210 (Va.1931); Mich.Comp.Laws § 556.130.

**66.** Uniform Probate Code § 2–603(b). *See also* Cal.Prob.Code §§ 673–74; *Restatement (Second) of Property (Donative Transfers)* § 18.6 (1984).

appoint to "one or more of my descendants" was held not to include an adult which the son had adopted.[67] Most courts would not permit appointment to a grandchild if the power says "children,"[68] although this conclusion is hard to square with the liberal construction of anti-lapse statutes just described. A power to appoint among the donee's "issue" was held not to allow an appointment to grandchildren whose parents were alive.[69] This seems wrong. Ordinarily it makes sense to exclude children of living parents in distributing a gift to "issue,"[70] but a donee who elects to appoint to them presumably considered that the advantages outweighed the possible disadvantages.

Appointments in trust, or the creation of further powers of appointment, are sometimes held invalid. When a will directed the trustee to pay the funds "free from trust, to and among [the] children and issue [of the testator's daughter] as she may appoint," the daughter was not permitted to use the power to create a trust for her children.[71] The Restatement, however, presumes that the donee is intended to have "the same breadth of discretion in appointment to objects that he has in the disposition of his owned property."[72]

If a power is construed to be "non-exclusive" the donee must include every object of the power in an appointment. This requirement seems inconsistent with the very idea of a power, yet a surprising number of cases have construed powers to be "non exclusive."[73] Can the donee satisfy the requirement by a nominal appointment or must each object of the power receive a substantial share? The Restatement and some statutes avoid this problem by providing that powers are "exclusive" unless the donor specifies a minimum share which each object must receive.[74] Most recent cases have construed questionable powers as being exclusive.[75]

An appointment to a permissible appointee may be invalid when the donee's motive was to benefit a non-object of the power. Thus if a donee has a power to appoint among her issue, her appointment to a child who has agreed to give part of the property to the donee's sister may be disallowed as a "fraud on the power."[76] However, the donee's use of the power need not be totally disinterested. An appointment to a child "because of the attention and kindness she has always shown to me" is permitted even if the power is special.[77]

The drafter of the donee's will should note any limits on the power. A donee who wishes to benefit a non-object of the power should use property of

**67.** Cross v. Cross, 532 N.E.2d 486 (Ill.App. 1988). For the inclusion of adoptees in class gifts generally see Section 2.10, note 19 et seq.

**68.** Equitable Trust Co. v. Foulke, 40 A.2d 713 (Del.Ch.1945); *Restatement (Second) of Property (Donative Transfers)* § 20.1, illus. 4 (1984).

**69.** Kramer v. Freedman, 346 So.2d 1216 (Fla.App.1977).*Contra, Restatement (Second) of Property (Donative Transfers)* § 24.2, comm. d (1984).

**70.** See Section 2.2, at note 5 et seq.

**71.** Loring v. Karri–Davies, 357 N.E.2d 11 (Mass.1976).

**72.** *Restatement (Second) of Property (Donative Transfers)* § 19.3, comm a, illus 4 (1984). *See also* Cal.Prob.Code § 650; Matter of Moore, 493 N.Y.S.2d 924 (Sup.1985).

**73.** 5 *Amer.Law of Prop.* § 23.57.

**74.** *Restatement (Second) of Property (Donative Transfers)* § 21.1 (1984); Wis.Stat. § 702.07; Cal.Prob.Code § 652.

**75.** Ferrell–French v. Ferrell, 691 So.2d 500 (Fla.App.1997); First Nat. Bank v. First Nat. Bank, 348 So.2d 1041 (Ala.1977).

**76.** *Restatement (Second) of Property (Donative Transfers)* § 20.2 (1984); Horne v. Title Ins. & Trust Co., 79 F.Supp. 91 (S.D.Cal.1948).

**77.** *Restatement (Second) of Property (Donative Transfers)* § 20.2, comm. h, illus. 16 (1984).

her own to do this. When a donee appointed property to a son-in-law, who was not an object of the power, he successfully sued the drafter of the donee's will who might have thus avoided the problem.[78] The exercise of a power is sometimes validated by "marshalling" after the donee has died. For example, a donee with a power to appoint to her heirs appointed to a trust which could be used to pay claims against the donee's estate. The appointment was upheld by utilizing the appointive assets exclusively for donee's issue by "selective allocation or marshalling," while using the donee's own property to fulfill objects not authorized by the power.[79]

Marshalling does not work if donee has not sufficient property of her own to satisfy the gifts to non-objects. If under these circumstances she had appointed half the assets to an object of the power and the other half to a non-object, courts usually give effect to the valid part of the appointment,[80] but not always. When the donee of a power to appoint among her children appointed to a trust for her children and their issue, the appointment to her issue was void. Only two of the donee's five children survived her. If the appointment to them was given effect they would "get not only their shares under the appointment but * * * would also take one fifth of the part illegally appointed." The court held that the donee would have preferred to have her appointment fail altogether, so that all her children's families would get equal shares under the gift in default of appointment.[81]

### *Failure to Effectively Appoint*

A well-drafted power should include a gift in default of appointment. Even if it does not, if the power is special, a gift in default of appointment to the objects of the power is usually implied. For example, a trust called for distribution as the settlor might appoint by will among seven named persons. When the settlor failed to exercise the power, the assets were equally divided among the seven objects of the power.[82] However, such a gift is not implied when the class of permissible appointees is very large.[83]

If the donee of a general power fails to exercise it and no gift in default of appointment is expressed, the appointive assets revert to the donor's estate.[84] However, an ineffective appointment by the donee may "capture" the assets, and may even override a gift in default of appointment. For example, a man

**78.** Merrick v. Mercantile–Safe Deposit & Trust Co., 855 F.2d 1095 (4th Cir.1988).

**79.** Dollar Savings & Trust Co. v. First Nat. Bank, 285 N.E.2d 768, 772 (Ohio Com.Pl. 1972). *See also Restatement (Second) of Property (Donative Transfers)* § 22.2 (1984).

**80.** *Restatement (Second) of Property (Donative Transfers)* § 23.1 (1984); First Nat. Bank v. First Nat. Bank, 348 So.2d 1041 (Ala. 1977); N.Y. EPTL § 10–6.6; Cal.Prob.Code § 670.

**81.** Equitable Trust Co. v. Foulke, 40 A.2d 713, 718–19 (Del.Ch.1945). *See also Restatement (Second) of Property (Donative Transfers)* § 23.1, illus. 6 (1984).

**82.** Schroeder v. Herbert C. Coe Trust, 437 N.W.2d 178, 182 (S.D.1989). *See also* Loring v. Marshall, 484 N.E.2d 1315 (Mass.1985); In re Spencer's Estate, 232 N.W.2d 491 (Iowa 1975); *Restatement (Second) of Property (Donative Transfers)* § 24.2 (1984). When the implied gift is to "issue" the shares are not necessarily equal. Children whose parents are living may be excluded, as in an express devise to "issue." *Id.*, comm. d (1984).

**83.** *Id.* comm. c. In California the implied gift applies only to "imperative powers," which are defined (somewhat circularly) as those where "the creating instrument manifests an intent that the permissible appointees be benefited even if the donee fails to exercise the power." Cal.Prob.Code §§ 613, 671; *cf.* N.Y. EPTL § 10–6.8.

**84.** *Restatement (Second) of Property (Donative Transfers)* § 24.1 (1984); Cal.Prob.Code § 672.

gave his wife a general testamentary power with a gift in default of appointment to his son. The wife's will left her property, including the appointive assets, to devisees who all predeceased her without issue so the appointment lapsed. The son's estate claimed the property under the gift in default of appointment,[85] but the court awarded it to the donee's heirs instead. "When the donee of a general power of appointment makes an ineffective appointment * * * the appointive property passes to the donee or his estate if the instrument of appointment manifests an intent to assume control of the property for all purposes." This intent "is most commonly manifested by provisions * * * which blend the property owned by the donee with the property subject to the power." The donee's will had done this by disposing of "all of the property I own including * * * any property over which I have a power of appointment."[86]

### *Choice of Law*

Since the rules governing powers vary in different states, choice of law may be crucial. The logic of the relation back theory suggests that the law of the donor's domicile should control, and many cases so hold,[87] but recent cases have applied the law of the donee's domicile. The donee's will "should be construed according to the laws under which his will was drafted and with which he was most familiar, those of his own domicile."[88] The Restatement also looks to the donee's domicile in selecting among conflicting antilapse statutes.[89]

Choice of law can also be an issue when the law has changed. A husband gave his wife a general testamentary power of appointment at a time when a statute presumed that a devise of all the testator's property exercised a power. Prior to the wife's death the statute was altered to reverse the presumption. The wife's will did not mention the power. The court held that she had not exercised it, saying "the law in effect at the time of the exercise of a power of appointment controls its exercise, rather than the law in effect at its creation."[90]

### *Powers and Planning: Creation of Powers*

**85.** The son failed to survive the donee, but a gift in default of appointment is usually construed as vested subject to divestiture only if the power is exercised. *Restatement (Second) of Property (Donative Transfers)* § 24.2, illus. 8 (1984).

**86.** Estate of Eddy, 176 Cal.Rptr. 598, 610–11 (App.1981). *See also Restatement (Second) of Property (Donative Transfers)* § 23.2 (1984); Cal.Prob.Code § 672(b); *Restatement (Second) of Trusts* § 426 (1959). Capture does not apply to special powers. *Id.* § 427. As to capture when an appointment violates the rule against Perpetuities see Section 11.5, at note 19 et seq.

On rehearing this case, the court held that the donee had not satisfied a specific reference requirement in the donor's will and so had not exercised the power, and thus the gift passed under the gift in default of appointment after all. Estate of Eddy, 184 Cal.Rptr. 521 (App. 1982).

**87.** Beals v. State Street Bank & Trust Co., 326 N.E.2d 896, 899–900 (Mass.1975); Will of Brown, 466 N.Y.S.2d 988, 991 (Surr.1983); Dollar Savings & Trust Co. v. First Nat. Bank, 285 N.E.2d 768, 776 (Ohio Com.Pl.1972); First Nat. Bank v. First Nat. Bank, 348 So.2d 1041, 1045 (Ala.1977).

**88.** White v. United States, 680 F.2d 1156, 1159 (7th Cir.1982). *See also* Toledo Trust Co. v. Santa Barbara Foundation, 512 N.E.2d 664, 667 (Ohio 1987); *cf.* First Nat. Bank v. Ettlinger, 465 F.2d 343 (7th Cir.1972).

**89.** *Restatement (Second) of Property (Donative Transfers)* § 18.6, comm. d (1984).

**90.** Hund v. Holmes, 235 N.W.2d 331, 334 (Mich.1975). *See also* Cal.Prob.Code § 601; Matter of Moore, 493 N.Y.S.2d 924, 927 (Sup. 1985).

Powers of appointment provide flexibility to deal with changing conditions.[91] If a husband, for example, gives his wife a power, she can, for example, adjust their estate plan to account for circumstances which arise after his death. As one lawyer has noted:

> Drafters should recognize that circumstances can change dramatically in the time between the husband's death and the wife's later death, and should provide for a means of adjustment. For example, it may appear best that the children not share equally. Perhaps there is a richly deserving person, such as a daughter-in-law or son-in-law, who would not share in the boilerplate remainder given to 'my then living descendants.' Perhaps the surviving spouse would choose to make a charitable bequest. Perhaps the interest of one descendant should be sheltered by a continuing trust.
>
> The same argument for flexibility applies if the husband, not the wife survives.[92]

Ownership also provides flexibility. If the husband leaves property to his wife outright she can dispose of it in the light of the circumstances existing when she dies. Powers have some advantages over ownership, however. Various types of power are appropriate for different purposes. If the husband wishes to keep property out of his wife's taxable estate and still allow her to alter the disposition at her death, he can give her a *special* power. A donor may also wish to use a special power in order to limit the donee's choices for non-tax reasons, *e.g.,* allow her to provide for their issue but not to give the property to her other relatives or to a second husband.

The donor may have absolute confidence that the donee will intelligently dispose of the property at death but fear that he will dissipate it during his lifetime if he owns it outright. If so, a spendthrift trust with a general *testamentary* power is the solution; a *presently exercisable* power would not achieve the donor's objective in this case.

Even if a donor has full confidence in the donee's ability to handle property and is unconcerned with avoiding taxation in the donee's estate, the donor may prefer to put property in trust (1) to free the donee from the burden of managing it and (2) to avoid the non-tax costs of passing assets through the donee's probate estate.[93] In *this* situation a presently exercisable general power may be useful. It would allow the donee to take the property out of trust if the trustee is not doing a good job.[94] A presently exercisable power also allows the donee to make gifts which may reduce the donee's taxable estate.[95]

A parent may also wish to give children powers of appointment, particularly if property which will be held in trust for their lifetimes, since the likelihood of a change of circumstances after the donor's death is even greater

**91.** Bolich, *The Power of Appointment: Tool of Estate Planning and Drafting,* [1964] Duke L.J. 32, 39–40; Halbach, *The Use of Powers of Appointment in Estate Planning,* 45 Iowa L.Rev. 691, 692 (1960).

**92.** Gardner, *Designing wills and trust instruments to provide maximum flexibility,* 18 Est.Plan. 138 (1991).

**93.** For the advantages of avoiding probate see Section 9.1, note 5 et seq.

**94.** Another alternative is to give the beneficiary power to remove the trustee and appoint another one.

**95.** As to the possible tax advantages of inter-vivos gifts see Chapter 15.

than in the case of spouses. Even if the children's trusts terminate when they reach an age like 30, it may be desirable to allow them to appoint the property to a spouse or a trust if they die prior to termination, since any issue of the child in this situation would almost certainly be minors.

If the children are given *general* powers, the assets will be taxable in their estates. This is not necessarily a disadvantage; without any power the property may be subject to a generation-skipping tax which is higher than the estate tax.[96] On the other hand, the donor may wish the children only special powers in order to keep the property in the family.

Powers of appointment have one disadvantage as compared with ownership. The Rule against Perpetuities in most states starts to run at the donor's death as to interests created by the donee's exercise of a power, whereas if the donee owns the property outright, she can use lives in being at *her* death as measuring lives.[97]

Many persons who decide to confer a testamentary power require that the donees refer to the power specifically in their wills in order to exercise it in order to avoid disputes as to the donee's intent to exercise the power. A donee may exercise a power inadvertently by a general devise of "all my property," or may violate the Rule against Perpetuities or exceed the limits of the power. These risks are diminished if the donor requires a specific reference.

The donor may also wish to require that the power be exercised by a will executed subsequent to donor's death. Powers are designed to enable the donee to alter arrangements in the light of changing circumstances, but unless restricted they can be exercised by a will executed before the donor dies.

The donor may also wish to require that any instrument exercising the power be filed with the trustee in order that the trustee will know whether the power has been exercised and can distribute the assets immediately after the donee dies without risking liability for a distribution to the wrong person.

Beware of drawing special powers too narrowly. Allowing appointment only to "children" precludes appointment to the issue of a deceased child. Many testators would want their children to be able to appoint to their spouse as well as their issue. A non-exclusive power makes no sense.[98] The donee should be authorized to make appointments in trust and to create further powers.

### *Dealing with Powers*

If you are drafting a will for the donee of a power of appointment, the client must first decide whether or not to exercise it. A key factor in this decision is the gift in default of appointment. The donee may be happy to let the assets pass under the gift in default, but she may prefer to leave the property to someone else, or to put assets into a trust which would otherwise

**96.** See Schwab, *General Powers of Appointment May Cause Unexpected Tax*, 19 Est. Plan. 75, 80 (1992). In Matter of Will of Lewis, 544 N.Y.S.2d 719 (Sur.1989), the court reformed a trust by adding a general power in order to qualify for a GST exemption. As to the generation-skipping tax, see Section 15.4.

**97.** *See* Section 11.5, at note 2.

**98.** See note 73 *supra*.

pass outright. If there is no gift in default of appointment in the instrument creating the power, or if it is ambiguous, exercising the power is desirable.

Exercising a power can put the assets in the donee's taxable estate or subject them to an otherwise avoidable state inheritance tax, or to claims of the donee's creditors. These adverse consequences of exercise do not often apply, since exercise of a power has the same effect as nonexercise on death taxes in most situations.[99] Avoiding creditors' claims is relevant only if 1) the donee is insolvent and 2) the governing law makes the rights of the donee's creditors depend on exercise.

If donee does wish to exercise a testamentary power, the donee's will should specifically refer to it. The drafter should carefully ascertain the limits of the power, and beware of violating the Rule against Perpetuities.

Often lawyers draft wills for clients who have no powers of appointment (that they know of), but who may acquire one later. Should a will expressly exercise or *refrain from* exercising unknown powers? Professor Rabin argues in favor of exercise. "The testator-donee ordinarily wishes to benefit his legatees to the maximum extent of his ability. * * * A failure to dispose of unknown or after-acquired appointive property is as unnatural as a failure to dispose of unknown or after-acquired owned property."[100] Others warn that such a blind exercise is "likely to violate some limitation on the power or to produce a violation of the rules regulating perpetuities."[101]

**99.** The federal estate tax is the most important or only death tax in most estates, and exercise or nonexercise is relevant for this purpose only for general powers created before 1942, rarely encountered today. Even if the donee has such a power, she may wish to exercise it because the estate tax cost may be offset by the income tax advantage of a step-up in basis given to assets included in her estate. Halbach, *supra* note 1, at 724.

**100.** Rabin, *Blind Exercise of Powers of Appointment*, 51 Cornell L.Q. 1, 2 (1965). *See also* Martin, *The Draftsman Views Wills for a Young Family*, 54 N.C.L.Rev. 277, 294 (1976).

**101.** *Use and Drafting of Powers of Appointment,* 1 Real Prop., Prob. and Trust L.J. 307, 318 (1966).

# Chapter 11

# THE RULE AGAINST PERPETUITIES

*Analysis*



---

## § 11.1 History and Policy of the Rule

### *The Fee Tail*

The first "perpetuity" so-called in the law was created by the Statute de Donis of 1285 which provided that if land was conveyed "to A and the heirs of his body," A could not alienate it. When courts began to allow such a fee tail to be barred by a process known as a common recovery,[1] landowners looked for new ways to keep land tied up in the hands of their families. One method was to attach to a fee tail a proviso that an attempt to bar it would cause a forfeiture. Courts refused to give effect to such provisos, calling them "perpetuities" and "utterly void and against the law."[2]

### *Destructibility of Contingent Remainders*

Landowners also used contingent remainders to keep land in the family. This was frustrated by the judicially created doctrine of destructibility of contingent remainders. For example, a testator devised land to his son Robert "for his life, and afterwards to the next heir male of Robert."[3] Robert's conveyance of the land to a stranger was held to destroy the remainder in his heir, since contingent remainders had to vest when (or before) the preceding estate ended. Robert's conveyance of a fee put an immediate end to his life estate,[4] and Robert's "next heir male" could not be ascertained until Robert

§ 11.1

1. See Section 10.2, note 43.

2. Corbet's Case, 76 Eng.Rep. 187 (1599).

3. Use of the word "heir" in place of "heirs" in the will avoided the rule in Shelleys Case (see Section 10.2, note 47) which would have given Robert a fee tail, because in England courts the Rule in Shelley's Case applied only when the whole line of heirs in successive generations was designated, not just the person(s) who inherited when the life tenant died. Re Rynard, 31 O.R.2d 257 (1980).

4. This rule was originally designed to protect future interests but it later had the opposite effect. McGovern, *The Historical Concep-*

died.[5] Contingent remainders could also be destroyed even when the preceding interest did not end prematurely. A remainder given "to Robert's children who survive to the age of 21," would be destroyed if his children were under 21 when Robert died.[6]

The destructibility of contingent remainders was viewed as a way to prevent "perpetuities." A leading case on destructibility was called "the Case of Perpetuities" and the report alludes to the "inconveniences" arising from "these perpetuities."[7] But the destructibility of contingent remainders operated "arbitrarily"[8] because there were so many exceptions. It did not apply to trusts.[9] A form of trust to preserve contingent remainders was devised in the 17th century "in order to secure in family settlements a provision for the future children of an intended marriage, who before were usually left to the mercy of the particular tenant for life."[10] Destructibility, like the Rule in Shelley's Case,[11] fostered alienability to some extent but placed "a premium on the drafting skills" of lawyers who knew how to avoid it.[12]

The destructibility of contingent remainders still operates occasionally,[13] but it has been abolished by statute in many states,[14] and some courts have rejected it even without a statute as "a relic of the feudal past, which has no justification or support in modern society."[15]

### *Executory Interests*

Lawyers of the 17th century came up with various other ways to avoid the destructibility of contingent remainders. A father with two sons, William and Thomas, devised land "to Thomas and his heirs," with a proviso that if Thomas died without issue, William should have the land. Thomas suffered a common recovery (the traditional device for breaking a fee tail), but this was ineffective because Thomas had a fee *simple*; the land was "devised to him *and his heirs*." Also, since Thomas had a fee simple, William's interest was not a remainder, because "one fee cannot be in remainder after another." The interest in Thomas was an "executory devise," and executory devises, unlike remainders, were not destructible.[16] One judge thought that executory interests *should* be destructible "for otherwise it would be a mischievous kind of perpetuity," but he was outvoted by his colleagues.[17] As Blackstone later "explained"

*tion of a Lease for Years,* 23 UCLA L.Rev. 501, 517 (1976).

**5.** Archer's Case, 76 Eng.Rep. 146 (1597).

**6.** Festing v. Allen, 12 Mees & W. 279 (1843).

**7.** Chudleigh's Case, 76 Eng.Rep. 270, 322 (1595).

**8.** Abo Petroleum Corp. v. Amstutz, 600 P.2d 278, 281 (N.M.1979).

**9.** Abbiss v. Burney, 17 Ch.Div. 211 (Ct. App. 1881).

**10.** 2 W. Blackstone, *Commentaries* *171–72 (1765).

**11.** See Section 10.2, note 47.

**12.** Abo Petroleum Corp. v. Amstutz, 600 P.2d 278, 280 (N.M.1979).

**13.** Belleville Nat. Bank v. Trauernicht, 445 N.E.2d 958 (Ill.App.1983) (statutory abolition of destructibility in 1921 was prospective, so remainder in life tenant's heirs created in a 1913 deed was destroyed when life tenant conveyed her interest).

**14.** 1 *Amer.Law of Prop.* § 4.63.

**15.** Abo Petroleum Corp. v. Amstutz, 600 P.2d 278, 281 (N.M.1979).

**16.** Alabama put an end to the destructibility of contingent remainders by turning them all into executory interests. Ala.Code § 35–4–212; King v. William M. King Family Ent. Inc., 515 So.2d 1241, 1243 (Ala.1987).

**17.** Pells v. Brown, 78 Eng.Rep. 504 (1620).

> If a man devises land to A. and his heirs, but if he dies before the age of twenty-one to B and his heirs, this remainder, though void in a deed [because no "remainder" can follow a fee simple], is good by executory devise. Such an executory devise * * * cannot be barred by a recovery suffered before it commences.[18]

Later in the 17th century a trust for the Duke of Norfolk came before Chancellor Nottingham. The basic plan involved another gift to a younger son if his elder brother died without issue. The common-law judges whom Nottingham consulted advised him that the limitation was void[19] but Nottingham did not wish to frustrate the father's intent to provide for his younger son. He and the judges agreed that the same rule should apply in law and in Equity. This distinguishes the Rule against Perpetuities from the destructibility of contingent remainders which did not apply to trusts. Nottingham also agreed with the judges that "perpetuities" were undesirable because they "fight against God, for they pretend to such a Stability in human Affairs as the Nature of them admits not of." But as to where the line should be drawn, the Chancellor had no clear answer: "I will stop wherever any visible Inconvenience doth appear, for the just Bounds of a Fee-simple upon a Fee-simple are not yet determined." He rejected the technical distinctions which had heretofore prevailed in the common law. "These are Words, and but Words, there is not any real Difference at all, but the Reason of Mankind will laugh at it. * * * Pray let us so resolve Cases here, that they may stand with the Reason of Mankind when they are debated abroad."

### *Lives in Being, Plus 21 Years*

The Duke of Norfolk's case actually held only that "where it is within the Compass of one Life, that the Contingency is to happen, there is no Danger of a Perpetuity." The details of the modern Rule were worked out during the succeeding century and a half. The "one Life" was expanded to many lives, on the ground that this did not greatly expand the restraint: "let the lives be never so many, there must be a survivor, and so it is but the length of that life for Twisden [J.] used to say, the candles were all lighted at once."[20] The persons used as measuring lives did not have to be beneficiaries of the interest, because the Rule was designed to avoid keeping "property for too great a length of time out of commerce. The length of time will not be greater or less, whether the lives taken have any interest, vested or contingent, or have not." Children in gestation when a testator died could be used as measuring lives because "the space of time between the death of the father and the birth of the posthumous son was so short that no inconvenience could ensue."[21] A period of gestation might be used "at both ends," *i.e.,* not only could posthumous children be used as measuring lives, but also a descendant who had been conceived but not born when the trust terminated could take.

Twenty one years was added to the period of the Rule in a case involving a devise to the "eldest son of my daughter Mary who attains the age of twenty

**18.** 2 W. Blackstone, *Commentaries* *173–74 (1765).

**19.** 22 Eng.Rep. 931, 940 (1685). For a fuller discussion of this case see Haskins, *Extending the Grip of the Dead Hand,* 126 U.Pa. L.Rev. 19, 35 (1977).

**20.** Scatterwood v. Edge, 91 Eng.Rep. 203 (1699).

**21.** Thellusson v. Woodford, 32 Eng.Rep. 1030, 1040–41 (H.L. 1805).

one years." The son's interest was not certain to vest during any life in being at the testator's death since he might be under 21 when Mary died. Nevertheless this did not restrain "the power of alienation * * * longer than the law would restrain it viz. during the infancy of" Mary's son, who could not make a conveyance so long as he was a minor.[22] This reasoning suggests that a postponement of vesting beyond lives in being must be connected with the minority of a beneficiary, but the law soon came to permit an absolute term of 21 years.[23] The period of gestation, on the other hand, is limited to actual children in gestation; a limitation which postpones vesting for 21 years and nine months without reference to any actual child is invalid.[24]

The modern Rule against Perpetuities has thus moved from Nottingham's general idea of "stopping when any visible inconvenience doth appear" to a more precise rule:

> No interest in property shall be valid unless it must vest, if at all, not later than twenty-one years after one or more lives in being at the creation of the estate and any period of gestation involved.[25]

The Rule against Perpetuities is more comprehensive than its predecessor, the destructibility of contingent remainders. It applies to trusts and legal interests, to real and personal property, and to executory interests as well as remainders. However, it has the same unfortunate quality of being a trap for unskilled drafters, though recent reforms make it much less so than it once was.[26]

### *Policy Behind the Rule: Alienability*

Early cases attributed the Rule to the public interest in keeping property alienable, or "in commerce." Perpetuities were defined as limitations which make "an estate unalienable, though all mankind join in the conveyance."[27] More recently a court said that the "purpose of the Rule Against Perpetuities [is] to facilitate the free alienation of property which in turn helps assure its proper maintenance and changing use as dictated by the changing circumstances of its various owners and of society as a whole."[28] Even persons who refuse to equate the operations of a free market with society's best interests should support the Rule, because it favors "free marketability versus restrictions imposed by an erratic testator; not free enterprise versus governmental regulation."[29]

Consider a farm which the present occupants wish to sell to a buyer who wants to use the land for a shopping center. The land could be sold for a high price, thus indicating that society's "best use" for it is as a shopping center. If

22. Stephens v. Stephens, 25 Eng.Rep. 751, 752 (1736).

23. *Restatement, Second, of Property (Donative Transfers)* § 1.1, comm. a (1981).

24. Cadell v. Palmer, 6 Eng.Rep. 956 (1833); *Restatement of Property* § 374 comm. o (1944); 6 *Amer.Law of Prop.* § 24.15.

25. N.Y. EPTL § 9–1.1(b).

26. These reforms are discussed in Section 11.4.

27. Scatterwood v. Edge, 91 Eng.Rep. 203 (1699).

28. Klugh v. United States, 588 F.2d 45, 53 (4th Cir.1978). *See also* Norton v. Georgia R.R. Bank & Trust Co., 322 S.E.2d 870, 873 (Ga. 1984) ("to prevent property from being tied up for an unreasonable length of time and to prohibit unreasonable restraints on alienation"). However, there is a separate rule dealing with unreasonable restraints on alienation. Section 11.8.

29. L. Simes, *Public Policy and the Dead Hand* 38 (1955).

a will gave an interest in the farm to the occupant's great-grandchildren, it could not be sold "though all mankind join in the conveyance"; *i.e.*, a deed signed by everyone alive could be upset by a later-born great-grandchild.

A New York statute invalidates any suspension of the power of alienation which lasts longer than lives in being plus 21 years. The power of alienation is "suspended" within the meaning of this statute "when there are no persons in being by whom an absolute fee * * * can be conveyed."[30] Similar statutes in some other states replace the Rule against Perpetuities,[31] but in New York interests may be invalid under the Rule against Perpetuities even though they do not suspend the power of alienation. For example, a perpetual option was held invalid under the Rule even though it did not suspend the power of alienation, because the optionor and optionee could join to convey the land.[32] Even though sale is theoretically possible when all interests in property are held by living, identifiable persons, the owners are not likely to join in a sale if their individual interests are contingent because they will not be able to agree on how to allocate the sales proceeds.[33]

### *Trusts*

Concerns about alienability are reduced when property is held in trust where the trustee normally has a power of sale. Some states do not apply the Rule to trusts if the trustee can sell the trust assets.[34] In most states, however, a trustee's power to sell property does not take the case out of the Rule against Perpetuities.[35] Professor Simes suggests the reason is that trustees "cannot invest the funds as freely as a person who owns it beneficially." Trustees are not supposed to speculate with trust assets, but society needs "risk investments to further social and economic advancement."[36] However, as Professor Haskell as observed

> Family trusts constitute a very small portion of available investment capital. Pension trusts * * * constitute a much larger portion * * * and are exempted from the Rule Against Perpetuities by statute as they must be if they are to function. * * * There is no shortage of risk capital. If a shortage of risk capital should develop, family trusts would be a very small part of the problem.[37]

Even if getting property out of trust is a goal worth pursuing, the Rule against Perpetuities does not accomplish it. The Rule allows trusts to last forever if all the beneficial interests are vested.[38] For example, a trust that

**30.** N.Y. EPTL § 9–1.1(a).

**31.** Idaho Code § 55–111; Wis. Stat.§ 700.16.

**32.** Buffalo Seminary v. McCarthy, 451 N.Y.S.2d 457 (A.D.1982).

**33.** Simes, *supra* note 29, at 37–38. *See also* J. Morris & W. Leach, *The Rule Against Perpetuities* 14 (1962); *Restatement of Property* § 370, comm. i (1944).

**34.** Wis.Stat. § 700.16(3); In re Walker's Will, 45 N.W.2d 94 (Wis.1950); S.D.Code § 43–5–1; *cf.* Del.Stat.tit. 25, § 503 (Rule not applicable to trusts but they must terminate after 110 years).

**35.** *Restatement of Property* § 370, comm. p (1944); Simes, *supra* note 29, at 55.

**36.** *Id.* at 60. (Simes, writing in 1955, used nuclear energy as an example.) *See also* In re Chun Quan Yee Hop's Estate, 469 P.2d 183, 186 (Haw.1970) (Rule channels wealth "into open commerce without subjecting it to the limited discretion of a trustee"). As to investments by trustees see Section 12.7.

**37.** Haskell, *A Proposal for a Simple and Socially Effective Rule against Perpetuities*, 66 N.C.L.Rev. 545, 558–59 (1988).

**38.** However, after the period of the Rule, the beneficiaries can compel termination of the trust. *Restatement (Second) of Property (Donative Transfers)* § 2.1 (1983); *Restatement (Second) of Trusts*, § 62, comm. o (1959). Thus the

allowed the trustee to retain shares of the testator's great-grandchildren until they reached age 25 was upheld. The challenge to the trust was based on

> an apparent misunderstanding as to when an interest vests. In general, the word "vest" is used to mean either a vesting in possession or a vesting in interest. * * * Vesting in possession connotes an immediate right of present enjoyment, while vesting in interest implies a presently fixed right to future enjoyment. * * * For an interest to vest within the meaning of the rule the interest [need only] be vested in interest.

Thus the "possibility that the great grandchildren will not obtain actual possession of the trust principal" within the period allowed by the Rule did not matter, since they would have "an absolute right to ultimately receive a share."[39]

### *Wealth Concentration*

Morris and Leach assert that the Rule against Perpetuities prevented "enormous concentrations of land in the hands of a very few and thereby brought it about that England never suffered unbearably from those conditions which elsewhere have produced violent social revolution."[40] Allowing wealthy parents to tie up property may prevent their children from dissipating it. The Rule, by freeing up property, may allow the rich to lose their wealth. A similar argument praises the Rule for assuring "the normal operation of the competitive struggle," preventing "persons less fit" from retaining property disproportionate to their skills.[41] But the role of the Rule in promoting social Darwinism or in preventing undue concentration of wealth is small. Morris and Leach themselves concede that the existence of progressive taxation today would "render the Rule (if this is its sole object) quite unnecessary."[42]

The estate tax depends to some extent on the Rule. If persons had unlimited freedom to do so they might create successive life estates in their children, grand-children, great-grandchildren, etc., and so avoid the estate tax for centuries to come. The Rule against Perpetuities prevents this. However, tax law does really not need the Rule. Today the generation-skipping tax reaches successive interests even before the period allowed by the Rule runs out.[43]

Perhaps the Rule no longer serves a useful function, but even Professor Leach, an effective advocate of reforming the Rule, did not propose its abolition. He concluded that "on the whole the Rule does more good than

*Claflin* rule, see Section 9.6, note 51, no longer applies as of that point.

**39.** Brown v. American Fletcher Nat. Bank, 519 N.E.2d 166, 168 (Ind.App.1988). *See also* May v. Hunt, 404 So.2d 1373 (Miss.1981) (trust created in 1973 to last until 2022 was valid because remainder was vested in settlor's children). *See also* Schuyler, *The Statute Concerning Perpetuities,* 65 Nw.U.L.Rev. 3, 6–7 (1970); *Restatement of Property* § 378 (1944); *Restatement (Second) of Trusts* § 62, comm. n (1959).

**40.** Morris & Leach, *supra* note 33, at 11–12.

**41.** *Restatement of Property,* Int. Note p. 1440 (1944). This "exaltation of self-reliance * * * is today an axiom that most thinkers reject." Hirsch & Wang, *A Qualitative Theory of the Dead Hand*, 68 Ind.L.J. 1, 44 (1992).

**42.** Morris & Leach, *supra* note 33, at 15.

**43.** For the generation-skipping tax see Section 15.4. As to the uneasy relationship between the GST and the Rule see Bloom & Dukeminier, *Perpetuities Reformers Beware: the USRAP Tax Trap,* 25 Real Prop. Trust J. 203 (1990).

harm, though the policy considerations undergoing it are much weaker than they were 300 or 100 years ago."[44]

### *Fair Balance Between Generations*

The most persuasive argument for the Rule today is that it "strikes a fair balance between the desires of members of the present generation, and similar desires of succeeding generations to control the property."[45] If parents could tie up their property in perpetuity, their descendants would have no power over it, and their claim to control property is as strong as that of their forbears. Furthermore, long-term arrangements for controlling property often become inappropriate as conditions change. Benjamin Franklin's 200-year charitable trust[46] turned out to be unsuited to the 20th-century. If noncharitable trusts were allowed to go on so long a period, they would present similar problems. As Chancellor Nottingham said, perpetuities "pretend to such a Stability in human Affairs as the Nature of them admits not of."

Arguably the Rule is too lax. Is it really a "fair balance" between generations when parents can tie up property so that their descendants who are lives in being have no power over it?[47] The Rule's limits have been explained on the ground that a "father could realistically and perhaps wisely, assess the capabilities of *living* members of his family" but "could know nothing of unborn persons. Hence, the father was permitted control only so long as his judgment was informed with an understanding of the capabilities and needs of persons alive when the judgment was made."[48] However, increasing life spans have stretched lives-in-being-plus 21 years to about a century. Can testators really be familiar with the capacities of even descendants in being at their death for such a long time? Professor Waggoner thinks that the Rule is "overpermissive" in allowing "donors in some cases to extend control through or into generations completely unknown and unseen by them," but he adds that there is almost "no enthusiasm" among knowledgeable persons "for tightening up" the Rule to make it coincide more precisely with its rationale.[49] This would be a difficult task, and not worth the effort, since few testators seek to exert dead hand control to the extent allowed by the Rule. Most testators use the permissiveness of the Rule simply as a "safety valve" to secure quite reasonable estate plans.

John Chapman Grey, who wrote an often-cited treatise on the Rule at the end of the nineteenth century, delighted in the Rule's precision. On most legal issues "there is no exact standard to which appeal can be made," but the Rule was different.

> If a decision agrees with [the Rule] it is right; if it does not agree with it, it is wrong. * * * If the answer to a problem does not square with the multiplication table one may call it wrong, although it be the work of

44. Morris & Leach, *supra* note 33, at 18. *See also* 5A R. Powell, *Real Property* ¶ 762.

45. Simes, *supra* note 29, at 58. *See also* *Restatement (Second) of Property (Donative Transfers)* Part I, Int. Note p. 8 (1983); Matter of Estate of Anderson, 541 So.2d 423, 428 (Miss.1989).

46. See Section 9.7, note 107.

47. Wiedenbeck, *Missouri's Repeal of the Claflin Doctrine—New View of the Policy Against Perpetuities* 50 Mo.L.Rev. 805, 828 (1985).

48. Dukeminier, *A Modern Guide to Perpetuities,* 74 Cal.L.Rev. 1867, 1870 (1986). *See also* Wiedenbeck, *supra* note 47, at 832–33.

49. Waggoner, *The Uniform Statutory Rule Against Perpetuities,* 21 Real Prop.Prob. and Trust L.J. 569, 586–89 (1987).

Sir Isaac Newton; and so if a decision conflicts with the Rule Against Perpetuities, one may call it wrong, however learned and able the court that has pronounced it.[50]

This characteristic of the Rule has delighted or baffled generations of law students, depending on their affinity for such reasoning. It has also had an unfortunate effect on the Rule as an instrument of policy, causing many trusts to fail, even though they did not violate the policy behind the Rule. On the other hand, those who know the Rule well can violate its spirit while complying with the letter.[51]

## § 11.2 Operation of the Rule

### *Starting Point*

The Rule is easy to memorize, but difficult to apply in practice. In testing an instrument for a Rule violation one should first determine when the period begins to run. For wills this is the time of the testator's death, regardless of when the will was executed. For irrevocable trusts or deeds, one starts counting at the time of execution of the instrument (or delivery if required).[1] Some perpetuities violations occur because the drafter overlooked this difference between wills and inter-vivos transfers. An irrevocable trust which was by its terms to last "until the death of the last surviving grandchild of the Grantor who shall be living *at the time of his death*." This would have been all right had this been a will or a revocable trust, but since the trust in this case was irrevocable, a grandchild born after its execution could not be used as a measuring life, and so the Rule was violated.[2]

After determining the starting date, one applies a two-step analysis. First, determine whether there is any possibility that the trust in question[3] will continue beyond lives in being at the starting date plus 21 years. If not, there is no problem.[4]

### *Is It Possible for the Trust to Continue Beyond Lives in Being Plus 21 Years?*

Any possibility, however remote, that the trust will continue beyond lives in being plus 21 years raises the specter of an infraction of the Rule in its traditional form.[5] Five types of cases occur with some frequency.

*(1) Period in Gross*

A testamentary trust was to continue for twenty-five years after the testator's death, following which the assets were to be distributed to the then living descendants of her husband's brothers and sisters. This violated the

50. J. Gray, *The Rule Against Perpetuities* xi (4th ed. 1942).

51. Morris & Leach, *supra* note 33, at 13.

§ 11.2

1. *See Restatement, Second, of Property (Donative Transfers)* § 1.2 (1983).

2. Ryan v. Ward, 64 A.2d 258 (Md.1949).

3. The Rule applies also to legal interests, but most modern cases involve trusts so it is convenient to use them as examples.

4. Even if the trust may last beyond lives in being plus 21 years, there is still no violation if the beneficiaries' interests will vest within the permitted period, even though they will not get possession until the trust terminates. See note 26 *infra*.

5. *Restatement of Property* § 370, comm. k (1944). This has been changed today in many states by the adoption of "wait and see." *See* Section 11.4, note 2 et seq.

Rule because there was the possibility of vesting after a life in being plus twenty-one years.[6] This case shows how the letter and the spirit of the Rule often diverge. A valid trust can be drafted in which the drafter designates a group of lives in being and provides that 21 years after the death of the survivor of them the trust will terminate. Such a trust will probably endure for about a century, and will not violate the Rule, but one which is certain to last for 25 years does.

*(2) Age Contingencies*

A testamentary trust provided that "when the youngest living child of my son has reached age of twenty-five years," the assets should be distributed to the son's then living descendants. Since it was possible that the son's youngest child would not reach 25 until more than 21 years after everyone alive at the testator's death had died, the Rule was violated.[9] Infractions like this are not unusual, since many testators do not want their grandchildren to receive property as soon as they reach 21, believing that they will not be ready to handle property at that age. Some have suggested that the 21–year–period allowed by the Rule should be increased so as not to "prematurely force capital into the hands of persons not mature enough to handle it."[10]

A trust to last until all the testator's grandchildren (or other class which includes potential after-born persons) complete their education seems like a sensible arrangement, but may create a Rule violation.[11]

Even an interest which vests when the youngest *child of the testator* reaches 25 may violate the Rule a) in an irrevocable trust[12], or b) in a will if the child in question is under 4 when the testator dies and the language is construed to postpone vesting until the child would have reached 25; this is equivalent to a period in gross of more than 21 years.[13] An interest which vests at age 21 may also violate the Rule if it involves grandchildren of a living person.[14] On the other hand, age designations in excess of 21 years are permissible when they relate to a class which contains only living persons. A testamentary trust which was to terminate when "the youngest of my grandnephews and grandnieces is fifty years old" did not violate the Rule because it was construed to mean only those grandnieces and grandnephews who were alive when the testator died.[15]

*(3) Two-generation Trust*

**6.** However, the court saved the trust by reducing the term to 21 years. Berry v. Union Nat. Bank, 262 S.E.2d 766 (W.Va.1980). See Section 11.3, note 21 et seq.

**9.** Hagemann v. National Bank and Trust Co., 237 S.E.2d 388 (Va.1977). *See also* Merrill v. Wimmer, 481 N.E.2d 1294 (Ind.1985).

**10.** Schuyler, *The Statute Concerning Perpetuities,* 65 Nw.U.L.Rev. 3, 19 (1970). *See also* J. Morris & W. Leach, *The Rule Against Perpetuities* 69 (1962); 6 *Amer.Law of Prop.* § 24.16.

**11.** Sheats v. Johnson, 189 S.E.2d 856 (Ga. 1972) (trust terminates when youngest grandchild completes education).

**12.** *Cf.* Second Bank–State Street Trust Co. v. Second Bank–State Street Trust Co., 140 N.E.2d 201 (Mass.1957) (trust to terminate when settlor's youngest child reached 21).

**13.** In re Lattouf's Will, 208 A.2d 411, 415 (N.J.Super.App.Div.1965). As to the various possible meanings of "when the youngest reaches ... years" see Section 10.3, note 6 et seq.

**14.** Ward v. Van der Loeff, [1924] A.C. 653 (remainder to nieces and nephews of testator who reached 21 invalid when testator's parents were living when he died).

**15.** Estate of Grove, 138 Cal.Rptr. 684 (App.1977). *See also* Underwood v. MacKendree, 251 S.E.2d 264 (Ga.1978).

Many Rule violations arise from trusts which are designed to last for two generations, *e.g.*, the lives of the testator's children and grandchildren. Such trusts may infringe the Rule even if the testator has no after-born grandchildren because some might have been born.

> At the time of his death the testator was survived by three children and five grandchildren. * * * There remained the possibility that another grandchild would be born. * * * The law looks forward from the time the limitation is made to see what may be, not backward to see what has been. It regards the possible, not the actual.[16]

However, if the testator's children all predecease him, such a trust does not violate the Rule since the possibility of an after born grandchild is eliminated even when one "looks forward from the time the limitation is made."[17]

Sometimes a trust is saved by construing it to exclude after-born class members. When a testator created a trust to terminate "upon the death of my last surviving grandchild," the court held that he meant only those grandchildren whom he had named previously in the will. Since they were lives in being the Rule was not violated.[18]

Sometimes courts rely on the circumstances to reach this result, *e.g.* the testator's children were so old when the will was drafted that they were unlikely to have further children.[19] This construction is questionable, however, because of the class gift language; if the testator had meant only grandchildren then living wouldn't the will have named them instead of referring generally to grandchildren?[20] Thus most courts construe such trusts to include any grandchildren born after the testator's death, even when this creates a perpetuities violation.[21]

*(4) Unborn Widow*

A will provided an income interest "to the wife of my son," followed by a contingent remainder at her death. The court held that since the son might marry a woman who was unborn when the testator died, it violated the Rule.[22]

Some courts avoid the Rule by construing the will to refer only to the spouse at the time the will was executed or took effect,[23] but this construction is subject to the objection that if the testator meant that, the will would have said so or named the wife instead of using the general term "widow."

**16.** Connecticut Bank & Trust Co. v. Brody, 392 A.2d 445, 450 (Conn.1978).

**17.** *Restatement of Property* § 374, comm. j, § 384, illus. 3 (1944); 6 *Amer.Law of Prop.* § 24.24.

**18.** Southern Bank & Trust Co. v. Brown, 246 S.E.2d 598 (S.C.1978). *See also* Cotham v. First Nat. Bank, 697 S.W.2d 101 (Ark.1985); Newick v. Mason, 581 A.2d 1269 (Me.1990); Abrams v. Templeton, 465 S.E.2d 117 (S.C.App.1995).

**19.** *Restatement of Property* § 377, illus. 3, 4 (1944); Morris & Leach, *The Rule Against Perpetuities* 79 (1962); 6 *Amer.Law of Prop.* § 24.22.

**20.** *Cf.* Sheats v. Johnson, 189 S.E.2d 856, 859 (Ga.1972); In re Ghiglia's Estate, 116 Cal. Rptr. 827, 831 (App.1974).

**21.** *E.g.*, Fleet National Bank v. Colt, 529 A.2d 122, 126 (R.I.1987).

**22.** Pound v. Shorter, 377 S.E.2d 854, 856 (Ga.1989). *See also* Dickerson v. Union Nat. Bank, 595 S.W.2d 677 (Ark.1980).

**23.** Matter of Chemical Bank, 395 N.Y.S.2d 917 (Surr.1977) (irrevocable trust for settlor's "widow" meant his present wife so Rule not violated).

*(5) Administrative Contingencies*

When a will created a trust which was to terminate five years after the distribution of the testator's estate, the heirs claimed that the Rule was violated because the distribution might be delayed beyond the allowed period.[24] Some courts find that the Rule is not violated by such a provision because the law requires administration to proceed expeditiously, so it cannot possibly last for more than 21 years after the testator dies. Others reject this reasoning on the ground that the Rule requires "absolute certainty," and distribution of a decedent's estate is subject to many possible delays.[25]

### *Are the Interests Vested?*

Even if a trust might continue beyond lives in being, the Rule is not violated if the interests vest in time. For example, a trust for the testator's daughters and their children was to last "until each of said grandchildren shall reach the age of 25 years, when [such] grandchild shall receive his or her share of the principal." This did not violate the Rule.

> Another grandchild could conceivably been born and been less than four years old at [the death of the lives in being. However] the testator's will can be construed to intend vesting in each grandchild immediately at birth, with only distribution delayed until age 25.[26]

In a similar trust there was a further provision that if any grandchild died before reaching 25, the share should be distributed to the grandchild's descendants. This gift over was held to violate the Rule, but the preceding clause which provided for distribution to the grandchildren at age 25 was upheld. In other words, the invalidity of the divestiture clause left the grandchildren with an indefeasibly vested remainder.[27]

### *Class Closing*

A class gift is not "vested" for purposes of the Rule so long as more persons can become members of the class.[28] For example, a testamentary trust was to last until all the testator's grandnieces and grandnephews reached 35, whereupon the assets would be distributed to them. Their interest was not conditioned on survival, but it violated the Rule, since it was not certain to vest within lives in being; the testator's brother survived him, and he could have had after-born children who produced more grandnieces and grandnephews. The class would not close until distribution was made, and that was not certain to occur in time.[29]

**24.** The trust beneficiaries made a substantial payment to the heirs to settle this claim and sought reimbursement from the attorney who had drafted the questionable will. Lucas v. Hamm, 364 P.2d 685 (Cal.1961).

**25.** Prime v. Hyne, 67 Cal.Rptr. 170, 173 (App.1968); Waggoner, *Perpetuity Reform,* 81 Mich.L.Rev. 1718, 1741 (1983).

**26.** Foley v. Evans, 570 N.E.2d 179, 181 (Mass.App.1991). *See also* White v. National Bank & Trust Co., 186 S.E.2d 21 (Va.1972) (25 year trust valid because remainder to John's "heirs" vested when John died); Deiss v. Deiss, 536 N.E.2d 120, 124 (Ill.App.1989); Brown v. American Fletcher National Bank, 519 N.E.2d 166 (Ind.App.1988).

**27.** Thornhill v. Riegg, 383 S.E.2d 447, 452 (N.C.App.1989). *See also* Lanier v. Lanier, 126 S.E.2d 776 (Ga.1962). This result turns on the way the will is worded. As to the distinction between contingent remainders and vested subject to divestment, see Section 10.1, note 7 et seq.

**28.** Morris & Leach, *supra* note 10, at 1; *Restatement of Property* § 371(1)(b), § 383 (1944).

**29.** Abram v. Wilson, 220 N.E.2d 739 (Ohio Prob.1966). As to when a class closes, see Section 10.3.

Any gift to the grandchildren (or more remote issue) of living persons poses a risk of violation, but it may be saved by the rule of convenience. For example, a devise to the testator's daughter for life, remainder to his great grandchildren was upheld; even though more great-grandchildren might be born after lives in being, the rule of convenience would close the class when the daughter died.[30] Normally a class remains open until the time for distribution, but courts sometimes construe gifts more narrowly so as to avoid perpetuities violations. They can do this because the rule of convenience is only a presumption of what the testator intended. For example, a devise of an annuity to the "issue of *N*" was construed to mean only *N*'s issue living at testator's death; this validated the devise.[31]

### *Effect of the Rule on Construction*

The mathematical certainty of the Rule against Perpetuities often evaporates when it is applied to actual instruments because the question whether the Rule was violated turns on cloudy constructional questions, such as when "heirs" are determined, or when a class closes, or whether there was a condition of survival. If the Rule is violated under one construction but not under another, should this affect the way a court resolves the construction question? According to John Chipman Grey, "every provision in a will or settlement is to be construed as if the Rule did not exist and then to the provision so construed the Rule is to be remorselessly applied."[32] Many modern courts disagree. For example, a court construed a will to refer only to grandnieces and grandnephews alive when the testator died because "a document should be interpreted if feasible to avoid the conclusion that it violates the rule against perpetuities."[33]

Much depends on how ambiguous the instrument is. No one can claim that "25" is ambiguous and really means "21."[34] (*Reforming* 25 to 21 is another matter which we shall discuss later).[35] But "grandnephews" can mean "grandnephews alive at my death" if other language in the will or the circumstances indicate the testator had this in mind.

### *Effect of Rule Violation*

Infractions of the Rule usually appear in the residuary clause of a will and result in property passing intestate. Therefore claims that the Rule was violated are typically raised by the testator's heirs in the hopes of getting property outright which was left in trust. This effort may fail even if a rule violation is found because normally the violation does not invalidate the income interests of the trust but only remainder interests which were to vest in the distant future.[36]

**30.** In re Greenwood's Will, 268 A.2d 867 (Del.1970). *See also* Austin v. Dobbins, 252 S.E.2d 588, 593 (Va.1979).

**31.** In re Trust of Criss, 329 N.W.2d 842 (Neb.1983). Normally such periodic payments do not close the class under the rule of convenience. Section 10.3, at note 10.

**32.** Quoted in Hagemann v. National Bank and Trust Co., 237 S.E.2d 388, 393 (Va.1977). *See also* First Alabama Bank v. Adams, 382 So.2d 1104, 1107 (Ala.1980).

**33.** Estate of Grove, 138 Cal.Rptr. 684, 688 (1977). *See also* Southern Bank & Trust Co. v. Brown, 246 S.E.2d 598, 601 (S.C.1978); *Restatement of Property* § 375 (1944).

**34.** *Id.* comm. a (will must be "ambiguous" and the construction "possible").

**35.** See Section 11.4, at note 21 et seq.

**36.** "The rule against perpetuities voids only those interests vesting beyond the perpetuities period. The remaining valid interests

If the violation appears in a pre-residuary clause, the property simply falls into the residue.[37] In an inter-vivos trust invalidity of an interest may create a resulting trust for the settlor which means that the property passes under the settlor's will if the settlor had one.[38] A Georgia statute providing that a Rule violation resulted in "vesting the fee in the last taker under the legal limitations" caused a person designated as a life beneficiary to get the remainder as well.[39] This avoids a distribution to the testator's heirs long after the testator's death.[40]

When application of the Rule produces an intestacy, this may not seriously disrupt the testator's estate plan. Many wills create a trust for the testator's heirs, and a successful invocation of the Rule simply gives them their inheritance outright rather than in trust. But sometimes the beneficiaries of the challenged will are not the testator's heirs; in this situation the distortion of the testator's wishes can be extreme.[41]

Courts sometimes use a doctrine called "infectious invalidity" to strike down interests which are valid in order to better effectuate the testator's intent when the Rule is violated. For example, a will created trusts for the testator's three children. The termination provision for two of them violated the Rule; the third child's trust did not but the court struck it down also.

> Even if the provisions for Walter be valid, * * * they cannot be permitted to stand alone, because such would result in significant distortion or defeat of the Testator's underlying objectives. * * * The underlying plan of the Testator was for his three children to have equal shares * * * If the provisions for Walter are permitted to stand, * * * Walter will share equally with Judith and Denis under the laws of intestate succession * * * while also receiving the income for life in the remaining one-third—a grossly distorted result.[42]

When a remainder is held to violate the Rule, preceding income interests may also be stricken as "inextricably intertwined" with them.[43] If the trust was created in order to avoid property being taxed in the estates of the testator's children, and if the Rule violation causes the remainder to pass to the children as intestate property, why should the trusts be established? On the other hand, the testator may have had another purpose for the trust which is inconsistent with early termination. When a remainder after a life estate in the testator's grandson was held invalid under the Rule, the court declined to void the life estate itself. A spendthrift provision in the trust showed that "the testator's obvious purpose was to protect the [grandson] against his own improvidence," and this would be frustrated by an outright distribution to him.[44]

take effect." White v. Fleet Bank of Maine, 739 A.2d 373, 378 (Me.1999).

**37.** Brownell v. Edmunds, 209 F.2d 349 (4th Cir.1953); *Restatement of Property* § 403, comm. c (1944).

**38.** Ryan v. Ward, 64 A.2d 258 (Md.1949).

**39.** Pound v. Shorter, 377 S.E.2d 854 (Ga. 1989). This statute was repealed in 1990, but 20 Pa.Stat. § 6105(c) is similar.

**40.** For the disadvantages of such a distribution see Section 10.1, at note 55.

**41.** Berry v. Union Nat. Bank, 262 S.E.2d 766 (W.Va.1980).

**42.** Merrill v. Wimmer, 481 N.E.2d 1294, 1299–1300 (Ind.1985). *See also Restatement of Property* § 402, illus. 3 (1944).

**43.** Connecticut Bank & Trust Co. v. Brody, 392 A.2d 445, 451 (Conn.1978).

**44.** In re Estate of Davis, 297 A.2d 451, 455 (Pa.1972). *See also Restatement of Property* § 386, illus. 5 (1944). *Compare* Section 9.6, at note 61.

### *Separability of Class Gifts*

Most infractions of the Rule involve class gifts. Courts generally refuse to sever them to hold the interests of some members valid. For example, a will left property to the testator's grandchildren who attained the age of 25. He had five grandchildren when he died and three more were born thereafter. The interest of the grandchildren who were alive when the testator died was certain to vest, if at all, in time because they were lives in being. The interest of the after-born grandchildren might vest too late. The court refused to distinguish between the two groups. The testator thought that he could "include after-born grandchildren and also postpone the vesting till twenty-five. But if he had been informed that he could not do both, can I say that the alteration he would have made would have been to leave out the after-born grandchildren * * * I should think quite the contrary."[45] This decision established the "all-or-nothing" rule under which if a gift is bad as to one class member it is bad as to all.[46]

Gifts to "sub-classes" are treated differently. For example, a trust provided for the testator's daughter and grandchildren, with a remainder to remoter issue upon the death of each grandchild. When one grandchild died, the remainder was challenged under the Rule.[47] The court invoked "the doctrine of vertical separability" under which the remainder to the issue of any grandchild who was alive at the testator's death was separable from the remainder to the issue of an after-born grandchild. "Because Heil Macklin was a life in being at the time of the will's [taking effect], the remainder to his issue was valid and any possible void remainder interest to [issue of] after-born children of his mother * * * was separable."[48] But in another case in which life estates in the testator's grandchildren were followed by a remainder to their descendants, the court refused to separate the remainders because the will did

> not indicate any intention that each of his grandchildren should have a separate life estate in a separate share and that each such separate share should vest separately at the death of such grandchild in the issue of that grandchild. Rather the entire corpus of the trust * * * was to be held for the benefit of his grandchildren as a class until the last of them should die at which time the same undivided corpus should, as a remainder, vest in his great-grandchildren per capita.[49]

**45.** Leake v. Robinson, 35 Eng.Rep. 979, 989 (1817).

**46.** *Restatement of Property* § 371, comm. a (1944); In re Ghiglia's Estate, 116 Cal.Rptr. 827 (App.1974); Abram v. Wilson, 220 N.E.2d 739 (Ohio Prob.1966); *cf.* Carter v. Berry, 140 So.2d 843 (Miss.1962).

**47.** The challenge was made by the widow of the deceased grandchild. She was not included in the remainder, but as the grandchild's devisee she would take under the Pennsylvania statute cited at note 39 *supra* if the remainder was invalid.

**48.** In re Estate of Weaver, 572 A.2d 1249, 1256 (Pa.Super.1990). *See also* First Alabama Bank v. Adams, 382 So.2d 1104 (Ala.1980).

**49.** Connecticut Bank and Trust Co. v. Brody, 392 A.2d 445, 452 (Conn.1978). *See also* North Carolina Nat. Bank v. Norris, 203 S.E.2d 657, 659 (N.C.App.1974); *Restatement of Property* § 376, illus. 2 (1944). Even if distribution is postponed until the last grandchild died if a per stirpes rather than per capita distribution is called for, the gift may be considered separable. *Id.* § 389, comm. g; Second Bank–State Street Trust Co. v. Second Bank–State Street Trust Co., 140 N.E.2d 201, 206 (Mass. 1957).

Separability is an appealing way to avoid the Rule if no after born beneficiaries have actually materialized.[50] But when after-born grandchildren actually appear, courts are reluctant to treat subclasses differently. For example, a trust for the children of testator's daughter provided that at the death of each child, the principal from which the child had been receiving income should go to his or her issue. The daughter had five children, one of whom was born after the testator died. The remainder to his issue was held invalid. When two of his elder brothers later died, even though they were lives in being when the testator died, the remainders to their issue were also stricken, because to separate these remainders from the one which had previously been held invalid would distort the testator's plan for "absolute equality on a stirpital basis" among his descendants. This differed from cases in which separability led to a "perfect result * * * because all grandchildren were born in testator's lifetime and [so] the whole of testator's disposition could be sustained."[51]

### *Alternative Contingencies*

A Rule violation is sometimes avoided if the instrument expresses alternate contingencies. For example, a trust was to last until the death of the settlor's two sons, or until their youngest child reached 25, "whichever event shall occur last." The youngest grandchild might not reach 25 until after lives in being plus 21 years, but the court refused to hold the trust invalid. "Where a limitation is made to take effect on two alternative events, one of which is too remote and the other valid, * * * the gift * * * will be allowed to take effect on the happening of the [valid] one."[52] If the youngest grandchild was 25 when the sons died the trust would terminate under the first alternative which was valid, the sons being lives in being. If the youngest grandchild was not then 25, the second alternative would apply and the remainder would be invalid.

This avenue of escape from the Rule is available only if the instrument expresses alternative contingencies. A trust which was to end upon the death of the beneficiaries, including the "widow" of the testator's son, was held invalid because the will did not *say* that the trust was to terminate "upon the death of my son, *or* upon the death of his widow," even though what the will said was equivalent to this.[53] Thus Chancellor Nottingham's dictum that "real Differences" rather than "Words" should be determinative does not always characterize the modern Rule.[54]

## § 11.3 Planning to Avoid the Rule

### *Bad Ways to Avoid the Rule*

Some lawyers distort sensible estate plans in order to avoid Rule violations, so the Rule has an impact on drafting even though it produces relatively

**50.** *Cf. Restatement of Property* § 389, comm. a (1944).

**51.** In re Morton's Estate, 312 A.2d 26, 27 (Pa.1973). *See also Restatement (Second) of Property (Donative Transfers)* § 1.5, comm. g (1983).

**52.** Application of Wolfsohn, 339 N.Y.S.2d 755, 759 (A.D.1973). *See also* Earle v. International Paper Co., 429 So.2d 989, 997 (Ala.1983) (concurring opinion); *Restatement (Second) of Property (Donative Transfers)* § 1.4, comm. *o* (1983).

**53.** Easton v. Hall, 154 N.E. 216, 220 (Ill. 1926). *See also Restatement of Property* § 377, illus. 3 (1944).

**54.** Section 11.1, after note 19.

few reported cases. Some suggested "prescriptions for avoiding violation of the Rule"[1] are questionable. For example:

"Beware of gifts to grandchildren," especially in irrevocable trusts or devises to grandchildren of a person who survives the testator. Such gifts may be desirable if settlors do not want property to pass outright to their children, for tax or other reasons.

"Describe beneficiaries by name rather than by class designation." This may exclude after-born grandchildren, a result most testators would want to avoid.

"Beware of gifts contingent upon the taker attaining an age over twenty-one." A distribution at age 21 may be premature. How many fortunes have been dissipated after they were distributed to beneficiaries at age 21 in order to avoid the Rule?

"Avoid gifts conditioned on the survival of the 'widow' of a named person." Surely it would be unfortunate if all widows (and widowers) were excluded from wills because of the Rule. Naming a relative's current spouse avoids the Rule, but excluding a later spouse may produce a questionable result.

### *Savings Clauses*

A savings clause avoids Rule violations without producing undesirable side effects, such as exclusion of after-born children or premature distribution.[2] For example, it saved a trust for the testator's daughter and her children which provided that each child's share vested at age 30. The trial court reduced the age to 21 in order to avoid violating the Rule, but the appellate court reversed, because this change

> creates possibilities that the trust property could pass out of the decedent's family or that a beneficiary could gain either absolute ownership or control over the disposition of the property earlier than was intended by the decedent. * * [A savings clause made this unnecessary. It] provides that all trusts created by the will are to terminate on the date limited by the applicable Rule against Perpetuities * * * and any remaining corpus is to be distributed to those persons then entitled to receive income from the trust.[3]

Savings clauses have two parts: a termination provision, and a direction for distribution. The termination clause in the foregoing case was imperfect since it failed to make clear what "the date limited" by the Rule is. Lives in being plus 21 years, of course, but *what* lives? The court found the relevant measuring life was the testator's daughter, so the trust would have to end no later than 21 years after she died. However, the Rule allows more than one measuring life, and so a well-drafted savings clause should specify a reasonable number of measuring lives. Vesting cannot be postponed "until the death

§ 11.3

1. Link, *The Rule against Perpetuities in North Carolina,* 57 N.C.L.Rev. 727, 817 (1979). *See also* 6 *Amer.Law of Prop.* § 24.7.

2. McGovern, *Perpetuities Pitfalls and How Best to Avoid Them,* 6 Real Prop., Prob. and Trust L.J. 155, 175 (1971).

3. In re Estate of Burrough, 521 F.2d 277, 280 (D.C.Cir.1975). *See also* Norton v. Georgia R.R. Bank & Trust, 322 S.E.2d 870, 875 (Ga. 1984) (trust for testator's children, grandchildren and great grandchildren valid under savings clause).

of the last survivor of all persons who shall be living at my death." The administrative difficulty of determining the date of death of the survivor of very large groups has led courts to hold clauses like this void.[4] An English court allowed a clause which used the "descendants of Queen Victoria alive at my death," even though these numbered 120 when the testator died (in 1926), and they were "scattered over the entire continent of Europe," and some had fallen into "penury and obscurity," which made tracing extremely difficult.[5]

No testator should use such a large group as measuring lives and very few do.[6] A trust which goes on for "as long as the law allows" imposes dead-hand control on an unforeseeable future, although to some extent this objection can be obviated by giving the trustee and/or beneficiaries broad discretionary powers. Savings clauses can usefully prevent frustration of a more limited objective, such as holding property in trust until grandchildren reach age 30. A savings clause makes this valid because if the unlikely event happens (expiration of lives in being plus 21 years before the grandchildren reach 30), the trust terminates. A well-drafted savings clause might say "unless sooner terminated in accordance with its provisions, this trust shall terminate 21 years after the death of the last survivor of my spouse and my issue who are living at the time of my death." A testator with no spouse or issue could designate "the issue of my parents who are living at the time of my death" (or some other comparable group) instead. An irrevocable trust should refer to "issue now living," or name the measuring lives.

If the trust terminates under the savings clause, to whom should distribution be made? If this is not made clear, the clause may be ineffective.[7] Many savings clauses provide that upon termination the assets should be "distributed to the persons then entitled to the income."[8] In most situations this makes sense. For example, a trust for children and grandchildren, with a remainder to their issue might still be operating for an after-born grandchild 21 years after the designated measuring lives expired. Distribution to the after-born grandchild would come close to the testator's plan, since the grandchild who receives the property under the clause would probably leave it to his or her children at death. However, if the income beneficiary at the time of termination under the savings clause is an "unborn widow," giving the trust assets to her outright may frustrate a settlor's wish to keep property in the family.[9]

**4.** In re Moore, [1901] 1 Ch. 936. According to *Restatement (Second) of Property (Donative Transfers)* § 1.3, comm. a (1983), if "the number of lives specified in the savings clause is unreasonable" a court may select "a reasonable number" out of the specified group, rather than avoiding the clause.

**5.** In re Villor, [1929] 1 Ch. 243. One of these descendants was Anastasia, Czar Nicholas' daughter, the date of whose death remains unclear. J. Morris & W. Leach, *The Rule against Perpetuities* 61 (1962).

**6.** Dukeminier, *The Uniform Statutory Rule Against Perpetuities: Ninety Years in Limbo,* 34 UCLA L.Rev. 1023, 1030 (1987). However, some lawyers tout trusts as a "unique opportunity to create a family asset pool which may be enjoyed by the creator's family into perpetuity without shrinkage caused by transfer taxes or loss due to divorce or other creditor claims." Oshins & Blattmachers, *The Megatrust: An Ideal Family Wealth Preservation Tool,* 130 Trusts & Estates (Nov. 1991) 20, 30.

**7.** Hagemann v. National Bank & Trust Co., 237 S.E.2d 388, 392 (Va.1977).

**8.** *E.g.,* In re Burrough's Estate, 521 F.2d 277, 279 (D.C.Cir.1975).

**9.** See McGovern, *supra* note 2, at 159; Farr & J. Wright, *An Estate Planner's Handbook* 400 (4th ed. 1979).

***Duration of Trusts***

Although the Rule allows trusts to continue beyond lives in being plus 21 years, knowledgeable estate planners do not try to keep trusts going beyond the period of the Rule.[10] Courts occasionally misunderstand the Rule and erroneously hold invalid trusts simply because they last too long.[11] Also, most trusts give the trustee discretion to accumulate income, or invade principal, or sprinkle income among a group of beneficiaries. This makes the beneficiaries' interest contingent upon the trustee's discretion. Thus the income interests as well as the remainder are invalid if such a trust continues beyond the period of the Rule.[12]

A savings clause, therefore, ought to terminate any trust which is still operating when the period of the Rule ends. This will be unfortunate if any distributee is then a minor, but in most cases the trust will actually terminate not under the savings clause but at a time when all the distributees are mature.[13]

## § 11.4 Modern Reforms

***Wait and See***

Late in his career, Professor Leach became a zealous crusader for reforming the Rule.[1] He attacked its focus on possibilities rather than the actual facts. "The public interest is not damaged by a tying up of property that *might have* exceeded the period of perpetuities." Therefore, courts should "wait and see" whether the contingency happens within the period of the Rule.[2]

This idea had already been adopted in a Pennsylvania statute which provided that the Rule should be "measured by actual rather than possible events."[3] Since then it has been accepted in some judicial decisions. A court upheld a devise to collateral relatives "if my grandchildren shall" die without issue in a case in which no grandchildren were born after the testator died. The court, citing Leach and the Pennsylvania statute, said "there is no logical justification for deciding the problem * * * on facts that might have happened rather than the facts which actually happened."[4] Another court upheld a 25 year trust because when it decided the case (about 5 years after the testator

**10.** McGovern, *supra* note 2, at 176; Link, *supra* note 1, at 818; Farr & Wright, *supra* note 9, at 401.

**11.** Burton v. Hicks, 136 S.E.2d 759 (Ga. 1964) (25 year trust "void" under Rule even though interests vested).

**12.** Arrowsmith v. Mercantile–Safe Deposit, 545 A.2d 674, 677 (Md.1988); Abram v. Wilson, 220 N.E.2d 739, 742 (Ohio Prob.1966); *Restatement (Second) of Trusts* § 62, comm. q (1959); Bolich, *The Power of Appointment: Tool of Estate Planning and Drafting,* [1964] Duke L.J. 32, 61–62; J. Morris & W. Leach, *The Rule Against Perpetuities* 143–44 (1962). This is ironic, since such flexible trusts are less subject to the objections against dead hand control. Hirsch & Wang, *A Qualitative Theory of the Dead Hand*, 68 Ind.L.J. 1 (1992).

**13.** A clause like Uniform Statutory Will Act § 9 for retaining in trust the share of any distributee under disability may be desirable for this remote possibility, and *ought not* to violate the Rule, since the interest retained in trust is vested.

§ 11.4

**1.** Leach's previous articles about the Rule were principally descriptive. Leach, *Perpetuities in a Nutshell,* 51 Harv.L.Rev. 638 (1938); *cf.* Leach, *The Rule against Perpetuities and Gifts to Classes,* 51 Harv.L.Rev. 1329 (1938) (attacking Leake v. Robinson).

**2.** Leach, *Perpetuities in Perspective: Ending the Rule's Reign of Terror,* 65 Harv.L.Rev. 721, 729–30 (1952) (emphasis added).

**3.** 20 Pa.Stat. § 6104(b).

**4.** Merchants Nat. Bank v. Curtis, 97 A.2d 207, 212 (N.H.1953). The court also relied on the "alternative contingencies" rationale, see Section 11.2, note 52, which can be regarded as a precursor of "wait and see."

died), the trust had less than 20 years to run and there were then "a host of" persons alive who were born before the testator died.[5]

### *Time of Decision*

The court in these cases did not actually *wait* to see what would happen; by the time the litigation arose it had become clear that there were no after-born grandchildren or that the trust would not last beyond twenty one years plus lives in being. Would the court have waited to see what would happen if the will had been challenged just after the testator died? This raises an issue which is related to, but distinct from wait and see: should courts decide whether a remainder is valid before the time comes to distribute it? Leach argued that they should not. Because remainders are usually given to persons who are unborn, under age or unascertained, an early decision requires that these persons be represented by a guardian ad litem, whereas if the court postpones the decision, the remaindermen can choose their own advocate.[6] Other knowledgeable authorities disagreed with Leach.[7] Postponing decision keeps title uncertain, and seems unfair to the challengers to say "the property may belong to you, but we will not decide this until you are dead and *then* you will get your property."

Even if the time of decision is not deliberately postponed, often no one raises the perpetuities question until after the relevant facts have become clear. When a decision as to validity is postponed, distributions may already have taken place. The English Perpetuities Act provides that any ultimate determination of invalidity will not affect previous distributions.[8]

### *Who Are the Measuring Lives?*

Many courts have rejected "wait and see."[9] The great difficulty with the concept is determining the appropriate measuring lives. Professor Simes illustrated the problem by a hypothetical: a devise "to my descendants living 120 years after my death." At the end of 120 years should a court uphold the devise if it discovers some person who was alive at the testator's death who died at age 100?[10] Simes' hypothetical has not appeared in a reported case, but the way in which courts have answered an analogous problem suggest that they would reject the 120 year trust. A testator who died in 1929 created a trust which was to last "for as long a period as is legally possible." The court held that the measuring lives for this trust were the testator's children, not including the testator's grandchildren alive at his death even though they

**5.** Matter of Estate of Anderson, 541 So.2d 423, 433 (Miss.1989). *See also* Hansen v. Stroecker, 699 P.2d 871, 875 (Alaska 1985).

**6.** Leach, *supra* note 2, at 729. *See also* Trust Agreement of Westervelt v. First Interstate Bank, 551 N.E.2d 1180, 1183 (Ind.App. 1990); Dewire v. Haveles, 534 N.E.2d 782, 785 (Mass.1989) (declining to decide possible invalidity of remainder under the Rule).

**7.** Mechem, *Further Thoughts on the Pennsylvania Perpetuities Legislation,* 107 U.Pa. L.Rev. 965, 979–80 (1959); Simes, *Is the Rule against Perpetuities Doomed?,* 52 Mich.L.Rev. 179, 183 (1953).

**8.** English Perpetuities and Accumulations Act, 1964, § 3(1). *See also* Uniform Statutory Rule Against Perpetuities § 1, comment. Perhaps courts would reach this result even without such a statute. Powell, *Florida's Statutory Rule Against Perpetuities,* U.Fla.St.U.L.Rev. 767, 813n (1984). As to the recovery of property erroneously distributed to a beneficiary see Section 12.10, at note 47 et seq.

**9.** Pound v. Shorter, 377 S.E.2d 854, 856 (Ga.1989).

**10.** Simes, *supra* note 7, at 187. *See also* Mechem, *supra* note 7, at 981–82.

were beneficiaries of the trust. As a result the trust would end after 78 years.[11]

The "possibilities" approach of the common-law Rule avoids the dilemma of picking measuring lives. Even a *25-year* postponement of vesting (without a savings clause) violates the common-law Rule because *whoever* is picked as a measuring life in advance *may* die within 4 years. Taking advantage of hindsight under "wait and see" can considerably lengthen the time during which property is tied up even though the period of the Rule remains nominally the same unless the measuring lives are limited in some way.

A Kentucky statute attempts to solve this problem by providing that "the period shall not be measured by any lives whose continuance does not have a causal relationship to the vesting or failure of the interest."[12] Is this clear? Professor Dukeminier believes that it is. He "had no trouble in identifying the causally-related measuring lives" in the standard perpetuities hypotheticals.[13] But Professor Waggoner finds "the simple one-sentence statute that Dukeminier touts as *the* solution to wait-and-see leaves so many questions in doubt" that it will breed much litigation.[14]

A Uniform Statutory Rule Against Perpetuities, promulgated in 1986 and now adopted in about 25 states, accepts wait and see but rejects the use of measuring-lives because of the difficulty of defining and keeping track of them. Instead USRAP validates any interest which "either vests or terminates within 90 years after its creation."[15] The 90-year period was selected as

> a reasonable approximation of * * * the period of time that would on average, be produced through the use of a set of actual measuring lives identified by statute and then adding the 21 year tack-on period after the death of the survivor.[16]

Professor Dukeminier characterizes the statute as

> a quantum leap toward extended dead-hand rule. * * * The statute invites lawyers unconversant with the law of future interests to create long-term ninety-year trusts. These trusts may lack the flexible powers an experienced estate planner gives to the trustee and beneficiaries to deal with changing circumstances over a long period of years.[17]

Professor Fellows, on the other hand, after studying how the USRAP would have affected perpetuities cases decided during the period 1984–89, concluded that the statute

**11.** Matter of Estate of Holt, 857 P.2d 1355 (Hawaii 1993). *See also* In re Burrough's Estate, 521 F.2d 277, 280 (D.C.Cir.1975) (testator's daughter used as measuring life under similar clause); *cf.* White v. Fleet Bank of Maine, 739 A.2d 373, 379 (Me.1999) (grandchildren and great-grandchild living at testator's death used).

**12.** Ky.Rev.Stat. § 381.216. *See also* R.I.Gen.Stat. § 34–11–38.

**13.** Dukeminier, *Perpetuities: The Measuring Lives,* 85 Colum.L.Rev. 1648, 1674 (1985). *See also* Fleet Nat. Bank v. Colt, 529 A.2d 122, 130 (R.I.1987) (2 generation trust sustained because grandchildren alive when testator died were still living when interest vested).

**14.** Waggoner, *Perpetuities: A Perspective on Wait-and-See,* 85 Colum.L.Rev. 1714, 1724 (1985). *See also* Maudsley, *Perpetuities: Reforming the Common–Law Rule–How to Wait and See,* 60 Cornell L.Rev. 355, 375 (1975).

**15.** Uniform Statutory Rule Against Perpetuities § 1(a)(2). Interests which would be valid under the common-law Rule continue to be valid under the statutory rule.

**16.** *Id.* Prefatory Note.

**17.** Dukeminier, *A Modern Guide to Perpetuities*, 74 Cal.L.Rev. 1867, 1886 (1986). *See also* Dukeminier, *The Uniform Statutory Rule Against Perpetuities: Ninety Years in Limbo,* 34 UCLA L.Rev. 1023 (1987).

> avoids unwarranted interference with a transferor's estate plan while guaranteeing that a trust does not last too long. * * * Only in unusual family situations in which adult children [of the testator] had not yet had their own children [when the testator died] did the ninety year rule result in a substantially longer perpetuity period. * * * This is a small cost to pay for the administrative simplicity obtained by the ninety-year rule.[18]

Legislatures should not worry that drafters will use the statute to establish "dynastic trusts." She cites the example of Wisconsin which abolished the rule in 1969, but has not become a "perpetuity haven," having less than the national average of trust assets per capita.[19]

### *Cy Pres*

Leach also espoused a second reform of the Rule, often called cy pres by analogy to the doctrine which allows courts to modify charitable trusts to meet changing circumstances.[20] "If a gift in the will or trust threatens to tie up property for too long a period, why should we invalidate it in toto? Why not cut it down to size?"[21] Cy pres extends the idea that ambiguous instruments should be *construed* so as to avoid violating the Rule, allowing unambiguous terms to be reformed, *e.g.*, changing "age 40" to "age 21." This idea had already been adopted by a court in 1891 which cured a perpetuities violation by reducing the age from 40 to 21 in a trust for the testator's grandchildren.[22]

A New York statute providing for this result[23] saved a trust for the testator's grandchildren by reducing the age of distribution from 35 to 21. The court in this case rejected "wait and see;" while it was possible that the gifts would be distributed within the perpetuities period, "the 'what might have been' doctrine * * * requires us to consider all possibilities as of the testator's death."[24]

Some statutes give courts a more general authorization to reform instruments, not limited to reducing a designated age to 21.[25] Others combine cy pres with wait and see. The Uniform Statutory Rule adopts this approach.[26] Wait and see is applied first. In most cases, this renders alteration in the instrument unnecessary,[27] but not always. A will purported to create a "perpetual" trust for scholarships "to any blood heirs of my husband or myself."[28] The court apparently assumed that "blood heirs" was not limited to descendants living at the testator's death, and held that the "perpetual" limitation barred the trustee from distributing principal from the trust. Thus

**18.** Fellows, *Testing Perpetuity Reforms: A Study of Perpetuity Cases 1984–89*, 25 Real Prop.Prob. and T.J. 597, 598 (1991).

**19.** *Id.*, pp. 602, 653.

**20.** See Section 9.7, at note 88 et seq.

**21.** Leach, *supra* note 2, at 734–35.

**22.** Edgerly v. Barker, 31 A. 900 (N.H. 1891).

**23.** N.Y. EPTL § 9–1.2. *See also* 765 ILCS § 305/4(c)(2). A similar provision appeared in the English Law of Property Act, 1925, § 163.

**24.** Matter of Estate of Kreuzer, 674 N.Y.S.2d 505, 508 (A.D.1998).

**25.** Mo.Stat. § 442.555(2); Tex.Prop.Code art. 5.043.

**26.** Uniform Statutory Rule Against Perpetuities § 3. *See also* Ky.Rev.Stat. § 381.216; Ohio Rev.Stat. § 2131.08(c); Iowa Code § 558.68(3).

**27.** Uniform Statutory Rule Against Perpetuities § 3, comment. *See also* Fellows, *supra* note 18, at 610.

**28.** Matter of Estate of Keenan, 519 N.W.2d 373, 375 (Iowa 1994). Because of the limitation to relatives, the trust could not qualify as charitable. See Section 9.7, note 20.

the trust might go on forever. The court said that although the statutory reformation provisions "are not triggered unless 'wait and see' fails to validate the challenged interest," reformation was necessary here because wait and see could not avoid the perpetuities problem.[29] The reformation consisted in authorizing the trustee to distribute principal, and directing that any remaining principal be distributed "twenty one years after the death of the last heir of the testator or her husband who was living at the time of the testator's death."[30]

Some courts have reformed wills to avoid a Rule violation even without statutory authority,[31] but others have refused to do so.[32] Some criticize the idea as too vague.[33] For instance, in a case involving an age contingency over 21, a court might reduce the specified age to 21, or it might confine the recipient class to persons born before the testator's death,[34] or it might leave the specified distribution date and class intact but make the interests vest prior to the trust termination.[35] Perhaps the testator would have preferred to do *nothing* and let the interests fail rather than modify the will.[36] Professor Waggoner regards cy pres as "an unwarranted distortion of the donor's intention" which can be avoided by wait and see.[37]

Professor Browder suggested that the best way to reform a will was to insert a perpetuities savings clause.[38] This would allow any reasonable estate plan to be carried out unchanged. If cy pres is used to insert a savings clause, it is virtually the same as wait and see.[39]

An Illinois statute has a general saving provision for trusts[40] which violate the Rule. It terminates the trust 21 years after the death of the last to die of all the beneficiaries alive when the trust began. The current income beneficiaries receive the present value of their interest and the heirs of the settlor or

**29.** Query, if none of the heirs living at the testator's death had issue, wouldn't the trust terminate within lives in being?

**30.** Matter of Estate of Keenan, 519 N.W.2d 373, 375 (Iowa 1994). Distribution was to be "to the testator's heirs at law." Presumably this means those who would have been the testator's heirs had she then died. Cf. 10.2, note 8 et seq.

**31.** Berry v. Union Nat. Bank, 262 S.E.2d 766, 771 (W.Va.1980) (25 year trust reduced to 21 years); In re Chun Quan Yee Hop's Estate, 469 P.2d 183 (Haw.1970) (30 years reduced to 21); Carter v. Berry, 140 So.2d 843 (Miss. 1962).

**32.** Hagemann v. National Bank and Trust Co., 237 S.E.2d 388, 392n (Va.1977). Later, however, the Virginia legislature adopted it. Va.Code § 55-13.3(B).

**33.** Schuyler, *The Statute Concerning Perpetuities,* 65 Nw.U.L.Rev. 3, 24 (1970); Powell, *The Rule against Perpetuities and Spendthrift Trust in New York,* 71 Colum.L.Rev. 688, 694 (1971); Simes, *Public Policy and the Dead Hand* 78 (1955).

**34.** Estate of Grove, 138 Cal.Rptr. 684, 689 (App.1977).

**35.** Foley v. Evans, 570 N.E.2d 179, 181 (Mass.App.1991).

**36.** McGovern, *Facts and Rules in the Construction of Wills,* 26 UCLA L.Rev. 285, 312–14 (1978); University of Louisville v. Isert, 742 S.W.2d 571 (Ky.App.1987) (refusing to apply reformation statute).

**37.** Waggoner, *The Uniform Statutory Rule Against Perpetuities: The Rationale of the 90–Year Waiting Period*, 73 Cornell L.Rev, 157, 158n (1988).

**38.** Browder, *Construction, Reformation, and the Rule Against Perpetuities*, 62 Mich. L.Rev. 1, 6 (1962). *See also* Uniform Statutory Rule Against Perpetuities § 5, comment.

**39.** Waggoner, *Perpetuity Reform,* 81 Mich. L.Rev. 1718, 1781 (1983) (the Restatement version of wait and see "automatically interjects a well-conceived saving clause into every instrument").

**40.** The drafters believed that wait and see would make property inalienable for too long unless a trustee had power to sell during the waiting period. Schuyler, *supra* note 33, at 22.

testator get the balance.[41] In most situations this will produce a desirable result, but not if the trust beneficiaries were not heirs of the testator.[42]

The Uniform Statutory Rule is only prospective with respect to wait and see, whereas it provides for reformation even of existing instruments.[43] A case arose under the statute involving a 1915 will which devised land to the testator's son and his children for their lives with a remainder to the testator's great grandchildren. The son had no further children after the testator died. The court could not take note of this fact directly, since the wait and see provisions of USRAP did not apply to this 1915 will, but the court did what amounted to the same thing: reformed the will to restrict the grandchildren to those "who are alive at the time of my death."[44]

## § 11.5 Powers and the Rule

### *Exercise of Power–Starting Point*

The starting point for determining the validity under the Rule of interests created by the exercise of a power of appointment depends on the type of power; general powers which are presently exercisable are differentiated from other types. For example, a trust gave the settlor's son a testamentary power of appointment which he exercised by creating a trust for his children for their lives with remainder to their issue. The court, following the traditional conception of "relation back,"[1] held that the terms of the donee's will must be considered as if they had been contained in the deed of trust creating the power. "The period of the rule is calculated from the date of the deed of trust creating the power and not from the exercise of the power by the will."[2] This rendered the trust created by the appointment invalid, since his children had been born after the trust which conferred the power was executed. Since the power was was not presently exercisable, even had it been a general power, the appointive assets would not be treated as belonging to the donee for purposes of the Rule.[3] There is some contrary authority with respect to general testamentary powers,[4] but the Uniform Statutory Rule agrees with most authorities that an interest given by the exercise of a power is deemed to have been created when the power was created, unless the power allows the donee "to become the unqualified beneficial owner."[5] This exception for

41. 765 ILCS § 305/5. The heirs are determined as of the date of distribution rather than at the testator's death.

42. For another situation in which the Illinois statute would produce an odd result see McGovern, *Perpetuities Pitfalls and How Best to Avoid Them,* 6 Real Prop., Prob. and T.L.J., 155, 167 (1971). A general *cy pres* power may allow a better solution. See *Restatement (Second) of Property (Donative Transfers)* § 1.5, illus. 8 (1983); Uniform Statutory Rule Against Perpetuities § 3, comment, example 2.

43. Uniform Statutory Rule Against Perpetuities § 5. For a general discussion of retroactivity of Perpetuities reform statutes see Section 1.3, note 58 et seq.

44. Abrams v. Templeton, 465 S.E.2d 117 (S.C.App.1995).

§ 11.5

1. See Section 10.4, at note 11.

2. Arrowsmith v. Mercantile–Safe Deposit, 545 A.2d 674, 678 (Md.1988).

3. Second Nat. Bank v. Harris Trust and Savings Bank, 283 A.2d 226 (Conn.Sup.1971); In re Bird's Estate, 37 Cal.Rptr. 288 (App. 1964); N.Y. EPTL § 10–8.1(a); *Restatement (Second) of Property (Donative Transfers)* § 1.2, comm. d (1983).

4. Industrial Nat. Bank v. Barrett, 220 A.2d 517 (R.I.1966); Wis.Stat. § 700.16(c); S.D.Laws § 43–5–5.

5. Uniform Statutory Rule § 2. The starting date for the Rule is postponed only if the general power is unlimited. A "5 and 5 power" allowing a trust beneficiary to invade corpus to the extent of $5,000 or 5% has no effect on the Rule. Comment, ex. 4.

presently exercisable general powers applies also at common law. For example, in a case like the foregoing one, the donee of a power exercised it to create trusts which were to terminate 21 years after "the death of the survivor of her issue in being at the time of her [the donee's] death." Because the donee had been given power to withdraw the assets from the trust during her lifetime, the trusts she created were valid.

> Where a trust beneficiary is granted * * * an unqualified lifetime power to withdraw for his own use * * * the trust principal, the period of the rule with respect to non-vested interests which may be created by his exercise of [a] testamentary power does not begin to run until the termination of his unqualified power of withdrawal * * * even though (as appears to have been the case here) such beneficiary may make little use of his lifetime power of withdrawal.[6]

As to interests created by exercise of special powers, almost all states agree that the period of the Rule starts when the power was created.[7] This is consistent with the tax avoidance rationale of the Rule,[8] since *special* powers do not normally cause the appointive assets to be taxable in the donee's estate.[9] In Delaware, however, interests created by exercise of any power, whether general or special, are "deemed to have been created at the time of the exercise and not at the time of the creation of such power of appointment."[10] The tax evasion possibilities of this statute inspired a special provision of the Internal Revenue Code to deal with the problem.[11]

### *Second Look*

All jurisdictions allow a "second-look" at the facts when a power of appointment of any kind is exercised, even though the starting period for the Rule is the date on which the power was created.

> When the permissible period of the rule against perpetuities must be computed from the time of the creation of the power of appointment, facts and circumstances existing on the effective date of the instrument exercising the power shall be taken into account in determining the validity of the interests created by the instrument exercising the power.[12]

If, for example, a donee exercises a special or general testamentary power given by a parent by creating trusts for the lives of the donee's children, the second look will validate the trusts if the donee's children were born before the power was created because they would have been lives in being at the

**6.** Matter of Moore, 493 N.Y.S.2d 924, 928 (Surr.1985).

**7.** United Cal. Bank v. Bottler, 94 Cal.Rptr. 227 (App.1971); N.Y. EPTL § 10–8.1(a)(2); Wis.Stat. § 700.16(c); S.D.Laws § 43–5–5; *Restatement, Second, of Property (Donative Transfers)* § 1.2, illus. 11 (1983).

**8.** See Section 11.1, note 43.

**9.** See Section 10.4, note 14.

**10.** Del.Code tit. 25, § 501. An ambiguous Ohio statute also might be read to change the rule but it was interpreted otherwise in Dollar Savings & Trust Co. v. First Nat. Bank, 285 N.E.2d 768, 778 (Ohio Com.Pl.1972); Johnson & Williams, *Application of the Rule Against Perpetuities to Powers of Appointment: Ohio Style,* 5 U.Day L.Rev. 39 (1980).

**11.** Int.Rev.Code § 2041(a)(3) (exercise of a power is taxable if it creates another power which can postpone vesting beyond the period of the Rule). This statute fails to fit exactly the Delaware loophole at which it was directed. Bloom, *Transfer Tax Avoidance,* 45 Albany L.Rev. 261, 283 (1981).

**12.** N.Y. EPTL § 10–8.3. *See also* Wis.Stat. § 700.16(c).

starting date. The second look is a limited form of "wait and see,"[13] but even opponents of wait and see favor the second look. A decision on the validity of interests created by exercise of a power must inevitably be postponed until the donee exercises the power. Therefore, "it would be silly for a court to refuse to look at the course of events during this unavoidable interval" in determining whether the Rule was violated.[14]

Second look does not go as far as wait and see. If the donee exercises a power to create trusts which uses persons who were born after the power was created as measuring lives, the second look does no good.[15] Under wait and see, however, such a trust would be valid if the after-born persons happened to die within 21 years after the death of the last to die of the lives in being when the power was created, (or within 90 years of creation of the power under the Uniform Statutory Rule).[16]

Courts take a second look in passing on gifts in default of appointment as well as interests created by exercise, because "where there is a power, whether it be exercised or not, * * * until the opportunity for its exercise ceases to exist" the determinative provisions cannot be known.[17]

### *Capture*

The consequences of a rule violation have special features when powers of appointment are involved. When an appointment violates the Rule, the property may pass under a gift in default of appointment in the instrument which created the power.[18] But some courts have avoided this result by invoking "capture." For example, when the donee exercised a power attempting to create trusts for children born after the power was created, the invalid remainders in the trusts were replaced by a gift to the donee's heirs, on the theory that the donee "has manifested an intent wholly to withdraw the appointive property from the operation of the instrument creating the power."[19]

Capture applies only to general powers. If a special power is invalidly exercised, the property passes to the takers in default of appointment. For example, a father gave his son a special power which he exercised to create a trust for his daughter for life with remainder to her issue. The daughter was born after the power was created and so the "second look" did not help and the remainder was invalid under the Rule, but not the daughter's life interest which vested when the donee-son died. After the daughter's death, the property was to pass under the gift in default of appointment to the son's issue. Since the power was special the court did not apply capture, but the

**13.** In fact some courts use the terms interchangeably. Harrison v. Marcus, 486 N.E.2d 710, 715n (Mass.1985).

**14.** 5A R. Powell, *Real Property* § 788(3). Professor Powell opposed wait and see.

**15.** Second Nat. Bank v. Harris Trust and Savings Bank, 283 A.2d 226 (Conn.Sup.1971); United California Bank v. Bottler, 94 Cal.Rptr. 227 (App.1971).

**16.** *Restatement (Second) of Property (Donative Transfers)* § 1.4, comm. *l* (1983).

**17.** Sears v. Coolidge, 108 N.E.2d 563, 566 (Mass.1952). *See also* In re Frank, 389 A.2d 536, 541 (Pa.1978).

**18.** Matter of Will of Grunebaum, 471 N.Y.S.2d 513, 515 (Surr.1984); Arrowsmith v. Mercantile–Safe Deposit and Trust Company, 545 A.2d 674, 677 (Md.1988).

**19.** Amerige v. Attorney General, 88 N.E.2d 126, 131 (Mass.1949). *See also Restatement, Second, of Property (Donative Transfers)* § 23.2 (1983); Cal.Prob.Code § 672(b). For other examples of "capture," see Section 10.4, at note 86.

result was the same, since the daughter was both the taker in default of appointment and the donee's heir.[20]

### *Choice of Law*

The law in effect at the date a power is exercised determines the validity of the exercise. This has allowed courts to use modern reform statutes to avoid or soften the consequences of a Rule violation.[21]

### *Planning*

What can the creator of a power do to prevent the donee from violating the Rule in exercising it?[22] A requirement that the donee specifically refer to the power may help, since some violations of the Rule arise from an donee's inadvertent exercise. Donees who deliberately exercise a power may forget that the period began to run at the time the power was created. A reminder in the power itself might avoid this mental lapse, since the drafter of the donee's will normally examines the terms of the power when providing for its exercise.[23]

Finally, the donor should consider giving the donee a presently exercisable general power, so that the Rule will not begin to run until the donee's death. This solution is unsuitable, however, if the donor is using a special power in order to keep the assets out of the donee's taxable estate, or fears that the donee might use a presently exercisable power to squander the trust assets.[24]

In drafting a will for the donee of a power, the perpetuities savings clause must refer to lives in being when the power was created,[25] not the usual clause referring to the testator (donee's) death. A donee who has substantial property of her own and who wishes to create trusts for persons who were born after the power was created, should use the power to pay claims or make outright bequests (if the power allows this) and use her own property for the trusts. If the donee fails to do this, a court may sometimes be able to do this by marshalling.[26]

## § 11.6 Gifts to Charity; Reversionary Interests

### *Duration of Trusts*

Charitable trusts can be perpetual. The reason is that courts can utilize their cy pres power to modify terms of charitable trusts which become

**20.** United California Bank v. Bottler, 94 Cal.Rptr. 227, 232 (App.1971). The daughter was the taker in default and thus ended up with both the life estate and the remainder. She argued that the life estate and remainder were so "inseparably blended that the whole should be declared ineffective" and the property given to her outright, but the court disagreed. Compare Section 11.2, note 43.

**21.** Dollar Savings & Trust Co. v. First Nat. Bank, 285 N.E.2d 768 (Ohio Com.Pl. 1972); In re Morgan Guaranty Trust Co., 269 N.E.2d 571, 573 (N.Y.1971). *See also* Section 10.4, note 90.

**22.** See generally, McGovern, *Perpetuities Pitfalls and How Best to Avoid Them,* 6 Real Prop., Prob. and T.L.J. 155, 168–70 (1971).

**23.** 6 *Amer.Law of Prop.* § 24.7.

**24.** For further discussion of the use of various kinds of powers in planning see Section 10.4, at note 91 et seq.

**25.** H. Tweed & W. Parsons, *Lifetime and Testamentary Estate Planning* 121–22 (10th ed. 1988).

**26.** *Restatement, Second, of Property (Donative Transfers)* § 22.1 (1983); Section 10.4, note 79.

obsolete.[1]

### *Vesting*

Gifts to charity must vest within the period prescribed by the Rule against Perpetuities.[2] For example, a woman who died in 1976 left her estate to a trust which was to accumulate the income for her son, who had never returned from action in World War 2; if the son did not appear by the year 2020, the trustees were to establish a foundation for cruelly treated animals with the trust funds. The court upheld this charitable gift only because a statute allowed testators to substitute 80 years in place of the Rule's lives in being plus 21 years.[3]

If the charity's interest "vests" in time, it need not actually receive the gift within the period of the Rule. The same rule applies to private trusts,[4] but courts are especially prone to treat charitable gifts as "vested." For example, a trust for the lives of the testator's grandchildren and their children, provided a gift at their death to Mt. Zion Methodist Church and "to an orphan or childrens home or homes selected" by the trustee. The charitable remainders were held valid because they vested at the testator's death.[5] This is clear as to the gift to Mt. Zion Methodist Church, but to say that the homes to be selected by the trustee had "vested" interests is questionable.[6] A devise in trust for a hospital "to be organized" after the testator's death did not infringe the Rule; the "organizational details" were not considered conditions precedent and so the gift was vested.[7]

The public interest in supporting charities is sometimes said to justify a more liberal application of the Rule to charitable gifts.[8] However, the Rule has been applied to frustrate charitable gifts or provisions connected with them.

### *Executory Interests Following Charitable Gift*

Immediate gifts to charity followed by a gift over to an individual if the charity ceases to use the property have been held to violate the Rule. For example, a testator who died in 1931 left money in trust for a hospital; if the hospital ceased to operate, the funds were to "become the absolute property of my friend George Green." When the hospital ceased to operate in 1975, the provision for George Green was held invalid. "Where property is given in trust for charitable purposes, and it is provided that on the happening of a designated event the property shall go to a noncharity, the gift over is subject

**§ 11.6**

1. See Sections 9.7, note 86 et seq. as to cy pres. As to the time limits on trusts for noncharitable purposes ("honorary" trusts) see Section 9.7, at note 58.

2. *Restatement (Second) of Property (Donative Transfers)* § 1.6 (1983); J. Morris & W. Leach, *The Rule Against Perpetuities* 186–88 (2d ed. 1962) Several American statutes appear to exempt charitable gifts from the Rule altogether, but it is not clear whether they go beyond the common law described in the text. *E.g.*, Mich.Comp.Laws § 554.351(1) (no gift for charitable uses "shall be invalid * * * by reason of the same contravening any statute or rule against perpetuities").

3. In re Green's Will Trusts, [1985] 3 All E.R. 455 (1984).

4. See Section 11.2, at note 26 et seq.

5. Burt v. Commercial Bank & Trust Co., 260 S.E.2d 306, 310 (Ga.1979).

6. *Compare* Arrowsmith v. Mercantile–Safe Deposit and Trust Co., 545 A.2d 674, 677 (Md. 1988) (income interests in individuals not vested because distributions were discretionary).

7. Rice v. Stanley, 327 N.E.2d 774 (Ohio 1975). *See also Restatement (Second) of Trusts* § 401, comm. j (1959).

8. Matter of Estate of Kirk, 907 P.2d 794, 805–06 (Idaho 1995).

to the rule against perpetuities and will be void unless it vests within the period of the rule.[9]"

A wait and see approach might have changed this result; under the Uniform Statutory Rule, for example, since the gift to George Green actually vested within 90 years, it would have been valid.[10] However, under the Uniform Trust Code a provision in a charitable trust for distribution to a noncharitable beneficiary can only be given effect "if fewer than 21 years have elapsed" since the trust was created.[11]

If the gift over in this case had been to another charity instead of an individual, it would be valid under a special exception to the Rule,[12] based "on the public interest that is served by a charitable gift."[13] Some commentators have questioned this exception, since it applies even if an event unrelated to charity causes the shift from one charity to another, *e.g.*, a gift for UCLA, but if it "should neglect to keep the testator's grave in repair the property" should go to USC.[14]

### *Effect of Invalid Executory Interest*

If the gift to an individual following a charitable gift is invalid, what happens to the property? Several answers are possible. Some cases have allowed the charitable donee to keep the property free of the restriction on the theory that when a divesting condition is invalid under the Rule, the prior interest becomes absolute.[15] For example, land was given to a city for a park, with a gift over to the donor's heirs if the land was not used as a park. The heirs' interest was invalid under the Rule, so the city was held to have "an absolute fee simple title to the property * * * devoid of all conditions and restrictions."[16] A court is not likely to reach this result, however, when property is being held by a non-charitable institution in trust, as distinguished from a public entity like a city.

Another possibility is an order compelling the trustee to comply with the terms of the trust. A trust "for the relief of aged needy and deserving women and couples" provided that if the funds were not used for this purpose, they should go to named individuals. When the trust ceased to operate, the gift to the individuals was held invalid, and the court appointed new trustees to carry out the testator's charitable intent.[17] Even in cases where the Rule is not involved, courts sometimes refuse to treat language of "condition" literal-

9. Nelson v. Kring, 592 P.2d 438, 442 (Kan. 1979). *Accord, Restatement (Second) of Property (Donative Transfers)* § 1.6, comm. c (1983).

10. As to the Uniform Statutory Rule see Section 11.4, note 15. In Harrison v. Marcus, 486 N.E.2d 710, 715 (Mass.1985) the court used wait and see to avoid a similar perpetuities problem.

11. Unif.Trust Code § 412. The comment to this section notes that most charitable trusts are designed to get a tax deduction and so the application of the limitation will be rare.

12. *Restatement (Second) of Property (Donative Transfers)* § 1.6 (1983); *Restatement (Second) of Trusts* § 401, comm. f (1959); Uniform Statutory Rule Against Perpetuities § 4(5).

13. *Restatement (Second) of Property (Donative Transfers)* § 1.6, comm. a (1983).

14. *Restatement (Second) of Trusts* § 401, illus. 3 (1959). *See also* Morris & Leach, *supra* note 2, at 194.

15. Compare cases holding that the invalidity of a divestiture clause makes the preceding interest indefeasibly vested. Section 11.2, note 27.

16. Standard Knitting Mills, Inc. v. Allen, 424 S.W.2d 796, 800 (Tenn.1967); *Restatement, Second, of Property (Donative Transfers)* § 1.5, comm. b (1983).

17. Davenport v. Attorney General, 280 N.E.2d 193, 198 (Mass.1972).

ly, when they think the donor used it simply in order to compel the performance of a duty.[18]

Where compliance with the terms of a gift is impossible, *e.g.* land given for a park is taken to build a highway, the court may apply the proceeds to a related purpose under *cy pres*.[19] This requires a finding that the testator had a "broader charitable intent" beyond the specified purpose.[20]

### *Possibility of Reverter*

Sometimes the invalidity of the gift to a third person causes property revert to the donor/testator or his or her successors.[21] This does not violate the Rule because future interests reserved by the grantor or testator, as distinguished from those given to third persons, are not subject to the Rule.[22] Modern commentators have argued that interests reserved by the grantor tie up property "in precisely the manner which the Rule against Perpetuities was designed to prevent."[23] Reversionary interests, unlike interests in unborn children, do not suspend the power of alienation since the grantor can join in a conveyance of the property affected, but that is also true of many executory interests which are invalid under the Rule.[24] Nevertheless the second Restatement of Property reaffirms the exemption for reversionary interests and the Uniform Statutory Rule leaves it undisturbed.[25]

The desire to support charity may explain this, since reversionary interests are often linked to charitable gifts. "The public benefits from our determination not to apply the rule here," because otherwise "grantors would not freely give their land for public use."[26] Also, the Rule period of lives in being plus 21 years is not appropriate for such interests, as distinguished from trusts for children and grandchildren or other individuals. Leach himself, although he attacked the exemption of reversionary interests, suggested that a special rule for them was a better solution than subjecting them to the common-law Rule.[27]

**18.** Section 4.6, note 76.

**19.** State v. Rand, 366 A.2d 183 (Me.1976).

**20.** Nelson v. Kring, 592 P.2d 438, 444 (Kan.1979) (rejecting cy pres because no such intent). See Section 9.7, note 114.

**21.** *Restatement, Second, Trusts* § 401, comm. d (1959); Nelson v. Kring, 592 P.2d 438, 444 (Kan.1979). For an 16th century statement of this idea see St. Germain, *Doctor and Student* (91 Sel.Soc.) 219 (1974).

**22.** Howson v. Crombie St. Congregational Church, 590 N.E.2d 687, 689 (Mass.1992); Nelson v. Kring, 592 P.2d 438, 442 (Kan.1979); Commerce Union Bank v. Warren County, 707 S.W.2d 854 (Tenn.1986); City of Klamath Falls v. Bell, 490 P.2d 515 (Or.App.1971).

**23.** Morris & Leach, *supra* note 2, at 213. *See also* Chaffin, *The Rule Against Perpetuities as Applied to Georgia Wills,* 16 Ga.L.Rev. 235, 318 (1982); L. Simes, *Public Policy and the Dead Hand* 70 (1955); Fellows, *Testing Perpetuities Reforms: A Study of Perpetuites Cases 1984–89,* 25 Real Prop.Prob. and T.J. 597, 667 (1991).

**24.** Section 11.1, note 32.

**25.** *Restatement (Second) of Property (Donative Transfers)* § 1.4, comm. c (1983); Uniform Statutory Rule Against Perpetuities § 4, comment, subsection 7. However, possibilities of reverter and rights of entry are subject to the Rule in England. Perpetuities and Accumulations Act, 1964, § 12.

**26.** Central Del. Cty. Auth. v. Greyhound Corp., 563 A.2d 139, 145 (Pa.Super.1989). (This decision was later reversed, 588 A.2d 485 (Pa.1991). For the rationale of the reversal see Section 11.7, note 3.) Some statutes which restrict possibilities of reverter make an exception for conveyances to charity. Fla.Stat. § 689.18(5); Mich.Comp.Laws § 554.64. However, at common law "the exemption from the Rule is equally applicable where the determinable fee is given to a non-charity." 6 *Amer.Law of Prop.* § 24.18, at 56.

**27.** Leach, *Perpetuities in Perspective: Ending the Rule's Reign of Terror,* 65 Harv.L.Rev. 721, 745 (1952). See also *Restatement, Second, of Property (Donative Transfers)* § 1.4, comm. c (1983); Uniform Statutory Rule § 4, comment.

### *Reverter Statutes*

Leach cited as a model an Illinois statute which provides that possibilities of reverter and rights of entry for breach of a condition shall be valid for only 40 years.[28] Unlike the Rule against Perpetuities, the statute does not invalidate an interest completely if it is too remote, but rather cuts it down to 40 years.

The statute applies to interests previously created. Some courts have held that retroactive statutes amount to an unconstitutional taking from persons who owned such reversionary interests when the statute was enacted.[29] However, the Illinois Supreme Court upheld the Illinois statute on the ground that possibilities of reverter were not property but only "an expectation."[30] If the statute were not applied retroactively, possibilities would remain as "clogs on title," making property unmarketable. This inconvenience outweighed the slight value of these interests to their owners.[31]

Some legislatures have enacted statutes which apply to existing interests unless the owner records a reservation of rights within a brief period after the statute is passed. Many owners, being unaware of such statutes, have failed to record their claims and thus lost them. Courts have upheld such statutes.[32] As one court said, "the requirement that a holder of a reversionary interest file a notice of intent to preserve that interest creates a minimal burden. * * * The benefit to the state is great in that marketability of title is improved."[33]

The Massachusetts statute eliminates the common law's disparate treatment of reversionary interests and executory interests, allowing 30 years for both.[34] It has been held not to apply to a trust where the trustee holds title in fee simple absolute, subject to an equitable obligation to return the property to the settlors.[35]

### *Transfers of Possibilities and Rights of Entry*

The common law distinction between executory interests (subject to the Rule) and reversionary interests (exempt from the Rule) becomes strained to the point of absurdity when a grantor transfers a reversionary interest. For example, a woman conveyed land to a church for use as a parsonage; if the church ceased to use the land for religious purposes, it was to "revert to me, or if I should be deceased, then to the persons who at such time would be

**28.** 765 ILCS § 330/4.

**29.** Biltmore Village v. Royal Biltmore Village, 71 So.2d 727 (Fla.1954). Followed in Board of Education v. Miles, 207 N.E.2d 181 (N.Y.1965). Florida courts, however, have applied the statute to a possibility of reverter created *after* its enactment. J.C. Vereen & Sons, Inc. v. City of Miami, 397 So.2d 979 (Fla.App.1981).

**30.** Compare the idea that "expectancies" are not "property" and so cannot be gratuitously transferred. Section 4.5, note 82. As to the transferability of possibilities of reverter see note 40 et seq. *infra*.

**31.** Trustees of Schools of Township No. 1 v. Batdorf, 130 N.E.2d 111, 114–15 (Ill.1955). *See also* Hiddleston v. Nebraska Jewish Education Soc'y., 186 N.W.2d 904 (Neb.1971).For a general discussion of retroactive legislation see Section 1.3.

**32.** Brookline v. Carey, 245 N.E.2d 446 (Mass.1969); Presbytery of Southeast Iowa v. Harris, 226 N.W.2d 232 (Iowa 1975); Kilpatrick v. Snow Mountain Pine Co., 805 P.2d 137 (Or.App.1991).

**33.** Walton v. City of Red Bluff, 3 Cal. Rptr.2d 275, 285 (App.1991). However, the court in this case did not actually apply the statute because it had not been properly pleaded.

**34.** Oak's Oil Serv. v. Massachusetts Bay Transp. Auth., 447 N.E.2d 27, 30 (Mass.App. 1983).

**35.** Harrison v. Marcus, 486 N.E.2d 710 (Mass.1985).

entitled to the residue of my estate."[36] The successors to the grantor's residuary devisees were able to recover the land after it ceased to be used for religious purposes. Their interest did not violate the Rule because they took as devisees of the grantor's right of entry.[37] The grantor's right was valid under the exception for interests reserved by the grantor, and since the grantor was dead the right passed under the residuary clause of her will.[38] In other words, the Rule barred the persons from taking the executory interest in the deed, but the same persons could take as devisees of the grantor. Here the Rule seems to turn on "mere words," rather than "real differences,"[39] which make sense to non-lawyers.

The result reached in a case like this depends on the transferability of reversionary interests. In the 15th century, rights of entry could not be assigned. If the grantor attempted to do so, they were destroyed, on the theory that the assignee could not enforce them (because they were non-assignable) and neither could the grantor because he had given the interest away.[40] The first Restatement of Property distinguished between rights of entry, which were not assignable, and possibilities of reverter which were.[41] This distinction raises difficult questions of classification because many deeds use language which does not clearly fit into either category.[42]

In many states modern statutes make even rights of entry alienable in keeping with the trend to make allow transfer of all interests,[43] but an Illinois statute goes in the other direction by making *both* possibilities of reverter and rights of entry inalienable.[44] This statute has been said to reduce the "nuisance value" of such interests,[45] but why making them inalienable makes them less a clog to marketability is unclear, unless an attempt to alienate destroys the interest.

## § 11.7 Commercial Transactions

The Rule against Perpetuities was not applied to commercial transactions until late in its history. In recent years, however, the reported cases involving

**36.** Howson v. Crombie St. Congregational Church, 590 N.E.2d 687, 688 (Mass.1992).

**37.** *Id.* at 689 n. The court did not attempt to uphold the interest under the Uniform Statutory Rule even though less than 90 years had passed, because the deed took effect before the statute was passed. See Section 13.5, note 42. A statute limiting reverters was inapplicable because the deed preceded the statute and the grantor had protected her interest by recording. Cf. note 35 supra.

**38.** See also Nelson v. Kring, 592 P.2d 438, 444 (Kan.1979); *Restatement of Property* § 403, illus. 2 (1944). *But cf.* Dukeminier, *Cleansing the Stables of Property,* 65 Iowa L.Rev. 151, 174 (1979) (testator should not be allowed "by one clause [to] retain a possibility of reverter and subsequently transfer it by another clause").

**39.** The result to which Chancellor Nottingham objected in the Duke of Norfolk's Case. See Section 11.1, note 19.

**40.** T. Littleton, *Tenures* § 347.

**41.** *Restatement of Property* §§ 159–60 (1936). The rule that a purported assignment destroyed a right of entry appeared originally in § 160, comm. c, but this was changed in 1947. See 1 *Amer.Law of Prop.* § 4.69. The idea reappears as an alternative holding in Kilpatrick v. Snow Mountain Pine Co., 805 P.2d 137, 139 (Or.App.1991).

**42.** Fennell v. Foskey, 225 S.E.2d 231, 233 (Ga.1976) (deed created an alienable possibility of reverter rather than an inalienable right of entry).

**43.** *Restatement of Property* § 160, comm. d (1936); 1 *Amer.Law of Prop.* § 4.68; Cal.Civ. Code § 1046; Oak's Oil Serv., Inc. v. Massachusetts Bay Transp. Auth., 447 N.E.2d 27 (Mass.App.1983).

**44.** 765 ILCS § 330/1. *See also* Neb.Rev. Stat. § 76–299.

**45.** 1 *Amer.Law of Prop.* § 4.68. *See also Restatement of Property* § 160, comm. a (1936).

the Rule in commercial transactions has outnumbered those in donative transfers,[1] perhaps because lawyers who handle commercial transactions are less familiar with the Rule and the ways to avoid it.

### *Options*

The Rule applies only to property, not to contracts to pay money. Thus a provision in a land sale requiring the buyer to pay the seller 10% of the gross sale price if he ever resold the land did not infringe the Rule, which

> does not affect the making of contracts which do not create rights of property. Thus a promise to A to pay him or his executors or administrators a sum of money on a future event is good, although such event may not happen within twenty one years after lives in being [even if] the covenant * * * can * * * be enforced by or against other persons than the original parties.[2]

Options to buy land or unique goods, on the other hand, because they give the optionee a right to specific performance even against third persons, create property interests and thus are subject to the Rule. The option is invalid if it might have been exercised beyond the period of the Rule.[3] This includes options to repurchase given to a seller, despite the general exemption from the Rule for interests reserved by a grantor.[4]

Options are frequently denied enforcement under the Rule even though the optionee seeks to exercise it only a few years after the option was created. Some courts have applied "wait and see" to make the option enforceable,[5] but others have refused to do so.[6] Other theories have been used to validate options. One is to imply a time limit for exercise of the option.

> Where the parties have explicitly fixed a period of time [for exercise] longer than that permitted by the rule, a reasonable time cannot be implied. * * * Use of a general term, however such as "any time" does not necessarily preclude the implication of a reasonable time. * * * A contrary interpretation is disfavored because it would create a perpetuities problem unnecessarily, * * * enabling the [promissors] to escape the enforcement of a contract they entered into freely.[7]

§ 11.7

1. Bloom, *Perpetuities Refinement: There Is an Alternative,* 62 Wash.L.Rev. 23, 76 (1987).

2. Kerley v. Nu–West, Inc., 762 P.2d 631, 637 (Ariz.App.1988).

3. Stuart Kingston, Inc. v. Robinson, 596 A.2d 1378 (Del.1991); Symphony Space v. Pergola Properties, 669 N.E.2d 799 (N.Y.1996); Low v. Spellman, 629 A.2d 57 (Me.1993) (right of repurchase); Mizell v. Greensboro Jaycees, 412 S.E.2d 904 (N.C.App.1992) (25 year right of first refusal).

4. All the cases in the previous note involved rights reserved by a seller. *cf.* Dukeminier, *A Modern Guide to Perpetuities,* 74 Cal. L.Rev. 1867, 1909 (1986) ("not easy to explain" why a grantor who must pay to reenter is subject to the Rule). As to the exemption of reserved interests see Section 11.6, note 22.

5. Colby v. Colby, 596 A.2d 901 (Vt.1990); Gartley v. Ricketts, 760 P.2d 143 (N.M.1988). As to "wait and see" see Section 11.4, at note 2 et seq.

6. Symphony Space v. Pergola Properties, 669 N.E.2d 799, 808 (N.Y.1996) (no wait and see statute); Low v. Spellman, 629 A.2d 57 (Me.1993) (conveyance was prior to wait and see statute); Buck v. Banks, 668 N.E.2d 1259, 1261 (Ind.App.1996).

7. Peterson v. Tremain, 621 N.E.2d 385, 387 (Mass.App.1993). *See also* Byke Const. Co., Inc. v. Miller, 680 P.2d 193 (Ariz.App.1984); Ryland Group, Inc. v. Wills, 331 S.E.2d 399 (Va.1985); Robroy Land Co., Inc. v. Prather, 622 P.2d 367 (Wash.1980). This argument can backfire; if the optionee has waited more than a reasonable time to sue, enforcement will be denied for that reason. Lawson v. Redmoor Corp., 679 P.2d 972 (Wash.App.1984).

This construction is particularly appealing if the jurisdiction has a statute requiring courts to construe or reform instruments so as to avoid violations of the rule.[8] However, some courts have rejected the inference of a reasonable time limit on the ground that if the parties had intended to impose one they would have said so in the contract.[9]

Sometimes an option is so expressed that a court can separate valid from invalid parts. For example, a lease gave the lessee the right to demand additional space "after the fifth, tenth, fifteenth, twentieth or twenty-fifth anniversary of the commencement of the lease." The court viewed this as five options and the first four were valid.[10] However, a single option will not be divided into annual components so as to make it valid for 21 years.[11]

Options are often saved by finding that they were "personal" to the optionor or optionee, so they will expire within a life in being. For example:

> The fact that the agreement is made binding on the heirs and assigns of [the optionor] but not on the heirs and assigns of [the optionee] supports the conclusion that the parties * * * intended [it] * * * to expire on [the optionee's] death. * * * Where there are two possible constructions of an instrument, one which renders it valid under the rule against perpetuities and the other which renders it invalid, preference will be accorded to the construction which upholds its validity.[12]

But this construction was rejected as to an option which by its terms extended to the heirs and assigns of both parties.[13]

### *Leases and Covenants*

Long term leases which give the lessee an option to purchase have been held not to infringe the Rule. Whereas options unconnected with a lease deter "the free marketability of the real estate and the possibility of its development," an option in a lease gives the lessee an incentive to develop the property fully. To hold it invalid under the Rule "could very well have a reverse effect."[14] By similar reasoning perpetual options to renew a lease do not violate the Rule,[15] but an option to buy additional land *is* subject to the Rule.[16]

**8.** Matter of Estate of Crowl, 737 P.2d 911, 914 (Okl.1987). As to construing or reforming instruments so as to avoid perpetuities violations see Section 11.4, at note 20 et seq.

**9.** Shaffer v. Reed, 437 So.2d 98 (Ala.1983); Buffalo Seminary v. McCarthy, 451 N.Y.S.2d 457 (A.D.1982).

**10.** Crossroads Shopping Center v. Montgomery Ward & Co., Inc., 646 P.2d 330 (Colo. 1981).

**11.** Certified Corp. v. GTE Products Corp., 467 N.E.2d 1336 (Mass.1984).

**12.** Stratman v. Sheetz, 573 N.E.2d 776, 779 (Ohio App.1989). *See also* Gore v. Beren, 867 P.2d 330 (Kan.1994); Morrison v. Piper, 566 N.E.2d 643 (N.Y.1990); Marcy v. Markiewicz, 599 N.E.2d 1051, 1058 (Ill.App.1992).

**13.** Buck v. Banks, 668 N.E.2d 1259 (Ind. App.1996); Shaffer v. Reed, 437 So.2d 98 (Ala. 1983).

**14.** St. Regis Paper Co. v. Brown, 276 S.E.2d 24, 25 (Ga.1981). *See also* Coomler v. Shell Oil Co., 814 P.2d 184 (Or.App.1991); Stenke v. Masland Development Co., Inc., 394 N.W.2d 418 (Mich.App.1986); Leach, *Perpetuities in Perspective,* 65 Harv.L.Rev. 721, 738 (1952).

**15.** Camerlo v. Howard Johnson Co., 710 F.2d 987 (3d Cir.1983); Dixon v. Rivers, 245 S.E.2d 572 (N.C.App.1978); *Restatement of Property* § 395 (1944).

**16.** Crossroads Shopping Center v. Montgomery Ward & Co., Inc., 646 P.2d 330 (Colo. 1981).

Restrictive covenants limiting the use of land are also exempt from the Rule.[17] The policy against dead-hand control is here effectuated by refusing to enforce covenants which have become out of date.[18]

### *Policy Analysis; USRAP*

Some have questioned whether the Rule is appropriate in commercial cases. It is troubling to let a party get out of a bargain for which he received valuable consideration because of the Rule.[19] In one case a seller who had sold property below its market value in return for an option to repurchase attempted to rescind the transaction when the option was held invalid. Rescission was denied on the ground that "it would lead to the same result as enforcing the option"[20] and so the buyer got a windfall.

The Rule may be considered necessary to limit foolish dispositions by a capricious testator, but when two parties with conflicting interests make a contract, their self-interest should protect against unreasonable restrictions.[21] The Uniform Statutory Rule Against Perpetuities exempts interests "arising out of a nondonative transfer" from the Rule on the ground that the period of the Rule is "not suitable" for them. The drafters acknowledged that options may restrain alienability or "provide a disincentive to improve the property" and their duration could be controlled by a special statute like one in Illinois which imposes a 40 year limit on options while exempting them from the Rule.[22]

One court has invoked USRAP in upholding a contract provision challenged for infringing the Rule, finding that "neither the Legislature nor this court can perceive any danger * * * requiring continued application of the rule to nondonative commercial transactions."[23] On the other hand, another court struck down an option on the theory that the USRAP exemption left the transaction subject to the common-law Rule.[24]

## § 11.8 Restraints on Alienation

### *History and Rationale*

Closely related to the Rule against Perpetuities is a much older rule against restraints on alienation. It appeared in the 15th century, almost two hundred years before the Duke of Norfolk's Case.[1]

**17.** State v. Reece, 374 S.W.2d 686 (Tex. Civ.App.1964); Lowry v. Norris Lake Shores Development Corp., 203 S.E.2d 171 (Ga.1974); *Restatement of Property* § 399 (1944).

**18.** *Id.* comm. d; Nutis v. Schottenstein Trustees, 534 N.E.2d 380, 385 (Ohio App.1987) (residence restriction no longer enforceable because of change in character of neighborhood); Lacer v. Navajo County, 687 P.2d 404, 411 (Ariz.App.1983).

**19.** Morris & Leach, *The Rule Against Perpetuities* 224 (2d ed. 1962); Fellows, *Testing Perpetuities Reforms: A Study of Perpetuities Cases 1984–89*, 25 Real Prop.Prob. and T.J. 597, 665 (1991); *cf.* Martin v. Prairie Rod and Gun Club, 348 N.E.2d 306, 310 (Ill.App.1976). Perhaps if the consideration paid for the option was clearly identifiable it could be recovered to avoid unjust enrichment, but it is usually an inseparable part of a larger transaction.

**20.** Symphony Space v. Pergola Properties, 669 N.E.2d 799, 809 (N.Y.1996).

**21.** Morris & Leach, *supra* note 19, at 224; 6 *Amer. Law of Prop.* § 24.56, at 144.

**22.** Uniform Statutory Rule Against Perpetuities § 4(1), Comment; 765 ILCS § 305/4(7).

**23.** Juliano & Sons v. Chevron, U.S.A., 593 A.2d 814, 819 (N.J.Super.App.Div..1991).

**24.** Buck v. Banks, 668 N.E.2d 1259 (Ind. App.1996).

**§ 11.8**

1. See Section 11.1, at note 19.

> If a feoffment is made on condition that the feoffee not alienate the property to anyone, the condition is void, for when a man is enfeoffed of lands or tenements, he has power to alienate them to anyone by law [so] if this condition were good, the condition would take away the power which the law gives him, which would be against reason.[2]

The rule is often stated in the same conclusory terms today: "the power of alienation is necessarily incident to every estate in fee, and a condition in a devise of lands altogether preventing alienation, is repugnant to the estate and void."[3] This "rationale" for the rule begs the question why the power of alienation is "necessarily incident to" a fee simple, even though the person who created the fee simple intended otherwise. The repugnancy rationale can be turned on its head. When a provision in a deed giving the seller the right to repurchase property if the buyer ever offered it for sale was claimed to be "repugnant" to the buyer's fee, the court disagreed, saying that the buyer's estate was not "a fee simple absolute" but only a "a fee simple defeasible."[4]

Reconciling the cases requires an understanding of the policy behind the rule. It is commonly said that the rule is designed to keep property alienable in order to allow "the utilization of land in the most effective manner."[5] Since this policy also underlies the Rule against Perpetuities,[6] courts sometimes examine a provision under both rules,[7] but the conclusion is not always the same. For example, a provision in a deed requiring the grantor's consent to sell the land was held not to violate the Rule under a "wait and see" statute, but the provision was nevertheless invalid as an unreasonable restraint.[8] Conversely, a provision may violate the Rule but not constitute an invalid restraint.

### *Reasonableness*

Although courts sometimes say that even "reasonable" restraints on alienation are invalid,[9] there are many decisions upholding restraints which seem to rest, either expressly or implicitly, on the idea of reasonableness. The second Restatement of Property says that in general a restraint is valid if "under the circumstances of the case, [it] is found to be reasonable."[10] Two factors determine whether a restraint is reasonable. First, does it serve a purpose which the court finds worthy? Thus one court found an restraint invalid which served "no worthwhile purpose * * * other than to allow [the grantor] to 'keep property in the family,' "[11] while another court upheld a

2. T. Littleton, *Tenures* § 360. In the 13th century, Bracton regarded such conditions as valid. 2 H. Bracton, *De Legibus* 146 (Woodbine ed.).

3. Hankins v. Mathews, 425 S.W.2d 608, 610 (Tenn.1968).*See also* Holien v. Trydahl, 134 N.W.2d 851, 855 (N.D.1965); Kenney v. Morgan, 325 A.2d 419, 422 (Md.App.1974); Cast v. National Bank, 183 N.W.2d 485, 489 (Neb.1971); Cal.Civ.Code § 711 (conditions restraining alienation are void "when repugnant to the interest created").

4. Floyd v. Hoover, 234 S.E.2d 89 (Ga.App. 1977).

5. 6 *Amer. Law of Prop.* § 26.3.

6. See Section 11.1, note 28.

7. Colby v. Colby, 596 A.2d 901 (Vt.1990) (repurchase option valid under both analyses); Low v. Spellman, 629 A.2d 57 (Me.1993) (repurchase option invalid under both analyses).

8. Gartley v. Ricketts, 760 P.2d 143 (N.M. 1988).

9. White v. White, 251 A.2d 470, 473 (N.J.Super.Ch.Div.1969); Andrews v. Hall, 58 N.W.2d 201, 203 (Neb.1953); *Restatement of Property* § 406, comm. p (1944).

10. *Restatement, Second, of Property (Donative Transfers)* § 4.2(3) (1981).

11. Gartley v. Ricketts, 760 P.2d 143, 146 (N.M.1988).

provision which was "reasonably designed to attain or encourage accepted social or economic ends."[12] A second factor is how substantial a bar to alienability the restraint presents. Courts balance these factors. "The greater the quantum of restraint that results from enforcement of a given clause, the greater must be the justification for that enforcement."[13]

(1) *Partial Restraints.* A restraint which simply forbids alienation to one person, or a small group, is valid.[14] But a restraint is not valid simply because it allows the land to be transferred to a small group, such as the testator's descendants.[15] The size of the group is not necessarily determinative. If the prohibited group contains the probable purchasers of the land, even though a small number, the restraint is invalid, and the converse is also true.[16] At one time restraints on alienation to minority groups, such as blacks, were held to be reasonable, but in 1948 the Supreme Court invalidated them under the 14th Amendment.[17]

(2) *Restraints on Use.* Courts distinguish between restraints on alienation and covenants which restricts use.[18] When land was deeded land to a Lodge with a stipulation that if the grantee failed to use the land or sold it, the land should revert to the grantor, the court held that the restraint on sale was invalid, but the condition on use was not.[19] Although restraints are prohibited because they deter the optimal *use* of land, restraints on use are exempt because they cease to be enforceable when they become obsolete. Sometimes, however, restrictions on use are held invalid because their practical effect is to restrain alienation. Provisions which require a devisee to occupy property as his residence have been held to be invalid on this reasoning.[20]

3. *Life Estates.* A restraint is not valid just because it is limited in time,[21] but restraints on alienation of a *limited interest* such as a life estate are permitted. For example, a devise to the testator's children, with the proviso that none could convey his or her interest "during the lifetime of any of my children * * * and after the death of the last of my children, the said property shall be owned by my grandchildren," was upheld as a restraint on a life estate; although the will did not expressly devise a life estate to the children, that was its effect.[22] Life estates differ from a fee simple because they are hard

**12.** Kerley v. Nu–West, Inc., 762 P.2d 631, 635 (Ariz.App.1988).

**13.** Carma Developers (California), Inc. v. Marathon Development California, Inc., 826 P.2d 710, 716 (Cal.1992).

**14.** T. Littleton, *Tenures* § 361; Pritchett v. Turner, 437 So.2d 104 (Ala.1983) (forfeiture if devisees convey land to testator's ex-wife); *Restatement (Second) of Property (Donative Transfers)* § 4.2, illus. 3 (1983).

**15.** Wise v. Poston, 316 S.E.2d 412, 415 (S.C.App.1984).

**16.** *Restatement (Second) of Property (Donative Transfers)* § 4.2, comm. r (1983).

**17.** Shelley v. Kraemer, 334 U.S. 1 (1948); *Cf. Restatement of Property* § 406, illus. 1 (1944). ("In states where the social conditions render desirable the exclusion of the racial or social group involved from the area in question, the restraint is reasonable and hence valid.")

**18.** *Restatement (Second) of Property (Donative Transfers)* § 3.4 (1983).

**19.** Mountain Brow Lodge No. 82 v. Toscano, 64 Cal.Rptr. 816 (App.1967).

**20.** Cast v. National Bank of Commerce, 183 N.W.2d 485 (Neb.1971); *Restatement (Second) of Property (Donative Transfers)* § 3.4, illus. 4 (1983).

**21.** Beauchamp v. Beauchamp, 574 So.2d 18 (Miss.1990) (restraint on sale for lives plus 30 years invalid); *Restatement (Second) of Property (Donative Transfers)* § 4.1, illus. 3, § 4.2, illus. 14 (1983).

**22.** Wise v. Poston, 316 S.E.2d 412 (S.C.App.1984). *See also* Johnson v. Girtman, 542 So.2d 1033 (Fla.App.1989).

to sell anyway—few purchasers want to buy an interest which will end when the seller dies.[23]

The Restatement distinguishes between forfeiture and disabling restraints in this connection. A provision that simply says "the grantee shall not alienate the land" is a disabling restraint; one which says the grantee shall lose the land if he tries to alienate it is a forfeiture restraint. As to a fee simple, both types of restraint are invalid. As to life estates, forfeiture restraints are permitted, but disabling restraints are not,[24] "because if effective they enable the person restrained to deny the validity of such person's own transfer."[25] Some courts, however, allow even disabling restraints on a life estate.[26] Spendthrift trusts are disabling restraints on equitable interests, and are permitted in nearly all states.[27] Some courts obliterate the distinction between disabling and forfeiture restraints by *implying* a forfeiture provision whenever a will restrains alienation by a life tenant.[28]

4. *Future Interests.* Restraints on the alienation of future interests are often upheld,[29] because "a future interest from its very nature is not as marketable as a present interest."[30] Also, the restraint serves to protect against improvident dispositions, since future interests are often sold at a large discount.[31]

5. *Contract for Deed; Lease.* Contracts to sell land often allow the buyer to get possession and pay the price in installments. Such contracts usually prohibit the buyer from transferring his interest without the seller's consent. These provisions are upheld, because of the seller's legitimate concern with possible waste committed by an unreliable assignee while the price remains unpaid.[32]

The law allows restraints on assignment by a lessee for years for similar reasons. However, many courts hold that a lessor may not "unreasonably" withhold consent to an attempted assignment.[33] Others disagree. [34]

**23.** *Restatement (Second) of Property (Donative Transfers)* § 4.2, comm. c (1983).

**24.** *Restatement (Second) of Property (Donative Transfers)* § 4.1 (disabling restraints), § 4.2 (forfeiture restraint); Carma Developers v. Marathon Dev., 826 P.2d 710, 718 (Cal.1992) (forfeiture restraints are viewed more favorably than comparable disabling restraints).

**25.** *Restatement, Second, of Property (Donative Transfers)* § 4.1, comm. a (1983).

**26.** In re Kelly's Estate, 193 So.2d 575, 578 (Miss.1967).

**27.** See Section 13.1, at note 37. Compare the "protective trust" which operates as a forfeiture restraint, and which is allowed even where spendthrift provisions are not. *Id.* note 57.

**28.** Atkinson v. Kish, 420 S.W.2d 104, 109 (Ky.1967); *cf. Restatement of Property* § 419 (1944) (ambiguous restraint construed not to be disabling).

**29.** *E.g.*, Lowrance v. Whitfield, 752 S.W.2d 129 (Tex.App.1988).

**30.** *Restatement (Second) of Property (Donative Transfers)* § 4.2, comm. u (1983).

**31.** 6 *Amer. Law of Prop.* § 26.54; Section 13.1, at note 16 et seq.

**32.** Carey v. Lincoln Loan Co., 998 P.2d 724, 732 (Or.App.2000).

**33.** *Restatement (Second) of Property, Landlord and Tenant* § 15.2(2) (1976); Newman v. Hinky Dinky Omaha–Lincoln Inc., 427 N.W.2d 50 (Neb.1988); Bert Bidwell Inv. v. LaSalle and Schiffer, 797 P.2d 811 (Colo.App. 1990); *cf.* Cheney v. Jemmett, 693 P.2d 1031 (Idaho 1984) (seller under land sale contract cannot unreasonably withhold consent to assignment); Carey v. Lincoln Loan Co., 998 P.2d 724, 732 (Or.App.2000) (seller's right to refuse to consent to assignment is "tempered by the duty of good faith").

**34.** First Federal Sav. Bank v. Key Markets, 559 N.E.2d 600 (Ind.1990); 21 Merchants Row Corp. v. Merchants Row, 587 N.E.2d 788 (Mass.1992). In Carma Developers (California), Inc. v. Marathon Development California, Inc., 826 P.2d 710 (Cal.1992) the court held it was not unreasonable for a lessor to invoke such a clause "in order to appropriate to itself the increased rental value of the property."

6. *Transfer with Consent.* According to the first Restatement of Property, a restraint is objectionable even if it allows transfer with another's consent; otherwise, all forfeiture restraints would be valid because the person to whom property would pass upon forfeiture can always consent to forego his claim.[35] The second Restatement, however, says that a restraint which allows alienation with another's consent is valid if reasonable. For example, if a father gives property to his son and requires consent by a family friend to any transfer until the son reaches 40, this restraint is considered to serve a reasonable purpose and is allowed.[36]

7. *Preemptive Rights.* Options are sometimes held invalid as unreasonable restraints on alienation.[37] However, preemptive provisions giving "a right of first refusal" if property is offered for sale, are not regarded as restraints if their terms are reasonable as to price and other conditions.[38] But when a deed provided that if the grantee wished to sell the land, the grantor could repurchase it for the price the grantee had paid plus the cost of any subsequent improvements, this was held to be an invalid restraint. Although "a repurchase option at market or appraised value" is permissible, a "fixed price" option is not because it "discourages any improvements of the land by the existing property owner."[39] However, some courts have upheld even fixed-price options[40], while others have invalidated preemptive rights which were based on current value.[41]

8. *Trusts.* Reasonable restraints against the alienation of trust property by the trustee are valid.[42] However, such restraints may be overridden, if, owing to a change of circumstances "the purpose of the trust would be defeated or substantially impaired unless the property is sold."[43]

Courts do not as a general rule cut down unreasonable restraints so as to make them reasonable. However, when a will leaving land to a daughter for life, remainder to her children, provided that the land was not to be sold until the children reached 45, the court, by analogy to cy pres in perpetuities cases,[44] held that the restriction was invalid only to the extent that it continued beyond the daughter's lifetime.[45]

**35.** *Restatement of Property* § 406, illus. 1 (1944). *See also* Gartley v. Ricketts, 760 P.2d 143 (N.M.1988) (clause requiring grantor's consent to transfer invalid).

**36.** *Restatement (Second) of Property (Donative Transfers)* § 4.1, illus. 11 (1983). *See also* id. § 4.2, comm. p.

**37.** Low v. Spellman, 629 A.2d 57 (Me. 1993) (option to repurchase); Urquhart v. Teller, 958 P.2d 714 (Mont.1998). They may also be held to violate the Rule against Perpetuities. See Section 11.7, note 3 et seq.

**38.** *Restatement, Second, of Property (Donative Transfers)* § 4.4 (1981). *See also* Wildenstein & Co., Inc. v. Wallis, 595 N.E.2d 828 (N.Y.1992); Lorentzen v. Smith, 5 P.3d 1082, 1086 (N.M.App.2000).

**39.** Iglehart v. Phillips, 383 So.2d 610, 615 (Fla.1980). *See also Restatement, Second, of Property (Donative Transfers)* § 4.4, illus. 4 (1981).

**40.** McDonald v. Moore, 790 P.2d 213 (Wash.App.1990); Colby v. Colby, 596 A.2d 901 (Vt.1990).

**41.** Holien v. Trydahl, 134 N.W.2d 851 (N.D.1965); Atchison v. City of Englewood, 463 P.2d 297 (Colo.1969).

**42.** Ohio Society for Crippled Children & Adults, Inc. v. McElroy, 191 N.E.2d 543 (Ohio 1963); *Restatement (Second) of Trusts* § 190 (1959).

**43.** *Id.* § 190, comm. f. *See also* Section 9.6, at note 11 et seq.

**44.** See Section 11.4, note 21 et seq.

**45.** In re Kelly's Estate, 193 So.2d 575 (Miss.1967). *But see* Beauchamp v. Beauchamp, 574 So.2d 18 (Miss.1990) (applying Wisconsin law making restraint totally void).

### *Planning*

Some cases suggest that for commercial transactions the rule against restraints should completely replace the Rule against Perpetuities.[46] Insofar as restraints on alienation are upheld where "reasonable" instances of a mechanical application of the rule which undercuts its policy are infrequent. Perhaps for this reason, the trend to soften the Rule against Perpetuities in order to avoid the ill effects of inexpert drafting, has not gone nearly so far with regard to restraints on alienation.

The rule against restraints on alienation may frustrate a reasonable plan if the drafter is not sophisticated. When a restraint on alienation is held invalid, often the objective could have been accomplished by use of a trust, as to which the limits are more generous. For example, a will which provided that land devised to the testator's wife and children should not be "sold, given away or in any way disposed of" for 20 years was held to be an invalid restraint. The court acknowledged that spendthrift trusts are valid, but said that this rule did not apply when the will "fails to create a 'trust' in unmistakable terms."[47]

## § 11.9 Accumulations

### *Common Law*

*Thelluson v. Woodford*[1] is the leading case on the legality of accumulations of income. It involved a trust which directed that the income be accumulated for nine lives. The House of Lords saw no policy objection to this and upheld the trust. "The rents and profits are not to be locked up, and made no use of. * * * The effect is only to invest them from time to time in land: so that the fund is not only in a constant course of accumulation, but also in a constant course of circulation."[2] Some have objected that because of limitations of trust investments, "there is not the same freedom of the use of such income in the economy in the hands of a the trustee as there would be in the hands of the trust beneficiaries."[3] Also, accumulations of income in a trust may allow huge fortunes to be amassed contrary to the law's policy against extreme inequality of wealth.[4] However, as with the Rule against Perpetuities itself, this problem can be dealt with by tax law.[5] Present law, for example, discourages accumulating income in a trust by taxing it at higher rates than those imposed on income distributed to beneficiaries.[6]

46. Metropolitan Transp. Auth. v. Bruken Realty Corp., 492 N.E.2d 379, 384 (N.Y.1986); Hartnett v. Jones, 629 P.2d 1357, 1363 (Wyo. 1981). *See also* Uniform Statutory Rule Against Perpetuities § 4, comment.

47. Baskin v. Commerce Union Bank, 715 S.W.2d 350, 352 (Tenn.App.1986).

§ 11.9

1. 32 Eng.Rep. 1030 (1805).

2. *Id.* at 1044. *See also* Macey, *Private Trusts for the Provision of Private Goods*, 37 Emory L.J. 295, 311 (1988).

3. *Restatement (Second) of Property (Donative Transfers)* § 2.2, comm. e (1983). *See also* Section 11.1, note 36 et seq.

4. *Restatement (Second) of Property (Donative Transfers)* § 2.2, comm. e (1983). In fact, Thelluson's trust grew far less than had been predicted, partly because of the costs of litigation. "The legal profession, mindful as always of the public weal, did its best to ensure that the accumulation did not exceed reasonable limits." W. Morris & W. Leach, *The Rule Against Perpetuities* 267 (2d ed. 1962).

5. See Section 11.1, at note 40 et seq.

6. Under Int.Rev.Code § 1 a married individual filing a joint return reaches the maximum rate (39.6%) at $250,000. The corresponding figure for trusts is only $7,500.

Even before the House of Lords rendered its decision upholding the Thelluson trust, Parliament passed a statute which prospectively imposed stringent time limits on accumulations.[7] Some American states followed suit,[8] but nearly all these American statutes have since been repealed. Commentators have generally condemned the statutes. The Thelluson Act "has proved to be one of the most difficult Acts on the Statute Book to apply. It has produced a vast mass of intricate case law" and "frustrates the quite reasonable dispositive schemes of settlors."[9] In criticizing a former New York statute, Professor Powell noted that "directions for the accumulation of income often serve desired and justifiable purposes ... It is often most unsuitable to have income of a trust fund accumulated until a child becomes twenty one,[10] and then to have the funds so accumulated dumped into the inexperienced hands of this child on his twenty-first birthday."[11]

Today virtually all states allow income to be accumulated in a trust for the period of the rule against perpetuities but no longer.[12] According to the Restatement an accumulation "is valid until the period of the rule * * * expires" and only "any accumulation thereafter is invalid." Any income released by the invalidity of the direction to accumulate is to be applied cy pres to effectuate the settlor's intent to the extent possible.[13] But a recent case, relying on a 19th century precedent, held that the direction to accumulate was void ab initio, and the income should pass intestate.[14]

Trusts which call for excessive accumulations usually also create contingent interests which violate the Rule. For example, a trust provided for paying 70% of the income to the settlor's daughter and 30% was to be accumulated; when the daughter died, or when her youngest child reached 23, whichever occurred last, the trust assets were to be distributed to the daughter's then living issue. Because of the possibility that the daughter might have an afterborn child, the trust violated both rules, but by modifying the trust so it would terminate when the daughter died, both the accumulation provision and the remainder were saved.[15] Probably no such modification of the trust would have been necessary under the second Restatement, which applies wait and see to accumulations.[16] However, a court recently refused to apply a "wait and see" statute to save a provision for accumulation in a trust.[17]

### *Presumption Against Accumulation*

The hostility of many courts to accumulation of income in a trust may affect construction of a trust. For example, a court construed an ambiguous

7. 39 & 40 Geo. 3, c. 98 (1800).

8. 6 *Amer. Law of Prop.* § 25.100; 5A R. Powell, *Real Property* ¶ 834.

9. Morris & Leach, *supra* note 4, at 304. *See also* L. Simes, *Public Policy and the Dead Hand* 100 (1955).

10. Even under the restrictive statutes, accumulation of income for a minor was permitted, since otherwise the income in excess of the minor's needs would have to be administered by a guardian.

11. Quoted in Will of Cheney, 379 N.Y.S.2d 346, 348 (Surr.1976).

12. *Restatement (Second) of Property (Donative Transfers)* § 2.2(1) (1983). *See also* In re Freeman's Estate, 404 P.2d 222 (Kan.1965); 6 *Amer. Law of Prop.* § 24.65.

13. *Restatement, Second, of Property (Donative Transfers)* § 2.2(3) (1983).

14. White v. Fleet Bank of Maine, 739 A.2d 373 (Me.1999).

15. In re Foster's Estate, 376 P.2d 784 (Kan.1962).

16. *Restatement, Second, of Property (Donative Transfers)* § 2.2(1) (1983).

17. White v. Fleet Bank of Maine, 739 A.2d 373, 380 (Me.1999).

trust as authorizing the trustee to distribute income rather than accumulating it because of "the general policy against accumulations."[18] Nevertheless, courts often find an implied direction to accumulate trust income. For example, a direction to pay the testator's grandchildren as much income as was needed for their support was held to imply that income in excess of their needs should be accumulated.[19]

### *Charitable Trusts*

An accumulation in a charitable trust can continue beyond the period of the Rule against Perpetuities.[20] This is justified by the social utility of charities, and the thought that gifts to charity will be encouraged if prospective givers can determine the details of the gift.[21] Also, the common-law rule based on measuring lives makes little sense in a charitable trust.

Courts will not allow an "unreasonable" accumulation even in a charitable trust. A settlor who believed that endowments for government could replace taxation created a trust to accumulate income for 500 years; in the year 2444 the principal and accumulated income was to go to the state of Pennsylvania. This was held to be "unreasonable, contrary to public policy, and void."[22] Other courts have simply whittled down directions for excessive accumulation. A trust to accumulate income until the funds were large enough to build a 40–bed rest home was modified by reducing the size of the rest home so as to allow an earlier distribution.[23]

It is not easy to predict when courts will find a provision for accumulation is "unreasonable." One court upheld a trust which required 25% of the income to be accumulated *forever*.[24] A reasonable purpose for an accumulation, such as a desire to have funds adequate for a project, is relevant.[25] Views of what is reasonable may alter as conditions change. When "continued accumulation no longer furthers the purpose of the trust" courts may order it to cease.[26]

**18.** Matter of Trust Estate of Daoang, 953 P.2d 959, 968 (Haw.App.1998). *See also* Rogerson v. Wheeling Dollar Sav. & Trust Co., 222 S.E.2d 816 (W.Va.1976); Matter of Estate of Krebs, 483 A.2d 919 (Pa.Super.1984).

**19.** Will of Cheney, 379 N.Y.S.2d 346, 348 (Surr.1976). *See also* Godfrey v. Chandley, 811 P.2d 1248 (Kan.1991); Jones v. Heritage Pullman Bank & Trust Co., 518 N.E.2d 178 (Ill. App.1987) (income in excess of annuity).

**20.** *Restatement (Second) of Property (Donative Transfers)* § 2.2(2) (1983); Estate of Puckett, 168 Cal.Rptr. 311 (App.1980); Matter of Booker, 682 P.2d 320 (Wash.App.1984).

**21.** *Restatement of Property* § 442, comm. a (1944).

**22.** Trusts of Holdeen, 403 A.2d 978 (Pa. 1979). *See also Restatement (Second) of Property (Donative Transfers)* § 2.2(2) (1983).

**23.** Matter of Booker, 682 P.2d 320 (Wash. App.1984).

**24.** Mercantile Trust Co. Nat. Ass'n v. Shriners' Hosp., 551 S.W.2d 864 (Mo.App. 1977).

**25.** In re James' Estate, 199 A.2d 275, 279 (Pa.1964). *But see* note 23.

**26.** Mercantile Trust Co. Nat. Ass'n v. Shriners' Hosp., 551 S.W.2d 864, 868 (Mo.App. 1977). *See also Restatement of Property* § 442, comm. a (1944).

# Chapter 12

# PROBATE AND ADMINISTRATION

*Analysis*



## § 12.1 Probate

A will may be contested, *e.g.* on the ground that the testator lacked capacity, or was subject to undue influence, or the will failed to satisfy the formal requirements imposed by the law. The court which hears such challenges in most states is called the probate court, from the Latin *probare,* to prove. However, the general trend is to unify the various courts under one head. In California, for example, the "Superior Court" has jurisdiction under the Probate Code over the administration of decedents' estates, thus rejecting "the [heretofore existing] limitations on the powers of the probate court ... while preserving the division of business among different departments of the superior court."[1]

### *Necessity for Probate*

Until a will is admitted to probate, it has no legal effect. Thus when a widower seeking custody of his stepchild tried to introduce the will of the child's mother nominating him as guardian, the court refused to consider the will because it had never been admitted to probate. "Without probate, no determination of testamentary capacity, freedom from undue influence, or due execution have been made."[2] These issues could not be resolved by the court in the custody proceedings.

The notion that only a specialized "probate" court can determine the validity of a will goes back to the time when there were many courts each

**§ 12.1**

1. Cal.Prob.Code § 7050.

2. Matter of Guardianship and Conservatorship of Slemp, 717 P.2d 519, 521 (Kan.App. 1986). *See also* Ohio Rev.Code § 2107.61; Mass.Ann.Laws c. 191 § 7; Simes, *The Function of Will Contests,* 44 Mich.L.Rev. 503, 512 (1946); 3 *Amer. Law of Prop.* § 14.36.

with limited competence. Jurisdiction over wills of personal property belonged to the ecclesiastical courts, the ancestor of today's probate court. They had no jurisdiction over land, and so wills of land were not probated; their validity was determined in ordinary actions to try title, such as ejectment.[3] The will of a person who died in England before 1857 was probated in an ecclesiastical court, but probate had no effect on any devise of land in the will; an heir could assert that the will was invalid even though it had been probated.[4]

Having two courts pass on the validity of the same will made no sense.[5] In keeping with the modern trend to assimilate the rules for land and personal property, a statute of 1857 made the probate of a will, or a decree that a will was invalid, binding as to all the testator's property.[6] The assimilation of land and personal property might have been accomplished in the opposite way, *i.e.* by abolishing probate altogether, and having the validity of wills tried in any court whenever it became relevant in a proceeding.[7] Other forms of transfer are so handled. If person conveys a home by deed, no probate of the deed is necessary. Why then should the beneficiaries of a *will* have to establish its validity in special court proceedings? Why not wait and see if anyone complains and decide the matter then?

Relatively few wills are contested,[8] but the probate system may actually promote efficiency. Since a will often affects many persons, it could give rise to many lawsuits between heirs and devisees, whereas a single probate proceeding binds them all. "A will contest is a proceeding in rem, the res being the estate of the deceased ... The principle ... is to determine in one proceeding ... who is entitled to inherit the property."[9]

### *Multi-State Probate*

Because probate is an *in rem* proceeding, a decree admitting a will to probate binds persons who live in other states, assuming the court has jurisdiction.[10] A will can be probated either in the state where the testator was domiciled at death or where assets of the testator are located.[11] For example, a Wisconsin court had jurisdiction to probate the will of a testator who was domiciled in Arizona because he owned property in Wisconsin.[12]

Determinations of domicile can be problematic. Was a decedent who had been residing in a nursing home for 8 years when he died domiciled in the county where the nursing home was located? No, because there was no evidence that he had intended to abandon his domicile in the place where his will stated that he was domiciled.[13] Is a court's decision as to where a decedent

3. *Id.* § 14.35; Simes, *supra* note 2, at 506.

4. Ash v. Calvert, 170 Eng.Rep. 1193 (1810).

5. However, as we shall see, something similar can happen today when a testator has property in different states. See notes infra.

6. Statute, 1857, 20 & 21 Vict. c. 77, § 62.

7. A commission had so recommended in 1836. Simes, *supra* note 2, at 510.

8. "Will contests rarely occur, perhaps on the order of one in a hundred or so cases." Schoenblum, *Will Contests: An Empirical Study*, 22 Real Prop. Prob. and Trust J. 607, 614 (1987).

9. Green v. Higdon, 891 S.W.2d 220, 222 (Tenn.App.1994).

10. 3 *Amer. Law of Prop.* § 14.37, at 720.

11. *Restatement (Second) of Conflict of Laws* § 314 (1971); Scoles & Hay, *Conflict of Laws* §§ 22.1–.2 (2d ed. 1992); Uniform Probate Code § 3–201(a).

12. Matter of Estate of Warner, 468 N.W.2d 736 (Wis.App.1991).

13. Matter of Estate of Brown, 587 N.E.2d 686, 690 (Ind.App.1992). *See also* Le Sueur v. Robinson, 557 N.E.2d 796 (Ohio App.1988); Matter of Estate of Burshiem, 483 N.W.2d 175 (N.D.1992) (trial court's finding of domicile

was domiciled binding on other courts? Yes, at least as to persons who were parties to the first proceeding.[14] If proceedings are commenced in two states involving inconsistent claims of domicile, the court in which proceedings were later instituted generally stays them until the question of domicile is resolved.[15]

The location of property, the second basis of probate jurisdiction, can also be unclear. An Oregon court refused to probate the will of a testator domiciled in Massachusetts on the basis of a note which the testator held secured by a mortgage on Oregon land; because the note was personal property, its situs was the decedent's domicile.[16] But the Uniform Probate Code says that debts evidenced by paper are located where "where the instrument is."[17]

Even though probate operates in rem, proceedings in two states may be necessary,[18] and they may reach different outcomes. For example, the heirs of a woman whose will had been probated in Florida were allowed to contest her will in Kentucky where she owned land. "A contest of a foreign will in another state, where the real estate affected by the will is located, does not violate full faith and credit required under the Federal Constitution."[19] The result might have been different if the dispute had involved personal property, or if the contestants had been served in the Florida proceedings.[20] Some states recognize foreign probate decrees even as to local land. The Uniform Probate Code makes a final order determining testacy by a court of the decedent's domicile determinative elsewhere.[21] According to the comment, this "adds nothing to existing law as applied to cases where the parties ... were also personally before the local court," but it "extends present law" in cases involving "local land." California has a similar provision for wills established in a foreign country, except one which does not "provide impartial tribunals" or "due process of law."[22] Both California and the UPC provisions apply only if the other probate was in the state of the decedent's domicile,[23] and only if all interested persons were given notice and an opportunity to contest the will.[24]

reversed for failure to give weight to recital in decedent's will). Similar questions arise with respect to choice of law insofar as it depends on domicile. See Section 1.2, at note 44 et seq.

**14.** In re Estate of Tolson, 947 P.2d 1242 (Wash.App.1997); *Restatement (Second) of Conflict of Laws* § 317(4) (1971).

**15.** Uniform Probate Code § 3–202; Collins v. Truman, 783 P.2d 813 (Ariz.App.1989) (Arizona proceedings stayed because Pennsylvania proceedings preceded them).

**16.** West v. White, 758 P.2d 424, 426 (Or. App.1988).

**17.** Uniform Probate Code § 3–201(d). See also Section 1.2, at note 32 et seq.

**18.** Cooper v. Tosco Corp., Lion Oil Div., 613 S.W.2d 831 (Ark.1981) (probate in Louisiana not effective as to Arkansas land).

**19.** Marr v. Hendrix, 952 S.W.2d 693, 695 (Ky.1997). *See also* Estate of Reed, 768 P.2d 566 (Wyo.1989); In re Roberg's Estate, 396 So.2d 235 (Fla.App.1981).

**20.** Estate of Waitzman, 507 So.2d 24 (Miss.1987) (contest of will probated in Florida not permitted because personal property involved); *Restatement, Second, Conflict of Laws* § 317 (1971).

**21.** Uniform Prob.Code § 3–408.

**22.** Cal.Prob.Code §§ 12522–23.

**23.** In re Estate of Stein, 896 P.2d 740 (Wash.App.1995) (Oregon probate binding only as to assets in Oregon, since decedent was domiciled in Washington); Matter of Reed's Estate, 664 P.2d 824 (Kan.1983) (probate in Indiana no bar to contest in Kansas where testator resided).

**24.** In re Estate of Farley, 397 N.W.2d 409 (Minn.App.1986) (Texas probate decree not binding when only "posted courthouse notice given").

### *Notice of Probate*

Historically, there were two forms of probate, "common" in which no notice to the testator's heirs was given, and "solemn" which did require notice. This dual system still prevails in many states.[25] The Georgia Code, for instance, provides that "the probate of a will may be in either common or solemn form." Common form probate occurs "without notice to anyone" and "is not conclusive upon anyone" until four years have elapsed. Solemn form probate, on the other hand, "requires due notice to all the heirs of the testator" and "is conclusive upon all parties notified."[26] The Uniform Probate Code provides similar options, but uses the terms "informal" and "formal" to describe them.[27] Orders in formal proceedings are "final as to all persons,"[28] whereas wills which have been informally probated may be contested for 12 months thereafter or up to 3 years after the decedent's death, whichever is later.[29] Even if a will is informally probated, the personal representative must notify the heirs after the appointment.[30]

Some state courts have held that any probate of a will without notice to the heirs which limits their right to contest the will is an unconstitutional denial of due process. Notice by publication suffices as to heirs who are not reasonably ascertainable, such as a distant relative whom the decedent had never mentioned,[31] but not as to heirs whose identity is known to the executor of the will.[32] Other courts have rejected the due process argument on the basis that heirs have a "mere expectancy" which is "not entitled to constitutional protection,"[33] but this was said of a statute which allowed a probated will to be contested for 5 months after the decree was entered. A statute which purported to make a probate decree immediately binding without prior notice to affected ascertainable heirs would probably be held invalid.

Although informal probate is not immediately conclusive, it has legal consequences other than triggering a limitation period. One who deals with the executor under an informally probated will in good faith, *e.g.* purchases property of the estate, is protected even if the probate of the will is later set aside.[34] A critic has argued that informal probate allows "a clean out of estate assets at the expense of creditors and beneficiaries" by the proponents of an invalid will.[35] But the drafters of the Uniform Probate Code retained informal probate because it had been proved satisfactory by "accumulated experience." They feared that people would avoid probate altogether if it was made "more awkward than non-probate alternatives which are freely available" such as joint tenancy.[36] In order to deter "misuse [of] the no-notice feature of informal

**25.** Chaffin & Barwick, *The Probate and Establishment of Domestic and Foreign Wills,* 13 Ga.L.Rev. 133, 141 (1978).

**26.** Ga.Code Ann. §§ 53-5-15-53-5-22.

**27.** Uniform Prob.Code §§ 3-301, 3-401.

**28.** Uniform Probate Code § 3-412; Matter of Estate of Gaines, 830 P.2d 569 (N.M.App. 1992) (proponent bound by order in formal proceeding finding will invalid).

**29.** Uniform Probate Code § 3-108(a)(3); Vieira v. Estate of Cantu, 940 P.2d 190 (N.M.App.1997) (informally probated will may be challenged as being made under undue influence).

**30.** Uniform Probate Code § 3-705.

**31.** Matter of Estate of Daily, 555 N.W.2d 254 (Iowa App.1996).

**32.** Estate of Beck v. Engene, 557 N.W.2d 270 (Iowa 1996).

**33.** Matter of Estate of Wilson, 610 N.E.2d 851, 858 (Ind.App.1993).

**34.** Ky.R.S. § 395.330; Cal.Prob.Code § 8272(b).

**35.** Parker, *No-Notice Probate and Non-Intervention Administration under the Code,* 2 Conn.L.Rev. 546, 556 (1970).

**36.** Wellman, *The Uniform Probate Code: Blueprint for Reform in the 70's,* 2 Conn.L.Rev. 453, 497-99 (1970).

proceedings," applicants must file a verified statement that they believe that the will being offered was validly executed and was the decedent's last will.[37] The rules of professional conduct provide a sanction against abuse by lawyers. A lawyer who filed a will for probate without disclosing the existence of a later will was suspended from practice for violating the Code of Professional Responsibility. "All judges regularly rely on the candor, honesty and integrity of the lawyer in handling ex parte matters which are presented to them ... Judges must be able to rely on the integrity of the lawyer."[38]

### *Will Contests*

Some states allow wills to be contested even after they have been probated with notice to the heirs. In Ohio, for example, a will which has been probated can be contested for up to four months. In such a contest the probate decree is only "prima facie evidence" that the will is valid.[39] Professor Simes calls this "a procedural anomaly." Legislators who allow this "appear to have lost sight of the only reason justifying a contest after probate, the absence of notice and the summary character of the first probate."[40]

Allowing wills which have been probated to be contested may reflect lack of confidence in probate judges,[41] who in some states are lay persons, whereas will contests take place in a court of general jurisdiction.[42] Under the Uniform Probate Code informal probate is handled by a Registrar, who is not necessarily a judge,[43] whereas formal testacy proceedings are heard by a judge who has "the same qualifications as a judge of the court of general jurisdiction."[44]

The ecclesiastical courts which probated wills of personal property did not use jury trial, whereas devises of land were tried in actions at law in which juries were used.[45] Most courts hold today that state constitutional provisions preserving the right to jury trial do not apply to will contests.[46] Nevertheless, many states provide for jury trial in will contests.[47] In others jury trial is discretionary, or the verdict is only advisory.[48]

Some commentators suggest that juries in will contests are "more disposed to work equity for the disinherited" than to follow the law.[49] Professor Schoenblum's empirical study suggested that "whether judgment was reached by a judge or jury, it was more likely than not to be in favor of the proponent" of the will, but jury trials "appear to improve materially the [contestants']

**37.** Uniform Probate Code § 3–301, comment.

**38.** In re Conduct of Hedrick, 822 P.2d 1187, 1190 (Or.1991). *See also* Cincinnati Bar Ass'n v. Lowery, 567 N.E.2d 1038 (Ohio 1991); Model Rules of Professional Conduct 3.3(d) (in ex parte proceedings "a lawyer shall inform the tribunal of all material facts known to the lawyer").

**39.** Ohio Rev.Code §§ 2107.71, 2107.76.

**40.** Simes, *supra* note 2, at 561. *See also* Chaffin & Barwick, *The Probate and Establishment of Domestic and Foreign Wills,* 13 Ga. L.Rev. 133, 147 (1978).

**41.** *Ibid.*

**42.** Simes, *supra* note 2, at 541; Mo.Rev. Stat. § 473.083(5).

**43.** Uniform Prob.Code §§ 1–307, 3–301.

**44.** *Id.* §§ 1–309, 3–401.

**45.** Brooke v. Warde, 73 Eng.Rep. 702 (1573).

**46.** Rantru v. Unger, 700 P.2d 272 (Or. App.1985); Petition of Atkins, 493 A.2d 1203 (N.H.1985); State ex rel. Kear v. Court of Common Pleas, 423 N.E.2d 427 (Ohio 1981); Matter of Suesz' Estate, 613 P.2d 947 (Kan.1980); In re Shaughnessy's Estate, 648 P.2d 427 (Wash.1982).

**47.** Mo.Rev.Stat. § 473.083(7); Matter of Estate of Ruther, 631 P.2d 1330, 1332 (N.M.App.1981).

**48.** Uniform Prob.Code § 1–306(b).

**49.** Langbein, *Living Probate: The Conservatorship Model,* 77 Mich.L.Rev. 63, 65 (1978).

chances for success."[50] This is sometimes advanced as a reason for the use of will substitutes.

### *Time Limits on Contest*

The time limits for contest of a probated will are typically quite short, *e.g.* Ohio allows only four months from the date of probate.[51] These short limitations provide a counter argument to the common advice to avoid probate in order to minimize the risk of a successful contest. "If circumstances suggest the possibilities of such a contest, the commencement of probate proceedings is advisable to bar the right of contest[52]." Some statutes provide comparable short limits to contests of living trusts. Under the Uniform Trust Code, for example, contests of a revocable trust after the settlor dies can be barred after 120 days by a notice from the trustee of the time allowed for contest, accompanied by a copy of the trust instrument.[53]

Some courts allow an untimely contest in cases of fraud. For example, the proponent of a will sent a notice of probate to the testator's heirs, but told their mother that "everything was fine—-he and the lawyer were handling the matter, and the boys' interests were well represented." He neglected to tell her that the will being probated gave him most of the estate. The court set aside the probate even though the statutory period for will contests had expired, because of the proponent's "extrinsic fraud," defined as fraud which prevents a party "from presenting all of his case to the court."[54] The Uniform Probate Code allows relief "whenever fraud has been perpetrated in connection with any proceeding" under the Code, if proceedings are brought within 2 years of discovery of the fraud.[55]

Some courts give contestants relief on a tort or constructive trust theory after the time for contest is over. For example, a court allowed an heir to sue the beneficiaries of a will for "tortious interference * * * and fraud, and undue influence in procuring the will," rejecting the objection that this was "collateral attack" on a duly probated will after the time for contest had expired. The statute of limitations for actions for tortious interference with a bequest began to run only when the tort was discovered.[56] Other courts have held that tort claims "alleging improper conduct concerning [a] will" are precluded by a probate decree,[57] or have rejected them on the ground that a will contest provides an adequate remedy for the plaintiff's claim.[58]

**50.** Schoenblum, *supra* note 8, at 626–27.

**51.** Ohio Rev.Code § 2107.76.

**52.** Parks, *Varied Duties Face the Successor Trustee of a Revocable Trust*, 19 Est.Plann. 203, 206 (1992).

**53.** Unif.Trust Code § 604(a)(2). *See also* Cal.Prob.Code § 16061.8.

**54.** Estate of Sanders, 710 P.2d 232 (Cal. 1985). *See also* Anderson v. Marquette Nat. Bank, 518 N.E.2d 196 (Ill.App.1987); Carrell v. Ellingwood, 423 N.E.2d 630 (Ind.App.1981). *But cf.* Rush v. Rush, 360 So.2d 1240 (Miss. 1978) (assurances to heir that she would be "taken care of" did not estop devisee from asserting bar to contest); Matter of Estate of Taylor, 675 P.2d 944 (Mont.1984) (no untimely probate on ground of estoppel; devisee's only remedy is to sue heir).

**55.** Uniform Probate Code § 1–106.

**56.** Barone v. Barone, 294 S.E.2d 260 (W.Va.1982). *But see* Robinson v. First State Bank, 454 N.E.2d 288, 294 (Ill.1983). A tort suit can be based on undue influence, but not on the testator's incapacity. Griffin v. Baucom, 328 S.E.2d 38 (N.C.App.1985).

**57.** Hadley v. Cowan, 804 P.2d 1271, 1276 (Wash.App.1991). *See also* Jurgensen v. Haslinger, 692 N.E.2d 347 (Ill.App.1998) (no tort action lies against witnesses who allegedly testified falsely in probate proceedings).

**58.** Minton v. Sackett, 671 N.E.2d 160 (Ind. App.1996); Geduldig v. Posner, 743 A.2d 247, 257 (Md.App.1999).

It is possible at least in some states to use a tort rationale to recover punitive damages for an attempt to probate a false will. For example, a wife who was found to have forged her husband's name to a will and a power of attorney was held liable, together with her attorney and a witness to the "will," for punitive damages. The court cited the Restatement of Torts which gives an action inter alia for forging a will. "On a showing in a tort action that a defendant acted wilfully, maliciously, fraudulently, or with gross negligence, there may be a recovery of exemplary damages, in addition to compensatory damages."[59]

Expiration of the time limit on will contests does not bar raising questions of will construction,[60] or even claims that a will provision is invalid on policy grounds.[61] A claim that a devise to the testator's spouse was revoked by divorce was held not covered by the limit on contests,[62] but another court held that a claim that the testator's marriage revoked the will was barred.[63]

Courts are divided as to whether an attempt to probate a later-discovered after an earlier one has been probated amounts to a "contest" of the prior will within the meaning of the time limit.[64] The Uniform Probate Code allows even a formal testacy order to be modified if proponents of a later will show that "they were unaware of its existence at the time of the earlier proceeding."[65] In California the later will may be admitted to probate, but it cannot "affect property previously distributed."[66]

### *Ante-Mortem Probate*

Courts generally refuse to determine the validity of a will while the testator is alive.[67] Many have argued that such determinations should be permitted so that the testator's capacity can be better evaluated by the fact finder.[68] The question may become moot if the testator later revokes the will or dies without an estate, but declaratory judgments of issues which may become moot are generally permitted if the potential benefits of a decision outweigh the costs.[69] Three states have enacted statutes allowing ante-mortem probate.[70]

These statutes require that all "the testator's present intestate successors" shall be made parties.[71] These may not turn out to be the testator's heirs, *e.g.* if another child is born thereafter. But often the testators "present heirs" would have the same interest with respect to a will as those in being at

**59.** King v. Acker, 725 S.W.2d 750, 755 (Tex.App.1987).

**60.** Matter of Estate of Worsham, 859 P.2d 1134 (Okl.App.1993).

**61.** Hall v. Eaton, 631 N.E.2d 805, 807 (Ill.App.1994).

**62.** In re Marriage of Duke, 549 N.E.2d 1096, 1101 (Ind.App.1990).

**63.** Martin v. Kenworthy, 759 P.2d 335 (Or.App.1988).

**64.** *Compare* Coussee v. Estate of Efston, 633 N.E.2d 815 (Ill.App.1994) *with* In re Will of Fields, 570 So.2d 1202 (Miss.1990); Matter of Estate of Brown, 587 N.E.2d 686, 690 (Ind. App.1992).

**65.** Uniform Prob.Code § 3–412(a)(1).

**66.** Cal.Prob.Code § 8226(b).

**67.** Burcham v. Burcham, 1 P.3d 756 (Colo. App.2000); Conservatorship of Bookasta, 265 Cal.Rptr. 1 (App.1989) (determination of invalidity reversed); Lawver v. Lawvor, 740 P.2d 1220 (Or.App.1987).

**68.** Fink, *Ante-Mortem Probate Revisited*, 37 Ohio St.L.J. 264, 266 (1978); Langbein, *supra* note 49, at 67.

**69.** Fink, *supra* note 68, at 278–79.

**70.** N.D.Code § 30.1–081; Ohio Rev.Code § 2107.081; Ark.Code § 28–40–201.

**71.** N.D.Code § 30.1–08.1–02. *See also* Ohio Rev.Code § 2107.081(A); Ark.Code § 28–40–202(b).

the testator's death. The Uniform Probate Code as to litigation after the testator's death allows unborn or unascertained persons to be bound by a decree "to the extent that [their] interest is adequately represented by another party having a substantially identical interest;" if this is not possible, a guardian ad litem may be appointed to represent them.[72]

The North Dakota and Ohio statutes imply that a finding *against* a will in ante-mortem probate proceedings would be "admissible", but not binding if the will were again offered for probate after the testator dies.[73] It seems unfair that a decree favorable to the contestants has less effect than one for the proponents of a will. But even if an adjudication of invalidity were made binding, the testator could circumvent it by executing a new will or by disposing of the estate by non-probate transfers. Conversely, heirs might be able to contest a will which had been declared valid on the ground that the testator was later prevented from revoking it by undue influence.[74]

Despite its potential advantages, ante-mortem probate raises many problems. Many testators do not want to disclose the contents of their will during their lifetime, but a proceeding to approve a will would be unfair unless the contents were revealed since they may constitute relevant evidence.[75] The existing statutes do not allow heirs to institute proceedings for a declaration that a will is invalid.[76] Use of ante-mortem probate even in states that allow it does not appear to be common.

### *Binding Effect on Persons not Sui Juris*

Heirs under disability often get additional time to file a contest. In Ohio, for example, probate of a will becomes binding after four months "except as to persons under any legal disability" who are allowed "four months after such disability is removed."[77] This may leave the disposition of an estate in doubt for a considerable time. The Uniform Probate Code circumvents this problem by providing for binding parties non sui juris by representation. For example, orders against a trustee in probate proceedings bind the trust beneficiaries "to the extent that there is no conflict of interest between them."[78] The Code also facilitates compromise of controversies concerning wills by providing for court approval thereof,[79] which makes the agreement binding even on persons "unborn, unascertained or who could not be located." Minor children can be bound by the agreement of their parents. Where the interests of children and

**72.** Uniform Probate Code § 1–403. *See also* Estate of Mayfield v. Estate of Mayfield, 680 N.E.2d 784, 787 (Ill.App.1997) (children bound by their parent's agreement not to contest will).

**73.** N.D.Code § 30.1–08.1–04; Ohio Rev. Code § 2107.085. Apparently a finding of invalidity in Arkansas would have no effect. Ark. Code § 28–40–203 speaks only of findings of validity.

**74.** Fellows, *The Case Against Living Probate*, 78 Mich.L.Rev. 1066, 1080, 1095 (1978).

**75.** Fink, *supra* note 68, at 290. As to the relevance of the "naturalness" of will provisions in determinations of incapacity and undue influence see Sections 7.1, at note 27 et seq.

**76.** Corron v. Corron, 531 N.E.2d 708 (Ohio 1988).

**77.** Ohio Rev.Code § 2107.76. *See also* 58 Okl.Stat. § 67; N.C.Gen.Stat. § 31–32.

**78.** Uniform Probate Code § 1–403(2). *See also* Fifth Third Bank v. Fifth Third Bank, 602 N.E.2d 325, 328 (Ohio App.1991). *But cf.* Schlosser v. Schlosser, 578 N.E.2d 1203 (Ill. App.1991) (default judgment against trustee not binding on beneficiaries who were not made parties).

**79.** An agreement between persons sui juris does not require court approval. Matter of Estate of Grimm, 784 P.2d 1238 (Utah App. 1989). However, oral agreements are not effective. Estate of Webster, 920 S.W.2d 600 (Mo. App.1996).

parents conflict, the agreement may be approved by a guardian ad litem for the children.[80] The court before approving an agreement must find that its effect on persons "represented by fiduciaries or other representatives is just and reasonable."[81]

### *Time Limits on Probate*

Time limits on *contesting* a probated will should not be confused with the time within which a will must be probated after the testator dies. A will which was discovered 5 years after the testator died could not be probated under the Uniform Probate Code which requires that probate proceedings be commenced within three years of the testator's death, regardless of when the will is discovered.[82] Another statute barring probate of a will more than three years after the testator died was held to render void a probate decree entered after that period, even though the decree was not contested within the period allowed for contests, on the theory that "when an order admitting a will to probate is void on its face, it may be attacked at any time."[83]

Some states, on the other hand, allow a will to be probated at any time. An Oklahoma court allowed a will to be probated 12 years after the testator died; Kansas, where the testator died, would not have allowed it, but Oklahoma had no time limitation and the law of the situs was controlling.[84]

Delay in probating a will may mislead third parties. Many statutes protect bona fide purchasers or mortgagees from an heir if a will is not probated or recorded within a specified time after the testator's death.[85] Courts have upheld the rights of bona fide purchasers in this situation even without a statute.[86] Even before a long time has elapsed, court proceedings based on the assumption that a person died intestate may lead purchasers to think that his heirs have title. Under the Uniform Probate Code a will cannot be probated after a court enters a decree of distribution to the heirs,[87] but this is not the case in all states.[88]

### *Standing*

In order to discourage "strike" suits by persons seeking to extract money by threatening costly litigation, courts allow wills to be contested only by

**80.** In re Estate of Truhn, 394 N.W.2d 864 (Minn.App.1986).

**81.** Uniform Probate Code §§ 1–1101–1102. *See also* Hunter v. Newsom, 468 S.E.2d 802, 807 (N.C.App.1996) (denying approval to settlement as "unfair to the remainder interests of the unborn and unknown heir").

**82.** Matter of Estate of Wood, 710 P.2d 476 (Ariz.App.1985). *See also* Martin v. Martin, 883 P.2d 673 (Haw.App.1994); Matter of Estate of Thompson, 962 P.2d 564 (Kan.App.1997). *But cf.* Matter of Estate of McGrew, 906 S.W.2d 53 (Tex.App.1995) (5 year limit on probate not applicable when proponent not "in default" for not offering it earlier).

**83.** In re Estate of Troxel, 720 N.E.2d 731 (Ind.App.1999).

**84.** Mitchell v. Cloyes, 620 P.2d 398 (Okl. 1980). *See also* In re Estate of Schafroth, 598 N.E.2d 479 (Ill.App.1992) (will probated 8 years after testator died).

**85.** N.C.Stat. § 31–39; Ohio Rev.Code § 2107.47; Kan.Stat. § 59–618. In Cooper v. Tosco Corp., Lion Oil Div., 613 S.W.2d 831 (Ark.1981), a similar statute was held to protect a purchaser from an heir even though he was not *bona fide*.

**86.** Thomas v. Harper, 218 S.E.2d 832 (Ga. 1975); Eckland v. Jankowski, 95 N.E.2d 342 (Ill.1950).

**87.** Matter of Estate of Chasel, 725 P.2d 1345 (Utah 1986), based on Uniform Prob. Code § 3–412(3)(i). *See also* In re Estate of Killinger, 448 So.2d 1187 (Fla.App.1984).

**88.** Gross v. Slye, 360 So.2d 333 (Ala.1978); Matter of Estate of Cornelius, 465 N.E.2d 1033 (Ill.App.1984); 3 *Amer. Law of Prop.* § 14.39, at 733.

persons with a financial interest in the contest. For example, a contest by the testator's grandchild was dismissed on the ground that she was not a "person interested;" she was not an heir, since the testator's children had survived him. An earlier will of the testator, which the will she challenged had revoked, would only have given her income in the discretion of the executor, "a mere expectancy, not a legally ascertainable right."[89] A devisee under an earlier will has standing to contest a later one,[90] but not if both wills leave her the same amount.[91] The testator's heirs may have standing, even if the testator left more than one will disinheriting them.[92] But one court rejected a contest by an heir.

> That there had been previous wills of the decedent which also excluded appellant was not by itself necessarily determinative of her lack of standing as an heir at law to contest the will ... But when an at least facially valid previous will is before the court, the burden is on the potential heir at law who wishes to contest a will to show that the previous will which excluded the contestant was invalid .. [93]

Sometimes courts hold a preliminary hearing to determine whether a contestant has standing.[94]

The state can contest the will of a testator who died without relatives in order to claim an escheat.[95] Courts are split on the question whether creditors of an heir can contest a will if the heir does not. Professor Hirsch suggests that this should depend on whether the state allows heirs to disclaim over the objection of their creditors.[96] An heir's right to contest a will survives and passes to his heirs or devisees.[97]

An heir who accepts devised property or appointment as a fiduciary is estopped from contesting the will.[98]

Fiduciaries have been held to have standing to contest wills in some cases but not in others. John Paul Getty's will left his estate to trustees for a

**89.** Martone v. Martone, 509 S.E.2d 302, 306 (Va.1999). *See also* Taylor v. Estate of Taylor, 770 P.2d 163 (Utah App.1989) (testator's brother has no standing since he was not his heir); York v. Nunley, 610 N.E.2d 576 (Ohio App.1992) (child raised but not adopted by testator).

**90.** Spicer v. Estate of Spicer, 935 S.W.2d 576 (Ark.App.1996); Estate of Malcolm, 602 N.E.2d 41 (Ill.App.1992); Estate of Auen, 35 Cal.Rptr.2d 557 (App.1994).

**91.** Miller v. Todd, 447 S.E.2d 9 (W.Va. 1994).

**92.** In re Estate of Powers, 106 N.W.2d 833 (Mich.1961); Rienhardt v. Kelly, 917 P.2d 963 (N.M.App.1996).

**93.** Cates v. Fricker, 529 So.2d 1253 (Fla. App.1988).

**94.** Jones v. LaFargue, 758 S.W.2d 320, 323 (Tex.App.1988); Estate of Lind, 257 Cal.Rptr. 853, 858 (App.1989).

**95.** In re Moll's Estate, 495 P.2d 854 (Ariz. App.1972); Matter of Estate of Barnhart, 339 N.W.2d 28 (Mich.App.1983).

**96.** Hirsch, *The Problem of the Insolvent Heir*, 74 Cornell L.Rev. 587, 645–51 (1989); *cf.* In re Bentley, 120 B.R 712 (Bktcy S.D.N.Y. 1990) (heir's trustee in bankruptcy has standing to contest will but refused to do so because no basis for a contest); Matter of Estate of Oelberg, 414 N.W.2d 672 (Iowa App.1987) (judgment creditor of devisee can challenge appointment of executor).

**97.** Sheldone v. Marino, 501 N.E.2d 504 (Mass.1986); Kinsella v. Landa, 600 S.W.2d 104 (Mo.App.1980). *But see* In re Estate of Davis, 467 N.E.2d 402 (Ill.App.1984) (right to contest is not assignable inter-vivos); Matter of Will of Calhoun, 267 S.E.2d 385 (N.C.App.1980) (legatee of legatee cannot contest later will); Matter of Estate of Pearson, 319 N.W.2d 248 (Iowa 1982) (heir's wife cannot contest will).

**98.** Matter of Estate of Joffe, 493 N.E.2d 70 (Ill.App.1986); Marine v. Johnson, 437 A.2d 694 (Md.App.1981); Matter of Estate of McDaniel, 935 S.W.2d 827 (Tex.App.1996). In In re Beglinger Trust, 561 N.W.2d 130 (Mich. App.1997), the court applied a similar rule to one who had accepted benefits from a trust and then sought to challenge its validity.

museum. A later codicil eliminated the trust and left the residue directly to the museum. A trustee designated in the will was not permitted to challenge, since the codicil did not affect the beneficial interest of the museum. The wish to manage the trust and receive trustee's fees did not give her standing.[99] However, personal representatives have been allowed to contest a will on behalf of the heirs or beneficiaries of an earlier will.[100] But the Uniform Probate Code does not allow executors to seek probate of a will if all the devisees object.[101] Trustees have been denied standing to appeal an order determining the rights of beneficiaries inter se because of their duty to deal impartially with all beneficiaries.[102]

### *Attorney's Fees*

A successful contestant of a will may recover attorneys' fees from the estate. Normally in the United States the prevailing party in a lawsuit does not recover attorney fees absent a special provision therefor, but if attorney fees were not paid from the estate, distributees who benefited from the contest without participating in it would be unjustly enriched.[103]

The Uniform Probate Code allows personal representatives to be reimbursed for attorney fees from the estate for any proceeding prosecuted or defended "in good faith" regardless of the outcome.[104] Many states have similar statutes, under which even if a will is rejected, the proponent can be reimbursed for attorney fees.[105] Some courts deny attorney fees to an executor who tried to probate a will which was rejected for undue influence on the ground that this "imports a finding of bad faith."[106] Some courts deny fees for attorneys hired by beneficiaries as distinguished from a personal representative,[107] but the fact that an executor was also a beneficiary did not preclude his recovery of fees.[108]

**99.** Matter of Estate of Getty, 149 Cal.Rptr. 656 (App.1978). *But see* Arrowsmith v. Mercantile–Safe Deposit, 545 A.2d 674, 677 (Md.1988) (trustee's loss of commissions from will construction gives him standing to appeal).

**100.** Toon v. Gerth, 735 N.E.2d 314, 320 (Ind.App.2000) (executor of earlier will); Matter of Estate of Beal, 769 P.2d 150, 152 (Okl. 1989); Matter of Estate of Campbell, 673 P.2d 645, 649 (Wyo.1983). *But see* Matter of Reed's Estate, 664 P.2d 824, 833 (Kan.1983) (administrator has no standing).

**101.** Uniform Prob.Code § 3–720, comment. *See also* Matter of Estate of Wise, 890 P.2d 744 (Kan.App.1995) (executor cannot challenge settlement reached by testator's heir and devisee); In Estate of Broadhurst, 737 S.W.2d 504 (Mo.App.1987) (personal representative cannot appeal an order allowing the testator's widow to elect against a will).

**102.** First Nat. Bank v. Yancey, 826 S.W.2d 287 (Ark.App.1991).

**103.** Matter of Estate of Foster, 699 P.2d 638 (N.M.App.1985). If the contestants are the sole beneficiaries this rationale is inapplicable. Rogers v. Rogers, 691 P.2d 114 (Or.App.1984).

**104.** Uniform Probate Code § 3–720.

**105.** In re Estate of Austin, 553 N.W.2d 632 (Mich.App.1996); Dunnuck v. Mosser, 546 N.E.2d 1291 (Ind.App.1989) (devisee who unsuccessfully contested later will awarded fees); Matter of Estate of Killen, 937 P.2d 1375 (Ariz. App.1996). In Estate of Clark v. Foster & Good, 568 N.E.2d 1098 (Ind.App.1991) attorneys fees were awarded to both sides in a will contest.

**106.** In re Estate of Herbert, 979 P.2d 1133, 1136 (Haw.1999); cf. Fields v. Mersack, 577 A.2d 376 (Md.App.1990).

**107.** In re Estate of Zonas, 536 N.E.2d 642 (Ohio 1989).

**108.** Matter of Estate of Killen, 937 P.2d 1375 (Ariz.App.1996). *See also* In re Estate of Dawson, 689 N.E.2d 1008 (Ohio App.1996) (executor who was also beneficiary can get attorney fees for opposing claim of contract to make a will).

### *Forfeiture Clauses*

Many commentators have deplored will contests. Few are successful. The testator's memory is often besmirched by attempts to show incapacity. The cost of litigation may force a settlement even when a contest has no merit. Some testators seek to forestall these evils by a clause in the will providing that a devisee who contests the will loses any interest thereunder. Under the Uniform Probate Code such a provision is unenforceable "if probable cause exists for instituting proceedings."[109] "Probable cause" has been construed to require a reasonable, not merely a good faith belief that the will is invalid.[110] Many cases apply a similar test,[111] but some courts enforce the clause even if the contestant had probable cause.[112] (If the will is actually invalid, the forfeiture clause fails along with the rest of the will.) Conversely in some states forfeiture clauses are ineffective in all cases.[113]

The question what acts are covered by a forfeiture provision has occasioned much litigation. They have been applied not only to the person who brought the contest but to others who aided the contestant.[114] A clause that by its terms covered any beneficiary who "directly or indirectly initiates legal action to contest or attack the validity of this will" has been held to cover an attempt to probate a later will.[115] But no forfeiture was imposed on a beneficiary who merely filed a contest to prevent the statute of limitation running while negotiating a settlement of his claim.[116]

A claim to assets in the testator's estate, *e.g.* that land was held in joint tenancy and so did not pass under the will, does not constitute a contest of the will.[117] Nor is a suit to construe a will a "contest" within the meaning of a forfeiture clause.[118]

Forfeiture provisions are narrowly construed,[119] but a broadly drafted one will be given effect (subject to the probable cause limitation). Thus an "extremely broad no contest clause prohibiting not only a 'contest' of the trust" but also "seeking 'otherwise' to . . . nullify . . . its provisions" was held

**109.** Uniform Probate Code § 3–905; In re Estate of Mumby, 982 P.2d 1219 (Wash.App. 1999) (clause effective where bad faith found). See also *Restatement (Third) of Property (Wills and Other Donative Transfers)* § 8.5 (Prel.Dft. 2000).

**110.** In re Estate of Shumway, 3 P.3d 977, 986 (Ariz.App.1999). On appeal, however, the supreme court found that the contestant had probable cause. Rodriguez v. Gavette, 9 P.3d 1062 (Ariz.2000).

**111.** *Restatement, Second, of Property (Donative Transfers)* § 9.2 (1983); Matter of Estate of Campbell, 876 P.2d 212 (Kan.App. 1994); Hannam v. Brown, 956 P.2d 794 (Nev. 1998) (no forfeiture when contestant had probable cause); Hammer v. Powers, 819 S.W.2d 669 (Tex.App.1991) (clause enforced when contestant fails to prove probable cause).

**112.** Larson v. Naslund, 700 P.2d 276 (Or. App.1985); Briggs v. Wyoming Nat. Bank, 836 P.2d 263 (Wyo.1992) (revocable trust). Under Cal.Prob.Code §§ 21303, 21306 "probable cause" prevents a forfeiture under a clause only if the contest is based on certain grounds; not, for example, a claim that the testator was incapacitated.

**113.** Ind.Code § 29–1–6–2; Fla.Stat. § 732.517.

**114.** In re Estate of Simpson, 595 A.2d 94, 100 (Pa.Super.1991); *Restatement (Second) of Property (Donative Transfers)* § 9.1, comm. f (1983).

**115.** In re Estate of Peppler, 971 P.2d 694, 696 (Colo.App.1998).

**116.** In re Estate of Mank, 699 N.E.2d 1103 (Ill.App.1998). *See also Restatement, Second, of Property (Donative Transfers)* § 9.1, comm. e (1983).

**117.** Jacobs–Zorne v. Superior Court (Swonetz), 54 Cal.Rptr.2d 385 (App.1996); Matter of Ikuta's Estate, 639 P.2d 400 (Haw. 1981).

**118.** Reed v. Reed, 569 S.W.2d 645 (Tex. Civ.App.1978).

**119.** Cal.Prob.Code § 21304 ("a no-contest clause shall be strictly construed"); Haley v. Pickelsimer, 134 S.E.2d 697, 702 (N.C.1964); *Restatement (Third) of Property (Wills and Other Donative Transfers)* § 8.5, comm. d (Prel.Dft. 2000).

to cover a claim that property characterized in a trust as separate was actually community property.[120] Probable cause in this situation is no defense. Indeed, even if the claim is upheld, the devisee may be forced to elect between claiming the property or taking under the will.[121]

No contest clauses have been held inapplicable to attacks on a fiduciary named in a will, *e.g.* attempts to remove an executor.[122] But a clause specifically directed to such attacks will be enforced unless the beneficiary had probable cause for it.[123]

Some clauses simply charge a contestant with the expenses of a proceeding instead of voiding the devise altogether. The Restatement applies the same rule to such provisions[124] but this seems questionable. A penalty which exceeds the harm caused by the wrongful conduct offends our sense of justice, but it does not seem unfair to charge costs to the person who caused them.[125] Some courts have deducted expenses caused by frivolous claims against the person asserting the claim even without a provision for this in the will.[126] A malicious prosecution suit against a person who brought a groundless will contest has been upheld.[127]

## § 12.2 Necessity for Administration

### *Probate and Administration*

When a will is admitted to probate, the court appoints an executor to administer the testator's estate. Probate and administration are thus closely connected. But probate of a will usually takes little time whereas administration of an estate typically lasts for many months or even years. Therefore, the widespread desire to "avoid probate"[1] is more appropriately directed at administration.

The connection between probate and administration is not inevitable:

> A proceeding to probate the will is distinct from a proceeding to administer the estate of a decedent. The fact that the latter is customarily carried on in connection with the former, at the same time, and in the same court, is likely to lead to the conclusion that the two constitute a single proceeding. Historically and functionally, however, they are sepa-

**120.** Estate of Pittman, 73 Cal.Rptr.2d 622, 631 (App.1998).

**121.** See Section 3.8, note 66.

**122.** McLendon v. McLendon, 862 S.W.2d 662, 678 (Tex.App.1993); Estate of Wojtalewicz, 418 N.E.2d 418 (Ill.App.1981) ("good faith" challenge to appointment of executor); Matter of Estate of Zarrow, 688 P.2d 47 (Okl. 1984) (clause not intended to apply to suit against executor for breach of fiduciary duty); Jackson v. Braden, 717 S.W.2d 206 (Ark.1986); Snook v. Sessoms, 350 S.E.2d 237 (Ga.1986).

**123.** *Restatement, Second, of Property (Donative Transfers)* § 9.2 (1983).

**124.** *Id.* § 9.1, comm. b.

**125.** 6 *Amer. Law of Prop.* § 27.5, at 622.

**126.** Matter of Estate of Leslie, 886 P.2d 284 (Colo.App.1994). *See also* Cal.Prob.Code §§ 8906, 11003 (costs of bad faith contest of an account or attempt to remove executor); Webbe v. First Nat. Bank, 487 N.E.2d 711 (Ill.App. 1985) (beneficiary who made groundless claim against trustee charged with trustee's counsel fees). *But see* Matter of Buckner's Estate, 609 P.2d 1285 (Okl.1980); Matter of Estate of Croft, 734 P.2d 59 (Wyo.1987); Estate of Rosen, 520 A.2d 700 (Me.1987) (error to charge unsuccessful contestant with attorney fees).

**127.** Crowley v. Katleman, 881 P.2d 1083 (Cal.1994).

**§ 12.2**

1. See Section 9.1, at note 5 et seq.

rate. * * * A will may be probated without being followed by administration.[2]

Conversely, administration is usually necessary even if there is no will to probate. The person appointed to administer an intestate estate is called an administrator, but an executor and an administrator have virtually the same function, except that executors have a will to carry out ("execute") whereas an administrator's distribution of the estate is controlled by the law of intestacy. The term "personal representative" includes both executors and administrators.

### *History and Comparative Law*

Administration is designed to assure that claims against the decedent are paid before the assets are distributed to the heirs or devisees. As Blackstone put it, a "legacy is not perfect without the assent of the executor; * * * it is his business first of all to see whether there is a sufficient fund left to pay the debts of the testator; the rule of equity being, that a man must be just before he is permitted to be generous."[3]

In Blackstone's day only personal property went to the executor; land passed directly to the devisees or heirs without administration. But just as England extended probate to devises of land in 1857,[4] administration was extended to land in 1897 by a statute which provided that land as well as chattels should vest in the decedent's personal representative.[5]

In some American states vestiges of the old distinction between land and personal property with respect to administration still exist. The practical effects are not much different from the English system, however: "title" to land may pass directly to the decedent's heirs or devisees but this is "a mere empty shell" because of the extensive powers over land which modern statutes confer on personal representatives.[6] In Tennessee, for example,

> The real property of an intestate decedent shall vest immediately upon the death of the decedent in the heirs * * * Upon qualifying, the personal representative shall be vested with the personal property of the decedent for the purpose of * * * the payment of * * * obligations of the decedent. * * * If the decedent's personal property is insufficient, * * * the personal representative may utilize the decedent's real property.[7]

When a will devised land to the testator's children, the Surrogate (New York's counterpart to the probate court) declined to order a sale of the land in a suit for partition.

> Title to the subject real property passed directly to the decedent's children at the time of her death. Accordingly the Surrogate properly

2. Basye, *Dispensing with Administration,* 44 Mich.L.Rev. 329, 424 (1945); *cf.* Uniform Prob.Code § 3–401 (petition for probate "may, but need not, involve a request for appointment of a personal representative").

3. 2 W. Blackstone, *Commentaries* *512 (1765).

4. See Section 12.1, note 6.

5. Land Transfer Act, 1897, 60 & 61 Vict. c. 65, § 1; 3 *Amer.Law of Prop.* § 14.6.

6. 3 *Amer.Law of Prop.* § 14.7, at 578.

7. Tenn.Code § 31–2–103. *Contrast* Wisc. Stat. § 857.01 (personal representative succeeds to all of decedent's property).

The historical idea that a decedent's personal property should be exhausted prior to land in paying debts of the decedent has been abandoned in most states. See Section 8.2, at note 23.

> declined to retain jurisdiction over any issue concerning the partition or sale of the specifically devised property since it was not part of the administrable estate.[8]

However, the same opinion cites a New York statute which would allow the land to be sold if this had been necessary to pay claims against the decedent. In another case an executor was allowed to collect rentals on real estate of the decedent during administration. Even though land "immediately passes to ... the heirs and devisees, ... it was in the best interest of the estate for [the executor] to collect all rents" and account for them in settling the estate.[9]

Administration is not the only possible way for the law might assure that a decedent's creditors are paid. Creditors could be allowed to sue the debtor's heirs or devisees, just as they did in Blackstone's day if the decedent debtor's personal estate was insufficient to pay claims.[10] However, such suits give rise to problems. If, for example, an intestate has several heirs, must creditors seek a proportionate amount from each, or can they collect the whole from any heir?[11] If the decedent died insolvent, his heirs and devisees should not be personally liable for his debts. Creditors should share the decedent's assets in a rational order; certain claims have priority, and creditors in the same class should get the same share. The Uniform Probate Code, for example, divides claims into 6 classes, and allows no preference in paying claims within the same class.[12] Conversely, devises are abated in a prescribed order in order to pay claims against a testator.[13] Without administration this might require a series of lawsuits. Before 1897 in England a creditor might "upset the order of assets" by suing an heir of the debtor who was only secondarily liable; this had to "be put right by marshalling," *i.e.* a suit for contribution from other successors.[14] Such multiple litigation can be avoided in administration in which the personal representative, like a trustee in bankruptcy, carries out the prescribed order of abatement among devisees and follows the prescribed order in distributing the assets of an insolvent estate to creditors.

In such situations, administration is necessary to handle the payment of claims fairly. In the great majority of cases, however, the decedent is not insolvent, and administration is a needless expense. Inefficiency in the system breeds general disrespect for law and lawyers, since the only direct contact which many persons have with our legal system involves administration of decedents' estates.[15]

**8.** Matter of Torricini, 671 N.Y.S.2d 115 (A.D.1998). *See also* Howe v. Johnston, 660 N.E.2d 380 (Mass.App.1996) (suit to set aside deed properly brought against grantee's heir, since title passed to her at death); Estate of Bond, 104 T.C. 652, 668 (1995) ("no administration of the estate is necessary to vest title to real property in a devisee").

**9.** Lucas v. Mannering, 745 S.W.2d 654, 656 (Ky.App.1987).

**10.** 2 W. Blackstone, *Commentaries* *243–44, 340, 378 (1765). For the history of the liability of heirs and executors see McGovern, *Contract in Medieval England: Wager of Law and the Effect of Death,* 54 Iowa L.Rev. 19, 38–48, 52–57 (1968).

**11.** 3 *Amer.Law of Prop.* § 14.20, at 644; Rheinstein, *European Methods for the Liquidation of Debts of Deceased Persons,* 20 Iowa L.Rev. 431, 444, 448 (1935).

**12.** Uniform Probate Code § 3–805.

**13.** See Section 8.2.

**14.** F. Maitland, *Equity* 211 (1913).

**15.** Link, *Probate and Administration of Small Estates in Georgia,* 6 Ga.L.Rev. 74, 75 (1971); Merrill, *The Proposed Model Small Estates Act,* 5 Okl.L.Rev. 49 (1952). However, popular satisfaction with the work of lawyers in this field actually is high. Stein & Fierstein, *The Role of the Attorney in Estate Administration,* 68 Minn.L.Rev. 1107, 1224 (1984).

The civil law system of continental Europe usually dispenses with administration.

> The countries of the continent of Europe are usually regarded as being fond of paternalistic governmental interference with private affairs, while in this country the traditional hostility to governmental meddling has tended to keep state supervision of private matters at a minimum. Yet, with respect to the transfer of property upon death, the roles are curiously reversed. While in Europe judicial or judicially supervised administration of decedent's estates constitutes a comparatively rare exception it is in this country, at least theoretically, required in every case.[16]

Louisiana follows the civil law system and "probably has the least expensive system in the nation" for succession.[17] Heirs may seek administration in order to avoid personal liability when the decedent was insolvent, but this is infrequent.[18] If creditors fear that lack of administration will jeopardize their rights, they can apply for appointment of an executor or administrator, but this also rarely happens, because "creditors have encountered few problems in collecting their claims."[19] Creditors in other states have shown a similar lack of concern about the use of will substitutes in order to avoid probate and administration.[20]

### *Practical Problems in Avoiding Administration*

Usually the heirs or devisees can enjoy a decedent's tangible personal property without bothering to have the estate administered, but they cannot collect choses in action like a bank account or securities registered in the decedent's name. For example, a suit by a decedent's children against their father's former partner for their father's share of the business was dismissed for lack of standing. "The executor or administrator of a decedent's estate has standing to file suit on behalf of a decedent, but the legatees, heirs, and devisees have no such standing," because the court cannot be sure that they are the sole claimants to the estate.[21] It would make no difference if the heirs claimed that administration was unnecessary because they had paid all the decedent's debts; since "the decedent's creditors, if any, are not parties to the action, the non-existence of debts can only be judicially determined by an official administration."[22]

Persons who owe money to a decedent sometimes voluntarily pay the decedent's successors without administration,[23] but in doing this they run a risk that an administrator for the estate will later sue them on the same obligation. Payment to the decedent's heirs is no defense to such a suit.[24] Thus

**16.** Rheinstein, *The Model Probate Code: A Critique,* 48 Colum.L.Rev. 534, 538 (1948).

**17.** Sarpy, *Probate Economy and Celerity in Louisiana,* 34 La.L.Rev. 523, 524 (1974). The low cost is attributable to the absence of an executor's fee and a reduction in attorney's fees. *Id.* at 528.

**18.** *Id.* at 528.

**19.** *Id.* at 535.

**20.** See Section 13.2, note 6.

**21.** McGill v. Lazzaro, 416 N.E.2d 29, 31 (Ill.App.1980). *See also* Gronowicz v. Leonard, 109 F.R.D. 624 (S.D.N.Y.1986) (plaintiff's wife cannot be substituted when he dies unless she is appointed administrator); Dalton v. McLaughlin, 635 P.2d 863, 866 (Ariz.App.1981) (widow can't exercise option to renew in lease to husband "unless and until she was acting as representative of the estate").

**22.** Basye, *supra* note 2, at 395.

**23.** *Id.* at 399, 405.

**24.** *Id.* at 334. But courts will deny a second recovery where the estate has ample funds to pay debts. *Id.* at 398.

persons who owed money to a decedent have standing to petition for administration of the estate so they will know whom to pay.[25]

Heirs or devisees may be able to take possession of the decedent's land without having the estate administered, but if they want to sell or mortgage it, third persons are usually reluctant to deal with them, for good reason.[26] For example, a mortgage executed by an heir was later held to be subject to a claim by a creditor of the decedent.[27]

Lapse of time may give heirs or devisees marketable title without administration, and some cases have allowed heirs to sue debtors of the decedent on the theory that "the non existence of creditors [of the decedent] will be presumed from the mere lapse of time."[28]

### *Small Estates*

The expense of administration is particularly burdensome for small estates because the cost represents a larger percentage of the estate,[29] and the beneficiaries are usually needier. If an estate is smaller than statutory exemptions,[30] the rationale for administration—protection of creditors—does not apply. Therefore, many states exempt small estates from administration. Since many estates are small, these statutes cover a large proportion of them. The provisions are of two types, "collection by affidavit" and "summary distribution."

Collection by affidavit requires no court action.[31] Suppose a man's will leaves his entire estate to his wife. When he dies he had a small bank account in his own name[32] and a claim for unpaid wages. The widow would have to wait thirty days after the husband died before attempting to collect these claims. This waiting period allows the decedent's creditors to initiate administration if they think it necessary. Then the widow could execute an affidavit stating that she was entitled to payment and that the estate was less than $5,000. If the bank and employer pay the widow when she produces the affidavits, they are discharged from liability, even if the facts asserted in the affidavit turn out to be untrue.[33] If they refuse to pay the widow when she produces the affidavit, she can sue them.[34] If a creditor of the decedent later initiates proceedings to have the estate administered, the widow will have to account for the money she received.

**25.** Matter of Windholz, 809 S.W.2d 30 (Mo.App.1991).

**26.** Costigan, *Problems Preliminary to Administration,* [1951] U.Ill.L.F. 357, 361; Siedel v. Snider, 44 N.W.2d 687 (Iowa 1950) (heir does not have marketable title without administration).

**27.** Janes v. Commerce Federal Savings & Loan Ass'n, 639 S.W.2d 490 (Tex.App.1982). *See also* 3 *Amer.Law of Prop.* § 14.22.

**28.** Basye, *supra* note 2, at 397. In Parsons v. Tickner, 37 Cal.Rptr.2d 810 (App.1995), the court allowed an heir to sue years after the estate had been closed.

**29.** Merrill, *supra* note 15, at 49; Link, *supra* note 15, at 79.

**30.** See Section 3.4, at note 33 et seq.

**31.** Sections 3–1201 and 3–1202 of the Uniform Probate Code allow this. They have influenced legislation in states which have not adopted the whole Code. Johnson, *Wills, Trusts & Estates,* 68 Va.L.Rev. 521, 529 (1982).

**32.** If the account was a joint account with the wife, she could collect it as a surviving party.

**33.** Uniform Prob.Code § 3–1202; Clark v. Unknown Heirs of Osborn, 782 P.2d 1384 (Okl. 1989).

**34.** Uniform Prob.Code § 3–1202. Some statutes only *allow* the debtor to pay without administration. Basye, *supra* note 1, at 402. As a practical matter, if the debtor insists on the estate being administered it may be cheaper to comply than to sue. Johnson, *supra* note 31, at 530.

In many states the ceiling on "small estates" for which this procedure is available is much higher; California allows an estate of up to $100,000 to be collected in this way.[35] On the other hand, some statutes cover only particular kinds of property, such as bank accounts, for no apparent reason except that they were promoted by banks so they could more easily "clear their books."[36] The Uniform Probate Code covers all assets, other than land, and can be used by any successor, whereas in some states only the decedent's spouse and children can collect by affidavit.[37]

The affidavit procedure is open to abuse. An heir (or alleged heir) could execute a false affidavit, collect the money and disappear.[38] A Missouri statute requires the distributee to file a bond conditioned on paying claims.[39] In Arkansas the affidavit must be filed with the clerk of the probate court.[40]

The affidavit procedure allowed by the Uniform Probate Code does not cover land, even if its value is small. The drafters believed it was unnecessary "since the appointment of a personal representative may be obtained easily under the Code."[41] California, on the other hand, provides a similar affidavit procedure for clearing title to land worth less that $20,000.[42]

The Uniform Probate Code also allows summary distribution in certain cases after administration has begun. Suppose a widow has the decedent's will probated, is appointed executor, and files an inventory of the estate assets which shows that the estate is so small that nothing would be left for ordinary creditors after paying the family allowance and other exemptions and preferred claims like funeral expenses. On these facts she can distribute the estate immediately.[43] Many states have similar provisions, though they often require that a court determine the relevant facts before any distribution.[44]

### *Larger Estates*

Some states allow even large estates to escape administration. If an estate consists entirely of community property which passes to the surviving spouse, in several states no administration would be necessary.[45] In California, even separate property need not be administered if the spouse gets it outright.[46] A spouse who receives property without administration becomes personally liable for the decedent spouse's obligations to the extent of the property received.[47] In order to avoid such personal liability, the spouse can elect to

**35.** Calif.Prob.Code § 13100. The ceiling refers only to the probate estate; thus property can be collected by affidavit even if the decedent had $500,000 which passed outside probate, *e.g.* joint tenancy. *Id.* § 13050.

**36.** Basye, *supra* note 2, at 401; Link, *supra* note 15, at 87.

**37.** Uniform Probate Code § 3–1201, comment; 20 Pa.Stat. § 3101 (spouse, child, parents, or siblings); Ohio Rev.Code § 2113.04 (spouse, adult children, or parents).

**38.** Basye, *supra* note 1, at 370. *See also* Sullivan & Hack, *Streamlining Probate,* 51 Marq.L.Rev. 150, 153 (1967).

**39.** Mo.Stat. § 473.097.

**40.** Ark.Code § 28–41–101. Notice is published if the estate includes real property.

**41.** Uniform Probate Code § 3–1201, Comment.

**42.** Cal.Prob.Code § 13200.

**43.** Uniform Probate Code § 3–1203.

**44.** 20 Pa.Stat. § 3102; Fla.Stat. § 735.301; Ark.Code § 28–41–103.

**45.** Basye, *supra* note 2, at 382–84.

**46.** Calif.Prob.Code § 13500.

**47.** *Id.* §§ 13550–51. This liability is subject to the same defenses as would be available if the claim were asserted in probate proceedings, such as the one year limitation running from the date of the death of the decedent spouse. Collection Bureau of San Jose v. Rumsey, 6 P.3d 713 (Cal.2000).

have the property administered.[48]

The Uniform Probate Code has provisions modeled on the civil law which allow the heirs or residuary devisees to become "universal successors" by assuming personal liability for claims against the decedent.[49] Heirs and devisees who agree to become universal successors become fully responsible for claims against the estate, but each successor's liability is proportional to his or her share of the estate.[50] Multiple suits to collect against several universal successors are not necessary, since creditors can join them all in one proceeding. All heirs or residuary devisees who are *sui juris* must join an application to become universal successors and they thereby become subject to the jurisdiction of the court.[51]

## § 12.3 Ancillary Administration

### *Rationale*

In the previous section we saw that even if a will leaves the entire estate to the testator's wife, for example, she may be unable to collect assets which belonged to her husband without a court appointment certified by "letters testamentary" that she is his executor. If she is acting as administrator, the letters would be called "letters of administration."[1] The problem is further complicated if the decedent owned assets in several states. Suppose that he was a resident of Maryland, but owned land in Georgia, a bank account in Virginia, stock in a Pennsylvania corporation, and had a tort claim against a resident of Illinois. If a Maryland court appoints the wife executor of the will,[2] she may be unable to collect assets in other states without ancillary administration. For example, an executor appointed by a court in Louisiana, the state of the testator's domicile, was not allowed to sue in Texas to collect a debt owed to the decedent, because personal representatives are "clothed with authority to administer only such assets as are within the jurisdiction of the court" which appoints them.[3] The result would have been the same even in a federal court, since capacity to sue is determined by state law.[4]

This limitation on the powers of personal representatives is usually explained by the need to protect local creditors of the decedent; creditors of the decedent in Texas should not be forced to go to Louisiana to collect their claims if the decedent had assets in Texas.[5] But Texas could not under the

**48.** Cal.Prob.Code § 13502.

**49.** Uniform Prob.Code § 3–312.

**50.** Uniform Prob.Code § 3–321.

**51.** *Id.* § 3–312, comment, § 3–318.

§ 12.3

**1.** Uniform Probate Code § 3–103: "Administration of an estate is commenced by the issuance of letters."

**2.** Even if the wife was the sole devisee, she would not necessarily be appointed executor. As to the choice of executors and administrators see Section 12.4.

**3.** Eikel v. Burton, 530 S.W.2d 907, 508 (Tex.Civ.App.1975). *See also* Matter of Estate of Widmeyer, 741 S.W.2d 758 (Mo.App.1987); Cal.Code Civ.Proc. § 1913(b). In Eikel, the defendant's failure to object to the plaintiff's standing in the trial court was held to be irrelevant, since "the question is fundamental, going to the jurisdiction of the court," but in Shaw v. Stutchman, 771 P.2d 156 (Nev.1989), the court held that the defence was waived by failure to raise it in time.

**4.** Blum v. Salyer, 299 F.Supp. 1074 (W.D.Mo.1969).

**5.** Eikel v. Burton, 530 S.W.2d 907, 909 (Tex.Civ.App.1975); Chaffin & Barwick, *The Probate and Establishment of Domestic and Foreign Wills,* 13 Ga.L.Rev. 133, 173 (1978); *Restatement (Second) of Conflict of Laws* § 354, comm. a (1971).

constitution prefer its own citizens if the decedent was insolvent.[6] Thus the only legitimate interest of local creditors requiring ancillary administration is the convenience of being able to file claims in their own state. Many have questioned whether this is enough to justify the burden of ancillary administration. Professor Currie called it "a feeble argument."[7] Professor Basye called ancillary administration "a wasteful expenditure of time, effort and expense."[8] Often there are no local creditors in the state of ancillary administration, or they are quickly paid and need no protection.[9] One cannot dispense with ancillary administration, however, by asserting that no local creditors exist, since one function of administration is to ascertain by publication of notice whether there are creditors.[10]

The Uniform Probate Code obviates the need for ancillary administration by giving personal representatives appointed in the state of the decedent's domicile standing to sue in the courts of any other jurisdiction.[11] They acquire "all powers of a local personal representative," including the right to sue, by filing a copy of their appointment.[12] By taking this action "a foreign personal representative submits personally to the jurisdiction of the Courts of this state."[13] This makes them subject to suit by local creditors without making ancillary administration necessary.

### *Particular Assets*

In practice, the need for ancillary administration depends upon (1) the type of asset, and (2) the state where it is located.

1. *The Stock of a Pennsylvania Corporation.* If the decedent's interest is represented by a stock certificate in the executor's possession, even if it is registered in the decedent's name, the executor can have it transferred without ancillary administration in Pennsylvania. A Pennsylvania statute limits the powers of foreign fiduciaries, but the limits do not apply to stock.[14] The Restatement of Conflicts allows corporations to transfer shares on their books "to any executor or administrator of the decedent who surrenders [the]

**6.** *Id.* § 344, comm. a; Currie, *The Multiple Personalty of the Dead,* 33 U.Chi.L.Rev. 429, 432 (1966); Uniform Probate Code § 3–815(b) (if estate is insolvent each creditor "in this state or elsewhere ... is entitled to receive payment of an equal portion of his claim").

**7.** *Id.* at 431. A state may insist on ancillary administration in order to collect taxes. In order to insure "proper administration of its tax laws, Louisiana has for many years required ancillary probate proceedings when a non-resident dies leaving property situated in this state." St. Charles Land Trust v. St. Amant, 217 So.2d 385 (La.1968). Louisiana would have difficulty in collecting its tax in other states since states do not usually help other states to collect taxes. Alford, *Collecting a Decedent's Assets Without Ancillary Administration,* 18 Sw.L.J. 329, 337–38 (1964). However, requiring ancillary administration is not the only way to collect. A Pennsylvania statute allows foreign fiduciaries to exercise their powers within the Commonwealth on condition that they pay all taxes due to Pennsylvania. 20 Pa.Stat. § 4101(4).

**8.** Basye, *Dispensing With Administration,* 44 Mich.L.Rev. 329, 409 (1945). *See also* E. Scoles & P. Hay, *Conflict of Laws* § 22.14 (2d ed. 1992).

**9.** Atkinson, *The Uniform Ancillary Administration and Probate Acts,* 67 Harv.L.Rev. 619, 623 (1954).

**10.** *Restatement (Second) of Conflict of Laws* § 354, comm. e (1971).

**11.** Uniform Probate Code § 3–703(c). An ancillary administrator, who was appointed by a state in which the decedent was not domiciled but had property, cannot sue to collect property in other states. Matter of Stern, 696 N.E.2d 984 (N.Y.1998).

**12.** This applies only if no local administration is pending. Uniform Probate Code § 4–204.

**13.** Uniform Prob.Code § 4–301. *See also Restatement (Second) of Conflict of Laws* § 358, comm. g (1971).

**14.** 20 Pa.Stat. § 4102(a).

share certificate." The executor or administrator can sue any corporation which refuses to transfer the shares.[15]

2. *Virginia Bank-account.* An ordinary bank account is not represented by a significant document like a stock certificate, so the executor will not possess anything apart from her Maryland appointment to show her right to the account. If the bank pays the money in the account to her voluntarily, a Virginia ancillary administrator might later force it to pay again. There are uncertainties of both law and fact in evaluating this risk, comparable to those incurred by a debtor in paying a debt to the creditor's heir or devisee.[16] The bank may not know whether there are local creditors who might institute ancillary administration, and the extent to which a payment made to a foreign executor legally discharges a debtor is unclear in many states. The Restatement says such payment discharges a debtor "in the absence of knowledge of the appointment of a local executor or administrator,"[17] but not all cases agree.[18] Under the Uniform Probate Code the bank could safely pay the executor if it waited 60 days after the testator died and got an affidavit from the executor that no local administration was pending.[19] Virginia has a similar statute but it requires publication of notice if the amount exceeds $10,000.[20]

3. *Georgia Land.* The executor may be able to take possession of the land without dealing with a third party like a bank or the transfer agent of a corporation. If so, she can sue trespassers without ancillary administration. Because of her possession the cause of action would be regarded as belonging to her as an individual.[21] If she tried to sell the land, however, prospective purchasers might question her title.[22] A Georgia statute now allows foreign executors to sell land in the state if no ancillary administration is pending.[23]

4. *Illinois Tort Claim.* If the tortfeasor residing in Illinois disputes his liability, the executor may seek to be appointed ancillary administrator there in order to pursue the claim. The executor of a Florida decedent who wished to pursue a claim against an Illinois resident was appointed ancillary administrator by an Illinois court on the theory that the decedent had property in Illinois. "The situs of intangible personal estate is ... where the debtor resides, if there is no instrument evidencing the ... chose in action[24] ... A 'cause of action' against an Illinois resident, though of presently undetermined value, may constitute an asset of an estate."[25] If the tortfeasor resided

**15.** *Restatement (Second) of Conflict of Laws* § 324, comm. c (1971). *See also* Va.Code § 64.1–129.

**16.** Section 12.2, note 24.

**17.** *Restatement (Second) of Conflict of Laws* § 329 (1971).

**18.** Atkinson, *supra* note 9, at 620.

**19.** Uniform Probate Code § 4–201. Compare the affidavit procedure for collecting assets in small estates without any administration. Section 12.2, note .

**20.** Va.Code § 64.1–130.

**21.** Currie, *supra* note 6, at 432. Currie adds that this is "arrant nonsense" given the rationale of ancillary administration-protecting local creditors, but the distinction is well settled. *Restatement (Second) of Conflicts* § 330 (1971).

**22.** Allen v. Amoco Production Co. 833 P.2d 1199 (N.M.App.1992) (deed by Colorado executor ineffective as to New Mexico land); Leggett v. Church of St. Pius, 619 S.W.2d 191 (Tex.Civ.App.1981) (deed to Texas mineral interest by Minnesota executor ineffective); Bell v. King Phipps & Assoc., P.C., 337 S.E.2d 364 (Ga.App.1985) (Florida executor "had no authority to convey" Georgia land—but see note 23).

**23.** Ga.Code Ann. §§ 53–5–42, 53–5–44 (effective 1/1/98).

**24.** *See also* Uniform Probate Code § 3–201(d).

**25.** In re Estate of Hoffman, 286 N.E.2d 103, 104 (Ill.App.1972). *See also* De Garza v. Chetister, 405 N.E.2d 331 (Ohio App.1978).

in another state, even if he was subject to suit in Illinois because he had property there, Illinois could not have appointed an ancillary administrator.[26] A California resident had a suit pending in Texas against the United States for an income tax refund when he died. A Texas court's appointment of an ancillary administrator to pursue the suit was rejected. The decedent's claim against the United States was not Texas property because claims against the government, unlike ordinary claims, are situated at the domicile of the *creditor,* not the debtor.[27]

### *Identity of Ancillary Administrator*

The burden of ancillary administration is reduced if the domiciliary representative can also act as the ancillary administrator, but some states require that administrators be residents of the appointing state. The cost of ancillary administration is increased when different persons must be appointed in each state.[28] The Uniform Probate Code simplifies ancillary administration, when it is necessary, by giving an executor appointed by the decedent's domicile priority in being appointed ancillary representative.[29]

### *Claims Against a Decedent*

Suppose that a resident of Michigan has a claim against a person who died domiciled in Maryland. She could file her claim in Maryland,[30] but she might prefer to litigate in Michigan. As a creditor of the decedent, she could begin ancillary administration in Michigan if the decedent owned property there. For example, a New York resident was allowed to initiate administration there in order to pursue a malpractice claim against the estate of a doctor who had died domiciled in Florida. The fact that the doctor was insured by a carrier doing business in New York did not of itself satisfy the "minimum contacts" needed to give New York jurisdiction. But "the occurrence of the allegedly tortious action within New York," where the doctor was domiciled and practiced medicine at the time, gave New York a substantial enough "nexus" to justify the ancillary proceedings there.[31]

Even if the tort claimant can initiate ancillary administration in Michigan this might not be her best strategy. If decedent does not have enough assets in Michigan to satisfy the claim, a Michigan judgment may be worthless in other states. "A judgment against one executor or administrator does not make the facts found by the court in the action res judicata in an action against another executor or administrator of the same decedent."[32] This rule has been much criticized and is changed by the Uniform Probate Code which treats a multistate estate as a unit: "an adjudication rendered in any jurisdiction in favor of

**26.** Leve v. Doyle, 177 N.Y.S.2d 617 (Sup. 1958) (ancillary administrator cannot collect debt due from a nonresident not served in ancillary jurisdiction).

**27.** Diehl v. United States, 438 F.2d 705, 710 (5th Cir.1971).

**28.** Currie, *supra* note 6, at 433.

**29.** Uniform Prob.Code §§ 3–203(g), 3–611(b).

**30.** But the Maryland court might stay proceedings on the claim if it could be tried more conveniently in the state where the tort occurred. V–1 Oil Co. v. Ranck, 767 P.2d 612 (Wyo.1989).

**31.** In re Estate of Muscillo, 527 N.Y.S.2d 20 (A.D.1988). *See also* In re Gardinier's Estate, 191 A.2d 294 (N.J.1963).

**32.** *Restatement (Second) of Conflict of Laws* § 356, comm. b (1971).

or against any personal representative of the estate is as binding on the local personal representative as if he were a party.''[33]

### *Suit Against Foreign Representative*

Claimants can not sue a personal representative of a decedent outside the state which appointed the representative unless a statute provides otherwise. For example, a suit was pending in Missouri when the defendant, a resident of Texas, died. A bank appointee by a Texas court as the defendant's executor could not be substituted as defendant in the Missouri proceedings.[34] Statutes in many jurisdictions change this rule. The Uniform Probate Code allows domiciliary personal representatives to be sued in any state in which the decedent could have been sued at death.[35]

### *Distribution of Ancillary Assets*

If a decedent had assets in another state and an ancillary administrator collects them, should the administrator after paying local creditors remit the balance to the domiciliary executor for distribution there? Yes, under the Uniform Probate Code with certain exceptions, *e.g.* if the decedent's successors ''are identified pursuant to the local law of'' the state of ancillary administration.[36] An Oklahoma court ordered the ancillary administrator of a Texas decedent to distribute the Oklahoma assets directly to the decedent's widow who claimed an elective share of the estate, on the ground that transmitting them to the Texas executor for distribution under to the decedent's will ''would defeat the public policy of'' Oklahoma.[37] The Restatement of Conflicts gives the court in this situation discretion, but says that ''unless there are special circumstances making local distribution desirable,'' assets collected in ancillary administration should be remitted to the domiciliary representative.[38]

### *Planning*

The inconvenience of ancillary administration is sometimes advanced as an argument for using will substitutes.[39] However, the planner should consider whether it will really be a problem in the particular estate. Depending on the nature and location of the client's assets, ancillary administration may be no great inconvenience, or not necessary at all even for assets passing through probate if the relevant states have statutes like the Uniform Probate Code.

**33.** Uniform Probate Code § 4–401. *See also* Beacham v. Palmer, 523 N.E.2d 1007 (Ill. App.1988) (dismissal of suit against ancillary administrator bars suit against domiciliary).

**34.** State ex rel. Mercantile Nat. Bank v. Rooney, 402 S.W.2d 354 (Mo.1966). *Accord, Restatement (Second) of Conflict of Laws* § 358, comm. b (1971); K L Cattle Co. v. Bunker, 491 F.Supp. 1314 (S.D.Tex.1980); In re Estate of Reynolds, 970 P.2d 537 (Kan.1998) (appearance of Kansas executor in New York court did not give it jurisdiction).

**35.** Uniform Probate Code § 3–703(c). *See also* Moore v. Healy, 745 F.Supp. 791 (D.Mass. 1990) (Florida executor subject to suit in Massachusetts under a statute).

**36.** Uniform Probate Code § 3–816.

**37.** Estate of Miller v. Miller, 768 P.2d 373, 377 (Okl.App.1988). Under the UPC § 2–202, however, the state of the decedent's domicile (Texas) would have governed the widow's elective share, even as to realty in another state.

**38.** *Restatement (Second) of Conflict of Laws* § 364 (1971).

**39.** Keydel, *Funding the Revocable Trust*, 14 Prob.Notes 98, 105 (1988). A trustee of a living trust is not normally appointed by a court, and even a trustee who is so appointed can sue outside the state of appointment. 4 A. Scott, *Trusts* § 280.6 (4th ed. 1987).

## § 12.4 Choice of Fiduciary

A fiduciary is a person who is entrusted with another's property; the word comes from the Latin *fiducia,* trust. We are primarily concerned in this book with two types: personal representatives of a decedent (executors and administrators) and trustees. Agents under a power of attorney, custodians under the Uniform Transfers to Minors Act, and conservators similar perform functions and are subject to many of the same rules.[1]

### *Court Appointment*

Personal representatives acquire their powers by court appointment.[2] Conservators of the property of a minor or adult incompetent are also appointed by a court,[3] but trustees under a living trust need no court appointment, nor do agents under a power of attorney or custodians under the Transfers to Minors Act. Some statutes provide for court appointment of testamentary trustees, but many do not.[4]

Even where a court is not involved in the initial designation of a fiduciary, court proceedings may be necessary 1/ to remove a fiduciary, or 2/ to designate a successor when the original fiduciary is unable or unwilling to continue to serve, for example, a trustee dies.[5] Rarely does the death of a trustee cause a trust to terminate, so a court may need to appoint a successor.[6] Court proceedings may be unnecessary, however, if the trust instrument designates a successor,[7] or provides a procedure for doing so. Because court proceedings are time consuming and expensive, many wills and trusts provide such a procedure. The Uniform Statutory Will Act, for example, provides that if a trustee designated in the will is unable or unwilling to serve, the personal representative "may appoint, without court order, a qualified person" to act.[8] The Uniform Transfers to Minors Act allows a custodian to designate a successor by a written instrument.[9] However, there is no general rule allowing personal representatives or trustees to designate successors unless the terms of the governing instrument authorize it.[10]

Another possible way to designate a new fiduciary is to empower the beneficiaries to do so. Such an empowerment is sometimes restricted, *e.g.* the designated beneficiary(ies) can only name a corporate trustee. This prevents

§ 12.4

1. As to powers of attorney and custodianships see Section 9.2.

2. *E.g.*, Uniform Prob.Code § 3–103.

3. Uniform Probate Code § 5–401. As to the differing uses of the words "conservator" and "guardian" see Section 1.1, note 8 et seq.

4. *Restatement, Third, of Trusts* § 34(1) (1999 (except as required by statute, trustee needs no court appointment).

5. The common-law rule that a trustee's title passed to his heirs at death has been generally superseded. Creel v. Martin, 454 So.2d 1350 (Ala.1984) (court appoints successor trustee, title does not pass to heirs of original trustee). *But see* Rohleder v. French, 675 S.W.2d 8 (Ky.App.1984) (deed of heir of original trustee is valid).

6. *Restatement, Third, of Trusts* § 31 (1999).

7. Barnett First Nat. Bank v. Cobden, 393 So.2d 78 (Fla.App.1981) (error to appoint a successor trustee when trust instrument designated one); Rose v. O'Reilly, 841 P.2d 3 (Or. App.1992) (error not to appoint successor trustee designated in will).

8. Uniform Statutory Will Act § 12(c); *cf.* In re Trust of Selsor, 468 N.E.2d 745 (Ohio App.1983) (cotrustees authorized to recommend successor to deceased trustee).

9. Uniform Transfers to Minors Act § 18(b).

10. Cal.Prob.Code § 8422 (executor cannot designate a successor unless the will so provides).

them from naming an individual subservient to their wishes.[11] Absent authorization in the instrument beneficiaries are not entitled at common law to name a new fiduciary,[12] although courts in selecting a fiduciary generally give weight to the beneficiaries' wishes.[13] Often some beneficiaries of a trust or estate are minors or unascertained persons who cannot act. California gets around this difficulty by allowing a vacancy in the office of trustee to be filled by "agreement of all adult beneficiaries who are receiving ... income under the trust or [would be entitled] to receive a distribution of principal if the trust were terminated at the time."[14] A provision in the Uniform Statutory Will allows either the testator's spouse or "a majority of the adult children of the testator" to fill vacancies in the office of trustee or personal representative.[15]

### *Administrators and Executors*

State statutes provide priorities for the choice of an administrator when someone dies intestate. The Uniform Probate Code gives priority to the decedent's spouse, but permits a court to depart from the statute and appoint "any suitable person." Persons eligible for appointment may instead nominate another.[16] Under a similar statute, a court chose the decedent's brother as administrator instead of his widow because her claim to certain property in the estate "created a conflict of interest that rendered her unfit."[17] Under these circumstances the trial court's choice was not an "abuse of discretion." (Appellate courts commonly defer to the determinations of lower courts in the appointment and removal of fiduciaries.[18]) Another court appointed a nominee of the decedent's mother over the decedent's father who was poorly educated.[19] In an estate where the decedent's heirs were all minor children, the court appointed her ex-spouse as administrator even though he was not an heir.[20]

When a will fails to designate an executor, or the designated executor cannot or will not serve, the court appoints an administrator "with will annexed" (sometimes designated in Latin: *cum testamento annexo*). Under the Uniform Probate Code, the devisees under the will have priority over heirs in seeking appointment, or in nominating an administrator with will annexed.[21]

Executors are by definition nominated in a will to carry out its terms. They too must be appointed by a court, but courts normally appoint the

**11.** In Matter of Schroll, 297 N.W.2d 282 (Minn.1980) the court blocked an attempt by the beneficiaries to evade such a restriction. But in In re Estate of Coleman, 317 A.2d 631, 633 (Pa.1974), the court refused to give effect to a provision requiring trustees to be Protestants because this was "unrelated to any proper trust purpose."

**12.** *Restatement, Third, of Trusts* § 34, comm. c (1999). *But cf.* Uniform Transfers to Minors Act § 18(d) (minor who has attained age 14 can designate successor custodian).

**13.** *Restatement, Third, of Trusts* § 34, comm. f (1999); Cal.Prob.Code § 15660(d).

**14.** Cal.Prob.Code § 15660(c). *See also* Unif.Trust Code § 704(c)(1) (vacancy in trusteeship to be filled by "unanimous agreement of the qualified beneficiaries").

**15.** Uniform Statutory Will Act § 12(d).

**16.** Uniform Probate Code § 3–203(b).

**17.** Ayala v. Martinez, 883 S.W.2d 270, 272 (Tex.App.1994).

**18.** In re Estate of Posey, 548 N.E.2d 1205, 1207 (Ind.App.1990) (appointment of bank rather than decedent's brother); In re Estate of Pfahler, 581 N.E.2d 602, 603 (Ohio App.1989) (refusal to appoint designated executor).

**19.** Estate of Robinson, 816 S.W.2d 896 (Ark.App.1991).

**20.** In re Estate of Robertson, 498 N.E.2d 206 (Ohio App.1985). *See also* Courtney v. Lawson, 631 A.2d 102 (Md.App.1993) (sister appointed when heirs were minor children).

**21.** Uniform Probate Code § 3–203(a); *cf.* Calif.Prob.Code § 8441.

person named in the will unless the nominee is disqualified. Similarly in appointing a conservator, deference is given to persons "nominated by the protected person" if the latter is over 14 and "of sufficient mental capacity to make an intelligent choice."[22]

A trial court's refusal to appoint the executor named in a will because of a potential conflict of interest was reversed because this was not a ground of disqualification under the governing statute.[23] The statutory grounds were 1/ being under the age of majority,[24] 2/ conviction of a felony,[25] and 3/ incompetence by virtue of "want of integrity or understanding." The Uniform Probate Code uses the broader term "unsuitable" as the controlling standard.[26] Under this standard courts may remove or refuse to appoint an executor or trustee because of a conflict of interest. For example, an executor was removed because his firm represented persons with claims against the estate.[27]

### *Conflicts of Interest*

A conflict does not always disqualify a fiduciary, especially if it was obvious to the testator or settlor who nominated the fiduciary. For example, when a will designated the testator's child by a prior marriage as a trustee as well as remainderman, the court held it was an error not to appoint the child.

> [The] remaindermen have interests antagonistic to those of [the testator's wife, the life beneficiary]. Because of the discretionary power conferred upon them in deciding whether to invade the corpus of the trust, * * * they might be tempted to favor themselves unduly in the administration of the trust. * * * Nevertheless, * * * [these] problems were known to the settlor and in spite of them he named [the remainderman] as trustee, * * * [so the trustee should be] permitted to act until it should appear that he was not properly exercising the discretion conferred upon him.[28]

On the other hand, a conflict which was "unknown to the settlor at the time of the designation, or that came into being at a later time" presents a stronger case for removal or refusal to appoint.[29] Also potential conflicts can

**22.** Uniform Probate Code § 5–409(a)(1). *See also* Cal.Prob.Code § 1810; Guardianship of Smith, 684 N.E.2d 613 (Mass.App.1997) (error not to appoint guardian nominated in ward's durable power of attorney).

**23.** Wolzinger v. Eighth Judicial Dist. Court, 773 P.2d 335, 341 (Nev.1989). *See also* Matter of Estate of Ringwald, 905 P.2d 833 (Okl.App.1995).

**24.** *See also* Cal.Prob.Code § 8402(a)(1); Uniform Probate Code § 3–203(f)(1). Minors cannot act as trustees initially, *Restatement, Third, of Trusts* § 32, comm. c (1999), but they can do so as soon as they come of age. Farmers State Bank of Yuma v. Harmon, 778 F.2d 543, 545 (10th Cir.1985).

**25.** *Cf.* 29 U.S.C. § 1111(a) (conviction of various listed felonies a bar to serving as fiduciary under ERISA plan for designated period); Smith v. Christley, 684 S.W.2d 158 (Tex.App. 1984) (one convicted of possessing drugs disqualified even though appeal pending); LaGrange v. Hinton, 603 A.2d 1385 (Md.App. 1992) (engaging in oral sex); In re Estate of Roy, 637 N.E.2d 1228 (Ill.App.1994) (statute barring convicted felon from serving as guardian of estate may be unconstitutional).

**26.** Uniform Probate Code § 3–203(f)(2).

**27.** In re Estate of Fogleman, 3 P.3d 1172 (Ariz.App.2000). *See also* District Attorney v. Magraw, 628 N.E.2d 24 (Mass.1994); Gockel v. Eble, 648 N.E.2d 539 (Ohio App.1994); Estate of Hammer, 24 Cal.Rptr.2d 190 (App.1993) (husband of devisee removed as executor when involved in a divorce with her).

**28.** Lovett v. Peavy, 316 S.E.2d 754, 757 (Ga.1984). *See also* Deal v. Huddleston, 702 S.W.2d 404 (Ark.1986); Schildberg v. Schildberg, 461 N.W.2d 186, 192 (Iowa 1990); Symmons v. O'Keeffe, 644 N.E.2d 631, 638n (Mass. 1995); *Restatement, Third, of Trusts* § 37, comm. f (1999).

**29.** *Restatement, Third, of Trusts* § 37, comm. f (1999); Estate of Hammer, 24 Cal. Rptr.2d 190 (App.1993) (husband of devisee

be determinative in a court's choice of fiduciaries when none is designated by the testator or settlor.[30]

A conflict of interest can be removed without completely disqualifying the fiduciary, *e.g.* by restricting the fiduciary's powers. A Wisconsin statute bars trustees from making discretionary distributions to themselves unless the trust instrument provides otherwise. The discretionary power may be exercised by other trustees, if any, or "by a special trustee appointed by the court."[31] When a conflict of interest arose between a trustee and the beneficiaries with respect to particular litigation, a court "suspended the trustee's powers regarding only the litigation and appointed a 'trustee ad litem' with limited powers to conduct the litigation."[32]

Even if a testator or settlor is convinced that a family member is sufficiently fair-minded to overlook his or her selfish interests, putting them in a position of conflict of interest may present income tax problems. Under Internal Revenue Code Section 678, anyone who has "a power solely exercisable by [herself] to vest the corpus or the income" of a trust in herself is taxed on income even if it was distributed to others or accumulated in the trust.[33] Use of a family member as trustee can also have adverse estate tax consequences. If a trust is used to keep property out of a beneficiary's taxable estate,[34] this objective will be defeated if as trustee or otherwise the beneficiary can distribute corpus to herself unless the power is limited "by an ascertainable standard relating to [the beneficiary's] health, education, support or maintenance."[35] The broad powers of custodians under the Uniform Transfers to Minors Act cause the property to be included in the taxable estate of a donor who acts as the custodian and dies during the custodianship.[36]

### *Other Grounds for Removal or Refusal to Appoint*

Another ground for removing or not appointing a designated executor or trustee is hostility between the fiduciary and the beneficiaries. For example, a court refused to appoint the executor designated in a will because he had acted so abrasively toward the testator's wife and children that "there was no way" they could get along with him. The "mere fact that the heirs of the testator have a feeling of hostility toward the designated executor and do not

later involved in acrimonious divorce with her); Shriners Hospitals v. Gardiner, 733 P.2d 1110, 1114 (Ariz.1987).

**30.** *Restatement, Third, of Trusts* § 37, illus. 8 (1999).

**31.** Wisc.Stat. § 701.19(10). *See also* N.Y. EPTL § 10–10.1; Uniform Principal and Income Act (1997) § 104(c)(d) (trustee's power to make adjustments between principal and income does not apply if trustee is a beneficiary); First Union Nat. Bank v. Cisa, 361 S.E.2d 615 (S.C.1987) (beneficiary trustee cannot participate in decisions to distribute to herself); Wiggins v. PNC Bank, 988 S.W.2d 498 (Ky.App. 1998).

**32.** Getty v. Getty, 252 Cal.Rptr. 342, 346 (App.1988). *See also* Matter of Sauter's Estate, 615 P.2d 875 (Mont.1980) (special administrator appointed to handle claim involving conflict of interest); Stilwell v. Estate of Crosby, 519 So.2d 68, 69 (Fla.App.1988); *Restatement, Third, of Trusts* § 37, comm. g (1999).

**33.** Rev.Rul. 67–268, 1967–2 Cum.Bull. 226.

**34.** See Section 9.3.

**35.** Internal Revenue Code § 2041(b); *cf.* Estate of Vissering v. Commissioner, 990 F.2d 578 (10th Cir.1993) (power to invade for "comfort" is not a general power). If a remainderman is named as trustee, a distribution of corpus to another may be a taxable gift by the remainderman. Treas. Reg. § 25.2511–1(g)(2).

**36.** Exchange Bank & Trust Co. v. United States, 694 F.2d 1261 (Fed.Cir.1982).

want him appointed is not alone a sufficient reason," because a testator "may recognize that dissension and division exist among his heirs" and choose "a person as executor who has the fortitude to administer his estate even in the face of such animosity." But when the antagonism "would probably result in prolonged and unnecessary difficulty or expense" the designated executor should not be appointed.[37] If a trustee has broad discretion in making distributions, hostility between the trustee and a particular beneficiary may make the trustee unsuitable.[38] However, hostility between a trustee and beneficiaries is not always grounds for removal. "There are many trusts in which no trustee could fully perform his duty without incurring the hostility of some of the beneficiaries."[39] Trial courts have wide discretion on this issue[40] so it is hard to reconcile all the cases, but the extent of the hostility and the reason for it are important factors.[41]

A change of circumstances after a will or trust is executed may throw in question the suitability of the designated fiduciary. "Clients with young children will often nominate a corporate fiduciary," but when the children are older the client may wish to give them the job.[42] In most states, when a testator marries or has a child after executing a will, the new spouse or child get a share of the estate despite the will,[43] but unless the statute revokes a will in this situation the named executor is still appointed.[44] If the testator divorces a spouse who is designated as a fiduciary in an instrument, however, the divorce revokes the designation under the Uniform Probate Code.[45]

If an executor or trustee becomes insolvent, his creditors can not reach property which he holds as fiduciary, but there is a risk that assets will become confused. Therefore, courts often remove a fiduciary who is insolvent.[46]

**37.** Matter of Petty's Estate, 608 P.2d 987, 995 (Kan.1980). *See also* Kerper v. Kerper, 780 P.2d 923, 938 (Wyo.1989); In re Estate of Pfahler, 581 N.E.2d 602 (Ohio App.1989).

**38.** Shear v. Gabovitch, 685 N.E.2d 1168, 1193 (Mass.App.1997); Matter of Brecklein's Estate, 637 P.2d 444, 452 (Kan.App.1981); In re Nassar's Estate, 356 A.2d 773, 776 (Pa. 1976).

**39.** Edinburg v. Cavers, 492 N.E.2d 1171, 1181 (Mass.App.1986). *See also Restatement (Third) of Trusts* § 37, comm. e (1999); Pontrello v. Estate of Kepler, 528 So.2d 441, 444 (Fla.App.1988) (error to refuse to appoint designated executor on grounds of hostility of testator's family). In Holst v. Purdy, 844 P.2d 229 (Or.App.1992), the court refused to remove a designated executor-trustee, but ordered him to post a bond.

**40.** Matter of Trust Created by Hill, 499 N.W.2d 475, 486 (Minn.App.1993) *But cf.* Rennacker v. Rennacker, 509 N.E.2d 798 (Ill.App. 1987) (abuse of discretion not to remove trustee because of extreme hostility); Matter of Estate of Robbin, 747 P.2d 869 (Mont.1987) (abuse of discretion to remove executor who had divorced legatee).

**41.** In Akin v. Dahl, 661 S.W.2d 911, 914 (Tex.1983), the court refusing to remove a trustee, noted that the "hostility was primarily created by the beneficiaries."

**42.** Mabley, *How and When to Conduct a Review of a Client's Estate Plan*, 16 Est.Plan. 162, 166 (1989).

**43.** See Sections 3.6, 3.7.

**44.** Matter of Bowman's Estate, 609 P.2d 663, 666 (Idaho 1980) (error to appoint testator's husband whom she married after will executed when will named another executor). *See also* State ex rel. First Nat. Bank v. Skow, 284 N.W.2d 74 (Wis.1979) (even though testator's children were minors when will executed but are now of age bank designated as executor in will should be appointed).

**45.** Uniform Probate Code § 2–804(b). *See also* Calif.Prob.Code § 6122 (wills), § 4154 (power of attorney); McClinton v. Sullivan, 438 S.E.2d 71 (Ga.1994) (refusal to appoint spouse as administrator when action for divorce pending at death). Homicide also negates the killer's nomination as fiduciary. Uniform Probate Code § 2–803(c)(1); Cal.Prob.Code § 250(b)(3).

**46.** In re Quinlan's Estate, 273 A.2d 340 (Pa.1971); *Restatement (Third) of Trusts* § 37, comm. e (1999); Calif.Prob.Code § 15642(b)(2).

Trustees and executors can also be removed for misconduct in office.[47] The Restatement of Trusts lists as grounds for removing a trustee, inter alia, "repeated or flagrant failure or delay in providing accountings or information to the beneficiaries, gross or continued under performance of investments," and "unwarranted preference" toward certain beneficiaries or "a pattern of indifference" toward others.[48] Such misconduct may involve other matters, *e.g.* an executor was removed for mishandling the testators' property while acting under a power of attorney and as their conservator.[49] Courts do not remove fiduciaries who have been guilty of only minor wrongs,[50] but the Uniform Trust Code allows removal simply for lackluster performance: "persistent failure to administer the trust effectively."[51]

Some trusts give designated beneficiaries the right to remove a trustee with whom they are dissatisfied. In this case no ground for the removal is necessary.[52] Even without such a provision in the instrument the Uniform Trust Code calls for a removal if the beneficiaries unanimously request it and the court finds this "serves the best interests of all the beneficiaries and is not inconsistent" with a material purpose of the trust."[53]

One way to obviate the need for court proceedings to remove a trustee who has become incompetent is a provision making the certificate of designated individuals, *e.g.* psychiatrists, conclusive that the trustee is no longer qualified to serve.[54]

### *Nonresidents*

Sometimes a will designates a person residing in another state as a fiduciary. Usually nonresidence is not disqualifying, but under a few statutes it is.[55] These statutes are of various types. For example, California disqualifies persons not resident in the United States from serving as administrator, but not as executor, presumably out of respect for the wishes of the testator.[56] Some states have reciprocity provisions; a foreign bank can be appointed only if its home state would do the same in the converse situation.[57] Others

**47.** Altshuler v. Minkus–Whalen, 579 N.E.2d 1369 (Mass.App.1991) (administrator removed for failure to tell court of the existence of other heirs); Smith v. Underwood, 437 S.E.2d 512, 517 (N.C.App.1993) (trustee removed for failure to file accounts, commingling); Matter of Estate of Townsend, 793 P.2d 818 (Mont.1990).

**48.** *Restatement, Third, of Trusts* § 37, comm. e (1999).

**49.** Matter of Estate of Stoskopf, 954 P.2d 712 (Kan.App.1998). *See also* Matter of Estate of Jones, 492 N.W.2d 723, 726 (Iowa App. 1992).

**50.** *Restatement, Third, of Trusts* § 37, comm. e (1999); In re Estate of Ehlers, 911 P.2d 1017 (Wash.App.1996) (trustee not removed for delay in filing account).

**51.** Unif.Trust Code § 706(b)(3).

**52.** *Restatement, Third, of Trusts* § 37, comm. c (1999); First Nat. Bank v. State, Office of Public Advoc., 902 P.2d 330, 334 (Alaska 1995) (guardian acting on behalf of incompetent settlor with power of removal); Mucci v. Stobbs, 666 N.E.2d 50, 56 (Ill.App.1996).

**53.** Unif.Trust Code § 706(b)(4).

**54.** Buchanan & Buchanan, *Strategies for Clients Residing in Nursing Homes*, 20 Est. Plann. 27, 30 (1993). In Manning v. Glens Falls Nat. Bank, 697 N.Y.S.2d 203 (A.D.1999) a similar clause was used to nullify a settlor's attempted exercise of a power to remove a trustee while the settlor was in a nursing home.

**55.** *Restatement, Third, of Trusts* § 32,- comm. d (1999); In re Farnsworth's Estate, 241 A.2d 204 (N.H.1968) (trust assets distributed to N.Y. bank); Grasty v. Clare, 168 S.E.2d 261 (Va.1969) (executor); Munford v. Maclellan, 373 S.E.2d 368 (Ga.1988) (refusal to remove nonresident trustee).

**56.** Cal.Prob.Code § 8402; In re Estate of Damskog, 1 Cal.Rptr.2d 653 (App.1991) (heir residing in Norway cannot even nominate administrator).

**57.** Matter of Estate of Westpfal, 531 N.Y.S.2d 81 (Surr.1988) (appointment of Florida bank for land in New York upheld); Ohio Rev. Code § 2109.21B.

condition the appointment of a nonresident on the naming of a resident cofiduciary.[58] Some allow only nonresident fiduciaries who are related to the decedent by blood or marriage. A Florida statute of this type was upheld, but several judges dissented on the ground that the statute was "arbitrary and irrational" since "a close personal advisor" was "a far more rational choice by the decedent than the choice of remote [relatives] which the statute would allow."[59]

Extreme forms of parochialism have been held unconstitutional. A South Carolina court struck down a statute which barred foreign corporations "licensed to business in a state contiguous to the State of South Carolina" from serving as testamentary trustees.[60] But other restrictions have been upheld against constitutional challenge.[61]

A fiduciary ought to be subject to process in the state of appointment so that the fiduciary can easily be brought to account, but this can be accomplished simply by requiring out-of-state fiduciaries to consent to local jurisdiction.[62] Thus, a Louisiana court in appointing an Arkansas resident as trustee, noted that "the Long Arm Statute would be available for the purpose of service of process."[63]

Distance between the fiduciary and the beneficiaries or the property which the fiduciary administers is sometimes a factor in determining the appropriateness of a particular fiduciary. An Arkansas court removed a resident of New York City as trustee of a trust operating a farm in Arkansas, saying she was "not qualified to make farming decisions."[64] A New York court approved a transfer of the situs of a trust to California after the beneficiaries had moved to that state.[65] The Uniform Probate Code provides for such transfers, which may involve "removal of the trustee and appointment of a trustee in another state."[66]

### *Corporations*

A corporation, usually a bank,[67] is frequently appointed as executor, or

58. Estate of White, 509 N.Y.S.2d 252 (Surr.1986) (nondomiciliary alien can act as trustee only if a N.Y. resident also serves); Matter of Estate of Oelberg, 414 N.W.2d 672 (Iowa App.1987) (resident co-executor appointed).

59. In re Greenberg's Estate 390 So.2d 40, 51 (Fla.1980).

60. Dunn v. North Carolina Nat. Bank, 277 S.E.2d 143 (S.C.1981). *See also* In re Fernandez' Estate, 335 So.2d 829 (Fla.1976) (citizenship requirement unconstitutional).

61. In re Guardianship of Coller, 599 N.E.2d 292 (Ohio App.1991) (residence requirement for guardians of the person upheld).

62. Uniform Probate Code § 3–602; Cal. Prob.Code § 8572; Md. Estates and Trusts Code § 5–105(6).

63. Succession of Batton v. Prince, 384 So.2d 506 (La.App.1980). *See also* Unif.Trust Code § 202(a) (by accepting trusteeship trustee submits to court's jurisdiction).

64. Ashman v. Pickens, 674 S.W.2d 4, 5 (Ark.App.1984). *See also* Matter of Estate of Ikuta, 639 P.2d 400 (Haw.1981) (appointing a resident of Hawaii, where trust had property, as cotrustee where existing trustee lived in California).

65. In re Weinberger's Trust, 250 N.Y.S.2d 887 (A.D.1964).

66. Uniform Probate Code § 7–305. *See also* Unif.Trust Code § 110. *Restatement, Third, of Trusts* § 37, comm. e (1999) lists "geographic inconvenience" as a possible ground of removal of a trustee.

67. The connection between banking and trust business is somewhat accidental. The earliest corporate trustees were often insurance companies. 2 A.Scott, *Trusts* § 96.5, at 31–32 (4th ed. Fratcher 1987). Municipal corporations sometimes operate as trustees of charitable trusts. *Restatement, Third, of Trusts* § 33, comm. d (1999); Cohen v. City of Lynn, 598 N.E.2d 682 (Mass.App.1992) (conveyance of land to city for a park creates a trust).

trustee,[68] or conservator. Many states impose special regulations on corporate trustees. In California, for example, a corporation cannot engage in the trust business unless it obtains a certificate of authority and deposits security with the state treasurer.[69] A corporation not so licensed is subject to removal.[70] National banks engaging in the trust business are regulated by the Comptroller of Currency, who can order a bank to discontinue its trust business because of bad practices.[71]

Whereas individual fiduciaries may die or become incompetent before the job is over, this is not a problem with corporations, so instruments often name a bank as successor fiduciary if a designated individual(s) cannot act. If a bank merges with another, normally the successor bank assumes the fiduciary functions of the predecessor without a formal new appointment.[72] However, although "from a legal sense" banks provide continuity, personnel changes at a particular bank may create a "lack of communications continuity in the eye of the customer."[73]

Banks charge for their services, whereas individual family members often do not.[74] This may push toward the choice of an individual.[75] On the other hand, executors' and trustees' fees are deductible for tax purposes, so part of the cost is actually borne by the government. In small estates, however, this tax deduction is useless and a professional's fee may be prohibitive. Professionals generally charge a minimum fee to discourage small estates and trusts, or refuse to handle them altogether.[76] The cost-saving in using a family member may be offset by the need for professional advice. As one court noted when appointing the testator's daughter as administrator, "most testators appoint a loved one, a relative or a trust friend as a fiduciary [and] assume the fiduciary will hire the experts necessary."[77] If an individual fiduciary has to hire an investment counselor, its fee may be equivalent to that of a professional trustee who provides investment expertise as part of the job.[78]

If a corporate fiduciary mismanages a trust or estate, it usually can pay for any losses. An individual is more likely to be judgment-proof. This risk can be avoided by having the individual give a bond with sureties, but the cost of such a bond reduces the cost-advantage of an individual fiduciary.

**68.** Often the same individual or corporation serves as both executor of a will and trustee of a testamentary trust created by the will. This is allowed despite a potential conflict of interest when the executor's accounts are approved. Lindsey v. Ogden, 406 N.E.2d 701 (Mass.App.1980).

**69.** Cal.Financial Code § 1500.

**70.** Erwin & Erwin v. Bronson, 844 P.2d 269 (Or.App.1992); Ozee v. American Council on Gift Annuities, 888 F.Supp. 1318 (N.D.Tex. 1995).

**71.** Central Nat. Bank v. U.S. Dept. of Treasury, 912 F.2d 897 (7th Cir.1990).

**72.** 12 U.S.C. § 215(e) (consolidated national bank continues to hold fiduciary offices without court order).

**73.** Buchanan, *Choosing Executors and Trustees*, 119 Trust & Estates (Aug 1980) 26, 27.

**74.** Family members, however, are legally entitled to claim a fee. For a more detailed discussion of fees, see Section 12.5.

**75.** Matter of Estate of Wasson, 453 N.E.2d 120, 123 (Ill.App.1983) (upholding choice of family member over bank because of concern over fees). Cal.Prob.Code § 15642(a)(5) lists as a ground for removal "where the trustee's compensation is excessive."

**76.** Olsen & Sharman, *Practical and Tax Considerations in Deciding Who Should Be a Trustee,* 8 Est.Plann. 214, 219 (1981).

**77.** In re Estate of Tyler, 716 N.E.2d 1239, 1240 (Ohio Com.Pl.1999).

**78.** Bromberg & Fortson, *Selection of a Trustee: Tax and Other Considerations*, 19 Sw. L.J. 523, 530 (1965). As to the right of a fiduciary to hire agents with trust funds see Section 12.5, at note 76 et seq.

Professional fiduciaries are expected to be experts in making investments and are held to higher standards than individuals.[79] "Serving as executor or trustee is neither an honor, nor a game for beginners to play. [It] requires technical skills [and] experience."[80] Banks have these qualities, but they also have a reputation for conservatism. A settlor who wants the trust to follow a more adventurous investment course may prefer to designate an individual trustee. If the trust is to operate a business, an individual familiar with the business may be a better choice for trustee than a bank.[81]

One way want to avoid the conflicts of interest which arise when a beneficiary is named trustee is to name a corporation instead, particularly when the conflict presents tax problems.[82] But Professor Pennell has questioned the "common belief among estate planners, often perpetrated by corporate fiduciaries, that * * * a trust beneficiary should never serve as trustee. * * * By using proper precautions in planning, coupled with precise drafting, the estate planner may feel safe in employing whomever is best suited for a particular circumstance."[83]

### *Multiple Fiduciaries*

It may be desirable to have more than one fiduciary.[84] Multiple fiduciaries may allow the particular skills of various persons to be utilized. A corporate trustee may be best suited to handle records and to perform routine administration while a business associate may have desirable investment skills and a family friend or relative may be the best person to exercise discretion over distributions.[85] Using a family member as co-trustee may also have psychological benefits. A spouse or child may resent a testator's putting "his or her" inheritance in a trust. This resentment can be reduced if the beneficiary is named as co-trustee.[86]

Multiple fiduciaries also have disadvantages. Unless the additional executors or trustees serve without compensation, the total fees may be higher.[87] If the co-fiduciaries disagree, court proceedings may be needed to resolve the deadlock.[88] The chance of such a deadlock can be reduced by designating an uneven number of fiduciaries and providing that in case of disagreement, the majority's decision will control. Absent such a provision the result is unclear. According to the second Restatement of Trusts if there are two or more trustees, all of them must agree to exercise their powers,[89] but the third

**79.** See Section 12.7, at note 40.

**80.** Mceachern, *Corporate Fiduciaries Can Be an Attoney's Best Friend*, 128 Trusts & Estates (April 1989) p. 30.

**81.** Bromberg & Fortson, *supra* note 78, at 532.

**82.** See notes 33–35 *supra*.

**83.** Pennell, *Estate Planning Considerations in Employing Individual Trustees*, 60 N.C.L.Rev. 799, 820 (1982).

**84.** This is not possible in custodianships, since the Uniform Transfers to Minors Act allows only one custodian to serve at a time. Uniform Transfers to Minors Act § 10.

**85.** Bromberg & Fortson, *supra* note 78, at 547.

**86.** *Id.* at 533. Co-trustees may also avoid having income attributed to a beneficiary-trustee under Section 678 of the Internal Revenue Code. However, naming a co-trustee will not be enough to keep the assets out of the trustee's taxable estate under Internal Revenue Code § 2041 unless the co-trustee has a "substantial interest in the property * * * which is adverse to exercise of the power," *e.g.*, a person with an interest in the remainder.

**87.** See Section 12.5, at note 109 et seq.

**88.** *Restatement, Third, of Trusts* § 39, comm. e (1999).

**89.** *Restatement (Second) of Trusts* § 194, comm. a (1959). *See also* Calif.Prob.Code § 15620. For charitable trusts, majority rules. *Restatement (Second) of Trusts* § 383 (1959).

Restatement and many statutes provide for majority rule.[90] At common law, each executor could exercise many powers without the others' concurrence,[91] but the Uniform Probate Code provides that all personal representatives must concur in an action unless the will provides otherwise.[92] This can create problems even if there is no actual disagreement among the fiduciaries, since the failure of all fiduciaries to join may invalidate a transaction.[93] When all fiduciaries have to sign every document, efficient administration is impaired.[94] This can be avoided by authorizing fiduciaries to delegate routine matters to a co-fiduciary. The Uniform Probate Code's requirement that all personal representatives must concur in exercising powers does not apply one of them has been delegated to act for the others, or "when the concurrence of all cannot be readily be obtained in the time reasonably available for emergency action."[95]

If a will names more than one fiduciary, it is usually assumed that if one ceases to act the others can continue without any need to appoint a successor. The Uniform Probate Code, for example, allows the personal representatives "remaining after the appointment of one or more is terminated * * * [to] exercise all the powers incident to the office."[96] The Restatement of Trusts says that when one of several trustees ceases to act a "replacement trustee is required, only if the settlor manifested an intention, or it is conducive to the proper administration of the trust that the number of trustees be maintained."[97]

### *Resignation*

A person will not be appointed executor or trustee over his or her objection.[98] A trustee who has not accepted the office may reject it,[99] but once accepting the office a fiduciary needs court approval in order to resign unless the trust instrument provides otherwise or all the beneficiaries consent.[100] Some trust instruments allow a trustee to resign simply by giving notice to

**90.** 760 ILCS § 5/10; N.Y. EPTL § 10–10.7; Uniform Trustees' Powers Act § 6(a); Unif. Trust Code § 703(a); *Restatement, Third, of Trusts* § 39 (1996); Edwards v. Edwards, 71 Cal.Rptr.2d 653 (App.1998) (majority controls as to voting stock under Corporations Code which trumps Probate Code).

**91.** F. Maitland, *Equity* 93–94 (1913); 2 W. Blackstone, *Commentaries* *510 (1765). *But cf.* 3 *Amer. Law of Prop.* § 14.28, at 689.

**92.** Uniform Probate Code § 3–717.

**93.** Walter E. Wilhite Revocable Living Trust v. Northwest Yearly Meeting Pension Fund, 916 P.2d 1264, 1271 (Idaho 1996); Farmers State Bank v. Harmon, 778 F.2d 543 (10th Cir.1985) (guarantee signed by one of two trustees is ineffective).

**94.** Fratcher, *Trustees' Powers Legislation,* 37 N.Y.U.L.Rev. 627, 640 (1962).

**95.** Uniform Probate Code § 3–717. *See also Restatement, Third, Trusts* § 39, comm. c, d (1999); *cf.* Cal.Prob.Code § 15622 (when a trustee is "unavailable" others may act). For further discussion of delegation see Section 12.8, at note 74 et seq.

**96.** Uniform Probate Code § 3–718. *See also* Calif.Prob.Code § 8521; N.Y. EPTL § 11–1.1(b)(11).

**97.** *Restatement, Third, of Trusts* § 34, comm. d (1999). *See also* Uniform Trustees' Powers Act § 6(b); Unif.Trust Code § 703(b); Rubinson v. Rubinson, 620 N.E.2d 1271, 1278 (Ill.App.1993) (act by remaining trustee was valid).

**98.** McCarthy v. Poulsen, 219 Cal.Rptr. 375 (App.1985) (error to force settlors to become trustees); In re Estate of Cavalier, 582 A.2d 1125 (Pa.Super.1990).

**99.** *Restatement, Third, of Trusts* § 35(2) (1999); Unif.Trust Code § 701(b).

**100.** *Restatement (Third) of Trusts* § 36 (1999). *But cf.* Uniform Transfers to Minors Act § 18(c) (custodian can resign by giving notice); Calif.Prob.Code § 15640 (consent of adult income beneficiaries sufficient for resignation); Unif.Trust Code § 705 (trustee may resign by giving 30 day notice to "qualified beneficiaries").

the current income beneficiaries.[101] This obviates the need for court proceedings which are wasteful since requests to resign are usually approved.[102] However, a court refused to allow a trustee to resign when no suitable successor had been found even though the trust instrument allowed resignation without court approval. "In some cases * * * the words of a will putting the acts of a trustee beyond review are not to be taken literally."[103]

### *Successor's Powers*

The powers conferred by an instrument on a fiduciary are usually not construed as personal to the original trustee or executor, *i.e.*, a successor can also exercise them. For example, a will authorized the "trustee named herein" to invade principal for any beneficiary. The named trustee refused to serve and a successor was appointed. The court held that the successor also had this power. "Useful in determining whether a particular power was intended to be personal to a named individual trustee is a consideration of the purpose of the settlor and the effect upon the realization of that purpose that a failure of the power would have." Given the needs of the testator's son the court refused to "conclude that the trustee's power to invade corpus * * * was rendered inoperative by the renunciation by the named trustee."[104] Many statutes presume that successor fiduciaries were intended to have the same powers.[105] The Uniform Probate Code gives a successor personal representative the same powers as the original except for any power "expressly made personal to the executor named in the will."[106] The Restatement of Trusts similarly allows successor trustees to exercise powers conferred on the original trustee unless the trust provides otherwise, but such a restrictive intent can be inferred from the circumstances; for example, the relationship between the settlor and the named trustee may show "an intention to place confidence in him and only in him."[107]

### *Attorneys' Role*

Testators and settlors often ask attorneys for advice as to who should be named as executor or trustee. A designation of the attorney who drafted the will as a fiduciary is sometimes challenged for undue influence or as a violation of the rules of professional conduct.[108]

**101.** T. Shaffer, *The Planning and Drafting of Wills and Trusts* 235 (2d ed. 1979); H.Tweed and W.Parsons, *Lifetime and Testamentary Estate Planning* 102 (10th ed 1988).

**102.** In re White, 484 A.2d 763, 766 (Pa. 1984); Oregon Bank v. Hendricksen, 515 P.2d 1328 (Or.1973) (trustee allowed to resign because stipulated compensation was too low).

**103.** Matter of Sherman B. Smith Family Trust, 482 N.W.2d 118, 119 (Wis.App.1992). *See also Restatement, Third, of Trusts* § 36, comm. a (1999).

**104.** Estate of Bowling, 93 T.C. 286, 295–96 (1989) (applying Georgia law). *See also* Matter of Estate of Webb, 832 P.2d 27, 29 (Okl. App.1991) (administrator cta can exercise power of sale conferred on executor).

**105.** Fratcher, *Trustees' Powers Legislation*, 37 N.Y.U.L.Rev. 627, 638 (1962); Uniform Trusts Act § 10; N.Y. EPTL § 11–1.1(b)(12); Wisc.Stat. § 701.17(3); *cf.* Cal.Prob.Code § 8442 (administrator cta has same powers as executor except as to "discretionary powers not conferred by law").

**106.** Uniform Probate Code § 3–716.

**107.** *Restatement (Second) of Trusts* § 196 (1959). *See also Restatement (Second) of Property (Donative Transfers)* § 18.1(3) (1984).

**108.** McGovern, *Undue Influence and Professional Responsibility*, 28 Real Prop.Prob. and T.J. 643, 670 (1994); Section 7.4, at note 30. In Matter of Bales, 608 N.E.2d 987 (Ind. 1993) a lawyer who drafted a will which named her executor and provided a high fee was reprimanded. A drafter-executor to whom the will gave discretion to distribute the estate to charities of his choice was held to be a "substantial beneficiary" thus raising a presumption of un-

Knowledgeable estate attorneys disagree about the propriety of attorneys serving as executors. Robert Stein suggests that it is "usually more efficient than the ordinary division of labor" between the personal representative and the estate's attorney; "potential communication difficulties are obviated. The attorney-representative is in a position to act quickly because it is unnecessary to wait for a lay representative to be informed and to participate." On the other hand, many time-consuming tasks of a personal representative require no legal expertise,[109] while others require skills which many lawyers lack. An "attorney who becomes a fiduciary must become financially sophisticated with investments and capable of evaluating the competence and prudence of [any] in-house or advisory service."[110] The trend to allow trustees to delegate investment functions experts may lead to a greater willingness on the part of lawyers to serve as trustees.[111]

Even lawyers who do not serve as fiduciaries profit from being chosen as attorneys for the executor or trustee. A provision in a will directing the executor to hire a particular attorney is usually held unenforceable on the ground that the executor, like any other client, should have "unfettered discretion to select an attorney."[112] Corporate executors typically hire the attorney who drafted the will to handle administration, a practice which has been described as a "conspiracy between corporate executors and lawyers to exploit the client by recommending that the testator name a bank as executor in exchange for assurance that the executor, once appointed, will retain the attorney to assist in the probate of the testator's estate."[113] A California court took a more favorable view of the practice when refusing to remove as executor a bank which had hired the drafter of the will as attorney for the estate.

> There is no doubt that economic self interest is a factor which motivates a corporate fiduciary to retain the same lawyer who drafts the will. Nevertheless, where the testator's selection of the executor is free and voluntary, his wish may not be annulled except on a clear showing the best interests of the estate require it. * * * Presumably, the lawyer with familiarity of the testator's property is a reasonable choice.[114]

Dean Price has suggested that lawyers who are asked to recommend an executor should not suggest their own appointment, or that of "an institution with which the lawyer has some connection. A corporate fiduciary should be recommended * * * only when in the best interests of the client. Even then

due influence. Allen v. Estate of Dutton, 394 So.2d 132 (Fla.App.1980).

**109.** Stein & Fierstein, *The Role of the Attorney in the Administration of the Estate*, 68 Minn.L Rev. 1107, 1164 (1984).

**110.** *Draft Statement of Principles Attorneys Acting as Other Fiduciaries*, 127 Trusts and Estates (Dec. 1988) p. 27.

**111.** Langbein, *The Uniform Prudent Investor Act and the Future of Trust Investing*, 81 Iowa L.Rev. 641, 666 (1996).

**112.** In re Estate of Deardoff, 461 N.E.2d 1292, 1293 (Ohio 1984). *See also* Johnston, *An Ethical Analysis of Common Estate Planning Practices*, 45 Ohio St.L.J. 57, 105 (1984); Hawaiian Trust Co., Ltd. v. Hogan, 623 P.2d 450 (Haw.App.1981). *But see* In re Devroy's Estate, 325 N.W.2d 345 (Wis.1982) (condition on appointment of X as executor that he retain Y as attorney upheld); La.Rev.Stat. § 9:2448 (designation of attorney in will is binding on executor); Kelley v. Marlin, 714 S.W.2d 303 (Tex. 1986) (direction to employ X as broker is binding).

**113.** Johnston, *supra* note 112, at 115. *See also* C. Wolfram, *Modern Legal Ethics* § 8.12.4 (1986).

**114.** Matter of Estate of Effron, 173 Cal. Rptr. 93, 102 (App.1981). *But cf.* Wis.Stat. § 856.31 (beneficiaries can select attorney for a corporate executor).

* * * the lawyer would do well to recommend more than one institution. * * * The lawyer should tell the client about any practices that corporate fiduciaries have of retaining the lawyer who prepared an instrument that names it as fiduciary."[115]

## § 12.5 Fees

An important factor in choosing a fiduciary is cost. In this section we will discuss the fees of personal representatives, trustees, their attorneys, and other related costs, such as bond and appraisal fees. It is convenient to talk about fiduciary fees in general, but dangerous to assume that the rules are the same for all fiduciaries. In California, for example, the fees of personal representatives and their attorneys are based on a percentage of the estate,[1] but the statutes governing the fees of trustees, custodians and conservators simply provide for "reasonable" compensation.[2] A donor who acts as custodian under the Uniform Transfers to Minors Act can receive no compensation,[3] but there is no such limitation on the settlor of a trust who acts as trustee.

### *Size of the Estate*

In many states fiduciary fees are based on the size of the estate or trust. New York, for example, allows personal representatives commissions on a sliding scale, starting at 5% of the first $100,000 down to 2% of property in excess of $5,000,000.[4] Trustees are entitled to annual fees of $10.50 per $1,000 of principal up to $400,000, $4.50 per $1,000 for the next $600,000, and $3 per $1,000 for the rest.[5] Note that fees for larger trusts are higher in amount, but smaller in proportion to the trust assets. Many trustees charge a minimum fee for each trust handled. This may make the use of a professional trustee uneconomical for a small trust, and may be a reason to consolidate smaller trusts with the same beneficiaries.[6]

The California provision for personal representatives is similar except that for estates over $25 million, a "reasonable amount" is substituted for a percentage.[7] The fees of personal representatives are typically based only on the probate estate.[8] They often exclude land on the theory that real estate passes outside administration.[9] On the other hand, executors fees based on a

**115.** J. Price, *Contemporary Estate Planning* 6–7 (1983).

§ 12.5

**1.** Cal.Prob.Code §§ 10800, 10810.

**2.** Cal.Prob.Code §§ 15681 (trustee), 3915(b) (custodian), 2640 (guardian and conservator).

**3.** Uniform Transfers to Minors Act § 15(b).

**4.** N.Y.Surr.Ct.Proc. Act § 2307.

**5.** N.Y.Surr.Ct.Proc.Act § 2309. In addition trustees receive 1% for all principal paid out. For charitable trusts the fees amount to 6% of the trust income.

**6.** See Section 9.6, at notes 21–25.

**7.** Cal.Prob.Code §§ 10800, 10810. These limitations apparently were inspired by the Getty estate the size of which produced (under the then prevailing rule) fees totalling over $27,000,000. Estate of Getty, 191 Cal.Rptr. 897, 898 (App.1983).

**8.** In re Estate of Preston, 560 A.2d 160, 164 (Pa.Super.1989) (error to include assets held in joint tenancy in computing executor's fee); Matter of Will of Staud, 529 N.Y.S.2d 978 (Surr.1988); *cf.* Iowa Code § 633.197–8 (2% of gross estate, excluding joint tenancy and life insurance paid to named beneficiary).

**9.** Arkansas includes real estate in the fee base for attorneys but not for personal representatives unless the latter performs "substantial services with respect to" it. Sloss v. Farmers Bank and Trust Co., 719 S.W.2d 273 (Ark. 1986); *cf.* Matthews v. Watkins, 373 S.E.2d 133, 139 (N.C.App.1988) (when land sold proper to include sale proceeds in computing executor's fee).

gross estate of $2.4 million were allowed even though the probate estate was only $20,000, when the will so provided.

> The statute denies executor's commissions on assets * * * passing outside the will on the theory that such assets vest automatically and are not received or paid out by the executor. Often, perhaps most often, this is a fiction. In actuality, the executor may have substantial responsibilities with regard to such * * * such property. Mr. Grant in his will, recognized this reality.[10]

The Uniform Probate Code does not base fiduciary fees on a percentage of the estate but rather provides for "reasonable compensation."[11] The Restatement of Trusts and Uniform Trust Code use the same language for trustees, as does the Uniform Transfers to Minors Act for custodians.[12] On the other hand, some states provide a statutory fee schedule for trustees based on the income and principal of the trust.[13]

Is there a substantial practical difference between a "reasonable fee" and a percentage of the estate? A Florida court reversed an award of administrator's fees based on a percentage of the estate under a "reasonable compensation" statute, saying that the "the amount of the probate estate * * * was not intended to be the sole controlling factor."[14] The Florida legislature thereafter reinstated a fee schedule based on a percentage of the estate, but this statute, like most percentage fee provisions, also allows "further compensation" for "any extraordinary services" provided by the fiduciary.[15] Some statutory percentage fees are expressed as a maximum. Arkansas, for example, allows personal representatives "reasonable compensation not to exceed" specified percentages.[16]

Reasonable compensation usually takes custom into account,[17] and courts often rely on expert testimony in passing on fees.[18] Professional trustees customarily base their fees on a percentage of the income and principal of the trust.[19] A termination fee of 2% of the trust assets was upheld under a

**10.** Will of Grant, 600 N.Y.S.2d 423, 425 (Surr.1993). See also Martin, *Professional Responsibility and Probate Practices*, 1975 Wis. L.Rev. 911, 946 (attorney and personal representative should be compensated for services performed on nonprobate property).

**11.** Uniform Probate Code § 3–719 (personal representatives), § 5–413 (conservators). *See also* Ind.Code. § 29–1–10–13.

**12.** *Restatement, Third, of Trusts* § 38 (1999); Uniform Transfers to Minors Act § 15(b); Unif.Trust Code § 708.

**13.** Md. Estates and Trusts Code § 14–103; Ky.R.S. § 386.180; note 5 supra.

The fee base for personal representatives often includes income of the estate. Matter of Estate of Schuldt, 428 N.W.2d 251, 254 (S.D. 1988); Estate of Sanchez, 39 Cal.Rptr.2d 141 (App.1995) ("receipts" means net income, not gross receipts).

**14.** In re Estate of Platt, 586 So.2d 328, 336 (Fla.1991). *See also* Ford v. Peoples Trust and Sav. Bank, 651 N.E.2d 1193 (Ind.App. 1995) (fees in large estate excessive given the time required).

**15.** Fla.Stat.§ 733.617. *See also* Cal.Prob. Code § 10801; Wis.Stat. § 857.05(2); Matter of Estate of Barber, 779 P.2d 477, 488 (Mont. 1989) (additional fees for extraordinary services of attorney).

**16.** Ark.Code § 28–48–108. *See also* Iowa Code § 633.197; Md. Estates and Trusts Code § 7–601(b); Estate of Stone, 768 P.2d 334 (Mont.1989) (fee claim based on statutory maximum disallowed).

**17.** *Restatement, Third, of Trusts* § 38, comm. c (1999); Appeal of Wickersham, 594 N.E.2d 498, 502 (Ind.App.1992) (attorney fees "higher than those customarily charged" reduced).

**18.** Estate of McClenahan v. Biberstein, 671 N.E.2d 482, 484 (Ind.App.1996) (attorneys fee).

**19.** *Restatement (Second) of Trusts* § 242, comm. b (1959); Jack, *Fiduciary Fees: Variations and Complexities*, 112 Trusts & Estates 622 (1973).

"reasonable compensation" statute. "In determining what is reasonable a trial court should look to the practices of other trust institutions in the state," most of which charged such a fee.[20]

State and local bar associations used to issue fee schedules which based lawyers' fees for administering estates on the size of the estate[21] until the Supreme Court held that such fee schedules violated the antitrust laws.[22] This decision contributed to a trend to base fees on factors other than the size of the estate.[23] On the other hand, a California court upheld that state's statutory percentage fee system for executors and attorneys. The anti-trust laws did not apply because the statute constituted state action. The legislature "after expending enormous energy" studying the issue had concluded that its system was "both cost effective and fair," because it saved judicial time which would otherwise be spent verifying fees,[24] favored small estates, and encouraged the efficient use of time.

The Restatement of Trusts lists the "amount and character of the trust property" as a factor in determining a reasonable fee along with the "responsibility and risk assumed in administering the trust."[25] A court said in determining a reasonable attorney's fee, "the size of the estate is relevant because it technically defines the attorney's exposure to liability [and] * * * it may also help to forecast the extent of the work to be performed, but clearly without any degree of certainty."[26] For example, holding on to a block of stock in a big company may involve little effort in comparison to managing a small business.[27] One court reversed a fee award based on a percentage of the estate, noting that the estate "contained liquid assets of a readily ascertainable value."[28]

Basing trustee's fees on the value of the trust principal may be justified as rewarding trustees who make shrewd investments, just as the compensation of mutual fund managers is often based on the value of the fund.[29] But percentage formulas also create perverse incentives. In California, personal representatives' fees are based on "the appraisal value of property in the inventory, plus gains over the appraisal value on sales,"[30] which gives them an

**20.** Matter of Trusts Under Will of Dwan, 371 N.W.2d 641, 642–43 (Minn.App.1985). *See also* Estate of Rosen, 520 A.2d 700, 702 (Me. 1987) (fee was reasonable and "consistent with what would be charged by other corporate fiduciaries in the community").

**21.** *Fiduciary and Probate Counsel Fees in the Wake of Goldfarb*, 13 Real Prop., Prob. & Trust L.J. 238 (1978) (hereinafter cited as *Fiduciary Fees* ).

**22.** Goldfarb v. Virginia State Bar, 421 U.S. 773 (1975).

**23.** In re Estate of Secoy, 484 N.E.2d 160, 164 (Ohio App.1984) (noting a "general retreat from fee schedules" following *Goldfarb*).

**24.** Estate of Effron, 173 Cal.Rptr. 93, 99 (App.1981). *See also* Stein & Fierstein, *The Role of the Attorney in Estate Administration*, 68 Minn.L.Rev. 1107, 1178 (1984) (lawyers' time in justifying fee may increase cost of administration).

**25.** *Restatement, Third, of Trusts* § 38, comm. c (1999).

**26.** Estate of Randeris v. Randeris, 523 N.W.2d 600, 607 (Iowa App.1994).

**27.** Matter of Trusts Under Will of Dwan, 371 N.W.2d 641, 643–44 (Minn.App.1985) (dissent); Martin, *supra* note 9, at 944.

**28.** In re Estate of Secoy, 484 N.E.2d 160, 164 (Ohio App.1984).

**29.** However, trustees' fees are not as "performance based" as those of some investment advisors. Gordon, *The Puzzling Persistence of the Constrained Prudent Man Rule*, 62 N.Y.U.L.Rev. 52, 82 (1987).

**30.** Cal.Prob.Code § 10800(b); Estate of Downing, 184 Cal.Rptr. 511, 515–16 (App. 1982) (unrealized appreciation in estate not counted in computing administrator's fee).

incentive to sell appreciated property.[31] Lawyers whose fees are based on the size of the probate estate have an incentive not to advise clients to avoid probate.[32]

Robert Stein has observed, "folklore in some legal communities suggests * * * that attorneys price estate planning services cheaply in the expectation that they will later be retained to provide the more profitable estate administration services."[33] Such "loss leader" pricing has tax advantages for clients, since fees for drafting instruments are not generally tax deductible,[34] whereas fees paid to the attorney for an estate are.[35] However, for lawyers the system has the disadvantage that full compensation is postponed until the client dies and may be lost altogether if, for example, the client moves to another jurisdiction or for some other reason the deceased client's personal representative selects another lawyer to handle the estate.[36] In any event, Stein's study found that "whatever the historical pattern, * * * estate planning services are now priced similarly to estate administration and other legal services performed by the attorney." The study also found that fees in California based on a percentage of the estate were comparable to fees charged in states with a reasonable compensation system.[37]

### *Other Factors*

What factors other than the size of the estate are relevant in determining a reasonable fee? The Restatement of Trusts mentions "the time devoted to trust duties."[38] The ABA Model Rules of Professional Conduct also make "the time and labor required" a factor in determining the reasonableness of a lawyer's fee.[39] An attorney was reprimanded for charging a fee which was not justified by "sufficient work on an hourly basis."[40] A fee claimed by a personal representative was rejected on the ground that "there was no evidence of the time spent in performing the claimed services."[41] Another court rejected fees

**31.** *Cf.* Matter of Will of Staud, 529 N.Y.S.2d 978 (Surr.1988) (executor cannot swell fees by electing to have deferred compensation benefits paid to probate estate).

**32.** In Matter of Tobin, 628 N.E.2d 1268 (Mass.1994) a lawyer was suspended inter alia for advising probate of an estate where all the assets were held in joint tenancy.

**33.** Stein & Fierstein, *supra* note 24, at 1193. *See also* Johnston, *An Ethical Analysis of Common Estate Planning Practices—Is Good Business Bad Ethics?* 45 Ohio St.L.J. 57, 102 (1984); *Developments Regarding the Professional Responsibility of the Estate Planning Lawyer: the Effect of the Model Rules of Professional Conduct*, 22 Real Prop.Prob. and Trust J. 1, 5 (1987).

**34.** Luman, 79 T.C. 846, 855 (1982).

**35.** Int.Rev.Code § 2053.

**36.** Tate, *Strategies for Establishing a Fair Rate of Compensation for Planning a Client's Estate,* 13 Est.Plan. 194, 196 (1986); Fox, *The State of Estate Planning: Meet Challenges and Prosper*, Trusts & Estates (Sept. 1992) 20. As to the practice of corporate fiduciaries to hire the attorney who drafted a will see Section 12.4 note 113 et seq.

**37.** Stein & Fierstein, *supra* note 24, at 1188, 1193.

**38.** *Restatement, Third, of Trusts* § 38, comm. c (1999).

**39.** Rule 1.5(a)(1). *See also* ABA Model Code of Professional Responsibility DR 2–106(B)(1); Minn.Stat. § 525.515.

**40.** Office of Disciplinary Counsel v. Burkhart, 581 N.E.2d 540 (Ohio 1991). *See also* Matter of Tobin, 628 N.E.2d 1268, 1269–70 (Mass.1994) (lawyer suspended for unreasonable fee based on former fee schedule "and not on time spent" of which he kept no records).

**41.** Noble v. McNerney, 419 N.W.2d 424, 430 (Mich.App.1988); Estate of Stone, 768 P.2d 334, 336 (Mont.1989) (claim for fees by attorney-executor who kept no time logs rejected); Matter of Estate of Konopka, 498 N.W.2d 853 (Wis.App.1993). *But see* In re Estate of Salus, 617 A.2d 737, 743 (Pa.Super.1992) (trustee awarded fee despite lack of time records); Estate of McClenahan v. Biberstein, 671 N.E.2d 482, 486 (Ind.App.1996) (same for attorney); Andrews v. Gorby, 675 A.2d 449, 455 (Conn. 1996).

claimed by a lawyer and a personal representative on the ground that the "equivalent hourly rates" ($561 for the bank and $836 for the lawyer) were unreasonable.[42] On the other hand, Bleak–House type fees exceeding the assets remaining in an estate were allowed in a case where "although an inordinate amount of time was spent by the attorneys for the estate, the time spent was reasonable and necessary" under the circumstances.[43] However, no statute fixes fees on a per hour basis, and courts have also resisted this notion. A claim for attorneys' fees based on 364.5 hours of work in administering an estate was rejected because "a number of routine matters had occupied an inordinate amount" of time. An expert testified that only "48 hours of a legal assistant's time and 131 hours of a lawyer's time" were reasonable for this estate. The attorney's primary area of practice was personal injury, and "clients should not be expected to pay for the education of a lawyer when he spends excessive amounts of time on tasks which, with reasonable experience, become matters of routine."[44] Moreover, "an attorney is not entitled to fees at professional legal rates for tasks that should be performed by staff, such as depositing checks in a bank." This is a common theme in cases in which the attorney also serves as executor, or the executor is a family member who lets the lawyer do all the work.[45]

Family members and friends who act as trustees are entitled to reasonable compensation as well as professionals, but usually at a lower rate under a reasonable compensation standard which takes into account "the trustee's skill, experience and facilities."[46] For attorney fees, "the experience, reputation, and ability of the lawyer" are relevant.[47] A court reduced the fee claimed by an accountant who "did not possess the 'specialized skills' or 'requisite level of expertise' to advise the estate in tax matters."[48]

Poor performance may cause a reduction or even total loss of fees. An executor was denied all compensation because of unjustified delays in closing an estate.[49] The fees of a trustee which had improperly left cash in a checking account were reduced by 10% in addition to surcharging the trustee for the loss suffered by the trust. "Whether and to what extent, a trustee should be ordered to refund commissions is within the discretion of the trial court if a trustee has been guilty of a serious breach of trust."[50] The Restatement includes "the quality of the trustee's performance" in its list of relevant

**42.** Ford v. Peoples Trust and Sav. Bank, 651 N.E.2d 1193, 1195 (Ind.App.1995).

**43.** In re Estate of Schaffer, 656 N.E.2d 368, 372 (Ohio App.1995).

**44.** Matter of Estate of Larson, 694 P.2d 1051, 1055–59 (Wash.1985). *See also* In re Estate of Miller, 556 N.E.2d 568, 571 (Ill.App. 1990); Matter of Estate of Quinn, 830 P.2d 282, 285 (Utah App.1992).

**45.** Estate of Coughlin, 633 N.Y.S.2d 610 (A.D.1995); Matter of Estate of Mathwig, 843 P.2d 1112, 1113 (Wash.App.1993).

**46.** *Restatement, Third, of Trusts* § 38, comm. c (1999). *See also* Shear v. Gabovitch, 685 N.E.2d 1168, 1192 (Mass.App.1997) (proper to disallow claim by individual trustee to fees based on a corporate fiduciary fee schedule).

**47.** ABA Model Rule 1.5. *See also* Code of Prof.Resp. DR 2–106.

**48.** In re Estate of Wallace, 829 S.W.2d 696, 702 (Tenn.App.1992).

**49.** Estate of Heller, 9 Cal.Rptr.2d 274 (App.1992). *See also* Lowery v. Evonuk, 767 P.2d 489 (Or.App.1989) (trustee).

In In re Estate of McCool, 553 A.2d 761 (N.H.1988) an executor was denied compensation because he had a conflict of interest as lawyer for persons with claims against the estate.

**50.** Maryland Nat'l Bank v. Cummins, 588 A.2d 1205, 1219–20 (Md.1991). In In re Consupak, Inc., 87 B.R. 529 (Bktcy.N.D.Ill.1988), a bankruptcy trustee was surcharged for leaving money in a checking account and the fee of the attorney for the trustee was reduced for failure to advise the trustee of his duty.

considerations in determining compensation.[51] The fee may be reduced even if the amount of loss to the estate or trust cannot be determined.[52] But fiduciaries who acted in good faith and performed valuable services may receive a fee despite a breach of duty.[53]

### *Contract*

Fees of fiduciaries or the attorney for an estate are often not discussed at the time a will or trust is drafted,[54] even though this would be a desirable practice.[55] ABA Model Rule 1.5(b) says that "the basis or rate of the [lawyer's] fee shall be communicated to the client * * * before or within a reasonable time after commencing the representation,"[56] but this does not apply to the fee of the attorney for the estate who is not necessarily the testator's client.

When an instrument does state what a fiduciary or lawyer is to receive, this provision may preclude a claim for more. For example, a trust provided that the trustee was to receive annual commissions on income "at the rates allowed * * * under the laws of the State of New York at the date hereof." New York law was thereafter amended to give trustees more compensation, and normally the statute in effect when compensation is claimed controls, regardless when the trust was created,[57] but the trustee was not allowed the higher compensation because of the provision in the trust instrument.[58] According to the Restatement of Trusts, a trustee's compensation is "ordinarily governed" by such a provision, but if the amount specified "is or becomes unreasonably high or unreasonably low, the court may allow a smaller or higher compensation."[59] Such relief is denied, however, if a trustee has agreed with the settlor to act for a certain compensation, and such an agreement is normally inferred when a trustee accepts a trust which contains such a provision.[60] Even in this case, however, a "substantial and unanticipated change" in the circumstances may warrant ignoring it.[61]

**51.** *Restatement, Third, of Trusts* § 38, comm. c (1999).

**52.** Matter of Kingseed's Estate, 413 N.E.2d 917 (Ind.App.1980).

**53.** Burch v. Dodge, 608 P.2d 1032 (Kan. App.1980) (since surcharge will make estate whole, no abuse of discretion to award trustee a fee); Matter of Estate of Bartlett, 680 P.2d 369 (Okl.1984) (fee should be reduced only if administrator failed to perform duties, not for an improper sale); Matter of Trust of Grover, 710 P.2d 597 (Idaho 1985) (family member trustee gets compensation despite failure to keep records).

**54.** Martin, *supra* note 10, at 942.

**55.** McGovern, *Undue Influence and Professional Responsibility*, 28 Real Prop.Prob. and Trust J. 643, 672 (1994). Massachusetts encourages this practice by requiring fiduciaries who know that someone intends to designate them to provide the customer with a statement of their current charges. Mass.Ann. Laws c. 203, § 4B. As to cases where the drafter is designated as fiduciary see Section 12.4, note 110.

**56.** ABA Model Rules of Professional Conduct 1.5(b).

**57.** *Restatement, Third, of Trusts* § 38, comm. c (1999).

**58.** Lehman v. Irving Trust Co., 432 N.E.2d 769 (N.Y.1982). *See also* Estate of Scheid, 657 N.E.2d 311 (Ohio App.1995) (executor bound by will provision that she was to get no compensation). *But cf.* Matter of Indenture Agreement of Lawson, 607 A.2d 803 (Pa.Super.1992) (provision that trustee's "total compensation" shall be 4% of trust income does not bar customary fee on principal at termination of trust).

**59.** *Restatement, Third, of Trusts* § 38, comm. e (1999). *See also* Cal.Prob.Code § 15680(b)(2); Unif.Trust Code § 708(b).

**60.** For cases enforcing such a contractual limitation on compensation *outside* the instrument, *see* Lowy v. Kessler, 522 So.2d 917 (Fla. App.1988) (executor); Rutanen v. Ballard, 678 N.E.2d 133, 142 (Mass.1997) (trustee).

**61.** Compare other cases of deviations from the terms of a trust when circumstances change. Section 9.6, note 10 et seq.

Under the Uniform Probate Code "if a will provides for compensation of the personal representative and there is no contract regarding compensation, he may renounce the provision before qualifying and be entitled to reasonable compensation."[62] A court held that a personal representative was bound by an agreement over fees even though the testator had misrepresented the complexities of the estate. When the personal representative

> learned the truth about the estate she could have exercised her right to rescind the agreement; instead, she undertook to perform it. * * * [Such] acquiescence in the contract after learning of the true facts concerning the estate estops her from seeking any fee other than that called for by the contract.[63]

A stipulation in a will about the compensation of the attorney for the estate may not be binding on the ground that "it is the [personal] representative who contracts for the services, not the testator."[64]

Agreements to serve without any compensation have been held unenforceable for lack of consideration,[65] but under the Uniform Probate Code a personal representative "may renounce his right to all or any part of the compensation," presumably without consideration.[66] Since fiduciaries have a right to take their fee before the assets of a trust or estate are distributed,[67] a trustee who distributes assets without deducting a fee may be deemed to have waived any claim to one.[68]

A provision for an unreasonably *high* fee for a fiduciary may be valid as a devise or gift,[69] but is subject to attack for undue influence. An attorney who drafted a will that named him as executor with a designated fee was limited to reasonable compensation because of the "fiduciary relationship" between lawyer and client.[70] New Jersey does not allow trustees commissions in excess of those fixed by statute unless the will refers to the statute and "expressly authorizes" payment of higher commissions.[71] Presumably this does not apply to a devise to a family member which exceeds the statutory fee.

**62.** Uniform Probate Code § 3–719. However, a comment to the Code says that "if a will provision is framed as a condition on the nomination, it could not be renounced."

**63.** Lowy v. Kessler, 522 So.2d 917, 918 (Fla.App.1988). *See also* In re Estate of Grimm, 705 N.E.2d 483, 491 (Ind.App.1999). But in Estate of Craft, 68 T.C. 249 (1977), an executor after serving was allowed more compensation than that provided in the will.

**64.** Matter of Estate of Schuldt, 428 N.W.2d 251, 255 (S.D.1988). Compare the idea that the will cannot control the executor's choice of an attorney. Section 12.4, note .

**65.** Riddleberger v. Goeller, 282 A.2d 101 (Md.1971); *cf.* Graddick v. First Farmers and Merchants Nat. Bank, 453 So.2d 1305 (Ala. 1984) (trustee's promise to waive fee enforceable because beneficiary acted in reliance).

**66.** Uniform Probate Code § 3–719.

**67.** *Restatement, Third, of Trusts* § 38, comm. b (1999).

**68.** *Restatement, Third, of Trusts* § 38, comm. g (1999); Rutanen v. Ballard, 678 N.E.2d 133, 142 (Mass.1997); McCormick v. McCormick, 536 N.E.2d 419, 435 (Ill.App. 1988). However, mere failure to claim a fee prior to termination of a trust was held not to be a waiver in In re Estate of Salus, 617 A.2d 737, 741 (Pa.Super.1992).

**69.** If the will is ambiguous on the point, the Restatement presumes that a devise to a person who is also designated as a fiduciary is in addition to compensation, and is not conditioned on the devisee's acceptance of the trusteeship. *Restatement, Third, of Trusts* § 38, comm. e (1999).

**70.** Andrews v. Gorby, 675 A.2d 449, 454 (Conn.1996); *cf.* Matter of Bales, 608 N.E.2d 987 (Ind.1993) (lawyer reprimanded for drafting a will providing high compensation for her services as executor and attorney). As to will provisions for the drafter see Section 7.4, note 11 et seq.

**71.** N.J.Stat. § 3B: 18–31.

The classification of such provisions can have estate and income tax consequences; for devises there is no deduction to the estate and no income to the recipient, whereas fees are deductible to the estate but taxable income to the recipient.[72] It may be advantageous taxwise for a family member to take a fee, since the deduction to the estate may be larger than the income tax to the recipient.[73]

Sometimes a fiduciary or attorney contracts with the beneficiaries of an estate for a higher than normal fee. For example, devisees hired lawyers to represent them for a contingent fee in a will contest. The probate court awarded them only $3,000 from the estate "as the reasonable amount for legal services rendered to the estate," but this did not preclude them from collecting the balance of the contracted fee from the devisees.[74] Stein notes that attorneys may properly charge a fee to the recipients of the nonprobate assets rather than burdening the probate estate with the fee for the attorney's services.[75] The Restatement allows trustees to contract for an enlarged fee from the trust beneficiaries if they "disclose all the relevant circumstances" and the agreement is not "unfair."[76]

### *Compensation of Agents*

Fiduciaries often seek reimbursement for the cost of hiring others to assist them. For example, a trustee hired a realty company to manage rental property held by the trust. A court allowed the trustee to pay the company's fees from the trust assets since "many ministerial details in renting this kind of property which could best be handled by someone in the real estate business."[77] The Restatement allows trustees indemnity from the trust for expenses properly incurred. This may include a reasonable fee paid to an investment advisor if the trustee is serving without compensation.[78] If, however, the trustee receives normal compensation, the trustee's right to reimbursement depends on "how the advisor's employment relates to the responsibilities reasonably expected of" the trustee.[79] Thus a court approved an arrangement whereby a bank trustee delegated its investment function to an investment advisor and charged only a considerably reduced "custody account fee."[80] In another case the fees of an accountant were charged against the executor's commission rather than the estate on the theory that

**72.** Peat and Willbanks, *Federal Estate and Gift Taxation* 168 (1991); Treas.Reg. § 20.2053–3(b)(2). Delay in renouncing the right to take a fee may cause the fiduciary to be taxed on the theory of constructive receipt.

**73.** H. Tweed & W. Parsons, *Lifetime and Testamentary Estate Planning* 104 (10th ed 1988).

**74.** In re Estate of Whitmore, 468 N.E.2d 769, 770 (Ohio App.1983). *See also* Matter of Baehm, 442 N.Y.S.2d 755 (Surr.1981).

**75.** Stein & Fierstein, *supra* note 23, at 1179.

**76.** *Restatement, Third, of Trusts* § 38, comm. f (1999). Under Cal.Prob.Code § 16004(c) the general suspicion of contracts between trustees and beneficiaries does not apply to contracts for the trustee's compensation. But Cal.Prob.Code § 10803 makes an agreement between a personal representative and devisees or heirs for higher compensation void. *See also* Haw.Rev.Stat. § 607–18(c) (agreement for higher compensation for trustee is void); Matter of Estate of Konopka, 498 N.W.2d 853 (Wis.App.1993) (fee contract between beneficiary of estate and attorney rejected as "unreasonable").

**77.** Corpus Christi Bank and Trust v. Roberts, 597 S.W.2d 752, 754 (Tex.1980). *See also* Matter of Estate of Cook, 529 N.E.2d 853 (Ind. App.1988) (broker hired by executor).

**78.** *See also* Chase v. Pevear, 419 N.E.2d 1358, 1364–65 (Mass.1981).

**79.** *Restatement, Third, of Trusts* § 38, illus. 1 (1999). *See also* Unif.Prud.Inv.Act § 9, Comment.

**80.** Matter of Estate of Younker, 663 N.Y.S.2d 946 (Surr.1997).

"if one hires a professional to assist in carrying out one of the ordinary duties of being a personal representative," the latter's fees should be adjusted accordingly.[81]

### *Attorneys' Fees*

Trustees and personal representatives can be indemnified for reasonable attorneys fees, but only if the services benefited the trust or estate rather than the fiduciary personally. The line between the two is sometimes fuzzy. For example, an executor who was also a principal beneficiary of a contested will, was denied reimbursement for her attorney fees in an appeal from a decree rejecting the will because "the appeal promoted only the [executor's] personal interests."[82] A trustee was not allowed reimbursement for attorney fees it had incurred in a will construction suit on the ground that its participation in the suit violated its "duty to deal impartially with all beneficiaries."[83] After a trustee was surcharged and removed, his claim for attorney fees in the proceedings was rejected with the comment that it "raises chutzpa to a new and astonishing level."[84] On the other hand, a trustee who successfully resisted an attempt to remove and surcharge it was awarded its attorney fees. "A trustee is entitled to reasonable attorney fees incurred in good faith in defending its administration of the trust."[85] Partial reimbursement of attorney fees may be allowed when trustees prevail as to part but not all of the claims made against them.[86] The Uniform Probate Code, allows personal representatives reasonable attorney fees when they "defend or prosecute any proceeding in good faith, whether successful or not."[87]

Some courts deny attorney fees incurred in litigation over the amount of the fiduciary's compensation,[88] but others disagree, reasoning that if fiduciaries and attorneys are not compensated for such expenses, "the compensation for the underlying services may be effectively diluted."[89]

Courts sometimes award attorneys' fees from an estate to beneficiaries who are not fiduciaries. For example, attorneys for two heirs recovered fees

**81.** In re Estate of Billings, 278 Cal.Rptr. 439, 442 (App.1991).

**82.** Matter of Estate of Jones, 492 N.W.2d 723, 727 (Iowa App.1992). *See also* In re Estate of Meyer, 802 P.2d 148, 154 (Wash.App.1990). *But see* Shepherd v. Mazzetti, 545 A.2d 621, 623–4 (Del.1988) (executor-devisee entitled to attorney fees in unsuccessfully resisting claim against the estate); In re Estate of Dawson, 689 N.E.2d 1008 (Ohio App.1996) (same).

**83.** Northern Trust Co. v. Heuer, 560 N.E.2d 961, 964 (Ill.App.1990).

**84.** Marzocco v. Titus, 665 N.E.2d 294 (Ohio App.1995). *See also* Matter of Estate of McCart, 847 P.2d 184 (Colo.App.1992); Conservatorship of Lefkowitz, 58 Cal.Rptr.2d 299 (App.1996) (conservator).

**85.** Matter of Trust Created by Hill, 499 N.W.2d 475, 494 (Minn.App.1993). *See also* Lucas v. Mannering, 745 S.W.2d 654 (Ky.App. 1987); Morrison v. Watkins, 889 P.2d 140 (Kan.App.1995). But in In Matter of Estate of Morris, 949 P.2d 401, 403 (Wash.App.1998), the court denied a similar claim by an executor on the ground that since estate administration is relatively short-term, the executor's desire to keep the job did not provide "a substantial benefit" to the estate.

**86.** Leigh v. Engle, 858 F.2d 361, 369 (7th Cir.1988) (ERISA); Matter of Estate of Cassity, 165 Cal.Rptr. 88, 91 (App.1980).

**87.** Uniform Probate Code § 3–720; *cf.* In re Estate of Stowell, 595 A.2d 1022 (Me.1991) (this does not allow a fiduciary to recover fees from "litigation that results from the fiduciary's misconduct"). Payment may be made even prior to the conclusion of the proceedings in question. National Wildlife Federation v. Foster, 575 A.2d 776, 781–83 (Md.App.1990).

**88.** Matter of Trust of Grover, 710 P.2d 597, 602 (Idaho 1985); Matter of Estate of Larson, 694 P.2d 1051 (Wash.1985) (attorney can't charge estate for time spent in justifying his own fee); In re Estate of Inlow, 735 N.E.2d 240, 250 (Ind.App.2000) (same).

**89.** In re Estate of Trynin, 782 P.2d 232, 238 (Cal.1989).

from the estate, under the "common fund" theory; there would otherwise be "an unfair advantage to the other [heirs] who are entitled to share in the fund and who should bear their share of the burden of the recovery."[90] Attorney fees have been denied where the suit benefited only the beneficiaries who sued or when an attempt to surcharge the fiduciary failed.[91] When beneficiaries proved a breach of duty by trustees but unreasonably continued the litigation in a fruitless quest for large damages, the court only allowed part of their fees, saying that their "folly * * * should not be rewarded."[92] Fees to attorneys for both sides in a will construction have been allowed on the theory that resolution of an ambiguity in the will benefited the estate.[93] The cases on attorney fees are hard to reconcile, because trial courts have much discretion on the question.[94]

Attorney fees are sometimes charged against persons who raise frivolous claims.[95] Fees of attorneys for beneficiaries who successfully sued a fiduciary have been charged to the fiduciary on the theory that they were a loss to the estate resulting from the fiduciary's breach.[96]

### *Attorney as Executor or Trustee*

Can an executor or trustee who is a lawyer receive compensation both as fiduciary and as attorney? English courts refuse to compensate trustees for any legal services they render to the trust on the ground that this involves self-dealing: "to permit a trustee to be compensated for rendering extraordinary services would tempt him to create a job for which there was no need or to employ himself to do services for which others would be better qualified."[97] California permits attorneys who act as personal representative to take compensation in both capacities only if a court finds that this is in the "best

**90.** In re Keller, 584 N.E.2d 1312, 1317 (Ohio App.1989). *See also* In re Estate of Pfoertner, 700 N.E.2d 438 (Ill.App.1998); Malachowski v. Bank One, 682 N.E.2d 530, 532 (Ind.1997) (error to deny attorney fees to beneficiaries who successfully sued to remove trustees). *But see* duPont v. Shackelford, 369 S.E.2d 673, 677 (Va.1988) (common fund rationale inapplicable when all beneficiaries had their own counsel).

**91.** Matter of Estate of Niehenke, 818 P.2d 1324, 1333 (Wash.1991); Matter of Ward, 360 N.W.2d 650 (Minn.App.1985); Hatcher v. United States Nat. Bank, 643 P.2d 359 (Or.App. 1982). *But see* Matter of Kirkman's Estate, 273 S.E.2d 712 (N.C.1981) (fees awarded to attorney for widow in suit to establish elective share).

**92.** Leigh v. Engle, 858 F.2d 361, 370 (7th Cir.1988).

**93.** Landmark Trust Co. v. Aitken, 587 N.E.2d 1076, 1086 (Ill.App.1992); Segal v. Levine, 489 So.2d 868 (Fla.App.1986); Matter of Will of Daniels, 799 P.2d 479, 485 (Kan.1990). *But see* In Matter of Campbell's Trusts, 258 N.W.2d 856 (Minn.1977) (attorneys' fees denied because trust was "not ambiguous"); Matter of Estate of Greatsinger, 492 N.E.2d 751 (N.Y.1986) (unsuccessful contender in will construction denied counsel fees because acting in his own interest).

**94.** Matter of Estate of Mathwig, 843 P.2d 1112, 1115 (Wash.App.1993) (statute allows court "in its discretion" to award attorney fees); Diemer v. Diemer, 717 S.W.2d 160, 163 (Tex.App.1986); Rennacker v. Rennacker, 509 N.E.2d 798, 801 (Ill.App.1987).

**95.** Matter of Estate of Barber, 779 P.2d 477, 489 (Mont.1989); In re Estate of Kerr, 949 P.2d 810 (Wash.1998) (attorney fees against beneficiary who unsuccessfully sought executor's removal); Cal.Prob.Code § 11003 (bad faith contest or opposition to contest of account by personal representative); Estate of Ivey, 28 Cal.Rptr.2d 16, 19–20 (App.1994).

**96.** In re Estate of Stowell, 595 A.2d 1022, 1026 (Me.1991). *See also* Lincoln Nat. Bank v. Shriners Hospitals, 588 N.E.2d 597 (Ind.App. 1992); Matter of Estate of Dyniewicz, 648 N.E.2d 1076 (Ill.App.1995) (fees of GAL charged to guardian whose conduct made suit necessary).

**97.** Hallgring, *The Uniform Trustees' Powers Act and the Basic Principles of Fiduciary Responsibility*, 41 Wash.L.Rev. 801, 819 (1966). As to self-dealing in sales and investment see Section 12.9.

interests of the estate."[98] A similar statute for conservators was held to bar compensation claimed by the conservator's spouse as her attorney. "In order to recover attorney fees, an attorney who is a conservator or related to a conservator must show * * * that his representation, as opposed to representation otherwise available, benefited the conservatorship estate."[99]

However, some courts allow dual compensation, citing the efficiencies involved in having the same individual act in both capacities.[100] "Usually money will be saved to an estate because, although the fee for the representative for dual services will be larger than would be a fee for only nonlegal services, it will be smaller than the combined fee for a separate representative and attorney."[101]

The Uniform Probate Code allows personal representatives to employ attorneys "even if they are associated with the personal representative."[102] The Restatement of Trusts uses more guarded language; trustees can be compensated for services to the trust as an attorney "when it is advantageous that the trustee rather than another perform those services."[103]

Self-hiring is not limited to lawyers. A California court held that the prohibition against "attorney-executor self-dealing" did not extend to persons other than attorneys, and allowed an fee to an accounting firm in which an executor was a partner.[104] A similar problem arises when an estate or trust owns a company which employs the fiduciary. For example, a will named Chambers as co-executor and trustee. Chambers, who was then serving as general counsel in a company owned by the estate, thereafter became the president and received several salary increases, for which he was late surcharged. "Even attributing to Chambers an astute talent for business management one would be overly naive not to think that his position as * * * trustee did not assist him in ascending to the presidency * * * A trustee, or one acting in a fiduciary capacity, is not permitted to place himself in such position that the interest of the beneficiaries and his own personal interest do or may conflict."[105] The Restatement, however, allows a trustee to receive a salary as an officer of a company controlled by the trust so long as the trustee "performs necessary services * * * and receives no more than proper compensation."[106] Perhaps courts should simply take the salary into account in

**98.** Cal.Prob.Code § 10804. In Mississippi any compensation paid to a personal representative as attorney must be "in lieu of" a fee as fiduciary. Miss.Code § 91-7-281. *But see* Ind. Code § 29-1-10-13; N.Y.Surr.Ct.Proc.Act § 2307.

**99.** Conservatorship of Bryant, 52 Cal. Rptr.2d 755, 759 (App.1996); Cal.Prob.Code § 2645. A similar provision applies to trustees. *Id.*, § 15687.

**100.** Section 12.4, note 109. Not surprisingly, individuals do not commonly serve in both capacities in states where they are limited to a single fee. Stein & Fierstein, *supra* note 24, at 1169.

**101.** Matter of Estate of Hackett, 366 N.E.2d 1103, 1106 (Ill.App.1977). *See also* Matter of Brown's Estate, 653 P.2d 928 (Okl.1982).

**102.** Uniform Probate Code § 3-715(21). This language is borrowed from the Uniform Trustees' Powers Act § 3(c)(24).

**103.** *Restatement, Third, of Trusts* § 38, comm. d (1999). *See also* Lembo v. Casaly, 361 N.E.2d 1314, 1317 (Mass.App.1977).

**104.** Estate of Haviside, 162 Cal.Rptr. 393 (App.1980).

**105.** Schmidt v. Chambers, 288 A.2d 356, 370-71 (Md.1972). *See also* Childs v. National Bank, 658 F.2d 487, 493 (7th Cir.1981).

**106.** *Restatement (Second) of Trusts* § 170, comm. o (1959). *See also* Ferber v. American Lamp Corp., 469 A.2d 1046 (Pa.1983); Harper v. Harper, 491 So.2d 189 (Miss.1986) (salary "commensurate with prior amounts" paid); Bartlett v. Dumaine, 523 A.2d 1 (N.H.1986) (reasonable compensation).

assessing the reasonableness of the trustee's total compensation.[107]

### *Multiple Fiduciaries*

When a will or trust names more than one executor or trustee, does each collect a full fee or do they divide a single fee?[108] The answer varies in different states. In California, if there are two or more personal representatives, the compensation is apportioned among them "according to the services actually rendered by each."[109] In Missouri, on the other hand, the ordinary fee of the personal representative can be doubled if two or more serve, and in New York the fee can be tripled.[110] The Restatement of Trusts says that the aggregate fees for several trustees may reasonably exceed those of a single trustee because the "normal duty of each trustee to participate in all aspects of administration" may "result in some duplication of effort."[111]

Often one fiduciary is an individual and the other is corporate. In this situation, the latter usually gets a larger share.[112] In a case where an individual served as cotrustee with a bank, the testimony "overwhelmingly established that 'normal compensation' for a fully active individual cotrustee is, at most, 50 percent of the corporate cotrustee's fee."[113] But in another case a court held that a corporate co-trustee was bound by its agreement to charge half its normal fee for a charitable trust because "the individual co-trustee has the lion's share of the responsibilities of management as compared with the bank's responsibilities of reinvestment and accounting."[114]

A similar apportionment problem arises when a single fiduciary is unable to complete the job and a successor does so.[115]

Fees can often be saved by designating the same person as executor and trustee, since many corporate trustees do not charge an acceptance fee if they also serve as executor.[116] The Restatement allows an executor-trustee "such compensation as is reasonable in view of all the duties performed."[117] One court denied compensation to a trustee, in part because his fee as a personal representative had "adequately compensated him for his services as trustee."[118] Many people use living trusts to avoid the cost of executor's fees based on the probate estate, but some trust companies take account of this by a special charge "for services performed by the bank which are similar to those usually performed by an Executor."[119]

**107.** Hughes, *Trust Principles and the Operation of a Trust-controlled Corporation,* 30 U.Tor.L.J. 151, 176–77 (1980).

**108.** Sometimes an estate hires more than one attorney. In re Estate of Knott, 615 N.E.2d 357, 360 (Ill.App.1993) held that it was proper for the estate to hire a second attorney for litigation in this "age of specialization".

**109.** Calif.Prob.Code § 10805. A similar rule applies to trustees *Id.*, § 15683.

**110.** Mo.Stat. § 473.153(2); N.Y.Surr.Ct. Proc.Act § 2307(5). *See also* N.J.Stat. § 3B: 18–15.

**111.** *Restatement, Third, of Trusts* § 38, comm. i (1999).

**112.** Jack, *supra* note 18, at 623.

**113.** Fred Hutchinson Cancer Research Center v. Holman, 732 P.2d 974, 978–79 (Wash.1987).

**114.** Estate of Ingram v. Ashcroft, 709 S.W.2d 956, 959 (Mo.App.1986).

**115.** *Restatement, Third, of Trusts* § 38, comm. j (1999); Ga.Code § 53–12–173(c)(2).

**116.** Jack, *supra* note 19, at 623.

**117.** *Restatement, Third, of Trusts*§ 38, comm. h (1999).

**118.** In re Estate of Stowell, 595 A.2d 1022, 1027 (Me.1991).

**119.** Quoted in G. Bogert, *The Law of Trusts and Trustees* § 975, at 26 (2d rev. ed. 1983).

### *Court Review*

In most states prior court approval is required before fees can be paid to personal representatives or their attorneys. Lawyers have been disciplined for taking attorney fees from an estate without obtaining prior court approval.[120] The Uniform Trustees' Powers Act, on the other hand, allows trustees to pay themselves without court authorization,[121] and this is the prevailing practice in living trusts which are freer of court supervision than decedent's estates. California, for example, "the administration of trusts is intended to proceed expeditiously and free of judicial intervention," although courts have jurisdiction to review the reasonableness of a trustee's compensation.[122] The Uniform Probate Code follows this model even for decedent's estates, permitting personal representatives to "fix their own fees and those of estate attorneys." However, "any interested person can get judicial review of fees," and one who has received "excessive compensation" may be ordered to refund it.[123]

When fee questions come before courts, appellate courts very often affirm trial courts' determinations if they find no "abuse of discretion." Some lower court decisions, however, are reversed on appeal. For example, an appellate court reversed a trial court's approval of a fees with the comment:

> The failure to articulate reasons for a discretionary action is an abuse of discretion. * * * Although we must uphold a discretionary decision if there are facts of record to support it, even if the trial court's reasons for it are not given, * * * there is no basis in the record from which we can conclude that * * * [the personal representative] rendered 'extraordinary services' so that a fee in excess of [the statutory base of] two percent was reasonable.[124]

### *Bond*

Another expense in many estates is caused by the requirement that the personal representatives file a bond. The California Probate Code is typical.

> Every person appointed as personal representative shall, before letters are issued, give a bond approved by the court * * * conditioned on the personal representative's faithful execution of the duties of the office.[125]

**120.** In re Altstatt, 897 P.2d 1164, 1169 (Or.1995) (lawyer suspended). *See also* Murray v. State Bar, 709 P.2d 480 (Cal.1985); Office of Disciplinary Counsel v. Burkhart, 581 N.E.2d 540 (Ohio 1991); Harper v. Harper, 491 So.2d 189, 203 (Miss.1986) (executor removed *inter alia* for paying attorney's fee without court approval).

**121.** Uniform Trustees' Powers Act § 3(a), (c)(20). *See also* N.J.Stat. § 3B: 18–17 (can take annual allowance without court action).

**122.** Cal.Prob.Code §§ 17200(b)(9), 17209. Trustees who increase fees during a trust's operation, must give advance notice to the beneficiaries who can petition a court to challenge this. *Id.* § 15686. Testamentary trusts created before 1977 are subject to "continuing court jurisdiction" but this can be removed on petition. *Id.* §§ 17350 *et seq.*

**123.** Uniform Probate Code § 3–721, comment. *See also id.* § 7–205 (review of fees of trustee); Vogt v. Seattle–First Nat. Bank, 817 P.2d 1364 (Wash.1991) (trustee to refund excessive fees with interest).

**124.** Matter of Estate of Anderson, 432 N.W.2d 923, 928 (Wis.App.1988). *See also* Duggan v. Keto, 554 A.2d 1126, 1142 (D.C.App. 1989) (remand for an explanation of fee award); Matter of Estate of Shull, 693 N.E.2d 489 (Ill.App.1998) (same); In re Estate of York, 727 N.E.2d 607, 614 (Ohio App.1999).

**125.** Calif.Prob.Code § 8480. A similar requirement is imposed on conservators. *Id.* § 2320.

The amount of the bond is generally based on the value of the personal property of the estate, because real estate is not subject to administration, but if land is sold the bond is increased.[126] The bond must have sureties, since the executor or administrator may be unable to pay a surcharge imposed for mismanagement, in which case the sureties are liable to the extent of the bond, with a right of reimbursement against the fiduciary.[127] The sureties naturally charge a fee for this, the cost of which is born by the estate.[128] No bond is required when a corporation is the fiduciary, since corporations must have substantial assets in order to be licensed to act as fiduciaries.[129]

A will can waive bond, but even if it does, a court may "for good cause" require one.[130] The testator's confidence in the designated executor may prove to be mistaken, or the fiduciary designated in the instrument may not actually serve.[131] Also, executors have duties to the testator's creditors as well as to the devisees, and the testator cannot "waive" protection to which creditors are entitled.

The business of acting as surety for bonds is substantial, and in many states sureties have lobbied for retaining the bond requirement.[132] Most estate planners believe a bond is usually not worth the expense.[133] The Uniform Statutory Will Act waives it.[134] The Uniform Probate Code rejects "the idea that a bond always should be required of a probate fiduciary, or required unless a will excuses it."[135] It allows courts to dispense with a bond if it is not necessary, even if the will does not waive it.[136]

Bond requirements tend to be more relaxed for trustees. In California executors must give a bond unless the will waives it whereas trustees do not have to give a bond unless the trust instrument requires one.[137] This is also the rule of the Restatement.[138] In New York, however, testamentary trustees must file a bond unless the will excuses it.[139] Trustees of living trusts do not usually give bonds, nor do custodians under the Uniform Transfers to Minors Act.[140] On the other hand, even the Uniform Probate Code provides for bonds for conservators; here the beneficiary of the arrangement (the conservatee) is incapable of waiving the requirement.[141]

### *Appraisal*

**126.** *Id.* § 8482.

**127.** *Id.* § 8488; Uniform Probate Code § 3–606; In re Estate of Berger, 520 N.E.2d 690 (Ill.App.1987); Gardner v. Cox, 843 P.2d 469, 471 (Or.App.1992).

**128.** Calif.Prob.Code § 8486.

**129.** Calif.Prob.Code § 301; Unif.Trust Code § 702(c).

**130.** Calif.Prob.Code § 8481 (personal representatives), § 15602(a)(2) (waiver of bond for trustee is ineffective if a bond is "necessary to protect the beneficiaries").

**131.** Cal.Prob.Code § 15602(a)(3) (waiver of bond ineffective as to "a trustee not named in the instrument").

**132.** Wellman, *Recent Developments in the Struggle for Probate Reform*, 79 Mich.L.Rev. 501, 523 (1981).

**133.** J. Price, *Contemporary Estate Planning* 198 (1983); J. Farr & Wright, *An Estate Planner's Handbook* 444–45 (4th ed. 1979); H Tweed & W Parsons, *Lifetime and Testamentary Estate Planning* 136 (10th ed. 1988).

**134.** Uniform Statutory Will Act § 14.

**135.** Uniform Probate Code § 3–603, comment.

**136.** *See also* Unif.Trust Code § 702(a).

**137.** Calif.Prob.Code § 15602.

**138.** *Restatement, Third, of Trusts* § 34(3) (1999).

**139.** N.Y.Surr.Ct.Prac.Act § 806. *See also* Texas Prop.Code § 113.058(b).

**140.** Uniform Transfers to Minors Act § 15(c).

**141.** Uniform Probate Code § 5–410.

Personal representatives in most states must file with the court an inventory listing the assets in the estate soon after they are appointed.[142] The Uniform Probate Code also requires an inventory, but the personal representative can simply mail it to the interested parties rather than file it in court so that the information does not become public.[143]

In California the assets in the estate must be appraised by a court-appointed "probate referee" unless a court waives this requirement "for good cause."[144] Referees get a fee of one tenth of one percent of the total value of the assets appraised.[145] The appraisal system has been attacked as "a needless and expensive formality which rarely serves any useful purpose."[146] It may be necessary to know the value of assets in an estate for tax purposes[147] and (in some states) the fees of the personal representative and attorney, but many assets do not require a professional appraiser. "If an estate consists solely of cash, bank and savings and loan deposits, obligations of the United States, life insurance policies, and securities listed with a recognized securities market or exchange, anyone with an adding machine and a back issue of the *Wall Street Journal* can appraise it."[148] The Uniform Probate Code makes use of an appraiser optional with the personal representative.[149]

### *Conclusion*

The avoidance of probate which has assumed such large proportions during the past fifty years has been motivated to some extent by the costs of administration. Often these costs reflect payment for unnecessary services or overcompensation of the persons who provide them. Reforms introduced by the Uniform Probate Code have diminished the advantages of avoiding probate, but they have not eliminated them completely.

## § 12.6 Sales by Fiduciaries

### *Power of Sale*[1]

Can an executor or administrator or trustee sell assets of the estate or trust or must they be preserved for distribution in kind to the beneficiaries when the estate is closed or the trust terminated? This may depend upon the terms of the governing instrument. Many wills and trusts confer broad powers of sale on the executor or trustee. Knowledgeable estate planners so recom-

**142.** *E.g.*, Cal.Prob.Code § 8800.

**143.** Uniform Probate Code § 3–706.

**144.** Calif.Prob.Code § 8902–03.

**145.** Calif.Prob.Code § 8961.

**146.** Smith, *Appraisers and Appraisements Under the Texas Probate Code*, 45 Texas L.Rev. 842 (1967). Under present Texas law appraisers are appointed only if deemed necessary by the court or requested by an interested person. Texas Prob.Code § 248.

**147.** U.S.Treas.Reg. § 20.2031–6 (expert appraisal required for household goods worth over $3,000). Even if no estate tax is payable, an appraisal is needed to establish the basis of assets for income tax purposes. Int.Rev.Code § 1014.

**148.** Smith, *supra* note 146, at 850. California exempts certain items, such as bank accounts, from appraisal by the referee. Calif.Prob.Code § 8901.

**149.** Uniform Probate Code § 3–707; Matter of Estate of Wagley, 760 P.2d 316, 319 (Utah 1988) (error to order appraisal by court's own appraiser).

**§ 12.6**

**1.** The question whether a fiduciary has a "power of sale" can be misleading. A sale may be effective to transfer title to a bona-fide purchaser for value, even if the fiduciary was not authorized to make it. Cowley v. Kaechelle, 696 P.2d 1354 (Ariz.App.1984) (purchaser gets title even though sale not approved by court as required by statute); Section 12.8, at note 164 et seq.

mend.[2] The Uniform Statutory Will Act, for example, gives the trustee power to

> sell, exchange or otherwise dispose of property at public or private sale on terms the trustee determines ... The personal representative, in the administration of the estate, has all the powers of a trustee.[3]

Some instruments are silent on this question, however, and for conservatorships, no governing instrument serves as a source of powers. A statute may then give the answer. The Uniform Probate Code allows personal representatives, unless restricted by will, to "dispose of an asset, including land" so long as they act "reasonably for the benefit of the interested persons."[4] Similar powers are conferred on conservators.[5] The Uniform Trustee's Powers Act has similar provisions for trustees.[6] Many statutes, however, are more restrictive. In Illinois, for example, trustees have broad powers of sale,[7] but a personal representative can sell property only "by leave of court and upon such terms as the court directs" unless the will gives a power of sale.[8]

The Third Restatement of Trusts implies a power of sale for trustees unless the terms of the trust or the circumstances indicate "that assets of the trust are to be retained in specie."[9] This is somewhat broader than the Second Restatement which implied a power of sale when it was "necessary or appropriate to carry out the purposes of the trust." Operating under the earlier version a court invalidated a deed by a trustee on the ground that no power of sale was conferred in the trust instrument, "nor was any evidence adduced to indicate that the sale was necessary or appropriate to carry out the purpose of the trust."[10] Even where a trust instrument gave the trustee broad power to "sell any property" in the trust, a court refused to authorize the sale of a farm. "Such a sale would defeat the express purpose of the trust ... Plaintiffs have shown no very convincing need to sell the ... farm." The trust had enough liquid assets and income to provide for the foreseeable needs of the income beneficiaries. Sale of the farm would frustrate a direction in the instrument that the farm be sold to a designated beneficiary when the trust terminated.[11] Another court set aside a sale by a trustee who had sold the property "without a valid reason, that is, without any expected benefit to the trust or its beneficiaries."[12]

Courts are reluctant to allow personal representatives to sell property which the will specifically devised. For example, a father left land which had been the family home place for over 100 years to his daughters. Although the will gave the executor power "to sell any part of my estate" the court enjoined the sale; "the mere lodgement of a discretionary power of sale in an executor can not destroy * * * the estate in fee of a devisee where there are no debts

**2.** *E.g.*, H.Tweed & W.Parsons, *Lifetime and Testamentary Estate Planning* 108 (10th ed. 1988).

**3.** Uniform Statutory Will Act § 13(a)(4), (b).

**4.** Uniform Probate Code § 3–715.

**5.** *Id.* § 5–423(c)(7).

**6.** Uniform Trustees' Power Act § 3(a)(7). *See also* Unif.Trust Code § 816.

**7.** 760 ILCS § 5/4.01.

**8.** 755 ILCS §§ 5/20–4(a), 20–15.

**9.** *Restatement (Third) of Trusts* § 190 (1990).

**10.** Schaneman v. Wright, 470 N.W.2d 566, 576 (Neb.1991). The court noted that the sale occurred before the state's adoption of the Trustees' Powers Act.

**11.** Matter of Heisserer, 797 S.W.2d 864, 871–72 (Mo.App.1990). *See also* Matter of Wood, 581 N.Y.S.2d 405 (App.Div.1992)

**12.** McNeely v. Hiatt, 909 P.2d 191, 196 (Or.App.1996).

or necessity of sale."[13] In many states the statutory power of sale given to personal representatives allows only sales which are needed to raise money to pay debts.[14] The Uniform Probate Code is not so restricted, but it provides that "the distributable assets of a decedent's estate shall be distributed in kind to the extent possible."[15] Similarly under the Restatement of Trusts, the beneficiaries can compel the trustee to transfer the trust property in kind to them when the trust terminates even if the trust instrument authorizes or even directs the trustee to sell it and distribute the proceeds.[16]

Courts may find justification for a sale in various situations. The asset may be a bad investment. Thus an executor's sale of stock was upheld despite the absence of claims against the estate on the ground that the stock "was subject to rapid fluctuation in value, . . . and the return on the stock was not sufficient" to warrant its retention.[17] Similarly trustees may have a power (as well as a duty) to sell trust assets in order to carry out an appropriate investment program.[18]

A trust which authorizes the trustee to support a beneficiary implies a power to sell trust assets in order to accomplish this.[19] A power to sell property given for charitable purposes can also be implied. A transfer of land to a bishop "for the use of St. Mary's Parish" was held to allow the land to be sold. "The charitable asset given, land, could be turned into another form of asset more useable by the designated charity, viz., cash."[20]

A sale may be necessary to effectuate distribution when an estate or trust terminates. For example, an executor was permitted to sell land even though the will said "it is my desire that the farm land which I own remain in the family." The court found that the "desire" was merely precatory, and that a sale would be "in the best interests of the estate;" the children to whom the land was devised did not get along so shared ownership would be inconvenient.[21] Another court allowed an executor to sell a residence, since it could not be divided among the devisees and the estate was not large enough to allow the residence to be assigned to one beneficiary and the remaining assets to the others so as to "effect an equal distribution as the will required."[22] A sale can

**13.** Lowell v. Bouchillon, 271 S.E.2d 498, 499 (Ga.1980). *See also* Maier v. Henning, 578 A.2d 1279, 1282 (Pa.1990); Diana v. Bentsen, 677 So.2d 1374 (Fla.App.1996) (error to order sale of specifically devised stock where not needed to pay debts); Koch v. James, 616 N.E.2d 759 (Ind.App.1993) (same).

**14.** 3 *Amer.Law of Prop.* § 14.27; In re Bettis' Estate, 340 A.2d 57 (Vt.1975) (sale of land by administrator voided because not necessary to pay debts); Duffy v. Heffernan, 459 N.E.2d 898 (Ohio App.1983) (where sale not needed to pay debts, 50% of interested persons must consent).

**15.** Uniform Probate Code § 3–906.

**16.** *Restatement, Second, Trusts* § 347, comm. o (1959). *See also* Matter of Wood, 581 N.Y.S.2d 405, 408 (A.D.1992).

**17.** McInnis v. Corpus Christi Nat. Bank, 621 S.W.2d 451, 453 (Tex.Civ.App.1981).

**18.** *Restatement, Third, of Trusts* § 190, comm. d (1990). As to investments by trustees see Section 12.7.

**19.** Estate of Wells v. Sanford, 663 S.W.2d 174, 177 (Ark.1984); *Restatement, Third, of Trusts* § 190, comm. c (1990).

**20.** Hillman v. Roman Cath. Bishop of Fall River, 508 N.E.2d 118, 120 (Mass.App.1987).

**21.** Matter of Estate of Zimbleman, 539 N.W.2d 67, 70 (N.D.1995). *See also* Matter of Estate of Kunzler, 699 P.2d 1388 (Idaho 1985). In Huntington Nat. Bank v. Wolfe, 651 N.E.2d 458, 462 (Ohio App.1994) the court upheld a decision by trustees to sell shares in lieu of distributing them to a beneficiary who might "manage it in a way that would be hostile" to the interests of a company.

**22.** Estate of Barthelmess, 243 Cal.Rptr. 832, 834 (App.1988). *See also* Lloyds Bank v. Duker, [1987] 3 All E.R. 193 (Ch. 1987) (stock sold to avoid disadvantage to devisees who would be minority shareholders).

take place after the termination date of a trust, since trustees' powers continue for a reasonable period to allow "winding up" of the trust.[23]

Courts' willingness to infer a power to sell may depend on the type of property involved. The Restatement suggests distinctions between land occupied as a residence and land purchased as an investment, and between securities in general and stock in a family corporation.[24] A court refused to authorize a transfer of a ward's home by her guardian, saying that "transfers of a ward's real property should be disfavored. While we do not go so far as to hold that a ward's personal estate must be exhausted before a court may approve transfer of any real estate, the transfer of the ward's home should not be the first alternative considered."[25]

The concept of prudence, to be discussed in more detail in the next section, governs sales as well as investments. For example, the Uniform Trustees' Powers Act gives trustees broad powers but they must be those "which a prudent man would perform for the purposes of the trust .. with due regard for his obligation as a fiduciary."[26] Similarly the powers conferred on personal representatives by the Uniform Probate Code are coupled with the duty of "acting reasonably for the benefit of the interested persons."[27] A sale may be imprudent because of its collateral consequences. For example, a guardian was surcharged for selling the ward's residence when the sale "resulted in unnecessary dissipation of estate assets" because the proceeds rendered her ineligible for public welfare.[28] Similarly an executor was surcharged for selling property without adequate consideration of the tax consequences.[29]

Some wills and trusts prohibit sale. Such restrictions are valid,[30] but courts may overrule them when the circumstances have changed.[31] Even without such an unanticipated change of circumstances, courts may order a deviation if the restriction is contrary to public policy, *e.g.*, because it hurts neighboring property.[32]

Normally fiduciaries are not required to notify or get the consent of beneficiaries before selling property.[33] But such a requirement, or one for consultation with or consent of an advisor may be found in the terms of an instrument.[34] Certainly it is good policy for fiduciaries to consult the beneficia-

**23.** Cal.Prob.Code § 15407(b); *Restatement, Second, Trusts* § 344 (1959). *But see* In re Nathan Trust, 638 N.E.2d 789 (Ind.1994).

**24.** *Restatement, Third, of Trusts* § 190, comm. d (1990).

**25.** In re Guardianship of Mabry, 666 N.E.2d 16, 21–22 (Ill.App.1996).

**26.** Uniform Trustee's Powers Act § 3(a)(b).

**27.** Uniform Probate Code § 3–715. Section 5–423(c) uses similar language for conservators. As to custodians see Uniform Transfers to Minors Act § 12(b).

**28.** Matter of Guardianship of Connor, 525 N.E.2d 214, 216 (Ill.App.1988).

**29.** In re Estate of Anderson, 196 Cal.Rptr. 782, 793 (App.1983). *But cf.* Estate of Fales, 431 N.Y.S.2d 763 (Surr.1980) (sale approved despite capital gains tax consequences where benefits exceeded the cost).

**30.** See Section 11.8, note 42.

**31.** See Section 9.6, at note 11 et seq.

**32.** Colonial Trust Co. v. Brown, 135 A. 555 (Conn.1926); *Restatement (Second) of Trusts* § 166, illus. 5 (1959).

**33.** In re Estate of Hughes, 641 N.E.2d 248, 251 (Ohio App.1994) (will conferred a power of sale); Shear v. Gabovitch, 685 N.E.2d 1168, 1189 (Mass.App.1997) (judgment as to propriety of a sale lies "with the trustees, not with the beneficiaries").

**34.** Taylor v. Crocker National Bank, 252 Cal.Rptr. 388, 395 (App.1988) (ordered not to be officially published); Papiernik v. Papiernik, 544 N.E.2d 664 (Ohio 1989) (refusal to remove requirement of advisor's consent to a sale).

ries about the sale of a major asset. One commentator has observed that most investment problems involving fiduciaries can be traced to ineffective communication between the fiduciary and the beneficiaries.[35]

### *Leases and Options*

The Uniform Probate Code allows personal representatives to "lease any real or personal property of the estate," and the Uniform Trustees' Powers Act gives a similar power to trustees.[36] Some statutes are more restrictive, on the theory that the beneficiaries should not be saddled with a lease which extends beyond the closing of the estate or trust. New York allows personal representatives to execute leases for up to three years and trustees for up to ten.[37] The Restatement of Trusts allows leases for a term which will not extend "beyond the probable period of the trust," but under proper circumstances courts can approve longer leases.[38]

Fiduciaries may lack power to grant an option. For example, guardians leased property of their ward, the lease giving the lessees an option to purchase. When they attempted to exercise the option, the guardians resisted. The court reversed a summary judgment for the lessees because "a fiduciary's authority to sell real estate does not normally include authority to grant an option to purchase it" unless "inclusion of an option agreement in a lease is clearly necessary to make the most advantageous arrangement."[39] Other courts, however, have assumed with little discussion that a power to sell or lease included a power to grant options.[40] The Uniform Probate Code permits personal representatives to execute leases "with or without option to purchase or renew."[41] Under the Uniform Trustees' Powers Act trustees can grant options, in connection with a lease or otherwise,[42] but some statutes are more restrictive.[43]

### *Terms of Sale*

A power of sale does not necessarily permit sale on credit. Although a will authorized trustees to sell stock, their contract to sell it for a price payable in installments over eight years was enjoined because the testator "intended

**35.** Willis, *Steps to Protect the Fiduciary from Liability for Investment Decisions*, 16 Est. Plan 228, 229 (1989); Gallagher, *The Trustee's Role in Selling a Closely Held Business*, Trust & Estates (Sept. 1990) 35, 40. In Allard v. Pacific Nat. Bank, 663 P.2d 104, 110 (Wash. 1983), the court in surcharging a trustee for an improper sale said that it should have consulted the beneficiaries, even though their consent was not required.

**36.** Uniform Probate Code § 3–715(23); Uniform Trustees' Powers Act § 3(c)(10); Unif. Trust Code § 816(9).

**37.** N.Y. EPTL § 11–1.1(b)(5)(C). A court may grant broader powers. *Id.* § 11–1.1(c). *See also* 20 Pa.Stat. § 7142 (trustee may grant leases for up to 5 years); Cal.Prob.Code §§ 9941, 9947 (lease for up to 1 year by personal representative allowed without court order, even with court order lease over 10 years not allowed if heir or devisee objects); Estate of Biewald, 468 N.E.2d 1321, 1325 (Ill.App.1984) (lease by administrator without court approval is voidable).

**38.** *Restatement (Second) of Trusts* § 189, comm. c, d (1959).

**39.** Nelson v. Maiorana, 478 N.E.2d 945, 948 (Mass.1985).

**40.** Jost v. Burr, 590 N.E.2d 828, 832 (Ohio App.1990). *See also* Aloha Lumber Corp. v. University of Alaska, 994 P.2d 991, 1000 (Alaska 1999) (upholding trustee's grant of right of first refusal).

**41.** Uniform Prob.Code § 3–715(9).

**42.** Uniform Trustees' Powers Act § 3(c)(10), (12).

**43.** 20 Pa.Stat. § 3354 (testamentary power of sale does not include granting an option without court order); N.Y. EPTL § 11–1.1(b)(7) (fiduciaries can grant options for up to 6 months).

that [any sale] be a complete sale and that a substantial portion of the proceeds would be immediately available and that proper safeguards would be incorporated into any agreement sufficient to protect the trustees and beneficiary."[44] The Third Restatement of Trusts says "it is proper and not unusual for a trustee to sell property partly for cash and partly for a secured promissory note of investment quality."[45] It does not include a sentence in the Second Restatement that "the trustee cannot properly sell trust property on credit taking the unsecured obligation of the purchaser," but in many circumstances such a sale would probably be deemed imprudent. Many statutes expressly authorize executors and trustees to sell on credit,[46] but some impose special requirements for this.[47]

Sales can be challenged because the price is too low. For example, a trustee who had sold an asset of the trust to a private purchaser was surcharged.

> A trustee when selling trust assets [must] try to obtain the maximum price ... A trustee may determine the best possible price ... either by obtaining an independent appraisal of the property or by 'testing the market' to determine what a willing buyer would pay ... None of these actions was taken by the defendant.[48]

Another trustee was surcharged for leasing property at less than its rental value.[49] A court refused to approve a sale by an personal representative because the property had not been adequately appraised. Although the sale was subject only to the "prudent person standard," this required such an appraisal.[50] On the other hand, an executor who delayed selling stock pending an appraisal was held to have been imprudent; the stock "was subject to rapid deterioration in value ... It may be that a 'blue ribbon' appraisal could not have been obtained in less than six months. But this case called for an appraisal under these extraordinary circumstances to be made as soon as possible."[51]

Prudence does not always require a fiduciary to accept the highest offer. A court upheld a trustee's rejection of a higher offer in a timber sale.

> A high dollar figure could not overcome operating difficulties in remote, mountainous terrain, could not make an otherwise inexperienced operator into a suitable operator, and could not ensure compliance with the strict environmental and other land and water protections.[52]

**44.** In re Gould's Will, 234 N.Y.S.2d 825, 827 (A.D.1962).

**45.** *Restatement, Third, of Trusts* § 190, comm. j (1990).

**46.** Uniform Probate Code § 3–715(23); Uniform Trustees' Powers Act § 3(c)(7); Unif. Trust Code § 816(2).

**47.** Cal.Prob.Code §§ 10257–28 (on credit sale of personal property buyer must pay 25% down, but court may waive this if to the advantage of the estate), § 10315 (on credit sale of land, buyer's note must be secured by mortgage on the property).

**48.** Allard v. Pacific Nat. Bank, 663 P.2d 104, 111 (Wash.1983). *See also* Murphy v. Central Bank and Trust Co., 699 P.2d 13 (Colo. App.1985); Estate of Blouin, 490 A.2d 1212 (Me.1985) (executor surcharged for sale at inadequate price); In re Estate of Hughes, 515 A.2d 581 (Pa.Super.1986) (injunction against executor's sale at too low a price); Hatcher v. United States Nat. Bank, 643 P.2d 359 (Or. App.1982)

**49.** Mest v. Dugan, 790 P.2d 38 (Or.App. 1990).

**50.** Carroll v. Carroll, 903 P.2d 579, 585–86 (Alaska 1995).

**51.** In re Estate of McCool, 553 A.2d 761, 768 (N.H.1988).

**52.** Aloha Lumber Corp. v. University of Alaska, 994 P.2d 991, 1000 (Alaska 1999).

It may even be prudent for a trustee to abandon property. The Uniform Trust Code allows trustees to abandon or disclaim property which is "of insufficient value to justify its ... continued administration" or because it "may have environmental liability attached to it."[53]

An fiduciary may be bound to accept a below-market price set by the terms of the will, or by an option given by the testator while living.[54]

Many states require sales by personal representatives to be confirmed by a court.[55] In California, no private sale of land by a personal representative can be confirmed unless the price is at least 90 percent of the value found by an appraisal made no more than a year prior to the sale.[56] Sometimes fiduciaries contract to sell property, and before the sale is confirmed by the court another buyer offers a higher price. Some courts refuse to confirm the sale when this occurs,[57] but others hold that if the sale was for a "reasonable value" it should be confirmed despite the later offer because "a confirmation proceeding is not a public auction."[58]

Whether court proceedings to confirm sales perform a useful function in avoiding sales for an inadequate price is questionable. The Uniform Probate Code allows personal representatives to "proceed expeditiously" in administering an estate "without adjudication, order or direction of the Court," although they may invoke the Court's jurisdiction "to resolve questions."[59] This is also true of trustees in most states.[60] Thus a court refused to surcharge a trustee for selling stock which later increased in value. The trustee "did not act improperly in failing to obtain Probate court approval for the" sale, even though "such proceedings would have been helpful because of circumstances which raised legitimate questions" about its propriety.[61] Even California provides an option for "independent administration" of estates. This allows sales to take place without court approval provided that prior notice is given to affected parties.[62]

## § 12.7 Investments

Fiduciaries have a power and a duty to invest. They can be surcharged or removed for failure to invest and for making improper investments. This Section will discuss the basic rules pertaining to investing; remedies against

**53.** Unif.Trust Code § 816(12)(13); *cf.* Unif.Trustees' Powers Act § 3(c)(7); *Restatement, Second, Trusts* § 192, comm. c (1959) (abandonment of claims); Seven G Ranching Co. v. Stewart Title, 627 P.2d 1088, 1090 (Ariz. App.1981).

**54.** Carr v. Huber, 557 A.2d 548 (Conn. App.1989) (will); Colorado Nat. Bank v. Friedman, 846 P.2d 159 (Colo.1993) (partnership agreement).

**55.** Matter of Estate of Ostrander, 910 P.2d 865 (Kan.App.1996) (sale of trailer without court approval set aside); *cf.* In re Estate of Hughes, 641 N.E.2d 248, 251 (Ohio App.1994) (no court approval needed when will confers a power of sale).

**56.** Calif.Prob.Code § 10309. Trustees, however, can sell without court approval. *Id.* § 16200.

**57.** Kapur v. Scientific Gas Products, Inc., 454 N.E.2d 1294 (Mass.App.1983) (court refused to approve executor's sale after higher bid received). *See also* Calif.Prob.Code § 10311 (substantially higher bid precludes confirmation).

**58.** Stanton v. Sayre, 461 N.E.2d 3, 7 (Ohio App.1983). *See also* In re Estate of Hughes, 538 A.2d 470 (Pa.1988) (sale for $42,000 approved despite later offer of $60,000).

**59.** Uniform Probate Code § 3–704. As to the extent to which a fiduciary who gets court approval of a transaction is protected thereby see Section 12.8, at note 88 et seq.

**60.** Uniform Trustees' Powers Act § 3(a); Unif.Trust Code § 815.

**61.** Malachowski v. Bank One, 667 N.E.2d 780 (Ind.App.1996).

**62.** Cal.Prob.Code § 10503.

fiduciaries who have acted improperly in investing or otherwise will be treated in the following Section.

### *Different Fiduciaries*

The rules which govern trustees, personal representatives, conservators,[1] custodians under the Uniform Transfers to Minors Act, and directors of charitable corporations[2] are similar but not identical. For example, a custodian was surcharged for investing a minor's funds improperly. The trial court assumed that the fiduciary duties of a trustee and a custodian were the same.[3] The state supreme court disagreed, because the relevant statutes were differently worded, but this did not affect the result.[4] Some state statutes on investments apply to all "fiduciaries,"[5] but the Restatement of Trusts says that the "investment authority and responsibilities" of personal representatives are generally "more limited than those of trustees."[6] The Uniform Prudent Investor Act covers only trustees, but the drafters suggest that states may adapt it to "other fiduciary regimes, taking account of such changed circumstances as the relatively short duration of most executorships."[7] California has adopted the Act, but has a more restricted rule for investments by personal representatives which limits them (with exceptions) to "short term fixed income obligations."[8] When an executor was sued for failing to diversify the holdings of an estate, a court held it was improper to instruct the jury under the prudent investor standard for trustees because of the "basic distinctions" between executors and trustees. "It was not the executors who had a duty to diversify the assets, it was the trustee. The executor's duty was to close out the estate as quickly as possible."[9]

Many wills give the same investment powers to the executor and the trustee.[10] But in California executors can exercise any expanded powers

§ 12.7

1. In In re Estate of Swiecicki, 477 N.E.2d 488 (Ill.1985), the court said that the relationship between a guardian and ward [conservator and conservatee] was "equivalent to the relationship between a trustee and a beneficiary." However, the bank-guardian was not allowed to take advantage of a statute applicable to investments by personal representatives.

2. See *Restatement, Second, Trusts* § 389, comm. b (1959); Lynch v. John M. Redfield Foundation, 88 Cal.Rptr. 86, 89 (App.1970). Today these are in most states governed by the Uniform Management of Institutional Funds Act.

Agents are also fiduciaries, but they differ from trustees in that they generally must follow the instructions of the principal. McGovern, *Trusts, Custodianships and Durable Powers of Attorney*, 27 Real Prop.Prob. and T.J. 1, 28–30 (1992).

3. Buder v. Sartore, 774 P.2d 1383, 1385 (Colo.1989).

4. *Id.* at 1388. *See also* In re Estate of Swiecicki, 477 N.E.2d 488, 490 (Ill.1985) (fiduciary duties of guardian and trustee are similar); Uniform Probate Code §§ 5–416 (conservators shall "observe the standards of care applicable to trustees"), 3–703(a) (same for personal representatives).

5. Matter of Estate of Janes, 681 N.E.2d 332, 336 (N.Y.1997) (imposing liability on an executor under such a statute).

6. *Restatement (Third) of Trusts* § 5, comm. c (1996).

7. Unif.Prud.Inv.Act, Prefatory Note.

8. Cal.Prob.Code § 9730. Compare the authorization in Uniform Probate Code § 3–715(6) to invest in "federally insured interest-bearing accounts, readily marketable secured loan arrangements or other prudent investments which would be reasonable for use by trustees generally." The expansive latter part of this provision seems inconsistent with the opening phrases.

9. Matter of Estate of Pirie, 492 N.E.2d 884, 893 (Ill.App.1986). *See also* Hamilton v. Nielsen, 678 F.2d 709, 712 (7th Cir.1982). *But see* Matter of Estate of Donner, 626 N.E.2d 922 (N.Y.1993) (executor surcharged for failure to sell stock in declining market).

10. Uniform Statutory Will Act § 13(b).

conferred by a will only after the debts of the estate are paid, since the testator's wishes are subject to the obligation to pay claims.[11]

### *Terms of the Instrument*

The will or trust instrument is a primary source of the rules controlling investments. The investment powers which the Uniform Probate Code gives to personal representatives apply "except as restricted * * * by the will."[12] The Uniform Prudent Investor Act also provides "a default rule, [which] may be expanded, restricted eliminated or otherwise altered by the provisions of a trust."[13] The Restatement of Trusts requires trustees to "conform to the terms of the trust directing or restricting investments."[14] However, as we have seen, courts may authorize trustees to ignore such terms when circumstances have changed, and trustees may even have a duty to seek such authorization.[15] Also, provisions dealing with investments in a will may be regarded as merely precatory. For example, a trustee was not surcharged for selling stock which the settlor had "requested" be retained, because, in contrast to this "request," the settlor had "unambiguously expressed his mandatory intentions throughout the remainder of his will, using such words as 'I direct' and 'the trustee shall'."[16]

Sometimes fiduciaries invoke a term in the instrument to justify what would otherwise be an improper investment. For example, a complaint that a trustee had failed to diversify investments and invested in speculative securities was dismissed because the will authorized the trustee to invest "in any type of real or personal property * * * regardless of diversification or state laws;" this was held to "waive the application of the prudent man rule."[17] However, such provisions are ordinarily construed not to override the obligation to diversify.[18] For example, a will authorized a trustee to retain securities in a named company "even though they may constitute a considerable portion of the trust property" and "any investment made or retained by the trustee in good faith shall be proper although not conforming to the rules of law." Nevertheless a claim that retention of the designated securities was improper was upheld because the instrument also required the trustee to "act so as to protect the interests of the beneficiaries."[19]

### *Court Approval*

Prior court approval for investments by trustees is not usually required.

**11.** Cal.Prob.Code § 9732.

**12.** Uniform Probate Code § 3–715.

**13.** Unif.Prud.Inv.Act § 2(b). *See also* Unif. Man.Inst.Funds Act § 4.

**14.** *Restatement, Third, of Trusts* § 228(b) (1990). *See also* Dardaganis v. Grace Capital Inc., 889 F.2d 1237, 1240 (2d Cir.1989) (pension fund trustees liable for exceeding the limit on equity investments in agreement).

**15.** *Restatement, Third, of Trusts* § 228, comm. e (1990); Section 9.6, at note 11 et seq.

**16.** Stevens v. National City Bank, 544 N.E.2d 612, 620 (Ohio 1989).

**17.** Hoffman v. First Virginia Bank, 263 S.E.2d 402, 407 (Va.1980).

**18.** *Restatement (Third) of Trusts* § 228, comm. f (1990).

**19.** Goddard v. Continental Illinois Nat. Bank & Trust, 532 N.E.2d 435, 438 (Ill.App. 1988). *See also* First Alabama Bank v. Spragins, 475 So.2d 512 (Ala.1985); Jewett v. Capital Nat. Bank, 618 S.W.2d 109 (Tex.Civ.App. 1981) (trustee authorized to make "speculative" investments can be surcharged for failure to diversify); Rutanen v. Ballard, 678 N.E.2d 133, 139 (Mass.1997) (general authorization to retain property does not warrant retention of underproductive asset).

Such a requirement for conservators is common,[20] but the Uniform Probate Code allows them "without Court authorization or confirmation [to] invest and reinvest funds of the estate as would a trustee."[21]

The need for court approval may turn on the type of investment in question. The Uniform Probate Code generally allows personal representatives to invest without court order, but court approval is needed to continue operating an unincorporated business for more than four months.[22] Conversely, even where conservators are closely supervised, they may be allowed to make certain kinds of investment without prior court approval.[23]

Even when it is not required, fiduciaries may seek court approval for a questionable investment decision. Thus a court in holding that a trustee "did not act improperly in failing to obtain Probate Court approval for diversification," added that "such a proceeding would have been helpful because of * * * legitimate questions concerning" its propriety.[24] Even though the administration of trusts is supposed to proceed "free of judicial intervention," courts are open to instruct trustees in doubtful questions.[25] However, excessive resort to courts, because it is costly, is discouraged. A trustee can get instructions only "if there is a reasonable doubt as to the extent of his powers or duties," and courts "will not instruct him how to exercise his discretion."[26]

### *Legal List v. "Prudent Man (Person)"*

Historically the law has followed one of two approaches to controlling investments, the legal list and the "prudent man (person)" rule. Legal lists vary, but they tend to be conservative ever since the disastrous burst of the South Sea Bubble in the early 18th century, following which Chancellors "developed a restricted list of presumptively proper trust investments, initially government bonds, later well-secured first mortgages. Only in 1961 was the English statute amended to allow trustees to invest in equities ... subject to a ceiling of half the trust fund."[27] In America each state had its own rules but the predominant view has been the one in the second Restatement of Trusts: absent a statute or trust terms providing otherwise, trustee could

> make such investments as a prudent man would make of his own property having in view the preservation of the estate and the amount and regularity of the income to be derived.[28]

This formula goes back to a 19th century Massachusetts case.[29] It has been adapted with variations in many statutes, such as the Uniform Transfers to

**20.** Cal.Prob.Code §§ 2570 (conservator may invest "after authorization by court"), 17209 (administration of trusts "free of judicial intervention"); Conservatorship of Coffey, 231 Cal.Rptr. 421, 424 (App.1986) (conservator surcharged for allowing policy to lapse without court approval).

**21.** Uniform Probate Code § 5–423(b).

**22.** *Id.* § 3–715(24). *See also* Calif.Prob.Code § 16222.

**23.** Cal.Prob.Code § 2574 (government bonds, listed securities).

**24.** Malachowski v. Bank One, 667 N.E.2d 780, 788 (Ind.App.1996).

**25.** Cal.Prob.Code § 17200, 17209.

**26.** *Restatement, Second, Trusts* § 259 (1959).

**27.** Langbein, *The Uniform Prudent Investor Act and the Future of Trust Investing*, 81 Iowa L.Rev. 641, 643 (1996). For a similar American statute see Ohio Rev.Code § 2109.37–.371.

**28.** *Restatement, Second, Trusts* § 227(a) (1959). Even when governed by a legal list, a trustee was supposed to use prudence in selecting among investments on the list. *Id.*, comm. p.

**29.** Harvard College v. Amory, 26 Mass. (9 Pick.) 446 (1830).

Minors Act, where the "prudent man" dealing with "his own property" became "a prudent person dealing with the property of another."[30]

Studies have showed that the return on trust investments in "prudent man/person" states, which generally allow investment in common stocks,[31] was almost double those controlled by legal lists. As a result, most states have abandoned legal lists, at least for trustees.[32] "During the depression years of 1930–1940, bonds and mortgages [included on most legal lists] suffered as well as common stocks [often excluded or limited], but unlike stocks, bonds and mortgages failed to recover their value once conditions improved."[33]

### *Fiduciary's Expertise*

The "prudent person" standard is used in many contexts. The broad grant of powers to trustees in the Uniform Trustees' Powers Act, covering investments and much else, is limited to those "which a prudent man would perform for the purposes of the trust."[34] The Uniform Trust Code requires trustees to "administer the trust as a prudent person would."[35] The Uniform Probate Code uses a similar formula for personal representatives,[36] as does ERISA for managers of pension funds.[37] The standard is objective. For example, trustees of a pension fund who loaned $2 million to a bank which failed were surcharged, even though "none of the trustees had an accounting or banking background" and were thus "wholly unequipped personally to analyze the figures presented to them" which showed the bank's "serious financial problems."[38] Similarly, a family member who served as trustee without compensation was surcharged for failing to invest funds despite her "good faith."[39]

A higher standard is imposed on professional fiduciaries. The Uniform Probate Code and Uniform Prudent Investor Act agree that "if the trustee has special skills or is named trustee on the basis of representations of special skills or expertise, he is under a duty to use those skills."[40]

**30.** Uniform Transfers to Minors Act § 12(b). The Uniform Prudent Investor Act rejects any distinction between a person "investing for another and investing on his or her own account." Unif.Prud.Inv.Act § 2, Comment.

**31.** *Restatement, Second, Trusts* § 227, comm. m (1959). King v. Talbot, 40 N.Y. 76 (1869) had held otherwise.

**32.** Begleiter, *Does the Prudent Investor Really Need the Uniform Prudent Investor Act—An Empirical Study of trust Investment Practices*, 51 Me.L.Rev. 27, 32 (1999). The dichotomy between "legal lists" and "prudent person" states is somewhat misleading, since some legal lists allow a broad range of investments, and conversely, "prudence" can be narrowly interpreted.

**33.** Fleming, *Prudent Investments,* 12 Real Prop., Prob. and Trust L.J. 243, 244–45 (1977). *See also* Gordon, *The Puzzling Persistence of the Constrained Prudent Man Rule,* 62 N.Y.U.L.Rev. 52, 87 (1987).

**34.** Uniform Trustees' Powers Act § 3(a). The Uniform Principal and Income Act (1962) uses similar language in § 2(a)(3), but the 1997 version rejects it as unhelpful. § 103, Comment.

**35.** Unif.Trust Code § 804.

**36.** Uniform Probate Code § 3–703, referring to § 7–302.

**37.** 29 U.S.C. § 1104(a)(1)(B).

**38.** Katsaros v. Cody, 744 F.2d 270 (2d Cir.1984).

**39.** Witmer v. Blair, 588 S.W.2d 222 (Mo. App.1979). *See also* Cal.Prob.Code § 16041 (standard of care not affected by lack of compensation); Buder v. Sartore, 774 P.2d 1383 (Colo.1989) (father acting as uncompensated custodian surcharged for losing investment). *But see* Section 12.8, at note 59 et seq.

**40.** Uniform Probate Code § 7–302; Uniform Prud.Inv.Act § 2(f). *See also Restatement (Third) of Trusts* § 227, comm. d (1990); Estate of Knipp, 414 A.2d 1007 (Pa.1980); Matter of Estate of Dwight, 681 P.2d 563 (Haw.1984).

### *Speculation*

Prudence is sometimes regarded as a question of fact with deference given to a trial court's findings on the issue.[41] But courts operating under the standard have tended to formulate specific sub-rules for determining prudence, *e.g.*, trustees should not invest in second mortgages or buy land for resale.[42]

Although prudent persons make often make speculative investments if the possible rewards outweigh the risk, fiduciaries were not supposed to do this. The second Restatement of Trusts barred "purchase of securities for speculation" and "in new and untried enterprises."[43] Many statutes included express prohibitions against speculation in their formulations of prudence. A court surcharged fiduciaries for buying real estate investment trusts (REITs) because they had existed "for only a short period" and so "there was no solid history of a productive return" to show they were safe investments. The prospectuses had said that REITs "were subject to substantial risks," whereas "the primary objective of a trustee should be preservation of the trust."[44] Another court surcharged a trustee for investing in REITs and other investments which failed to meet its criteria of prudence: "a minimum of $100 million in annual sales" and "earnings stability (positive earnings for the last ten years)".[45]

Fiduciaries who followed the crowd were considered prudent. The second Restatement of Trusts said trustees could invest in stocks which "prudent men in the community are accustomed to invest in."[46] A court refused to surcharge a trustee for investing in Penn Central despite its disastrous performance because "the stock was widely held * * * by financial institutions and common trust funds." Another losing investment was upheld because "33 common trust funds" held the same stock.[47]

This aversion to "speculation" and penchant for sticking to well-trodden paths has disappeared in the Third Restatement which expressly approves speculative and "unconventional" investments.[48] A Uniform Prudent Investor Act was promulgated in 1994 and has been widely adopted.[49] The drafters of this Act and the third Restatement shared the same philosophy.[50] The Act

**41.** Matter of Trusts Created by Hormel, 504 N.W.2d 505, 512 (Minn.App.1993); Matter of Estate of Donner, 626 N.E.2d 922, 927 (N.Y. 1993); Malachowski v. Bank One, 667 N.E.2d 780, 788 (Ind.App.1996).

**42.** *Restatement, Second, Trusts* § 227, comm. f, h (1959); F. Maitland, *Equity* 98–99, 102 (1913); In re Estate of Munger, 309 A.2d 205 (N.J.1973) (investment in real estate improper); Matter of Estate of Collins, 139 Cal. Rptr. 644, 648 (App.1977) (junior mortgage); Langbein & Posner, *Market Funds and Trust Investment Law,* [1976] Amer.Bar Found.R.J. 1, 3.

**43.** *Restatement (Second) of Trusts* § 227, comm. f (1959).

**44.** Matter of Newhoff's Will, 435 N.Y.S.2d 632, 636 (Surr.1980). *See also* Matter of Goldstick, 581 N.Y.S.2d 165, 171 (A.D.1992) (investment in company with no earnings history).

**45.** First Ala. Bank v. Martin, 425 So.2d 415, 419–22 (Ala.1982). *See also* (English) Trustee Investments Act, 1961, First Schedule Part IV § 3 (company must have paid dividends for preceding five years); Buder v. Sartore, 774 P.2d 1383, 1386 (Colo.1989) (custodian surcharged for "highly speculative" investment in "penny stocks").

**46.** *Restatement, Second, Trusts* § 227, comm. m (1959).

**47.** Chase v. Pevear, 419 N.E.2d 1358, 1368–69 (Mass.1981).

**48.** *Restatement, Third, of Trusts* § 227, comm. e (1990).

**49.** 28 adopting states are listed in 7B Uniform Laws Annotated 57 (1999 pocket part).

**50.** John Langbein and Robert Stein served on both groups. The Act's debt to the Restatement is acknowledged in the Prefatory Note.

allows trustees to invest "in any kind of property or type of investment," and "disavows the emphasis in older law on avoiding 'speculative' or 'risky' investments."[51]

### *Diversification*

The Act requires that in investing trustees "exercise caution"[52] but the Act's answer to risk is not to avoid "speculative" investments but to diversify. Trustees "shall diversify the investments of the trust."[53] This emphasis on diversification "responds to one of the central findings of Modern Portfolio Theory that there are huge and essentially costless gains to diversifying the portfolio thoroughly."[54]

A requirement of diversification was already present in earlier law, *e.g.* the second Restatement of Trusts[55] and ERISA.[56] It remains to be seen how much weight courts will give to the increased emphasis on diversification in the third Restatement and the Act. A court in 1997 recognized that trustees had a duty to diversify, but refused to surcharge a trustee who had failed to dispose of real property which constituted the bulk of a trust's assets.

> While the trustee did not expressly prohibit the trustee from selling the land, the trustee could properly have considered the fact that the subject land was placed in the trust by the settlor and comprised a majority of the trust, thus indicating the settlor's intent that the land remain the primary asset of the trust.[57]

On the other hand, another court in the same year surcharged executors who delayed selling a block of Kodak stock which made up 71% of the portfolio.

> Maintaining a concentration of Kodak stock * * * violated certain critical obligations of a fiduciary in making investment decisions under the prudent person rule. * * * Even high quality growth stocks, such as Kodak, possess some degree of volatility because their market value is tied so closely to earnings projections. * * * The investment risk from that volatility is significantly exacerbated when a portfolio is heavily concentrated in one such growth stock.[58]

Most cases of underdiversification involve portfolios which the fiduciary received in this condition, and so the need to diversify must be balanced against possible reasons for retaining an asset. Even the Prudent Investor Act does not require diversification if "the trustee reasonably determines that,

**51.** Unif.Prud.Inv.Act § 2(e) and Comment thereto.

**52.** *Id.* § 2(a).

**53.** *Id.* § 3.

**54.** Langbein, *supra* note 27, at 647. This theory is briefly summarized in this article and in more detail in Langbein & Posner, *Market Funds and Trust investment Law*, [1976] Amer.Bar. Found.R.J 1. Begleiter, *supra* note 32, at 56 suggests that the Act's use of "prudent investor" rather than "prudent man/person" reflects the drafters' intention "to embrace modern investment theory."

**55.** *Restatement, Second, Trusts* § 228 (1959); Matter of Estate of Collins, 139 Cal. Rptr. 644, 649 (App.1977). The idea now appears in *Restatement, Third, of Trusts* § 227(b) (1990).

**56.** 29 U.S.C. § 1104(a)(1)(C); Brock v. Citizens Bank of Clovis, 841 F.2d 344 (10th Cir. 1988) (pension trustee's investing over 65% of assets in real estate mortgages violated Act).

**57.** Matter of Estate of Maxedon, 946 P.2d 104, 109 (Kan.App.1997). *See also* Matter of Trusts Created by Hormel, 504 N.W.2d 505 (Minn.App.1993); United States Trust Co. v. Bohart, 495 A.2d 1034 (Conn.1985).

**58.** Matter of Estate of Janes, 681 N.E.2d 332, 338 (N.Y.1997). *See also* Matter of Estate of Cooper, 913 P.2d 393 (Wash.App.1996) (trustee surcharged for investing 87% in bonds).

because of special circumstances the purposes of the trust would be better served without diversifying." The Comment suggests as a possible special circumstance the tax costs of selling low-basis stock in order to diversify.[59] A weak market for an asset may be another. A court recently refused to surcharge trustees for failure to sell realty in an undiversified portfolio because the absence of a strong market meant that a sale would have been at a sacrifice.[60]

Many statutes and judicial opinion apply different standards to new investments and retention of received asset.[61] The Uniform Probate Code allows personal representatives to "retain assets owned by the decedent * * * which are otherwise improper for trust investment."[62] The Management of Institutional Funds Act allows a board "to hold property given by the donor even though it may not be the best investment."[63] The second Restatement of Trusts, on the other hand, required trustees to dispose of assets which would be improper investments "within a reasonable time," but an authorization in the trust instrument to retain property (a common provision)[64] could be construed as abrogating the requirement of diversification.[65] The third Restatement and the Uniform Prudent Investor Act are less approving of fiduciaries' maintaining the status quo. Trustees must "within a reasonable time" review the portfolio and bring it into compliance with the Act.[66] A general authorization in a trust to retain investments "does not ordinarily abrogate the trustee's duty with respect to diversification." Even an authorization to retain a specific investment ("my XYZ stock") does not control "if retention would otherwise be imprudent."[67]

How far does the duty to diversify extend? The Restatement leaves this open. One of its illustrations approves a portfolio of 20 carefully selected stocks, noting that diversification "is not simply a matter of numbers."[68] But it also touts the advantages of investing in index funds which match the performance of the market as a whole.[69] Langbein predicts that trustees will make increasing "use of pooled investment vehicles," because "studies have found that professionally managed institutional portfolios as a group actually underperformed the broad stock market averages such as the Standard and

**59.** Unif.Prud.Inv.Act § 3 and Comment. See also *Restatement, Third, of Trusts* § 229, comm. a (1990). Langbein, however, suggests that fiduciaries can use "derivatives" to reduce risk in an underdiversified portfolio without realizing capital gains. Langbein, *supra* note 27, at 661.

**60.** In re Estate of Cavin, 728 A.2d 92, 100 (D.C.App.1999).

**61.** Gardner v. Cox, 843 P.2d 469, 471–72 (Or.App.1992) (distinguishing between buying and retaining a "speculative" investment); Estate of Weingart, 182 Cal.Rptr. 369, 375 (App. 1982).

**62.** Uniform Probate Code § 3–715(1). *See also* Uniform Transfers to Minors Act § 12(b). Under Uniform Trustees' Powers Act § 3(c)(1) the trustee has broad discretion to retain assets, but this is subject to the general requirement of prudence.

**63.** Unif.Man.Inst.Funds Act § 4, comment.

**64.** Uniform Statutory Will Act § 13 (a)(1) [Alternative B].

**65.** *Restatement, Second, Trusts* § 230, comm. j (1959).

**66.** Unif.Prud.Inv.Act § 4.

**67.** *Restatement, Third, of Trusts* § 229, comm. d (1990). *See also* Rutanen v. Ballard, 678 N.E.2d 133, 139 (Mass.1997) (authorization to retain property does not allow retention of underproductive asset).

**68.** *Restatement, Third, of Trusts* § 227, illus. 14 (1990). *See also* Unif.Prud.Inv.Act § 3, Comment:"there is no automatic rule for identifying how much diversification is enough."

**69.** *Restatement, Third, of Trusts* § 227, comm. h (1996).

Poor's 500 stock index."[70] This is so because stock markets are efficient; since everything knowable about a publicly traded security is already reflected in its price,[71] research in attempting to pick the "best" stocks is a waste of money.[72] On the other hand, there are also "inefficient" markets, like real estate, where investment without prior inquiry would be imprudent.[73] Assets of this type should not be rejected because "vigorous research and investigation to introduce assets from less efficient markets into the trust portfolio can ... contribute to its overall diversification."[74]

A small portfolio is hard to diversify. Many banks have established "common trust funds" which pool the assets of many small trusts to facilitate diversification. Mutual funds provide another way to diversify investments. This investment delegates the trustee's responsibility to the manager of the mutual fund, but this objection has been considered "of relatively trivial importance compared to the virtues which may be gained by" such funds.[75] The Prudent Investor Act and the third Restatement reject the idea that delegation is improper, in part because of the advantages of mutual funds, and in part because prudent investments in new areas beyond the expertise of the typical trustee may require reliance on the expertise of others.[76]

### *Adapting Investments to the Circumstances*

One reason for the modern rejection of the traditional aversion to "speculation" is the recognition that the situations of beneficiaries differ widely. Some persons are more risk averse than others, partly because they are in varying financial situation. Prudence requires fiduciaries to consider *inter alia* a beneficiary's "ability to absorb losses in the event an investment is unsuccessful."[77] Not all trust beneficiaries are poor widows and orphans. The third Restatement recognizes that "trusts differ considerably in their risk-bearing capacities."[78] A trust "to support an elderly widow of modest means will have a lower risk tolerance than a trust to accumulate for a young scion of great wealth."[79]

The goal of prudent investing in the second Restatement was "preservation of the estate and the amount and regularity of the income."[80] But many beneficiaries (not only "scions of great wealth") are more concerned about protecting against inflation than about a regular income, and prefer non-dividend-paying growth stocks to high-yield bonds. Investments of this type were not allowed by the second Restatement, which only permitted trustees to invest in stock which paid "regular dividends."[81] On similar principles a

**70.** Langbein, *supra* note 27, at 655.

**71.** *Id.* at 657. *See also* Halbach, *Trust Investment Law in the Third Restatement*, 27 Real Prop.Prob. and Trust.J. 407, 425 (1992).

**72.** *Id.* at p. 447.

**73.** Langbein, *supra* note 27, at 658; Matter of Estate of Dwight, 681 P.2d 563, 566 (Haw. 1984) (trustee bought land "without proper investigation").

**74.** *Restatement, Third, of Trusts* § 227, comm. h (1990).

**75.** Farr & Wright, *An Estate Planner's Handbook* 208 (4th ed. 1979).

**76.** Unif.Prud.Inv. Act § 9; *Restatement, Third, of Trusts* § 227, comm. j (1990).

**77.** Erlich v. First Nat'l Bank, 505 A.2d 220, 235 (N.J.Super.Law Div.1984) (imprudent to invest in a single stock for a person who had little income and few assets apart from investment).

**78.** *Restatement, Third, of Trusts* § 227, comm. e (1990).

**79.** Unif.Prud.Inv.Act § 2. Comment.

**80.** *Restatement, Second, Trusts* § 227 (1959).

**81.** *Id.*, comm. m.

trustee was ordered to sell a farm which was worth $1.5 million but produced only $1,265 in income.[82]

The third Restatement recognizes that in many trusts today distributions are made without regard to the trust's income and so the trustee should be free "to disregard income productivity in managing investments."[83] By the same token, the Uniform Management of Institutional Funds Act allows managers of such funds to make "investments with favorable growth prospects" despite a "low current yield" and use capital appreciation to meet the institution's needs.[84] Even in private trusts where income is important to some beneficiaries, it is the trust estate as a whole, not any particular investment that must be productive. The Prudent Investor Act requires that individual investments "be evaluated not in isolation but in the context of the trust portfolio as a whole."[85] This allows trustees to hold one or more non-income producing investments if the portfolio as a whole produces a reasonable income.

Investments which are expected to appreciate even if they produce no income are easier to justify than failure to invest at all, *e.g.* leaving money in a checking account. Many fiduciaries have been surcharged for this, including a bank did not invest cash receipts until they amounted to $1,000, even though they could have been placed in money market funds. The court rejected the bank's claim that it was following "the universal practice of the trust industry," saying that "reasonable persons do not, as a matter of policy leave uninvested sums up to $999."[86] Even executors have been surcharged for leaving estate funds in a checking account.[87] On the other hand, liquidity can be a legitimate concern for fiduciaries.[88] California allows trustees to keep amounts "reasonably necessary for the orderly administration of the trust" in a checking account.[89]

The beneficiaries of a trust often have conflicting interests with respect to investments, *e.g.* income beneficiaries who wish the trust to produce more income and remaindermen who are concerned only with the principal. Trustees are supposed to keep these interests in balance, to be "impartial" in such conflicts. The third Restatement and Prudent Investor Act reiterate this idea.[90] A trustee was surcharged for investing 87% of the assets in bonds because "the prudent investor standard requires that the trustee maintain a balance between the rights of the income beneficiaries with those of the remainderman."[91] But another court refused to surcharge a trustee for failure

**82.** Sturgis v. Stinson, 404 S.E.2d 56 (Va. 1991). *See also* Perfect Union Lodge v. Interfirst Bank, 748 S.W.2d 218 (Tex.1988) (order to sell land which produced less than 1% in income); Rutanen v. Ballard, 678 N.E.2d 133 (Mass.1997) (trustee surcharged for retaining underproductive property).

**83.** *Restatement, Third, of Trusts* § 227, comm. i (1990); *cf.* Shear v. Gabovitch, 685 N.E.2d 1168, 1185 (Mass.App.1997) (proper for trustee to hold stock paying no dividends since settlor implicitly authorized this).

**84.** Unif.Man.Inst.Funds Act, Prefatory Note, § 2 (allowing use of appreciation), § 4(1) (allowing investment in property "whether or not it produces a current return").

**85.** Unif.Prud.Inv.Act § 2(b).

**86.** Maryland Nat'l Bank v. Cummins, 588 A.2d 1205, 1210–12 (Md.1991).

**87.** Cooper v. Jones, 435 N.Y.S.2d 830, 834 (A.D.1981).

**88.** Unif.Prud.Inv. Act § 2(c)(f).

**89.** Cal.Prob.Code § 16225(e).

**90.** *Restatement, Third, of Trusts* § 227, comm. c (1990); Unif.Prud.Inv.Act § 6. The duty of impartiality is not limited to investments. Unif.Trust Code § 803.

**91.** Matter of Estate of Cooper, 913 P.2d 393, 398 (Wash.App.1996).

to "make growth investments to protect the principal against inflation," saying that "the trustees could not sacrifice income in order to increase the value of principal."[92]

The Prudent Investor Act directs trustees to consider *inter alia* the "tax consequences of investment decisions;" for example, "it may be prudent for the trust to buy lower-yielding tax-exempt securities for high tax-bracket taxpayers." However, such choices may have different impact on beneficiaries in different tax situations and so the trustee must balance.[93] In some cases tensions can be reduced by dividing trusts. One court reformed a large trust by splitting it into portions, some of which qualified for exemption from the generation skipping tax. This permitted the trustees to "allocate fixed income investments to the unprotected trusts and investments selected for growth to the tax protected trusts."[94] Another court divided a trust in order to accommodate the different investment wishes of two beneficiaries.[95]

The second Restatement listed "preservation of the estate" (along with production of income) as the goal of trust investment, but under the new rules, preservation of the estate in the traditional sense is not enough. The Prudent Investor Act speaks of "total return from income and the appreciation of capital."[96] The third Restatement describes the goal as preservation of the "real value" of the trust property, *i.e.* "seeking to avoid the loss of the trust estate's purchasing power as a result of inflation."[97] The same attitude is reflected in a recent case surcharging a trustee under whose management a portfolio had increased by $226,000.

> This figure represented a 22.23 percent return on those investments, or a 2.15 percent increase per year between 1978 and 1987. Inflation averaged 6 percent a year during that same period. The purchasing power of those assets decreased then just under 4 percent a year.[98]

### *Family Business*

Retention of a family business may subject fiduciaries to surcharge. The administrator of the estate of the sole shareholder of a company was surcharged for continuing to operate the business at a loss. "A personal representative breaches his trust if he continues to operate a trade or business on behalf of an estate in the absence of testamentary direction."[99] The success of such a business often depends on the ability of its manager, and so it may be imprudent to continue the business after he or she dies.[100]

**92.** Tovrea v. Nolan, 875 P.2d 144, 149 (Ariz.App.1993).

**93.** Unif.Prud.Inv.Act § 2(c)(3), and Comment; *cf.* In re Estate of Feinstein, 527 A.2d 1034, 1038 (Pa.Super.1987) (upholding trustee's investment in tax-free bonds over objection of charitable remaindermen).

**94.** Matter of Will of Kaskel, 549 N.Y.S.2d 587, 590 (Surr.1989).

**95.** In re Siegel, 665 N.Y.S.2d 813 (Surr.1997).

**96.** Unif.Prud.Inv.Act § 2(c)(5).

**97.** *Restatement, Third, of Trusts* § 227, comm. e (1990).

**98.** Matter of Estate of Cooper, 913 P.2d 393, 397–98 (Wash.App.1996). *See also* Dennis v. Rhode Island Hosp. Trust Nat. Bank, 744 F.2d 893, 899 (1st Cir.1984) (surcharge based on consumer price index because proper investments would have "preserved the real value" of the principal).

**99.** In re Kurkowski's Estate, 409 A.2d 357, 361 (Pa.1979). *See also* Estate of Baldwin, 442 A.2d 529 (Me.1982).

**100.** Fortune v. First Union Nat. Bank, 359 S.E.2d 801, 805 (N.C.App.1987).

Some courts apply this rule only to *unincorporated* businesses which, because their unlimited liability, may deplete the whole estate. A court refused to surcharge an executor who continued a to operate a company without court approval on the ground that a statute requiring approval for continuing a "business" did not apply to an incorporated business.[101] The Uniform Probate Code requires court approval to continue an unincorporated business for more than 4 months, but an incorporated business can be operated "throughout the period of administration" if no potential distributee objects.[102]

The Uniform Prudent Investor Act indicates that "interests in closely held enterprises" may be permissible trust investments, and "the wish to retain a family business" may even override the duty to diversify.[103] The language of the third Restatement is less favorable. A trustee cannot continue a business of the settlor "unless authority to do so is expressly or impliedly granted by terms of the trust, or unless ... it is prudent to do so."[104] A lawyer whose client owns a business should make special provision for this in any will or trust. A sale of the business may be the best solution, but a mere authorization (or direction) to sell may be hard to carry out after the client dies, so the client or lawyer testator may need to negotiate a "buy-out" agreement with others associated with the business.

### *Evaluating Performance*

Relatively few reported decisions have appeared since the promulgation of the third Restatement and the Prudent Investor Act, so it remains to be seen how courts will interpret them. The idea of diversification which they stress was already present in prior law, but older decisions surcharging fiduciaries for speculative investments now seem obsolete. Older decisions have also said that the fact that a portfolio showed substantial overall increase in value "does not insulate the trustee from responsibility for imprudence with respect to individual investments."[105] Such statements cannot be squared with the Prudent Investor Act's instruction that trustees' decisions "must be evaluated not in isolation, but in the context of the trust portfolio as a whole."[106]

The Act also says that a trustee's actions must not be judged "by hindsight;" the fact that a portfolio has gone down in value does not *ipso facto* mean that the trustee has been imprudent.[107] But how then is a fiduciary's prudence to be assessed? Langbein noted that the cases "give great weight to the trustee's internal procedures for investing and monitoring investments; ... the courts have sometimes been willing to treat this paper trail as presumptive evidence of prudence."[108] For example, a trial court surcharged trustees for a failure to sell real estate, saying that they had "simply rubber-stamped ('mindlessly reaffirmed') their initial decisions to retain it." The

**101.** Harper v. Harper, 491 So.2d 189, 195 (Miss.1986). *See also* Matter of Estes' Estate, 654 P.2d 4, 13 (Ariz.App.1982).

**102.** Uniform Probate Code § 3–715(24).

**103.** Unif.Prud.Inv.Act § 2(c)(4), § 3, Comment.

**104.** *Restatement, Third, of Trusts* § 229, comm. e (1990).

**105.** In re Bank of New York, 323 N.E.2d 700, 703 (N.Y.1974); Chase v. Pevear, 419 N.E.2d 1358, 1366 (Mass.1981).

**106.** Unif.Prud.Inv.Act § 2(b). *See also Restatement, Third, of Trusts* § 227(a) (1990).

**107.** Unif.Prud.Inv.Act § 8. *See also Restatement, Third, of Trusts* § 227, comm. b (1990); Pillsbury v. Karmgard, 27 Cal.Rptr.2d 491, 502 (App.1994).

**108.** Langbein, *supra* note 27, at 662.

surcharge was set aside on appeal because the trustees had "evaluated each offer that came in to determine whether it was a prudent sale opportunity."[109]

Langbein suggests that under the Prudent Investor Act a "paper trail" cannot excuse a seriously underdiversified portfolio, and a trustee who "persistently underperforms" comparable funds may be found imprudent.[110] Is this consistent with the command not to use "hindsight" in evaluating trustees? The Act requires trustees to have "an overall investment strategy."[111] But presumably the absence of a defensible strategy, *e.g.* using a "blindfolded chimpanzee throwing darts at the stock tables" (who, according to Langbein can perform as well as the funds managed by experts), will not cause a trustee whose investment performance was above average to be surcharged. It is not clear whether under the Act surcharges of trustees will be more or less frequent than they were heretofore. In any event the risk of surcharge is not the only incentive for fiduciaries to perform well; "gross or continued underperformance of investments" is grounds for removal of a trustee.[112] However courts interpret the Act, it will probably change the investment practices of trustees by opening up a broader range of investments.[113]

## § 12.8 Remedies

In this Section we will discuss the remedies available to beneficiaries against fiduciaries for breach of their duties in administering an estate or trust. We will focus primarily on personal representatives and trustees, but similar principles also apply to custodians, conservators/guardians and managers of pension plans under ERISA.

### *Jurisdiction*

The court which appoints a fiduciary may have exclusive jurisdiction over claims against the fiduciary for breach of trust. When beneficiaries of a will probated in Ohio sued the executor in federal court for "irregularities" in her administration, their suit was dismissed on the ground that federal courts have no probate jurisdiction, and can entertain actions to redress wrongs in the administration of an estate only if the state allowed such actions to be pursued in a court of general jurisdiction. Ohio gave exclusive jurisdiction of probate matters to its probate court.[1] On the other hand, another federal court upheld a similar suit arising from Illinois on the ground that Illinois did *not* give its probate court exclusive jurisdiction.[2]

A Massachusetts court entertained a suit against an executor who had been appointed in Greece, saying "the fact that a fiduciary will be made to account for his administration in a court of probate jurisdiction does not deprive an equity court of jurisdiction." Its assumption of jurisdiction would not derogate from the authority of the domiciliary court, but rather assist it

**109.** In re Estate of Cavin, 728 A.2d 92, 98 (D.C.App.1999).

**110.** Langbein, *supra* note 27, at 662.

**111.** Unif.Prud.Inv.Act § 2(b)

**112.** *Restatement, Third, of Trusts* § 37, comm. e (1999).

**113.** Begleiter, *supra* note 32.

**§ 12.8**

**1.** Bedo v. McGuire, 767 F.2d 305 (6th Cir. 1985).

**2.** Hamilton v. Nielsen, 678 F.2d 709 (7th Cir.1982). *See also* Dinger v. Gulino, 661 F.Supp. 438 (E.D.N.Y.1987).

"by securing and preserving estate property."[3] However, even if a court has jurisdiction it may decline to proceed if another court offers a more convenient forum. Thus a New Hampshire court declined to render a judgment concerning a Massachusetts trust, saying

> The administration of a trust is ordinarily governed by the law of the state of primary supervision, and the rights of the parties should not be dependent on the fact that a court of some other state happens to have acquired jurisdiction. That court may ... attempt to apply the law of the primary jurisdiction but mistake that law.[4]

On the other hand, a Minnesota court dismissed on grounds of forum non conveniens a suit involving a trust which was governed by Minnesota law but which had been administered for years in the District of Columbia where all the concerned parties and witnesses lived.[5]

A state continues to have jurisdiction over fiduciaries who move to another state. For example, a trustee of a trust registered in Wisconsin died as a resident of Illinois, naming his wife as his successor. A trust beneficiary was allowed to sue the trustee's wife in Wisconsin, because her husband was "deemed to have consented to the jurisdiction of the Wisconsin court" with respect to liabilities relating to the trust.[6]

### *Form of Trial*

Since historically trusts were enforced in equity, there is usually no right to trial by jury in a suit for a breach of trust,[7] or in a suit against a conservator or personal representative.[8] However, a beneficiary or successor trustee can sue a trustee at law for money which is presently due to the claimant. For example, when the settlor of a revocable trust revoked it before he died, and his executor sued the trustee for damages for negligence, jury trial was allowed because this was a suit for immediate payment to the plaintiff, not one to compel the trustee to put money into the trust for all the beneficiaries.[9]

The historical distinction between courts of law and equity does not bar a state legislature from extending jury trial to trusts, as Michigan, for example, has done. Nevertheless that state's Supreme Court has held that the issue of

**3.** Kaltsas v. Kaltsas, 497 N.E.2d 26 (Mass. App.1986). *See also* Cocke v. Duke University, 131 S.E.2d 909 (N.C.1963) (N.C. has jurisdiction over trust created by resident of N.J.); Israel v. National Board of Y.M.C.A., 369 A.2d 646 (R.I.1977) (N.Y. judgment regarding Rhode Island testamentary trust is valid).

**4.** Bartlett v. Dumaine, 523 A.2d 1, 15 (N.H.1986).

**5.** Matter of Cary, 313 N.W.2d 625, 628 (Minn.1981). *See also Restatement (Second) of Conflict of Laws* § 267, comm. e (1971).

**6.** Norton v. Bridges, 712 F.2d 1156, 1162 (7th Cir.1983). *See also* Uniform Probate Code §§ 3–602, 7–103 (personal representative submits to jurisdiction by accepting appointment); Calif.Prob.Code § 17003; *Restatement (Second) of Conflict of Laws* § 361 (1971); *Restatement (Second) of Trusts* § 199, comm. f (1959).

**7.** Matter of Trust Created by Hill, 499 N.W.2d 475, 490 (Minn.App.1993); Kann v. Kann, 690 A.2d 509 (Md.1997); Mest v. Dugan, 790 P.2d 38, 39 (Or.App.1990); *Restatement (Second) of Trusts* § 197 (1959); Calif.Prob.Code § 17006.

**8.** Estate of Grove v. Selken, 820 P.2d 895, 900 (Or.App.1991); Kaitz v. District Court, 650 P.2d 553 (Colo.1982); Conservatorship of Estate of Coffey, 231 Cal.Rptr. 421, 427 (App. 1986).

**9.** Jefferson Nat. Bank v. Central Nat. Bank, 700 F.2d 1143 (7th Cir.1983). *See also Restatement (Second) of Trusts* § 198 (1959); *cf.* Levinson v. Citizens Nat. Bank, 644 N.E.2d 1264, 1267 (Ind.App.1994) (suggesting that whenever damages are sought trial is by jury); Fortune v. First Union Nat. Bank, 371 S.E.2d 483 (N.C.1988).

the trustee's prudence remains an issue for the court, because "to allow a jury to determine the issue would potentially subject a trustee to the whim of every impatient or dissatisfied beneficiary who is displeased with the trustee's business decisions."[10]

### *Equitable Remedies*

The traditional equitable remedies are often invoked against fiduciaries. Courts can enjoin them from making an improper investment or sale, or order them to sell property.[11] An improper sale which has already taken place can be vacated,[12] but not if the buyer was a bona-fide purchaser. Thus when trustees made a lease for an inadequate rent, the trustee was surcharged but the court refused to rescind the lease because the lessee could reasonably have thought that it lease was proper.[13] A trustee who has wrongfully sold property to a bona fide purchaser can be compelled to buy a replacement if this is reasonably possible.[14]

The beneficiaries can also elect to affirm a wrongful purchase if the property later rises in value, or may affirm an improper sale if the property declines in value.[15] This allows beneficiaries to speculate at the fiduciary's expense, but delay may bar their remedy under the idea of laches.[16] When some of a trustee's improper investments are profitable while others are not, can the trustee deduct the gain from the profitable investments from the loss on the others? This depends on whether the breaches of trust are regarded as "distinct." In a case in which a trustee made 12 improper investments, seven of them were regarded as distinct because they were made at different times. But as to five which were made at the same time the gains realized on some could be used to offset losses incurred by the others.[17] The refusal to allow gains from "distinct" breaches as an offset is not inconsistent with the portfolio approach to investments, which deals with "the question whether a breach of trust has occurred" rather than the "amount of liability for multiple breaches."[18]

**10.** In re Messer Trust, 579 N.W.2d 73, 79 (Mich.1998).

**11.** Donovan v. Bierwirth, 680 F.2d 263 (2d Cir.1982) (injunction against trustees of pension fund); Matter of Estate of Rolczynski, 349 N.W.2d 394 (N.D.1984) (executor ordered to sell land); In re Estate of Feeney, 189 Cal.Rptr. 84 (App.1983); Lowell v. Bouchillon, 271 S.E.2d 498 (Ga.1980) (TRO against sale of land); In re Estate of Hughes, 515 A.2d 581 (Pa.Super.1986); *Restatement (Second) of Trusts* § 199 (1959).

**12.** Matter of Estate of Ostrander, 910 P.2d 865 (Kan.App.1996) (unauthorized sale by administrator set aside); Smiley v. Johnson, 763 S.W.2d 1 (Tex.App.1988) (constructive trust imposed on buyers from agent); Cohen v. City of Lynn, 598 N.E.2d 682, 684 (Mass.App.1992); Walter E. Wilhite Revocable Living Trust v. Northwest Yearly Meeting Pension Fund, 916 P.2d 1264 (Idaho 1996) (transfer rescinded but transferee reimbursed for liens removed from property).

**13.** Jarrett v. U.S. National Bank, 725 P.2d 384, 388 (Or.App.1986).

**14.** Application of Kettle, 423 N.Y.S.2d 701 (A.D.1979); *Restatement, Third, of Trusts* § 208 (1990). For further discussion of bona-fide purchasers see note 163 et seq. *infra.*

**15.** *Restatement, Third, of Trusts* § 208 (election to affirm a sale), § 210(b) (election to affirm an improper investment) (1990).

**16.** For further discussion of laches see note 119 et seq. *infra.*

**17.** Ramsey v. Boatmen's First Nat. Bank, 914 S.W.2d 384, 390 (Mo.App.1996).

**18.** *Restatement, Third, of Trusts* § 213 (1990). As to the portfolio approach see Section 12.7, note 85.

### *Damages*

Sometimes damages are the only appropriate remedy. These may be based on profits arising to the fiduciary from a breach. For example, when a trustee used trust assets to secure a loan with which he made a profitable purchase for himself, the court awarded damages even though the trust suffered no loss. "Any benefit or profit inures to the trust estate, even though no injury was intended and none was in fact done to the trust estate."[19] In another case administrators of an estate sold land to a corporation which they owned. The sale could not be rescinded because the company had later resold the land. Had the company resold the land without improving it, the estate would be entitled to any profit made on the resale,[20] but not if the profit was due to improvements which the company had placed on the land; thus it was necessary to ascertain whether the company had paid fair market value for the land.[21]

Any profits claimed against a fiduciary must be shown with reasonable certainty. A bank which wrongfully invested trust funds in its own passbook accounts was not charged with its profits from use of the funds since they could not accurately be determined; instead it had to pay interest at the legal rate on the amounts (less the interest already paid to the trust) as damages.[22] Another court refused to hold a trustee accountable for any profit it had earned on excessive fees it had taken because "other than the amount of the fees themselves, no profit from the fees was traceable ... they simply became part of the bank's general operating revenues."[23]

Even if a fiduciary makes no profit from a breach, damages may be recovered for any loss suffered by the trust.[24] If a sale was proper but the price was too low, damages are based on the value of the property when it was sold, *i.e.* the difference between what the trustee received and what the buyer should have paid.[25] But when a trustee sells an asset which should have been retained, the damages are based on the present value of the asset, since the loss of appreciated value of the sold asset constitutes "an actual loss" to the trust.[26] Dividends paid on stock after it was improperly sold (reduced by interest received on the sales proceeds) are also awarded.[27]

**19.** Coster v. Crookham, 468 N.W.2d 802, 806–07 (Iowa 1991). *See also Restatement, Third, of Trusts* § 205(a) (1990); In re Estate of Stowell, 595 A.2d 1022 (Me.1991); 29 U.S.C. § 1109(a) (ERISA).

**20.** *Restatement, Third, of Trusts* § 206, comm. b (1990).

**21.** Stegemeier v. Magness, 728 A.2d 557, 566 (Del.1999).

**22.** Stephan v. Equitable Savings and Loan Association, 522 P.2d 478, 492 (Or.1974); *cf.* Maryland Nat'l Bank v. Cummins, 588 A.2d 1205, 1217 (Md.1991).

**23.** Nickel v. Bank of America Nat. Trust & Sav. Ass'n, 991 F.Supp. 1175, 1182–83 (N.D.Cal.1997).

**24.** *Restatement, Third, of Trusts* § 205(b) (1990).

**25.** *Id.* § 205, comm. d. *See also* Hatcher v. United States Nat. Bank, 643 P.2d 359 (Or. App.1982); *cf.*Matter of Guardianship of Eisenberg, 719 P.2d 187, 192 (Wash.App.1986) (surcharge based on difference between fair rental value and rent received); Murphy v. Central Bank and Trust Co., 699 P.2d 13 (Colo.App. 1985) (surcharge based on higher price received by buyers on resale).

Conversely when a fiduciary pays too much for a proper investment, damages are based on the excess payment. *Restatement, Second, Trusts* § 205, comm. e (1959); *cf.* McCormick v. McCormick, 455 N.E.2d 103, 110 (Ill.App.1983) (trustees used a more expensive method of financing than necessary).

**26.** Taylor v. Crocker National Bank, 252 Cal.Rptr. 388, 397 (App.1988) (not officially published). *See also Restatement, Third, of Trusts* § 208 (1990); Progressive Land Developers v. Exchange National Bank, 641 N.E.2d 608, 614 (Ill.App.1994); Estate of Rothko, 372 N.E.2d 291, 297 (N.Y.1977) (executors).

**27.** Matter of Donald E. Bradford Trust, 538 So.2d 263, 268 (La.1989); *Restatement, Third, of Trusts* § 208, illus. 2 (1990).

Trustees may also be surcharged for failing to sell assets which are improper investments. Trustees who had failed to sell property when they were offered $1.64 million for it had to pay damages based on "what the net sales proceeds would have been had the offers ... been accepted ... less the value of the property when it was transferred" to the remaindermen.[28] An executor who unduly delayed selling stock while its value dropped was charged the value of the stock on the date it should have been sold less "the proceeds from the sale of the stock [when sold] or, if the stock is still retained, the value of the stock at the time" of trial.[29]

In this case the trial court added to the damages so computed prejudgment interest at the legal rate, compounded from the date when the sale should have occurred. This was held to be within the trial court's discretion.[30] This is consistent with the second Restatement of Trusts, but the third Restatement in place of interest speaks of "an appropriate additional amount to compensate for the loss of return" on the amount lost. This can be "based on total return experience (positive or negative) for other investments of the trust," or "portfolios of other trusts having comparable objectives and circumstances."[31] A trustee who made excess payments to a beneficiary was charged compound interest on the amounts paid at a rate of 9.16 percent, because "had the trust retained those payments they would have generated a return of 9.16 percent compound interest."[32] Fiduciaries who exceeded a 50% limit on equity investments imposed by the terms of a pension plan were held liable for the difference between the actual earnings of the plan and "what the earnings would have been if the 50% limit had been observed," based on the assumption the remaining money would have "earned a rate of return equal to the non-equity securities held by the fund."[33] Conversely a bank which invested solely for the benefit of the income beneficiaries without regard to the growth of corpus for the remaindermen had to pay damages based on the rate of appreciation realized by its common equity funds.[34] A custodian who had invested minors' funds in "penny stocks" was required to buy them back at the price paid and also to compensate the minors "for the loss of

**28.** Rutanen v. Ballard, 678 N.E.2d 133, 137 (Mass.1997).

**29.** Matter of Estate of Janes, 681 N.E.2d 332, 339 (N.Y.1997). *See also* Estate of Lindberg, 424 N.E.2d 1161 (Ill.App.1981).

**30.** Matter of Estate of Janes, 681 N.E.2d 332, 339–40 (N.Y.1997). The dividends which the estate received from the improperly retained stock were deducted from the interest awarded. *See also* Jarrett v. U.S. National Bank, 768 P.2d 936, 938 (Or.App.1989) (proper to charge trustee with interest on damages); Lincoln Nat. Bank v. Shriners Hospitals, 588 N.E.2d 597, 600 (Ind.App.1992); McLaughlin v. Cohen, 686 F.Supp. 454, 458 (S.D.N.Y.1988) (simple interest at Treasury rate in ERISA case).

**31.** *Restatement, Third, of Trusts* §§ 209(1), 205, comment a (1990). *See also* Estate of Wilde, 708 A.2d 273, 275 (Me.1998) (damages based on the value of trust assets "had they been managed by a prudent trustee").

**32.** Austin v. U.S. Bank of Washington, 869 P.2d 404, 415 (Wash.App.1994). *See also* Dunkley v. Peoples Bank & Trust Co., 728 F.Supp. 547, 563–64 (W.D.Ark.1989); *cf.* In re Testamentary Trust of Hamm, 707 N.E.2d 524, 530 (Ohio App.1997) (trustee is charged "only" with interest at the usual rate of return for trust investments and not the legal rate absent "wilful misconduct").

**33.** Dardaganis v. Grace Capital Inc., 889 F.2d 1237, 1243 (2d Cir.1989). *See also* Gillespie v. Seymour, 823 P.2d 782, 796 (Kan.1991) (damages based on rate of return for other trust funds).

**34.** Noggle v. Bank of America, 82 Cal. Rptr.2d 829, 836 (App.1999). *See also Restatement, Third, of Trusts* § 211 (1990). *But see* Nickel v. Bank of America Nat. Trust & Sav. Ass'n, 991 F.Supp. 1175, 1183 (N.D.Cal.1997) (granting interest on excessive fees charged by trustee but rejecting loss of profit to trust as "too speculative"); Gillespie v. Seattle–First Nat. Bank, 855 P.2d 680, 694 (Wash.App. 1993).

appreciation of the funds."[35] The opinion does not indicate how this "loss of appreciation" was measured; presumably it was based on the funds' "blue-chip" investments.

Courts refuse to impose a surcharge if they find no causal link between the breach of trust and the loss. For example, a trustee which was authorized to invest in bonds with AAA or AA ratings bought some with only an A rating. They declined in value but the decline in higher rated bonds was even greater. The court refused to surcharge the trustee because the loss would have occurred in the absence of the breach.[36] Another court refused to surcharge an executor when a loss in the estate was "caused by the decline of the stock market rather than by the lack of diversification of the estate's holdings."[37] But a trustee who buys an asset from himself which declines in value is surcharged even though the same decline would have occurred if he had bought the asset from someone else.[38] Perhaps the trustee would not have bought the asset at all without the conflict of interest, so there may in fact be a causal connection between the breach and the loss in this case.

### *Punishment*

Historically it was not a crime for trustees to misappropriate property,[39] but this is no longer true.[40] Lawyers who engage of breach of duty as fiduciaries are subject to discipline under the rules of the profession, *e.g.* attorneys have been disbarred for stealing money from a trust of which they were the trustee.[41]

Traditionally, courts did not award punitive damages for breach of trust, because equity which did not give punitive damages.[42] The terms "equitable or remedial relief" in ERISA are usually held not to encompass punitive damages.[43] Some more recent cases, however, have awarded punitive damages against trustees who acted in "bad faith or conscious indifference to the rights of the beneficiaries."[44]

Courts may also use contempt procedures against recalcitrant fiduciaries. However, an order to imprison a guardian until he turned over funds which he had dissipated was reversed. The guardian

**35.** Buder v. Sartore, 774 P.2d 1383, 1390 (Colo.1989).

**36.** Fort Myers Mem. Gardens v. Barnett Banks, 474 So.2d 1215, 1218 (Fla.App.1985).

**37.** Hamilton v. Nielsen, 678 F.2d 709, 713 (7th Cir.1982). *See also Restatement (Second) of Trusts* § 205, comm. f (1959).

**38.** Matter of Guardianship of Eisenberg, 719 P.2d 187, 191 (Wash.App.1986); *Restatement, Second, Trusts* § 206, comm. d (1959). For a further discussion of the duty of loyalty see Section 12.9.

**39.** F. Maitland, *Equity* 47 (1913).

**40.** Commonwealth v. Garrity, 682 N.E.2d 937 (Mass.App.1997) (executor convicted of embezzlement from an estate).

**41.** Matter of Stern, 682 N.E.2d 867 (Mass. 1997); People v. Rouse, 817 P.2d 967 (Colo. 1991).

**42.** Kohler v. Fletcher, 442 N.W.2d 169 (Minn.App.1989); Kaitz v. District Court, 650 P.2d 553 (Colo.1982); *cf.* Bank of America Nat. Trust v. Superior Court, 226 Cal.Rptr. 685, 693 (App.1986) (guardian of the estate).

**43.** Diduck v. Kaszycki & Sons Contractors, Inc., 974 F.2d. 270, 286 (2d Cir.1992).

**44.** Cartee v. Lesley, 350 S.E.2d 388, 390 (S.C.1986). *See also* Citizens and Southern Nat. Bank v. Haskins, 327 S.E.2d 192 (Ga. 1985) (jury instructed on punitive damages but refuses to grant them); InterFirst Bank Dallas v. Risser, 739 S.W.2d 882 (Tex.App.1987) ($2.6 million in punitive damages awarded); Melvin v. Home Federal Sav. & Loan Ass'n, 482 S.E.2d 6 (N.C.App.1997).

was imprisoned without a jury trial and without any of the traditional procedural protections afforded criminal defendants ... Consequently his incarceration is proper only if it qualifies as a sanction based on civil coercive contempt ... The court's inherent power to impose sanctions for civil contempt [applies only for] ... the omission or refusal to perform an act which is yet in the power of a defendant to perform.[45]

Beneficiaries of a trust have an advantage over ordinary creditors if a trustee becomes insolvent; they "retain their equitable interests in the trust property if it can be identified, or in its product if it can be traced into the product."[46] If the trust property can no longer be identified or traced, the trustee remains personally liable for damages. Claims arising out of "fraud or defalcation while acting in a fiduciary capacity" are not dischargeable in bankruptcy.[47]

### *Defenses: Standing*

We shall now turn to possible defenses of a fiduciary against the remedies just discussed. A suit may be dismissed for lack of standing. A testator's children were not allowed to challenge the fees paid to his personal representative because they had no interest in the question since the will had disinherited them.[48] Even a beneficiary of an estate or trust has no standing to challenge actions which do not affect the beneficiary's interest; thus remaindermen under a trust were not permitted to question a loan made by the trustee at an interest below the market rate, because any increased income generated from the loan would not go to them but to the income beneficiary.[49] On the other hand, the fact that a trust beneficiary's interest is contingent does not deprive the beneficiary of standing to sue.[50] The fact that the beneficiary may take nothing under the trust (*e.g.* a remainderman whose interest is contingent on surviving the income beneficiary) does not matter, since the recovery goes to the trust itself for eventual distribution under its terms.[51] A class action against a trustee administering a common trust fund on behalf of beneficiaries of many trusts has also been allowed.[52]

Courts are liberal about standing when the interests of incapacitated persons are at stake. An attorney was allowed to challenge a conservator's accounts even though "there is some question whether [she] was the children's guardian ad litem," since "any person may petition the court as the next friend of the children to bring the conservator's conflict of interest to the

**45.** Matter of Elder, 763 P.2d 219, 221–22 (Alaska 1988).

**46.** *Restatement, Third, of Trusts* § 5, comm. k (1990).

**47.** 11 U.S.C. § 523(a)(4).

**48.** Estate of Miles v. Miles, 994 P.2d 1139, 1145 (Mont.2000). *See also* In re Estate of Burgeson, 516 N.E.2d 590 (Ill.App.1987) (decedent's former guardian lacks standing to attack acts of attorney for the estate).

**49.** Regan v. Uebelhor, 690 N.E.2d 1222, 1226 (Ind.App.1998); *Restatement, Second, Trusts* § 214, comm. b (1959) *But see* Jarrett v. United States Nat. Bank, 725 P.2d 384, 389 (Or.App.1986) (remaindermen damaged by failure to maximize income because it "would reduce the potential need to invade the corpus" to provide for needs of income beneficiary).

**50.** Giagnorio v. Emmett C. Torkelson Trust, 686 N.E.2d 42, 45 (Ill.App.1997).

**51.** Claims concerning a trustee's misconduct in running a company in which the trust owns shares belong to the company and must be asserted in a stockholder's derivative suit. Symmons v. O'Keeffe, 644 N.E.2d 631, 638 (Mass.1995).

**52.** Bank One Indianapolis, NA v. Norton, 557 N.E.2d 1038 (Ind.App.1990).

court's attention."[53] The Uniform Probate Code allows "any person interested in the welfare" of a conservatee to petition for relief against the conservator.[54]

Co-trustees have standing to sue their fellow trustees, and successor trustees can sue the predecessor (or the personal representative of the estate in the case of a testamentary trust) for breaches by the latter.[55] Public officials have standing in some cases, the state attorney general for charitable trusts and the Secretary of Labor for funds subject to ERISA.[56] However, a settlor who has reserved no interest in the trust has no standing.[57] Courts on their own motion may raise questions about a fiduciary's conduct.[58]

### *Good Faith*

Occasionally a court refuses to impose liability on a trustee who has committed a breach of trust in good faith. For example, when a trust authorized payments to the settlor's older children only in case of "emergency or hardship," a court refused to require the trustees to repay sums they had disbursed "grounded on a good faith, albeit erroneous, interpretation of the hardship clause of the trust document."[59] The Uniform Trusts Act allows courts to "excuse a trustee who has acted honestly and reasonably from liability for violations" of the Act,"[60] and the Restatement of Trusts says that even without a statute "it would seem that a court of equity may have power to excuse a trustee" under such circumstances.[61] But the Restatement also says that a trustee who makes a mistake in interpreting the law or the instrument is not immune from liability "merely because he acts in good faith," because in doubtful cases "he can protect himself by obtaining instruction from the court."[62]

### *Exculpatory Clauses*

Clauses which exculpate a fiduciary from liability are sometimes given effect. For example, a trust provided that the trustee "shall not be liable if [the trust powers] are exercised in good faith." A judgment surcharging the trustee for imprudent transactions was reversed, because the lower court had "incorrectly used the prudent man standard" whereas the "administration of the trust was fully consistent with the good faith standard which must be used to test her management of the trust."[63] Often, however, exculpatory

**53.** Matter of Conservatorship of L.M.S., 755 P.2d 22, 25 (Kan.App.1988). *See also Restatement, Second, Trusts* § 214, comm. a (1959).

**54.** Uniform Probate Code § 5–415.

**55.** In Axelrod v. Giambalvo, 472 N.E.2d 840, 846 (Ill.App.1984), the court held that a good faith determination by successor trustees not to pursue a possible claim against a former trustee barred the beneficiaries from doing so.

**56.** 29 U.S.C. § 1132(a). As to charitable trusts see Section 9.7, note 63.

**57.** *Restatement, Second, Trusts* § 200 (1959).

**58.** Estate of Kerns v. Western Surety Co., 802 P.2d 1298 (Okl.1990); *Restatement, Second, Trusts* § 200, comm. h (1959).

**59.** Griffin v. Griffin, 463 So.2d 569, 574 (Fla.App.1985).

**60.** Uniform Trusts Act § 19. *See also* Cal. Prob.Code § 16440(c).

**61.** *Restatement, Second, Trusts* § 205, comm. g (1959). (Although this section was revised in 1990, comment g was not changed.)

**62.** *Id.*, § 201, comm. b, § 226, comm. b. *See also* Nat. Academy of Sciences v. Cambridge Trust Co., 346 N.E.2d 879, 885 (Mass. 1976) (trustee liable for payment to beneficiary in ignorance of her remarriage, which by the terms of the trust disqualified her).

**63.** Kerper v. Kerper, 780 P.2d 923, 930–31 (Wyo.1989). *See also* Jewish Hospital v. Boatmen's Nat. Bank, 633 N.E.2d 1267, 1280 (Ill. App.1994); Barnett v. Barnett, 424 So.2d 896 (Fla.App.1982); Boston Safe Deposit and Trust Co. v. Boone, 489 N.E.2d 209, 213 (Mass.App. 1986).

clauses are held not to bar imposition of liability. Thus a trustee was held liable for a wrongful distribution despite a clause holding the trustee harmless for actions taken "except in the case of fraud." Although the trustee's actions were not "wanton or malicious" (so no punitive damages were awarded), it had "acted with reckless indifference" and hence was liable for compensatory damages.[64] A New York statute invalidates even clauses which exonerate an executor or testamentary trustee from liability for ordinary negligence.[65] Courts are particularly averse to such clauses when they are invoked by professional fiduciaries. One held that to give effect to an exculpatory clause "would violate public policy" if applied to defendants who had "held themselves out to be professional investment advisors."[66] Lawyers who attempt to limit their liability for malpractice by an exculpatory clause may run afoul of the rules of professional conduct.[67]

An exculpatory clause will be disregarded if it was "improperly inserted" in the instrument, *e.g.* when a lawyer who drafted a trust in which he was named trustee failed to bring the clause to the settlor's attention and explain its implications, the settlor being 70 years old and "in questionable health."[68] However, in another case the court upheld such a clause even though the trustee drew the instrument and suggested the clause. The drafter said he had discussed the clause with the testator who "was competent in financial matters" and thus there was no "abuse of a the fiduciary relationship."[69]

### *Throwing the Blame on Others*

Fiduciaries sometimes try to shift the responsibility for a breach to others, with mixed results. A court surcharged a personal representative for penalties incurred by the estate for a late tax return despite her claim that "she reasonably relied on the advice of her accountant who * * * reasonably informed her that the return had been timely filed." The court said that she was not justified in leaving "all tax matters to the accountant."[70] Another court rejected a guardian's defense that his failure to sell the ward's home after the ward moved into a nursing home was made on the advice of an attorney; in some situations "an administrator should be exonerated because of a loss due to the mistakes" of his counsel, but in this matter "the primary responsibility rests upon the administrator himself."[71] On the other hand, an executor who filed an improper estate tax return was exonerated because it had relied on the advice of the lawyer for the estate. "The Bank had a right to hire an attorney to handle the legal affairs of the estate, and . . . to rely on the attorney's advice, unless the Bank knowingly chose incompetent counsel or

**64.** Feibelman v. Worthen Nat. Bank, N.A., 20 F.3d 835, 836 (8th Cir.1994), following *Restatement, Second, Trusts* § 222(2) (1959). *See also* Cal.Prob.Code § 16461(b); Lincoln Nat. Bank v. Shriners Hospitals, 588 N.E.2d 597, 600 (Ind.App.1992).

**65.** N.Y. EPTL § 11–1.7(a). In Estate of Lubin, 539 N.Y.S.2d 695 (Surr.1989), a lawyer was criticized for inserting an exculpatory clause which because of its invalidity might mislead fiduciaries and beneficiaries.

**66.** Erlich v. First Nat'l Bank, 505 A.2d 220, 233 (N.J.Super.Law Div.1984).

**67.** ABA Model Code of Prof.Resp. DR 6–102; ABA Model Rules of Prof.Cond. 1.8(h).

**68.** Rutanen v. Ballard, 678 N.E.2d 133, 141 (Mass.1997), citing *Restatement, Second, Trusts* § 222, comm. d (1959).

**69.** Marsman v. Nasca, 573 N.E.2d 1025, 1032–33 (Mass.App.1991).

**70.** Gudschinsky v. Hartill, 815 P.2d 851, 855 (Alaska 1991).

**71.** In re Guardianship of McPheter, 642 N.E.2d 690, 695 (Ohio App.1994).

had some reason to know that the advice given was not sound."[72] A trustee which delayed selling stock because its "market advisory service * * * had opined the market would recover" was found to have acted prudently.[73]

The second Restatement of Trusts said that trustees had a duty "not to delegate to others the doing of acts which the trustee can reasonably be required to perform personally."[74] This rather open-ended formula was reformulated in the third Restatement to reflect a more favorable attitude toward delegation; indeed trustees may now be deemed imprudent for *failure* to delegate in some situations.[75] The Uniform Trustees' Powers' Act authorizes trustees to employ investment advisors and other agents and "to act without independent investigation upon their advice."[76] A similar approval of delegation appears in ERISA[77] and the Uniform Management of Institutional Funds Act.[78] Most recently the Uniform Prudent Investor Act "reverses the much-criticized rule that forbad trustees to delegate investment and management functions." Trustees must exercise reasonable skill in selecting the agent and "periodically reviewing the agent's actions."[79] If they do this, they are not liable for the agent's actions, but the *agent* has a duty to exercise reasonable care in carrying out the delegated duties.[80]

A similar problem arises when there are multiple fiduciaries and one takes a leading role. An attempt by a co-trustee to escape liability for the failure to sell a trust asset was rejected.

> A cotrustee must 'participate in the administration of the trust and use reasonable care to prevent a co-trustee from committing a breach of trust ... If one trustee refuses to exercise a power that the trustees are under a duty to exercise, the other trustees are not justified in merely acquiescing ... It is their duty to apply to the court ... Baylis ... largely abandoned his duties of administering the trust to Ballard ... [He] never advised her ... that her failure to sell ... constituted a breach of her fiduciary duties.[81]

In such situations each fiduciary is jointly liable for the whole loss, but has a right of contribution against the other(s) if the beneficiary sues only one of the fiduciaries.[82] A fiduciary who is substantially more at fault than the

72. Jewish Hospital v. Boatmen's Nat. Bank, 633 N.E.2d 1267, 1281 (Ill.App.1994).

73. Matter of Wiese's Estate, 257 N.W.2d 1, 2–3 (Iowa 1977). *See also* Estate of Knipp, 414 A.2d 1007, 1008 (Pa.1980) (executor "respected outside sources of information and advice").

74. *Restatement, Second, Trusts* § 171 (1959).

75. *Restatement, Third, of Trusts* § 171, comm. a (1990). *See also id.*, comm. g (trustee may "be virtually compelled by considerations of efficiency" to delegate), § 227, comm. j.

76. Uniform Trustees' Powers Act § 3(c)(19).

77. 29 U.S.C. § 1103(a)(2).

78. Unif.Man.Inst.Funds Act § 5.

79. *Cf.* Whitfield v. Cohen, 682 F.Supp. 188 (S.D.N.Y.1988) (ERISA trustee liable for failure to exercise care in selecting investment advisor and monitoring its performance).

80. Unif.Prud.Inv.Act § 9.

81. Rutanen v. Ballard, 678 N.E.2d 133, 140 (Mass.1997) (quoting *Restatement, Second, Trusts* § 184 (1959)). *See also* Ramsey v. Boatmen's First Nat. Bank, 914 S.W.2d 384, 388 (Mo.App.1996). The same principles apply to co-executors. Matter of Estate of Donner, 626 N.E.2d 922, 926 (N.Y.1993). Uniform Trustees' Powers Act § 6(a), on the other hand, provides that "a trustee who has not joined in exercising a power is not liable ... for the consequences of the exercise."

82. In re Estate of Chrisman, 746 S.W.2d 131, 134–35 (Mo.App.1988); Gbur v. Cohen, 155 Cal.Rptr. 507 (App.1979).

other is not entitled to contribution and the other can get full indemnity from the fiduciary primarily at fault.[83]

Similar rules appear in ERISA, but they do not "preclude any agreement, authorized by the trust instrument, allocating specific responsibilities ... among trustees" which may limit the liability of particular trustees.[84] The more liberal attitude of the third Restatement of Trusts toward delegation by trustees apparently encompasses delegation to a co-trustee, at least when authorized by the terms of the trust.[85] It is not clear how delegation among trustees differs from delegation to agents, but Uniform Prudent Investor Act § 9 only speaks of delegation to an "agent."

Some trust instruments allow a person other than the trustee to control investments. Such a provision may affect the trustee's liability. If the power is for the sole benefit of its holder, the trustee's only obligation is to follow directions, but if the holder is "subject to fiduciary obligations" the trustee may be liable for complying with improper directions, just as if the power holder were a co-trustee.[86] For example, even though a trust did not permit the trustee to alter investments without the settlor's consent, the trustee was surcharged for failure to diversify the portfolio. The settlor's power over investments was "for the benefit of the beneficiaries," so he was "just as much a fiduciary as the trustee" and the trustee was obligated "to submit a reinvestment plan to the settlor and, if rejected, to seek instructions from the court."[87]

### *Res judicata*

Fiduciaries frequently claim to be protected from liability by a prior judgment. A trustee, for example, who gets court instructions as to the propriety of an action should be protected for actions taken in compliance with the instructions received.[88] Even transactions involving a conflict of interest are allowed when they are "approved by the Court after notice to interested persons."[89] However, this protection does not preclude relief from a judgment under the general rules of civil procedure. Thus a judgment approving fees was set aside for "excusable neglect" by devisee who had "no prior experience with the probate system .. and no idea what an estate attorney's fees should have been."[90] Nor does res judicata extend to questions which were not covered by the decree. For example, an order approving a executor's sale of property at a specified price, did not bar a later claim that the executor had "mishandled the business in such a manner that the value [of the

83. *Restatement, Second, Trusts* § 258 (1959); In re Mueller's Trust, 135 N.W.2d 854, 866 (Wis.1965) (contribution but not indemnity given).

84. 29 U.S.C. § 1105. Some courts have recognized a right of contribution among ERISA fiduciaries, even though the statute does not provide for it. Chemung Canal Trust Co. v. Fairway Spring Co., 939 F.2d 12 (2d Cir.1991).

85. *Restatement, Third, of Trusts* § 171, comm. i (1990).

86. *Restatement (Second) of Trusts* § 185, comms. d, e (1959).

87. Steiner v. Hawaiian Trust Co., 393 P.2d 96, 107 (Haw.1964).

88. Estate of Fales, 431 N.Y.S.2d 763, 765 (Surr.1980) (order approving sale "protects the trustee against even a claim of liability"); Harper v. Harper, 491 So.2d 189, 199 (Miss.1986) (challenge to action which court had approved rejected).

89. Uniform Probate Code § 3-713. *See also* Uniform Trustees' Powers Act § 5; *Restatement (Second) of Trusts* § 170, comm. f (1959); In re Scarborough Properties Corp., 255 N.E.2d 761 (N.Y.1969).

90. Johnson v. Doris, 933 P.2d 1139, 1143 (Alaska 1997).

property had] decreased significantly during the period after [the testator] died." This issue was "clearly distinct" from the question whether the sales price adequately reflected the value of the business at the time of the sale.[91]

The effect of court approval of a fiduciary's accounts is often at issue. For example, after trustees filed annual accounts for several years, beneficiaries claimed that they had wrongfully retained an under-productive asset. A statute expressly made a trustee's *final* account conclusive, but no such language appeared in the provision requiring intermediate accounts.[92] The court nevertheless gave summary judgment to the trustees.

> Most jurisdictions conclude that a judicial settlement of a trustee's accounts, as to persons who receive notice and are subject to the court's jurisdiction, bars subsequent litigation seeking to raise defaults or defects with the matters shown or disclosed in the accountings. It is a modified kind of res judicata * * * because * * * the beneficiaries are barred from questioning later matters which are disclosed by the accounting, but *not* those *not* disclosed. In traditional res judicata, a party is barred from raising not only issues which were litigated, but those that might have been discovered and litigated. * * *
>
> Whether retention of the [under productive] asset was a breach of the trustee's fiduciary duty appears to us to be barred by the accountings, because retention was fully disclosed.[93]

Under the Uniform Probate Code a conservator's intermediate account only "adjudicates as to liabilities considered in connection therewith," but a final account "adjudicates as to all previously unsettled liabilities."[94] The approval of an administrator's final account has been held a "bar not only to issues which were actually raised but to causes of action which could have been litigated," at least where the devisees "were aware of the facts giving rise to their collateral attack."[95]

The res judicata effect of the approval of an intermediate account is necessarily limited. For example, it did not preclude later challenges to a trustee's retention of a stock, but "a challenger in a subsequent accounting period must ... show that changed circumstances make that investment strategy no longer prudent."[96]

Even a final account may leave some issues open. A woman left property in trust to her husband. Approval of his final account as executor showing

**91.** First of America Trust v. First Illini Bancorp, 685 N.E.2d 351, 358 (Ill.App.1997).

**92.** *See also* Uniform Prob.Code § 7–307 (trustee protected by "final account or other statement * * * showing termination of the trust relationship").

**93.** Fraser v. Southeast First Bank, 417 So.2d 707, 710–12 (Fla.App.1982). *See also* Matter of Estate of Aschauer, 544 N.E.2d 71, 75 (Ill.App.1989); Matter of Trust Created by Hill, 499 N.W.2d 475, 489 (Minn.App.1993); Matter of Conservatorship of Holman, 849 P.2d 140 (Kan.App.1993); *Restatement (Second) of Trusts* § 220, comm. a (1959).

**94.** Uniform Probate Code § 5–418.

**95.** Goldberg v. Frye, 266 Cal.Rptr. 483, 486 (App.1990). *See also Restatement, Second, Trusts* § 220, comm. a (1959) ("matters which were open to dispute, whether or not actually disputed"); Fried v. Polk Bros., Inc., 546 N.E.2d 1160, 1167 (Ill.App.1989) (heirs estopped to challenge approved sale when they "had a full opportunity to litigate the valuation" but did not do so).

**96.** Matter of Trusts Created by Hormel, 504 N.W.2d 505, 510–11 (Minn.App.1993). *See also* Matter of Estate of Dawson, 641 A.2d 1026, 1034 (N.J.1994) (treatment of stock distributions in prior accountings had no res judicata effect as to later distributions).

distribution to himself did not preclude a later claim to the assets by the designated remainderman under the trust. "The approval of the final report in the probate proceedings did not determine the capacity in which the assets, which should have been in the trust, were received" or relieve the husband of his fiduciary duties as trustee.[97] Courts have even allowed the beneficiaries of a testamentary trust to surcharge executor-trustees for actions during the administration of the probate estate after the executor's final account had been approved on the theory that in its capacity as trustee the bank had improperly failed to question its own account as executor. Trustees have an obligation to pursue claims against a prior fiduciary, even if this requires them to question their own conduct.[98]

Sometimes court approval is held not binding because the court was not informed of a relevant fact. The Restatement allows an account to be reopened if the trustee "was guilty of misrepresentation or concealment" in presenting it.[99] The Uniform Probate Code protects personal representatives from claims not brought within 6 months after filing of a "closing statement," but not if there was "fraud, misrepresentation, or inadequate disclosure."[100] A conservator was held liable for allowing an insurance policy to lapse even though his final account had been approved because the account did not reveal the policy lapse.[101] When an administrator sold land to his step-daughter, a court approved the sale without being aware of the relationship. The approval was later revoked.[102]

Not all claims of "fraud" are sufficient to avoid res judicata, however. A claim that a bank "fraudulently misrepresented its skill" as an investor was not enough to allow an account to be reopened, since "it had no effect on [the ward's] ability to attend the hearing of which she received notice and to litigate ... her claims of wrongdoing by Bank." [103]A guardian ad litem sought to surcharge a trustee for violating a "well-recognized rule of practice" that corporate trustees should hold no more than five per cent of the stock of any company. The guardian argued that approval of the trustee's accounts was not binding because they had not disclosed its aggregate holdings of the stock, but the court disagreed, saying local practice had never required fiduciaries to list their aggregate holdings in an account.[104]

**97.** Kemper v. Kemper, 532 N.E.2d 1126, 1128 (Ill.App.1989).

**98.** Matter of Irrevocable Inter Vivos Trust, 305 N.W.2d 755, 762 (Minn.1981). *See also* Pepper v. Zions First Nat. Bank, 801 P.2d 144, 151 (Utah 1990); *Restatement (Second) of Trusts* § 177, comm. a (1959); Calif.Prob.Code § 16403 (successor trustee liable for failure to redress predecessor's breach). *But cf.* In re Will of Scheele, 517 N.E.2d 418, 427 (Ind.App. 1987).

**99.** *Restatement (Second) of Trusts* § 220, comm. a (1959).

**100.** Uniform Probate Code § 3–1005.

**101.** Conservatorship of Coffey, 231 Cal. Rptr. 421, 424 (App.1986). *See also* Altshuler v. Minkus–Whalen, 579 N.E.2d 1369 (Mass.App. 1991) (approval of administrator's account revoked because she failed to disclose the existence of other heirs).

**102.** Satti v. Rago, 441 A.2d 615 (Conn. 1982). *See also* Matter of Guardianship of Eisenberg, 719 P.2d 187, 192 (Wash.App.1986).

**103.** Bank of America Nat. Trust v. Superior Court, 226 Cal.Rptr. 685, 690 (App.1986). *See also* Matter of Herbert M. Dowsett Trust, 791 P.2d 398, 406 (Haw.App.1990) (claim of fraud is barred by res judicata); Hooks v. Bonner, 543 N.E.2d 953 (Ill.App.1989).

**104.** Roche v. Boston Safe Deposit and Trust Co., 464 N.E.2d 1341, 1346 (Mass.1984). *See also* In re Poulsen's Estate, 194 N.W.2d 593 (Wis.1972) (listing stock at its appraised value when it was worth considerably less was "a customary practice although misleading to a layperson").

In order for a judgment to have res judicata effect, the court which rendered it must have had jurisdiction. An Oklahoma court rejected a guardian's attempt to rely on a Michigan court's judgment approving withdrawals from an estate, because "the Michigan court never acquired jurisdiction over the guardianship assets."[105] An approved account can bind beneficiaries who live outside the jurisdiction but only if they are given notice and an opportunity to appear. In a leading case involving the accounts of a trustee the United States Supreme Court held that

> The interests of each state in providing means to close trusts ... is so insistent and rooted in custom as to establish beyond doubt the right of its courts to determine the interests of all claimants, resident or nonresident, provided its procedure accords full opportunity to appear and be heard.[106]

Notice by publication was sufficient for those beneficiaries whose interests or addresses were unknown to the trustee, but as to those whose addresses were on the trustee' books "a serious effort to inform them personally of the accounting at least by ordinary mail to the record addresses" was constitutionally required.[107] Court-approved transactions can be set aside for failure to comply with statutory notice requirements.[108]

Court orders are not binding on incompetent beneficiaries unless they are adequately represented. For example, an order authorizing a conservator to use assets of the estate to pay a claim was held not binding because no guardian ad litem had been appointed.[109] Appointing a guardian ad litem for incompetent beneficiaries is costly because they are entitled to compensation and reimbursement of attorney fees from the estate.[110] Commentators have argued that guardians ad litem should be appointed only when there is no other way to protect the incompetent. "Where a necessary party who is adult and competent has interests substantially identical to those of a * * * minor or incompetent, the court should be reluctant to burden the estate with the expenses of a guardian ad litem."[111] The Uniform Probate Code requires appointment of a GAL only where "representation of the interest would otherwise be inadequate,"[112] and allows, for example, parents to represent their minor children when there is no conflict of interest between them. This concept has been recognized in judicial decisions as well. For example, after a sale by personal representatives was approved, the remaindermen under a

**105.** In re Estate of LaRose, 1 P.3d 1018, 1023 (Okl.Civ.App.1999).

**106.** Mullane v. Central Hanover Bank & Trust Co., 339 U.S. 306, 313 (1950). *See also* Unif.Trust Code § 202(b).

**107.** *Id.* at 318. *See also Restatement (Second) of Trusts* § 220, comm. c, d (1959).

**108.** Hawkins v. Walker, 281 S.E.2d 311 (Ga.App.1981) (approval of sale vacated for failure publish notice). *But see* Bohl v. Haney, 671 P.2d 991 (Colo.App.1983) (bona fide purchaser at court-approved sale protected despite failure to give notice).

**109.** Matter of Conservatorship of L.M.S., 755 P.2d 22, 25 (Kan.App.1988). *See also* Matter of Estate of Bomareto, 757 P.2d 1135 (Colo. App.1988) (child not bound by order because he was not made a party in proceedings). *Compare* Matter of Estate of Nuyen, 443 N.E.2d 1099, 1104 (Ill.App.1982) (minor bound by order when he was represented by a GAL). Even when a guardian was appointed, the judgment may not be binding when the minor was "so poorly represented that there was no substantial representation of his case." *Restatement, Judgments* § 123; In re Will of Wickman, 289 So.2d 788, 790 (Fla.App.1974).

**110.** Cal.Prob.Code § 1003(c); Matter of Estate of Trotalli, 366 N.W.2d 879 (Wis.1985).

**111.** Martin, *Professional Responsibility and Probate Practices*, 1975 Wis. L.Rev. 911, 948.

**112.** Uniform Probate Code § 1–403. *See also* Unif.Trust Code § 305.

testamentary trust sued to set the sale aside because they had received no notice of the proceedings. The court rejected their claim, saying that they had been adequately represented by the trustee named in the will.[113] On the other hand, the approval of a trustee's accounts was held not to bind remaindermen who were minors at the time because no guardian ad litem had been appointed for them. Here virtual representation was not accepted because there was a conflict of interest between the life beneficiaries and their children; the former's interest was to maximize trust income rather than preserve trust corpus.[114] Similarly when a will named a bank as executor and co-trustee, approval of the bank's accounts as executor was set aside for failure to comply with a statute which required notice to all "persons whose interests are not represented." Notice to a trustee was sufficient to bind the trust beneficiaries where no conflict of interest existed, but here there was such a conflict because the accounting executor was one of the trustees.[115]

Requiring court approval of transactions may not be an adequate safeguard against abuses because often "the proceeding is not adversary, and there is no thorough investigation into the desirability of the transaction."[116] Court scrutiny of fiduciary accounts tends to be superficial.[117] Therefore the Uniform Probate Code allows personal representatives and trustees to dispense with court approval of accounts; they are protected from claims for breach of fiduciary duty 6 months after they simply file a closing statement which adequately discloses their handling of the estate.[118]

### *Laches and Standing*

According to the second Restatement of Trusts most states have "no Statute of Limitations applicable to equitable claims" but they may be barred by "laches of the claimant." Laches depends on a variety of factors in addition to the mere lapse of time, such as the reason (if any) for the plaintiff's delay in bringing suit, and the extent of hardship to the defendant if relief were given despite the delay.[119] For example, a complaint that a bank trustee committed a breach of trust in selling certain stock was held to be barred by laches when the trustee began selling the stock in 1958 but the beneficiary did

**113.** Matter of Estate of Jones, 770 P.2d 1100 (Wyo.1989). *See also* Uniform Probate Code § 1–403(2)(ii) (orders binding a trustee bind beneficiaries of the trust in proceedings to probate a will); Fifth Third Bank v. Fifth Third Bank, 602 N.E.2d 325 (Ohio App.1991); People v. Progressive Land Developers, 602 N.E.2d 820, 826 (Ill.1992) (Attorney General's interests in a charitable trust were adequately represented by the Nation of Islam in prior proceeding).

**114.** Matter of Will of Maxwell, 704 A.2d 49, 58 (N.J.Super.App.Div.1997). *See also* Matter of Herbert M. Dowsett Trust, 791 P.2d 398, 403 (Haw.App.1990).

**115.** Azarian v. First Nat. Bank of Boston, 423 N.E.2d 749 (Mass.1981). *See also* Norris v. Estate of Norris, 493 N.E.2d 121 (Ill.App.1986) (trust beneficiaries entitled to notice of probate proceedings); Harper v. Harper, 491 So.2d 189, 202 (Miss.1986) (notice to trustee insufficient because of conflict of interest with beneficiaries). Under Uniform Probate Code § 1–403 an order binding a trustee also binds beneficiaries, but "notice *may* be given both to a person and to another who may bind him." Probably "may" should be read as "must" in cases like *Azarian* in which the trustee and executor are the same.

**116.** Fratcher, *Trustees' Powers Legislation,* 37 NYU L.Rev. 627, 662 (1962).

**117.** Wellman, *Recent Developments in the Struggle for Probate Reform,* 79 Mich.L.Rev. 501, 516 (1981).

**118.** Uniform Probate Code § 3–1005; Tovrea v. Nolan, 875 P.2d 144, 148 (Ariz.App. 1993); Meryhew v. Gillingham, 893 P.2d 692 (Wash.App.1995). Uniform Probate Code § 7–307 is similar as to trustees, but § 5–418 requires court accountings for conservators.

**119.** *Restatement, Second, Trusts* § 219, comm. a (1959).

not complain about it until 1977. The trustee's quarterly reports showed the sales, so the beneficiary "had or should have had knowledge ... of the trustee's conduct for nearly nineteen years before filing suit."[120] Furthermore,

> the trustee was prejudiced by the delay ... During the nineteen-year delay, the trustee's personnel responsible for the Crider trust changed hands, and it seems various records were misplaced or destroyed ... More importantly, the amount of potential damages increased greatly during this period and the ability of the trustee to reverse its actions by repurchasing the stock became more difficult.[121]

On the other hand, a court rejected the laches defense asserted against two beneficiaries, one of whom was a minor. "Laches cannot be imputed to a person during his or her minority."[122] As to the other beneficiary, even though usually plaintiffs must be diligent in ascertaining the facts underlying a claim, "when a fiduciary has a duty to disclose certain facts to the plaintiff but fraudulently fails to do so, the plaintiff's failure to discover the facts is excused and the time begins to run when the fraud is actually discovered."[123]

In most recent cases, the discussion turns on a statute of limitations rather than laches. Such statutes provide a fixed period rather than leaving it to the court's discretion,[124] but the statutes raise issues similar to those involved in laches, including a "balancing test to weigh the hardship imposed on the claimant by the application of the statute of limitations against any prejudice to the defendant resulting from the passage of time."[125] For example, a trustee invoked a two-year statute of limitations when sued for an allegedly improper sale of stock.[126] Even though the sale took place more than 2 years before the suit was filed, the court rejected the defence on the basis of another statute which postponed commencement of the limitation period "when the defendant has concealed the existence of the cause of action from the plaintiff ... Usually, to invoke the protection provided by this statute, the wrongdoer must have actively concealed the cause of action and the plaintiff is charged with the responsibility of exercising due diligence to discover the claims ... However, when the parties are in a fiduciary relationship ... a mere failure to disclose ... may be sufficient to toll the statute."[127] In another

**120.** *Cf.* Boston Safe Deposit & Trust Co. v. Wilbur, 728 N.E.2d 264, 272 (Mass.2000) (remand to determine when beneficiary learned of claim so as to pass on laches defence).

**121.** Stevens v. National City Bank, 544 N.E.2d 612, 621 (Ohio 1989); *cf.* First Ala. Bank v. Martin, 425 So.2d 415, 424 (Ala.1982) (laches defense rejected because no showing of prejudice to the defendant). The death of crucial witnesses may constitute sufficient prejudice for laches. Murphy v. Emery, 629 S.W.2d 895, 898 (Tenn.1981).

**122.** Kurtz v. Solomon, 656 N.E.2d 184, 192 (Ill.App.1995). *Accord, Restatement, Second, Trusts* § 219, comm. d (1959) (no laches while beneficiary is under incapacity).

**123.** Kurtz v. Solomon, 656 N.E.2d 184, 192 (Ill.App.1995).

**124.** *E.g.*, McDonald v. U.S. National Bank, 830 P.2d 618 (Or.App.1992) (trustee protected by 2 year statute); Mack v. American Fletcher Nat. Bank, 510 N.E.2d 725, 739 (Ind.App. 1987); Vorholt v. One Valley Bank, 498 S.E.2d 241 (W.Va.1997).

**125.** Snow v. Rudd, 998 P.2d 262, 266 (Utah 2000).

**126.** Another statute barred actions 3 years after the trustee filed a final account. *Cf.* Uniform Probate Code § 7-307. The court held that this limitation was not exclusive, since otherwise a trustee would have no protection before the trust terminated. Malachowski v. Bank One, Indianapolis, 590 N.E.2d 559, 562 (Ind.1992).

**127.** Malachowski v. Bank One, Indianapolis, 590 N.E.2d 559, 563 (Ind.1992). *See also* Hagney v. Lopeman, 590 N.E.2d 466 (Ill.1992); Condon v. Bank of California, 759 P.2d 1137, 1139 (Or.App.1988).

case a trustee made a bad investment in 1985 and the beneficiaries brought suit in 1989. The trustee invoked a 3 year statute of limitation which ran "from the earlier of the time the alleged breach was discovered or should have been discovered .. or the time of termination of the trust."[128] The trust provided that it would terminate on the death of the life beneficiary who had died more than three years before the action was brought, but the court held "termination" under the statute "refers to when the trustee winds up the trust affairs and distributes the trust assets" and this had occurred less than 3 years before the action was filed. The discovery branch of the statute did not help the defendant either, because the beneficiaries "although generally aware by May 1986 that [the investment] was losing money, did not know that this was not merely a 'temporary setback' until [later] when it became clear that something was seriously wrong."[129]

When a defendant denies the very existence of a trust, the statute of limitations (or laches) begins to run when the trustee "repudiates the trust to the knowledge of the beneficiary."[130]

### *Consent*

Beneficiaries may be prevented from challenging a fiduciary's action by their consent. For example, an attempt to surcharge trustees for "having pursued an aggressive, risky investment policy" failed because the beneficiaries had signed a form by which they "acknowledge the high degree of economic risk associated with these investments" and nevertheless approved them.[131] In this case the approval was in writing but this is not necessary.[132] According to the Restatement of Trusts mere failure to object does not amount to consent,[133] but there are many cases to the contrary, *e.g.* one in which a trustee had abused its discretion in making distributions, but "there had never been any objection" by the disfavored beneficiaries, whose "inaction for so many years acted as a ratification of SNB's conduct."[134] (The rules on consent before or at the time of an act are essentially the same as those for a later affirmance).[135] Consent and laches sometimes overlap. Beneficiaries who sought to upset an executor's sale of mineral interests were held to have "ratified" the sale by accepting checks arising therefrom. Furthermore, because of the "violent fluctuations of value" in mineral interests, "there is no class of cases in which the doctrine of laches has been more relentlessly enforced."[136]

**128.** Compare Morrison v. Watkins, 889 P.2d 140, (Kan.App.1995) applying the "continuing representation" idea to a trustee-lawyer with the result that the statute was tolled so long as he continued to serve as trustee.

**129.** Gillespie v. Seattle–First Nat. Bank, 855 P.2d 680, 688, 690 (Wash.App.1993).

**130.** *Restatement, Second, Trusts* § 219(2) (1959); Goodman v. Goodman, 907 P.2d 290, 294 (Wash.1995).

**131.** Beyer v. First Nat. Bank, 843 P.2d 53, 56 (Colo.App.1992).

**132.** *Restatement, Second, Trusts* § 216 (1959); Cal.Prob.Code § 16463 ; Brent v. Smathers, 547 So.2d 683, 685 (Fla.App.1989) (all referring generally to consent).

**133.** *Restatement, Second, Trusts* § 216, comm. a (1959).

**134.** In re Estate of Winograd, 582 N.E.2d 1047, 1050 (Ohio App.1989). *See also* In re Higgins' Trust Estate, 162 N.W.2d 768 (S.D. 1968); Matter of Trusts Under Will of Dwan, 371 N.W.2d 641, 643 (Minn.App.1985) (failure to object for years "constituted a waiver").

**135.** *Restatement, Second, Trusts* §§ 216–17 (1959); Cal.Prob.Code §§ 16463–64.

**136.** Jackson v. Braden, 717 S.W.2d 206, 208 (Ark.1986).

When one beneficiary has consented but others have not, courts will give a remedy to the nonconsenting beneficiaries. For example, the fact that the settlor's daughter, a beneficiary and co-trustee of a trust had participated in making improper investments did not preclude her children from recovering from the other trustees. The plaintiffs' interests "do not arise or flow through [their mother]. Even assuming [she] might be estopped to bring an action against ... her cotrustee, this cannot affect plaintiffs rights to bring this action."[137] The result would have different if the trust had provided (as some do) that children are bound by their parents' consent.[138] Consent by a person with a general power of appointment may bar relief for the persons designated to take in default of appointment.[139] When a will gave a remainder to the testator's "children if living, or their surviving issue," the children's consent was held to exonerate the executors. The children as "presumptive takers" represented their issue "in the absence of any demonstrable conflict of interest."[140]

A spendthrift trust beneficiary can effectively consent but not an incapacitated beneficiary, or one of "limited understanding."[141] Even though a beneficiary "acquiesced" when the trustee invested in passbook accounts, the trustee was liable because it had not "clearly explained to [the beneficiary], an elderly woman whose schooling had ended at age 10," that it would profit from the investment.[142] But a trustee who reasonably believed that a beneficiary was capable of consenting may be protected. When the settlor authorized withdrawals from a revocable trust, a claim that she was incompetent at the time was irrelevant if "the trustee did not know or have any reason to believe" this.[143]

Consent given by a beneficiary without knowledge of relevant facts does not bar relief. A beneficiary who consented to a trustee buying land from the trust for $40,000 without knowing that the property had been appraised at $500,000 was allowed to have the sale vacated. Consent is binding only when "given voluntarily after full disclosure by the trustees of all the facts, * * * and the burden is on the fiduciary to show that the transaction was fair."[144] According to the Restatement of Trusts the requirement that the bargain be "fair" is limited to cases "where the trustee has an adverse interest in the transaction."[145]

**137.** Gillespie v. Seymour, 823 P.2d 782, 790 (Kan.1991). *See also Restatement (Second) of Trusts* § 216, comm. g. (1959).

**138.** Beyer v. First Nat. Bank, 843 P.2d 53, 62 (Colo.App.1992).

**139.** *Restatement (Second) of Trusts* § 216, comm. h (1959). *Contra,* Pinzino v. Vogel, 424 N.E.2d 371, 374 (Ill.App.1981). If the consenting beneficiary has a general *inter-vivos* power, the consent binds the takers in default under Uniform Prob.Code § 1–108. Cal.Prob.Code § 16462 exonerates trustees for acts performed "pursuant to written directions from the person holding the power to revoke."

**140.** Matter of Estate of Lange, 383 A.2d 1130, 1140 (N.J.1978). *But cf.* Jones v. Heritage Pullman Bank & Trust, 518 N.E.2d 178, 182 (Ill.App.1987).

**141.** *Restatement (Second) of Trusts* § 216, comm.e, m (1959).

**142.** Stephan v. Equitable Savings and Loan Ass'n, 522 P.2d 478, 489 (Or.1974).

**143.** Cloud v. United States Nat. Bank, 570 P.2d 350, 355 (Or.1977). Under *Restatement, Second, Trusts* § 216(2) (1959) and Cal.Prob. Code § 16463(b), however, a trustee's reasonable belief is relevant as to the beneficiary's knowledge of material facts, but not as to the beneficiary's capacity.

**144.** Ford City Bank v. Ford City Bank, 441 N.E.2d 1192, 1195 (Ill.App.1982). Uniform Probate Code § 3–713 simply refers to consent "after fair disclosure."

**145.** *Restatement, Second, Trusts* § 216 (1959).

***Remedies Against Third Parties***

Beneficiaries of an estate or trust may also have remedies against persons other than the fiduciary. Trust beneficiaries were allowed to sue accountants hired by the trustees, because a beneficiary

> as equitable owner of the trust res has the right that third persons shall not knowingly join with the trustee in a breach of trust ... Mere knowledge by a third person that a breach of trust is in process, coupled with a failure to notify the beneficiary or to interfere with the action of the trustee does not amount to participation in a breach ... On the other hand if the third party by any act whatsoever assists the trustee in wrongfully transferring the benefits of the trust property to the trustee, [or] another person ... liability can be [imposed] ... [146]

Applying this standard, the court allowed a claim that the accountants had overcharged the trust, but rejected another that they had failed to report improper investments made by the trustees. According to the Restatement a stockbroker who handles a purchase of stock by a trustee, knowing that the purchase is in breach of trust, is liable for participating in the breach.[147] A court upheld a claim against a law firm which allegedly "performed legal services intended to prevent [the beneficiary] from discovering the dissipation of trust assets and the trustee's inappropriate investments" in order to "keep receiving a greater amount of fees."[148] But another court rejected a suit against the attorneys for trustees who had allegedly rejected an advantageous offer to buy a trust asset. It was not enough that the lawyers "knew of the breach and failed firmly to advise the trustees" to avoid it; the plaintiff had to show that the defendants had "actively participated" in the breach.[149]

Officers of a corporate trustee who cause the trustee to commit a breach of trust have also been held liable for the loss caused thereby.[150] The Uniform Prudent Investor Act imposes on agents exercising a delegated function a duty of reasonable care to the trust.[151] According to the Restatement, a person who has power by the terms of a trust power to control the trustee's actions may be deemed a fiduciary and "liable for any loss resulting to the trust estate from a breach of his duty as fiduciary."[152]

Normally actions against third persons who injure trust property must be brought by the trustee, but a beneficiary can sue a third party when "the beneficiary's interests are hostile to those of the trustee,"[153] *e.g.* when the third party and trustee have participated in a breach of trust. Suit may also

**146.** Gillespie v. Seymour, 796 P.2d 1060, 1065 (Kan.App.1990) (quoting Bogert, *Trusts and Trustees* § 901). *See also Restatement, Second, Trusts* § 326 (1959).

**147.** *Id.* comm. a. *See also* Anderson v. Dean Witter Reynolds, Inc., 841 P.2d 742 (Utah App.1992). *But see* Hosselton v. First American Bank N.A., 608 N.E.2d 630 (Ill.App. 1993) (stock broker not liable for participating in stock sale by guardian without court order as required by statute).

**148.** Wolf v. Mitchell, Silberberg & Knupp, 90 Cal.Rptr.2d 792, 798 (App.1999).

**149.** Spinner v. Nutt, 631 N.E.2d 542, 546 (Mass.1994).

**150.** Seven G Ranching Co. v. Stewart Title, 627 P.2d 1088, 1091 (Ariz.App.1981); *cf.* Dardaganis v. Grace Capital Inc., 889 F.2d 1237, 1242 (2d Cir.1989) (president of investment advisor liable as a "fiduciary" under ERISA).

**151.** Unif.Prud.Inv.Act § 9(b).

**152.** *Restatement, Second, Trusts* § 185, comm. h (1959).

**153.** Anderson v. Dean Witter Reynolds, Inc., 841 P.2d 742, 745 (Utah App.1992); *cf. Restatement, Second, Trusts* § 282(2) (1959) (beneficiary can sue when trustee improperly neglects to sue).

be brought be a co- or successor fiduciary.[154] A fiduciary who has been surcharged for an improper distribution may claim indemnification from the recipient.[155]

### *Banks*

Banks are often sued for participating in a breach of trust. According to the Restatement they are liable for permitting a withdrawal of trust funds "with notice of a breach of trust."[156] But banks which had no actual knowledge of the breach are usually protected by a statute. For example, a trustee stole thousands of dollars from a trust checking account by issuing checks to himself. The trustee was unable to reimburse the trust so the beneficiaries sued the bank. Their claim was rejected. The bank would be liable only if it knew that the withdrawals were a breach of fiduciary duty and there was no evidence of such knowledge. "The issue is not whether First Interstate exercised reasonable care with regard to the trust account. Rather the issue is whether first Interstate had knowledge the [the trustee] was violating the trust."[157]

Banks have been held liable for paying a depositor's money to an "agent" under a forged power of attorney.[158] But in order to encourage banks to deal with agents under durable powers, many states have passed statutes like the Uniform Probate Code which protect third persons who deal with an agent "in good faith" despite defects in the agent's power.[159] A similar statute was successfully invoked by a savings and loan association which had allowed an agent under a durable power to withdraw over $135,000 from the principal's account. The principal's administrator claimed that the principal had been incompetent when she executed the power, but the court held that the defendant had no duty to investigate this absent "actual knowledge."

> As a practical matter, how could the Capitol Federal employee, responding to the attorney in fact's request for withdrawal of funds make such a determination? ... Every working day it has over 500 transactions involving an agency or power of attorney relationship. The practical effect of requiring such a determination would be to eliminate the power of attorney as a useful tool in the transaction of business ...
>
> Where an agent draws checks on his principal's bank account, payable to himself, and deposits them to his own account, the mere form of the transaction ... is not sufficient to put the depositing bank on notice of the agent's fraud.[160]

**154.** Hosselton v. K's Merchandise Mart, 617 N.E.2d 797 (Ill.App.1993) (suit against store which had accepted guardianship funds from plaintiff's predecessor); Matter of Estate of Ostrander, 910 P.2d 865 (Kan.App.1996) (suit to recover property sold by plaintiff's co-administrator).

**155.** *Restatement, Second, Trusts* § 254 (1959).

**156.** *Restatement, Second, Trusts* § 324 (1959).

**157.** Heilig Trust and Benef. v. First Interstate, 969 P.2d 1082, 1085 (Wash.App.1998). *See also* Hosselton v. First American Bank N.A., 608 N.E.2d 630 (Ill.App.1993) (bank not liable for cashing check made out to guardian); Heffner v. Cahaba Bank & Trust Co., 523 So.2d 113 (Ala.1988) (bank not liable for checks drawn by embezzling executor); Wetherill v. Bank IV Kansas, N.A., 145 F.3d 1187 (10th Cir.1998).

**158.** In re Estate of Davis, 632 N.E.2d 64 (Ill.App.1994).

**159.** For discussion of various statutes on this issue see McGovern, *Trusts, Custodianships, and Durable Powers of Attorney*, 27 Real Prop., Prob. and Trust J. 1, 39–40 (1992).

**160.** Bank IV, Olathe v. Capitol Federal S & L, 828 P.2d 355, 357–58, 363 (Kan.1992). *See also* Johnson v. Edwardsville Nat. Bank &

The second Restatement of Trusts imposed liability on corporations who registered transfers of securities "with notice" that they were in breach of trust, but added that "experience indicates that the rule stated in the Section ... has not been very effective" in preventing breaches of trust, and should be abolished by statute.[161] This was accomplished by a widely adopted Uniform Act for the Simplification of Fiduciary Security Transfers, which is based on the principle that "the responsibility of corporations to inquire into the propriety of transfers of their shares is ... anachronistic."[162]

### *Bona–Fide Purchase*

When property of an estate or trust has been transferred, bona-fide purchasers of the property are protected even if the fiduciary was acting improperly. For example, an administrator leased property of the estate even though the terms of his appointment did not authorize him to make the lease.[163] The court upheld the lessee's rights under Uniform Probate Code § 3–714 which protects persons who deal with a personal representative "in good faith for value."[164] A trial was necessary to determine whether the lessee "had actual knowledge of the limitations" on the administrator's authority.[165]

Persons claiming to be bona-fide purchasers often flounder on the issue of good faith. One who knows *or should know* of the breach of trust does not qualify.[166] In a state which required a court order for all sales by personal representatives, a buyer at a sale without such an order was not a bona fide purchaser.[167] A guarantee given to a bank by one of two trustees was ineffective despite a statute protecting third persons who had no "actual knowledge that the trustee is exceeding the trustee's powers," because a bank officer had read the trust instrument and someone who "has actual knowledge of what a trust says is charged with actual knowledge of what it means."[168] A lessee was not allowed to exercise an option in a lease because the trustees had no power to give it and "persons dealing with [a fiduciary] are bound to know the extent of his powers."[169]

Traditionally purchasers could rarely be in "good faith" if they knew they were dealing with a fiduciary. Whether or not they knew this might depend on how title to the property was held. If land was conveyed "to *X*" in trust, but without designating *X* as trustee in the deed, *X* might be treated as the

Trust Co., 594 N.E.2d 342, 345 (Ill.App.1992) (bank protected where principal incompetent when power executed); *Restatement, Second, Trusts* § 324, comm. g (1959) (trustee making check to self from trust account does not create duty of inquiry on bank); Unif.Fid.Act § 6 (same).

**161.** *Restatement, Second, Trusts* § 325 (1959).

**162.** Unif.Fid.Sec.Trans.Act, Prefatory Note.

**163.** Although Uniform Probate Code § 3–715(9) generally authorizes personal representatives to enter into leases, this may be restricted by court order.

**164.** The same principle applies to persons dealing other fiduciaries. *Restatement, Second, Trusts* § 284 (1959); Uniform Trustees' Powers Act § 7. As to custodians see Uniform Transfers to Minors Act § 16. As to conservators see Uniform Probate Code § 5–422.

**165.** AgAmerica, FCB v. Westgate, 931 P.2d 1, 4 (Idaho App.1997). *See also* Cowley v. Kaechelle, 696 P.2d 1354 (Ariz.App.1984).

**166.** *Restatement (Second) of Trusts* § 297 (1959); Nozik v. McDonald, 650 N.E.2d 923, 927 (Ohio App.1994).

**167.** Matter of Estate of Ostrander, 910 P.2d 865, 868 (Kan.App.1996).

**168.** Farmers State Bank of Yuma v. Harmon, 778 F.2d 543, 547 (10th Cir.1985). *See also Restatement, Second, Trusts* § 297, comm. j (1959) (one who knows the terms of a trust "is chargeable with notice of the legal effect of those terms").

**169.** Adler v. Adler, 118 S.E.2d 456, 458 (Ga.1961).

outright owner as to persons "dealing with *[X]* in good faith and for a valuable consideration."[170] But if trust beneficiaries were in possession of the land, this might give purchasers "constructive notice" of the trust, thus negating their "good faith."[171]

Transactions in securities could be facilitated if title was registered in a way which did not reveal that the registered owner was a trustee, but at common law trustees were supposed "to see that trust property is designated as property of the trust."[172] Modern trusts, however, often expressly allow the trustee to hold property in the name of a nominee rather than "as trustee."[173] Many statutes, such as the Uniform Trustees' Powers Act, also permit this.[174] The Uniform Probate Code has a similar provision for personal representatives and conservators.[175]

Historically, the liability of third parties was often needed to make the beneficiaries whole, since their remedies against a defaulting trustee were "apt to be of little value."[176] Today fiduciaries are usually solvent (or bonded), and modern law tends to protect purchasers to a greater extent so as not to deter them from dealing with fiduciaries. For example, a successor executor was not allowed to repudiate a sale made by his predecessor on the ground that the price was too low. In order to "facilitate prompt and economic administration of estates" third parties should "be able to deal with personal representatives without concern for [their] authority or duty to the beneficiaries ... The beneficiaries' remedy is not to void the transaction but to seek damages for the personal representative's breach of his fiduciary duty."[177]

The Restatement imposed on purchasers from a trustee a duty "to inquire as to the terms of the trust,"[178] but the Uniform Probate Code relieves third parties who deal with personal representatives from any duty "to inquire into the existence of a power or the propriety of its exercise."[179] A similar provision appears in the Uniform Trustees' Powers Act.[180] Under the Uniform Commercial Code, even if a security is registered in the name of a fiduciary, a purchaser has no duty of inquiry into the rightfulness of the transfer.[181]

Even a person who does not qualify as a bona fide purchaser may obtain some relief in order to prevent unjust enrichment. Thus even though lessees knew that a lease made by an administrator was unauthorized, they were

**170.** Cal.Prob.Code § 18103.

**171.** In re Sale Guaranty Corp., 220 B.R. 660 (9th Cir.BAP (Cal.) 1998); American Nat. Bank and Trust v. Vinson, 653 N.E.2d 13, 16 (Ill.App.1995); *Restatement, Second, Trusts* § 297, comm. e (1959).

**172.** *Id.* § 179.

**173.** *Id.* comm. e.

**174.** Uniform Trusts Act § 9; Uniform Trustees' Powers Act § 3(c)(16); N.Y. EPTL § 11.1-1(b)(10); Wisc.Stat. § 701.19(6).

**175.** Uniform Probate Code § 3-715(14), 5-423(17). *But see* Uniform Transfers to Minors Act § 12(d) (custodian "shall keep custodial property ... in a manner sufficient to identify it clearly as custodial property").

**176.** Maitland, *supra* note 39, at 171.

**177.** Wittick v. Miles, 545 P.2d 121, 126 (Or.1976). Even if the consideration for a purchase is below the value of the property, the buyer may still be a bona fide purchaser for value. *Restatement, Second, Trusts* § 298, comm. i (1959).

**178.** *Restatement, Second, Trusts* § 297, comm. f (1959).

**179.** Uniform Probate Code § 3-714.

**180.** Uniform Trustees' Powers Act § 7. *See also* Calif.Prob.Code § 18100. The terms of a trust sometimes expressly protect third parties who deal with the trustee. ITT Commercial Finance v. Stockdale, 521 N.E.2d 417 (Mass.App.1988).

**181.** Uniform Commercial Code § 8-304.

allowed to recover for improvements which they placed on the property and rental payments in excess of the rental value for the period of their occupancy.[182]

### *Creditors*

Creditors of a trustee sometimes seek to reach trust property on the ground that they had no notice that it was held in trust. For example, creditors of Paul King attempted to claim land which was held in the names of "Paul King and [another], Trustees of the [designated] Trust" on the basis of a Colorado statute, designed to facilitate transactions, which provided that deeds to a trustee must "name the beneficiary so represented and define the trust; ... otherwise the description of the grantee in any such representative capacity ... shall not be notice of a trust."[183] Similar statutes in other states had been held to "prevent the undisclosed beneficiaries from contesting the interest of subsequent takers who relied" on the deed in assuming that the title holder owned the land.

> Some states have specifically legislated that only purchasers, lessees, mortgagees, or assignees of the trust property, and not a trustee's individual creditors, may rely on the non-conforming instrument ... When statutes mention creditors, the benefit of the statute is limited to creditors who relied on the trustee's apparent ownership of the property to extend credit.[184]

The court interpreted this statute the same way, despite its general language, and rejected the creditors' claim; since they had lent the money prior to the recording of the noncomplying deed, they had not relied on the property in making the loan.

### *Donees*

A donee is not a bona fide purchaser for value even if he had no inkling that the transfer was a breach of the fiduciary's duty. "If the trustee in breach of trust transfers trust property and no value is given for the transfer, the transferee does not hold the property free of the trust, although he had no notice of the trust."[185] This is not the case, however, if the donee has "so changed his position that it would be inequitable to compel him to restore" the property.[186] Similarly when a fiduciary pays a beneficiary more than the beneficiary is entitled to, the recipient must restore the money unless the "overpaid beneficiary has so changed his position as to make it inequitable to enforce payment."[187] This allowed a conservator who had been surcharged for

**182.** AgAmerica, FCB v. Westgate, 931 P.2d 1, 5 (Idaho App.1997); cf. *Restatement, Second, Trusts* § 291, comm. o, p (1959) (transferee credited with payments on the price unless they were misappropriated by trustee, and for improvements unless made with knowledge of the breach of trust).

**183.** *Cf. Restatement, Second, Trusts* § 297, comm. d (1959) (the word "trustee" in an instrument imposes a duty on purchaser to "make inquiry").

**184.** Lagae v. Lackner, 996 P.2d 1281, 1286 (Colo.2000).

**185.** Kampschroeder v. Kampschroeder, 887 P.2d 1152, 1158 (Kan.App.1995); *Restatement, Second, Trusts* § 289 (1959).

**186.** *Id.* § 292(1).

**187.** Brent v. Smathers, 547 So.2d 683, 686 (Fla.App.1989). *See also Restatement, Second, Trusts* § 254 (1959); Uniform Probate Code § 3–909.

improper distributions to indemnification from the recipients, even though they had "acted fairly and in good faith."[188]

## § 12.9 Duty of Loyalty

Trustees must "administer the trust solely in the interest of the beneficiary."[1] This so-called "duty of loyalty" also applies to other fiduciaries, such as agents under a power of attorney.[2] Similar language in ERISA governs fiduciaries of pension plans.[3]

The duty applies most often to situations in which the fiduciary's personal interests conflict with those of the beneficiaries, *e.g.* when a trustee sells the trustee's own property to the trust or buys an asset of the trust. For example, a trustee-executor was removed because he sold an asset of the estate to his son. A trustee may not thus "place himself in a position where his interests conflict with those of the trust beneficiaries." It did not matter that the land was sold at a public auction for a fair price.[4] Even if no bad faith is present, a trustee's duty did not permit "the faintest appearance of impropriety."[5] The Uniform Probate Code makes voidable "any transaction which is affected by a substantial conflict of interest on the part of the personal representative."[6]

It does not matter that a disinterested co-fiduciary approved the transaction.[7] In this respect trustees differ from directors of corporations, even though the latter also have fiduciary duties. A court approved a transaction whereby a charitable corporation exchanged stock with a company which had the same directors. For corporations such transactions are valid if approved by disinterested directors, or if the directors establish the fairness of the transaction. The court refused to apply the same rules to charitable corporations and charitable trusts. "The founder of a charitable trust ... imposes upon its trustees the strict and unyielding rules principles of trust law. By contrast, the founder of a charitable corporations ... invokes the far more flexible and adaptable principles of corporate law."[8]

Although there is general agreement about the basic duty of loyalty, there is some uncertainty around the edges. A court refused to void an executor's sale of property to his daughter, saying that the ban applied to sales to the fiduciary or the fiduciary's spouse but not "to other persons who bear a close family relationship."[9] The Restatement of Trusts also distinguishes between a

**188.** In re Estate of Berger, 520 N.E.2d 690, 709 (Ill.App.1987). *See also* Matter of Estate of Olson, 332 N.W.2d 711, 714 (S.D.1983) (recipient of excess distribution from estate liable also for interest thereon); Lee v. Barksdale, 350 S.E.2d 508 (N.C.App.1986).

**§ 12.9**

**1.** *Restatement, Second, Trusts* § 170(1) (1959).

**2.** First Nat. Bank v. Cooper, 312 S.E.2d 607 (Ga.1984) (agent cannot use principal's property to secure loan to agent).

**3.** 29 U.S.C. § 1104(a)(1).

**4.** *Restatement, Second, Trusts* § 170, comm. b (1959).

**5.** Matter of Estate of Hawley, 538 N.E.2d 1220, 1222 (Ill.App.1989).

**6.** Uniform Probate Code § 3–713. *See also* Williamson v. Williamson, 714 N.E.2d 1270 (Ind.App.1999) (sale by executor to himself set aside).

**7.** Matter of Garwood's Estate, 400 N.E.2d 758 (Ind.1980) (sale by co-executors to one of them voided).

**8.** Oberly v. Kirby, 592 A.2d 445, 466–67 (Del.1991). *See also* Stegemeier v. Magness, 728 A.2d 557 (Del.1999) (sale by estate to company owned by an administrator is voidable although approved by a disinterested administrator).

**9.** In re Estate of Hughes, 641 N.E.2d 248, 251 (Ohio App.1994). *See also* Culbertson v. McCann, 664 P.2d 388, 390 (Okl.1983) (sale to executor's sister).

trustee's spouse and other relatives,[10] but the Uniform Trusts Act bars purchases and sales "from or to a relative" which is defined to include a spouse, ancestor, descendant or sibling.[11] The Uniform Probate Code's ban on "any transaction which is affected by a substantial conflict of interest" has been held to cover a sale to the executor's son.[12]

The duty of loyalty is also applied when a personal representative or trustee has ties to a company which deals with the estate. A sale of stock by an executor to a company of which he was an officer and director was set aside under a statute barring executors from buying estate property "directly or indirectly."[13] A trustee was surcharged for making investments in companies of which he was the president.[14] However, some conflicts of interest are deemed too insubstantial to matter. Thus a court vacated a sale of stock by a corporate trustee to its president but not a sale to a stockholder of the trustee.[15]

Lawyers who represent a family with a business may also encounter conflicts of interest. A lawyer was the executor and his firm represented the estate of an officer of a company which the lawyer represented and which claimed the right to buy the decedent's stock. The lawyer and his firm were denied fees for their services to the estate. "An attorney who violates our rules of professional conduct by engaging in clear conflicts of interest . . . may receive neither executor's nor legal fees for services he renders an estate."[16] Another lawyer who represented an estate was held liable for a below-market-value sale made by the estate to a client of the lawyer; the lawyer had recommended the sale without disclosing the conflict of interest.[17] Lawyers involved in self dealing while acting as fiduciaries have been subjected to discipline under the rules of professional conduct.[18]

### *Exceptions to the Rule: Court Approval*

Probably the most often quoted passage in a judicial opinion about trustees dealt with the duty of loyalty. "A trustee is held to something stricter than the morals of the market place . . . Uncompromising rigidity has been

**10.** *Restatement, Second, Trusts* § 170, comm. e (1959).

**11.** Uniform Trusts Act §§ 1(3), 5.

**12.** Cudworth v. Cudworth, 312 N.W.2d 331 (N.D.1981). *See also* Matter of Estate of Engels, 692 P.2d 400, 405 (Kan.App.1984) (executor surcharged for allowing son to live in house owned by estate); note 5 supra.

**13.** In re Estate of Martin, 86 Cal.Rptr.2d 37 (App.1999). *See also* Furr v. Hall, 553 S.W.2d 666 (Tex.Civ.App.1977); Lincoln Nat. Bank v. Shriners Hospitals, 588 N.E.2d 597 (Ind.App.1992) (sale to company whose president was a director of trustee).

**14.** Wheeler v. Mann, 763 P.2d 758 (Utah 1988). *See also* In re Estate of Stowell, 595 A.2d 1022 (Me.1991) (loans by executor to companies in which he was interested).

**15.** Steiner v. Hawaiian Trust Co., 393 P.2d 96, 104 (Haw.1964). As to transactions between a bank trustee and its commercial customers *compare* Brock v. Citizens Bank, 841 F.2d 344 (10th Cir.1988) (loan by trustee to persons who had borrowed from bank allowed) *with* InterFirst Bank Dallas, N.A. v. Risser, 739 S.W.2d 882 (Tex.App.1987) (sale of stock at inadequate price to commercial customer of trustee warrants punitive damages).

**16.** In re Estate of McCool, 553 A.2d 761, 769 (N.H.1988). *See also* In re Estate of Halas, 512 N.E.2d 1276 (Ill.App.1987).

**17.** Kelly v. Foster, 813 P.2d 598 (Wash. App.1991).

**18.** In re Conduct of Carey, 767 P.2d 438 (Or.1989) (lawyer reprimanded for lending money as guardian to his secretary); Office of Disciplinary Counsel v. Kurtz, 693 N.E.2d 1080 (Ohio 1998) (lawyer-trustee suspended for lending trust funds to self); In re Gordon, 524 N.E.2d 547 (Ill.1988) (attorney for estate suspended for lending estate funds to a person for whom he had guaranteed a loan); In re Cohen, 8 P.3d 429 (Colo.1999) (lawyer suspended for loan of trust funds to company which lawyer represented).

the attitude of courts of equity when petitioned to undermine the rule of undivided loyalty by ... particular exceptions."[19] In fact, however, the "rule of undivided loyalty" has been qualified, if not "undermined" by particular exceptions. Otherwise, the rule would pose serious difficulties for estates or trusts which hold property for which there is an inadequate market, like a family corporation, where the fiduciary may be the most likely buyer.[20] Because the duty of loyalty can hinder efficiency, self dealing may be allowed (1) when approved by a court in a particular case, (2) when authorized by the governing instrument, (3) or in some situations by a special statute.

The Uniform Probate Code allows self-dealing if "the transaction is approved by the Court after notice to interested person."[21] The Uniform Trustees' Powers Act has a similar provision.[22] Courts approve such transactions only when the advantages are clear, *e.g.* if "there are no other available purchasers willing to pay the same price the trustee is willing to pay."[23] The court approval need not precede the transaction. For example, a conservator's sale of a house to his daughter, though not approved by a court at the time, was not subject to challenge because "his acts as conservator ... were approved by the court in its orders approving his annual accountings."[24] In another case an executor had lent money to the estate which "was unable to obtain a bank loan for the payment of estate taxes" since it consisted mostly of undeveloped land. The executor was allowed interest on the loan which was "slightly greater" than he would have received from a bank, since the loan "was essential for the protection of the estate."[25]

### *Authorization in Instrument*

Self dealing is proper if it is authorized by the terms of a will or trust,[26] but even a broadly drafted power does not necessarily permit self-dealing. A court set aside sales by an executor to himself despite a clause in the will allowing the executor to sell to "any purchaser."[27] Even an explicit authorization for self dealing does not permit a trustee to "act in bad faith."[28] For example, even though a trust allowed the trustees to lease trust property to their automobile dealership, they were surcharged for making the lease without any "determination whether the rental rates were reasonable in the current market."[29] However, sales which are personally advantageous to the

**19.** Meinhard v. Salmon, 164 N.E. 545, 546 (N.Y.1928) (Cardozo J.). Actually the parties in this case were coventurers rather than trustees but this made no difference to Cardozo J. Compare the contrast made in Oberly v. Kirby, note 8 *supra*, between trustees and directors.

**20.** Wellman, *Punitive Surcharges Against Disloyal Fiduciaries,* 77 Mich.L.Rev. 95, 114 (1978).

**21.** Uniform Probate Code § 3–713.

**22.** Uniform Trustees' Powers Act § 5(b). *See also Restatement (Second) of Trusts* § 170, comm. f (1959).

**23.** Wachovia Bank and Trust Co. v. Johnston, 153 S.E.2d 449, 460 (N.C.1967).

**24.** Matter of Conservatorship of Holman, 849 P.2d 140, 142 (Kan.App.1993). For circumstances when court approval of an account is not a defence to a breach of fiduciary duty see Section 12.8, at note 90 et seq.

**25.** Miller v. Miller, 734 N.E.2d 738 (Mass. App.2000).

**26.** Uniform Probate Code § 3–713; *cf.* Ohio Rev.Code § 2109.44 (court approval necessary).

**27.** Powell v. Thorsen, 322 S.E.2d 261, 263 (Ga.1984). *See also* Furr v. Hall, 553 S.W.2d 666, 672 (Tex.Civ.App.1977).

**28.** *Restatement (Second) of Trusts* § 170, comm. t (1959).

**29.** Mest v. Dugan, 790 P.2d 38, 41 (Or. App.1990). *See also* Estate of Blouin, 490 A.2d 1212 (Me.1985) (sale by executor to himself at below market value set aside).

fiduciary may be found to have been authorized, *e.g.,* when the will or a contract gave an executor an option to buy property at a favorable price.[30]

Authorization for self-dealing can be inferred from the circumstances. For example, a court upheld a sale by trustees of stock to a company of which a trustee was officer and director. The settlor

> was fully aware of his brother's interest in the closely-held family corporations. Yet he chose to name his brother ... as Co–Trustee of trusts whose primary assets were stock in those same corporations [and] ... provided his Co–Trustees with wide discretion as to selling that stock ... Included within that wide discretion was the possibility of selling the Trust's stock back to those corporations of which [the brother] was part of the management ... The settlor must have understood that his Co–Trustee would take into consideration the interests of the corporation as well as the interest of the beneficiary in making any decisions concerning the family corporations' stock held by the Trusts.[31]

### *Statutory Exceptions*

According to the Restatement a bank serving as trustee cannot deposit trust funds in its own banking department,[32] but the Uniform Trustees' Powers Act and many state statutes allow this.[33] Nevertheless, a court surcharged a bank trustee for keeping excessive sums on self-deposit. "A bank-trustee does not commit a per se breach of trust by depositing with itself ... cash which it holds as trustee," but it should not leave cash unproductive except for overriding liquidity needs. The court refused to accept as a defence "the practices of even a majority of commercial banks which operated trust departments because of the inherent conflicts of interest" in this situation.[34]

A corporate trustee holding its own stock in the trust also raises conflict of interest problems; the trustee may hold on to the stock in order to avoid depressing its value, or to bar a take-over by a purchaser who plans to install a new management.[35] The Restatement does not allow a corporate trustee to purchase its own shares for the trust or even to "retain shares of its own stock which it has received from the settlor * * * unless such retention is expressly or impliedly authorized by the terms of the trust or by statute,"[36]

**30.** Matter of Gaylord's Estate, 552 P.2d 392 (Okl.1976); Matter of Estate of Hensley, 413 N.E.2d 315 (Ind.App.1980); Calif.Prob.Code § 9885.

**31.** Huntington Nat'l Bank v. Wolfe, 651 N.E.2d 458, 464 (Ohio App.1994). *See also* Goldman v. Rubin, 441 A.2d 713 (Md.1982).

**32.** *Restatement (Second) of Trusts* § 170, comm. m (1959).

**33.** Uniform Trustees' Powers Act § 3(c)(6); Cal.Prob.Code § 16225; Tex.Prop. Code § 113.007; 12 Code Fed.Reg. § 9.10(b) (governing national banks). *See also* Uniform Probate Code § 5–423(c)(6) (conservators).

**34.** Maryland Nat'l Bank v. Cummins, 588 A.2d 1205, 1213 (Md.1991). *See also* Cal.Prob. Code § 9705 (trust company which self deposits must pay the prevailing rate of interest on such deposits).

**35.** Hallgring, *The Uniform Trustees' Powers Act and the Basic Principles of Fiduciary Responsibility,* 41 Wash.L.Rev. 801, 813 (1966). *See also* Donovan v. Bierwirth, 754 F.2d 1049 (2d Cir.1985) (trustee used pension fund to buy stock to block a takeover). Federal law prohibits national banks which hold their own stock as trustee from voting it in the election of directors. 12 U.S.C. § 61.

**36.** *Restatement (Second) of Trusts* § 170, comm. n (1959); First Ala. Bank v. Spragins, 515 So.2d 962 (Ala.1987) (trustee surcharged for retaining its own stock). *Contra,* Elmhurst Nat. Bank v. Glos, 241 N.E.2d 121 (Ill.App. 1968). A general authorization to retain investments may be held to include the trustee's own stock. In re Heidenreich's Will, 378 N.Y.S.2d 982 (Surr.1976).

but many statutes allow corporate trustees to retain, but not to purchase their own shares.[37] The Uniform Trustees' Powers Act allows trustees to retain any "assets received from a trustor," including those "in which the trustee is personally interested."[38]

### *Self-Hiring*

Some states do not allow the same person to get compensation as both personal representative and attorney, but the advantages in this arrangement have induced many states to allow it.[39] The Uniform Probate Code permits personal representatives to employ attorneys "even if they are associated with the personal representative."[40] This language is borrowed from a similar provision in the Uniform Trustees' Powers Act.[41]

Many statutes authorize corporate fiduciaries to use mutual funds which they manage for a fee as a vehicle for investments for a trust or estate.[42]

### *Fiduciaries Acting in Two Capacities*

Often the same fiduciary acts in two capacities for the same beneficiaries, *e.g.* as executor and trustee, or as trustee of several trusts for the same family. Can the ABC Bank as trustee of an insurance trust buy assets from itself as the executor of the insured's probate estate? Allowing such a transaction can provide a market for hard to sell assets, and the potential conflict of interest is attenuated since the Bank has no personal interest in the matter. The California Probate Code allows sales and exchanges between two trusts where the same trustee administers both if the transaction is "fair and reasonable with respect to the beneficiaries of both trusts" and the beneficiaries are properly notified.[43] The Uniform Trustees' Powers Act, however, requires court approval regardless whether a conflict involves the trustee's "individual interest or his interest as trustee of another trust."[44]

### *Contracts Between Fiduciary and Beneficiary*

In dealings between a fiduciary and a competent beneficiary, the beneficiary can protect his or her own interests and so an absolute prohibition is unnecessary. Therefore, contracts between a beneficiary and a fiduciary are not *ipso facto* voidable; an executor, for example, can buy stock from a legatee.[45] But often the parties do not deal on equal terms, *e.g.* the very reason

**37.** Tex.Prop.Code § 113.055; Ky.Rev.Stat. § 386.025; Mo.Stat. § 362.550(5). *But cf.* Ind. Code § 30–4–3–7(a)(4) (trustee cannot purchase or retain own stock).

**38.** Uniform Trustees' Powers Act § 3(c)(1). *See also* Uniform Probate Code § 3–715(a)(1); Rev.Code Wash. § 11.100.060; Cal. Prob.Code § 16220. Uniform Trusts Act § 7 bars a trustee from purchasing its own stock, but is silent about retention.

**39.** See Section 12.4, note 109.

**40.** Uniform Probate Code § 3–715(21).

**41.** Unif.Trustees' Powers Act § 3(c)(24). The Restatement of Trusts uses more guarded language; trustees can be compensated for services to the trust as an attorney "when it is advantageous that the trustee rather than another perform those services." *Restatement, Third, of Trusts* § 38, comm. d (1999). *See also* Lembo v. Casaly, 361 N.E.2d 1314, 1317 (Mass. App.1977).

**42.** *E.g.*, Estate of Vail v. First of America Trust, 722 N.E.2d 248, 252 (Ill.App.1999) (upholding such an investment as authorized by statute).

**43.** Cal.Prob.Code § 16002. *See also* Ind. Code § 30–4–7(c); 760 ILCS § 5/4.15; 12 Code Fed.Regs. § 9.10(d); *cf.* Texas Prop.Code § 113.054 (where U.S. obligations sold for current market price).

**44.** Uniform Trustees' Powers Act § 5(b).

**45.** Matter of Winslow's Estate, 636 P.2d 505 (Wash.App.1981); In re Estate of Neisewander, 474 N.E.2d 1378 (Ill.App.1985).

why the settlor put property in trust was doubt about the beneficiary's business acumen. Therefore the Restatement of Trusts requires trustees who contract with a beneficiary "on the trustee's own account" to "deal fairly" and communicate to the beneficiary all material facts in connection with the transaction.[46] The Restatement of Contracts also makes contracts between a fiduciary and beneficiary voidable by the latter unless they are on "fair terms" and the beneficiary fully understands the relevant facts.[47] For example, an agreement between an executor and his siblings that he should receive $56,000 in settlement of his claims against the estate was set aside because the executor had "abuse[d] his fiduciary relationship" in failing to advise his siblings, over whom he enjoyed "total domination," that his claims were barred because they had not been filed in time.[48]

These restrictions only apply to contracts which are "within the scope of the fiduciary relationship." In some cases it is difficult know where to draw the line. A trustee sold property to a beneficiary for more than it was worth. The property was not a trust asset, but the trustee took an assignment of the beneficiary's interest in the trust as security. The court allowed the beneficiary to set aside the sale, saying that the use of the beneficiary's interest in the trust as security was sufficient to extend the fiduciary duty to the transaction.[49] On the other hand, the requirement of "fair terms" in transactions between a beneficiary and trustee did not prevent a court from upholding a beneficiary's gift of her interest to the trustee (her mother).[50]

### *Social Investing*

Scott argued that in choosing investments trustees could avoid securities of corporations whose actions were "contrary to fundamental and generally accepted ethical principles. They may consider such matters as pollution, race discrimination, fair employment and consumer responsibility," just as directors of corporations could contribute corporate funds to charity.[51] Langbein and Posner on the other hand argue that any consideration of social objectives is inconsistent with the trustees' duty "to administer the trust *solely* in the interest of the beneficiary."[52] They particularly objected pension funds divesting their holdings in companies which did business in South Africa this would leave the portfolio less than optimally diversified.[53] Scott's view was cited with

**46.** *Restatement, Second, Trusts* § 170(2) (1959).

**47.** *Restatement, Second, Contracts* § 173 (1981).

**48.** Matter of Hamilton, 637 P.2d 542, 545 (N.M.1981). *See also* delaVergne v. delaVergne, 514 So.2d 186 (La.App.1987) (executor's purchase of property from devisee voided).

**49.** Smith v. First Nat. Bank, 624 N.E.2d 899, 908 (Ill.App.1993). *Compare* McCormick v. McCormick, 455 N.E.2d 103, 112 (Ill.App.1983) (release given by beneficiary to former trustee is "not subject to the presumption of fraud" because "the fiduciary relationship no longer existed").

**50.** Gross v. Gross, 625 S.W.2d 655, 666–70 (Mo.App.1981).

**51.** 3 A. Scott, *Trusts* § 227.17 (4th ed. Fratcher 1987). *See also* Ravikoff & Curzan, *Social Responsibility in Investment and the Prudent Man Rule,* 68 Calif.L.Rev. 518 (1980); Dobris, *Arguments in Favor of Fiduciary Divestment of "South African" Securities,* 65 Neb.L.Rev. 209 (1986).

**52.** Langbein & Posner, *Social Investing and the Law of Trusts,* 79 Mich.L.Rev. 71, 96–98 (1979). *See also* Cowan v. Scargill (1984) 2 All E.R. 750 (Ch) (pension fund for coal miners cannot eschew investments in competing sources of energy).

**53.** Langbein & Posner, *supra* note 52, at 85.

approval by a court in upholding a city ordinance that required pension trustees to divest their South Africa holdings.

> Given the vast power that pension trust funds exert in American society, it would be unwise to bar trustees from considering the social consequences of investment decisions in any case in which it would cost even a penny more to do so ... If, as in this case, the cost of investing in accordance with social conditions is *de minimis,* the duty of prudence is not violated.[54]

The court's interpretation of "*de minimis*" was generous, since the estimated cost of divestiture exceeded $1 million annually, but this amounted to a small percentage of the funds' assets.

On the other hand, the third Restatement of Trusts, accepting the Langbein/Posner view, says that a trustee's investment decisions "must not be motivated by a purpose of advancing or expressing the trustee's personal views concerning social or political issues."[55] The same idea appears in a comment in the Prudent Investor Act, the text of which reiterates the trustee's duty to manage the trust "solely in the interest of the beneficiaries."[56]

Discussion on this issue focus primarily on pension funds, perhaps because of their vast size.[57] Most pension funds are governed by ERISA which, like trust law, requires fiduciaries to act "solely in the interests of the participants and beneficiaries."[58] ERISA does not apply to pension funds for state employees, but many states, including California, have similar provisions.[59] Nevertheless in 1986 the California legislature ordered state pension funds to divest from companies doing business in South Africa, as "both fiscally imprudent, given the political and economic instability of South Africa, and inconsistent with the moral and political values of the people of California."[60]

Charitable trusts differ from private trusts because social benefits *are* their objective and they have no private beneficiaries. However, money which is given for one charitable purpose cannot be diverted to another, and any investing decision must be justified "on grounds of advancing" one of the trust purposes.[61]

**54.** Board of Trustees v. City of Baltimore, 562 A.2d 720, 727, 737 (Md.1989).

**55.** *Restatement, Third, of Trusts* § 227, comm. c (1990).

**56.** Unif.Prud.Inv.Act § 5, Comment, which says that proponents of social investing generally argue only that "particular schemes of social investing may not result in below-market returns."

**57.** "There has been little pressure on trustees of individual trusts to adopt social investing." Langbein & Posner, *supra* note 52, at 75.

**58.** 29 U.S.C. § 1104(a)(1).

**59.** Cal.Const. art. 16, § 17.

**60.** Cal.Gov.Code § 16640. The statute was repealed after apartheid ended in South Africa, but Gov.Code § 20194 requires one pension fund to direct 25% of its new investments to loans on realty within the state.

**61.** *Restatement, Third, of Trusts* § 227, comm. c (1990); Langbein & Posner, *supra* note 52, at 108.

## § 12.10 Accounting and Distribution

### *Accounting to Beneficiaries*

Fiduciaries have a duty to keep the beneficiaries informed upon request about the property they are managing for them and the terms of the governing instrument.[1] Trustees must also "keep and render clear and accurate accounts with respect to the administration of the trust."[2] A beneficiary can compel a trustee to account without alleging any wrongdoing by the defendant.[3] Even contingent beneficiaries and persons to whom the trustee is authorized but not required to make distributions can sue for an accounting.[4] However, the beneficiaries of a revocable trust are not entitled to an accounting so long as the settlor with a power to revoke is still alive.[5] Indeed, it may be a breach of the trustee's duty to disclose information to them in this situation.[6]

A provision in a trust instrument relieving the trustee from any duty to account has been held invalid as against public policy, assuming that a true trust was intended rather than a gift to the "trustee."[7] Thus a statement in a trust that "trustees need keep no accounts" did not preclude a court from ordering the trustees to account, because a "settlor who attempts to create a trust without any accountability in the trustee is contradicting himself."[8]

### *Accounting in Court*

Accounting to the beneficiaries must be distinguished from accounting in court. Guardians/conservators must file accounts in court; in California, for example, they must "not less frequently than biennially" present an account to the court for settlement.[9] Custodians under the Uniform Transfers to Minors Act, on the other hand, may be compelled to account in a suit by the minor or someone on the minor's behalf, or the custodian may ask for a court accounting, but otherwise a court accounting is not required.[10]

Many states require court accountings for personal representatives. In Texas, for example, they must present "a complete account of receipts and disbursements" annually.[11] The account is then approved by a judge, or

§ 12.10

1. *Restatement, Second, Trusts* § 173 (1959); Cal.Prob.Code § 16060; Fletcher v. Fletcher, 480 S.E.2d 488 (Va.1997); Karpf v. Karpf, 481 N.W.2d 891, 896–7 (Neb.1992). Trustees may, however, withhold from beneficiaries an opinion of counsel which they have obtained for their own protection. Symmons v. O'Keeffe, 644 N.E.2d 631, 639–40 (Mass.1995); Huie v. DeShazo, 922 S.W.2d 920 (Tex.1996). *But cf.* Moeller v. Superior Court (Sanwa Bank), 947 P.2d 279, 283 (Cal.1997) (attorney-client privilege passes to successor trustee and cannot be invoked by predecessor).

2. *Restatement (Second) of Trusts* § 172 (1959). *See also* Calif.Prob.Code § 16062; Texas Prop.Code § 113.151; Uniform Probate Code § 7–303(c); *cf.* Uniform Transfers to Minors Act § 12(d) (custodians shall keep records and make them available for inspection).

3. Zuch v. Connecticut Bank & Trust Co., Inc., 500 A.2d 565 (Conn.App.1985); McCormick v. McCormick, 455 N.E.2d 103 (Ill.App. 1983); Cox v. Cox, 357 N.W.2d 304, 306 (Iowa 1984).

4. Goodpasteur v. Fried, 539 N.E.2d 207 (Ill.App.1989).

5. Montrone v. Valley Bank and Trust Co., 875 P.2d 557 (Utah App.1994); Cal.Prob.Code § 16064(b).

6. Cal.Fin.Code § 1582(e) (authorizing disclosure to beneficiary of an *irrevocable* trust).

7. Briggs v. Crowley, 224 N.E.2d 417 (Mass.1967); *Restatement (Second) of Trusts* § 172, comm. d (1959). As to whether words in an instrument actually create a trust or are merely precatory, see Section 4.6, note 65 et seq.

8. Raak v. Raak, 428 N.W.2d 778, 780 (Mich.App.1988).

9. Cal.Prob.Code § 2620. *See also* Uniform Probate Code § 5–418.

10. Uniform Transfers to Minors Act § 19(c) (court "may require or permit the custodian to account").

11. Texas Prob.Code § 399. These provisions do not apply to estates under "independent administration."

"corrected" if erroneous.[12] A final account is approved when the estate is closed.[13] In California, even an "independent" executor or administrator must get court approval of accounts.[14] Under the Uniform Probate Code, on the other hand, if administration is not "supervised," the personal representative can close an estate simply by filing a statement that he has given an account to the affected distributees.[15] A direction for supervised administration in the will may be ignored if "circumstances bearing on the need for supervised administration" changed after the will was signed. Conversely, a direction for unsupervised administration is not binding if supervision is found to be necessary to protect interested persons.[16] Cautious fiduciaries may seek the "greater protection" afforded by court approval of accounts even when it is not required.[17] However, court approval of an account does not always protect a fiduciary from claims for surcharge.[18]

Many states require court accounting by testamentary trustees. In Delaware they must submit accounts for court approval every two years. On the other hand, trustees of living trusts can be compelled to account in court only "for cause shown."[19]

Court supervision of testamentary trusts has come under attack. Some trustees charge higher fees for testamentary trusts because of the cost of court accountings, which also focus "unwanted publicity" on the beneficiaries' financial affairs. These disadvantages are not justified by the protection they afford.[20] Also, it is hard to justify the distinction between living and testamentary trusts.[21]

Many states have reduced or eliminated periodic judicial review of trustees' accounts. The Uniform Probate Code makes trust administration "free of judicial intervention."[22] Beneficiaries are entitled to an annual account, but copies do not have to be filed in court.[23] Courts have jurisdiction, however, when it is "invoked by interested parties" to "review and settle interim or final accounts."[24]

Even states which require court accountings allow the interested parties to waive them,[25] but beneficiaries cannot approve or waive accounts if they are unborn, unascertained, or minors. The fee of a guardian ad litem to represent such beneficiaries can be a significant cost. Under the Uniform Probate Code

**12.** Texas Prob.Code § 401.

**13.** *Id.* §§ 405, 408.

**14.** Calif.Prob.Code § 10501(a)(3).

**15.** Uniform Probate Code § 3–1003(a). The personal representative or any interested person can ask for court review of an account. *Id.* § 3–1001.

**16.** *Id.* § 3–502.

**17.** *Id.* § 3–1005, comment. In Massachusetts fiduciaries must "file" accounts but there is no legal requirement that they be "presented for allowance." Nevertheless, surety companies press fiduciaries to do so in order to limit their liability. Kehoe, *Allowance of Probate Accounts,* 59 Mass.L.Q. 315 (1975).

**18.** See Section 12.8, at note 90 et seq.

**19.** 12 Del.Code Ann. § 3521. *See also* Bartlett v. Dumaine, 523 A.2d 1 (N.H.1986) (inter-vivos trustee not required to account regularly in court); Coster v. Crookham, 468 N.W.2d 802, 808 (Iowa 1991).

**20.** Westfall, *Nonjudicial Settlement of Trustees Accounts,* 71 Harv.L.Rev. 40, 49–50 (1958).

**21.** Uniform Probate Code, Article VII, comment.

**22.** Uniform Probate Code § 7–201(b). *See also* Calif.Prob.Code § 17209.

**23.** Uniform Probate Code § 7–303, comment.

**24.** Uniform Probate Code § 7–201. *See also* Cal.Prob.Code § 17200(a)(5).

**25.** Calif.Prob.Code § 10954 (waiver of account by personal representative); Ohio Rev. Code § 2109.30(B).

guardians ad litem are appointed only if "representation of the interest otherwise would be inadequate."[26]

A provision in the trust instrument allowing one or more adult beneficiaries to approve accounts can avoid the cost of a guardian ad litem. Approval by a designated beneficiary discharges the trustee, but only if it is given "in good faith."[27]

### *Decree of Distribution*

Normally when a court approves a final account it also enters a decree of distribution.[28] Partial distributions may also be authorized during administration, if the estate is clearly solvent, though in some cases a bond may be required of the distributees.[29]

The Uniform Probate Code allows personal representatives to distribute assets of the estate without court authorization,[30] but many states do not; even in independent administration California requires court supervision for preliminary and final distributions.[31] No such order is generally required for distributions by trustees,[32] but a beneficiary can get a court order if a distribution is improperly made or withheld. A trustee in doubt as to the propriety of a distribution can seek instructions from the court.[33]

A decree of distribution may supersede the terms of a will or trust. For example, a court rejected a claim that a distribution by the executors of a will was "void because it was not in conformity with [the] will." This claim was deemed an impermissible "collateral attack ... on a judgment rendered by a court of competent jurisdiction."[34] However, a decree of distribution which was made without proper notice to interested parties does not bind them. "A formal proceeding which is to be effective on all interested persons must follow reasonable notice to such persons ... Notice is effected by publication only if the address or identity of the person is unknown and cannot be obtained with reasonable diligence. In this case, the names and addresses of the omitted heirs were known prior to the hearing on the petition for order of distribution. Yet, no notice of any kind was given to the omitted heirs," so the

**26.** Uniform Probate Code § 1–403(4). As to "virtual representation" see Section 12.8, note 112.

**27.** *Restatement (Second) of Trusts* § 172, comm. d (1959).

**28.** *E.g.*, Calif.Prob.Code § 11641 (personal representative may distribute estate "when an order settling a final account and for distribution is entered"). A trustee can withhold final distribution until its accounts are approved. First Midwest Bank/Joliet v. Dempsey, 509 N.E.2d 791 (Ill.App.1987).

**29.** Calif.Prob.Code § 11612; Uniform Prob.Code § 3–505. A trial court's order granting or denying a petition for partial distribution will be affirmed absent an abuse of discretion. Matter of Estate of Barber, 699 P.2d 90 (Mont.1985) (denial affirmed when estate tax liability unsettled); In re Estate of Beard, 84 Cal.Rptr.2d 276, 293–94 (App.1999) (partial distribution with bond approved).

**30.** Unless the administration is "supervised." Uniform Probate Code §§ 3–504, 3–704.

**31.** Calif.Prob.Code § 10501(a)(4).

**32.** Trust administration is to proceed "free of judicial intervention." *Id.* § 17209. In California, testamentary trusts created before 1977 are subject to continuing court jurisdiction, but they can petition for removal therefrom. *Id.* §§ 17300, 17351.

**33.** *Id.* § 17200. As to petitions for instructions see *Restatement, Second, Trusts* § 259 (1959).

**34.** First Hawaiian Bank v. Weeks, 772 P.2d 1187, 1191 (Haw.1989). *See also* Baker v. Baker, 813 S.W.2d 116 (Mo.App.1991); Black v. Unknown Creditors, 155 N.W.2d 784 (S.D. 1968).

court which issued the order was "without jurisdiction" as to them.[35] This also applies to persons unborn at the time of the decree who had a future interest under a will or trust.[36]

Even a minor who was represented by a guardian may sometimes get relief against a decree. A will left one third of the testator's estate to his wife, two thirds in trust for his minor sons. A guardian ad litem appointed for the sons raised no questions when the executors distributed more than a third of the estate to the wife. The guardian's "compensation was $100, indicative of a minimum effort involved in checking the documents for their facial regularity." The sons after they came of age were allowed to sue the trustees for failing to obtain their proper share of the estate. "Equitable relief from a valid judgment will be granted to a party to the action injured thereby if there was no fair trial because he was subject to an incapacity and was so poorly represented that there was no substantial presentation of his case."[37]

A decree can also be attacked on the ground that it purported to determine title to property which did not belong to the decedent. "A probate court may only determine who takes property owned by the decedent."[38] However, the Uniform Probate Code, in keeping with a trend to expand the limits of the probate court's jurisdiction allows it "to determine title to property alleged to belong to the estate."[39]

Some courts refuse to be bound by a mistaken decree if the court which rendered it failed to focus on the relevant issue. A will left land to the testator's wife for life, remainder to his son. The decree of distribution of the testator's estate gave the land to wife in fee. When the mistake was discovered after she died, the court imposed a constructive trust on the wife's devisee in favor of the testator's son. Collateral attack on a judgment was barred if "the court had actually construed a will, albeit erroneously" but in this case, "the court did not erroneously construe a will but made an obvious mistake."[40] Another will left property to the testator's husband in trust for his life. A decree of distribution to the husband did not bar a claim by the trust remaindermen because it "did not determine the capacity in which" he took the assets.[41]

Finally, a decree of distribution has been set aside for "extrinsic fraud" when the applicant for an estate failed to reveal the existence of a closer heir of the decedent.[42]

**35.** Matter of Estate of Hoffas, 422 N.W.2d 391, 395 (N.D.1988).

**36.** In re Estate of Evans, 80 N.W.2d 408, 415 (Wis.1957).

**37.** In re Wickman's Will, 289 So.2d 788 (Fla.App.1974). *Cf.* Lowinger v. Herlihy, 472 N.E.2d 676 (Mass.App.1985) (guardian ad litem's false statement that he had examined account constitutes fraud warranting reopening it). Perhaps the proper defendant in this case was the guardian ad litem. "A number of decisions solemnly declare that he is liable to his ward for negligence in the performance of [his] duty [to assert claims] but it is difficult to find decisions in which liability was in fact imposed." Westfall, *supra* note 20, at 45.

**38.** Apple v. Kile, 457 N.E.2d 254, 258 (Ind. App.1983).

**39.** Uniform Probate Code § 3–105.

**40.** Loberg v. Alford, 372 N.W.2d 912, 918 (N.D.1985). *See also* Harvey v. Harvey, 524 P.2d 1187, 1192 (Kan.1974) (invalidity of restraint on alienation can be asserted because issue "was not raised in the probate court").

**41.** Kemper v. Kemper, 532 N.E.2d 1126, 1128 (Ill.App.1989).

**42.** Estate of McGuigan, 99 Cal.Rptr.2d 887 (App.2000).

### *Liability for Improper Distribution*

Fiduciaries can be held liable for making distributions to the wrong person. When a trust gave the settlor's wife the income so long as she remained unmarried, and she remarried and failed to notify the trustee which continued to pay her the income, the trustee was held liable to the remaindermen for these payments. "When a trustee makes payment to a person other than the beneficiary entitled to receive the money, he is liable to the proper beneficiary to make restitution."[43] Some statutes protect trustees who make erroneous distributions without knowledge of a relevant fact like marriage, divorce, or death.[44] The Restatement, however, holds a trustee liable even though "he makes the payment under a reasonable mistake of law or fact," because if in doubt, a trustee can apply to court for instructions.[45] But the Restatement protects trustees who make payments under a trust which is later held invalid unless they knew "or should have had reasonable doubt as to its validity."[46] Similarly, under the Uniform Probate Code personal representatives are not surcharged for a distribution which "was authorized at the time" *e.g.*, a distribution of apparently intestate assets to the heirs when a will is later probated. And a trustee of a revocable trust is not liable to the settlor's creditors for distributing property to the beneficiaries unless the trustee has written notice of the creditors' claim.[47]

Whether or not a personal representative who makes an erroneous distribution is protected, the person who receives it is liable under the Uniform Probate Code unless the distribution can "no longer can be questioned because of adjudication, estoppel, or limitation."[48] Thus a personal representative who was forced to pay estate taxes personally was allowed to get reimbursement from a distributee; the defendant's claim of laches was rejected because he was not substantially prejudiced by the delay.[49] The Restatement of Trusts has a similar provision for trustees.[50] Thus a court decree surcharging a trustee for excessive payments to a beneficiary included a provision directing the recipient to return to the money improperly distributed to him.[51]

### *Distributions to Incompetents*

**43.** National Academy of Sciences v. Cambridge Trust Co., 346 N.E.2d 879, 884 (Mass. 1976).

**44.** Texas Prop.Code § 114.004; Wash.Rev. Code § 11.98.100. Such claims may also be limited by a statute of limitations. Toombs v. Daniels, 361 N.W.2d 801, 810 (Minn.1985) (claim of wrongfully excluded beneficiary limited to last 6 years' income).

**45.** *Restatement (Second) of Trusts* § 226, comm. a, § 345, comm. j (1959); Alderman v. Cooper, 185 S.E.2d 809, 813 (S.C.1971); Estate of Sewell, 409 A.2d 401 (Pa.1979).

**46.** *Restatement (Second) of Trusts* § 226A (1959); *cf.* Wilcox v. Waldman, 744 P.2d 444 (Ariz.App.1987) (filing suit not enough to create reasonable doubt as to validity of trust).

**47.** Uniform Probate Code §§ 3–703, 6–102(i)(2).

**48.** Uniform Probate Code § 3–909. *See also* Matter of Olson's Estate, 332 N.W.2d 711 (S.D.1983); Lee v. Barksdale, 350 S.E.2d 508 (N.C.App.1986).

**49.** Quintana v. Quintana, 802 P.2d 488, 491 (Idaho App.1990); *cf.* Matter of Estate of Meyer, 774 P.2d 839 (Ariz.App.1989) (similar action against distributee's estate time-barred).

**50.** *Restatement (Second) of Trusts* § 254 (1959). *See also* Texas Prop.Code § 114.031(a)(3); In re Estate of Berger, 520 N.E.2d 690 (Ill.App.1987) (conservator's surety).

**51.** Dunkley v. Peoples Bank & Trust Co., 728 F.Supp. 547, 564 (W.D.Ark.1989); Brent v. Smathers, 547 So.2d 683, 686 (Fla.App.1989).

Fiduciaries who make distributions to persons who are legally incapacitated run a serious risk. For example, when an insured died, the insurer paid the proceeds to the designated beneficiary, an 11 year old niece of the insured. Her father misappropriated the money, and the insurer had to pay again when the niece came of age. "Since she was legally incapable of discharging [the insurer, it] is still contractually liable to plaintiff * * * It is without consequence that [the insurer] had no knowledge that plaintiff was a minor or that it acted in good faith."[52] On similar principles a trustee was surcharged for permitting an incompetent settlor to withdraw funds from a revocable trust when "the trustee should have known of the settlor's incompetency." However, the trustee was not liable for earlier distributions, since "the facts do not indicate that the bank knew or should have known" that the distributee was incompetent at the time.[53]

Executors and administrators usually must distribute the share of a minor heir or devisee to a guardian or conservator,[54] but many states have "facility of payment" statutes to avoid the need for guardianship for minors when only small amounts are involved.[55] The Uniform Probate Code allows "any person under a duty to pay or deliver money or personal property to a minor" to do so "in amounts not exceeding $5,000 a year" by paying "any person having the care and custody of the minor with whom the minor resides." The recipient must apply the money for the minor's support and turn over any balance to the minor at majority, but the payor "is not responsible for the proper application" of the money.[56] The Uniform Trustees' Powers Act authorizes trustees to pay any amount distributable to a beneficiary "under legal disability" to the beneficiary, or, if there is no appointed guardian, "to a relative" for the beneficiary's use.[57] An Illinois statute covers not only a beneficiary under legal disability, but anyone who "in the opinion of the trustee is unable properly to manage his affairs." It also permits the trustee to distribute to a custodian under the Uniform Transfers to Minors Act, or use the property "directly for the benefit of the beneficiary."[58] The Transfers to Minors Act itself allows personal representatives and trustees to transfer property to a custodian for the benefit of a minor, but court authorization is required for amounts over $10,000, on the theory that for larger amounts "stricter investment standards" may be appropriate.[59]

Even without a statute, trustees can apply income for the benefit of an incapacitated beneficiary instead of paying it to the beneficiary. Further, according to the Third Restatement of Trusts,

**52.** Iverson v. Scholl, Inc., 483 N.E.2d 893, 898 (Ill.App.1985). The insurer would have been protected if the minor had still had the funds which had been distributed to her. *Restatement, Second, Contracts* § 14, comm. c (1971).

**53.** Cloud v. United States Nat. Bank, 570 P.2d 350, 355–56 (Or.1977). Compare the distinction in *Restatement, Second, Contracts* §§ 14–15 (1979) between minors and adult incompetents.

**54.** Matter of Estate of Roberts, 426 N.E.2d 269, 272 (Ill.App.1981) (trustee directed to distribute to conservator of incompetent beneficiary).

**55.** Uniform Probate Code § 5–101, comment.

**56.** *Id.* § 5–101.

**57.** Uniform Trustees' Powers Act § 3(c)(22).

**58.** 760 ILCS § 5/4.20. *See also* Texas Prop.Code § 113.021; Calif.Prob.Code § 16245.

**59.** Uniform Transfers to Minors Act § 6(c), comment. *See also* Unif.Cust.Trust Act § 5(a).

if the trustee has good-faith doubt concerning a beneficiary's practical or legal capacity to handle funds, distributions to which the beneficiary is entitled may be retained and managed by the trustee as a separate fund belonging to the beneficiary subject to a continuing right of withdrawal by or on behalf of the beneficiary. Thus, it will ordinarily be unnecessary for a personal fiduciary (guardian, conservator, or the like) to be appointed for the beneficiary.[60]

The terms of the trust or will often confer broad powers to deal with this problem. For example, a will authorized the executor to deliver any sum due to a minor "to the then living parents of such minor, without bond." A court order directing distribution to a guardian for the minors was reversed because it would "thwart the expressed intention of the testatrix and will result in additional expense which the testatrix sought to avoid."[61]

### *Distribution in Kind*

Distributions are sometimes made in cash, sometimes in kind. The Uniform Probate Code provides that assets of an estate "shall be distributed in kind to the extent possible" but a pecuniary or a residuary devisee can object to such distribution.[62]

Distributions in kind can raise problems of valuation when used to satisfy pecuniary devises. Suppose a will leaves $10,000 to the testator's sister and the executor proposes to satisfy this by distributing XYZ stock. The stock must be valued to know how many shares the sister should get. Assets are valued for this purpose at the date of distribution.[63] If the assets of an estate appreciate or depreciate during administration, the benefit or burden of the change falls on the residuary and specific devisees, not pecuniary devisees.[64] The distinction gives rise to questions of interpretation as to the character of an ambiguous gift.[65]

When heirs or residuary devisees are entitled to fractional shares, can a fiduciary make non-prorata distributions, *e.g.*, all the XYZ stock to one, and other assets of comparable value to the others? The California Probate Code authorizes trustees to make such non-pro-rata distributions,[66] but the Uniform Probate Code gives each residuary beneficiary a right "to his proportionate share of each asset constituting the residue."[67] Non-pro-rata distributions may be desirable to avoid divided ownership, but they raise valuation problems. For example, a will left one third of the estate to the testator's widow, and 2/3 to a trust for his sons. The executors made a non-prorata distribution, using the probate inventory valuation in allocating assets which were "worth

**60.** *Restatement, Third, of Trusts* § 49, comm. c (1999).

**61.** In re Estate of Tate, 543 S.W.2d 588, 590 (Tenn.1976). *See also* Uniform Statutory Will Act § 9.

**62.** Uniform Probate Code § 3–906. *See also* Estate of Lindberg, 388 N.E.2d 148, 156 (Ill.App.1979) (executor has a duty to sell when residuary legatee objects to distribution in kind); *Restatement, Second, Trusts* § 346 (1959) (beneficiary can control whether distribution is in cash or kind).

**63.** Uniform Probate Code § 3–906(a)(2)(ii); Van Schaack v. AmSouth Bank, NA, 530 So.2d 740, 744 (Ala.1988). When distributions are made in installments, multiple valuations are necessary. Williams v. Harrington, 460 So.2d 533 (Fla.App.1984).

**64.** Rev.Rul. 90–3, 1990–1 Cum.Bull. 174.

**65.** See Section 8.2, at note 17.

**66.** Calif.Prob.Code § 16246. *See also* In re Estate of Meyer, 802 P.2d 148, 153 (Wash.App. 1990).

**67.** Uniform Probate Code § 3–906, comment.

substantially more" at the time of distribution. This was held to be improper despite a provision in the will that the values placed on property by the executors in making distribution "shall be final and conclusive." This provision did not absolve them "of their obligation to act in good faith."[68]

### *Delay in Distribution*

One of the most common complaints about lawyers and the legal system is delay in distribution of assets in administration.[69] This is also a commonly cited reason for the widespread popular desire to avoid probate.[70] Some states penalize personal representative who unduly delay distribution. Illinois, for example, charges them 10% interest per year on the value of any assets not distributed two years after their appointment unless good cause for the delay is shown.[71] In California courts can reduce the personal representatives' compensation for such delays.[72] Delays have also been the basis for disciplining attorneys who were responsible for them.[73] However, on this point courts have shown their customary deference to reasonable decisions by fiduciaries.[74]

**68.** In re Will of Wickman, 289 So.2d 788, 790 (Fla.App.1974). *See also* Pastan v. Pastan, 390 N.E.2d 253, 256 (Mass.1979); *Restatement, Second, Trusts* § 347, comm. h (1959); N.Y. EPTL § 11–1.7(a)(2) (contrary to public policy to allow executor or trustee to fix value conclusively for distribution). In this connection it is appropriate to apply a discount to undivided fractional interests in light of the difficulty in selling them. In re Estate of Ehlers, 911 P.2d 1017, 1022 (Wash.App.1996).

**69.** Link, *Developments Regarding the Professional Responsibility of the Estate Administration Lawyer: The Effect of the Model Rules of Professional Conduct*, 26 Real Prop.Prob. and Trust L.J. 1, 17–19 (1991).

**70.** See Section 9.1, note 19.

**71.** 755 ILCS 5/24–10.

**72.** Cal.Prob.Code § 12205; Estate of Heller, 9 Cal.Rptr.2d 274, 276 (App.1992).

**73.** Committee of Pro. Ethics v. Winkel, 415 N.W.2d 601 (Iowa 1987) (attorney reprimanded for allowing an estate to remain open for seven years).

**74.** Estate of Vail v. First of America Trust, 722 N.E.2d 248 (Ill.App.1999) (finding of good cause for delay in distributing estate upheld); Shriners Hospitals v. Robbins, 450 So.2d 798, 802 (Ala.1984) (refusal to impose liability on trustee for delay in distribution).

# Chapter 13

# RIGHTS OF CREDITORS

*Analysis*



## § 13.1 Creditors' Remedies against Trusts

Generally speaking, creditors of a trustee have no rights against the trust property, which in equity belongs to the beneficiaries.[1] The question of other creditors' rights to reach interests in a trust to satisfy their claims can be divided into two categories: creditors of the settlor, and those of beneficiaries other than the settlor.

### *Creditors of Settlor*

Creditors can in general only reach property which belongs to their debtor. If *S* creates a trust which requires the trustee to pay the income and principal to others, *S*'s creditors have no right to reach the trust, unless the creation of a trust involved a fraudulent conveyance. For example, creditors of a man were allowed to reach an irrevocable trust which the debtor had created for his children on the basis of a statute providing that "every conveyance made * * * by a person who is, or will thereby be rendered, insolvent is fraudulent as to creditors" if the conveyance was made without "fair consideration."[2] Most states have similar statutes, some of them based on an English statute of 1571, others on a more recent Uniform Fraudulent Transfer Act.[3] These statutes cover all gratuitous transfers, including the creation of trusts.

Even when the creation of a trust did not involve a fraudulent conveyance, if the settlor reserves the right to revoke the trust, most states allow the settlor's creditors to reach the trust, either by virtue of a statute[4] or by case law.[5] The Third Restatement of Trusts agrees.[6] Even after the settlor has died

**§ 13.1**

1. Unif.Trust Code § 507. For limited exceptions see Section 6.4, at note 95 et seq.

2. Territorial Sav. & Loan Ass'n v. Baird, 781 P.2d 452 (Utah App.1989).

3. *Restatement, Second, of Property (Donative Transfers)* § 34.3, Statutory Note (1990).

4. Ind.Code § 30–1–9–14; Ala.Code § 35–4–290(b); Calif.Prob.Code § 18200; Unif.Trust Code § 505(1).

5. McGoldrick v. Walker, 838 P.2d 1139 (Utah 1992) (interpreting a statute); Soto v. First Gibraltar Bank, 868 S.W.2d 400 (Tex. App.1993) (Totten trust).

and the power to revoke has expired, many authorities allow the settlor's creditors to reach the trust assets, at least if the settlor's probate estate is insufficient to satisfy claims.[7] The Restatement of Property agrees, provided that creditors assert their claims "within a reasonable time after the [settlor's] death."[8] The California Probate Code imposes time limits on presentation of claims against a revocable trust analogous to the nonclaim statutes governing claims against a deceased debtor's probate estate.[9]

Even if a trust is irrevocable, creditors of the settlor can reach any interest in the trust which the settlor has reserved. Thus if a trust provides that the trustee shall pay the income to the settlor for her life, remainder to her children, her creditors can reach her income interest. They can also reach the principal if the trustee has discretion to distribute it to the settlor. According to the Restatement, where the trustee

> has discretionary authority to pay to the settlor * * * as much of the income and principal as the trustee may determine appropriate, creditors of the settlor can reach the maximum amount the trustee, in the proper exercise of fiduciary discretion, could pay to * * * the settlor.[10]

Courts generally interpret this rule to give the settlor's creditors access to all the trust principal, presumably on the theory that the trustee could properly pay all of a settlor's debts under such a power.[11]

If several persons contribute property to a trust, each is treated as the settlor of a portion which reflects his or her particular contribution. Thus when a woman created a trust with other members of her family and later went bankrupt, the property which she had put into the trust, but not assets contributed by others, was included in her bankruptcy estate, because the trust authorized the trustee to use principal for her support.[12]

### *Beneficiaries Other Than the Settlor*

Creditors of beneficiaries other than the settlor traditionally were required to resort to "equitable" remedies, and show that their legal remedies were inadequate in order to reach the beneficiary's interest.[13] In accordance with the traditions of equity, courts have discretion in deciding how to use the beneficiary's interest to satisfy claims. The Uniform Trust Code says that the court may award a creditor "such relief as is appropriate under the circum-

**6.** *Restatement, Third, of Trusts* § 25, comm. e (1996). *See also Restatement, Second, of Property (Donative Transfers)* § 34.3, comm. h (1990). *Contra, Restatement (Second) of Trusts* § 330, comment *o* (1959).

**7.** Cal.Prob.Code § 19001; Uniform Probate Code § 6–102 (1998); Matter of Estate of Nagel, 580 N.W.2d 810 (Iowa 1998); Unif.Trust Code § 505(3); *Restatement, Third, of Trusts* § 25, comm. e (1996).

**8.** *Restatement, Second, of Property (Donative Transfers)* § 34.3, comm. i (1990).

**9.** Cal.Prob.Code § 19100; *cf.* Uniform Probate Code § 6–201(h) (1998) (one year from death of debtor). As to the nonclaim statutes see Section 13.3, note .

**10.** *Restatement, Third, of Trusts* § 60, comm. f (1999). Similar language appeared in *Restatement, Second, Trusts* § 156 (1959) and is found in Unif.Trust Code § 505(2).

**11.** In re Robbins, 826 F.2d 293 (4th Cir. 1987) (bankruptcy); State v. Hawes, 564 N.Y.S.2d 637 (App.Div.1991); Giles v. Ingrum, 583 So.2d 1287 (Ala.1991) (claim allowed after settlor's death).

**12.** Matter of Shurley, 115 F.3d 333 (5th Cir.1997). *See also Restatement, Third, of Trusts* § 60, comm. f (1999); Cal.Prob.Code § 15304(b); Unif.Trust Code § 505(2).

**13.** This has been changed by statute in many states. *Restatement (Second) of Trusts* § 147, comment c (1959).

stances."[14] Thus where the debtor-beneficiary is entitled to the trust income "the court will normally direct the trustee to make the payments to the creditor until the claim * * * is satisfied," but it may order less than all the income to be paid to the creditor, leaving some for the basic needs of the beneficiary. The court may alternatively order a sale of the beneficiary's interest, particularly when it is a future interest which produces no current income.[15] Unfortunately, however, contingent future "interests upon forced sale typically fail to fetch even their full risk-adjusted value, given the absence of an established market in these nonhomogeneous assets."[16] The law takes account of this fact; if "the uncertainty or remoteness of the interest [is] such that its forced sale would produce little relative to its value to the beneficiary," the court may simply give creditors "a lien on the beneficiary's interest, to be realized if and when it falls into possession."[17] One court held that a husband's contingent remainder interests in a trust "were mere expectancies, comparable to future inheritances, which are not sufficient property interests" to be divided upon his divorce because of the "administrative hardships inherent in the valuation of expectant interests or in the requirement of continued court supervision" of a "future award on an 'if and when' basis."[18]

If the trustee has discretion to pay principal or income to a debtor other than the settlor, the creditor's rights are limited. For this reason it may be necessary to determine who the settlor of a trust was. For example, a will left property to the testator's nieces and nephews, one of whom, Martha, was developmentally disabled. Martha's siblings decided to establish a discretionary trust for her. A state agency which had been supporting Martha sought reimbursement from the trust assets. The court had to determine whose funds were used to create the trust. Where "the beneficiary has no right to a disbursement from the trust other than what the trustee in his sole discretion chooses to distribute, the beneficiary's creditors cannot compel the trustee to pay," but (as we have seen) "where the settlor is a beneficiary of the trust, the creditors can reach the maximum amount that the trustee could pay to the beneficiary."[19]

Even a tax lien has been held not to attach to a discretionary trust created by someone other than the beneficiary, because the beneficiary "does not have 'property' or any 'right to property' in nondistributed trust property before the trustees have exercised their discretionary powers of distribution."[20] However, creditors can get an order directing the trustee to pay them rather than the beneficiary if the trustee decides to exercise the discretion in

**14.** Unif.Trust Code § 501.

**15.** *Restatement, Third, of Trusts* § 56, comm.e (1999).

**16.** Hirsch, *Spendthrift Trusts and Public Policy: Economic and Cognitive Perspectives,* 73 Wash.U.L.Q. 1, 58 (1995).

**17.** *Restatement, Third, of Trusts* § 56, comm. e (1999). *See also* Cal.Code Civ.Proc. § 709.010; United States v. Riggs Nat. Bank, 636 F.Supp. 172, 177 (D.D.C.1986) (income paid to claimant until claim satisfied); First City Nat. Bank v. Phelan, 718 S.W.2d 402 (Tex.App.1986) (same).

**18.** Williams v. Massa, 728 N.E.2d 932, 941 (Mass.2000).

**19.** In re Johannes Trust, 479 N.W.2d 25, 28 (Mich.App.1991). *See also* In re Estate of McInerny, 682 N.E.2d 284 (Ill.App.1997) (creditor of daughter cannot reach discretionary trust created by her father).

**20.** United States v. O'Shaugnessy, 517 N.W.2d 574, 578 (Minn.1994). *See also* Landmark First Nat. Bank of Fort Lauderdale v. Haves, 467 So.2d 839 (Fla.App.1985).

the beneficiary's favor; a trustee who makes distributions to a beneficiary in disregard of such an order will be liable to the beneficiary's creditors.[21]

The Second Restatement of Trusts drew a distinction between "trusts for support" and "discretionary trusts;" certain classes of creditors were allowed to reach the beneficiary's interest in a support trust, for example, those who had supplied "necessaries" to the beneficiary.[22] Courts have had difficulty in applying this distinction,[23] since many trusts direct the trustee to support a beneficiary, but they give the trustee discretion in determining the appropriate level of support. The Third Restatement rejects the distinction; it gives creditors of a beneficiary of a discretionary trust, like the beneficiary him/herself, "judicial protection from abuse of discretion by the trustee."[24] This view has some judicial support. A court reversed the dismissal of an attempt by a beneficiary's creditor to reach her interest in a discretionary trust.

> When a trustee has the absolute discretion to withhold from the beneficiary all payments, * * * the trust * * * is beyond the reach of his creditors who stand in his shoes. * * * [But here] the wording of the trust requires the trustee to pay to [the beneficiary] as much of the trust income as is necessary to maintain her 'in accordance with her station in life.' * * * Because [the beneficiary] can demand payment from the trustee, so may her creditors who 'stand in her shoes.'[25]

The Uniform Trust Code, on the other hand, does not allow creditors to compel a trustee to make a discretionary distribution even if the trustee "has abused the discretion." The beneficiary can get judicial relief in such cases, but not creditors of the beneficiary, unless the claim is for support by a child, spouse or former spouse of the beneficiary, in which case the court may direct the trustee to distribute "such amount as is equitable under the circumstances."[26]

In any event, courts are unlikely to find that a trustee has abused discretion when the issue is raised by a beneficiary's creditors, particularly if the trustee's discretion is not controlled by a standard like support. Courts tend to defer to the trustee's decisions in any event, and even under the third Restatement "a trustee's refusal to make distributions might not constitute an abuse against * * * a creditor even when * * * a decision to refuse distributions to the beneficiary might have constituted an abuse."[27]

The Restatement gives creditors more rights when the beneficiary by the terms of the trust has authority, as trustee or otherwise, "to determine his or her own benefits" even if this authority is restricted by a standard. In this situation the beneficiary's creditors, like the creditors of the settlor, can reach

**21.** Wilcox v. Gentry, 867 P.2d 281 (Kan. 1994); Cal.Prob.Code § 15303(b); *Restatement, Third, of Trusts* § 60, comm. c (1999).

**22.** *Restatement, Second, Trusts* §§ 154, 155, 157 (1959).

**23.** Smith v. Smith, 517 N.W.2d 394 (Neb. 1994); State ex rel. Sec'y of SRS v. Jackson, 822 P.2d 1033 (Kan.1991).

**24.** *Restatement, Third, of Trusts* § 60, comm. e (1999).

**25.** Goforth v. Gee, 975 S.W.2d 448, 450 (Ky.1998). *See also* Sisters of Mercy Health v. First Bank, 624 N.E.2d 520 (Ind.App.1993); *cf.* Cal.Prob.Code § 15306(a)(3) (court may order trustee of discretionary trust to satisfy claims for public support furnished to a beneficiary who is "the spouse or a minor child of the settlor"). As to judicial review of discretionary decisions by trustees see Section 9.5, at note 8 et seq.

**26.** Unif.Trust Code § 504.

**27.** *Restatement, Third, of Trusts* § 60, comm. e (1999).

"the maximum amount" which the beneficiary can properly take.[28] Case support this rule is thin;[29] some courts hold that a beneficiary's power is not reachable by creditors if the beneficiary does not choose to exercise it.[30]

### *Spendthrift Provisions*

Most states do not allow most creditors to reach a beneficiary's interest in a trust if it contains a spendthrift provision. Such provisions, despite the commonly used name, rarely contain the word "spendthrift." A typical provision says:

> Every beneficiary hereof is hereby restrained from anticipating, assigning, selling or otherwise disposing of his or her interest in the Trust, and none of the interests of the beneficiaries hereunder shall be subject to the claims of creditors or other persons.[31]

But under the Uniform Trust Code, a settlor can avoid beating around the bush and simply say "this is a spendthrift trust."[32]

Some state statutes make all trusts spendthrift. Washington, for example, exempts from execution "property held in trust for a judgment debtor" unless the debtor created the trust.[33] In most states, however, if the trust instrument contains no spendthrift provision, beneficiaries' interests which are not dependent on the trustee's discretion are subject to claims of their creditors.[34]

England does not give effect to spendthrift provisions,[35] but most American states do.[36] In the states which recognize them, spendthrift provisions keep the beneficiary's interest out of bankruptcy.[37]

Debate has raged over spendthrift trusts ever since they first appeared a little over a century ago. One commonly used argument for their validity focuses on the settlor's intent.

> A property owner should have the right to dispose of her property as she chooses. * * * A beneficiary owns no greater interest in the trust proper-

**28.** *Restatement, Third, of Trusts* § 60, comm. g (1999). The rule does not apply if the power is held jointly by the beneficiary and another.

**29.** *Compare* Morrison v. Doyle, 582 N.W.2d 237 (Minn.1998); (beneficiary's powers do not allow his creditor's to reach his interest) *with* In re Baldwin, 142 B.R. 210 (Bktcy.S.D.Ohio 1992) (spendthrift provision ineffective when beneficiary had power to replace the trustee and control investments).

**30.** University Nat. Bank v. Rhoadarmer, 827 P.2d 561 (Colo.App.1991). See Section 10.4, note 17 et seq.

**31.** Council v. Owens, 770 S.W.2d 193, 194–95 (Ark.App.1989).

**32.** Unif.Trust Code § 502(b).

**33.** Rev.Code Wash. § 6.32.250. These provisions go back to a New York statute of 1828. E. Griswold, *Spendthrift Trusts* §§ 64, 73.

**34.** Henderson v. Collins, 267 S.E.2d 202 (Ga.1980); Chandler v. Hale, 377 A.2d 318 (Conn.1977); *Restatement (Third) of Trusts* § 56 (1999). However, an intent to impose a spendthrift restriction can be inferred; it need not be stated expressly. *Id.*, § 58, comm. b; *cf.* Morrison v. Doyle, 582 N.W.2d 237 (Minn. 1998).

**35.** Brandon v. Robinson, 34 Eng.Rep. 379 (1811).

**36.** Knight v. Knight, 589 N.Y.S.2d 195 (A.D.1992) (assignment of corpus invalid because of spendthrift provision); Scott v. Bank One Trust Co., 577 N.E.2d 1077 (Ohio 1991); *Restatement (Third) of Trusts* § 58 (1999); Cal. Prob.Code § 15300–01; R.I.Gen.Laws § 18–9.1–1.

**37.** First Northwestern Trust Co. v. Internal Rev. Serv., 622 F.2d 387 (8th Cir.1980); Matter of Shurley, 115 F.3d 333 (5th Cir.1997); 11 U.S.C. § 541(c)(2).

ty than the settlor has given him. In the case of a spendthrift trust, the settlor has not given the beneficiary an alienable interest.[38]

The premise of this reasoning is questionable, since the right of property owners to dispose of property is limited by "public policy," which has traditionally curtailed the ability of transferors to restrict alienation.[39] Another rationale for spendthrift trusts compares them to laws exempting a portion of a debtor's property from execution.[40] This analogy has been challenged on the ground that exemption laws "apply equally to all members of society" whereas spendthrift trusts are a privilege of the few who have relatives with enough property to create trusts. Also, exemption laws only keep debtors "from absolute poverty" and allow creditors to reach the balance of their property, whereas spendthrift trusts "permit the children of rich men to live in debt and luxury at the same time."[41]

A New York statute which has been copied in several states attempts to meet this objection by allowing creditors to reach trust income in excess of the amount necessary for the beneficiary's support.[42] This statute has been construed to exempt large amounts of income from execution on the ground that they were necessary to support the beneficiary's "station-in-life."[43] Some states limit spendthrift provisions more strictly. Oklahoma, for example, makes all trust income in excess of $5000 a year subject to garnishment.[44] Most states have no such limits, however. In revising the Bankruptcy Code in 1978 Congress considered, but ultimately deleted, a provision that would have made spendthrift trusts valid in bankruptcy only to the extent necessary for the debtor's support.[45]

Spendthrift trusts have also been justified by analogy to the protection which the law confers on minors and incapacitated adults. A spendthrift provision allows a settlor to secure "the object of his affection * * * from * * * his own improvidence, or incapacity for self-protection."[46] However, spendthrift provisions are inserted in many trusts without regard to the beneficiaries' actual capacity for self-protection, and often apply to persons whom the settlor never knew.[47] In a recent case a court construed a spendthrift clause to cover the settlor's great grandchildren, who began to receive trust income over 60 years after the trust was created. Surely the settlor was in no position to assess their "capacity for self-protection" after this length of time.[48] Perhaps such provisions should be allowed only for beneficiaries who

**38.** Scott v. Bank One Trust Co., 577 N.E.2d 1077, 1082, 1084 (Ohio 1991). *See also* Erickson v. Bank of California, 643 P.2d 670 (Wash.1982); Lundgren v. Hoglund, 711 P.2d 809 (Mont.1985).

**39.** Emanuel, *Spendthrift Trusts: It's Time to Codify the Compromise*, 72 Neb.L.Rev. 179, 192–94 (1993). As to restraints on alienation generally see Section 11.8.

**40.** Nichols v. Eaton, 91 U.S. 716, 726 (1875). See Section 3.4, at note 32.

**41.** Bushman, *The (In)Validity of Spendthrift Trusts*, 47 Ore.L.Rev. 304, 312 (1968). *See also* Alexander, *The Dead Hand and the Law of Trusts in the Nineteenth Century*, 37 Stan.L.Rev. 1189, 1247 (1985).

**42.** N.Y.EPTL § 7–3.4. *See also* Calif.Prob.Code § 15307; *cf.* Lundgren v. Hoglund, 711 P.2d 809 (Mont.1985) (similar statute held to apply only to trust of real property).

**43.** Griswold, *supra* note 34, §§ 378, 379; Powell, *The Rule Against Perpetuities and Spendthrift Trusts in New York*, 71 Colum.L.Rev. 688, 699 (1971).

**44.** 60 Okl.Stat. § 175.25. *See also* Va. Code § 55–19 (spendthrift trust corpus cannot exceed $1 million).

**45.** Matter of Goff, 706 F.2d 574, 582 (5th Cir.1983).

**46.** Nichols v. Eaton, 91 U.S. at 727.

**47.** Hirsch, *supra* note 16, at 44.

**48.** Schreiber v. Kellogg, 50 F.3d 264 (3d Cir.1995).

need protection, but the law does not so restrict them. "Spendthrift protection is not limited to beneficiaries who are legally incompetent or who, as a practical matter, lack the ability to manage their finances in a responsible manner."[49]

It is often said that creditors have no reason to complain about spendthrift provisions because they can have notice of them. This has been challenged on the ground that inter vivos trusts of personal property are not matters of public record,[50] but Adam Hirsch doubts that "in the computer age" a spendthrift restriction will "escape notice by a credit rating agency."[51] The paucity of legislation restricting spendthrift trusts suggests that in the real world, creditors, who are not slow to seek favorable legislation on other issues, do not regard them as a serious problem.

Spendthrift restraints may secure an income beneficiary's means of support, but future interests in a trust supply no current support. At one time the validity of spendthrift restraints on future interests was doubted, but modern authorities make no distinction between income and principal in this regard.[52]

After income or principal from a spendthrift trust has actually been distributed to a beneficiary it becomes subject to creditors' claims.[53] Even if distribution has not yet taken place, but by the terms of the trust the beneficiary has the right to demand it—*e.g.* she has reached the age specified in the trust instrument for distribution but the money is still in the hands of the trustee, the beneficiary's creditors can reach it despite the spendthrift provision.[54] Thus *eventually* the money in a spendthrift trust becomes subject to claims, so the objections to (and advantages of) a spendthrift provision are limited. However, it may be hard for creditors to collect money after it reaches the beneficiary's hands, particularly if the beneficiary is actually a spendthrift. As Adam Hirsch notes, creditors can reach the money after distribution "assuming they can find it, for in practice what may follow is a game of hide and seek."[55]

### *Protective Trusts*

Perhaps creditor groups have not vigorously opposed spendthrift trusts because the alternative is no better for them. Jurisdictions which do not allow spendthrift trusts permit "protective" trusts, which provide that if a creditor seeks to reach a beneficiary's interest it is forfeited, or it becomes discretion-

**49.** *Restatement, Third, of Trusts* § 58, comm. a (1999). Adam Hirsch argues that beneficiaries under a spendthrift restraint should have "the right to petition for their termination on grounds of manifest unsuitability or unforeseen conditions." Hirsch, *supra* note 16, at 48.

**50.** Bushman, *supra* note 41, at 315; Wicker, *Spendthrift Trusts*, 10 Gonz.L.Rev. 1, 3 (1974); Emanuel, *supra* note 39, at 194.

**51.** Hirsch, *supra* note 16, at 64–65.

**52.** *Restatement (Third) of Trusts* § 58, comm. a (1959); Cal.Prob.Code § 15301; In re Vought's Estate, 250 N.E.2d 343 (N.Y.1969) (transfer of principal invalid because of spendthrift clause); Matter of Newman, 903 F.2d 1150, 1152 (7th Cir.1990).

**53.** *Restatement (Third) of Trusts* § 58, comm. d (1999); De Mille v. Ramsey, 254 Cal. Rptr. 573 (App.1989). *But cf.* Matter of Newman, 903 F.2d 1150, 1153 (7th Cir.1990) (distributions from living trust not covered by Act and so not includable in bankruptcy).

**54.** *Ibid.*; Unif.Trust Code § 506; Brent v. State Cent. Collection Unit, 537 A.2d 227 (Md. 1988). However, a trust does not terminate for this purpose until after the trustee has had a reasonable time to make distribution. Shannon v. Johnson, 741 S.W.2d 791 (Mo.App.1987).

**55.** Hirsch, *supra* note 16, at 2.

ary with the trustee whether to pay the beneficiary.[56] Opponents of the spendthrift trust object that it allows debtors not to pay creditors and still retain their property. This is not true of a protective trust, but the distinction makes little practical difference to creditors.

### *Special Claims*

Some claims override spendthrift provisions. Creditors who supply necessaries to a beneficiary can reach the beneficiary's interest despite a spendthrift clause.[57] Both the settlor and society have an interest in having beneficiaries provided with necessaries, and this might not happen if those who furnished them could not collect from the trust. Similar reasoning underlies an exception for persons who have rendered services to protect the beneficiary's interest in the trust. For example, an attorney who represented a beneficiary in a suit to surcharge the trustee was allowed to reach the beneficiary's interest to collect his fee despite a spendthrift provision.[58]

The Restatement, as well as many cases and statutes, allow claims for alimony and child support to be asserted against a spendthrift trust.[59] The exception is sometimes predicated on the settlor's probable intent,[60] but this is questionable at least as to alimony, the recipient of which is usually not related to the settlor. The Restatement bases the exception "on policy considerations;" the settlor's intent "is neither the rationale nor the limit of this exception."[61] Some say that a spouse and children "are in quite a different position from ordinary creditors who have voluntary extended credit." Furthermore, "unless the interest of the beneficiary can be reached, the state may be called upon for their support."[62] The *beneficiary* may also become dependent on state support if the spendthrift trust is dissipated, but alimony and child support are based in part upon the extent of the beneficiary's resources, so they will not leave the beneficiary destitute, as might happen with ordinary claims. Support claims can be satisfied from a spendthrift trust only after taking account of "the beneficiary's need for some part of the distributions."[63]

**56.** *Restatement, Third, of Trusts* § 57 (1999); N.C.Stat § 36A–115; (English) Trustee Act, 1925, § 33. Scott v. Bank One Trust Co., 577 N.E.2d 1077 (Ohio 1991), involved a protective trust, since Ohio had previously disapproved spendthrift trusts, but in this case the court changed its mind. Protective provisions are also effective in bankruptcy. In re Fitzsimmons, 896 F.2d 373 (9th Cir.1990). As to the distinction between "forfeiture" and "disabling" restraints see Section 11.8, at note 24 et seq.

**57.** Sisters of Mercy Health v. First Bank, 624 N.E.2d 520 (Ind.App.1993); Erickson v. Bank of California, 643 P.2d 670 (Wash.1982); Matter of Dodge's Estate, 281 N.W.2d 447 (Iowa 1979); *Restatement (Third) of Trusts* § 59(b) (1999).

**58.** Schreiber v. Kellogg, 50 F.3d 264 (3d Cir.1995); Evans & Luptak v. Obolensky, 487 N.W.2d 521 (Mich.App.1992); *Restatement (Third) of Trusts* § 59(b) (1999); Unif.Trust Code § 503(a).

**59.** Albertson v. Ryder, 621 N.E.2d 480 (Ohio App.1993) (child support from pension plan); Ex parte Boykin, 656 So.2d 821 (Ala.Civ. App.1994) (child support but not alimony in gross); Council v. Owens, 770 S.W.2d 193 (Ark. App.1989) (alimony); *Restatement (Third) of Trusts* § 59(a) (1999); Cal.Prob.Code § 15305; Unif.Trust Code § 503(a).

**60.** Howard v. Spragins, 350 So.2d 318, 322 (Ala.1977); Hurley v. Hurley, 309 N.W.2d 225, 228 (Mich.App.1981).

**61.** *Restatement, Third, of Trusts*, 59, comm. b (1999). *See also* Council v. Owens, 770 S.W.2d 193, 196 (Ark.App.1989).

**62.** *Id.* at 197.

**63.** *Restatement (Third) of Trusts* § 59, comment b (1999). *See also* Calif.Prob.Code § 15305(b) ("to the extent that the court deems it reasonable"); Council v. Owens, 770 S.W.2d 193, 197 (Ark.App.1989).

If the trust itself has a claim against a beneficiary, *e.g.*, for defalcations while the beneficiary was serving as a trustee, the beneficiary's interest can be reached to satisfy the claim despite a spendthrift provision.[64]

The question whether tort claims should be subject to a spendthrift provision has been discussed in the literature, but there is little case law, perhaps because of the prevalence of liability insurance. In a recent case in which the beneficiary of a spendthrift trust had seriously injured a man by drunken driving, the court held that the spendthrift provision did not immunize the beneficiary's interest. It cited a tort victim's lack of opportunity to investigate the tortfeasor's credit,[65] and the policy reflected in the federal Bankruptcy Act, which denies discharges for claims "based on 'willful and malicious' injuries."[66] The Restatement approves the result in this case, but the Reporter's Note suggests that the case was overturned by later legislation in the state allowing spendthrift provisions with a stated exception only for self-settled trusts.[67] A recurring problem in interpreting statutes is whether a reference to *some* situations where spendthrift provisions are not recognized precludes courts from creating other exceptions. The United States Supreme Court, when a union sought to reach the pension funds of an official who had stolen money from the union, refused "to approve any generalized equitable exception-either for employee malfeasance or for criminal misconduct—to ERISA's prohibition on the assignment or alienation of pension benefits."[68] The exceptions listed in the Restatement for spendthrift trusts, on the other hand, are expressly stated to be "not exclusive," because "special circumstances or evolving policy may justify recognition of others."[69]

Liens for unpaid federal taxes are held generally to override a spendthrift or protective provision.[70] The Restatement refers generally to "governmental claimants * * * to the extent provided by federal law or an applicable state statute."[71]

### *Self-Settled Trusts*

Creditors can reach any interest of the settlor of a trust notwithstanding a spendthrift provision. This is well-settled by case law, and many statutes so provide.[72] Dean Griswold questioned why the law "allows a man to hold the bounty of others free from the claims of his creditors, but denies the same immunity to his interest in property which he has accumulated by his own

**64.** *Restatement (Third) of Trusts* § 59, comment a (1999).

**65.** Hirsch suggests that "unsophisticated trade creditors-plumbers and small service providers * * * may reasonably be categorized as involuntary creditors" also entitled to break through a spendthrift restraint. Hirsch, *supra* note 16, at 82.

**66.** Sligh v. First Nat. Bank of Holmes County, 704 So.2d 1020, 1028 (Miss.1997). Ga. Code Ann. § 53–12–28(c) exempts "tort judgments" generally from the bar of a spendthrift provision.

**67.** *Restatement, Third, of Trusts* § 59, comm. a, Reporter's Note (1999).

**68.** Guidry v. Sheet Metal Workers Nat'l Pension Fund, 493 U.S. 365, 376 (1990).

**69.** *Restatement, Third, of Trusts* § 59, comm. a (1999).

**70.** United States v. Grimm, 865 F.Supp. 1303 (N.D.Ind.1994); Bank One Ohio Trust Co., N.A. v. United States, 80 F.3d 173 (6th Cir.1996).

**71.** *Restatement, Third, of Trusts* § 59, comm. a (1999). *See also* Cal.Prob.Code § 15306(a) (reimbursement of the state or local public entity for support furnished the beneficiary); Ga.Code Ann. § 53–12–28(c) ("governmental claims"); Unif.Trust Code § 503(b).

**72.** *Restatement (Third) of Trusts* § 58(2) (1999); Calif.Prob.Code § 15304; Matter of Shurley, 115 F.3d 333 (5th Cir.1997); Speed v. Speed, 430 S.E.2d 348 (Ga.1993); Wilson v. Dixon, 598 N.E.2d 158 (Ohio App.1991).

efforts."[73] Perhaps "self-settled spendthrift trusts would offer a socially desirable means of self-protection * * * to persons who suddenly acquire unaccustomed wealth."[74] The reasons generally advanced for not allowing them—*e.g.* a debtor should not be allowed to "have his cake and eat it too"[75]—apply equally to *all* spendthrift trusts, so the special status of self-settled trusts is puzzling, particularly since the ERISA's immunity of pension plans from creditors includes plans built up by contributions of the employee-beneficiary.[76]

Perhaps the divergent treatment of self-settled trusts and those created by others arises from the fact that the latter do not withdraw assets from the reach of creditors which would otherwise be available to them. If spendthrift trusts were not allowed, settlors could disinherit improvident relatives and their creditors would be no better off. But if potential settlors, because they are not allowed to provide spendthrift protection for themselves, refrain from creating the trust, the property would remain available to their creditors.

The special rule for self-settled trusts occasionally gives rise to the question "who *was* the settlor of the trust?" Form is not determinative. For example, an employee who had been injured in an accident settled his claim with an insurance company which gave him an unassignable annuity. When the employee later went into bankruptcy, the annuity was held to be part of his bankruptcy estate.

> The settlor cannot create a spendthrift trust for his own benefit. * * * Instead of pursuing his claim for personal injuries, Ronald Jordan agreed to exchange his cause of action for cash payments [and] * * * agreed that the money owing to him under the settlement be placed in a trust that was beyond the reach of his creditors. * * * He was the settlor of the trust. 'One who furnishes the consideration necessary to induce another to create a trust is the settlor of the trust when it is created.'[77]

However, this reasoning has not been extended to spouses who accept a spendthrift trust created by the other spouse's will instead of taking an elective share of the testator's estate.[78]

The general refusal to allow self-settled spendthrift trusts is not world wide. "More than a half-dozen nations compete for foreign investment by ... providing havens for judgment debtors from their foreign creditors ... by validating self-settled spendthrift trusts." According to one estimate "this

**73.** Griswold, *supra* note 33, § 474. *See also id.* § 557. However, Griswold's model statute restates the general rule. *Id.* § 565.

**74.** Note, 64 Colum.L.Rev. 1323, 1332 (1964). *See also* Costigan, *Those Protective Trusts Which are Miscalled 'Spendthrift Trusts,'* 22 Calif.L.Rev. 471, 492 (1934); Hirsch, *supra* note 16, at 83 (restriction on self-settled spendthrift trust "makes no sense").

**75.** Matter of Shurley, 115 F.3d 333, 337 (5th Cir.1997).

**76.** Patterson v. Shumate, 504 U.S. 753 (1992) (exemption under ERISA does not depend on plan qualifying as spendthrift trust under state law). *See also* Ga.Code Ann. § 53–12–28(d) (spendthrift provision in a pension trust is valid "even if the beneficiary is also the settlor of the trust"); Ind.Code § 30–4–3–2(c).

**77.** In re Jordan, 914 F.2d 197, 198–99 (9th Cir.1990). *See also* Speed v. Speed, 430 S.E.2d 348 (Ga.1993); Wilson v. Dixon, 598 N.E.2d 158 (Ohio App.1991); *Restatement, Third, of Trusts* § 58, comm. f (1999).

**78.** American Security and Trust Co. v. Utley, 382 F.2d 451 (D.C.Cir.1967). *Restatement, Third, of Trusts* § 58, comm. f agrees, but suggests that in community property states the result may be different, and that an heir may be deemed the settlor of a spendthrift trust created to settle a will contest.

offshore trust industry already administers a trillion dollars in assets." The author discusses various strategies creditors might invoke to reach such assets but concludes that they are not likely to succeed.[79]

### *Voluntary Transfers*

Interests in a trust without a spendthrift provision are normally transferable by the beneficiaries; if the interest does not expire at the beneficiary's death (as would an interest for the beneficiary's life), it passes by testate or intestate succession just like a legal interest owned by a decedent.[80]

Spendthrift provisions typically bar transfers by the beneficiary as well as claims by the beneficiary's creditors. According to the Restatement, "for reasons of policy, a spendthrift restraint that seeks only to prevent creditors from reaching the beneficiary's interests, while allowing the beneficiary to transfer the interest, is invalid."[81] There is case law to the contrary, however.[82] Even the Restatement allows beneficiaries of spendthrift trusts to disclaim or release their interest[83] on the theory that because the disposition of the released interest is "supplied by the settlor, * * * not by the renouncing beneficiary," releases do not "involve the type of risks that concern a settlor."[84] A release can give beneficiaries "flexibility * * * to deal with changing circumstances."[85] For example, a spendthrift restraint may prevent a beneficiary who later falls into a high tax bracket from giving away her interest in order to reduce income taxes.[86] New York and Delaware have alleviated this problem by statute. New York allows beneficiaries, despite a spendthrift clause, to assign income in excess of $10,000 a year to a spouse or relatives.[87] A Delaware statute allows the beneficiary of a spendthrift trust to assign up to 50% of the income to charity.[88]

If a beneficiary purports to assign an unassignable interest, the assignment can be revoked, but if the beneficiary does so, a trustee who has been paying to the assignee is protected from liability for such prior payments.[89]

### *Planning*

**79.** LoPucki, *The Death of Liability*, 106 Yale L.J. 1, 33 (1996).

**80.** *Restatement, Third, of Trusts* § 51, 55 (1996). *But see* In re Raymond W. George Trust, 986 P.2d 427 (Mont.1999), holding that an apparently vested remainder was not transmissible because a statute said that "beneficiaries take no interest in the [trust] property."

**81.** *Restatement, Third, of Trusts* § 58, comm. b (1999). *See also* Unif.Trust Code § 502(a).

**82.** Bank of New England v. Strandlund, 529 N.E.2d 394 (Mass.1988). *See also* Hirsch, *supra* note 16, at 8 (rights of creditors and voluntary alienation "raise different policy concerns and ought to be addressed independently").

**83.** *Restatement, Third, of Trusts* § 58, comm. c (1999). As to disclaimers see also Uniform Probate Code § 2–801(a); Cal.Prob. Code § 286.

**84.** An attempt by a beneficiary to transfer his interest to another can not qualify as a renunciation. Lundgren v. Hoglund, 711 P.2d 809, 814 (Mont.1985). See also Section 2.8, note 63.

**85.** *Restatement, Third, of Trusts* § 58, Rep. note.

**86.** Howard v. Chapman, 241 N.E.2d 492 (Ill.App.1968) (refusing to allow the beneficiary of a spendthrift trust with an income of over $200,000 to assign her interest).

**87.** N.Y.EPTL § 7–1.5(b)(1). A broader power to assign income may be given by the terms of the trust. *Id.* § 7–1.5(a)(1).

**88.** Wilmington Trust Co. v. Carpenter, 168 A.2d 306 (Del.1961).

**89.** *Restatement (Third) of Trusts* § 58, comment d (1999); Matter of Will of Link, 462 N.Y.S.2d 582 (Surr.1983).

Many lawyers routinely insert spendthrift provisions in all trusts.[90] This is a questionable practice, because it may prevent a desirable transfer of income by a beneficiary in a high income tax bracket. On the other hand, the provision can serve to prevent improvident transfers and the unwise use of credit. It is difficult to resolve these competing considerations, since settlors of long-term trusts cannot know whether the beneficiaries—*e.g.*, young children or others still unborn—will turn out to be spendthrifts.

The choice of whether or not to use a spendthrift clause should depend upon the purpose of the trust. If a settlor wants property to be managed by a trustee for children until they reach age 30, a spendthrift provision prevents a child from frustrating this goal by selling his interest before the trust terminates. On the other hand, when assets are put in trust only in order to keep them out of the beneficiary's estate at death, a spendthrift provision may serve no useful purpose, and prevent a desirable termination of the trust if circumstances change.[91]

A discretionary trust may better achieve the settlor's goals than a fixed income spendthrift trust. Discretionary trusts may be effective against claims like alimony which prevail over a spendthrift provision.[92] They also avoid the problem of an unassignable income interest held by a beneficiary in a high tax bracket, since the trustee of a discretionary trust can take account of tax consequences in deciding how to distribute income.

### *Insurance and Pensions*

The common law generally held that provisions barring alienation of property were against public policy. Spendthrift trusts are (in America) considered distinguishable because the trustee in this situation normally has a power of sale over the property in the trust, and so it is not kept out of commerce.[93]

Benefits paid in installments under insurance policies, including annuities, are not technically trusts[94] but they have many similar characteristics and purposes. "Just as a restraint on the alienation of the interest of a beneficiary under a trust may be valid, * * * so a restraint on the interest of the interest of the beneficiary of an insurance policy may be valid" since the same policy applies to both.[95] An anti-assignment provision in an annuity has been held effective despite the UCC's general prohibition of terms in a contract barring assignment because the UCC excepts insurance.[96]

**90.** J. Farr & J. Wright, *An Estate Planner's Handbook* 451 (4th ed. 1979); Hirsch, *supra* note 16, at 3.

**91.** As to the effect of a spendthrift provision in barring trust termination see Section 9.6, at note 61 et seq.

**92.** Compare Cal.Prob.Code § 15305 (b) and (c).

**93.** Broadway Nat. Bank v. Adams, 133 Mass. 170 (1882). *See also Restatement (Second) of Property (Donative Transfers)* Introductory Note to Chapter 4 (1983). However, if a "trustee" has "no active responsibilities and hence is purely a passive holder of the legal title," the special exemption for trusts does not apply. *Id.* § 4.1, comm. c. For further discussion of restraints on alienation see Section 11.8, on a trustee's power of sale, Section 12.6.

**94.** *Restatement, Third, of Trusts* § 5, comm. k (1996).

**95.** *Restatement, Second, Trusts* 12, comm. k (1959). *See also* N.Y.EPTL § 7–1.5(a)(2). In Drewes v. Schonteich, 31 F.3d 674 (8th Cir. 1994), a nonassignable annuity was held to be a "trust" and thus excludable from the annuitant's bankruptcy estate.

**96.** Henderson v. Roadway Express, 720 N.E.2d 1108 (Ill.App.1999); Green v. Safeco Life Ins. Co., 727 N.E.2d 393 (Ill.App.2000). The annuities in these cases arose out of structured settlements, and are hard to distinguish from self-settled trusts.

Of particular importance, in view of the vast number of persons entitled to pension benefits, is the federal Employee Retirement Income Security Act of 1974 (ERISA) which covers most pension plans and requires that benefits under the plan may not be assigned.[97] The limitations on spendthrift trusts as to claims for alimony and child support have counterparts with respect to pensions; for example, ERISA allows spouses to garnish pension benefits in order to collect a maintenance obligation.[98] The protection against creditors does not extend to money after it is distributed to the beneficiary.[99] However, the ineffectiveness of spendthrift provisions as to the settlor of a trust is not matched by a like restriction on pension plans to which a beneficiary has contributed.

## § 13.2 Joint Tenancy and Insurance

### *Joint Tenancy*

Traditionally, property in joint tenancy can not be reached by creditors of a deceased tenant, even those with liens. For example, a husband owned land in joint tenancy with his wife. After a creditor obtained a judgment against the husband and attached the property, the husband died. Since the creditor's judgment lien attached only to the husband's interest, it terminated when he died.[1] The result would have been the same in many states even if the husband had mortgaged or pledged the property,[2] although this rule has been changed by statute in some states.[3] If a lien is foreclosed by sale before the joint tenant dies, this severs the joint tenancy so the creditor prevails.[4]

This rule seems unfair to creditors, but sophisticated creditors can protect themselves by getting all joint tenants to sign a note when they extend credit.[5] Professor Langbein has written

> Will substitutes do impair the mechanism by which probate protects creditors ... Whereas probate directs all assets and all claimants into a common pot, the nonprobate system disperses assets widely and facilitates transfer without creditors' knowledge. If modern creditors had needed to use probate very much, they would have applied their considerable political muscle to suppress the nonprobate system. Instead, they

**97.** 29 U.S.C. § 1056(d).

**98.** 29 U.S.C. § 1056(d)(3); Albertson v. Ryder, 621 N.E.2d 480 (Ohio App.1993); Hogle v. Hogle, 732 N.E.2d 1278 (Ind.App.2000).

**99.** Brosamer v. Mark, 561 N.E.2d 767 (Ind.1990).

§ 13.2

**1.** Irvin L. Young Foundation, Inc. v. Damrell, 511 A.2d 1069 (Me.1986). *See also* Sherman County Bank v. Lonowski, 289 N.W.2d 189 (Neb.1980); Park State Bank v. McLean, 660 P.2d 13 (Colo.App.1982); Matter of Clancy, 425 N.W.2d 772 (Mich.App.1988). *But see* Granwell v. Granwell, 228 N.E.2d 779 (N.Y. 1967) (treating joint account as a fraudulent conveyance); Rupp v. Kahn, 55 Cal.Rptr. 108 (App.1966).

**2.** Webster v. Mauz, 702 P.2d 297 (Colo. App.1985); Harms v. Sprague, 473 N.E.2d 930 (Ill.1984); In re Certificates of Deposit, 569 N.E.2d 484 (Ohio 1991); Kalk v. Security Pacific Bank Washington, 894 P.2d 559 (Wash. 1995). *Contra*, Heffernan v. Wollaston Credit Union, 567 N.E.2d 933, 939 (Mass.App.1991).

**3.** Wis.Stat. § 700.24; Conn.Gen.Stat. § 47–14e. If a state follows the theory that execution of a mortgage conveys "title" to the mortgagee, the mortgage severs the joint tenancy even if it is later paid off. Mattis, *Joint Tenancy: Notice of Severance; Mortgages and Survivorship,* 7 N.Ill.U.L.Rev. 41, 47–48 (1986).

**4.** Jolley v. Corry, 671 P.2d 139 (Utah 1983).

**5.** Bahler v. Doenges, 499 N.E.2d 35 (Ohio App.1986) (land held by the entireties subject to liens against both spouses).

have acquiesced without a struggle ... [because] the data processing revolution has virtually eliminated the problem toward which much of the debt-resolving phase of probate procedure has been oriented.[6]

Nevertheless, the claim-avoiding effect of joint tenancy seems particularly unjust to tort claimants who have no chance to protect themselves by getting security.[7] The original Uniform Probate Code subjected joint and other multiple party bank accounts to creditors' claims if the decedent debtor's probate estate was insufficient to satisfy them.[8] This provision was not extended to securities registered in TOD form when the Code authorized this form of nonprobate transfer in 1989.[9] Thus a distinction was drawn between an account with a bank and one with a stock broker.[10]

In 1998 a new provision was added, Uniform Probate Code § 6–102 which subjects more beneficiaries of nonprobate transfers to liability to the extent of the property received if the debtor's probate estate is insufficient to satisfy claims. The protection given to creditors by this provision is not as extensive as that given to disinherited spouses because "creditors are better able to fend for themselves than financially disadvantaged mates."[11] For example, survivorship interests in joint tenancy in real estate are expressly excluded from the reach of creditors of a deceased joint tenant.

Creditors who wish to invoke this provision cannot do so directly; they must notify the personal representative to proceed on their behalf. This prevents a free-for-all among creditors and allows the statutory priorities in paying claims of an insolvent estate to control.[12]

Subjecting nonprobate transfers to creditors' claims can have unpleasant consequences for the nonprobate transferees. Suppose, for example, the surviving party to a joint bank account withdraws and spends the funds without notice that the decedent died insolvent. This is unlikely to happen when property passes through probate, because the property usually stays in administration until all claims against the estate are ascertained and paid.[13] To guard against undue hardship to nonprobate transferees, the UPC imposes a limit of one year from the decedent's death on claim enforcement against a non-probate transfer.[14]

**6.** Langbein, *The Nonprobate Revolution and the Future of the Law of Succession,* 97 Harv.L.Rev. 1108, 1124–25 (1984). *See also* Prefatory Note to Uniform Probate Code § 6–102 (1998) ("commercial creditors ... have demonstrated lack of interest in probate law protections").

**7.** Effland, *Rights of Creditors in Non-Probate Assets,* 48 Mo.L.Rev. 431–32 (1983).

**8.** Uniform Prob.Code § 6–107. Section 6–215 of the 1989 version is similar.

**9.** McGovern, *Nonprobate Transfers under the Revised Uniform Probate Code,* 55 Alb. L.Rev. 1329, 1347 (1992).

**10.** Estate of Reed, 681 A.2d 460 (Me.1996) (UPC does not allow creditors to reach funds in decedent's brokerage account); Berg v. D.D.M., 603 N.W.2d 361, 365 (Minn.App.1999). But in Russell v. Posey County Dept. of Pub. Welf., 471 N.E.2d 1209 (Ind.App.1984), a creditor was allowed to reach payments due under a payable-on-death provision in a land sale contract.

**11.** Uniform Probate Code § 6–102, Comment. As to the augmented estate for the spouse's elective share under the UPC see Section 3.7, at note 29 et seq.

**12.** As to these see Section 13.3, at note 5 et seq.

**13.** However, Uniform Probate Code § 3–909 contemplates recovery from a distributee when property is improperly distributed. Cal. Prob.Code § 11622 allows courts to require a bond from persons who receive an early distribution "conditioned on payment of the distributee's proper share of the debts of the estate."

**14.** Uniform Probate Code § 6–102(h). Cal. Prob.Code § 19100 allows the trustee of a revocable trust to cut off claims after 30 days by appropriate notice to creditors, by analogy to the non-claim statutes governing claims in probate. See the next section.

***During Lifetime***

Claims of creditors to assets held in joint tenancy have also been a source of problems while all the parties are still living. Suppose that a husband puts some of his money in a joint account with his wife who contributes nothing to the account. Can her creditors reach the account? Under the Uniform Probate Code a joint account belongs to the parties "in proportion to the net contributions by each to the sums on deposit, unless there is clear and convincing evidence of a different intent."[15] This provision has been widely copied even in states which have not enacted the UPC as a whole.[16] It assumes that persons who put money into a joint account normally do not intend to make a present gift of the funds but use it rather as a will substitute. Therefore creditors of a non-contributing party should have no more claim to the account while the depositor is still living than creditors of a devisee under a will of a testator who is still alive. Most courts have reached this result without a statute,[17] but the result is not always clear. The government was allowed to reach an account in the names of "Roy or Ruby or Neva Reeves" to satisfy a claim for taxes owed by Roy even though it was uncertain whether any money in the account belonged to him. Because each party was authorized to draw on the account, the court held that Roy had a "right to property" sufficient to support a levy under the Internal Revenue Code.[18]

In another case a wife's creditor attached funds in a joint account in the names of the wife and her husband. Because the wife was authorized to withdraw all the funds from the account, they were remitted to the creditor. The husband then sued the bank, but the court rejected his claim that the bank had "a duty to determine the net contributions that each party had made to the account." By putting his wife's name on the account, the husband had "assumed the risk that his wife would have unpaid bills that her creditors would satisfy by court action." The court bemoaned the fact that "all too frequently the parties entering into this type of contractual arrangement ... are not really apprised of all the ramifications."[19] In community property states, use of the joint tenancy form may create a presumption that the property is community and thus available to any creditor of the community.[20] The Uniform Probate Code presumes that when parties are married, their contributions to the account were equal,[21] but omits to state a presumption when the parties are not married to each other. However, when the bank itself has a claim against a party, the parties are presumed to have equal shares absent contrary proof.[22] Some courts presume that the account belongs entirely to the debtor, in the absence of proof that the other party contributed to it, since the depositors "are in a much better position than the judgment creditor to know the pertinent facts."[23]

**15.** Uniform Prob.Code § 6–211(b).

**16.** *E.g.* Cal.Prob.Code § 5301.

**17.** General Motors Acceptance Corp. v. Deskins, 474 N.E.2d 1207 (Ohio App.1984); Yakima Adjustment Service, Inc. v. Durand, 622 P.2d 408 (Wash.App.1981); *cf.* Beehive State Bank v. Rosquist, 484 P.2d 1188 (Utah 1971).

**18.** United States v. National Bank of Commerce, 472 U.S. 713 (1985).

**19.** Ingram v. Hocking Valley Bank, 708 N.E.2d 232, 239 (Ohio App.1997).

**20.** Swink v. Fingado, 850 P.2d 978 (N.M. 1993). *See also* Cal.Prob.Code § 5305 (when parties to a joint account are married, it is presumed to be community property).

**21.** Uniform Probate Code § 6–211(b).

**22.** *Id.* § 6–227. *See also* Wilson v. Morrison, 703 P.2d 314 (Wash.App.1985).

**23.** Browning & Herdrich Oil Co., Inc. v. Hall, 489 N.E.2d 988 (Ind.App.1986). *See also* Baker v. Baker, 710 P.2d 129 (Okl.App.1985); Hancock v. Stockmens Bank & Trust Co., 739

The creation of a joint tenancy in land is more likely to be viewed as a present gift to a tenant who does not contribute to the cost of acquisition.[24] When a mother bought land and put title in the names of herself and her sons, a creditor of one of the sons was allowed to execute on his interest. The mother's claim that "she never intended to give her sons any present interest in the property [but] only for them to take the property upon her death" did not matter, since either party can destroy a joint tenancy by severance; an execution on the son's interest "would sever the joint tenancy, which would be converted into a tenancy in common."[25]

### *Tenancy By the Entirety*

In some states when land is held jointly by two spouses as tenants by the entirety, creditors of one spouse cannot reach it. For example, when a couple owned their home as "tenants by the entirety," even after the home was sold, the husband's creditors could not reach the proceeds. Indiana law governed and Indiana still recognizes tenancy by the entirety in which neither spouse's interest can be seized by his or her creditors.[26] "This is also true of the proceeds from the sale of property so held, as long as they are left intact * * * although normally there can be no tenancy by the entirety in personalty."[27] Some states no longer recognize tenancy by the entirety,[28] and it is recognized, if at all, only between spouses.[29]

### *Insurance*

Many states exempt insurance policies in whole or in part from claims of the insured's creditors. In this respect insurance has advantages over trusts in some cases. If I create a revocable trust, in most states my creditors can reach the trust assets during my lifetime and at the time of my death.[30] But if I use the same assets to buy insurance on my life, even though I retain the right to alter the policy, my creditors are restricted in reaching the cash surrender value during my life[31] or the proceeds at my death in many states. For example, a man took out insurance on his life, designating a girl friend as the beneficiary. He died insolvent and his administrator (his widow) sought to reach the proceeds to pay claims against the estate. A statute provided:

> All proceeds payable because of the death of the insured* * * to a wife or husband of the insured, or to a child, parent or other person dependent

P.2d 760 (Wyo.1987); Traders Travel Intern., Inc. v. Howser, 753 P.2d 244, 248 (Haw.1988).

**24.** See Section 5.5, at note 42 et seq.

**25.** Remax of Blue Springs v. Vajda & Co., Inc., 708 S.W.2d 804, 806 (Mo.App.1986). *See also* Jones v. Conwell, 314 S.E.2d 61 (Va.1984) (creditor of one joint tenant can compel partition).

**26.** *See also* Central Nat. Bank v. Fitzwilliam, 465 N.E.2d 408 (Ohio 1984); Hinchee v. Security Nat. Bank, 624 P.2d 821 (Alaska 1981); Matter of Savage's Estate, 650 S.W.2d 346 (Mo.App.1983); Effland, *Creditors and Non–Probate Assets,* 48 Mo.L.Rev. 431, 437 (1983).

**27.** Matter of Agnew, 818 F.2d 1284 (7th Cir.1987). *But see* Diss v. Agri Business Intern., Inc., 670 N.E.2d 97, 99 (Ind.App.1996) (half of rental income from entirety property is subject to claims of a spouse's creditors); Coraccio v. Lowell Five Cents Sav. Bank, 612 N.E.2d 650 (Mass.1993) (husband can mortgage property held by the entireties, subject to wife's right of survivorship).

**28.** Lurie v. Sheriff of Gallatin County, 999 P.2d 342 (Mont.2000).

**29.** Traders Travel Intern., Inc. v. Howser, 753 P.2d 244, 247 (Haw.1988).

**30.** See Section 13.1, at note 4 et seq.

**31.** In re Marriage of Gedgaudas, 978 P.2d 677 (Colo.App.1999) (cash surrender value of insurance exempt up to $25,000).

> upon the insured, whether the power to change the beneficiary is reserved to the insured or not, * * * shall be exempt from execution * * * for the debts of the insured* * *[32]

It did not matter that the designated beneficiary here (the insured's girl friend) was not covered by the statute, since "proceeds of life policies payable to a named beneficiary are free from the claims of creditors of the insured apart from any statute."[33] Most states have similar exemptions but many are not so generous. In California, for example, the loan value of unmatured life insurance policies is exempt from creditors only up to $8,000, and the proceeds of matured policies only "to the extent reasonably necessary for the support of the judgment debtor and the spouse and dependents of the judgment debtor."[34] The Uniform Probate Code allows creditors to reach "nonprobate transfers" when the probate estate is insufficient to pay claims, but this is subject to any statutory exemptions for insurance.[35]

When insurance proceeds are paid to the estate of the insured rather than a named beneficiary they usually become fully subject to claims of creditors of the estate.[36] But in some states the privileged position of insurance vis a vis creditors can be preserved if it is paid to a trustee designated in the insured's will.[37]

### *Promises Made at Divorce*

The following situation frequently arises: At the time of a divorce *H* promises to designate *W* or his children or both as beneficiary(ies) of an insurance policy on his life to assure their continued support if he dies. He later remarries and, in violation of his agreement, changes the beneficiary of the policy to his second wife, who, after he dies, tries to bar the contractual claim of the first family to the proceeds by citing an exemption of insurance proceeds from creditors of the insured. Courts usually avoid the exemption, and impose a constructive trust on the proceeds.

> Most courts have concluded that a promise, made as part of a separation agreement, to maintain a policy of insurance designating either spouse or children as beneficiaries vests in such spouse or children an equitable interest in the policy which is superior to that of a stranger to the agreement who was subsequently named gratuitously as beneficiary. * * * Although the second wife who was named beneficiary was innocent throughout, * * * no person shall be unjustly enriched at the expense of another.[38]

32. In re Estate of Grigg, 545 N.E.2d 160, 161 (Ill.App.1989). The statute also covers the cash value of the policy during the insured's lifetime but contains an exception for "premiums paid in fraud of creditors."

33. In re Estate of Grigg, 545 N.E.2d 160, 161 (Ill.App.1989).

34. Cal.Code Civ.Proc. § 704.100; *Cf.* 11 U.S.C. § 522(d)(8) (federal exemption in bankruptcy of loan value of unmatured policy up to $4,000). In Citizens Nat. Bank of Evansville v. Foster, 668 N.E.2d 1236 (Ind.1996), the court limited the validity of a similar statute because the state constitution only authorized exemptions of a "reasonable amount."

35. Uniform Probate Code § 6–102(b) and comment, par. 2.

36. Estate of Chiesi v. First Citizens Bank, 613 N.E.2d 14 (Ind.1993).

37. Cal.Prob.Code § 6324.

38. Bailey v. Prudential Ins. Co. of America, 705 N.E.2d 389, 392–93 (Ohio App.1997). *See also* Aetna Life Ins. Co. v. Bunt, 754 P.2d 993 (Wash.1988); IDS Life Ins. Co. v. Sellards, 527 N.E.2d 426 (Ill.App.1988). For the rights of trust beneficiaries against donees from the trustee see Section 12.8, at note 185 et seq.

Similar reasoning has been applied to death benefits under a pension plan in order to avoid an exemption from attachment of such benefits by ordinary creditors.[39]

The constructive trust rationale presents difficulties if the agreement does not refer to a specific policy,[40] or if the promisor simply lets the designated policy lapse, since a trust requires an identifiable *res*.[41] However, many courts are not meticulous about this. For example, a husband agreed to maintain his "present insurance on his life" and to designate his wife as beneficiary. When he died, his second wife was the designated beneficiary of another policy which the husband took out after the divorce. The court held that the "mere substitution of policies, or even substitutions of insurance companies did not defeat the first wife's equitable interest."[42]

Such agreements are sometimes unclear as to the rights of the parties when the insurance proceeds exceed the insured's support obligation at the time of his death. For example, an agreement required a father to name his daughter as beneficiary "until she attains the age of twenty-two (22) years for the purpose of insuring her education." The daughter was 18 when her father died. The court held, over a dissent, that "since the agreement in this case unambiguously stated the purpose (as education) for which the insurance proceeds would be provided," any funds not needed for this purpose would pass to the beneficiary whom the father had later designated.[43] But an agreement that the husband should maintain "at all times" an insurance policy with his daughter as beneficiary was held to be enforceable by the daughter even though she was 32 when her father died. "In this case it was clear that the parties intended that the Daughter's benefit extended beyond emancipation."[44]

One court made an "equitable adjustment" in an agreement involving a policy geared to the insured's salary. After the divorce he remarried, had another child and received a promotion, thus raising the value of the insurance proceeds. The court held that if the husband had

> received an increase in salary by reason of a promotion or reassignment or by undertaking additional work duties after the date of divorce, * * * the consequent enhancement of value in his life insurance benefit * * * [was] attributable to his second marriage rather than his first. It follows that the benefit of such an enhancement should inure to the spouse and child of the second marriage.[45]

39. Smithberg v. Illinois Mun. Retirement Fund, 735 N.E.2d 560 (Ill.2000).

40. Sullivan for Herald v. Aetna Life & Cas., 764 P.2d 1390 (Wash.App.1988). *But see* Bernal v. Nieto, 943 P.2d 1338 (N.M.App. 1997).

41. Oregon Pacific State Ins. Co. v. Jackson, 986 P.2d 650 (Or.App.1999); Weiner v. Goldberg, 306 S.E.2d 660 (Ga.1983).

42. Appelman v. Appelman, 410 N.E.2d 199 (Ill.App.1980). *See also* Zobrist v. Bennison, 486 S.E.2d 815 (Ga.1997)

43. Aetna Life Ins. Co. v. Hussey, 590 N.E.2d 724, 728 (Ohio 1992). *See also* Bainter v. Bainter, 590 N.E.2d 1134 (Ind.App.1992) (adult children have no claim to proceeds); Will of Tanenblatt, 609 N.Y.S.2d 532 (Sur.1994) (even though insurance beneficiary not changed, insured's estate can recover amount in excess of support obligation which it was intended to secure).

44. Miller v. Partridge, 734 N.E.2d 1061, 1065 (Ind.App.2000). *See also* Thomas v. Studley, 571 N.E.2d 454 (Ohio App.1989) (agreement *not* limited to securing the insured's support obligation.

45. Della Terza v. Estate of Della Terza, 647 A.2d 180, 182 (N.J.Super.A.D.1994). Compare the problem of the rights of a second spouse of the promisor in a contractual will. Section 4.9, at note 42 et seq.

The constructive trust rationale used in these cases may be superseded by federal law if the insured was a federal employee. The United States Supreme Court held that a serviceman's former wife and children could not enforce a promise to give them the proceeds of a policy because "Congress has insulated the proceeds of SGILA insurance from attack or seizure by any claimant other than the beneficiary designated by the insured."[46] This reasoning has been extended to policies of civilian employees of the federal government.[47]

## § 13.3 Probate Estate

### *Survival*

The death of one of the parties sometimes terminates a claim. For example, a man hired to be "musical director" for a singer for one year was not allowed to claim the balance of his salary when the singer died during the year. "Where one engages another to render services to him personally for a specified period of time, his death before the end of the agreed time terminates the contract."[1] In some states claims for punitive damages do not survive the tort feasor's or the victim's death.[2] Most claims survive death, however. Thus a tenant's estate is liable for rent if the tenant dies during the term of a lease.[3] In some states there are special evidentiary hurdles that must be overcome to establish a claim against a decedent's estate.[4] The rest of this section assumes the existence of an otherwise enforceable claim.

### *Priorities and Preferences*

One of the primary duties of a personal representative is to pay claims against the estate. If its assets are insufficient to pay all claims, the law establishes priorities among creditors. Section 3–805 of the Uniform Probate Code, for example, requires payment in the following order: (1) expenses of administration, (2) funeral expenses, (3) debts and taxes preferred under federal law,[5] (4) medical expenses of the decedent's last illness,[6] (5) claims preferred under other state laws, (6) other claims. The execution of judgments against a decedent are stayed by death, but not the enforcement of mortgages or other liens,[7] which come ahead of even administration expenses.[8] If the lien

**46.** Ridgway v. Ridgway, 454 U.S. 46, 63 (1981). *See also* Concepcion v. Concepcion, 722 N.E.2d 176, 182 (Ohio App.1999).

**47.** Dean v. Johnson, 881 F.2d 948 (10th Cir.1989); Metropolitan Life Ins. Co. v. Potter, 533 So.2d 589 (Ala.1988); Mercier v. Mercier, 721 F.Supp. 1124 (D.N.D.1989). *But cf.* Rollins v. Metropolitan Life Ins. Co., 912 F.2d 911 (7th Cir.1990) (constructive trust prevails when new spouse not specifically named as beneficiary of FEGLI policy).

§ 13.3

1. Farnon v. Cole, 66 Cal.Rptr. 673, 675 (App.1968). *See also Restatement (Second) of Contracts* § 262 (1981).

**2.** Doe v. Colligan, 753 P.2d 144 (Alaska 1988); Lohr v. Byrd, 522 So.2d 845 (Fla.1988); *Restatement (Second) of Torts* § 925, comm. d (1979). *But cf.* Portwood v. Copper Valley Elec. Ass'n, 785 P.2d 541 (Alaska 1990) (wrongful death claim for punitive damages allowed).

**3.** Sherman v. Carlin, 546 N.E.2d 433 (Ohio App.1988).

**4.** Kohler v. Armstrong, 758 P.2d 407, 409 (Or.App.1988) (claim must be corroborated by independent evidence).

**5.** The preference for administrative and funeral expenses has been upheld despite a federal statute giving priority to federal claims. Martin v. Dennett, 626 P.2d 473 (Utah 1981).

**6.** In In re Estate of McVietty, 727 N.E.2d 653 (Ill.App.2000), a nursing home was not allowed a priority higher than the one allotted by statute with respect to insurance payable to the decedent to cover nursing home care.

**7.** Uniform Probate Code § 3–812; Lundgren v. Gaudiane, 782 P.2d 285, 288 (Alaska 1989).

**8.** Estate of Lammerts v. Heritage Bank, 663 N.E.2d 1174 (Ind.App.1996).

is insufficient to satisfy the claim, the mortgagee can claim the balance as a general creditor.[9]

Historically, personal representatives had to follow a similar set of priorities, but within each class they could prefer one creditor over another, *e.g.*, pay their own claims first.[10] Today, however, claims in the same class must receive an equal pro-rata share.[11]

Normally neither the heirs and devisees nor the personal representative are personally liable for claims against the estate.[12] However, a personal representative may incur such liability by neglecting the specified priorities, *i.e.* paying claims "due to negligence or wilful default ... in such manner so as to deprive the injured claimant of priority."[13] The distributees of an insolvent estate may be held liable to the extent of the property they received in the distribution.[14]

### *Non-Claim Statutes*

Personal representatives need to know how many claims exist against an estate; otherwise they may pay a claim in full or distribute to an heir or devisee and later discover that there are not enough assets in the estate to satisfy all claims. An English statute of 1859 allowed them to notify creditors "to send in * * * their Claims against the Estate" within a specified time, after which they could distribute the estate without being liable for claims of which they had no notice.[15]

American states have similar "non-claim" statutes. The Uniform Probate Code allows personal representatives to publish in a newspaper of general circulation a notice to creditors to present their claims within four months "or be forever barred."[16] Such statutes were typical in the United States until 1989 when the Supreme Court in Tulsa Professional Collection Services, Inc. v. Pope,[17] held a similar statute unconstitutional because it barred claims without giving adequate notice. Statutes of limitations bar claims without any notice to the claimant, but they are "self-executing," whereas non-claim statutes are triggered by "significant state action," the probate court's appointment of an executor. Creditors are often unaware of the debtor's death or of the probate proceedings and are unlikely to see "an advertisement in small type inserted in the back pages of a newspaper." Such notice by publication is sufficient only for creditors who are not "reasonably ascertainable" by the personal representative.

**9.** Uniform Probate Code § 3–809.

**10.** F. Maitland, *Equity* 197–98 (1913); W. Blackstone, *Commentaries* *511 (1769). When administration was handled by the church courts, apparently the personal representative had discretion as to the order of paying claims. Helmholz, *Bankruptcy and Probate Jurisdiction Before 1571,* 48 Mo.L.Rev. 415, 425 (1983).

**11.** Uniform Probate Code § 3–805(b).

**12.** Bailey v. Cherokee County Appraisal Dist., 862 S.W.2d 581 (Tex.1993) (heirs not personally liable for property taxes on decedent's property during the period of administration).

**13.** Uniform Probate Code § 3–807(b); *cf.* Estate of Starkweather, 75 Cal.Rptr.2d 766 (App.1998) (administrator liable for failure to notify claimant). Compare the liability of fiduciaries for improper distributions to beneficiaries. Section 12.10, at note 43 et seq.

**14.** Gumm, 93 T.C. 475 (1989); Estate of Berg, 398 N.Y.S.2d 948 (Surr.1977); Uniform Probate Code § 3–909; *cf.* Farm Credit Bank v. Woodring, 851 P.2d 532 (Okl.1993) (distribution by trustee treated as a fraudulent conveyance to beneficiary).

**15.** 22 & 23 Vict. ch. 35, § 29 (1859).

**16.** Uniform Probate Code § 3–801(a).

**17.** 485 U.S. 478 (1988).

On remand, the court decided that the claimant in the case, the hospital in which the decedent died, was reasonably ascertainable.[18] Personal representatives must make "a good-faith search of decedent's personal and business financial records ... The focus should not be on the actual knowledge of the claim by" the personal representative, but rather "on the efforts expended ... in attempting to discover claims."[19] Some unnotified claimants have been barred despite *Tulsa* on the ground that they were not reasonably ascertainable.[20] Other late claims have been rejected because the claimant, although not given notice, had actual knowledge of the administration proceedings.[21] On the other hand, mere knowledge of the decedent's death has been held insufficient to bar a claimant who was not notified of the time within which the claim had to be filed.[22]

The drafters of the Uniform Probate Code responded to the *Tulsa* decision by making the traditional publication of notice to creditors optional, on the ground that it "is quite expensive in some populous areas" and under *Tulsa* "is useless except as to bar unknown creditors."[23] The Code provides for notice "by mail or other delivery" to creditors. Such notice bars creditors within 60 days "after the mailing or other delivery."

The UPC also bars all claims, whether or not notice was given, one year after the decedent's death.[24] In may seem odd that a bar which operates without any notice at all is less objectionable than one which provides inadequate notice, but of course one year is longer than 4 months. In any event, courts have routinely upheld statutes cutting off claims one year after death without regard to notice.[25]

There are several exceptions to the non-claim bar.

1. *Suit Pending.* A claimant who had a suit pending against the decedent at the time of the decedent's death need not present the claim in the estate proceedings under the Uniform Probate Code.[26] Some courts have held otherwise, however, on the ground that personal representatives should not be forced to search the court records to discover suits against the deceased.[27]

If a claimant files suit during the non-claim period, service of process on the personal representative can satisfy the non-claim statute.[28] But creditors

**18.** Matter of Estate of Pope, 808 P.2d 640 (Okl.1990).

**19.** Matter of Estate of Anderson, 615 N.E.2d 1197, 1206 (Ill.App.1993).

**20.** Matter of Estate of Ragsdale, 879 P.2d 1145 (Kan.App.1994); In re Estate of Thompson, 484 N.W.2d 258 (Minn.App.1992).

**21.** Venturi v. Taylor, 41 Cal.Rptr.2d 272, 276 (App.1995); Matter of Estate of Sutherland, 593 N.E.2d 955 (Ill.App.1992).

**22.** In re Estate of Malone, 556 N.E.2d 678 (Ill.App.1990); Matter of Estate of Anderson, 821 P.2d 1169 (Utah 1991). *But see* In re Estate of Reynolds, 970 P.2d 537, 545 (Kan. 1998).

**23.** Uniform Probate Code § 3–801, Comment.

**24.** Uniform Probate Code § 2–803(a).

**25.** Burnett v. Villaneuve, 685 N.E.2d 1103 (Ind.App.1997); In re Estate of Ongaro, 998 P.2d 1097 (Colo.2000); Estate of Kruzynski, 744 A.2d 1054 (Me.2000); In re Estate of Beider, 645 N.E.2d 553 (Ill.App.1994).

**26.** Uniform Probate Code § 3–804(2); Reese v. Reese, 637 P.2d 1183 (Mont.1981).

**27.** In re Worrell's Estate, 442 N.E.2d 211 (Ill.1982). *See also* Fox v. Woods, 382 So.2d 1118 (Ala.1980) (suit pending in a foreign jurisdiction). *But cf.* Berke v. First Nat. Bank & Trust Co., 397 N.E.2d 842 (Ill.1979) (substitution of executor for defendant in pending action satisfies statute).

**28.** Mathe v. Fowler, 469 N.E.2d 89 (Ohio App.1983). *But see* Dodson v. Charter Behav. Health System, 983 S.W.2d 98, 106 (Ark.1998); Cloud ex rel Cloud v. Summers, 991 P.2d 1169, 1176 (Wash.App.1999).

can also "present" a claim so as to satisfy the non-claim bar without filing suit; presentation simply requires delivering or mailing to the personal representative, or filing in court, a written statement of the claim.[29]

2. *Claims arising after death.* Claims which arise after the decedent's death are governed by a special rule. Under the Uniform Probate Code they can be presented within 4 months after performance is due (contracts) or the claim arises (other claims).[30] For example, one Kirkendall had agreed while alive to convey land suitable for the construction of single family residences. His personal representatives conveyed the land after Kirkendall died. Eleven months thereafter the conveyee claimed the land was not suitable. This claim was held not subject to the non-claim limit, because "at the time of Kirkendall's death the contract ... was still executory" and no right of action existed at that time.[31]

Claims which are only potential at the time of the decedent's death are troublesome. For example, a partner guaranteed the debt of a partnership. The partnership defaulted after the partner died. The court allowed a claim on the guaranty after the non-claim period had run, saying:

> The filing of a contingent claim permits the personal representative to set aside assets for future distribution should the claim become absolute; however, the representative is not required to do so.... To reserve against such contingencies may greatly impede the full distribution of an estate ... contrary to the policy of speedy and efficient administration of estates.[32]

Many non-claim statutes, however, expressly apply to claims "whether due, or to become due, absolute or contingent."[33] This requires contingent claims to be *presented,* but they are not necessarily *paid* during administration because it is difficult to ascertain the amount due. Under the Uniform Probate Code the claimant may accept the present value of the claim "taking any uncertainty into account," or can insist on an arrangement for future payment, such as a bond from the distributees of the estate.[34]

3. *Governmental Claims.* The Uniform Probate Code nonclaim provision expressly includes claims by the state or its agencies,[35] but some states treat

**29.** In Caldwell v. Brown, 672 N.E.2d 1037 (Ohio App.1996), a letter sent to the executor's attorney was held to satisfy a similar statute. *See also* In re Estate of Tollison, 463 S.E.2d 611 (S.C.App.1995). But not a letter sent to the decedent under the assumption that he was still alive. In re Estate of Beider, 645 N.E.2d 553 (Ill.App.1994).

**30.** Uniform Probate Code § 3–803(b); In Matter of Estate of Scott, 735 P.2d 924 (Colo. App.1986) (claim for reformation of deed given by executor "arises" only when mistake is discovered).

**31.** Cardwell v. Estate of Kirkendall, 712 N.E.2d 1047, 1049 (Ind.App.1999). *See also* In re Estate of Knott, 615 N.E.2d 357, 359 (Ill. App.1993) (fees of attorney for the estate).

**32.** Security S & L v. Estate of Kite, 857 P.2d 430, 433 (Colo.App.1992). *See also* In re Estate of Morrow, 501 N.E.2d 998 (Ill.App. 1986) (contingent claim not allowable against estate); Priestman v. Elder, 646 N.E.2d 234, 237 (Ohio App.1994) (contingent claims need not be presented until they accrue). *But see* Poleson v. Wills, 998 P.2d 469 (Colo.App.2000) (malpractice claim against lawyer for failure to shield client from liability which arose after lawyer died barred by non-claim statute).

**33.** Uniform Probate Code § 3–803(a).

**34.** Uniform Probate Code § 3–810(b); *cf.* Ind.Code § 29–1–14–8 (if contingent claim becomes absolute after estate distributed creditor can sue distributees); Iowa Code § 633.427 (same); *cf.* Cohen v. Cronin, 346 N.E.2d 524 (N.Y.1976) (fund to pay contingent claim retained when balance of estate distributed).

**35.** Uniform Probate Code § 3–803(a).

them as exceptions.[36] The federal government is not subject to state non-claim statutes,[37] but the Internal Revenue Code contains comparable provisions discharging personal representatives from liability for unpaid taxes for the decedent of which they are not notified within nine months of a request therefor.[38]

4. *Recoupment.* If an estate sues on a claim due to the estate, many courts allow the debtor to assert by recoupment a claim against the estate even if the period allowed by the non-claim statute has expired,[39] but there is also contrary authority.[40]

5. *Insurance.* Most non-claim statutes apply to tort as well as contract claims, but if the tort is covered by liability insurance a special rule applies. Since claims which are "to be satisfied by the insurance proceeds do not affect the interests of the beneficiaries under the estate, ... a failure to file within the statutory period bars only the right to enforce any liability of the estate beyond the limits of the insurance policy."[41]

6. *Devises.* Devisees do not have to file claims to preserve their rights. The line between creditors and devisees is sometimes fuzzy. A claim against an estate for services rendered during the testator's last illness was rejected as untimely even though the will directed the executor "to pay the expenses of my last sickness * * * and all of my other just debts." A creditor does not have to present a claim if a will directs it be paid, but "a general direction in a will for the payment of debts was not enough."[42] On the other hand, a direction in a will that any "property in my name and that of another as joint tenants" pass to the survivor was held to make a person fitting this description a devisee who was not subject to the non-claim statute.[43]

7. *Property.* If an executor erroneously inventories property which did not belong to the testator, the actual owner need not file a claim within the non-claim period to protect her property.[44] The "property" exception has been held to cover claims for specific performance of contracts,[45] including contracts to devise property,[46] and even a claim for rescission by a purchaser who could

**36.** Matter of Estate of Thomas, 743 S.W.2d 74 (Mo.1988); cf. State ex rel. Department of Human Resources v. Payne, 970 P.2d 266 (Or.App.1998) (time limit on suit after rejection of claim by personal representative not applicable to claim by state agency); Cal. Prob.Code §§ 9200 et seq (special time periods prescribed for claims by various "public entities").

**37.** United States v. Summerlin, 310 U.S. 414 (1940).

**38.** Internal Revenue Code §§ 2204, 6905; *cf.* Bank of Kansas City v. District Director, 721 S.W.2d 226 (Mo.App.1986).

**39.** Estate of Ruehl v. Ruehl, 623 N.E.2d 741 (Ohio Mun.1993); In re Estate of Massie, 353 N.W.2d 735 (Neb.1984).

**40.** Imbesi v. Carpenter Realty, 744 A.2d 549 (Md.2000); In re Estate of Kremer, 546 N.E.2d 1047, 1052 (Ill.App.1989).

**41.** Corlett v. Smith, 763 P.2d 1172, 1174–75 (N.M.App.1988). *See also* Matter of Daigle's Estate, 634 P.2d 71 (Colo.1981). *But cf.* Turner v. Lo Shee Pang's Estate, 631 P.2d 1010 (Wash.App.1981) (even claim covered by insurance is barred after 18 months); Scott v. Scott, 918 P.2d 198 (Wyo.1996).

**42.** Matter of Bachand's Estate, 307 N.W.2d 140 (S.D.1981). *See also* Farm Credit Bank v. Brown, 577 N.E.2d 906, 912 (Ill.App. 1991).

**43.** Matter of Estate of Powers, 552 N.W.2d 785, 787 (N.D.1996).

**44.** In re Estate of Kolbinger, 529 N.E.2d 823, 827 (Ill.App.1988); Lewis v. Steinreich, 652 N.E.2d 981, 984 (Ohio 1995); Gottwig v. Blaine, 795 P.2d 1196, 1199 (Wash.App.1990).

**45.** Hackmann v. Dawley, 663 N.E.2d 1342 (Ohio App.1995).

**46.** Matter of Shepley's Estate, 645 P.2d 605 (Utah 1982); O'Steen v. Wineberg's Estate, 640 P.2d 28 (Wash.App.1982); L.G. v. F.G.H., 729 S.W.2d 634 (Mo.App.1987). *But see* Young v. Wheeler, 676 P.2d 748 (Kan.1984); Grossman v. Selewacz, 417 So.2d 728 (Fla.App.1982) (promise to sell unidentifiable property).

trace the price paid.[47] Also, persons holding mortgages and other security interests in estate assets are not required to present their claims unless their security is insufficient and they wish to collect the deficiency from the decedent's other assets.[48]

8. *Estoppel* Sometimes a personal representative is held to be "estopped" to raise the non-claim bar, *e.g.* "where an estate * * * makes representations to the claimant which lead the claimant to believe that it is not necessary to protect his claim by filing a creditor's claim."[49] Other courts, however, have rejected such claims on the ground that "the personal representative is a trustee of the estate for the benefit of its creditors and heirs, and as such cannot by his conduct waive any provision of a statute affecting their substantial rights."[50] The Uniform Probate Code allows personal representatives to "waive any defense of limitations available to the estate" only "with the consent of all whose interests would be affected."[51]

In many respects the non-claim statutes operate more harshly than ordinary statutes of limitations. The latter often do not run until a claimant has reason to know of the claim, or are tolled while a claimant is unable to sue. For example, a prison inmate brought suit against the estate of a guard over three years after the alleged tort occurred, and a few months after the non-claim period expired. The three year statute of limitations was extended due to the plaintiff's imprisonment and so did not bar his claim, but the non-claim statute did, since "there is no extension provided by law for persons having a statutory 'disability.' "[52]

### *Statute of Limitations*

Non-claim statutes resemble statutes of limitations but they have different purposes and each operates independently. A claim which is presented within the limits of a non-claim statute may be dismissed because the statute of limitations has run and vice-versa. If a claim is not yet due—*e.g.,* a note payable in 2005, the non-claim period may expire even before the statute of limitations starts to run, because the former is designed "not to prevent the litigation of stale claims, but to facilitate the speedy settlement of estates."[53]

Special provisions apply to cases where a debtor dies while the statute of limitations is running, since the creditor has no one to sue in this situation until administration of the debtor's estate begins. The Uniform Probate Code, for example, suspends the running of any statute of limitations for 4 months following the decedent's death. Presentation of a claim is treated as "equivalent to commencement of a proceeding," so the statute of limitations stops

**47.** Pay Less Drug Stores v. Bechdolt, 155 Cal.Rptr. 58 (App.1979).

**48.** Uniform Probate Code § 3–803(c)(1); WYHY Federal Credit Union v. Burchell, 643 P.2d 471 (Wyo.1982); Estate of Ripley v. Mortgage One Corp., 16 S.W.3d 593 (Mo.App.1999) (mortgagee entitled to lien on proceeds of sale of mortgaged property despite failure to file claim in time).

**49.** Boyer v. Sparboe, 867 P.2d 1116, 1119–20 (Mont.1994).

**50.** In re Estate of Ongaro, 998 P.2d 1097, 1104 (Colo.2000). *See also* Estate of Decker v. Farm Credit Services, 684 N.E.2d 1137 (Ind. 1997) (court is without power to extend limits of nonclaim statute).

**51.** Uniform Probate Code § 3–802(a).

**52.** In re Estate of Allen, 843 P.2d 781, 784 (Mont.1992). *See also* Matter of Estate of Watson, 896 P.2d 401, 403 (Kan.App.1995) (lack of knowledge of claim does not prevent the non-claim bar).

**53.** State v. Goldfarb, 278 A.2d 818, 821 (Conn.1971).

running when a claim is presented.[54] On the other hand, the Code imposes another limitation: if the personal representative "disallows" a claim which has been timely presented, the claimant must bring proceedings on it within 60 days.[55]

### *Court Approval*

In some states courts closely supervise the payment of claims by personal representatives, like other aspects of administration. In Mississippi claims against an estate must be "registered, probated, and allowed" in court. A personal representative may be surcharged for paying an otherwise valid claim because it was not "probated, allowed and registered."[56] The Uniform Probate Code, on the other hand, in keeping with its goal to simplify administration, allows personal representatives to "pay any just claim which has not been barred, with or without presentation."[57] They can compromise claims if it appears to be "for the best interest of the estate."[58]

Personal representatives may be surcharged for paying an invalid claim,[59] but the Code allows them to "satisfy written charitable pledges of the decedent" even if they are not binding obligations or properly presented "if in the judgment of the personal representative the decedent would have wanted the pledges completed."[60] A will can by appropriate language provide for the payment of other "moral obligations" of the testator which are not legally binding. Some of the most famous cases in contract law involve suits against the promisor's estate which could have been avoided by including such a provision in the decedent's will.[61]

Many states make special provisions for claims of personal representatives against the estate because of the conflict of interest involved. In Ohio personal representatives cannot pay any claims they may have against the estate until the claim has been "proved to and allowed by the probate court" after notice to the decedent's heirs and devisees.[62]

## § 13.4 Claims Arising During Administration

### *Contracts*

**54.** Uniform Probate Code § 3–802. *See also* Brown v. Eiguren, 628 P.2d 299 (Nev. 1981) (can sue within one year of appointment of personal representative if claim not barred when decedent dies); Shearer v. Pla–Boy Inc., 538 N.E.2d 247 (Ind.App.1989).

**55.** Uniform Probate Code § 3–806. *See also* First Interstate Bank v. Haynes, 699 P.2d 1168 (Or.App.1985); Matter of Estate of Levine, 700 P.2d 883 (Ariz.App.1985); Matter of Estate of Mayfield, 771 P.2d 179 (N.M.1989).

**56.** Miss.Code §§ 91–7–151, 91–7–155; Harper v. Harper, 491 So.2d 189 (Miss.1986).

**57.** Uniform Probate Code § 3–807(b). However, they risk being personally liable if they pay before the non-claim period expires and the estate is insolvent.

**58.** Uniform Probate Code § 3–813; Matter of Estate of Vertin, 352 N.W.2d 200 (N.D. 1984). Trustees have a similar power. Uniform Trustees' Powers Act § 3(c)(19); *Restatement (Second) of Trusts* §§ 178, 192 (1959).

**59.** Estate of Sturm, 246 Cal.Rptr. 852 (App.1988) (claims paid which were time-barred); *cf. Restatement (Second) of Trusts* § 178 (1959) (trustee has duty to defend trust against actions).

**60.** Uniform Probate Code § 3–715(4).

**61.** *E.g.*, Webb v. McGowin, 168 So. 196 (Ala.App.1935); Hamer v. Sidway, 27 N.E. 256 (N.Y.1891).

**62.** Ohio Rev.Code §§ 2117.01, 21107.02. *See also* Ind.Code § 29–1–14–17; Iowa Code § 633.431. Compare the need for court authorization for other types of self-dealing. Section 12.9, at note 21 et seq.

A personal representative who makes a contract on behalf of the estate may be personally liable on it. For example, an executor who leased land owned by the estate was subject to suit for breach of an obligation in the lease. A contract made by an executor or administrator "is his personal contract upon which he becomes personally liable * * * even though the debt was incurred for the benefit of the estate and the representative described himself in the contract as an 'executor' or 'administrator.' "[1] Trustees are also personally liable on contracts they make in administering a trust, even though in making the contract they were properly performing their duties.[2] They can avoid such personal liability by an express provision in the contract, but simply signing the contract "as trustee" is not enough according to the Restatement of Trusts, nor is the fact that the trust instrument provides that the trustee shall not be personally liable on such a contract.[3]

Trustees and executors can get reimbursement from the trust or estate for their liability if the contract was properly made, but if the estate is insufficient to cover their liability they may be left "holding the bag."[4]

If a trustee is personally insolvent, the claimant will want to reach the assets of the trust estate. The Restatement allows them to do so "to the extent to which the trustee is entitled to exoneration out of the trust estate."[5] This limitation bars relief to claimants if the trustee is liable to the trust in an amount which exceeds the trustee's right of exoneration. Professor Scott criticized this.

> Where the trustee exceeded his powers in incurring the liability * * * it seems unobjectionable to deny a creditor a right to reach the trust estate. But where the trustee acted within his powers * * * it seems unjust to the creditor to deny him a recovery out of the trust estate merely because in some other matter the trustee has committed a breach of trust subjecting him to a surcharge. * * * The creditor is in no way responsible for that.[6]

The modern trend is to treat trustees like agents who are themselves not liable on contracts which they make on behalf of a principal, but who subject the principal to liability if the agent acted within the scope of his or her authority.[7] The drafters of the Uniform Trusts Act attributed the restriction on trust creditors reaching trust assets to "the ancient distinction between law and equity" and removed it in order to facilitate collection of claims.[8] If a trustee makes a contract "within his powers," the other party can get a

§ 13.4

1. Sanni, Inc. v. Fiocchi, 443 N.E.2d 1108, 1111 (Ill.App.1982). *See also* Corpus Christi Bank & Trust v. Cross, 586 S.W.2d 664 (Tex. Civ.App.1979).

2. *Restatement (Second) of Trusts* § 262 (1959); Matter of Estate of Burke, 492 N.Y.S.2d 892 (Surr.1985); First Eastern Bank, N.A. v. Jones, 602 N.E.2d 211, 216 (Mass. 1992).

3. *Restatement, (Second) of, Trusts* § 263 (1959). *But cf.* Church v. First Union Nat. Bank, 304 S.E.2d 633, 635 (N.C.App.1983) (trustee not liable on note signed "in our fiduciary capacity but not individually").

4. *Restatement, (Second), of Trusts* § 246, comm. a, § 262, comm. b(1959).

5. *Id.* § 268.

6. 3A A. Scott, *Trusts* § 268.2, at 478 (4th ed. (Fratcher) 1988).

7. *Restatement (Second) of Trusts* § 271A, comm. a (1959). Sometimes it is not clear whether a person in a transaction was acting as agent or as trustee. Botwood Investments Ltd v. Johnson, 36 O.R.2d 443 (1982) (defendant liable if Field was acting as agent rather than as trustee for him)

8. Uniform Trusts Act, Prefatory Note.

judgment collectible out of the trust property without proving that the trustee could have secured reimbursement. The Act preserves the personal liability of trustees if the contract does not exclude it, but "the words 'as trustee' after the signature of a trustee to a contract shall be deemed *prima facie* evidence of an intent to exclude the trustee from personal liability."[9] The Uniform Probate Code is similar: "a trustee is not personally liable on contracts properly entered into in his fiduciary capacity * * * unless he fails to reveal his representative capacity and identify the trust estate in the contract."[10] This is restricted to "contracts properly entered;" a trustee who makes an *unauthorized* contract may still incur personal liability.[11] Similar provisions apply to personal representatives and conservators,[12] and to custodians under the Uniform Transfers to Minors Act.[13]

When creditors try to reach trust assets both they and the trustee have an incentive to argue that the contract was within the trustee's powers since this (a) allows the creditor to reach the trust assets, and (b) negates any personal liability of the trustee.[14] This creates a conflict of interest between the trustee and the beneficiaries, and so one court appointed a "trustee ad litem" to conduct the litigation in this situation.[15] The Uniform Trusts Act requires that the trust beneficiaries be notified before any judgment is entered against the trust assets so they can raise the question of the trustee's authority.[16] The Uniform Probate Code allows the beneficiaries to intervene in any litigation against the trustee.[17]

### *Tort Claims*

Similar rules govern tort claims. For example, the manager of a farm operated by a trust collided with a car while driving on farm business. The passengers in the car recovered a judgment against the trustee, but he was permitted to satisfy the judgment out of the trust assets. He was not personally at fault, but "a trustee is personally liable for torts committed by an agent or employee in the course of the administration of the trust."[18] This rule is harsh if the trust estate is insufficient to indemnify the trustee, but trustees can protect themselves by buying liability insurance and paying the premiums from the trust. Since they are in a better position than a tort victim

**9.** *Id.* § 12.

**10.** Uniform Probate Code § 7–306.

**11.** *Restatement, Second, Trusts* § 263(2) (1959). But not when the other party had reason to know the trustee was exceeding his authority. Gerhardt Const. Co. v. Wachter Real Estate Trust, 306 N.W.2d 223 (N.D.1981).

**12.** Uniform Probate Code §§ 3–808, 5–428. *See also* N.Y. EPTL § 11–4.7; 20 Pa.Stat. § 3331.

**13.** Uniform Transfers to Minors Act § 17.

**14.** Johnston, *Developments in Contract Liability of Trusts and Trustees*, 41 N.Y.U.L.Rev. 483, 517 (1966).

**15.** Getty v. Getty, 252 Cal.Rptr. 342 (App. 1988).

**16.** Uniform Trusts Act § 12(2). Professor Johnston argues that such notification may be more "expensive and time-consuming" than it is worth, because in the absence of litigation "trustees routinely discharge all obligations incurred on behalf of the trust out of trust funds." If they do so improperly, the trustee's bond protects the beneficiaries. Johnston, *supra* note 14, at 518, 495–97.

**17.** Uniform Probate Code § 7–306, comment.

**18.** *Accord, Restatement (Second) of Trusts* § 264 (1959); Uniform Trusts Act § 14(4); Evans v. Johnson, 347 N.W.2d 198 (Mich.App. 1984) (executor). In McCarthy v. Poulsen, 219 Cal.Rptr. 375 (App.1985) a trust owned land which created a risk of substantial liability for mud slides. For fear of liability the trustee resigned and no one could be found to agree to succeed him. The court ordered a *receiver* appointed instead because a receiver "is not personally liable for torts committed in the performance of his receivership duties."

to get insurance, they should bear the "risk of insolvency of the trust estate."[19] The plaintiffs' claim that the trust beneficiary was also personally liable was denied. Trust beneficiaries are usually not personally liable for torts committed by the trustee in administering the trust.[20]

The Uniform Probate Code treats trustees and personal representatives as if they were agents of the trust or estate for purposes of tort as well as contractual liability. They are not liable for torts committed in the course of administration of the estate unless they are "personally at fault."[21] The tort victim can reach the assets of the estate or trust directly if the tort was "committed in the course of administration of the estate."[22]

A type of liability of great recent concern to fiduciaries is that arising out of land ownership. To illustrate, a bank as trustee succeeded to ownership of a landfill which it later sold to a city. The city thereafter sued the bank under CERCLA (Comprehensive Environmental Response, Compensation and Liability Act) to recover costs it had incurred in cleaning up hazardous substances deposited on the land while it was in the trust. The bank cited the Restatement of Trusts which makes a trustee as holder of title to property liable as such "only to the extent to which the trust estate is sufficient to indemnify him."[23] The court, however, held that if the trustee "had the power to control the use of the property at the time it was contaminated," it would be personally liable under the Restatement "regardless of the trust's ability to indemnify him."[24] Presumably the result would be the same under the Uniform Probate Code which imposes personal liability on a trustee "for obligations arising out of the ownership or control of property of the trust estate ... if he is personally at fault.[25]

**19.** Cook v. Holland, 575 S.W.2d 468, 472 (Ky.App.1978).

**20.** *Restatement (Second) of Trusts* § 276 (1959). This is also true of contractual liability, *id.* § 275; Abraham Zion Corp. v. Lebow, 761 F.2d 93, 103 (2d Cir.1985), but not if the trustee acts under the control of the beneficiaries as their agent. Kessler, Merci, and Lochner, Inc. v. Pioneer Bank & Trust Co., 428 N.E.2d 608, 611 (Ill.App.1981).

**21.** Uniform Probate Code §§ 3–808(b), 7–306(b). *See also* N.Y. EPTL § 11–4.7(b); Cal. Prob.Code § 18002.

**22.** Uniform Probate Code §§ 3–808(c), 5–428(c), 7–306(c). *See also* N.Y. EPTL § 11–4.7(c) (estates); Uniform Trusts Act § 14; Vance v. Myers' Estate, 494 P.2d 816 (Alaska 1972).

**23.** *Restatement, Second, Trusts* § 265 (1959).

**24.** City of Phoenix v. Garbage Services Co., 827 F.Supp. 600, 604–5 (D.Ariz.1993) (citing *Restatement, Second, Trusts* § 264)

**25.** Uniform Probate Code § 7–306(b).

# Chapter 14

# LIVING WILLS AND DURABLE HEALTH CARE POWERS OF ATTORNEY

*Analysis*



---

## § 14.1 Introduction

"Every human being of adult years and sound mind has a right to determine what shall be done with his own body."[1] These oft-quoted words of Judge (later Justice) Benjamin Cardozo have become the foundation for the law of "informed consent." Under the doctrine of informed consent an adult competent patient, at least in a non-emergent situation, has the right to have the risks and benefits of proposed medical treatment explained to her before that treatment is provided, and the right to either refuse or accept medical treatment. The right to refuse or accept medical treatment can be grounded in either the common law, statute or state constitutions, and, in *Cruzan v. Director, Missouri Department of Health*[2] all of the Justices of the United States Supreme Court, excepting Justice Scalia, either stated or strongly implied that the right of a competent adult patient to refuse medical treatment was a constitutionally protected "liberty" interest.

The ethical and moral dilemmas surrounding the right to refuse medical treatment, whatever its source, were not severely tested until medical technologies made it possible to physically sustain the life of a person in a persistent (or permanent)vegetative state.[3]

The dilemmas were first publicly sharpened in the oft-cited case of *In the Matter of Quinlan*.[4] Karen Ann Quinlan, age 22, stopped breathing for at least

§ 14.1

**1.** Scholendorff v. Society of New York Hospital, 105 N.E. 92, 93 (N.Y.1914).

**2.** 497 U.S. 261, 278 (1990)(hereinafter cited as "Cruzan"). See, Cruzan at 287 (O'Connor concurring); Cruzan at 304–05 (Brennan, Marshall and Blackmun dissenting); Cruzan at 331 (Stevens dissenting).

**3.** "The distinguishing feature of a patient in a persistent vegetative state is wakefulness without awareness. These patients commonly make sporadic movements, spontaneously blink their eyes and have heightened reflex responses, but they cannot voluntarily respond to stimuli." Mack v. Mack, 618 A.2d 744, 746 (Md.1993).

**4.** 355 A.2d 647 (N.J.1976).

two 15 minute periods. As a result, the flow of blood to her brain ceased, destroying her cortex but not her brain stem. She was diagnosed as being in a persistent vegetative state "with the capacity to maintain the vegetative parts of neurological function but"[5] no longer having any cognitive function. Karen was connected to a respirator to assist her in breathing and to feeding tubes to provide her with food and hydration. Karen's doctors believed that she had no reasonable hope of recovery and, in all likelihood, would die if she were removed from the respirator.[6] Her father sought to be appointed her legal guardian for the purpose, among other things, of directing her health care providers to remove her from the respirator. The New Jersey court found that Karen had a constitutionally protected right of privacy which would have permitted her, had she been competent, to demand that the life-sustaining procedures be withdrawn even if withdrawal would result in her death. Because, in the court's view, this right of privacy is not extinguished because Karen became incompetent, it could be exercised on her behalf by her father, who was her legally appointed guardian.[7] The court did not engage in any extended discussion of the standards to be used by her guardian in determining whether the respirator should be removed. Rather, the court concluded that the guardian had the right to require the removal of the respirator if Karen's attending physicians, with the consent of an appropriate ethics committee, were of the view that there was "no reasonable possibility of Karen's ever emerging from her present comatose condition to a cognitive, sapient state."[8]

Later cases from New Jersey and many other states have attempted to develop standards to guide decision makers. In addition, Quinlan sparked a national interest in both living wills and durable health care powers of attorney (sometimes called "advance directives")which has ultimately led to the adoption of statutes throughout the country designed to empower patients to have health care decisions made on their behalf consistent with their wishes.

When patients are unable to express their own health care decisions, those decisions may be expressed by a so-called "surrogate" or "agent."[9] For example, in *Quinlan* the surrogate was Karen's guardian. Generally, surrogate's make decisions by complying with either the substituted judgement or the best interest standard.

Under the "substituted judgment" standard, the surrogate is expected to make that decision the patient would have made if the patient had decision making capacity. To do this, the surrogate should take into account the patient's previously expressed preferences, if any, as well as the patient's

5. Id. at 24, 355 A.2d at 654.

6. Karen's father did seek the removal of the feeding tubes.

7. In some jurisdictions, a conservator rather than a guardian would be appointed to represent the patient.

8. Id. at 55, 355 A.2d at 671.

9. As used in this chapter, a "surrogate" could be either a family member to whom by custom health care providers look to for guidance in making medical decisions for a patient lacking decision making capacity or a person authorized by statute, the courts or under a durable health care power to make decisions on behalf of a patient.

Where there have been a number of well publicized cases involving surrogate decision-making in the health care arena, overwhelming decisions to withdraw life support are made at the bedside by physicians working closely with patients, if able, and their families. The reported cases should not create the impression that this matters are frequently litigated.

known values and interests.[10] The substituted judgement standard presumes that the patient had once been competent to express his or her preferences and values.

A surrogate's decision might be challenged on the grounds that the patient's preferences cannot be ascertained. This was the core of the dispute in *Cruzan v. Director, Missouri Department of Health.*[11] Nancy Cruzan was in a persistent vegetative state unable to breath or be nourished without the use of a respirator and feeding tube. Her parents, after some considerable period of time, asked that the feeding tube be withdrawn, knowing that, if it were withdrawn, Nancy would die. The employees at the state hospital where Nancy resided refused to honor that request. Her parents then sued in state court.

The *Cruzan* trial court found that Nancy had a "fundamental right" under state and federal law to "refuse or direct the withdrawal of 'death prolonging procedures.' " It also found that in at least one conversation Nancy had with a friend she evidenced her intent not to be maintained on life sustaining technologies. This, in the trial court's view, was sufficient to permit her parents to exercise substituted judgement.

On appeal from an order in the parents' favor, the Missouri Supreme Court reversed. It held that any decision to withdraw life support from Nancy must be based upon clear and convincing evidence that withdrawal would be consistent with Nancy's intent.[12] The parents appealed that decision to the United States Supreme Court which held that the Constitution did not proscribe the Missouri Supreme Court from imposing the heightened "clear and convincing" standard to the facts. Said the Court: "[w]e believe that Missouri may permissibly place an increased risk of an erroneous decision on those seeking to terminate an incompetent individual's life-sustaining treatment. An erroneous decision not to terminate results in a maintenance of the status quo; the possibility of subsequent developments such as advancements in medical science, the discovery of new evidence regarding the patient's intent, changes in the law, or simply the unexpected death of the patient despite the administration of life-sustaining treatment, at least create the potential that a wrong decision will eventually be corrected or its impact mitigated. An erroneous decision to withdraw life-sustaining treatment, however, is not susceptible of correction."[13]

While the Court did not decide whether a person had a constitutional right to die or a right to direct the withholding or withdrawal of life-sustaining treatment, it stated in dicta that "for purposes of this case, we assume that the United States Constitution would grant a competent person a constitutionally protected right to refuse lifesaving hydration and nutrition."[14]

**10.** See generally, In re Fiori, 673 A.2d 905 (Pa.1996); Barry R. Furrow, Thomas L. Greaney, Sandra H. Johnson, Timothy Stoltzfus Jost & Robert Schwartz, Health Law, vol. 2, § 17–18 (1995) (hereinafter "Furrow").

**11.** 497 U.S. 261 (1990).

**12.** But see, Conservatorship of Drabick, 245 Cal.Rptr. 840 (App.1988)(conservator has authority to remove life support without court permission and can make a decision on behalf of patient without need for evidence of intent to be "clear and convincing.")

**13.** Id. at 263.

**14.** Id. at 278.

On the other hand, state courts have held that such protection can be found or grounded either in state constitutions or state statutes.

*Cruzan* is important because is emphasizes the importance of planning for end-of-life decisions making. *Cruzan* implicitly supports the need for persons to clearly express their end-of-life decisions through the execution of either living wills or durable health care powers.[15]

Both *Quinlan* and *Cruzan* focused on the substituted judgement standard. Use of the substituted standard may be illogical and thus inappropriate in cases where the patient *never* had decision making capacity. This, for example, could be the true in the case of infants, young minors, or severely retarded persons. The substituted judgement standard may also be inappropriate to use where there is little or no evidence that a patient who once had decision making capacity had any preferences, values or interest that would inform the decision to be made. For such patients the best interest standard is more appropriate.

The best interest standard seeks what is best for the patient without regard to what the patient would have preferred. However, some courts find the use of a best interest test inappropriate because "it lets another make a determination of the patient's quality of life, thereby undermining the foundation of self-determination and inviolability of the person upon which the right to refuse medical treatment stands."[16]

Because of the respect and deference given to a once-competent patient's expressed wishes respecting medical procedures and treatment, lawyers are keenly aware of the importance of having their clients communicate their wishes and desires respecting the health care they receive when they no longer are able to communicate themselves, particularly in the context of what has come to be called "end-of-life decision making." Lawyers also know that state statutes frequently give adults the power to designate agents or surrogates to make health care decisions on their behalf when they are no longer capable of making their own decisions. Thus, lawyers, and particularly lawyers who practice in the area of estate planning, invariably discuss with their clients both living wills and durable health care powers and prepare appropriate legal documents reflecting their clients' wishes. The statutory law surrounding these documents is rapidly evolving. While the following sections rely on the available uniform acts,[17] most of the issues raised in the discussion can be resolved in each state by resort to the local statutes.

**15.** Justice O'Connor opined that states might be required to respect the decisions of duly-designated surrogate decision makers. She stated: "In my view, such a duty may well be constitutionally required to protect the patient's liberty interest in refusing medical treatment. Few individuals provide explicit oral or written instructions regarding their intent to refuse medical treatment should they become incompetent. States which decline to consider any evidence other than such instructions may frequently fail to honor a patient's intent. Such failures might be avoided if the State considered an equally probative source of evidence: the patient's appointment of a proxy to make health care decisions on her behalf. Delegating the authority to make medical decisions to a family member or friend is becoming a common method of planning for the future. Id. at 289

**16.** Mack v. Mack, 618 A.2d 744, 758 (Md. 1993) quoting from In re Estate of Longeway, 549 N.E.2d 292, 299 (Ill.1989)

**17.** The two principal acts are the Uniform Health–Care Decisions Act, and the Uniform Rights of the Terminally Ill Act of 1989. See also, Uniform Rights of the Terminally Act of 1985.

## § 14.2 End-of-life Decision Making for the Competent Patient[1]

State case law or statutes or state constitutions generally recognize the right of competent persons to accept or reject medical treatment, including treatment that may be life-sustaining. The right to refuse medical treatment is closely aligned with the law of battery which recognizes the right of persons to be free of any unwanted touching.[2] *Bouvia v. Superior Court*[3] is illustrative. Elizabeth, a 28–year old woman, was a quadriplegic who suffered from severe cerebral palsy. She was completely bed-ridden, essentially immobile, constantly in pain and totally dependent on others to assist her with her all of her activities of daily living. Elizabeth had to be spoon fed. Elizabeth, who was fully mentally competent, refused to eat because she wanted to starve herself to death, primarily because she believed her life to be intolerable. To keep her alive, therefor, the health care providers at the publicly owned hospital inserted a feeding tube into her body against her will. With the feeding tube, Elizabeth had a life expectancy of 15–20 years. Elizabeth sued to have the tube removed.

The court held that Elizabeth had the right to refuse medical treatment, including medical treatment needed to sustain her life. The question for the court was whether the state had any countervailing interests that would trump Elizabeth's right to refuse life-sustaining treatment. The court noted that the state might assert up to four countervailing interests. These were the state's interest in (1) preserving life, (2) preventing suicide, (3) protecting the interest of third parties, and (4) maintaining the integrity and ethical standards of the medical profession.[4] But the court found that none of these interests trumped Elizabeth's right, as an exercise of her personal autonomy, to determine whether to receive medical treatment. The exercise of her personal rights are not dependent on her motives, even if those motives include a desire to die. Said the court: "it certainly is not illegal or immoral to prefer a natural, albeit sooner, death than a drugged life attached to a mechanical device."[5]

In so holding, the court relied on its earlier holding that a competent terminally-ill man had a right to require the removal of life-sustaining medical treatment even over the objections of the pro-life hospital where he was a patient.[6]

The court further stated that even though the removal of the feeding tube was opposed by the public hospital which no longer wanted to participate in her care, because, as a public hospital it was required to accept her as a patient, it could not deny her relief from pain and suffering while she starved

§ 14.2

1. The use of the phrase "competent patient" is misleading. The notion here is that the patient has decision making capacity, however that might be generally determined in interactions between the patient and the patient's health care providers.

2. See generally, Schloendorff v. Society of New York Hospital, 105 N.E. 92, 93 (N.Y. 1914).

3. 225 Cal.Rptr. 297 (App.1986).

4. See also, Superintendent of Belchertown State School v. Saikewicz, 370 N.E.2d 417 (Mass.1977).

5. Bouvia, *supra* note 3, 225 Cal.Rptr. at 306.

6. Bartling v. Superior Court, 209 Cal.Rptr. 220 (App.1984).

to death.[7] However, in *Brophy v. New England Sinai Hospital, Inc.*[8] the Massachusetts court, while upholding the right of a family to have a feeding tube removed from a patient in a persistent vegetative state, also held that, where the hospital had an ethical objection to doing so, the patient's family could be required to remove the patient to a facility more receptive to the family's request. Thus, courts are divided over whether the health care provider's objections to a decision to remove life-sustaining have to be accommodated. It may be, however, that greater accommodation may be required when the hospital is a private rather than a public hospital.

## § 14.3 End-of-life Decision Making for the Adult Incompetent Patient[1]

With respect to incompetent patients, distinctions are drawn between those patients who were never legally competent, such as minors, and those patients who were once competent but no longer are. Additionally, distinctions are drawn between those once competent patients who have signed living wills, advanced directives, or durable health care powers and those who have not.

For adult patients who were never competent, surrogate decision makers are expected to apply what is called the "best interest" test rather than the "substituted judgement" test. For such patients, application of the "substituted judgement" test where the decision maker would, in theory, make that decision the patient would have made if the patient could make a decision, is logically impossible. Under the "best interest" test, the decision maker makes whatever decision he believes is in the patient's best interest. Account is not taken, in theory, of what choice the patient might have made because the patient had never been able to make a rationale choice. However, this makes the most sense only for infants and young minors and for persons with profound mental retardation. But for mature minors and persons with less severe mental retardation, it is quite possible that they could rationalize a health care decision and, thus, it would be entirely appropriate to take their views into account using a substituted judgement approach. Furthermore, at least one influential court has held that even for adult patients who had never been competent, health care decisions made on their behalf must take their wants into account. Joseph Saikewicz[2] was an adult mentally retardate with the mental age of a 2 year, 8 month old infant who suffered from leukemia. Leukemia aside, he was generally in good health. He could not communicate verbally but would resort to gestures and grunts to communicate his wishes. His disease was invariably fatal. His guardian ad litem refused to consent to Joseph receiving chemotherapy because that would cause significant adverse

7. But see, Conservatorship of Morrison, 253 Cal.Rptr. 530 (App.1988)(where hospital staff had a moral objection to removing life support, was willing to transfer patient to a facility which would and conservator failed to show no physician would remove tube, hospital could refuse to remove life support system)

8. 497 N.E.2d 626 (Mass.1986).

§ 14.3

1. The use of the phrase "incompetent patient" is misleading. The notion is that the patient lacks decision making capacity as determined by the health care provider, not that the patient has been judicially declared incompetent. Of course, minors and judicially declared incompetents as a matter of law cannot make legally binding medical decisions. Even so, health care providers will often respect the decisions of "mature minors."

2. Superintendent of Belchertown State School v. Saikewicz, 370 N.E.2d 417 (Mass. 1977).

side effects and discomfort and would cause Joseph, who was incapable of understanding the purpose of the treatment, fear and pain. The guardian concluded that the limited benefits of the treatment did not outweigh the burdens of treatment. The trial judge agreed with that assessment. The appellate court heard the appeal even though Joseph died in the interim because of the importance of the issue for future patients.

Although the court recognized that Joseph could never have made a rationale decision, use of a best interest standard to determine whether he'd receive chemotherapy, in the court's view, was not appropriate. Rather the guardian should "ascertain the incompetent person's actual interests and preferences ... and the decision ... should be that which would be made by the incompetent person, if that person were competent, but taking into account the present and future incompetency of the individual as one of the factors which would necessarily enter in the decision-making process of the competent person."[3] This standard, in the court's view, recognizes that the autonomy interest of the incompetent is as deserving of protection as the autonomy interest of competent persons.

Other courts, however, have been less concerned about protecting the autonomy interests of adult persons who are profoundly disabled and believe it is only appropriate to apply a best interest standard to such persons. For example John Storar[4] was a 52–year old profoundly mentally retardate. He had terminal bladder cancer which his doctors wanted to treat with radiation therapy at a local hospital. After a period of time, John's mother, his guardian, withdrew her permission to treat John because he found the treatments disagreeable, distressful and painful. The treatment center then brought an action to compel treatment arguing that without treatment he would die within a few weeks. The court ordered the treatments stating that while a parent or guardian ordinarily has the right to consent to the ward's medical treatment, "the parent ... may not deprive a child of life saving treatment, however well intentioned."[5] As the court saw it, sustained life is always in the ward's best interest—life is better than death. It appears that it was for this belief that the *Storar's* court approach was rejected in *Saikewicz.* The *Saikewicz* court expressed concern that a best interest standard mandates "an unvarying responsibility by the courts to order necessary medical treatment for an incompetent person facing an immediate and sever danger to life."[6]

For an adult incompetent who were once competent, almost all courts adopt the substituted judgement standard as the appropriate standard to protect the patient's autonomy interest. What judgement the patient would have made may be ascertained from any oral or written instructions communicated by the patient through a living will, durable health care power, or otherwise, such as direct communication with a physician or family members. If a surrogate's decision using substituted judgement is based on the patient's statements, the decision is more likely to be upheld, if challenged, if the court finds that the patient's statements were made (1) consistently, (2) on serious occasions, (3) by a mature person with an understanding of the consequences

**3.** 370 N.E.2d at 431.

**4.** In re Storar, 420 N.E.2d 64 (N.Y.1981).

**5.** Id at 73.

**6.** Superintendent of Belchertown State School v. Saikewicz, § 14.2 *supra* note 4 at 427.

of the decision, (4) shortly before the treatment, and (4) with some specificity in relation to the patient's actual condition.[7] While courts do not require all four conditions, the more of these conditions that are met the more likely the court will respect the decision. Courts also look to see if the statements attributed to the patient are consistent with other known values of the patient.[8] Courts will consider other evidence of a patient's intent including the patient's religious convictions, value structure, attitude generally about health care, prior interactions with the health-care system, reaction generally to illness, reaction to disease in others, and relationship to friends and family.[9]

The New Jersey courts have assumed a leadership role in this area. Consider the case of Claire Conroy.[10] Claire was a 84 year old woman with serious and irreversible physical and mental impairments who had been declared mentally incompetent. She resided in a nursing home where her life was maintained by the artificial administration of food and hydration because of her inability to swallow sufficient amounts of these nutrients. All doctors agreed that if her tubes were removed she would die of dehydration within one week. The evidence was inconclusive regarding whether she was experiencing pain. She was not in a coma. Her nephew sought the removal of her feeding tubes. The trial court granted his request finding that Claire's "intellectual functioning had been permanently reduced to a very primitive level, that her life had become impossibly and permanently burdensome, and that removal of the feeding tube should . . . be permitted."[11] The intermediate appellate court reversed believing that the withdrawal of the tubes "would be tantamount to killing [Claire]–not simply letting her die–and that such active euthanasia was ethically impermissible." The New Jersey Supreme Court reversed.

The New Jersey court developed a series of rules to be applied to determine under what circumstances life sustaining treatment could be withdrawn from incompetent patients incapable of making medical decisions. First, and in recognition of the patient's autonomy rights, the court stated that life-sustaining treatment could be withdrawn or withheld "when it is clear that the particular patient would have refused the treatment under the circumstances involved."[12] The patient's intent may be evidenced by a living will, oral declarations, a durable health care power, the patient's reactions to the medical treatment others received or deduced from the patient's religious beliefs or from other decisions the patient might have made with respect to his or medical treatment. The probative value of the evidence could vary depending upon a number of factors, including, the "remoteness, consistency, and thoughtfulness of the prior statements or actions and the maturity of the person at the time of the statements or acts."[13] For persons who had never clearly expressed their wishes but who are suffering a prolonged and painful death, the court adopted two additional tests–the limited objective best interest test and the pure objective best interest test.

**7.** Furrow, § 14.2, *supra*, note 10, vol. 2, at § 17.25 at 369–370.

**8.** Id. at 370.

**9.** Id. at 371.

**10.** In re Matter of Conroy, 486 A.2d 1209 (N.J.1985).

**11.** Id. at 1209.

**12.** Id. at 1229.

**13.** Id. at 1230.

Under the limited objective best interest test, life support may be withheld or withdrawn where "there is some trustworthy evidence that the patient would have refused the treatment, and the decision-maker is satisfied that it is clear that the burdens of the patient's continued life with the treatment outweigh the benefits of that life for him."[14] This test allows for the termination of treatment when the patient's intent expressed before he or she became incompetent is ambiguous but it is clear that the life sustaining treatment would merely prolong the patient's suffering.

Absent any trustworthy evidence of the patient's intent or any evidence of the patient's intent, the decision maker employs the pure objective test. Here again there is a balance between the net burdens of treatment and the benefits. If the burdens outweigh the benefits, treatment can be withdrawn if "the recurring, unavoidable and severe pain of the patient's life with the treatment ... [are such] that the effect of administering the life-sustaining treatment would be inhumane."[15]

In a subsequent case, the New Jersey court backed away from this test in the case of patient's in a persistent vegetative state who are incapable of feeling pain. For such patient the court held that the decision of close and caring family members or a close friend should control and their right to decide is not circumscribed by any balancing of benefits and burdens.[16]

## § 14.4 End-of-life Decision Making for Minors

As a general proposition, the right to make health care decisions for minors, including decisions to withhold or withdraw life support, are made by the minor's parents. However, the right of a parent to make health care decisions for a minor child is not absolute. Parental authority may be limited in at least three cases: (1) where the parents are in violation of child abuse laws, (2) where the minor is a "mature minor," and (3) the parents disagree.

Child abuse and neglect statutes prohibit parents from, among other things, depriving their children of necessary medical care. When parents deprive their children of appropriate medical care, the state may step in, take custody of the child, and direct medical decisions for the child. In the context of end-of-life decision making, the issue is whether the parents judgement to withhold or withdraw treatment is neglect or abuse. While some courts have held that a parental decision to withhold or withdraw life support is neglect *per se*, many courts have used a balancing test to make that determination.

Colin Newmark was a three years old with terminal cancer. His parents were Christian Scientists who wanted to reject a proposed radical form of chemotherapy with a 40% chance of success, preferring to rely on prayer and spiritual aid as the means to cure Colin. The trial court held that the parents' decision constituted neglect. The Supreme Court held that whether the parents approach to treatment was neglect depended on a balancing of factors. Factors to be taken into account included: (1) family primacy in medical decision making for minor children, (2) the state's parens patriae power exercisable to protect the health and safety of children, (3)the child's best interests taking into account the prognosis with or without treatment,

**14.** Id. at 1231.

**15.** Id. at 1232.

**16.** In re Jobes, 529 A.2d 434 (N.J.1987)

the risks of the treatment, the invasiveness of the treatment, the burdens of the treatment, and the chances of success.

Where the prognosis is good but parents refuse treatment, courts are more likely to step in to overrule a parent's decision to withhold treatment. Where the prognosis is grim or less certain and the child is likely to experience much pain and discomfort, courts are less prone to overrule a decision to withhold treatment.

Often courts are asked to overturn parents' decisions where those decisions are based upon the parents' religious views. This is typical with Jehovah's Witnesses and Christian Scientists. The extent of respect accorded parental decisions motivated by their religious views varies. For example, religiously-based decisions to withhold blood transfusions that would save a child's life are typically not respected by the courts. As noted in *Prince v. Massachusetts,*[1] "parents may be free to become martyrs themselves. But it does not follow they are free, in identical circumstances, to make martyrs of their children before they have reached the age of full and legal discretion when they can make that choice for themselves."[2]

In the case of mature minors, wider latitude is given to permit the minor to participate in his or her own health care decisions although if push comes to shove health care providers are most unlikely to follow a minor's directive when it conflicts with that of the minor's parents.

## § 14.5 Living Wills and Durable Powers

Almost all states now have statutes permitting persons over the age of 18 to execute both living wills (sometimes called "advance directives" or "advance health-care directive") and durable health care powers (sometimes called "power of attorney for health care").[1] The formalities necessary to execute these instruments also vary widely. Typically, these documents must be evidenced by a writing, but the Uniform Health-Care Decisions Act (unlike most statutes) permits an advance directive to be oral.[2] While the Uniform Health-Care Decisions Act does not expressly require that any directive or durable power be witnessed or notarized, most states impose at least one of these requirements. It is often common for the state statute to prohibit certain health care professionals from being a witness to a living will.

Some states also provide that a living will validly executed in another state is valid in the state where the patient is currently residing.

The living will typically becomes effective when it is executed, although the Uniform Rights of the Terminally Act provides that the living will becomes operative after it is communicated to the attending physician and the declarant is determined to have a terminal condition and no longer capable of making decisions regarding the use of life-sustaining procedures.[3] It is not

§ 14.4

1. 321 U.S. 158 (1944).

2. Id. at 170.

§ 14.5

1. See Appendix A at end of chapter for model forms.

2. Unif. Health-Care Decisions Act (hereafter UHDA) § 2(a) & (b).

3. Unif. Rights of the Terminally Ill Act, § 3.

uncommon, however, for a state law to suspend the operation of a living will during the declarant's pregnancy.

Living wills usually are easy to revoke. They can be revoked orally or by a writing and often without regard to the declarant's mental or physical condition. However, to protect health care providers, it is generally provided that a revocation is effective "upon its communication to the attending physician or other health-care provider by the declarant or a witness to revocation."[4]

While state laws differ, a typical living will usually provides that, if the maker has an "incurable and irreversible" condition that will result in death within "a relatively short time"[5] or, as some states add, if the maker becomes "unconscious and, to a reasonable degree of medical certainty ... will not regain consciousness,"[6] then life-sustaining or life-prolonging procedures be withheld or withdrawn.[7] The quoted phrases are fraught with ambiguity, although there is little case law to suggest that they have become the subject of much litigation. The language of living will statutes necessarily clothes the physician with a lot of authority to determine whether the declarant has a medical condition described in the living will.

Once the living will becomes operative, life-sustaining treatment can be withheld or withdrawn. State laws differ regarding whether artificial nutrition and hydration are included within the concept of life-sustaining or life-prolonging procedures.

Interestingly, the typical living will is at best precatory although some states provide that they shall govern decisions regarding the administration of life-sustaining procedures. Where merely precatory, physicians and other health care providers are not required to honor them. On the other hand, the typical statute provides that if the living will is honored and the patient dies as a result of the withdrawal or withholding of life support, the patient's death is not treated as a suicide or homicide.

A 1997 study published in the Journal of the American Medical Association found a high incidence of physicians' failing to abide by patients' living wills. This study appears to confirm anecdotal information that lawyers often hear and underlies, as well, the movement to enable persons to sign durable health care powers.

The durable power is conceptually broader in scope than the living will in that it permits an agent designated by the principal to make any health-care decision for the principal whenever the principal is unable to make a health care decision for himself.[8] Durable powers generally become operative whenever the principal is incapable of making a health-care decision. They are not limited to cases where the principal has a terminal condition.

Generally, the agent can be any competent adult although there are often prohibitions on the principal's physician or an employee of the physician being designated as an agent.

**4.** Id. at § 4.

**5.** Unif. Health Care Decisions Act § 4; Unif. Rights of the Terminally Ill Act § 2. In some jurisdictions the living will becomes operative if death is likely to occur within 6 months.

**6.** Id. § 4.

**7.** Id.

**8.** Id.at §§ 2(b) & 4

Whether the principal is capable of making a health-care decision is determined by the principal's primary physician.[9]

Under UHDA, the decision of the agent should comport with the principal's expressed instructions or other wishes to the extent known, or, if there are none, then in accordance with the agent's judgement of the principal's best interest.[10] Given that the agent's first duty is to make a decision consistent with the principal's wishes, it is important that the durable power adequately reflect the desires of the principal, or that those desires be communicated to the principal by some other means. The agent's powers can be limited in most any way by the terms of the durable power, although often a principal will want the agent to act in all cases where the principal is unable to act to the fullest extent possible. Thus, a principal may not expressly limit the agent's authority agent to act on his or her behalf.

Lawyers who prepare these health care documents for their clients often combine the living will and health care power. A combination document provides a written expression of the principal's intent, particularly when end-of-life decision making is required, that not only guides the agent but also helps assuage possible psychological concerns that an agent might have in making a decision that could end the principal's life.

## § 14.6 Family Consent Laws

Because most patients have not executed either living wills or durable health care powers, physicians and other health care providers must often look to family members as alternative decision makers. In the absence of express statutory authority empowering family members to make health care decisions for a loved one, there is a concern whether physicians expose themselves to risk by relying on the family member's decisions. These concerns are eliminated in jurisdictions that have adopted some form of family consent rules.[1] Some of these statutes apply only to end-of-life decision making, while others apply to all health care decisions. The typical statute provides that, absent an effective living will or durable power, health care decisions can be made on behalf of a patient who the attending physician has determined is incapable of making a health-care decision by a designated family member or family members. The typical priority among family members is spouse, then adult child, or if more than one, a majority of them, parents, adult siblings or a majority of them. Often, these statutes permit close friends to make decisions where family members are unavailable. If the patient had designated a surrogate decision maker or had a judicially appointed guardian, the surrogate or guardian, topically in that order, would be empowered to make the decision.

### UNIFORM HEALTH–CARE DECISIONS ACT

### OPTIONAL FORM

The following form may, but need not, be used to create an advance health-care directive. The other sections of this [Act] govern the effect of this

9. Id. at §§ 2(c) & 4.

10. Id. at § 2(e).

§ 14.6

1. See, e.g., Iowa Code § 144A.7.

or any other writing used to create an advance health-care directive. An individual may complete or modify all or any part of the following form:

ADVANCE HEALTH–CARE DIRECTIVE

Explanation

You have the right to give instructions about your own health care. You also have the right to name someone else to make health-care decisions for you. This form lets you do either or both of these things. It also lets you express your wishes regarding donation of organs and the designation of your primary physician. If you use this form, you may complete or modify all or any part of it. You are free to use a different form.

Part 1 of this form is a power of attorney for health care. Part 1 lets you name another individual as agent to make health-care decisions for you if you become incapable of making your own decisions or if you want someone else to make those decisions for you now even though you are still capable. You may also name an alternate agent to act for you if your first choice is not willing, able, or reasonably available to make decisions for you. Unless related to you, your agent may not be an owner, operator, or employee of [a residential long-term health-care institution] at which you are receiving care.

Unless the form you sign limits the authority of your agent, your agent may make all health-care decisions for you. This form has a place for you to limit the authority of your agent. You need not limit the authority of your agent if you wish to rely on your agent for all health-care decisions that may have to be made. If you choose not to limit the authority of your agent, your agent will have the right to:

(a) consent or refuse consent to any care, treatment, service, or procedure to maintain, diagnose, or otherwise affect a physical or mental condition;

(b) select or discharge health-care providers and institutions;

(c) approve or disapprove diagnostic tests, surgical procedures, programs of medication, and orders not to resuscitate; and

(d) direct the provision, withholding, or withdrawal of artificial nutrition and hydration and all other forms of health care.

Part 2 of this form lets you give specific instructions about any aspect of your health care. Choices are provided for you to express your wishes regarding the provision, withholding, or withdrawal of treatment to keep you alive, including the provision of artificial nutrition and hydration, as well as the provision of pain relief. Space is also provided for you to add to the choices you have made or for you to write out any additional wishes.

Part 3 of this form lets you express an intention to donate your bodily organs and tissues following your death.

Part 4 of this form lets you designate a physician to have primary responsibility for your health care.

After completing this form, sign and date the form at the end. It is recommended but not required that you request two other individuals to sign as witnesses. Give a copy of the signed and completed form to your physician, to any other health-care providers you may have, to any health-care institution at which you are receiving care, and to any health-care agents you have named. You should talk to the person you have named as agent to make sure that he or she understands your wishes and is willing to take the responsibility.

You have the right to revoke this advance health-care directive or replace this form at any time.

PART 1

POWER OF ATTORNEY FOR HEALTH CARE

(1) DESIGNATION OF AGENT: I designate the following individual as my agent to make health-care decisions for me:

______________________________________

(name of individual you choose as agent)

______________________________________

(address) (city) (state) (zip code)

______________________________________

(home phone) (work phone)

OPTIONAL: If I revoke my agent's authority or if my agent is not willing, able, or reasonably available to make a health-care decision for me, I designate as my first alternate agent:

______________________________________

(name of individual you choose as first alternate agent)

______________________________________

(address) (city) (state) (zip code)

______________________________________

(home phone) (work phone)

OPTIONAL: If I revoke the authority of my agent and first alternate agent or if neither is willing, able, or reasonably available to make a health-care decision for me, I designate as my second alternate agent:

______________________________________

(name of individual you choose as second alternate agent)

______________________________________

(address) (city) (state) (zip code)

______________________________________

(home phone) (work phone)

(2) AGENT'S AUTHORITY: My agent is authorized to make all health-care decisions for me, including decisions to provide, withhold, or withdraw artificial nutrition and hydration and all other forms of health care to keep me alive, except as I state here:

[Insert Instructions]

(3) WHEN AGENT'S AUTHORITY BECOMES EFFECTIVE: My agent's authority becomes effective when my primary physician determines that I am unable to make my own health-care decisions unless I mark the following box. If I mark this box [ ], my agent's authority to make health-care decisions for me takes effect immediately.

(4) AGENT'S OBLIGATION: My agent shall make health-care decisions for me in accordance with this power of attorney for health care, any instructions I give in Part 2 of this form, and my other wishes to the extent known to my agent. To the extent my wishes are unknown, my agent shall make health-care decisions for me in accordance with what my agent determines to be in my best interest. In determining my best interest, my agent shall consider my personal values to the extent known to my agent.

(5) NOMINATION OF GUARDIAN: If a guardian of my person needs to be appointed for me by a court, I nominate the agent designated in this form. If that agent is not willing, able, or reasonably available to act as guardian, I nominate the alternate agents whom I have named, in the order designated.

PART 2

INSTRUCTIONS FOR HEALTH CARE

If you are satisfied to allow your agent to determine what is best for you in making end-of-life decisions, you need not fill out this part of the form. If you do fill out this part of the form, you may strike any wording you do not want.

(6) END-OF-LIFE DECISIONS: I direct that my health-care providers and others involved in my care provide, withhold, or withdraw treatment in accordance with the choice I have marked below:

"[ ] (a) Choice Not To Prolong Life

I do not want my life to be prolonged if (i) I have an incurable and irreversible condition that will result in my death within a relatively short time, (ii) I become unconscious and, to a reasonable degree of medical certainty, I will not regain consciousness, or (iii) the likely risks and burdens of treatment would outweigh the expected benefits, OR

"[ ] (b) Choice To Prolong Life

I want my life to be prolonged as long as possible within the limits of generally accepted health-care standards.

(7) ARTIFICIAL NUTRITION AND HYDRATION: Artificial nutrition and hydration must be provided, withheld, or withdrawn in accordance with the choice I have made in paragraph (6) unless I mark the following box. If I mark this box [ ], artificial nutrition and hydration must be provided regardless of my condition and regardless of the choice I have made in paragraph (6).

(8) RELIEF FROM PAIN: Except as I state in the following space, I direct that treatment for alleviation of pain or discomfort be provided at all times, even if it hastens my death:

(9) OTHER WISHES: (If you do not agree with any of the optional choices above and wish to write your own, or if you wish to add to the instructions you have given above, you may do so here.) I direct that:

[Insert Instructions]

PART 3

DONATION OF ORGANS AT DEATH (OPTIONAL)

(10) Upon my death (mark applicable box)

[ ] (a) I give any needed organs, tissues, or parts, OR

[ ] (b) I give the following organs, tissues, or parts only

_______________________________________________

(c) My gift is for the following purposes (strike any of the following you do not want)

(i) Transplant

(ii) Therapy

(iii) Research

(iv) Education

PART 4

PRIMARY PHYSICIAN

(OPTIONAL)

(11) I designate the following physician as my primary physician:

_______________________________

(name of physician)

_______________________________

(address)(city) (state) (zip code)

_______________________________

(phone)

OPTIONAL: If the physician I have designated above is not willing, able, or reasonably available to act as my primary physician, I designate the following physician as my primary physician:

_______________________________

(name of physician)

_______________________________

(address)(city) (state) (zip code)

_______________________________

(phone)

(12) EFFECT OF COPY: A copy of this form has the same effect as the original.

(13) SIGNATURES: Sign and date the form here:

__________ ____________________

(date) (sign your name)

__________ ____________________

(address) (print your name)

_______________________________

(city) (state)

(Optional) SIGNATURES OF WITNESSES:

First witness Second witness

__________ ____________________

(print name) (print name)

____________ ________________________

(address) (address)

____________ ________________________

(city) (state) (city) (state)

____________ ________________________

(signature of witness) (signature of witness)

____________ ________________________

(date) (date)

# Chapter 15

# OVERVIEW OF THE FEDERAL TAX LAWS RELATING TO ESTATES AND TRUSTS

*Analysis*



## § 15.1 Income Taxation of Gifts and Bequests and Basis of Gifted and Inherited Property

Section 102 of the Internal Revenue Code excludes from gross income for income tax purposes the amount of property received by a donee or beneficiary as either a lifetime gift or a testamentary bequest.[1] This exclusion does not apply, however, to income on gifts or bequests.[2]

Section 102 fails to define the meaning of a gift or bequest. Thus, the definition of a gift or bequest is largely left to state law. Likewise section 102 does not delineate how a gift or bequest excluded from gross income should be distinguished from the income on a gift or bequest which should be included in gross income. For outright gifts or bequests, this is also left to state law, For gifts or bequests in trust, however, the delineation is essentially provided by the rules of Subchapter J.

For outright gifts or bequests the operation of section 102 is fairly straight forward. For example, if Oscar gives Sally 100 shares of X Corporation, common stock, the value of the stock on the date of the gift is excluded from Sally's gross income. On the other hand, all dividends paid by X Corporation to Sally after the date of the gift are included in Sally's gross income.

The making of a gift is not a taxable event for income tax purposes. Thus, if a donor gives appreciated stock to a donee, the donor realizes no capital gain as a result of the gift. On the other hand, the basis of gifted property in

§ 15.1

1. Likewise, section 101 excludes from gross income the proceeds of any life insurance payable by reason of an insured's death from the beneficiary's gross income.

2. I.R.C. § 102(b).

the donee's hands is the donor's adjusted basis[3] increased by the gift tax paid, if any, on the difference between the donor's basis and the property's fair market value on the date of the gift.[4] The adjustment for gift taxes paid is determined by multiplying the gift tax paid by a fraction. The numerator of the fraction is the difference between the property's fair market value and the donor's adjusted basis immediately before the gift; the denominator is the value of the gift.[5] For example, suppose Orville gives Harry property valued at $10. In Orville's hands, the property had an adjusted basis of $2. Orville pays a gift tax of $4 on the transfer. The basis of the property in Harry's hands is $2 plus 80% of the $4 gift tax, or $5.20. If no gift tax was paid with respect to the gift, then the donee's basis equals the donor's basis.

If the donor's adjusted basis in gifted property is greater than the property's fair market value at the time of the gift, then for purposes of determining loss on a sale or exchange of the property, its basis equals its fair market value on the date of the gift.[6]

This "transferred basis" rule means that any appreciation on gifted property is taxed in the donee's hands, not the donor's hands, and, of course, only when the donee disposes of the gifted property during the donee's life. For example, suppose Anna gives John 100 shares of Y Corporation, common stock having a value of $1,000 on the date of the gift. Suppose further that Anna paid $100 for this stock. Anna realizes no gain on this gift even though at the time of the gift the stock had appreciated by $900 over what Anna had paid for it. If two years later, John sells the stock for $1,500, John realizes a capital gain of $1,400. This amount is the difference between the amount he realized and the transferred basis of $100.

For property acquired by bequest or inheritance, the basis of the property in the beneficiary's hands is the property's estate tax value in the case of property that was included in a decedent's estate tax return.[7] The property's estate tax value is its fair market value as of decedent's death or its fair market value determined under the alternate valuation method.[8] Because the basis of inherited property, is "stepped up" to its estate tax value, to the extent that value exceeds decedent's basis in the property[9], such excess avoids being taxed for income tax purposes. The "stepped up" basis rule provides a powerful incentive to hold property until death rather than sell the property during life and incur a potential tax on capital gains, or gift the property to a donee who, under section 1015, would acquire the donor's basis in the property.[10] For example, Alice buys Blackacre for $50,000. It is worth

3. Ordinarily the donor's adjusted basis in the gift property equals the donor's cost. I.R.C. § 1012. In certain cases, the donor's cost basis will have to be adjusted. See, *e.g.*, I.R.C. § 1016.

4. I.R.C. § 1015(a), (d)(6).

5. *Id.*

6. I.R.C. § 1015(a).

7. I.R.C. § 1014.

8. See, § 15.3, infra. If decedent's estate was not required to file an estate tax return, then the property's basis is its fair market value on the date of the decedent's death.

9. Decedent's basis usually equals the cost of the asset in the decedent's hand. See generally, I.R.C. § 1012.

10. Proposals to eliminate the estate tax also include repeal of the stepped up basis rule, at least for larger estates, in favor of a transferred or carryover basis which would cause the inherited property's basis in the beneficiary's hands to be determined by reference to the decedent's basis. A proposal to this effect was adopted by Congress in 2000 but vetoed by President Clinton. To some extent Democrats also support repeal or modification of the transfer tax laws and with the election of Pres-

$450,000 when she dies. Under her will she bequeaths Blackacre to Chris. In Chris' hands the basis of Blackacre is $450,000 which means that if Chris immediately sells Blackacre for $450,000 Chris realizes no gain on the sale because his basis in Blackacre is $450,000. Thus, the $400,000 of appreciation occurring during Alice's lifetime wholly escapes the income tax.[11]

As noted the stepped up basis rule applies to property acquired by bequest or inheritance. It also applies to property otherwise included in a decedent's gross estate that is acquired by the donee by means other than a bequest or inheritance. For example, if Bob transferred stock into a revocable trust which Bob acquired for $5,000, the basis of the stock in the trustee's hand is $5,000 under section 1015. When Bob later dies, the trust assets will be included in Bob's gross estate because of his retained power of revocation and subject to the federal estate tax.[12] If, at Bob's death, the stock is worth $50,000 and it then becomes distributable to Jim, the remainder person of the trust, Jim's basis in the property will be $50,000. Likewise, suppose Nancy purchases Blackacre for $5,000 and takes title in the name of herself and Drew as joint tenants with right of survivorship. At Nancy's death, Blackacre will be included in her gross estate for federal estate tax purposes.[13] At her death Blackacre is worth $150,000. The basis of Blackacre in Drew's hands is $150,000.

## § 15.2 Gift Tax

Federal law imposes a transfer tax upon the privilege of transferring property by gift, bequest or inheritance. This transfer tax takes the form of a gift tax in the case of completed lifetime gifts[1] and an estate tax in the case of property owned by the decedent at the time of death, certain lifetime transfers, annuities, joint tenancy property, property over which decedent had, exercised or released a general power of appointment, life insurance and certain qualified terminable interest property.[2]

Generally, gifted property is not included in the donor's gross estate but this is not always the case. However, where gifted property is included in the donor's estate, available credits assure that only the increase in value of the gifted property between the date of the gift and the date of the donor's death is effectively subject to the estate tax. For example, suppose Helen transfers property with a gift tax value of $500,000 to a trust and retains the income for life with a remainder to her children. This property is worth $750,000 when Helen dies and is included in her gross estate because of her retained life estate.[3] While at face value it might appear that at least $500,000 of the property's value is subject to both the gift and estate tax, in fact and because of the gift tax credit against the estate tax, only the property's $500,000 value is subject to the gift tax; the balance of $250,000 is subject to the estate tax.

ident Bush it is expected that some significant changes will occur in the tax.

**11.** See also, § 15.3, and notes 11 et. seq. and accompanying text.

**12.** I.R.C. § 2038. The step up in basis is available even if Bob's estate is too small to warrant the filing of an estate tax return, although in such case the property tax basis will equal its fair market value on Bob's death, not its estate tax value. See generally, I.R.C. § 1014.

**13.** I.R.C. § 2040.

§ 15.2

**1.** See notes 34 *infra* and accompanying text.

**2.** See § 15.3, *infra*.

**3.** I.R.C. § 2036.

Gift and estate taxes are computed on the progressive unified rate schedule set forth in Section 2001 of the Internal Revenue Code with rates ranging from 18% to 55%. The tentative tax computed under that section is reduced by a number of credits. The two more important of these are the unified credit and the state death tax credit which is applicable only to the estate tax. The unified credit when fully phased in by 2006 will be $345,800[4] which is the amount of tax payable on $1,000,000. Thus, aggregate lifetime and deathtime transfers under $1,000,000 are effectively exempt from transfer taxes.

The state death tax credit equals the lesser of the actual amount of state death taxes payable by reason of the decedent's death or the scheduled credit in Section 2011.

For estates of persons dying after December 31, 1987 and gifts made after that date, the benefits of both the unified credit and the graduated transfer tax rate structure are minimized or eliminated once aggregate lifetime and testamentary transfers exceed $10,000,000. This occurs because of the assessment under Section 2001(c)(3) of a 5% surcharge on the taxable amount between $10,000,000 and $21,040,000. In these cases once the value of the taxable base equals or exceeds the ceiling amount on the surcharge bracket, each dollar is taxed at the 55% maximum transfer tax rate.

The rates of tax are applied against cumulative lifetime and death time transfers with double taxation avoided by appropriate credits for transfer taxes paid on transfers previously subject to a transfer tax.

### *The Meaning of Taxable Gift*

A federal gift tax is imposed on the value of lifetime gifts. For gift tax purposes a gift is defined as the transfer of property for less than adequate and full consideration in money or money's worth, other than a transfer in the "ordinary course of business."[5]

Most transfers that meet the common law definition of a gift also are gifts for gift tax purposes but certain lifetime transfers may not be gifts for state property law purposes that nonetheless are gifts for gift tax purposes. This can result from the fact that the consideration necessary to support a contract under state law may not be sufficient to avoid a gift under federal tax law.

For gift tax purposes, consideration that cannot be expressed in money or money's worth is ignored. Thus, if the consideration received does not replace the value of the donor's personal wealth that has been transferred to another, then, for gift tax purposes, the transfer was not for adequate consideration in money or money's worth. For example, if John transfers Blackacre, valued at $100,000, to his daughter, Mary, for cash in the amount of $100,000, John receives adequate and full consideration in money or money's worth. Both before and after the transfer John's personal wealth is valued at least at $100,000. On the other hand, suppose John promises to pay Mary $20,000 if Mary does not smoke for a year. Mary stops smoking for one year and John

4. I.R.C. § 2001.

5. A transfer is in the "ordinary course of business" if it is a bona fide arms' length transaction free of any donative intent. For example, when a department store has a sale and sells goods at a price that is less than the marked price, no gift results because of the ordinary business transaction exception.

pays her $20,000. John makes a gift to Mary of $20,000 of which, after the annual exclusion, only $10,000 is taxed. While Mary's performance may be sufficient consideration under state law to support the enforcement of John's promise, it is not consideration in money or money's worth because it does not replenish the value of John's personal estate which has been depleted by $20,000.

A transfer in consideration for the donee's release of dower or curtesy or a statutory right in lieu thereof is not consideration in money or money's worth.[6] On the other hand, a transfer to a spouse in consideration for the spouse's release of a support obligation is a transfer for adequate and full consideration in money or money's worth.[7]

According to the Treasury Regulations "the terms 'taxable gifts' means the 'total amount of gifts' made by the donor during the 'calendar period' * * * less the deductions" allowable under Sections 2522 and 2523 for certain charitable and interspousal transfers. The term "total amount of gifts" means the sum of the values of gifts during the calendar period less any available annual exclusion.

The annual exclusion equals the value of present interest[8] gifts to any donee each year up to the amount of $10,000.[9] To illustrate, suppose Mary gave Alice $100,000 in cash. With respect to this gift both the "total amount of gift" and the "taxable gift" is $90,000. On the other hand, suppose the gift had been made to Mary's husband, George. In this case the "total amount of gift" is $90,000 but the "taxable gift" is $0 because of the availability of the gift tax marital deduction.[10]

The amount of a donor's taxable gift is also affected by the so-called "split gift" rule,[11] under which a married donor's gifts can be treated for gift tax purposes as having been made half by the donor and half by the donor's spouse if the donor and the donor's spouse so elect. Thus, if Mary gives Alice $20,000 and Mary and her husband, George, elect to split the gift for gift tax purposes, then for purposes of computing the taxable gifts of Mary and George, each of them is deemed to have given Alice $10,000. Since each of them is entitled to an annual exclusion for present interest gifts up to $10,000, each of them make a taxable gift of $0 to Alice. The split gift rules permit electing married couples to double up on their annual exclusions and unified credits. Thus, between them they can make gifts of $20,000 annually to any donee gift tax free, and gifts in excess of that amount can be shielded from transfer tax by the use of their individual unified credits.

**6.** Merrill v. Fahs, 324 U.S. 308 (1945), rehearing denied 324 U.S. 888 (1945); I.R.C. § 2043. *But see* I.R.C. § 2516 and note 80 *infra* and accompanying text.

**7.** See, *e.g.,* Glen v. C.I.R., 45 T.C. 323 (1966).

**8.** See notes 13, 14 & 27 *infra* and accompanying text (relating to present and future interests).

**9.** For gifts made after 1998, the amount of the $10,000 annual exclusion is subject to increase for an inflation adjustment in multiples of $1,000. See I.R.C. § 2503((b)(2). In the text, the annual exclusion will continue to be referred to as $10,000.

**10.** See notes 74–76 *infra* and accompanying text.

**11.** I.R.C. § 2513. The split gift option is designed to equalize the treatment of gifts for married persons whether they live in common law property states or community property states.

### *Valuation of Gifted Property*

Gifted property is valued at its fair market value on the date of the gift.[12] Fair market value is the "price at which [gifted] * * * property would change hands between a willing buyer and a willing seller, neither being under any compulsion to buy or to sell, and both having reasonable knowledge of relevant facts."[13]

Where the gifted property is an annuity, life estate or remainder or reversion, the value of the property from which the annuity, life estate, remainder or reversion is carved must first be valued under the willing seller-willing buyer test. This value is then multiplied by the appropriate factor set forth in the Treasury regulations[14] taking account of the age of the relevant beneficiary or the term for which the interest is payable. To illustrate, suppose Mary transfers Blackacre to Alice for life, remainder to Bernie. In order to value the gifts to Alice and Bernie Blackacre first must be valued. Assume that under the willing seller-willing buyer test, Blackacre is valued at $100,000. Alice's interest, under the appropriate valuation table, is valued at $98,198; Bernie's interest is valued at $1,934. In computing the amount of Mary's gift tax liability, Mary is deemed to have made a gift of $98,198 to Alice and a transfer of $1,934 to Bernie. However, the gift to Alice is a present interest[15] and qualifies for a $10,000 annual exclusion but the gift to Bernie is a future interest[16] and does not qualify for the annual exclusion.

If the donor retains an interest in gifted property, then the value of the gift must be reduced by the value of the donor's retained interest. However, under section 2702 in most cases where the donor transfers property in trust for the benefit of a family member and retains any interest in the trust, the value of the donor's retained interest will be deemed to be zero. This results in the transferred property's entire value being subject to the gift tax notwithstanding that under state law the donor has retained an interest in the transferred property. For example, suppose Oscar transfers $100,000 to T in trust to pay the income to Oscar for life, remainder to Oscar's daughter. Under the appropriate valuation tables, Oscar's retained interest is worth $62,000 and the daughter's remainder interest is worth $38,000. Nonetheless, section 2702 provides that Oscar's retained interest is to be valued at zero Since Oscar's taxable gift equals the difference between the amount transferred and the value of his retained interest and under section 2702 Oscar's retained interest is valued at zero, he makes a taxable gift of $100,000. Section 2702 does not apply to otherwise completed gifts if the donor's retained interest is in the form of a (a) guaranteed annuity (pay Oscar $8,000 per year), (b) a unitrust interest (pay Oscar an annual payment equal to 6% of the value of the trust principal valued on the first day of each calendar year, or (c) a remainder interest in a trust in which another has either an annuity or unitrust interest. Section 2702 also is inapplicable to trusts of a qualified

**12.** A gift is deemed made when the gift is complete. See notes 34–61, *infra* and accompanying text.

**13.** Treas.Reg. § 25.2512–1.

**14.** Treas.Reg. § 25.2512–5.

**15.** A present interest for gift tax purposes is an "unrestricted right to the immediate use, possession, or enjoyment of property or the income from property." Treas.Reg. § 25.2503–3(b).

**16.** A future interest for gift tax purposes is "a legal term, and includes reversions, remainders, and other interests or estates, whether vested or contingent, and whether or not supported by a particular interest or estate, which are limited to commence in use, possession, or enjoyment at some future date or time." Treas.Reg. § 25.2503–3(a).

personal residence. Under this exception it remains possible to transfer the remainder interest in a personal residence and have the value of the donor's retained life estate reduce the amount of the gift. However any transfer tax savings would be lost as the entire residence would be included in the donor's gross estate under section 2036. On the other hand, if the donor retained only a term interest in the residence, the value of the donor's retained interest reduces the amount of the gift and, if the donor outlives the term, the residence would not be included in the donor's gross estate and thus future appreciation would have escaped transfer taxes.

Even if section 2702 is inapplicable, if the donor's retained interest cannot be valued by recognized actuarial methods, then its value is presumed to be zero.[17]

### *Calculation of Gift Tax and Payment of Tax*

The amount of gift taxes payable on taxable gifts for the calendar year is determined by first calculating a tentative gift tax on the aggregate value of taxable gifts for the calendar year and all prior calendar years, and then reducing this tentative tax by a tax computed on the aggregate value of taxable gifts for all prior years.[18] The resulting tax is then reduced by the remaining amount of the taxpayer's unified credit.[19] Prior years gifts are taken into account in calculating the gift tax payable on the current year's gifts to assure progressivity in the gift tax. To illustrate, suppose Harry makes a gift of $300,000 to Andrea in 1996. Harry and his wife, Joan, elect to split this gift for gift tax purposes. Harry's aggregate taxable gifts for years prior to 1996 equal $550,000. In computing the gift taxes thereon in prior years Harry used $174,300 of his unified credit. The amount of his 1996 gift tax liability is $37,000 determined as follows:

| | | |
|---|---|---|
| 1996 Gift | | $300,000 |
| Portion deemed made by Joan | | 150,000 |
| Harry's 1996 taxable gift | | $150,000 |
| Harry's prior years' gifts | | 550,000 |
| Harry's total gifts | | |
| Tax on $700,000 | | $229,800 |
| Tax on $550,000 | | 174,300 |
| Difference | | $ 55,500 |
| Unified Credit | $192,800 | |
| Previously Used | 174,300 | |
| Remaining Credit | | 18,500 |
| Gift tax due | | $ 37,000 |

This method of calculation assures progressivity in the computation of gift taxes with respect to gifts made over a donor's lifetime. Therefore, the same amount of gift taxes is payable by a donor who makes total taxable gifts of $700,000 over more than one year and a donor who makes $700,000 of taxable gifts only in one year if one ignores the benefits of multiple annual exclusions if the gifts had been made over multiple calendar years.

17. Robinette v. Helvering, 318 U.S. 184 (1943).

18. I.R.C. § 2502.

19. I.R.C. § 2505. See also Chart II at end of chapter.

The gift tax payable on gifts made during a calendar year is payable on or before April 15 following the close of the calendar year.[20]

### *Identity of the Donee*

Since the gift tax is imposed on the value of property transferred by a donor, rather than upon the value of property received by a donee, ordinarily the identity of a donee is not important to the assessment of the gift tax. In certain cases, however, the identity of the donee or the nature of the interest received by the donee rather than the nature of the interest transferred by the donor may be important.

If the donee is a charity, gifts to the donee can qualify for a gift tax charitable deduction.[21] If the donee is the donor's spouse, the gift can qualify for a gift tax marital deduction.[22] If the interest passing to the donee is a "present interest," the value thereof qualifies for the annual exclusion. Lastly, if transfers are made in trust, the donee is the person or persons entitled to the beneficial interests in the trust, not the trustee. This can be important in determining not only the availability of a charitable or marital deduction but also the value of the donated interest from the valuation tables published in the Treasury Regulations[23] and the amount, if any, that qualifies for the annual exclusion.

### *The Annual Exclusion and Medical and Tuition Payment Exclusion*

Section 2503(b) provides an annual exclusion not to exceed $10,000 for gifts of a present interest to any donee in each calendar year. Gifts of a future interest do not qualify for the exclusion.[24] An unrestricted right to the use, possession or enjoyment of property or the income therefrom is a gift of a present interest.[25] Gifts of discretionary income interests even if limited by a standard do not qualify for the annual exclusion. Similarly, gifts of reversions and remainders do not qualify for the annual exclusion as they are gifts of a future interest.

Use of the annual exclusion to avoid gift taxes on annual transfers can result in a significant shift of wealth from one generation to another without any transfer tax cost. For example, if $10,000 is given annually to a child for 20 years, $200,000 of tax free gifts can be made to that child over a 20 year period. For married couples utilizing the split gift rules, annual gifts to any donee of $20,000 can be made gift tax free. Gifts shielded from tax by the annual exclusion do not result in any further use of the donor's unified credit. For large families the potential to shift wealth from one generation to another at little or no transfer tax cost using only the annual exclusion to fully shield gifts from tax can be significant.

A transfer to a minor that does not meet the ordinary definition of a present interest can qualify for the annual exclusion if the transfer qualifies as a present interest under Section 2503(c). Under Section 2503(c) no part of

**20.** I.R.C. §§ 6075(b); 6151.

**21.** See notes 70–73, *infra* and accompanying text.

**22.** See notes 74–77, *infra* and accompanying text.

**23.** Treas.Reg. § 25.2512–5(f).

**24.** I.R.C. § 2503(b).

**25.** Treas.Reg. § 25.2503–3(b).

a gift is considered to be a gift of a future interest if the gift is made to a person under age 21 and if the gifted property and the income therefrom may be paid to, or applied towards the benefit of, the donee prior to the donee attaining age 21, and such property and the income will pass to the donee when the donee attains age 21 or, if the donee dies prior to attaining age 21, such property and the income is payable to either the donee's estate or as the donee may appoint pursuant to a general power of appointment.

This statute has led to the creation of so-called Section 2503(c) trusts under the terms of which income in the trustee's discretion may be paid to the donee prior to the donee attaining age 21 or accumulated for distribution to the donee when the donee attains age 21. These Section 2503(c) trusts must also provide that (1) when the donee attains age 21, the principal and any accumulated income shall be paid to the donee, or (2) if the donee dies under age 21, the principal and any accumulated income will be paid to his estate.[26] Many donors prefer to provide that if the donee dies under age 21 the principal and accumulated income will be paid to such persons as the donee appoints pursuant to a general testamentary power of appointment and then designate takers in default of appointment in the event (which is quite likely) the donee's general power is unexercised. If the trustee's power to pay income to the donee is substantially restricted, the gift will not qualify as a present interest under Section 2503(c).[27] A trustee's discretion is not substantially restricted if payments are limited to providing for the donee's "support," "care," or "education."[28]

Gifts to minors under Uniform Gifts (Transfers) to Minors Act qualify for the annual exclusion under the Section 2503(b) exception.[29]

In lieu of a Section 2503(c) trust donors may qualify transfers in trust for the annual exclusion even though the donee's interest is not described in Section 2503(c) by the use of so-called "Crummey" powers.[30] A Crummey power is a species of a general power that enables the donee of the power to appoint the property subject to the power to himself for a limited period of time, at the end of which, the power lapses if, in fact, it is not exercised. Since the donee has a general power, albeit, for a limited period, it qualifies as a present interest and the property over which the power is exercisable qualifies for the annual exclusion. To illustrate, suppose Bob transfers $10,000 in trust to pay the income to Sandy, or, in the trustee's discretion, to accumulate the trust income. The trust will terminate when Sandy dies or attains age 40 when the trust principal is payable to Sandy, if living, or otherwise to Sandy's issue. Sandy is age 17. On its face the trust does not qualify for the annual exclusion under Section 2503(c). If Bob also granted Sandy a Crummey power exercisable only for the first three months after the contribution to the trust, then the annual exclusion would be allowable because the Crummey power vests Sandy with a present interest in the trust. It is irrelevant that Sandy

**26.** It is possible to qualify the value of the under age 21 income interest as a present interest even if the trust corpus is not payable to the donee when the donee attains age 21. See Herr v. Comm'r, 35 T.C. 732 (1961), affirmed 303 F.2d 780 (3d Cir.1962); Estate of Levine v. C.I.R., 63 T.C. 136 (1974), reversed 526 F.2d 717 (2d Cir.1975).

**27.** Treas.Reg. § 25.2503–4(b)(1).

**28.** See Rev. Rul. 67–270, 1967–2 C.B. 349.

**29.** Rev. Rul. 59–357, 1959–2 C.B. 212. See generally, § 9.2, note 5 et. seq. for a discussion of these acts.

**30.** Crummey v. C.I.R., 397 F.2d 82 (9th Cir.1968).

lets the power lapse. Crummey powers work so long as (i) the donee receives notice of the contribution and a reasonable opportunity to exercise the power,[31] and (ii) in the Service's but not the courts' view, the holder of the power has either a current income interest or a vested remainder.[32]

Payments made on behalf of a person's tuition at an educational institution or for such person's medical care are not taxable gifts. This exclusion is not available if the payments are made to the intended donee who then pays the tuition or medical expense.[33] The wording of the statute places a premium on direct payments to the educational institution or health care provider as payments through the student do not qualify for the exclusion.

### *Complete and Incomplete Gifts*

The gift tax is imposed only upon so-called completed gifts. A transfer for less than adequate and full consideration in money or money's worth is a completed gift for gift tax purposes only if the enjoyment of the transferred property is placed beyond the donor's dominion and control. The dominion and control test is explained as follows:[34]

> As to any property, or part thereof or interest therein, of which the donor has so parted with dominion and control as to leave in him no power to change its disposition, whether for his own benefit or for the benefit of another, the gift is complete. But if upon the transfer of property (whether in trust or otherwise) the donor reserves any power over its disposition, the gift may be partially complete and partially incomplete, depending upon all the facts in the particular case.

If the donor transfers property outright and the transferred property is beyond the donor's dominion and control, the gift is complete for gift tax purposes. Alternatively, if the donor retains any power to regain possession or ownership of the property or retains the power to determine who shall enjoy the benefits of the property, the gift is incomplete[35] and no taxable gift is made until the donor's dominion and control terminates over the transferred property. In many cases, however, the donor's dominion and control will not terminate in the donor's lifetime. In this case, more likely than not, the property will be included in the donor's gross estate for estate tax purposes[36] and not be included in the donor's gift tax base. For example, if Mary transfers property into a revocable trust, no gift occurs when the trust is created because Mary retains dominion and control over the transferred property. If two years later Mary releases the power of revocation, a gift occurs at that time since after the release Mary no longer has dominion and

**31.** See Rev. Rul. 81–7, 1981–1 C.B. 474.

**32.** See Tech. Adv. Mem. 96–28–004 (7/12/96). Crummey power granted to persons with no underlying interest in the trust are called "naked powers." The Tax Court rejects the Service's view. See, e.g, Kohlsaat v. C.I.R., 73 T.C.M (CCH) ¶ 2732 (1997); Cristofani v. C.I.R., 97 T.C. 74 (1991).

**33.** I.R.C. § 2503(e).

**34.** Treas.Reg. § 25.2511(b).

**35.** An apparent exception is found in Treas.Reg. § 25.2511–2(d) where it is provided that if the donor retains the power only to affect the time and manner of enjoyment of property, the gift is complete for gift tax purposes. For example, if the donor transfers property to T in trust to pay the income to A until A attains age 21 when the trust terminates and the corpus is distributable to A, the gift is complete even though the donor retains the power to direct trust income be accumulated until A attains age 21 and distributed to A at that time.

**36.** See § 15.3, *infra* notes 49 et. seq. and accompanying text.

control.[37] If Mary fails to release the power during her life and dies in possession of the power, the property in the trust is included in Mary's gross estate.[38]

Mary is deemed to retain dominion and control even though the power she retains cannot be exercised for her pecuniary benefit. For example, suppose Mary transfers property in trust to pay the income to such of Alice, Bob and Charlie as Mary from time to time directs. Upon Mary's death the trust terminates and the principal is distributable to Alice, Bob and Charlie. In this case, Mary retains dominion and control over the income interest[39] but no dominion and control over the value of the remainder interest. Thus, the gift of the income interest is incomplete; the gift of the remainder interest is complete. In other words, in measuring whether there is a completed gift, each interest in the trust is considered separately. In this case, the trust property will also be included in Mary's gross estate because Mary retained a power to control the beneficial enjoyment of the income interest. When the estate tax is computed on Mary's estate, however, appropriate credit will be allowed for the gift tax paid on the value of the completed gift of the remainder interest.[40]

An incomplete gift may become complete for gift tax purposes because the property that is the subject of the gift is distributed to a beneficiary free of a donor's retained power. For example, suppose John creates a revocable trust for the primary benefit of Alice and transfers $100,000 to the trustee. This transfer is not a completed gift because of John's retained dominion and control. The following year the trustee distributes the trust's entire income for that year to Alice. In Alice's hands the income is no longer subject to John's power of revocation. The distribution of income to Alice results in John making a taxable gift of that income to Alice even though with respect to the trust the gift continues to be incomplete.[41]

Whether a gift is complete or incomplete for gift tax purposes does not determine whether the gifted property is included or excluded from the donor's gross estate. The taxability of any transfer is separately determined under rules governing each tax. In those cases where a gift is incomplete for gift tax purposes the entire gift or some portion thereof will be included in the donor's gross estate. Counterintuitively, however, gifts that are wholly complete for gift tax purposes may also be included in the donor's gross estate. One example is where property is transferred in trust to pay the income to Alice until she attains age 21 when any accumulated income and principal is to be paid to her. John, the grantor, retains the power to direct the trustee to accumulate the income rather than pay it to Alice. This gift is complete for gift tax purposes[42] but the entire trust also is included in John's gross estate if John dies before Alice reaches age 21.[43]

**37.** Treas.Reg. § 25.2511–2(f).

**38.** I.R.C. § 2038.

**39.** Treas.Reg. § 25.2511–2(c).

**40.** See I.R.C. § 2036.

**41.** Treas.Reg. § 25.2511–2(f). To the extent the amount of income payable to Alice is less than the available annual exclusion, it is not a taxable gift.

Under I.R.C. § 676 John will include the income paid to Alice in his gross income. Section 676 treats John as the owner of any portion of a trust with respect to which John has a power of revocation. When the income is distributed to Alice, she receives it income tax free. I.R.C. § 101.

**42.** Treas.Reg. § 25.2511–2(d).

**43.** I.R.C. § 2036. This is precisely what happens when the donor acts as custodian under either the Uniform Gifts or Transfers to Minors Acts.

A more common example occurs where a donor retains a power over transferred property that is exercisable only with the consent of an adverse person. Under the gift tax, if a donor retains a power over transferred property that is exercisable only with the consent of an adverse person, the gift of the interest in which there is adversity is complete. For example, if Doris transfers property in trust to pay the income to Lauren for life, remainder to Arthur, and Doris retains the power to accumulate the income for ultimate distribution to Arthur, for gift tax purposes the gift of the income interest is incomplete because of Doris' retained power; the gift of the remainder, however, is complete.[44] Furthermore, the entire trust is included in Doris' gross estate under Section 2036 because of her retained power. If, however, Doris' power to accumulate income was exercisable only with Lauren's consent, the gift of the income and remainder interests would be complete.[45] The gift of the remainder interest is complete because Doris retains no dominion and control over that interest; the gift of the income interest is complete because Doris' power is exercisable only with Lauren's consent and Lauren has an interest that would be adversely affected if Doris exercised the power. Nonetheless, the entire trust is included in Doris' gross estate under Section 2036 because of her co-held power to accumulate the income.[46]

A substantial adverse interest exists only if there is a substantial economic interest that could be prejudiced or destroyed if the power over the interest was exercised. No adverse interest exists in a property interest in which the co-holder of power has no economic benefits. For example, suppose Mary creates a revocable trust under which income is payable to Allan and the remainder is distributable to Betty. Mary retains the power to revoke the trust but only with Allan's consent. In this case there is a completed gift only of the income interest. Allan has no economic interest in the remainder interest distributable to Betty when he dies. Admittedly, if Allan joined with Mary in terminating the trust in favor of Mary, Allan's income interest would terminate. However he could be persuaded to join with Mary in revoking the trust by an agreement that Mary pay him the present value of his income interest.

If a donor declares himself trustee, or transfers property to himself and another as trustees, retains no beneficial interest in the property but retains a fiduciary power the exercise of which is limited by an ascertainable standard which would permit him to change beneficiaries, the gift is complete for gift tax purposes.[47] For example, if Bob creates a trust to pay so much of the income to Pat and Jenny as they need for their support and upon the death of Bob to distribute the corpus to Emily, the gift of the income interest is complete even though Bob is a trustee.[48] The retention of a power limited by an ascertainable standard is not the equivalent of a discretionary power and

**44.** Doris' power to increase to value of the remainder interest by directing an accumulation of income is effectively a power to make additions, not a power to alter Arthur's initial interest in the trust.

**45.** Treas.Reg. § 25.2511–2(e).

**46.** In computing the estate tax liability on Doris' estate credit will be allowed for any gift tax paid on this transfer.

**47.** Treas.Reg. § 25.2511–2(g).

**48.** See the discussion of the ascertainable standard exception under the estate tax law at § 15.3, *infra*, notes 65 & 97, and accompanying text.

does not amount to the retention of dominion and control such that the gift is incomplete.

### *Subject Matter of A Gift*

The gift tax is assessed against transfers of property. Property includes real and personal property, tangible and intangible property.[49] The tax applies whether a legal or equitable interest in property is transferred.[50] A gift can be made of a present or a future interest, a vested or a contingent interest.[51] An income interest can be the subject of a gift. Thus, if John creates a trust under which Alice is entitled to the income for life and subsequently Alice transfers her income interest to Bob, Alice makes a gift to Bob equal to the value of her income interest at the time of the transfer measured by reference to her life expectancy.[52]

A gift of a check is complete at the earlier of the date on which the donor no longer has the power to change it disposition, or the date when the donee deposits the check or cashes the check.[53]

Property applied towards the benefit of another rather than paid to him can constitute a gift. Thus, if Don owes Arnie $5,000 and Oscar gratuitously pays Don's debt to Arnie, Oscar makes a gift to Don, not Arnie. This fact may be important for purposes of the $10,000 annual exclusion.

The forgiveness of a debt is a gift.[54]

Life insurance can be the subject matter of a gift although the value of the gift, if the insured is living, is necessarily less than the face value of the policy.[55] A gift of a life insurance policy can be made by its irrevocable assignment to another.[56] However, the designation of someone as the beneficiary of a life insurance policy is not a gift if the owner retains the right to change the beneficiary as is usually the case. Likewise an irrevocable beneficiary designation would not result in the making of a gift under the dominion and control test if the owner retained the power to cancel the policy or surrender the policy for its cash surrender value. The proceeds of gifted life insurance are included in the insured's gross estate if the insured dies within three years of the gift.[57]

The gift tax does not apply to a gift of personal services by the donor regardless of value.[58] If the donor pays a third person to perform a personal service for another, the amount paid is a gift.[59] Thus, if Scott pays Nancy $15,000 to perform a medical procedure on Tom, Scott makes a gift to Tom of $15,000.

**49.** I.R.C. § 2511(a).

**50.** Treas.Reg. § 25.2511–1(g)(1).

**51.** Goodwin v. McGowan, 47 F.Supp. 798 (W.D.N.Y.1942).

**52.** See, *e.g.,* Lockard v. C.I.R., 166 F.2d 409 (1st Cir.1948).

**53.** Rev. Rul. 96–56, 1996–2 C.B. 161. If the donor dies before the donee cashes the check, the value of the checks is included in the donor's gross estate. See McCarthy v. United States, 806 F.2d 129 (7th Cir.1986); § 4.5, supra, note 36.

**54.** Treas.Reg. § 25.2511–1(a).

**55.** See Treas.Reg. § 25.2511–6 for the valuation of gifted life insurance policies.

**56.** Treas.Reg. § 25.2511–1(h)(8).

**57.** I.R.C. § 2035. Gifts of life insurance can be an effective way to transfer significant wealth at little or no transfer tax cost. See § 15.3, *infra,* and note 143, and accompanying text.

**58.** *See generally,* C.I.R. v. Hogle, 165 F.2d 352 (10th Cir.1947); Rev.Rul. 64–225, 1964–2 C.B. 15, Rev.Rul. 66–167, 1966–1 C.B. 20, Rev. Rul. 70–237, 1970–1 C.B. 13.

**59.** Regs. § 25.2511–1(h)(3).

### *Powers of Appointment*

Section 2514 governs the gift taxation of general powers of appointment that have been exercised or released during the donee's lifetime.[60] For gift tax purposes a general power of appointment is a power under which the donee can appoint to himself, "his estate, his creditors, or the creditors of his estate."[61] Under Section 2514 if a donee of a general power exercises or releases the power, the donee is deemed to have made a transfer. Whether this transfer results in the making of a taxable gift further depends upon whether, as a result of the exercise or release, the donee has surrendered dominion and control over the property that was subject to the power.

Suppose Olive transfers property in trust to pay the income to Cecil for life, remainder to Cecil's surviving issue. Olive grants Cecil a general inter vivos power to appoint the property to himself or anyone else. Two years later Cecil exercises the power and appoints the entire trust principal to Jack. The exercise of the power results in a transfer of the trust property from Cecil to Jack. Since Cecil retains no dominion and control over the transferred property, the exercise of the power also results in his making a taxable gift.

Similarly, suppose that Cecil exercises the power by directing that the trustee hold the property in trust to pay the income to Jack for life, remainder to Jack's children. In this case Cecil also makes a transfer under Section 2514 and a gift because he retains no dominion and control. But, suppose that when exercising this power, Cecil provided that he could revoke the appointment in trust for the benefit of Jack and Jack's children. In this case Cecil makes a transfer under Section 2514 because he exercised the power. However, no gift results from the exercise of the power in this manner because Cecil retained dominion and control by retaining a power of revocation.

If Cecil does not exercise the power but rather releases the power, Cecil also makes a transfer of the property subject to the power under Section 2514. Of course, since a person cannot make a gift to himself, this release/transfer results in a gift of the remainder interest only. This gift would not qualify for any annual exclusion because it is a gift of a future interest. Cecil's release of the general power does not result in the termination of his income interest.[62]

The lapse of a general power is considered to be a release of a power.[63] A lapse of a power occurs when the donee fails to exercise the power within a time period specified in the instrument creating the power. Thus, if Oscar grants Felix a general inter vivos power exercisable prior to January 1, 1990 and Felix fails to exercise the power by that date, on January 1, 1990 when the power lapses Felix is deemed to have released the power. This "lapse equals a release" rule is tempered by a special provision that the lapse of a power during any calendar year is treated as a release of a power in that year

60. Section 2514 distinguishes between general powers created on or before October 21, 1942 (so-called "pre–42 powers" ) and powers created after October 21, 1942 (so-called "post–42 powers".) The discussion in the text is limited to post–42 powers. See also, § 10.4, note 6 for a discussion of powers.

61. I.R.C. § 2514(c). This broad definition of a general power is subject to a number of refinements. These are discussed in § 15.3 *infra*. The distinction is similar to the one drawn between general and special powers of appointment for non-tax purposes. See § 10.4, *supra*, note 6.

62. While Cecil's makes a gift only of the remainder interest, the value of that interest will equal the value of trust corpus since the value of Cecil's retained interest is zero under section 2702.

63. I.R.C. § 2514(e).

"only to the extent that the property which could have been appointed by exercise of such lapsed powers exceeds in value the greater of "$5,000 or 5% of the aggregate value of the assets out of which, or the proceeds of which, the exercise of the lapsed powers could be satisfied."[64] This so-called "5 and 5" rule has lead to the development of an important estate planning tool.

Under the "5 and 5 rule" a donee may be granted a general power, exercisable annually, to withdraw from the principal of a trust an amount equal to the greater of $5,000 or 5% of trust principal valued annually. If the donee exercises the power there is no gift because a person cannot make a gift to herself. If the donee permits the power to lapse, no release (and therefore no transfer) occurs because of the 5 and 5 rule. This type of power is attractive because it permits the donee to withdraw trust principal to the dollar limits of the power for any reason whatsoever and without the approval of any other person.[65]

If a donee is given an annual withdrawal power measured by a fixed dollar amount which exceeds the 5 and 5 limits, the lapse of the power results in a release of the power *only to the extent of the excess*. For example, suppose Dolly has an annual withdrawal power exercisable in the amount of $15,000 with respect to a trust that at all times is valued at $150,000. In any year Dolly exercises the power in full, there is no gift tax consequence. (Remember, Dolly can't make a gift to herself). In any year in which there is a lapse of the power in an amount of $7,500 or less, there is no gift tax consequence because the lapsed power is valued under the 5 and 5 limits. However, in any year there is a lapse of the power in excess of $7,500, the excess is deemed to have been transferred by Dolly and subject to gift tax unless she retains dominion and control over the property. For example, suppose Dolly, in addition to having a $15,000 withdrawal power, possessed a testamentary special power to appoint the property among her children. A lapse of the power results in a transfer of $7,500 ($15,000 − $7,500) but no gift because Dolly retains dominion and control over the property subject to the lapsed power because of her testamentary special power. If, on the other hand, Dolly did not have the testamentary special power, the lapse of the power would result in a gift of the remainder interest in $7,500, assuming Dolly was the income beneficiary of the trust. This would be a gift of a future interest and would not qualify for the annual exclusion.[66] Any tax on the remainder interest, however, could be avoided by the use of Dolly's unified credit.

### *Transfers Pursuant to a Property Settlement Agreement*

Section 2516 sets forth special rules relating to the gift tax consequences of property transfers made pursuant to the terms of a property settlement agreement. If a married couple executes a written agreement relating to their marital and property rights and the parties are divorced within a three year period beginning on a date that is one year prior to when the agreement is made, transfers of property or interests in property pursuant to the terms of the agreement to either spouse in settlement of the spouse's marital or

**64.** I.R.C. § 2514(e).

**65.** See also § 15.32, *infra,* notes 128–132 and accompanying text.

**66.** *See also* notes 24–33, *supra* and accompanying text. The fact that the 5 & 5 rule is not coextensive with the $10,000 annual exclusion can result in possible adverse tax consequence if the donee of a Crummey power permits it to lapse. See, notes 43–49, *supra* and accompanying text.

property rights or to provide a reasonable allowance for the support of the issue of the marriage during minority are deemed to be transfers for adequate and full consideration in money or money's worth.[67] Section 2516 applies even though the agreement is not approved by the divorce decree.

### *Qualifying Income Interest for Life*

If a person transfers a qualifying income interest for life in any property, the transferor is deemed to have made a transfer of the remainder interest as well.[68] A more thorough discussion of this provision is contained in the section on qualified terminable interest property.[69]

### *Gifts to Charity or to the Donor's Spouse*

Gifts to qualified[70] charitable organizations qualify for an unlimited charitable deduction.[71] Special rules apply when gifts are made in trust for the benefit of both charities and private individuals.[72] These special rules are more fully discussed in the section on the estate tax charitable deduction.[73]

A gift to the donor's spouse qualifies for an unlimited marital deduction[74] so long as the gift is not disqualified for the deduction under the nondeductible terminable interest rule.[75] The marital deduction rules are more fully discussed in the section on the estate tax marital deduction.[76]

## § 15.3 The Estate Tax

A federal estate tax, in common with the federal gift tax, is a tax on the right of transferring property at death.[1] The tax is measured against a tax base that includes not only the assets of decedent's probate estate[2] but also certain gifts by the decedent during life that are deemed to be the equivalent of testamentary transfers because decedent retained either an interest or power over the gift. Items included in a decedent's gross estate are reduced by other items to calculate decedent's taxable estate.

The gross estate is computed by taking into account the following:

1. Property owned at death.[3]
2. Certain property transferred within three years of death.[4]

**67.** I.R.C. § 2516.

**68.** I.R.C. § 2519.

**69.** See § 15.3, *infra,* notes 174–178 and accompanying text.

**70.** I.R.C. § 2522(a). The definition of "charitable" for tax purposes, while similar, is not identical to its definition for "trust law" purposes. See § 9.7, *supra,* note 5 et. seq.; § 15.3, *infra.*

**71.** I.R.C. § 2522.

**72.** I.R.C. § 2522(c).

**73.** See § 15.3 *infra,* notes 153–161, and accompanying text.

**74.** I.R.C. § 2523.

**75.** I.R.C. § 2523(b).

**76.** See § 15.3, *infra,* notes 162–180 and accompanying text.

**§ 15.3**

**1.** See, Hodel v. Irving, 481 U.S. 704 (1987)(holding that the complete abolition of both the devise and descent of property can be an unconstitutional taking).

**2.** Probate estate property is limited to property capable of passing by a decedent's will or under the laws of intestate succession. Thus, it excludes such property as joint tenancy property, life insurance and annuities payable to a named beneficiary. For possible, non-tax advantages to keeping property out of the probate estate, see § 9.1, *supra.*

**3.** I.R.C. § 2033.

**4.** I.R.C. § 2035.

3. Lifetime transfers in which decedent retained an interest for life.[5]

4. Certain lifetime transfers taking effect at the decedent's death.[6]

5. Revocable transfers.[7]

6. Annuities.[8]

7. Joint tenancy property.[9]

8. General powers of appointment.[10]

9. Life insurance.[11]

10. Qualified Terminable Interest Property.[12]

The deductions available to compute the decedent's taxable estate are:

1. Debts, expenses and taxes.[13]

2. Losses.[14]

3. Charitable deduction.[15]

4. Marital deduction.[16]

5. The family-owned business interest deduction.[17]

In order to assure that cumulative lifetime and testamentary transfers are taxed in accordance with the progressive unified rate schedule, the estate tax base also includes the value of decedent's adjusted taxable gifts.[18] A tentative estate tax is then computed against this base which is then reduced by the gift taxes payable on adjusted taxable gifts. The resulting tax is then reduced by a unified credit which, when fully phased in by 2006, will be $345,800 (the equivalent of a $1,000,000 exemption)[19] and, if applicable, the credit for state death taxes,[20] the credit for pre–1977 gift taxes,[21] the tax on prior transfers,[22] and the foreign death tax credit.[23]

To illustrate, suppose John dies in 1995 when the unified credit was $192,800, leaving a gross estate of $2,500,000, deductions of $300,000, and adjusted taxable gifts of $800,000. The estate tax on John's estate is $1,008,000 determined as follows:

| | |
|---|---|
| Gross estate | $2,500,000 |
| Less: Deductions | 300,000 |

5. I.R.C. § 2036.
6. I.R.C. § 2037.
7. I.R.C. § 2038.
8. I.R.C. § 2039.
9. I.R.C. § 2040.
10. I.R.C. § 2041.
11. I.R.C. § 2042.
12. I.R.C. § 2044.
13. I.R.C. § 2053.
14. I.R.C. § 2054.
15. I.R.C. § 2055.
16. I.R.C. § 2056.
17. I.R.C. § 2057.
18. Adjusted taxable gifts are gifts made after December 31, 1976 that are not included in the decedent's gross estate. I.R.C. § 2001(b). While "adjusted taxable gifts" are added to the taxable estate to assure progressivity in the calculation of the estate tax, that should not suggest there is not benefit in the making of lifetime gifts. That is because, once a lifetime gift is made subsequent appreciation on that gift is excluded from both the donor's gift and estate tax base.
19. I.R.C. § 2010. *See also* Chart I at the end of the chapter.
20. I.R.C. § 2011.
21. I.R.C. § 2012.
22. I.R.C. § 2013.
23. I.R.C. § 2014.

| | |
|---|---|
| Taxable estate | $2,200,000 |
| Adjusted taxable gifts | 800,000 |
| Estate tax base | $3,000,000 |
| Tax on base | $1,275,800 |
| Tax on adjusted taxable gifts | 75,000 |
| Difference | $1,200,800 |
| Unified Credit | 192,800 |
| Federal estate tax | $1,008,000 |

### *Valuation and Income Tax Basis; Due Date of the Return*

Two separate questions must be kept clearly in mind when calculating the value of the gross estate. The first is whether a particular asset is included in the gross estate; the second is what is the included asset's value. An included asset's value is determined under one of three sections of the estate tax law.

Section 2031 provides that assets included in the gross estate are valued at the "fair market value" on the date of the decedent's death. In common with the gift tax, fair market value is determined under the willing seller-willing buyer test.[24]

In lieu of the date of death valuation method, the executor may elect on the estate tax return[25] to value all[26] of the estate assets under the alternate valuation method. This valuation method is available only if as a result of the election (1) the value of the gross estate will be less than its value based upon date of death values and (2) the amount of the estate tax will be less than it would be if estate tax values were determined on decedent's date of death.[27] This provision prevents the use of the alternate valuation method merely for the purpose of obtaining higher estate tax values and therefor a higher income tax basis where there would be no estate tax cost. This might occur where the estate qualified for an unlimited marital deduction.

Under the alternate valuation method gross estate assets are valued on the sixth month anniversary of the decedent's date of death or, if any asset is sold, distributed, exchanged or otherwise disposed of between the date of decedent's death and the sixth month anniversary thereof, on the date of its sale, distribution, exchange, or other disposition.

To illustrate if Harry owned Asset A valued at $100 at his death and $50 on the sixth month anniversary of his death, Asset A would be valued at $100 if date of death values were used or at $50 if the alternate valuation method was used. If between Harry's death and the sixth month anniversary thereof Asset A were sold for $65 and Harry's estate was valued under the alternate valuation method, Asset A would be valued at $65.

Under Section 2032A, certain qualifying real estate can be valued under the so-called "special use" valuation method.[28] Under this method, value is not determined by reference to the property's highest and best use but at its

**24.** Treas.Reg. § 20.2031–1(b).

**25.** Ordinarily the estate tax return is due on or before the ninth month anniversary of the decedent's death. *But see,* I.R.C. § 2032(d).

**26.** Treas.Reg. § 20.2032–1(b)(2).

**27.** I.R.C. § 2032(c).

**28.** I.R.C. § 2032A.

actual value taking account of its farming or business use. Section 2032A is exceptionally complicated by rules designed to assure that the statutory benefits are available only to committed, long-time farm and small-business owners.

The income tax basis of inherited property equals its estate tax value determined as of date of death or under the alternate or special use valuation methods.[29] Thus, decedent's income tax basis in the property is ignored in favor of a basis that is "stepped up" (or "stepped down") to the property's estate tax value.

This rule applies even though decedent's estate was too small to require the filing of an estate tax return. In such case, however, the property's fair market value on the date of decedent's death controls since the alternate valuation method is only available for estates for which an estate tax return must be filed.[30] Section 1014 applies with respect to all property included in the gross estate.[31]

The effect of Section 1014 is to assure that increases in the value of property between the time decedent acquired the property and the time the decedent dies escapes income tax. Similarly, losses in value between those dates go unrecognized.

The federal estate tax return, and any tax payable thereon, is due nine months after the date of the decedent's death[32] unless the time has been extended.

### *Property Owned at Death*

The gross estate includes the value of all interests in property owned by the decedent at the time of death,[33] including real property, tangible and intangible personal property, such as stocks, bonds, notes and cash. The decedent's property interest must have been a beneficial interest.[34] Thus if decedent owned property merely as a trustee at the time of his death, the property is not included in the decedent's gross estate.[35] Decedent's property interest can be a future interest.[36] While literally read property owned at death would include property interests which simultaneously expired with the decedent's death, such as a life estate measured by decedent's life, a contingent remainder, or a joint tenancy, only those interests capable of passing from the decedent by the laws of intestate succession or by decedent's will are included in the decedent's gross estate under the provision relating to property owned at death.[37] Thus if decedent's life estate terminates at decedent's death it is not included in the decedent's gross estate.[38]

**29.** I.R.C. § 1014. See also § 15.1, *supra*, notes 7–13 and accompanying text.

**30.** See Rev.Rul. 56–60, 1956–1 C.B. 443; Treas.Reg. § 20.2032–1(b)(1).

**31.** An important exception to this rule is Section 1014(c) providing that the general basis rule of Section 1014 does not apply to income in respect of a decedent. *See also* I.R.C. § 691.

**32.** I.R.C. §§ 6075(a); 6151.

**33.** I.R.C. § 2033.

**34.** See, *e.g.* Reed v. C.I.R., 36 F.2d 867 (5th Cir.1930).

**35.** *Id.*

**36.** Adriance v. Higgins, 113 F.2d 1013 (2d Cir.1940).

**37.** *But see* I.R.C. § 2040 relating to joint tenancies.

**38.** In some cases not all of the income due the decedent was paid to the decedent prior to his death. Any accrued or undistributed income due the decedent would be included in the decedent's probate and gross estates. See,

Generally, whether decedent has a property interest is determined under state law[39] but a state law characterization of an interest may not control for federal estate tax purposes. This fact is well illustrated by the case of *Commissioner v. Bosch's Estate.*[40] After Mr. Bosch died his estate claimed a marital deduction for property passing to Mrs. Bosch under the terms of a revocable trust that was included in Mr. Bosch's gross estate. The availability of that deduction depended upon whether Mrs. Bosch possessed a general power of appointment over the trust.[41] While the case was pending in the Tax Court the executor of Mr. Bosch's estate initiated a state court proceeding for the settlement of certain accounts. In that proceeding, to which the federal government was not a party, it was held that Mrs. Bosch had a general power. The Tax Court accepted that judgement as controlling and a divided Court of Appeals affirmed. The Service contended that the federal courts did not have to accept the correctness of the state court determination since the government had not been a party to the state court proceeding. The Supreme Court, in reversing the lower court decisions, held that the federal courts were required only to give the state court determination "proper regard;" a state trial court decision should be given some weight; its intermediate appellate court decision should be given greater weight and its highest court's decision should be followed.

Property owned at death includes property that under state law is distributable to the decedent's spouse as dower, curtesy or a statutory right in lieu thereof.[42] It does not include the surviving spouse's share of community property, if applicable. If the spouse's interest qualifies for the estate tax marital deduction,[43] it is excluded from the decedent's taxable estate.

### *Transfers Within Three Years of Death*

The gross estate includes the value of all life insurance policies transferred by the decedent within three years of the decedent's death for less than adequate and full consideration in money or money's worth.[44] For example, if Mary gratuitously transfers to Andy a life insurance policy having a cash value on the date of transfer of $5,000 and a face value of $100,000 and dies within three years of the transfer, $100,000 is included in Mary's gross estate. If, on the other hand, Andy paid Mary $5,000 for the transfer, the policy is excluded from Mary's gross estate because the lifetime transfer was for adequate and full consideration in money or money's worth.

The gross estate also includes the amount of any gift taxes paid by the decedent or the decedent's estate on gifts made by the decedent or the decedent's spouse after December 31, 1976 and within the three year period immediately preceding the decedent's death.[45] Inclusion of such gift tax in the decedent's gross estate is not dependent upon the gift subject to that tax being included in the decedent's gross estate. This section prevents the

*e.g.,* Corbett v. C.I.R., 12 T.C. 163 (1949); § 9.4, *supra,* note 61. While property may not be included in the income beneficiary's estate, the property may be subject to the generation skipping transfer tax at the income beneficiary's death.

**39.** Blair v. C.I.R., 300 U.S. 5 (1937).

**40.** 387 U.S. 456 (1967), on remand 382 F.2d 295 (2d Cir.1967).

**41.** I.R.C. § 2056(b)(5). *See also* notes 119–127, *infra* and accompanying text.

**42.** I.R.C. § 2034.

**43.** I.R.C. § 2056.

**44.** I.R.C. § 2035(a)(2).

**45.** I.R.C. § 2035(b).

making of substantial gifts within three years of death for the purposes (intended or not) of removing the gift tax thereon from the donor's estate tax base. The estate tax is a so-called "gross up" tax meaning that the estate tax base includes funds that will be used to pay the estate tax. The gift tax, on the other hand, is not grossed up. The gift tax is computed on the value of the gift, not the value of the gift increased by the amount of gift tax thereon. However, gifts within three years of death cannot be used to avoid the "gross up" effect of the estate tax with respect to gifts within the three year period.[46]

Lastly, the gross estate includes the value of any interest in property transferred by the decedent within three years of death or the value of any property over which the decedent relinquished a power within three years of death if the value of such property would have been included in the decedent's gross estate under section 2036 (relating to retained life estates), 2037 (relating to transfers taking effect at death) and 2038 (relating to revocable transfers) had the transfer or relinquishment not occurred.[47] However, this rule does not apply to distributions from, or powers relinquished over, trusts if the trust was revocable and the grantor was treated as the owner of the trust under section 676 for income tax purposes.[48] For example, suppose Gary creates a revocable trust and two years before he died he exercised his power of revocation and directed the trustee to distribute $50,000 of trust principal to Anita. For gift tax purposes, Gary makes a taxable gift of $40,000 after taking account of the annual exclusion. The $50,000 is not included in his gross estate. If Gary's power was exercisable only with the consent of persons having an adverse interest, then for purposes of section 676 Gary is not treated as the owner of the trust. In this case, the $50,000 would be included in his gross estate since section 2038 applies without regard to whether the grantor had a power of revocation exercisable only with the consent of another.

### *Transfers with a Retained Life Estate*

The gross estate includes the value of all property to the extent of the decedent's interest therein transferred by the decedent during life, in trust or otherwise, for less than adequate and full consideration in money or money's worth[49] under which the decedent retained (1) for his life, (2) for any period not ascertainable without reference to decedent's death,[50] or (3) for any period that does not in fact end before the decedent's death,[51] either (1) the possession or enjoyment of, or the right to receive the income from, the transferred property, or (2) the right to designate the persons who shall enjoy the transferred property or the income therefrom.

**46.** I.R.C. 2035(c).

**47.** I.R.C. § 2035(a).

**48.** I.R.C. § 2035 (e).

**49.** If decedent received partial consideration for the transfer, then the amount that would otherwise be included in the decedent's gross estate under Section 2036 is reduced by the amount of the partial consideration received. *See generally,* I.R.C. § 2043.

**50.** For example, if decedent retained the income for a period that would end three months before his death, Section 2036 applies because the period of time for which decedent retained the income cannot be determined without reference to his death.

**51.** For example, suppose decedent retained the income from the property transferred in trust for 10 years and decedent died three years after the transfer was made. Decedent retained an interest that did not in fact end before his death. If decedent outlived the 10 years period, Section 2036 is inapplicable.

Unless otherwise stated and for convenience purposes, all three time periods are simply referred to as "retained for life."

The most common example of a retained life estate transfer that is included in the decedent's gross estate occurs where a decedent transferred property in trust and retained the income interest in the trust for life.[52] Similarly, if decedent transferred real property and retained a legal life estate in the property expressly or impliedly (as evidenced by continued residence), then at death the real estate would be included in the decedent's gross estate.[53]

A transfer with a retained life estate also occurs where the decedent retained the right to have the income used to discharge decedent's legal obligations, such as the support of the decedent's dependents.[54]

There has been much litigation focusing on whether decedent's right must be expressly retained or whether it is sufficient that decedent's right arises from an implied understanding. Where payments to the decedent are wholly discretionary and there has been no implied understanding to make payments to the decedent, Section 2036 may not apply.[55] Where, however, payments to the decedent were to be wholly discretionary but there had been actual payments of income to the decedent during his life, receipt may give rise to an inference of an implied understanding. It would seem that the more regularized the "discretionary" income payments are, the greater the inference.[56]

Decedent is deemed to have retained the use or enjoyment or the right to income from transferred property if decedent retained the right to vote share of controlled corporation stock[57] even though decedent retained no right to the dividends paid on the stock.

**52.** I.R.C. § 2036(a)(1).

**53.** See, *e.g.,* Tubbs v. United States, 348 F.Supp. 1404 (N.D.Tex.1972), judgment affirmed 472 F.2d 166 (5th Cir.1973), cert. denied 411 U.S. 983 (1973). Rapelje's Estate v. C.I.R., 73 T.C. 82 (1979). But see, Gutchess v. C.I.R., 46 T.C. 554 (1966), acq. 1967–1 C.B. 2 (Section 2036 inapplicable to case where husband transfers family home to wife and continues to live in home as incident of the marital relationship.)

**54.** See C.I.R. v. Douglass' Estate, 143 F.2d 961 (3d Cir.1944), acq. 1971–1 C.B. 2; Estate of Chrysler v. C.I.R., 44 T.C. 55 (1965), reversed 361 F.2d 508 (2d Cir.1966), acq. in result only, 1970–2 C.B. xix; National Bank of Commerce in Memphis v. Henslee, 179 F.Supp. 346 (M.D.Tenn.1959); Exchange Bank & Trust of Fla. v. United States, 82–2 USTC ¶ 13,505 (Fed.Cir.1982).

In those cases where decedent's right to income is limited to either decedent's support or the support of a dependent, it may be relevant for valuation purposes to consider the level of support due the decedent or decedent's dependent. See Pardee's Estate v. C.I.R., 49 T.C. 140, 148 (1967).

**55.** See Skinner's Estate v. United States, 316 F.2d 517 (3d Cir.1963). *See also* McNichol's Estate v. C.I.R., 265 F.2d 667 (3d Cir. 1959), cert. denied,361 U.S. 829 (1959). See also Estate of German v. United States, 55 AFTR2d 85–1577 (Cl.Ct.1985). But see, Estate of Uhl v. C.I.R., 25 T.C. 22 (1955), rev'd, 241 F.2d 867 (7th Cir.1957) (in dicta concluding that if under local law the creditors of the grantor of a wholly discretionary trust could reach the trust assets, trust included in gross estate because grantor could reach trust assets merely by incurring debt). Cf., Outwin v. Commissoner, 76 T.C. 153 (1981)(grantor of discretionary trust makes incomplete gift where, under state law, grantor's creditors could reach the trust assets to satisfy grantor's debts accruing after trust created.

**56.** *See generally,* Lowndes, Kramer & McCord, *Federal Estate and Gift Taxes,* 3rd Ed. § 9.12.

**57.** I.R.C. § 2036(b). A corporation is a controlled corporation if at any time after the transfer of the corporation's stock and within three years of the decedent's death the decedent owned (using family attribution rules under Section 318) or had the right to vote alone or in conjunction with another stock possessing 20% or more of the total combined voting power of all classes of the corporation's stock.

This statutory section legislatively overturns the holding in United States v. Byrum, 408 U.S. 125 (1972) rehearing denied 409 U.S. 898 (1972).

Transfers with a retained life estate also include transfers in which decedent did not retain any economic benefits but retained the power, exercisable alone or in conjunction with any other person, to designate the persons who shall possess or enjoy the transferred property or the income therefrom.[58] Thus, if John creates a trust for the primary benefit of Alice, Bob and Charlie and retains the power to determine their respective shares of the income for his life, the trust is included in John's gross estate.

The statute also applies where there is one or more income beneficiaries and the decedent retained the power to direct that income be accumulated for ultimate distribution to the remainderman of the trust.[59] For example, if Mary creates a trust to pay the income to John, remainder to John's children and retains the power to accumulate and capitalize the income, the trust is included in Mary's gross estate because her retained power permits her to shift the enjoyment of the income from John to his children.

There is some disagreement, however, whether a power to accumulate income is a power to designate under Section 2036 where there is only one income beneficiary who will ultimately receive the accumulated income at the termination of the trust. Suppose John created a trust for the primary benefit of Alice to terminate when Alice dies or reaches age 25, whichever first occurs. Upon the termination of the trust the corpus and any accumulated income would be paid to Alice or her estate. John retained a power exercisable prior to Alice attaining age 25 to pay the income to Alice or accumulate the income for ultimate distribution to her. If John dies before Alice attains age 25, is the trust included in his gross estate under Section 2036?[60] Arguably Section 2036(a)(2) is inapplicable because it requires a power to designate among "persons" and in this case there is only one beneficiary, namely, Alice.[61] Therefore, the decedent's power is only a power that affects Alice's time of enjoyment of the trust income, not who shall enjoy the income.[62]

Section 2036(a)(2) is inapplicable if decedent retained only managerial powers over the transferred property, such as the power to allocate receipt and disbursements between income and principal or the power to make investments.[63] Furthermore, the statute is inapplicable if the power to designate is controlled by an ascertainable standard and the beneficiaries are not dependents of the decedent.[64] An ascertainable standard is a standard relating to health, education, or support. It does not include a power to pay for mere comfort or happiness.[65]

Section 2036(a)(2) applies even though decedent's power is exercisable only in conjunction with a person having a substantial adverse interest in its

**58.** I.R.C. § 2036(a)(2).

**59.** Cf., United States v. O'Malley, 383 U.S. 627 (1966).

**60.** The value of Alice's income interest would be included in the decedent's gross estate under Section 2038. See Treas.Reg. § 20.2038–1.

**61.** *But see* Struthers v. Kelm, 218 F.2d 810 (8th Cir.1955) holding to the contrary apparently on the belief that Lober v. United States, 346 U.S. 335 (1953), decided under the predecessor to Section 2038, controlled.

**62.** Walter v. United States, 341 F.2d 182 (6th Cir.1965). *See also* Lowndes, Kramer & McCord, *Federal Estate and Gift Taxes,* 3rd ed. § 8.13.

**63.** See, *e.g.*, Old Colony Trust Co. v. United States, 423 F.2d 601 (1st Cir.1970).

**64.** See, *e.g.*, Jennings v. Smith, 161 F.2d 74 (2d Cir.1947); Leopold v. United States, 510 F.2d 617 (9th Cir.1975).

**65.** See Old Colony Trust Co. v. United States, *supra* note 63. *See also* Estate of Cutter v. C.I.R., 62 T.C. 351 (1974).

exercise.[66] Thus, even though the gift of the interest is complete for gift tax purposes, the transferred property is still in the donor-decedent's gross estate. Of course, since a gift tax credit is allowable in computing the federal estate tax on the donor-decedent's estate, effectively only the value of the appreciation, if any, between the time of the gift and the donor-decedent's date of death is subject to estate tax.

Section 2036(a)(2) applies even if the decedent retained the power to designate who shall enjoy the income from the transferred property in a fiduciary capacity. Furthermore, even if the decedent did not retain the power directly but granted it exclusively to a third party trustee, if the decedent retained the power to fire the trustee and appoint a successor trustee, including himself, Section 2036 applies.[67] The statute also applies if decedent could name himself trustee only if the independent trustee resigned, died or was removed from office.[68]

Section 2036 can apply even though the decedent was not the formal creator of the trust. For example, suppose John creates a trust to pay the income to Mary for life, remainder to their children. Mary also creates a trust to pay the income to John for life, remainder to their children. Formally, neither John nor Mary is the creator of the trust of which he or she is the income beneficiary. Nonetheless, Section 2036 could apply causing the trust formally created by John of which Mary is the income beneficiary to be included in Mary's gross estate (and the trust formally created by Mary of which John is the income beneficiary to be included in John's gross estate) if a court concluded that the trusts were reciprocal.[69] The basic notion underlying the reciprocal trust doctrine, as originally formulated,[70] was that if two trusts were created in consideration of each other, the grantors of each trust would be switched for estate tax purposes to the effect that each would be deemed to be the substantive grantor of the trust formally created by the other. This initial test was based upon subjective intent. In *United States v. Grace's Estate*[71] the Court held that application of the reciprocal trust doctrine did not depend upon a finding that the trusts were created in consideration of each other. Rather, "the application of the * * * doctrine requires only that the trusts be interrelated, and that the arrangement, to the extent of mutual value, leaves the settlors in approximately the same economic position as they would have been in had they created trusts naming themselves as life beneficiaries."[72]

If Section 2036 applies then the entire trust, not merely the value of the decedent's retained interest, generally is included in the decedent's gross

**66.** Treas.Reg. § 20.2036–1(b)(3).

**67.** Treas.Reg. § 20.2036–1(b)(3).

**68.** Estate of Farrel v. United States, 213 Ct.Cl. 622, 553 F.2d 637 (1977). The statute is inapplicable if the original trustee was a corporate trustee and decedent could fire the corporate trustee and appoint only another corporate trustee. See Rev. Rul. 95–58, 1995–2 C.B. 191.

**69.** The reciprocal trust doctrine can also apply to Section 2037 and Section 2038 transfers. See also § 13.1, note 77 (application of self-settled spendthrift trust rules to cases where formal designation of settlor is not always controlling).

**70.** See Lehman v. C.I.R., 109 F.2d 99 (2d Cir.1940), cert. denied 310 U.S. 637 (1940).

**71.** 395 U.S. 316 (1969), rehearing denied 396 U.S. 881 (1969).

**72.** United States v. Grace's Estate, 395 U.S. 316, 324 (1969), rehearing denied 396 U.S. 881 (1969). See also § 14.4 *supra*, note 93. For a further discussion of *Grace* see, Lowndes, Kramer & McCord, Federal Estate and Gift Taxes, 3d ed. § 9.8.

estate.[73] However, if decedent retained only a portion of the income interest or the right to designate only a portion of the income, then only a like portion would be included in the decedent's gross estate under Section 2036. For example, if decedent created a trust and retained only one-half of the income, then only one-half of the trust would be included in the decedent's gross estate.[74]

Also, if decedent created an interest in property preceding decedent's retained interest, the value of that interest is excluded from the decedent's gross estate. For example, suppose George created a trust to pay the income to Ann for life, then to George for life, remainder to Barney, and George dies survived by Ann and Barney. The value of Ann's income interest is excluded from George's gross estate.[75] Apparently, only the value of the preceding estate being enjoyed at George's death is excluded from his gross estate. Thus, if George transferred property in trust to pay the income to Ann for life, then to Barney for life, then to George for life and then to Don, and George died survived by both Ann and Barney, only the value of Ann's life estate would be excluded from George's gross estate. The rationale for this rule, however, is wholly unclear.

### *Transfers Taking Effect at Death*

Section 2037 provides that the gross estate includes the value of all property transferred by the decedent during life for less than adequate and full consideration in money or money's worth if (1) possession or enjoyment of the property transferred by the decedent can only be obtained by the transferee surviving the decedent *and* (2) immediately before the decedent's death, decedent had a reversionary interest retained at the time of transfer valued at more than 5% of the transferred property.[76] However, Section 2037 will not apply if possession or enjoyment could have been obtained by a beneficiary during the decedent's life through the exercise of a general power of appointment that was exercisable immediately before the decedent's death.[77]

The statute applies only if both the survivorship test and the reversionary interest test are satisfied. If the decedent has a reversion in the property but Section 2037 is inapplicable, the value of the reversion is included in decedent's gross estate under Section 2033.[78]

The survivorship test relates to whether a beneficiary can obtain possession or enjoyment of the transferred property *only* by surviving the decedent. If John transfers property to Amy for life, remainder to Amy's children who survive her, Section 2037 is inapplicable even though John has a reversionary

**73.** Treas.Reg. § 20.2036–1. *Cf.* I.R.C. § 2038 where only interests subject to a power to revoke, alter, amend or terminate are included in the decedent's gross estate. This would also include any income accumulated as a result of the decedent's lifetime directions. See United States v. O'Malley, *supra* note 59.

**74.** Treas.Reg. § 20.2036–1(a). If the decedent retained the right to a specific dollar amount of income, then only such percentile of the trust necessary to produce that amount of income is included in the decedent's gross estate. See United States National Bank v. United States, 188 F.Supp. 332 (D.Or.1960). *Cf.*, Industrial Trust Co. v. C.I.R., 165 F.2d 142 (1st Cir.1947).

**75.** See Marks v. Higgins, 213 F.2d 884 (2d Cir.1954). *See also,* Treas.Reg. § 20.2036–1(a).

**76.** If decedent received partial consideration for the transfer, then the amount otherwise included under Section 2037 is reduced by the amount of partial consideration received. *See generally,* I.R.C. § 2043.

**77.** I.R.C. § 2037(b).

**78.** See Graham v. C.I.R., 46 T.C. 415 (1966).

interest because neither Amy nor her children must survive John to obtain possession or enjoyment of their interest. On the other hand, if John transfers property to Amy for life, remainder to such of Amy's children as survive John, Section 2037's survivorship test is met and, if John's reversion exceeds 5% of the value of the trust immediately before his death, the value of the remainder is included in his gross estate.

The survivorship test relates to the possession or enjoyment of the property not the vesting of a property interest. For example, suppose Arnold creates a trust to pay the income to Agnes for life, remainder to Dick, or if Dick predeceases Agnes then to Arnold, or if he is not then living to Zelda or Zelda's estate. Zelda cannot obtain personal possession and enjoyment of the property without surviving Arnold even though her interest vests (for property law purposes) if Dick and Arnold predecease Agnes.[79] Thus Section 2037 applies even though Zelda's interest can vest without Zelda surviving Arnold. It applies because Zelda cannot personally obtain possession or enjoyment without surviving Arnold.

The survivorship test applies if a beneficiary can obtain possession or enjoyment only by surviving the decedent *and* another event. According to the regulations, it also applies if the beneficiary can obtain possession by surviving the decedent *or* some other event if the other event is unreal and, in fact, the decedent dies before the other event occurs.[80] For example, suppose Arthur creates a trust to accumulate the income for 12 years or until Arthur dies, if earlier, at the end of which time all accumulated income and principal shall be paid to Andrea. Five years later Arthur dies. Andrea's possession and enjoyment was dependent upon either the running of 12 years or Arthur's death. If at the time of transfer Arthur had a life expectancy of more than 12 years and was then in good health, Andrea is considered able to possess or enjoy the property without having to survive Arthur. On the other hand, if at the time of transfer Arthur's life expectancy was less than 12 years or he was terminally ill, Andrea is not considered able to possess or enjoy the property without surviving Arthur.[81] If Andrea could obtain possession at the later of 12 years or Arthur's death, Section 2037 applies since possession and enjoyment can only be obtained by surviving both events.

Under the reversionary test, decedent must have retained a reversionary interest valued at more than 5% immediately before death using the appropriate valuation methods and tables. A reversionary interest includes any possibility that the transferred property will return to the decedent or to the decedent's estate or that the property will be subject to decedent's power of disposition.[82] A power of disposition need not be a general power.[83] It is irrelevant whether the reversionary interest arises under the express terms of the governing instrument or by operation of law.[84] Therefore, Section 2037

**79.** *See also* Treas.Reg. § 20.2037–1(e) ex. 4.

**80.** Treas.Reg. § 20.2037–1(e) ex. 5.

**81.** *Id.*

**82.** A power of disposition does not include the possibility that the income from the property alone will be subject to the power. I.R.C. § 2037(b). If decedent had such a power either Section 2036 or 2038 would apply. The possibility the decedent might receive back the property by inheritance through the estate of another person is not a reversionary interest. Treas.Reg. § 20.2037–1(c)(2).

**83.** See Costin v. Cripe, 235 F.2d 162 (7th Cir.1956).

**84.** *But see* Treas.Reg. § 20.2037–1(f).

can apply if Herb transfers property to Beverly for life, remainder to Beverly's children who survive Herb, or if none, then to Herb (express reservation of a reversion) as well as where Herb transfers property to Beverly for life, remainder to her children who survive Herb (Herb's reversion arises by operation of law).

The value of the reversionary interest must exceed 5%. In determining whether the more than 5% test is met, the reversionary interest is valued immediately before the decedent's death on the assumption that the estate assets are valued under the date of death valuation method only.[85] The value of the reversionary interest is compared to the value of the entire property not merely the value of the interest dependent upon survivorship.[86] For example, suppose Elaine created a trust valued at $100,000 immediately before her death which provided that the income should be paid to Peter for life, then to his children who survive Elaine. Peter's life estate is valued at $60,000; his children's remainder is valued at $40,000. If Elaine's reversion is valued at $5,000 or under, Section 2037 is inapplicable even though were it valued at anywhere between $2,000 and $5,000, it would be valued at more than 5% of the value of the children's remainder interest. If Elaine's reversion is valued at more than $5,000, Section 2037 applies and the value of the remainder interest is included in her gross estate.

Even if both the reversionary interest and survivorship tests are met Section 2037 is inapplicable if possession or enjoyment of the property could be obtained by a beneficiary during decedent's life through exercise of a general power of appointment.[87] Suppose Sam creates a trust to pay the income to Betsy for life, remainder to her children who survive Sam. Sam grants Betsy a general inter vivos power to appoint the property to anyone. In this case even though Sam's reversionary interest meets the more than 5% test, Section 2037 is inapplicable because Betsy has a general power.[88]

If Section 2037 applies the amount included in the decedent's gross estate is the value of the interest whose possession or enjoyment is dependent upon surviving the decedent. Thus, if Section 2037 applies to John's transfer to Alice for life, remainder to Alice's children who survive John, only the children's interest is included in John's gross estate. If both the income interest and remainder interest are dependent upon surviving the decedent, then the entire property is included in the decedent's gross estate. For example, suppose Ginny transfers property in trust to accumulate the income during her life and at her death to distribute the accumulated income and principal to Walter if he survives Ginny, or if he predeceases her, to her estate. In this case, the entire trust is included in Ginny's gross estate.

### *Revocable Transfers*

The gross estate includes the value of all interests in property transferred by the decedent during life for less than adequate and full consideration in

**85.** Treas.Reg. § 20.2037-1(c)(3). For Section 2037 purposes, the valuation tables should be used exclusively. The actual circumstances surrounding the decedent's death should be ignored. See Roy's Estate v. C.I.R., 54 T.C. 1317 (1970). *Contra,* Hall v. United States, 353 F.2d 500 (7th Cir.1965).

**86.** Treas.Reg. § 20.2037-1(c)(4).

**87.** I.R.C. § 2037(b).

**88.** See notes 119-127, *infra* for a discussion of a general power.

money or money's worth which at the time of the decedent's death are subject to a power, exercisable by the decedent alone or in conjunction with any other person, to alter, amend, revoke or terminate.[89] If decedent had a power of revocation that was relinquished within three years of decedent's death, the property interest subject to such power also is included in the decedent's gross estate.[90]

In order for Section 2038 to apply the decedent must have been possessed of the power of revocation at the time of death or relinquished the power within three years of death. It is irrelevant whether the decedent's power was exercisable in a fiduciary capacity. If the power of revocation was only exercisable by someone other than the decedent, Section 2038 is inapplicable. However, if the decedent possessed the power to fire the trustee and hire himself as trustee, all the trustee's powers are attributable to the decedent and, if the trustee possessed a power of revocation, decedent will be deemed to possess it as well.[91]

Section 2038 applies even though decedent had only a co-held power and even though the co-holder of the power has a substantial adverse interest in the exercise of the power.[92] Thus if Jim creates a trust to pay the income to Priscilla for life, remainder to Bonny and Jim reserves a power exercisable only with Priscilla's consent to revoke the trust, the trust is included in Jim's gross estate even though Priscilla must join in the exercise of the power. Suppose, however, the trust provides that Jim can revoke the trust only with the consent of both Priscilla and Bonny. In *Helvering v. Helmholz*[93] the Court held that a trust that could be revoked only with the consent of all beneficiaries of the trust was not a revocable trust because even in the absence of the revocation clause they could, under state law, revoke the trust in any event. Therefore, the clause did not enhance the rights of the grantor.[94]

Section 2038 applies even though the deceased transferor did not retain the power at the time of the transfer. This conclusion is based upon the statutory parenthetical directing that the source of the power is irrelevant.[95] For example, suppose John creates a trust that a trustee is empowered to alter or amend and names Mary as trustee. Ten years later Mary resigns and the court having jurisdiction of the trust appoints John as successor trustee. John dies in possession of the power to alter or amend. The trust is included in John's gross estate.

In order for Section 2038 to apply decedent must have possessed a power to alter, amend, revoke or terminate at decedent's death. The distinction between a power to revoke and a power to terminate is unclear. Both appear

**89.** I.R.C. § 2038. If decedent received partial consideration for the transfer, the entire value less the amount of partial consideration received would be included in the gross estate. See I.R.C. § 2043. In most states, inter vivos trusts are irrevocable unless the grantor expressly retains a power of revocation. However, in some states, the opposite rule applies. In those states it is essential to expressly provide in the trust instrument that the trust is irrevocable to avoid section 2038.

**90.** I.R.C. § 2038(a)(1). *See also* I.R.C. § 2035(d)(2).

**91.** Treas.Reg. § 20.2038–1(a)(3). *See also* notes 64–65, supra and accompanying text.

**92.** Helvering v. City Bank Farmers Trust Co., 296 U.S. 85 (1935).

**93.** 296 U.S. 93 (1935).

**94.** Accord, Treas.Reg. § 20.2038–1(a)(2). *See also* § 9.6, *supra*, note 74.

**95.** The statutory language overturns the Supreme Court decision in White v. Poor, 296 U.S. 98 (1935).

to address a power permitting the decedent, through exercise of the power, to regain title or possession of the trust property. A power to alter or amend contemplates a power that affects the enjoyment of the trust property or some interest therein without revoking or terminating the trust. It does not include powers to administer or manage the trust property, such as a power to control investments or allocate receipts between income and principal.[96] If the power to alter or amend is limited by an ascertainable standard relating to health, support, education or maintenance (sometimes called nondiscretionary powers), it is not a power to alter or amend for Section 2038 purposes unless the exercise of the power would permit the deceased transferor to enjoy the economic benefits of the trust.[97]

Section 2038 applies only if the deceased transferor possessed a power of revocation at death or the power was relinquished within three years of death.[98] If the decedent's power was subject to a contingency beyond the decedent's control such that it was not exercisable at the time of the decedent's death then Section 2038 is inapplicable if the contingency had not occurred prior to the decedent's death.[99] For example, if John transfers property subject to his power to revoke the trust if Alice survives Bob and at the time of John's death both Alice and Bob are living, the trust is not included in John's gross estate under section 2038 because the power was not in existence at his death. A power is deemed to be in existence when decedent dies even though the decedent was incompetent to exercise the power.[100]

If the exercise of the power is subject to a precedent giving of notice that was not given at the time of the decedent's death, the power is deemed to be in existence at the time of the decedent's death although proper adjustment "shall be made representing the interests which would have been excluded from the power if the decedent had lived, and for such purpose, if the notice has not been given or the power has not been exercised on or before the date of his death, such notice shall be considered to have been given, or the power exercised, on the date of his death."[101] For example, suppose Ron creates a trust revocable only upon the giving of one year's notice. Ron dies without having given such notice. The trust is included in Ron's gross estate but the amount included in the gross estate is reduced by a one year term certain to take account of the fact that if Ron had given the notice on the date of his death, he could not have received the economic benefit of next year's income.

Only the value of the interest subject to the power of revocation is included in the gross estate under Section 2038. If decedent possessed the power to revoke the entire trust, then the value of the entire trust is included

**96.** See also, note 63–65, *supra* and accompanying text.

**97.** See Jennings v. Smith, *supra* note 61. There has been much litigation concerning whether the language attached to a power limiting its exercise causes the power to be limited by an ascertainable standard. *See generally,* Lowndes, Kramer & McCord, *Federal Estate and Gift Taxes,* 3rd ed. § 8.9.

**98.** But see I.R.C. § 2035(e)(three-year rule inapplicable to transfers from a revocable trust where grantor was the owner of the trust under I.R.C. § 676.

**99.** Treas.Reg. § 20.2038–1(b). On the other hand, the contingent power may be taxable under Section 2036 if the power is a right to designate who shall possess or enjoy the property or the income therefrom. See Treas.Reg. § 20.2036–1(b)(3)(iii).

**100.** Hurd v. C.I.R., 160 F.2d 610 (1st Cir. 1947). As to whether a conservator can exercise a power to revoke when the settlor is incompetent, see § 7.2, *supra*, notes 35–36.

**101.** I.R.C. § 2038(b).

in the gross estate. If decedent only possessed to power to revoke the income interest, then only the value of that interest is included in the gross estate under Section 2038 although, since the power to revoke is also a right to designate who shall enjoy the income, the whole trust is included in the gross estate under Section 2036. If the power to revoke affects only the remainder interest, then only the value of that interest is included in the gross estate under Section 2038. For example, suppose Ron creates a trust to pay the income to Nancy for life, remainder to Bob. If Ron reserves the power to direct payment of income to Sue rather than Nancy, then under Section 2038 the value of the income interest is included in Ron's gross estate although under Section 2036(a)(2) the entire trust is included in Ron's gross estate. If Ron reserves no power over the income but reserves a special testamentary power to designate a remainderman other than Bob, then the value of the remainder interest only is included in Ron's gross estate under Section 2038 and Section 2036 is inapplicable.[102] Suppose Ron only possessed the power to invade the trust principal on behalf of Nancy. Clearly, the value of the remainder interest is included in Ron's gross estate since the invasion power is a power to shift the enjoyment of the remainder interest from Bob to Nancy. Would this power also cause the income interest to be included in Ron's gross estate? The answer should be no.[103]

As suggested by the preceding discussion there are some cases in which either Section 2038 or Section 2036(a)(2) or both could apply to decedent's lifetime transfer. Most transfers that are taxable under one of those provisions are taxable under the other, but there are important exceptions. Furthermore, the amount that is included in the gross estate can differ depending upon which of the statutes governs. For example, if decedent possesses a power at death that she retained at the time of the transfer to alter the interests of two or more beneficiaries in trust income, both sections apply. However, under Section 2036(a)(2) the entire trust is included in the gross estate whereas under Section 2038 only the income interest subject to the power would be included in the gross estate. If decedent did not retain the power at the time of the transfer but acquired the power thereafter, Section 2036 could not apply; Section 2038 would. Contingent powers are taxable under Section 2036 but not under Section 2038.

### *Annuities*

Under Section 2039 annuities with survivorship benefits can be included in a decedent's gross estate. More particularly, Section 2039(a) provides that the value of decedent's gross estate includes the value of an annuity or other payment (other than life insurance)[104] that is receivable by any beneficiary by reason of surviving the decedent under the terms of a contract or agreement[105] if, under the terms of the same contract or agreement, an annuity or other

**102.** See, *e.g.,* C.I.R. v. Bridgeport City Trust Co., 124 F.2d 48 (2d Cir.1941), cert. denied 316 U.S. 672 (1942).

**103.** See Walter v. United States, 341 F.2d 182 (6th Cir.1965); Rev. Rul. 70–513, 1970–2 C.B. 194. *But see* In re Inman's Estate, 203 F.2d 679 (2d Cir.1953).

**104.** This phrase refers to one or more payments that extend over a period of time whether the payments are equal or unequal, conditional or unconditional, periodic or sporadic. Treas.Reg. § 20.2039–1(b).

**105.** A contract or agreement includes any arrangement, understanding or plan, or any combination thereof, written or oral. Treas. Reg. § 20.2039–1(b).

payment had been payable to the decedent at the time of death or the decedent had the right to receive an annuity or other payment,[106] alone or in conjunction with another person, for life or for a period not ascertainable without reference to decedent's death or for a period that did not in fact end before the decedent's death.

Section 2039 cannot apply to a single life annuity payable to the decedent that terminates at the decedent's death but it does apply to a common commercial annuity contract providing benefits to the decedent and then to another upon the decedent's death. It is irrelevant if the beneficiary was also entitled to benefits while the decedent was living. It also applies to annuity arrangements between employers and employees, such as deferred compensation agreements.

The value of the survivor's interest is determined under Treasury Regulation § 20.2031–8 which provides that value equals the cost of a comparable annuity purchased from the annuity company on the life of the survivor with benefits equal to those payable to the survivor under the contract. Replacement cost, however, is unavailable if the survivor's interest is not payable under the terms of a commercially available contract. For such contracts, the annuity tables[107] apply. If decedent did not contribute the entire purchase price for the annuity, the amount included in the gross estate equals replacement cost or value under the tables, whichever is applicable, multiplied by a fraction. The numerator of the fraction equals decedent's contribution; the denominator is the total purchase price. For example, suppose Harry purchases a joint and survivor annuity contract for himself and his wife, Dorothy, at a cost of $100. At Harry's death the entire value of Dorothy's survivorship interest is included in Harry's gross estate. If, however, Dorothy predeceases Harry, nothing is included in her gross estate.

If decedent's employer made contributions towards the contract or other agreement, they are deemed to have been made by the decedent if they were made "by reason of [decedent's] employment."[108]

Section 2039 also applies to many common pension and profit sharing arrangements and IRAs to which contributions during the decedent's life were deductible for income tax purposes. These tax deferred plans are not only included in the decedent's gross estate but also the recipient-beneficiary's gross income as income in respect of a decedent under Section 691. Thus the aggregate income and estate tax liabilities associated with these assets are quite significant. The impact of assessing both an income and estate tax on "income in respect of a decedent" is ameliorated to some extent by allowing the person including income in respect of a decedent in her gross income to claim a deduction for the estate tax attributable to such income.[109]

### *Marital Joint Tenancies*

If husband and wife own property as joint tenants with right of survivorship or as tenants by the entirety, then upon the death of the first of them to

**106.** This language contemplates the case where decedent had a right to receive an annuity in the future without regard to whether decedent was receiving payments at the time of his death. Treas.Reg. § 20.2039–1(b)(1).

**107.** Treas.Reg. § 20.2031–5.

**108.** I.R.C. § 2039(b).

**109.** I.R.C. § 691(c).

die, one-half of the property's estate tax value is included in the decedent's gross estate.[110] The entire value of the property is included in the survivor's estate under Section 2033 unless transferred or consumed during the survivor's lifetime. Section 2040 is inapplicable to tenancies in common. With respect to a tenancy in common, each co-tenants undivided interest is included in his or her gross estate under Section 2033. Since only one-half of the property is included in the gross estate of the first spouse to die, only that half receives a step-up in basis for income tax purposes. For example, John and Mary purchase Blackacre for $50,000 as joint tenants with right of survivorship. John dies ten years later when Blackacre is worth $150,000. One-half of Blackacre's value is included in John's gross estate such that in Mary's hands Blackacre has a basis of $100,000 ($75,000 attributable to the half included in John's gross estate and $25,000 attributable to Mary's one-half cost basis in the property).[111] If John and Mary owned Blackacre as community property, only one-half of its value would be included in John's gross estate but both John and Mary's community halves would get a step-up in basis by virtue of a special rule in section 1014 inapplicable to marital joint tenancies.

### *Other Joint Tenancies*

Under Section 2040(a) a decedent's gross estate includes the entire value of all non-marital joint tenancy property in which the decedent had an interest at the time of his death, except to the extent the surviving joint tenancy can prove that he contributed part of the property or consideration for the property. If the decedent and the survivor acquired the joint tenancy property by gift, bequest or inheritance, the value of the property included in the gross estate of the first joint tenant to die is determined by multiplying that value by the number of joint tenants.

To illustrate, suppose Andrea and Becky own Blackacre as joint tenants. Andrea dies survived by Becky. Blackacre's entire value is included in Andrea's gross estate unless Becky can prove that she contributed towards the acquisition of Blackacre or that they acquired Blackacre by gift, bequest or inheritance. In that case, none or less than all of Blackacre's value is included in Andrea's gross estate.

If Becky can establish that she contributed towards the acquisition of Blackacre, then a proportionate part of Blackacre's value is excluded from Andrea's gross estate. For example suppose they acquire Blackacre as joint tenants. Of the $5,000 purchase price, Andrea contributed $2,000 and Becky contributed $3,000. At Andrea's death, 40% of the value of Blackacre is includible in her gross estate; if Becky predeceases Andrea, then 60% of Blackacre's value is included in Becky's gross estate.[112] Section 2040(c) applies even though the joint tenants who make unequal contributions towards the acquisition and maintenance of the property have agreed to equal ownership.

**110.** I.R.C. § 2040(b).

**111.** See I.R.C. § 1014(b0(6).

**112.** *But see,* Peters' Estate v. C.I.R., 386 F.2d 404 (4th Cir.1967). In *Peters* the surviving joint tenant did not contribute to the acquisition of joint tenancy property. Rather the survivor contributed towards an improvement to the property. The court held that the value of the joint tenancy property less the amount of the contribution towards the improvement was included in the decedent's estate. No appreciation in the value of the property subsequent to the improvement was credited to the survivor's contributions. See also § 6.4, *supra,* note 66.

The survivor's contribution must not have been acquired from the decedent for less than adequate and full consideration in money or money's worth. For example, suppose Andrea gives Blackacre to Becky. Thereafter Becky reconveys Blackacre to Andrea and herself as joint tenants. Andrea dies survived by Becky. The entire value of Blackacre is included in Andrea's gross estate.[113] On the other hand, joint tenancy property acquired by the survivor with the income from property the survivor received from the decedent is deemed to be the survivor's contribution.[114] Therefore, if Becky, in the preceding example, retained the title to Blackacre in her own name but deposited the rents from Blackacre into a joint bank account in the name of Andrea and herself, at Andrea's death survived by Becky, no portion of that bank account would be included in Andrea's gross estate.[115] The survivor's contribution towards the joint tenancy property can take the form of the assumption of liability on a mortgage. For example, in *Bremer v. Luff.*[116] Louis and Emma acquired Blackacre as joint tenants. Each assumed joint and several liability on the purchase money mortgage. The court held that each was deemed to have contributed one half of the mortgage liability towards acquisition of the property.[117] Their percentage contributions remain unchanged if the mortgage is discharged with income from the joint tenancy property. However, if either Louis or Emma uses personal funds to discharge the mortgage debt, their respective contributions on account of the mortgage must be readjusted.[118]

### *Powers of Appointment*

The gross estate includes the value of all property over which the decedent:

1. Possessed at the time of his death a general power of appointment,[119] or

2. During life exercised or released a general power of appointment[120] if, as a result of such exercise or release, decedent retained the income from the property subject to the exercised or released power or the right to designate who would possess or enjoy the income therefrom

**113.** Treas.Reg. § 20.2040–1(c) ex. 4. *See also* Dimock v. Corwin, 305 U.S. 593 (1939).

**114.** Treas.Reg. § 20.2040–1(c)(5).

**115.** *See also* Harvey v. United States, 185 F.2d 463 (7th Cir.1950); Swartz v. United States, 182 F.Supp. 540 (D.Mass.1960) (gain from sale of property acquired by survivor from decedent; the survivor's contribution equals the gain attributable to appreciation in value of property between time survivor acquired property from decedent and time of decedent's death.

If the survivor contributes stock dividends on stock acquired from the decedent in a joint tenancy, the courts are divided whether the contribution falls within the income exception. *Compare* McGehee v. C.I.R., 260 F.2d 818 (5th Cir.1958) with In re Schlosser's Estate, 277 F.2d 268 (3d Cir.1960), cert. denied 364 U.S. 819 (1960).

**116.** 7 F.Supp. 148 (N.D.N.Y.1933).

**117.** Accord, Rev. Rul. 79–302, 1979–2 C.B. 328, Rev. Rul. 81–183, 1981–2 C.B. 180, Rev. Rul. 81–184, 1981–2 C.B. 181.

**118.** See Estate of Awrey v. C.I.R., 5 T.C. 222 (1945).

**119.** I.R.C. § 2041.

**120.** The textual discussion relates only to general powers created after October 21, 1942. Property subject to a general powers created on or before that date is included in the decedent's gross estate only if the decedent exercised the power by will or in a disposition that if made by the decedent with his own property would cause that disposition to be included in the decedent's gross estate under Sections 2036, 2037 or 2038.

or decedent retained the power to alter, amend, revoke or terminate any interest resulting from the exercise or release.[121]

For example, if Ruth held a general power of appointment over the principal of a trust created by another and later exercised her general power by directing the trustee to hold the trust assets in a revocable trust for the primary benefit of Andy, this trust is included in Ruth's gross estate if Ruth retained the power to revoke the trust at the time of her death or released such power within the three year period ending with her death.[122] On the other hand, if during life Ruth exercised a general power by appointing the property outright to Andy and Ruth retained no interest in, or power over, the appointive assets, then the property would not be included in her gross estate, although the exercise would be a transfer for gift tax purposes.[123]

A general power of appointment is a power that enables the donee of the power to appoint the assets subject to the power to the donee, the donee's estate, the donee's creditors *or* the creditors of the donee's estate.[124] It does not include a power to consume, invade or appropriate property for the donee if the donee's power is limited by an ascertainable standard relating to the donee's health, education, support or maintenance.[125] Special rules apply if decedent could exercise the general power only with the consent of another. These rules are:

1. If the donee could only exercise the general power with the consent of the donor of the power, the power is not a general power for estate or gift tax purposes.[126]

2. If the donee could only exercise the general power with the consent of another person who has a substantial interest in the property subject to the power adverse to the donee's exercise of the power, the donee's power is not a general power.[127] For this purpose if the co-holder of the power would have a general power to appoint the property to himself after the donee's death, such person is deemed to have a substantial adverse interest. For example, suppose Frank creates a trust to pay the income to Eleanor for life, remainder to Ruth for life, remainder to Charles. Frank grants Eleanor a general power to appoint the property to herself which is exercisable only with Ruth's consent. Since Ruth has a substantial adverse interest in the exercise of the power, no portion of this trust is included in Eleanor's gross estate. If Eleanor's power was exercisable only with the consent of Dan who had no interest in the trust except that he could appoint the property to himself after Eleanor died, the trust would not be included in Eleanor's gross estate because Dan has a substantial adverse interest.

**121.** I.R.C. § 2041(a)(2). Additionally, the gross estate includes property over which decedent exercised or released a general power in such manner that if the property subject the power had been transferred by the decedent it would have been included in his gross estate under Section 2037 relating to transfers taking effect at death.

**122.** *Cf.* I.R.C. § 2038.

**123.** I.R.C. § 2514. Even if the decedent exercised or released the power in a manner that would cause the property to be included in the decedent's gross estate, decedent's exercise or release could result in a transfer for gift tax purposes. *Id.* In such case, credit for gift taxes paid as a result of the exercise or release would be available in computing the estate tax on the decedent's estate.

**124.** I.R.C. § 2041(b)(1).

**125.** I.R.C. § 2041(b)(1)(A). See § 9.5, *supra*, note 23 et. seq. (standard on a trustee's exercise of a discretionary power to distribute trust assets).

**126.** I.R.C. § 2041(b)(1)(C)(i).

**127.** I.R.C. § 2041(b)(1)(C)(ii).

3. If the donee of the general power can exercise the power with the consent of another in whose favor the power can also be exercised, then the power is deemed to be a general power only with respect to a fractional part of the property. The fraction is determined by dividing the property's value by the number of persons who must join in the exercise and in whose favor the power can be exercised. Thus if John transfers property in trust to pay the income to Alice for life, remainder to Benny, and John grants Alice a general power to appoint the property to anyone exercisable only with Larry's consent, Alice has a general power but only one-half of the value of the property subject to the power is included in her gross estate.

The lapse of a power is treated as the release of a power.[128] A lapse of a power occurs when the right to exercise the power terminates upon the passage of time or the happening of an event, other than the donee's death. Thus, if Jerry grants Betty a general power exercisable on or before January 1, 1990 and Betty fails to exercise the power by that date, then on that date the power lapses and Betty is deemed to have released the power. However, during any calendar year the lapse of a power is a release of a power "only to the extent that the property, which could have been appointed by exercise of such lapsed power, exceeded in value, at the time of such lapse, the greater of "$5,000 or 5% of the aggregate value at the time of the lapse of the property, or the proceeds of the property, out of which the power could have been satisfied."[129] Thus, if the donee possessed an annual noncumulative power to draw down from the principal of a trust an amount limited to the greater of $5,000 or 5%, the annual lapse of the power would not result in a release. Even if the donee's power exceeded the 5 and 5 standard, only annual lapses valued *in excess of the greater of $5,000 or 5%* are taxable releases. For example, suppose Mary had the power to withdraw up to $25,000 annually from a $200,000 trust. If in any year she exercised the power and drew down $25,000, there is no lapse.[130] If Mary permitted the power to lapse in any calendar year, there would be a release of only $15,000, the difference between $25,000 and 5% of $200,000. If Mary exercised the power and drew down $10,000, there would be a lapse of $15,000 but a release of only $5,000, being $15,000 less 5% of $200,000.

Where a lapse results in a taxable release, the amount that is included in the donee's gross estate because of the release is determined by computing what percentage of the trust the donee is deemed to own because of the release and applying that percentage to the value of the trust as determined for estate tax purposes. In the preceding example Mary withdrew $10,000 from the trust and let her power lapse over $15,000. She made a taxable release of $5,000. This represents 1⁄40 of a $200,000 trust. Assuming no further releases, then 1⁄40 of the trust is included in Mary's gross estate valued at Mary's death. If there had been releases in more than one calendar year, Mary's percentage ownership interest in the trust for each year is aggregated for the purpose of computing the amount included in the donee's gross estate.

**128.** I.R.C. § 2041(b)(2).

**129.** I.R.C. § 2041(b)(2)(A) & (B).

**130.** Of course the withdrawn funds could find their way into the donee's gross estate under Section 2033 if, for example, the donee deposited the funds into her personal bank account.

Thus, if in the second year Mary released an additional $5,000, her percentage interest would increase from 1/40 to 2/40.[131]

The 5 and 5 rule applies only to calendar years in which the power lapsed and the donee survived. If the donee dies during any calendar year without having exercised the power and prior to the lapse of the power, the entire amount the donee could have withdrawn that year is included in the donee's gross estate because with respect to such amounts the donee died in possession of a general power.[132]

### *Life Insurance*

The gross estate includes the value of all life insurance payable to the insured's estate.[133]

The gross estate also includes the value of all life insurance on the decedent's life payable to a named beneficiary if, at the time of the insured's death, the insured possessed any incidents of ownership with respect to the life insurance exercisable alone or in conjunction with any other person.[134]

The phrase "incidents of ownership" is not limited to ownership in the strict sense. Rather it refers to the ability of the insured to affect who shall enjoy any of the economic benefits of the policy. Thus, incidents of ownership include, among other things, the right to change the beneficiary, the right to cancel the policy or borrow against it, and the right to pledge the policy as security for a loan.[135] The term "incident of ownership" also includes certain reversionary interests the decedent might have in a life insurance policy.[136]

Under certain circumstances the incidents of ownership held by a corporation may be attributed to the insured. If the deceased insured was the sole or controlling shareholder of a corporation, the corporation's incidents of ownership are deemed possessed by the insured unless the insurance proceeds are payable to, or for the benefit of, the corporation.[137] If policy proceeds are not payable to, or for the benefit of, the corporation and thus are ignored in valuing the corporation for estate tax purposes, the corporation's incidents of ownership are attributable to the deceased insured.[138] The decedent is a controlling shareholder if decedent owned stock possessing more than 50% of the total combined voting power of the corporation.[139]

There has been much litigation concerning whether Section 2042 applies where the insured possessed incidents of ownership over policies on the insured's life that were exercisable by the insured only in a fiduciary capacity. Some courts hold the capacity in which the incidents of ownership are exercisable is irrelevant;[140] other courts hold that Section 2042 applies only if the insured fiduciary could exercise the incidents of ownership for his own economic benefit.[141] The Internal Revenue Service has adopted the latter position.[142]

**131.** See Treas.Reg. § 20.2041–3(d)(5).

**132.** Treas.Reg. § 20.2041–3(d)(3).

**133.** I.R.C. § 2042(1). Insurance payable to the estate would include insurance payable to the insured's creditors in discharge of the decedent's debts. Treas.Reg. § 20.2042–1(b)–1.

**134.** I.R.C. § 2042(2).

**135.** Treas.Reg. § 20.2042–1(c)(2).

**136.** I.R.C. § 2042(2); Treas.Reg. § 20.2042–1(c)(3).

**137.** Treas.Reg. § 20.2042–1(c)(6).

**138.** *Id.*

**139.** *Id.*

**140.** See, *e.g.*, Rose v. United States, 511 F.2d 259 (5th Cir.1975).

**141.** See, *e.g.*, Estate of Skifter v. C.I.R., 468 F.2d 699 (2d Cir.1972).

**142.** See Rev. Rul. 84–179, 1984–2 C.B. 195.

Insurance on the insured's life transferred by the insured within three years of death is included in the insured's gross estate even though the insured possessed no incidents of ownership over the policy at the time of this death.[143] Insurance transferred by the insured more than three years before death is excluded from the insured's gross estate if the insured retained no incidents of ownership and the proceeds were not payable to the insured's estate. These rules have resulted in a popular estate planning device—the irrevocable life insurance trust. Abe transfers a $1,000,000 term life insurance policy to a trust for his wife, Mary, remainder to their children. At the time of this transfer the policy has no value and therefore is not subject to gift tax. If Abe dies within three years the insurance is in his gross estate. If Abe survives three years, the policy is not included in his gross estate. In either case the proceeds are not included in Mary's gross estate and thus pass to the children transfer tax free at her death. If the proceeds are also excluded from Abe's gross estate then ultimately the children have received $1,000,000 transfer tax free. If is also possible to create a life insurance trust that is excluded from the gross estate even though the insurance proceeds payable to the trustee at the insured's death can be used for the payment of the debts, expenses, and taxes of the insured's estate. This can occur so long as the use of the insurance proceeds for such purposes is wholly discretionary with the trustee of the insurance trust. However, if the trustee is required to use the insurance proceeds for such purposes, then to that extent the proceeds are included in the insured's gross estate under section 2033 even though the they would have been excluded under both sections 2042 and 2035.

### *Qualified Terminable Interest Property*

The gross estate includes the value of all property in which the decedent possessed a qualified income interest for life at the time the decedent died so long as Section 2519 did not apply to such property as a result of a disposition made by the decedent during life. The rules relating to such property are discussed in a subsequent section of this chapter.[144]

### *The Taxable Estate*

The federal estate tax is computed against an estate tax base equal to the sum of the taxable estate and decedent's adjusted taxable gifts. Adjusted taxable gifts are taxable gifts[145] made by the decedent after December 31, 1976, other than gifts that are included in the decedent's gross estate. The taxable estate equals the value of the gross estate less the deductions allowed under Section 2053 for debts, expenses and taxes, Section 2054 for losses, Section 2055 for transfers to charity, Section 2056 for transfers to the surviving spouse and Section 2056 for family-owned business interests.

### *Deductible Debts, Expenses and Taxes*

In computing the value of the taxable estate a deduction is allowed against the gross estate for decedent's funeral expenses, expenses incurred in

**143.** I.R.C. § 2035(a)(2).

**144.** See notes 174–178, *infra,* and accompanying text.

**145.** See note 118, *supra* and accompanying text.

the administration of the estate,[146] claims against the estate,[147] and unpaid mortgages and other indebtedness against property where decedent's interest therein is included in the gross estate at a value that does not take the mortgage or other indebtedness into account.[148]

Additionally, a deduction is allowed for expenses incurred in administering "property not subject to claims" that is included in the gross estate[149] to the extent such expenses would be deductible if such property had been subject to claims if such expenses are paid before the running of the statute of limitations on the decedent's estate tax return.[150]

The deduction under Section 2053 for claims, unpaid mortgages or any other indebtedness founded upon a promise or agreement are limited to the extent that they were incurred bona fide and for adequate and full consideration in money or money's worth.[151] Thus, if John promised to pay Mary $50,000 if she stopped smoking and John owed Mary this amount when he died, no deduction is allowed for this claim because it was not a promise for adequate and full consideration in money or money's worth.

***Losses***

Losses incurred during the administration of the estate arising from fire, storm, shipwreck, or other casualty or from theft that are not compensated for by insurance or otherwise are deductible in computing the value of the taxable estate.[152]

***Swing Deduction Rule***

Section 642(h) provides that administration expenses and losses allowable as deductions in computing the value of decedent's taxable estate can not be allowed as a deduction for income tax purposes or as offsets for the purpose of computing gain or loss on sales for income tax purposes, unless the right to have such expenses, losses or offsets allowed as an estate tax deduction is waived.

Ordinarily the executor will claim such items as deductions (or offsets) on whichever return results in the greatest tax savings. For example, if the estate is in the marginal estate tax bracket of 38% but the marginal income tax bracket of 28%, it would ordinarily be most beneficial to claim these "swing deductions" as an estate tax deduction since overall estate and income taxes will be reduced by an additional 10%. Of course, if the estate is not subject to any estate tax liability, it would be advisable to claim swing deductions as an income tax deduction or offset.[153]

**146.** This would include attorneys' fees and executors' fees. See generally, Treas.Reg. § 20.2053–3.

**147.** Claims would include decedent's unpaid federal and state income, gift and property taxes. It would not include the federal estate tax payable on the decedent's estate. *See generally,* Treas.Reg. § 20.2053–6.

**148.** I.R.C. § 2053(a).

**149.** This would include property transferred during the decedent's life that is included in the decedent's gross estate which under state law is immune from claims against the decedent's estate. *See generally,* Treas.Reg. § 20.2053–8. See also, § 13.2 (joint tenancy and insurance) and § 13.1, *supra,* note 4 et. seq. (revocable trust) regarding the extent to which non-probate property is exempt from the claims of the decedent's creditors.

**150.** I.R.C. § 2053(b).

**151.** I.R.C. § 2053(c).

**152.** I.R.C. § 2054.

**153.** See also § 12.5, *supra,* note 73.

### *Charitable Transfers*

In computing the value of the decedent's taxable estate an unlimited deduction is allowable for outright transfers to charity. For purposes of both the gift and estate tax laws, charities include the federal and state governments and subdivisions thereof and most organizations engaged in religious, charitable, scientific, literary, or educational activities.

If decedent bequeaths her entire estate to charity, decedent's taxable estate would be zero. The amount of the charitable deduction cannot exceed the value of the property transferred to charity that is included in the decedent's gross estate. Property passing to charity as a result of the decedent's death that is not included in the decedent's gross estate cannot qualify for a charitable deduction.

For purposes of Section 2055 transfers include property passing to charity as a result of a bequest, legacy, devise and inter vivos dispositions that are included in the decedent's gross estate.[154] For example, if decedent created a revocable inter vivos trust providing that upon her death the remainder would be paid to charity, the property passing to charity at decedent's death qualifies for the estate tax charitable deduction because the revocable trust is included in the decedent's gross estate. On the other hand, if George grants Martha a special testamentary power of appointment enabling Martha to appoint the trust property to her issue and to charity, property Martha appoints to charity does not qualify for the estate tax charitable deduction because it is not included in Martha's gross estate.

To the extent that the property passing to charity is subject to the payment of any death tax, the charitable deduction must be reduced by the amount of that tax.[155]

If property passes in a form that benefits both individuals and charity, special and complex rules apply to the allowance of the charitable deduction for charity's interest in the transfer. If the transfer is in the form of a trust in which the remainder interest passes to charity, no deduction is allowed for the charitable remainder interest unless the trust qualifies as either a charitable remainder annuity trust or a charitable remainder unitrust.[156]

Generally a charitable remainder annuity trust is a trust providing that an annuity in an amount at least equal to at least 5% of the initial value of the trust principal shall be paid to the individual beneficiary or beneficiaries for their lives or for a term of years not in excess of 20 years, from which no amount, other than the annuity, can be paid to the noncharitable beneficiaries, and upon the termination of which the remainder will pass to charity.[157]

A charitable remainder unitrust is a trust providing that a fixed percentage, not less than 5% of the value of the trust assets determined annually and no other amounts,[158] be paid to the noncharitable beneficiary for life or for a

**154.** It has been held that property passing to a state because decedent died intestate does not qualify for the deduction because it does not pass to charity as the result of decedent's transfer. See Senft v. United States, 319 F.2d 642 (3d Cir.1963).

**155.** Reg. § 20.2055–3(a).

**156.** I.R.C. § 2055(d)(2)(A). See § 9.4, *supra*, note 73 (non-tax reasons for using an annuity or unitrust)

**157.** See I.R.C. § 664(d)(1).

**158.** An income pay out exception is available for the unitrust. See I.R.C. § 664(d)(3).

term of years not to exceed 20 years and that upon the termination of the trust the remainder shall pass to charity.[159]

Under the unitrust, the amount paid to the noncharitable beneficiary varies each year and rises or falls as the value of the trust principal rises or falls over the life of the trust. With an annuity trust, the amount the noncharitable beneficiary receives remains constant.

A charitable deduction is also available for so-called charitable "lead" trusts which provide for payment of an annuity or unitrust amount to charity for a term certain or a term measured by the life of an individual and a remainder to a noncharitable beneficiary.[160]

Similar rules apply in the case of the unlimited gift tax charitable deduction.[161]

The split-interest charitable trust provides some significant estate planning opportunities for many taxpayers by generating some large charitable deductions while preserving substantial assets for family members. These trusts have become common estate and financial planning tools not only for their potential to avoid or reduce transfer taxes but also to minimize the donor's income taxes to the extent these trusts qualify for an income tax deduction under section 170 of the Code.

### *Marital Deduction*

An unlimited deduction is allowed in computing the value of the taxable estate for the value of all property included in the decedent's gross estate passing[162] from the decedent to the decedent's surviving spouse. This is the most important deduction available to married couples wishing to minimize the transfer taxes on their property. This deduction reflects a strongly held policy that it is inappropriate to assess transfer taxes on transfers of property between spouses.

The marital deduction is available only for a deductible interest passing from the decedent to the surviving spouse. A deductible interest is a property interest passing to the spouse that is not made nondeductible by the so-called "nondeductible terminable interest rule."[163] Under the nondeductible terminable interest rule, a property interest passing from the decedent to the surviving spouse is not deductible if, upon the happening of an event or contingency or upon the lapse of time, the spouse's interest will terminate, and upon such termination the interest or the property from which the interest is carved passes to someone other than the spouse for less than adequate and full consideration in money or money's worth.[164] For example, if John bequeaths $100,000 in trust to pay the income to Abagail for 20 years, remainder to John, Jr., Abagail's term interest is nondeductible because (1) it will terminate upon the lapse of 20 years, and (2) upon the termination of that interest the trust will pass to John, Jr. for less than adequate and full consideration in money or money's worth. On the other hand, if John

**159.** I.R.C. § 664(d)(2).

**160.** I.R.C. § 2055(d)(2)(B).

**161.** See I.R.C. § 2522.

**162.** See I.R.C. § 2056(c) (broadly defining passing to include all interests included in the decedent's gross estate whether or not the interest was included in the decedent's probate estate.)

**163.** I.R.C. § 2056(b).

**164.** I.R.C. § 2056(b)(1).

bequeaths Abagail his remaining term interest in a copyright, the interest passing to Abagail qualifies for the marital deduction. While Abagail's interest terminates at the end of the copyright term, upon the termination of her interest no interest passes to any other person for less than adequate and full consideration in money or money's worth.

The nondeductible terminable interest rule essentially assures that property passing from one spouse to another escapes tax only if such property is transferred in such a way that it will be included in the surviving spouse's gift or estate tax base unless consumed by the surviving spouse during the spouse's lifetime.

The nondeductible terminable interest rule is subject to a number of important exceptions. First, if the spouse's interest will terminate because the gift to the spouse is conditioned upon the spouse surviving the decedent by six months or less, or upon the spouse and the decedent not dying as the result of a common accident or disaster, and in fact the spouse's interest does not terminate, the property passing to the spouse qualifies for the marital deduction.[165]

Second, if the property passing from the decedent passes in form such that (1) the spouse is entitled to all of the income[166] from the property, or a specific portion thereof,[167] for life payable at least annually, (2) the spouse has a power to appoint the property either to herself or to her estate[168] which is exercisable alone and in all events[169] and (3) no person, except the spouse, has a power to appoint the property to any person other than the spouse, the property passing from the decedent qualifies for the marital deduction.[170] To illustrate, suppose Dolly creates a $100,000 trust to pay the income to James for life, remainder to such persons, including James' estate, as he appoints by will and in default of appointment to Allan. Dolly's estate is entitled to a marital deduction in the amount of $100,000. The same marital deduction would be allowable even though James had a special inter vivos power of appointment exercisable in favor of his issue, in addition to his testamentary general power. Likewise, the trust would qualify for a $100,000 marital deduction even if the trustee of the trust could invade the trust corpus for James. However, if the trustee could invade the corpus for the benefit of another person, other than James' dependent and in satisfaction of his legal obligation of support, the trust would not qualify for the marital deduction.

Property qualifying for the marital deduction under the life estate/power of appointment exception is included in the surviving spouse's transfer tax

**165.** I.R.C. § 2056(b)(3). The six-months clause obviously is consistent with the 120 hours survivorship rules under the Uniform Probate Code. For the problem of simultaneous death and the planning considerations relevant thereto, see § 8.3, *supra*, note 85 et. seq.

**166.** Treas.Reg. § 20.2056(b)–5(f).

**167.** The specific portion can be either a specific portion of the income from the entire trust, or all of the income from a specific portion of the trust. *See generally,* Treas.Reg. § 20.2056(b)–5(a)(1).

**168.** Treas.Reg. § 20.2056(b)–5(g). The terms of this general power are not coterminous with the definition of a general power in Section 2041. Under Section 2041 a general power includes a power to appoint to the donee, the donee's estate, the donee's creditors or the creditors of the donee's estate.

**169.** *Id.* Thus, co-held powers do not qualify for the Section 2056(b)(5) exception and a general power that is not exercisable from the date of the decedent's death until the date of the surviving spouse's death either as an inter vivos power or a testamentary power does not qualify under Section 2056(b)(5).

**170.** I.R.C. § 2056(b)(5).

base either because the spouse exercises or releases the general power during life[171] or possessed the general power at the time of his death.[172]

Third, property transferred to the spouse for life, remainder to the spouse's estate qualifies for the marital deduction even if the spouse is not entitled to the income for life or the income may be paid to the spouse or accumulated. This transfer is not disqualified by the nondeductible terminable interest rule because no one but the spouse's alter ego—her estate—is entitled to the property at the termination of the spouse's life interest.[173]

Fourth, under Section 2056(b)(7) qualified terminable interest property passing from the decedent to the surviving spouse qualifies for the marital deduction. Qualified terminable interest property ("QTIP") is property in, or with respect to, which (1) the spouse is entitled to all of the income for life payable at least annually,[174] (2) no person, including the spouse, has the power to appoint any of the property to someone other than the spouse during the spouse's lifetime[175] and (3) the executor has made an election that the property should qualify for the marital deduction. To illustrate, a transfer from Helen in trust to pay the income to William for life, remainder to Helen's issue qualifies as QTIP if the executor of Helen's estate elects to treat the property as QTIP so long as no one can appoint the property to someone other than William during his life. This type of devise is often used by spouses who have children from a prior marriage and who do not wish to risk the loss of property for their children by the other spouse's exercise of a power of appointment.

Since the negative power rule applies only to powers exercisable during the spouse's life, the surviving spouse can be granted a special testamentary power of appointment.

To assure that QTIP enters into the surviving spouse's transfer tax base either under the gift or the estate tax law, Section 2519 and Section 2044 were enacted. If a person with a qualifying income interest for life in QTIP transfers[176] that income interest to another, the person is deemed to also have transferred the remainder interest.[177] If the transfer of the income interest is for less than adequate and full consideration in money or money's worth, the transfer results in the making of a taxable gift of that income interest.[178] Whether or not the transfer of the income interest is a transfer for less than adequate and full consideration in money or money's worth, a transfer of that interest also results in a transfer of the remainder under Section 2519. Of course, whether there is a gift of the remainder interest depends upon whether the transferor surrendered dominion and control over that remainder. Thus, suppose Grace transfers $100,000 in trust to pay the income to Cal

**171.** I.R.C. §§ 2514; 2041.

**172.** I.R.C. § 2041. Although it does not matter for tax purposes, whether the spouse exercised the power is a question frequently litigated when the takers in default of appointment differ from the beneficiaries named in the spouse's will. See, § 10.4, *supra*, note 45 et. seq.

**173.** Treas.Reg. § 20–2056(e)–2(b).

**174.** QTIP also includes property in which the spouse has a usufruct interest for life. I.R.C. § 2056(b)(7)(B)(ii). An annuity can be treated as an income interest. I.R.C. § 2056(b)(7)(B).

**175.** *Cf.* I.R.C. § 2056(b)(5) discussed *supra* at notes 169–171, and accompanying text.

**176.** A transfer may be by sale, gift or otherwise.

**177.** I.R.C. § 2519.

**178.** See I.R.C. § 2511.

for life, remainder to Jim. Grace elects to treat the $100,000 as QTIP and the transfer qualifies for the gift tax marital deduction. Five years later when Cal's life estate is worth $40,000, he transfers it to Bert who therefore acquires a life estate in the property measured by Cal's life. Whether the transfer of the life estate results in a taxable gift is determined under general gift tax principles. The transfer of the life estate also results in Cal making a transfer of the $60,000 remainder interest under Section 2519. This transfer is a gift unless Cal received adequate and full consideration for the transfer of the remainder (an unlikely event) or retained dominion and control over the remainder interest. For example, if Cal had a special testamentary power over the remainder interest deemed transferred under Section 2519, there would be no gift of that interest but it would be included in his gross estate.

When the spouse who possesses a qualifying income interest in QTIP dies, the QTIP is included in the spouse's gross estate under Section 2044 unless during the spouse's life a Section 2519 transfer occurred. Thus, in the preceding example, if Cal died never having transferred the income interest, the trust is included in his gross estate under Section 2044. Any estate tax attributable to the inclusion of QTIP in Cal's gross estate is payable from the trust unless the trust instrument or Cal's will otherwise provides. If Cal made a Section 2519 disposition with respect to that trust, nothing would be included in his gross estate under Section 2044.

Fifth, section 2056(b)(8) creates an additional exception to the nondeductible terminable interest rule for charitable remainder trusts[179] in which the surviving spouse has an annuity or unitrust interest. This exception is necessary to qualify the spouse's interest for the marital deduction because, of necessity, the spouse's interest is not otherwise deductible under Section 2056(b)(5) or Section 2056(b)(7) since such trusts do not give the spouse all of the income for life. If the decedent's surviving spouse is the only noncharitable beneficiary of a charitable remainder trust, the spouse's interest qualifies for the marital deduction and the remainder interest qualifies for the charitable deduction. Thus, the entire value of the property passing into the charitable remainder trust is excluded from decedent's taxable estate. The utility of this exception is questionable because similar tax consequences can result through the use of a QTIP trust of which charity is the remainderman which, unlike the charitable remainder trust, could permit the trustee to invade the corpus for the benefit of the spouse.

Section 2523 contains comparable provisions for the gift tax marital deduction, including a gift tax nondeductible terminable interest rule,[180] a life estate power of appointment[181] and a QTIP[182] exception to that rule and a special rule for gifts to a charitable remainder trust.[183]

### *Marital Deduction Planning*

Use of the unlimited marital deduction may result in higher aggregate transfer taxes on the estates of both spouses than might otherwise be payable. This can result from the first spouse to die failing to take full advantage of

**179.** See notes 155–159, *supra* and accompanying text.

**180.** I.R.C. § 2523(b).

**181.** I.R.C. § 2523(e).

**182.** I.R.C. § 2523(f).

**183.** I.R.C. § 2523(g).

the unified credit. Mary has a personal estate of $2,000,000 which she is prepared to leave to John, her husband, in the full expectation that he will bequeath it to their children. If Mary dies in 2002 bequeathing all of this to John who has not property of his own, no estate taxes are payable on her estate because of the unlimited marital deduction. When John dies in 2003, however, $551,000 in estate taxes are payable on the $2,000,000 bequeathed to the children. Alternatively, if Mary created a $700,000 trust for John with a remainder to their children and the remaining $1,300,000 outright to John, then no estate taxes would be payable on her taxable estate of $700,000 and only $239,000 of estate taxes would be payable on his taxable estate of $1,400,000. If Mary divides her estate in that way $312,000 of estate taxes are saved. The difference in result arises because through proper planning Mary utilized her unified credit and did not avoid its tax saving potential by avoiding all estate taxes on her estate by the use of an unlimited marital deduction. Even if Mary and John lived in a community property state such that only $1,000,000 was included in Mary's estate, it would continue to be advisable for her to maximize the use of the unified credit by sheltering $700,000 from John's estate such that only $1,300,000 ($300,000 from Mary and $1,000,000 of his community share) is included in his gross estate at his death.

The terms of the trust for John that bypasses his estate when he dies can be as broad or restrictive as Mary wishes so long as John does not have a general power which would cause the trust to be included in his gross estate when he died. Similarly, Mary's estate can claim the $1,400,000 marital deduction not only for an outright bequest to John but also for a life estate/power of appointment or QTIP trust created for John's benefit. Which of those transfers Mary prefers depends, among other things, on how well John manages money and how much power Mary wishes to give John to determine the ultimate takers of the property.

In determining how much Mary should bequeath to John to take optimum advantage of both the unified credit and the marital deduction, she could use a marital deduction formula clause. These clauses are used because changes in the value and composition of Mary's assets, how much debt she owes to others, and the amount of the available unified credit can change between the time the will is executed and the time she dies.[184] Under these clauses the exact amount passing to or for the benefit of the surviving spouse is not determined until the deceased spouse's death when the precise value of the decedent's assets, as well as the amount of debts and expenses and the allowable unified credit, is known.

Proper marital deduction planning should also take into account the advisability of lifetime interspousal gifts. If Mary failed to make gifts to John and John predeceased Mary, then Mary's estate would not benefit from the marital deduction and the $2,000,000 she bequeathed to her children would be subject to a tax of $588,000.

**184.** *See generally,* Kurtz, *The Impact of the Revenue Act of 1978 and the 1976 Tax Reform Act on Estate Tax Marital Deduction Formulas,* 64 Iowa L.Rev. 739 (1979); Kurtz, *Marital Deduction Estate Planning Under the Economic Recovery Tax Act of 1981: Opportunities Exist, But Watch the Pitfalls,* 34 Rutgers L.Rev. 591 (1982). Such formula gifts should make clear whether the spouse shares in appreciation and depreciation on estate assets.

### *Family-owned Business Interest*

If the decedent's estate includes a so-called "qualified family-owned business interest," the estate is entitled to a deduction in an amount equal to the lesser of the adjusted value of such interest or $675,000.[185] However, if an estate is entitled to this deduction, the amount of the unified credit to which it would otherwise be entitled is reduced. If the family-owned business interest deduction is $675,000, the unified credit is limited to $202,050.[186] If the deduction is less than $675,000, the unified credit is increased by an amount provided in the statute.

The definition of a qualified family-owned business interest is quite complex and to some extent parallels the rules relating to "special use" valuation.[187] The section only applies if the value of the business exceeds 50% of the value of the adjusted gross estate[188] and the executor makes an appropriate election.[189]

### *Disclaimers*

Under Section 2518(a), if a person makes a qualified disclaimer which satisfies the provision of Section 2518(b) with respect to any interest in property, the estate tax shall be computed as if the disclaimed interest had not been transferred to the disclaimant. For example, if T bequeaths $100,000 to spouse S who disclaims the bequest in the statutory manner, and by reason of the disclaimer the bequest passes to friend F, the legacy is treated as not passing from T to S and does not qualify for the estate tax marital deduction. Likewise, it would not be treated as a taxable gift from S to F.[190] Alternatively, if T bequeaths $100,000 to Child A who timely disclaims and as a result of the disclaimer the property passing to T's spouse who is the residuary legatee, the property is deemed to pass from T to the spouse and qualifies for the marital deduction.

Under Section 2518(b), a qualified disclaimer is an irrevocable and unqualified refusal by a disclaimant to accept an interest in property if:

1. The refusal is in writing;[191]

2. The writing is received by the transferor of the disclaimed interest, by his legal representative or by the holder of the legal title to the property from which the disclaimed interest is carved, not later than nine months after the day on which the transfer creating the interest is made.[192] However, in no event will the period for making the disclaimer expire until nine months after the day on which the disclaimant attains age twenty-one.[193] Accordingly, if T bequeaths $10,000 to child A who is twenty years and nine months old at T's death, A may disclaim the interest one year after T's death and not nine

**185.** I.R.C. § 2057.

**186.** I.R.C. § 2057(a)(3).

**187.** I.R.C. § 2032A.

**188.** The "adjusted gross estate" is the value of the gross estate less deductions only for debts and expenses. I.R.C. § 2057(c).

**189.** I.R.C. § 2057(b).

**190.** I.R.C. § 2518.

**191.** I.R.C. 2518(b)(1).

**192.** I.R.C. § 2518(b)(2)(A). See also § 2.8, *supra*, note 30 (relating to longer times allowed to make disclaimers for future interests under the Uniform Probate Code and other state laws)

**193.** The possibility of a child disclaiming several years later after the child reaches age 21 may present problems if one seeks to disclaim in order to increase the marital deduction. With respect to the possibility of a guardian disclaiming on behalf of the child, see § 2.8, *supra*, note 52 et. seq.

months after T's death because A may in all events timely disclaim within nine months after A attains age twenty-one. Similarly, if T establishes a testamentary trust to pay the income to A for life and upon A's death to pay the corpus to A's children, A's children would have at least until nine months after they attained age twenty-one to disclaim the interest. If this event occurs prior to A's death, they must disclaim before A dies and not after.[194] If decedent dies testate, it appears that a transfer is made as of decedent's death and that no qualified disclaimer is possible if the will is probated and an interest is disclaimed more than nine months after decedent's death;

3. The disclaimant has not accepted the interest or any of its benefits prior to the disclaimer;[195] and

4. The disclaimed interest must pass as a result of the disclaimer and without any direction on the part of the disclaimant to either the decedent's spouse or to a person, other than the disclaimant.[196] Thus, a decedent's spouse may effectively disclaim an interest passing to the spouse under the decedent's will even though the disclaimed interest would then pass into a trust of which the spouse is the income beneficiary.

In order to assure uniformity for the treatment of disclaimers under federal law which might not otherwise be possible because of Section 2518(b)(4)'s requirements effectively incorporating various state laws in the federal statute, Section 2518(c)(3) provides that a written transfer of the transferor's entire interest in property within the time limits provided in Section 2518 and before the transferor accepts any benefits in the transferred property is treated as a qualified disclaimer if the transferee is a person who would have received the property had the transferor made a qualified disclaimer.

A disclaimer of an undivided portion of an interest is treated as a qualified disclaimer of the portion of the interest if the disclaimer otherwise satisfies the foregoing four requirements.[197]

## § 15.4 Generation Skipping Transfer Tax

The federal estate tax does not apply to property passing as the result of the termination of an interest of a beneficiary in a trust having beneficiaries of different generations unless the beneficiary whose interest terminates has a general power of appointment.[1] Transfer taxes on property passing into a trust providing benefits to beneficiaries of different generations generally are payable only when the trust is created. This permits persons of substantial wealth to avoid transfer taxes at each generation level through the use of so-called generation skipping trusts. To illustrate, suppose John bequeaths his personal estate of $5,000,000 to daughter Carol who, in turn, bequeaths her entire estate that she inherited from John to her daughter, June. Upon John's death in 1985, $2,083,000 of estate taxes were paid, and Carol received $2,917,000. Upon Carol's death in 1995 an additional $1,041,500 of estate taxes were paid and June inherited $1,875,500. Thus a total of $3,124,500 of

194. I.R.C. § 2518(b)(2)(B).

195. I.R.C. § 2518(b)(3).

196. I.R.C. § 2518(b)(4). As to what happens to disclaimed property under state law, see § 2.8, *supra*, note 52 et. seq.

197. I.R.C. § 2518(c)(1).

§ 15.4

1. I.R.C. §§ 2041; 2514.

estate taxes are paid as John's property wound its way down to June who received only $1,875,500. On the other hand, if John had created a trust to pay the income to Carol for life, remainder to June, only $2,083,000 of estate taxes would have been paid and June would ultimately receive $2,917,000.

In 1976 Congress enacted Chapter 13 of the Internal Revenue Code for the purpose of minimizing the opportunities to avoid transfer taxes through the use of such trusts. The initial provisions of Chapter 13 were, however, retroactively repealed by the Internal Revenue Code of 1986 and in lieu thereof the provisions of Chapter 13 discussed below were enacted.

### *Critical Definitions:*
### *Transferor*

With one exception[2] the transferor, in the case of a transfer that is included in the transferor's gross estate under chapter 11 of the Code is the decedent.[3] In the case of a transfer that is included in the transferor's gift tax base under chapter 12, the transferor is the donor.[4] Two special rules relate to the determination of who is the transferor. First, if one spouse makes a lifetime transfer to someone, other than the other spouse, and the spouses elect, under Section 2513 to split this gift for gift tax purposes,[5] then for purposes of Chapter 13 each spouse is deemed the transferor of one-half of the gift even though under state property law rules only one of the spouses was in fact the donor.[6]

Second, if a donor spouse or a deceased spouse transfers property to the other spouse in a form that qualifies for the estate or gift tax marital deduction as qualified terminable interest property,[7] the donor spouse or the estate of the deceased spouse may elect, for purposes of Chapter 13, not to treat such property as qualified terminable interest property.[8] If no such election is made, then the donee spouse of qualified terminable interest property is treated as the transferor of such property.[9] If an election is made, then the deceased spouse or the donor spouse is treated as the transferor for Chapter 13 purposes even though the property is later included in the transfer tax base of the donee spouse.[10] This election assists married persons in assuring that each spouse can be a transferor under Chapter 13 and possibly claim the benefits of available deductions and exclusions.

2. I.R.C. § 2653(a).

3. I.R.C. § 2652(a)(1)(A).

4. I.R.C. § 2652(a)(1)(B).

5. Under Section 2513 if spouses elect to split a gift made by one spouse to a third person, then for gift tax purposes, each spouse is deemed the donor of one half of the gift. For example, if Wife gives $100,000 to Child A and Wife and Husband elect to split this gift for gift tax purposes, then Wife and Husband, for gift tax purposes, are each treated as having made a $50,000 gift to A. In calculating the amount of gift tax payable on this transfer, both Wife and Husband are entitled to claim the $10,000 annual exclusion against the gift each of them is deemed to have made to A. I.R.C. § 2503(b). Additionally, each of them is fully entitled to claim his or her remaining unified credit against any tentative gift tax computed on the taxable gift of $40,000 each is deemed to have made to A. I.R.C. § 2505.

6. I.R.C. § 2652(a)(2).

7. I.R.C. §§ 2056(b)(7); 2523(f). *See also* § 15.3, notes 174–177, *supra.*

8. I.R.C. § 2652(a)(3).

9. See Id.

10. No similar election is available for property qualifying the marital deduction under the life estate/power of appointment exceptions in I.R.C. §§ 2056(b)(5) and 2523(e).

### *Interest*

Under Chapter 13 it may be important at certain times to determine whether a person has an interest in a trust. Ordinarily the time a determination is to be made is when some other person's interest has terminated.[11] A person has an interest in a trust if the person has a present right to receive the income or corpus of the trust[12] or is a permissible *current* recipient of either the income or corpus of the trust.[13] However, the person with this permissible interest cannot be a charity[14] unless the trust[15] is either a charitable remainder trust[16] or a pooled income fund.[17] A charitable beneficiary of a charitable remainder trust or a pooled income fund has an interest even though the interest is only a future interest. An interest which is created primarily to avoid the Chapter 13 tax is disregarded.[18]

### *Skip Person and Non-skip Person*

A "skip person" is a person who is assigned to a generation that is at least two generations below the transferor's generation.[19] A trust can be a skip person if (i) all present interests in the trusts are held by skip persons or (ii) no person holds a present interest in the trust and after the transfer no distribution, including terminating distributions, can be made to a non-skip person from the trust.[20] A non-skip person is a person who is *not* a skip person.[21] To illustrate suppose Amy creates a trust to pay the income to her son, Bernie, for life, remainder to his children (grandchildren of Amy). This trust is *not* a skip person because Bernie, who is assigned to the first generation below Amy and therefore is not a skip person, has the present interest in trust. Bernie's children, however, are skip persons.[22] But if Amy transfers property in trust to pay the income to her grandchildren for their lives remainder to her great-grandchildren the trust is a skip person.[23] Suppose the trust provided that if none of Amy's great-grandchildren survived Amy's grandchildren, then upon the death of the survivor of them, the corpus would be distributed to Amy's nieces and nephews. The nieces and nephew are in the first generation below the grantor's generation and thus are non-skip persons. The trust is a skip person because all present interests (which by definition excludes future interests)[24] are held by skip persons.

**11.** See I.R.C. § 2612(a). *See also* notes 42–53, 293, *infra* and accompanying text.

**12.** I.R.C. § 2652(c)(1)(A). A trust includes a legal life estate followed by a remainder and similar trust equivalents. I.R.C. § 2652(b)(1).

**13.** *Id.* Presumably the "current" requirement means that a person who will only be a permissible recipient in the future has no interest in the trust.

**14.** For this purpose a charity is an organization described in I.R.C. § 2055(a).

**15.** I.R.C. § 2652(c)(1)(C).

**16.** I.R.C. § 664.

**17.** I.R.C. § 642(c)(5).

**18.** I.R.C. § 2652(c)(2).

**19.** I.R.C. § 2613(a)(1). See notes 25–41, *infra* and accompanying text for a discussion of the generation assignment rules. Under prior law such a person was called a "younger generation beneficiary." Former I.R.C. § 2613(c). However, under prior law a younger generation beneficiary also could include a person assigned to the first generation below the grantor's generation.

**20.** I.R.C. § 2613(a)(2). An example of this trust would be a transfer to T in trust to accumulate the income for 15 years and at the end of the term to distribute the corpus and accumulated income to the grantor's then living grandchildren and more remote descendants.

**21.** I.R.C. § 2613(b).

**22.** The fact that a trust is not a skip person does not mean it or its beneficiaries are not subject to the generation skipping transfer tax.

**23.** I.R.C. § 2613(a)(2).

**24.** I.R.C. § 2652(c).

### *Assignment of Generations*

Chapter 13 sets forth detailed rules to determine a person's generation assignment.[25] These rules fall into three categories: rules relating to the generational assignments of lineal descendants of the transferor,[26] rules relating to the generational assignment of persons related to the transferor by marriage,[27] and rules relating to the generational assignment of persons who are not related to the transferor.[28] These rules are:

1. The transferor's children are assigned to the first generation below the transferor,[29] the transferor's grandchildren are assigned to the second generation below the transferor, the transferor's great-grandchildren are assigned to the third generation below the transferor and so forth. The transferor's siblings are assigned to the transferor's generation; nieces and nephews are assigned to the first generation below the transferor, grandnieces and grandnephews are assigned to the second generation below the transferor and so forth.

2. A lineal descendant of the grandparents of the transferor's spouse, other than the transferor's spouse who is always assigned to the same generation as the transferor,[30] is assigned to the generation resulting from comparing the number of generations between the lineal descendant and the grandparent and the number of generations between the grandparent and the transferor's spouse.[31]

3. In determining the generation assignments of lineal descendants of the grandparents of the transferor or the transferor's spouse, relationships created by adoption are treated as relationships by blood[32] and relationships by half-blood are treated as relationships by whole blood.[33]

4. A person who at any time was married to the transferor is assigned to the transferor's generation.[34] A person who at any time was married to a lineal descendant of the grandparents of either the transferor or the transferor's spouse is assigned to the same generation as that lineal descendant.[35]

5. If none of the foregoing rules apply, a person born no more than 12½ years after the transferor is assigned to the transferor's generation, a person born more than 12½ years after the birth of the transferor but not more than 37½ years after the transferor is assigned to the first generation below the transferor and every person in the next successive 25 year period is assigned to the next younger generation.[36]

**25.** I.R.C. § 2651.

**26.** I.R.C. § 2651(b).

**27.** I.R.C. § 2651(c).

**28.** I.R.C. § 2651(d).

**29.** Determined by subtracting the number of generations between the transferor and his grandparents (2) from the number of generations the transferor's children are removed from the transferor's grandparents(3).

**30.** I.R.C. § 2651(c)(1).

**31.** I.R.C. § 2651(b)(2). There was no comparable provision under prior law.

**32.** I.R.C. § 2651(b)(3)(A).

**33.** I.R.C. § 2651(b)(3)(B). Half-bloods unlike whole bloods are related to each other only through one common ancestor. For example, if H and W have Child A, H dies and W remarries H–2 with whom she has Child B, Child A and Child B are half bloods. Only W is the parent they have in common. See also § 2.2, *supra* note 54.

**34.** I.R.C. § 2651(c)(1).

**35.** I.R.C. § 2651(c)(2).

**36.** I.R.C. § 2651(d). This is identical to the provisions under prior law. Former I.R.C. § 2611(c)(5).

6. If, in applying the foregoing rules, a person could be assigned to more than one generation, such person shall be assigned to the youngest such generation.[37] For example, suppose Harry adopts his grandchild, Allan, who but for the adoption would be assigned to the second generation below Harry. Under the general rule relating to the generation assignment of adopted persons, Allan would be in the first generation below Harry. However, under the rule of Section 2652(e)(1) Harry is assigned to the second generation.[38]

7. If the transferee is a lineal descendant of the parent of the transferor (or the transferor's spouse or former spouse) and (i) the transferee's parent is dead at the time of the transfer from which the transferee's interest is either established or derived, (ii) such transfer was subject to the estate or gift tax upon the transferor or his estate, then the generation assignment of the transferee shall be either 1 generation below that of the transferor, or, if lower, that generation of the transferee's youngest living ancestor who is also a descendant of the transferor's parent (or the parent of the transferor's spouse or former spouse.[39] However, this provision shall not apply to a person who is a collateral relative of the transferor if at the time of the transfer the transferor had any living relatives.[40]

7. If an entity[41] has an interest in property, every person having a beneficial interest in that entity is treated as having an interest in the property.[42] Each such person is then assigned to a generation under the foregoing rules.[43]

### *Generation Skipping Transfers and Multiple Skips*

There are three types of generation skipping transfers. They are taxable terminations, taxable distributions and direct skips.

### *Taxable Termination*

**37.** I.R.C. § 2651(e)(1). This provision is identical to Former I.R.C. § 2611(b)(6). The Service is authorized to adopt exceptions to this rule by regulation.

**38.** Under the proposed regulations to former chapter 13 it was provided that the rule relating to the person who might be assigned to two different generations "does not apply to the adoption of an unrelated person by the grantor or any beneficiary, or the marriage of an unrelated person to the grantor or any beneficiary. In these cases the * * * [rules relating to the generation assignment of lineal descendants] apply. Prop.Treas.Reg. § 26.2611–3(c).

**39.** I.R.C. § 2651(e)(1).

**40.** I.R.C. § 2651(e)(2).

**41.** An entity includes an estate, trust, partnership, corporation or other entity. I.R.C. § 2651(f)(2).

**42.** I.R.C. § 2651(f)(2).

**43.** Proposed regulations under the prior statute provided that (i) a person was a beneficiary of a trust if that person had an interest in either an estate or trust that was the beneficiary of the trust, (ii) both general and limited partners of partnerships interested in a trust were treated as beneficiaries of the trust, (iii) and shareholders of corporations having interests in trusts were treated as beneficiaries of the trust. Prop.Treas.Reg. § 26.2611–3(e). This proposal seems overly broad. For example, suppose O transfers property to T in trust to pay the income to D for ten years, remainder to X. D dies five year later leaving an estate of $500,000. Under the terms of D's will D leaves $10,000 to A and the residue of his estate to B. Under the proposed regulations both A and B are beneficiaries of the trust and that appears to be so even though A's interest in D's estate is limited to $10,000 and D's estate is more than adequate to fully fund that bequest.

Organizations described in Section 511(a)(2) and charitable trusts described in Section 511(b)(2) are assigned to the transferor's generation. I.R.C. § 2651(e)(3). This provision incorporates prior law. See Former I.R.C. § 2611(c)(7).

A taxable termination means "the termination (by death, lapse of time, release of power, or otherwise) of an interest in property held in a trust *unless*—

(A) immediately after such termination, a non-skip person has an interest in such property, or

(B) at no time after such termination may a distribution (including distributions on termination) be made from such trust to a skip person."[44]

The amount taxed generally equals the value of property with respect to which the taxable termination has occurred.[45] The tax is payable by the trustee of the trust.[46]

For example, suppose Bess creates a trust to pay the income to her husband, Harry, for life, remainder to their surviving children, or to the survivors or survivor of them,[47] for their lives and upon the death of the survivor of them to distribute the corpus equally to their surviving grandchildren. Harry is assigned to Bess's generation and is a non-skip person, their children are assigned to the first generation below Bess. They are also non-skip persons. The grandchildren are assigned to the second generation below Bess and are skip persons. Harry dies survived by two children, Ann and Billy. No taxable termination then occurs, even though Harry's interest terminates because immediately after this termination non-skip persons, Ann and Billy, have interests in the trust. Likewise if Ann dies survived by Billy, no taxable termination then occurs because Billy, who has the continuing present interest, is a non-skip person. When Billy dies survived by Bess's grandchildren, a taxable termination occurs.[48] If, at Bess' death, all of her children had predeceased her, then no taxable termination would occur at Harry's death even though the principal then became distributable to her grandchildren, because, under Section 2651(e)(1) such grandchildren would have been assigned to generation #1 and would not be skip persons. On the other hand, if Bess' children survived her, then died in Harry's lifetime, the distribution to the grandchildren at Harry's death would be a taxable termination because Section 2651(e)(1) would not apply and the grandchildren would be assigned to generation #2 and, therefore, be skip persons.

Suppose Rhoda creates a trust to pay the income to her child Andy for life, remainder to Andy's surviving children. Andy is assigned to the first generation below Rhoda; his children are assigned to the second generation. Andy, accordingly, is a non-skip person; his children are skip persons. Since Andy is entitled to the trust income he has an interest in the trust.[49] This interest terminates by reason of Andy's death. Since immediately after the termination of Andy's interest no non-skip person has an interest in the trust and distributions from the trust can be made to a skip person (Andy's

**44.** I.R.C. § 2612(a) (emphasis added). This is essentially similar to the definition of a taxable termination under prior law. I.R.C. § 2613(b).

**45.** I.R.C. § 2621.

**46.** I.R.C. § 2603(a)(2).

**47.** See § 10.1, *supra* note 141 et. seq. (discussion of cross remainders).

**48.** This definition of a taxable termination represents a significant simplification of the prior definitions and eliminates the need for the numerous provisions under prior law deferring the time at which a taxable termination is deemed to occur. *See generally,* Former I.R.C. § 2613(b).

**49.** I.R.C. § 2652(c)(1)(A).

children), a taxable termination occurs at Andy's death.[50] If Andy had a special power to appoint the property during his life among his children, his children would have interests in the trust because they are permissible recipients of current income should Andy exercise the power. If Andy exercises the power during his life by appointing the corpus outright to his child Bernie, Andy's interest terminates and a taxable termination occurs.[51] If Andy exercises the power and appoints only the remainder interest in the trust to Bernie, no taxable termination occurs because immediately after the exercise of the power, Andy, a non skip person, has an interest in the trust.[52] Lastly, if Andy releases the special power terminating the interest of his children as permissible recipients of current income or corpus, no taxable termination occurs. While the children's interest (as objects of Andy's special power) terminates, immediately thereafter Andy, a non skip person, continues to have an interest in the trust.

### *Taxable Distribution*

A taxable distribution means any distribution, including distributions of income from a trust to a skip person (other than a taxable termination).[53] In the case of a taxable distribution, the taxable amount is generally the value of the property received by the transferee.[54] The tax on a taxable distribution is paid by the transferee.[55] To illustrate, suppose Martha creates a trust to pay the income among her children and grandchildren and their spouses living at Martha's death in such shares as the trustee deems advisable. Upon the death the survivor of them, the corpus is distributable to Martha's surviving issue per stripes. The children and their spouses are assigned to the first generation below Martha and, therefore, they are non skip persons. The grandchildren and their spouses and Martha's more remote descendants are assigned to the second and lower generations. Only the children, grandchildren and their spouses, however, have an interest in the trust.[56] Distributions of income or corpus to Martha's children and their spouses are not taxable distributions because the children are non skip persons. Discretionary distributions of income or principal to the grandchildren or their spouses are taxable distributions because they are skip persons.

### *Direct Skip*

A "direct skip" is a transfer to a skip person that is subject to the estate or gift tax.[57] In the case of a direct skip the taxable amount is the value of the property received by the transferee.[58] In the case of a direct skip, other than a

**50.** The fact that a taxable termination occurs, however, does not mean a generation skipping transfer tax is payable. As will be discussed below there are a number of reasons why this taxable termination may not actually result in the payment of a tax. See notes 61–71, *infra* and accompanying text.

**51.** A taxable termination occurs not because the exercise of the power terminates the power; rather it occurs because Andy's income interest has terminated.

**52.** This is true even though the exercise of the power to appoint the remainder interest is deemed to be a termination of the interest of Andy's children as permissible objects of the power.

**53.** I.R.C. § 2612(b).

**54.** I.R.C. § 2622.

**55.** I.R.C. § 2603(a)(1).

**56.** I.R.C. § 2652(c).

**57.** I.R.C. § 2612(c). A direct skip would not include aggregate gifts to any donee in any year less than the amount of the annual exclusion.

**58.** I.R.C. § 2623.

direct skip from a trust, the generation skipping tax is paid by the transferor.[59] In the case of a direct skip from a trust, the tax is paid by the trustee.[60]

For purposes of determining whether a transfer is a direct skip, if the transfer is to the grandchild of either the transferor or the transferor's present or former spouse and the parent of such grandchild is not living, the grandchild is treated as if she was a child of the transferor or the transferor's spouse.[61] The issue of such grandchild (great-grandchildren of the transferor or the transferor's spouse) are treated as if they were grandchildren of the transferor or the transferor's spouse.[62] The most obvious example of a direct skip is an outright gift from grandparent to a grandchild whose parent who is the donor's child is living. If the grandchild's parent is not living at the time of the transfer, the transfer is not a direct skip.

### *Multiple Skip*

A special rule applies in the case of so-called multiple skips to assure that the generation skipping tax is assessed only once at each generation. If immediately after a generation skipping transfer the property is held in trust, for purposes of applying Chapter 13 (except the rules relating to the assignment of generation) to subsequent transfers from the portion of the trust representing a generation skipping transfer, the trust will be treated as if the transferor was assigned to the first generation above the highest generation of any beneficiary having an interest in the trust immediately after the transfer.[63] Two illustrations are helpful to illustrate the operation of this provision.

Suppose Oscar creates a discretionary trust to pay income and corpus among his daughter, Dolly, his grandson, Felix and his great-granddaughter, Greta. The trust will terminate upon the death of the survivor of them at which time the corpus and any accumulated income is payable to Greta's surviving issue. If Dolly dies survived by Felix and Greta a taxable termination occurs. Since following the termination of Dolly's interest, the property continues to be held in trust, Section 2653 applies. Felix is the person with an interest in the trust assigned to the highest generation; therefore the transferor is presumed to be assigned to Dolly's generation. Accordingly any distribution of income or corpus to Felix, who is now a non-skip person, is not a taxable distribution although distributions to Greta, who continues to be a skip person, would be taxable distributions. Furthermore, upon Felix's death, another taxable termination would occur.

Suppose Allen transfers property to a trust to pay the income to grandchild, George, for life, remainder to George's surviving issue. At the time of the transfer George's parents are living. The transfer to the trust is a direct skip. George is assigned to the highest generation level and therefore after the direct skip someone in George's parent's generation is deemed to be the transferor and George is a non-skip person. Thus, distributions to George during the term of the trust are not taxable distributions. At George's death, however, a taxable termination occurs. If the trust provided that upon George's death the corpus should be paid to his sibling, John, no taxable

**59.** I.R.C. § 2603(a)(3).

**60.** I.R.C. § 2603(a)(2).

**61.** I.R.C. § 2612(c)(2). See also I.R.C. § 2652(e)(2).

**62.** *Id.* A similar increase in generational levels applies to descendants more remote than great-grandchildren.

**63.** I.R.C. § 2653.

termination would occur at George's death since John is also a non-skip person.

### *The $1,000,000 Exemption*

Every person is allowed an aggregate $1,000,000 so-called "GST exemption."[64] If married persons elect to split their gifts, each spouse is entitled to a GST exemption of $1,000,000 and may allocate the exemption to any property with respect to which the person is deemed to be the transferor.[65] Generally, lifetime allocations are made on a timely filed gift tax return;[66] allocations on behalf of a decedent are made by the executors on the decedent's estate tax return.[67]

If the entire exemption is allocated to a $1,000,000 transfer, then the entire transfer is exempt from the Chapter 13 tax for all times even though at a later time the property's value exceeds $1,000,000. For example, suppose Oscar transfers $1,000,000 in trust to pay the income to son, Sam, for life, remainder to grandchild, Eddie, for life, remainder to Eddie's surviving issue. Oscar allocates his entire GST exemption to this transfer. When Sam dies the trust property is worth $10,000,000. It is worth $15,000,000 when Eddie dies. No generation skipping transfers occur upon the deaths of Sam or Eddie. On the other hand, if only $400,000 of Oscar's GST exemption had been allocated to the transfer, 40% of the property is exempt from the Chapter 13 tax and upon the deaths of Sam and then Eddie, 40% of the trust's value at that time would be subject to the Chapter 13 tax. It is advisable to allocate the exemption to transferred assets that are expected to increase significantly in value, such as a life insurance trust or closely held corporate stock.

### *Exemption Planning with the Marital Deduction*

For wealthy persons, integrating the marital deduction with the generation skipping transfer tax exclusion is extremely important. For example, if the decedent's basic plan also includes creating a trust to take advantage of the unified credit, it often is advisable to create a bypass trust along with two separate shares set aside in some manner to qualify for the marital deduction. For example, suppose Charlie has an estate of $5,000,000. If Charlie dies in 2007, he can set aside $1,000,000 into a bypass trust, and the balance could be disposed of in a manner that qualified for the marital deduction. The tax on the $1,000,000 would be zero because of the available unified credit. While Charlie could leave the remaining $4,000,000 outright or in trust for this spouse Lise in a manner that qualifies for the marital deduction, and, if left in trust, even allocate his $1,000,000 to that trust such that 1/4 of it would not be subject to the generation skipping transfer tax, Charlie might be better advised to create two separate funds that qualify for the marital deduction. For example, he could bequeath $3,000,000 directly to Lise or into a QTIP trust for her benefit, and the other $1,000,000 to a separate trust for her benefit that also qualifies for the marital deduction. If Charlie were to then allocate his entire $1,000,000 GST exemption to this latter trust, it would

**64.** I.R.C. § 2631. For persons dying or gifts made after 1997, the $1,000,000 exemption is subject to an inflation adjustment in multiples of $10,000. See I.R.C. § 2631(c).

**65.** *Id.* See I.R.C. § 2632 for special rules relating to the allocation of the GST exemption.

**66.** I.R.C. §§ 2632(a); 2642(b)(1) & (b)(3).

**67.** I.R.C. § 2632(a).

never be subject to the generation skipping transfer tax. Putting the marital deduction qualifying property into two separate trusts may have administrative and investment advantages.

### *Computation of the Tax*

The Chapter 13 tax on a transfer equals the "taxable amount" multiplied by the "applicable rate."[68] The taxable amount in the case of taxable distribution is generally the value of property received by the transferee;[69] in the case of a taxable termination, it is generally the value of the property with respect to which a taxable termination occurs;[70] with respect to a direct skip it is the value of property received by the transferee.[71] Generally, values are determined at the time the generation skipping transfer occurs and in certain cases an alternate valuation method is available.[72]

The "applicable rate" equals the maximum federal estate tax rate (50% after 1993) times the inclusion ratio.[73] The inclusion ratio equals 1 minus the "applicable fraction."[74] The applicable fraction is determined as follows: The numerator of this fraction is the amount of the GST exemption allocated to the trust or to the direct skip; the denominator is generally the value of the property transferred to the trust or involved in the direct skip.[75]

To illustrate, in 1994 suppose John transfers $5,000,000 in trust to pay the income to daughter, Sally, for life, remainder to Sally's daughter, Roz, for life, remainder to Roz's issue. No portion of John's GST exemption is allocated to this trust. Therefore the applicable fraction is zero and the inclusion ratio is 1 (1–0). With respect to the generation skipping transfers occurring at the death of Sally and then Roz, the applicable rate applied to the value of the property at the time the transfers occurs would be 50%. Thus, if the $5,000,000 value remains unchanged, then at Sally's death, the Chapter 13 tax is $2,500,000; at Roz's death it is $1,250,000.

Suppose, however, that John allocated $500,000 of his GST exemption to this trust. In this case the applicable fraction for this trust is $500,000/$5,000, 000 or 10%; the inclusion ratio is 90% (1–.10) and the applicable rate would be 45% (50% times 90%).[76] At the termination of the trust the amount of the generation skipping transfer valued at that time is taxed at the rate of 45%.

### *Other Exemptions*

Chapter 13 is inapplicable to transfers from a trust that if made by an individual would not be subject to gift tax because of the exclusion for payments of tuition or medical expenses.[77] For example, if Mary creates a trust to apply the income towards the medical expenses of her children and grandchildren, such payments are not generation skipping transfers.

**68.** I.R.C. § 2602.

**69.** I.R.C. § 2621.

**70.** I.R.C. § 2632.

**71.** I.R.C. § 2623.

**72.** See I.R.C. § 2624.

**73.** I.R.C. § 2641.

**74.** I.R.C. § 2642(a).

**75.** I.R.C. § 2642(a)(2). This value is reduced by the sum of federal and state death tax attributable to the property and recovered from the trust and any gift or estate tax charitable deduction with respect to the property. *Id.*

**76.** *But see* I.R.C. § 2653(b) directing an adjustment of the inclusion ratio in the case of multiple skips.

**77.** I.R.C. § 2611(b). *See also,* I.R.C. § 2503(e).

Transfers to or for the benefit of an individual that are exempt from the gift tax because of the annual exclusion or the exclusion for certain tuition and medical payments also are exempt from the Chapter 13 tax.

## § 15.5 Income Taxation of Estates and Trusts

### *The Subchapter J Estate*

Both estates and trusts are separate entities for income tax purposes, just as corporations and partnerships are entities for income tax purposes. The income taxation of estates and trusts is governed by the provisions of Subchapter J of the Internal Revenue Code and particularly the provisions of sections 641 through 663.

The so-called Subchapter J estate (the property subject to taxation under Subchapter J) is not co-extensive with the property of a decedent subject to the federal estate tax. The estate tax reaches property in a decedent's probate estate as well as certain lifetime-transferred property, joint tenancy property and life insurance.[1] In the case of a decedent, however, the Subchapter J estate is limited to the decedent's probate estate. For income tax purposes, the Subchapter J estate terminates when the decedent's estate terminates.

With respect to lifetime or testamentary trusts, the Subchapter J estate includes the value of the trust property in the hands of the trustee and lasts so long as the trust is in existence.

At one time there was a significant income tax advantage in creating a trust, not distributing all of the trust's income, and having undistributed income taxed in the hands of the trust for ultimate income-tax free distributions to the trust beneficiaries. This advantage has largely dissipated because of the current income tax rates for estates and trusts which escalate from 15% for taxable income up to $1,500 to 39.6% once taxable income reaches $7,500.[2] Under current law it is often advisable to have the trust's income taxed in the hand of the beneficiaries rather than the hands of the trust because the rate of tax on the income in the beneficiary's hands is significantly lower.

### *The Purpose of Subchapter J*

The primary purpose of Subchapter J is to provide a vehicle by which it can be determined whether the estate or its beneficiaries, or a trust or its beneficiaries, is taxable on the entities' income for any particular taxable year. Subchapter J is designed to assure that either the entity or its beneficiaries, but not both, are taxed on the entity's income in each year. Estates and trusts are taxed differently than corporations and partnerships. Net income of a corporation is taxed at both the corporate and shareholder level because the corporation is not entitled to any deduction for dividends paid to shareholders. Partnerships don't pay taxes; all partnership income is deemed distributed to the partners and taxed to them even if the income is actually retained by the partnership.

**§ 15.5**

1. See § 15.3, *supra*.

**2.** I.R.C. § 1(f). For unmarried individuals the 39.6% rates kicks in once taxable income reaches $79,772 and for married taxpayers $250,000.

### *The Distributions Deduction and the Beneficiary Gross Income Inclusion*

The starting point in the analysis is that the gross income of an entity is determined in the same manner as an individual's gross income is determined. For entities, this generally means that gross income includes dividends, interests, rents and capital gains. Entities are also entitled to certain deductions in calculating their taxable income. One of these deductions, unavailable to individuals, is the "distributions deduction."[3]

The distribution deduction equals the amount during the taxable year actually that is distributed to, or set aside for the benefit of, the beneficiaries. Amounts distributed include both cash and property distributed in kind, such as securities. If property in kind is distributed, it is valued, for purposes of computing the distributions deduction, at its fair market value on the date of distribution.[4] The flip side of this deduction is that the beneficiaries must include in their gross income amounts that the entity claimed as a distribution deduction.[5]

It is the combination of the entity's distribution deduction and the beneficiaries' gross income inclusion that assures that the income received by the entity is taxed to the entity or to the beneficiary but not both. Needless to say, there are many nuances that complicate how the taxable income of the entity and its beneficiaries is calculated but these nuances do not substantially change the above picture.

### *Specific Bequest Rule*

For estates, and to a limited extent for trusts, certain distributions can be made which do not generate either a distributions deduction for the estate or a gross income inclusion for the beneficiary. These distributions are described in section 663 and generally are referred to as specific bequests. Specific bequests include both specific bequests as defined by state law[6] as well as general legacies, typically of a specific sum of money. They do not include distributions to residuary legatees.

For example, if, in the year 2000, the estate has gross income of $20,000 and pays $5,000 to John in satisfaction of a general legacy the estate is not entitled to any deduction in computing its taxable income for the amount of the distribution to John and none of the $5,000 is included in John's gross income. On the other hand, if the $5,000 had been distributed to a residuary legatee, the estate would have been entitled to a distributions deduction of $5,000 and $5,000 would have been included in the gross income of the residuary beneficiary. Thus, of the estate's $20,000 of income, $15,000 is taxed to the estate and $5,000 to the residuary legatee.

**3.** I.R.C. §§ 651; 661.

**4.** Treas. Reg. § 1.661(a)–2(f)(2). If property is distributed in kind to a residuary legatee or remainderman, no gain or loss is realized by the entity as a result of this distribution even though the fair market value of the distributed property differs from the property's income tax basis. On the other hand, if property is distributed in kind in satisfaction of a right to receive a specific dollar amount, gain or loss can result to the entity from the distribution. Treas. Reg. § 1.661(a)–2(f)(1).

**5.** I.R.C. §§ 652; 662

**6.** Typically, these are bequests of specific, identifiable property. The distinction discussed in § 8.1, *supra,* note 9 et. seq. between specific and general devises for ademption purposes is not determinative in interpreting section 663.

### *Distributable Net Income*

Unlike trusts, an estate is rarely required to make distributions to beneficiaries until it terminates. As a result, estate distributions, except in the year of the estate's termination, are essentially discretionary. Trusts, on the other hand, are often required to make distributions, and, like estates, are required to make distributions to the beneficiaries when they terminate. Also, trustees often are permitted to make discretionary distributions.[7] It is not uncommon, for example, for a trust to mandate required distributions and authorize discretionary distributions. To illustrate, suppose Rhonda transfers property to Bank in trust. The trust instrument directs Bank to distribute all of the trust's income to Able and authorizes Bank to invade corpus in its discretion for the benefit of Able and Able's children. Here, there are both required and possible discretionary distributions.

Under Subchapter J, all required and discretionary distributions, other that distributions in payment of a specific bequest, most likely will, but may not necessarily, generate a distributions deduction for the entity as well as a gross income inclusion for the beneficiary. To sort out the possibilities, Congress created the concept of distributable net income (DNI), which has no counterpart in the income taxation of corporations, partnerships, or individuals.

Essentially, DNI[8] equals the entity's gross income plus the entity tax exempt income,[9] if any, less net gains included in its gross income, deductions, other than the distributions deduction, and the entity's personal exemption.[10] For example, assume the entity has $20,000 of rents, $5,000 of capital gains, and $8,000 of tax-exempt municipal bond interest. It paid $4,000 in state income taxes last year. Its DNI equals $24,000, which includes the rents and the municipal bond interest less the state income taxes. DNI excludes the capital gains.[11]

In the income taxation scheme for estates and trusts, DNI serves both a qualitative and quantitative function. Qualitatively, DNI preserves the characterization of items included in DNI as either rents, dividends, interests, tax exempt income and, when applicable, capital gains. This assures that to the extent such items are entitled to any special tax benefits, the benefits are achieved regardless of whether they are ultimately taxed at the entity or beneficiary level.

Quantitatively, DNI is the uppermost ceiling on the entity's distributions deduction and the amount that can be included in a beneficiary's gross income because of a distribution from the entity. Amounts distributed to beneficiaries that exceed DNI do not qualify for a distributions deduction and are not

**7.** These distinctions are reflected in the fact the sections 651 and 652 apply exclusively to trusts required to distribute all of their income currently whereas sections 661 and 662 apply to all other trusts as well as estates.

**8.** I.R.C. § 643.

**9.** I.R.C. § 103 (tax-exempt interest is interest payable on state and municipal bonds).

**10.** An estate is entitled to a $600 personal exemption; trusts are entitled to either a $100 or a $300 exemption. See I.R.C. § 642(b).

**11.** Capital gains are included in DNI if they are required to be distributed. I.R.C. § 643(a)(3). Usually this only occurs in the taxable year the entity terminates when all of its income is required to be distributed as capital gains are not treated as income for trust accounting purposes. See § 9.4, *supra*, note 11.

included in the beneficiary's gross income. They are effectively income-tax free gifts and inheritances.

To the extent DNI is characterized as including amounts of tax-exempt income, no deduction is allowable to the estate for that item and no amount of that item is included in the beneficiary's gross income.[12] If the amounts distributed are less than DNI, then it is these amounts that serve as the ceiling on the distributions deduction and beneficiary gross income inclusion. However, in that case, the distribution that is less than DNI also must be characterized in proportion to DNI to assure that no deduction is allowable for and no gross income inclusions result for amounts deemed to be tax-exempt income.

For example, suppose the entity has $20,000 of rents, $5,000 of capital gains, and $8,000 of tax-exempt municipal bond interest. DNI equals $28,000.[13] If more than $28,000 is actually distributed to the beneficiary, then the entity is entitled to a distributions deduction of $20,000 and that amount, characterized as rents, is included in the beneficiary's gross income. On the other hand, suppose only $7,000 actually is distributed to the beneficiary. This distribution is deemed to include a portion of rents and a portion of tax-exempt income. The portion is determined by reference to DNI. Since 5/7th of DNI was rents and 2/7th was tax exempt, so too, 5/7th or $5,000 of the $7,000 distribution is characterized as rents and 2/7th or $2,000 is characterized as tax exempt income. The estate gets a distributions deduction of $5,000 which amount also in included in the beneficiary's gross income.

### *The Tier Structure*

For purposes of Subchapter J a distinction is made between distributions of income which by state law are required to be distributed in the current taxable year and all other distributions, whether discretionary income distributions or principal distributions. While the entity is entitled to an income tax deduction for the smaller of the amount of DNI or the sum of distributions of both income required to be distributed and discretionary distributions,[14] the distributees of income required to be distributed[15] include DNI, to the extent of the required income distribution in their gross income but subject to characterization in the event tax exempt income is included in DNI. Only if there is an excess of DNI, do the distributees of the other distributions include any amounts in their gross income.

For example, suppose a trustee is required to distribute $500 of income to A and also makes a $4,000 distribution of principal to B. DNI equals $2,000 and is wholly characterized as rents. A includes $500 in A's gross income; B includes $1,500 in B's gross income (thus exhausting DNI) and B receives the balance income tax free. If the trustee had been required to distribute $2,000 of income to A, then $2,000 of income would be included in A's gross income and nothing would be included in B's gross income.

**12.** I.R.C. §§ 651; 661.

**13.** Capital gains are excluded from DNI.

**14.** Excluding items characterized as tax-exempt income.

**15.** Income required to be distributed is also called "state law income" and means that amount of income to which a beneficiary is entitled under state law. Typically, the amount of such income is determined by reference to applicable income and principal statutes. See, e.g., Unif. Inc. & Prin. Act.

The tier structure places the beneficiaries of discretionary distributions in a favored position over beneficiaries of income required to be distributed because beneficiaries of discretionary distributions only include amounts distributed to them in their gross income to the extent the beneficiaries of income required to be distributed have not exhausted DNI. For estates, however, this is of little consequence because, for years prior to termination there are rarely, if ever, beneficiaries to whom income is required to be distributed, and for the year of termination all of the residuary legatees are beneficiaries of income and other amounts required to be distributed. Thus, they include the distributions in their gross income to the extent of their proportionate share of DNI.

***Terminating Distributions–Excess Deductions***

In the year in which an entity terminates, if the entity has deductions, other than a distributions deduction and personal exemption, that exceed its gross income, the excess deduction is allowable as a deduction on the personal tax returns of the persons succeeding to the entities property.[16] For example, Alice's estate is about to terminate. In the year of termination it has gross income of $12,000 and pays the deductible attorney fee of $15,000. The $3,000 excess can be claimed as a deduction on the residuary legatee's personal income tax return. The deduction is allowable only in computing taxable income, not adjusted gross income, and, thus, is unavailable to beneficiaries claiming the standard deduction.[17]

***Charitable Deduction for Entity***

Estates and trusts, like individuals, are entitled to a charitable deduction but the deduction available to estates and trusts differs in a two important respects from that available to an individual. First, the deduction is unlimited.[18] It is not subject to a percentage limitation as it is with individuals. Thus, if all of the estate or trust's income is paid to charity, all of it qualifies for the charitable deduction. Second, only estate or trust income distributable or set aside for charity pursuant to the terms of the governing instrument qualify for the charitable deduction.[19] Thus, no deduction is available to intestate estates which escheat as there is no governing instrument.

## § 15.6 Income Taxation of Grantor Trusts

Sections 671 through 677 set forth a series of rule under which a grantor of an inter vivos trust may be required to include in her gross income either the trust's ordinary income or capital gains or both. Generally, these rules apply whenever the grantor has retained an economic interest or "too much power over" either the income interest or the remainder interest or both. The most important of the provisions are as follows:

***Grantor Retains a Reversionary Interest***

The grantor is treated as the owner of any portion of a trust (that is the income interest or the remainder) in which the grantor has a reversionary interest if the value of the grantor's reversionary interest exceeds 5% of the

**16.** I.R.C. § 642(h).

**17.** I.R.C. § 1.642(h)–2(a).

**18.** I.R.C. § 642(c).

**19.** Id.

value of such portion.[1] Harry creates a trust to pay the income to Able for life, and when Able dies, to pay the trust corpus to distribute the corpus to Harry. Harry's owns the entire reversion in this trust. Thus all of the trust's capital gains are included in Harry's gross income under section 673. Section 673 does not apply to the grantor's reversion in a trust in which any lineal descendant has a present interest, such as the right to receive the income, if the grantor's reversion would take affect solely because the lineal descendant were to die under age 21.[2] Thus, if grantor has a reversion in a section 2503(c) trust[3] which would become possessory should the grantor's lineal descendant die under age 21, the trust's capital gains would not be included in the grantor's gross income.

***Power to Control Beneficiary Enjoyment or Retains Administrative Control***

Section 674 and 675 apply when the grantor, whether or not in the capacity of trustee, *or a nonadverse party* retains the power to control the beneficial enjoyment of the trust power or retains certain administrative powers over the trust. It bears emphasis that section 674 and 675 can apply even if the grantor has no retained power and the only "tainted" power is held by a nonadverse party.

In particular, section 674 treats the grantor as the owner of the portion of any trust over which the grantor or a nonadverse party has a "power of disposition." A power of disposition is a power "to dispose of the beneficial enjoyment of the corpus or income unless the power"[4] is specifically excepted under the provisions of either section 674(b), (c) or (d). The exceptions to the general rule of section 674, all of which are highly nuanced and thus capable of being inapplicable absent careful planning and drafting relate to the following: (1) power to apply income to support a dependent, (2) power exercisable only the occurrence of an event, (3) testamentary power, (4) power affecting charities, (5) power to distribute corpus, (6) power to withhold income temporarily, (7) power to withhold income during the beneficiary's disability, (8) powers exercisable by certain independent trustees and (9) powers limited by an ascertainable standard.

Section 675 applies to powers held by the grantor or a nonadverse party without the consent of an adverse party (1) permitting the grantor or any other person to deal with the trust assets for less and adequate and full consideration, (2) enabling the grantor to borrow trust assets without adequate interest or security, (3) permitting the exercise of certain powers of administration.

Because the rules of section 674 and 675 are highly nuanced and not easily committed to memory, whenever an attorney prepares an inter vivos trust in which the grantor has any retained power, the attorney would be well-advised to carefully scrutinize sections 674 and 675 to assure that the power held by the grantor or a nonadverse party will not result in any adverse income tax consequences to the grantor.

§ 15.6

1. I.R.C. § 673(a).
2. I.R.C. § 673(b).
3. See § 15.2, note 39 and accompanying text.
4. Treas. Reg. § 1.674(a)–1(b).

### *Revocable Trust*

Under section 676 the grantor is treated as the owner of any portion of a trust where the title to the portion can be revested in the grantor by a power exercisable by the grantor or a nonadverse power. The typical trust to which section 676 applies is the revocable trust. Thus, is Ralph transfers property into a revocable trust to pay the income to Sally for life, remainder to Don and Ralph retains the power to revoke the trust, or the trust on its face is irrevocable but the trustee-bank can distribute income or corpus to Ralph, all of the trusts ordinary income and capital gains will be included in Ralph's gross income.

### *Trust's Whose Income Payable to Grantor*

With some limited exceptions, the grantor is treated as the owner of any portion of a trust the income from which is, or may be, distributed to the grantor or the grantor's spouse or held or accumulated for future distribution to the grantor or the grantor's spouse.[5] In addition, the grantor is treated as the owner of any portion of a trust the income from which is, or may be applied, applied towards to payment of premiums on life insurance policies on the grantor or grantor spouse's life.[6]

The typical section 677 trust includes the trust where either the grantor or the grantor's spouse is entitled to the income for life. But it also includes trusts where the trustee has discretion to distribute income or corpus to the grantor or the grantor's spouse. Thus, if Carrie creates a trust to pay the income to Mary for life, remainder to Jo and empowers the trustee to distribute the corpus to the grantor, all of the ordinary income and capital gains will be included in the grantor's gross income even if the trust income in the particular taxable year is actually distributed to Mary and all of the gains are retained by the trustee as part of the principal of the trust. Carrie includes these in gross income because the trustee could have distributed them to her. It is irrelevant that the trustee did not do so.

In common with the fact that not all completed gifts in trust are necessarily excluded from the grantor's gross estate, not all completed gifts in trust necessarily result in the income from the gifted property being excluded from the grantor's gross income. For example, suppose George creates $100,000 trust to pay the income to Donna for life, remainder to Sam. The trustee decides to purchase a life insurance policy on George's life either in the trustee's exercise of its discretion to make trust investments or because the trust instrument expressly directed that such investment be made. The trustee anticipates paying the insurance premiums with trust income and deducting those premiums from the amount of income otherwise payable to Donna. While the gift of the $100,000 is a completed gift for gift tax purposes, to the extent trust income can be used to purchase the life insurance policy once acquired on George's life, it is includible in his gross income. Because of this rule, it is not uncommon for life insurance trusts to be unfunded such that the trust has no income that could be included in the grantor's gross income. Of course, this necessitates other ways for the trustee to acquire funds to pay premiums, such as subsequent year gifts from the grantor.

5. I.R.C. § 677(a).

6. Id.

### *Income Taxation of Beneficiary's With a General Power of Appointment*

Among the grantor trust provisions of the Code is a provision treating the holder of a general power of appointment exercisable during the donee's life (as distinguished from solely by the donee's will) as the owner of the portion of the trust over which the lifetime general power is exercisable.[7] Thus, suppose Patricia creates a trust to pay the income to Don for life, remainder to Alice. The trustee is granted the discretion to accumulate income rather than pay it to Don. However, Don is granted a lifetime general power to distribute the trust corpus to himself. Under section 678 all of the trust income and gains are included in Don's gross income even though none of the income or gains are actually distributed to Don. Because of section 678, persons creating marital deduction qualifying trusts by coupling the spouse's income interest with a general power of appointment often prefer to grant the spouse a general testamentary, rather than a general inter vivos, power of appointment.

**7.** I.R.C. § 678.

## CHART I

## Computation of Federal Estate Tax Due For Decedents Dying After December 31, 1981

| | |
|---|---|
| GROSS ESTATE | § 2031(a) (valuation at date of death). |
| | § 2032 (alternate valuation method). |
| | § 2032A (special use valuation method). |
| | § 2033 Property interests owned at death including under § 2034 |
| MINUS | the surviving spouse's dower or curtesy interest or an estate in lieu thereof. |
| | § 2035 Transfers within 3 years of death. |
| | § 2036 Transfers with retained life estates. |
| | § 2037 Transfers conditioned on surviving decedent. |
| | § 2038 Revocable Transfers. |
| | § 2039 Annuities. |
| | § 2040 Jointly-owned property. |
| | § 2041 Property subject to general power of appointment. |
| | § 2042 Life insurance on decedent's life. |
| | § 2044 Qualified Terminable Interest Property. |
| | § 2046 Disclaimers. |
| | § 2053 Funeral, debts, expenses and taxes. |
| DEDUCTIONS FROM GROSS ESTATE | § 2054 Losses incurred during administration. |
| | § 2055 Unlimited charitable deduction. |
| EQUALS | § 2056 Unlimited marital deduction. |
| | § 2057 Family-owned business deduction. |
| TAXABLE ESTATE | Defined § 2051. |
| PLUS | |
| ADJUSTED TAXABLE GIFTS | (post-1976 gifts in excess of annual exclusion, other than those gifts includible in gross estate.) |
| EQUALS | |
| TAX BASE | |
| APPLY TAX RATES (§ 2001) | |
| TENTATIVE TAX BEFORE CREDITS | |
| MINUS | |
| GIFT TAX PAYABLE ON POST-1976 GIFTS | § 2001(b)(2). |
| | § 2010 Unified Credit. |
| MINUS | § 2011 State death tax credit. |
| OTHER CREDITS | § 2012 Gift tax credit on pre-1977 gifts. |
| | § 2013 Credit for tax on prior transfers. |
| EQUALS | § 2014 Foreign death tax credit. |
| | § 2015 Credit for death tax on remainder. |
| FEDERAL ESTATE TAX DUE BEFORE SURCHARGE | |
| PLUS | § 2001(c)(3) Phaseout of graduated rates and unified credit. |
| FEDERAL ESTATE TAX DUE | |

# CHART II

## Computation of Federal Gift Tax Due on post-1981 transfer

| | |
|---|---|
| GIFTS DURING CALENDAR YEAR | § 2511 Defined generally. |
| | § 2512 Valuation of gifts. |
| MINUS | § 2513 Gifts attributable from spouse. |
| | § 2514 Powers of appointment. |
| | § 2516 Property settlement agreements. |
| | § 2517 Annuities. |
| | § 2518 Disclaimers. |
| | § 2519 Qualifying income interest for life. |
| GIFTS ATTRIBUTABLE TO SPOUSE | § 2513 Gift by husband or wife to third party. |
| EQUALS | |
| GIFTS DURING CALENDAR YEAR BEFORE DEDUCTIONS AND EXCLUSIONS | |
| MINUS | |
| DEDUCTIONS AND EXCLUSIONS | § 2503(b), (c) & (e) Annual exclusion of $10,000 per donee for present interests. |
| EQUALS | (Must be claimed first); gifts of certain educational and medical expenses. |
| | § 2522 Unlimited charitable deduction. |
| | § 2523 Unlimited marital deduction. |
| TAXABLE GIFTS FOR CALENDAR YEAR | § 2503(a) Defined. |
| PLUS | |
| TAXABLE GIFTS FOR PRIOR YEARS | § 2504 Defined. |
| APPLY TAX RATES (§ 2502) | |
| TAX ON TOTAL GIFTS | |
| MINUS | |
| TAX ON GIFTS FOR PRIOR PERIODS | |
| EQUALS | |
| TAX BEFORE UNIFIED CREDIT | |
| MINUS | |
| UNIFIED CREDIT | § 2505 Defined. |
| EQUALS | |
| GIFT TAX DUE BEFORE SURCHARGE | |
| PLUS | § 2001(c)(3) Phaseout of graduated rates and unified credit. |
| FEDERAL GIFT TAX DUE | |

*

# Appendix

# RESEARCHING WILLS, TRUSTS AND ESTATES LAW ON WESTLAW

*Analysis*



## Section 1. Introduction

*Wills, Trusts and Estates* provides a strong base for analyzing even the most complex problem involving wills, trusts and estates law. Whether your research requires examination of case law, statutes, expert commentary or other materials, West books and Westlaw are excellent sources of information.

To keep you abreast of current developments, Westlaw provides frequently updated databases. With Westlaw, you have unparalleled legal research resources at your fingertips.

### Additional Resources

If you have not previously used Westlaw or have questions not covered in this appendix, call the West Group Reference Attorneys at 1–800–REF–ATTY (1–800–733–2889). The West Group Reference Attorneys are trained, licensed attorneys, available 24 hours a day to assist you with your Westlaw search questions. To subscribe to Westlaw, call 1–800–344–5008 or visit the West Group Web site at **www.westgroup.com**.

### Section 2. Westlaw Databases

Each database on Westlaw is assigned an abbreviation called an *identifier*, which you use to access the database. You can find identifiers for all databases in the online Westlaw Directory and in the printed *Westlaw Database Directory*. When you need to know more detailed information about a database, use Scope. Scope contains coverage information, lists of related databases and valuable search tips. To access Scope, click **Scope** after you access the database.

The following chart lists Westlaw databases that contain information pertaining to wills, trusts and estates law. For a complete list of wills, trusts and estates law databases, see the online Westlaw Directory or the printed *Westlaw Database Directory*. Because new information is continually being added to Westlaw, you should also check Welcome to Westlaw and the Westlaw Directory for new database information.

**Selected Wills, Trusts and Estates Law Databases on Westlaw**

| Database | Identifier | Coverage |
|---|---|---|
| **Federal and State Case Law Combined** | | |
| Federal & State Case Law | ALLCASES | Begins with 1945 |
| Federal & State Case Law–Before 1945 | ALLCASES–OLD | 1789–1944 |
| **Federal Case Law** | | |
| Federal Case Law | ALLFEDS | Begins with 1945 |
| Federal Case Law–Before 1945 | ALLFEDS–OLD | 1789–1944 |
| **State Case Law** | | |
| State Case Law | ALLSTATES | Begins with 1945 |
| State Case Law Before 1945 | ALLSTATES–OLD | 1821–1944 |
| Multistate Estate Planning & Probate Cases | MEPP–CS | Varies by state |
| Individual State Estate Planning & Probate Cases | XXEPP–CS (where XX is a state's two-letter postal abbreviation) | Varies by state |
| **State Statutes, Regulations and Court Rules** | | |
| State Statutes–Annotated | ST–ANN–ALL | Varies by state |
| Individual State Statutes–Annotated | XX–ST–ANN (where XX is a state's two-letter postal abbreviation) | Varies by state |

| Database | Identifier | Coverage |
|---|---|---|
| **State Statutes, Regulations and Court Rules** | | |
| State Administrative Code Multibase | ADC–ALL | Varies by state |
| Individual State Administrative Code | XX–ADC (where XX is a state's two-letter postal abbreviation) | Varies by state |
| Individual State Court Rules | XX–RULES (where XX is a state's two-letter postal abbreviation) | Varies by state |
| **Legal Periodicals, Texts and Practice Materials** | | |
| American Jurisprudence Legal Forms 2d | AMJUR–LF | Current through June 2000 cumulative supplement |
| American Jurisprudence Pleading and Practice Forms Annotated | AMJUR–PP | Current through April 2000 supplement |
| Asset Protection: Domestic and International Law and Tactics | ASSETP | Current through 2000–2002 supplement |
| Bellatti: Estate Planning for Farms and Other Family–Owned Businesses | WGL–FARM | Current edition |
| Bittker & Lokken: Federal Taxation of Income, Estates and Gifts | WGL–IEG | Current edition |
| California Civil Practice–Probate and Trust Proceedings | CCP–PROB | Current through October 1999 cumulative supplement |
| California Estate Planning and Probate | CA–EPP | Varies by source |
| California Transaction Forms–Estate Planning and Probate | CTF–EP | Current data |
| Colliton: Charitable Gifts | WGL–CHARIT | Current edition |
| Colorado Forms Legal and Business | CO–LF | Current data |
| Elder Law Journal | ELDLJ | Full coverage begins with 1993 (vol. 1) |
| Esperti & Peterson: Irrevocable Trusts: Analysis with Forms | WGL–IRREVTR | Current edition |
| Estate Planning | WGL–ESTPLN | Full coverage begins with 1985 (vol. 12) |
| Estate Planning & Probate–Law Reviews, Texts & Bar Journals | EPP–TP | Varies by source |
| Family Estate Planning Guide | FAMEPGD | Current through October 2000 cumulative supplement |
| Federal Tax Practice (Casey) | CASEY | Current data |

| Database | Identifier | Coverage |
|---|---|---|
| **Legal Periodicals, Texts and Practice Materials** | | |
| Florida Legal and Business & Pleading and Practice Forms Combined | FL–LFPP | Current data |
| Florida Jur Forms Legal and Business | FL–LF | Current data |
| Florida Pleading and Practice Forms | FL–PP | Current data |
| Forms–All | FORMS–ALL | Varies by source |
| Frolik: Residence Options for Older or Disabled Clients | WGL–RESID | Current edition |
| Georgia Forms Legal and Business | GA–LF | Current data |
| Harrington, Plaine & Zaritsky: Generation–Skipping Transfer Tax | WGL–GENSKIP | Current edition |
| Henkel: Estate Planning & Wealth Preservation: Strategies & Solutions | WGL–WEALTH | Current edition |
| Illinois Forms Legal and Business | IL–LF | Current data |
| Kasner: Post–Mortem Tax Planning | WGL–POSTMORT | Current edition |
| Koren–Estate and Personal Financial Planning | KOREN–EPFP | Current through August 2000 update |
| Madden: Tax Planning for Highly Compensated Individuals | WGL–HICOMPI | Current edition |
| Michigan Legal Forms | MI–LF | Current data |
| Michigan Pleading and Practice | MI–PP | Current data |
| New Jersey Legal and Business & Pleading and Practice Forms–Combined | NJ–LFPP | Current data |
| New Jersey Forms Legal and Business | NJ–LF | Current data |
| New Jersey Pleading and Practice Forms | NJ–PP | Current data |
| New York Forms Legal and Business | NY–LF | Current through November 1999 supplement |
| Ohio Legal and Business & Pleading and Practice Forms Combined | OH–LFPP | Current through September 1999 supplement |
| Ohio Forms Legal and Business | OH–LF | Current through September 1999 supplement |
| Ohio Jurisprudence Pleading and Practice Forms | OH–PP | Current through 1998 supplement |
| Peschel & Spurgeon: Federal Taxation of Trusts, Grantors & Beneficiaries | WGL–TAXTRUST | Current edition |

| Database | Identifier | Coverage |
|---|---|---|
| **Legal Periodicals, Texts and Practice Materials** | | |
| PLI Tax Law and Estate Planning: Estate Planning & Administration Course Handbook Series | PLI–EST | Begins with February 1985 |
| Probate & Property | PROBPROP | Selected coverage begins with 1987 (vol. 1) |
| Quinnipiac Probate Law Journal | QPROBLJ | Selected coverage begins with 1989 (vol. 4); full coverage begins with 1993 (vol. 8) |
| Real Property, Probate and Law Journal | REALPPTJ | Selected coverage begins with 1982 (vol. 17) |
| Restatement of the Law–Trusts | REST–TRUST | *Restatement of the Law Second–Trusts* (1959 and updating appendixes); *Restatement of the Law Third–Trusts (Prudent Investor Rule)* (1992); *Restatement of the Law Third–Trusts* (Tentative Draft Nos. 1, 1996, and 2, 1999) |
| RIA Estate Checklists | RIA–ESTC | Current data |
| RIA Estate Client Letters | RIA–ESTCL | Current data |
| RIA Estate Filled In Forms | RIA–ESTF | Current data |
| RIA Estate IRS Sample Correspondence | RIA–ESTIRS | Current data |
| RIA Estate Planners Alert | RIA–ESTPA | Current data |
| RIA Estate Planning | RIA–ESTP | Current data |
| RIA Estate Planning Analysis | RIA–ESTA | Current data |
| RIA Estate Planning Collection Complete | RIA–EST | Current data |
| RIA Estate State Summaries | RIA–ESTS | Current data |
| RIA International Estate Tax Treaties and Explanations | RIA–ESTTEX | Current data |
| RIA Wills & Trust Forms & Clauses | RIA–ESTW & T | Current data |
| The Rutter Group–California Practice Guide: Probate | TRG–CAPROBTE | 2000 edition |
| South Carolina Legal and Business Forms | SC–LF | Current data |
| Spero: Asset Protection: Forms & Checklists | WGL–ASSETFORMS | Current edition |
| Spero: Asset Protection: Legal Planning & Strategies | WGL–ASSETPRO | Current edition |

| Database | Identifier | Coverage |
|---|---|---|
| **Legal Periodicals, Texts and Practice Materials** | | |
| Stephen, Maxfield, Lind & Calfee: Federal Estate & Gift Taxation | WGL–GIFTAX | Current edition |
| Streng: Tax Planning for Retirement | WGL–RETIRE | Current edition |
| Streng: U.S. International Estate Planning | WGL–INTLEP | Current edition |
| Tax Management Estates, Gifts and Trusts Journal | TM–EGTJ | Begins with January/February 1987 |
| Tax Management Portfolios–Estates, Gifts and Trusts Series | TM–EGT | Active portfolios |
| Taxation–Law Reviews, Legal Texts & Bar Journals | TX–TP | Varies by publication |
| Tennessee Legal and Business Forms | TN–LF | Current data |
| Texas Jurisprudence Pleading and Practice Forms 2d | TX–LFPP | Current data |
| Texas Forms Legal and Business | TX–LF | Current data |
| Texas Jurisprudence Pleading and Practice Forms 2d | TX–PP | Current data |
| Texas Practice Guide: Probate | TXPG–PROB | 2000 edition |
| Trusts and Trustees 2d (Bogert) | BOGERT | Current through 2000 pocket part |
| Westfall & Mair: Estate Planning Law & Taxation | WGL–EPTAX | Current edition |
| Westlaw Topical Highlights–Estate Planning & Probate | WTH–EPP | Current data |
| West's® McKinney's® Forms | NY–FORMS | Current data |
| West's McKinney's Forms–All Forms Indices | NYFORMSIDX–ALL | Current through January 1999 |
| West's McKinney's Forms–Estates and Surrogate Practice Index | NYFORMSIDX–ESP | Current through January 1999 |
| WGL Combined Estate Planning and Estate Taxation Treatises | WGL–TAXTEST | Current editions |
| Will Contests, Second Edition | WILLCONTESTS | Current data |
| Wisconsin Legal Forms | WI–LF | Current data |
| Wisconsin Pleading and Practice Forms | WI–PP | Current data |
| Zaritsky: Tax Planning for Family Wealth Transfers: Analysis with Forms | WGL–FAMTRAN | Current edition |

| Database | Identifier | Coverage |
|---|---|---|
| **Legal Periodicals, Texts and Practice Materials** | | |
| Zaritsky & Aucutt: Structuring Estate Freezes: Analysis with Forms | WGL–ESTFREEZ | Current edition |
| Zaritsky & Lane: Federal Income Taxation of Estates and Trusts | WGL–TAXET | Current edition |
| Zaritsky & Leimberg: Tax Planning with Life Insurance: Analysis with Forms | WGL–LIFEINS | Current edition |
| **West Legal Directory®** | | |
| West Legal Directory–Estate Planning | WLD–EP | Current data |

## Section 3. Retrieving a Document with a Citation: Find and Hypertext Links

### 3.1 Find

Find is a Westlaw service that allows you to retrieve a document by entering its citation. Find allows you to retrieve documents from anywhere in Westlaw without accessing or changing databases. Find is available for many documents, including case law (state and federal), the *United States Code Annotated®*, state statutes, administrative materials, and texts and periodicals.

To use Find, simply access the Find service and type the citation. The following list provides some examples:

| To Find This Document | Access Find and Type |
|---|---|
| *U.S. v. Hemme*, 106 S. Ct. 2071 (1986) | **106 sct 2071** |
| *Jones v. Barnett,* 619 N.W.2d 490 (N.D. 2000) | **619 nw2d 490** |
| 26 U.S.C.A. § 2041 | **26 usca s 2041** |
| 26 C.F.R. § 20.2031–1 | **26 cfr s 20.2031–1** |
| Minn. Stat. Ann. § 500.08 | **mn st s 500.08** |
| 72 Pa. Cons. Stat. Ann. § 7305 | **pa st ti 72 pa csa s 7305** |

For a complete list of publications that can be retrieved with Find and their abbreviations, consult the Publications List after accessing Find.

### 3.2 Hypertext Links

Use hypertext links to move from one location to another on Westlaw. For example, use hypertext links to go directly from the statute, case or law review article you are viewing to a cited statute, case or article; from a headnote to the corresponding text in the opinion; or from an entry in a statutes index database to the full text of the statute.

## Section 4. Searching with Natural Language

**Overview:** With Natural Language, you can retrieve documents by simply describing your issue in plain English. If you are a relatively new Westlaw user, Natural Language searching can make it easier for you to retrieve cases that are on point. If you are an experienced Westlaw user, Natural Language gives you a valuable alternative search method.

When you enter a Natural Language description, Westlaw automatically identifies legal phrases, removes common words and generates variations of terms in your description. Westlaw then searches for the concepts in your description. Concepts may include significant terms, phrases, legal citations or topic and key numbers. Westlaw retrieves the 20 documents that most closely match your description, beginning with the document most likely to match.

### 4.1 Natural Language Search

Access a database, such as Multistate Estate Planning & Probate Cases (MEPP–CS). In the text box, type a Natural Language description such as the following:

**standard of proof in a will contest**

### 4.2 Next Command

Westlaw displays the 20 documents that most closely match your description, beginning with the document most likely to match. If you want to view additional documents, use the Next command, click the **Document** or **Doc** arrow at the bottom of the page, or click the right arrow in the left frame.

### 4.3 Natural Language Browse Commands

**Best Mode:** To display the best portion (the portion that most closely matches your description) of each document in your search result, click the **Best Section** or **Best** arrow at the bottom of the window or page.

**Standard Browsing Commands:** You can also browse your Natural Language search result using standard Westlaw browsing commands, such as citations list, Locate and term mode.

## Section 5. Searching with Terms and Connectors

**Overview:** With Terms and Connectors searching, you enter a query, which consists of key terms from your issue and connectors specifying the relationship between these terms.

Terms and Connectors searching is useful when you want to retrieve a document for which you know specific details, such as the title or the fact situation. Terms and Connectors searching is also useful when you want to retrieve documents relating to a specific issue.

### 5.1 Terms

**Plurals and Possessives:** Plurals are automatically retrieved when you enter the singular form of a term. This is true for both regular and irregular plurals (e.g., **child** retrieves *children*). If you enter the plural form of a term, you will not retrieve the singular form.

If you enter the nonpossessive form of a term, Westlaw automatically retrieves the possessive form as well. However, if you enter the possessive form, only the possessive form is retrieved.

**Automatic Equivalencies:** Some terms have alternative forms or equivalencies; for example, *5* and *five* are equivalent terms. Westlaw automatically retrieves equivalent terms. The *Westlaw Reference Manual* contains a list of equivalent terms.

**Compound Words, Abbreviations and Acronyms:** When a compound word is one of your search terms, use a hyphen to retrieve all forms of the word. For example, the term **along-side** retrieves *along-side, alongside* and *along side.*

When using an abbreviation or acronym as a search term, place a period after each of the letters to retrieve any of its forms. For example, the term **n.l.r.b.** retrieves *nlrb, n.l.r.b., n l r b* and *n. l. r. b.* Note: The abbreviation does *not* retrieve *national labor relations board,* so remember to add additional alternative terms to your query such as **"national labor relations board"**.

**The Root Expander and the Universal Character:** When you use the Terms and Connectors search method, placing the root expander (!) at the end of a root term generates all other terms with that root. For example, adding the ! to the root *notif!* in the query

**contest /s notif!**

instructs Westlaw to retrieve such terms as *notified, notification, notifying* and *notifies.*

The universal character (*) stands for one character and can be inserted in the middle or at the end of a term. For example, the term

**withdr*w**

will retrieve *withdraw* and *withdrew.* Adding three asterisks to the root *elect*

**elect* * ***

instructs Westlaw to retrieve all forms of the root with up to three additional characters. Terms such as *elected* or *election* are retrieved by this query. However, terms with more than three letters following the root, such as *electronic,* are not retrieved. Plurals are always retrieved, even if more than three letters follow the root.

**Phrase Searching:** To search for an exact phrase, place it within quotation marks. For example, to search for references to *condition precedent,* type **"condition precedent"**. When you are using the Terms and Connectors search method, you should use phrase searching only if you are certain that the terms in the phrase will not appear in any other order.

### 5.2 Alternative Terms

After selecting the terms for your query, consider which alternative terms are necessary. For example, if you are searching for the term *admissible,* you might also want to search for the term *inadmissible.* You should consider both synonyms and antonyms as alternative terms. You can also use the Westlaw thesaurus to add alternative terms to your query.

### 5.3 Connectors

After selecting terms and alternative terms for your query, use connectors to specify the relationship that should exist between search terms in your retrieved documents. The connectors are described below:

| Use: | To retrieve documents with: | Example: |
|---|---|---|
| & (and) | both terms | **interest & income** |
| or (space) | either term or both terms | **principal corpus** |
| /p | search terms in the same paragraph | **convey! /p deed** |
| /s | search terms in the same sentence | **interpret! discern! /s intent** |
| +s | the first search term preceding the second within the same sentence | **constructive +s trust** |
| /n | search terms within "n" terms of each other (where "n" is a number) | **gift /3 tax** |
| +n | the first search term preceding the second by "n" terms (where "n" is a number) | **contingent +3 remainder** |
| " " | search terms appearing in the same order as in the quotation marks | **"undue influence"** |
| **Use:** | **To exclude documents with:** | **Example:** |
| & (but not) | search terms following the % symbol | **age % gender** |

## 5.4 Field Restrictions

**Overview:** Documents in each Westlaw database consist of several segments, or fields. One field may contain the citation, another the title, another the synopsis and so forth. Not all databases contain the same fields. Also depending on the database, fields with the same name may contain different types of information.

To view a list of fields for a specific database and their contents, see Scope for that database. Note that in some databases not every field is available for every document.

To retrieve only those documents containing your search terms in a specific field, restrict your search to that field. To restrict your search to a specific field, type the field name or abbreviation followed by your search terms enclosed in parentheses. For example, to retrieve a California case titled *Osswald v. Anderson,* access the California Estate Planning & Probate Cases database (CAEPP–CS) and search for your terms in the title field (ti):

**ti(osswald & anderson)**

The fields discussed below are available in Westlaw databases you might use for researching estate planning and probate law issues.

**Digest and Synopsis Fields:** The digest (di) and synopsis (sy) fields, added to case law databases by West's attorney-editors, summarize the main points of a case. The synopsis field contains a brief description of a case. The digest field contains the topic and headnote fields and includes the complete hierarchy of concepts used by West's editors to classify the headnotes to specific West digest topic and key numbers. Restricting your search to the synopsis and digest fields limits your result to cases in which your terms are related to a major issue in the case.

Consider restricting your search to one or both of these fields if

- you are searching for common terms or terms with more than one meaning, and you need to narrow your search; or
- you cannot narrow your search by using a smaller database.

For example, to retrieve New York cases that discuss the validity of a holographic will, access the New York Estate Planning & Probate Cases database (NYEPP–CS) and type the following query:

**sy,di("holographic will" /s valid!)**

**Headnote Field:** The headnote field (he) is part of the digest field but does not contain topic numbers, hierarchical classification information or key numbers. The headnote field contains a one-sentence summary for each point of law in a case and any supporting citations given by the author of the opinion. A headnote field restriction is useful when you are searching for specific statutory sections or rule numbers. For example, to retrieve headnotes from Minnesota cases that cite Minn. Stat. Ann. § 524.3–806, access the Minnesota Estate Planning & Probate Cases database (MNEPP–CS) and type the following query:

**he(524.3–806)**

**Topic Field:** The topic field (to) is also part of the digest field. It contains hierarchical classification information, including the West digest topic names and numbers and the key numbers. You should restrict search terms to the topic field in a case law database if

- a digest field search retrieves too many documents; or
- you want to retrieve cases with digest paragraphs classified under more than one topic.

For example, the topic Trusts has the topic number 390. To retrieve cases that discuss trusts in the context of discretionary trusts, access the Multistate Estate Planning & Probate Cases database (MEPP–CS) and type a query like the following:

**to(390) /p "discretionary trust"**

To retrieve cases classified under more than one topic and key number, search for your terms in the topic field. For example, to retrieve recent cases discussing life estates, which may be classified to Deeds (120), Estates in Property (154), Life Estates (240), or Wills (409), among other topics, access the Multistate Estate Planning & Probate Cases database (MEPP–CS) and type a query like the following:

**to(life /5 estate) & da(aft 1998)**

For a complete list of West digest topics and their corresponding topic numbers, access the Key Number Service.

> *Note:* Slip opinions, cases not reported by West and cases from topical services do not contain the digest, headnote and topic fields.

**Prelim and Caption Fields:** When searching in a database containing statutes, rules or regulations, restrict your search to the prelim (pr) and caption (ca) fields to retrieve documents in which your terms are important enough to appear in a section name or heading. For example, to retrieve Illinois statutes concerning guardians and guardianships in probate proceedings, access the Illinois Statutes–Annotated database (IL–ST–ANN) and type the following:

**pr,ca(guardian! & probate)**

### 5.5 Date Restrictions

You can use Westlaw to retrieve documents *decided* or *issued* before, after or on a specified date, as well as within a range of dates. The following sample queries contain date restrictions:

**da(1999) & "testamentary capacity"**

**da(aft 1995) & inter-vivos /3 transfer!**

**da(12/27/2000) & spend-thrift**

You can also search for documents *added to a database* on or after a specified date, as well as within a range of dates. The following sample queries contain added-date restrictions:

**ad(aft 1995) & terminat! /5 joint! /5 tenan!**

**ad(aft 2/1/1998 & bef 5/15/1998) & trustee /s breach! /5 fiduciary /5 duty**

## Section 6. Searching with Topic and Key Numbers

To retrieve cases that address a specific point of law, use topic and key numbers as your search terms. If you have an on-point case, run a search using the topic and key number from the relevant headnote in an appropriate database to find other cases containing headnotes classified to that topic and key number. For example, to search for cases containing headnotes classified under topic 409 (Wills) and key number 703 (Evidence), access the Multistate Estate Planning & Probate Cases database (MEPP–CS) and enter the following query:

**409k703**

For a complete list of West digest topic and key numbers, access the Key Number Service.

> *Note:* Slip opinions, cases not reported by West and cases from topical services do not contain West topic and key numbers.

## Section 7. Verifying Your Research with Citation Research Services

**Overview:** A citation research service is a tool that helps you ensure that your cases are good law; helps you retrieve cases, legislation or articles that cite a case, rule or statute; and helps you verify that the spelling and format of your citations are correct.

### 7.1 KeyCite

KeyCite is the citation research service from West Group.

**KeyCite for cases** covers case law on Westlaw, including unpublished opinions.

**KeyCite for statutes** covers the *United States Code Annotated* (USCA®), the *Code of Federal Regulations* (CFR) and statutes from all 50 states.

**KeyCite Alert** monitors the status of your cases or statutes and automatically sends you updates at the frequency you specify when their KeyCite information changes.

KeyCite provides the following:

- Direct appellate history of a case, including related references, which are opinions involving the same parties and facts but resolving different issues
- Negative indirect history of a case, which consists of cases outside the direct appellate line that may have a negative impact on its precedential value
- The title, parallel citations, court of decision, docket number and filing date of a case
- Citations to cases, administrative decisions and secondary sources on Westlaw that have cited a case
- Complete integration with the West Key Number System® so you can track legal issues discussed in a case
- Links to session laws amending or repealing a statute
- Statutory credits and historical notes
- Citations to pending legislation affecting a federal statute or a statute from California or New York
- Citations to cases, administrative decisions and secondary sources that have cited a statute or federal regulation

### 7.2 Westlaw As a Citator

For citations not covered by KeyCite, including persuasive secondary authority such as restatements and treatises, use Westlaw as a citator to retrieve cases that cite your authority.

For example, to retrieve cases citing the law review article "Ademption and the Testator's Intent," 74 Harv. L. Rev. 741 (1961), access the Multistate Estate Planning & Probate Cases database (MEPP–CS) and type a query like the following:

**ademption /s testator /s 74 /s 741**

## Section 8. Researching with Westlaw—Examples

### 8.1 Retrieving Law Review Articles

Recent law review articles are often a good place to begin researching a legal issue because law review articles serve 1) as an excellent introduction to a new topic or review for a stale one, providing terminology to help you formulate a query; 2) as a finding tool for pertinent primary authority, such as rules, statutes and cases; and 3) in some instances, as persuasive secondary authority.

Suppose you need to gather background information on the use of no-contest clauses in wills and trusts.

*Solution*

- To retrieve recent law review articles relevant to your issue, access the Estate Planning & Probate–Law Reviews, Texts & Bar Journals database (EPP–TP). Using the Natural Language search method, enter a description like the following:

**no-contest clause**

- If you have a citation to an article in a specific publication, use Find to retrieve it. For more information on Find, see Section 3.1 of this appendix. For example, to retrieve the article found at 50 Syracuse L. Rev. 625, access Find and type

**50 syracuse l rev 625**

- If you know the title of an article but not which journal it appeared in, access the Estate Planning & Probate–Law Reviews, Texts & Bar Journals database (EPP–TP) and search for key terms using the title field. For example, to retrieve the article "Public Policy and the Probate Pariah: Confusion in the Law of Will Substitutes," type the following Terms and Connectors query:

**ti(pariah & will /5 substitute)**

### 8.2 Retrieving Case Law

Suppose you need to retrieve state case law dealing with durable powers of attorney.

*Solution*

- Access the Multistate Estate Planning & Probate Cases database (MEPP–CS). Type a Natural Language description such as the following:

**durable power of attorney**

- When you know the citation for a specific case, use Find to retrieve it. For more information on Find, see Section 3.1 of this appendix. For example, to retrieve *In re Guardianship of Lee*, 982 P.2d 539 (Okla. Ct. App. 2000), access Find and type

**982 p2d 539**

- If you find a topic and key number that is on point, run a search using that topic and key number to retrieve additional cases discussing that point of law. For example, to retrieve cases containing headnotes classified under topic 390 (Trusts) and key number 119 (Evidence to Aid Construction), type the following query:

**390k119**

- To retrieve cases written by a particular judge, add a judge field (ju) restriction to your query. For example, to retrieve cases written by Judge Pariente of the Florida Supreme Court that contain headnotes classified under topic 409 (Wills), access the Florida Estate Planning & Probate Cases database (FLEPP–CS) and type the following query:

**ju(pariente) & to(409)**

### 8.3 Retrieving Statutes

Suppose you need to retrieve sections from the Internal Revenue Code (Title 26), specifically addressing gift taxes.

*Solution*

- Access the United States Code Annotated database (USCA). Search for your terms in the prelim and caption fields using the Terms and Connectors search method:

  **pr,ca("title 26" & "gift tax")**

- When you know the citation for a specific statute, use Find to retrieve it. For example, to retrieve 26 U.S.C.A. § 2035, access Find and type

  **26 usca 2035**

- To look at surrounding sections, use the Table of Contents service. Click a hypertext link in the prelim or caption field, or click the **TOC** tab in the left frame. You can also use Documents in Sequence to retrieve the section following § 2035, even if that subsequent section was not retrieved with your search or Find request.
- When you retrieve a statute on Westlaw, it will contain a message if legislation amending or repealing it is available online. To display this legislation, click the hypertext link in the message.

> Because slip copy versions of laws are added to Westlaw before they contain full editorial enhancements, they are not retrieved with the update feature. To retrieve slip copy versions of laws, access the United States Public Laws database (US-PL) or a state's legislative service database (XX-LEGIS, where XX is the state's two-letter postal abbreviation). Then type **ci(slip)** and descriptive terms, e.g., **ci(slip) & fiduciary**. Slip copy documents are replaced by the editorially enhanced versions within a few working days. The update feature also does not retrieve legislation that enacts a new statute or covers a topic that will not be incorporated into the statutes. To retrieve this legislation, access US-PL or a legislative service database and enter a query containing terms that describe the new legislation.

### 8.4 Using KeyCite

Suppose one of the cases you retrieve in your case law research is *In re Estate of Novak*, 458 N.W.2d 221 (Neb. 1990). You want to determine whether this case is good law and to find other cases that have cited this case.

*Solution*

- Use KeyCite to retrieve direct history and negative indirect history for *In re Estate of Novak*.
- Use KeyCite to display citing references for *In re Estate of Novak*.

### 8.5 Following Recent Developments

As the wills, trusts and estates law specialist in your firm, you are expected to keep up with and summarize recent legal developments in this area of the law. How can you do this efficiently?

*Solution*

One of the easiest ways to stay abreast of recent developments in wills, trusts and estates law is by accessing the Westlaw Topical Highlights–Estate Planning & Probate database (WTH–EPP). The WTH–EPP database contains summaries of recent legal developments, including court decisions, legislation and materials released by administrative agencies in the area of wills, trusts and estates law. Some summaries also contain suggested queries that combine the proven power of West's topic and key numbers and West's case headnotes to retrieve additional pertinent cases. When you access WTH–EPP, you will automatically retrieve a list of documents added to the database in the last two weeks.

# Table of Cases

## A

Anderson, Matter of Estate of, 541 So.2d 423 (Miss.1989)—**§ 11.1, n. 45; § 11.4, n. 5.**
Anderson, Matter of Estate of, 147 Wis.2d 83, 432 N.W.2d 923 (Wis.App.1988)—**§ 12.5, n. 124.**
Anderson, Matter of Estate of, 359 N.W.2d 479 (Iowa 1984)—**§ 2.10, n. 72; § 6.1, n. 13.**
Andrews v. Gorby, 237 Conn. 12, 675 A.2d 449 (Conn.1996)—**§ 12.5, n. 41, 70.**
Andrews v. Hall, 156 Neb. 817, 58 N.W.2d 201 (Neb.1953)—**§ 11.8, n. 9.**
Andrews v. Troy Bank and Trust Co., 529 So.2d 987 (Ala.1988)—**§ 4.5, n. 30; § 4.8, n. 8.**
Anello, Estate of v. McQueen, 953 P.2d 1143 (Utah 1998)—**§ 5.5, n. 66.**
Angier, In re Estate of, 381 Pa.Super. 114, 552 A.2d 1121 (Pa.Super.1989)—**§ 6.1, n. 52.**
Angleton v. Estate of Angleton, 671 N.E.2d 921 (Ind.App.1996)—**§ 2.7, n. 3, 7, 30, 35.**
Annan v. Wilmington Trust Co., 559 A.2d 1289 (Del.Supr.1989)—**§ 1.3, n. 52; § 2.9, n. 79.**
Anthony's Estate, In re, 423 Pa. 401, 223 A.2d 857 (Pa.1966)—**§ 9.4, n. 40.**
Antonopoulos, In re Estate of, 268 Kan. 178, 993 P.2d 637 (Kan.1999)—**§ 1.3, n. 54; § 2.11, n. 47; § 3.7, n. 13, 32, 39, 45; § 5.5, n. 46.**
**Appeal of (see name of party)**
Appelman v. Appelman, 87 Ill.App.3d 749, 43 Ill.Dec. 199, 410 N.E.2d 199 (Ill.App. 1 Dist. 1980)—**§ 13.2, n. 42.**
Apple v. Kile, 457 N.E.2d 254 (Ind.App. 2 Dist. 1983)—**§ 12.10, n. 38.**
**Application of (see name of party)**
Aragon v. Rio Costilla Co-op. Livestock Ass'n, 112 N.M. 152, 812 P.2d 1300 (N.M.1991)—**§ 4.6, n. 49.**
Aranda v. Camacho, 122 N.M. 763, 931 P.2d 757 (N.M.App.1997)—**§ 2.7, n. 15, 22.**
Araneo, Matter of, 211 N.J.Super. 456, 511 A.2d 1269 (N.J.Super.L.1985)—**§ 6.1, n. 55.**
Archer's Case, 76 Eng.Rep. 146 (1597)—**§ 11.1, n. 5.**
Arch, Ltd. v. Yu, 108 N.M. 67, 766 P.2d 911 (N.M.1988)—**§ 3.8, n. 58.**
Arens' Trust, In re, 41 N.J. 364, 197 A.2d 1 (N.J.1964)—**§ 1.3, n. 11; § 9.4, n. 23, 25.**
Arman v. Bank of America, N.T. & S.A., 88 Cal.Rptr.2d 410 (Cal.App. 2 Dist.1999)—**§ 9.7, n. 80.**
Armendaris Water Development Co. v. Rainwater, 109 N.M. 71, 781 P.2d 799 (N.M.App. 1989)—**§ 6.4, n. 96.**
Armijo, In re Estate of, 128 N.M. 565, 995 P.2d 487 (N.M.App.1999)—**§ 4.9, n. 5.**
Armington v. Meyer, 103 R.I. 211, 236 A.2d 450 (R.I.1967)—**§ 9.5, n. 74.**
Armstrong v. Bray, 64 Wash.App. 736, 826 P.2d 706 (Wash.App. Div. 2 1992)—**§ 2.7, n. 44.**
Arrowsmith v. Mercantile–Safe Deposit and Trust Co., 313 Md. 334, 545 A.2d 674 (Md. 1988)—**§ 11.3, n. 12; § 11.5, n. 2, 18; § 11.6, n. 6; § 12.1, n. 99.**
Artope, In re Will of, 144 Misc.2d 1090, 545 N.Y.S.2d 670 (N.Y.Sur.1989)—**§ 6.1, n. 63.**
Artz, Estate of v. Artz, 198 N.J.Super. 585, 487 A.2d 1294 (N.J.Super.A.D.1985)—**§ 2.7, n. 29.**
Aschauer, Matter of Estate of, 188 Ill.App.3d 63, 135 Ill.Dec. 714, 544 N.E.2d 71 (Ill.App. 4 Dist.1989)—**§ 12.8, n. 93.**
Ascherl, Matter of Estate of, 445 N.W.2d 391 (Iowa App.1989)—**§ 3.9, n. 35.**
Ash v. Calvert, 170 Eng.Rep. 1193 (1810)—**§ 12.1, n. 4.**
Ashbaugh v. Ashbaugh, 222 Ga. 811, 152 S.E.2d 888 (Ga.1966)—**§ 6.4, n. 77.**
Ashe, Matter of Estate of, 114 Idaho 70, 753 P.2d 281 (Idaho App.1988)—**§ 4.5, n. 56.**
Ashkenazy v. Ashkenazy's Estate, 140 So.2d 331 (Fla.App. 3 Dist.1962)—**§ 8.2, n. 26.**
Ashman v. Pickens, 12 Ark.App. 233, 674 S.W.2d 4 (Ark.App.1984)—**§ 12.4, n. 64.**
Ashton v. Ashton, 733 P.2d 147 (Utah 1987)—**§ 6.4, n. 94.**
Atchison, In re, 925 F.2d 209 (7th Cir.1991)—**§ 2.8, n. 14.**
Atchison v. City of Englewood, 170 Colo. 295, 463 P.2d 297 (Colo.1969)—**§ 11.8, n. 41.**
Atkins, Petition of, 126 N.H. 577, 493 A.2d 1203 (N.H.1985)—**§ 12.1, n. 46.**
Atkinson v. Kish, 420 S.W.2d 104 (Ky.1967)—**§ 11.8, n. 28.**
Auen, Estate of, 35 Cal.Rptr.2d 557 (Cal.App. 1 Dist.1994)—**§ 7.4, n. 28; § 12.1, n. 90.**
Ault, In re Estate of, 80 Ohio App.3d 399, 609 N.E.2d 568 (Ohio App. 12 Dist.1992)—**§ 4.5, n. 22.**
Aurora Nat. Bank v. Old Second Nat. Bank, 59 Ill.App.3d 384, 16 Ill.Dec. 671, 375 N.E.2d 544 (Ill.App. 2 Dist.1978)—**§ 10.4, n. 11.**
Ausley, Matter of Estate of, 818 P.2d 1226 (Okla.1991)—**§ 5.2, n. 4; § 5.3, n. 4.**
Austin, In re Estate of, 218 Mich.App. 72, 553 N.W.2d 632 (Mich.App.1996)—**§ 12.1, n. 105.**
Austin v. Dobbins, 219 Va. 930, 252 S.E.2d 588 (Va.1979)—**§ 11.2, n. 30.**
Austin v. United States Bank of Washington, 73 Wash.App. 293, 869 P.2d 404 (Wash.App. Div. 2 1994)—**§ 9.5, n. 9, 17; § 12.8, n. 32.**
Awrey, Estate of v. Commissioner, 5 T.C. 222 (Tax Ct.1945)—**§ 15.3, n. 118.**
Axelrod v. Giambalvo, 129 Ill.App.3d 512, 84 Ill.Dec. 703, 472 N.E.2d 840 (Ill.App. 1 Dist. 1984)—**§ 12.8, n. 55.**
Ayala v. Martinez, 883 S.W.2d 270 (Tex.App.-Corpus Christi 1994)—**§ 4.4, n. 20; § 12.4, n. 17.**
Azarian v. First Nat. Bank of Boston, 383 Mass. 492, 423 N.E.2d 749 (Mass.1981)—**§ 12.8, n. 115.**
Azcunce v. Estate of Azcunce, 586 So.2d 1216 (Fla.App. 3 Dist.1991)—**§ 3.5, n. 14.**

# B

Bachand's Estate, Matter of, 307 N.W.2d 140 (S.D.1981)—**§ 13.3, n. 42.**
Bacot, Succession of, 502 So.2d 1118 (La.App. 4 Cir.1987)—**§ 4.4, n. 12, 18; § 6.1, n. 34.**

## C

# D

# E

# F

## G

# H

Hardenbergh v. Commissioner, 198 F.2d 63 (8th Cir.1952)—**§ 2.8, n. 46.**

Hardin v. McPhearson, 569 So.2d 319 (Ala. 1990)—**§ 9.4, n. 5.**

Harding v. DeAngelis, 39 Mass.App.Ct. 455, 657 N.E.2d 758 (Mass.App.Ct.1995)—**§ 2.9, n. 65.**

Hardman v. Feinstein, 195 Cal.App.3d 157, 240 Cal.Rptr. 483 (Cal.App. 1 Dist.1987)—**§ 9.7, n. 69.**

Hargrove v. Taylor, 236 Or. 451, 389 P.2d 36 (Or.1964)—**§ 2.7, n. 41.**

Harms v. Sprague, 105 Ill.2d 215, 85 Ill.Dec. 331, 473 N.E.2d 930 (Ill.1984)—**§ 13.2, n. 2.**

Harmston v. Harmston, 680 P.2d 751 (Utah 1984)—**§ 6.4, n. 18.**

Harper v. Harper, 491 So.2d 189 (Miss.1986)—**§ 12.5, n. 106, 120; § 12.7, n. 101; § 12.8, n. 88, 115; § 13.3, n. 56.**

Harper v. Martin, 552 S.W.2d 690 (Ky.App. 1977)—**§ 2.10, n. 49.**

Harper v. Prudential Ins. Co. of America, 233 Kan. 358, 662 P.2d 1264 (Kan.1983)—**§ 2.7, n. 10.**

Harper v. Springfield, 578 S.W.2d 824 (Tex. Civ.App.-Waco 1979)—**§ 10.2, n. 53.**

Harper, Estate of v. Commissioner, 93 T.C. No. 32, 93 T.C. 368 (U.S.Tax Ct.1989)—**§ 3.7, n. 50; § 6.2, n. 23, 33.**

Harper, Matter of Estate of, 138 Ill.App.3d 571, 93 Ill.Dec. 194, 486 N.E.2d 295 (Ill. App. 4 Dist.1985)—**§ 4.9, n. 43.**

Harrell v. McDonald, 90 S.D. 482, 242 N.W.2d 148 (S.D.1976)—**§ 2.10, n. 9.**

Harrell, Appeal of, 104 Or.App. 332, 801 P.2d 852 (Or.App.1990)—**§ 9.6, n. 5.**

Harrington, Matter of Estate of, 850 P.2d 158 (Colo.App.1993)—**§ 4.4, n. 9; § 6.2, n. 16.**

Harris v. Rock, 799 S.W.2d 10 (Ky.1990)—**§ 3.7, n. 24.**

Harris, Matter of Estate of, 151 Mich.App. 780, 391 N.W.2d 487 (Mich.App.1986)—**§ 3.1, n. 38.**

Harrison v. Bird, 621 So.2d 972 (Ala.1993)—**§ 5.2, n. 31.**

Harrison v. Marcus, 396 Mass. 424, 486 N.E.2d 710 (Mass.1985)—**§ 11.5, n. 13; § 11.6, n. 10, 35.**

Harrison, Matter of Estate of, 25 Kan.App.2d 661, 967 P.2d 1091 (Kan.App.1998)—**§ 3.7, n. 36.**

Harrison, Matter of Estate of, 738 P.2d 964 (Okla.App.1987)—**§ 4.3, n. 16.**

Harris Trust and Sav. Bank v. Beach, 118 Ill.2d 1, 112 Ill.Dec. 224, 513 N.E.2d 833 (Ill.1987)—**§ 10.1, n. 18; § 10.2, n. 16, 67.**

Harris Trust and Sav. Bank v. Beach, 145 Ill.App.3d 682, 99 Ill.Dec. 438, 495 N.E.2d 1173 (Ill.App. 1 Dist.1986)—**§ 10.1, n. 64, 83.**

Harris Trust and Sav. Bank v. Donovan, 145 Ill.2d 166, 163 Ill.Dec. 854, 582 N.E.2d 120 (Ill.1991)—**§ 2.9, n. 81.**

Harris Trust & Sav. Bank v. MacLean, 186 Ill.App.3d 882, 134 Ill.Dec. 597, 542 N.E.2d 943 (Ill.App. 1 Dist.1989)—**§ 9.4, n. 13.**

Hart v. Connors, 85 Ill.App.2d 50, 228 N.E.2d 273 (Ill.App. 1 Dist.1967)—**§ 9.5, n. 35, 49.**

Hart, Estate of, 165 Cal.App.3d 392, 209 Cal. Rptr. 272 (Cal.App. 4 Dist.1984)—**§ 2.10, n. 51.**

Hart, Estate of, 135 Cal.App.3d 684, 185 Cal. Rptr. 544 (Cal.App. 4 Dist.1982)—**§ 2.7, n. 53.**

Hartford Nat. Bank and Trust Co. v. Thrall, 184 Conn. 497, 440 A.2d 200 (Conn.1981)—**§ 2.2, n. 34.**

Hartford Nat. Bank & Trust Co. v. Birge, 159 Conn. 35, 266 A.2d 373 (Conn.1970)—**§ 10.1, n. 50.**

Hartnett v. Jones, 629 P.2d 1357 (Wyo.1981)—**§ 11.8, n. 46.**

Hartzell, Estate of v. Commissioner, T.C. Memo. 1994-576 (U.S.Tax Ct.1994)—**§ 9.5, n. 26.**

Harvard College v. Amory, 26 Mass. 446 (Mass. 1830)—**§ 12.7, n. 29.**

Harvey v. Harvey, 215 Kan. 472, 524 P.2d 1187 (Kan.1974)—**§ 12.10, n. 40.**

Harvey, Succession of, 573 So.2d 1304 (La.App. 2 Cir.1991)—**§ 4.3, n. 17.**

Harvey v. United States, 185 F.2d 463 (7th Cir.1950)—**§ 15.3, n. 115.**

Hastings v. Bridge, 86 N.H. 247, 166 A. 273 (N.H.1933)—**§ 6.2, n. 9.**

Hatcher v. Hatcher, 188 Ariz. 154, 933 P.2d 1222 (Ariz.App. Div. 1 1996)—**§ 3.8, n. 7, 41.**

Hatcher v. Southern Baptist Theological Seminary, 632 S.W.2d 251 (Ky.1982)—**§ 9.6, n. 82.**

Hatcher v. United States Nat. Bank of Oregon, 56 Or.App. 643, 643 P.2d 359 (Or.App. 1982)—**§ 12.5, n. 91; § 12.6, n. 48; § 12.8, n. 25.**

Hatfield, Matter of Estate of, 46 Wash.App. 247, 730 P.2d 696 (Wash.App. Div. 3 1986)—**§ 8.1, n. 63.**

Hatton v. Meade, 23 Mass.App.Ct. 356, 502 N.E.2d 552 (Mass.App.Ct.1987)—**§ 4.6, n. 12.**

Hauck v. Seright, 290 Mont. 309, 964 P.2d 749 (Mont.1998)—**§ 7.1, n. 25, 33.**

Haugk's Estate, In re, 91 Wis.2d 196, 280 N.W.2d 684 (Wis.1979)—**§ 5.2, n. 9.**

Hauseman v. Koski, 259 Mont. 498, 857 P.2d 715 (Mont.1993)—**§ 5.5, n. 27.**

Haviside, Estate of, 102 Cal.App.3d 365, 162 Cal.Rptr. 393 (Cal.App. 1 Dist.1980)—**§ 12.5, n. 104.**

Hawaiian Trust Co., Ltd. v. Hogan, 1 Haw. App. 560, 623 P.2d 450 (Hawai'i App. 1981)—**§ 12.4, n. 112.**

Hawes v. Hawes, 95 Eng.Rep. 552 (1747)—**§ 4.8, n. 10.**

Hawes, State v., 169 A.D.2d 919, 564 N.Y.S.2d 637 (N.Y.A.D. 3 Dept.1991)—**§ 13.1, n. 11.**

Hawkins v. Walker, 158 Ga.App. 562, 281 S.E.2d 311 (Ga.App.1981)—**§ 12.8, n. 108.**

Hawkins' Estate, In re, 213 N.Y.S.2d 188 (N.Y.Sur.1961)—**§ 2.7, n. 40.**

Hawley, Matter of Estate of, 183 Ill.App.3d 107, 131 Ill.Dec. 664, 538 N.E.2d 1220 (Ill. App. 5 Dist.1989)—**§ 12.9, n. 5.**

Hayes v. Hammond, 336 Mass. 233, 143 N.E.2d 693 (Mass.1957)—**§ 10.1, n. 96.**
Haynes v. Williams, 686 S.W.2d 870 (Mo.App. W.D.1985)—**§ 8.3, n. 45.**
Hearst, Estate of, 67 Cal.App.3d 777, 136 Cal. Rptr. 821 (Cal.App. 2 Dist.1977)—**§ 9.1, n. 14.**
Heater, In re Estate of, 266 Ill.App.3d 452, 203 Ill.Dec. 734, 640 N.E.2d 654 (Ill.App. 4 Dist. 1994)—**§ 2.8, n. 44.**
Heath by Heath v. Heath, 143 Ill.App.3d 390, 97 Ill.Dec. 615, 493 N.E.2d 97 (Ill.App. 2 Dist.1986)—**§ 6.3, n. 23.**
Hecht v. Superior Court, 20 Cal.Rptr.2d 275 (Cal.App. 2 Dist.1993)—**§ 10.3, n. 14.**
Heck v. Archer, 23 Kan.App.2d 57, 927 P.2d 495 (Kan.App.1996)—**§ 6.4, n. 36; § 7.3, n. 30.**
Hedrick v. West One Bank, Idaho, N.A., 123 Idaho 803, 853 P.2d 548 (Idaho 1993)—**§ 9.4, n. 61.**
Heffernan v. Wollaston Credit Union, 30 Mass. App.Ct. 171, 567 N.E.2d 933 (Mass.App.Ct. 1991)—**§ 13.2, n. 2.**
Heffner v. Cahaba Bank and Trust Co., 523 So.2d 113 (Ala.1988)—**§ 12.8, n. 157.**
Hegel, In re Estate of, 76 Ohio St.3d 476, 668 N.E.2d 474 (Ohio 1996)—**§ 8.1, n. 35.**
Heggstad, Estate of, 20 Cal.Rptr.2d 433 (Cal. App. 1 Dist.1993)—**§ 3.6, n. 22; § 4.6, n. 4.**
Heidenreich's Will, In re, 85 Misc.2d 135, 378 N.Y.S.2d 982 (N.Y.Sur.1976)—**§ 12.9, n. 36.**
Heilig Trust and Beneficiaries v. First Interstate Bank of Washington, 93 Wash.App. 514, 969 P.2d 1082 (Wash.App. Div. 2 1998)—**§ 12.8, n. 157.**
Heiman v. Parrish, 262 Kan. 926, 942 P.2d 631 (Kan.1997)—**§ 5.5, n. 8.**
Heimbach, Matter of Estate of, 847 P.2d 824 (Okla.App. Div. 3 1993)—**§ 3.4, n. 36.**
Heim, Estate of v. Commissioner, 914 F.2d 1322 (9th Cir.1990)—**§ 6.1, n. 42.**
Hein v. Hein, 214 Mich.App. 356, 543 N.W.2d 19 (Mich.App.1995)—**§ 9.6, n. 74.**
Heinzman v. Mason, 694 N.E.2d 1164 (Ind. App.1998)—**§ 2.7, n. 57.**
Heirship of McLeod, Matter of, 506 So.2d 289 (Miss.1987)—**§ 1.3, n. 34; § 2.11, n. 43.**
Heisserer, Matter of, 797 S.W.2d 864 (Mo.App. S.D.1990)—**§ 12.6, n. 11.**
Heller, Estate of, 9 Cal.Rptr.2d 274 (Cal.App. 2 Dist.1992)—**§ 12.5, n. 49; § 12.10, n. 72.**
Heller's Estate, In re, 39 Wis.2d 318, 159 N.W.2d 82 (Wis.1968)—**§ 3.10, n. 36.**
Hellums v. Reinhardt, 567 So.2d 274 (Ala. 1990)—**§ 3.6, n. 21.**
Helmer v. Voss, 646 S.W.2d 738 (Mo.1983)—**§ 8.3, n. 53.**
Helmholz, Helvering v., 296 U.S. 93, 56 S.Ct. 68, 80 L.Ed. 76 (1935)—**§ 15.3; § 15.3, n. 93.**
Helton v. Helton, 114 Ohio App.3d 683, 683 N.E.2d 1157 (Ohio App. 2 Dist.1996)—**§ 5.5, n. 42.**
**Helvering v. _____ (see opposing party)**
Hempe v. Hempe, 54 Or.App. 490, 635 P.2d 403 (Or.App.1981)—**§ 2.11, n. 32.**
Henderson, Matter of, 590 N.Y.S.2d 836, 605 N.E.2d 323 (N.Y.1992)—**§ 7.4, n. 33.**
Henderson v. Collins, 245 Ga. 776, 267 S.E.2d 202 (Ga.1980)—**§ 13.1, n. 34.**
Henderson v. Millis, 373 N.W.2d 497 (Iowa 1985)—**§ 1.3, n. 62.**
Henderson v. Parker, 728 S.W.2d 768 (Tex. 1987)—**§ 8.3, n. 64.**
Henderson v. Roadway Exp., 308 Ill.App.3d 546, 242 Ill.Dec. 153, 720 N.E.2d 1108 (Ill. App. 4 Dist.1999)—**§ 13.1, n. 96.**
Hendricks v. Hendricks, 109 Or.App. 80, 817 P.2d 1339 (Or.App.1991)—**§ 3.3, n. 14.**
Hendrickson, Matter of Estate of, 248 Kan. 72, 805 P.2d 20 (Kan.1991)—**§ 2.11, n. 10.**
Hendrickson v. Minneapolis Federal Sav. & Loan Ass'n, 281 Minn. 462, 161 N.W.2d 688 (Minn.1968)—**§ 5.5, n. 47.**
Hengst v. Hengst, 491 Pa. 120, 420 A.2d 370 (Pa.1980)—**§ 4.5, n. 48.**
Henkle v. Henkle, 75 Ohio App.3d 732, 600 N.E.2d 791 (Ohio App. 12 Dist.1991)—**§ 6.4, n. 9, 12.**
Henley v. Henley, 95 Wash.App. 91, 974 P.2d 362 (Wash.App. Div. 2 1999)—**§ 5.5, n. 75.**
Hensley, Matter of Estate of, 413 N.E.2d 315 (Ind.App. 1 Dist.1980)—**§ 12.9, n. 30.**
Herbert, In re Estate of, 979 P.2d 1133 (Hawai'i 1999)—**§ 12.1, n. 106.**
Herbert, In re Estate of, 979 P.2d 39 (Hawai'i 1999)—**§ 6.1, n. 6; § 7.3, n. 16.**
Herbert M. Dowsett Trust, Matter of, 7 Haw. App. 640, 791 P.2d 398 (Hawai'i App. 1990)—**§ 12.8, n. 103, 114.**
Hering, Estate of, 108 Cal.App.3d 88, 166 Cal. Rptr. 298 (Cal.App. 2 Dist.1980)—**§ 5.3, n. 21.**
Herman v. Herman, 42 Wash.App. 6, 707 P.2d 1374 (Wash.App. Div. 1 1985)—**§ 4.7, n. 8.**
Hermitage Methodist Homes of Virginia, Inc. v. Dominion Trust Co., 239 Va. 46, 387 S.E.2d 740 (Va.1990)—**§ 9.7, n. 43, 123.**
Hermon, Estate of, 46 Cal.Rptr.2d 577 (Cal. App. 1 Dist.1995)—**§ 5.4, n. 12.**
Herr v. Commissioner, 35 T.C. 732 (Tax Ct.1961)—**§ 15.2, n. 26.**
Herron v. Underwood, 152 Ill.App.3d 144, 105 Ill.Dec. 105, 503 N.E.2d 1111 (Ill.App. 5 Dist.1987)—**§ 4.5, n. 57.**
Hess v. Whitsitt, 257 Cal.App.2d 552, 65 Cal. Rptr. 45 (Cal.App. 2 Dist.1967)—**§ 2.9, n. 18.**
Hessenflow, Matter of Estate of, 21 Kan. App.2d 761, 909 P.2d 662 (Kan.App.1995)—**§ 3.7, n. 56; § 3.9, n. 12.**
Hettinga v. Sybrandy, 126 Idaho 467, 886 P.2d 772 (Idaho 1994)—**§ 1.1, n. 7.**
Hewitt v. Hewitt, 77 Ill.2d 49, 31 Ill.Dec. 827, 394 N.E.2d 1204 (Ill.1979)—**§ 2.11, n. 63.**
Heyer v. Flaig, 70 Cal.2d 223, 74 Cal.Rptr. 225, 449 P.2d 161 (Cal.1969)—**§ 3.6, n. 23.**
Hickman v. Trust of Heath, House and Boyles, 310 Ark. 333, 835 S.W.2d 880 (Ark.1992)—**§ 4.6, n. 55.**
Hickox v. Wilson, 269 Ga. 180, 496 S.E.2d 711 (Ga.1998)—**§ 4.2, n. 21.**
Hicks v. Boshears, 846 S.W.2d 812 (Tenn. 1993)—**§ 2.7, n. 42.**

## K

Kinney v. Ewing, 83 N.M. 365, 492 P.2d 636 (N.M.1972)—**§ 5.5, n. 57.**
Kinney v. Shinholser, 663 So.2d 643 (Fla.App. 5 Dist.1995)—**§ 2.8, n. 11.**
Kinsella v. Landa, 600 S.W.2d 104 (Mo.App. E.D.1980)—**§ 12.1, n. 97.**
Kintzinger v. Millin, 254 Iowa 173, 117 N.W.2d 68 (Iowa 1962)—**§ 4.5, n. 34.**
Kirk, Matter of Estate of, 127 Idaho 817, 907 P.2d 794 (Idaho 1995)—**§ 3.10, n. 7; § 9.1, n. 21; § 11.6, n. 8.**
Kirkeby v. Covenant House, 157 Or.App. 309, 970 P.2d 241 (Or.App.1998)—**§ 3.7, n. 70; § 4.1, n. 30; § 4.3, n. 37; § 5.3, n. 8.**
Kirkman's Estate, Matter of, 302 N.C. 164, 273 S.E.2d 712 (N.C.1981)—**§ 12.5, n. 91.**
Kirksey v. Teachers' Retirement System of Georgia, 250 Ga. 884, 302 S.E.2d 101 (Ga. 1983)—**§ 3.6, n. 22.**
Kitchen v. Estate of Blue, 498 N.E.2d 41 (Ind. App. 3 Dist.1986)—**§ 4.9, n. 2, 31.**
Klamath Falls, City of v. Bell, 7 Or.App. 330, 490 P.2d 515 (Or.App.1971)—**§ 11.6, n. 22.**
Klassen v. Klassen, 5 W.W.R. 746 (Sask.Q.B.1986)—**§ 9.5, n. 71, 75, 79; § 9.7, n. 50.**
K L Cattle Co. v. Bunker, 491 F.Supp. 1314 (S.D.Tex.1980)—**§ 12.3, n. 34.**
Klein v. Shaw, 109 Idaho 237, 706 P.2d 1348 (Idaho App.1985)—**§ 6.4, n. 32.**
Klein, Matter of Estate of, 434 N.W.2d 560 (N.D.1989)—**§ 6.1, n. 49; § 10.1, n. 95.**
Kleinman, In re Estate of, 970 P.2d 1286 (Utah 1998)—**§ 4.4, n. 9, 18.**
Klinkner, Estate of, 85 Cal.App.3d 942, 151 Cal.Rptr. 20 (Cal.App. 2 Dist.1978)—**§ 9.7, n. 124.**
Klugh v. United States, 588 F.2d 45 (4th Cir. 1978)—**§ 11.1, n. 28.**
Knickerbocker, In re Estate of, 912 P.2d 969 (Utah 1996)—**§ 5.5, n. 37.**
Knight v. Knight, 182 A.D.2d 342, 589 N.Y.S.2d 195 (N.Y.A.D. 3 Dept.1992)—**§ 1.2, n. 35; § 13.1, n. 36.**
Knipp, Estate of, 489 Pa. 509, 414 A.2d 1007 (Pa.1980)—**§ 12.7, n. 40; § 12.8, n. 73.**
Knott v. Garriott, 784 S.W.2d 603 (Ky.App. 1989)—**§ 3.6, n. 3.**
Knott, In re Estate of, 245 Ill.App.3d 736, 185 Ill.Dec. 798, 615 N.E.2d 357 (Ill.App. 5 Dist. 1993)—**§ 12.5, n. 108; § 13.3, n. 31.**
Knupp v. District of Columbia, 578 A.2d 702 (D.C.1990)—**§ 6.1, n. 8.**
Koch v. James, 670 N.E.2d 113 (Ind.App. 1996)—**§ 8.2, n. 20.**
Koch v. James, 616 N.E.2d 759 (Ind.App. 1 Dist.1993)—**§ 12.6, n. 13.**
Koch, In re Estate of, 297 Ill.App.3d 786, 232 Ill.Dec. 189, 697 N.E.2d 931 (Ill.App. 3 Dist. 1998)—**§ 6.4, n. 55, 75.**
Koch, Matter of Estate of, 18 Kan.App.2d 188, 849 P.2d 977 (Kan.App.1993)—**§ 7.4, n. 7.**
Koeninger v. Toledo Trust Co., 49 Ohio App. 490, 197 N.E. 419 (Ohio App. 6 Dist.1934)—**§ 6.2, n. 20.**
Kohler v. Armstrong, 92 Or.App. 326, 758 P.2d 407 (Or.App.1988)—**§ 13.3, n. 4.**
Kohler v. Fletcher, 442 N.W.2d 169 (Minn.App. 1989)—**§ 12.8, n. 42.**
Kohlsaat, Estate of v. Commissioner, T.C. Memo. 1997-212 (U.S.Tax Ct.1997)—**§ 15.2, n. 32.**
Kokjohn, Matter of Estate of, 531 N.W.2d 99 (Iowa 1995)—**§ 5.5, n. 80, 87.**
Kolacy, In re Estate of, 332 N.J.Super. 593, 753 A.2d 1257 (N.J.Super.Ch.2000)—**§ 10.3, n. 14.**
Kolbinger, In re Estate of, 175 Ill.App.3d 315, 124 Ill.Dec. 842, 529 N.E.2d 823 (Ill.App. 2 Dist.1988)—**§ 8.1, n. 37; § 13.3, n. 44.**
Kolodney v. Kolodney, 6 Conn.App. 118, 503 A.2d 625 (Conn.App.1986)—**§ 9.5, n. 10, 18, 24.**
Konopka, Matter of Estate of, 175 Wis.2d 100, 498 N.W.2d 853 (Wis.App.1993)—**§ 12.5, n. 41, 76.**
Konow, Matter of Estate of, 154 Ill.App.3d 744, 106 Ill.Dec. 743, 506 N.E.2d 450 (Ill.App. 3 Dist.1987)—**§ 4.9, n. 21.**
Koors, Matter of Guardianship of, 656 N.E.2d 530 (Ind.App.1995)—**§ 3.5, n. 38.**
Korten v. Chicago City Bank and Trust Co., 178 Ill.App.3d 397, 127 Ill.Dec. 484, 533 N.E.2d 102 (Ill.App. 1 Dist.1988)—**§ 9.6, n. 30.**
Kosak v. MacKechnie, 24 Mass.App.Ct. 20, 505 N.E.2d 579 (Mass.App.Ct.1987)—**§ 2.11, n. 34.**
Kostelnik v. Roberts, 680 S.W.2d 532 (Tex. App.-Corpus Christi 1984)—**§ 3.4, n. 32; § 6.4, n. 81, 88.**
Kostick, In re Estate of, 514 Pa. 591, 526 A.2d 746 (Pa.1987)—**§ 3.1, n. 38.**
Kottke, In re Estate of, 6 P.3d 243 (Alaska 2000)—**§ 7.1, n. 7; § 7.3, n. 11, 28.**
Kotz, Estate of, 486 Pa. 444, 406 A.2d 524 (Pa.1979)—**§ 3.7, n. 38.**
Kradwell's Estate, In re, 44 Wis.2d 40, 170 N.W.2d 773 (Wis.1969)—**§ 9.5, n. 70.**
Kraft, In re Marriage of, 119 Wash.2d 438, 832 P.2d 871 (Wash.1992)—**§ 3.8, n. 86.**
Kraft's Estate, In re, 186 N.W.2d 628 (Iowa 1971)—**§ 8.2, n. 24.**
Kramer v. Freedman, 346 So.2d 1216 (Fla.App. 3 Dist.1977)—**§ 10.4, n. 69.**
Kramer v. Freedman, 272 So.2d 195 (Fla.App. 3 Dist.1973)—**§ 6.1, n. 66.**
Kramer, Matter of Guardianship of, 101 Misc.2d 782, 421 N.Y.S.2d 975 (N.Y.Sur. 1979)—**§ 2.8, n. 55.**
Kramme, Estate of, 143 Cal.Rptr. 542, 573 P.2d 1369 (Cal.1978)—**§ 2.7, n. 9.**
Krebs v. Krebs, 114 Idaho 571, 759 P.2d 77 (Idaho App.1988)—**§ 7.3, n. 38.**
Krebs, Matter of Estate of, 334 Pa.Super. 635, 483 A.2d 919 (Pa.Super.1984)—**§ 11.9, n. 18.**
Kreitman's Estate, In re, 68 Ill.App.3d 523, 25 Ill.Dec. 379, 386 N.E.2d 650 (Ill.App. 1 Dist. 1979)—**§ 2.6, n. 37.**
Kremer, In re Estate of, 190 Ill.App.3d 650, 137 Ill.Dec. 934, 546 N.E.2d 1047 (Ill.App. 5 Dist.1989)—**§ 4.5, n. 26, 56; § 13.3, n. 40.**
Kresser v. Peterson, 675 P.2d 1193 (Utah 1984)—**§ 4.5, n. 56; § 4.8, n. 8.**

# L

Lindsay, Matter of Estate of, 91 Wash.App. 944, 957 P.2d 818 (Wash.App. Div. 3 1998)—**§ 3.9, n. 56; § 4.3, n. 35.**
Lindsey v. Ogden, 10 Mass.App.Ct. 142, 406 N.E.2d 701 (Mass.App.Ct.1980)—**§ 12.4, n. 68.**
Lindsey v. Wilcox, 479 N.E.2d 1330 (Ind.App. 1 Dist.1985)—**§ 2.10, n. 64.**
Lindsey's Estate v. Taylor, 13 Ill.App.3d 717, 300 N.E.2d 572 (Ill.App. 5 Dist.1973)—**§ 8.1, n. 45.**
Linger v. Rohr, 181 W.Va. 643, 383 S.E.2d 825 (W.Va.1989)—**§ 6.4, n. 44.**
Lingscheit, Matter of Estate of, 387 N.W.2d 738 (S.D.1986)—**§ 3.7, n. 57.**
Linkins v. Protestant Episcopal Cathedral Foundation of the District of Columbia, 187 F.2d 357, 87 U.S.App.D.C. 351 (D.C.Cir. 1950)—**§ 5.3, n. 11.**
Linkous v. Candler, 270 Ga. 284, 508 S.E.2d 657 (Ga.1998)—**§ 9.6, n. 41.**
Link's Will, Matter of, 119 Misc.2d 181, 462 N.Y.S.2d 582 (N.Y.Sur.1983)—**§ 13.1, n. 89.**
Lint, Matter of Estate of, 135 Wash.2d 518, 957 P.2d 755 (Wash.1998)—**§ 2.11, n. 10; § 6.1, n. 61.**
Lipe v. Lipe, 728 P.2d 1124 (Wyo.1986)—**§ 3.3, n. 16.**
Little, Matter of Estate of, 106 Wash.2d 269, 721 P.2d 950 (Wash.1986)—**§ 2.2, n. 60.**
Little City Foundation v. Capsonic Group, Inc., 231 Ill.App.3d 122, 172 Ill.Dec. 867, 596 N.E.2d 146 (Ill.App. 1 Dist.1992)—**§ 4.5, n. 54.**
Little Red Schoolhouse for Special Children, Inc. v. Citizens & Southern Nat. Bank, 230 Ga. 393, 197 S.E.2d 342 (Ga.1973)—**§ 10.4, n. 58.**
Littleton v. Prange, 9 S.W.3d 223 (Tex.App.-San Antonio 1999)—**§ 2.11, n. 91.**
Littwin v. Littwin, 147 Ill.App.3d 1065, 101 Ill.Dec. 220, 498 N.E.2d 544 (Ill.App. 1 Dist. 1986)—**§ 10.1, n. 116.**
Livingston, In re Estate of, 999 S.W.2d 874 (Tex.App.-El Paso 1999)—**§ 4.3, n. 16, 69.**
Lloyd's Bank v. Duker, [1987] 3 All E.R. 193 (Ch.1987)—**§ 12.6, n. 22.**
Lober v. United States, 346 U.S. 335, 74 S.Ct. 98, 98 L.Ed. 15 (1953)—**§ 15.3, n. 61.**
Loberg v. Alford, 372 N.W.2d 912 (N.D.1985)—**§ 12.10, n. 40.**
Lockard v. Commissioner, 166 F.2d 409 (1st Cir.1948)—**§ 15.2, n. 52.**
Locken v. Locken, 98 Nev. 369, 650 P.2d 803 (Nev.1982)—**§ 6.4, n. 82.**
Lockwood v. Adamson, 409 Mass. 325, 566 N.E.2d 96 (Mass.1991)—**§ 2.10, n. 9, 21.**
Lockwood v. Killian, 179 Conn. 62, 425 A.2d 909 (Conn.1979)—**§ 9.7, n. 40.**
Lockwood v. Killian, 172 Conn. 496, 375 A.2d 998 (Conn.1977)—**§ 9.7, n. 27, 39.**
Loeser v. Talbot, 412 Mass. 361, 589 N.E.2d 301 (Mass.1992)—**§ 6.1, n. 41; § 6.3, n. 18, 21.**
Lohr v. Byrd, 522 So.2d 845 (Fla.1988)—**§ 13.3, n. 2.**
Lombardo, In re Guardianship of, 86 Ohio St.3d 600, 716 N.E.2d 189 (Ohio 1999)—**§ 9.6, n. 76.**
Lonergan v. Estate of Budahazi, 669 So.2d 1062 (Fla.App. 5 Dist.1996)—**§ 5.2, n. 26.**
Lones v. Winzer, 486 S.W.2d 758 (Tenn.Ct. App.1971)—**§ 10.1, n. 92.**
Long v. Buehler, 8 Kan.App.2d 23, 648 P.2d 270 (Kan.App.1982)—**§ 4.9, n. 36.**
Long, Matter of Estate of, 82 Wash.App. 609, 918 P.2d 975 (Wash.App. Div. 2 1996)—**§ 8.3, n. 93; § 10.1, n. 13.**
Longeway, In re Estate of, 133 Ill.2d 33, 139 Ill.Dec. 780, 549 N.E.2d 292 (Ill.1989)—**§ 14.1, n. 16.**
Longworth, In re, 222 A.2d 561 (Me.1966)—**§ 4.3, n. 19.**
Lopes, Estate of, 152 Cal.App.3d 302, 199 Cal. Rptr. 425 (Cal.App. 3 Dist.1984)—**§ 5.3, n. 9.**
Lopez, Matter of, 64 Haw. 44, 636 P.2d 731 (Hawai'i 1981)—**§ 2.2, n. 29; § 10.1, n. 114.**
Lopez v. Medford Community Center, Inc., 384 Mass. 163, 424 N.E.2d 229 (Mass.1981)—**§ 9.7, n. 76.**
Lord Dacre, In re, 93 Sel.Soc. 228 (1536)—**§ 3.2, n. 15.**
Lorentzen v. Smith, 129 N.M. 278, 5 P.3d 1082 (N.M.App.2000)—**§ 11.8, n. 38.**
Loring v. Karri–Davies, 371 Mass. 346, 357 N.E.2d 11 (Mass.1976)—**§ 10.4, n. 71.**
Loring v. Marshall, 396 Mass. 166, 484 N.E.2d 1315 (Mass.1985)—**§ 9.7, n. 65; § 10.4, n. 82.**
Los Angeles County Pioneer Soc., In re, 40 Cal.2d 852, 257 P.2d 1 (Cal.1953)—**§ 9.7, n. 65.**
Lotz v. Atamaniuk, 172 W.Va. 116, 304 S.E.2d 20 (W.Va.1983)—**§ 1.2, n. 37, 79.**
Loughmiller's Estate, Matter of, 229 Kan. 584, 629 P.2d 156 (Kan.1981)—**§ 1.2, n. 72; § 2.11, n. 6.**
Lourdes College of Sylvania, Ohio v. Bishop, 94 Ohio Misc.2d 51, 703 N.E.2d 362 (Ohio Com.Pl.1997)—**§ 5.5, n. 23.**
Lovett v. Peavy, 253 Ga. 79, 316 S.E.2d 754 (Ga.1984)—**§ 12.4, n. 28.**
Low v. Spellman, 629 A.2d 57 (Me.1993)—**§ 1.3, n. 59; § 11.7, n. 3, 6; § 11.8, n. 7, 37.**
Lowell v. Bouchillon, 246 Ga. 357, 271 S.E.2d 498 (Ga.1980)—**§ 12.6, n. 13; § 12.8, n. 11.**
Lowery v. Evonuk, 95 Or.App. 98, 767 P.2d 489 (Or.App.1989)—**§ 12.5, n. 49.**
Lowinger v. Herlihy, 19 Mass.App.Ct. 935, 472 N.E.2d 676 (Mass.App.Ct.1985)—**§ 12.10, n. 37.**
Lowney, Matter of Estate of, 152 A.D.2d 574, 543 N.Y.S.2d 698 (N.Y.A.D. 2 Dept.1989)—**§ 2.9, n. 51.**
Lowrance v. Whitfield, 752 S.W.2d 129 (Tex. App.-Hous. (1 Dist.) 1988)—**§ 11.8, n. 29.**
Lowry v. Norris Lake Shores Development Corp., 231 Ga. 549, 203 S.E.2d 171 (Ga. 1974)—**§ 11.7, n. 17.**

# M

# N

# O

## P

# Q



# R

# S

## T

## U

# V



# W

# Y

## Z



*

# Table of Uniform Probate Code Sections

UNIFORM PROBATE CODE

| Sec. | This Work Sec. | Note |
|---|---|---|
| 1-103 | 2.7 | |
| 1-103 | 3.9 | 26 |
| 1-106 | 12.1 | 55 |
| 1-106, Comment | 1.1 | 33 |
| 1-107(1) | 8.3 | 100 |
| 1-107(2) | 8.3 | 101 |
| 1-107(5) | 8.3 | 102 |
| 1-108 | 12.8 | 139 |
| 1-110 | 2.6 | 3 |
| 1-201 | 1.1 | 39 |
| 1-201 | 8.3 | 11 |
| 1-201(5) | 3.5 | 6 |
| 1-201(8) | 1.1 | 11 |
| 1-201(9) | 2.2 | 2 |
| 1-201(10) | 1.1 | 22 |
| 1-201(11) | 1.1 | 23 |
| 1-201(16) | 1.1 | 30 |
| 1-201(19) | 5.5 | 75 |
| 1-201(21) | 1.1 | 38 |
| 1-201(21) | 2.4 | 3 |
| 1-201(25) | 1.1 | 19 |
| 1-201(25) | 2.2 | 2 |
| 1-201(28) | 1.1 | 42 |
| 1-201(31) | 1.1 | 25 |
| 1-201(36) | 1.1 | 45 |
| 1-201(52) | 1.1 | 62 |
| 1-201(53) | 1.1 | 63 |
| 1-201(56) | 1.1 | 9 |
| 1-201(56) | 5.1 | 4 |
| 1-202(5) | 2.10 | 65 |
| 1-306(b) | 12.1 | 48 |
| 1-307 | 12.1 | 43 |
| 1-309 | 12.1 | 44 |
| 1-403 | 12.1 | 72 |
| 1-403 | 12.8 | 112 |
| 1-403 | 12.8 | 115 |
| 1-403(2) | 12.1 | 78 |
| 1-403(2)(ii) | 12.8 | 113 |
| 1-403(4) | 1.1 | 34 |
| 1-403(4) | 12.10 | 26 |
| 1-1101—1-1102 | 12.1 | 81 |
| Art. II | 1.1 | |
| Art. II, Pt. 1, | 2.3 | 2 |
| 2-101, Comment | 3.10 | 10 |
| 2-102 | 2.1 | 10 |
| 2-102 | 2.1 | 15 |
| 2-102 | 2.6 | 23 |
| 2-102 | 2.11 | 1 |
| 2-102 | 3.6 | 21 |
| 2-102(2) | 2.1 | 21 |
| 2-102(2) | 2.1 | 24 |
| 2-102, Comment | 2.3 | 2 |
| 2-102A | 3.6 | 21 |
| 2-102A | 3.8 | 3 |
| 2-102A(b) | 2.1 | 18 |
| 2-103 | 2.2 | 62 |
| 2-103(1) | 2.2 | |
| 2-103(1) | 2.2 | 51 |
| 2-103(2) | 2.2 | |
| 2-103(2) | 2.2 | 43 |
| 2-103(3) | 2.2 | |
| 2-103(4) | 2.2 | |
| 2-103(4) | 2.2 | 13 |
| 2-103(4) | 2.2 | 51 |
| 2-103, Comment | 2.2 | 17 |
| 2-104 | 2.2 | 6 |
| 2-104 | 8.3 | 86 |
| 2-104, Comment | 8.3 | 95 |
| 2-106 | 2.2 | 24 |
| 2-106 | 2.2 | 28 |
| 2-106 | 2.8 | |
| 2-107 | 2.2 | 58 |
| 2-108 | 2.2 | 5 |
| 2-108 | 10.3 | 13 |
| 2-109 | 2.6 | 2 |
| 2-109 | 2.6 | 3 |
| 2-109 | 2.6 | 26 |
| 2-109(2) | 2.9 | 28 |
| 2-109(a) | 2.6 | 13 |
| 2-109(b) | 2.6 | 29 |
| 2-109, Comment | 2.6 | 9 |
| 2-109, Comment | 2.6 | 20 |
| 2-109, Comment | 2.6 | 22 |
| 2-110 | 2.2 | 8 |
| 2-112 | 3.7 | 11 |
| 2-113 | 2.10 | 18 |
| 2-114 | 2.9 | 64 |
| 2-114 | 2.10 | |
| 2-114 | 2.10 | 35 |
| 2-114(a) | 2.9 | 4 |
| 2-114(a) | 2.9 | 33 |
| 2-114(a) | 2.9 | 41 |
| 2-114(b) | 2.10 | |
| 2-114(b) | 2.10 | 12 |
| 2-114(b) | 2.10 | 42 |
| 2-114(c) | 2.7 | 65 |
| 2-114(c) | 2.9 | 28 |
| Art. II, Pt. 2, General | 3.7 | 16 |
| Art. II, Pt. 2, General | 3.7 | 52 |
| Art. II, Pt. 2, General | 3.8 | 22 |
| 2-201 | 3.8 | 72 |
| 2-202 | 2.11 | 1 |

UNIFORM PROBATE CODE

| Sec. | This Work Sec. | Note |
|---|---|---|
| 2–510, Comment | 6.2 | 13 |
| 2–511 | 6.2 | 23 |
| 2–511 | 6.2 | 29 |
| 2–511(a) | 6.2 | 24 |
| 2–511(b) | 6.2 | 31 |
| 2–511(c) | 6.2 | 34 |
| 2–512 | 6.2 | 18 |
| 2–513 | 6.2 | 15 |
| 2–513 | 6.2 | 16 |
| 2–514 | 4.9 | 4 |
| 2–514 | 4.9 | 9 |
| 2–514, Comment | 4.9 | 11 |
| 2–515 | 5.2 | 35 |
| 2–601 | 2.10 | 32 |
| 2–601 | 6.1 | 22 |
| 2–601 | 8.3 | 86 |
| 2–602 | 8.3 | 2 |
| 2–603 | 2.10 | 23 |
| 2–603 | 8.3 | 9 |
| 2–603 | 8.3 | 16 |
| 2–603 | 8.3 | 18 |
| 2–603(a)(4) | 8.3 | 43 |
| 2–603(a)(4) | 8.3 | 46 |
| 2–603(b) | 10.4 | 66 |
| 2–603(b)(3) | 8.3 | 33 |
| 2–604 | 8.3 | 71 |
| 2–604 | 8.3 | 74 |
| 2–604(a) | 8.3 | 69 |
| 2–604(b) | 8.3 | 71 |
| 2–605 | 8.1 | 16 |
| 2–605 | 8.1 | 26 |
| 2–605(b) | 8.1 | 19 |
| 2–606 | 8.1 | 30 |
| 2–606 | 8.1 | 38 |
| 2–606 | 8.1 | 39 |
| 2–606(a)(1) | 8.1 | 21 |
| 2–606(a)(5) | 8.1 | 8 |
| 2–606(b) | 8.1 | 27 |
| 2–606(b) | 8.1 | 34 |
| 2–606(d) | 8.1 | 27 |
| 2–606(e) | 8.1 | 36 |
| 2–608 | 8.2 | 27 |
| 2–608 | 10.4 | 46 |
| 2–609 | 2.6 | 32 |
| 2–609 | 2.6 | 39 |
| 2–609 | 8.1 | 1 |
| 2–609 | 8.2 | 28 |
| 2–611 | 2.10 | 23 |
| 2–701 | 2.9 | 77 |
| 2–701 | 5.5 | 76 |
| 2–701 | 9.1 | 26 |
| 2–701 | 10.1 | 19 |
| 2–702 | 8.3 | 90 |
| 2–702(b) | 8.3 | 86 |
| 2–702(c) | 8.3 | 88 |
| 2–703 | 1.2 | |
| 2–703 | 1.2 | 8 |
| 2–703 | 1.2 | 11 |
| 2–703 | 1.2 | 16 |
| 2–704 | 10.4 | 51 |
| 2–704, Comment | 10.4 | 51 |
| 2–705 | 2.9 | 77 |
| 2–705 | 2.10 | 23 |
| 2–705 | 2.10 | 35 |

UNIFORM PROBATE CODE

| Sec. | This Work Sec. | Note |
|---|---|---|
| 2–705(a) | 2.2 | 61 |
| 2–705(a) | 10.1 | 51 |
| 2–705(c) | 2.10 | 45 |
| 2–705(c) | 2.10 | 50 |
| 2–706 | 2.10 | 50 |
| 2–706 | 8.3 | 26 |
| 2–706 | 8.3 | 35 |
| 2–706(b)(3) | 8.3 | 33 |
| 2–707 | 10.1 | |
| 2–707 | 10.1 | 71 |
| 2–707(b) | 8.3 | 25 |
| 2–707(b) | 10.1 | 19 |
| 2–707(b)(2) | 10.1 | 59 |
| 2–707(b)(3) | 10.1 | 86 |
| 2–707, Comment | 10.1 | 22 |
| 2–707, Comment | 10.1 | 85 |
| 2–708 | 2.2 | 16 |
| 2–708 | 2.2 | 30 |
| 2–709 | 2.2 | 37 |
| 2–710 | 10.2 | 65 |
| 2–711 | 1.3 | 53 |
| 2–711 | 2.2 | 30 |
| 2–711 | 2.4 | 1 |
| 2–711 | 2.4 | 4 |
| 2–711 | 2.4 | 6 |
| 2–711 | 2.4 | 14 |
| 2–711 | 2.4 | 20 |
| 2–711 | 2.4 | 26 |
| 2–711 | 10.1 | 55 |
| 2–711 | 10.2 | 12 |
| 2–711 | 10.2 | 22 |
| 2–711 | 10.2 | 27 |
| 2–801 | 1.1 | 65 |
| 2–801 | 2.8 | |
| 2–801(a) | 2.8 | |
| 2–801(a) | 2.8 | 40 |
| 2–801(a) | 2.8 | 47 |
| 2–801(a) | 2.8 | 50 |
| 2–801(a) | 9.6 | 69 |
| 2–801(a) | 13.1 | 83 |
| 2–801(b) | 2.8 | 24 |
| 2–801(b) | 2.8 | 28 |
| 2–801(b)(1) | 2.8 | 30 |
| 2–801(c) | 2.8 | 22 |
| 2–801(d) | 2.7 | 56 |
| 2–801(d) | 2.8 | |
| 2–801(d) | 2.8 | 52 |
| 2–801(d) | 2.8 | 58 |
| 2–801(d) | 3.10 | 11 |
| 2–801(d) | 8.3 | 82 |
| 2–801(d) | 9.6 | 40 |
| 2–801(d)(1) | 2.8 | 62 |
| 2–801(e) | 2.8 | 14 |
| 2–801(e) | 2.8 | 26 |
| 2–801(f) | 2.8 | 23 |
| 2–801, Comment | 2.8 | 57 |
| 2–802 | 3.7 | 13 |
| 2–802, Comment | 2.8 | 8 |
| 2–802, Comment | 2.11 | 31 |
| 2–803 | 2.7 | 56 |
| 2–803(a) | 13.3 | 24 |
| 2–803(b) | 2.7 | 24 |
| 2–803(c)(1) | 12.4 | 45 |
| 2–803(c)(2) | 2.7 | 43 |

UNIFORM PROBATE CODE

| Sec. | This Work Sec. | Note |
|---|---|---|
| 2–803(d) | 2.7 | 12 |
| 2–803(e) | 8.3 | 82 |
| 2–803(f) | 2.7 | 12 |
| 2–803(g) | 2.7 | 34 |
| 2–803(g) | 2.7 | 35 |
| 2–803(h) | 5.5 | 90 |
| 2–803(h)(1) | 2.7 | 62 |
| 2–803(i)(1) | 2.7 | 61 |
| 2–803, Comment | 2.7 | 14 |
| 2–803, Comment | 2.7 | 17 |
| 2–803, Comment | 2.7 | 46 |
| 2–804(a)(1) | 5.4 | 15 |
| 2–804(b) | 5.4 | 2 |
| 2–804(b) | 5.4 | 8 |
| 2–804(b) | 5.5 | 75 |
| 2–804(b) | 12.4 | 45 |
| 2–804(d) | 5.4 | 14 |
| 2–804(d) | 8.3 | 82 |
| 2–804(e) | 5.4 | 9 |
| 2–804(f) | 5.4 | 18 |
| 2–804(g) | 5.5 | 90 |
| 2–907(a) | 9.7 | 55 |
| 2–907(a) | 9.7 | 60 |
| 2–907(c)(4) | 9.7 | 56 |
| 2–907(c)(7) | 9.7 | 57 |
| 2–1003 | 4.2 | 1 |
| 2–1003 | 4.3 | 12 |
| 2–1003(b) | 4.3 | 39 |
| 2–1003(e) | 4.3 | 54 |
| 2–1004 | 4.2 | 17 |
| 2–1009 | 4.3 | 12 |
| 3–103 | 12.3 | 1 |
| 3–103 | 12.4 | 2 |
| 3–105 | 12.10 | 39 |
| 3–108(a)(3) | 12.1 | 29 |
| 3–201 | 1.1 | 27 |
| 3–201 | 1.1 | 60 |
| 3–201 | 1.2 | 31 |
| 3–201(a) | 12.1 | 11 |
| 3–201(d) | 1.2 | 32 |
| 3–201(d) | 12.1 | 17 |
| 3–201(d) | 12.3 | 24 |
| 3–202 | 1.2 | 48 |
| 3–202 | 12.1 | 15 |
| 3–203(a) | 2.11 | 1 |
| 3–203(a) | 12.4 | 21 |
| 3–203(b) | 12.4 | 16 |
| 3–203(f)(1) | 12.4 | 24 |
| 3–203(f)(2) | 12.4 | 26 |
| 3–203(g) | 12.3 | 29 |
| 3–301 | 12.1 | 27 |
| 3–301 | 12.1 | 43 |
| 3–301, Comment | 12.1 | 37 |
| 3–312 | 12.2 | 49 |
| 3–312, Comment | 12.2 | 51 |
| 3–318 | 12.2 | 51 |
| 3–321 | 12.2 | 50 |
| 3–401 | 12.1 | 27 |
| 3–401 | 12.1 | 44 |
| 3–401 | 12.2 | 2 |
| 3–406(a) | 4.3 | 5 |
| 3–406(b) | 4.3 | 67 |
| 3–407 | 5.2 | 20 |
| 3–408 | 12.1 | 21 |

UNIFORM PROBATE CODE

| Sec. | This Work Sec. | Note |
|---|---|---|
| 3–412 | 12.1 | 28 |
| 3–412(3)(i) | 12.1 | 87 |
| 3–412(a)(1) | 12.1 | 65 |
| 3–504 | 1.1 | 41 |
| 3–504 | 12.10 | 30 |
| 3–505 | 12.10 | 29 |
| 3–602 | 12.4 | 62 |
| 3–602 | 12.8 | 6 |
| 3–603, Comment | 12.5 | 135 |
| 3–606 | 12.5 | 127 |
| 3–611(b) | 12.3 | 29 |
| 3–703 | 12.7 | 36 |
| 3–703 | 12.10 | 47 |
| 3–703(a) | 12.7 | 4 |
| 3–703(c) | 12.3 | 11 |
| 3–703(c) | 12.3 | 35 |
| 3–704 | 12.6 | 59 |
| 3–704 | 12.10 | 30 |
| 3–705 | 12.1 | 30 |
| 3–706 | 12.5 | 143 |
| 3–707 | 12.5 | 149 |
| 3–709 | 2.8 | 41 |
| 3–713 | 12.8 | 89 |
| 3–713 | 12.8 | 144 |
| 3–713 | 12.9 | 6 |
| 3–713 | 12.9 | 21 |
| 3–713 | 12.9 | 26 |
| 3–714 | 12.8 | |
| 3–714 | 12.8 | 179 |
| 3–715 | 12.6 | 4 |
| 3–715 | 12.6 | 27 |
| 3–715 | 12.7 | 12 |
| 3–715(1) | 12.7 | 62 |
| 3–715(4) | 13.3 | 60 |
| 3–715(6) | 12.7 | 8 |
| 3–715(9) | 12.6 | 41 |
| 3–715(9) | 12.8 | 163 |
| 3–715(11) | 2.8 | 41 |
| 3–715(14) | 12.8 | 175 |
| 3–715(21) | 12.5 | 102 |
| 3–715(21) | 12.9 | 40 |
| 3–715(23) | 12.6 | 36 |
| 3–715(23) | 12.6 | 46 |
| 3–715(24) | 12.7 | 22 |
| 3–715(24) | 12.7 | 102 |
| 3–715(a)(1) | 12.9 | 38 |
| 3–716 | 12.4 | 106 |
| 3–717 | 12.4 | 92 |
| 3–717 | 12.4 | 95 |
| 3–718 | 12.4 | 96 |
| 3–719 | 12.5 | 11 |
| 3–719 | 12.5 | 62 |
| 3–719 | 12.5 | 66 |
| 3–720 | 12.1 | 104 |
| 3–720 | 12.5 | 87 |
| 3–720, Comment | 12.1 | 101 |
| 3–721, Comment | 12.5 | 123 |
| 3–801(a) | 13.3 | 16 |
| 3–801, Comment | 13.3 | 23 |
| 3–802 | 13.3 | 54 |
| 3–802(a) | 13.3 | 51 |
| 3–803(a) | 13.3 | 33 |
| 3–803(a) | 13.3 | 35 |
| 3–803(b) | 13.3 | 30 |

## UNIFORM PROBATE CODE



## UNIFORM PROBATE CODE

# Table of Restatement References

## RESTATEMENT 2ND AGENCY

| Sec. | This Work Sec. | Note |
|---|---|---|
| 120 | 7.2 | 40 |
| 122 | 7.2 | 40 |

## RESTATEMENT 2ND CONFLICT OF LAWS

| Sec. | This Work Sec. | Note |
|---|---|---|
| 23, Comm. b | 1.2 | 50 |
| 122 | 1.2 | 53 |
| 122, Comm. a | 1.2 | 54 |
| 133—134 | 1.2 | 56 |
| 136, Comm. f | 1.2 | 57 |
| 138 | 1.2 | 55 |
| 187 | 1.2 | 14 |
| 223 | 1.2 | 18 |
| 223, Comm. b | 1.2 | 22 |
| 223, Comm. e | 1.2 | 67 |
| 224(1) | 1.2 | 5 |
| 224, Comm. e | 1.2 | 13 |
| 224, Illus. 1 | 1.2 | 41 |
| 225 | 1.2 | 26 |
| 239 | 1.2 | 7 |
| 258 | 3.8 | 75 |
| 258, Comm. c | 3.8 | 74 |
| 259 | 3.8 | 75 |
| 260 | 1.2 | 34 |
| 260 | 1.2 | 49 |
| 263 | 1.2 | 7 |
| 263 | 1.2 | 34 |
| 263 | 1.2 | 49 |
| 263, Comm. c | 1.2 | 66 |
| 264 | 1.2 | 34 |
| 264 | 1.2 | 49 |
| 264(1) | 1.2 | 5 |
| 264, Comm. e | 1.2 | 13 |
| 264, Comm. f | 1.2 | 51 |
| 265 | 1.2 | 34 |
| 265 | 1.2 | 36 |
| 267, Comm. e | 12.8 | 5 |
| 268(1) | 1.2 | 5 |
| 268, Comm. b | 1.2 | 13 |
| 268, Comm. f | 1.2 | 51 |
| 269 | 1.2 | 7 |
| 270 | 1.2 | 7 |
| 270(2) | 1.2 | 59 |
| 270, Comm. b | 1.2 | 9 |
| 270, Comm. b | 1.2 | 13 |
| 270, Comm. c | 1.2 | 60 |
| 277—278 | 1.2 | 18 |
| 278, Comm. a | 1.2 | 18 |
| 278, Comm. e | 1.2 | 25 |
| 283(2) | 1.2 | 72 |

## RESTATEMENT 2ND CONFLICT OF LAWS

| Sec. | This Work Sec. | Note |
|---|---|---|
| 283, Comm. h | 1.2 | 71 |
| 283, Comm. i | 1.2 | 73 |
| 287, Comm. d | 1.2 | 74 |
| 290 | 2.10 | 52 |
| 314 | 1.2 | 31 |
| 314 | 12.1 | 11 |
| 317 | 1.2 | 47 |
| 317 | 12.1 | 20 |
| 317(4) | 12.1 | 14 |
| 324, Comm. c | 12.3 | 15 |
| 329 | 12.3 | 17 |
| 330 | 12.3 | 21 |
| 354, Comm. a | 12.3 | 5 |
| 354, Comm. e | 12.3 | 10 |
| 356, Comm. b | 12.3 | 32 |
| 358, Comm. b | 12.3 | 34 |
| 358, Comm. g | 12.3 | 13 |
| 361 | 12.8 | 6 |
| 364 | 12.3 | 38 |

## RESTATEMENT 2ND CONTRACTS

| Sec. | This Work Sec. | Note |
|---|---|---|
| 14—15 | 12.10 | 53 |
| 14, Comm. c | 12.10 | 52 |
| 15(2) | 7.2 | 23 |
| 17 | 4.5 | 6 |
| 27 | 4.4 | 22 |
| 86 | 4.9 | 25 |
| 90 | 4.5 | 75 |
| 90(2) | 4.5 | 76 |
| 95 | 4.5 | 75 |
| 110 | 4.5 | 15 |
| 124, Illus. 3 | 3.9 | 14 |
| 125 et seq. | 4.5 | 15 |
| 129, Illus. 4 | 4.5 | 17 |
| 129, Illus. 5 | 4.5 | 19 |
| 129, Illus. 10 | 4.9 | 14 |
| 133, Comm. c | 2.8 | 67 |
| 137 | 4.9 | 18 |
| 152, Illus. 12 | 6.1 | 53 |
| 155 | 6.1 | 2 |
| 155 | 6.3 | 17 |
| 155 | 6.3 | 19 |
| 155 | 6.4 | 11 |
| 155 | 6.4 | 89 |
| 155, Comm. a | 6.4 | 8 |
| 155, Comm. b | 6.4 | 14 |
| 155, Comm. c | 6.3 | 21 |
| 155, Comm. c | 6.4 | 67 |
| 155, Comm. d | 6.4 | 15 |

RESTATEMENT 2ND PROPERTY

## RESTATEMENT 2ND PROPERTY

| Sec. | This Work Sec. | Note |
|---|---|---|
| 26.1, Illus. 22—23 | 10.3 | 18 |
| 26.2, Comm. i | 9.6 | 39 |
| 26.2, Comm. m | 10.3 | 3 |
| 26.2, Comm. o | 10.3 | 7 |
| 26.2, Comm. o | 10.3 | 8 |
| 27.1(2) | 8.3 | 55 |
| 27.1, Comm. b | 8.3 | 62 |
| 27.1, Comm. e | 8.3 | 12 |
| 27.1, Comm. e | 8.3 | 24 |
| 27.1, Illus. 3 | 8.3 | 48 |
| 27.1, Illus. 6 | 8.3 | 32 |
| 27.1, Stat. Note | 8.3 | 9 |
| 27.1, Stat. Note 1 | 8.3 | 43 |
| 27.2, Illus. 4 | 8.3 | 46 |
| 27.3 | 10.1 | 50 |
| 27.3, Comm. b | 8.3 | 7 |
| 27.3, Comm. e, Illus. 1 | 10.1 | 105 |
| 27.3, Comm. f | 10.1 | 81 |
| 27.3, Rptr. Tax Note | 10.1 | 23 |
| 28.1 | 2.2 | 29 |
| 28.1, Comm. i | 10.1 | 62 |
| 28.2 | 8.3 | 49 |
| 28.2 | 10.1 | 66 |
| 28.2(2) | 2.2 | 16 |
| 28.2, Comm. b | 2.2 | 35 |
| 28.2, Stat. Note | 2.2 | 21 |
| 28.3 | 10.3 | 27 |
| 28.3 | 10.3 | 29 |
| 28.4, Illus. 4 | 8.3 | 41 |
| Ch. 29, Intro. Note | | |
| 29.1 | 2.4 | 1 |
| 29.1, Comm. b | 2.4 | 5 |
| 29.1, Comm. b | 2.4 | 6 |
| 29.1, Comm. e | 2.4 | 18 |
| 29.1, Comm. f | 2.4 | 17 |
| 29.1, Comm. g | 2.4 | 12 |
| 29.1, Comm. j | 2.4 | 13 |
| 29.1, Comm. j | 2.4 | 16 |
| 29.1, Comm. k | 2.4 | 26 |
| 29.2 | 2.4 | 21 |
| 29.3 | 10.2 | 31 |
| 29.3, Comm. a | 2.4 | 13 |
| 29.3, Comm. d | 1.3 | 53 |
| 29.4 | 10.2 | 11 |
| 29.4, Comm. c | 10.2 | 28 |
| 29.4, Comm. f | 10.2 | 21 |
| 29.4, Comm. g | 10.2 | 27 |
| 29.4, Comm. h | 10.2 | 26 |
| 29.4, Illus. 14 | 10.2 | 25 |
| 29.4, Illus. 15 | 10.2 | 33 |
| 29.6 | 2.2 | 30 |
| 29.6, Illus. 3 | 2.2 | 31 |
| 29.7, Comm. a | 10.2 | 37 |
| 30.1 | 10.2 | 54 |
| 30.1(3) | 10.2 | 56 |
| 30.1, Comm. a | 10.2 | 49 |
| 30.1, Comm. a | 10.2 | 51 |
| 30.1, Comm. g | 10.2 | 53 |
| 30.1, Stat. Note par. 7 | 10.2 | 44 |
| 30.2 | 10.2 | 63 |
| 30.2, Comm. a | 10.2 | 59 |
| 30.2, Comm. j | 10.2 | 60 |
| 30.2, Illus. 1 | 10.2 | 67 |
| 31.1 | 4.5 | 26 |

## RESTATEMENT 2ND PROPERTY

| Sec. | This Work Sec. | Note |
|---|---|---|
| 31.1 | 4.5 | 56 |
| 31.1, Comm. a | 4.5 | 29 |
| 31.1, Comm. b | 4.5 | 32 |
| 31.1, Comm. b | 4.5 | 47 |
| 31.1, Comm. k | 4.5 | 46 |
| 31.1, Illus. 1 | 4.5 | 54 |
| 31.1, Illus. 12 | 4.5 | 52 |
| 31.1, Illus. 16 | 5.5 | 45 |
| 31.2, Illus. 5—8 | 5.5 | 7 |
| 31.2, Illus. 10 | 4.5 | 53 |
| 31.2, Illus. 12 | 4.5 | 52 |
| 31.3 | 5.5 | 3 |
| 31.4, Comm. e | 4.5 | 19 |
| 32.1 | 4.5 | 13 |
| 32.1—32.2 | 4.5 | 27 |
| 32.1, Comm. b | 4.1 | 18 |
| 32.1, Illus. 4 | 4.5 | 79 |
| 32.2(2) | 2.8 | 27 |
| 32.2, Illus. 4 | 4.5 | 35 |
| 32.3(2) | 2.8 | 27 |
| 32.3, Comm. e | 2.8 | 17 |
| 32.4 | 4.5 | 63 |
| 33.1, Comm. c | 4.1 | 36 |
| 33.1, Comm. c | 4.2 | 18 |
| 33.1, Comm. c | 4.3 | 2 |
| 33.1, Comm. c | 4.3 | 41 |
| 33.1, Comm. c | 4.3 | 63 |
| 33.1, Comm. g | 4.1 | 17 |
| 33.1, Comm. g | 4.1 | 26 |
| 33.2, Comm. b | 5.1 | 12 |
| 34.1(2) | 3.7 | 29 |
| 34.1(3) | 3.6 | 22 |
| 34.1(3) | 3.7 | 22 |
| 34.1, Comm. h | 3.7 | 53 |
| 34.1, Comm. i | 3.7 | 53 |
| 34.1, Comm. j | 8.2 | 11 |
| 34.2(2) | 3.5 | 40 |
| 34.2(2), Comm. f | 3.5 | 18 |
| 34.2, Stat. Note | 3.5 | 5 |
| 34.3, Comm. h | 13.1 | 6 |
| 34.3, Comm. i | 13.1 | 8 |
| 34.3, Comm. j | 8.2 | 7 |
| 34.3, Stat. Note | 13.1 | 3 |
| 34.4, Comm. a | 7.1 | 1 |
| 34.5, Comm. b | 7.2 | 25 |
| 34.5, Comm. b | 7.2 | 26 |
| 34.7 | 6.4 | 5 |
| 34.7, Comm. a | 7.3 | 22 |
| 34.7, Comm. c | 6.1 | 59 |
| 34.7, Comm. d | 6.1 | 24 |
| 34.7, Comm. d | 6.4 | 6 |
| 34.7, Comm. d | 6.4 | 19 |
| 34.7, Comm. e, Illus. 9 | 6.1 | 56 |
| 34.7, Illus. 4 | 7.3 | 21 |
| 34.8, Comm. b | 2.7 | 56 |
| 34.8, Comm. c | 2.7 | 42 |
| 34.8, Illus. 1 | 2.7 | 23 |
| 34.8, Illus. 2 | 2.7 | 13 |
| 34.8, Stat. Note | 2.7 | 12 |
| 34.9 | 4.5 | 25 |

## RESTATEMENT 3RD PROPERTY

| Sec. | This Work Sec. | Note |
|---|---|---|
| 1.1 | 1.1 | |

## RESTATEMENT 3RD PROPERTY



## RESTATEMENT OF RESTITUTION



## RESTATEMENT 2ND TORTS



## RESTATEMENT OF TRUSTS



## RESTATEMENT 2ND TRUSTS



## RESTATEMENT 2ND TRUSTS

RESTATEMENT 2ND TRUSTS

RESTATEMENT 3RD TRUSTS

# INDEX

References are to Pages

References are to Pages

References are to Pages

References are to Pages

References are to Pages

References are to Pages

0–314–23815–8

90000

9 780314 238153